CHEVY & GMC

2- & 4-WHEEL DRIVE MID-SIZE

Super Shop Manual

S- & T-Series Pickups, Blazer & Jimmy • 1982-1986

Gas & Diesel

By
KALTON C. LAHUE

ALAN AHLSTRAND
Editor

JEFF ROBINSON
Publisher

CLYMER PUBLICATIONS

World's largest publisher of books devoted exclusively to do-it-yourself vehicle maintenance.

12860 MUSCATINE STREET • P.O. BOX 4520 • ARLETA, CALIFORNIA 91333-4520

FIRST EDITION
First Printing December, 1986

Printed in U.S.A.

ISBN: 0-89287-425-2

Production Coordinator, Lisa Colletta

Technical illustrations courtesy of General Motors Corporation. Additional art by Mitzi McCarthy. With thanks to Jack Wall Chevrolet, Pasadena, CA.
Special thanks to Mike Roeder, Mitchell Information Services, Inc.

CONTENTS

CHAPTER FOUR
4-CYLINDER ENGINE 77

CHAPTER FIVE
V6 ENGINE 131

CHAPTER SIX
FUEL, EXHAUST AND EMISSION CONTROL SYSTEMS 159

QUICK REFERENCE DATA

MAINTENANCE SCHEDULE (GASOLINE ENGINE)

Every 7,500 miles (12 months)	• Engine oil change * • Chassis/suspension lubrication * • Check manual transmission, transfer case and axles • Check brake lines • Check exhaust system
First 7,500 miles, then every 15,000 miles	• Check and rotate tires • Check disc brakes • Change oil filter * • Check and adjust drive belts
First 7,500 miles, then every 30,000 miles	• Check carburetor choke and hoses • Check carburetor/throttle body mounting torque • Check and adjust idle speed (carburetted engines only) • Change manual transmission fluid (4-speed only)
Every 15,000 miles	• Check cooling system ** • Check rear brakes • Check throttle linkage • Inspect fuel tank, cap and lines • Check crankcase vent system • Check and adjust valve clearance (1.9L engine only) • Change fuel filter
Every 30,000 miles	• Replace spark plugs * • Check and adjust ignition timing • Check ignition wiring • Drain/refill cooling system • Replace PCV valve (except 1.9L) • Clean PCV orifice (1.9L only) • Inspect manual steering gear seal • Check air cleaner system • Replace air cleaner filter • Replace crankcase vent filter • Check idle stop solenoid/dashpot (carburetted engine only) • Check EGR system operation • Repack and adjust wheel bearings *
Every 100,000 miles	• Change automatic transmission fluid and strainer

*** SEVERE SERVICE OPERATION: If the vehicle is operated under any of the following conditions, change engine oil @ 3,000 miles or 3 month intervals and oil filter @ alternate oil changes. Clean and regap spark plugs every 6,000 miles. Lubricate chassis and suspension every 6,000 miles. Change automatic transmission fluid and strainer every 15,000 miles. Repack wheel bearings every 15,000 miles.**

a. Extended idle or low-speed operation (short trips, stop-and-go driving).
b. Trailer towing.
c. Operation @ temperatures below 10° F for 60 days or more with most trips under 10 miles.
d. Very dusty or muddy conditions.

**** Check coolant protection and condition once a year.**

MAINTENANCE SCHEDULE (DIESEL ENGINE)

Every 7,500 miles (12 months)	• Engine oil and filter change * • Chassis/suspension lubrication * • Check manual transmission • Check brake lines • Check exhaust system
First 7,500 miles, then every 15,000 miles	• Check and rotate tires • Check disc brakes • Check and adjust drive belts
First 7,500 miles, then every 30,000 miles	• Check and adjust idle speed • Change manual transmission fluid (4-speed only)
Every 15,000 miles	• Check cooling system ** • Check rear brakes • Check throttle linkage • Inspect fuel tank, cap and lines • Check and adjust vacuum pump drive belt • Check and adjust valve clearance
Every 30,000 miles (24 months)	• Drain/refill cooling system
Every 30,000 miles	• Change fuel filter • Inspect manual steering gear seal • Check air cleaner system • Replace air cleaner filter • Repack and adjust wheel bearings *
Every 100,000 miles	• Change automatic transmission fluid and strainer

* SEVERE SERVICE OPERATION: If the vehicle is operated under any of the following conditions, change engine oil @ 3,000 miles or 3 month intervals and oil filter @ alternate oil changes. Clean and regap spark plugs every 6,000 miles. Change automatic transmission fluid and strainer every 15,000 miles. Repack wheel bearings every 15,000 miles.

a. Extended idle or low-speed operation (short trips, stop-and-go driving).
b. Trailer towing.
c. Operation @ temperatures below 10° F for 60 days or more with most trips under 10 miles.
d. Very dusty or muddy conditions.

** Check coolant protection and condition once a year.

RECOMMENDED LUBRICANTS

Engine crankcase	
Gasoline	API Service SF oil
Diesel	API Service SF/CC or SF/CD
Engine coolant	Prestone II or equivalent
Brake fluid	Delco Supreme 11 or other DOT 3 or DOT 4 fluid
Power steering pump	GM power steering fluid or equivalent
Manual steering gearbox	GM lubricant part No. 1051052 or equivalent
Transfer case	DEXRON II automatic transmission fluid
Manual transmission	DEXRON II automatic transmission fluid
Automatic transmission	DEXRON II automatic transmission fluid
Differential	SAE 80W GL-5 or 80W-90 GL-5 gear lubricant

(continued)

RECOMMENDED LUBRICANTS (continued)

Shift linkage	Engine oil
Front wheel bearings	GM lubricant part No. 1051344 or equivalent
Chassis lubrication	GM chassis grease meeting 6031-M specification
Hood latch, all hinges	Engine oil
Windshield wiper	GM Optikleen washer solvent or equivalent
Key lock cylinders	WD-40 or equivalent

APPROXIMATE REFILL CAPACITIES

	gal.	qt.	pt.
Engine crankcase			
Gasoline		4.0	
Diesel		6.0	
Automatic transmission			
200C			
After rebuild			19.0
After fluid change			7.0
700R4			
After rebuild			23.0
After fluid change			10.0
Manual transmission			
4-speed		2.5	
5-speed		3.25	
Transfer case		2.3	
Differential			3.5
Front axle		1.5	
Cooling system			
1.9L engine		9.5	
2.2L diesel		11.5	
All others		12.0	
Fuel tank			
Gasoline engine			
Standard			
Pickup	13		
Blazer/Jimmy	13.5		
Optional	20		
Diesel engine			
Standard	14		
Optional	20		

GASOLINE ENGINE OIL VISCOSITY

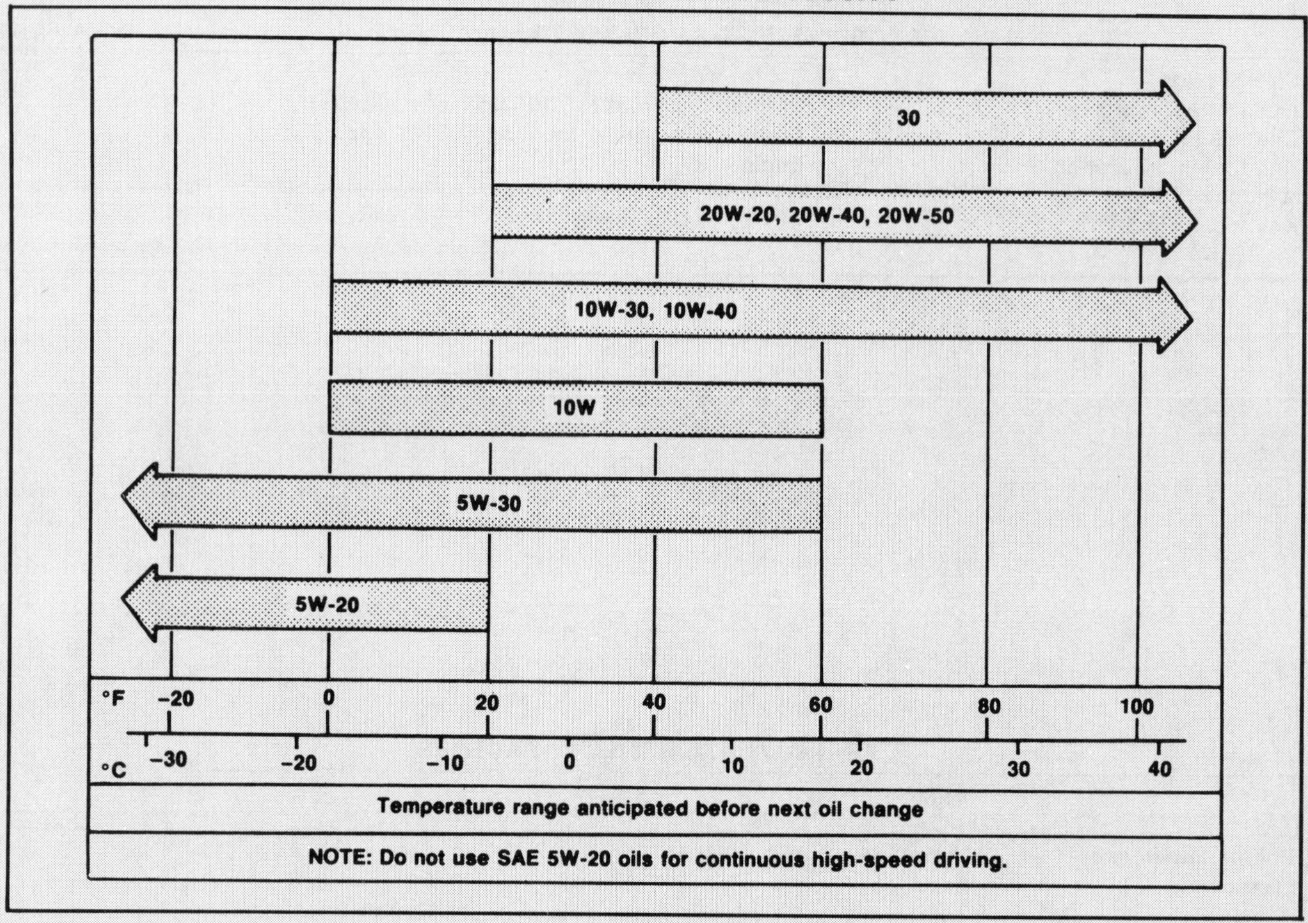

30
20W-20, 20W-40, 20W-50
10W-30, 10W-40
10W
5W-30
5W-20
°F -20 0 20 40 60 80 100
°C -30 -20 -10 0 10 20 30 40
Temperature range anticipated before next oil change
NOTE: Do not use SAE 5W-20 oils for continuous high-speed driving.

DIESEL ENGINE OIL VISCOSITY

SAE 30
*SAE 10W-30
°F -20 0 20 32 40 60 80 100
°C -30 -20 -10 0 10 20 30 40
Temperature range you expect before next oil change.
*For sustained high-speed driving above 32° (0° C) use SAE 30 grade.

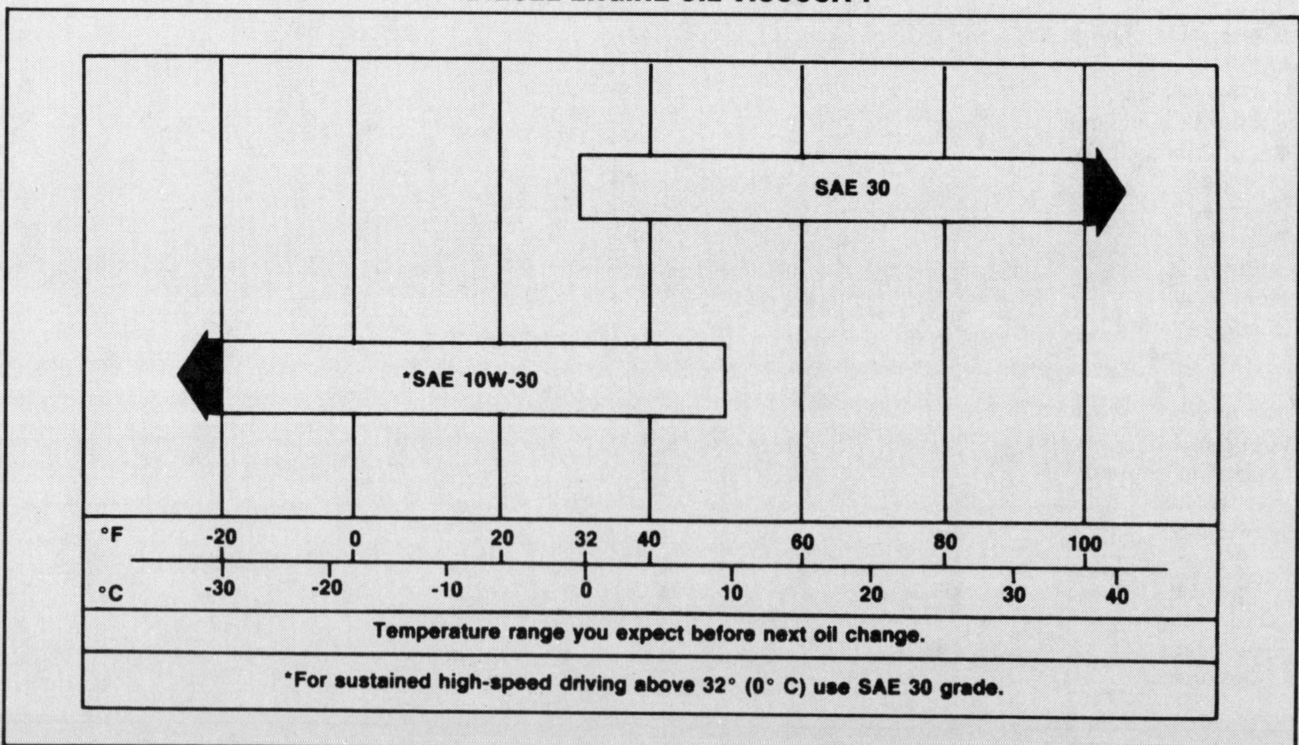

CHEVY & GMC

2- & 4-WHEEL DRIVE MID-SIZE

Super Shop Manual

S- & T-Series Pickups,
Blazer & Jimmy • 1982-1986

Gas & Diesel

INTRODUCTION

This detailed, comprehensive manual covers all 1982-1986 Chevy and GMC S- & T-series pickup, Blazer and Jimmy models. The expert text gives complete information on maintenance, repair and overhaul. Step-by-step instructions and hundreds of illustrations guide you through jobs ranging from simple maintenance to complete overhaul.

This manual can be used by anyone from a first-time do-it-yourselfer to a professional mechanic. Easy to read type, detailed drawings and clear photographs give you all thc information you nccd to do thc work right.

Where repairs are practical for the owner/mechanic, complete procedures are given. Where special tools are required and recommended, their designations are provided. Such tools may often be borrowed or rented or can be purchased directly from Kent-Moore Tool Division, 29784 Little Mack, Roseville, MI 48066.

Equally important, difficult jobs are pointed out. Such operations are usually more economically performed by a dealer or an independent garage.

A shop manual is a reference. You want to be able to find information fast. As in all Clymer books, this one is designed with that in mind. All chapters are thumb tabbed. Important items are indexed at the rear of the book. Finally, all the most frequently used specifications and capacities are summarized on the *Quick Reference* pages at the front of the book.

Keep this shop manual handy in your tool box and use it often. It can save you hundreds of dollars in maintenance and repair bills and keep your vehicle reliable and performing well.

CHAPTER ONE

GENERAL INFORMATION

Troubleshooting, tune-up, maintenance and repair are not difficult, if you know what tools and equipment to use and what to do. Anyone not afraid to get their hands dirty, of average intelligence and with some mechanical ability can perform most of the procedures in this manual.

Due to the number of vehicle/powertrain combinations used over the period covered by this manual, some of the procedures provided are rather general in nature and may require some interpretation. Every effort has been made, however, to be as specific as possible.

Some of the procedures require the use of special tools. The resourceful mechanic can, in many cases, think of acceptable substitutes for special tools—there is always another way. However, using a substitute for a special tool is not recommended as it can be dangerous to you and may damage the part.

MANUAL ORGANIZATION

This chapter provides general information useful to vehicle owners and mechanics. It also discusses the tools and techniques for preventive maintenance, troubleshooting and repair.

Chapter Two describes typical equipment problems and provides logical and specific troubleshooting procedures.

Following chapters describe specific systems, providing disassembly, repair, assembly and adjustment procedures in simple step-by-step form. Specifications concerning a specific system are included at the end of the appropriate chapter.

U.S. standards are used throughout and are accompanied by metric equivalents in parentheses where such reference might have practical value. Metric to U.S. conversion is given in **Table 1**.

NOTES, CAUTIONS AND WARNINGS

The terms NOTE, CAUTION and WARNING have specific meanings in this manual. A NOTE provides additional information to make a step or procedure easier or clearer. Disregarding a NOTE could cause inconvenience, but would not cause damage or personal injury.

A CAUTION emphasizes areas where equipment damage could occur. Disregarding a CAUTION could cause permanent mechanical damage; however, personal injury is unlikely.

A WARNING emphasizes areas where personal injury of even death could result from negligence. Mechanical damage may also occur. WARNINGS *are to be taken seriously.* In some cases, serious injury or death has resulted from disregarding such warnings.

SAFETY FIRST

Professional mechanics can work for years and never suffer a serious injury. If you follow a few rules of common sense and safety, you too can enjoy many safe hours servicing your vehicle. You can hurt yourself or damage the equipment if you ignore these rules.

1. Never use gasoline as a cleaning solvent.
2. Never smoke or use a torch near flammable liquids such as cleaning solvent. If you are working in your home garage, remember that your home gas appliances have pilot lights.
3. Never smoke or use a torch in an area where batteries are being charged. Highly explosive hydrogen gas is formed during the charging process.
4. Never arc the terminals of a battery to see if it is charged. The sparks can ignite the explosive hydrogen as easily as an open flame.
5. If welding or brazing is required on the vehicle, make sure that it is not in the area of the fuel tank or lines. In such cases, the work should be entrusted to a specialist.
6. Always use the correct size wrench for loosening and tightening fasteners. This will prevent damage to the fastener and possible injury to yourself.
7. When replacing a fastener, make sure to use one with the same measurements and strength as the old one. Incorrect or mismatched fasteners can result in damage to the vehicle and personal injury.
8. Keep your work area clean, uncluttered and well lighted.
9. Wear safety goggles during all operations involving drilling, grinding, use of a cold chisel or snap ring removal.
10. Never use worn tools or tools that are not appropriate to the job.
11. Keep an approved fire extinguisher nearby. Be sure it is rated for gasoline (Class B) and electrical (Class C) fires.
12. When drying bearings or other rotating parts with compressed air, never allow the air jet to rotate the bearing or part; the jet is capable of rotating them at speeds far in excess of those for which they were designed. The likelihood of a bearing or rotating part disintegrating and causing serious injury and damage is very great.

SERVICE HINTS

Time, effort and frustration can be saved by following the practices suggested here.

1. "Front," as used in this manual, refers to the front of the vehicle; the front of any component is the end closest to the front of the vehicle. The left side of the vehicle is the driver's side; the right side of the vehicle is the passenger side.
2. Never trust any jack, mechanical or hydraulic. Use jackstands to hold the vehicle when working under it. Always block the wheels that remain on the ground.
3. Disconnect the negative battery cable when working on or near the electrical system and before disconnecting any wires. On most batteries, the negative terminal will be marked with a minus (–) sign and the positive terminal with a plus (+) sign. Never run the engine with the battery disconnected, as this can cause serious damage to the alternator.
4. When disassembling a part or assembly, it is a good practice to tag the parts for location and mark all parts which mate together for relative position. Small parts, such as bolts, can be identified by placing them in plastic sandwich bags. Seal the bags and label them with masking tape and a marking pen. When reassembly will take place immediately, an accepted practice is to place the nuts and bolts in a cupcake tin or egg carton in the order of disassembly.
5. Finished surfaces should be protected from physical damage or corrosion. Keep gasoline and brake fluid off painted surfaces.
6. Use penetrating oil on frozen or tight bolts, then strike the bolt head a few times with a hammer and punch (use a screwdriver on screws). Avoid the use of heat where possible, as it can warp, melt or affect the temper of parts. Heat also ruins finishes, especially paint and plastics.
7. Keep flames and sparks away from a charging battery or flammable fluids and do not smoke in the area. It is a good idea to have a fire extinguisher handy in the work area. Remember that many gas appliances in home garages (water heater, clothes drier, etc.) have pilot lights.
8. No parts removed or installed in the procedures given in this manual should require unusual force during disassembly or assembly. If a part is difficult

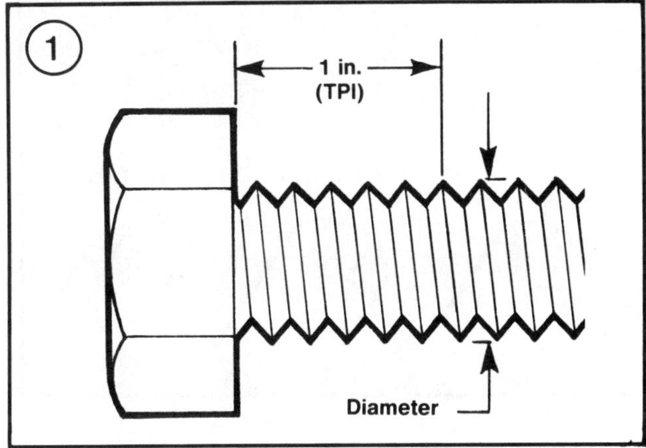

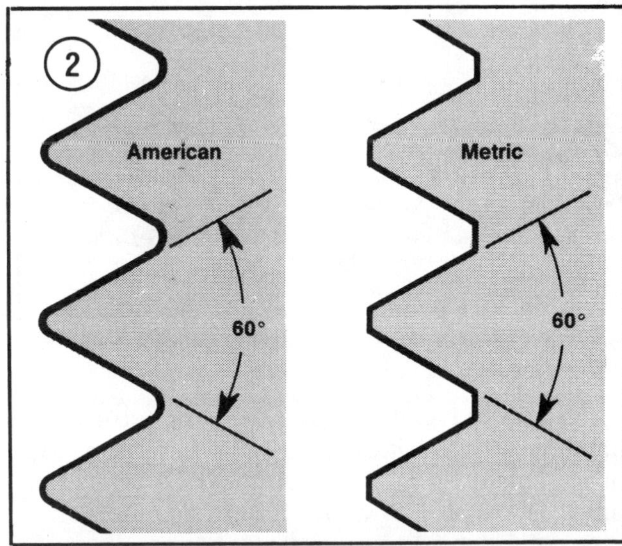

to remove or install, find out why before proceeding.

9. Cover all openings after removing parts or components to prevent dirt, small tools, etc. from falling in.

10. Read each procedure *completely* while looking at the actual parts before starting a job. Make sure you *thoroughly* understand what is to be done and then carefully follow the procedure, step by step.

11. Recommendations are occasionally made to refer service or maintenance to a dealer or a specialist in a particular field. In these cases, the work will probably be done more quickly and economically than if you performed the job yourself.

12. In procedural steps, the term "replace" means to discard a defective part and replace it with a new or exchange unit. "Overhaul" means to remove, disassemble, inspect, measure, repair, reassemble and install major systems and parts.

TORQUE SPECIFICATIONS

Torque specifications throughout this manual are given in foot-pounds (ft.-lb.) and Newton meters (N•m). Newton meters are being adopted in place of meter-kilograms in accordance with the International Modernized Metric System. Existing torque wrenches calibrated in meter-kilograms can be used by performing a simple conversion: move the decimal point one place to the right. For example, 4.7 mkg = 47 N•m. This conversion is accurate enough for mechanics' use even though the exact mathematical conversion is 3.5 mkg = 34.3 N•m.

FASTENERS

The materials and designs of the various fasteners used on automotive parts are not arrived at by chance. Fastener design determines the type of tool required to work with the fastener. Fastener material is carefully selected to decrease the possibility of physical failure.

Threads

Nuts, bolts and screws are manufactured in a wide range of thread patterns. In order for a nut and bolt to join, the diameter of the bolt and the diameter of the hole in the nut must be the same. It is just as important that the threads on both be properly matched.

The best way to tell if the threads on 2 fasteners are matched is to turn the nut on the bolt (or the bolt into the threaded hole in a piece of equipment) with fingers only. Be sure both pieces are clean. If much force is required, check the thread condition on each fastener. If the thread condition is good but the fasteners jam, the threads are not compatible.

Four important specifications describe every thread:

a. Diameter.
b. Threads per inch.
c. Thread pattern.
d. Thread direction.

Figure 1 shows the first 2 specifications. Thread pattern is more subtle. Italian and British standards exist, but the most commonly used by automotive manufacturers are American standard and metric standard. The threads are cut differently as shown in **Figure 2**.

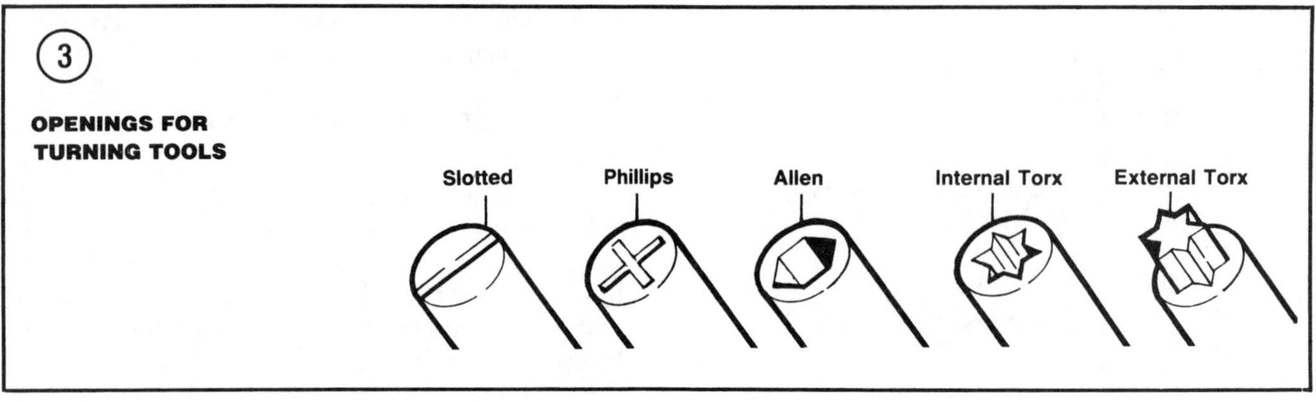

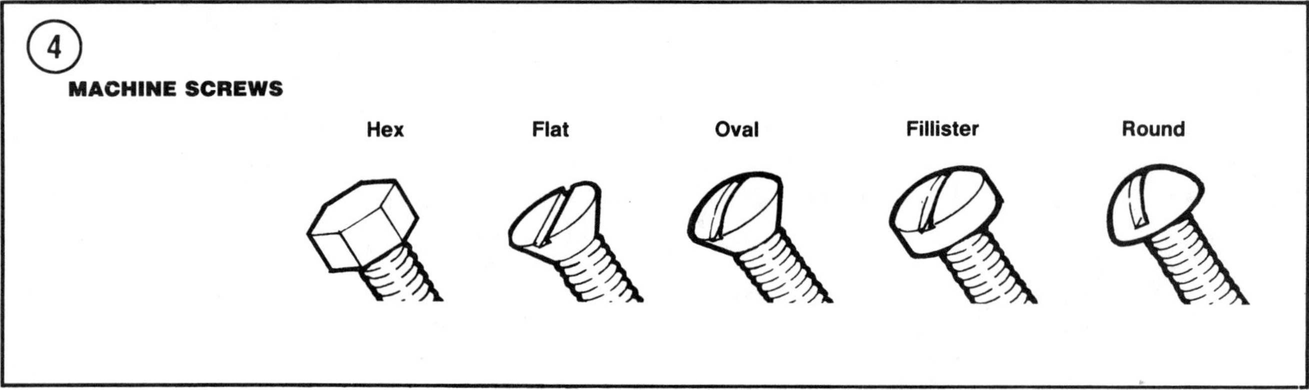

Most threads are cut so that the fastener must be turned clockwise to tighten it. These are called right-hand threads. Some fasteners have left-hand threads; they must be turned counterclockwise to be tightened. Left-hand threads are used in locations where normal rotation of the equipment would tend to loosen a right-hand threaded fastener.

Machine Screws

There are many different types of machine screws. **Figure 3** shows a number of screw heads requiring different types of turning tools. Heads are also designed to protrude above the metal (round) or to be slightly recessed in the metal (flat). See **Figure 4**.

Bolts

Commonly called bolts, the technical name for these fasteners is cap screw. They are normally described by diameter, threads per inch and length. For example, 1/4-20×1 indicates a bolt 1/4 in. in diameter with 20 threads per inch, 1 in. long. The measurement across 2 flats on the head of the bolt indicates the proper wrench size to be used.

Nuts

Nuts are manufactured in a variety of types and sizes. Most are hexagonal (6-sided) and fit on bolts, screws and studs with the same diameter and threads per inch.

Figure 5 shows several types of nuts. The common nut is generally used with a lockwasher. Self-locking nuts have a nylon insert which prevents the nut from loosening; no lockwasher is required. Wing nuts are designed for fast removal by hand. Wing nuts are used for convenience in non-critical locations.

To indicate the size of a nut, manufacturers specify the diameter of the opening and the threads per inch. This is similar to bolt specification, but without the length dimension. The measurement across 2 flats on the nut indicates the proper wrench size to be used.

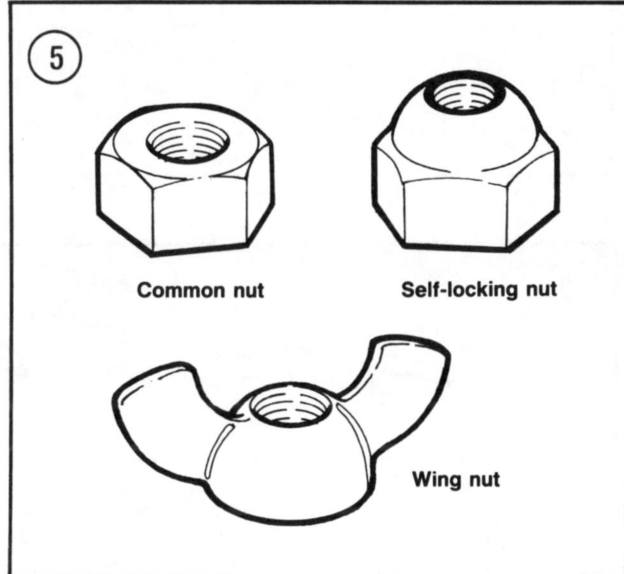

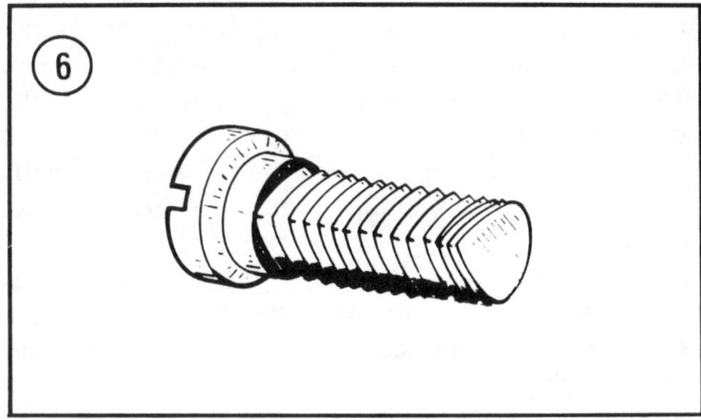

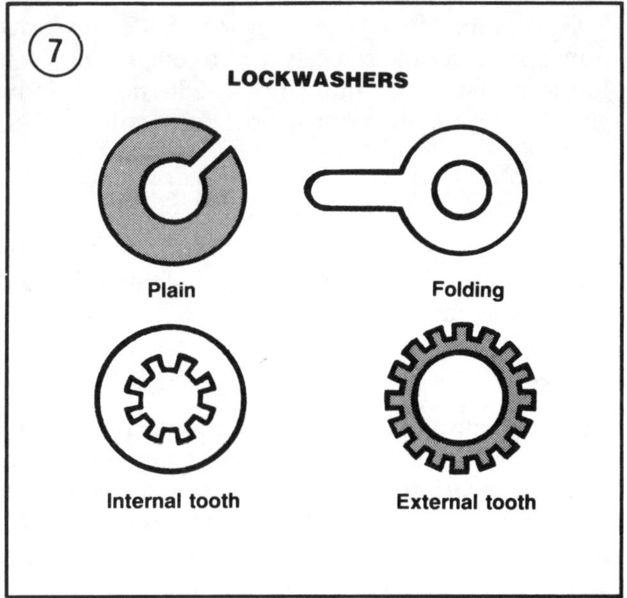

Prevailing Torque Fasteners

Several types of bolts, screws and nuts incorporate a system that develops an interference between the bolt, screw, nut or tapped hole threads. Interference is achieved in various ways: by distorting threads, coating threads with dry adhesive or nylon, distorting the top of an all-metal nut, using a nylon insert in the center or at the top of a nut, etc.

Prevailing torque fasteners offer greater holding strength and better vibration resistance and are commonly used on late-model vehicle components such as carburetors. Some prevailing torque fasteners can be reused if in good condition; others like the trilobial screw shown in **Figure 6** are thread-rolling screws which form their own threads when installed and cannot be removed without displacement of the thread pattern. For greatest safety, it is recommended that you install new prevailing torque fasteners whenever they are removed.

Washers

There are 2 basic types of washers: flat washers and lockwashers. Flat washers are simple discs with a hole to fit a screw or bolt. Lockwashers are designed to prevent a fastener from working loose due to vibration, expansion and contraction. **Figure 7** shows several types of washers. Note that flat washers are often used between a lockwasher and a fastener to provide a smooth bearing surface. This allows the fastener to be turned easily with a tool.

Cotter Pins

Cotter pins (**Figure 8**) are used to secure special kinds of fasteners. The threaded stud must have a

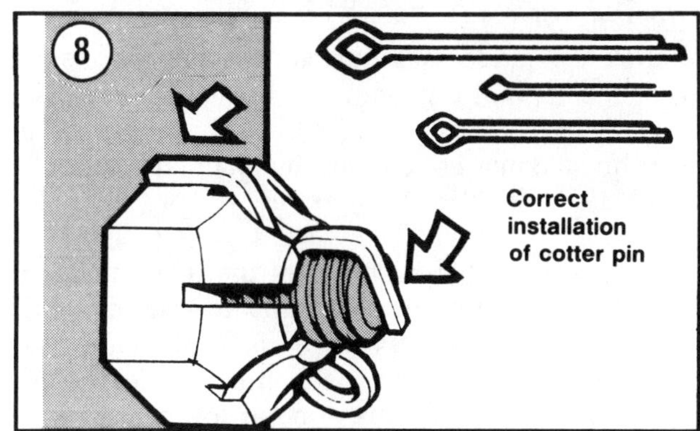

hole in it; the nut or nut lock piece has castellations around which the cotter pin ends wrap. Cotter pins should not be reused after removal.

Snap Rings

Snap rings can be an internal or external design. They are used to retain items on shafts (external type) or within tubes (internal type). In some applications, snap rings of varying thicknesses are used to control the end play of parts assemblies. These are often called selective snap rings. Snap rings can be reused if not distorted during removal, but it is a good idea to discard them and install new ones whenever possible.

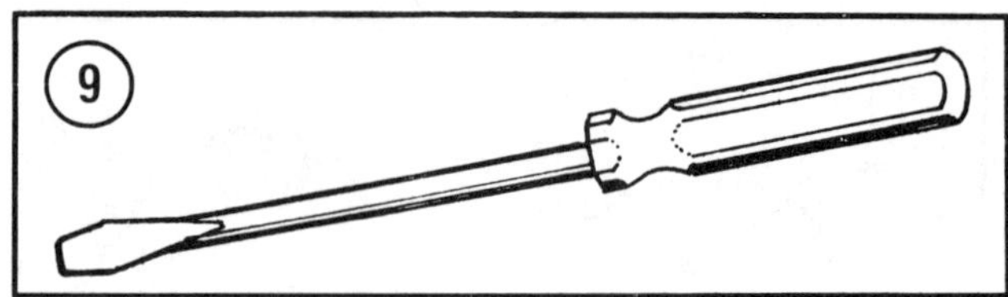

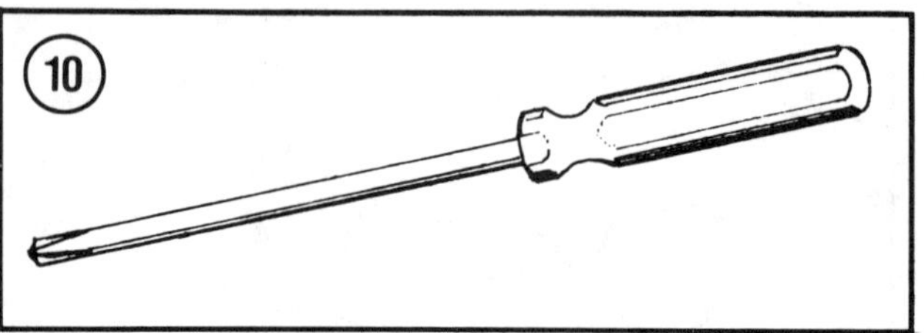

LUBRICANTS

Periodic lubrication assures long life for any type of equipment. The *type* of lubricant used is just as important as the lubrication service itself, although in an emergency the wrong type of lubricant is better than none at all. The following paragraphs describe the types of lubricants most often used on automotive equipment. Be sure to follow the manufacturer's recommendations for lubricant types.

Generally, all liquid lubricants are called "oil." They may be mineral-based (including petroleum bases), natural-based (vegetable and animal bases), synthetic-based or emulsions (mixtures). "Grease" is an oil to which a thickening base has been added so that the end product is a semi-solid. Grease is often classified by the type of thickener added; lithium soap is commonly used.

Engine Oil

Oil for automotive engines is graded by the American Petroleum Institute (API) and the Society of Automotive Engineers (SAE) in several categories. Oil containers display these ratings on the top or label.

API oil grade is indicated by letters; oils for gasoline engines are identified by an "S" while oils for diesel engines are identified by a "C." The gasoline engines covered in this manual require SF graded oil. The diesel engines use CC or CD graded oil.

Viscosity is an indication of the oil's thickness. The SAE uses numbers to indicate viscosity; thin oils have low numbers while thick oils have high numbers. A "W" after the number indicates that the viscosity testing was done at low temperature to simulate cold-weather operation. Engine oils fall into the 5W-30 and 20W-50 range.

Multi-grade oils (for example, 10W-40) are less viscous (thinner) at low temperatures and more viscous (thicker) at high temperatures. This allows the oil to perform efficiently across a wide range of engine operating conditions. The lower the number, the better the engine will start in cold climates. Higher numbers are usually recommended for engine running in hot weather conditions.

The label may also carry the words "energy conserving." This indicates that the oil has been formulated to reduce friction between moving engine parts.

Gear Oil

Gear lubricants are assigned SAE viscosity numbers under the same system as engine oil. Gear lubricant falls into the SAE 72-250 range. Some gear lubricants are multi-grade; for example, SAE 85W-90.

Various additives are incorporated in gear oils to tailor them for specific uses; these additive packages are graded by the API and identified by the letters "GL" and a number. GL-4 and GL-5 are the most commonly used.

Grease

Greases are graded by the National Lubricating Grease Institute (NLGI). Greases are graded by number according to the consistency of the grease; these ratings range from No. 000 to No. 6, with No. 6 being the most solid. A typical multipurpose grease is NLGI No. 2. For specific applications,

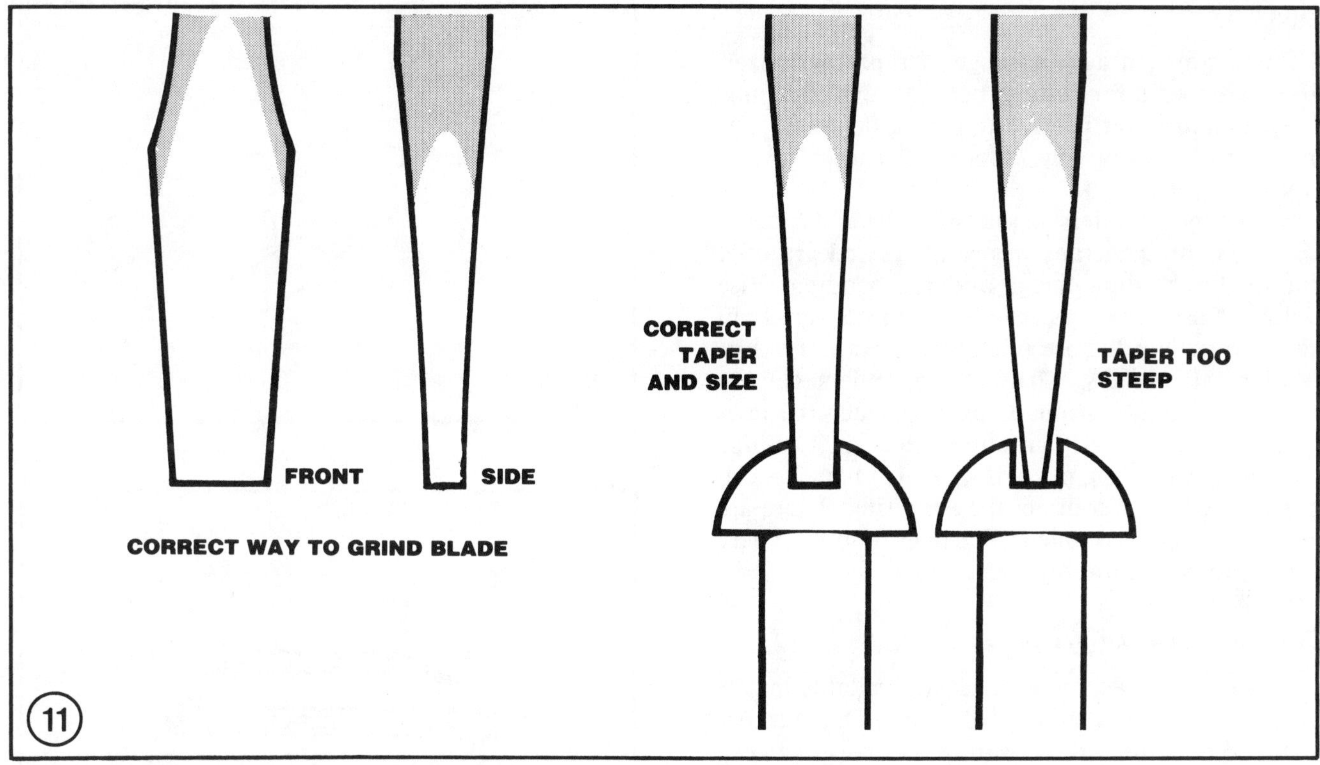

equipment manufacturers may require grease with an additive such as molybdenum disulfide (MOS2).

BASIC HAND TOOLS

Many of the procedures in this manual can be carried out with simple hand tools and test equipment familiar to the average home mechanic. Keep your tools clean and in a tool box. Keep them organized with the sockets and related drives together, the open-end and box wrenches together, etc. After using a tool, wipe off dirt and grease with a clean cloth and return the tool to its correct place.

The following tools are required to perform virtually any repair job. Each tool is described and the recommended size given for starting a tool collection. Additional tools and some duplicates may be added as you become more familiar with the equipment. You may need all English size tools, all metric size tools or a combination of both.

Screwdrivers

The screwdriver is a very basic tool, but if used improperly it will do more damage than good. The slot on a screw has a definite dimension and shape. A screwdriver must be selected to conform with that shape. Use a small screwdriver for small screws and a large one for large screws or the screw head will be damaged.

Two types of screwdrivers are required: a common (flat-blade) screwdriver (**Figure 9**) and Phillips screwdrivers (**Figure 10**).

Screwdrivers are available in sets which often include an assortment of common and Phillips blades. If you buy them individually, buy at least the following:

a. Common screwdriver—5/16×6 in. blade.
b. Common screwdriver—3/8×12 in. blade.
c. Phillips screwdriver—size 2 tip, 6 in. blade.

Use screwdrivers only for driving screws. Never use a screwdriver for prying or chiseling. Do not try to remove a Phillips or Allen head screw with a common screwdriver (unless the screw has a combination head that will accept either type); you can damage the head so that the proper tool will be unable to remove it.

Keep screwdrivers in the proper condition and they will last longer and perform better. Always keep the tip of a common screwdriver in good condition. **Figure 11** shows how to grind the tip to the proper shape if it becomes damaged. Note the symmetrical sides of the tip.

Pliers

Pliers come in a wide range of types and sizes. Pliers are useful for cutting, bending and crimping. They should never be used to cut hardened objects or to turn bolts or nuts. **Figure 12** shows several types of pliers.

Each type of pliers has a specialized function. Gas pliers are general purpose pliers and are used mainly for holding things and for bending. Vise Grips are used as pliers or to hold objects very tight like a vise. Needlenose pliers are used to hold or bend small objects. Channel lock pliers can be adjusted to hold various sizes of objects; the jaws remain parallel to grip around objects such as pipe or tubing. Snap ring pliers (**Figure 13**) have special tips to expand or contract the snap ring. There are many more types of pliers. The ones described here are the most commonly used.

Box and Open-end Wrenches

Box and open-end wrenches are available in sets or separately in a variety of sizes. The number stamped near the end refers to the distance between 2 parallel flats on the hex head bolt or nut.

Box wrenches (**Figure 14**) are usually superior to open-end wrenches (**Figure 15**). An open-end wrench grips the nut on only 2 flats. Unless it fits well, it may slip and round off the points on the nut. The box wrench grips all 6 flats. Both 6-point and 12-point openings on box wrenches are available. The 6-point gives superior holding power; the 12-point allows a shorter swing.

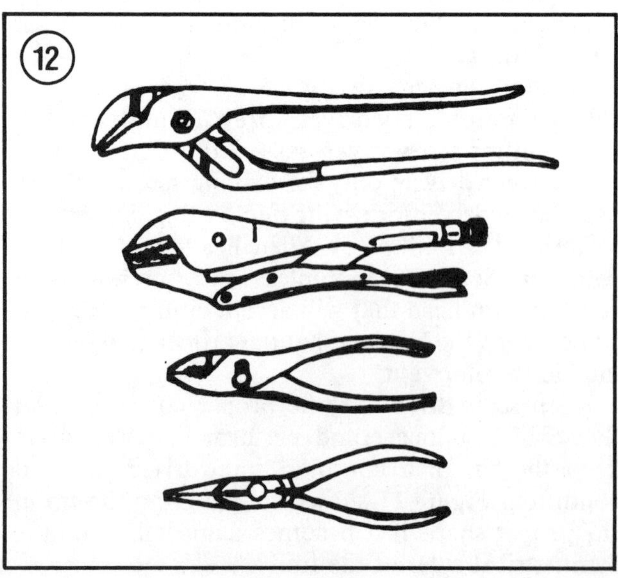
12

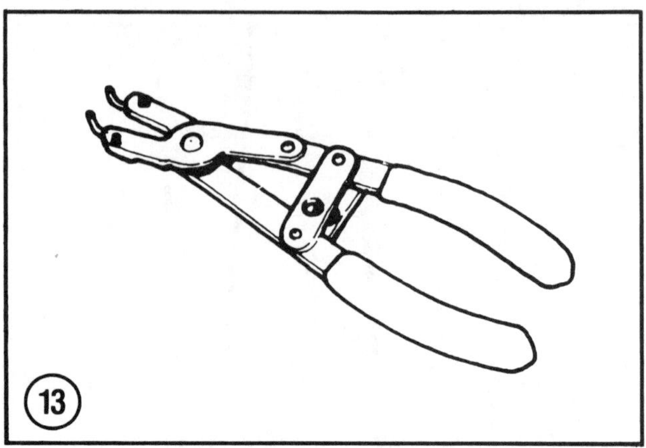
13

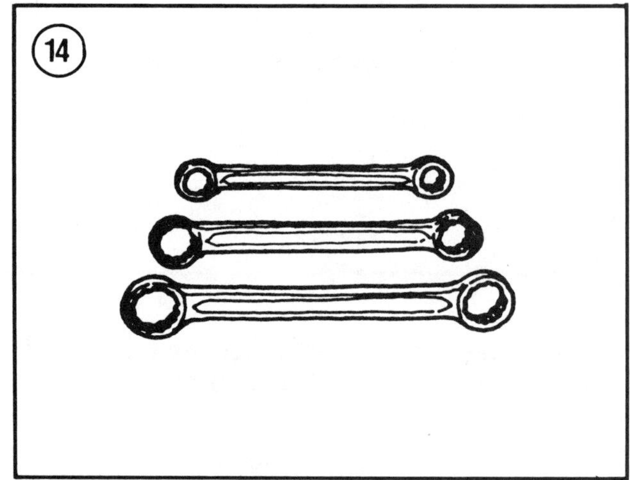
14

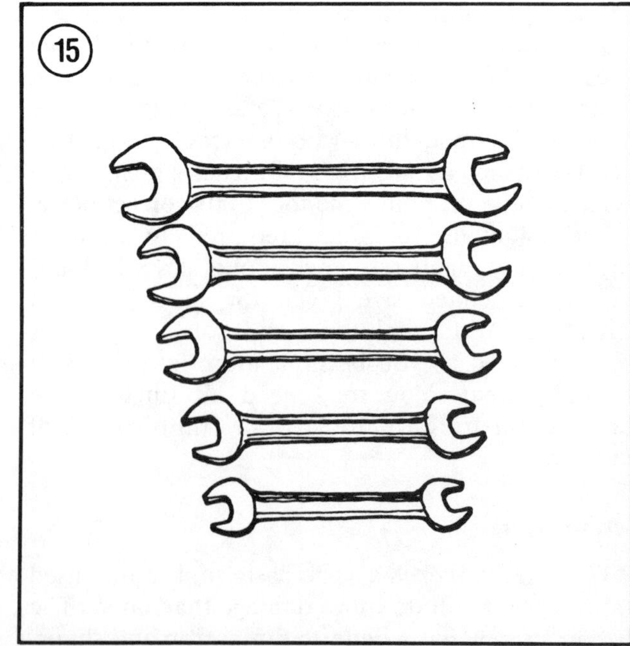
15

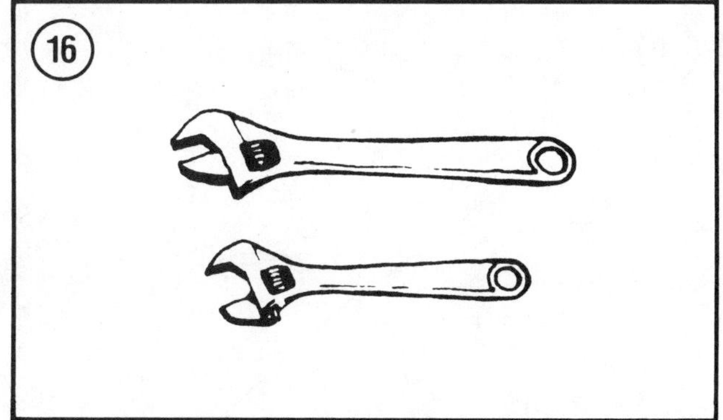

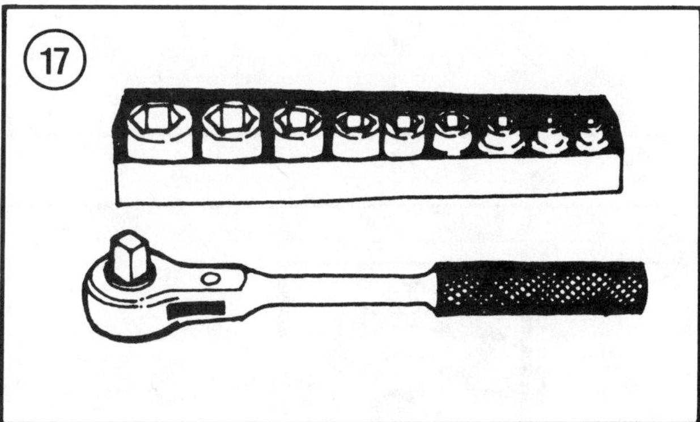

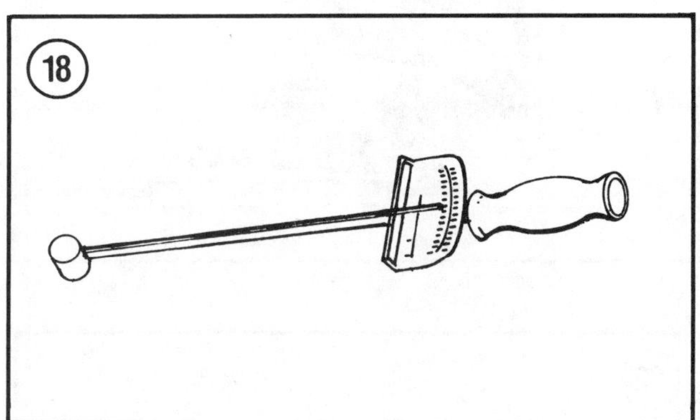

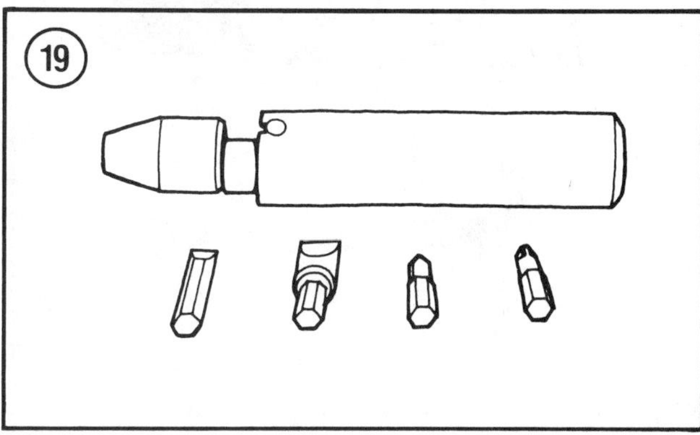

Combination wrenches which are open on one side and boxed on the other are also available. Both ends are the same size.

Adjustable (Crescent) Wrenches

An adjustable wrench (also called a crescent wrench) can be adjusted to fit a variety of nuts or bolt heads (**Figure 16**). However, it can loosen and slip, causing damage to the nut and perhaps to your knuckles. Use an adjustable wrench only when other wrenches are not available.

Crescent wrenches come in sizes ranging from 4-18 in. overall. A 6 or 8 in. wrench is recommended as an all-purpose wrench.

Socket Wrenches

This type is undoubtedly the fastest, safest and most convenient to use. Sockets which attach to a ratchet handle (**Figure 17**) are available with 6-point or 12-point openings and 1/4, 3/8 and 3/4 inch drives. The drive size indicates the size of the square hole which mates with the ratchet handle.

Torque Wrench

A torque wrench (**Figure 18**) is used with a socket to measure how tight a nut or bolt is installed. They come in a wide price range and with either 3/8 or 1/2 in. square drive. The drive size indicates the size of the square drive which mates with the socket. Purchase one that measures 0-140 N•m (0-100 ft.-lb.).

Impact Driver

This tool makes removal of tight fasteners easy and eliminates damage to bolts and screw slots. Impact drivers and interchangeable bits (**Figure 19**) are available at most large hardware and auto parts stores.

Hammers

The correct hammer is necessary for repairs. Use only a hammer with a face or head for rubber or plastic or the soft-faced type that is filled with buckshot. *Never* use a metal-faced hammer as severe damage will result in most cases. You can always produce the same amount of force with a soft-faced hammer.

Feeler Gauge

This tool has either flat or wire measuring gauges. See **Figure 20**. Wire gauges are used to measure spark plug gap; flat gauges are used for all other measurements. A non-magnetic (brass or plastic) gauge may be specified when working around magnetized parts.

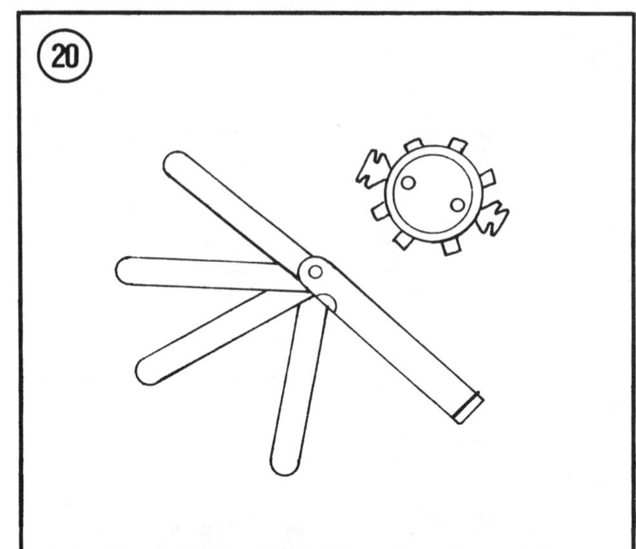
20

TEST EQUIPMENT

Voltmeter, Ammeter and Ohmmeter

A good voltmeter is required for testing ignition and other electrical systems. Voltmeters are available with analog meter scales or digital readouts. The digital readout voltmeter is recommended for troubleshooting HEI breakerless ignition systems. An instrument covering 0-20 volts is satisfactory. It should also have a 0-2 volt scale for testing relays, or individual contacts where voltage drops are much smaller. Accuracy should be ± 1/2 volt.

An ohmmeter measures electrical resistance. This instrument is useful in checking continuity (for open and short circuits) and testing fuses and lights. A self-powered 12-volt test light can often be used in its place.

The ammeter measures electrical current. Ammeters for automotive use should have scales covering 0-50 amperes and 0-250 amperes. These are useful for checking battery starting and charging currents.

Some manufacturers combine the 3 instruments into one unit called a multimeter or VOM. See **Figure 21**.

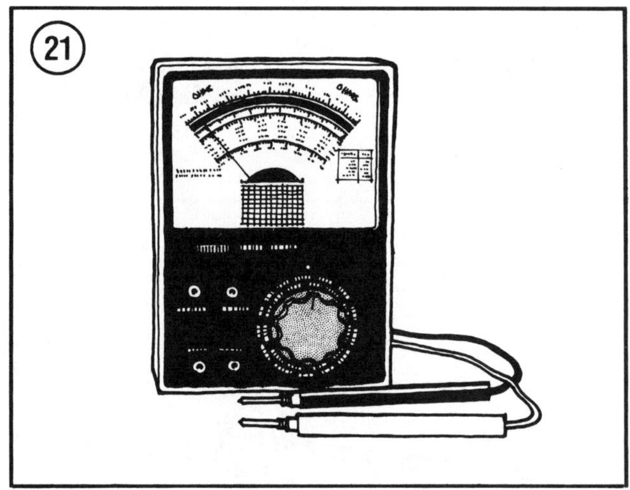
21

Strobe Timing Light

This instrument is necessary for checking ignition timing. By flashing a light at the precise instant the spark plug fires, the position of the timing mark can be seen. The flashing light makes a moving mark appear to stand still opposite a stationary mark.

Suitable lights range from inexpensive neon bulb types to powerful xenon strobe lights. See **Figure 22**. A light with an inductive pickup is recommended to eliminate any possible damage to ignition wiring.

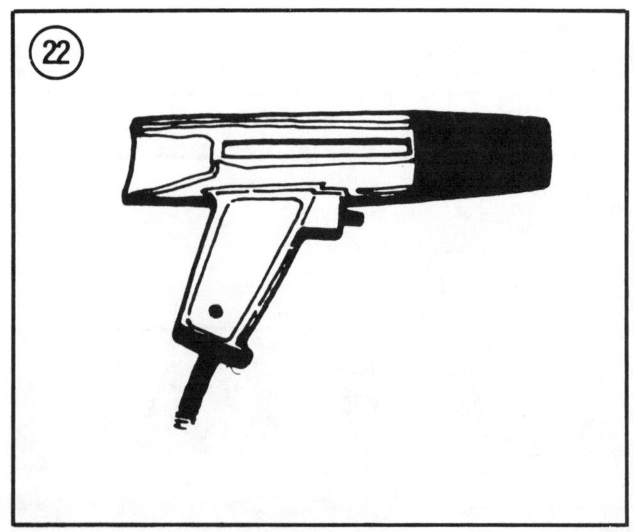
22

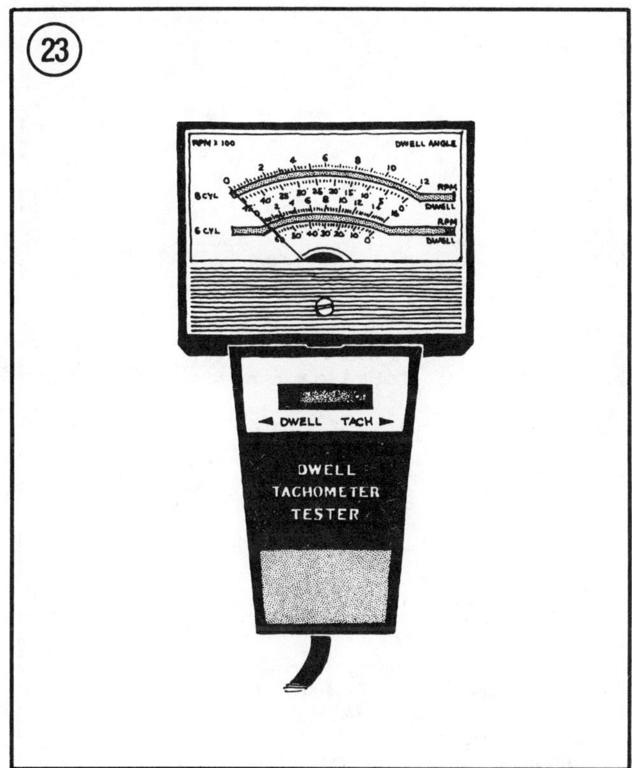

23

Tachometer/Dwell Meter

Dwell meters are often combined with a tachometer (**Figure 23**), another piece of necessary test equipment. The dwell meter is not necessary for the engines equipped with an HEI breakerless ignition. Dwell is determined by a solid state ignition module and cannot be changed.

The tachometer is useful when setting ignition timing and adjusting the carburetor, both of which must be performed at a specified idle speed. The best instrument for this purpose is one with a low range of 0-1,000 or 0-2,000 rpm and a high range of 0-4,000 rpm. Extended range (0-6,000 or 0-8,000 rpm) instruments lack accuracy at lower speeds. The instrument used should be capable of detecting changes of 25 rpm on the low range.

Compression Gauge

This tool measures the amount of pressure present in the engine's combustion chamber during the compression stroke. This indicates general engine condition. Compression readings can be interpreted along with vacuum gauge readings to pinpoint specific engine mechanical problems.

The easiest type to use has screw-in adaptors that fit into the spark plug holes (**Figure 24**). Press-in rubber-tipped types (**Figure 25**) are also available.

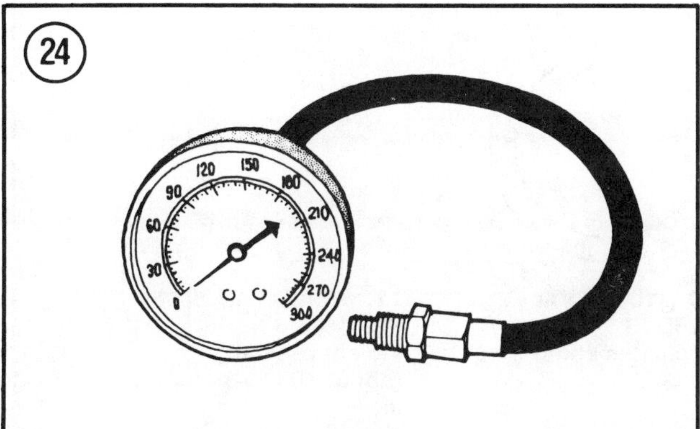

24

Vacuum Gauge

The vacuum gauge (**Figure 26**) measures the intake manifold vacuum created by the engine's intake stroke. Manifold and valve problems can be identified by interpreting the readings; when combined with compression gauge readings, other engine problems can be diagnosed.

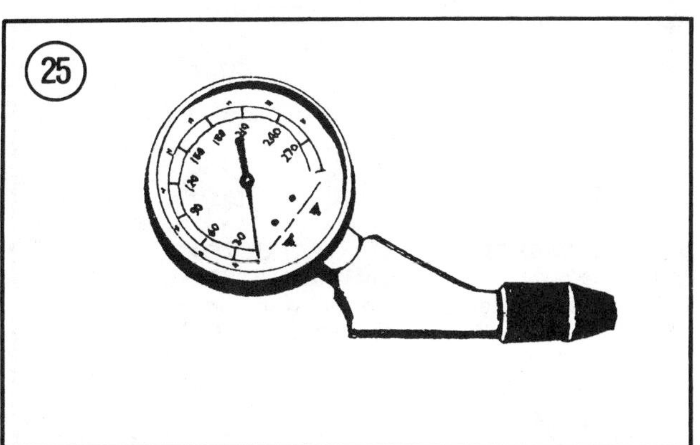

25

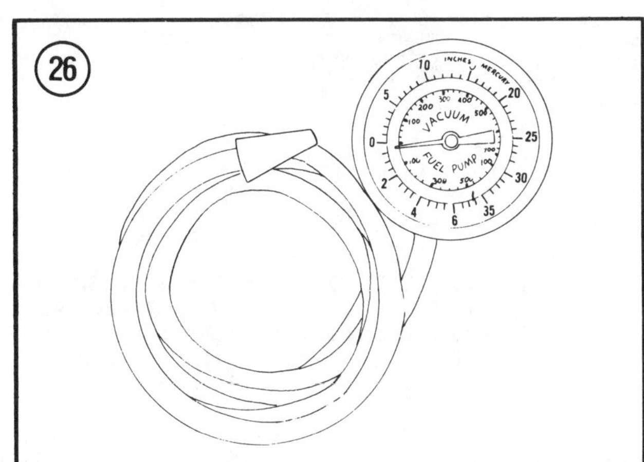

26

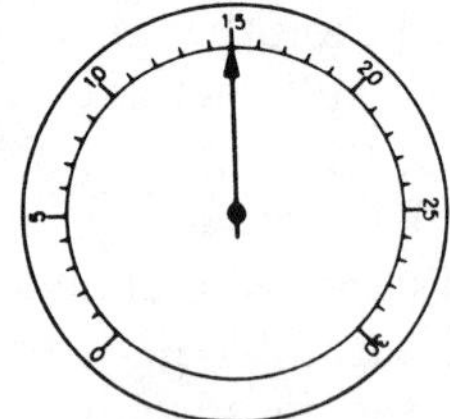

1. NORMAL READING.
Reads 15 in. at idle.

2. LATE IGNITION TIMING
About 2 inches too low at idle.

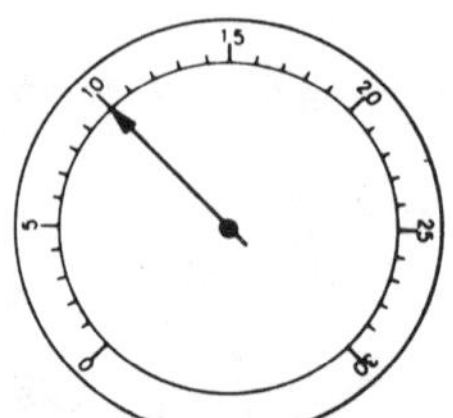

3. LATE VALVE TIMING
About 4 to 8 inches low at idle.

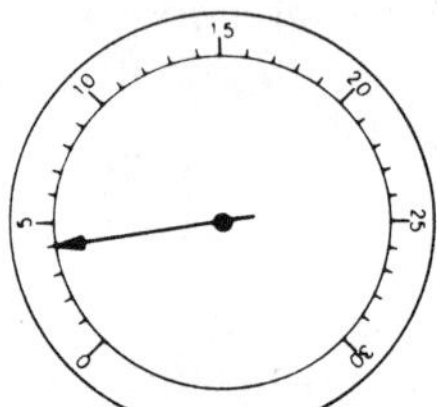

4. INTAKE LEAK
Low steady reading.

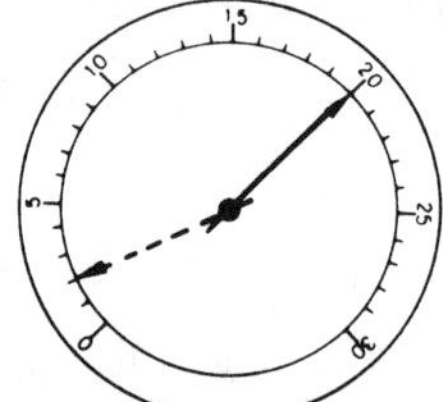

5. NORMAL READING
Drops to 2, then rises to 25 when accelerator is rapidly depressed and released.

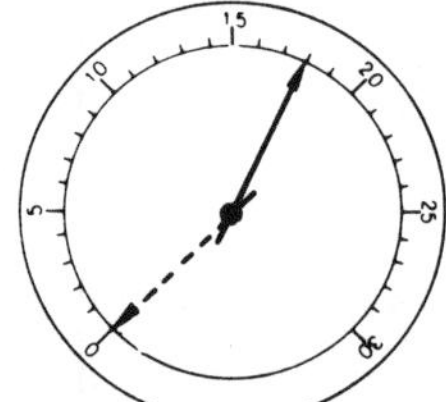

6. WORN RINGS, DILUTED OIL
Drops to 0, then rises to 18 when accelerator is rapidly depressed and released.

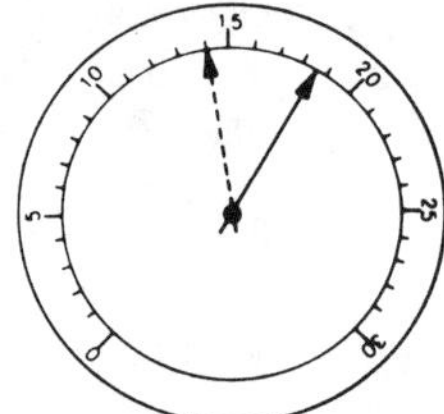

7. STICKING VALVE(S)
Normally steady. Intermittently flicks downward about 4 in.

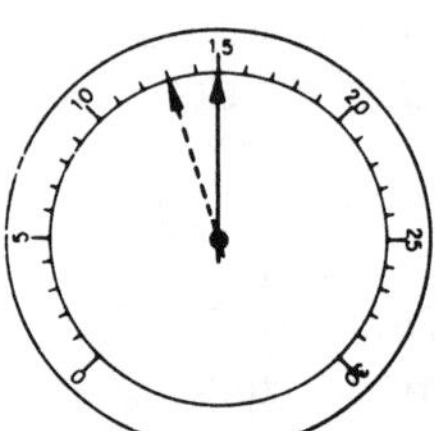

8. LEAKY VALVE
Regular drop about 2 inches.

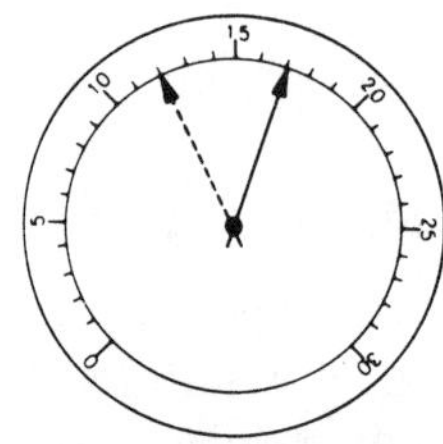

9. BURNED OR WARPED VALVE
Regular, evenly spaced down-scale flick about 4 in.

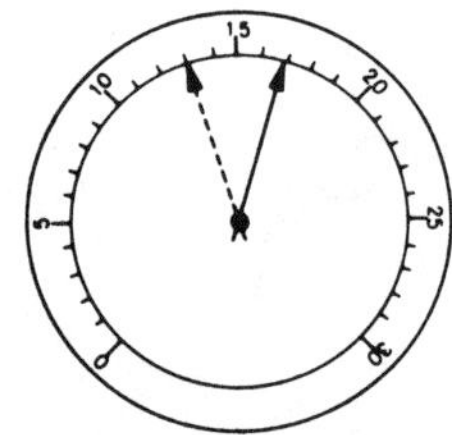

10. WORN VALVE GUIDES
Oscillates about 4 in.

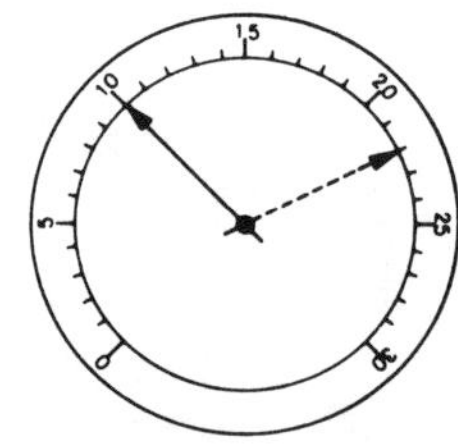

11. WEAK VALVE SPRINGS
Violent oscillation (about 10 in.) as rpm increases. Often steady at idle.

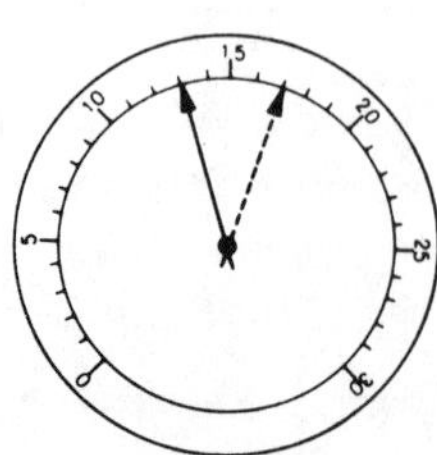

12. IMPROPER IDLE MIXTURE
Floats slowly between 13-17 in.

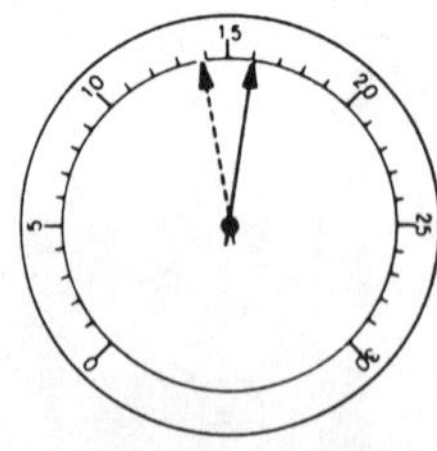

13. SMALL SPARK GAP or DEFECTIVE POINTS
Slight float between 14-16 in.

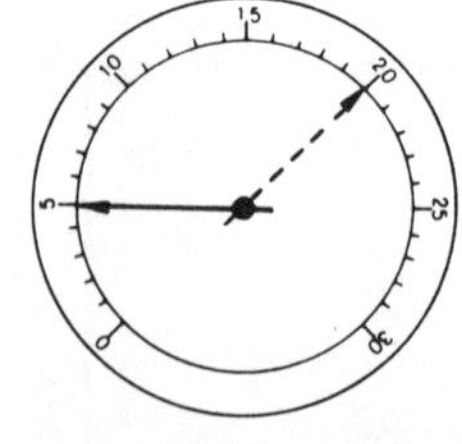

14. HEAD GASKET LEAK
Gauge floats between 5-19 in.

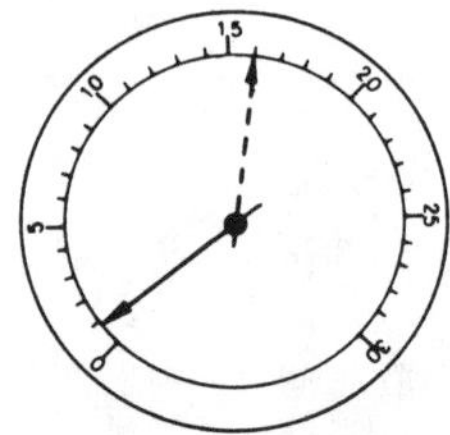

15. RESTRICTED EXHAUST SYSTEM
Normal when first started. Drops to 0 as rpm increases. May eventually rise to about 16.

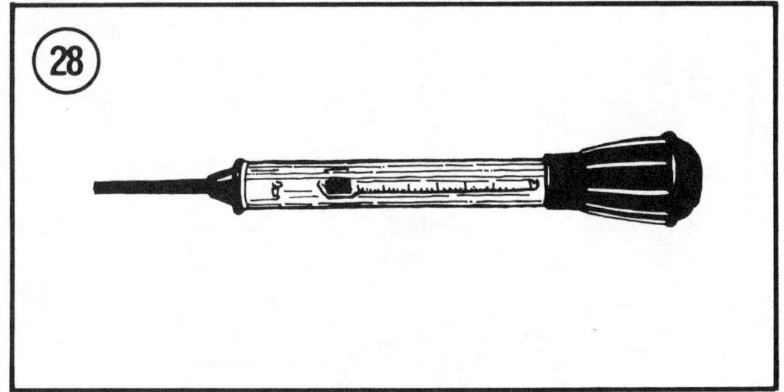

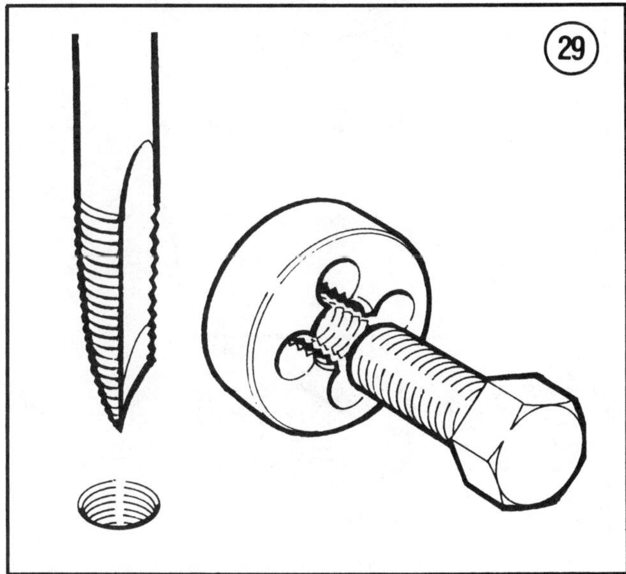

Figure 27 shows a number of typical vacuum gauge readings with interpretations.

Fuel Pressure Gauge

This instrument is needed for evaluating fuel pump performance. Usually, a vacuum gauge and a fuel pressure gauge are combined in one unit.

Hydrometer

Hydrometer testing is the best way to check the condition of unsealed batteries. The most efficient type is a temperature-compensated hydrometer with numbered gradations (**Figure 28**) from 1.100 to 1.300 rather than one with color-coded bands.

Remote Start Switch

An optional but convenient item of equipment, the remote starter switch connects to the starter relay and permits cranking the engine from outside the car. It eliminates the need for an assistant during certain procedures, such as checking compression.

Expendable Supplies

Certain expendable supplies are also required to correctly service your vehicle. These include greases, oil, gasket cement, shop rags, cleaning solvent and distilled water. Special fastener locking compounds and silicone lubricants are available from dealers or auto parts specialists to make maintenance simpler and easier. Solvent is available at auto parts stores and distilled water for the battery is available at most supermarkets.

MECHANIC'S TECHNIQUES

Removing Frozen Fasteners

When a fastener rusts and cannot be removed, several methods may be used to loosen it. First, apply penetrating oil such as Liquid Wrench or WD-40 (available at any hardware or auto supply store). Apply it liberally and let it penetrate for 10-15 minutes. Rap the fastener several times with a small hammer; do not hit it hard enough to cause damage. Reapply the penetrating oil if necessary.

For frozen screws, apply penetrating oil as described, then insert a screwdriver in the slot and rap the top of the screwdriver with a hammer. This loosens the rust so the screw can be removed in the normal way. If the screw head is too chewed up to use a screwdriver, grip the head with Vise Grip pliers and twist the screw out.

Avoid applying heat unless specifically instructed, as it may melt, warp or remove the temper from parts.

Remedying Stripped Threads

Occasionally, threads are stripped through carelessness or impact damage. Often the threads can be cleaned up by running a tap (for internal threads on nuts) or die (for external threads on bolts) through threads. See **Figure 29**.

Removing Broken Screws or Bolts

When the head breaks off a screw or bolt, several methods are available for removing the remaining portion.

If a large portion of the remainder projects out, try gripping it with Vise Grips. If the projecting portion is too small, file it to fit a wrench or cut a slot in it to fit a screwdriver. See **Figure 30**.

If the head breaks off flush, use a screw extractor. To do this, centerpunch the remaining portion of the screw or bolt. Drill a small hole in the screw and tap the extractor into the hole. Back the screw out with a wrench on the extractor. See **Figure 31**.

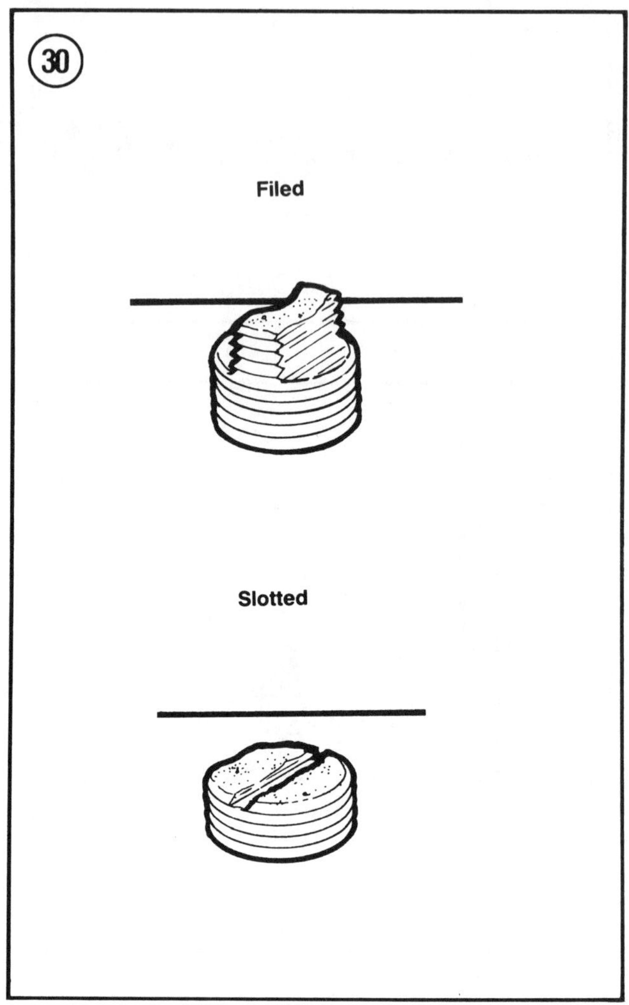

GASKET SEALANT

Gasket sealant is used instead of pre-formed gaskets between various engine, transmission, transfer case and axles mating surfaces. Two types of gasket sealant are used: room temperature vulcanizing (RTV) and anaerobic. Since these 2 materials have different sealing properties, they cannot be used interchangeably.

Room Temperature Vulcanizing (RTV) Sealant

This black silicone gel is supplied in tubes and is available from your GM dealer (part No. 1052366). Moisture in the air causes RTV to cure. Always place the cap on the tube as soon as possible when using RTV. RTV has a shelf life of one year and will not cure properly when the shelf life has expired. Check the expiration date on RTV tubes before using and keep partially used tubes tightly sealed.

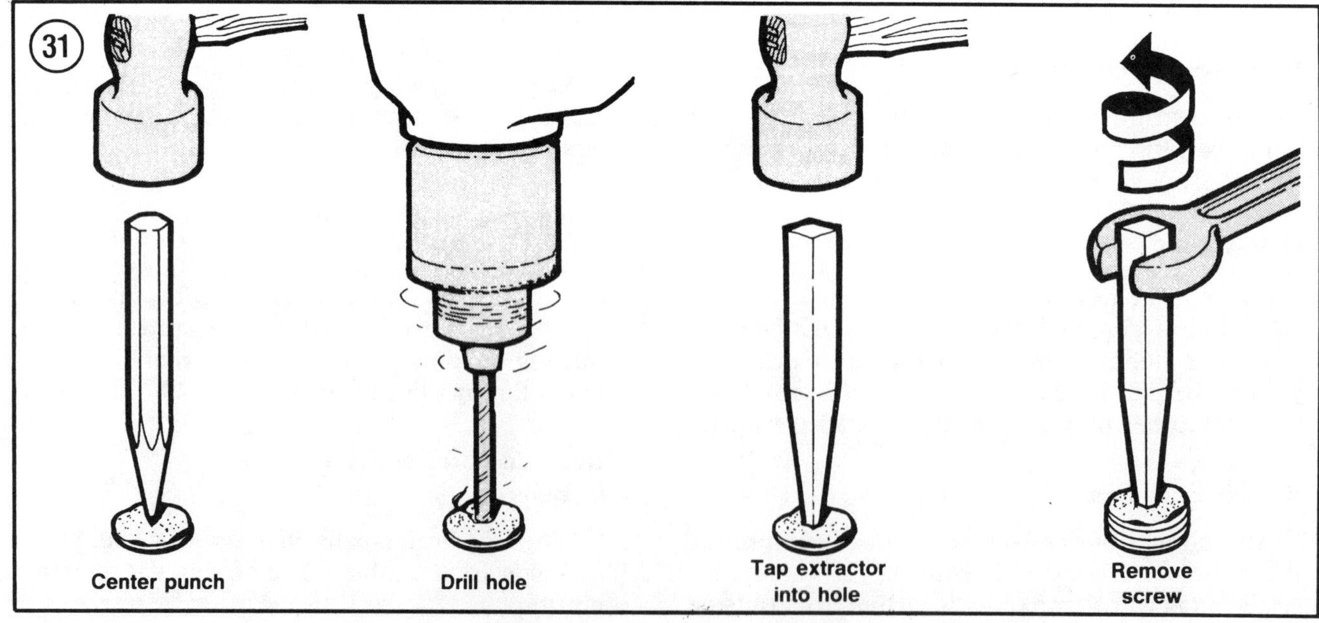

Applying RTV sealant

Clean all RTV residue from mating surfaces. They should be clean and free of oil and dirt. Remove all RTV gasket material from blind attaching holes, as it can cause a hydraulic effect and affect bolt torque.

Unless otherwise specified, apply RTV sealant in a continuous bead 3-5 mm (1/8-3/16 in.) thick. Apply the sealant on the inner side of mounting holes. Torque mating parts within 15 minutes after application.

Anaerobic Sealant

This is a red gel supplied in tubes and is available from your GM dealer. It cures only in the absence of air, as when squeezed tightly between 2 machined mating surfaces. For this reason, it will not spoil if the cap is left off the tube. It should not be used if one mating surface is flexible.

Applying Anaerobic Sealant

Clean all gasket residue from mating surfaces. They must be clean and free of oil and dirt. Remove all gasket material from blind attaching holes, as it can cause a hydraulic effect and affect bolt torque.

Unless otherwise specified, apply anaerobic gasket material in a 1 mm or less (0.04 in.) bead to one sealing surface. Apply the sealant on the inner side of all mounting holes. Torque mating parts within 15 minutes after application.

Table 1 DECIMAL AND METRIC EQUIVALENTS

Fractions	Decimal in.	Metric mm	Fractions	Decimal in.	Metric mm
1/64	0.015625	0.39688	33/64	0.515625	13.09687
1/32	0.03125	0.79375	17/32	0.53125	13.49375
3/64	0.046875	1.19062	35/64	0.546875	13.89062
1/16	0.0625	1.58750	9/16	0.5625	14.28750
5/64	0.078125	1.98437	37/64	0.578125	14.68437
3/32	0.09375	2.38125	19/32	0.59375	15.08125
7/64	0.109375	2.77812	39/64	0.609375	15.47812
1/8	0.125	3.1750	5/8	0.625	15.87500
9/64	0.140625	3.57187	41/64	0.640625	16.27187
5/32	0.15625	3.96875	21/32	0.65625	16.66875
11/64	0.171875	4.36562	43/64	0.671875	17.06562
3/16	0.1875	4.76250	11/16	0.6875	17.46250
13/64	0.203125	5.15937	45/64	0.703125	17.85937
7/32	0.21875	5.55625	23/32	0.71875	18.25625
15/64	0.234375	5.95312	47/64	0.734375	18.65312
1/4	0.250	6.35000	3/4	0.750	19.05000
17/64	0.265625	6.74687	49/64	0.765625	19.44687
9/32	0.28125	7.14375	25/32	0.78125	19.84375
19/64	0.296875	7.54062	51/64	0.796875	20.24062
5/16	0.3125	7.93750	13/16	0.8125	20.63750
21/64	0.328125	8.33437	53/64	0.828125	21.03437
11/32	0.34375	8.73125	27/32	0.84375	21.43125
23/64	0.359375	9.12812	55/64	0.859375	21.82812
3/8	0.375	9.52500	7/8	0.875	22.22500
25/64	0.390625	9.92187	57/64	0.890625	22.62187
13/32	0.40625	10.31875	29/32	0.90625	23.01875
27/64	0.421875	10.71562	59/64	0.921875	23.41562
7/16	0.4375	11.11250	15/16	0.9375	23.81250
29/64	0.453125	11.50937	61/64	0.953125	24.20937
15/32	0.46875	11.90625	31/32	0.96875	24.60625
31/64	0.484375	12.30312	63/64	0.984375	25.00312
1/2	0.500	12.70000	1	1.00	25.40000

CHAPTER TWO

TROUBLESHOOTING

Every automotive engine requires an uninterrupted supply of fuel and air, proper ignition and adequate compression. If any of these are lacking, the engine will not run.

Troubleshooting is a relatively simple matter when it is done logically. The first step in any troubleshooting procedure is to define the symptoms as fully as possible and then localize the problem. Subsequent steps involve testing and analyzing those areas which could cause the symptoms. A haphazard approach may eventually solve the problem, but it can be very costly in terms of wasted time and unnecessary parts replacement.

There are two axioms to remember about troubleshooting:

a. The source of the problem is seldom where you think it is.
b. When all else fails, go back to basics—simple solutions often solve complex-appearing problems.

Never assume anything. Don't overlook the obvious. If the engine suddenly quits when running or refuses to start, check the easiest and most accessible spots first. Make sure there is fuel in the tank, the spark plugs or glow plugs are properly connected and all wiring harnesses are properly connected. Something as simple as a loose terminal connection on the ignition coil can allow the primary wire to come off while driving, especially if the vehicle has been subjected to harsh or off-road driving. It is costly and embarrassing to call a tow truck in such a case.

You should be familiar enough with the engine compartment to know which wires go where. If a quick visual check of the obvious does not turn up the cause of the problem, look a little further. Learning to recognize and describe symptoms accurately will make repairs easier for you or a mechanic at the shop. Saying that "it won't run" isn't the same as saying "it quit at high speed and wouldn't start."

Gather as many symptoms together as possible to aid in diagnosis. Note whether the engine lost power gradually or all at once, what color smoke (if any) came from the exhaust and so on. Remember, the more complicated engine systems become, the easier it is to troubleshoot them because symptoms point to specific problems.

After the symptoms are defined, test and analyze those areas which could cause the problem(s). You don't need fancy or complicated test equipment to

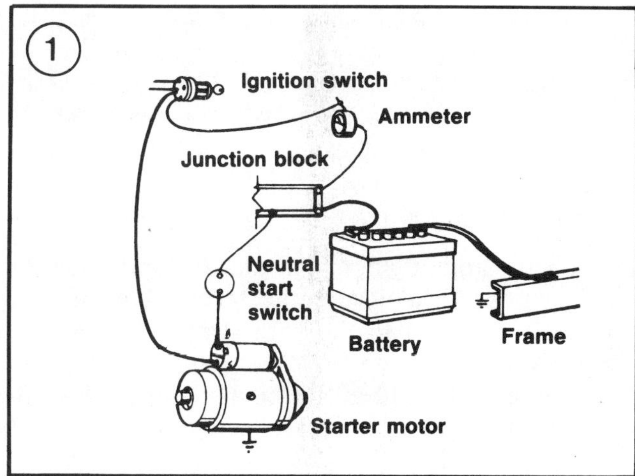

determine whether repairs can be attempted at home.

The electrical system is the weakest link in the chain. More problems result from electrical malfunctions than from any other source. Keep this in mind before you blame the fuel system and start making unnecessary carburetor adjustments. A few simple checks can keep a small problem from turning into a large one. They can also save a large repair bill and time lost while the vehicle sits in a shop's service department.

On the other hand, be realistic and don't attempt repairs beyond your abilities or with makeshift tools. Stripping the threads on a carburetor inlet while trying to change the fuel filter will cost you several hundred dollars for a new carburetor. Service departments also tend to charge heavily for putting together a disassembled engine or other component that may have been abused. Some won't even take on such a job—so use common sense and don't get in over your head or attempt a job without the proper tools.

Due to strict emission requirements, the vehicles covered in this manual are equipped with electronic engine control systems. A microprocessor determines idle speed, air-fuel ratio, EGR flow and many other aspects of engine operation. Amateur mechanics should not attempt to diagnose and service such systems. They require the use of special diagnostic testers and specialized training. System calibration differs according to engine, model year and geographical location in which the vehicle is sold. If you can localize the symptoms sufficiently to indicate that the electronic engine control system is at fault, leave the servicing of the system to your dealer.

Proper lubrication, maintenance and periodic tune-ups as described in Chapter Three will reduce the necessity for troubleshooting. Even with the best of care, however, an automotive engine is prone to problems which will eventually require troubleshooting.

This chapter contains brief descriptions of each operating system and troubleshooting procedures to be used. The troubleshooting procedures analyze common symptoms and provide logical methods of isolation. These are not the only methods. There may be several approaches to a problem, but all methods used must have one thing in common to be successful—a logical, systematic approach.

STARTING SYSTEM

The starting system consists of the battery, starter motor, starter solenoid, ignition switch, neutral start switch (automatic transmission) and connecting wiring. Some vehicles equipped with a manual transmission also have a neutral safety switch which requires that the transmission be placed in NEUTRAL before the starting circuit will operate. A Delco Remy direct drive starter with attached solenoid is used on all models. Vehicles equipped with the 2.2L diesel engine use a gear reduction starter with attached solenoid.

When the ignition switch is turned to START (automatic transmission in PARK or NEUTRAL, manual transmission in NEUTRAL), it transmits current from the battery to the starter solenoid which mechanically engages the starter with the engine flywheel. **Figure 1** is a schematic of the starter system.

Starting system problems are relatively easy to find. In most cases, the trouble is a loose or dirty electrical connection.

On-car Testing

Two of these procedures require a fully charged 12-volt battery to be used as a booster and a pair of jumper cables. Use the jumper cables as outlined in *Jump Starting*, Chapter Eight, following all of the precautions noted.

Engine cranks very slowly or not at all

1. Turn on the headlights. If the lights are very dim, the battery or connecting wires are most likely at fault. Check unsealed batteries with a

hydrometer. Check wiring for breaks, shorts and dirty connections. If the battery and wires are satisfactory, turn the headlights on and crank the engine. If the lights dim drastically, the starter is probably shorted to ground.

2. If the lights remain bright or dim only slightly when cranking, the trouble may be in the starter, starter solenoid, or wiring. If the starter spins, check the solenoid and wiring to the ignition switch.

3. Note whether the solenoid plunger is pulled into the solenoid when the starter circuit is closed (it should make a loud click).

   a. If the plunger is pulled in, the trouble is in the solenoid switch, starter motor or starter motor circuit. Remove the starter motor for repairs to either motor or switch.

   b. If the plunger is not pulled in, connect a jumper lead between the solenoid battery terminal and the terminal on the solenoid switch to which the purple lead wire is attached. If the starter now works, the solenoid is good. The problem is in the neutral start switch, ignition switch or in the wires or connections between the switches.

4. If the starter still will not crank properly, refer the problem to a dealer or automotive electrical specialist.

CLYMER QUICK TIP

Problem: After a trip of several hours duration on the freeway in hot weather, you pull into a service station for gas. When you're ready to leave, the starter will not turn the engine over. Your first thought is that the battery is dead.

Solution: Don't buy a new battery on the spot, even if the price is right. Engine heat has increased the resistance in the solenoid enough to prevent it from "kicking in" until it cools. To overcome this, many drivers have installed a Motorcraft relay in the starting circuit to bypass the ignition and neutral start switches, sending battery voltage directly to the starter solenoid. By eliminating the voltage drop across the switches, they hope the slightly higher voltage will overcome the higher solenoid resistance. This solution may prove satisfactory in borderline cases.

A more satisfactory method of eliminating (or preventing) this problem is to replace the spring in the starter solenoid with a weaker one (part No. 1978281). This reduces the amount of effort required to activate the starter drive mechanism. Once this is done, fabricate an aluminum heat shield to fit between the exhaust manifold or headers and the starter motor. This reduces the amount of heat that will affect the starter motor.

Starter solenoid clicks, starter does not crank

1. Clean and tighten all starter and solenoid connections. Make sure the terminal eyelets are securely fastened to the wire strands and are not corroded.

2. Remove the battery terminal clamps. Clean the clamps and battery posts. Reinstall the clamps and tighten securely.

3. If the starter does not crank, connect the 12-volt booster battery to the vehicle's battery with the jumper cables. If the starter still does not crank, replace it.

Starter solenoid chatters (no click), starter does not crank

1. Check the purple wire connection at the starter solenoid. Clean and tighten if necessary.

2. Place the transmission in PARK (automatic) or NEUTRAL (manual).

3. Disconnect the purple wire at the starter solenoid. Connect a jumper wire between this solenoid connector and the positive battery terminal.

4. Connect the 12-volt booster battery to the vehicle's battery with the jumper cables. Try starting the engine.

5. If the engine starts, check the ignition switch, neutral start switch or the system wiring for an open circuit or a loose connection. If the engine does not start, replace the starter solenoid.

Starter spins but does not crank

1. Remove the starter. See Chapter Eight.

2. Check the starter pinion gear. If the teeth are chipped or worn, inspect the flywheel ring gear for the same problem. Replace the starter and/or ring gear as required.

3. If the pinion gear is in good condition, disassemble the starter and check the armature shaft for corrosion. See *Brush Replacement*, in Chapter Eight for disassembly procedure.

4. If there is no corrosion, the starter drive assembly is slipping. Replace the starter with a new or rebuilt unit.

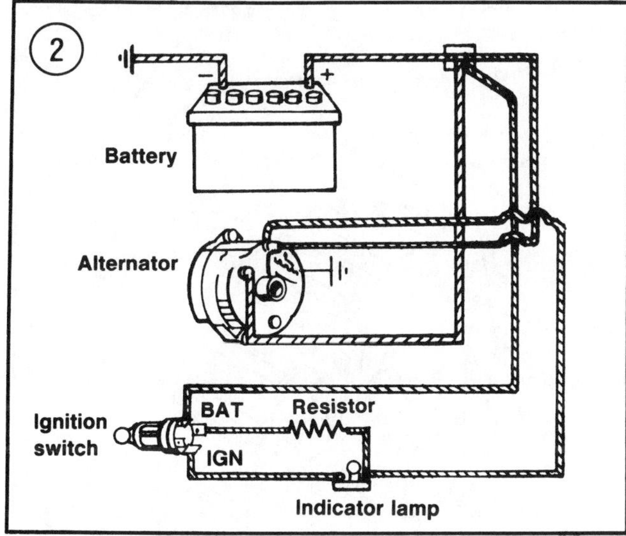

Starter will not disengage when ignition switch is released

This problem is usually caused by a sticking solenoid but the pinion may jam on the flywheel ring gear of high-mileage vehicles. If equipped with a manual transmission, the pinion can often be temporarily freed by rocking the vehicle in high gear.

Loud grinding noises when starter runs

This can be caused by improper meshing of the starter pinion and flywheel ring gear or by a broken overrunning clutch mechanism.

1. Remove the starter. See Chapter Eight.
2. Check the starter pinion gear. If the teeth are chipped or worn, inspect the flywheel ring gear for the same problem. Replace the starter and/or ring gear as required.
3. If the pinion gear is in good condition, disassemble the starter and check the overrunning clutch mechanism. See *Brush Replacement*, Chapter Eight for disassembly procedure.

CLYMER QUICK TIP

Problem: The engine starts fine when cold and restarts easily when used for short distance driving. After a drive of several miles duration, however, the starter will not crank and restart the hot engine. After the engine cools for 1-3 hours (depending upon ambient temperature), the starter works normally. An open-circuit test and hydrometer check of the battery indicates that it is in satisfactory condition.

Solution: Disregard helpful hints about resetting the ignition timing or mechanics who tell you that this is typical of GM vehicles. The key here is your battery, especially if it has been replaced recently. Check the cold cranking amperage rating of the battery installed in the vehicle and compare it to specifications. If a replacement battery has been installed, the odds are high that while the battery has sufficient power for a cold start, it is insufficient to cope with the high internal resistance in the starter and reduced engine operating tolerances which result from engine operation, especially in extremely warm weather.

Many drivers buy a replacement battery according to the length of the guarantee and their pocketbook. While a 12-month battery seems satisfactory (and the price is right), it does not have the power and stamina to handle the starting requirements of your engine.

CHARGING SYSTEM

The charging system consists of the alternator, voltage regulator, battery, ignition switch, ammeter or charge indicator light, fusible link and connecting wiring.

A drive belt driven by the engine crankshaft pulley turns the alternator, which produces electrical energy to charge the battery. As engine speed varies, the voltage output of the alternator varies. The regulator maintains the voltage to the electrical system within safe limits. The ammeter or charge indicator light signals when charging is not taking place.

All models use a 10-SI, 12-SI, 15-SI or 27-SI Delcotron alternator with an internal solid-state regulator. The output rating is stamped on the alternator frame. **Figure 2** shows a typical charging circuit.

Complete troubleshooting of the charging system requires test equipment and skills which the average home mechanic does not possess. However, there are basic tests which can be done to pinpoint most problems.

Charging system troubles are generally caused by a defective alternator, voltage regulator, battery or a blown fuse. They may also be caused by something as simple as incorrect drive belt tension.

The following are symptoms of problems you may encounter.

1. *Battery dies frequently, even though the ammeter indicates no discharge*—This can be caused by a

drive belt that is slightly loose. Grasp the alternator pulley with both hands and try to turn it. If the pulley can be turned without moving the belt, the drive belt is too loose. As a rule, keep the belt tight enough so that it can be deflected only about 1/2 in. under moderate thumb pressure applied between the pulleys. The battery may also be at fault; test the battery condition as described in Chapter Eight.

2. *Ammeter needle does not move or indicator light does not come on when ignition switch is turned ON*—This may indicate a defective ignition switch, battery, voltage regulator or ammeter/indicator light. Try to start the engine. If it doesn't start, check the ignition switch and battery.
   a. If equipped with an ammeter and the engine starts, remove and test the ammeter.
   b. If equipped with an indicator light and the engine starts, check for a blown bulb.
   c. If the problem persists, the alternator brushes may not be making contact.

3. *Ammeter needle fluctuates between "Charge" and "Discharge" or charge indicator lamp comes on and off*—This usually indicates that the charging system is working intermittently. Check drive belt tension first, then check all electrical connections in the charging circuit. As a last resort, check the alternator.

4. *Unsealed battery requires frequent addition of water or lamps require frequent replacement*—The alternator is probably overcharging the battery.

5. *Excessive noise from the alternator*—Check for loose mounting brackets and bolts. The problem may also be worn bearings or (in some cases) lack of lubrication. If an alternator whines, a shorted diode may be the problem.

CHARGING SYSTEM TROUBLESHOOTING

Charging System Test

A voltmeter with a 0-2-volt scale and an engine tachometer are required for an accurate charging system test.

1. Check the alternator drive belt tension. See Chapter Seven.
2. Check the battery terminals and cables for corrosion and/or loose connections. Clean and tighten as necessary.
3. Check all wiring connections between the alternator and engine.
4. Connect the positive voltmeter lead to the positive battery cable clamp. Connect the negative voltmeter lead to the negative battery cable clamp. Make sure the ignition and all accessories are off.
5. Record the voltage displayed on the voltmeter scale. This is the battery or base voltage.
6. Connect a tachometer to the engine according to manufacturer's instructions.
7. Start the engine and bring its speed up to about 1,500 rpm. The voltmeter reading should increase from that recorded in Step 5, but not by more than 2 volts.
8. If the voltage does not increase, perform the *Undercharge Test*. If the voltage increase is greater than 2 volts, remove the alternator and have it checked by a dealer or an automotive electrical shop for grounded or shorted field windings.

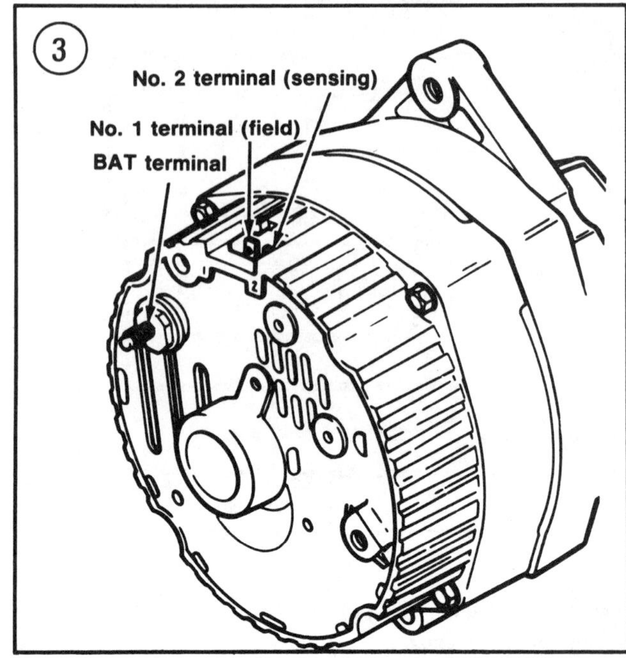

Undercharge Test

A voltmeter with a 0-20-volt scale, an ammeter and a carbon pile are require for this procedure. Refer to **Figure 3** for test points.

1. Turn the ignition switch ON. Make sure all electrical harness leads are properly connected.
2. Connect the negative voltmeter lead to a good engine ground. Connect the positive voltmeter lead in turn between ground and:
   a. BAT terminal.
   b. No. 1 terminal.
   c. No. 2 terminal.

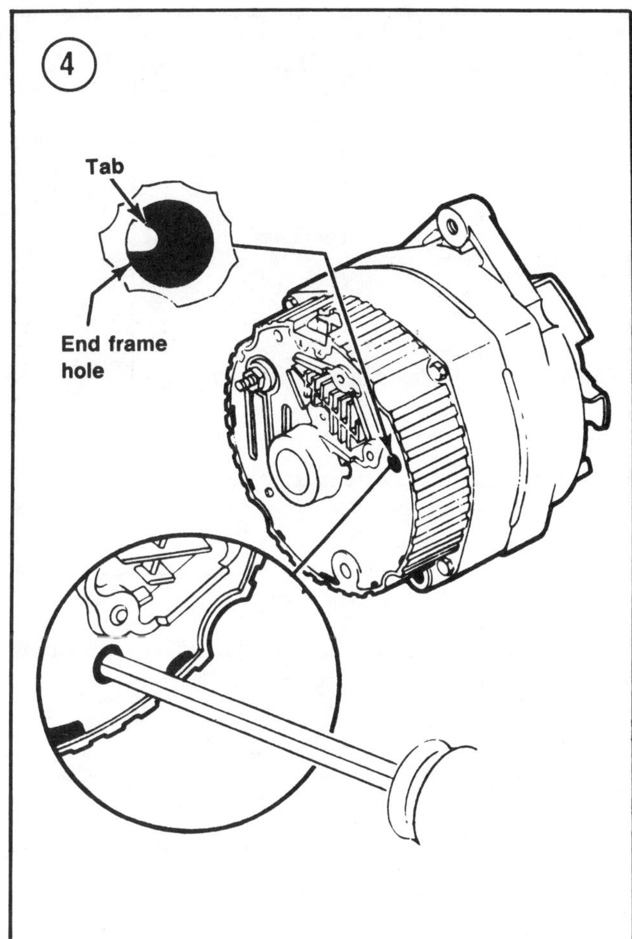

3. Read the voltmeter as each connection in Step 2 is made. A zero reading at any of the connections indicates an open circuit between the voltmeter connection and ground. Check the wiring if an open circuit is indicated.

CAUTION
An open in the No. 2 lead (sensing) circuit will cause uncontrolled voltage, battery overcharge and possible damage to the battery and accessories. Late-model alternators have a built-in feature to prevent these problems by not allowing the unit to turn on if there is an open in the No. 2 lead circuit. Such an open could occur between terminals, at the crimp between the harness wire or terminal, or in the wire itself.

4. Disconnect the voltmeter. Disconnect the negative battery cable.
5. Disconnect the alternator wiring connector at the BAT terminal. Connect an ammeter between the BAT terminal and the wiring connector.
6. Reconnect the negative battery cable. Turn on all accessories.
7. Connect a carbon pile across the battery posts.
8. Start the engine and run at approximately 2,000 rpm. Adjust the carbon pile to obtain the maximum current output.
9. If the ammeter reading is within 10 amps of the alternator's rated output, the unit is satisfactory.
10. If the ammeter reading is not within 10 amps of the rated output, locate the test hole in the end frame. If test hole is accessible, continue testing. If it is not accessible, remove the alternator and have it checked by your dealer or an automotive electrical shop.
11. Insert a thin screwdriver in the test hole to ground the tab inside to the end frame. See **Figure 4**. Since the tab is within 3/4 in. of the casting surface, the screwdriver should not be inserted into the end frame more than 1 inch.
12. Run the engine at approximately 2,000 rpm and adjust the carbon pile to obtain the maximum current output.
   a. If the output is now within 10 amps of the rated output, the problem is in the field winding, diode trio, rectifier bridge or regulator. Perform the *Regulator Test* in this chapter. If the regulator is good, remove the alternator and have it checked by your dealer or an automotive electrical shop.
   b. If the output is still not within 10 amps of the rated output, the problem is in the field winding, diode trio, rectifier bridge or stator. Remove the alternator and have it checked by your dealer or an automotive electrical shop.

Regulator Test

The solid-state voltage regulator can be tested on the vehicle. Connect a fast charger and voltmeter to the battery terminals, observing correct polarity. See **Figure 5**. Turn the ignition ON and slowly increase the charge rate. When the indicator lamp on the instrument panel starts to dim, read the voltmeter scale. The lamp should dim at a reading between 13.5-16 volts. If it dims at a voltage setting outside this range, the regulator is defective.

Charge Indicator Lamp

If the alternator and voltage regulator are operating satisfactorily and the charge indicator warning lamp remains on, the charge indicator relay located inside the voltage regulator may be defective. To determine the cause of the problem, perform the following procedure.

1. *Switch OFF, lamp on*—Disconnect the leads from the alternator No. 1 and No. 2 terminals. If the lamp remains on, there is a short circuit between the 2 leads. If the lamp goes out, the rectifier bridge is faulty and must be replaced, as this condition will result in an undercharged battery.
2. *Switch ON, lamp off, engine stopped*—This defect can be caused by the conditions listed in Step 1, by reversal of the No. 1 and No. 2 leads at these 2 terminals or by an open circuit. To determine where the open exists, proceed as follows:
   a. Connect a voltmeter between the No. 2 alternator terminal and ground. If a reading is obtained, proceed to the next step. If the reading is zero, repair the open circuit between the No. 2 alternator terminal and the battery. If the lamp comes on, no further check is required.

CAUTION
Do not ground the No. 2 lead or terminal in Step b.

   b. Disconnect the No. 1 and No. 2 terminal leads at the alternator. Turn the ignition switch ON and momentarily ground the No. 1 terminal.
   c. If the lamp does not come on, check for a blown fuse or fusible link, burned-out lamp bulb, defective lamp socket or an open in the No. 1 lead circuit between the alternator and ignition switch.
   d. If the lamp lights, remove the ground at the No. 1 terminal and reconnect the No. 1 and No. 2 wires to the alternator. Insert a screwdriver in the test hole (**Figure 4**) to ground the wiring.
   e. If the lamp does not go on, check the connection between the wiring harness and No. 1 alternator terminal. If the wiring is good, have the alternator brushes, slip rings and field winding checked.
   f. If the lamp lights, repeat the voltmeter check in the previous step. If a reading is now obtained, replace the regulator.
3. *Switch ON, lamp on, engine running*—Possible causes are improper drive belt tension, a defective or discharged battery, faulty wiring or an open circuit between the alternator and battery.

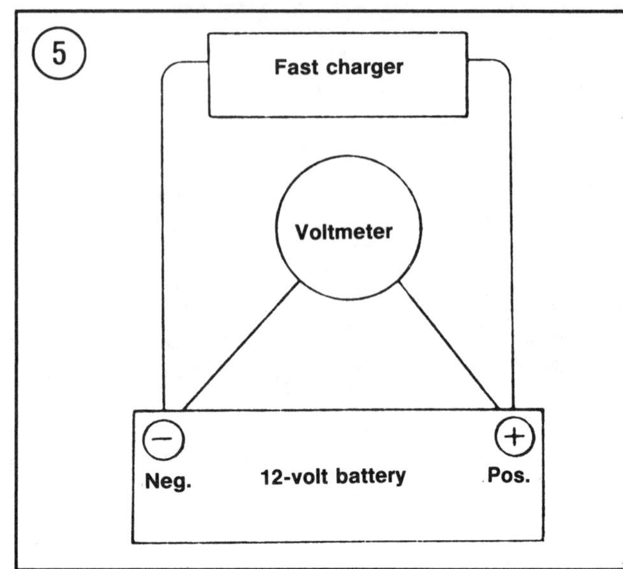

CLYMER QUICK TIP
Problem: The charging system seems to be working properly, but 1 or 2 cells of your unsealed battery require water quite frequently. A visual inspection of the battery and charging system turns up nothing and you suspect an overcharge condition.
Solution: Remove the battery from the engine compartment and check the case carefully for a crack before having the alternator tested. When only 1 or 2 cells are thirsty, the chances are good that the battery has been damaged from moving around in the battery case (especially if the vehicle has been used off-road) or from a battery hold-down that was tightened excessively.

IGNITION SYSTEM

All vehicles covered in this manual use a breakerless ignition. The 2.0L and V6 engines use the Delco High Energy Ignition (HEI). The 1.9L ignition system functions in essentially the same way, but the distributor components differ somewhat. See Chapter Eight.

Most problems involving a failure to start, poor driveability or rough running stem from trouble in the ignition system, particulary in breaker point systems. Many novice troubleshooters assume that these symptoms point to the fuel system instead of the ignition system (remember our axioms?).

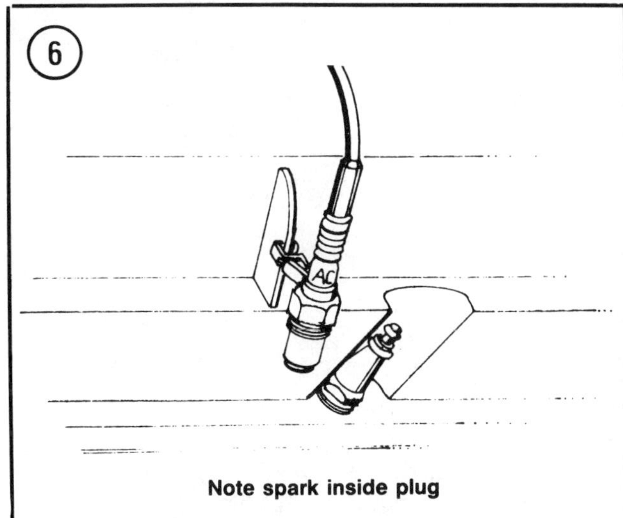

6 Note spark inside plug

Note the following driveability symptoms:

a. Engine misses.
b. Stumbles on acceleration (misfiring).
c. Loss of power at high speed (misfiring).
d. Hard starting (if at all).
e. Rough idle.

These symptoms may be caused by one of the following:

a. Spark plug.
b. Secondary wires.
c. Distributor cap and rotor.
d. Ignition coil.

Most of the symptoms can also be caused by a carburetor that is worn or improperly adjusted or a fuel pump that is about to fail. But considering the law of averages, the odds are far better that the source of the problem will be found in the ignition rather than the fuel system.

Ignition system troubles may be roughly divided between those affecting only one cylinder and those affecting all cylinders. If the problem affects only one cylinder, it can only be in the spark plug, secondary wiring or that part of the distributor associated with that cylinder. If the problem affects all cylinders (weak or no spark), then the trouble is in the ignition coil, rotor, distributor or associated wiring.

Breakerless Ignition Troubleshooting

The following basic tests are designed to quickly pinpoint and isolate problems in the primary circuit of the breakerless ignition.

1. If the engine cranks but will not start, connect a voltmeter between the BAT terminal lead on the distributor cap and a good engine ground. Turn the ignition switch ON. If the voltmeter reads zero, check the continuity of all wiring and terminal connections between the distributor and ignition switch. If the wiring and connections are good, replace the ignition switch.
2. If the meter reads battery voltage in Step 1, disconnect one spark plug lead and connect it to an AC Delco tester part No. ST-125 or equivalent. See **Figure 6**.
3. Disconnect the coil high tension lead at the distributor and connect it to a good engine ground with a jumper lead.
4. Connect a remote start switch according to manufacturer's instructions.
5. Crank the engine briefly and note the spark intensity:
   a. Strong spark—The spark plug or fuel system is at fault. Inspect the spark plug condition as described in Chapter Three.
   b. Weak or no spark—Repeat steps 2-5a with the remaining spark plug wires. A few sparks and then nothing is considered as no spark. Proceed to the component tests below.

Ignition Coil Test (1.9L Engine)

The 1.9L coil is bracket-mounted to the inner right-hand fender behind the battery. Refer to **Figure 7** for this procedure.

1. Disconnect the negative battery cable.
2. Disconnect the coil primary terminal connector.
3. Disconnect the secondary lead from the coil center tower.
4. Connect an ohmmeter between terminals B and A in the primary terminal connector as shown in **Figure 7**. If the meter reading is not 0.9-1.4 ohms, replace the coil.
5. Connect the ohmmeter between the primary terminal connector terminal A and the secondary tower as shown in **Figure 7**. If the reading is not 7,300-11,100 ohms, replace the coil.
6. Connect the ohmmeter between the primary terminal connector terminal B and the coil case as shown in **Figure 7** to check insulation resistance. If the meter does not read 10 megaohms without needle deflection, replace the coil. If the reading is within specifications but the needle wavers, the coil is poorly insulated and should be replaced.

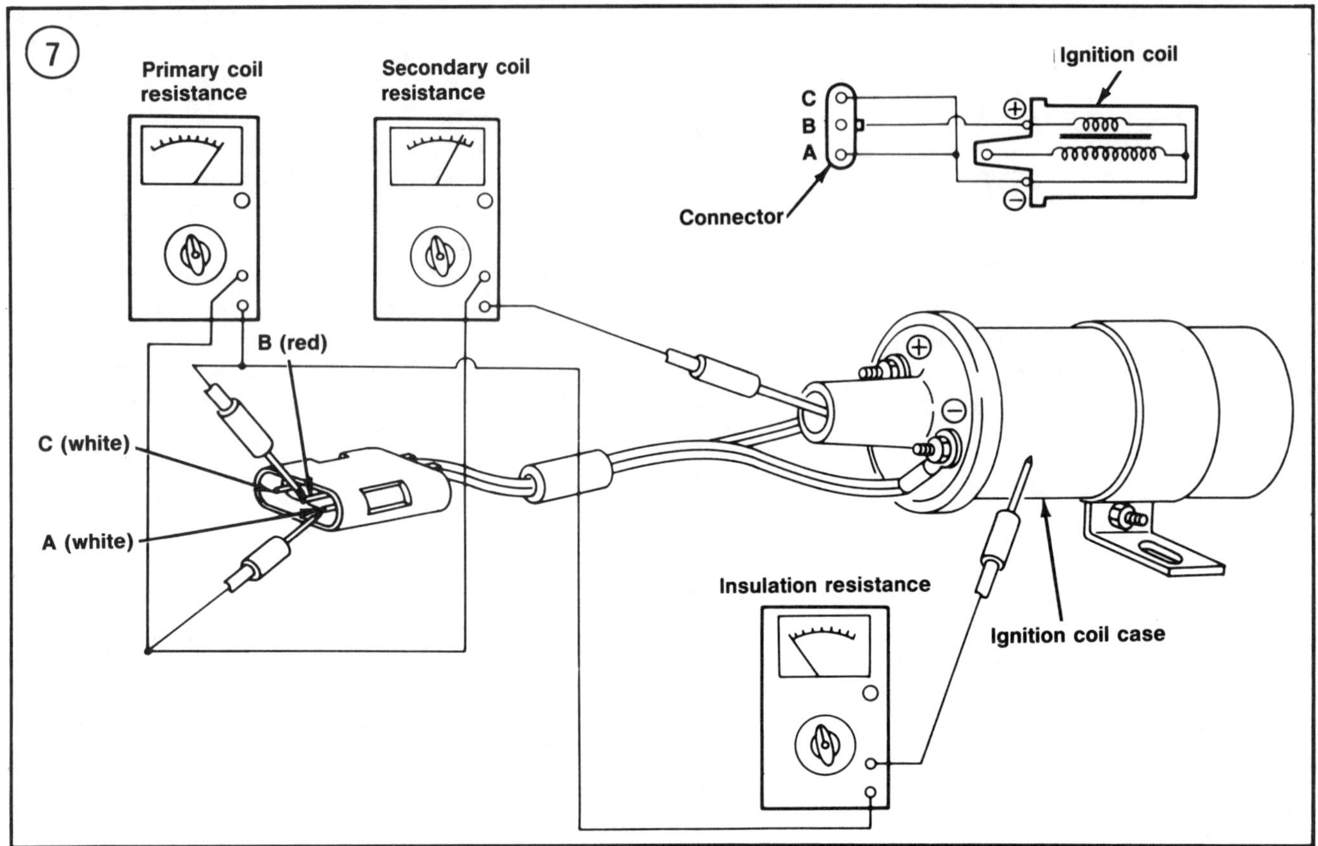

Ignition Coil Test (2.0L and V6 Engine)

The 2.0L coil is bracket-mounted under the intake manifold. The V6 coil is bracket-mounted on the right cylinder head.

1. Disconnect the distributor-to-coil connector, the battery feed connector and the coil-to-distributor high tension lead.
2. Set an ohmmeter on its low range scale and connect it between the No. 1 and No. 2 terminals on the coil. See **Figure 8**. If the meter does not read 0.3-1.0 ohm, replace the coil.
3. Set the ohmmeter on its high range scale and connect it between the No. 1 and No. 3 terminals. See **Figure 9**. If the meter does not read between 6,000-30,000 ohms, replace the coil.

Cranking Voltage Test

1. Connect the positive voltmeter lead to the coil primary No. 1 terminal and the negative lead to a good engine ground. See **Figure 10**.
2. Turn the ignition switch ON and note the voltmeter reading. If it reads less than battery

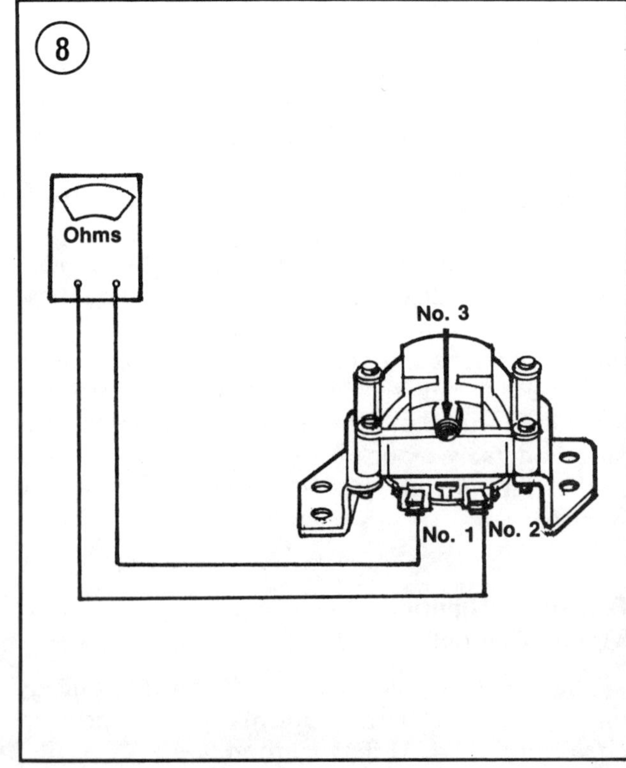

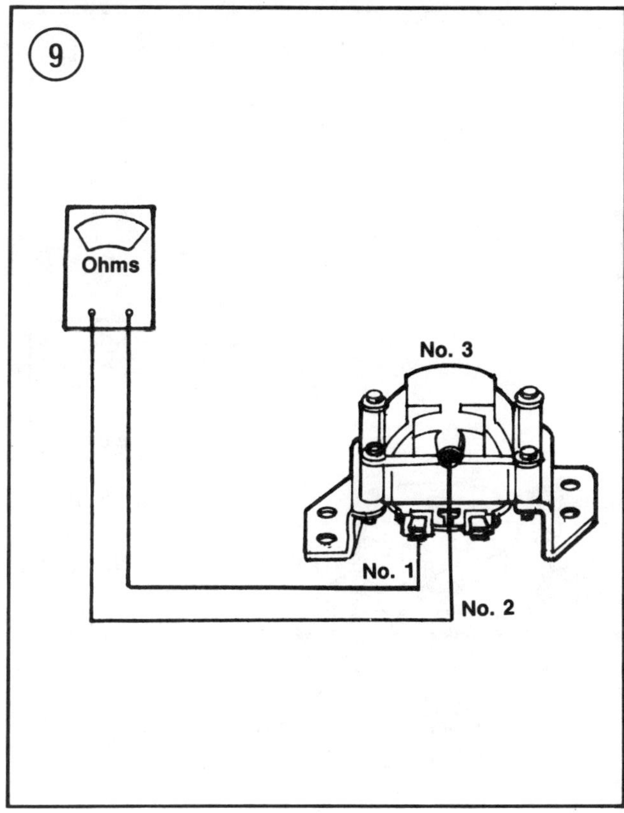

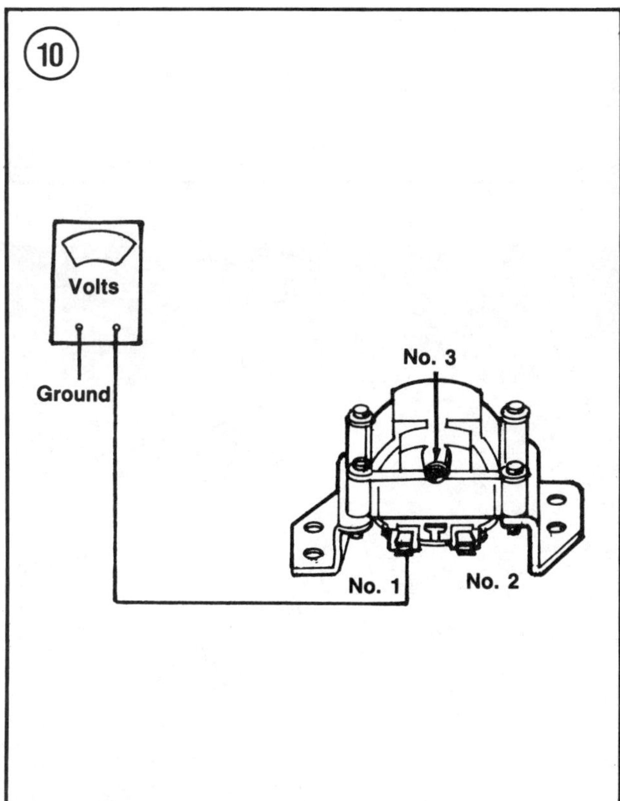

voltage, check the battery condition, battery cables, ignition switch and all wiring between the distributor and battery.

3. Disconnect the coil high tension lead at the distributor and connect it to a good engine ground with a jumper lead.

4. Connect a remote start switch according to manufacturer's instructions.

5. Crank the engine and note the voltmeter reading. If less than 9.6 volts, check the ignition switch and starter solenoid.

Pick-up Coil Test

1. Disconnect the distributor cap connector(s).

2. Depress and rotate the cap-to-distributor latches 90°, then remove the cap.

CAUTION

Pulling the leads from the module connectors in Step 3 can damage the wiring. On V6 distributors equipped with EST (see Chapter Eight), the wire colors may be different. If so, disconnect the 2-wire connector.

3. Disconnect the white and green pick-up coil leads from the module with needlenose pliers or a thin-blade screwdriver.

4. Set the ohmmeter at its mid-range position. Ground one lead and connect the other to one of the disconnected pick-up coil leads. See **Figure 11**. The meter should read infinity.

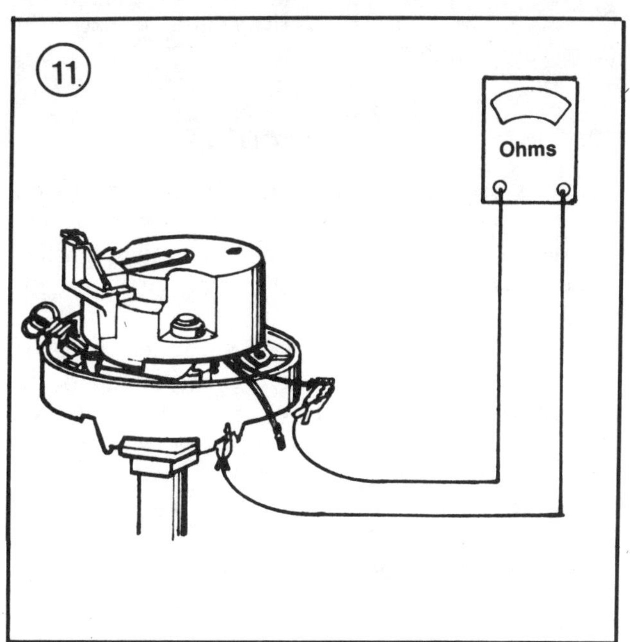

5. If the distributor is equipped with a vacuum advance mechanism, operate the linkage with a small screwdriver while watching the meter. The reading should not change when the vacuum advance is activated.
6. If distributor has no vacuum advance mechanism, flex the pick-up coil leads to check for an intermittent condition. The reading should not change while flexing the leads unless an intermittent condition is present.
7. Connect the ohmmeter leads between the 2 disconnected pick-up coil leads. See **Figure 12**. If the meter reading is not between 500-1,500 ohms, replace the pick-up coil.
8. Repeat Step 5.
9. Reconnect the pick-up coil leads to the module. Remove the test equipment and install the distributor cap.

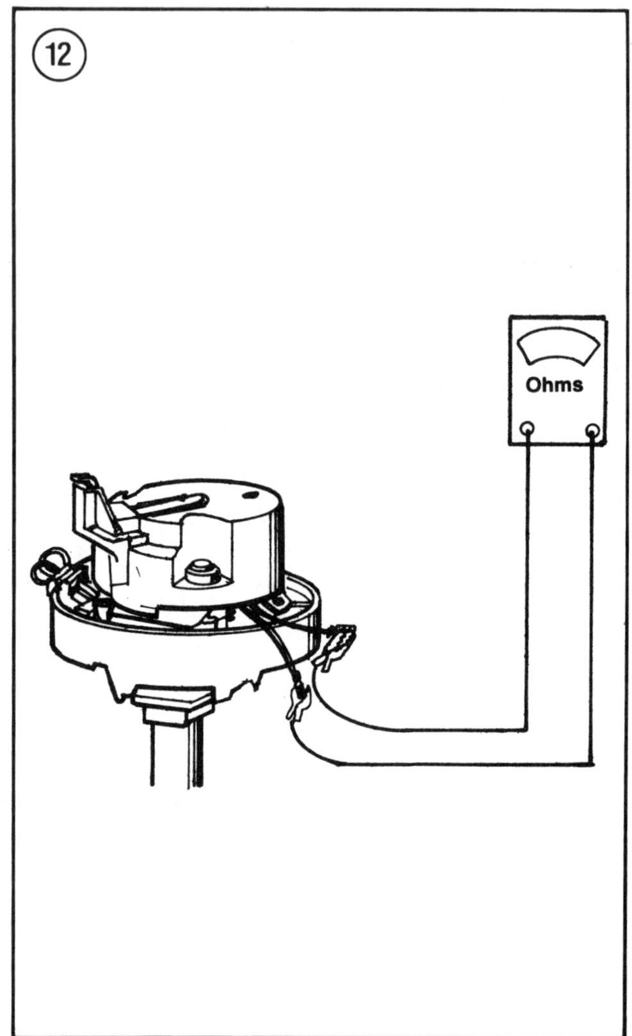

Dwell Test

If the engine runs poorly or suffers from heavy hesitation, check the dwell to see if the control module is defective.

1. Start the engine and warm to normal operating temperature.
2. Stop the engine. Connect a dwell meter between the ignition coil TACH terminal pigtail and ground.
3. Start the engine and note the meter scale while gradually increasing engine speed from idle to approximately 2,500 rpm. The dwell should increase smoothly from about 15° at idle to about 30° at 2,500 rpm. If it does not, replace the distributor module.

FUEL SYSTEM (CARBURETTED)

Fuel system problems should be isolated to the fuel pump, fuel lines, fuel filter or carburetor. The following procedures assume that the ignition system is working properly and is correctly adjusted.

1. *Engine will not start*—Make sure there is gas in the tank and that it is being delivered to the carburetor. Remove the air cleaner cover, look into the carburetor throat and operate the throttle linkage several times. See **Figure 13** (typical). There should be a stream of fuel from the accelerator pump discharge tube each time the linkage is moved. If not, check the fuel pump pressure as described in Chapter Six. Also check the float condition and adjustment. If the engine will not

start, check the automatic choke parts for sticking or damage. If necessary, rebuild or replace the carburetor as described in Chapter Six.

2. *Engine runs at fast idle*—Check the choke setting, idle speed and mixture adjustments.

3. *Rough idle or engine miss with frequent stalling*—Check choke linkage for proper adjustment. Check throttle stop screw adjustment. Check for sticking throttle plates. Set idle speed to specifications. Check float adjustment.

4. *Engine "diesels" (continues to run) when ignition is switched off*—Check idle mixture (probably too lean), ignition timing and idle speed (probably too fast). Check linkage to make sure the fast idle cam is not hanging up. Check for engine overheating.

5. *Stumbling when accelerating from idle*—Check accelerator pump action (Step 1). Check for a clogged fuel filter, low fuel pump volume, plugged bowl vents or a power valve that is stuck closed.

6. *Engine misses at high speed or lacks power*—This indicates possible fuel starvation. Check accelerator pump action (Step 1). Check float setting. Check for a plugged pump discharge nozzle or leaking nozzle gasket.

7. *Engine stalls on deceleration or during a quick stop*—Adjust idle speed to specifications. Check throttle positioner functioning. Check for leaking intake manifold or carburetor gasket(s).

8. *Engine will not reach wide-open throttle; top speed and power is reduced*—Check throttle linkage for binding. Check for low fuel pump volume, incorrect float drop, a clogged fuel filter, stuck power valve or an inoperative secondary system.

9. *Engine surges at cruising speed*—Check for a plugged fuel filter. Adjust float level and drop. Check for low fuel pump volume or pressure. Check fuel for contamination. Check for blocked air bleeds or leaking plugs/lead seals.

10. *Black exhaust smoke*—Check for an excessively rich mixture. Check idle speed adjustment and choke setting. Check for excessive fuel pump pressure, leaky float or worn needle valve.

11. *Excessive fuel consumption*—Check for an excessively rich mixture or misblended gasohol. Check choke operation. Check idle speed and mixture adjustments. Check for excessive fuel pump pressure, leaky float or worn needle valve.

CLYMER QUICK TIP

Problem: Contrary to what manufacturers would have you believe, the composition material used in floats ***does*** *gradually absorb fuel over a period of time. Such fuel absorption increases the weight of the float and prevents it from operating properly when set to correct specifications.*

Solution: To check a composition float for fuel absorption, remove it from the carburetor, hold it between a thumb and finger and gently press a fingernail into the surface. If moisture appears where your fingernail pressed, the float has started to absorb fuel.

Since floats are quite expensive, the best way to determine if fuel absorption has affected float performance is to weigh it with an inexpensive float scale available in most auto supply stores. The scale comes with weight specifications for all new floats and can immediately pinpoint a fuel system problem that's often overlooked.

CLYMER QUICK TIP

Problem: The engine stumbles during acceleration, misses at high speed and generally lacks power. The diagnosis is a malfunctioning accelerator pump in the carburetor but an overhaul does not cure the problem.

Solution: You are probably using a blended fuel (alcohol and gasoline). The alcohol in the fuel causes the accelerator pump to swell, restricting its travel in the pump bore. When the carburetor is removed and disassembled, the alcohol evaporates and the pump cup returns to normal size, allowing the pump to work properly. Carburetors with a tapered pump bore are especially prone to this problem. Look for tell-tale marks on the cup lip and pump bore which indicate cup scuffing. Installing a new pump cup will not solve this problem—the only real cure is to change the brand of gasoline used.

FUEL SYSTEM (FUEL INJECTED)

Troubleshooting a fuel injection system requires more thought, experience and knowledge than any other part of the vehicle. A logical approach and proper test equipment are essential in order to successfully find and fix these troubles.

Injectors and other injection system components are also very expensive. You cannot afford to troubleshoot the system by replacing all of the injectors on the chance that it will solve the problem. Since the injection system is electronically controlled by the CCC microprocessor, system operation is more complex. You cannot "adjust" components to perform as you would like them to if such adjustments are not within the parameters of the microprocessor program.

It is best to leave fuel injection troubles to your dealer. In order to isolate a problem to the injection system, make sure that the fuel and air cleaner filters are not clogged.

CLYMER QUICK TIP

The substitute additives now being used in place of lead in gasoline have a tendency to clog fuel injectors. Since each gasoline refiner uses a different combination of additives, the problem varies according to gasoline brand and area of the country in which it is sold. However, clogged injectors have become a fact of life for owners of fuel injected vehicle, who are quickly learning that injectors are expensive to replace.

Chevron markets a fuel injector cleaner (detergent) under its own brand name (Techron) and private-lables it for other companies. The cleaner is very efficient and used ***exactly*** *as directed on the container, will clean clogged injectors and keep them clean. Failure to follow the instructions properly and/or excessive use, however, can result in even more damage, as its detergent action will clean rust out of the fuel tank and send it to the injectors.*

If you have an injector problem, do not hesitate to use this cleaner, but do use it properly.

EMISSION CONTROL SYSTEMS

Major emission control systems used on virtually all of the models covered in this manual include the following:

a. Positive crankcase ventilation (PCV) system.
b. Heated air cleaner intake.
c. AIR (air injection) system.
d. Evaporative emission control (EEC) system.
e. Exhaust gas recirculation (EGR) system.

Emission control system operation varies considerably depending upon model year and engine application. Many of the systems and components are factory set and sealed. Without special and expensive test equipment, it is impossible to adjust the systems to meet state and Federal requirements.

Troubleshooting can also be difficult without special equipment. The procedures described in Chapter Six will help you find emission control components which have failed, but repairs may have to be entrusted to a dealer or other properly equipped repair shop.

ENGINE NOISES

Often the first evidence of an internal engine problem is a strange noise. That knocking, clicking or tapping sound which you never heard before may be warning you of impending trouble.

While engine noises can indicate problems, they are difficult to interpret correctly; inexperienced mechanics can be seriously misled by them.

Professional mechanics often use a special stethoscope (which looks like a doctor's stethoscope) for isolating engine noises. You can do nearly as well with a "sounding stick" which can be an ordinary piece of doweling, a length of broom handle or a section of small hose. By placing one end in contact with the area to which you want to listen and the other end near your ear, you can hear sounds emanating from that area. The first time you do this, you may be horrified at the strange sounds coming from even a normal engine. If you can, have an experienced friend or mechanic help you sort out the noises.

Clicking or Tapping Noises

Clicking or tapping noises usually come from the valve train and indicate excessive valve clearance. A sticking valve may also sound like a valve with excessive clearance. In addition, excessive wear in valve train components can cause similar engine noises.

Knocking Noises

A heavy, dull knocking is usually caused by a worn main bearing. The noise is loudest when the engine is working hard, such as accelerating at low speed. You may be able to isolate the trouble to a single bearing by disconnecting the spark plugs one at a time. When you reach the spark plug nearest the bearing, the knock will be reduced or disappear. Worn connecting rod bearings may also produce a knock, but the sound is usually more metallic.

As with a main bearing, the noise is worse during acceleration. It may increase just as you go from acceleration to coasting. Disconnecting the spark plugs will help isolate this knock as well.

A double knock or clicking usually indicates a worn piston pin. Disconnecting spark plugs will isolate this to a particular piston; however, the noise will *increase* when you reach the affected piston.

A loose flywheel and excessive crankshaft end play also produces knocking noises. While similar to main bearing noises, they are usually intermittent, not constant, and they do not change when spark plugs are disconnected. When caused by a loose flywheel or coupling, the noise is generally heard at idle or during rapid deceleration.

Some mechanics confuse piston pin noise with piston slap (excessive piston clearance). The double knock will distinguish piston pin noise. Piston slap will always be louder when the engine is cold.

GASOLINE ENGINE TROUBLESHOOTING

These procedures assume the starter cranks the engine over normally. If not, refer to the *Starter* section of this chapter.

Engine Won't Start

This can be caused by the ignition or fuel system. Refer to *Ignition System* section of this chapter and perform a spark intensity test. If sparks occur, the problem is more likely in the fuel system. If they do not occur, check the ignition system.

Engine Misses Steadily

Remove one spark plug wire at a time and ground the wire. If engine miss increases, that cylinder is working properly. Reconnect the wire and check another. When a wire is disconnected and engine miss remains the same, that cylinder is not firing. Perform a spark intensity test. If no spark occurs for the suspected cylinder, check the distributor cap, wire and spark plug. See Chapter Three. If a spark occurs properly, check cylinder compression and intake manifold vacuum (Chapter Three).

Engine Misses Erratically at All Speeds

Intermittent problems can be difficult to locate. This could be in the ignition system, exhaust system or fuel system. Start with the secondary ignition wiring and follow the troubleshooting procedures for each system to isolate the cause.

Engine Misses at Idle Only

The problem could be in the ignition system, carburetor idle adjustment or EGR system. Have the idle mixture adjustment checked and inspect idle circuit for restrictions.

Engine Misses at High Speed Only

Check the accelerator pump operation and fuel pump delivery. Look for a restricted fuel line. Check the spark plugs and wires.

Low Performance at All Speeds, Poor Acceleration

Usually an ignition or fuel system problem. May also be an intake manifold or carburetor vacuum leak.

CLYMER QUICK TIP

Problem: To check for a leaking V6 intake manifold gasket, use a garden hose to run water along the mating surface on each side with the engine idling. The V-design of the engine will allow enough water to accumulate to temporarily seal any leak. If the engine idle suddenly smooths out, the gasket is leaking.

Solution: Although oil or carburetor cleaner is often used to troubleshoot this problem, water is preferred, as it is both cleaner and safer. Water does not leave the messy residue of oil and is not dangerous like carburetor cleaner.

Tighten the bolts on a leaking intake manifold first to see if this eliminates the problem. However, tightening the manifold on engines which use a metal valley cover with laminated gasket sections will not work. The laminated gasket material is causing the leak and the entire valley cover will have to be replaced.

Excessive Fuel Consumption

Check for a plugged or restricted air cleaner filter element. If the engine uses a feedback carburetor, the mixture control solenoid may have failed. Misblended gasohol will also cause the problem, although there will be driveability problems at the same time.

A number of other seemingly unrelated factors can cause this problem. Check for clutch slippage (Chapter Nine), brake drag (Chapter Twelve), defective wheel bearings (Chapter Ten), poor front-end alignment (Chapter Ten), faulty ignition (Chapter Eight) and leaking fuel lines or gas tank.

Low Oil Pressure Indicated by Oil Pressure Gauge or Warning Light

Proper oil pressure to the engine is vital. If oil pressure is insufficient, the engine can destroy itself in a comparatively short time. The oil pressure warning circuit monitors oil pressure constantly. If pressure drops below a predetermined level, the warning light comes on. If it doesn't, there is trouble in the warning circuit, not the oil pressure system.

Once the engine is running, the warning light should stay off. If the warning light comes on or acts erratically, or if the oil pressure gauge shows low oil pressure (less than 6 psi) with the engine running, there is trouble with the engine oil pressure system. Stop the engine immediately and coast to a stop with the clutch disengaged.

The problem may be caused by low oil level, blockage in an oil line, a defective oil pump, overheated engine or a defective sending switch. Check the oil level and drive belt tension. Check for a shorted oil pressure sender with an ohmmeter (gauge) or by grounding the sender lead to the engine block (warning lamp). Do not restart the engine until you know why the low indication was given and are sure the problem has been corrected.

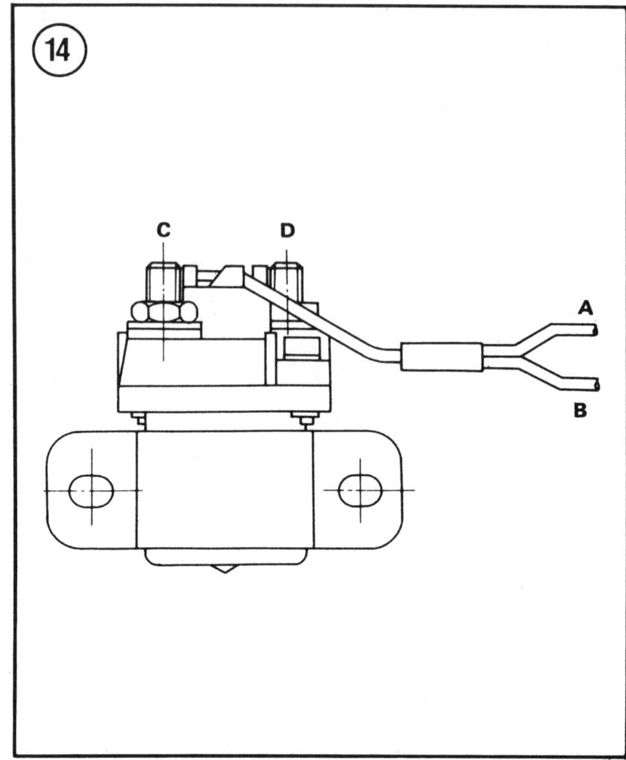

Engine Overheats

Usually caused by a cooling system problem, although late ignition or valve timing can be responsible. Check the coolant level in the recovery tank. If there is no fluid in the tank, check the radiator. Check the condition of the drive belt. Check the cooling system hoses for leaks and loose connections. Check the cooling fan operation (Chapter Seven).

Engine Stalls As It Warms Up

The choke valve may be stuck closed, the manifold heat control valve may be stuck, the engine idle speed may be set too low, or the PCV or EGR valve may be defective.

Engine Stalls After Idling or Slow-speed Driving

This can be caused by a defective fuel pump, overheated engine, incorrect float level or idle adjustment, or a defective PCV or EGR valve.

Engine Stalls After High-speed Driving

Vapor lock within the fuel lines caused by an overheated engine and/or hot weather is the usual cause of this trouble. Inspect and service the cooling system (Chapter Seven). If the problem persists, change to a different fuel or shield the fuel line from engine heat.

Engine Backfires

There are several possible reasons for this problem: incorrect ignition timing, overheating, excessive carbon, spark plugs with an incorrect heat range, hot or sticking valves and/or a cracked distributor cap.

Smoky Exhaust

Blue smoke indicates excessive oil consumption usually caused by worn piston rings. Black smoke indicates an excessively rich fuel mixture.

Excessive Oil Consumption

This can be caused by external leaks through broken seals or gaskets, or by burning oil in the combustion chambers. Check the oil pan and the front/rear of the engine for signs of oil leakage. If the oil is not leaking externally, valve stem clearances may be excessive, valve seals may be defective, piston rings may be worn, or cylinder walls may be scored.

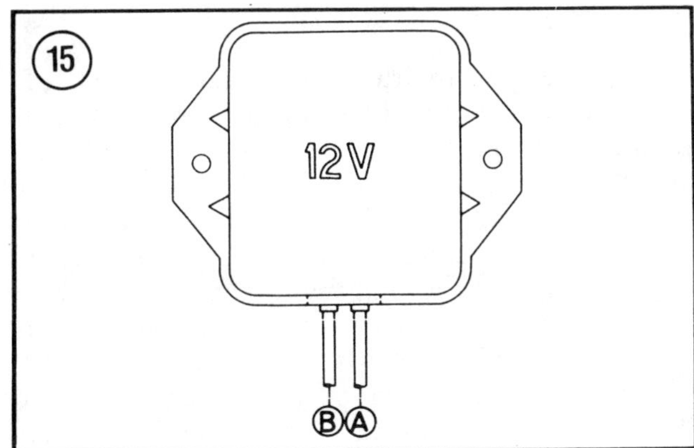

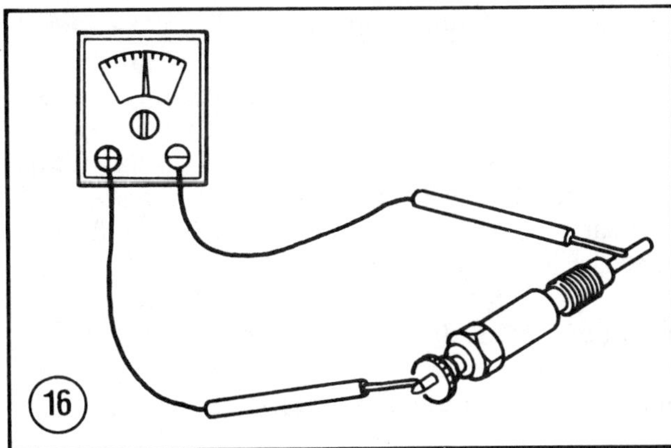

DIESEL ENGINE TROUBLESHOOTING

The following troubleshooting procedures apply only to diesel engine systems.

Incorrect or Uneven Idle Speed

The engine should be warmed to normal operating temperature (upper radiator hose hot) and all accessories turned OFF before attempting to discover the cause of the problem.

1. *Linkage adjustment*—Check for loose or incorrect idle screw setting. If necessary, adjust the idle screw to obtain the specified rpm. Check the throttle cable for looseness, tightness, binding, etc. and correct as required.
2. *Air in fuel system*—Drain the water separator to remove air or water from the fuel system. See *Diesel Engine Tune-up*, Chapter Three.
3. *Fuel restriction*—Check the system for blocked fuel lines, bent or kinked lines, over-tightened connections and a clogged fuel filter. Repair or replace, as required.
4. *Injection problems*—Have the injection pump timing checked. Also check for dirty or corroded injectors and incorrect fuel pressures. Correct or replace, as required.
5. *Engine mechanical problems*—Have valve clearance and engine compression checked. Also check engine for proper mounting.

Engine Will Not Start

Make sure that there is adequate fuel in the tank and that the starter is cranking the engine at a normal speed before proceeding.

1. *Defective throttle and engine stop controls*—Check all throttle controls for damage and lack of free movement. The throttle lever must reach the speed stop or top speed and power will be reduced. Readjust linkage, if necessary.
2. *Malfunctioning glow plug system:*
   a. Apply 12 volts across terminals A and B of glow plug relay No. 1. Check for continuity across terminals C and D of relay. See **Figure 14**. Replace relay if continuity is not shown. Repeat this step to test relay No. 2.
   b. Check for continuity between terminals A and B of the dropping resistor (**Figure 15**). Replace resistor if continuity is not shown.
   c. Remove and check each glow plug for continuity as shown in **Figure 16**. If there is no continuity, the heater wire is broken and the plug should be replaced.
3. *Fuel system problem*—Determine if fuel is being delivered to the injectors by loosening the fuel line to one injector and cranking the engine. Make sure that all fuel lines are connected to the proper injectors. Also check for leaking or blocked fuel lines and a clogged fuel filter. Drain the water-separator. See *Diesel Engine Tune-up*, Chapter Three.

Smoking Exhaust

Some smoke is normal and should be expected from a diesel engine.

   a. Black smoke usually indicates that excessive fuel is reaching the combustion system. It is more common at higher than at lower altitudes. If noted at idle or during normal driving conditions at low altitude, it should be diagnosed as soon as possible.
   b. Blue or gray smoke indicates burning oil.
   c. White smoke is usually water vapor (steam) and is generally noted during engine start-up.

It should disappear after a minute or so of engine operation but may return in cool weather during extended idling. White smoke can also result from a leak in the cooling system.

Visible exhaust gases that occur when the engine is cold but disappear when the engine warms up may be ignored, as a rule. The exhaust may also "smoke" when the engine is being "lugged down" in an incorrect gear. This "smoking" may also be ignored in most cases. Some common causes of visible exhaust from diesel engines are discussed below.

1. *Dirty air cleaner or fuel filter*—Clean or replace the air cleaner element or replace the fuel filter element as required.
2. *Injection system problem*—Have injection pump timing checked. Check maximum engine speed and adjust to specifications, if necessary. Have injection pressure and injector condition checked; injectors may be sticking, leaking or otherwise damaged.
3. *Engine mechanical problem*—Have valve clearance checked. Also check for leaking valves, defective valve stem seals and worn valve guides. A compression test will check for sticking or worn piston rings, worn cylinders and/or pistons or a leaking head gasket.
4. *Exhaust system problem*—Check for kinks or dents in the exhaust system. These will cause high backpressure, which results in high smoke levels and low power.

Excessive Fuel Consumption

One of the most frequent causes of excessive fuel consumption is a dirty air cleaner filter. Check the filter element and clean or replace as required before proceeding. Also check the fuel system for leaks and blockages. Correct any that are found.

1. *Injection system problem*—Perform the checks decribed in Step 2, *Smoking Exhaust* in this chapter.
2. *Engine mechanical problem*—Perform the checks described in Step 3, *Smoking Exhaust* in this chapter.
3. *External leakage*—Leakage will result in high consumption of fuel and oil. An air intake leak can also reduce engine service life, especially if the truck is driven under dusty conditions.

Lack of Power

A number of conditions can cause a lack of power. Before proceeding, make sure that the speedometer/odometer is in good working order, the vehicle is equipped with standard size wheels and tires that are properly inflated, the brakes are not binding, the clutch is in good condition and properly adjusted and that the throttle pedal, cable and injection pump linkage are not restricted, loose or improperly adjusted. Also check the air cleaner filter element and clean or replace as required. Check the exhaust system for kinks or dents that can cause high backpressure. Correct if necessary.

1. *Fuel system problem*—Check for clogged fuel lines, a clogged fuel filter, air in the fuel system, kinked injector lines, loose injector connections and improperly connected injector lines. Also check for system leaks. Correct as required.
2. *Injection system problem*—Have injector pump timing checked. Check and adjust fast idle speed, if necessary. Check for damaged injectors and/or a defective injection pump.
3. *Engine mechanical problem*—Have valve clearances checked. A compression test will check for sticking or worn piston rings, worn cylinders and/or pistons or a leaking head gasket.

CLUTCH TROUBLESHOOTING

Several clutch problems may be experienced. Usually the trouble is quite obvious and will fall into one of the following categories.

1. Slipping, chattering or grabbing when it is engaging.
2. Spinning or dragging when disengaged.
3. Clutch noises, clutch pedal pulsations and rapid clutch disc facing wear.

Clutch service procedures are covered in Chapter Nine.

Clutch Slips While Engaged

Clutch linkage is improperly adjusted, the pressure springs are weak or broken, the friction disc facings are worn or the disc is contaminated with grease or oil.

This problem is most noticeable when accelerating in a high gear at a relatively low speed. To check slippage, park the vehicle on a level surface with the parking brake set. Shift to 2nd gear and release the clutch as if driving off. If the clutch is good, the engine will slow and stall. If the clutch slips, continued engine speed will give it away.

Clutch Chatters or Grabs When Engaging

Clutch linkage is improperly adjusted, the friction disc facings are contaminated with grease or oil or clutch components are worn and/or damaged.

Clutch Spins or Drags When Disengaged

The clutch friction disc normally spins briefly after engagement and takes a moment to come to rest. This sound should not be confused with drag.

Drag is caused by the friction disc not being fully released from the flywheel or pressure plate as the clutch pedal is depressed. It usually causes difficult shifting and gear clash, especially when downshifting. This problem can be caused by misadjusted linkage or defective/worn clutch components.

Clutch Noises

Clutch noise is generally most noticeable when the engine is idling. Note whether the noise is heard when the clutch is engaged or disengaged. Clutch noises when engaged could be caused by a loose friction disc hub, loose disc springs and misalignment or looseness of the engine or transmission mounts. When disengaged, noises can be caused by a worn release bearing, defective pilot bearing or a misaligned release lever.

Clutch Pedal Pulsates

This problem is generally noticed when slight pressure is applied to the clutch pedal with the engine running. As pedal pressure is increased, the pulsation ceases. Possible causes include misalignment of the engine and transmission, a bent crankshaft flange, distortion or shifting of the clutch housing, a misaligned release lever, warped friction disc or a damaged pressure plate.

Rapid Friction Disc Facing Wear

This problem is caused by any condition that permits slippage between the facings and the flywheel or pressure plate. Probable causes are "riding" the clutch, slow releasing of the clutch after disengagement, weak or broken pressure springs, misadjusted pedal linkage and a warped clutch disc or pressure plate.

CLYMER QUICK TIP

Leaks under a vehicle indicate trouble ahead. The problem is two-fold: identifying the type of fluid leaking and determining where it came from. If you can correctly identify the type of fluid, it will narrow down the places to look for the leak considerably.

Manufacturers put dyes into various automotive fluids to help in identifying them, but after a period of use in the hot engine/transmission/cooling system, the dyes lose their potency and cannot be seen under certain conditions. For example, automatic transmission fluid contains a red dye. If the fluid is burned, however, the value of the dye is lost.

To troubleshoot a leak, blot a small amount of the fluid from the puddle under the vehicle on the edge of a clean paper towel. Remove each dipstick (crankcase, transmission, power steering, etc.) in turn and wipe a small amount of the fluid on the dipstick beside the leak blot on the paper towel. One of the fluids should be a near-perfect match for that found under the vehicle.

MANUAL TRANSMISSION TROUBLESHOOTING

Manual transmission problems are evident when one or more of the following symptoms appear:

a. Difficulty changing gears.
b. Gears clash when downshifting.
c. Slipping out of gear.
d. Excessive noise in NEUTRAL.
e. Excessive noise in gear.
f. Oil leaks.

Transmission troubles are sometimes difficult to distinguish from clutch problems. Eliminate the clutch as a source of the problem before installing a new or rebuilt transmission. Transmission service procedures are covered in Chapter Nine.

Hard Shifting Into Gear

Common causes of this problem include a clutch that does not release properly, misadjusted or insufficiently lubricated linkage, a stuck detent ball or synchro sleeves that are tight on the hub splines.

Transmission Slips Out of Gear

This problem can result from misadjusted linkage, transmission and engine misalignment, worn gear teeth, a gear that is too loose on the mainshaft, excessive mainshaft end play, worn bearings, a defective synchronizer or insufficient shift lever spring tension.

No Power Through Transmission

Look for a slipping clutch, stripped gear teeth, a damaged shift fork or shift fork linkage, a broken gear or shaft or a stripped drive key.

Transmission is Noisy in NEUTRAL

The transmission and engine are misaligned, bearings are worn or dry, the gears are worn, the countershaft is worn, bent or has excessive end play.

Transmission is Noisy in Gear

May result from a defective clutch disc, loose gears and the faults listed above.

Gears Clash During Shifting

This may be caused by a clutch that does not release properly, a defective synchronizer or gears that stick on the mainshaft.

Oil Leaks

The most common causes are foaming due to the use of the wrong lubricant or overfilling, broken gaskets, damaged oil seals, a loose drain plug or a cracked transmission case.

AUTOMATIC TRANSMISSION TROUBLESHOOTING

Most automatic transmission repairs require considerable specialized knowledge and tools. It is impractical for the home mechanic to invest in the tools, since they cost more than a properly rebuilt transmission.

Keep the linkage properly adjusted (Chapter Nine) and check the fluid level and condition frequently (Chapter Three) to help prevent future problems. If the fluid is brown or black in color or has a burned or varnish-like smell, it indicates that there is some type of damage or failure inside the transmission. Have the transmission serviced by your dealer or a competent automatic transmission service facility.

DIFFERENTIAL TROUBLESHOOTING

Noise is usually the first thing to draw attention to differential problems. It is not always easy to diagnose the trouble by determining the source of the noise and the operating conditions that produce it. Defective universal joints, wheel bearings, muffler and/or tires may be wrongly diagnosed as differential or axle problems.

Some clue as to the cause of the trouble may be gained by noting whether the noise is a hum, growl or knock; whether it is produced when the vehicle is accelerating under load or coasting; and whether it is heard when the vehicle is going straight or making a turn.

Differential service procedures are covered in Chapter Eleven.

Noise During Acceleration

This can result from insufficient lubricant, incorrect tooth contact between the drive gear and drive pinion, damaged or misadjusted bearings in axles or side bearings, a worn differential cross shaft or damaged gears.

Noise During Coasting

This can be caused by incorrect backlash between the drive gear and drive pinion gear, or from an incorrect adjustment of the drive pinion bearing.

Noise During A Turn

This is generally caused by loose or worn axle shaft bearings, pinion gears that are too tight on their shafts, a side gear jammed in the differential case or worn side gear and pinion thrust washers.

Driveline "Clunk" When Shifting From Forward Into Reverse, or Reverse Into Forward

This noise is usually caused by an idle speed that is too high or insufficient lubrication. Other possible causes include loose engine mounts, excessive backlash in the axle or transmission, defective shock absorbers or loose rear springs and loose or worn drive shaft components.

Other Noises

A humming noise in the differential is often caused by improper drive pinion or ring gear adjustment which prevents normal tooth contact between the gears. If ignored, rapid tooth wear will occur and the noise will become more like a growl. This should be corrected as soon as the noise is heard to prevent damage to the gears.

Tire noise varies considerably, depending upon the type of road surface and type of tread pattern. Differential noises will sound the same, regardless of road surfaces. If noises are heard, carefully listen to them over different road surfaces to help isolate the problem.

Broken Differential Parts

Insufficient lubrication, improper use of the clutch, excessive load, misadjusted bearings or gears, excessive backlash, loose bolts and case damage can all result in differential damage.

BRAKE SYSTEM TROUBLESHOOTING

Good brakes are vital to the safe operation of any vehicle. Perform the maintenance specified in Chapter Three to minimize brake system problems. Brake system service is covered in Chapter Twelve.

Brake Pedal Goes to the Floor

Worn linings or pads, air in the hydraulic system, a leaking master or wheel cylinder, or a leaking brake line or hose can cause this problem. Check for leaks. Check for worn brake linings or pads. Bleed and adjust the brakes. Rebuild a leaking master or wheel cylinder.

Spongy Brake Pedal

This problem is generally caused by air in the hydraulic system. Bleed and adjust the brakes.

Brakes Pull

Check brake adjustment and lining/pad wear. Check for contaminated linings/pads, leaking wheel cylinders and loose brake lines or hoses. Check front end alignment and look for suspension damage such as a broken front/rear spring or shock absorber. Check tire condition and pressure.

Brakes Squeal or Chatter

Check brake lining/pad thickness and brake drum/disc condition. Make sure that shoes are not loose. Clean off any dirt on shoes and drums. Disc brake squealing is more difficult to eliminate. Check to make sure that the anti-squeal or anti-rattle springs are properly installed and in good condition. As a last resort, use one of the aerosol sprays sold to minimize disc brake squeal.

Brakes Drag

Check brake adjustment, including the parking brake. Look for broken or weak shoe return springs, swollen rubber parts caused by contaminated or improper brake fluid. Check for a defective master cylinder.

Hard Pedal

Check for contaminated brake linings/pads. Check for brake line/hose restrictions.

High Speed Fade

Check for distorted or out-of-round drums/discs and contaminated linings/pads.

Pulsating Pedal

Check for distorted or out-of-round drums/discs with a dial indicator. If the drum/disc condition appears normal according to the dial indicator but the condition persists, have a light cut taken from the drums/discs by a dealer or machine shop.

This problem often occurs when the vehicle was equipped with organic brake linings/pads by the factory, but semi-metallic linings/pads are installed as replacements. The drums/discs furnished with organic pads do not have the ability to resist the high heat levels created by semi-metallic linings/pads and will often warp just enough to cause the problem yet provide no tell-tale signs of overheating or distortion.

COOLING SYSTEM TROUBLESHOOTING

Cooling system service is provided in Chapter Seven.

Engine Overheats

An overheating condition may be caused by insufficient coolant, use of plain water instead of water mixed with antifreeze, a loose or defective drive belt, a defective thermostat or water pump,

17

Underinflation—Worn more on sides than in center.

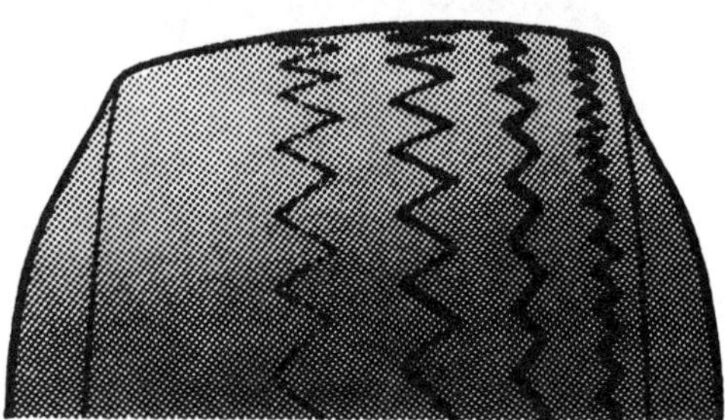

Wheel Alignment—Worn more on one side than the other. Edges of tread feathered.

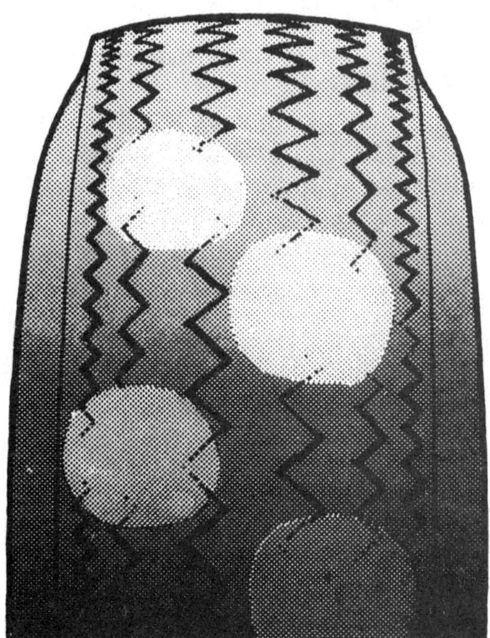

Wheel Balance – Scalloped edges indicate wheel wobble or tramp due to wheel unbalance.

Road Abrasion—Rough wear on entire tire or in patches.

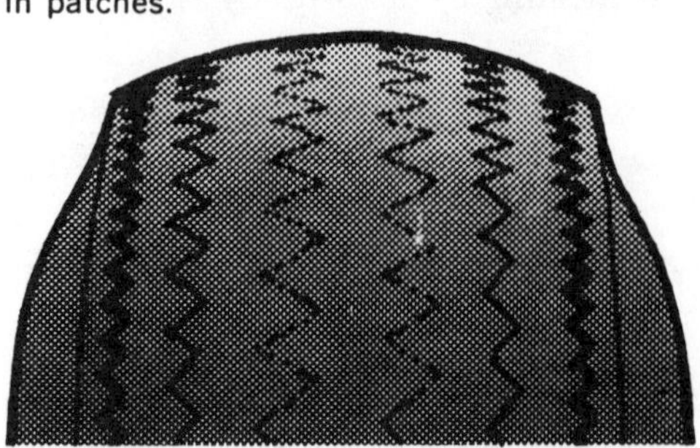

Overinflation—Worn more in center than on sides.

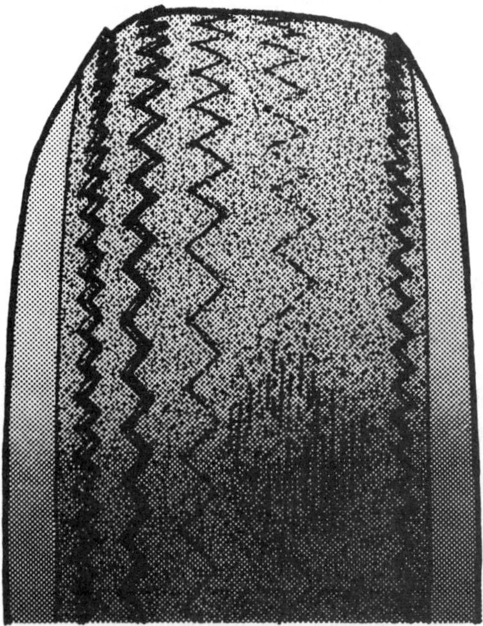

Combination—Most tires exhibit a combination of the above. This tire was overinflated (center worn) and the toe-in was incorrect (feathering). The driver cornered hard at high speed (feathering, rounded shoulders) and braked rapidly (worn spots). The scaly roughness indicates a rough road surface.

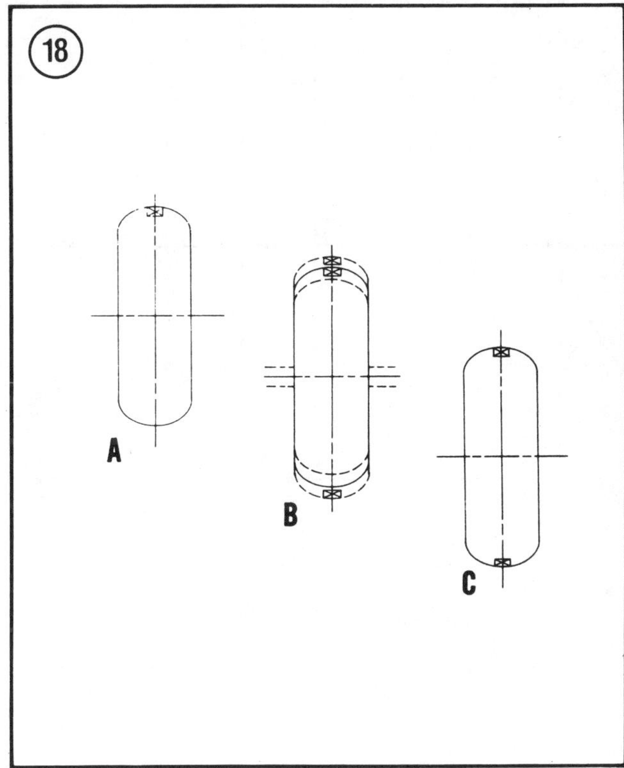

incorrect ignition timing and/or clogged, defective or loose coolant hoses.

Engine Does Not Warm Up

This condition generally results from a defective thermostat or extremely cold weather.

Coolant Loss

Radiator leaks, loose or defective coolant hoses, a defective radiator cap or water pump, a cylinder head gasket leak or a cracked cylinder head/engine block can cause this problem.

Noisy Cooling System

Cooling system noise is generally caused by defective water pump bearings, loose or bent fan blades, or a defective drive belt.

CLYMER QUICK TIP

Visually inspect metal radiator tanks periodically for traces of a greenish-gold appearance. This looks like a harmless fungus that has eaten through the radiator paint but will not wipe off. Called "mildew" or "solder bloom," it is caused by a chemical reaction between the solder used to construct the tank and the antifreeze. Once it appears, there is no way to stop it and the radiator will eventually have to be replaced.

STEERING AND SUSPENSION TROUBLESHOOTING

Steering and suspension system checks, adjustments and service are covered in Chapter Ten.

Problems in the suspension or steering are evident when any of the following occur:

a. Hard steering.
b. Vehicle pulls to one side.
c. Vehicle wanders or front wheels wobble.
d. Excessive play in steering.
e. Abnormal tire wear.

Unusual steering, pulling or wandering is usually caused by bent or misaligned suspension parts. If the problem seems to be excessive play, check wheel bearing adjustment first. Next, check the steering free play and ball-joints. Finally shake each wheel to check tie rod ends.

Tire Wear Analysis

Abnormal tire wear should always be analyzed to determine the cause. The most common is incorrect tire pressure, followed by improper driving, overloading, loose wheel bearings and incorrect wheel alignment. **Figure 17** identifies wear patterns and their most probable cause.

Wheel Balancing

All 4 wheels and tires must be in balance along 2 axes. To be in static balance (**Figure 18**), weight must be evenly distributed around the axis of rotation. (A) shows a statically unbalanced wheel. (B) shows the result—wheel tramp or hopping. (C) shows proper static balance.

To be in dynamic balance (**Figure 19**), the centerline of weight must coincide with the centerline of the wheel. (A) shows a dynamically unbalanced wheel. (B) shows the result—wheel wobble or shimmy. (C) shows the proper dynamic balance.

If wheel imbalance is indicated immediately after the vehicle has been subjected to hard, rough or off-road use, check the balance weights on both sides of each wheel. If any balance weights are missing, have the wheel rebalanced as soon as possible.

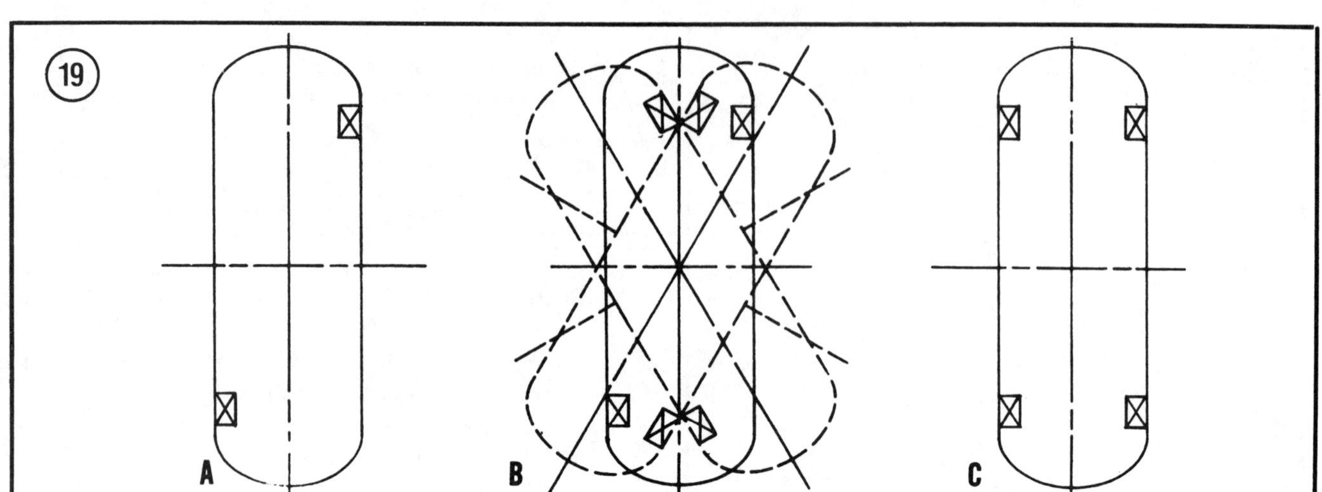
19
A
B
C

CHAPTER THREE

LUBRICATION, MAINTENANCE AND TUNE-UP

A careful program of lubrication, preventive maintenance and regular tune-ups will result in longer engine and vehicle life, ensuring good performance, dependability and safety. It will also pay dividends in fewer and less expensive repair bills. Such a program is especially important if the vehicle is used in remote areas, off-highway or on heavily traveled freeways where breakdowns are not only inconvenient but dangerous. Breakdowns are much less likely to occur if the vehicle has been well maintained.

Certain maintenance tasks and checks should be performed weekly. Others should be performed at certain time or mileage intervals. Still others should be done whenever certain symptoms appear. Some maintenance procedures are included in the *Tune-up* section at the end of this chapter. Detailed instructions will be found there. Other steps are described in the following chapters. Chapter references are included with these steps.

Scheduled maintenance requirements are provided in **Table 1** (gasoline) and **Table 2** (diesel). Oil viscosity recommendations are provided in **Table 3** (gasoline) and **Table 4** (diesel). Recommended lubricants are found in **Table 5**, with crankcase capacities given in **Table 6** and automatic transmission fluid (ATF) oxidation temperatures in **Table 7**. **Tables 1-7** are at the end of the chapter.

JACKING AND SUPPORTING THE VEHICLE

S- and T-series frames are a ladder channel section riveted type. The use of this design requires that special precautions be taken when raising the vehicle with a jack or a hoist and when positioning jackstands. Incorrect jack or jackstand placement can cause suspension or drive train damage. The service jack provided with the vehicle is intended only for emergency use in changing a flat tire. Refer to the Owner's Manual when using this jack. Do not use it to lift the vehicle up while performing other service.

When lifting one wheel of the vehicle, as when changing a tire, dismantling a hub or removing a brake drum, make sure the vehicle is resting as level as possible and firmly block the wheels at the opposite end of the vehicle. Set the parking brake and place the transmission in PARK (automatic transmission) or REVERSE (manual transmission). Position the jack carefully to provide maximum contact under axles or spring hangers. The jack should be as close as possible to the wheel being raised and positioned exactly vertical.

Raise the jack until it just begins to support the axle. Loosen all wheel lug nuts about 1/4 turn. Continue to raise the jack slowly until the wheel just clears the ground and will rotate freely.

Unscrew the lug nuts and remove the wheel. When reinstalling the wheel, tighten the lug nuts securely, lower the vehicle to the ground and remove the jack, then tighten all of the lug nuts to specifications.

When lifting the entire front of the vehicle, block the rear wheels, set the parking brake and place the transmission in PARK or REVERSE. Fit the head of the jack under the engine oil pan with a block of wood placed between the jack head and oil pan. If the vehicle weight is to be taken off the suspension, place the jack at the center of the front frame crossmember. Make sure the jack does not lift against or contact any sheet metal, suspension or steering components or the bottom of the radiator. Check to see that it does not touch electrical leads, hydraulic lines or oil/fuel lines.

When lifting the entire rear of the vehicle, block the front wheels and apply the head of the jack to the differential. After the vehicle has been lifted with the jack, support it on jackstands located under the frame rails or the rear axle. Do *not* run the engine when the rear wheels are jacked up if the vehicle is equipped with a limited-slip differential.

WARNING
Never work beneath the vehicle when it is supported only by a jack.

When raising the vehicle on a service station hoist, position the front hoist arms or lifting pads to provide maximum contact under the center of lower suspension arms or spring supports as near the wheels as possible, making sure they do not touch the steering linkage. The rear hoist arms or pads should be positioned beneath the rear axle housing or the spring mounting pads, but not allowed to touch the shock absorber mounting brackets.

WARNING
On vehicles equipped with an under-chassis mounted spare tire, remove the tire, wheel or tire carrier before raising the vehicle to a high-lift position. This will avoid any sudden weight release from the chassis that might affect vehicle positioning on the hoist.

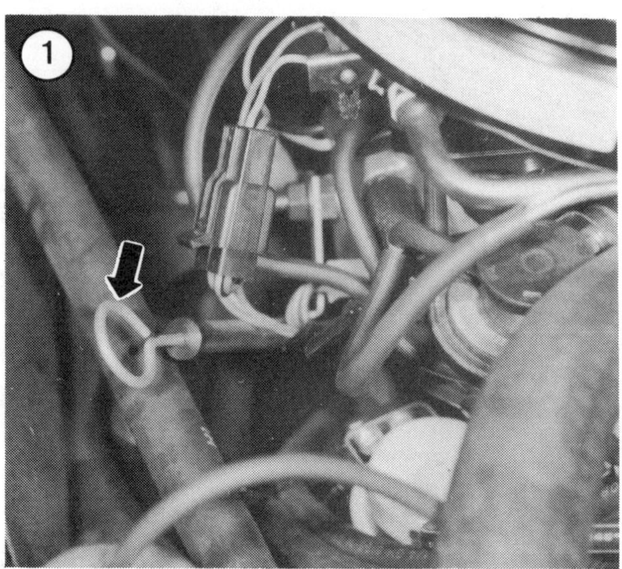

TOWING

CAUTION
Tow a vehicle only as described in this chapter and with a minimal load. Improper towing techniques can result in serious transmission damage.

As a general rule, the vehicles covered in this manual should be towed with their rear wheels off the ground. If the rear wheels cannot be raised, either disconnect the drive shaft or tow the vehicle with the aid of a dolly.

If the vehicle is towed with its front wheels on the ground, clamp the steering wheel in a straight-ahead position with a wheel clamping device designed for towing. Do *not* rely upon the steering column lock.

If the vehicle is towed with the front wheels off the ground, do not exceed speeds of 35 mph or distances of 50 miles unless the rear drive shaft is disconnected. Vehicles towed with the rear wheels off the ground should not exceed speeds of 35 mph (rough pavement) or 50 mph (smooth pavement).

WEEKLY CHECKS

Many of the following checks were once routinely made by service station attendants during a fuel stop. With the advent of the self-service station and the extra cost for "full-service," you may want to perform the checks yourself. Although simple to perform, they are important, as such checks give an indication of the need for other maintenance.

Engine Oil Level

Engine oil should be checked before the vehicle is started each day. At this time, all the oil is in the crankcase and the dipstick will give a true reading. If you find it necessary to check the oil after the engine has been started, let the vehicle sit for an hour to allow oil in the upper part of the engine to drain back into the crankcase.

To check engine oil level, remove the dipstick and wipe it clean with a cloth or paper towel. Reinsert the dipstick in the tube until it seats firmly. Wait a moment, then remove it again and read the oil level on the lower end. Reinsert the dipstick after taking the reading. See **Figure 1** for 4-cylinder engines and **Figure 2** for V6 engines.

Some dipsticks have "ADD" and "FULL" lines. Others read "ADD 1 QT." and "OPERATING RANGE." In either case, the oil level should be maintained above the "ADD" line on the dipstick. Oil should be added whenever the level drops below the "ADD" line. Do *not* overfill the engine. Too much oil can be as harmful to the engine as too little and may result in a front or rear seal leak.

Top up to the "FULL" or "OPERATING RANGE" line on the dipstick if necessary, using only an SF grade oil for gasoline engines or an SF/CC or SF/CD grade oil for diesel engines. See **Table 3** (gasoline) or **Table 4** (diesel) for oil viscosity requirements. Add oil through the hole in the 4-cylinder valve cover (**Figure 3**) or through the V6 oil filler tube (**Figure 4**).

Coolant Level and Condition

WARNING

Do not remove the radiator cap when the engine is warm or hot, especially if an air conditioner has been in use. You may be seriously scalded or burned.

Check coolant level by observing the liquid level in the translucent reservoir (**Figure 5**). The radiator cap should *not* be removed. Coolant should be at the "FULL COLD" mark on the reservoir with the engine coolant at ambient temperature or at the "FULL HOT" mark with the engine at operating temperature. If the tank is empty, check the radiator level as well.

WARNING

The radiator cap should not be removed when the engine is warm or hot. If this is unavoidable, cover the cap with a thick rag or wear heavy leather gloves. Turn the cap slowly counterclockwise against the first stop (about 1/4 turn). Let all pressure (hot coolant and steam) escape. Then press the cap down and turn counterclockwise to remove. If the cap is removed too soon, scalding coolant may escape and cause a serious burn.

Check the condition of the coolant. If it is dirty or rusty, drain the radiator and flush the cooling system, then refill it with fresh coolant as described in Chapter Seven.

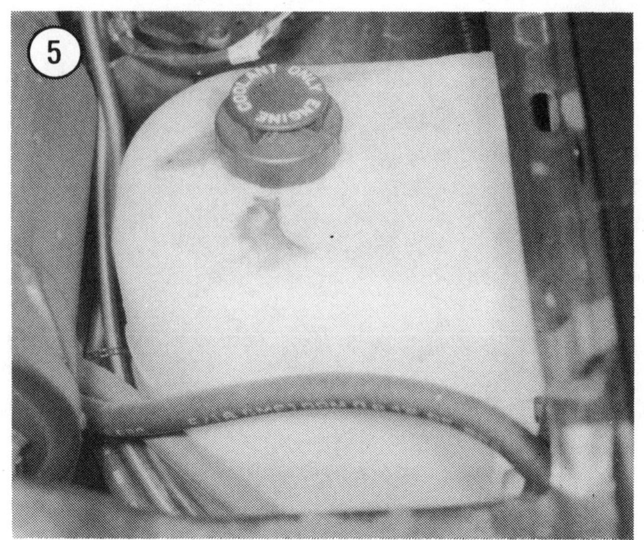

Battery Electrolyte Level

Unsealed batteries have individual cell vent caps or a bar with vented plugs which fits across 3 cells. To check electrolyte level with this type of battery, remove the vent caps or vent bars and observe the liquid level. With translucent batteries, it should be between the marks on the outside of the battery case (**Figure 6**). With black batteries, it should touch the bottom of the vent well (**Figure 7**).

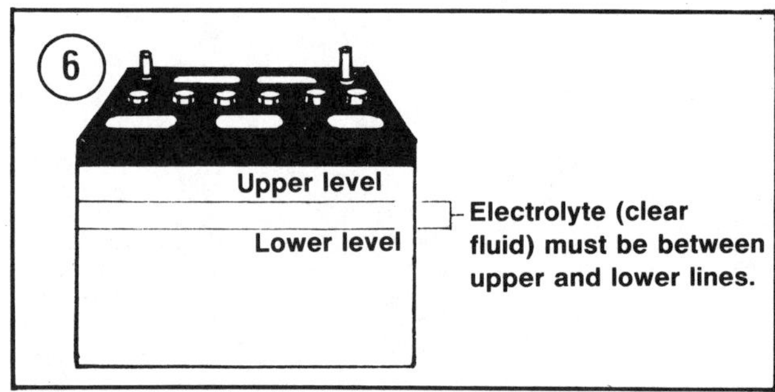

If the electrolyte level is not correct, add distilled water until the level is satisfactory. Do not overfill, as this will result in loss of electrolyte and shorten the battery life. Carefully wipe any spilled water from the battery top before reinstalling the vent caps or bars.

Periodic electrolyte level checks are not required on Freedom II or other sealed maintenance-free batteries.

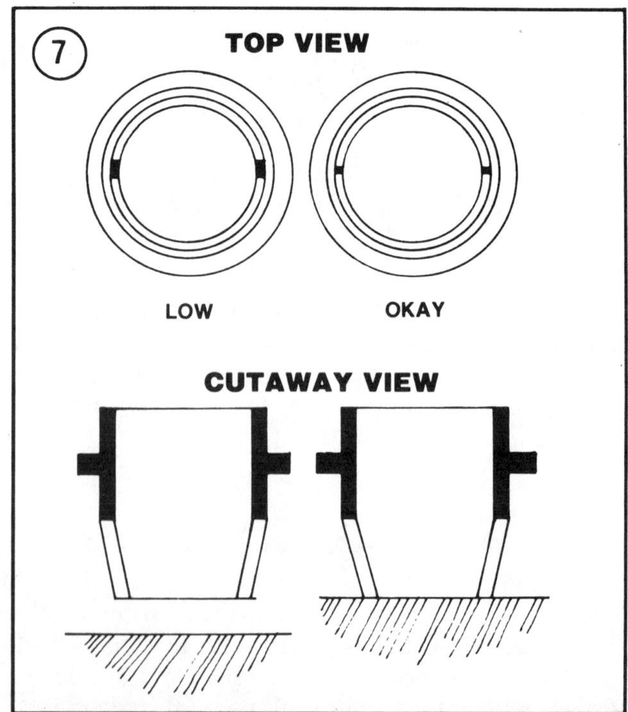

Windshield Wipers and Washers

Check the wiper blades for breaks or cracks in the rubber. Blade replacement intervals will vary with age, the weather, amount of use and the degree of chemical reaction from road salt or tar.

Operate the windshield washer and wiper blades. At the same time, check the amount and direction of the sprayed fluid. If the blades do not clean the

windshield satisfactorily, wash the windshield and the blades with a mild undiluted detergent. Rinse with water while rubbing with a clean cloth or paper towels.

If the wiper pattern is uneven and streaks over clean glass, replace the blades.

Fill the fluid reservoir (**Figure 8**) with a mixture of water and GM Optikleen windshield washer solvent or equivalent. A mixture of ammonia and water works equally well. In cold weather areas, do not fill the reservoir more than 3/4 full to allow for expansion in freezing weather. Never use radiator antifreeze in the windshield washer reservoir, as it can damage painted surfaces.

Brake Fluid Level

Clean the master cylinder housing and cover (**Figure 9**) to remove any possible contamination that might get into the fluid when the cover is removed. Grasp the cover tabs, depress the center of the cover and lift it off the reservoir (**Figure 10**). If the level is more than 1/4 in. below the lowest edge of each filler opening in either reservoir section, top up with a brake fluid marked DOT 3 and reinstall the cover.

CAUTION
Do not use fluid from a previously opened container that is only part full. Brake fluid absorbs moisture that can reduce braking efficiency.

Hydraulic Clutch Fluid Level

Check the fluid level in the clutch master cylinder reservoir located near the master cylinder (if so equipped). The fluid level can be seen inside the translucent reservoir and should be between the "FULL" and "ADD" lines. If not, top up with DOT 3 brake fluid.

Power Steering Fluid Level

Check the fluid level in the power steering pump reservoir (**Figure 11**), if so equipped. With the engine at normal operating temperature (upper radiator hose hot), turn the steering wheel from lock to lock several times, then shut the engine off and remove the power steering pump dipstick. Wipe the dipstick clean and reinsert. Remove the dipstick a second time. The fluid level should be between the "HOT" and "COLD" marks on the

3

dipstick (**Figure 12**). Top up if necessary with power steering fluid.

OWNER SAFETY CHECKS

The following simple checks should be performed on a daily basis during normal operation of the vehicle. Some are driveway checks. The others can be performed while driving. If any result in unsatisfactory operation, see your dealer to have the condition corrected.

Steering Column Lock

The ignition key should turn to LOCK position only when the transmission selector is in PARK (automatic transmission) or REVERSE (manual transmission).

Parking Brake and Transmission Park Mechanism

Check holding ability to setting the parking brake with the vehicle on a fairly steep hill. Check automatic transmission PARK mechanism by placing the transmission selector in PARK and releasing all brakes.

WARNING
You should not expect the PARK mechanism to hold the vehicle by itself even on a level surface. ***Always*** *set the parking brake after placing the transmission selector in PARK. When parking on an incline, you should also turn the wheels to the curb before shutting off the engine.*

Transmission Shift Indicator

Make sure the automatic transmission shift indicator accurately indicates the gear position selected.

Starter Safety Switch

The starter should operate only in PARK or NEUTRAL positions (automatic transmission) or in NEUTRAL with the clutch fully depressed (manual transmission, if equipped with starter safety switch).

Steering

With the vehicle on level ground, and with the front wheels lined up straight ahead, grasp the steering wheel and turn it from right to left and

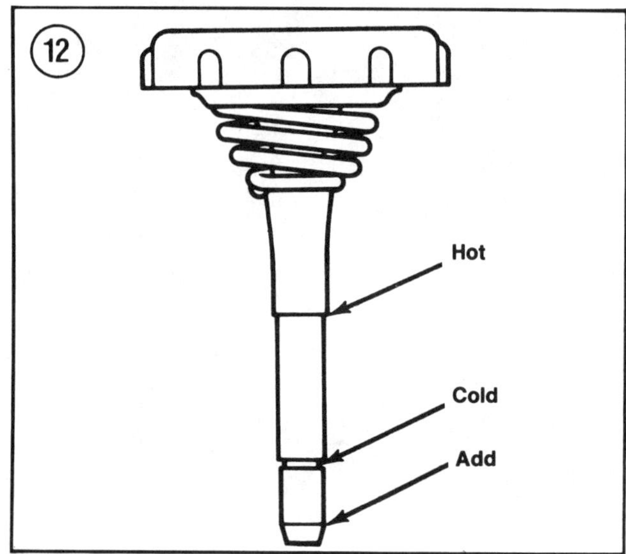

check for rotation free play. The free play should not be greater than about one inch (**Figure 13**). If it is, the front wheel bearings should be checked for condition and adjustment (see Chapter Ten), and the ball-joints, steering linkage and steering arm should be checked as possible causes of excessive play. These checks should be referred to a dealer.

Try to move the steering wheel in and out and check for axial play. If any play is felt, check the tightness of the steering wheel center nut.

Attempt to move the steering wheel from side to side without turning it. Movement is an indication of loose steering column mounting bolts or worn column bushings. Check and tighten the mounting bolts if necessary, and if the movement is still

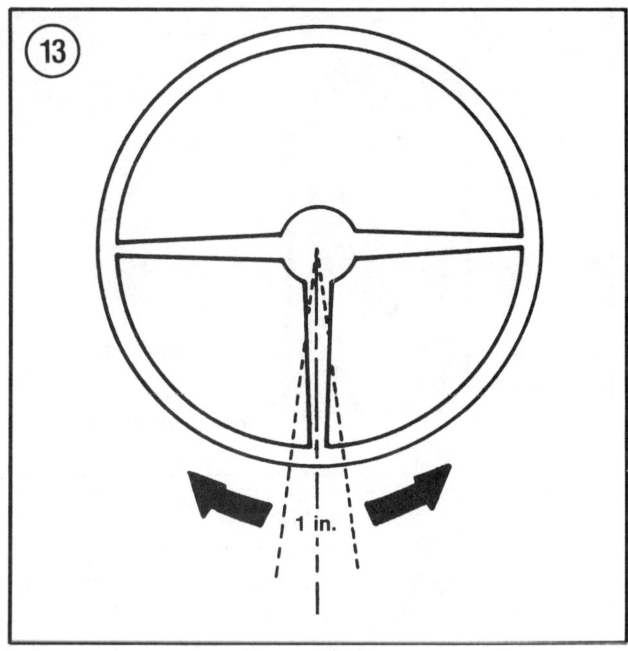

present, take the vehicle to a dealer or front-end specialist for corrective service.

Wheel Alignment and Balance

Wheel alignment and balance should be checked periodically by a dealer or an alignment specialist. Visually check the tires for abnormal wear. If the vehicle pulls either to the right or left on a straight, level road, an alignment problem is indicated. Excessive vibration of the steering wheel or front of the vehicle while driving at normal highway speeds usually indicates the need for wheel balancing.

Brakes

Observe brake warning light during braking action. Also check for changes in braking action, such as pulling to one side, unusual sounds or increased brake pedal travel. If the brake pedal feels spongy, there is probably air in the hydraulic system. Bleed the brakes (Chapter Twelve).

Exhaust System

Be alert to any smell of fumes in the vehicle or to any change in the sound of the exhaust system that might indicate leakage.

Defroster

Turn on the heater, then move the control to defrost (DEF) and check the amount of air directed to the windshield.

Rear View Mirror and Sun Visors

Make sure that the friction mounts are adjusted so that mirrors and visors stay in selected positions.

Horn

Check the horn to make sure that it works properly.

Lap and Shoulder Belts

Check all components for proper operation. Make sure that the anchor bolts are tight. Check the belts for fraying.

Head Restraints

If the seats are equipped with head restraints, check to see that they will adjust up and down properly and that no components are missing, loose or damaged.

Lights and Buzzers

Verify that all interior lights and buzzers are working. These include seat belt reminder light and buzzer, ignition key buzzer, interior lights, instrument panel illumination and warning lights.

Check all exterior lights for proper operation. These include the headlights, license plate lights, side marker lights, parking lights, turn or directional signals, backup lights and hazard warning lights.

Glass

Check for any condition that could obscure vision or be a safety hazard. Correct as required.

Door and Tailgate Latches

Verify positive closing, latching and locking action.

Fluid Leaks

Check under the vehicle after it has been parked for awhile for evidence of fuel, coolant or oil leaks.

Water dripping from the air conditioner drain tube after use is normal. Immediately determine and correct the cause of any leaking gasoline fumes or liquids to avoid possible fire or explosion.

Tires and Wheels

Inspect the tire tread and sidewall condition. Original equipment tires have tread wear indicators molded into the bottom of the tread grooves. Tread wear indicators will become visible as shown in **Figure 14** when tread depth becomes 1/16 in. Tires should be replaced at this point. Wear patterns are a good indicator of chassis and suspension alignment. If detected early, alignment problems can be corrected before the tires have worn severely.

Checking tire condition is particularly important following hard off-highway usage. Look for nails, cuts, excessive wear or other damage. Remove all stones or other objects wedged in the tread. Pay particular attention to signs of severe rock damage. This is usually found in the form of fractures and cuts in the tread and sidewalls. This type of damage presents an extreme driving hazard when the vehicle is operated at highway speeds. A damaged tire should be replaced as soon as possible.

CAUTION

For satisfactory operation, all 4 wheels must be equipped with the same size tires, of equal circumference and identical or near identical tread pattern. In addition, bias ply and radial tires should not be mixed; mixing will result in severe and even hazardous handling problems. Damage to the drive train components may also result.

Check the tire valve for air leaks; replace valve if necessary. Replace any missing valve caps. Check the tire pressures. This should be done when the tires are cold or after the vehicle has been parked for at least 3 hours after being driven less than one mile. When the tires heat up from driving, the air inside them expands and gives false high-pressure readings.

NOTE

If tire pressure must be checked when the tires are warm, it will be about 3 psi higher following a low-speed drive and about 7 psi higher following a high-speed drive.

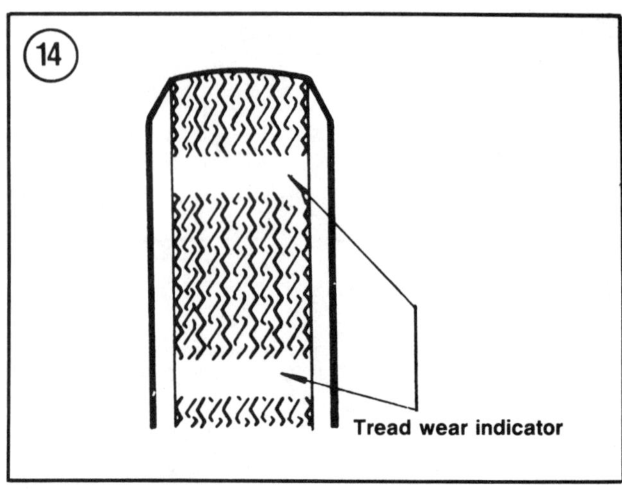

Use a reliable pressure gauge and adjust air pressure to agree with that specified for the tires. Pressure specifications for tires furnished with the vehicle are found on the tire placard attached to the rear edge of the driver's door lock pillar.

NOTE

Because of the variety of tire types and makes used on the vehicles covered in this manual, it is impractical to print all possible tire pressure ranges. When buying tires other than original equipment sizes, check with the manufacturer for recommended pressures. In all cases, never exceed the maximum pressure embossed on the side of the tire.

SCHEDULED MAINTENANCE (GASOLINE AND DIESEL ENGINES)

Various services are required at the intervals stated to assure that the emission control systems are maintained at the levels required by law.

The maintenance services and intervals provided in **Table 1** and **Table 2** are a compilation and simplification of the manufacturer's schedules designed to offer maximum protection. If you follow the appropriate table for your vehicle, it will receive periodic maintenance that will meet all Chevrolet and GMC requirements.

Engine Oil and Filter

For average use, the engine oil and filter should be changed at the intervals shown in the appropriate maintenance table at the end of this chapter. If driving is primarily short distances and in stop-and-go traffic, or if the vehicle is used

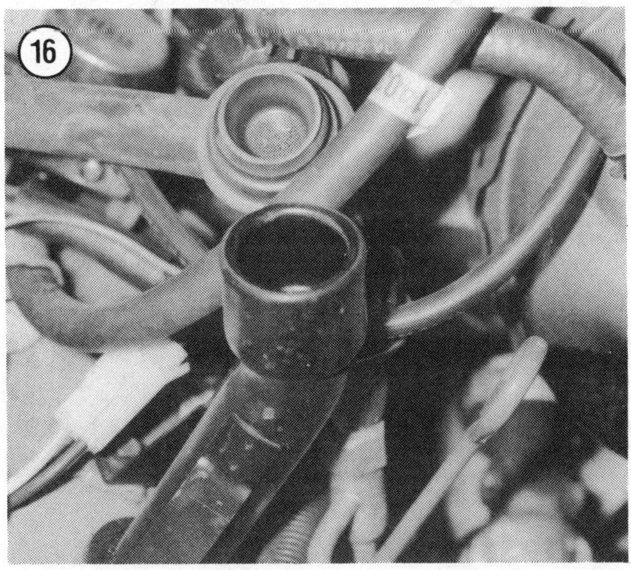

mainly off-highway, change the oil and filter twice as often as for average use. If the vehicle is only driven a few hundred miles each month, change the oil and filter every 6-8 weeks. If the vehicle is driven for long periods in extremely cold weather (when the temperature is frequently below 10° F), change the oil and filter twice as often as for average use.

CAUTION
Non-detergent, low quality oil should never be used. The use of oil additives is unnecessary and not recommended.

Engine oil should be selected to meet the demands of the temperatures and driving conditions anticipated. Refer to **Table 3** (gasoline) or **Table 4** (diesel) to select a viscosity that is appropriate for the temperatures you expect to encounter for the next maintenance interval. Chevrolet and GMC recommend the use of a high quality motor oil with an API classification of SF for all gasoline engines regardless of the model year or previous oil recommendations. An API designation of SF/CC or SF/CD is required for diesel engines. The rating and viscosity range are plainly marked on top of the can.

CAUTION
*While oil marked SF/CC or SF/CD can be used in gasoline engines when SF oil is not available, do **not** use an SF oil in diesel engines. It does not possess the necessary lubrication qualities to prevent serious engine damage.*

To drain the oil and change the filter, you will need:

a. Drain pan (6 quarts or more capacity).
b. Oil can spout or can opener and funnel.
c. Filter wrench.
d. Sufficient oil (See **Table 6**).
e. Adjustable wrench.
f. New oil filter.

There are several ways to discard the old oil safely. The easiest way is to pour it from the drain pan into a gallon bleach or milk container. The oil can then be taken to a service station for dumping or, where permitted, thrown in your household trash.

NOTE
Some service stations accept oil for recycling. Check local regulations before disposing of oil in trash. Never let oil drain on the ground.

The drain pan can be cleaned with solvent or paint thinner, if available. If not, hot water and dishwashing liquid will work.

1. With the vehicle on a level surface, warm the engine to operating temperature, then shut it off.
2. Set the parking brake and block the rear wheels.
3. Place a suitable container under the oil pan to serve as a drain pan.
4. Remove the oil filler cap (**Figure 15** or **Figure 16**) to promote faster draining.
5. Remove the dipstick (**Figure 1** or **Figure 2**) and wipe it clean with a cloth or paper towel.

6. Remove the drain plug. See **Figure 17** (typical).
7. Clean the drain plug and check its gasket. Replace the gasket if damaged.
8. Allow the oil to drain completely (10-15 minutes), then reinstall the plug.
9. Relocate the drain pan beneath the oil filter. **Figure 18** shows the gasoline engine filter; the diesel filter is installed in a vertical position on an oil cooler assembly bolted to the right side of the block near the flywheel.

NOTE
On V6 engines it will be necessary to use a grasp slide type filter wrench on the end of an 18 inch socket extension inserted through a flap provided in the left front wheelwell to remove the filler in Step 10.

10. Unscrew the filter counterclockwise. Use a filter wrench if the filter is too tight or too hot to remove by hand. Remove and discard the filter.
11. Wipe the engine mounting pad clean with a lint-free cloth or paper towel.
12. Coat the neoprene gasket on the new filter with a thin film of clean engine oil. Screw the filter in place *by hand* until it contacts the mounting pad surface. Tighten 3/4 turn further *by hand.* Do not overtighten, as this can cause an oil leak.
13. Fill the crankcase with oil through the filler cap hole. Wipe up any spills on the valve cover with a clean cloth and reinstall the filler cap.
14. Reinstall the dipstick. Wait a few seconds, then withdraw the dipstick. The oil level on the dipstick should be very close to the correct mark if the proper quantity of oil was used in Step 13.
15. Start the engine. The engine warning or oil pressure light will stay on for several seconds. Allow the engine to idle for several minutes.

CAUTION
Do not operate the engine at more than idle speed until the oil has had a chance to circulate throughout the engine or damage may result.

16. Check the area under and around the drain plug and filter for leaks while the engine is idling. Shut the engine off.

Air Cleaner

A disposable paper element filter is used. Service to a paper element filter consists of replacement only. Elements should not be cleaned with an air hose, tapped, washed or oiled. See Chapter Six for replacement procedure.

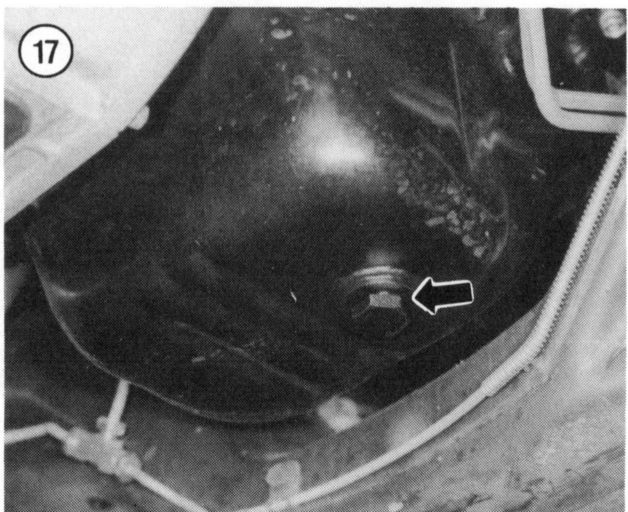

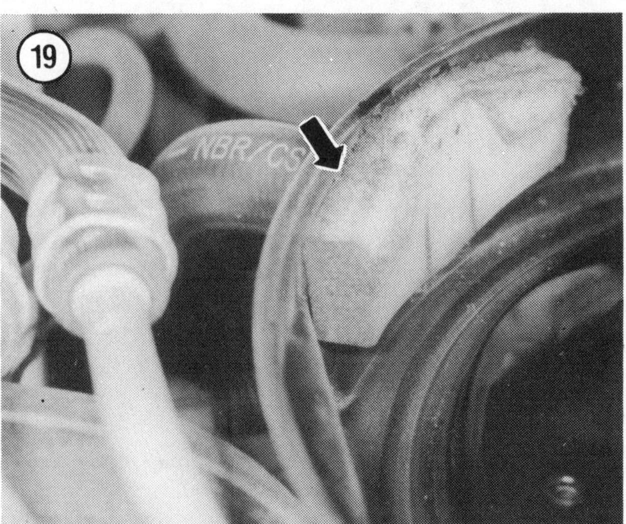

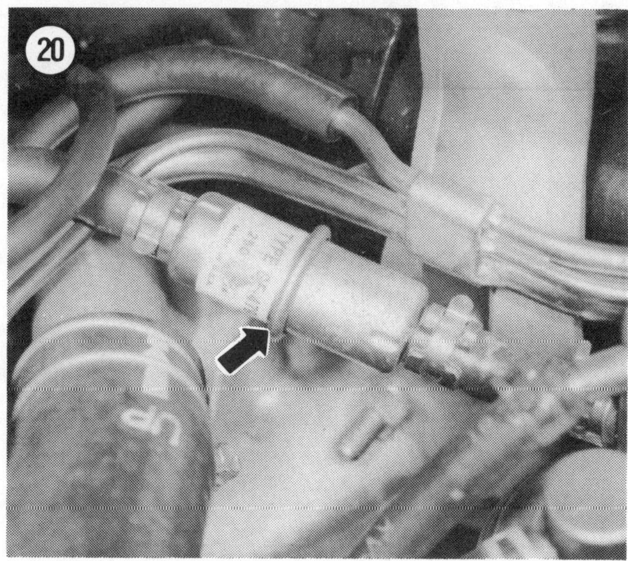

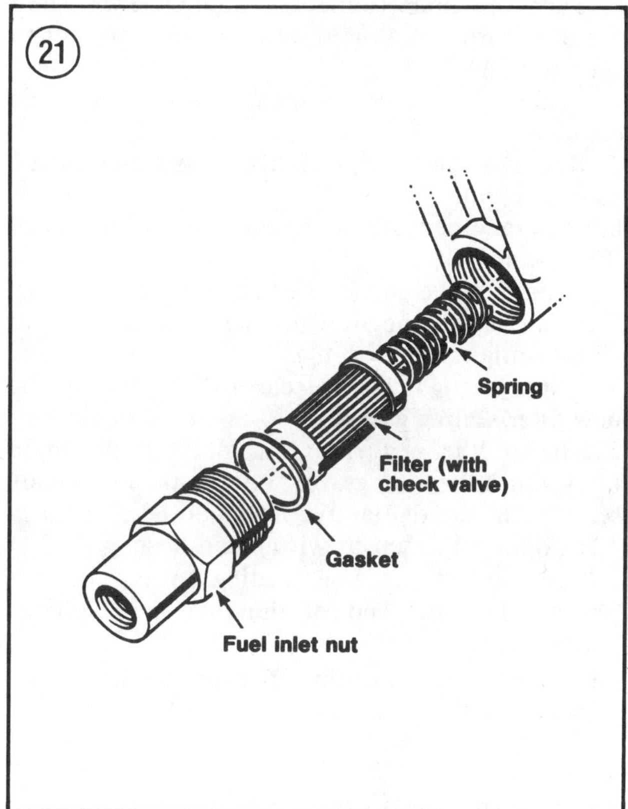

Check the air cleaner hoses and ducts when servicing the filter. Replace any hose or duct that is damaged. Check to make sure the air control valve in the air cleaner snorkel operates freely. Locate and correct any cause of valve binding or sticking. See Chapter Six.

Crankcase Ventilation Filter

The crankcase ventilation filter pack in the air cleaner housing (**Figure 19**) should be replaced each time the air cleaner filter is changed, if the air cleaner is so equipped. Disconnect the hose leading to the filter pack, slide the retaining clip off and remove the filter pack from inside the air cleaner housing. Install a new filter pack through the air cleaner housing hole, slide the retaining clip in place on the outside of the housing, making sure that it engages the groove in the filter pack tube and reconnect the hose.

3

Fuel Filter and Lines (Gasoline Engine)

1.9L engine

The 1.9L engine fuel filter is a disposable canister mounted in the fuel line between the fuel pump and carburetor (**Figure 20**). To replace the filter:

1. Compress the hose attaching clamps with a pair of pliers and slide the clamps off the filter nipples.
2. Disconnect the hoses from each end of the filter and remove.
3. Install the new filter with the arrow on the housing pointing toward the carburetor.
4. Attach the hoses to the filter nipples.
5. Compress the clamps and slide them back in position.

2.0L engine

The 2.0L 4-cylinder and carburetted V6 fuel filter is a pleated paper type installed in the carburetor float bowl behind the fuel inlet nut (**Figure 21**). To replace the filter:

1. Place one wrench on the fuel inlet nut and hold it from moving.
2. Place a second wrench on the fuel inlet fitting nut and loosen the nut.
3. Disconnect and plug the fuel line.
4. Remove the fuel inlet nut with the first wrench and remove the filter.
5. Install the new filter in the carburetor bowl.
6. Install and tighten the fuel inlet nut.
7. Install the fuel line to the fuel inlet nut.
8. Hold the inlet nut with the first wrench while tightening the inlet fitting nut with the second wrench.

2.5L and fuel injected V6 engines

The 2.5L and fuel injected V6 engines use a disposable inline filter canister (**Figure 22**). To replace the filter:

1. Relieve system pressure as described in Chapter Six.
2. Loosen the fuel inlet and outlet lines.
3. Loosen the bracket clamp screw.
4. Pull the filter from the bracket.
5. Install the new filter in the bracket with the arrow stamped on the canister facing in the direction of fuel flow.
6. Reconnect the lines to the canister and tighten securely.

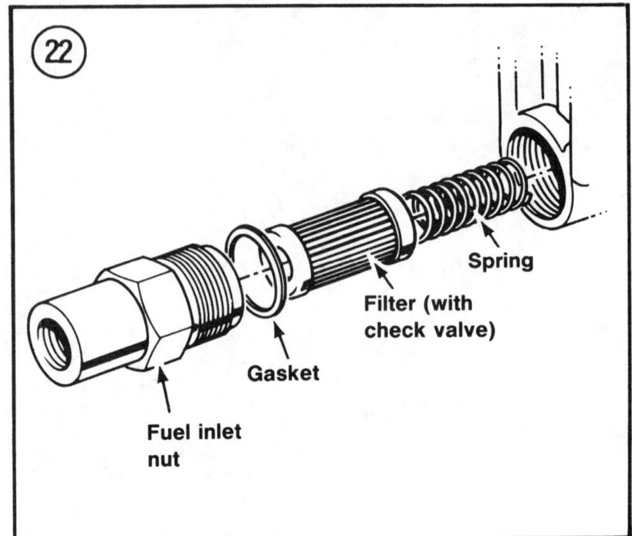

Fuel Filter and Water Separator (2.2L Diesel Engine)

The fuel filter strains contaminants from diesel fuel before it reaches the injection pump. The 2.2L diesel engine uses a combined filter/water separator unit (**Figure 23**) to filter the fuel, separate water from the fuel and sense the water level. A separate plug-in fuel control heater is mounted to the separator bracket.

Diesel fuel contains a small percentage of water. Additional moisture collects in the fuel during storage and shipment from the refinery to service stations. As long as the moisture remains in suspension, it will pass harmlessly through the injection pump.

A "water-in-fuel" module is incorporated in the 2.2L diesel electrical system. When the amount of moisture in the fuel tank exceeds a predetermined percentage, the module turns on a "Water-in-Fuel" lamp on the instrument panel. When the light illuminates, the separator should be drained to remove the accumulated water and prevent the possibility of damage to the fuel injection pump.

Diesel Fuel Filter Element Replacement

Refer to **Figure 23** and **Figure 24** for this procedure.

1. Disconnect the negative battery cable.
2. Disconnect the water sensor wiring connector.
3. Disconnect the hose between the main body and water sensor.
4. Pack shop cloths under the filter assembly to catch any spillage.
5. Turn the filter element counterclockwise and remove it from the main body, taking care not to spill any fuel.
6. Drain the filter element into a suitable container.
7. Remove the shop cloths from the engine compartment.
8. Unscrew the water and heater sensor unit from the bottom of the old filter.
9. Lubricate the sensor O-ring with clean diesel fuel and install the water and heater sensor unit with O-ring to the new filter.
10. Apply a light coat of clean diesel fuel to the new filter sealing gasket.
11. Install the new filter assembly to the main body. Once the filter gasket contacts the main body sealing surface, tighten the filter another 2/3 turn.
12. Connect the sensor wiring and hose.
13. Disconnect the line leading to the injector pump. Place the end of the line in a suitable container.
14. Operate the priming pump handle several times to fill the new filter element with fuel.
15. Reconnect the line leading to the injector pump.
16. Start the engine and check for leaks.

Diesel Water Separator Draining

Refer to **Figure 23** and **Figure 24** for this procedure.

1. Place a container under the end of the drain hose connected to the separator.

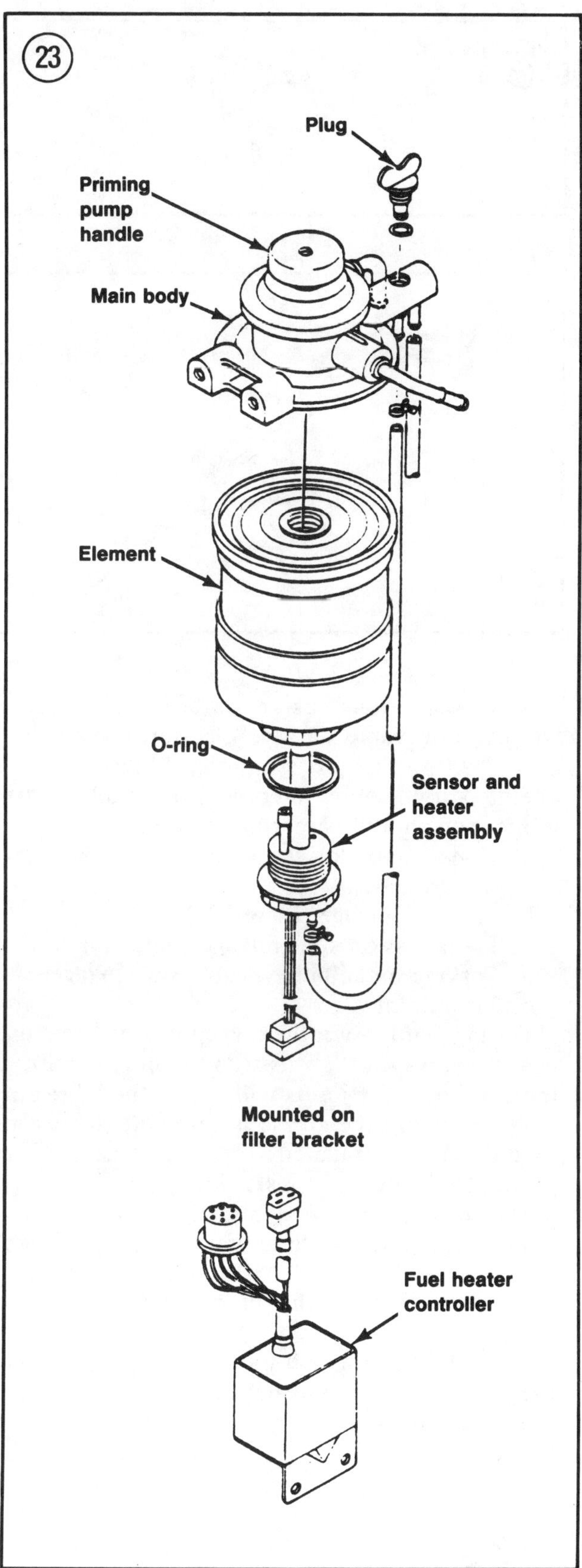

2. Turn the drain plug wing nut about 4 turns counterclockwise. Operate the priming pump handle until only clear diesel fuel is pumped from the drain hose.

3. Tighten the drain plug wing nut securely and operate the priming pump handle until you feel resistance.

4. Remove the container of diesel fuel and water from the engine compartment.

5. Start the engine and check for leaks. The "Watcr-in-Fuel" lamp on thc instrument panel should go off shortly after the engine starts running. If it does not, purge the fuel tank as described in this chapter.

3

Fuel Tank Purging (2.2L Diesel Engine)

This procedure must be performed whenever the "Water-in-Fuel" lamp on the instrument panel does not go out after the water separator is drained or whenever excessive moisture has accumulated in the tank itself.

1. Remove the fuel tank filler cap.

2. Disconnect the fuel return line from the injection pump.

3. Connect a pump or siphon to the return line.

4. Operate the pump or siphon until only clear diesel fuel is pumped out of the return line.

5. Remove the pump or siphon from the return line, then reconnect the line to the injection pump. Install the fuel tank filler cap.

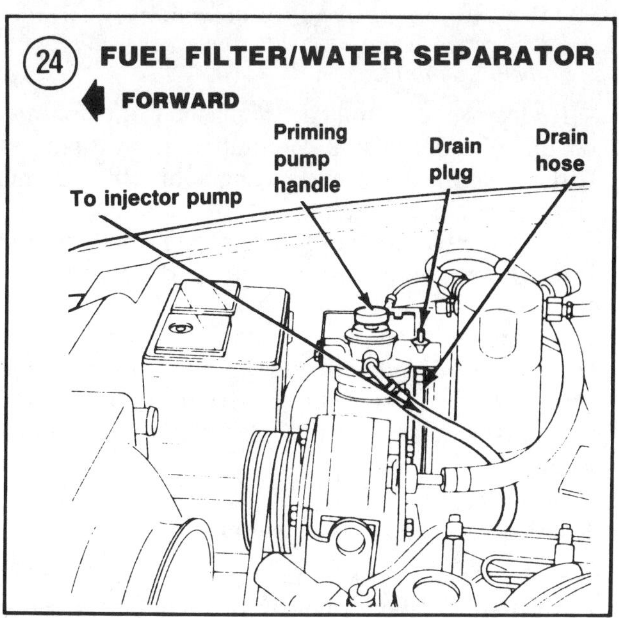

Battery (Unsealed)

Water is the only component of the battery which is lost as the result of charging and discharging. It must be replaced before the electrolyte level falls to the tops of the battery plates. If the plates become exposed, they may become sulfated. This will reduce performance and eventually ruin the battery. Also, the plates cannot take part in the battery action unless they are completely covered by the electrolyte. Add distilled water as often as necessary to keep the fluid level approximately 1/2 in. above the top of the battery plates or at the bottom of the filler vent wells. Do not overfill.

The charging action of a battery creates heat. A battery that requires frequent addition of water may be subject to overcharging. This is a signal to have the charging system checked to see if the alternator and voltage regulator are doing their job properly.

When working with batteries, use extreme care to avoid spilling or splashing the electrolyte. Battery electrolyte is sulfuric acid, which can destroy clothing and cause serious chemical burns. If any electrolyte is spilled or splashed on clothing or body, immediately neutralize it with a solution of baking soda and water, then flush the affected area with plenty of clean water.

WARNING

Electrolyte splashed into the eyes is extremely dangerous. Always wear safety glasses when working with batteries. If electrolyte is splashed into the eyes, call a physician immediately, force the eyes open and flood with cool, clean water for about 15 minutes.

If electrolyte is spilled or splashed onto painted or unpainted surfaces, neutralize it immediately with a baking soda and water solution and then rinse with clean water.

Keep the battery clean. Electrolyte which escapes through the vents will create a surface charge on the top of the battery which lowers battery performance. It also attacks metal surfaces such as the hold-down clamp and battery cable clamps. Periodically remove the battery from the engine compartment and clean it as described in Chapter Eight.

Chassis/Suspension Lubrication

Inspect and lubricate the following components or system. If the vehicle is driven under severe service conditions as described in **Table 1** (gasoline) or **Table 2** (diesel), perform this service every 3,000 miles or 3 months. If the vehicle is operated in deep water and/or mud, chassis lubrication should be performed daily.

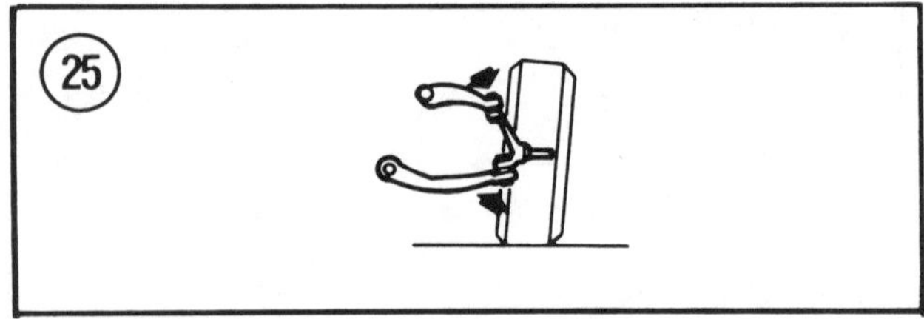

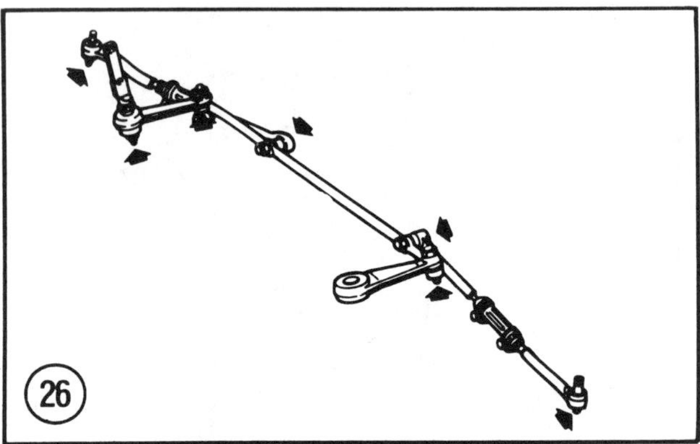

a. Upper and lower control arm ball-joints (**Figure 25**).
b. Steering linkage (**Figure 26**).
c. Transmission shift linkage contacting faces.
d. Parking brake pulley, cable and linkage.
e. Throttle linkage.

During winter weather, keep the vehicle in a heated garage for at least 30 minutes prior to lubrication so the joints will accept the lubricant.

Wipe around the grease fittings with a clean rag to remove accumulated dirt. On some vehicles, plugs may be installed instead of grease fittings. To lubricate such components, it is necessary to remove the plug and temporarily install a suitable grease or "zerk" fitting. When lubrication has been completed, remove the fitting and reinstall the plug.

When lubricating ball-joints, force lubricant into the joint until the joint boot can be felt or seen to swell slightly, indicating that the boot is full of lubricant.

CAUTION

Do not overfill until lubricant escapes from boot. This will destroy the weathertight seal.

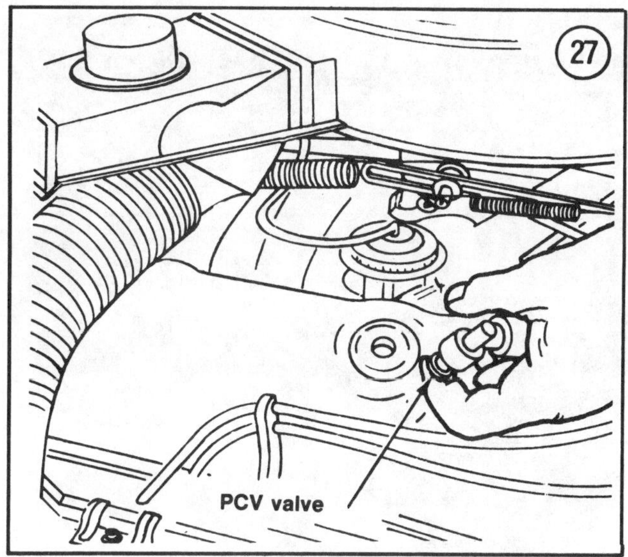

Any lubricants used should be applied sparingly and the excess wiped away to prevent it from attracting dirt which will also accelerate wear and contribute to difficult operation.

Body Lubrication

All hood, tailgate and door hinges, latches, locks and seat tracks should be lubricated periodically to ensure smooth operation and reduce wear. Recommended lubricants are given in **Table 5**.

1. Clean latch and hinge area of accumulated dirt or contamination.
2. Apply the specified lubricant sparingly, operating the mechanism several times to aid penetration.
3. Wipe off any excess lubricant with a clean, dry cloth to prevent it from attracting dirt and from soiling clothes, carpeting or upholstery.

Positive Crankcase Ventilation (PCV) System

The PCV system should be checked for proper operation at the interval stated in **Table 1**. More frequent checks and/or replacement should be made if the vehicle is operated under severe service conditions.

System Check

1. Start the engine and run at idle. Remove the PCV valve from the rocker cover. A hissing noise should be heard as air passes through the valve and a strong vacuum should be felt when a finger is placed over the end of the valve (**Figure 27**). If not, check for plugged hoses. See Chapter Six. If the hoses are not plugged, replace the valve as described in this chapter.
2. Reinstall the PCV valve and remove the crankcase breather cap, vent retainer or fresh air inlet hose from the valve cover (this is located on the opposite valve cover on V6 or V8 engines). Hold a piece of stiff paper, such as a parts tag or a 3×5 memo card, over the valve cover opening. Wait approximately 60 seconds for crankcase pressure to be reduced. Shortly thereafter, the paper should be sucked to the valve cover opening. If it is not, check for a plugged PCV hose. See Chapter Six.
3. Shut the engine off. Reinstall the breather cap, vent retainer or fresh air inlet hose and remove the PCV valve from the valve cover a second time. Shake the valve and listen for the rattle of the check needle in the valve. If no rattle is heard, replace the valve as described in this chapter.

PCV Valve Replacement

Chevrolet and GMC use PCV valves with different flow rates calibrated to the engine and model year. A new PCV valve should be of the same design and bear the same part number as the one being replaced.

1. Disconnect the hose from the PCV valve.
2. Remove the PCV valve from the valve cover grommet with an upward rotating motion. Discard the valve.

NOTE
Do not attempt to clean and reuse a plugged PCV valve.

3. Check the condition of the valve cover grommet and replace as required.
4. Install the new valve in the valve cover grommet with a downward rotating motion.
5. Position the valve with the vacuum nipple facing the PCV hose. Reconnect the hose to the valve.

Exhaust Gas Recirculation (EGR) System

The EGR valve is mounted on an adapter housing on the intake manifold on 1.9L engines. The 2.0L EGR valve is located beside the

3

thermostat housing. The 2.5L and V6 EGR valve is behind the carburetor on the intake manifold.

Test the system (Chapter Six) at the interval stated in **Table 1**. If the valve does not function as described, remove it and inspect the orifice hole for deposits. EGR valves should be replaced, not cleaned. At the same time, inspect and clean the EGR passages in the spacer and the intake manifold as required.

Evaporative Emission Canister

Canister size, design and location differ according to model year and engine application. **Figure 28** shows a typical design located in the engine compartment.

Inspect the canister lines and connections and the fuel tank filler cap when checking the evaporative emission control system as specified in **Table 1**.

Drive Belt Condition and Tension

Check the alternator, water pump, AIR pump, air conditioning and power steering pump drive belts for fraying, glazing or cracking of the contact surfaces. Belts that are damaged or deteriorated should be replaced (Chapter Seven) before they fail and cause serious problems from engine overheating, electrical system failure or reduction of steering and brake control.

Check and adjust (if necessary) the tension of all drive belts (Chapter Seven). A belt that is too loose will cause the driven components to operate at less than required efficiency. A belt that is adjusted too tightly will wear rapidly and place unnecessary side loads on the bearings of driven components, which can cause premature wear or failure.

Brake System

Check the brake master cylinder fluid level as described in this chapter.

Inspect all brake lines, hoses and fittings for abrasion, kinks, leakage and other damage and replace as necessary. This is particularly important following rough, off-highway usage where the likelihood of brush and rock damage is high. Any line that is less than perfect should be replaced immediately.

Check all connections for tightness and look for signs of leakage which may indicate a cracked or otherwise unserviceable connection. As with lines and hoses, any connections that are less than perfect should be replaced.

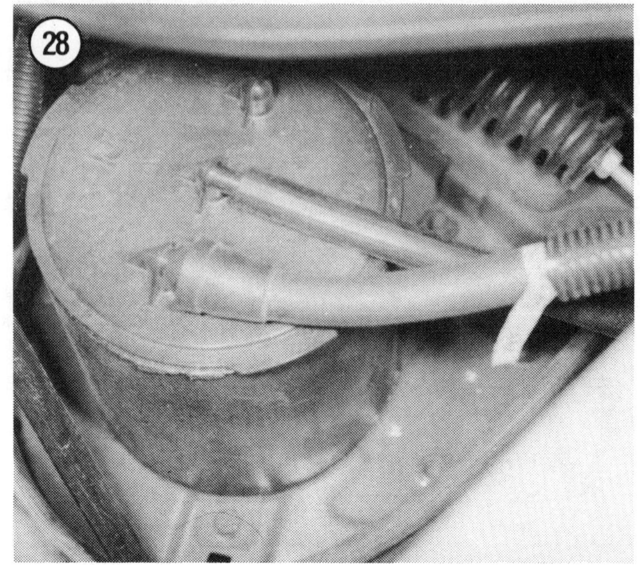

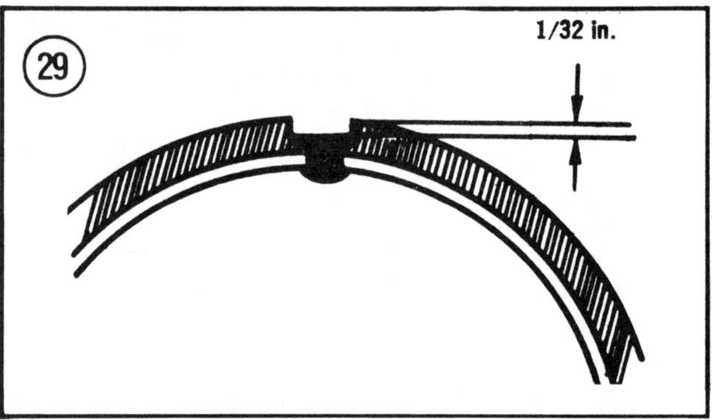

Always bleed the brakes after opening a system connection. See Chapter Twelve.

Check all brake shoe linings (disc and drum) for brake fluid, oil or grease contamination on the friction material. If any contamination is present, the linings must be replaced regardless of how much material remains.

Measure the linings to determine their serviceability. If any brake shoe lining (disc or drum) has worn down to within 1/32 in. of a rivet head (**Figure 29**) or the backing plate on bonded shoes, replace the linings on both wheels.

Power Steering

Check the power steering fluid in the pump reservoir as described in this chapter.

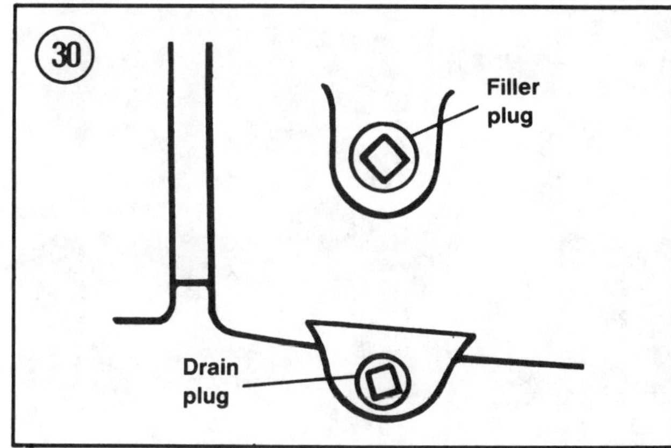

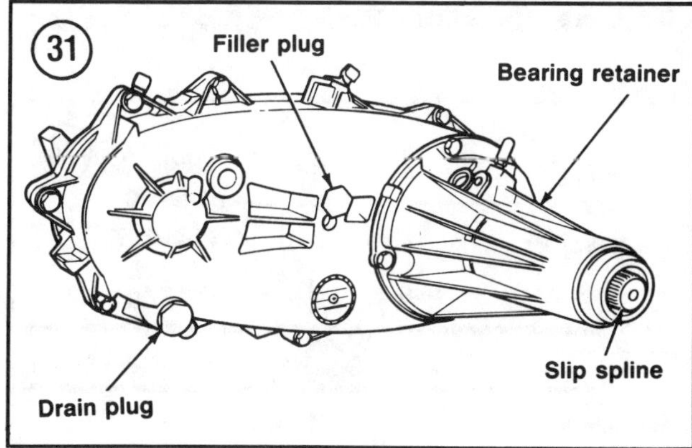

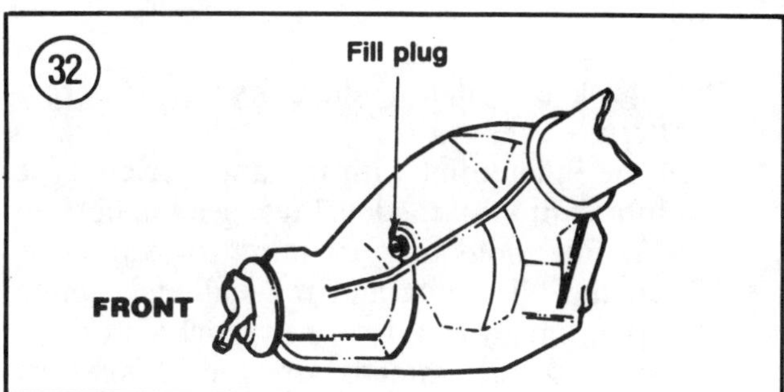

Check all power steering hoses and lines for proper connections, leaks and deterioration. If abrasion or excessive wear is evident, locate and correct the cause immediately.

Manual Steering Gearbox Seal

The steering gearbox is permanently lubricated and should require no service other than checking around the pitman arm and housing for seal leakage and oozing. Leakage (solid grease, not just an oily film) should be corrected immediately.

Cooling System

WARNING
Personal injury is possible. Perform cooling system service when the engine is cold.

3

Clean exterior of radiator and air conditioning condenser with compressed air and inspect radiator hoses at least once a year for cracks, checks, swelling or other signs of deterioration. Make sure that all hoses are correctly routed and installed and that all clamps are tight. Replace hoses at every coolant change.

Remove the radiator cap and check the condition of the coolant. If it is dirty or rusty, the system should be drained, flushed and refilled with fresh coolant regardless of the mileage. Replace the coolant every 24 months or 30,000 miles. See Chapter Seven.

Manual Transmission/Transfer Case/ Axle Lubricant Level

At each oil change, check fluid level of manual transmission, transfer case and axles. Top up if necessary with the recommended lubricant (**Table 5**).

1. Drive the vehicle several miles to bring the lubricant to normal operating temperature.
2. Set the parking brake and block the appropriate drive wheels.
3. Raise the front or rear of the vehicle as appropriate with a jack and place it on jackstands.
4. Clean all dirt and grease from the fill/level or fill plug. See **Figure 30** (manual transmission), **Figure 31** (transfer case), **Figure 32** (axle) for typical plug locations.
5. Unscrew and remove the fill/level or fill plug. The lubricant level should be even with the bottom of the fill/level plug hole (manual transmissions/transfer case) or within 3/8 in. of the bottom of the fill hole (axles). If not, top up with the recommended lubricant (**Table 5**) and install the plug. Wipe any excess lubricant from the transmission/transfer case or differential housing.
6. Remove the jackstands and lower the vehicle to the ground. Remove the blocks from the wheels.

Manual Transmission/Transfer Case/ Axle Lubricant Change

Vehicles equipped with a 4-speed manual transmission require periodic fluid changes. Other lubricant changes should be performed as needed.

If the vehicle is driven only a few hundred miles each month, the oil should be changed more frequently, as is the case if the vehicle is operated in extremely cold weather when the temperature is frequently below 10° F. Acids that form in the lubricant during short-haul driving or during operation in extremely cold weather are injurious to moving parts. In addition, lubricants should be changed whenever water has entered the component and contaminated the oil.

Positraction rear axles require a special lubricant (GM part No. 1051052) or equivalent. Drain and refill to level of fill plug hole at first specified interval, then maintain as a standard differential.

With limited slip rear axles, drain and refill to level of fill plug hole at first 7,500 miles. Change lubricant at 15,000-mile intervals when using vehicle to pull a trailer. Add 4 ounces of GM lubricant additive (part No. 1052358) or equivalent, then fill with GM gear lubricant (part No. 1052271, 1052272 or equivalent.

1. Drive the vehicle several miles to bring the lubricant to normal operating temperature.
2. Set the parking brake and block the appropriate drive wheels.
3. Raise the front or rear of the vehicle as appropriate with a jack and place it on jackstands.
4. Clean all dirt and grease from the fill/level or fill plug. See **Figures 30-32** as required.
5. Manual transmission/transfer case:
   a. Place a drain pan under the transmission or transfer case and remove the drain plug. Let the oil drain for 10-15 minutes.
   b. Clean and reinstall the drain plug snugly.
   c. Fill the transmission or transfer case with the recommended lubricant (**Table 5**). The level is correct when oil just starts to seep from the fill/level hole.
   d. Clean and reinstall the fill/level plug snugly.
   e. Wipe any excess lubricant from the transmission/transfer case.

6. Front/rear axle:
   a. Unscrew and remove the filler plug.
   b. Remove the old oil with a suction pump.
   c. If a suction pump is not available, place a drain pan under the differential and loosen the rear cover bolts several turns. Tap the edge of the cover with a mallet to break it loose and let the oil drain.
   d. Remove the cover and discard the gasket. Clean all gasket residue from the cover and differential flange. Reinstall the cover with a new gasket, tightening the bolts in a crisscross pattern.
   e. Fill the differential with the appropriate type of lubricant until the level reaches the bottom of the filler hole and just starts to seep out.
   f. Clean the filler plug and reinstall it. Tighten the plug snugly but do not overtighten or you may strip the threads on the differential housing. Wipe any excess lubricant from the differential housing.
7. Remove the jackstands and lower the vehicle to the ground.
8. After driving the vehicle about 100 miles, check for leaks around the drain plug. If leakage is found, correct the problem and recheck the oil level.

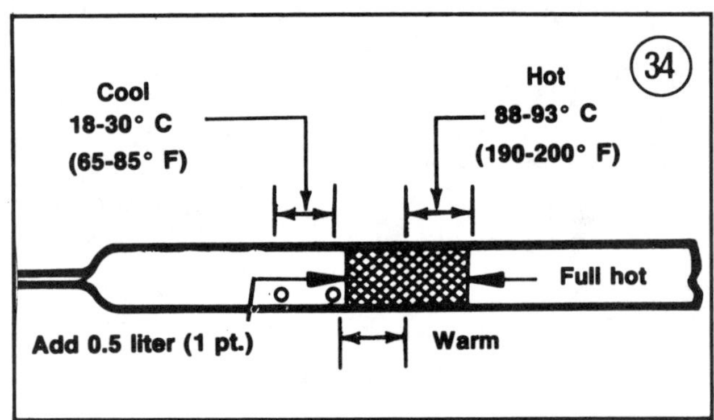

Automatic Transmission Service

Automatic transmission fluid will deliver 100,000 miles of service at normal operating temperature (approximately 175° F) before oxidation takes place. When a transmission

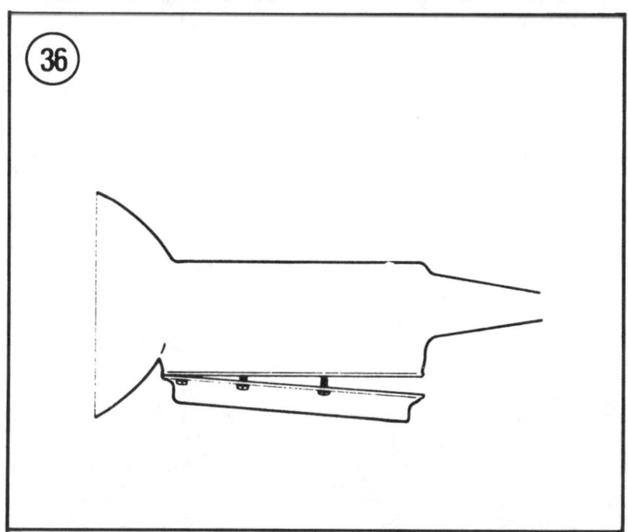

operates at above normal temperature, the service life of its fluid is cut in half with each 20° F increase in temperature. See **Table 7**.

If fluid operating temperature is allowed to reach 500° F, the metals inside the transmission will start to warp rapidly. For this reason, rocking a vehicle out of snow, mud or sand by rapidly shifting from FORWARD to REVERSE should be avoided if at all possible. If attempted, do not rock the vehicle for more than 1-2 minutes.

Level Check

1. Check the fluid level with the transmission at operating temperature, engine running and the vehicle parked on level ground with the parking brake set and the transmission selector in PARK.
2. Clean all dirt from the transmission dipstick cap. See **Figure 33**. Pull the dipstick from the tube, wipe with a clean, lint-free cloth and reinsert until the cap seats fully. Wait a few seconds, then remove the dipstick a second time and note the reading (**Figure 34**).
3. If the fluid level is low, add sufficient automatic transmission fluid of the recommended type (**Table 5**) to bring it to the proper level on the dipstick. Reinsert the dipstick and make sure it is fully seated in the tube.

CAUTION
Do not overfill the transmission. Too much fluid can cause damage to the transmission.

Fluid Change

Under normal circumstances, automatic transmission fluid is changed at 100,000-mile intervals. If the vehicle has been subjected to constant severe service such as those stated in **Table 1** or **Table 2**, drain and refill the fluid at 15,000-mile intervals.

1. Drive the vehicle several miles to bring the lubricant to normal operating temperature.
2. Set the parking brake and block the drive wheels.
3. Raise the front of the vehicle with a jack and place it on jackstands.
4. Place a drain pan under the transmission.
5. Loosen all pan attaching bolts (**Figure 35**) a few turns. Tap one corner of the pan with a rubber hammer to break it loose and let the fluid drain.
6. When the fluid has drained to the level of the pan flange, remove the pan bolts at the rear and along both sides of the pan (**Figure 36**). This will let the pan drop at one end and drain slowly.
7. When all fluid has drained, remove the pan and let the strainer drain.
8. Remove any gasket or sealant residue from the pan and transmission case mating flanges.
9. Discard the gasket and clean the pan thoroughly with solvent and lint-free cloths or paper towels.
10. Remove the strainer attaching screws (**Figure 37**). Remove the strainer from the transmission valve body. Check the attaching nipple on the strainer for an O-ring seal. If it is not on the strainer, remove it from the valve body bore.
11. Install a new O-ring on the new strainer nipple. Install the strainer to the valve body bore and tighten the attaching screws securely.

12. Apply a 1/16 in. bead of RTV sealant to the pan mounting flange. See **Figure 38**.

NOTE
If the pan flange has a raised rib as shown in ***Figure 39****, do not use RTV sealant. This pan design requires the use of a gasket.*

13. Install the pan on the transmission and tighten the attaching bolts to 10-13 ft.-lb. (14-18 N•m) in a crisscross pattern.
14. Insert a clean funnel containing a fine-mesh filter in the filler tube and pour approximately 4 quarts of fresh DEXRON II automatic transmission fluid into the transmission.
15. Start the engine and let it idle for 2 minutes with the gear selector in PARK. Increase the engine speed to approximately 1,200 rpm and let it run until it reaches normal operating temperature.
16. Depress and hold the foot brake. Slowly move the selector through each gear range, pausing long enough for the transmission to engage. Return to the PARK position.
17. Remove the dipstick and wipe it with a clean, lint-free cloth. Reinsert the dipstick in the filler tube until it seats completely.

CAUTION
Do not overfill the transmission. Too much fluid is harmful. If the fluid level is above the specified mark on the dipstick with the fluid at normal operating temperature, drain enough fluid to correct the level.

18. Remove the dipstick and check the fluid level. Add sufficient fluid as required to bring the fluid to the appropriate level on the dipstick (**Figure 34**).
19. Once the fluid level is correct, check for and correct any leaks at the filler tube connection and around the edge of the oil pan.
20. Road test the vehicle to make sure the transmission operates properly. After driving the vehicle approximately 100 miles, recheck the fluid level and correct, if necessary.

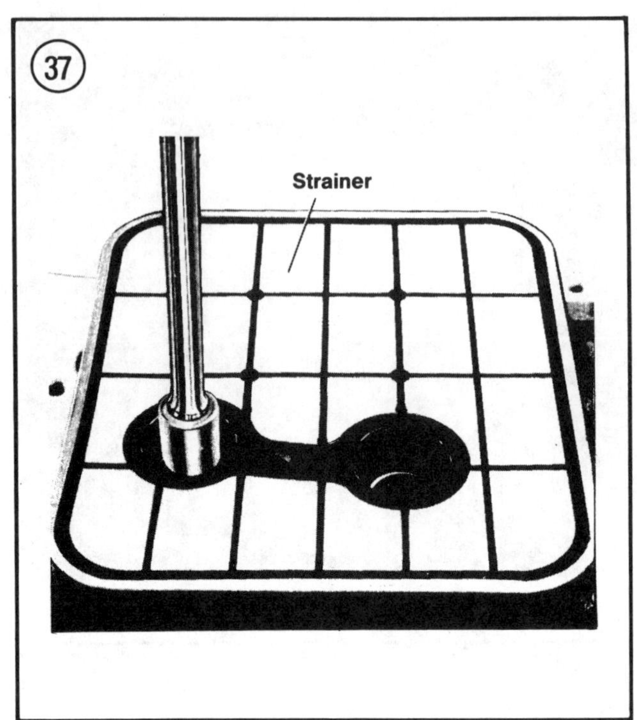

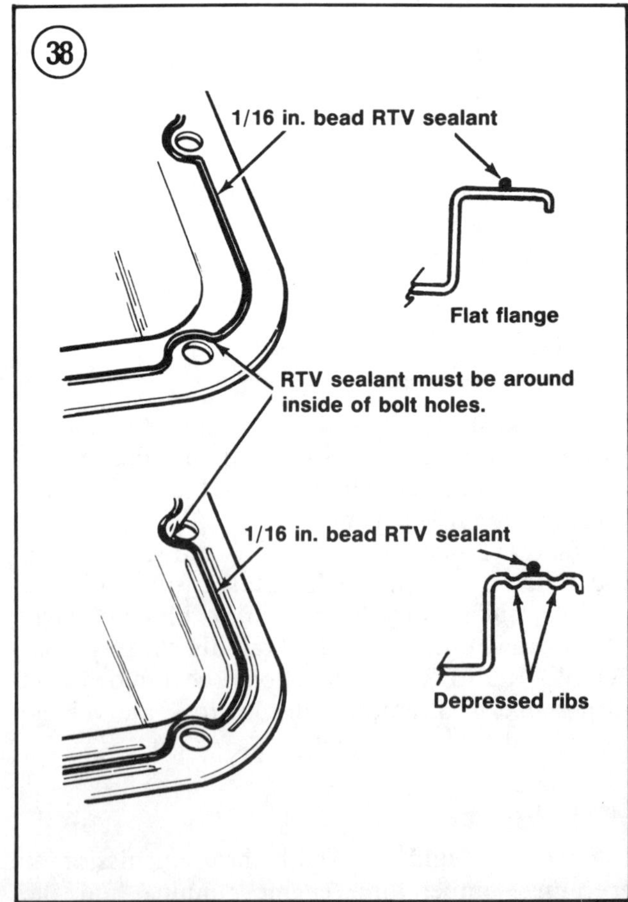

Carburetor Choke and Vacuum Lines

Make sure that the choke and vacuum break assembly work freely and properly. Spray choke shaft with choke cleaner to remove any gum or varnish buildup. Inspect vacuum lines for proper routing and connection. Check vacuum line

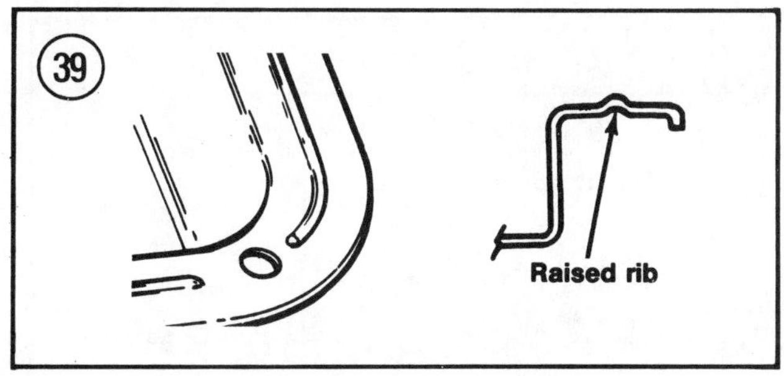

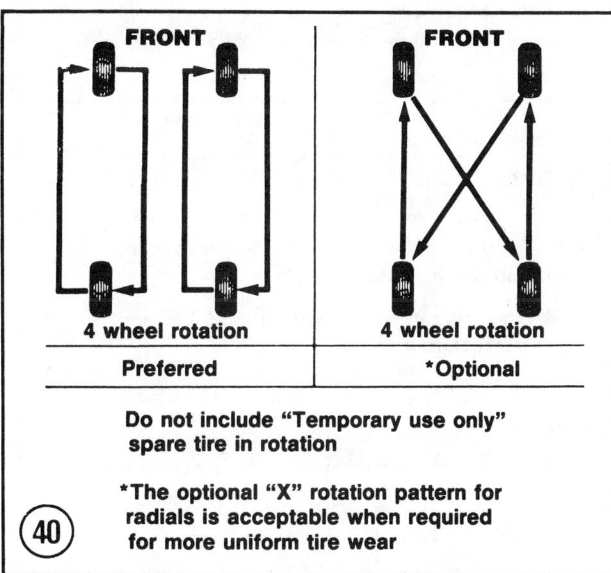

condition and replace any that are cracked, split or deteriorated.

Carburetor/Throttle Body Mounting Fasteners

Check mounting fastener torque. Tighten carburetor fasteners to 12 ft.-lb. (16 N•m) and throttle body fasteners to 10-14 ft.-lb. (14-19 N•m).

Idle Speed (Except Fuel-injected Engine)

Check and adjust to the specifications shown in the vehicle emission control information (VECI) label under the hood.

Exhaust System

Check the entire exhaust system from exhaust manifold to tailpipe(s). Look for broken, damaged, missing, corroded or misaligned components, open seams, holes, loose connections or any other defect that could allow exhaust gases to enter the cab (or bed area on pickups equipped with a camper shell).

Inspect the catalytic converter heat shields (if so equipped) for looseness or damage. Tighten or replace as required. Remove any debris that may have lodged or accumulated in or around the shields. Make sure there is adequate clearance between the exhaust system components and nearby body areas.

Whenever the muffler requires replacement, replace the exhaust pipe(s) and resonator to the rear of the muffler to maintain exhaust system integrity.

Tire Rotation

Inspect the tires for cracks, bumps, bulges or other defects. Look for signs of excessive wear. Rotate radial tires at the first 7,000 miles, then every 15,000 miles thereafter. Rotate bias belted tires every 6,000 miles. Refer to **Figure 40** for recommended rotation patterns.

Front Wheel Bearings

Clean, repack and adjust bearings. See Chapter Ten.

Oxygen Sensor

Replace the sensor as required. See Chapter Six.

Idle Stop Solenoid

Check idle stop solenoid operation on carburetted models, if so equipped.

1. Turn the ignition switch ON but do not start the engine. If equipped with air conditioning, turn the air conditioner on.
2. Open the throttle until the solenoid plunger fully extends, then close the throttle. Unplug the solenoid electrical lead and the plunger should move away from the throttle lever.
3. Reconnect the solenoid lead and the plunger should extend again until it touches the throttle lever. If it does not, connect a test lamp between the solenoid feed wire and ground.
   a. If the test lamp lights, replace the solenoid.
   b. If it does not light, look for an open circuit in the feed wire and correct the condition.

Fuel Tank, Cap and Lines

Inspect the fuel tank, cap and lines for leaks or damage. Remove the fuel cap and check the gasket for an even filler neck imprint.

Throttle Linkage

Check for damaged or missing parts. Work the throttle lever back and forth to check for interference or binding. Spray the linkage with carburetor cleaner and lubricate with WD-40.

GASOLINE ENGINE TUNE-UP

A tune-up consists of a series of inspections, adjustments and parts replacements to compensate for normal wear and deterioration of engine components. Regular tune-ups are important for proper emission control and fuel economy.

Since proper engine operation depends upon a number of interrelated system functions, a tune-up consisting of only one or two corrections will seldom give lasting results. For improved power, performance and operating economy, a thorough and systematic procedure of analysis and correction is necessary.

Always refer to the Vehicle Emission Control Information (VECI) decal on the valve cover or elsewhere in the engine compartment for tune-up specifications pertaining to your vehicle.

TUNE-UP SEQUENCE

Because different systems in an engine interact, the tune-up should be carried out in the following order.

a. Valve clearance adjustment (1.9L gasoline and 2.2L diesel only).
b. Compression check.
c. Ignition system work.
d. Carburetor inspection and adjustment.

Refer to the VECI label in the engine compartment for tune-up specifications.

VALVE CLEARANCE ADJUSTMENT

1.9L Gasoline Engine

Check and adjust valve clearance as follows:

1. Remove the valve cover. See Chapter Four.
2. Check torque on rocker arm shaft bracket nut. Tighten as required to 16 ft.-lb. (22 N•m) before adjusting the valve clearances.

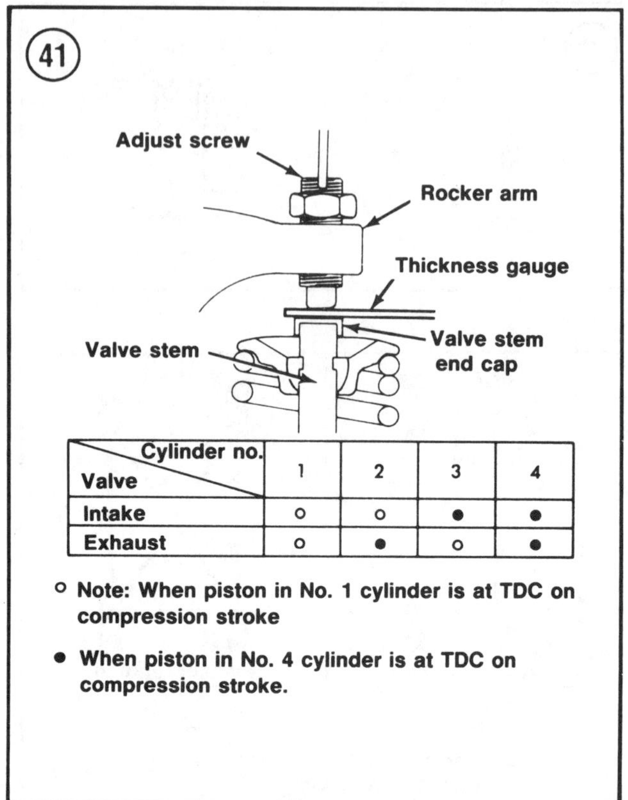

Valve \ Cylinder no.	1	2	3	4
Intake	o	o	•	•
Exhaust	o	•	o	•

o Note: When piston in No. 1 cylinder is at TDC on compression stroke

• When piston in No. 4 cylinder is at TDC on compression stroke.

3. Position the No. 1 cylinder at top dead center. To do this, place a socket wrench on the crankshaft pulley nut and rotate the crankshaft until the timing mark on the crankshaft pulley is aligned with the timing pointer. Remove the distributor cap and check the position of the rotor. If it does not point toward the No. 1 electrode in the distributor cap, the crankshaft must be rotated another full turn.
4. When the timing marks are aligned and the distributor rotor points to the No. 1 cap electrode, insert a feeler gauge between the valve stem end cap and rocker arm adjusting screw as shown in **Figure 41**. Adjust the No. 1 and No. 2 intake valves to 0.006 in. (0.15 mm). Adjust the No. 1 and No. 3 exhaust valves to 0.010 in. (0.25 mm).

NOTE
Intake valves are on the carburetor side of the engine. Exhaust valves are on the exhaust manifold side of the engine.

5. Rotate the crankshaft one full turn and repeat Step 4 to adjust the No. 3 and No. 4 intake valves and the No. 2 and No. 4 exhaust valves.
6. Install the valve cover. See Chapter Four.

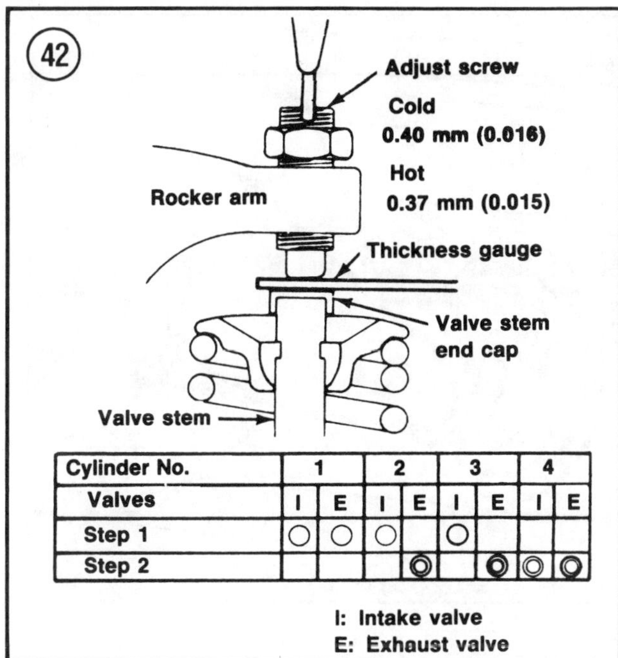

Cylinder No.	1		2		3		4	
Valves	I	E	I	E	I	E	I	E
Step 1	O	O	O		O			
Step 2				O		O	O	O

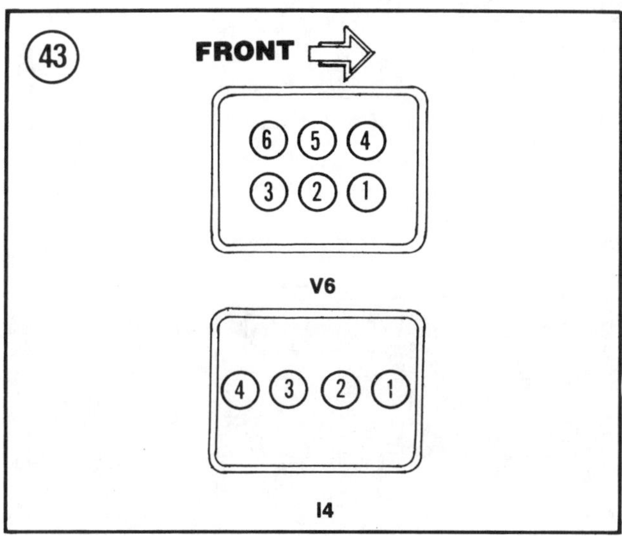

2.2L Diesel Engine

Check and adjust valve clearance as follows:

1. Disconnect the negative battery cable.
2. Remove the PCV pipe hose from the valve cover.
3. Remove the air cleaner.
4. Remove the 2 valve cover bolts. Remove the valve cover.
5. Check torque on rocker shaft bracket bolts. Tighten as required to 9-17 ft.-lb. (12-23 N•m) before adjusting the valve clearances.
6. Rotate the crankshaft until the No. 1 cylinder is at top dead center (TDC) on the compression stroke. In this position, the No. 1 intake and exhaust and the No. 2 and No. 3 intake valves will be closed and their clearance can be checked.
7. Insert a 0.016 in. (cold engine) or 0.015 in. (hot engine) flat feeler gauge between one valve stem end cap and rocker arm adjusting screw as shown in **Figure 42**. If adjustment is required, loosen the adjusting screw locknut and turn the screw in or out as required to obtain the specified clearance. Tighten the locknut and repeat this step for each of the 3 remaining valves.
8. Rotate the crankshaft one full turn and repeat Step 7 to check and adjust the clearance of the No. 4 intake and the No. 2, No. 3 and No. 4 exhaust valves.
9. Reverse Steps 1-4. Use a new valve cover gasket and tighten cover bolts to 9-13 ft.-lb. (12-17 N•m).

COMPRESSION TEST

An engine with low or uneven compression cannot be properly tuned. Whenever the spark plugs are removed from the engine, it is a good idea to run a compression test. A compression test measures the compression pressure built up in each cylinder. Its results can be used to assess general cylinder and valve condition. In addition, it can warn of developing problems inside the engine.

1. Warm the engine to normal operating temperature (upper radiator hose hot). Shut the engine off. Make sure the choke and throttle valves are wide open on carburetted models.
2. Remove all spark plugs as described in this chapter.

3A. 1.9L engine—Disconnect and ground the high tension lead between the distributor and coil.

3B. All other—Disconnect the pink wire between the HEI distributor and the ignition coil.

4. Connect a remote start switch to the starter solenoid according to manufacturer's instructions. Leave the ignition key in the OFF position.
5. Connect a compression tester to the No. 1 cylinder according to manufacturer's instructions.

NOTE

*The No. 1 cylinder is the front cylinder on the 4-cylinder engine and the front cylinder on the right (passenger side) bank on the V6. See **Figure 43**.*

6. Crank the engine at least 5 turns with the remote start switch or until there is no further increase in compression shown on the tester gauge.
7. Remove the compression tester and record the reading. Relieve the tester pressure valve.
8. Repeat Step 6 and Step 7 for each cylinder.

When interpreting the results, actual readings are not as important as the differences in readings. The lowest must be within 75 percent of the highest. A greater difference indicates worn or broken rings, leaking or sticking valves or a combination of these problems.

If the compression test indicates a problem (excessive variation in readings), isolate the cause with a wet compression test. This is done in the same way as the dry compression test, except that about 1 teaspoon of oil is poured down the spark plug hole before performing Steps 5-7. If the wet compression readings are much greater than the dry compression readings, the trouble is probably due to worn or broken rings. If there is little difference between the wet and dry readings, the problem is probably due to leaky or sticking valves. If 2 adjacent cylinders read low in both tests, the head gasket may be leaking.

SPARK PLUG REPLACEMENT

Spark plugs should be replaced every 30,000 miles.

CAUTION

Whenever the spark plugs are removed, dirt from around them can fall into the spark plug holes. This can cause expensive engine damage.

1. Blow out any foreign matter from around the spark plugs with compressed air. Use a compressor if you have one. Cans of compressed inert gas are available from photo stores.
2. Disconnect the spark plug wires by twisting the wire boot back and forth on the plug insulator while pulling upward (**Figure 44**). Pulling on the wire instead of the boot may cause internal damage to the wire. Wire removal with spark plug terminal pliers is recommended where there is enough clearance for their use.
3. Remove the plugs with a 5/8 in. spark plug socket. Keep the plugs in order so you know which cylinder they came from.
4. Examine each spark plug. Compare its condition with **Figure 45**. Spark plug condition indicates engine condition and can warn of developing trouble.
5. Discard the plugs. Although they could be cleaned, regapped and reused if in good condition, they seldom last very long. New plugs are inexpensive and far more reliable.
6. Remove the plugs from the box. Tapered plugs do not use gaskets. Some plug brands may have small end pieces that must be screwed on (**Figure 46**) before the plugs can be used.

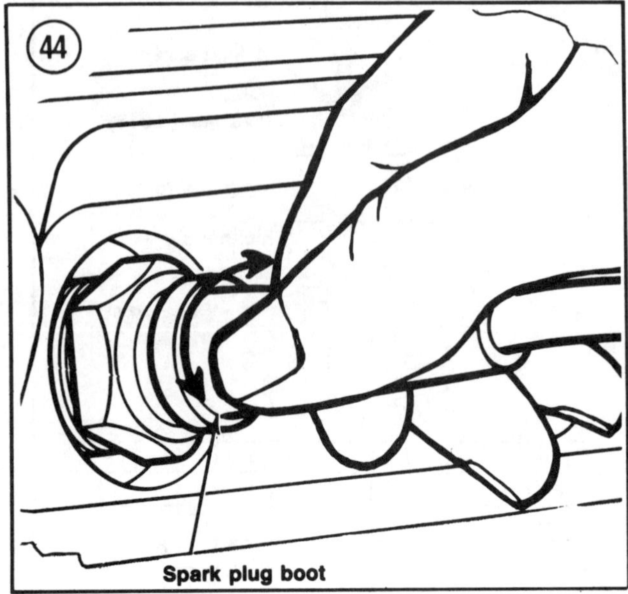

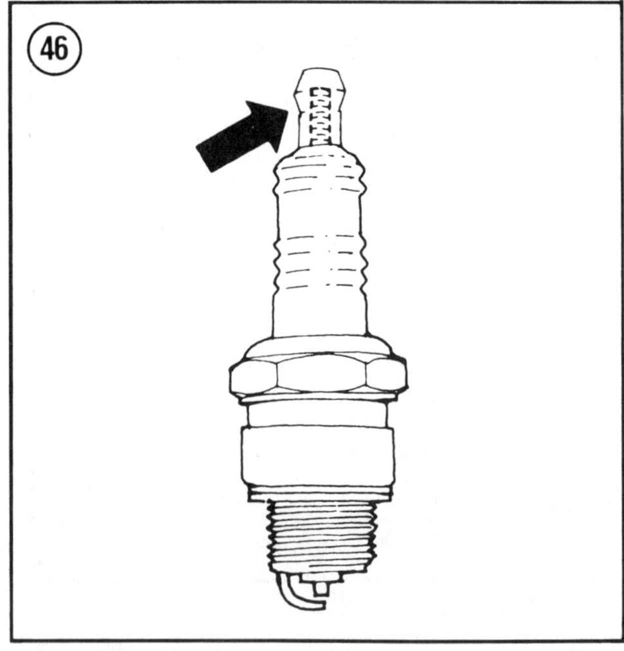

45

SPARK PLUG CONDITION

NORMAL

- Identified by light tan or gray deposits on the firing tip.
- Can be cleaned.

GAP BRIDGED

- Identified by deposit buildup closing gap between electrodes.
- Caused by oil or carbon fouling. If deposits are not excessive, the plug can be cleaned.

OIL FOULED

- Identified by wet black deposits on the insulator shell bore electrodes.
- Caused by excessive oil entering combustion chamber through worn rings and pistons, excessive clearance between valve guides and stems, or worn or loose bearings. Can be cleaned. If engine is not repaired, use a hotter plug.

CARBON FOULED

- Identified by black, dry fluffy carbon deposits on insulator tips, exposed shell surfaces and electrodes.
- Caused by too cold a plug, weak ignition, dirty air cleaner, too rich a fuel mixture, or excessive idling. Can be cleaned.

LEAD FOULED

- Identified by dark gray, black, yellow, or tan deposits or a fused glazed coating on the insulator tip.
- Caused by highly leaded gasoline. Can be cleaned.

WORN

- Identified by severely eroded or worn electrodes.
- Caused by normal wear. Should be replaced.

FUSED SPOT DEPOSIT

- Identified by melted or spotty deposits resembling bubbles or blisters.
- Caused by sudden acceleration. Can be cleaned.

OVERHEATING

- Identified by a white or light gray insulator with small black or gray brown spots and with bluish-burnt appearance of electrodes.
- Caused by engine overheating, wrong type of fuel, loose spark plugs, too hot a plug, or incorrect ignition timing. Replace the plug.

PREIGNITION

- Identified by melted electrodes and possibly blistered insulator. Metallic deposits on insulator indicate engine damage.
- Caused by wrong type of fuel, incorrect ignition timing or advance, too hot a plug, burned valves, or engine overheating. Replace the plug.

7. Determine the correct gap setting from the VECI label. Use a spark plug gapping tool to check the gap. **Figure 47** shows two common types. Insert the appropriate size wire gauge between the electrodes. If the gap is correct, there will be a slight drag as the wire is pulled through. If there is no drag or if the wire will not pull through, bend the side electrode with the gapping tool (**Figure 48**) to change the gap and then remeasure with the wire gauge.

NOTE

Never try to close the electrode gap by tapping the spark plug on a solid surface. This can damage the plug internally. Always use a spark plug tool to open or close the gap.

8. Check spark plug hole threads and clean with an appropriate size spark plug chaser if necessary before installing plugs. This will remove any corrosion, carbon build-up or minor flaws from the threads. Coat the chaser with grease to catch chips or foreign matter. Use care to avoid cross-threading.
9. Apply a thin film of engine oil or anti-seize compound to the spark plug threads and screw each plug in by hand until it seats. Very little effort is required. If force is necessary, the plug is cross-threaded. Unscrew it and try again.

NOTE

On some V6 engine installations, access to the rear cylinder spark plug wells is limited. To install such plugs more easily, slip a 10 in. length of fuel line hose over the end of the plug. This will serve as a flexible handle and allow you to screw the plugs in easily and quickly.

10. Tighten each spark plug by hand until it makes contact, then tighten an additional 1/4-3/8 turn. If you have a torque wrench, tighten to 7-15 ft.-lb. (10-20 N•m). Do not overtighten the plugs, as excessive torque may change the gap setting.
11. Inspect the spark plug wires before connecting installing them to their spark plugs. If the insulation is oil soaked, brittle, torn or otherwise damaged, replace the wires as a set.

IGNITION SERVICE

The Delco High Energy Ignition (HEI) system is used on all gasoline engines except the 1.9L. California V6 engines use Electronic Spark Timing (EST). The HEI-EST system differs from the standard HEI system used on Federal models in that the distributor has no vacuum or centrifugal

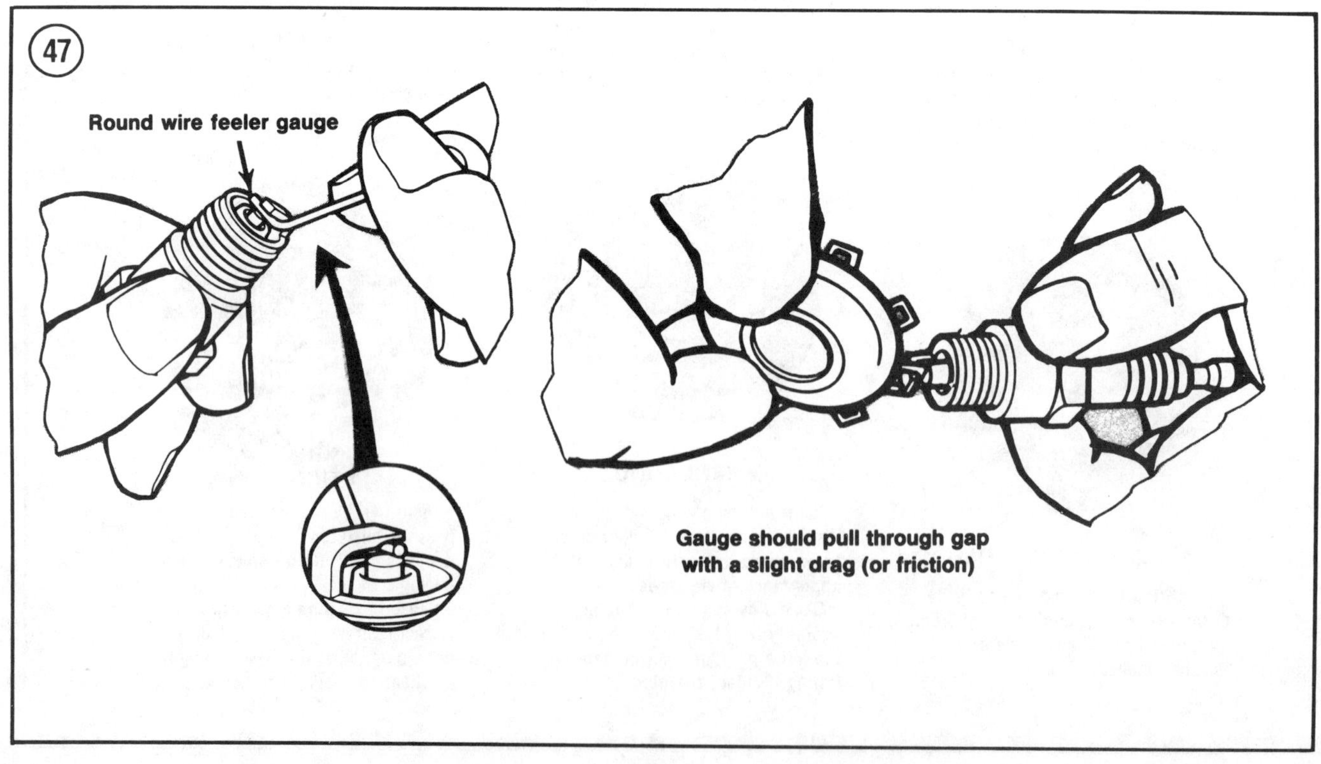

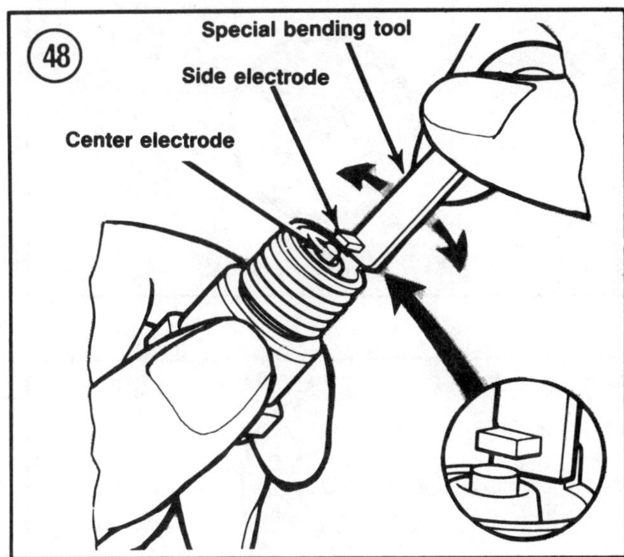

advance mechanisms. Spark timing is controlled directly by the electronic control module or ECM.

The HEI is a pulse-triggered, transistor controlled, inductive discharge system. Breaker points are not used. Principal system components are the ignition coil, electronic module, magnetic pickup assembly or Hall-effect switch and the centrifugal and vacuum advance mechanisms.

Ignition Coil

The HEI coil operates in basically the same way as a standard coil, but is smaller in size and generates a higher secondary voltage when the primary circuit is broken.

Electronic Module

The electronic module is contained within the distributor housing. Circuits within the module perform 5 basic functions: spark triggering, switching, current limiting, dwell control and distributor pickup. Modules used in EST distributors also control timing advance.

Magnetic Pickup Assembly or Hall-effect Switch

The magnetic pickup assembly consists of a rotating timer core with external teeth (one for each cylinder) rotated by the distributor shaft, a stationary pole piece with internal teeth and a pickup coil and magnet located between the pole piece and a bottom plate. The Hall-effect vane switch used in some late model distributors contains a stator assembly with one window in the vane for each engine cylinder.

System Operation

As the distributor shaft rotates the timer core out of alignment with the pole piece teeth, a voltage is created in the magnetic field of the pickup coil. The pickup coil sends this voltage to the electronic module, which determines from the rotational speed of the distributor shaft when to start building current in the ignition coil primary windings.

When the timer core teeth are again aligned with the pole piece teeth, the magnetic field is changed, creating a different voltage. This signal is sent to the electronic module by the pickup coil and causes the module to shut off the ignition coil primary circuit. This collapses the coil magnetic field and induces a high secondary voltage to fire one spark plug.

The Hall-effect switch uses the windows in the rotating stator assembly to signal the module when to start and stop primary current flow.

The electronic module limits the 12-volt current to the ignition coil to 5-6 amperes. The module also triggers the opening and closing of the primary circuit with zero energy loss. The efficiency of the triggering system allows 35,000 volts or more to be delivered through the secondary wiring system to the spark plugs.

The module circuit controlling dwell causes dwell time to increase as engine speed increases.

The 1.9L breakerless ignition system is essentially the same in function but the distributor components differ somewhat. Instead of a timer core and pole piece, the 1.9L distributor contains a toothed reluctor which revolves in front of a magnetic pickup. Movement of the reluctor teeth in front of the pickup creates the voltage signal to trigger the ignition module.

System Maintenance

Routine maintenance is not required for the breakerless ignition systems. If parts fail, they are serviced by replacement. However, the distributor cap and rotor should be visually inspected at periodic intervals. At the same time, inspect the spark plug wires for burned or cracked insulation or other damage. If it is necessary to replace ignition wires, disconnect and replace one wire at a time. This will prevent any confusion as to which spark plug and distributor cap terminal the wire should connect to.

The HEI system uses large (8 mm) diameter, silicone-insulated spark plug wires. While these are more heat resistant and less vulnerable to deterioration than standard wires, they should not be mistreated. When removing wires from spark plugs, pull on the boots. Twist the boot 1/2 turn in either direction to break the seal, then pull to remove. Use of spark plug pliers is recommended for wire removal.

The only adjustments possible on the HEI distributor are centrifugal and vacuum advance, both of which should be entrusted to a dealer or automotive ignition system specialist. On models equipped with EST, the distributor contains no advance mechanisms. Distributor advance is electronically controlled by the ignition module.

Suspected ignition trouble with the HEI or 1.9L breakerless ignitions should be referred to a dealer or ignition specialist. Testing beyond that described in Chapter Two requires special equipment and skills and an otherwise good electronic circuit can be damaged by an incorrect test connection.

Distributor Cap, Wires and Rotor

The distributor cap, wires and rotor should be inspected every 30,000 miles.

1A. 1.9L—Unsnap the 2 distributor cap clips. Lift the cap straight up and off to prevent rotor blade damage.

1B. All others—Depress the 2 distributor cap latch screws with a suitable screwdriver and turn 90°. Lift the cap straight up and off to prevent rotor blade damage.

2. Check the carbon button and electrodes inside the distributor cap for dirt, corrosion or arcing. Check the cap for cracks. Replace the cap and rotor as a set, if necessary.

3. Replace the wires if the insulation is melted, brittle or cracked.

4A. 1.9L—Grasp the rotor and pull it straight up and off the distributor shaft.

4B. All others—Loosen the 2 rotor screws. Lift the rotor straight up and off the distributor shaft.

5. Wipe the rotor with a clean, damp cloth. Check for burns, arcing, cracks or other defects. Replace the cap and rotor as a set, if necessary.

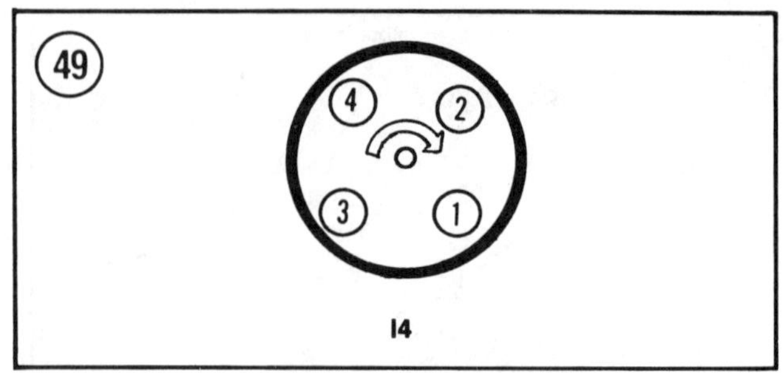

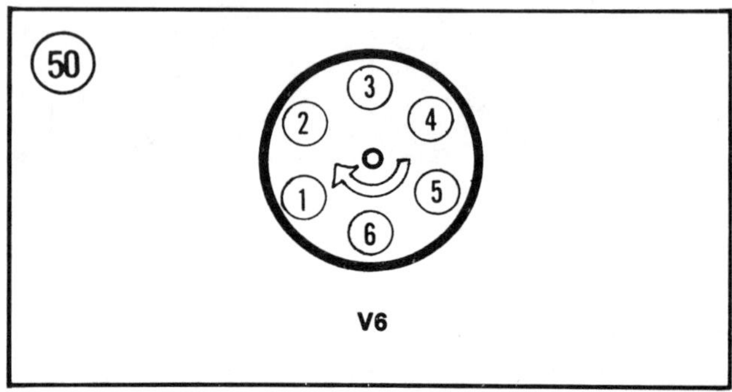

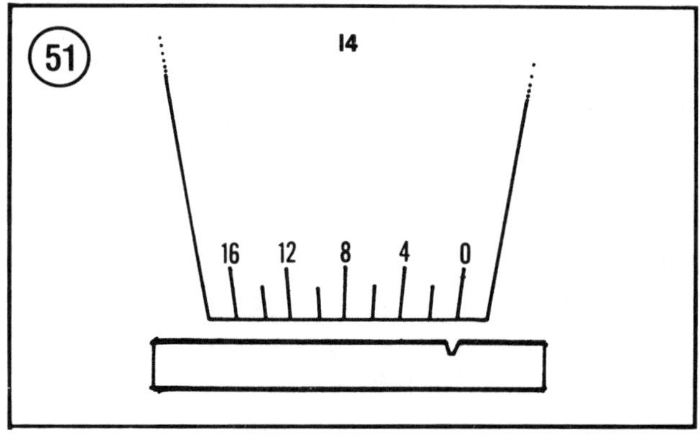

6. Reinstall the rotor. Tighten the attaching screws on the 2.0L, 2.5L and V6 rotor.

7. Reinstall the distributor cap. Snap the cap clips into place on the 1.9L distributor. Depress and rotate the cap latch screws 90° on all other models to lock the cap in place.

Ignition Timing

Ignition timing should be checked at every tune-up or at 30,000-mile intervals.

1. Connect a timing light and tachometer to the engine according to manufacturer's instructions. Refer to **Figure 49** for the I4 engine No. 1 cylinder plug wire. Refer to **Figure 50** for the V6 engine No. 1 cylinder plug wire.

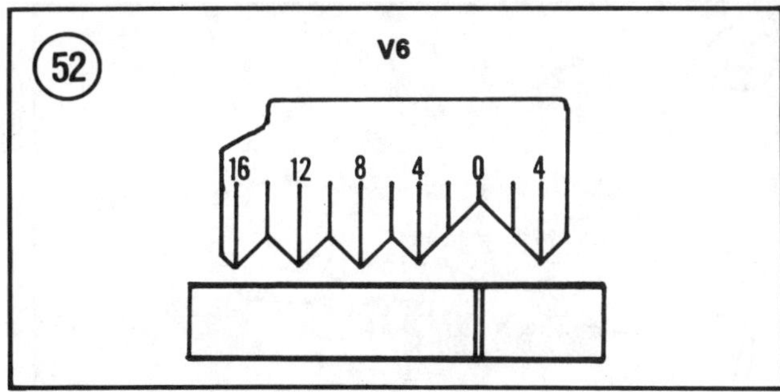

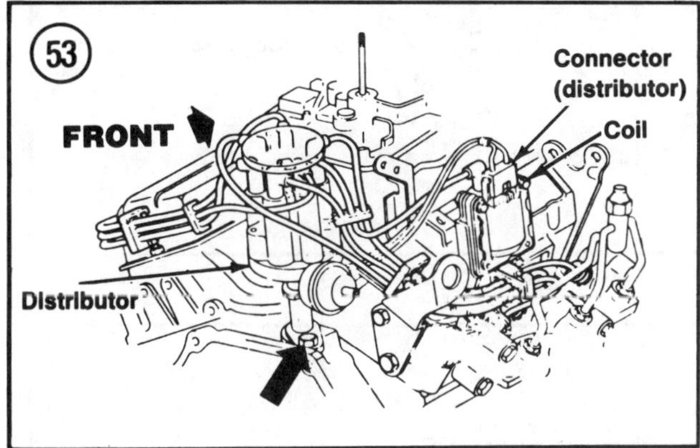

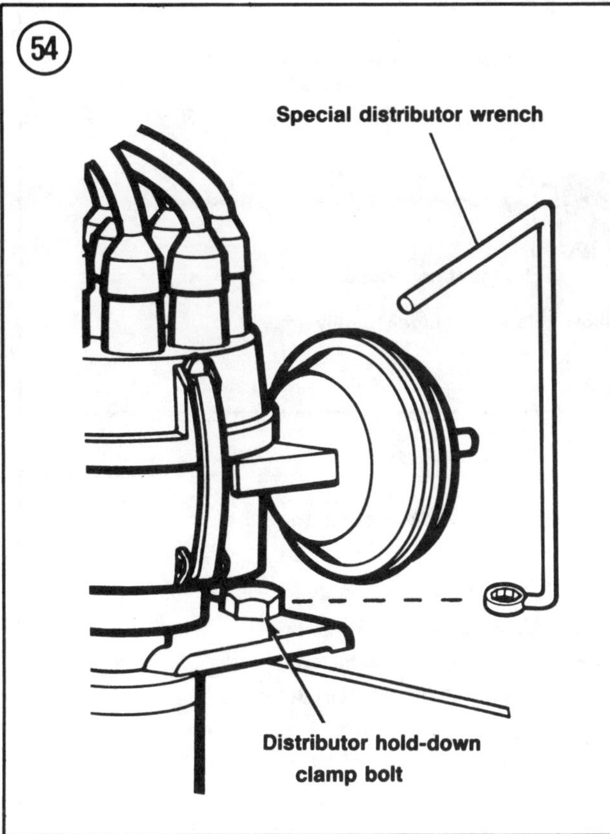

2. Check the idle speed and compare to the specification provided on the VECI label under the hood. If it is not correct on carburetted models, see *Idle Speed Adjustment* in this chapter. If idle speed is incorrect on fuel injected models, take the vehicle to a dealer (idle speed is computer-controlled).

3. Disconnect and plug the distributor vacuum advance line, if so equipped. Disconnect and plug the EGR vacuum line.

4. Locate the timing mark on the crankshaft pulley and mark it with white paint. See **Figure 51** (I4) or **Figure 52** (V6) for typical timing marks. Also mark the notch in the crankshaft pulley. The paint makes the marks easier to see under the timing light.

5. Start the engine and let it idle. Point the timing light at the marks. They will appear to stand still or waver slightly under the light.

WARNING
Keep your hands and hair clear of all drive belts and pulleys. Although they seem to be standing still, they are actually spinning at more than 10 times per second and can cause serious injury.

6. If the timing is incorrect, loosen the distributor hold-down bolt enough to rotate the distributor body. See **Figure 53** (V6 shown). On V6 installations, the use of a distributor wrench (**Figure 54**) is recommended.

WARNING
Never touch the distributor's thick wires when the engine is running. This can cause a painful shock, even if the insulation is in perfect condition.

7. Grasp the distributor cap and rotate the body clockwise or counterclockwise as required to align the timing marks. Tighten the distributor hold-down bolt snugly and recheck the timing.

8. Shut the engine off. Remove the test equipment. Reconnect the vacuum advance and EGR vacuum lines.

FUEL SYSTEM ADJUSTMENTS

Idle Speed Adjustment (Carburetted Engine)

1.9L 4-cylinder engine

Check ignition timing and valve clearances before adjusting idle speed.

1. Set the parking brake. Block the drive wheels. Place the transmission in NEUTRAL.
2. Start the engine and warm to normal operating temperature (upper radiator hose hot).
3. Disconnect the plug the distributor vacuum advance line, canister purge line and EGR valve vacuum line. Pinch off the idle compensator vacuum line.
4. Make sure the choke is open, the air cleaner installed and the air conditioner is OFF, if so equipped.
5. Connect a tachometer to the engine according to the manufacturer's instructions.
6. Check the VECI label under the hood for the correct idle speed setting. Adjust the idle speed screw (**Figure 55**) to obtain that specification.
7. If equipped with air conditioning:
   a. Turn the air conditioner on MAX COLD.
   b. Turn the blower on HIGH.

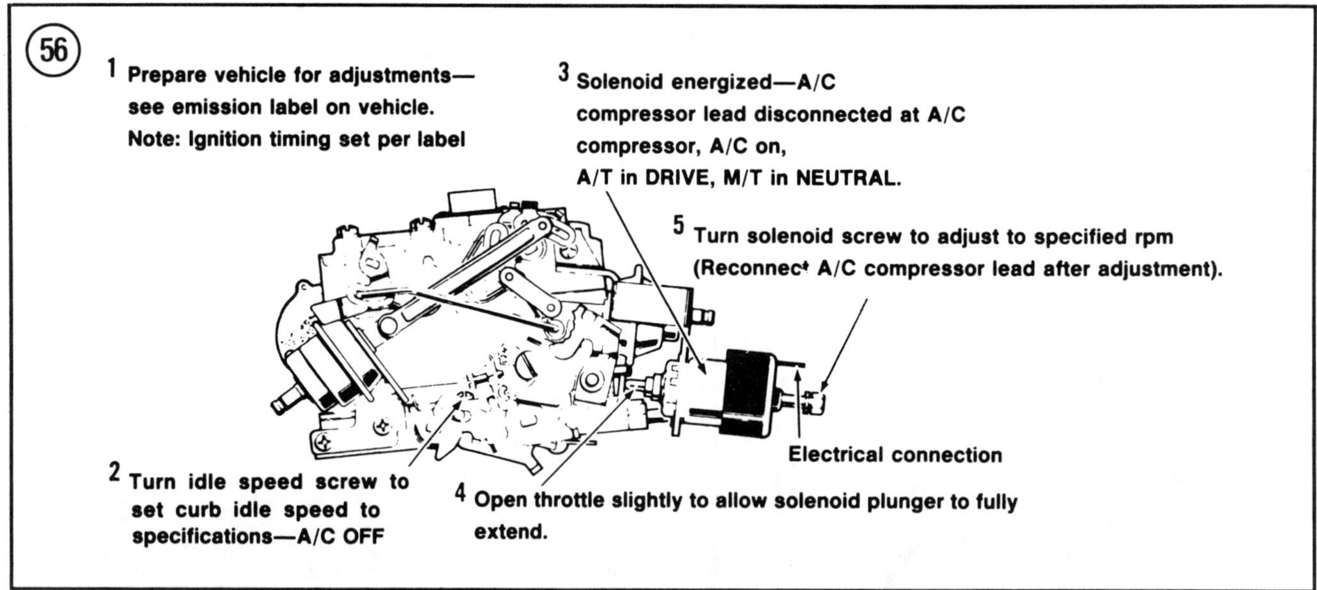

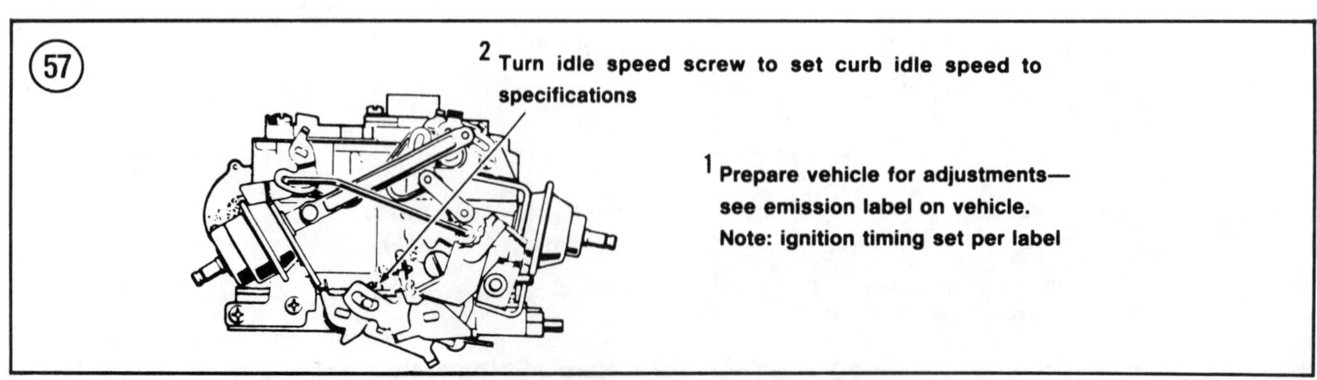

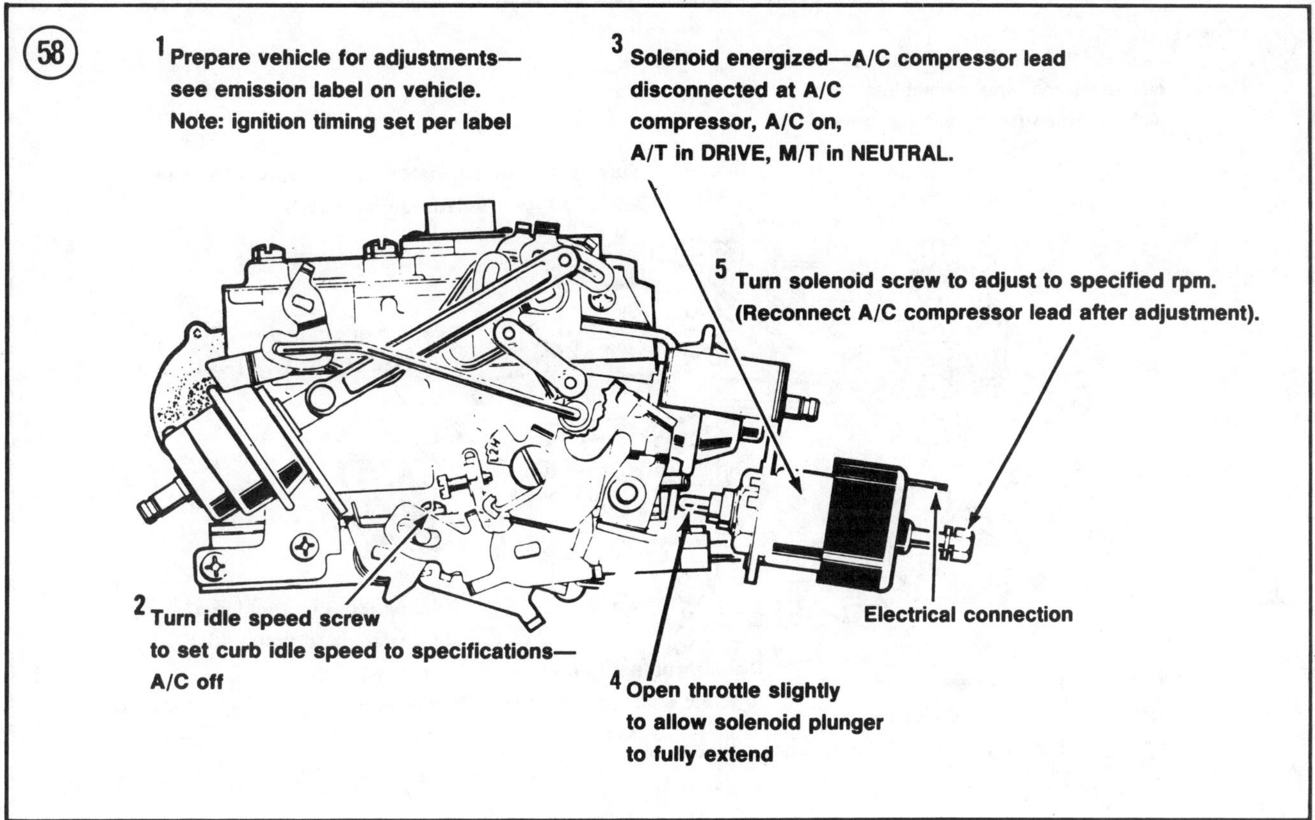

c. Open the throttle part way and let it close.
d. Adjust the air conditioning solenoid to set the idle speed to the "A/C rpm" setting specified on the VECI label.

8. Remove the test equipment.

2.0L and V6 engine
(2SE carburetor)

Refer to **Figure 56** for idle speed adjustment if equipped with air conditioning. Refer to **Figure 57** if not equipped with air conditioning.

2.0L and V6 engine
(E2SE carburetor)

Refer to **Figure 58** for idle speed adjustment if equipped with air conditioning. Refer to **Figure 59** if not equipped with air conditioning.

Idle Speed Adjustment (Fuel Injected Engine)

No attempt should be made to adjust the idle speed on engines equipped with fuel injection. An idle air control (IAC) assembly mounted on the throttle body maintains the correct idle speed according to electrical impulses from the electronic control module (ECM). Attempting to adjust the system will only make matters worse. If idle speed requires adjustment, see your Chevy or GMC dealer.

Idle Mixture Adjustment (All Engines)

The idle mixture screw is located under a plug seal on all carburetors in accordance with Federal regulations governing unauthorized adjustment. The carburetors are flow-tested and pre-set at the factory. Idle mixture on fuel injected engines is computer-controlled. If the idle mixture requires adjustment for any reason, see your Chevrolet or GMC dealer.

Fast Idle Speed Adjustment (Carburetted Engine)

1.9L engine

The fast idle speed is pre-set and cannot be adjusted.

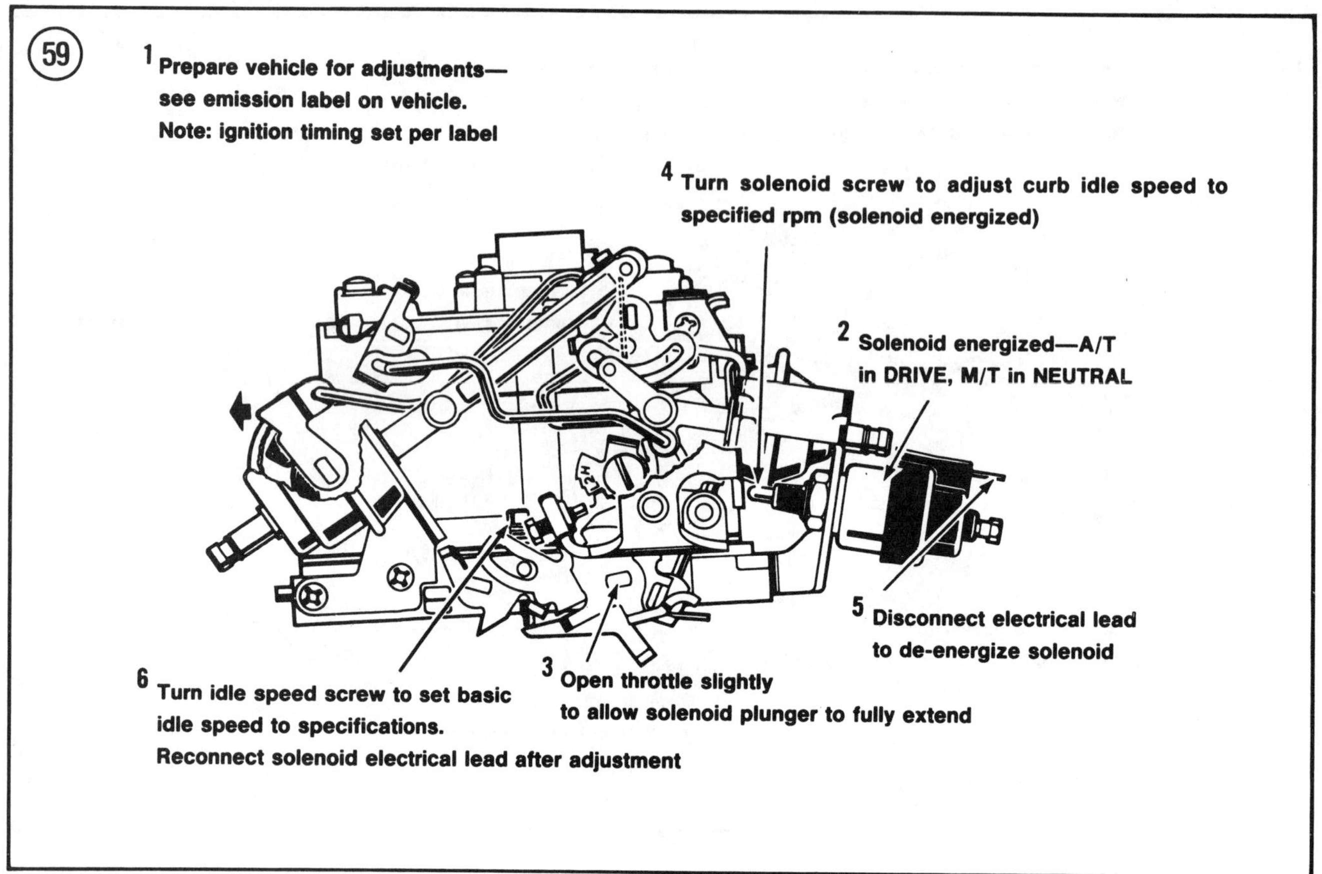

2.0L and V6 engine

Refer to **Figure 60**.

Fast Idle Speed Adjustment (Fuel-injected Engine)

The fast idle speed is controlled by the electronic control module and idle speed control assembly and cannot be adjusted.

DIESEL ENGINE TUNE-UP

Diesel engines do not require a tune-up in the same sense as a gasoline engine, primarily because the diesel engine uses compression for ignition instead of an electrical ignition system. Fewer maintenance tasks are required on a diesel engine, but the required tasks are just as important, if not more so, as the more extensive gasoline engine maintenance.

The required tasks and intervals at which they should be performed are given in **Table 2**. Owner maintenance on the diesel engine should be limited to the tasks listed in **Table 2**. Tampering by an unskilled mechanic, especially with the injection system, can lead to serious (and expensive) damage.

CAUTION
Do not wash the diesel engine. Washing a hot engine can cause damage to the injection pump. Washing the engine (hot or cold) can contaminate the timing belt with grease or road film and cause belt failure.

Idle Speed Adjustment

NOTE
A special magnetic tachometer (GM part No. J-26925-5 or equivalent) must be used on the 2.2L diesel engine. Most tachometers for gasoline engines operate from the electrical ignition system impulses and will not work on diesel engines.

Refer to **Figure 61** for this procedure.

1. Set the parking brake and block the drive wheels.
2. Place the transmission in NEUTRAL.

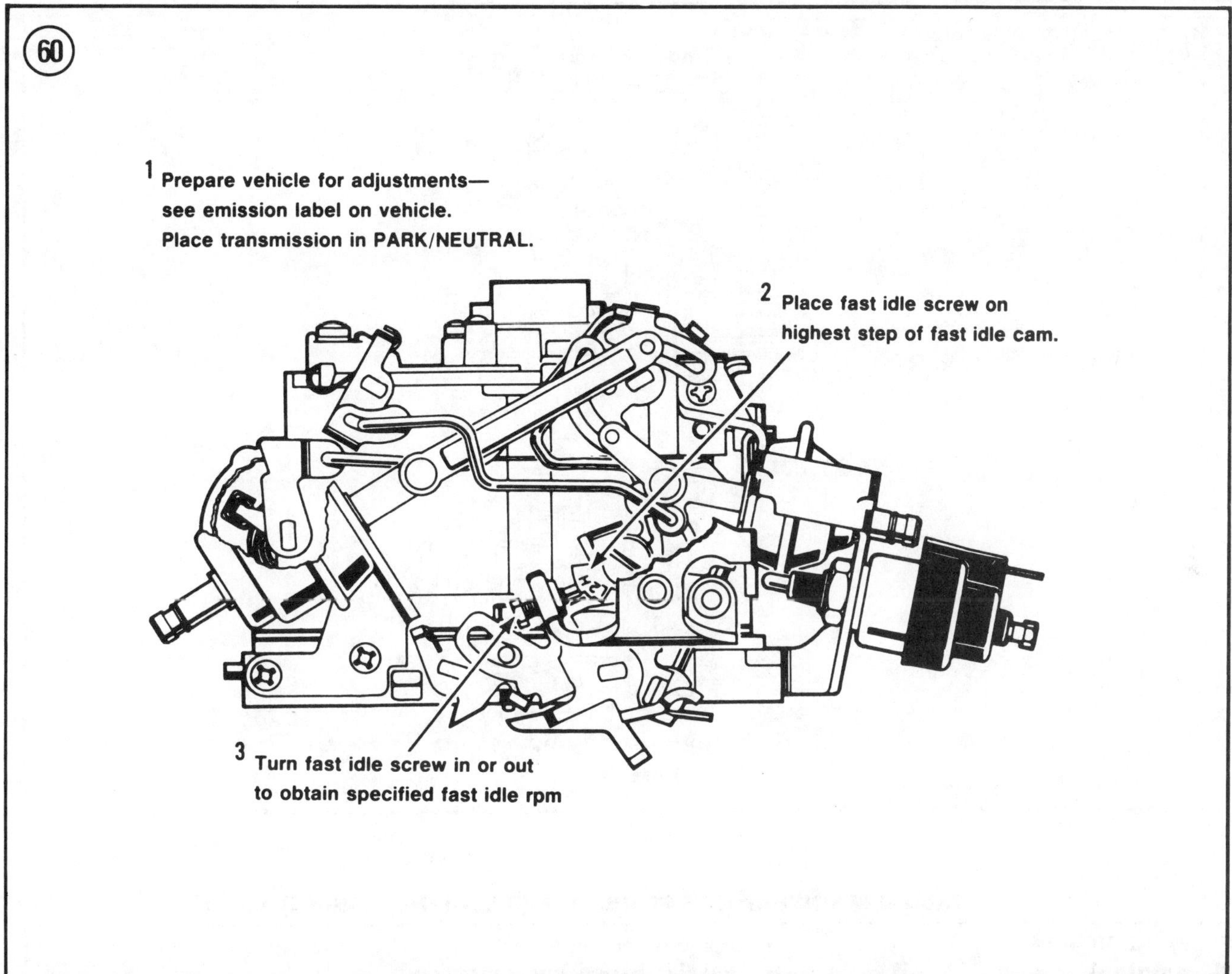

3. Connect the tachometer according to manufacturer's instructions.
4. Start the engine and warm to normal operating temperature (upper radiator hose hot).
5. If the idle speed shown on the tachometer is not within the range specified on the VECI decal in the engine compartment, loosen the idle adjusting screw locknut.
6. Adjust the idle screw as required to bring the engine speed within specifications and tighten the locknut without disturbing the idle screw setting.
7. Shut the engine off. Disconnect the tachometer.

Fast Idle Speed

Refer to **Figure 61** for this procedure.

1. Set the parking brake and block the drive wheels.
2. Place the transmission in NEUTRAL.
3. Connect the tachometer according to manufacturer's instructions.
4. Start the engine and warm to normal operating temperature (upper radiator hose hot).
5. Connect a hand vacuum pump to the fast idle actuator and apply 8-10 in. Hg vacuum.
6. If the fast idle speed shown on the tachometer is not within the range specified on the VECI decal in the engine compartment, loosen the fast idle adjusting screw locknut.
7. Adjust the knurled nut as required to bring the engine speed within specifications and tighten the locknut without disturbing the fast idle setting.
8. Shut the engine off. Disconnect the tachometer. Remove the hand vacuum pump.

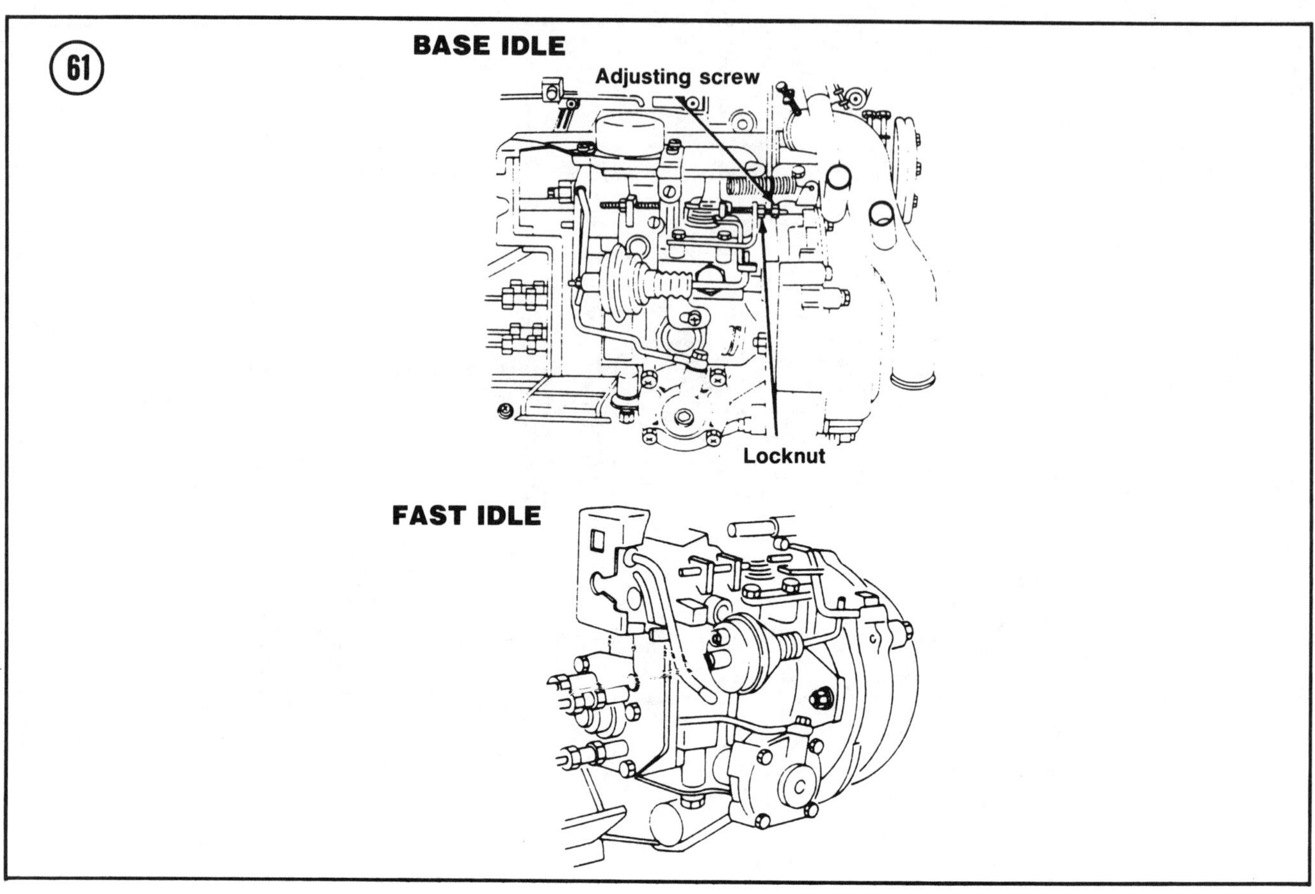

Table 1 MAINTENANCE SCHEDULE (GASOLINE ENGINE)

Interval	Service
Every 7,500 miles (12 months)	• Engine oil change * • Chassis/suspension lubrication * • Check manual transmission, transfer case and axles • Check brake lines • Check exhaust system
First 7,500 miles, then every 15,000 miles	• Check and rotate tires • Check disc brakes • Change oil filter * • Check and adjust drive belts
First 7,500 miles, then every 30,000 miles	• Check carburetor choke and hoses • Check carburetor/throttle body mounting torque • Check and adjust idle speed (carburetted engines only) • Change manual transmission fluid (4-speed only)
Every 15,000 miles	• Check cooling system ** • Check rear brakes • Check throttle linkage • Inspect fuel tank, cap and lines • Check crankcase vent system • Check and adjust valve clearance (1.9L engine only) • Change fuel filter

(continued)

Table 1 MAINTENANCE SCHEDULE (GASOLINE ENGINE) (continued)

Every 30,000 miles	• Replace spark plugs * • Check and adjust ignition timing • Check ignition wiring • Drain/refill cooling system • Replace PCV valve (except 1.9L) • Clean PCV orifice (1.9L only) • Inspect manual steering gear seal • Check air cleaner system • Replace air cleaner filter • Replace crankcase vent filter • Check idle stop solenoid/dashpot (carburetted engine only) • Check EGR system operation • Repack and adjust wheel bearings *
Every 100,000 miles	• Change automatic transmission fluid and strainer

* SEVERE SERVICE OPERATION: If the vehicle is operated under any of the following conditions, change engine oil @ 3,000 miles or 3 month intervals and oil filter @ alternate oil changes. Clean and regap spark plugs every 6,000 miles. Lubricate chassis and suspension every 6,000 miles. Change automatic transmission fluid and strainer every 15,000 miles. Repack wheel bearings every 15,000 miles.

a. Extended idle or low-speed operation (short trips, stop-and-go driving).
b. Trailer towing.
c. Operation @ temperatures below 10° F for 60 days or more with most trips under 10 miles.
d. Very dusty or muddy conditions.

** Check coolant protection and condition once a year.

Table 2 MAINTENANCE SCHEDULE (DIESEL ENGINE)

Every 7,500 miles (12 months)	• Engine oil and filter change * • Chassis/suspension lubrication * • Check manual transmission • Check brake lines • Check exhaust system
First 7,500 miles, then every 15,000 miles	• Check and rotate tires • Check disc brakes • Check and adjust drive belts
First 7,500 miles, then every 30,000 miles	• Check and adjust idle speed • Change manual transmission fluid (4-speed only)
Every 15,000 miles	• Check cooling system ** • Check rear brakes • Check throttle linkage • Inspect fuel tank, cap and lines • Check and adjust vacuum pump drive belt • Check and adjust valve clearance

(continued)

Table 2 MAINTENANCE SCHEDULE (DIESEL ENGINE) (continued)

Every 30,000 miles (24 months)	• Drain/refill cooling system
Every 30,000 miles	• Change fuel filter • Inspect manual steering gear seal • Check air cleaner system • Replace air cleaner filter • Repack and adjust wheel bearings *
Every 100,000 miles	• Change automatic transmission fluid and strainer

* SEVERE SERVICE OPERATION: If the vehicle is operated under any of the following conditions, change engine oil @ 3,000 miles or 3 month intervals and oil filter @ alternate oil changes. Clean and regap spark plugs every 6,000 miles. Change automatic transmission fluid and strainer every 15,000 miles. Repack wheel bearings every 15,000 miles.

a. Extended idle or low-speed operation (short trips, stop-and-go driving).
b. Trailer towing.
c. Operation @ temperatures below 10° F for 60 days or more with most trips under 10 miles.
d. Very dusty or muddy conditions.

** Check coolant protection and condition once a year.

Table 3 GASOLINE ENGINE OIL VISCOSITY

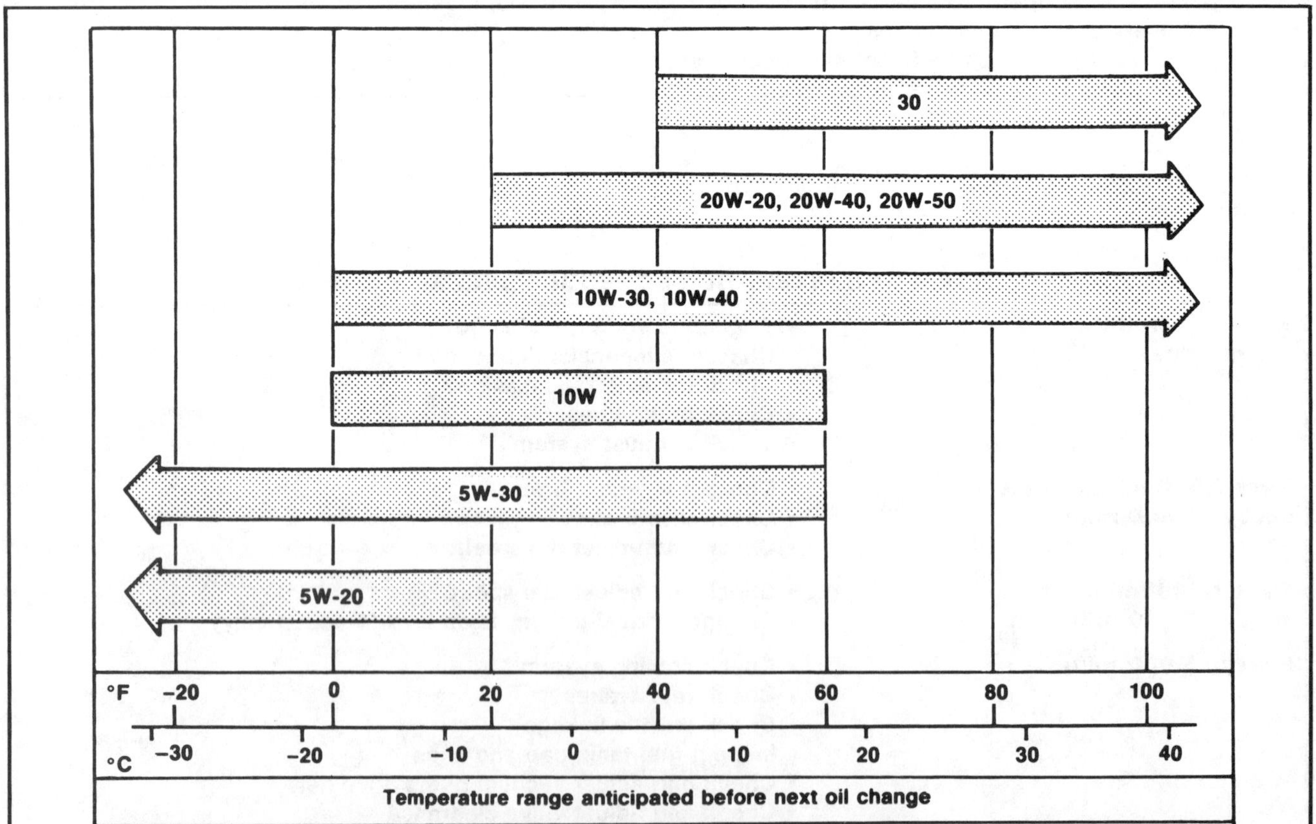

30

20W-20, 20W-40, 20W-50

10W-30, 10W-40

10W

5W-30

5W-20

°F −20 0 20 40 60 80 100

°C −30 −20 −10 0 10 20 30 40

Temperature range anticipated before next oil change

NOTE: Do not use SAE 5W-20 oils for continuous high-speed driving.

Table 4 DIESEL ENGINE OIL VISCOSITY

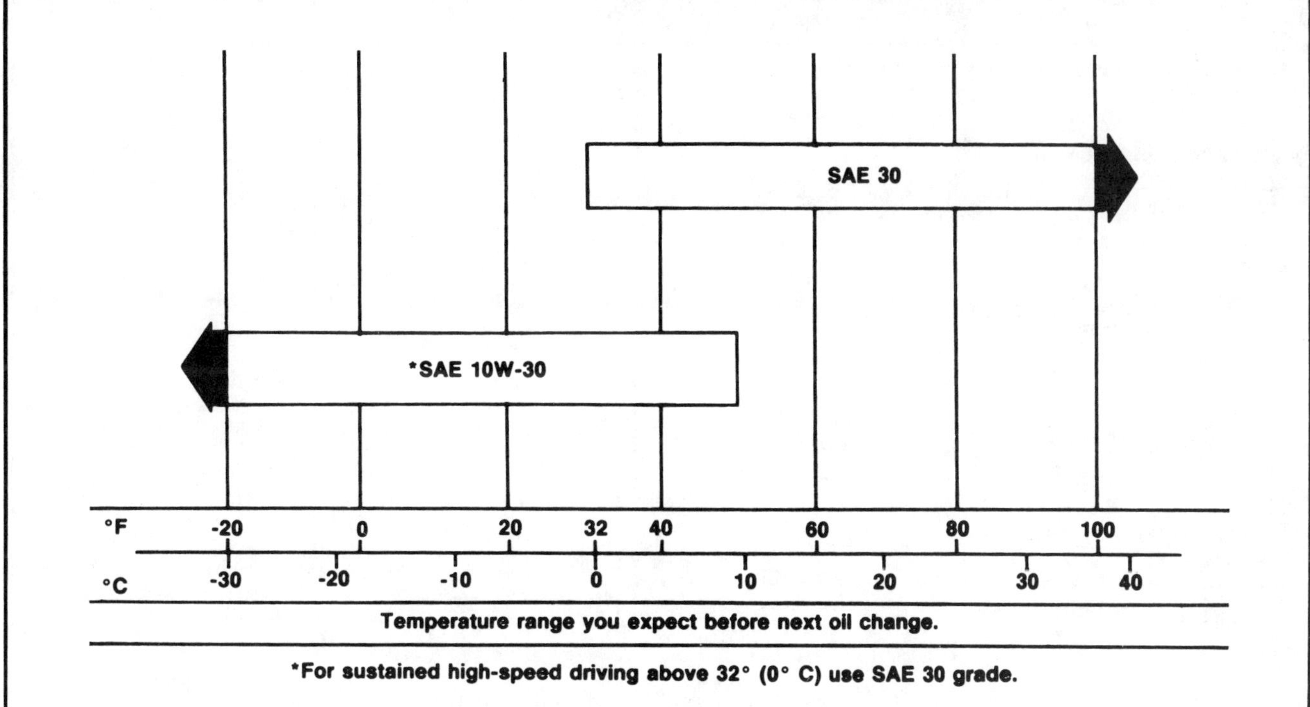

Table 5 RECOMMENDED LUBRICANTS

Engine crankcase	
Gasoline	API Service SF oil
Diesel	API Service SF/CC or SF/CD
Engine coolant	Prestone II or equivalent
Brake fluid	Delco Supreme 11 or other DOT 3 or DOT 4 fluid
Power steering pump	GM power steering fluid or equivalent
Manual steering gearbox	GM lubricant part No. 1051052 or equivalent
Transfer case	DEXRON II automatic transmission fluid
Manual transmission	DEXRON II automatic transmission fluid
Automatic transmission	DEXRON II automatic transmission fluid
Differential	SAE 80W GL-5 or 80W-90 GL-5 gear lubricant
Shift linkage	Engine oil
Front wheel bearings	GM lubricant part No. 1051344 or equivalent
Chassis lubrication	GM chassis grease meeting 6031-M specification
Hood latch, all hinges	Engine oil
Windshield wiper	GM Optikleen washer solvent or equivalent
Key lock cylinders	WD-40 or equivalent

Table 6 APPROXIMATE REFILL CAPACITIES

	gal.	qt.	pt.
Engine crankcase			
Gasoline		4.0	
Diesel		6.0	
Automatic transmission			
200C			
After rebuild			19.0
After fluid change			7.0
700R4			
After rebuild			23.0
After fluid change			10.0
Manual transmission			
4-speed		2.5	
5-speed		3.25	
Transfer case		2.3	
Differential			3.5
Front axle		1.5	
Cooling system			
1.9L engine		9.5	
2.2L diesel		11.5	
All others		12.0	
Fuel tank			
Gasoline engine			
Standard			
Pickup	13		
Blazer/Jimmy	13.5		
Optional	20		
Diesel engine			
Standard	14		
Optional	20		

Table 7 AUTOMATIC TRANSMISSION FLUID OXIDATION

Temperature (degrees F)	Life expectancy (in miles)
175	100,000
195	50,000
212	25,000
235	12,000
255	6,250
275	3,000
295	1,500
315	750
335	325
355	160
375	80
390	40
415	Less than 30 minutes

CHAPTER FOUR

4-CYLINDER ENGINE

The vehicles covered in this manual may be equipped with a 1.9L, 2.0L or 2.5L 4-cylinder gasoline engine, or an optional 2.2L diesel. All engines have a firing order of 1-3-4-2 (No. 1 is at the front of the engine). The 1.9L gasoline and 2.2L diesel engines are made by Isuzu. The 2.0L is a Chevrolet design and the 2.5L a Pontiac design. Complete specifications and tightening torques are listed in **Tables 1-8** at the end of the chapter.

1.9L 4-cylinder

The 1.9L (118.9 cid) overhead cam (OHC) Isuzu engine uses a 5-bearing crankshaft, with the No. 3 bearing providing the crankshaft thrust surface. The crankshaft is driven by a timing chain. A 2-piece tension and guide assembly maintains proper chain tension.

The aluminum cylinder head contains intake and exhaust valves mounted in a "V" arrangement with the spark plug at the center. Crossflow intake and exhaust ports increase efficiency. The double rocker arm system operates the intake and exhaust valves independently. Double-action type inner and outer springs improve valve action at high engine speed. The oil pump is mounted at the front of the engine block and driven by a crankshaft gear. Valve clearances must be adjusted at 15,000-mile intervals. See Chapter Three. Specifications (**Table 1**) and tightening torques (**Table 5**) are at the end of the chapter.

2.0L 4-cylinder

The 2.0L (122 cid) pushrod Chevrolet engine uses a 5-bearing camshaft mounted high in the block, with the No. 4 crankshaft bearing providing the crankshaft thrust surface. The crankshaft is driven by a double row 3/8 in. pitch roller chain. A 2-piece tension and guide assembly maintains proper chain tension.

The cast iron cylinder head contains intake and exhaust valves mounted in a vertical plane with positive valve stem-to-guide seals and integral valve seals. Rocker arms are retained on individual threaded studs. A ball pivot valve train is used, with camshaft motion transferred through the hydraulic lifters to the rocker arms by pushrods. The oil pump is mounted at the bottom rear of the engine block in a cast aluminum housing and is driven by the distributor shaft. Specifications (**Table 2**) and tightening torques (**Table 6**) are at the end of the chapter.

2.5L 4-cylinder

The 2.5L (151 cid) pushrod Pontiac Tech IV engine uses a 5-bearing crankshaft, with the No. 5 bearing providing the crankshaft thrust surface. The gear-driven camshaft is supported by 3 bearings.

The cast iron cylinder head contains intake and exhaust valves with integral valve guides. Rocker arms are retained on individual threaded shoulder bolts. A ball pivot valve train is used, with camshaft motion transferred through the hydraulic roller lifters to the rocker arms by pushrods. The oil pump is mounted at the bottom rear of the engine block and is driven by the distributor shaft. Specifications (**Table 3**) and tightening torques (**Table 7**) are at the end of the chapter.

2.2L 4-cylinder Diesel

The 2.2L (134 cid) Isuzu diesel engine uses a belt-driven camshaft located in the cast iron cylinder block with inline valves operated by pushrods and rocker arms. Valve clearances must be adjusted at 15,000-mile intervals. See Chapter Three.

Service by amateur mechanics to diesel engines, other than the maintenance and tune-up procedures provided in Chapter Three, is not recommended. A removal/installation procedure is provided so you can take the engine to a dealer or specialist for repairs. Specifications (**Table 4**) and tightening torques (**Table 8**) are at the end of the chapter.

ENGINE IDENTIFICATION

An engine identification number is located on a pad at the rear of the block below the exhaust manifold. The pad also contains the Vehicle Identification Number or VIN. **Figure 1** (1.9L) and **Figure 2** (2.5L) are typical locations. This information indicates if there are unique parts or if internal changes have been made during the model year. It is important when ordering replacement parts for the engine.

The engine code is the 8th digit/letter of the Vehicle Identification Number (VIN). The VIN is the official identification for title and vehicle registration. The VIN is stamped on a gray-colored plate fastened to the upper left corner of the instrument panel close to the windshield on the driver's side (**Figure 3**). It can be read from outside the vehicle.

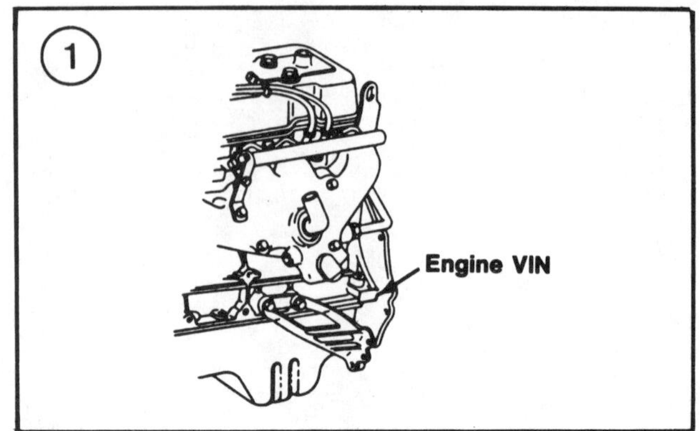

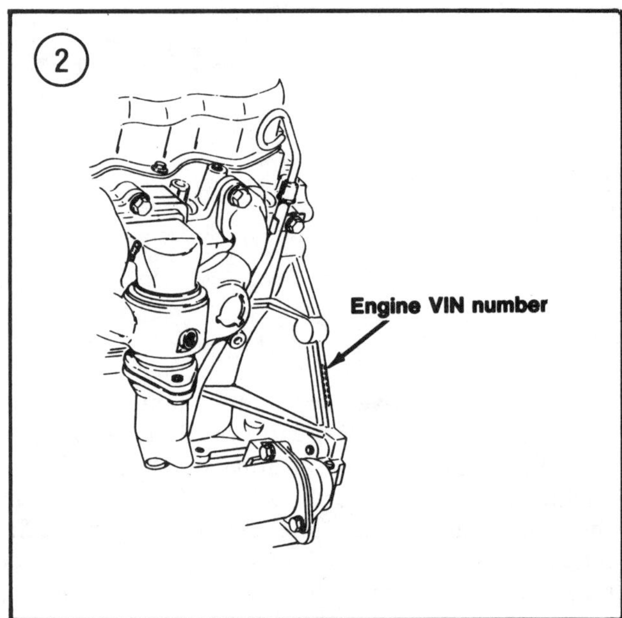

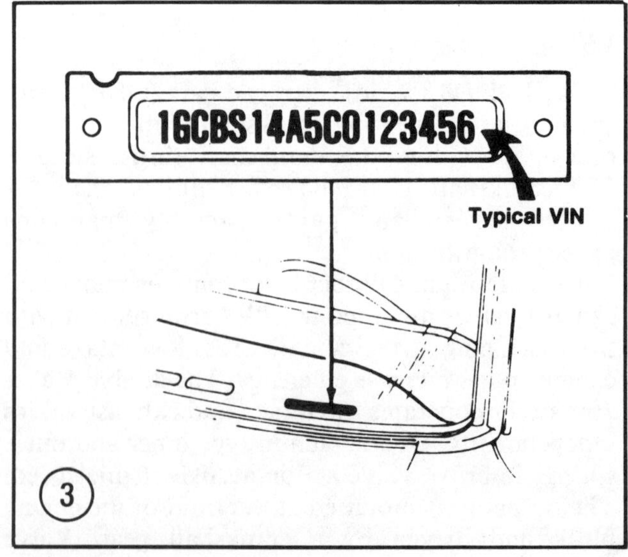

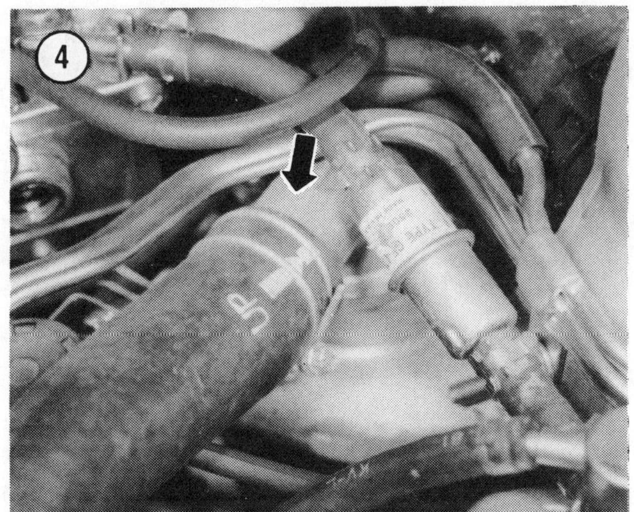

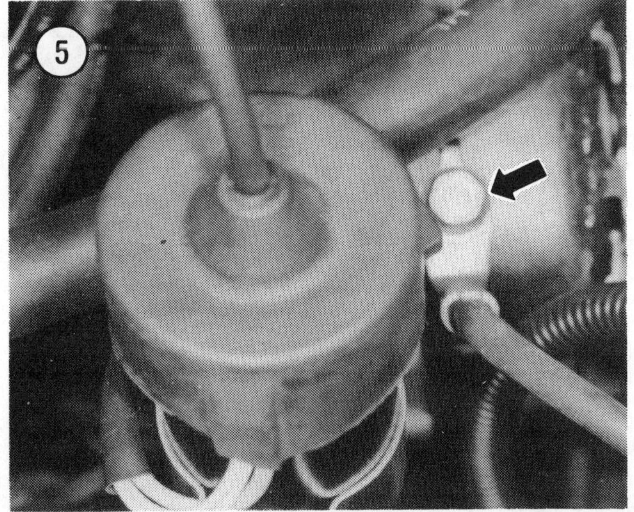

GASKET SEALANT

Gasket sealant is used instead of pre-formed gaskets between numerous mating surfaces on the engines covered in this chapter. See *Gasket Sealant*, Chapter One.

1.9L/2.0L ENGINE REMOVAL (2-WHEEL DRIVE)

WARNING
The engine is heavy, awkward to handle and has sharp edges. It may shift or drop suddenly during removal. To prevent serious injury, always observe the following precautions.
1. Never place any part of your body where a moving or falling engine may trap, cut or crush you.
2. If you must push the engine during removal, use a board or similar tool to keep your hands out of danger.
3. Be sure the hoist is designed to lift engines and has enough load capacity for your engine.
4. Be sure the hoist is securely attached to safe lifting points on the engine.
5. The engine should not be difficult to lift with a proper hoist. If it is, stop lifting, lower the engine back onto its mounts and make sure the engine has been completely separated from the vehicle.

If the vehicle is equipped with air conditioning, have the system discharged by a dealer or air conditioning shop before starting this procedure.

1. Disconnect the underhood lamp. Mark the location of the hinges and remove the hood.
2. Drain the cooling system. See Chapter Seven.
3. Disconnect the upper radiator hose at the thermostat housing (**Figure 4**). Disconnect the lower radiator hose at the water pump.
4. Drain the crankcase oil. See Chapter Three.
5. Disconnect the negative battery cable at the alternator shield (**Figure 5**) and battery. Remove the cable and battery from the engine compartment. See Chapter Eight.
6. Remove the power steering pump, if so equipped. See **Figure 6** (typical). Set pump to one side out of the way without opening any hydraulic line connections.
7. Remove the air cleaner assembly. See Chapter Six.
8. Remove the air conditioning relay bracket at the bulkhead connector, if so equipped.
9. Remove the bulkhead connector and separate the harness connections.

4

10. Remove the cruise control servo bracket, if so equipped.
11. Tag and disconnect all vacuum and electrical lines connecting the engine to other engine compartment components.

WARNING
Be sure to have the air conditioning system discharged by a professional before attempting the next step.

12. Disconnect the suction hose from the air conditioner compressor coupling.
13. Remove the master cylinder attaching nuts at the vacuum booster (**Figure 7**). Move the master cylinder to one side out of the way without disconnecting the fluid lines.
14. Remove the heater hose at the hot water pipe on the engine (**Figure 8**).
15. Disconnect the carburetor linkage (**Figure 9**).
16. Raise the front of the vehicle with a jack and place it on jackstands.
17. Disconnect the fuel line and heater hose at the intake manifold. Plug the fuel line to prevent leakage.
18. Remove the exhaust shield, if so equipped. Disconnect the exhaust pipe at the exhaust manifold.
19. Disconnect the starter electrical connections. Remove the starter. See Chapter Eight.
20. Disconnect the transmission linkage, speedometer cable and all electrical connections at the transmission.
21A. Manual transmission—Disconnect the clutch cable at the clutch fork (1982-1983) or remove the hydraulic clutch slave cylinder (1984-on). See Chapter Nine.
21B. Automatic transmission—Disconnect the oil cooler lines at the transmission. Plug the lines and cap the fittings to prevent leakage.
22. Place a jack under the engine and raise it slightly to take the engine weight off the mounts.
23. Remove the front engine mount nuts and retaining wire.
24. Remove the front mount-to-engine bracket.
25. Disconnect and remove the drive shaft.
26. Place a jack under the transmission and raise it slightly.

NOTE
At this point, there should be no hoses, wires or linkage connecting the engine to the vehicle. Recheck this to be sure nothing will hamper engine removal.

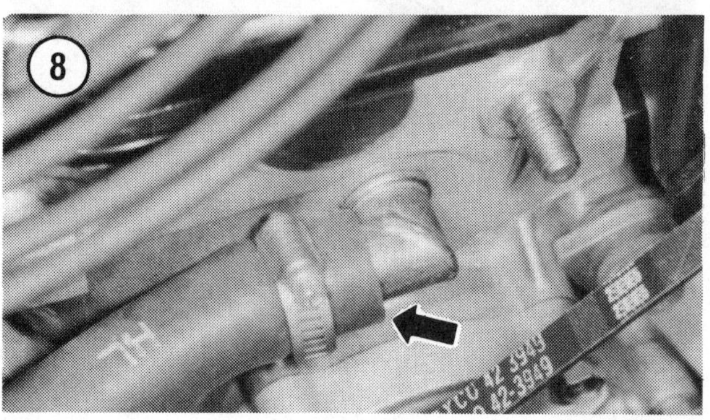

27. Attach an engine hoist to the engine lifting eye bracket.
28. Remove the rear mount under the transmission extension housing (**Figure 10**).
29. Lift the engine/transmission from the vehicle with the hoist. Remove the transmission-to-engine bolts. Separate the engine and transmission.

1.9L/2.0L ENGINE INSTALLATION (2-WHEEL DRIVE)

Engine installation is the reverse of removal, plus the following:

1. Lower the engine/transmission assembly into the vehicle. Leave the hoist attached and holding the engine weight until all mounts and mount bolts have been installed and tightened to specifications (**Table 5** or **Table 6**).
2. Fill the engine with an oil recommended in Chapter Three.
3. Fill the cooling system. See Chapter Seven.
4. Adjust the drive belts. See Chapter Three.
5. Adjust the clutch cable on 1982-1983 manual transmission vehicles. See Chapter Nine.
6. Fill the clutch master cylinder reservoir with DOT 3 brake fluid.

1.9L/2.0L ENGINE REMOVAL (4-WHEEL DRIVE)

WARNING

The engine is heavy, awkward to handle and has sharp edges. It may shift or drop suddenly during removal. To prevent serious injury, always observe the following precautions.

1. Never place any part of your body where a moving or falling engine may trap, cut or crush you.

2. If you must push the engine during removal, use a board or similar tool to keep your hands out of danger.

3. Be sure the hoist is designed to lift engines and has enough load capacity for your engine.

4. Be sure the hoist is securely attached to safe lifting points on the engine.

5. The engine should not be difficult to lift with a proper hoist. If it is, stop lifting, lower the engine back onto its mounts and make sure the engine has been completely separated from the vehicle.

1. Disconnect the negative battery cable at the battery and engine block. Disconnect the positive battery cable at the battery and frame.
2. Remove the console cover and shift lever boot.
3. Remove the transfer case shift lever.
4. Remove the transmission shift lever and shifter.
5. Disconnect the underhood lamp. Mark the location of the hinges and remove the hood.
6. Remove the air cleaner assembly. See Chapter Six.
7. Remove the upper fan shroud and fan. See Chapter Seven.
8. Drain the cooling system and remove the radiator. See Chapter Seven.
9. Disconnect the diverter valve at the air pump.
10. If equipped with power steering, remove the power steering pump without disconnecting any fluid lines. Place the pump out of the way.

WARNING

The air conditioning system contains pressurized refrigerant which can cause frostbite if it touches skin and blindness if it touches the eyes. If discharged near an open flame, the refrigerant forms poisonous gas. Never disconnect air conditioning system lines unless the system has been discharged and evacuated by a professional.

11. If equipped with air conditioning, disconnect the compressor electrical leads and remove the compressor without disconnecting any air conditioning lines. Place the compressor out of the way.
12. Drain the crankcase oil. See Chapter Three.
13. Disconnect the throttle cable at the carburetor. Disconnect the cruise control cable, if so equipped.
14. Tag and disconnect all vacuum and electrical lines connecting the engine to other engine compartment components. Disconnect the fuel hoses. Plug the fuel hoses to prevent leakage.
15. Disconnect the wiring harness and ground strap at the bulkhead.
16. Disconnect the heater hoses at the engine.
17. Raise the vehicle with a jack and place it on jackstands.
18. Remove the clutch bellcrank (1982-1983) or the hydraulic clutch slave cylinder (1984-on). See Chapter Nine.
19. Drain the transmission fluid. See Chapter Three.
20. Remove the front and rear skid plates.
21. Drain the transfer case.
22. Disconnect the exhaust pipe at the manifold and bellhousing hanger.
23. Disconnect and remove the drive shaft.
24. Disconnect the back-up light wires at the transmission.
25. Disconnect the parking brake cable.

26. Support the transmission with a jack and remove the transmission mount and catalytic converter hanger.
27. Remove the transfer case. Remove the transmission. See Chapter Nine.
28. Remove the left-hand body mount bolts and raise the body slightly with a jack.
29. Remove the front splash shield.
30. Remove the jackstands and lower the vehicle to the ground.

NOTE
At this point, there should be no hoses, wires or linkage connecting the engine to the vehicle. Recheck this to be sure nothing will hamper engine removal.

31. Attach an engine hoist to the engine lifting eye bracket.
32. Remove the motor mount through-bolts.
33. Lift the engine from the vehicle with the hoist.

1.9L/2.0L ENGINE INSTALLATION (4-WHEEL DRIVE)

Engine installation is the reverse of removal, plus the following:

1. Lower the engine into the vehicle. Leave the hoist attached and holding the engine weight until all mounts and mount bolts have been installed and tightened to specifications (**Table 5** or **Table 6**).
2. Fill the engine with an oil recommended in Chapter Three.
3. Fill the cooling system. See Chapter Seven.
4. Adjust the drive belts. See Chapter Three.
5. Adjust the clutch cable on 1982-1983 manual transmission vehicles. See Chapter Nine.
6. Fill the clutch master cylinder reservoir with DOT 3 brake fluid.

2.5L ENGINE REMOVAL (ALL MODELS)

WARNING
The engine is heavy, awkward to handle and has sharp edges. It may shift or drop suddenly during removal. To prevent serious injury, always observe the following precautions.
1. Never place any part of your body where a moving or falling engine may trap, cut or crush you.
2. If you must push the engine during removal, use a board or similar tool to keep your hands out of danger.
3. Be sure the hoist is designed to lift engines and has enough load capacity for your engine.
4. Be sure the hoist is securely attached to safe lifting points on the engine.
5. The engine should not be difficult to lift with a proper hoist. If it is, stop lifting, lower the engine back onto its mounts and make sure the engine has been completely separated from the vehicle.

WARNING
Before opening any fuel system lines on a fuel injected engine, relieve system pressure as described in Chapter Six.

1. Disconnect the negative battery cable.
2. Disconnect the underhood lamp. Mark the location of the hinges and remove the hood.
3. Disconnect the power steering reservoir at the fan shroud.
4. Remove the upper fan shroud and fan. Drain the coolant and remove the radiator. See Chapter Seven.
5. If equipped with power steering, remove the power steering pump without disconnecting any fluid lines. Place the pump out of the way.

WARNING
The air conditioning system contains pressurized refrigerant which can cause frostbite if it touches skin and blindness if it touches the eyes. If discharged near an open flame, the refrigerant forms poisonous gas. Never disconnect air conditioning system lines unless the system has been discharged and evacuated by a professional.

6. If equipped with air conditioning, disconnect the compressor electrical leads and remove the compressor without disconnecting any air conditioning lines. Place the compressor out of the way.
7. Drain the crankcase oil. See Chapter Three.
8. Remove the air cleaner assembly. See Chapter Six.
9. Disconnect the fuel line bracket at the fuel filter. Disconnect the fuel inlet and return lines at the flex hoses. Plug the lines to prevent leakage.
10. Disconnect all electrical connectors and vacuum lines at the TBI assembly. Disconnect the throttle cable and transmission TV cables at the TBI assembly. Disconnect the cruise control cable, if so equipped.
11. Disconnect the heater hoses at the engine.
12. Tag and disconnect all vacuum and electrical lines connecting the engine to other engine compartment components.

13. Raise the vehicle with a jack and place it on jackstands.
14A. 2-wheel drive—Remove the strut rods.
14B. 4-wheel drive:
  a. Remove the brake line clips at the crossmember, then remove the crossmember.
  b. Disconnect the transmission cooler lines at the flywheel cover.
  c. Disconnect the drive shaft at the front axle.
15. Disconnect the exhaust pipe at the manifold and catalytic converter hanger.
16. Remove the flywheel cover.
17. Remove the drive belt splash shield, if so equipped.
18. Remove the starter motor. See Chapter Eight.
19. Remove the flex plate-to-torque converter bolts.
20. Remove the 2 outer air dam bolts on the left side of the vehicle.
21. Remove the lower fan shroud.
22. Remove the left body mount bolts.
23. Raise the left side of the body with a floor jack and insert a suitable wooden block between the engine and mount.
24. Remove the upper bolts holding the transmission to the engine.
25. Remove the wooden block and lower the body with the floor jack.
26. Remove all remaining bolts holding the transmission to the engine.
27. Remove the motor mount through-bolts.
28. Remove the jackstands and lower the vehicle to the ground.
29. Position a floor jack with a block of wood under the transmission housing for support.
30. Attach an engine hoist to the engine lifting eye bracket.
31. Slowly lift the engine from the vehicle with the hoist. As the engine assembly comes out of the engine compartment, remove wire loom brackets and disconnect any remaining wires.

2.5L ENGINE INSTALLATION (ALL MODELS)

Engine installation is the reverse of removal, plus the following:
1. Lower the engine into the vehicle, attaching wire looms and ground leads as required. Leave the hoist attached and holding the engine weight until all mounts and mount bolts have been installed and tightened to specifications (**Table 7**).
2. Fill the engine with an oil recommended in Chapter Three.
3. Fill the cooling system. See Chapter Seven.
4. Adjust the drive belts. See Chapter Three.
5. Fill the clutch master cylinder reservoir with DOT 3 brake fluid.

2.2L DIESEL ENGINE REMOVAL

WARNING
The engine is heavy, awkward to handle and has sharp edges. It may shift or drop suddenly during removal. To prevent serious injury, always observe the following precautions.
1. Never place any part of your body where a moving or falling engine may trap, cut or crush you.
2. If you must push the engine during removal, use a board or similar tool to keep your hands out of danger.
3. Be sure the hoist is designed to lift engines and has enough load capacity for your engine.
4. Be sure the hoist is securely attached to safe lifting points on the engine.
5. The engine should not be difficult to lift with a proper hoist. If it is, stop lifting, lower the engine back onto its mounts and make sure the engine has been completely separated from the vehicle.

1. Disconnect the negative battery cable, then the positive cable.
2. Disconnect the exhaust pipe at the exhaust manifold.
3. Drain the cooling system and remove the radiator. Remove the cooling fan and lower fan shroud. See Chapter Seven.
4. Remove the power steering reservoir, if so equipped.
5. Disconnect the heater hoses at the engine.
6. Disconnect the PCV system hoses at the valve cover.
7. Remove the air cleaner assembly. See Chapter Six.

WARNING
The air conditioning system contains pressurized refrigerant which can cause frostbite if it touches skin and blindness if it touches the eyes. If discharged near an open flame, the refrigerant forms poisonous gas. Never disconnect air conditioning system lines unless the system has been discharged and evacuated by a professional.

8. If equipped with air conditioning, disconnect the compressor electrical leads and remove the compressor without disconnecting any air conditioning lines. Place the compressor out of the way.

9. If equipped with power steering, remove the power steering pump without disconnecting any fluid lines. Place the pump out of the way.
10. Tag and disconnect all vacuum and electrical lines connecting the engine to other engine compartment components.
11. Disconnect the injection pump fuel hoses. Plug the hoses to prevent leakage.
12. Disconnect the throttle cable at the injection pump.
13. Remove the rear air cleaner bracket.
14. Disconnect the starter electrical wires and remove the starter motor. See Chapter Eight.
15. Disconnect the underhood lamp. Mark the location of the hinges and remove the hood.
16. Remove the shift lever boot and shift lever.
17. Securely block the drive wheels so the truck will not roll in either direction. Raise the vehicle with a jack and place it on jackstands.
18. Remove the right-hand motor mount through-bolt.
19. Remove the clutch slave cylinder. See Chapter Nine.
20. Disconnect the back-up light wires and speedometer cable at the transmission.
21. Disconnect and remove the drive shaft.
22. Remove the transmission mount nut. Support the transmission with a jack and remove the transmission crossmember.
23. Remove the transmission-to-bellhousing bolts. Lower the jack carefully and remove the transmission.
24. Remove the bellhousing-to-engine bolts. Remove the bellhousing.
25. Remove the jackstands and lower the vehicle to the ground.

NOTE

At this point, there should be no hoses, wires or linkage connecting the engine to the vehicle. Recheck this to be sure nothing will hamper engine removal.

26. Attach an engine hoist to the engine lifting eye bracket.
27. Remove the left-hand motor mount through bolt.
28. Disconnect the negative battery cable ground at the engine block.
29. Lift the engine from the vehicle with the hoist.

2.2L DIESEL ENGINE INSTALLATION

Engine installation is the reverse of removal, plus the following:

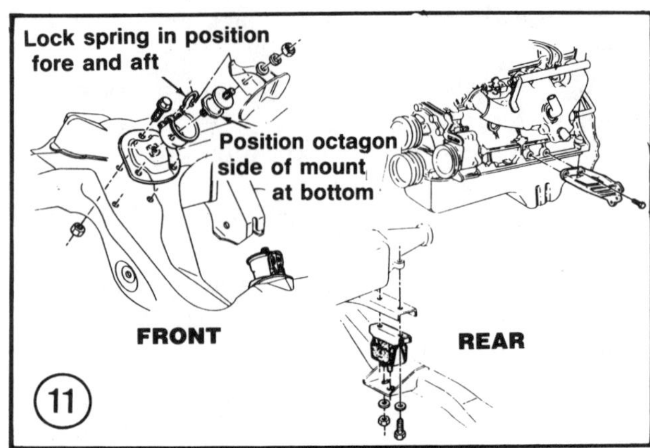

1. Lower the engine into the vehicle. Leave the hoist attached and holding the engine weight until all mounts and mount bolts have been installed and tightened to specifications (**Table 8**).
2. Fill the engine with an oil recommended in Chapter Three.
3. Fill the cooling system. See Chapter Seven.
4. Adjust the drive belts. See Chapter Three.
5. Fill the clutch master cylinder reservoir with DOT 3 brake fluid.

ENGINE MOUNTS AND SUPPORTS

Engine mounts are non-adjustable and rarely require service. Replace any broken or deteriorated mounts immediately to reduce strain on remaining mount and drive line components.

Checking Front Mounts

1. Attach a lifting device and raise the engine enough to remove its weight from the mount.
2. Check the rubber surface of the mount for:
   a. Heat check cracks.
   b. Separation from the metal plate.
   c. Splitting through the center.

NOTE

When one mount requires replacement, it is a good idea to replace all mounts at the same time.

3. If any of these defects are noted, replace the mount(s) as described in this chapter.

Checking Rear Mounts

1. Securely block the drive wheels so the truck will not roll in either direction. Raise the vehicle with a jack and place it on jackstands.

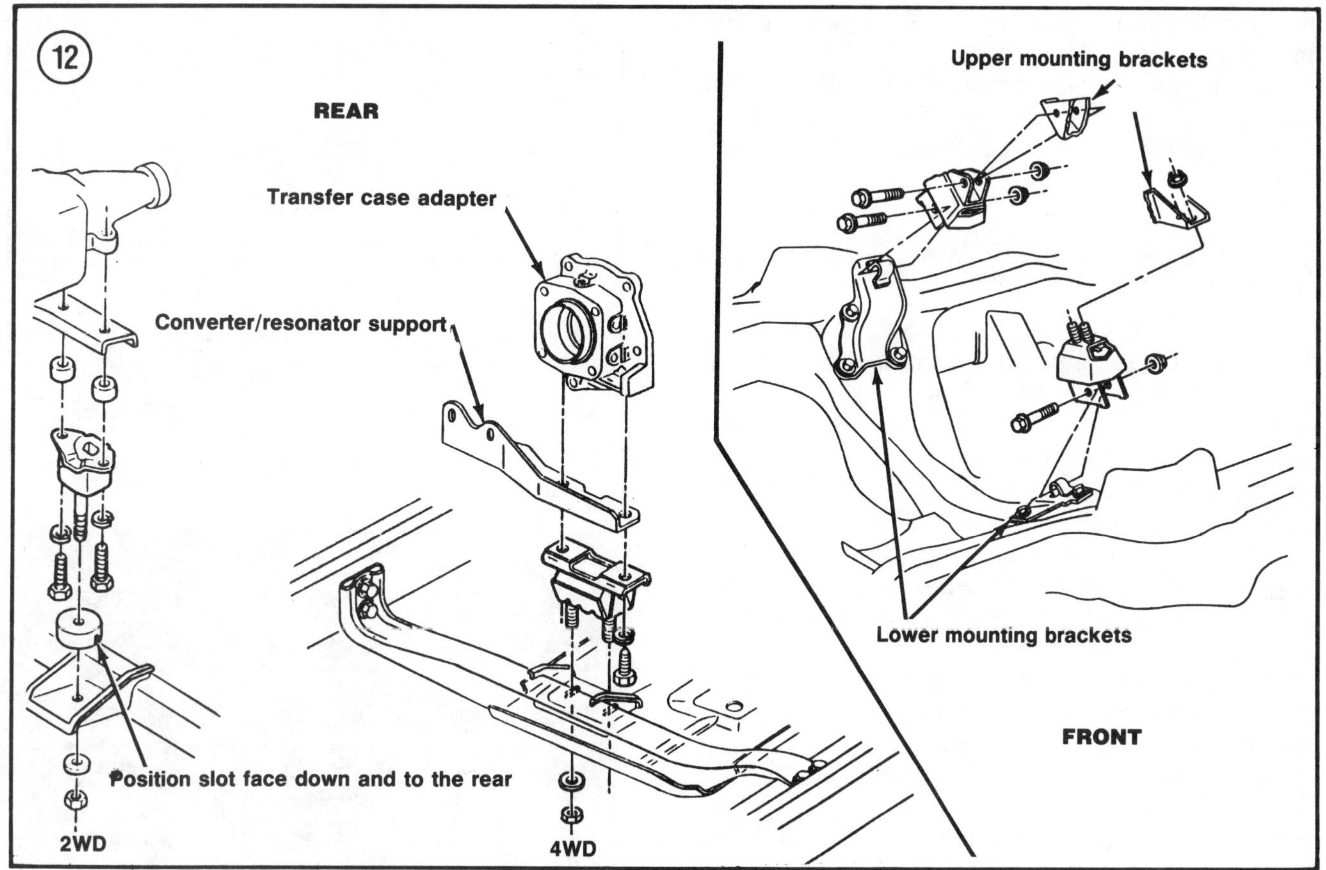

2. Watch the transmission mount while pushing up and pulling downward on the transmission extension housing. Replace the mount if the rubber separates from the metal plate or if the extension housing moves up but not downward.
3. If movement of the mount relative to the crossmember is noted during this procedure, retighten the mount fasteners.

Front Mount Replacement

1.9L engine

Refer to **Figure 11** for this procedure.

1. Disconnect the negative battery cable.
2. Remove the air cleaner duct.
3. Remove the upper half of the fan shroud.
4. Remove the engine mount nuts and retaining wire.
5. Securely block the drive wheels so the truck will not roll in either direction. Raise the vehicle with a jack and place it on jackstands.
6. Place a hydraulic jack under the engine oil pan. Insert a wooden block between the jack and oil pan, then raise the engine with the jack until its weight is removed from the mounts.
7. Remove the mount-to-engine bracket.
8. Remove the mount with tool part No. J25510.
9. Installation is the reverse of removal. Tighten all fasteners to specifications (**Table 5**).

2.0L and 2.5L engine

Refer to **Figure 12** for this procedure.

1. Disconnect the negative battery cable.
2. Remove the upper half of the fan shroud.
3. Securely block the drive wheels so the truck will not roll in either direction. Raise the front of the vehicle with a jack and place it on jackstands.

CAUTION

Raise the engine just enough in Step 4 to remove the mount. If raised too much, the distributor or EGR valve may be damaged from striking the cowl panel.

4. Place a hydraulic jack under the torsional damper and raise the front of the engine enough to

remove the mount-to-engine bolts. Remove the mount(s).
5. Installation is the reverse of removal. Tighten mount-to-frame fasteners to 35-47 ft.-lb. (48-65 N•m). Tighten all other fasteners to 29-39 ft.-lb. (40-54 N•m).

2.2L diesel engine

Refer to **Figure 13** for this procedure.
1. Disconnect the negative battery cable.
2. Remove the upper half of the fan shroud.
3. Securely block the drive wheels so the truck will not roll in either direction. Raise the front of the vehicle with a jack and place it on jackstands.
4. Place a hydraulic jack under the engine oil pan. Insert a wooden block between the jack and oil pan, then raise the engine with the jack until its weight is removed from the mounts. Remove the engine mount through-bolts.
5. Continue raising the engine until there is sufficient clearance to remove the mount-to-frame bracket bolts. Remove the mount.
6. Installation is the reverse of removal. Tighten mount-to-frame fasteners to 35-47 ft.-lb. (48-65 N•m). Tighten all other fasteners to 29-39 ft.-lb. (40-54 N•m).

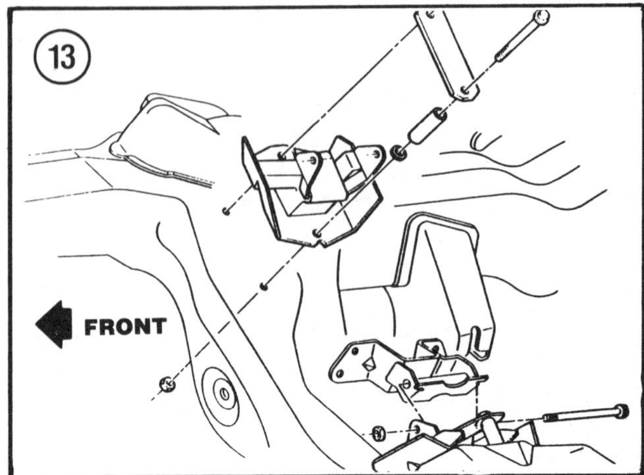

Rear Mount Replacement

Refer to **Figure 11** or **Figure 12** for this procedure.

1. Disconnect the negative battery cable.
2. Securely block the drive wheels so the truck will not roll in either direction. Raise the vehicle with a jack and place it on jackstands.
3. Place a jack under the engine and raise it enough to relieve the weight from the rear mount.
4. Remove the mount-to-transmission fasteners.
5. Remove the mount-to-crossmember fasteners. Remove the mount.
6. Install a new mount to the transmission. Tighten fasteners to 20-30 ft.-lb. (27-41 N•m).
7. Lower the engine slowly, aligning the mount-to-crossmember bolt holes. Install the mount-to-crossmember fasteners and tighten to 20-30 ft.-lb. (27-41 N•m).
8. Remove the jack from under the engine. Remove the jackstands and lower the vehicle to the ground. Reconnect the negative battery cable.

DISASSEMBLY CHECKLISTS

To use the checklists, remove and inspect each part in the order mentioned. To reassemble, go through the checklists backwards, installing the parts in order. Each major part is covered in its own section in this chapter, unless otherwise noted.

Decarbonizing or Valve Service

1. Remove the valve cover.
2. Remove the intake and exhaust manifolds.
3. Remove the rocker arms (and camshaft on overhead cam engines).
4. Remove the cylinder head.
5. Have valves removed and inspected. Have valve guides and seats inspected, repairing or replacing as required.
6. Assemble by reversing Steps 1-4.

Valve and Ring Service

1. Perform Steps 1-5 of *Decarbonizing or Valve Service.*

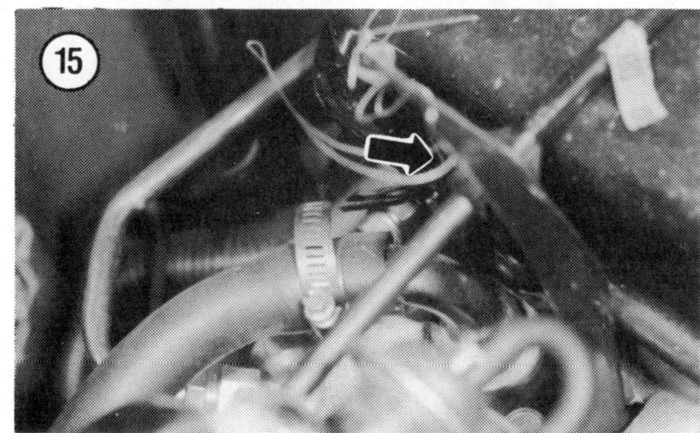

2. Remove the oil pan.
3. Remove the pistons with the connecting rods.
4. Remove the piston rings. It is not necessary to separate the pistons from the connecting rods unless a piston, connecting rod or piston pin needs repair or replacement.
5. Assemble by reversing Steps 1-4.

General Overhaul

1. Remove the engine. If equipped with the 1.9L/2.0L engine, remove the clutch and transmission from manual transmission vehicles or the torque converter and transmission from automatic transmission vehicles.
2. Remove the flywheel (manual) or drive plate (automatic).
3. Remove the mount brackets and oil pressure sending unit from the engine.
4. If available, mount the engine on an engine stand. These can be rented from equipment rental dealers. The stand is not absolutely necessary, but it will make the job much easier.
5. Check the engine for signs of coolant or oil leaks.
6. Clean the outside of the engine.
7. Remove the distributor. See Chapter Eight.
8. Remove all hoses and tubes connected to the engine.
9. Remove the fuel pump. See Chapter Six.
10. Remove the intake and exhaust manifolds.
11. Remove the thermostat housing. See Chapter Seven.
12. Remove the rocker arms.
13. Remove the crankshaft pulley, front hub, front cover, timing chain or gear and sprocket(s).
14. Remove the camshaft.
15. Remove the water pump. See Chapter Seven.
16. Remove the cylinder head.
17. Remove the oil pan and oil pump.
18. Remove the pistons and connecting rods.
19. Remove the crankshaft.
20. Inspect the cylinder block.
21. Assemble by reversing Steps 1-19.

VALVE COVER

Removal/Installation

1. Disconnect the negative battery cable.
2. Remove the air cleaner. See Chapter Six.
3. 1.9L/2.0L engine—Remove the distributor cap with plug wires attached. See *Tune-up*, Chapter Three.
4. Remove the plug wire clips from the valve cover (**Figure 14**). Place the wires to one side out of the way.
5. Disconnect all vacuum hoses, PCV hoses and pipes at the valve cover.
6. 2.5L engine—Remove the EGR valve. See Chapter Six.
7. 1.9L engine—Remove the evaporator pipe from the air manifold and engine lift bracket. Disconnect the throttle cable at the bracket (**Figure 15**).
8. 2.0L engine—Disconnect the oxygen sensor lead, carburetor choke lead and the bracket ground wires. Loosen the throttle linkage bracket.
9. 2.5L engine—Disconnect the vacuum lines at the intake manifold stud.
10A. 1.9L engine—Remove the 2 nuts and washers at each end of the valve cover. See **Figure 16**. Remove the cover.
10B. 2.0L/2.5L engine—Remove the valve cover bolts. Tap the end of the valve cover with a rubber mallet to break the RTV seal. Remove the cover.
11. Clean any gasket or RTV residue from the cylinder head and valve cover with degreaser.

CAUTION
Keep sealant out of bolt holes in Step 12 to prevent a hydraulic lock which could damage the cylinder head.

12. Apply a continuous bead of RTV sealant on the valve cover flange or sealing surface. Flow the RTV on the inside of the bolt holes. Use a 1/8 in. bead for 1.9L/2.0L engines and a 3/16 in. bead for 2.5L engines. See **Figure 17** (typical).
13. Install the valve cover while the RTV is wet. Tighten the attaching nuts snugly on the 1.9L engine. Tighten the 2.0L attaching bolts to 7 ft.-lb. (10 N•m) and the 2.5L bolts to 6 ft.-lb. (8 N•m).
14. Reverse Steps 1-9 to complete cover installation.

INTAKE MANIFOLD

The aluminum intake manifold is located on the right-hand (passenger) side of the engine. A coolant passage allows engine coolant to warm the manifold. An EGR passage is also provided.

Removal/Installation

1.9L engine

1. Disconnect the negative battery cable.

CAUTION
Drain the cooling system completely in Step 2. If coolant remains in the engine, it will flow into the cylinder head when the intake manifold is removed.

2. Drain the cooling system. See Chapter Seven.
3. Remove the air cleaner. See Chapter Six.
4. Tag and disconnect all vacuum lines, electrical lines and fuel lines to the carburetor. Plug the fuel lines to prevent leakage.
5. Disconnect the throttle cable at the carburetor.
6. Disconnect the heater hoses from the rear of the intake manifold and from the connector under the dashboard.
7. Disconnect the upper radiator hose from the front of the intake manifold.
8. Disconnect the vacuum hose at the intake manifold.
9. Disconnect the vacuum line at the distributor.
10. Disconnect the temperature sensor wiring at the connector.
11. Disconnect the PCV hose at the valve cover.
12. Unbolt the dipstick tube at the intake manifold.

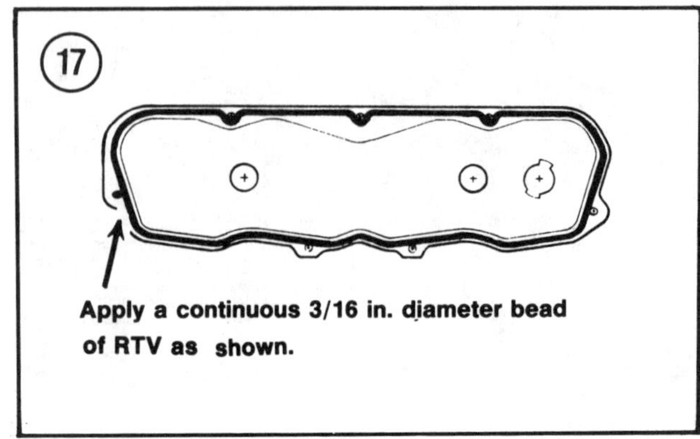

13. Disconnect the EGR pipe from the EGR valve adapter. Remove EGR valve and adapter.
14. Remove nut located under EGR valve. Disconnect the air pump hose from the 3-way joint.
15. Remove the 8 nuts holding the intake manifold. Remove the intake manifold.
16. Remove and discard the manifold gasket. Clean all gasket residue on the intake manifold and cylinder head sealing surfaces.
17. Installation is the reverse of removal. Use a new gasket. Start with the inner nuts and work to the outer fasteners, tightening to 16 ft.-lb. (20 N•m). Refill the cooling system (Chapter Seven).

2.0L engine

1. Disconnect the negative battery cable.

CAUTION
Drain the cooling system completely in Step 2. If coolant remains in the engine, it will flow into the cylinder head when the intake manifold is removed.

2. Drain the cooling system. See Chapter Seven.
3. Remove the air cleaner. See Chapter Six.
4. Tag and disconnect all vacuum lines, electrical lines and fuel lines to the carburetor. Plug the fuel lines to prevent leakage.
5. Disconnect the throttle cable at the carburetor.
6. Loosen the power steering pump and remove the belt. Remove the pump without disconnecting any lines or hoses and place to one side out of the way.
7. Remove the carburetor. See Chapter Six.
8. Remove the intake manifold nuts and bolts (**Figure 18**). Remove the intake manifold. Disconnect the heater hose and condensor at the bottom of the manifold.

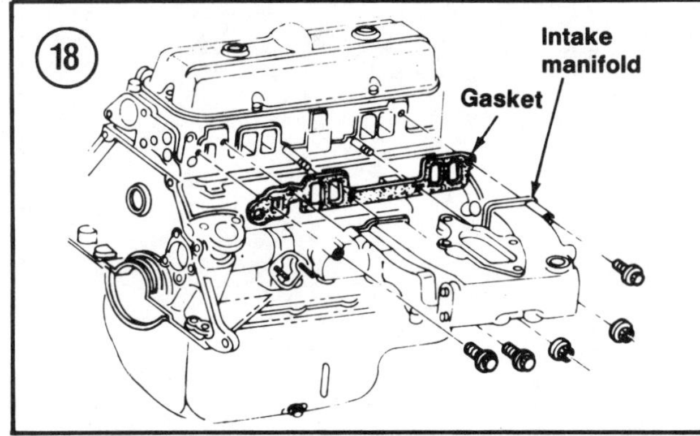

9. Remove and discard the manifold gasket. Clean all gasket residue from the intake manifold and cylinder head sealing surfaces.
10. Installation is the reverse of removal. Use a new gasket. Start with the inner nuts and work to the outer fasteners, tightening to 20-25 ft.-lb. (27-34 N•m). Refill the cooling system (Chapter Seven).

2.5L engine

1. Disconnect the negative battery cable.

CAUTION
Drain the cooling system completely in Step 2. If coolant remains in the engine, it will flow into the cylinder head when the intake manifold is removed.

2. Drain the cooling system. See Chapter Seven.
3. Remove the air cleaner. See Chapter Six.
4. Label and disconnect all vacuum lines and electrical connectors from the TBI (throttle body injection) assembly.

WARNING
Before opening any fuel system lines on a fuel injected engine, relieve system pressure as described in Chapter Six.

5. Disconnect the fuel line at the TBI assembly fuel inlet. Plug the line to prevent leakage.
6. Disconnect the TBI throttle cable and transmission TV (throttle valve) cable at the bellcrank.
7. Disconnect the bypass hose at the intake manifold.
8. Remove the rear alternator mounting bracket, then disconnect the alternator brace and move it to one side.
9. Disconnect the vacuum pipe hold-down at the thermostat housing.
10. Disconnect the heater hose and ignition coil at the intake manifold.
11. Remove the manifold bolts and studs. Remove the manifold.
12. Remove and discard the manifold gasket. Clean all gasket residue from the intake manifold and cylinder head sealing surfaces.
13. Installation is the reverse of removal. Use a new gasket. Refer to **Figure 19** and tighten bolts 1 and 2 to 28 ft.-lb. (38 N•m), bolts 3, 4, 5 and 6 to 25 ft.-lb. (34 N•m) and bolt 7 to 37 ft.-lb. (50 N•m). Refill the cooling system (Chapter Seven).

4

EXHAUST MANIFOLD

The exhaust manifold is a single take-down design of cast iron mounted on the left-hand (driver) side of the engine. It has a manifold cover to provide heated air to the air cleaner.

Removal/Installation

1.9L engine

1. Disconnect the negative battery cable.
2. Securely block the drive wheels so the truck will not roll in either direction. Raise the front of the vehicle with a jack and place it on jackstands.
3. Disconnect the exhaust pipe at the exhaust manifold.
4. Disconnect the EGR pipe at the exhaust manifold.
5. Remove the jackstands and lower the vehicle to the ground.
6. Remove the air cleaner attaching bolts. Lift the air cleaner housing enough to disconnect the hot air hose from the manifold cover.

WARNING
The air conditioning system contains pressurized refrigerant which can cause frostbite if it touches skin and blindness if it touches the eyes. If discharged near an open flame, the refrigerant forms poisonous gas. Never disconnect air conditioning system lines unless the system has been discharged and evacuated by a professional.

7. If so equipped, remove the air conditioning compressor and/or power steering pump without disconnecting any refrigerant or hydraulic lines. Place accessory unit(s) to one side out of the way.
8. Remove the bolts holding the manifold cover. Remove the cover.

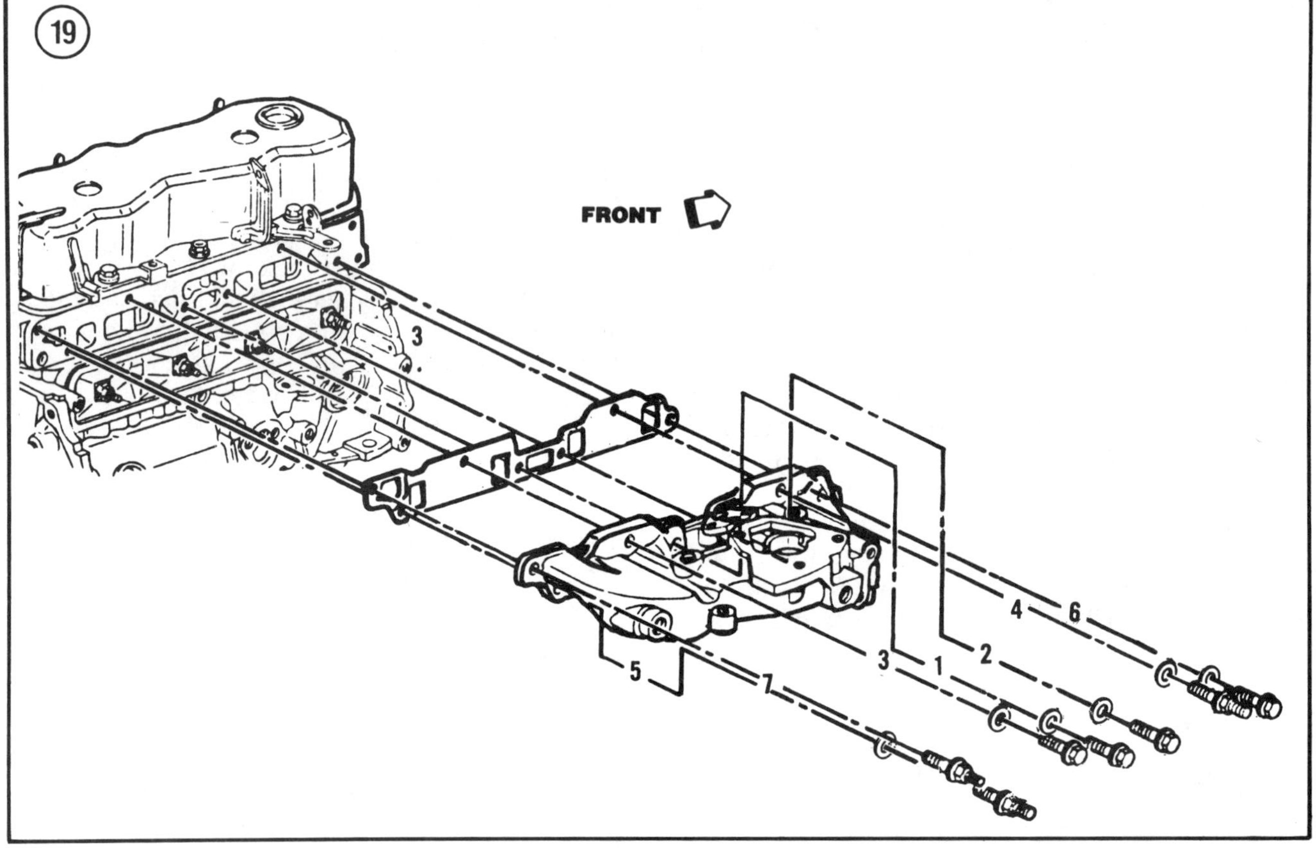

9. Disconnect the oxygen sensor lead, if so equipped.
10. Remove the nuts holding the exhaust manifold. Remove the manifold.
11. Installation is the reverse of removal. Tighten manifold nuts to 16 ft.-lb. (20 N•m) working from the inner to outer nuts.

2.0L engine

1. Disconnect the negative battery cable.
2. Remove the air cleaner. See Chapter Six.
3. Remove the exhaust manifold shield.
4. Securely block the drive wheels so the truck will not roll in either direction. Raise the front of the vehicle with a jack and place it on jackstands.
5. Disconnect the exhaust pipe at the manifold.
6. Disconnect the oxygen sensor lead.
7. Remove the alternator adjusting bolt. Loosen the pivot bolt. Remove the drive belt and move the alternator upward, then remove the alternator brace.
8. Disconnect the Pulsair pipe.

9. Remove the dipstick bracket bolt. Remove the exhaust manifold bolts. See **Figure 20**. Remove the exhaust manifold.
10. Installation is the reverse of removal. Tighten manifold fasteners to 22-28 ft.-lb. (30-38 N•m).

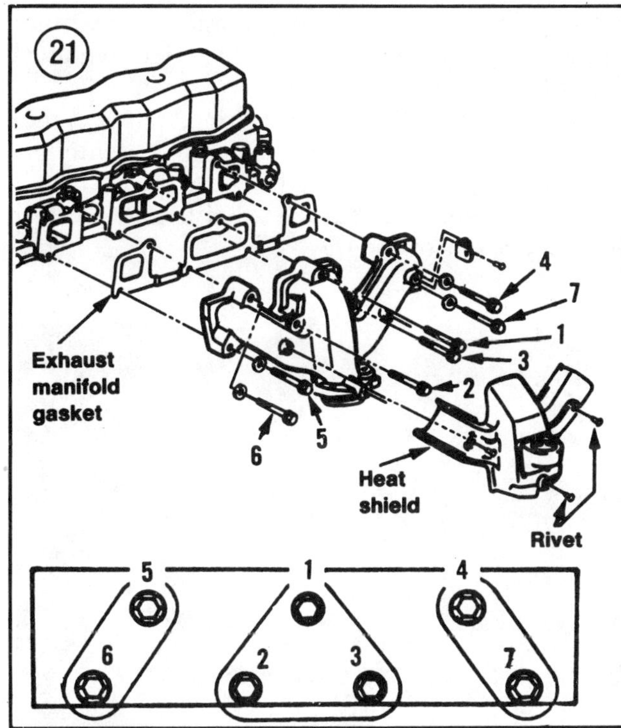

2.5L engine

1. Disconnect the negative battery cable.

WARNING
The air conditioning system contains pressurized refrigerant which can cause frostbite if it touches skin and blindness if it touches the eyes. If discharged near an open flame, the refrigerant forms poisonous gas. Never disconnect air conditioning system lines unless the system has been discharged and evacuated by a professional.

2. Remove the air conditioning compressor, if so equipped, and place to one side without disconnecting any refrigerant lines.
3. Remove the rear alternator mounting bracket.
4. Raise the vehicle with a jack and place it on jackstands.
5. Disconnect the exhaust pipe from the exhaust manifold.
6. Remove the jackstands and lower the vehicle to the ground.
7. Remove the air cleaner assembly. See Chapter Six.
8. Disconnect the oxygen sensor lead.
9. Remove the exhaust manifold bolts. Remove the manifold and gasket. Discard the gasket.
10. Clean any gasket residue from the cylinder head and manifold sealing surfaces.
11. Installation is the reverse of removal. Use a new gasket and tighten all fasteners to 44 ft.-lb. (60 N•m) in the sequence shown in **Figure 21**.

MANIFOLD INSPECTION

1. Check the intake and exhaust manifolds for cracks or distortion. Replace if distorted or if cracks are found.
2. Check the gasket surfaces for nicks or burrs. Small burrs may be removed with an oilstone.
3. Place a straightedge across the manifold flange/gasket surfaces. If there is any gap between the straightedge and the surface, measure it with a feeler gauge. Measure each manifold from end to end and from corner to corner.
   a. The 1.9L manifold gasket surface must be flat within 0.4 mm ±0.05 mm (0.0157 in. ±0.0020 in.) per foot of manifold length. If not, replace the manifold.
   b. The 2.0L/2.5L manifold gasket surface must be flat within 0.15 mm (0.006 in.) per foot of manifold length. If not, replace the manifold.

CRANKSHAFT PULLEY AND FRONT HUB

Removal/Installation

1.9L engine

1. Disconnect the negative battery cable.
2. Loosen the accessory units and remove all drive belts.
3. Securely block the drive wheels so the truck will not roll in either direction. Raise the front of the vehicle with a jack and place it on jackstands.
4. Drain the cooling system. Remove the cooling fan and radiator. See Chapter Seven.
5. Remove the center bolt from the crankshaft pulley. Remove the pulley and hub.
6. Installation is the reverse of removal. Tighten the crankshaft pulley bolt to 87 ft.-lb. (118 N•m). Adjust all drive belts (Chapter Three) and refill the cooling system (Chapter Seven).

2.0L engine

This procedure requires the use of a 3-legged puller (part No. J-24420) and hub installer (part No. J-29113).

1. Disconnect the negative battery cable.
2. Loosen the accessory units and remove all drive belts.
3. Securely block the drive wheels so the truck will not roll in either direction. Raise the front of the vehicle with a jack and place it on jackstands.

4

4. Remove the crankshaft pulley retaining bolts (**Figure 22**).
5. Remove the front hub (**Figure 23**) with tool part No. J-24420.
6. Lubricate the front cover seal contact area with SAE 30W engine oil.
7. Apply a small amount of RTV sealant to the hub keyway. Position the hub over the crankshaft key.
8. Pull hub into position with tool part No. J-29113.
9. Reverse Steps 1-4 to complete installation. Adjust all drive belts (Chapter Three).

2.5L engine

1. Disconnect the negative battery cable.
2. Loosen the accessory units and remove all drive belts.
3. Remove the crankshaft pulley bolt. Slide the pulley and hub from the crankshaft.
4. Installation is the reverse of removal. Tighten the crankshaft bolt to 160 ft.-lb. (212 N•m). Adjust all drive belts (Chapter Three).

CRANKCASE FRONT COVER

Removal/Installation

1.9L engine

1. Rotate the crankshaft until the timing pointer and crankshaft pulley marks align to position the No. 1 cylinder at TDC. Remove the distributor cap and check to make sure the rotor points to the No. 1 cap electrode. If not, rotate the crankshaft 360°.
2. Remove the cylinder head as described in this chapter.
3. Remove the oil pan as described in this chapter.
4. Remove the oil pickup tube from the oil pump (**Figure 24**).
5. Remove the crankshaft pulley and hub as described in this chapter.
6. Loosen the air pump pivot/mounting bolts. Remove the drive belt.

WARNING
The air conditioning system contains pressurized refrigerant which can cause frostbite if it touches skin and blindness if it touches the eyes. If discharged near an open flame, the refrigerant forms poisonous gas. Never disconnect air conditioning system lines unless the system has been discharged and evacuated by a professional.

7. If equipped with air conditioning, remove the compressor and place it to one side without disconnecting any refrigerant lines.
8. If equipped with power steering, remove the pump and place it to one side without disconnecting any hydraulic lines.
9. Remove the distributor cap (Chapter Three) and place it out of the way.

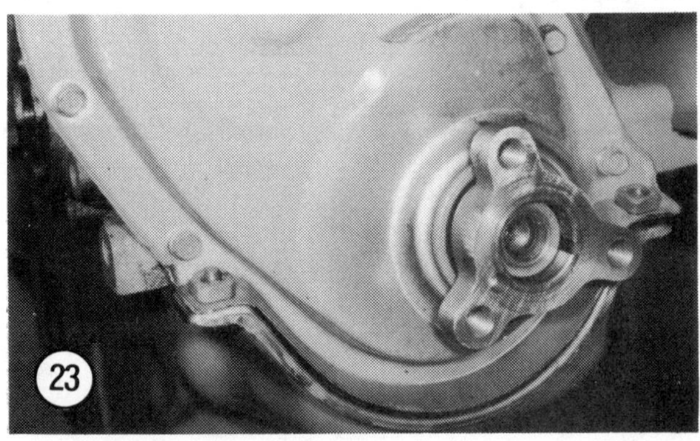

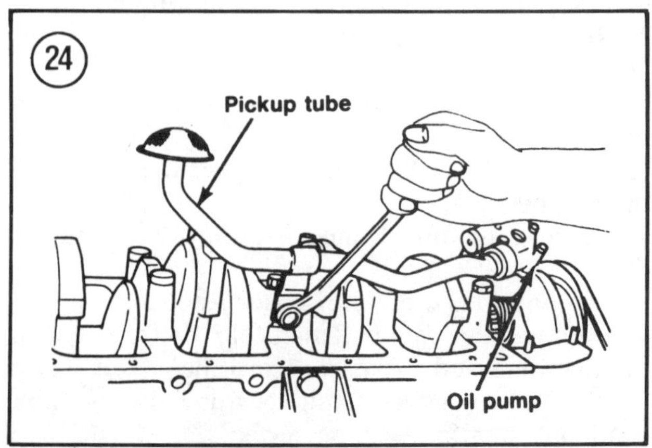

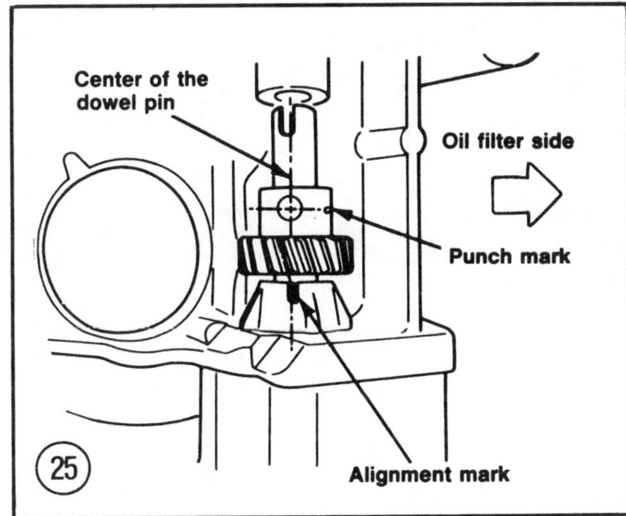

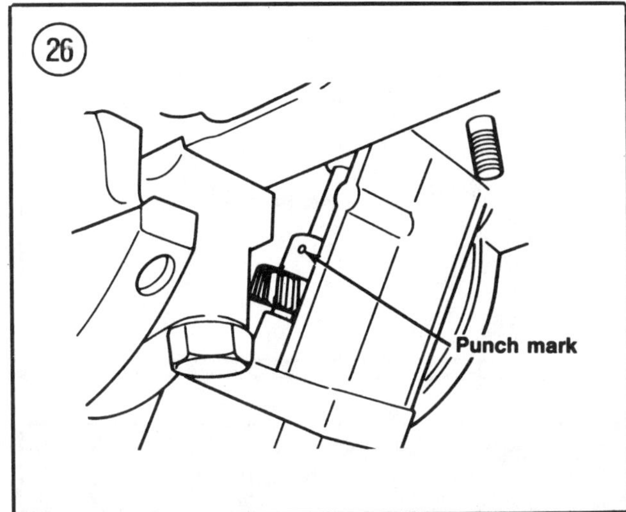

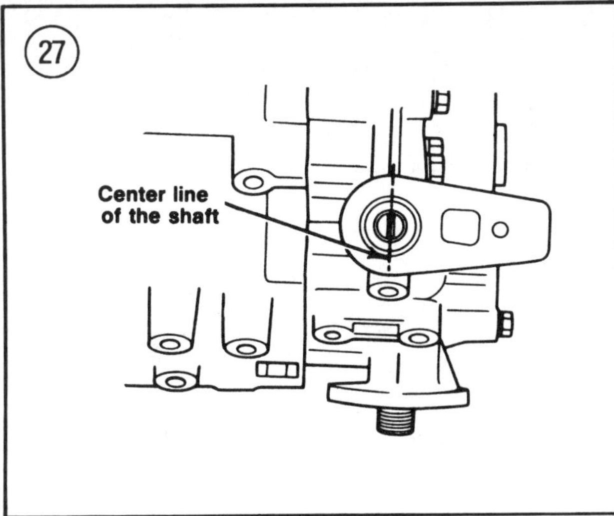

10. Loosen the distributor hold-down bolt and remove the distributor (Chapter Eight).
11. Remove the front cover attaching bolts. Remove the front cover. Remove and discard the gasket.
12. Clean the block and front cover sealing surfaces of all oil and grease. Install a new gasket on the block.
13. Align the punch mark on the oil pump drive gear with the oil filter side of the cover. Align the center of the dowel pin with the oil pump case alignment mark. See **Figure 25**.
14. Engage the pinion gear with the oil pump drive gear on the crankshaft. Install the front cover.
15. Make sure the punch mark on the oil pump drive gear is turned to the rear side, as seen through the gap between the front cover and cylinder block. See **Figure 26**.
16. Make sure the slit at the end of the oil pump is parallel with the front of the block and that it is offset to the front. See **Figure 27**.
17. Install and tighten the front cover bolts to 18 ft.-lb. (24 N•m).
18. Reverse Steps 1-10 to complete cover installation.

2.0L engine

Refer to **Figure 28** for this procedure.

1. Remove the crankshaft pulley and front hub as described in this chapter.

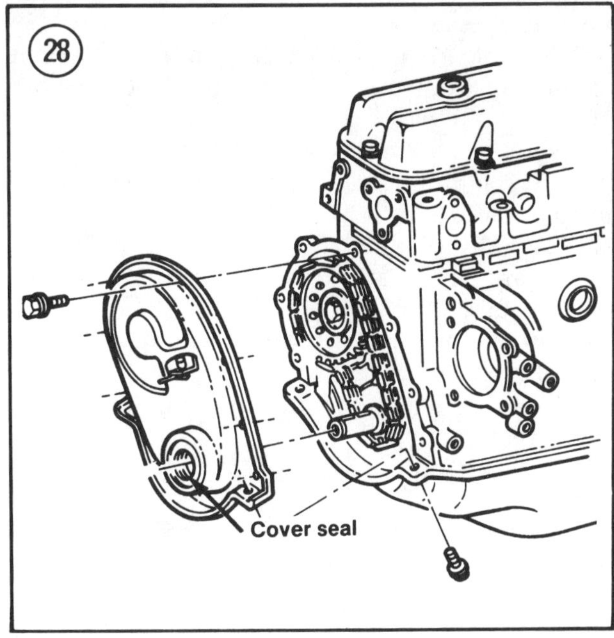

4

NOTE
The front oil pan attaching screws on each side of the pan also hold the base of the front cover in place. These must be removed to remove the front cover.

2. Remove the front cover bolts. Remove the front cover.
3. Clean the block and front cover sealing surfaces of all oil and grease. Apply a 2 mm (0.08 in.) bead of RTV sealant to the cover sealing surface. Install cover within 10 minutes of applying RTV.
4. Tighten cover screws to 6-9 ft.-lb. (8-12 N•m).
5. Install the front hub and crankshaft pulley as described in this chapter.

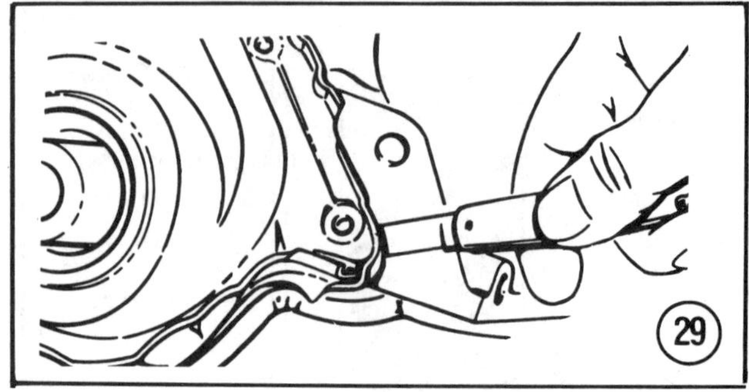
29

2.5L engine

1. Disconnect the negative battery cable.
2. Drain the cooling system. See Chapter Seven.
3. Remove the power steering reservoir at the fan shroud without disconnecting any hydraulic lines.
4. Remove the upper fan shroud, fan and pulley.
5. Loosen the accessory units and remove all drive belts.
6. Remove the alternator mounting brackets, brace and alternator. Place alternator to one side out of the way.
7. Remove the crankshaft pulley and hub as described in this chapter.
8. Disconnect the lower radiator hose at the water pump.
9. Remove the oil pan-to-front cover and front cover-to-block screws.
10. Pull the front cover slightly forward and cut the oil pan front seal flush with the block at both sides of the cover (**Figure 29**) with a sharp knife.
11. Remove the front cover with the cut portion of the oil pan front seal. Remove and discard the cover gasket.
12. Carefully pry the seal from the front cover. Work carefully to avoid bending or distorting the sheet metal cover.
13. Install a new seal with its helical lip facing the rear of the engine.
14. Clean all gasket residue from the block and front cover mating surfaces.
15. Cut a replacement oil pan front seal as shown in **Figure 30**.
16. Install the seal on the timing gear cover and press the tips into the cover holes.
17. Coat a new gasket with sealer and position it on the cover.

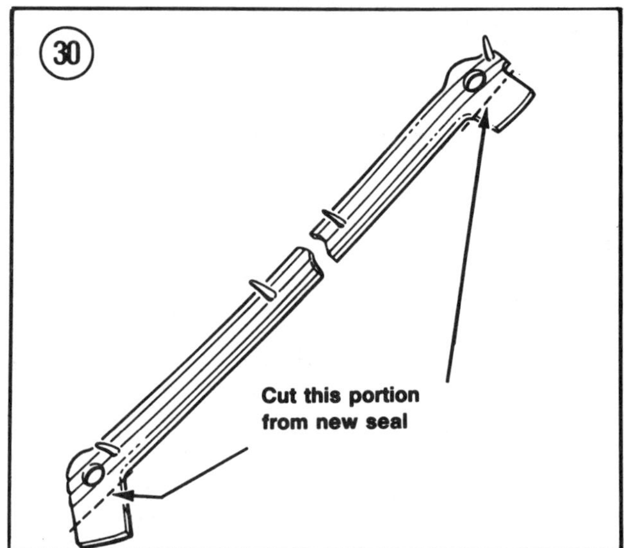

30

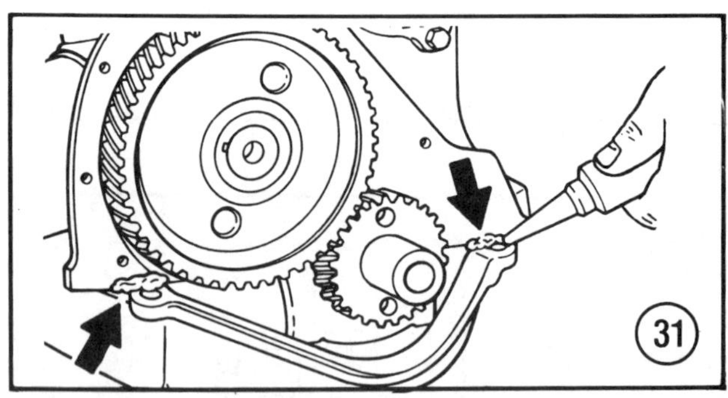
31

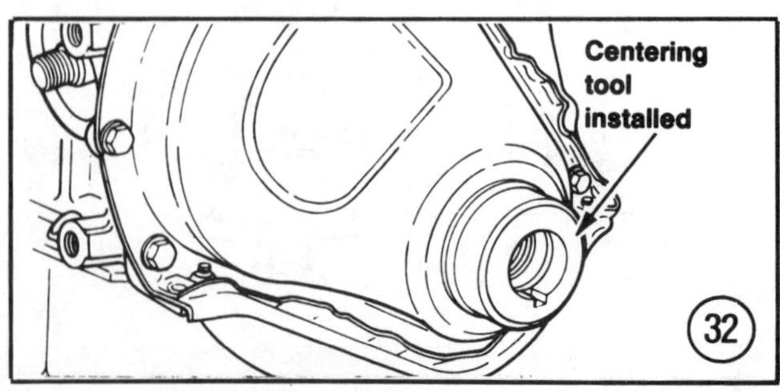

32

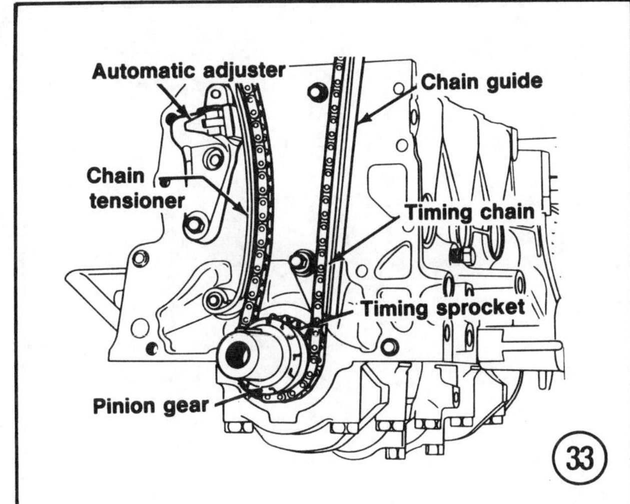

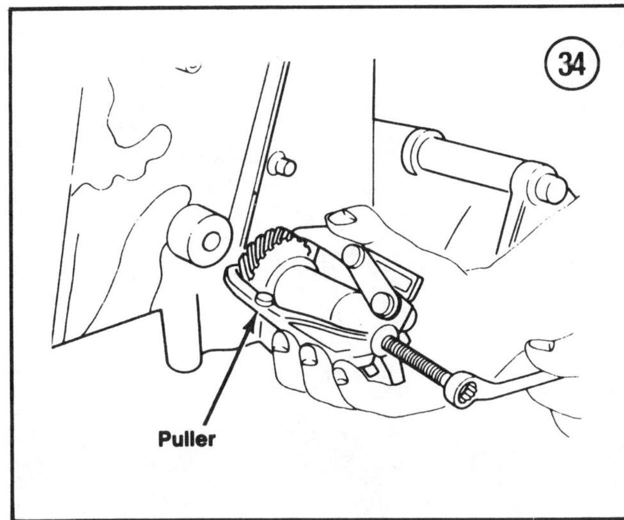

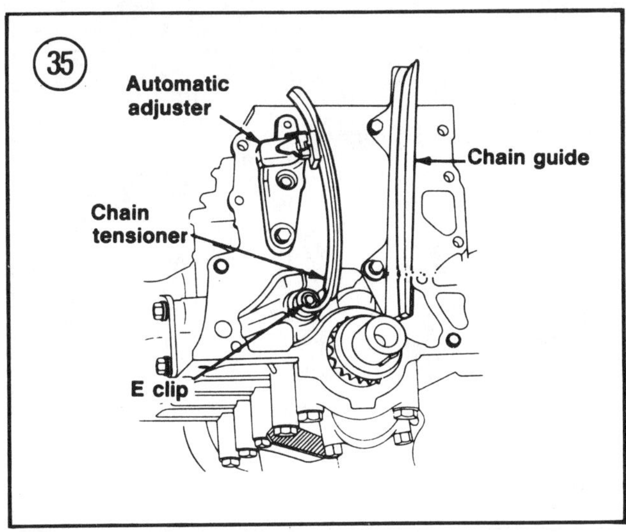

18. Run a 3 mm (1/8 in.) bead of RTV sealant along the joint formed at the oil pan and engine block. See **Figure 31**.

NOTE

The use of a centering tool in Step 19 is recommended to assure that the front cover is properly aligned. If it is not, the crankshaft pulley hub may damage the seal when it is installed.

19. Install centering tool part No. J-34995 in the front cover seal and position the cover on the block (**Figure 32**).
20. Install and partially tighten the 2 oil pan-to-front cover screws. Install the cover-to-block screws.
21. Tighten cover attaching screws to specifications (**Table 7**) and remove the centering tool.
22. Reverse Steps 1-8 to complete installation. Adjust the drive belts (Chapter Three) and refill the cooling system (Chapter Seven).

TIMING CHAIN AND SPROCKET (1.9L ENGINE)

Removal

Refer to **Figure 33** for this procedure.

1. Remove the spark plugs. See *Tune-up* in Chapter Three.
2. Remove the crankshaft pulley and front hub as described in this chapter.
3. Remove the front cover as described in this chapter.
4. Depress the adjuster lock lever to lock the adjuster shoe in a fully retracted position.
5. Remove the timing chain from the crankshaft sprocket.
6. Remove the chain from the camshaft sprocket.

NOTE

*If the crankshaft sprocket is not worn or damaged, it does not have to be removed for timing chain replacement. If removal is necessary, use a puller like the one shown in **Figure 34** and remove the sprocket and pinion gear.*

Inspection

1. Remove the automatic adjuster bolt. Remove the adjuster. See **Figure 35**.

2. Make sure the shoe locks when it is pushed in with the lock lever released.
3. Check the adjuster rack teeth (**Figure 36**). Replace the adjuster if the rack teeth are excessively worn.
4. Remove the E-clip (**Figure 35**). Remove the chain tensioner and inspect for wear or damage.
5. Check the tensioner pin for wear or damage.
   a. If replacement is necessary, use locking pliers to remove the pin.
   b. Lubricate a new pin with engine oil and start it in the block.
   c. Place the tensioner over the pin, install the E-clip and tap pin into block until the clip just clears the tensioner.
   d. Check tensioner and adjuster for free rotation on the pins.
6. Check the chain guide (**Figure 35**) for wear, damage or a plugged lower oil jet. If necessary, remove and replace the guide. Install lower oil jet and bolt with the oil port pointing toward the crankshaft, as shown in **Figure 37**.

Installation

1. Align the timing mark plate on the chain with the setting mark on the crankshaft timing sprocket and install as shown in **Figure 38**.
2. Install the camshaft timing sprocket with its timing mark facing forward. The triangular timing mark must align with the chain plate mark.
3. Install the automatic chain adjuster, if removed.
4. Depress the adjuster shoe to release the lock. Make sure the chain is tensioned when the lock is released.
5. Reverse Steps 1-3 of *Removal* in this chapter.

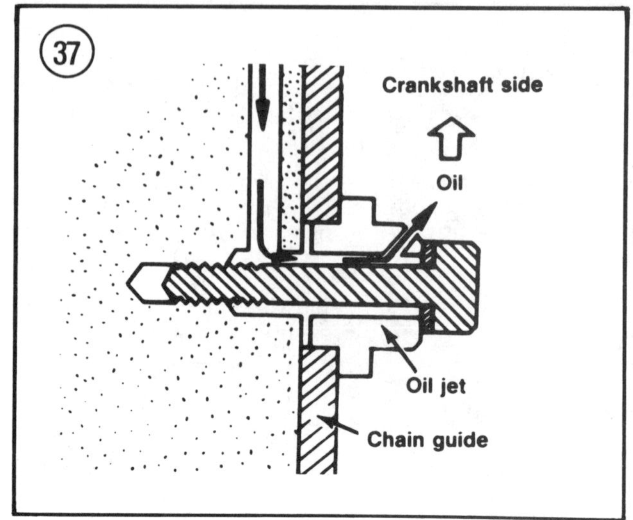

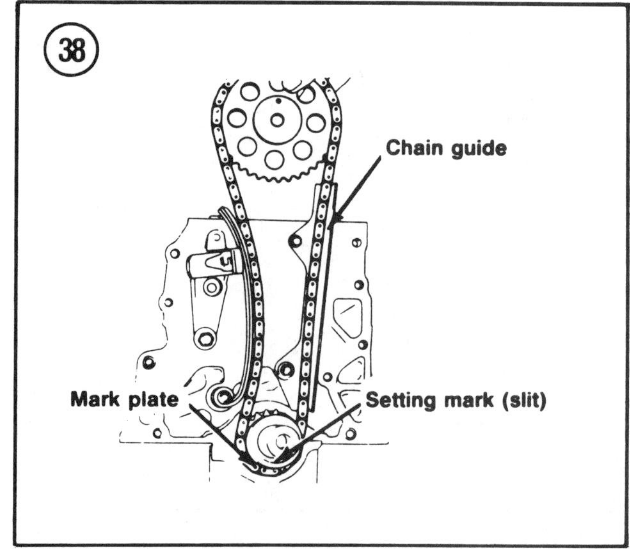

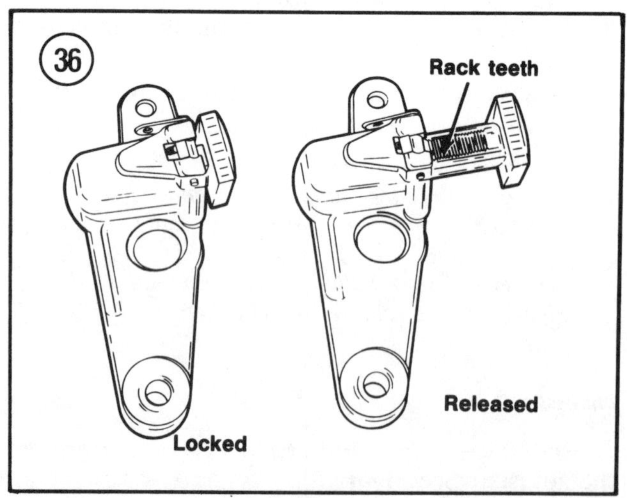

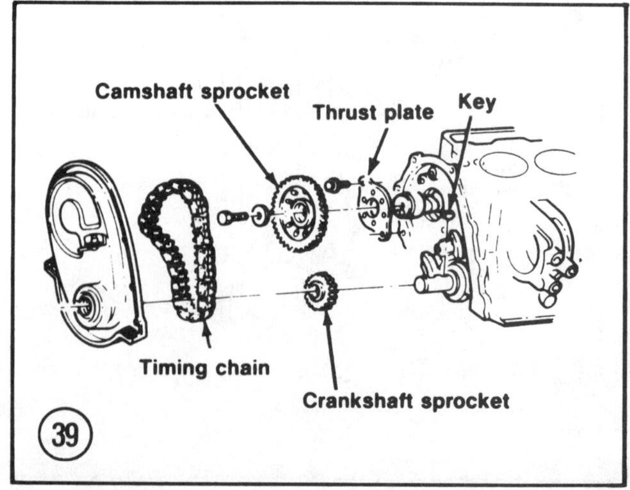

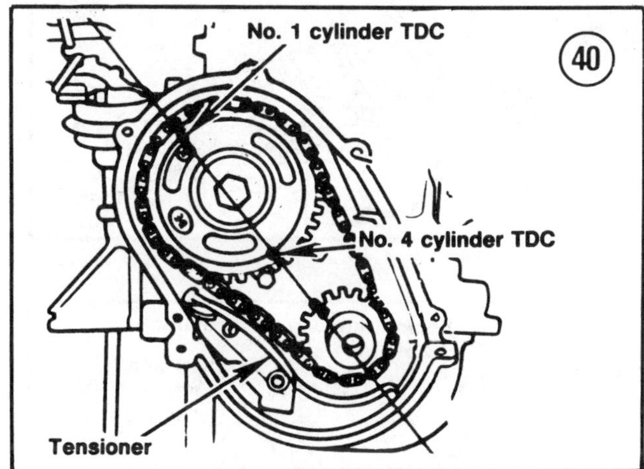

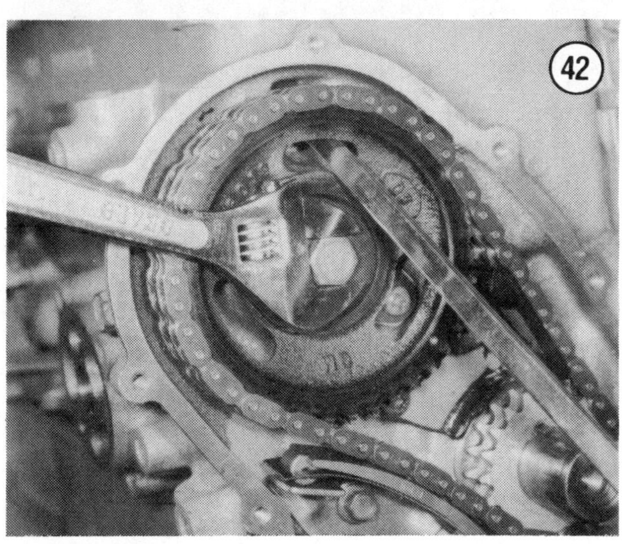

TIMING CHAIN AND SPROCKET (2.0L ENGINE)

Removal

Refer to **Figure 39** for this procedure.

1. Remove the spark plugs. See *Tune-up* in Chapter Three.
2. Remove the crankshaft pulley, front hub and front cover as described in this chapter.
3. Temporarily reinstall the crankshaft pulley bolt in the crankshaft sprocket.
4. Place a wrench on the pulley bolt and rotate the crankshaft to align the timing marks on the crankshaft and camshaft sprockets as shown in **Figure 40**.
5. Loosen the upper tensioner nut (A, **Figure 41**) as far as possible. Reach into the oil pan area with an open-end wrench and loosen the lower tensioner attaching nut (B, **Figure 41**). Remove the nut carefully with 2 fingers. If it slips out of your fingers, you will have to remove the oil pan to retrieve it.
6. Insert a large flat-blade screwdriver in the camshaft sprocket cutout as shown in **Figure 42**. Hold the sprocket from moving and remove the sprocket bolt.
7. Pull the sprocket from the camshaft locating dowel. Remove the sprocket and chain assembly.

Installation

Refer to **Figure 39** for this procedure.

1. Install the timing chain on the camshaft sprocket.
2. Loop the chain over the crankshaft sprocket. Position the camshaft sprocket so that its timing marks align as shown in **Figure 40**.
3. Align the camshaft dowel with the sprocket dowel hole and install the sprocket on the camshaft.
4. Install the camshaft sprocket bolt. Hold the sprocket from moving as shown in **Figure 42** and tighten the bolt to 66-85 ft.-lb. (90-115 N•m).
5. Lubricate the timing chain with SAE 30W engine oil.
6. Install the tensioner over the stud inside the oil pan area. Carefully thread the nut in place using 2 fingers and tighten with an open-end wrench. Tighten the upper tensioner nut.
7. Install the front cover, hub and crankshaft pulley as described in this chapter.
8. Install the spark plugs (Chapter Three).

TIMING GEAR REPLACEMENT (2.5L ENGINE)

1. Remove the camshaft as described in this chapter.

NOTE
Make sure the thrust plate is aligned with the Woodruff key in the camshaft before performing Step 2.

2. Install the camshaft in a press plate and use an arbor press to remove the camshaft from the gear.
3. Installation of the gear is the reverse of removal. Press the gear onto the camshaft until it bottoms against the gear spacer ring.
4. Check the thrust plate end clearance with a feeler gauge as shown in **Figure 43**. It should be 0.0015-0.0050 in. (0.038-0.127 mm). If less than 0.0015 in. (0.038 mm), replace the spacer plate. If greater than 0.0050 in. (0.127 mm), replace the thrust plate.

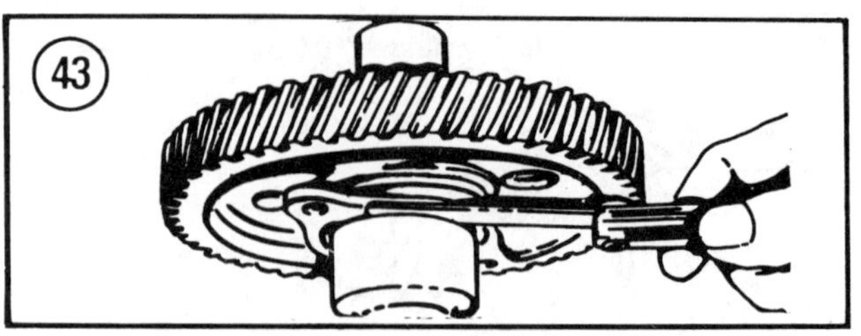

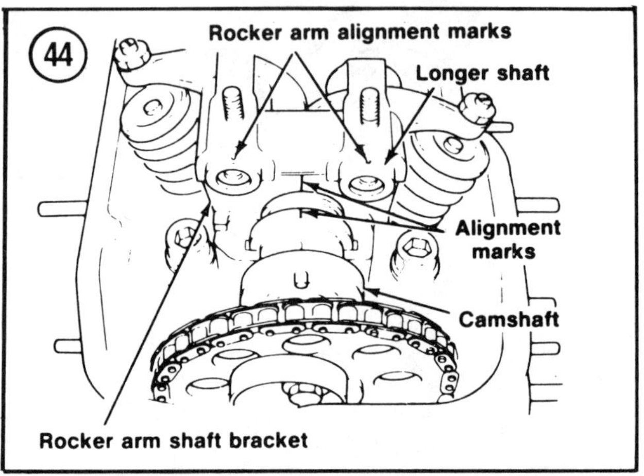

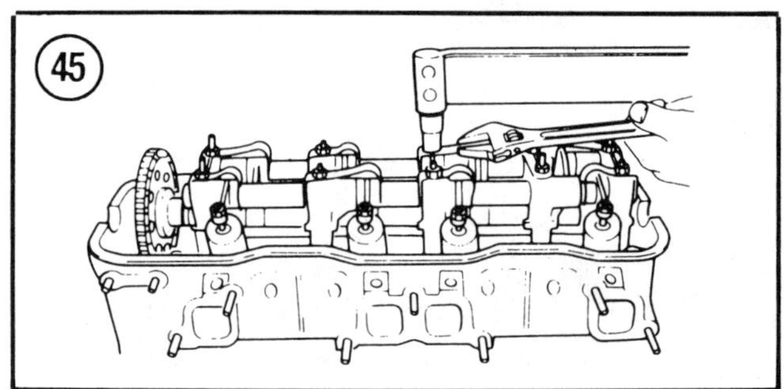

ROCKER ARMS (1.9L ENGINE)

Removal

1. Remove the valve cover as described in this chapter.
2. Loosen the rocker arm shaft bracket nuts a few turns at a time. Start with the outer bracket nuts and work in sequence toward the center nuts.
3. Remove the shaft bracket nuts. Remove the shaft assembly.
4. Remove the rocker arm shaft spring. Remove the rocker arm brackets and arms from the shaft.

Inspection

1. Place the rocker arm shaft on V-blocks and check for runout with a dial indicator. Replace the shaft if runout exceeds 0.0079 in. (0.2 mm).
2. Measure rocker arm shaft diameter at 4 points with a micrometer. Replace the shaft if less than 0.8012 in. (20.35 mm).
3. Measure the inner diameter of the rocker arms and compare with outer diameter of the shaft. If clearance exceeds 0.0078 in. (0.2 mm), replace the rocker arms and/or shaft.
4. Check the rocker arm faces for scoring or excessive wear. Minor wear can be corrected with an oil stone or valve refacer. Replace the rocker arm if wear is excessive.

Installation

1. Lubricate all rocker arms, valve stems and the rocker arm shaft with engine oil.
2. Install the longer shaft on the exhaust valve side and the shorter shaft on the intake side. Shaft alignment marks must face the front of the engine. See **Figure 44**.
3. Assemble the rocker arm shaft brackets and arms to the shafts. The cylinder number on the upper face of the bracket must point to the front of the engine.
4. Align the No. 1 shaft bracket mark with the mark on the valve side of the rocker arm shafts.
5. Install the shaft springs between the bracket and rocker arm.

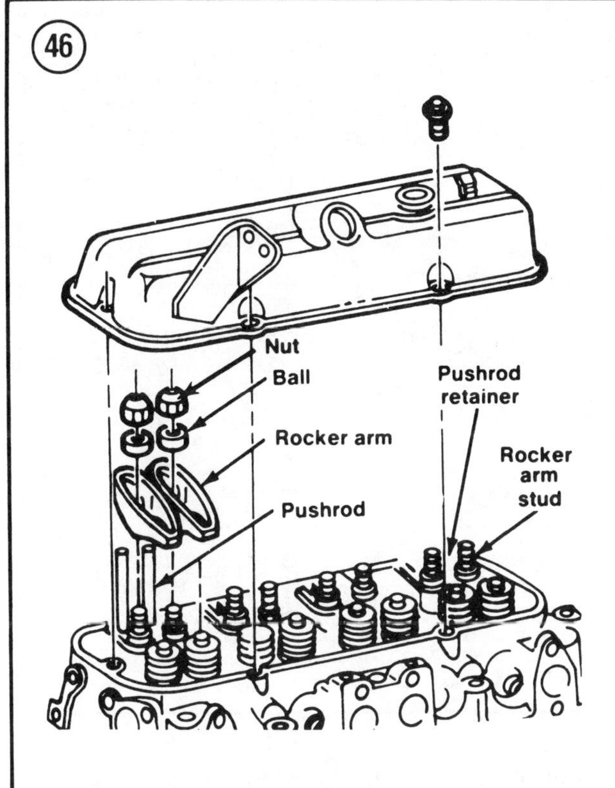

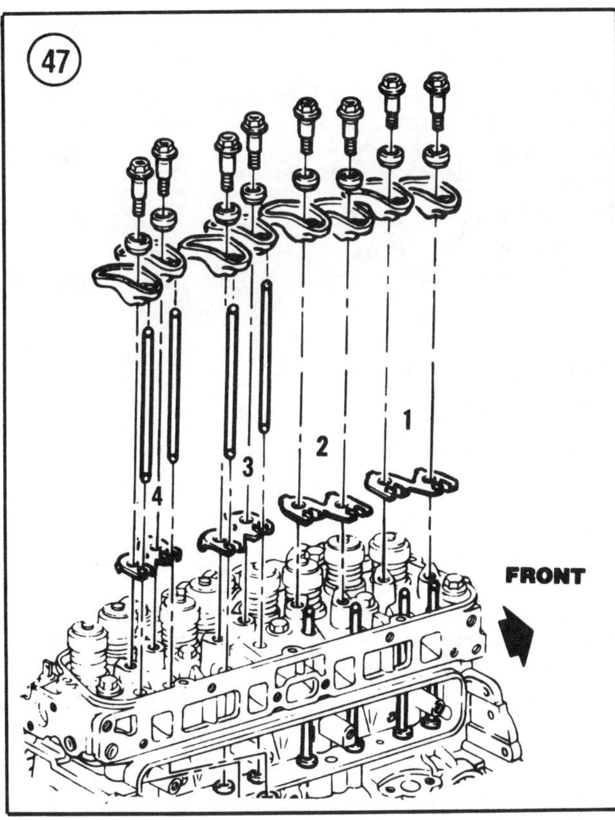

6. Make sure the rocker arm shaft punch mark faces up, then install the shaft bracket assembly to the cylinder head studs. Align the camshaft mark with the No. 1 rocker arm shaft bracket mark. See **Figure 44**.
7. Hold each rocker arm spring with an adjustable wrench (**Figure 45**) while tightening the stud nuts to 16 ft.-lb. (22 N•m). Start at the center bracket and work toward the outside.
8. Adjust valve clearance. See Chapter Three.
9. Install the valve cover as described in this chapter.

ROCKER ARMS (2.0L ENGINE)

Removal/Installation

Refer to **Figure 46** for this procedure.
1. Remove the valve cover as described in this chapter.
2. Remove the rocker arm nuts, rocker arm balls, rocker arms and pushrods.
3. Place each rocker arm and pushrod assembly in a separate container or use a rack to keep them separated for reinstallation in the same position as removed.
4. Remove the valve lifters with tool part No. J-29834. Do not pry lifters out with a screwdriver. If tool part No. J-29834 is not available, use a pencil-type magnet.

NOTE
When installing new valve lifters, rocker arms or rocker arm balls, coat the contact surface with Molykote or equivalent.

5. Install the valve lifters and pushrods. Seat each pushrod in its lifter and align in its retainer.
6. Install the rocker arms, rocker arm balls and rocker arm nuts. Tighten the nuts until all lash is removed.
7. Adjust the valves as described in this chapter.
8. Install the valve cover as described in this chapter.

ROCKER ARMS AND PUSHROD COVER (2.5L ENGINE)

Rocker Arm Removal/Installation

Each rocker arm moves on its own pivot ball. The rocker arm and pivot ball are retained by a capscrew. It is not necessary to remove the rocker arm for pushrod replacement; simply loosen the capscrew and move the arm away from the pushrod. Refer to **Figure 47** for this procedure.

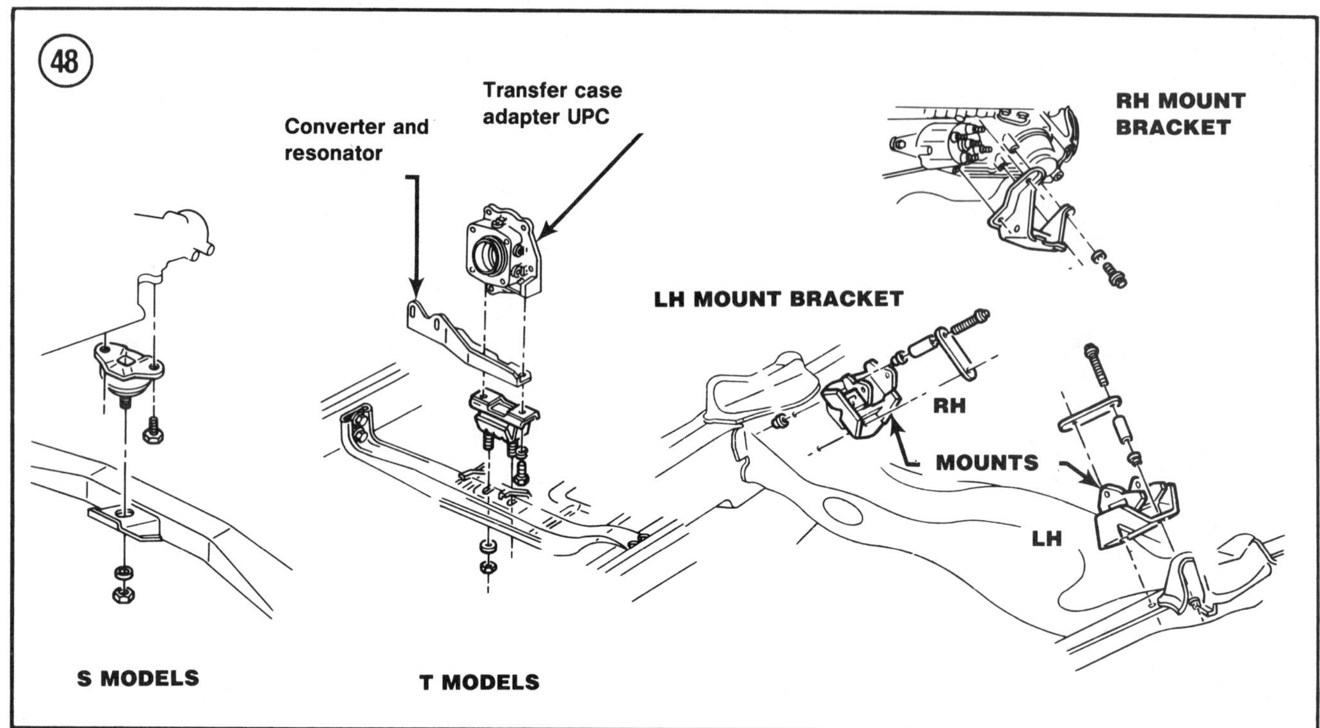

1. Remove the valve cover as described in this chapter.
2. Remove the rocker arm capscrew and ball.
3. Remove the rocker arm. Remove the pushrod.
4. Installation is the reverse of removal. Tighten the capscrew to 20 ft.-lb. (27 N•m).

Rocker Arm Inspection

Clean all parts with solvent and use compressed air to blow out the oil passage in each pushrod. Check each rocker arm, pivot ball and pushrod for scuffing, pitting or excessive wear. If the pushrod is worn from lack of oil, it will be necessary to replace the hydraulic valve tappet and rocker arm as well.

Pushrod Cover Removal/Installation

Refer to **Figure 48** for this procedure.

1. Disconnect the negative battery cable.
2. Remove the alternator and mounting bracket.
3. Remove the brace between the intake manifold and engine block.
4. Drain the cooling system. See Chapter Seven.
5. Disconnect the lower radiator and heater hoses at the engine.
6. Disconnect and remove the oil pressure sending unit.
7. Remove the wiring harness brackets from the pushrod cover.
8. Remove the pushrod cover attaching nuts. Remove the cover and gasket. Discard the gasket.
9. Clean all gasket residue from pushrod cover and cylinder block sealing surfaces.
10. Run a continuous 3/16 in. (5 mm) bead of RTV sealant along the pushrod cover flange as shown in **Figure 49**.
11. Install cover to block. Tighten attaching nuts to 75 in.-lb. (10 N•m).
12. Reverse Steps 1-7 to complete installation.

Hydraulic Valve Lifter Removal/Installation

Refer to **Figure 50** for this procedure.

1. Remove the valve cover as described in this chapter.
2. Remove the pushrod cover as described in this chapter.
3. Loosen the rocker arms and remove the pushrod as described in this chapter.
4. Remove the guide plate and clamp. Remove the valve lifter.
5. Installation is the reverse of removal. Make sure lifter fits into lifter boss before installing the guide plate and clamp.

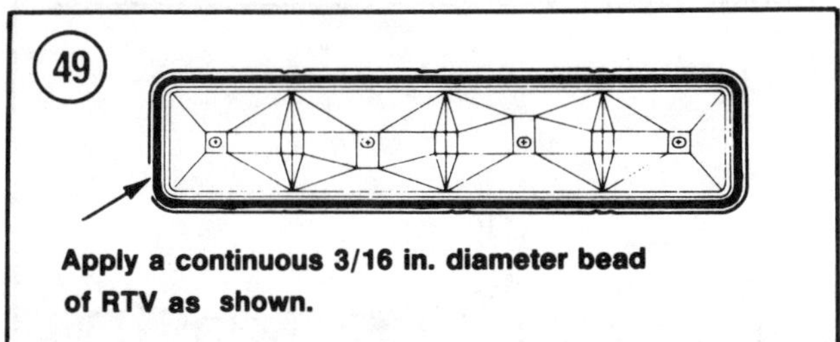

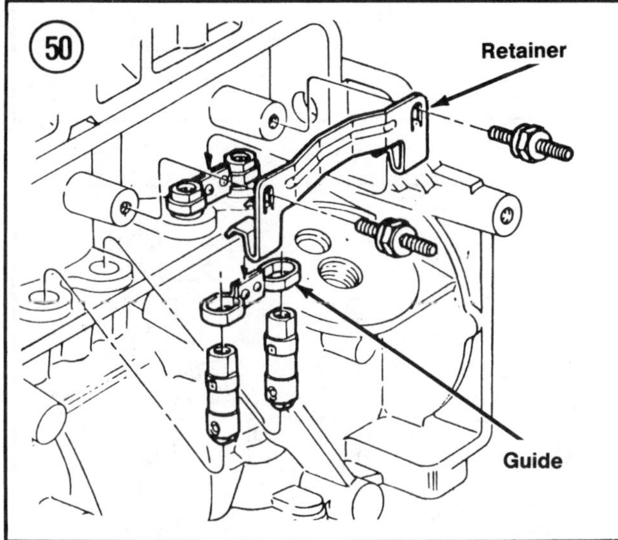

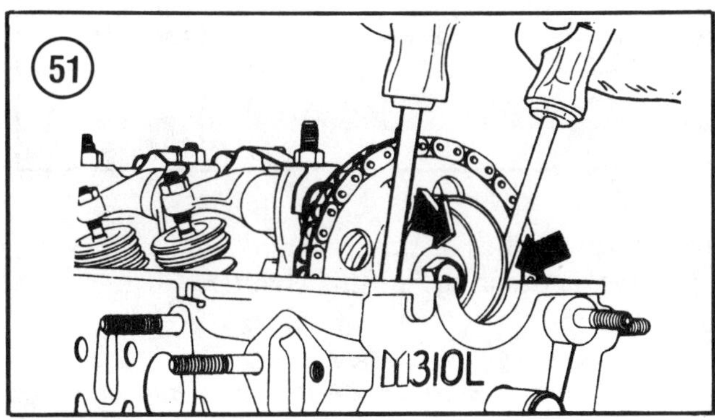

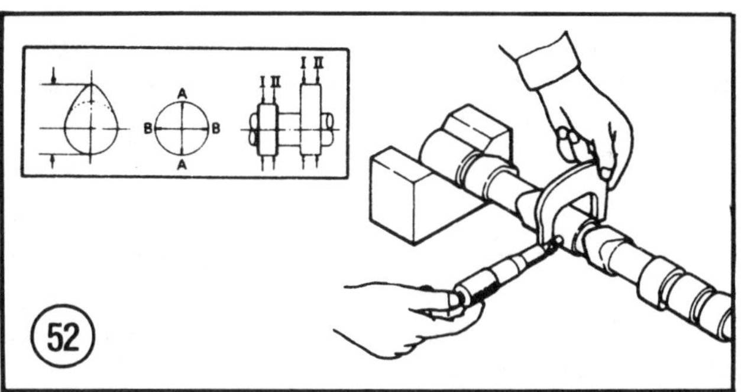

CAMSHAFT (1.9L ENGINE)

Removal

1. Remove the engine from the vehicle as described in this chapter.
2. Remove the valve cover as described in this chapter.
3. Rotate the crankshaft to position the No. 4 piston at TDC. When this occurs the crankshaft pulley timing mark will align with the O mark on the front cover. Remove the distributor cap and check to make sure the rotor points to the No. 4 cap electrode. If not, rotate the crankshaft another 360°. Mark the rotor-to-housing position and remove the distributor (Chapter Eight).
4. Remove the fuel pump. See Chapter Six.
5. Depress the adjuster lock lever with screwdrivers as shown in **Figure 51**. Make sure the chain is untensioned when the adjuster is locked.
6. Remove the camshaft sprocket bolt. Remove the sprocket and fuel pump drive cam from the camshaft. Do not remove chain from sprocket.
7. Remove the rocker arm assembly as described in this chapter.
8. Remove the camshaft.

Inspection

1. Check the journals and lobes for signs of wear or scoring. Lobe pitting in the toe area is not sufficient reason for replacement unless the lobe lift loss exceeds specifications.

NOTE
If you do not have precision measuring equipment, have Steps 2-5 done by a machine shop.

2. Measure the camshaft journal diameters with a micrometer (**Figure 52**). Replace the camshaft if the journals are less than 1.3307 in. (33.8 mm) in diameter or if the journals differ in size by more than 0.0020 in. (0.05 mm).
3. Install the rocker arm shaft brackets on the cylinder head and tighten bracket nuts to 16 ft.-lb. (22 N•m). Measure the inside diameter of the camshaft bearings with a cylinder bore gauge. Subtract camshaft journal diameter from inside diameter of bearing. If any journal/bearing has a clearance in excess of 0.0059 in. (0.15 mm), replace camshaft or cylinder head as required.

4. Place the camshaft on V-blocks and measure runout with a dial indicator (**Figure 53**). Replace if runout exceeds 0.0038 in. (0.1 mm).
5. Place the camshaft on the cylinder head and measure end play with a dial indicator as shown in **Figure 54**. Replace the camshaft if end play exceeds 0.0078 in. (0.2 mm).

Installation

1. Lubricate the camshaft and cylinder head journals with engine oil.
2. Install the camshaft in the cylinder head.
3. Make sure the No. 1 rocker arm shaft bracket is aligned with the camshaft mark (**Figure 44**). The crankshaft pulley groove should be aligned with the TDC timing mark.
4. Align the timing sprocket with the pin on the camshaft. Install the sprocket without disturbing the chain.
5. Install the fuel pump drive cam. Install the sprocket retaining washer and bolt.
6. Remove the semi-circular seal from the front end of the head. Tighten the bolt to 60 ft.-lb. (79 N•m). See **Figure 55**. Reinstall the seal.
7. Install the distributor. See Chapter Eight.
8. Depress the adjuster shoe with a screwdriver and check the timing chain tension to make sure the adjuster shoe has moved into place.
9. Check valve timing. The distributor rotor and mark on the housing (made during removal) should align when the No. 4 piston is at TDC on the compression stroke. The crankshaft pulley timing mark should align with the TDC mark on the front cover.
10. Install the distributor cap.
11. Install the valve cover as described in this chapter.

CAMSHAFT (2.0L ENGINE)

Removal

1. Remove the engine from the vehicle as described in this chapter.
2. Remove the valve cover, rocker arms and valve lifters as described in this chapter.
3. Remove the crankshaft pulley, hub and front cover as described in this chapter.
4. Mark the position of the distributor rotor relative to the engine block. Remove the distributor (Chapter Eight).
5. Remove the fuel pump. See Chapter Six.

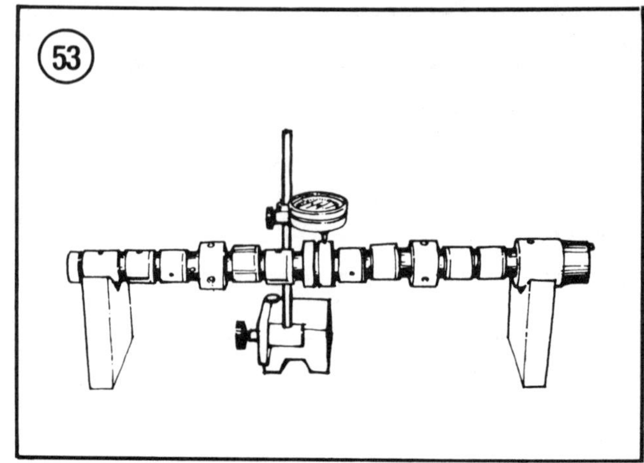

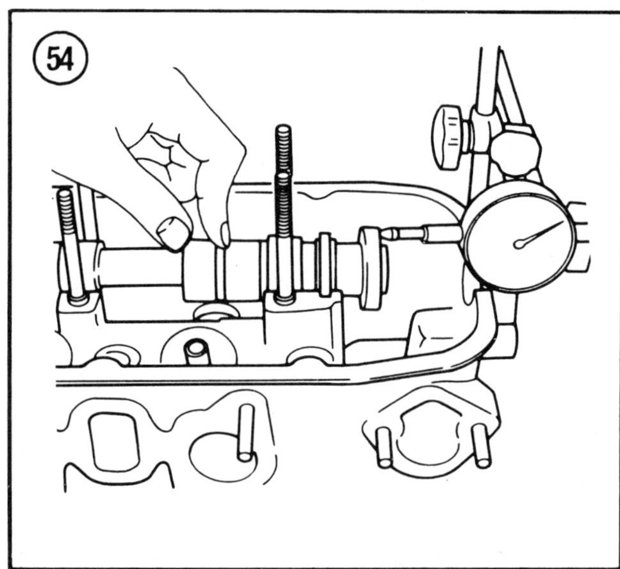

6. Remove the timing chain and camshaft sprocket as described in this chapter.

NOTE
All camshaft journals are the same diameter. Take care to prevent bearing damage while performing Step 7.

7. Remove the camshaft thrust plate. Withdraw the camshaft from the block with a slow, careful rotating motion.

Inspection

1. Check the journals and lobes for signs of wear or scoring. Lobe pitting in the toe area is not sufficient reason for replacement unless the lobe lift loss exceeds specifications.

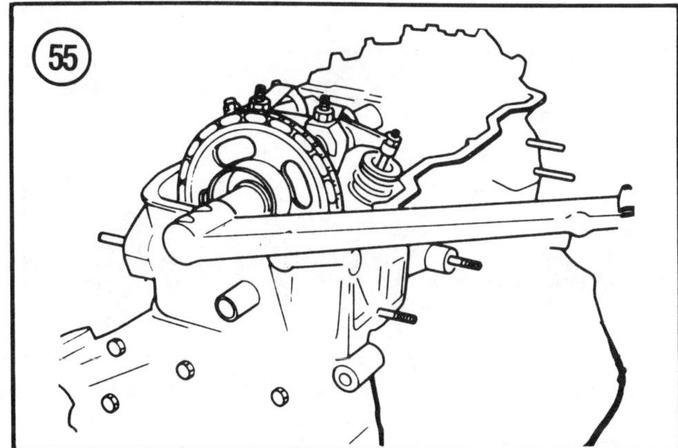

NOTE
If you do not have precision measuring equipment, have Step 2 done by a machine shop.

2. Measure the camshaft journal diameters with a micrometer (**Figure 52**) and compare to specifications (**Table 2**). Replace the camshaft if the journals are more than 0.0009 in. (0.025 mm) out-of-round.

Installation

NOTE
When installing a new camshaft, coat the lobes with GM EOS lubricant or equivalent.

1. Lubricate the camshaft journals with SAE 30W engine oil.
2. Install the camshaft with a slow, careful rotating motion. Install the thrust plate.
3. Reverse Steps 1-6 of *Removal* in this chapter to complete installation.

CAMSHAFT (2.5L ENGINE)

Removal

1. Remove the pushrod cover as described in this chapter.
2. Remove the front cover as described in this chapter.
3. Remove the distributor (Chapter Eight).
4. Remove the oil pump drive shaft and cover.
5. Remove the air cleaner assembly. See Chapter Six.
6. Remove the EGR valve.
7. Remove the valve cover as described in this chapter.
8. Remove the pushrods and hydraulic lifters as described in this chapter.
9. Drain the cooling system and remove the radiator. See Chapter Seven.
10. Remove the 2 camshaft thrust plate screws through the holes in the camshaft gear (**Figure 56**).
11. If equipped with air conditioning, remove the condenser baffles, then unbolt the condenser. Raise condenser enough to provide access and secure it in place.
12. Remove the head lamp bezel, grille and bumper filler panel.
13. Carefully withdraw the camshaft and gear assembly from the front of the engine block with a rotating motion.

Inspection

1. Check the journals and lobes for signs of wear or scoring. Lobe pitting in the toe area is not sufficient reason for replacement unless the lobe lift loss exceeds specifications.

NOTE
If you do not have precision measuring equipment, have Step 2 done by a machine shop.

2. Measure the camshaft journal diameters with a micrometer (**Figure 52**) and compare to specifications (**Table 3**). Replace the camshaft if the journals are more than 0.0009 in. (0.025 mm) out-of-round.

Installation

NOTE
When installing a new camshaft, coat the lobes with GM EOS lubricant or equivalent.

1. Lubricate the camshaft journals with SAE 30W engine oil.
2. Carefully install the camshaft in the engine block with a rotating motion.
3. Rotate the crankshaft and camshaft as required to align the valve timing marks on the gear teeth. See **Figure 57**. This places the No. 4 piston in its firing position.
4. Reverse Steps 1-12 of *Removal* in this chapter to complete installation. Tighten thrust plate screws to 75 in.-lb. (10 N•m).

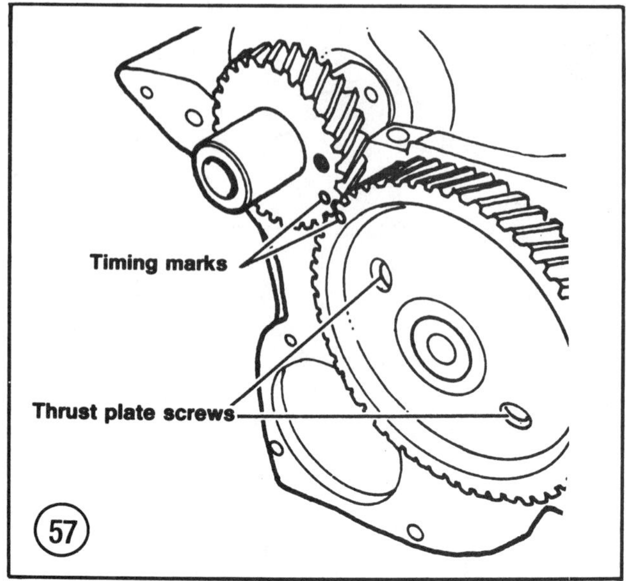

OIL PAN

Removal/Installation

1.9L engine

1. Disconnect the negative battery cable.
2. Securely block both rear wheels so the truck will not roll in either direction. Raise the vehicle with a jack and place it on jackstands.
3. Drain the crankcase. See Chapter Three.

NOTE
Since the steering linkage and crossmember interfere with oil pan removal, it is necessary at this point to either remove the engine from the vehicle or attach an engine hoist to the lifting bracket eye, disconnect the engine mounts and lift the engine sufficiently to remove the oil pan.

4. Remove the nuts/bolts holding the oil pan to the block and remove the oil pan. Remove the dipstick tube from the intake manifold and oil pan.
5. Clean any RTV or gasket residue from the oil pan rail on the engine block.
6. Apply a thin coat of Permatex No. 2 or equivalent sealer to the engine block mounting surfaces as shown in **Figure 58**. Install the pan with a new gasket and tighten the fasteners to 4 ft.-lb. (5.4 N•m).
7. Check the gasket edge and compare with **Figure 59**. If the gasket is not set in place properly, remove and reinstall the oil pan.
8. Install the engine in the vehicle, if removed. If not removed, reinstall the engine mounts and lower the engine in place. Install and tighten the engine mount bolts.
9. Lower the vehicle to the ground. Fill the crankcase with oil (Chapter Three) and connect the negative battery cable.

2.0L engine

1. Disconnect the negative battery cable.

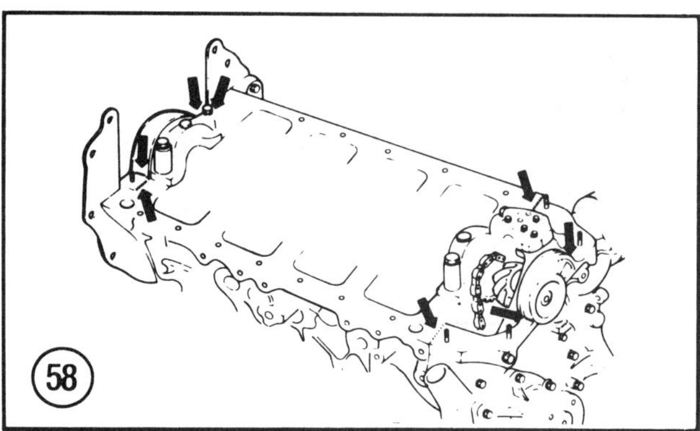

2. Securely block both rear wheels so the truck will not roll in either direction. Raise the vehicle with a jack and place it on jackstands.
3. Drain the crankcase. See Chapter Three.

NOTE
Since the steering linkage and crossmember interfere with oil pan removal, it is necessary at this point to either remove the engine from the vehicle or attach an engine hoist to the lifting bracket eye, disconnect the engine mounts and lift the engine sufficiently to remove the oil pan.

4. Remove the oil pan screws (**Figure 60**) and remove the oil pan. Remove the oil pan rear end seal.

NOTE
The 2.0L oil pump pickup tube and screen are a press fit in the pump housing and should not be removed unless replacement is required.

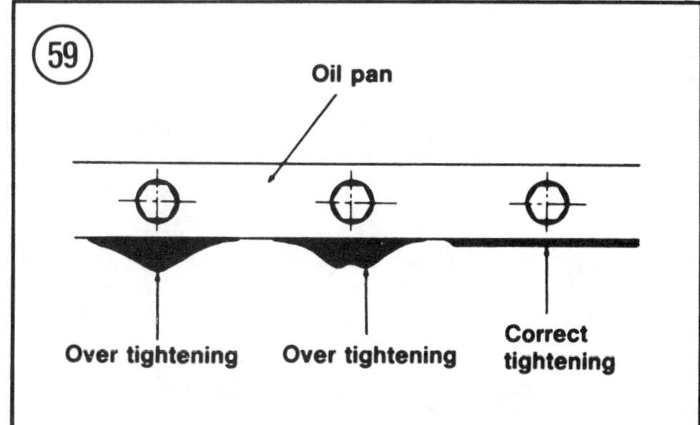

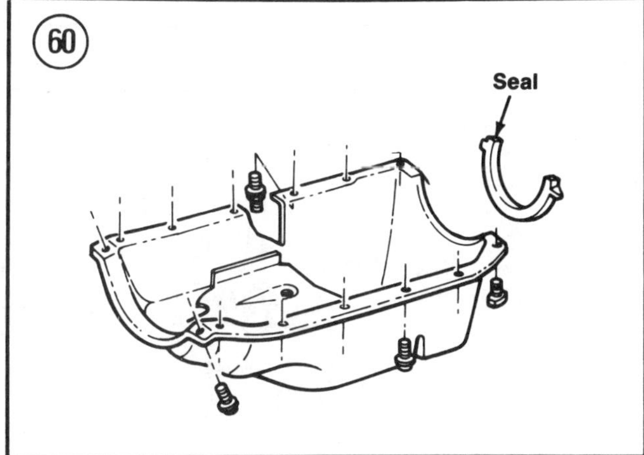

5. Clean any RTV or gasket residue from the oil pan rail on the engine block.
6. Apply a 0.008 in. (2 mm) bead of RTV sealant along the oil pan block sealing flanges. Install a new rear end seal and apply RTV sealant where the seal meets the block.
7. Install the oil pan and tighten the 2 front pan screws to 6-9 ft.-lb. (8-12 N•m). Tighten the remaining screws to 13-18 ft.-lb. (18-24 N•m).
8. Install the engine in the vehicle, if removed. If not removed, reinstall the engine mounts and lower the engine in place. Install and tighten the engine mount bolts.
9. Lower the vehicle to the ground. Fill the crankcase with oil (Chapter Three) and connect the negative battery cable.

2.5L engine (2-wheel drive)

1. Disconnect the negative battery cable.
2. Securely block both rear wheels so the truck will not roll in either direction. Raise the vehicle with a jack and place it on jackstands.
3. Drain the crankcase. See Chapter Three.
4. Remove the strut rods.
5. Remove the torque converter cover bolts.
6. Disconnect the exhaust pipe at the catalytic converter hanger.
7. Remove the torque converter cover.
8. Remove the starter motor. See Chapter Eight.
9. Disconnect the transmission oil cooler lines at the oil pan.
10. Remove the oil pan bolts. Remove the oil pan.
11. Clean any RTV or gasket residue from the oil pan rail on the engine block.
12. Apply a 0.012 in. (3 mm) bead of RTV sealant along the entire oil pan sealing flange.
13. Install the oil pan and tighten the pan bolts to 75 in.-lb. (6 N•m).
14. Reverse Steps 1-9 to complete installation.

2.5L engine (4-wheel drive)

1. Disconnect the negative battery cable.
2. Drain the crankcase. See Chapter Three.
3. Remove the power steering reservoir at the fan shroud without disconnecting any hydraulic lines.
4. Remove the upper fan shroud.
5. Remove the dipstick.
6. Securely block both rear wheels so the truck will not roll in either direction. Raise the vehicle with a jack and place it on jackstands.
7. Disconnect the brake line clips at the crossmember. Remove the crossmember.
8. Disconnect the transmission oil cooler lines at the torque converter cover.
9. Disconnect the exhaust pipe at the manifold.
10. Remove one bolt from the catalytic converter hanger and loosen the other.
11. Remove the torque converter cover.
12. Remove the drive shaft splash shield.
13. Mark the idler arm position for reinstallation, then remove the attaching bolts.
14. Remove the steering gearbox bolts. Pull the steering gearbox and linkage forward to provide clearance.
15. Remove the bolts from the differential bracket on the right side. Remove the bolts from the frame on the left side. Move the differential housing forward.
16. Remove the starter motor. See Chapter Eight.
17. Loosen the starter motor brace at the engine block.
18. Disconnect the front drive shaft.
19. Remove the motor mount through-bolts.

20. Remove the oil pan bolts.
21. Place a hydraulic jack under the engine block at a convenient point and raise the engine enough to remove the oil pan.
22. Clean any RTV or gasket residue from the oil pan rail on the engine block.
23. Apply a 0.012 in. (3 mm) bead of RTV sealant along the entire oil pan sealing flange.
24. Install the oil pan and tighten the pan bolts to 75 in.-lb. (6 N•m).
25. Reverse Steps 1-19 to complete installation.

Inspection

1. Clean the pan thoroughly in solvent.
2. Check the pan for dents or warped gasket surfaces. Straighten or replace the pan as required.
3. Check the pan for cracks. Repair or replace the pan as required.

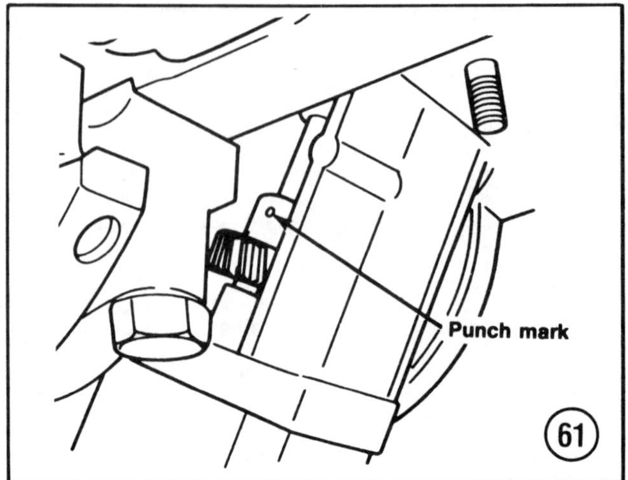

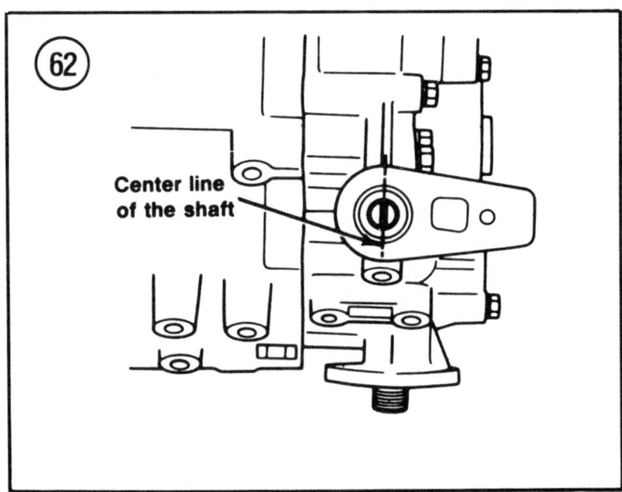

OIL PUMP (1.9L ENGINE)

Removal

1. Remove the oil pan as described in this chapter.
2. Remove the bolt holding the oil pickup tube to the block. Remove the tube from the oil pump.
3. Remove the oil pump mounting bolts. Remove the oil pump.
4. Remove the rubber hose and relief valve assembly from the oil pump.

Inspection

1. Measure the clearance between the drive and driven rotors with a flat feeler gauge. Replace the entire oil pump assembly if the clearance exceeds 0.0079 in. (0.20 mm).
2. Measure the clearance between the driven rotor and inner wall of the pump body with a flat feeler gauge. Replace the entire oil pump assembly if the clearance exceeds 0.0098 in. (0.25 mm).
3. Measure the clearance between the drive rotor, driven rotor and pump cover with a straightedge and flat feeler gauge. Replace the entire oil pump assembly if the measurement exceeds 0.0079 in. (0.20 mm).
4. Measure the outside diameter of the drive shaft and the inside diameter of the shaft hole in the pump cover. Compare the measured values to determine the clearance. Replace the entire oil pump assembly if the clearance exceeds 0.0098 in. (0.25 mm).
5. Check the oil pump rubber hose for deterioration or damage. Replace if necessary.
6. Check the relief valve and spring for wear, weakening or damage. Replace the entire oil pump assembly if defective.
7. Check the pump body, cover and drive gear for wear, cracking or damage. Replace as required.

Installation

1. Align the camshaft mark with the No. 1 rocker arm bracket mark. Align the crankshaft pulley notch with the TDC mark on the front cover. The No. 4 cylinder is now at TDC on its compression stroke.
2. Install the driven rotor with its alignment mark aligned with the drive rotor mark.
3. Engage the pinion gear with the crankshaft oil pump drive gear.

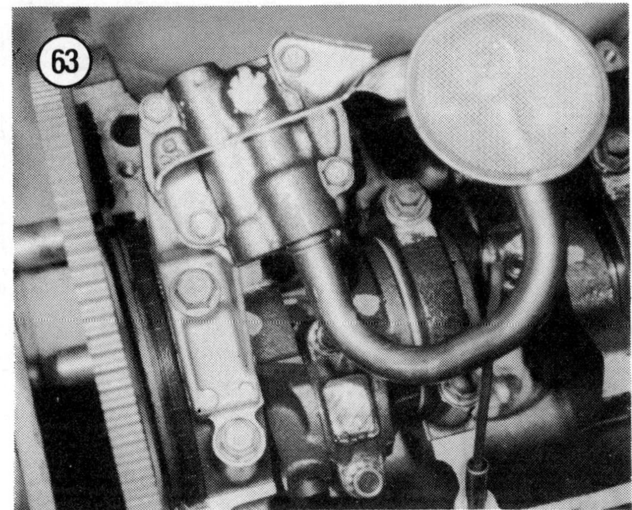

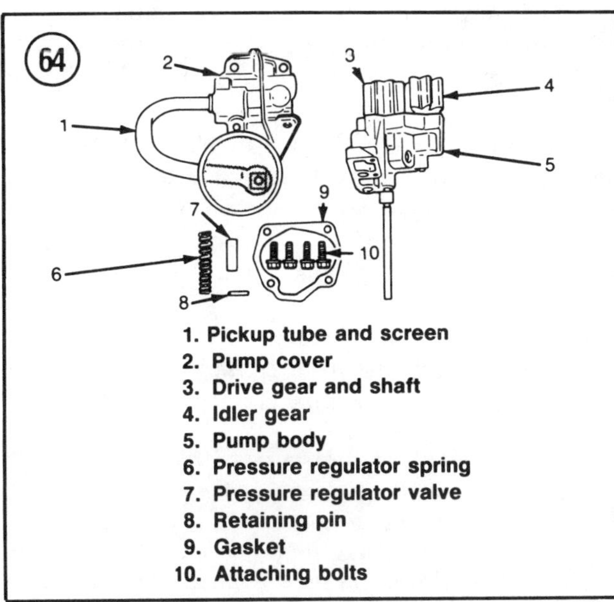

1. Pickup tube and screen
2. Pump cover
3. Drive gear and shaft
4. Idler gear
5. Pump body
6. Pressure regulator spring
7. Pressure regulator valve
8. Retaining pin
9. Gasket
10. Attaching bolts

4. Make sure the punch mark on the oil pump drive gear is turned to the rear side, as seen through the gap between the front cover and cylinder block. See **Figure 61**.
5. Make sure the slit at the end of the oil pump shaft is parallel with the front of the block and that it is offset to the front. See **Figure 62**.
6. Fit the pump cover to the dowel pins and install the mounting bolts.
7. Install the relief valve assembly and oil pipe rubber hose to the cover.
8. Connect the oil pipe to the rubber hose. Attach the oil pipe to the cylinder block.
9. Install the oil pan as described in this chapter.

OIL PUMP (2.0L ENGINE)

Removal/Installation

1. Remove the oil pan as described in this chapter.
2. Remove the bolt holding the pump to the rear main bearing cap (**Figure 63**). Remove the oil pump and drive shaft.
3. Installation is the reverse of removal.

Disassembly/Assembly

Refer to **Figure 64** for this procedure.

1. Remove the cover bolts and cover.
2. Remove the idler gear, drive gear and shaft from the pump body.
3. Remove the pressure regulator valve pin, spring and valve.
4. Remove the pickup tube/screen assembly *only* if it needs replacement. Secure the pump body in a soft-jawed vise and separate the tube from the cover.

CAUTION
Do not twist, shear or collapse the tube when installing it in Step 5.

5. If the pickup tube/screen assembly was removed, install a new one. Secure the pump body in a soft-jawed vise. Apply sealer to the new tube and tap in place with a plastic mallet.
6. Assembly is the reverse of disassembly. Use a new cover gasket and tighten cover bolts to 6-9 ft.-lb. (8-12 N•m).

Inspection

NOTE
The pump assembly and gears are serviced as an assembly. If one or the other is worn or damaged, replace the entire pump. No wear specifications are provided by GM.

1. Clean all parts thoroughly in solvent. Brush the inside of the body and the pressure regulator chamber to remove all dirt and metal particles. Dry with compressed air, if available.
2. Check the pump body and cover for cracks or excessive wear.
3. Check the pump gears for damage or excessive wear.
4. Check the drive gear shaft-to-body fit for excessive looseness.
5. Check the inside of the pump cover for wear that could allow oil to leak around the ends of the gears.

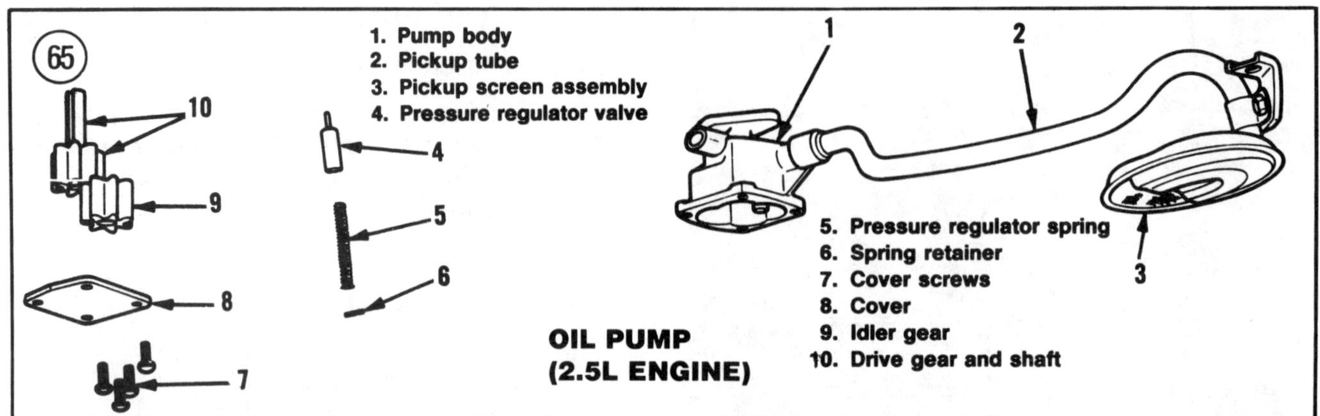

OIL PUMP (2.5L ENGINE)

6. Check the pressure regulator valve for a proper fit.

OIL PUMP (2.5L ENGINE)

Removal/Installation

1. Remove the oil pan as described in this chapter.
2. Remove the pickup tube support bracket nut.
3. Remove the 2 flange mounting bolts and the nut from the main bearing cap bolt. Remove the oil pump and pickup assembly as a unit.
4. Align pump gear shaft tang with pump drive shaft slot.
5. Install pump-to-block positioning bracket over the oil pump drive shaft lower bushing.

NOTE
The oil pump should slide into place easily. If it does not, remove the shaft and realign the slot.

6. Install the pump attaching bolts and nut. Tighten to 22 ft.-lb. (30 N•m).
7. Install the pickup tube support bracket nut. Tighten to 37 ft.-lb. (50 N•m).
8. Install the oil pan as described in this chapter.

Disassembly/Assembly

See *Oil Pump (2.0L Engine)* in this chapter. Refer to **Figure 65** for this procedure.

CYLINDER HEAD (1.9L ENGINE)

Removal

1. Disconnect the negative battery cable.
2. Drain the cooling system. See Chapter Seven.
3. Remove the valve cover as described in this chapter.
4. Securely block both rear wheels so the truck will not roll in either direction. Raise the front of the vehicle with a jack and place it on jackstands.
5. Remove the exhaust shield, if so equipped. Disconnect the exhaust pipe at the exhaust manifold.
6. Disconnect the heater hoses at the intake manifold and at the front of the cylinder head.
7. Remove the EGR pipe clamp bolt at the rear of the cylinder head.

WARNING
The air conditioning system contains pressurized refrigerant which can cause frostbite if it touches skin and blindness if it touches the eyes. If discharged near an open flame, the refrigerant forms poisonous gas. Never disconnect air conditioning system lines unless the system has been discharged and evacuated by a professional.

8. If so equipped, remove the air conditioning compressor and/or power steering pump without disconnecting any refrigerant or hydraulic lines. Place the units to one side out of the way.
9. Tag and disconnect all vacuum and electrical lines at the carburetor. Disconnect the spark plug wires.
10. Disconnect and plug the fuel line at the carburetor.
11. Rotate the crankshaft until the No. 1 cylinder is at TDC. Remove the distributor cap and mark the rotor-to-housing relationship.

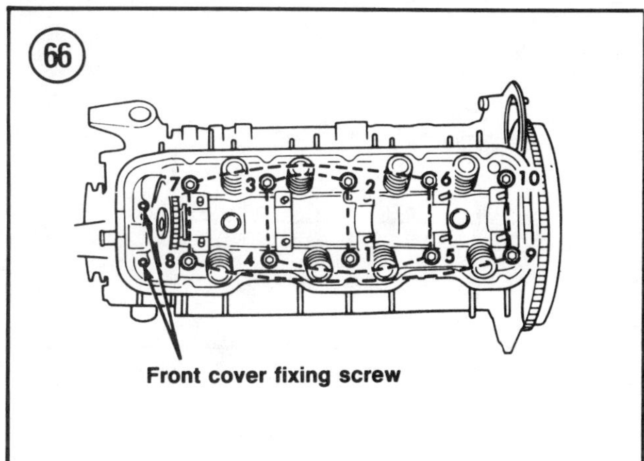

12. Remove the fuel pump. See Chapter Six.
13. Depress the timing chain adjuster lock lever with screwdrivers as shown in **Figure 51** to lock the adjuster shoe in place.
14. Remove the camshaft sprocket bolt. Remove the sprocket and fuel pump drive cam. Do not remove the sprocket from the chain.
15. Disconnect the air pump hose and check valve at the air injection manifold.
16. Remove the front cover fixing screws (**Figure 66**). Remove the head bolts in the reverse of the sequence shown in **Figure 66**.

NOTE

Place the head on its side in Step 17 to prevent damage to the spark plugs or head gasket surface.

17. With the help of an assistant, remove the head with the intake/exhaust manifolds attached.
18. Remove the intake/exhaust manifolds from the cylinder head, if required.
19. Remove and discard the head gasket. Clean any residue from the head and block surfaces.

Installation

1. Make sure the cylinder head and block gasket surfaces and bolt holes are clean. Dirt in the block bolt holes or on the head bolt threads will affect bolt torque.
2. Check all visible oil and water passages for cleanliness.
3. Reinstall the intake/exhaust manifolds, if removed.
4. Install a new head gasket on the cylinder block dowel pins with the word "TOP" facing up. Do not use gasket sealer on the head gasket.
5. Carefully lower the cylinder head in place on the dowel pins and gasket.
6. Coat the head bolt threads with sealing compound and install the bolts finger-tight.
7. Tighten the head bolts following the sequence shown in **Figure 66** to 60 ft.-lb. (85 N•m), then retighten in sequence to 70 ft.-lb. (100 N•m). Install the front cover screws.
8. Reverse Steps 1-15 of *Removal* in this chapter.

CYLINDER HEAD (2.0L ENGINE)

Removal

1. Disconnect the negative battery cable.
2. Drain the cooling system. See Chapter Seven.
3. Remove the air cleaner assembly. See Chapter Six.
4. Securely block both rear wheels so the truck will not roll in either direction. Raise the front of the vehicle with a jack and place it on jackstands.
5. Remove the exhaust shield and disconnect the exhaust pipe at the exhaust manifold.
6. Disconnect the heater hose at the fitting under the intake manifold.
7. Remove the jackstands and lower the vehicle to the ground.
8. Remove the engine lifting eye bracket (**Figure 67**).
9. Remove the distributor. See Chapter Eight.
10. Disconnect the vacuum lines at the intake manifold and thermostat housing.
11. Remove the Pulsair pipe.

12. Disconnect the throttle linkage at the carburetor and remove the linkage bracket.
13. Disconnect the upper radiator hose at the thermostat housing.
14. Remove the dipstick tube/hot water bracket bolt.
15. If so equipped, remove the power steering pump, drive belt and bracket. Set the pump to one side without disconnecting any hydraulic lines.
16. Disconnect the fuel line at the carburetor. Plug the line to prevent leakage.
17. Remove the alternator, alternator brace and upper bracket.
18. Remove the valve cover as described in this chapter.
19. Remove the thermostat housing/EGR valve adapter.
20. Remove the rocker arm assemblies as described in this chapter.
21. Loosen and remove the cylinder head bolts in the sequence shown in **Figure 68**.

NOTE
Place the head on its side in Step 22 to prevent damage to the spark plugs or head gasket surface.

22. With the help of an assistant, remove the head with the intake/exhaust manifolds attached.
23. Remove the intake/exhaust manifolds from the cylinder head, if required.
24. Remove and discard the head gasket. Clean any residue from the head and block surfaces.

Installation

1. Make sure the cylinder head and block gasket surfaces and bolt holes are clean. Dirt in the block bolt holes or on the head bolt threads will affect bolt torque.
2. Check all visible oil and water passages for cleanliness.
3. Reinstall the intake/exhaust manifolds, if removed.
4. Install a new head gasket on the cylinder block dowel pins.
5. Carefully lower the cylinder head in place on the dowel pins and gasket.
6. Coat the head bolt threads with sealing compound and install the bolts finger-tight.
7. Tighten the head bolts following the sequence shown in **Figure 68** to 65-75 ft.-lb. (88-107 N•m).
8. Reverse Steps 1-20 of *Removal* in this chapter.

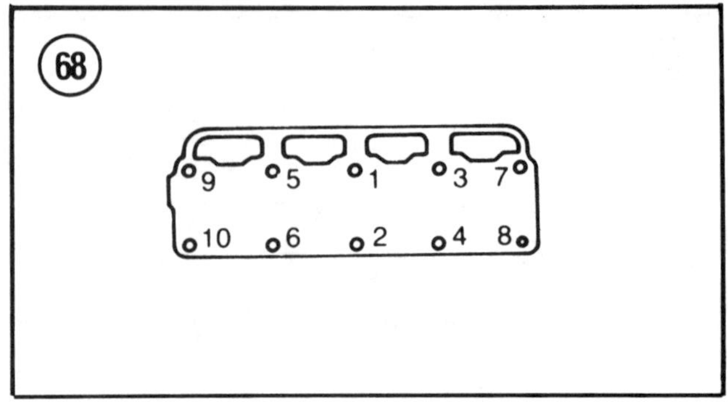

CYLINDER HEAD (2.5L ENGINE)

Removal

WARNING
Before opening any fuel system lines on a fuel injected engine, relieve system pressure as described in Chapter Six.

1. Disconnect the negative battery cable.
2. Remove the air cleaner assembly. See Chapter Six.
3. Drain the cooling system. See Chapter Seven.

WARNING
The air conditioning system contains pressurized refrigerant which can cause frostbite if it touches skin and blindness if it touches the eyes. If discharged near an open flame, the refrigerant forms poisonous gas. Never disconnect air conditioning system lines unless the system has been discharged and evacuated by a professional.

4. Remove the air conditioning compressor and bracket, if so equipped. Place to one side without disconnecting any refrigerant lines. Disconnect the air conditioning line hold-down.
5. Disconnect the PCV hose at the valve cover.
6. Remove the EGR valve.
7. Disconnect the spark plug wires at the plugs and remove the valve cover as described in this chapter.
8. Disconnect the throttle cable and transmission TV (throttle valve) cable at the TBI (throttle body injection) assembly. Disconnect the cruise control cable, if so equipped.
9. Remove the alternator brace.
10. Disconnect the bypass and heater hoses at the intake manifold.
11. Disconnect the exhaust pipe at the exhaust manifold.

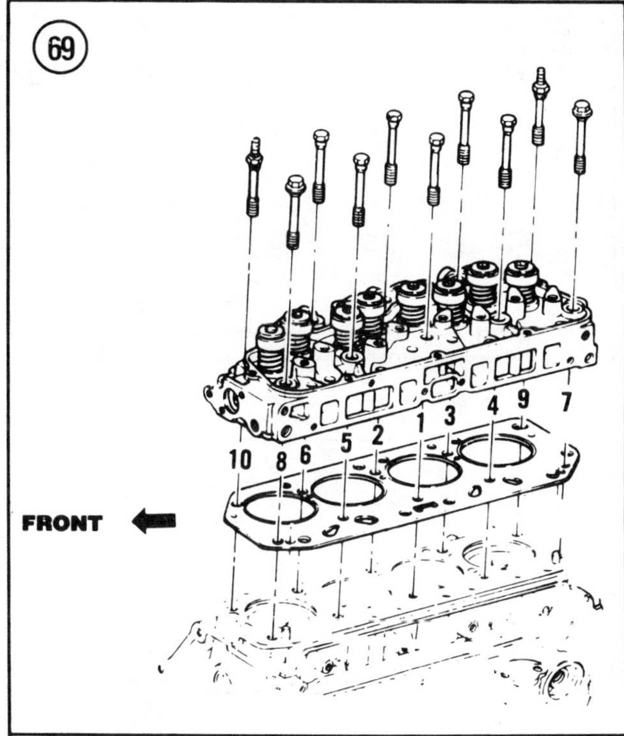

12. Remove the alternator.
13. Disconnect the upper radiator hose at the engine.
14. Disconnect the fuel line bracket at the fuel filter.
15. Remove the dipstick tube.
16. Disconnect the fuel and vacuum lines near the fuel filter. Plug the fuel lines to prevent leakage.
17. Tag and disconnect all vacuum lines and electrical connectors at the TBI assembly.
18. Disconnect the wiring harness bracket at the rear of the head.
19. Remove the ignition coil bracket from the cylinder head.
20. Back off the rocker arm capscrews and swivel the rocker arms to one side. Remove the pushrods.
21. Remove the brace between the intake manifold and block.
22. Loosen and remove the cylinder head bolts in the reverse of the sequence shown in **Figure 69**.

NOTE
Place the head on its side in Step 23 to prevent damage to the spark plugs or head gasket surface.

23. With the help of an assistant, remove the head with the intake/exhaust manifolds attached.
24. Remove the intake/exhaust manifolds from the cylinder head, if required.
25. Remove and discard the head gasket. Clean any residue from the head and block surfaces.

Installation

1. Make sure the cylinder head and block gasket surfaces and bolt holes are clean. Dirt in the block bolt holes or on the head bolt threads will affect bolt torque.
2. Check all visible oil and water passages for cleanliness.
3. Reinstall the intake/exhaust manifolds, if removed.
4. Install a new head gasket on the cylinder block dowel pins.
5. Carefully lower the cylinder head in place on the dowel pins and gasket.
6. Coat the head bolt threads with sealing compound and install the bolts finger-tight.
7. Tighten the head bolts following the sequence shown in **Figure 69** to 92 ft.-lb. (125 N•m).
8. Reverse Steps 1-21 of *Removal* in this chapter.

CYLINDER HEAD DECARBONIZING (ALL MODELS)

1. Without removing the valves, remove all deposits from the combustion chambers, intake ports and exhaust ports. Use a fine wire brush dipped in solvent or make a scraper from hardwood. Be careful not to scratch or gouge the combustion chambers.
2. After all carbon is removed from the combustion chambers and ports, clean the entire head in solvent.
3. Clean away all carbon on the piston tops. Do not remove the carbon ridge at the top of the cylinder bore.

CYLINDER HEAD INSPECTION (ALL MODELS)

1. Check the cylinder head for signs of oil or water leaks before cleaning.
2. Clean the cylinder head thoroughly in solvent. While cleaning, look for cracks or other visible signs of damage. Look for corrosion or foreign material in the oil and water passages.
3. Clean the passages with a stiff spiral brush, then blow them out with compressed air.
4. Check the cylinder head studs for damage and replace if necessary.

5. Check the flatness of the cylinder head-to-block surface with a straightedge and feeler gauge (**Figure 70**). Measure diagonally, as well as end to end. If the gap exceeds 0.0078-0.0157 in. (0.2-0.4 mm), have the head resurfaced by a machine shop. If the gap exceeds 0.0157 in. (0.4 mm) for 1.9L/2.0L heads or 0.004 in. (0.102 mm) for 2.5L heads, replace the head.

VALVES AND VALVE SEATS

Servicing the valves, guides and valve seats requires special knowledge and expensive machine tools. A general practice among those who do their own service is to remove the cylinder head, perform all disassembly except valve removal and take the head to a dealer or machine shop for inspection and service. Since the cost is low relative to the required effort and equipment, this is usually the best approach, even for experienced mechanics.

Valve Adjustment

The 1.9L and 2.2L diesel engines require valve lash adjustment at 15,000-mile intervals. See Chapter Three.

The 2.5L hydraulic lifters adjust automatically to maintain zero lash under all conditions.

The 2.0L engines require valve lash adjustment only when the cylinder head or valve train has been disassembled. Adjust the valves with the lifter on the base circle of the camshaft lobe.

1. Rotate the crankshaft until the pulley notch aligns with the zero mark on the timing tab. This positions the No. 1 cylinder at TDC. This position can be verified by placing a finger on the No. 1 rocker arms as the pulley notch nears the zero mark. If the valves are moving, the engine is in the No. 4 firing position. Rotate the crankshaft pulley one full turn to reach the No. 1 firing position.
2. With the engine in the No. 1 firing position, adjust the No. 1 and No. 3 exhaust valves and the No. 1 and No. 2 intake valves. See **Figure 71**. Back off the adjusting nut until lash is felt at the pushrod, then turn the nut to remove all lash. When lash has been removed, the pushrod will not rotate. Turn the nut in another 1 1/2 turns to center the lifter plunger.
3. Rotate the crankshaft pulley one full turn to realign the pulley notch and the timing tab zero mark in the No. 4 firing position. Adjust the No. 2 and No. 4 exhaust valves and the No. 3 and No. 4 intake valves. See **Figure 71**.

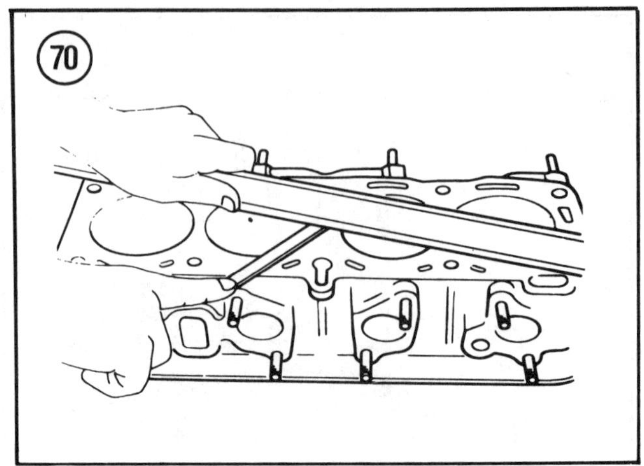

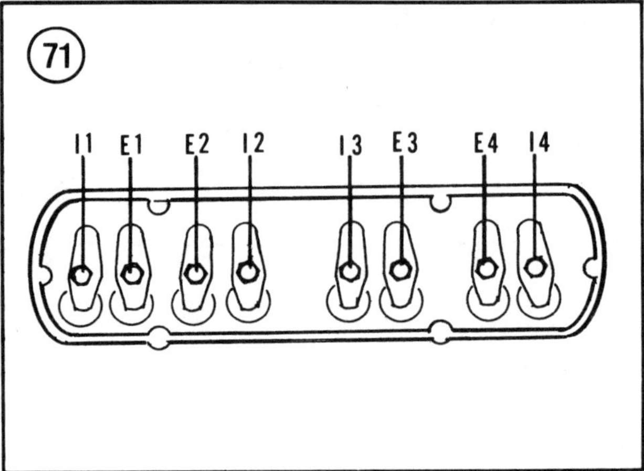

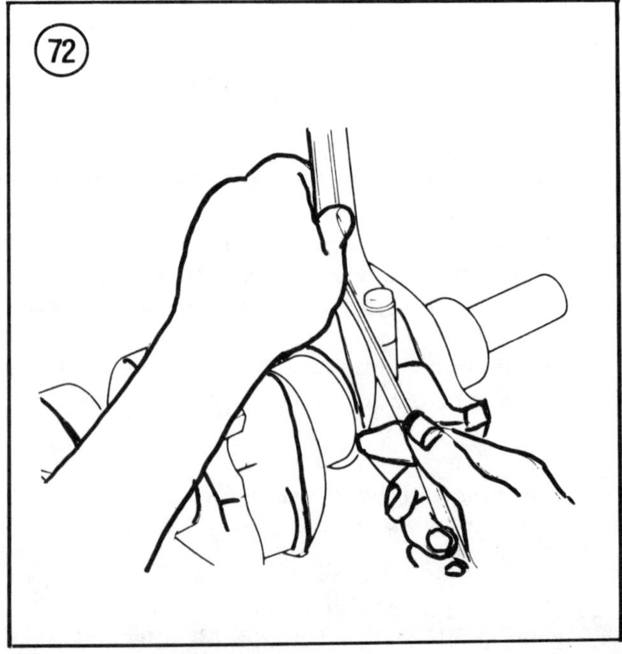

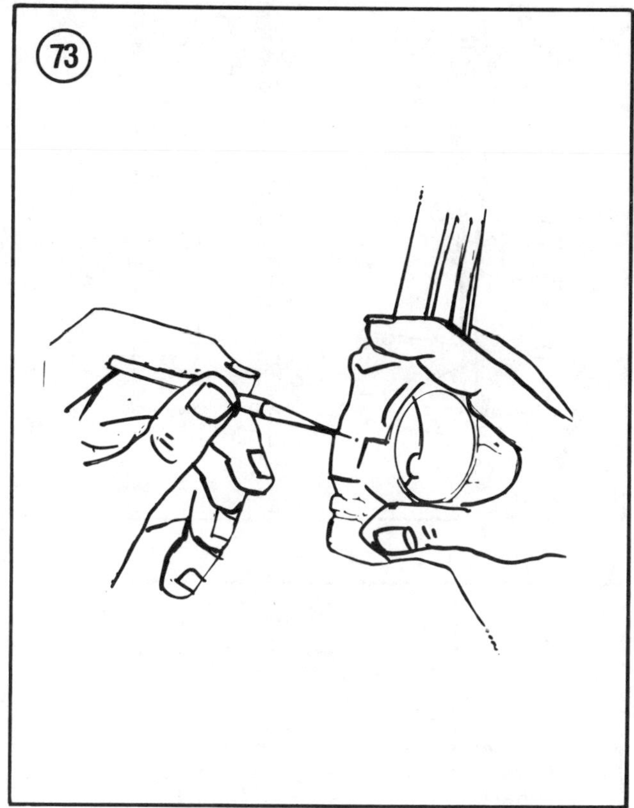

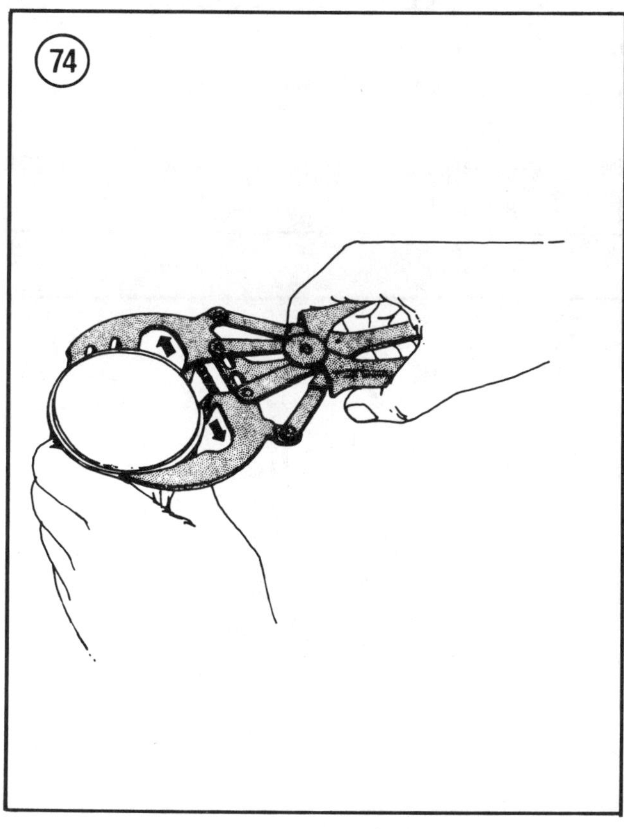

PISTON/CONNECTING ROD ASSEMBLY

Piston/Connecting Rod Removal

1. Remove the cylinder head and oil pan as described in this chapter.
2. Rotate the crankshaft until one piston is at bottom dead center. Pack the cylinder bore with clean shop rags. Remove the carbon ridge at the top of the cylinder bores with a ridge reamer. These can be rented for use. Vacuum out the shavings, then remove the shop rags.
3. Rotate the crankshaft until one connecting rod is centered in the bore. Measure the clearance between the connecting rod and the crankshaft with a feeler gauge (**Figure 72**). If the clearance exceeds 0.0137 in. (1.9L), 0.0235 in. (2.0L) or 0.022 in. (2.5L), replace the connecting rod during reassembly. Repeat this step for all connecting rods.

NOTE
*Mark the cylinder number on the top of each piston with quick-drying paint. Check for cylinder numbers or identification marks on the connecting rod and cap. If they are not visible, make your own (**Figure 73**).*

4. Remove the nuts holding the connecting rod cap. Lift off the cap, together with the lower bearing insert.

NOTE
If the connecting rod caps are difficult to remove, tap the studs with a wooden hammer handle.

5. Use the wooden hammer handle to push the piston and connecting rod from the bore.
6. Remove the piston rings with a ring remover (**Figure 74**).

Piston Pin Removal/Installation

The piston pins are press-fitted to the connecting rods and hand-fitted to the pistons. Removal requires the use of a press and support stand. This is a job for a dealer or machine shop equipped to fit the pistons to the pins, ream the pin bushings to the correct diameter and install the pistons and pins on the connecting rods.

Piston Clearance Check

Unless you have precision measuring equipment and know how to use it properly, have this procedure done by a machine shop.

4

1. Measure the piston diameter with a micrometer (**Figure 75**). Measure at a point 1.575 in. (40 mm) below the piston head in a direction at right angles to the piston pin.
2. Measure the cylinder bore diameter with a bore gauge (**Figure 76**). Measure at the top, center and bottom of the bore, in front-to-rear and side-to-side directions.
3. Subtract the piston diameter from the largest cylinder bore reading. If the clearance in any cylinder exceeds the specifications in **Table 1** (1.9L), **Table 2** (2.0L) or **Table 3** (2.5L), the cylinder must be rebored and an oversized piston installed.

NOTE

Obtain the new piston and measure it to determine the correct cylinder bore oversize dimension.

Piston Ring Fit/Installation

1. Check the ring gap of each piston ring. To do this, position the ring at the bottom of the ring travel area and square it by tapping gently with an inverted piston. See **Figure 77**.

NOTE

If the cylinders have not been rebored, check the gap at the bottom of the ring travel, where the cylinder is least worn.

2. Measure the ring gap with a feeler gauge as shown in **Figure 78**. Compare with specifications in Tables 1-3. If the measurement is not within specifications, the rings must be replaced as a set.

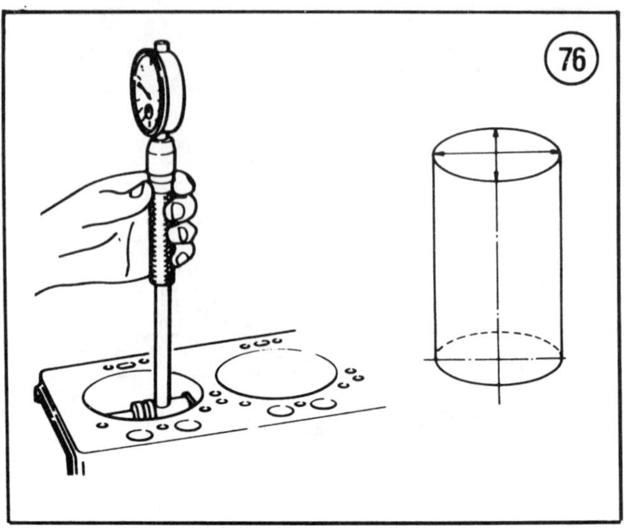

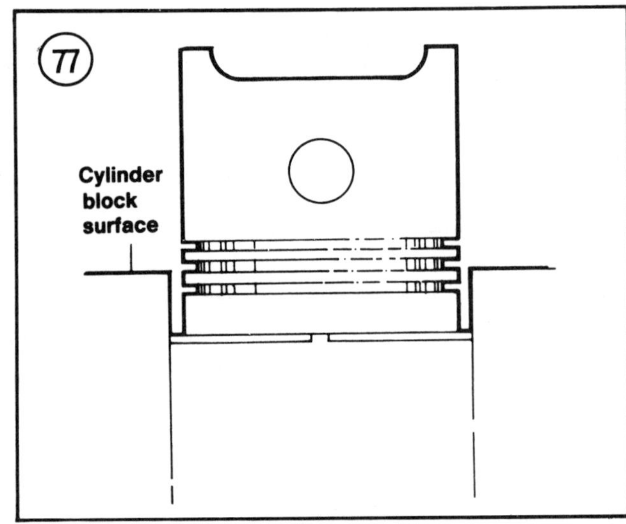

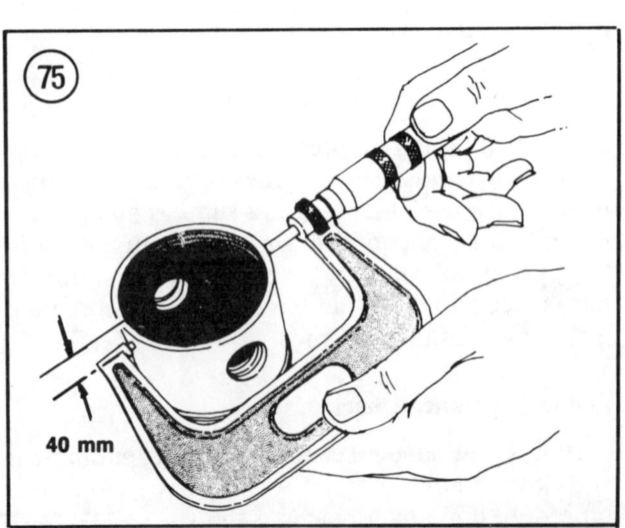

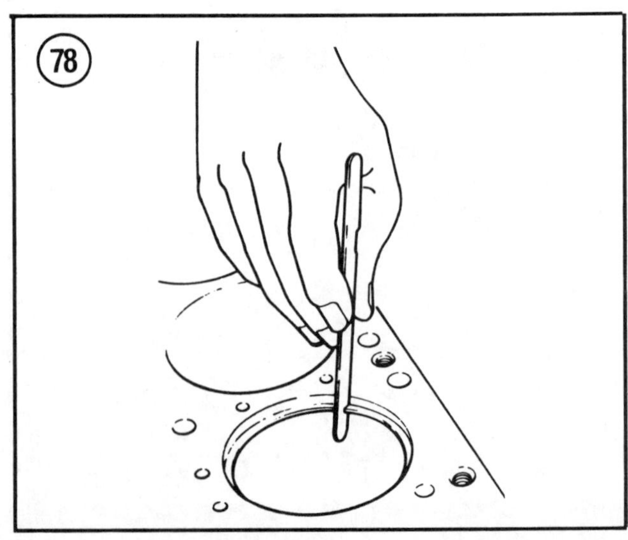

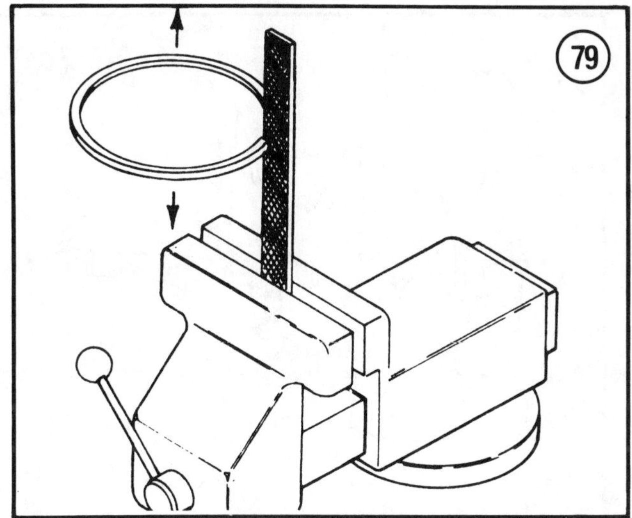

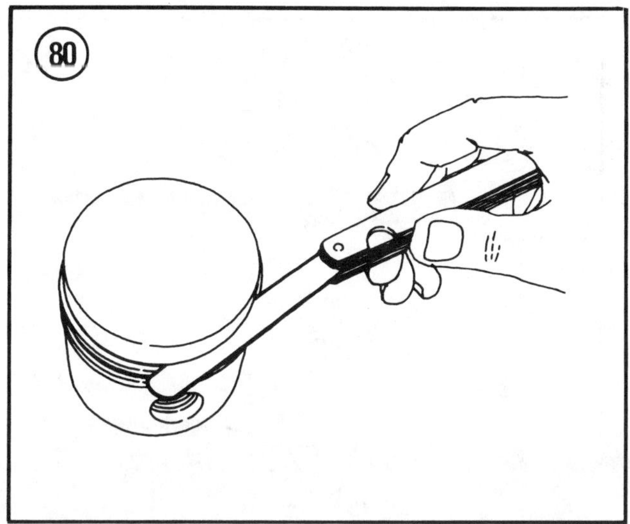

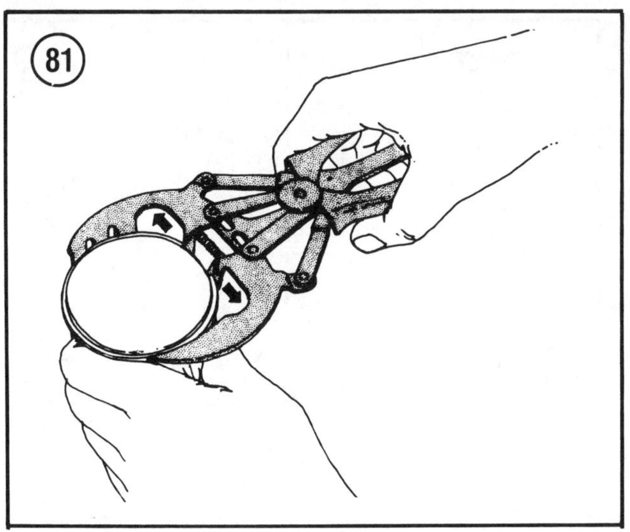

Check gap of new rings as well. If the gap is too small, file the ends of the ring to correct it (**Figure 79**).

3. Check the side clearance of the rings as shown in **Figure 80**. Place the feeler gauge alongside the ring all the way into the groove. If the measurement is not within specifications (**Tables 1-3**), either the rings or the ring grooves are worn. Inspect and replace as necessary.

4. Using a ring expander tool (**Figure 81**), carefully install the oil control ring, then the compression rings. Oil rings consist of 3 segments. The wavy segment goes between the flat segments to act as a spacer. Upper and lower flat segments are interchangeable. The second compression ring is tapered. The top of each compression ring is marked and must face up.

5. Position the ring gaps as shown in **Figure 82**.

4

Connecting Rod Inspection

Have the connecting rods checked for straightness by a dealer or a machine shop.

Connecting Rod Bearing Clearance Measurement

1. Place the connecting rods and upper bearing halves on the proper connecting rod journals.

2. Cut a piece of Plastigage the width of the bearing. Place the Plastigage on the journal, then install the lower bearing half and cap.

NOTE

Do not place Plastigage over the journal oil hole.

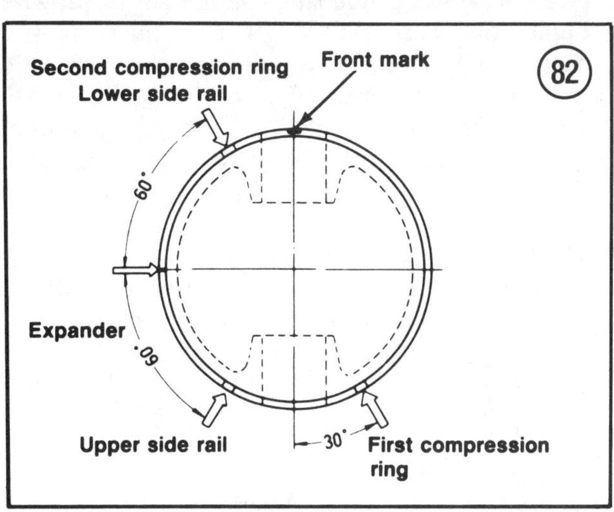

3. Tighten the connecting rod cap to specifications (**Tables 5-7**). Do not rotate the crankshaft while the Plastigage is in place.
4. Remove the connecting rod caps. Bearing clearance is determined by comparing the width of the flattened Plastigage to the markings on the envelope (**Figure 83**). If the clearance is excessive, the crankshaft must be reground and undersize bearings installed.

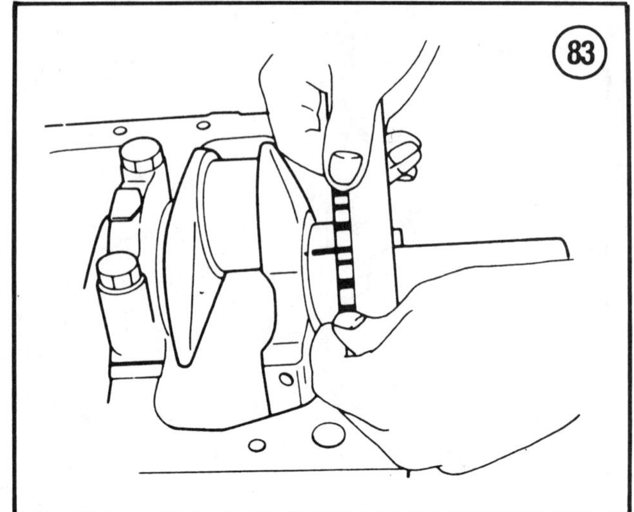

Piston/Connecting Rod Installation

1. Make sure the pistons are correctly installed on the connecting rods. The indentation on the top of the piston and the bearing recess in the connecting rod and cap must both face in the same direction. See **Figure 84**. When installed in the block, the indentation on the top of the piston must face toward the front of the engine. See **Figure 85**.
2. Make sure the ring gaps are positioned as shown in **Figure 82**.
3. Slip short pieces of hose over the connecting rod studs to keep them from nicking the crankshaft. Tape will work if you do not have the right diameter hose, but it is more difficult to remove.
4. Immerse the entire piston in clean engine oil. Coat the cylinder wall with oil.

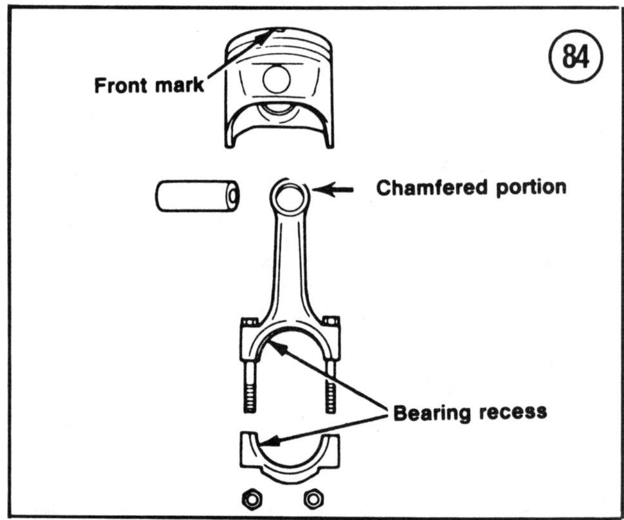

CAUTION
Use extreme care in Step 5 to prevent the connecting rod from nicking the crankshaft journal.

5. Install the piston/connecting rod assembly in its cylinder with a piston ring compressor as shown in **Figure 86**. Tap lightly with a wooden hammer handle to insert the piston. Be sure the indentation at the top of the piston (**Figure 85**) faces toward the front of the engine and that the piston number (painted on the top before removal) corresponds to the cylinder number, counting from the front of the engine.
6. Clean the connecting rod bearings carefully, including the back sides. Coat the journals and bearings with clean engine oil. Place the bearings in the connecting rod and cap.
7. Remove the protective hose or tape and install the connecting rod cap. Make sure the rod and cap marks align.
8. Lightly lubricate the connecting rod bolt threads with SAE 30W engine oil and install the rod caps.

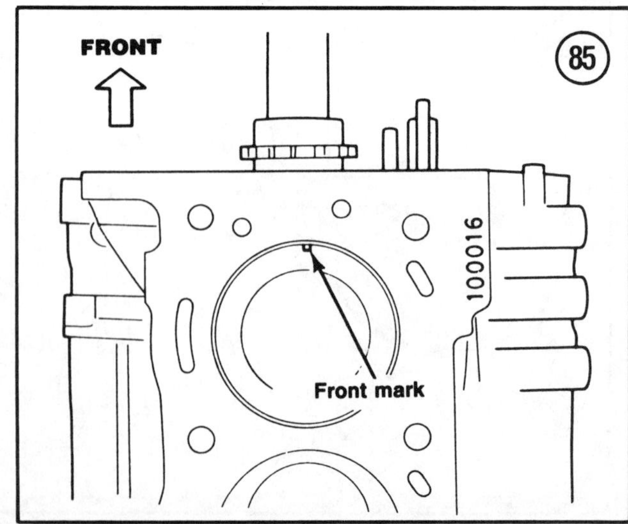

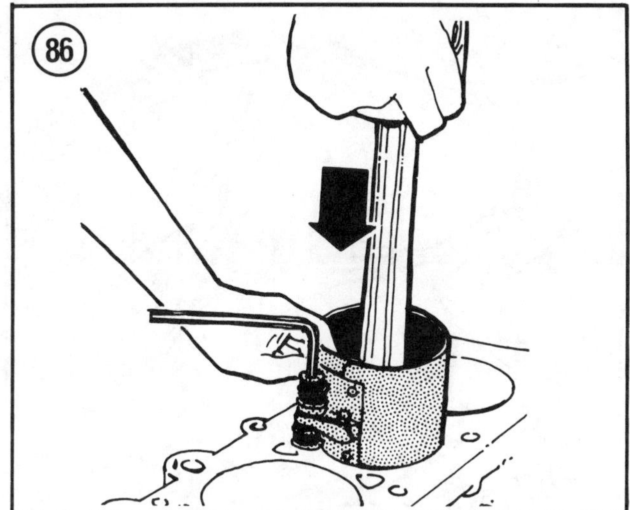

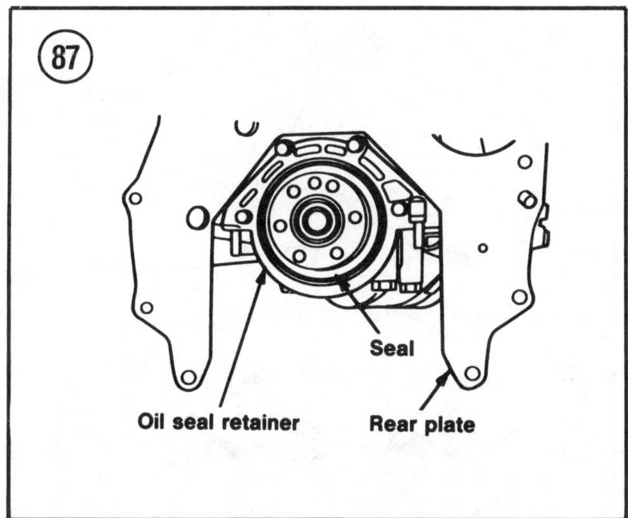

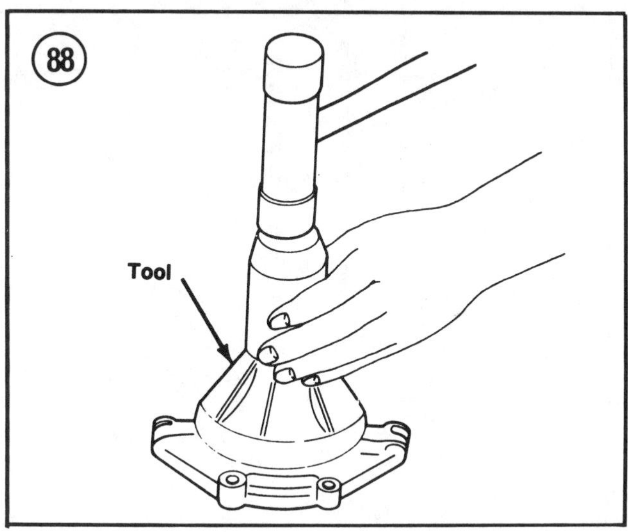

9. Install the cap nuts finger-tight, then tighten the nuts to specifications (**Tables 5-7**).

10. Check the connecting rod big-end play as described under *Piston/Connecting Rod Removal* in this chapter.

REAR MAIN OIL SEAL REMOVAL/INSTALLATION

1.9L Engine

The rear main oil seal is located under a seal retainer (**Figure 87**).

1. Remove the engine from the vehicle as described in this chapter.
2. Remove the oil pan as described in this chapter.
3. Remove the 4 seal retainer bolts. Remove the retainer and seal assembly.
4. Carefully pry the old seal from the retainer and discard it.
5. Fit a new seal in the retainer. Fill the space between the seal lips with grease. Lubricate the seal lip with engine oil.
6. Place the retainer on a clean, flat surface. Drive the seal in place with seal installer part No. J-22354 or equivalent (**Figure 88**).
7. Reverse Steps 1-3 to complete seal replacement.

2.0L Engine

A 2-piece rope type seal located under the rear main bearing cap is used on 1982-1983 engines. A 1-piece oil seal is used on 1984-1985 engines and as a replacement seal for 1983 engines. Two types of 1-piece seals are used: a thick seal and a thin seal. To determine which type is used in a given engine, refer to the identification mark shown in **Figure 89**.

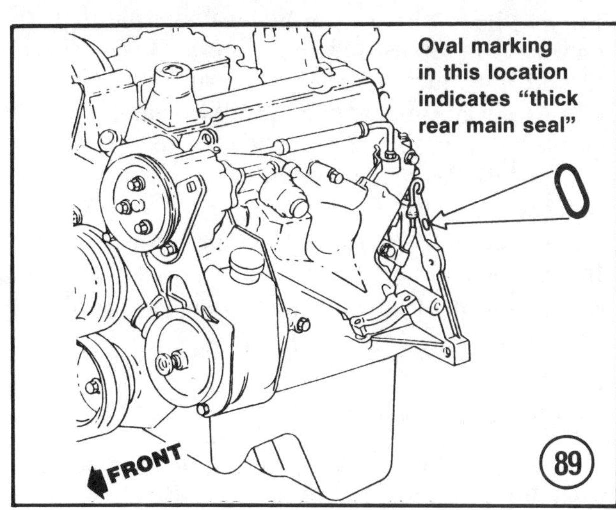

Rope seal

This procedure requires the use of tools part No. J-29114-1, part No. J-29114-2 and part No. J-29590 for replacement.

1. Remove the engine from the vehicle as described in this chapter.
2. Remove the oil pan and oil pump as described in this chapter.
3. Unbolt and remove the rear main bearing cap.
4. Tap one end of the upper seal half (in block) with a hammer and brass pin punch until the other end protrudes far enough to be pulled out with pliers. Remove the old seal half.
5. Carefully drive the new upper seal into the block groove about 1/4 in. on both sides with tool part No. J-29114-2 (**Figure 90**).
6. Measure how far the seal was driven up on one side and add 1/16 in. to the distance. Carefully pry the old seal from the main bearing cap and cut that amount off it. Repeat this step for the other side of the seal.
7. Install tool part No. J-29114-1 to the cylinder block (**Figure 91**). Use tool part No. J-29114-2 to work the short pieces cut in Step 6 onto tool part No. J-29114-1. Oil the short pieces and pack into the block groove.
8. Install a new seal half in the main bearing cap. Position the seal with tool part No. J-29590, rotate the tool slightly and cut off each seal end flush with the block. See **Figure 92**.
9. Check rear main bearing clearance with Plastigage. See *Main Bearing Clearance Measurement* in this chapter.
10. Clean Plastigage from the journal and bearing. If bearing clearance is out of specifications, recheck seal ends for fraying and correct as required.
11. Apply a thin coat of anaerobic sealant to the rear bearing cap as shown in **Figure 93**. The sealant should not touch the seal or bearing.
12. Apply a thin coat of SAE 30W engine oil to the crankshaft surface that touches the seal.
13. Install the rear main bearing cap and tighten bolts to 70 ft.-lb. (95 N•m).
14. Install the oil pump and oil pan as described in this chapter.
15. Install the engine in the vehicle as described in this chapter.

Thin one-piece seal

The new seal comes attached to a disposable installation tool.

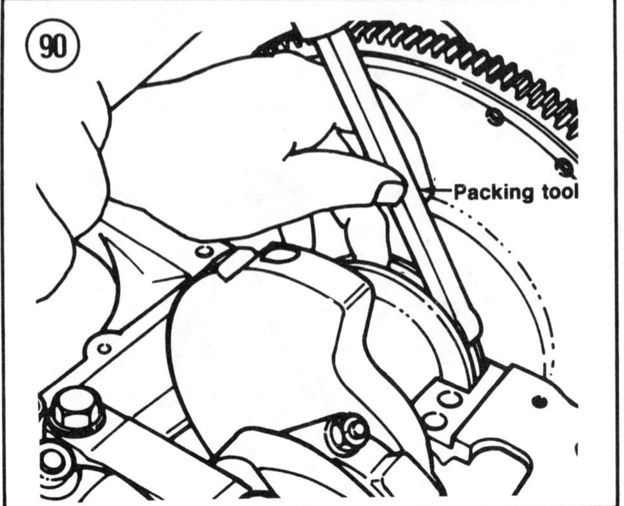

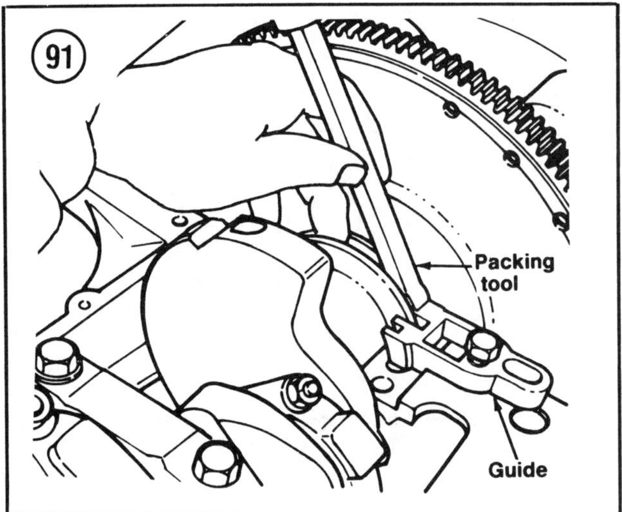

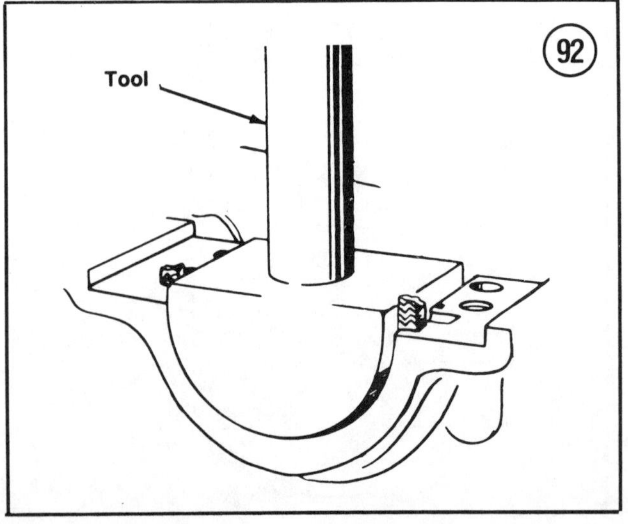

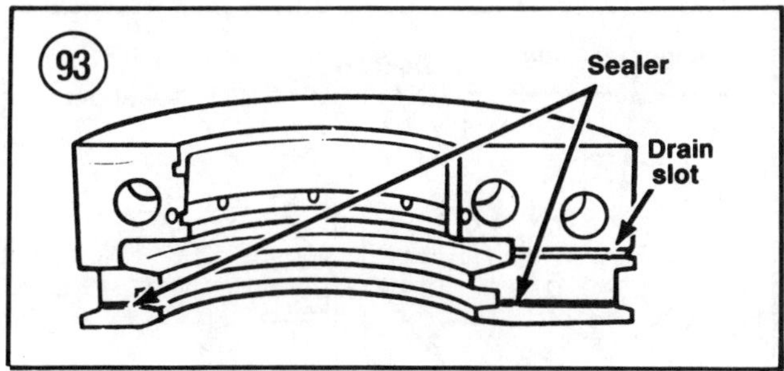

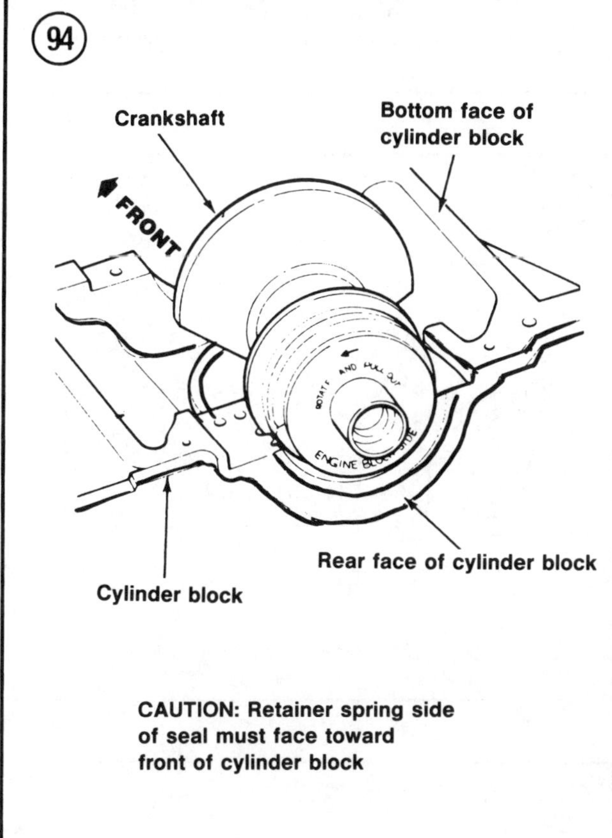

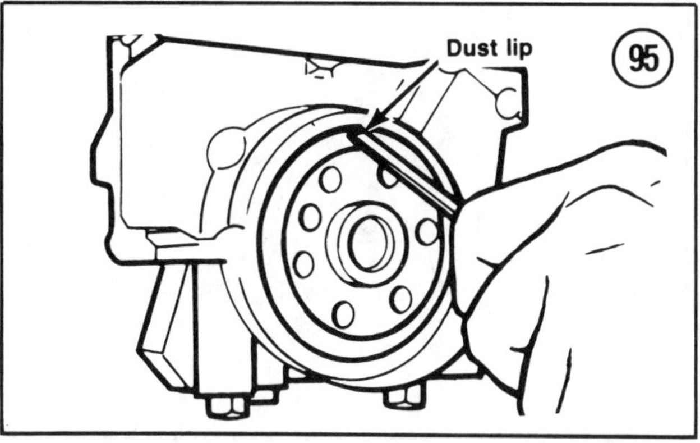

1. Remove the engine from the vehicle as described in this chapter.
2. Remove the oil pan and pump assembly.
3. Remove the front cover and lock the chain tensioner with a pin or punch.
4. Rotate the crankshaft to align the camshaft and crankshaft sprocket timing marks.
5. Remove the camshaft sprocket and timing chain.
6. Remove the crankshaft as described in this chapter.
7. Remove and discard the oil seal.
8. Clean all sealant residue from the cap, block and crankshaft seal area with solvent.
9. Coat the outer diameter of a new seal with a 0.04 in. (1 mm) bead of RTV sealant.
10. Install the seal installation tool on the rear of the crankshaft and align the tool so its arrow points as shown in **Figure 94**. Install crankshaft and tool in cylinder block, then remove and discard the tool.
11. Apply a 0.04 in. (1 mm) bead of RTV sealant along the split-line surface and install the rear main bearing cap with bearing insert. Install the remaining main bearing caps and tighten to specifications (**Table 6**).
12. Reverse Steps 1-5 to complete the installation.

Thick one-piece seal

This procedure can be performed with the engine in the vehicle.

1. Set the parking brake. Securely block both rear wheels so the truck will not roll in either direction. Raise the vehicle with a jack and place it on jackstands. Support the engine with a jack.
2. Remove the transmission. See Chapter Nine.
3. Remove the flywheel as described in this chapter.
4. Insert an awl or small screwdriver blade through the seal dust lip as shown in **Figure 95** and pry seal out with a revolving motion. Work carefully to prevent damage to the outer diameter of the crankshaft with the pry tool.
5. Check the inner diameter of the seal bore for nicks, burring or other defects. Correct as required.
6. Check crankshaft for burring or surface nicks on area which touches the seal. Repair or replace crankshaft as required.
7. Lubricate a new seal with clean engine oil and install seal on installer tool part No. J-34686. Slide

seal on installer mandrel until dust lip bottoms against tool collar. See **Figure 96**.

8. Align tool dowel pin with hole in crankshaft. Install tool to crankshaft and tighten attaching screws to 2-5 ft.-lb.
9. Rotate the installer handle so collar will push seal into the seal bore. Continue turning handle until collar fits tightly against the case, indicating that the seal has seated properly.
10. Loosen the installer handle and remove the tool.
11. Check that the seal is seated completely and squarely in the bore.
12. Reverse Steps 1-3 to complete the installation.

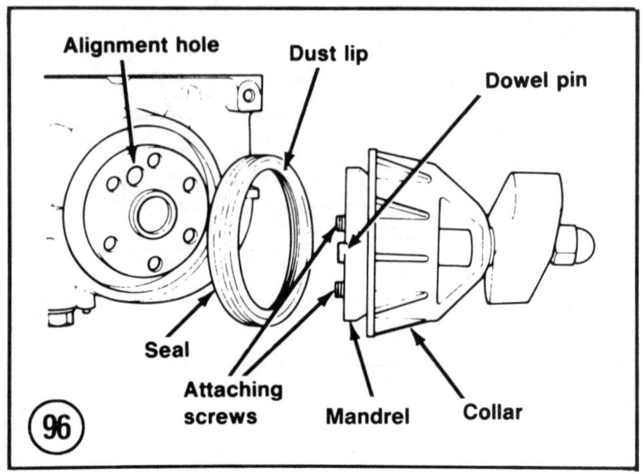

2.5L Engine

Refer to *2.0L Engine Thick, 1-piece Seal* in this chapter. Use seal installer part No. J-34924.

CRANKSHAFT

End Play Measurement

1. Pry the crankshaft to the front of the engine with a large screwdriver.
2. Measure the crankshaft end play at the front of the No. 3 (1.9L) main bearing, No. 4 main bearing (2.0L) or No. 5 main bearing (2.5L) with a flat feeler gauge (**Figure 97**). Compare to specifications in Tables 1-3 according to engine.
3. If the end play is excessive, replace the No. 3 main bearing (1.9L), No. 4 main bearing (2.0L) or No. 5 main bearing (2.5L). If less than specified, check the bearing faces for imperfections.

Removal

NOTE
*If it is necessary to remove the 1.9L crankshaft sprocket, use puller part No. J-25031 or equivalent (**Figure 98**). Use puller part No. J-22888-20 or equivalent to remove the 2.0L crankshaft sprocket.*

1. Check the caps for identification numbers or marks. If none are visible, clean the caps with a wire brush. If marks still cannot be seen, make your own with quick-drying paint.
2. Unbolt and remove the main bearing caps and bearing inserts.

NOTE
If the caps are difficult to remove, lift the bolts partway out, then pry them from side to side.

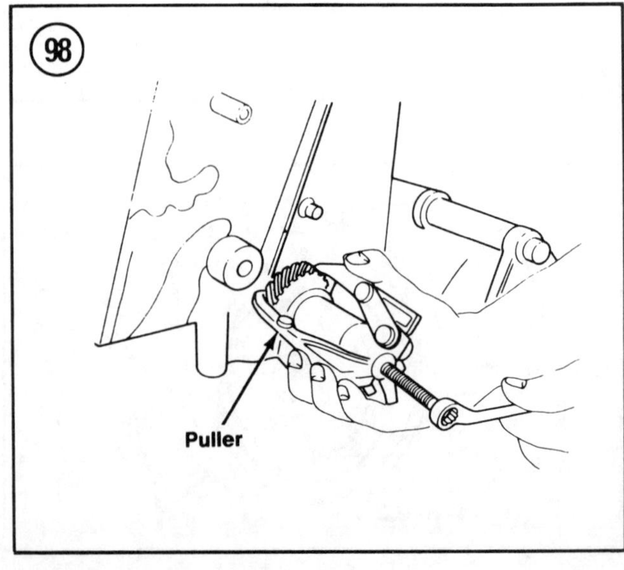

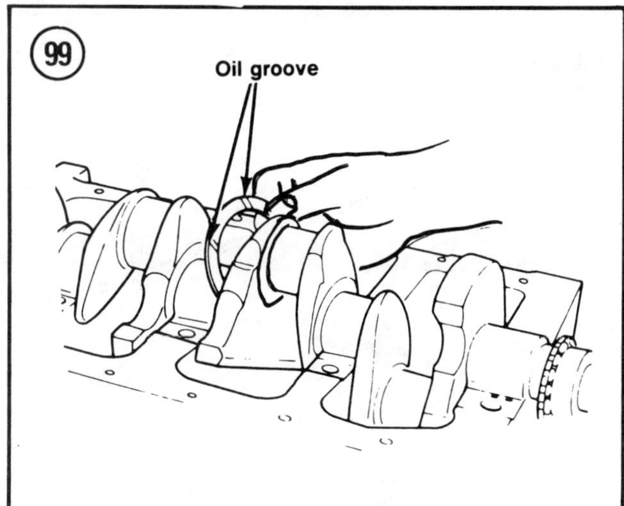

99

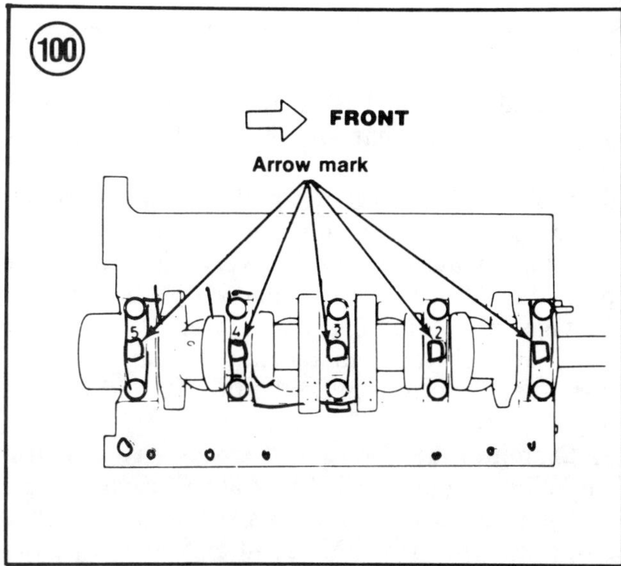

100

3. Lift the crankshaft from the engine block and place it on a clean workbench.
4. Remove the bearing inserts from the block. Place the bearing caps and inserts in order on a clean workbench.

Inspection

1. Clean the crankshaft thoroughly with solvent. Blow out the oil passages with compressed air.

NOTE
If you do not have precision measuring equipment, have a machine shop perform Step 2.

2. Check the crankpins and main bearing journals for wear, scoring and cracks. Check all journals against specifications (**Tables 1-3**) for out-of-roundness and taper. If necessary, have the crankshaft reground.

Main Bearing Clearance Measurement

Main bearing clearance is measured with Plastigage in the same manner as the connecting rod bearing clearance, described in this chapter. Excessive clearance requires that the bearings be replaced, the crankshaft be reground or both.

Installation

1. Install the main bearing inserts in the cylinder block. Bearing oil holes must align with block oil holes and bearing tabs must seat in the block tab slots.

NOTE
Check cap bolts for thread damage before reuse. If damaged, replace the bolts.

2. Lubricate the bolt threads with SAE 30W engine oil.
3. Install the cap bearing shells.
4. Install the crankshaft in the block.
5. On the 1.9L engine, install the thrust bearing as shown in **Figure 99** so that the side containing the oil groove is turned outward.
6. Install the bearing caps in their marked positions with the arrows pointing toward the front of the engine and the number mark aligned with the corresponding mark on the journals. See **Figure 100**.
7A. 1.9L Engine—Tighten the cap bolts snugly in 3-4-2-5-1 sequence. Rotate the crankshaft to seat the bearings. Tighten the bolts to 75 ft.-lb. (100 N•m).
7B. 2.0L engine—Tighten all bolts finger-tight, then tighten all main bearing caps *except* the No. 4 main cap bolts to 70 ft.-lb. (95 N•m). Tighten the No. 4 main cap bolts to 11 ft.-lb. (15 N•m). Tap crankshaft back and forth with a plastic mallet to align rear main bearing and crankshaft thrust surfaces. Retighten *all* cap bolts to 70 ft.-lb. (95 N•m).
7C. 2.5L engine—Tighten all bolts finger-tight. Recheck end play as described in this chapter, then tighten all bolts to to specifications (**Table 7**).

8. Rotate the crankshaft to make sure it turns smoothly at the flywheel rim. If not, remove the bearing caps and crankshaft and check that the bearings are clean and properly installed.

Pilot Bearing (1.9L/2.0L Engine)

The pilot bearing is located inside the rear end of the crankshaft. It supports the transmission input shaft on manual transmission vehicles.

1. Check the bearing for visible wear or damage. Turn the bearing with a finger and make sure it turns easily. If wear, damage or stiff movement are found, remove the bearing with a puller. These are available from rental dealers.
2. Tap a new bearing in place with a suitable drift until fully seated.

CAUTION
Do not tap too hard or you will damage the bearing.

FLYWHEEL/DRIVE PLATE

Removal/Installation

1. Remove the engine as described in this chapter.
2. Remove the clutch on manual transmission vehicles. See Chapter Nine.
3. Unbolt the flywheel or drive plate from the crankshaft. Remove the bolts gradually in a diagonal pattern.
4. Visually check the flywheel or drive plate surfaces for cracks, deep scoring, excessive wear, heat discoloration and checking. If the surface is glazed or slightly scratched, have the flywheel/drive plate resurfaced by a machine shop.
5. Inspect the ring gear for cracks, broken teeth or excessive wear. If severely worn, check the starter motor drive teeth for similar wear or damage. Replace as required.
6. Installation is the reverse of removal. Tighten bolts to specifications (**Tables 5-7**) in a crisscross pattern. Wipe all oil, grease and other contamination from the flywheel surface before installing the clutch on manual transmission vehicles.

CYLINDER BLOCK

Cleaning and Inspection

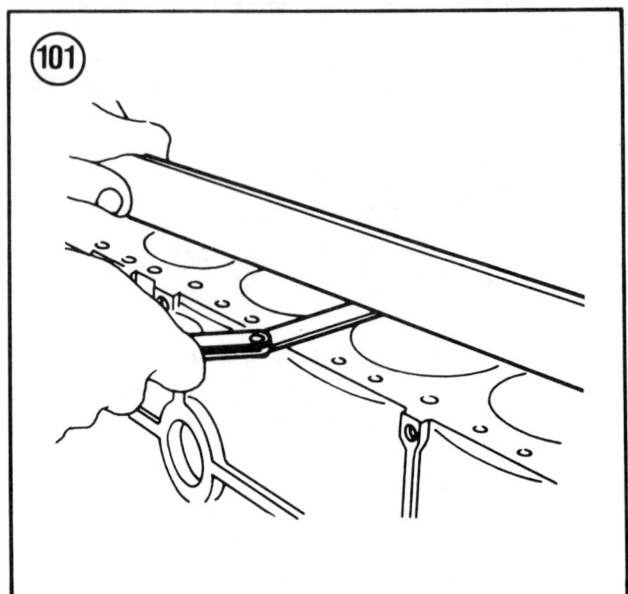

1. Clean the block thoroughly with solvent. Remove any RTV sealant residue from the machined surfaces. Check all core plugs for leaks and replace any that are suspect. See *Core Plug Replacement* in this chapter. Remove any plugs that seal oil passages. Check oil and coolant passages for sludge, dirt and corrosion while cleaning. If the passages are very dirty, have the block boiled out by a machine shop. Blow out all passages with compressed air. Check the threads in the head bolt holes to be sure they are clean. If dirty, use a tap to true up the threads and remove any deposits.
2. Examine the block for cracks. To confirm suspicions about possible leak areas, use a mixture of 1 part kerosene and 2 parts engine oil. Coat the suspected area with this solution, then wipe dry and immediately apply a solution of zinc oxide dissolved in wood alcohol. If any discoloration appears in the treated area, the block is cracked and should be replaced.
3. Check flatness of the cylinder block deck or top surface. Place an accurate straightedge on the block. If there is any gap between the block and straightedge, measure it with a feeler gauge (**Figure 101**). Measure from end to end and from corner to corner. Have the block resurfaced if it is warped more than 0.0078-0.0157 in. (0.2-0.4 mm) for 1.9L/2.0L engines or 0.004 in. (0.0102 mm) for 2.5L engines.
4. Measure the cylinder bores with a bore gauge for out-of-roundness or excessive wear as described in Step 2, *Piston Clearance Check* in this chapter. If the cylinders exceed maximum tolerances, they

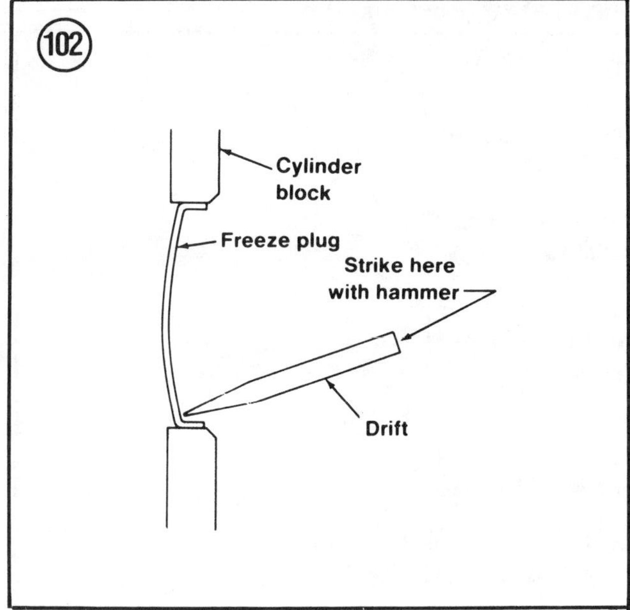

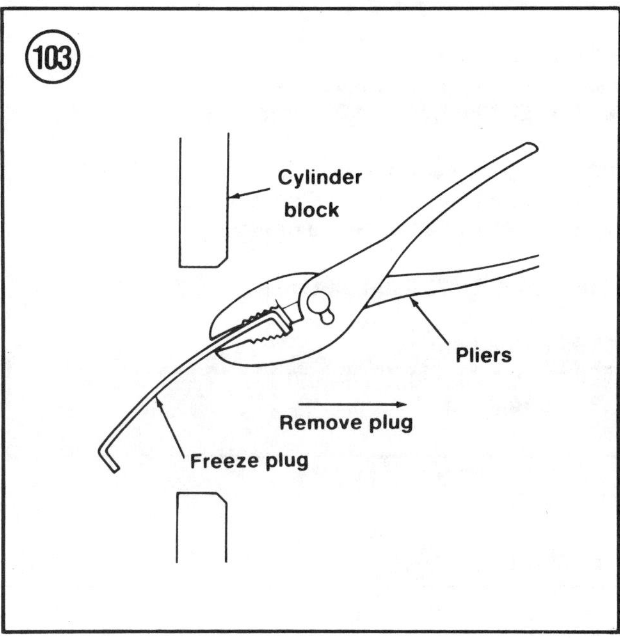

must be rebored. Reboring is also necessary if the cylinder walls are badly scuffed or scored.

NOTE
Before boring, install all main bearing caps and tighten the cap bolts to specifications in Tables 1-3.

CORE PLUG REPLACEMENT

The condition of all core plugs in the block should be checked whenever the engine is out of the vehicle for service. If any signs of leakage or corrosion are found around one core plug, replace them all.

Removal/Installation

CAUTION
Do not drive core plugs into the engine casting. It will be impossible to retrieve them and they can restrict coolant circulation, resulting in serious engine damage.

1. Tap the bottom edge of the core plug with a hammer and drift. Use several sharp blows to push the bottom of the plug inward, tilting the top out (**Figure 102**).
2. Grip the top of the plug firmly with pliers. Pull the plug from its bore (**Figure 103**) and discard.
3. Clean the plug bore thoroughly to remove all traces of the old sealer.
4. Apply a light coat of Loctite Stud N' Bearing Mount or equivalent to the plug bore.
5. Install the new core plug with an appropriate size driver or socket. The sharp edge of the plug should be at least 0.02 in. (0.5 mm) inside the lead-in chamfer.
6. Repeat Steps 1-5 to replace each remaining core plug.

Table 1 1.9L ENGINE SPECIFICATIONS

Type	4-cylinder OHC
Valve arrangement	V-type
Displacement	1.9 liter (118.9 cid)
Bore	3.43 in. (487 mm)
Stroke	3.23 in. (482 mm)
Cylinder arrangement (front to rear)	1-2-3-4
Firing order	1-3-4-2

(continued)

Table 1 1.9L ENGINE SPECIFICATIONS (continued)

Valve system	
Clearance	
Intake	0.006 in. (0.15 mm)
Exhaust	0.010 in. (0.25 mm)
Head diameter	
Intake	1.59 in. (40.4 mm)
Exhaust	1.34 in. (34.0 mm)
Stem diameter	
Intake	0.3102 in. (7.88 mm)
Exhaust	0.3091 in. (7.85 mm)
Seat angle	45°
Valve spring	
Tension	
Outer	32-37 lb. (143-164 N)
Inner	18-21 lb. (83-95 N)
Free height	
Outer	1.7874-1.8465 in. (45.4-46.9 mm)
Inner	1.7244-1.7835 in. (43.8-45.3 mm)
Camshaft	
End play	0.0020-0.0059 in. (0.05-0.15 mm)
Journal clearance	1.3362-1.3370 in. (33.94-33.96 mm)
Crankshaft	
Runout (maximum)	0.0038 in. (0.1 mm)
Journal clearance	0.0008-0.0025 in. (0.022-0.064 mm)
Crankpin clearance	0.0007-0.0030 in. (0.018-0.064 mm)
Journal/crankpin out-of-round	0.00028 in. (0.007 mm) max.
Journal diameter	2.2016-2.2022 in. (55.920-55.935 mm)
Crankpin diameter	1.9262-1.9268 in. (48.925-48.940 mm)
Piston-to-cylinder clearance	0.0018-0.0026 in. (0.045-0.065 mm)
Connecting rod	
Distortion (maximum)	0.0078 in. (0.2 mm)
Bending	0.0058 in. per 3.94 in. (0.15 mm per 100 mm)
Rod-to-crankpin clearance (maximum)	0.0137 in. (0.35 mm)

Table 2 2.0L ENGINE SPECIFICATIONS

Type	Inline 4-cylinder
Displacement	2.0 liter (122 cid)
Bore	3.50 in. (89 mm)
Stroke	3.15 in. (80 mm)
Cylinder arrangement (front to rear)	1-2-3-4
Firing order	1-3-4-2
Cylinder bore	
Diameter	3.5036-3.5067 in. (88.992-89.070 mm)
Out-of-round	0.001 in. (0.02 mm) max.
Taper (thrust side)	0.001 in. (0.02 mm) max.
Piston	
Clearance to cylinder	0.0007-0.0017 in. (0.017-0.043 mm)

(continued)

Table 2 2.0L ENGINE SPECIFICATIONS (continued)

Piston rings	
Ring groove clearance	
Top	0.001-0.003 in. (0.03-0.07 mm)
2nd	0.001-0.0035 in. (0.03-0.09 mm)
Oil	0.008 in. (0.20 mm) max.
Ring gap	
Compression	0.10-0.20 in. (0.25-0.50 mm)
Oil	0.02-0.06 in. (0.5-1.5 mm)
Piston pin	
Diameter	0.9051-0.9055 in. (22.99-23.00 mm)
Clearance	0.00026-0.00037 in. (0.007-0.009 mm)
Fit in rod	0.00078-0.0021 in. (0.020-0.053 mm)
Camshaft	
Lobe lift (intake and exhaust)	0.260 in. (6.65 mm)
Journal diameter	1.867-1.869 in. (47.44-47.49 mm)
Journal clearance	0.001-0.004 in. (0.026-0.101 mm)
Out-of-round	0.001 in. (0.025 mm)
Crankshaft	
Main journal	
Diameter	
No. 1, 2, 3, 4	2.4945-2.4954 in. (63.360-63.384 mm)
No. 5	2.4937-2.4946 in. (63.340-63.364 mm)
Taper	0.0002 in. (0.005 mm) max.
Out-of-round	0.0002 in. (0.005 mm) max.
Main bearing clearance	
No. 1, 2, 3, 4	0.0010-0.0022 in. (0.026-0.058 mm)
No. 5	0.0018-0.0030 in. (0.046-0.078 mm)
End play	0.002-0.008 in. (0.05-0.21 mm)
Crankpin	
Diameter	1.9983-1.9994 in. (50.758-50.784 mm)
Taper	0.0002 in. (0.005 mm) max.
Out-of-round	0.0002 in. (0.005 mm) max.
Connecting rod	
Bearing clearance	0.001-0.0031 in. (0.25-0.79 mm)
Side clearance	0.004-0.024 in. (0.10-0.61 mm)
Valve system	
Lifter	Hydraulic
Rocker arm ratio	1.5:1
Valve lash	1 1/2 turns from zero lash
Face angle	45°
Seat angle	46°
Seat runout	0.002 in. (0.05 mm)
Seat width	
Intake	0.049-0.059 in. (1.25-1.50 mm)
Exhaust	0.063-0.075 in. (1.60-1.90 mm)
Stem clearance	
Intake	0.0011-0.0026 in. (0.028-0.066 mm)
Exhaust	0.0014-0.0030 in. (0.035-0.078 mm)
Valve spring	
Free length	1.91 in. (48.5 mm)
Load	
Intake and exhaust	
Closed	72.8-81.0 lb.@ 1.60 in. (324-360 N @ 40.6 mm)
Open	176-188 lb. @ 1.33 in. (783-837 N @ 33.9 mm)

Table 3 2.5L ENGINE SPECIFICATIONS

Engine type	Inline 4-cylinder
Bore	4.00 in. (101.6 mm)
Stroke	3.00 in. (76.2 mm)
Displacement	2.5 liter (151 cid)
Firing order	1-3-4-2
Cylinder numbering (front to rear)	1-2-3-4
Cylinder bore	
Out-of-round (maximum)	0.0014 in. (0.0356 mm)
Taper (maximum)	0.0005 in. (0.0127 mm)
Valve system	
Clearance	
Intake	0.0010-0.0027 in. (0.0254-0.06858 mm)
Exhaust	
Top	0.0010-0.0027 in. (0.0254-0.06858 mm)
Bottom	0.0020-0.0037 in. (0.0508-0.09398 mm)
Head diameter	
Intake	1.72 in. (43.688 mm)
Exhaust	1.50 in. (38.1 mm)
Stem diameter	
Intake and exhaust	0.3418-0.3425 in. (8.68172-8.6995 mm)
Seat angle	
Intake	46°
Exhaust	45°
Face angle	45°
Installed height	1.69 in. (42.926 mm)
Valve spring load	
Closed	78-86 lb. @ 1.66 in.
Open	122-180 lb. @ 1.254 in.
Camshaft	
End play	0.0015-0.0050 in. (9.9381-0.127 mm)
Journal clearance	0.0007-0.0027 in. 0.1778-0.0685 mm)
Journal diameter	1.869 in. (47.4726 mm)
Crankshaft	
Main bearing journal	
Diameter	2.300 in. (59.182 mm)
Out-of-round (maximum)	0.0005 in.
Taper (maximum)	0.0005 in.
Clearance limit (new)	0.0005-0.0022 in. (0.05588 mm)
Crankshaft end play (new)	0.0035-0.0085 in. 0.889-0.2159 mm)
Rod bearing journal	
Diameter	2.000 in. (50.8 mm)
Out-of-round (maximum)	0.0005 in.
Taper (maximum)	0.0005 in.
Clearance limit (new)	0.0005-0.0026 in. (0.0127-0.06604 mm)
Rod side clearance	0.006-0.022 in. (0.1524-0.5588 mm)
Piston	
Clearance in bore	
Top	0.0025-0.0033 in. (0.635-0.838 mm)
Bottom	0.0017-0.0041 in. (0.043-0.1041 mm)
Piston-to-pin clearance	0.0003-0.0005 in. (loose)
Piston rings	
Clearance	
Compression	0.0015-0.0030 in. (0.0762-0.0381 mm)
Ring gap	
Top	0.010-0.022 in. (0.254-0.635 mm)
Second	0.010-0.0027 in. (0.254-0.4826 mm)
Oil	0.015-0.055 in. (0.381-1.397 mm)

Table 4 DIESEL ENGINE SPECIFICATIONS

Engine type	4-cylinder OHV
Valve arrangement	Inline
Displacement	2.2 liter (136.6 cid)
Bore	3.46 in. (88 mm)
Stroke	3.62 in. (92 mm)
Cylinder numbering (front to rear)	1-2-3-4
Firing order	1-3-4-2
Piston	
Diameter	2.547 in. (64.65 mm)
Clearance	0.0014-0.0022 in. (0.036-0.055 mm)
Piston rings	
Ring groove width	
Compression (top)	0.0018-0.0028 in. (0.045-0.070 mm)
Compression (2nd)	0.0012-0.0021 in. (0.030-0.055 mm)
Oil	0.0008-0.0021 in. (0.020-0.054 mm)
Ring end gap	
Compression (both)	0.079-0.0158 in. (0.2-0.4 mm)
Oil	0.079-0.0158 in. (0.2-0.4 mm)
Piston pin	
Diameter	1.0630 in. (27 mm)
Clearance	0.003-0.0007 in. (0.008-0.020 mm)
Camshaft	
Journal diameter	1.8898 in. (48 mm)
Journal clearance	0.0020 in. (0.05 mm) max.
Cam lobe height	1.5973 in. (40.57 mm)
Runout	0.0020 in. (0.05 mm) max.
End play	0.0032-0.0079 in. (0.08-0.20 mm)
Crankshaft	
Journal diameter	2.3591-2.3594 in. (59.92-59.93 mm)
Main bearing clearance	0.0011-0.0033 in. (0.029-0.085 mm)
End play	0.0018 in. (0.3 mm) max.
Runout	0.0023 in. (0.06 mm) max.
Crankpin diameter	2.0835-2.0839 in. (52.92-52.93 mm)
Connecting rod	
Runout	0.0078 in. (0.2 mm) max.
Bearing clearance	0.0016-0.0047 in. (0.04-0.12 mm)
Valve train	
Lifter	Hydraulic
Rocker arm shaft	
Diameter	0.7472-0.7480 in. (18.98-19.00 mm)
Runout	0.0079 in. (0.2 mm) max.
Shaft-to-bushing clearance	0.0.0016 in. (0-0.04 mm)
Stem diameter	0.314 in. (8 mm)
Seat and face angle	45°
Valve spring free length	
Inner	1.887 in. (47.9 mm)
Outer	1.864 in. (47.3 mm)

4

Table 5 1.9L ENGINE TIGHTENING TORQUES

Fastener	ft.-lb.	N•m
Connecting rod cap	45	60
Crankshaft pulley bolt	87	118
Cylinder head bolt	72	98
Exhaust manifold nuts	16	20
Flywheel bolt	76	103
Front cover bolt	18	24
Intake manifold nuts	16	20
Main bearing cap	75	100
Oil pan bolt	4	5
Rear plate bolt	36	48
Rocker arm shaft bracket nut	16	22
Timing sprocket bolt	58	79
Valve cover bolt	4	5

Table 6 2.0L ENGINE TIGHTENING TORQUES

Fastener	ft.-lb.	N•m
Air conditioning		
Bracket to block	26-37	36-50
Compressor to engine	26-37	36-50
Alternator		
Bracket to head	29-39	40-54
Brace to head	20-30	27-41
Adjusting bolt	20-25	27-34
Pivot bolt	29-39	40-54
Camshaft		
Sprocket	66-88	90-120
Rear cover	4-5	5-6.5
Thrust plate	4-13	6-18
Connecting rod cap	34-42	46-58
Crankshaft		
Pulley	29-44	40-60
Pulley hub	66-88	90-120
Main bearing caps	63-77	85-105
Cylinder head bolts	65-75	88-107
EGR valve	14-19	20-27
Exhaust manifold	19-29	26-40
Flywheel	45-59	61-80
Front cover	6-9	8-12
Fuel pump	15-22	20-30
Intake manifold	22-29	30-40
Oil filter	12-17	16-23
Oil filter adapter	12-20	16-27
Oil pan		
Two front screws	6-9	8-12
To side rail	4-9	6-12
To rear holes	11-17	15-24

(continued)

Table 6 2.0L ENGINE TIGHTENING TORQUES (continued)

Fastener	ft.-lb.	N•m
Oil pump		
Attaching bolts	26-38	35-52
Cover bolts	6-9	8-12
Oil drain plug	15-20	20-27
Rocker arm cover screws	3	4
Rocker arm nut	4-14	6-19
Spark plug	7-15	10-20
Starter motor	25-29	34-40
Thermostat housing	29-44	40-60
Transmission to engine	48-63	65-85
Water outlet	14-22	20-30
Water pump	14-22	20-30

Table 7 2.5L TIGHTENING TORQUES

Fastener	in.-lb.	ft.-lb.	N•m
Camshaft thrust plate		7	10
Connecting rod nut		32	44
Crankshaft hub bolt		160	212
Distributor hold-down bolt		22	30
EGR valve		10	14
Exhaust manifold		44	60
Flywheel bolt		44	60
Front cover bolts	90		10
Intake manifold		29	40
Main bearing cap bolt		70	95
Oil pan			
Attaching screws	75		10
Drain plug		25	34
Oil pump			
To block		22	30
Cover		10	14
Pushrod cover	90		10
Rocker arm bolt		20	27
Thermostat housing		20	27
Valve cover		6	8
Water pump		25	34

Table 8 DIESEL TIGHTENING TORQUES

Fastener	ft.-lb.	N•m
Camshaft sprocket	72-87	97-118
Connecting rod cap nuts	58-65	78-88
Crankshaft		
Pulley	10-17	14-23
Sprocket	124-151	168-204
Cylinder head bolts		
First stage	40-47	54-63
Second stage		
New bolt	54-61	73-82
Reused bolt	61-69	82-93
Exhaust manifold	10-17	14-23
Intake manifold	10-17	14-23
Main bearing cap bolts	116-130	157-176
Oil pan bolts	2-4	3-7
Rocker arm shaft bracket bolts	9-17	12-23
Valve cover bolts	9-13	12-17

CHAPTER FIVE

5

V6 ENGINES

A 2.8L (173 cid) V6 engine is optional in all vehicles. A carburetted version is used on 1982-1985 models; throttle body fuel injection replaced the carburetor on 1986 models. The cylinder banks are set at a 60° angle. The right (passenger side) bank is numbered 1, 3, 5; the left (driver side) bank is numbered 2, 4, 6. The firing order is 1-2-3-4-5-6.

The 4-journal camshaft mounted in the block is driven by a 3/8 in. pitch chain. A camshaft gear drives the distributor and oil pump. A camshaft eccentric operates the fuel pump on carburetted models.

The cast iron cylinder heads have individual intake and exhaust ports. Integral valve guides are used, with rocker arms held on individual threaded studs. A ball pivot valve train is used, with camshaft motion transferred through hydraulic lifters to the rocker arms by pushrods.

The oil pump is driven by the camshaft and is mounted at the bottom of the engine block.

The crankshaft is supported by 4 main bearings. The No. 3 bearing provides the crankshaft thrust surfaces.

The cylinder block is cast iron with full length water jackets around each cylinder.

All dimensions and fasteners are *metric.*

Specifications (**Table 1**) and tightening torques (**Table 2**) are at the end of the chapter.

ENGINE IDENTIFICATION

The Vehicle Identification Number (VIN) is the official identification for title and vehicle registration. It is located on a pad at the front of the block below the cylinder head in one of 2 locations, as shown in **Figure 1**.

The engine code is the 8th digit/letter of the VIN. The VIN is stamped on a gray-colored plate fastened to the upper left corner of the instrument panel close to the windshield on the driver's side (**Figure 2**). It can be read from outside the vehicle.

GASKET SEALANT

Gasket sealant is used instead of pre-formed gaskets between numerous mating surfaces on the V6 engine. See *Gasket Sealant,* Chapter One.

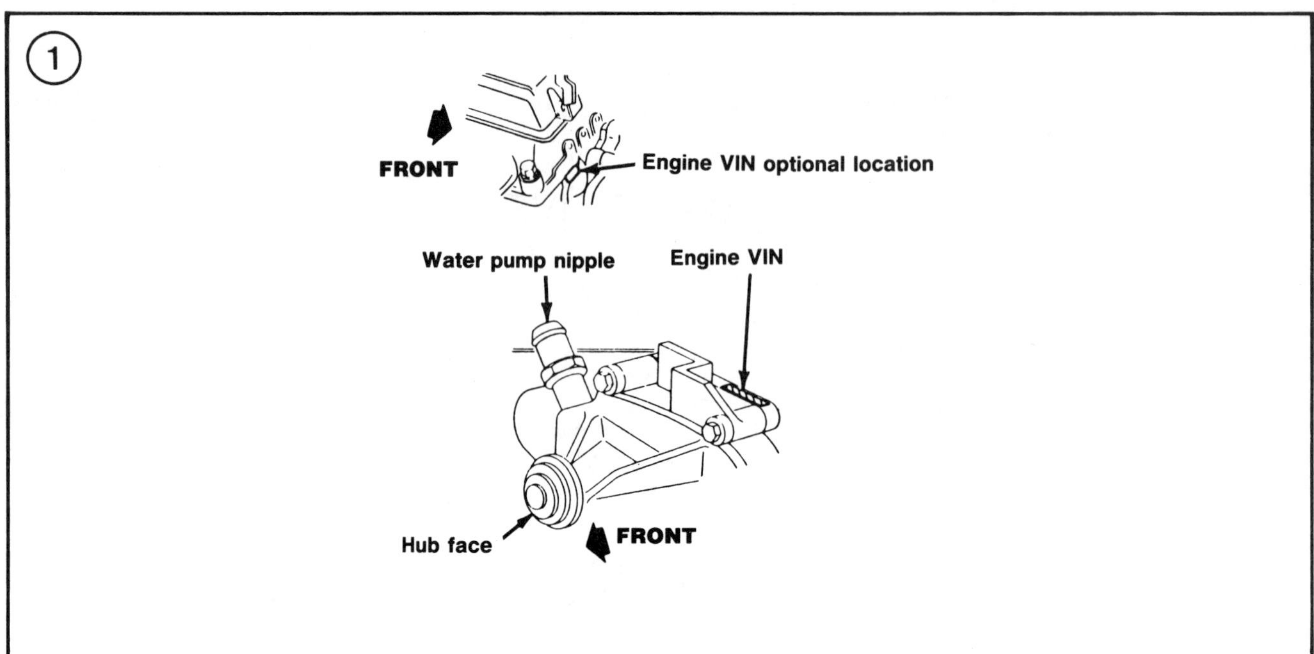

ENGINE REMOVAL (ALL 2-WHEEL DRIVE)

WARNING

The engine is heavy, awkward to handle and has sharp edges. It may shift or drop suddenly during removal. To prevent serious injury, always observe the following precautions.

1. Never place any part of your body where a moving or falling engine may trap, cut or crush you.

2. If you must push the engine during removal, use a board or similar tool to keep your hands out of danger.

3. Be sure the hoist is designed to lift engines and has enough load capacity for your engine.

4. Be sure the hoist is securely attached to safe lifting points on the engine.

5. The engine should not be difficult to lift with a proper hoist. If it is, stop lifting, lower the engine back onto its mounts and make sure the engine has been completely separated from the vehicle.

WARNING

Before opening any fuel system lines on a fuel injected engine, relieve system pressure as described in Chapter Six.

1. Disconnect the underhood lamp. Mark the location of the hinges and remove the hood.
2. Disconnect the negative battery cable.
3. Remove the air cleaner assembly. See Chapter Six.

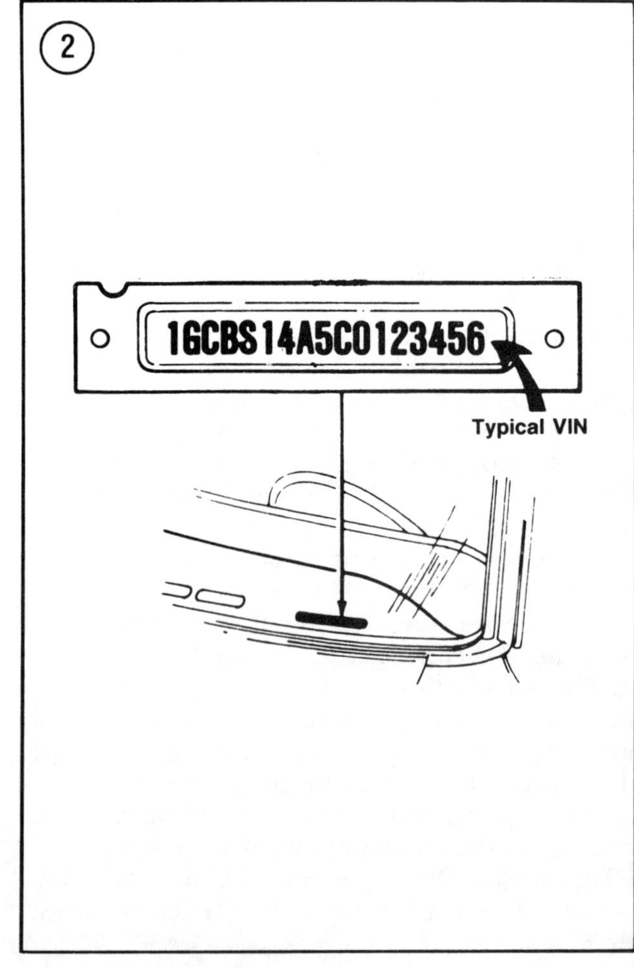

4. Drain the cooling system. Disconnect the heater hoses at the engine. Remove the upper fan shroud and radiator. See Chapter Seven.

WARNING
The air conditioning system contains pressurized refrigerant which can cause frostbite if it touches skin and blindness if it touches the eyes. If discharged near an open flame, the refrigerant forms poisonous gas. Never disconnect air conditioning system lines unless the system has been discharged and evacuated by a professional.

5. If equipped with power steering or air conditioning, remove the pump and/or compressor without disconnecting any hydraulic or refrigerant lines and place to one side out of the way.
6. Disconnect the wiring harness at the bulkhead. Disconnect any ground or main feed wires connecting the engine to the engine compartment.
7. Disconnect all electrical connectors and vacuum lines at the carburetor or TBI (throttle body injection) assembly. Disconnect the throttle cable at the carburetor or TBI assembly. Disconnect the transmission TV (throttle valve) cable or cruise control cable, if so equipped.
8. Remove the distributor cap.
9. Set the parking brake. Securely block the rear wheels so the truck will not roll in either direction. Raise the vehicle with a jack and place it on jackstands.
10. Disconnect the exhaust pipe at the catalytic converter and at each exhaust manifold. Remove pipe.
11. Remove the bellhousing strut rods.
12. Remove the flywheel cover.
13. Remove the flex drive-to-torque converter bolts, if equipped with an automatic transmission.
14. Remove the clutch bellcrank (1982-1983) or the hydraulic clutch cylinder (1984-on). See Chapter Nine.
15. Disconnect the shield at the rear of the catalytic converter and remove the converter hanger at the exhaust pipe.
16. Remove the lower fan shroud.
17. Disconnect the fuel lines at the fuel pump (carburetted) or flex hoses (TBI).
18. Remove the 2 outer air dam bolts and the left-hand body mount bolts.
19. Remove the bellhousing bolts and motor mount through-bolts.
20. Remove the jackstands and lower the vehicle to the ground.

NOTE
At this point, there should be no hoses, wires or linkage connecting the engine to the vehicle. Recheck this to be sure nothing will hamper engine removal.

21. Attach a hoist to the engine and support the transmission with a hydraulic floor jack.
22. Lift the engine from the vehicle with the hoist.

ENGINE INSTALLATION (2-WHEEL DRIVE)

5

Engine installation is the reverse of removal, plus the following:

1. Lower the engine into the vehicle. Leave the hoist attached and holding the engine weight until all mounts and mount bolts have been installed and tightened to specifications. See *Engine Mounts And Supports* in this chapter.
2. Fill the engine with an oil recommended in Chapter Three.
3. Fill the cooling system. See Chapter Seven.
4. Adjust the drive belts. See Chapter Three.
5. Fill the clutch master cylinder reservoir (if so equipped) with DOT 3 brake fluid.

ENGINE REMOVAL (4-WHEEL DRIVE MANUAL TRANSMISSION)

WARNING
The engine is heavy, awkward to handle and has sharp edges. It may shift or drop suddenly during removal. To prevent serious injury, always observe the following precautions.
1. Never place any part of your body where a moving or falling engine may trap, cut or crush you.
2. If you must push the engine during removal, use a board or similar tool to keep your hands out of danger.
3. Be sure the hoist is designed to lift engines and has enough load capacity for your engine.
4. Be sure the hoist is securely attached to safe lifting points on the engine.
5. The engine should not be difficult to lift with a proper hoist. If it is, stop lifting, lower the engine back onto its mounts and make sure the engine has been completely separated from the vehicle.

WARNING
Before opening any fuel system lines on a fuel injected engine, relieve system pressure as described in Chapter Six.

1. Disconnect the underhood lamp. Mark the location of the hinges and remove the hood.
2. Disconnect the negative battery cable.
3. Remove the air cleaner assembly. See Chapter Six.
4. Drain the cooling system. Disconnect the heater hoses at the engine. Remove the upper and lower fan shrouds and the radiator. See Chapter Seven.

WARNING

The air conditioning system contains pressurized refrigerant which can cause frostbite if it touches skin and blindness if it touches the eyes. If discharged near an open flame, the refrigerant forms poisonous gas. Never disconnect air conditioning system lines unless the system has been discharged and evacuated by a professional.

5. If equipped with power steering or air conditioning, remove the pump and/or compressor without disconnecting any hydraulic or refrigerant lines and place to one side out of the way.
6. Disconnect the fuel inlet and return lines at the fuel pump (carburetted) or flex hoses (TBI).
7. Disconnect all electrical connectors, vacuum lines and the throttle cable at the carburetor or TBI assembly. Disconnect the cruise control cable, if so equipped.
8. Disconnect the engine wiring harness, main feed wires and ground strap at the bulkhead.
9. Disconnect the negative battery cable at the engine.
10. Remove the distributor cap.
11. Remove the diverter valve.
12. Remove the console cover and shifter boot.
13. Remove the transfer case and transmission shifters.
14. Set the parking brake. Securely block the rear wheels so the truck will not roll in either direction. Raise the the vehicle with a jack and place it on jackstands.
15. Remove both skid plates and the front splash shield.
16. Drain the transfer case and transmission. See Chapter Three.
17. Disconnect and remove the rear drive shaft. Disconnect the front drive shaft at the transfer case.
18. Disconnect the speedometer cable, shift linkage and all vacuum hoses at the transfer case.
19. Disconnect the parking brake cable.
20. Remove the rear transmission mount and catalytic converter bracket.
21. Remove the transfer case. See Chapter Nine.
22. Place a jack under the transmission for support and remove the rear crossmember.
23. Disconnect the back-up light wire and clip at the transmission.
24. Remove the slave cylinder. See Chapter Nine.
25. Remove the transmission. See Chapter Nine.
26. Remove the clutch release bearing.
27. Remove the clutch housing inspection cover.
28. Remove the left-hand body mount bolts. Loosen the left-hand radiator bolt.
29. Raise the left side of the vehicle body with a jack and install a suitable wooden block to hold it in place while removing the bellhousing bolts. Remove the bellhousing. Remove the wooden block and jack from the left side of the vehicle.
30. Disconnect the exhaust pipe at the catalytic converter and at each exhaust manifold. Remove the pipe.
31. Disconnect the clutch cross shaft at the frame.
32. Remove the starter motor. See Chapter Eight.
33. Remove the motor mount through-bolts.

NOTE

At this point, there should be no hoses, wires or linkage connecting the engine to the vehicle. Recheck this to be sure nothing will hamper engine removal.

34. Attach a hoist to the engine and support the transmission with a hydraulic floor jack.
35. Lift the engine from the vehicle with the hoist.

ENGINE INSTALLATION (4-WHEEL DRIVE MANUAL TRANSMISSION)

Engine installation is the reverse of removal, plus the following:

1. Lower the engine into the vehicle. Leave the hoist attached and holding the engine weight until all mounts and mount bolts have been installed and tightened to specifications. See *Engine Mounts And Supports* in this chapter.
2. Fill the engine with an oil recommended in Chapter Three.
3. Fill the transfer case and transmission. See Chapter Three.
4. Fill the cooling system. See Chapter Seven.
5. Adjust the drive belts. See Chapter Three.
6. Fill the clutch master cylinder reservoir (if so equipped) with DOT 3 brake fluid.

ENGINE REMOVAL (4-WHEEL DRIVE AUTOMATIC TRANSMISSION)

WARNING

The engine is heavy, awkward to handle and has sharp edges. It may shift or drop suddenly during removal. To prevent serious injury, always observe the following precautions.

1. Never place any part of your body where a moving or falling engine may trap, cut or crush you.

2. If you must push the engine during removal, use a board or similar tool to keep your hands out of danger.

3. Be sure the hoist is designed to lift engines and has enough load capacity for your engine.

4. Be sure the hoist is securely attached to safe lifting points on the engine.

5. The engine should not be difficult to lift with a proper hoist. If it is, stop lifting, lower the engine back onto its mounts and make sure the engine has been completely separated from the vehicle.

WARNING

Before opening any fuel system lines on a fuel injected engine, relieve system pressure as described in Chapter Six.

1. Disconnect the underhood lamp. Mark the location of the hinges and remove the hood.
2. Disconnect the negative battery cable.
3. Set the parking brake. Securely block the rear wheels so the truck will not roll in either direction. Raise the vehicle with a jack and place it on jackstands.

4A. Blazer—Remove the body mounts.

4B. Chassis cab—Loosen and remove front 2 body mounts.

5. Remove the bolts at the ends of the front air dam.
6. Raise the vehicle body with a jack enough to provide access to the top transmission-to-engine mounting bolts. Remove the bolts and lower the body.
7. Remove the remaining transmission-to-engine bolts.
8. Remove the No. 2 crossmember.
9. Disconnect the exhaust pipe at the catalytic converter and at each exhaust manifold. Remove the pipe.
10. Disconnect the front drive shaft at the front axle.
11. Unbolt and remove the torque converter cover.
12. Disconnect the transmission cooler lines from the engine clips.
13. Remove the motor mount through-bolts.
14. Remove the drive plate-to-torque converter bolts.
15. Remove the front splash shield and lower fan shroud.
16. Remove the jackstands and lower the vehicle to the ground.
17. Drain the cooling system. Disconnect the heater hoses at the engine. Remove the upper fan shroud, fan and radiator. See Chapter Seven.
18. Remove the air cleaner assembly. See Chapter Six.

WARNING

The air conditioning system contains pressurized refrigerant which can cause frostbite if it touches skin and blindness if it touches the eyes. If discharged near an open flame, the refrigerant forms poisonous gas. Never disconnect air conditioning system lines unless the system has been discharged and evacuated by a professional.

19. If equipped with power steering or air conditioning, remove the pump and/or compressor without disconnecting any hydraulic or refrigerant lines and place to one side out of the way.
20. Disconnect the fuel inlet and return lines at the fuel pump (carburetted) or flex hoses (TBI).
21. Disconnect all electrical connectors, vacuum lines and the throttle and TV cables at the carburetor or TBI assembly. Disconnect the cruise control cable, if so equipped.
22. Disconnect the engine wiring harness, main feed wires and ground strap at the bulkhead.

NOTE

At this point, there should be no hoses, wires or linkage connecting the engine to the vehicle. Recheck this to be sure nothing will hamper engine removal.

23. Attach a hoist to the engine and support the transmission with a hydraulic floor jack.
24. Lift the engine from the vehicle with the hoist.

ENGINE INSTALLATION (4-WHEEL DRIVE AUTOMATIC TRANSMISSION)

Engine installation is the reverse of removal, plus the following:

1. Lower the engine into the vehicle. Leave the hoist attached and holding the engine weight until all mounts and mount bolts have been installed

and tightened to specifications. See *Engine Mounts And Supports* in this chapter.
2. Fill the engine with an oil recommended in Chapter Three.
3. Fill the cooling system. See Chapter Seven.
4. Adjust the drive belts. See Chapter Three.
5. Fill the clutch master cylinder reservoir (if so equipped) with DOT 3 brake fluid.

ENGINE MOUNTS AND SUPPORTS

Engine mounts are non-adjustable and rarely require service. Replace any broken or deteriorated mounts immediately to reduce strain on remaining mount and drive line components.

Checking Front Mounts

1. Attach a lifting device and raise the engine enough to remove its weight from the mount.
2. Check the rubber surface of the mount for:
   a. Heat check cracks.
   b. Separation from the metal plate.
   c. Splitting through the center.
3. If any of these defects are noted, replace the mount(s) as described in this chapter.

NOTE
When one mount requires replacement, it is a good idea to replace all mounts at the same time.

4. If movement of the mount relative to the frame is noted during this procedure, lower the engine to place its weight back on the mounts and retighten the mount fasteners.

Checking Rear Mounts

1. Securely block both front wheels so the truck will not roll in either direction. Raise the vehicle with a jack and place it on jackstands.
2. Watch the transmission mount while pushing up and pulling downward on the transmission extension housing. Replace the mount if the rubber separates from the metal plate or if the extension housing moves up but not downward.
3. If movement of the mount relative to the crossmember is noted during this procedure, retighten the mount fasteners.

Front Mount Replacement

Refer to **Figure 3** for this procedure.
1. Attach a lifting device to the engine.

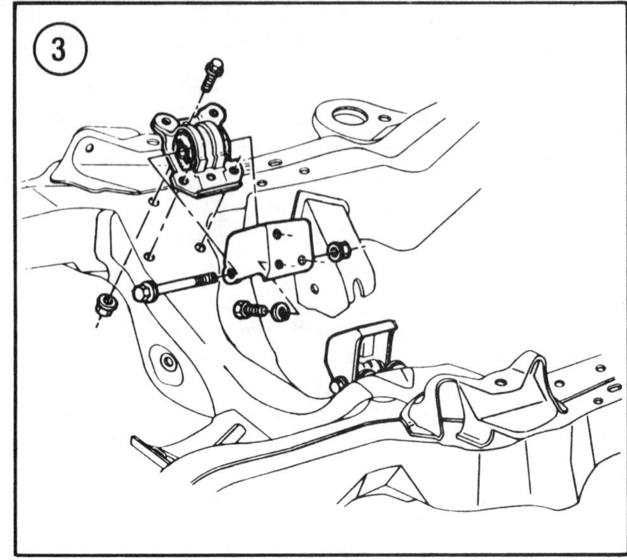

2. Disconnect the negative battery cable.
3. Remove the upper half of the fan shroud.
4. Raise the front of the engine and remove the engine mount through-bolts.

CAUTION
Raise the engine just enough in Step 5 to remove the mount. If raised too much, the distributor may be damaged from striking the cowl panel.

5. Continue raising the engine until there is sufficient clearance to remove the mount-to-frame bracket bolts. Remove the mount.
6. Install a new engine mount. Tighten mount-to-frame fasteners to 35-48 ft.-lb. (48-65 N•m) and bracket-to-block fasteners to 30-40 ft.-lb. (40-54 N•m).
7. Lower the engine until the through-bolt can be installed. Tighten the through-bolt to 53-66 ft.-lb. (72-90 N•m).
8. Remove the jackstands and lower the vehicle to the ground. Remove the lifting device. Install the upper half of the fan shroud and reconnect the negative battery cable.

Rear Mount Replacement

Refer to **Figure 4** for this procedure.
1. Disconnect the negative battery cable.
2. Raise the vehicle with a jack and place it on jackstands.
3. Place a jack under the engine and raise it enough to relieve the weight from the rear mount.
4. Remove the mount-to-transmission fasteners.

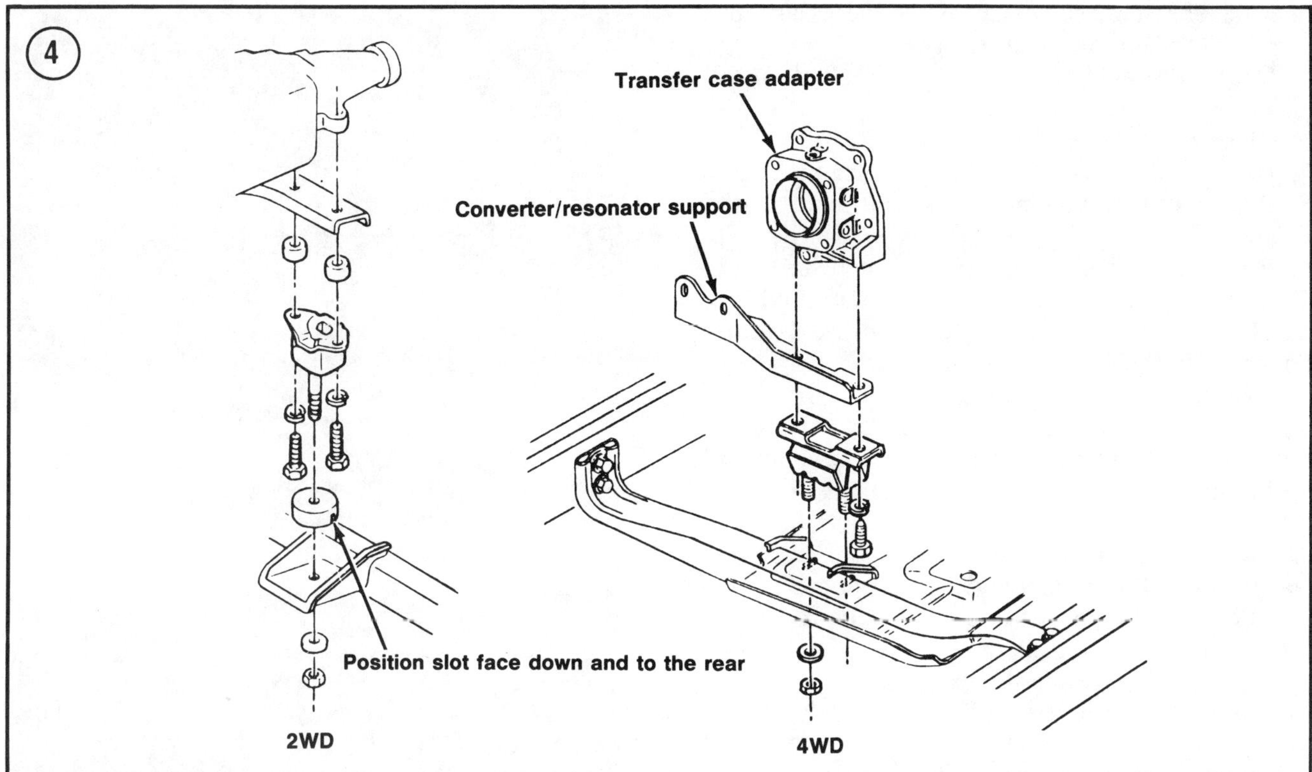

5. Remove the mount-to-crossmember fasteners. Remove the mount.
6. Install a new mount to the transmission. Tighten fasteners to 20-30 ft.-lb. (27-41 N•m).
7. Lower the engine slowly, aligning the mount-to-crossmember bolt holes. Install the mount-to-crossmember fastener and tighten to 20-30 ft.-lb. (27-41 N•m).
8. Remove the jack from under the engine. Remove the jackstands and lower the vehicle to the ground. Reconnect the negative battery cable.

DISASSEMBLY CHECKLISTS

To use the checklists, remove and inspect each part in the order mentioned. To reassemble, go through the checklists backwards, installing the parts in order. Each major part is covered in its own section in this chapter, unless otherwise noted.

Decarbonizing or Valve Service

1. Remove the rocker arm cover.
2. Remove the intake and exhaust manifolds.
3. Remove the rocker arms and camshaft.
4. Remove the cylinder heads.
5. Have valves removed and inspected. Have valve guides and seats inspected, repairing or replacing as required.
6. Assemble by reversing Steps 1-4.

Valve and Ring Service

1. Perform Steps 1-5 of *Decarbonizing or Valve Service.*
2. Remove the oil pan.
3. Remove the pistons with the connecting rods.
4. Remove the piston rings. It is not necessary to separate the pistons from the connecting rods unless a piston, connecting rod or piston pin needs repair or replacement.
5. Assemble by reversing Steps 1-4.

General Overhaul

1. Remove the engine. Remove the clutch from manual transmission vehicles.
2. Remove the flywheel (manual) or drive plate (automatic).
3. Remove the mount brackets and oil pressure sending unit from the engine.
4. If available, mount the engine on an engine stand. These can be rented from equipment rental

dealers. The stand is not absolutely necessary, but it will make the job much easier.

5. Check the engine for signs of coolant or oil leaks.
6. Clean the outside of the engine.
7. Remove the distributor. See Chapter Eight.
8. Remove all hoses and tubes connected to the engine.
9. Remove the fuel pump. See Chapter Six.
10. Remove the intake and exhaust manifolds.
11. Remove the thermostat housing. See Chapter Seven.
12. Remove the rocker arms.
13. Remove the crankshaft pulley, torsional damper, front cover, water pump, timing chain and sprockets.
14. Remove the camshaft.
15. Remove the cylinder heads.
16. Remove the oil pan and oil pump.
17. Remove the pistons and connecting rods.
18. Remove the crankshaft.
19. Inspect the cylinder block.
20. Assemble by reversing Steps 1-18.

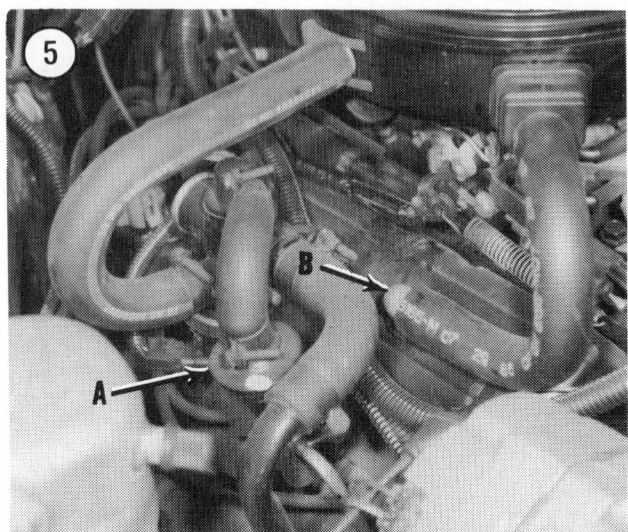

ROCKER ARM COVER

Removal/Installation

1. Disconnect the negative battery cable.
2. Remove the air cleaner. See Chapter Six.
3. Right cover:
   a. Disconnect all hoses at the air management valve (A, **Figure 5**).
   b. Remove the ignition coil (Chapter Eight).
   c. Disconnect the PCV hose (B, **Figure 5**).
4. Left cover:
   a. Disconnect the PCV hose (A, **Figure 6**).
   b. Remove all wires and the oil pipe bracket (B, **Figure 6**).
5. Remove the spark plug wires and clips from the retaining studs.
6. Right cover—Disconnect carburetor or TBI linkage from cover. **Figure 7** shows carburetor linkage; the TBI linkage is similar.

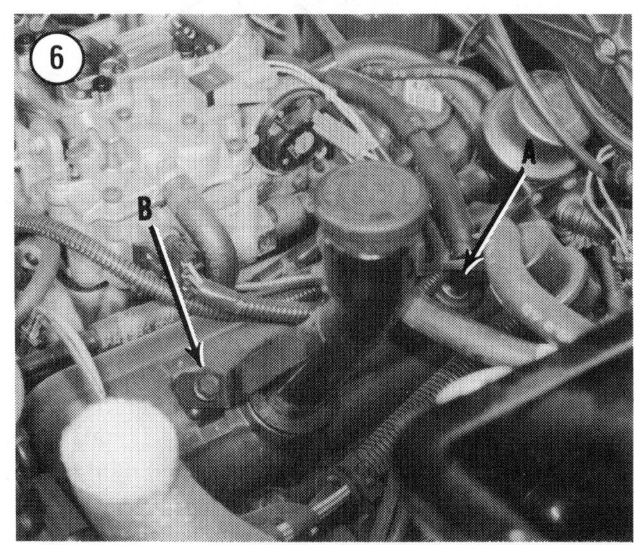

WARNING

Before opening any fuel system lines on a fuel injected engine, relieve system pressure as described in Chapter Six.

7. Left cover—Disconnect the fuel line at the carburetor or TBI assembly. Plug the line to prevent leakage.

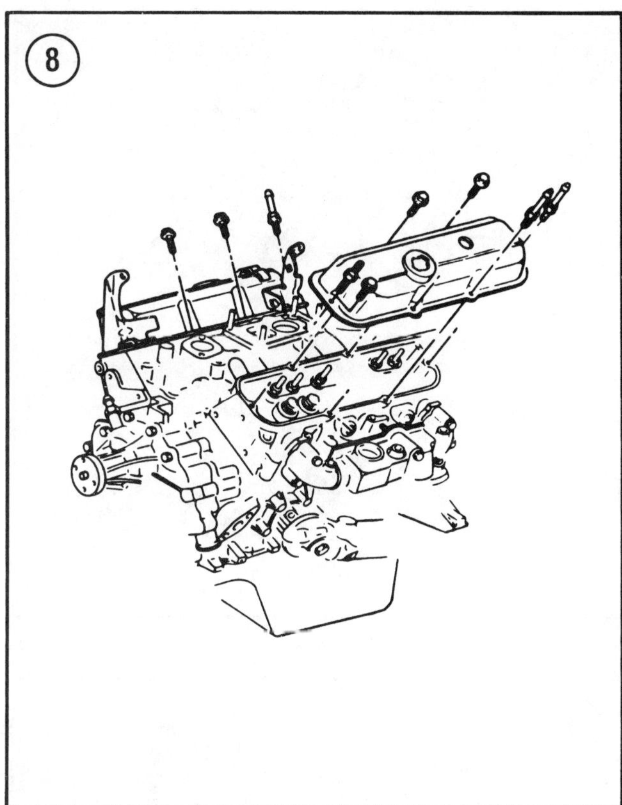

8. Remove the rocker arm cover bolts (**Figure 8**).

NOTE
If the cover refuses to come free in Step 9, bump the end with a rubber mallet. If this does not break the RTV seal, carefully pry the cover loose with a screwdriver. Use caution to prevent distorting the cover flange.

9. Remove the rocker arm cover. Clean any RTV residue from the cylinder head and rocker arm mating surfaces.

NOTE
Keep sealant out of bolt holes in Step 10 to prevent a hydraulic lock condition which could damage the cylinder head.

10. Run a 1/8 in. (3 mm) bead of RTV sealant around the rocker arm sealing surfaces. Flow the RTV on the inside of the bolt holes.
11. Install the rocker arm cover while the RTV is wet. Tighten the attaching bolts to specifications (**Table 2**).
12. Reverse Steps 1-7 to complete cover installation.

5

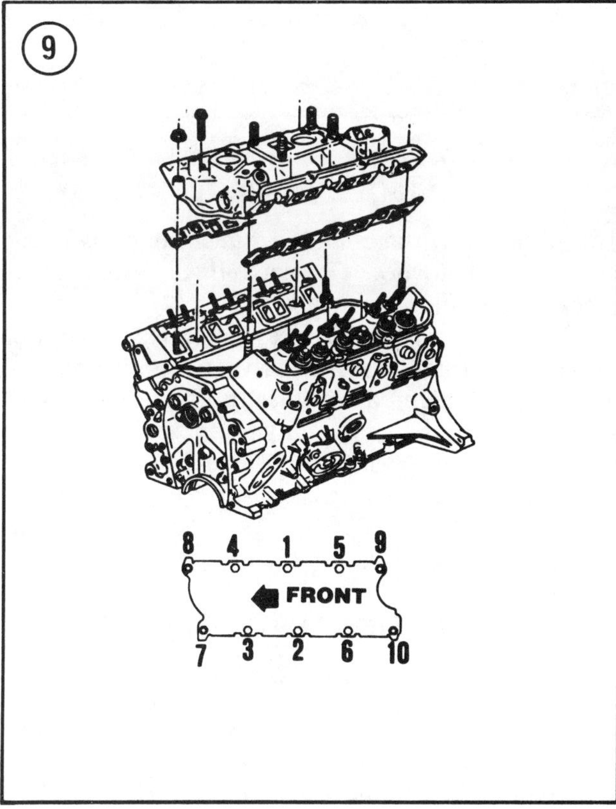

INTAKE MANIFOLD

The intake manifold is an aluminum single plane design. A coolant passage allows engine coolant to warm the manifold. An EGR passage is also provided.

Removal/Installation

WARNING
Before opening any fuel system lines on a fuel injected engine, relieve system pressure as described in Chapter Six.

Refer to **Figure 9** for this procedure.
1. Disconnect the negative battery cable.
2. Drain the cooling system. See Chapter Seven.
3. Remove the air cleaner. See Chapter Six.
4. Label and disconnect all vacuum lines, electrical connectors and fuel lines at the carburetor or TBI assembly.
5. Remove the distributor (Chapter Eight).
6. Disconnect the throttle cable.
7. Disconnect and remove the air management hoses.
8. Disconnect the canister lines. Remove tubing bracket from left rocker arm cover.

9. Remove the left rocker arm cover bolts. Remove the cover.
10. Remove the air management valve bracket.
11. Remove the right rocker arm cover.
12. Disconnect the upper radiator hose and heater hose at the engine.
13. Remove the air compressor belt, if so equipped. Rotate the compressor out of the way.
14. Disconnect all coolant switches.
15. Remove the manifold nuts and bolts.
16. Remove the manifold. Discard the gaskets. Remove all RTV residue from the front and rear of the block.
17. Clean the gasket sealing surfaces on the intake manifold and cylinder head.

NOTE

Gaskets are marked "Right Side" or "Left Side." Install as marked. Cut gaskets where indicated to install behind pushrods.

18. Run a 5 mm (3/16 in.) bead of RTV sealant at the front and rear block mating surfaces. Install gaskets and retain by extending the RTV bead 6 mm (7/32 in.) onto the gasket ends.
19. Install the intake manifold. Reverse Steps 1-15 to complete the installation. Tighten the bolts to specifications (**Table 2**) in the sequence shown in **Figure 9**.

EXHAUST MANIFOLDS

Removal/Installation

Refer to **Figure 10** for this procedure.

1. Disconnect the negative battery cable.
2. Set the parking brake. Securely block both rear wheels so the truck will not roll in either direction. Raise the front of the vehicle with a jack and place it on jackstands.
3. Disconnect the exhaust pipe at the manifold.
4. Left manifold—Remove 4 rear bolts and one nut.
5. Remove the jackstands and lower the vehicle to the ground.
6. Right manifold—Remove the attaching bolts.
7. Disconnect the air management valve hoses and any associated wiring.
8. Left manifold—Remove the power steering pump bracket.
9. Remove the manifold bolts. Remove the manifold.
10. Installation is the reverse of removal. Use a new exhaust pipe-to-manifold gasket. Tighten manifold bolts to specifications (**Table 2**).

10

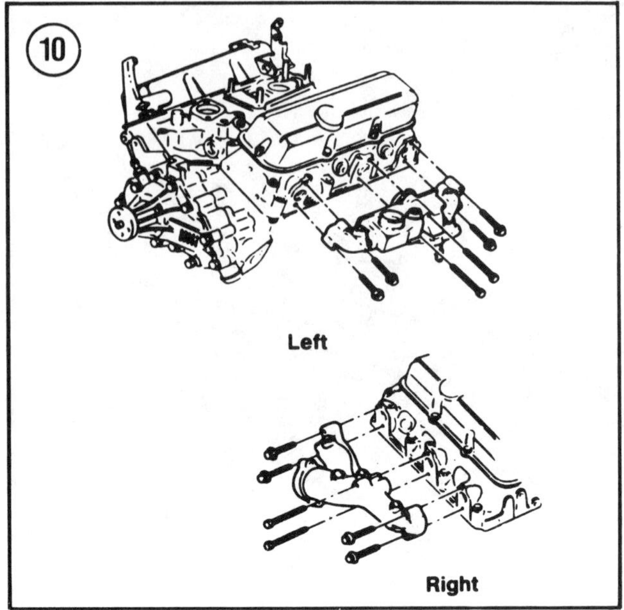

11

MANIFOLD INSPECTION

1. Check the intake and exhaust manifolds for cracks or distortion. Replace if distorted or if cracks are found.
2. Check the gasket surfaces for nicks or burrs. Small burrs may be removed with an oilstone.
3. Place a straightedge across the manifold gasket surfaces. If there is any gap between the straightedge and gasket surface, measure it with a flat feeler gauge. The gasket surface must be flat within 0.15 mm (0.006 in.) per foot of manifold length. If not, replace the manifold.

TORSIONAL DAMPER

CAUTION

The inertial weight section of the damper is assembled to the hub by a rubber sleeve. Follow the procedure below using the specified tools or you may destroy the damper tuning.

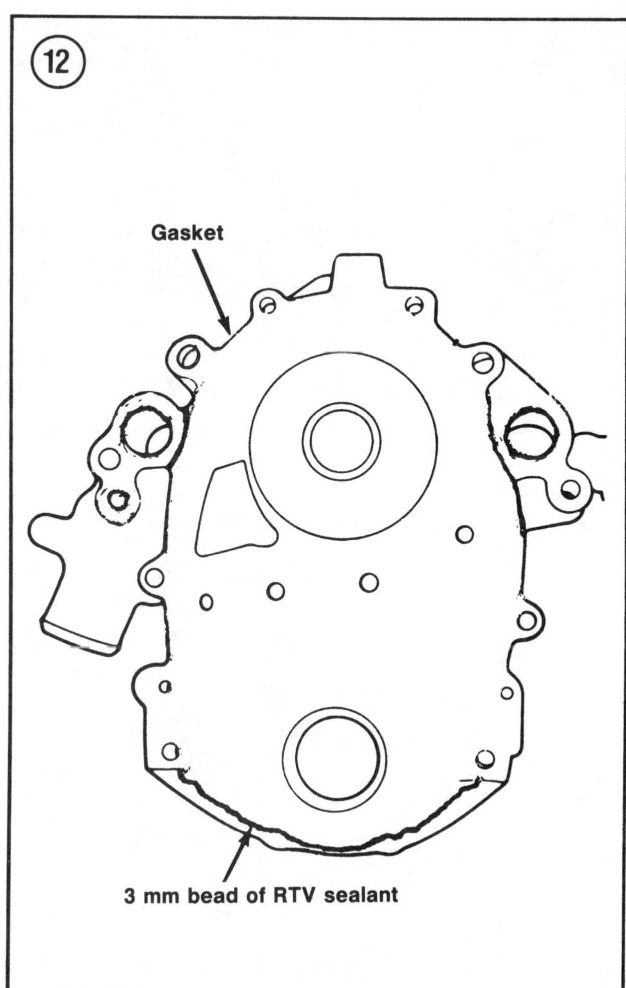

Removal/Installation

This procedure requires the use of a special puller (part No. J-23523) and installer (part No. J-29113).

1. Disconnect the negative battery cable.
2. Loosen the accessory units and remove all drive belts.
3. Set the parking brake. Securely block both rear wheels so the truck will not roll in either direction. Raise the front of the vehicle with a jack and place it on jackstands.
4. Remove the wheel/tire assembly on the passenger side.
5. Remove the inner fender splash shield.
6. Remove the accessory drive pulley. Remove the damper retaining bolt.
7. Remove the damper with tool part No. J-23523.
8. Lubricate the front cover seal contact area with SAE 30W engine oil.
9. Apply a small amount of RTV sealant to the hub keyway. Position the damper over the crankshaft key.
10. Install part No. J-29113 in the crankshaft so that at least 6 mm of the tool thread is engaged.
11. Pull the damper into position with tool part No. J-29113.
12. Reverse Steps 1-6 to complete installation. Adjust all drive belts. See Chapter Three.

CRANKCASE FRONT COVER

Removal/Installation

Refer to **Figure 11** for this procedure.

1. Remove the water pump. See Chapter Seven.

WARNING
The air conditioning system contains pressurized refrigerant which can cause frostbite if it touches skin and blindness if it touches the eyes. If discharged near an open flame, the refrigerant forms poisonous gas. Never disconnect air conditioning system lines unless the system has been discharged and evacuated by a professional.

2. If equipped with air conditioning, remove the compressor from the mounting bracket without disconnecting any lines. Place the compressor out of the way and remove the mounting bracket.
3. Remove the torsional damper as described in this chapter.
4. Disconnect the lower radiator hose at the front cover.
5. Remove the front cover bolts. Remove the front cover and gasket. Discard the gasket.
6. Clean the block and front cover sealing surfaces of all oil and grease.
7. Install a new gasket and run a 3 mm bead of RTV sealant as shown in **Figure 12**. Install the cover while the sealant is wet.
8. Install the stud bolt and bolts. Install water pump and tighten all fasteners to specifications (**Table 2**) within 5 minutes after installing the cover. If fasteners are not tightened within 5 minutes, remove the water pump, remove all traces of sealant, and install new sealant again.
9. Connect cooling system hoses, install torsional damper and reinstall air conditioning compressor, if so equipped.
10. Install and adjust accessory drive belts. See Chapter Seven.

TIMING CHAIN AND SPROCKET

Removal

Refer to **Figure 13** for this procedure.

1. Remove the spark plugs. See *Tune-up* in Chapter Three.
2. Remove the torsional damper and front cover as described in this chapter.
3. Rotate the crankshaft to position the No. 1 piston at TDC with the camshaft and crankshaft marks aligned as shown in **Figure 14**. The No. 4 piston will be at firing position.

NOTE
The camshaft sprocket is a light fit on the camshaft. A light blow with a plastic mallet on the lower sprocket edge should dislodge it.

4. Remove the camshaft sprocket bolts. Remove the sprocket and chain.

Installation

Refer to **Figure 13** and **Figure 14** for this procedure.

1. Install the timing chain on the camshaft sprocket. Lubricate the thrust surfaces with Molykote or equivalent.
2. Hold the sprocket vertically with the chain hanging down. Align the camshaft and crankshaft sprocket marks as shown in **Figure 14**.
3. Align the camshaft dowel with the sprocket hole. Install the sprocket on the camshaft.
4. Install the camshaft sprocket mounting bolts. Tighten bolts to draw sprocket on camshaft, then tighten bolts to specifications (**Table 2**).
5. Lubricate the timing chain with SAE 30W engine oil.
6. Install the front cover and torsional damper as described in this chapter.
7. Install the spark plugs. See *Tune-up* in Chapter Three.

ROCKER ARMS, VALVE LIFTERS AND CAMSHAFT

Rocker Arm and Valve Lifter Removal/Installation

Refer to **Figure 15** for this procedure.

1. Remove the rocker arm cover as described in this chapter.
2. Remove the rocker arm nuts, rocker arm balls, rocker arms and pushrods.

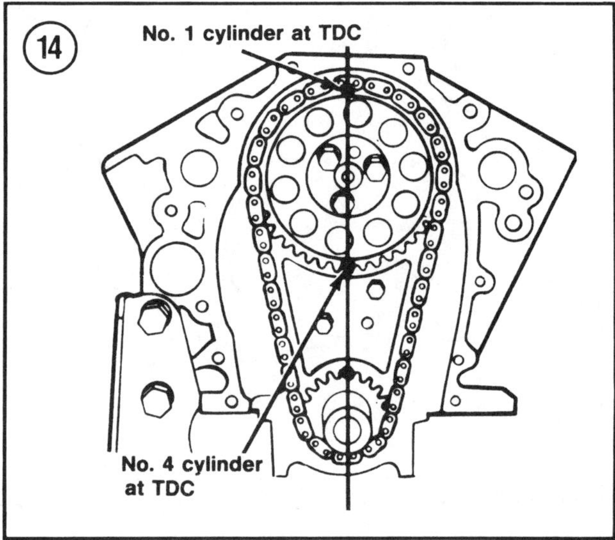

3. Place each rocker arm assembly in a separate container or use a rack to keep them separated for reinstallation in the same position as removed.
4. Remove the valve lifters with tool part No. J-29834. Do not pry lifters out with a screwdriver. If tool part No. J-29834 is not available, use a pencil-type magnet.

NOTE
When installing new valve lifters, rocker arms or rocker arm balls, coat the contact surfaces with Molykote or equivalent.

5. Install the valve lifters and pushrods. Seat each pushrod in its lifter and align in its retainer.
6. Install the rocker arms, rocker arm balls and rocker arm nuts. Tighten the nuts until all lash is removed.
7. Adjust the valves as described in this chapter.

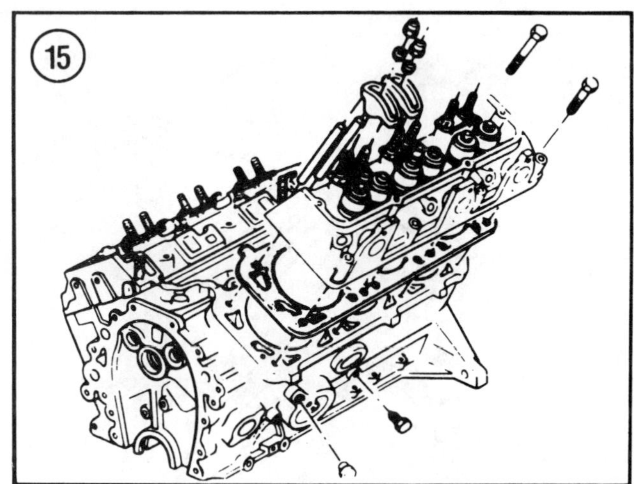

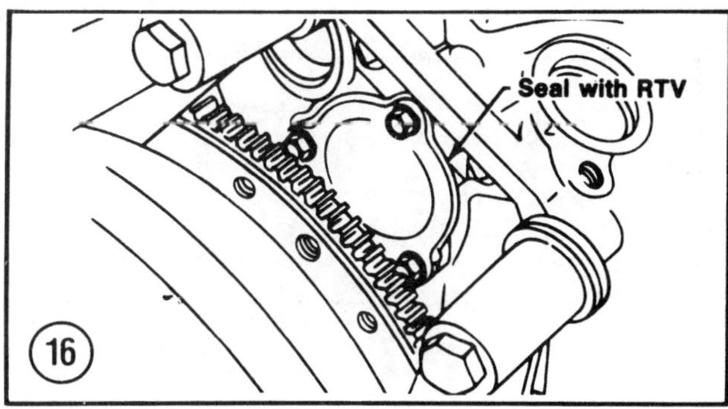

8. Install the rocker arm cover as described in this chapter.

Inspection

Keep the lifters in proper sequence for reinstallation in their original position. Clean lifters in solvent and wipe dry with a clean lint-free cloth.

If any lifter shows signs of pitting, scoring, galling, non-rotation or excessive wear, replace the entire lifter. Check the lifter foot. It must be slightly convex. If the bottom of the body is scuffed or worn, check the camshaft lobe. If the pushrod seat is scuffed or worn, check the pushrod and replace as required.

Camshaft Removal

1. Remove the engine from the vehicle as described in this chapter.
2. Remove the rocker arm covers as described in this chapter.
3. Remove the rocker arms and valve lifters as described in this chapter.
4. Remove the torsional damper and front cover as described in this chapter.
5. Remove the fuel pump and pushrod on carburetted engines. See Chapter Six.

NOTE
All camshaft journals are the same diameter. Care must be taken to prevent bearing damage while performing Step 6.

6. Carefully withdraw camshaft from the block with a slow rotating motion.

Camshaft Inspection

1. Check the journals and lobes for signs of wear or scoring. Lobe pitting in the toe area is not sufficient reason for replacement, unless the lobe lift loss exceeds specifications.

NOTE
If you do not have precision measuring equipment, have Step 2 done by a machine shop.

2. Measure the camshaft journal diameters with a micrometer. Replace the camshaft if the journals are more than 0.025 mm (0.0009 in.) out-of-round.

Camshaft Installation

NOTE
When installing a new camshaft, coat the lobes with GM EOS lubricant or equivalent.

1. Lubricate the camshaft journals with SAE 30W engine oil.
2. Install the camshaft with a slow, rotating motion.
3. Reverse Steps 1-5 of *Camshaft Removal* in this chapter to complete installation.

Camshaft Bearing Replacement

Camshaft bearings can be replaced without complete engine disassembly. Camshaft bearing remover/installer part No. J-6098 is required for bearing replacement.

1. Remove the camshaft and crankshaft as described in this chapter.
2. Remove the camshaft rear cover (**Figure 16**) from the block.
3. Install the nut and thrust washer to part No. J-6098. Index the tool pilot in the front cam bearing. Install the puller screw through the pilot.

4. Install tool part No. J-6098 with its shoulder facing the front intermediate bearing and the threads engaging the bearing.
5. Hold the puller screw with one wrench. Turn the nut with a second wrench until the bearing has been pulled from its bore.
6. Repeat Steps 3-5 to remove the other center bearing.
7. Remove the tool and index it to the rear bearing to remove the rear intermediate bearing from the block.
8. Remove the front and rear bearings by driving them toward the center of the block.
9. Installation is the reverse of removal. Use the same tool to pull new bearings into their bores. Place rear and intermediate bearing oil holes at the 2:30 position. Place the front bearing oil holes at the 1:00 and 2:30 positions.
10. Install the camshaft rear cover with a 1/8 in. bead of RTV sealant and tighten bolts immediately.

Camshaft Lobe Lift Measurement

Camshaft lobe lift is measured with the camshaft in the block and the cylinder heads in place. Refer to **Figure 17**.

1. Remove the rocker arm covers and rocker arm assemblies as described in this chapter.
2. Install a dial indicator with a ball socket adapter to fit over the pushrod.
3. Turn the crankshaft in the direction of rotation until the valve lifter seats on the heel of the cam lobe. This positions the pushrod at its lowest point.
4. Set the dial indicator to zero, then slowly rotate the crankshaft until the pushrod is in its fully raised position. Record the total lift.
5. Repeat Steps 2-4 for each pushrod. If all lobes are within specifications (**Table 1**), reinstall the rocker arm assemblies and adjust the valves as described in this chapter.
6. If one or more lobes are worn beyond specifications, replace the camshaft as described in this chapter.

OIL PAN AND PUMP

Oil Pan Removal

Refer to **Figure 18** for this procedure.

1. Drain the crankcase. See Chapter Three.
2. Remove the engine as described in this chapter.
3. Remove the oil pan.

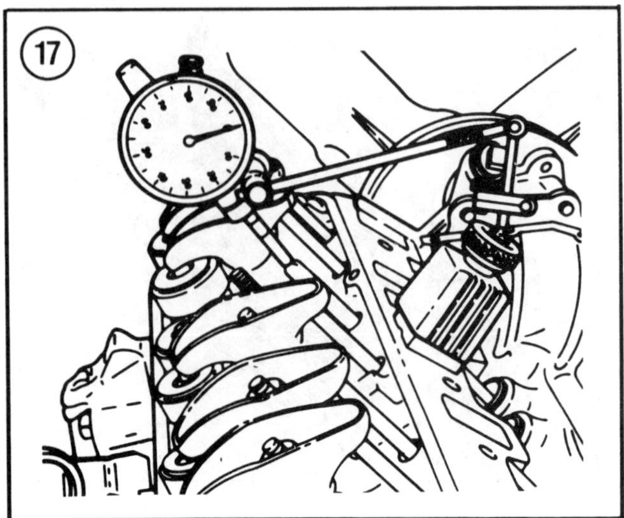

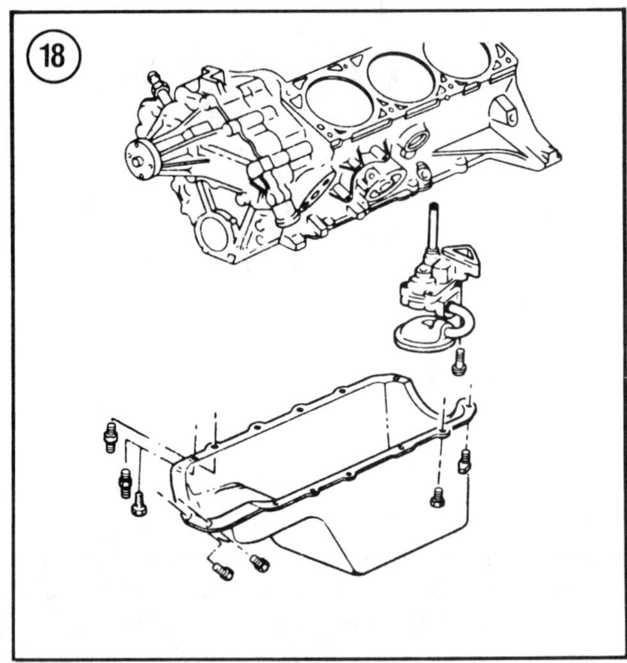

NOTE

The oil pump pickup tube and screen are a press fit in the pump housing and should not be removed unless replacement is required.

Inspection

1. Clean the pan thoroughly in solvent.
2. Check the pan for dents or warped gasket surfaces. Straighten or replace the pan as required.

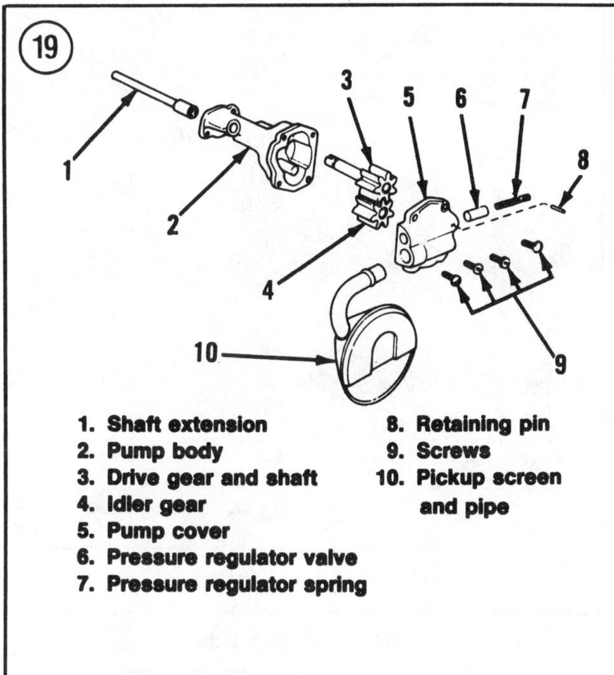

Oil Pan Installation

1. Clean any RTV residue from the oil pan rail on the engine block.
2. Run a 3 mm (1/8 in.) bead of RTV sealant along the oil pan sealing flanges on the engine block.
3. Install the oil pan and tighten bolts to specifications (**Table 2**).

Oil Pump Removal/Installation

1. Remove the oil pan as described in this chapter.
2. Remove the bolt holding the pump to the rear main bearing cap. Remove the oil pump and drive shaft.
3. Installation is the reverse of removal.

Disassembly/Assembly

Refer to **Figure 19** for this procedure.

1. Remove the cover bolts and cover.
2. Scribe a mark on the gear teeth for reinstallation indexing.
3. Remove the idler gear, drive gear and shaft from the pump body.
4. Remove the pressure regulator valve pin, spring and valve.
5. Remove the pickup tube/screen assembly *only* if it needs replacement. Secure the pump body in a soft-jawed vise and separate the tube from the cover.

NOTE
Do not twist, shear or collapse the tube when installing it in Step 6.

6. If the pickup tube/screen assembly was removed, install a new one. Secure the pump body in a soft-jawed vise. Apply sealer to the new tube and tap in place with a plastic mallet.
7. Assembly is the reverse of disassembly. Use a new cover gasket and tighten cover bolts to 6-9 ft.-lb. (8-12 N•m).

Inspection

NOTE
The pump body and gears are serviced as an assembly. If one or the other is worn or damaged, replace the entire pump. No wear specifications are provided by GM.

1. Clean all parts thoroughly in solvent. Brush the inside of the body and the pressure regulator chamber to remove all dirt and metal particles. Dry with compressed air, if available.
2. Check the pump body and cover for cracks or excessive wear.
3. Check the pump gears for damage or excessive wear.
4. Check the drive gear shaft-to-body fit for excessive looseness.
5. Check the inside of the pump cover for wear that could allow oil to leak around the ends of the gears.
6. Check the pressure regulator valve for a proper fit.

CYLINDER HEADS

Removal

1. Remove the intake manifold as described in this chapter.
2. Drain the cooling system. See Chapter Seven.
3. Set the parking brake. Securely block both rear wheels so the truck will not roll in either direction. Raise the front of the vehicle with a jack and place it on jackstands.
4. Disconnect the exhaust pipe at the exhaust manifold.
5. Left head—Remove the dipstick tube attachment.
6. Remove the jackstands and lower the vehicle to the ground.
7. Loosen the rocker arms. Swivel rocker arms off pushrods and remove pushrods.
8. Right head—Remove the alternator mounting bracket.

NOTE
Place the head on its side in Step 9 to prevent damage to the spark plugs or head gasket surface.

9. Loosen and remove the head bolts. Remove the head with the exhaust manifold attached.
10. Remove the exhaust manifold from the cylinder head, if required.
11. Remove and discard the head gasket. Clean any residue from the head and block surfaces.

Decarbonizing

1. Without removing the valves, remove all deposits from the combustion chambers, intake ports and exhaust ports. Use a fine wire brush dipped in solvent or make a scraper from hardwood. Be careful not to scratch or gouge the combustion chambers.
2. After all carbon is removed from the combustion chambers and ports, clean the entire head in solvent.
3. Clean away all carbon on the piston tops. Do not remove the carbon ridge at the top of the cylinder bore.

Inspection

1. Check the cylinder head for signs of oil or water leaks before cleaning.
2. Clean the cylinder head thoroughly in solvent. While cleaning, check for cracks or other visible damage. Look for corrosion or foreign material in the oil and water passages. Clean the passages with a stiff spiral brush, then blow them out with compressed air.
3. Check the cylinder head studs for damage and replace if necessary.
4. Check the threaded rocker arm studs for damaged threads and replace as required.

Installation

Refer to **Figure 20** for this procedure.

1. Make sure the cylinder head and block gasket surfaces and bolt holes are clean. Dirt in the block bolt holes or on the head bolt threads will affect bolt torque.
2. Check all visible oil and water passages for cleanliness.
3. Reinstall the exhaust manifold, if removed.

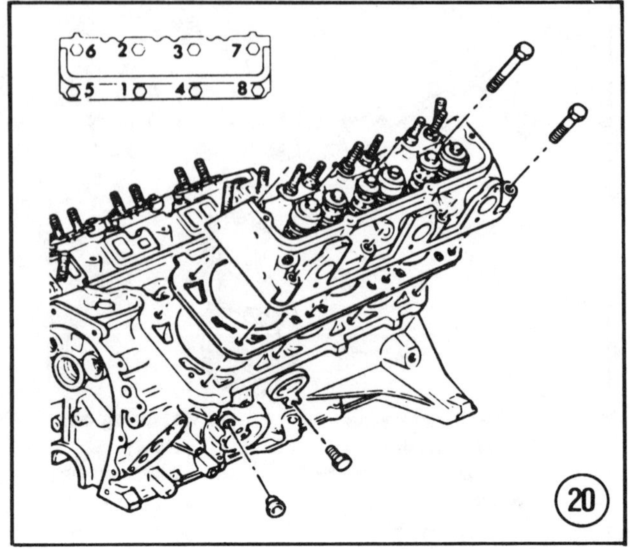

20

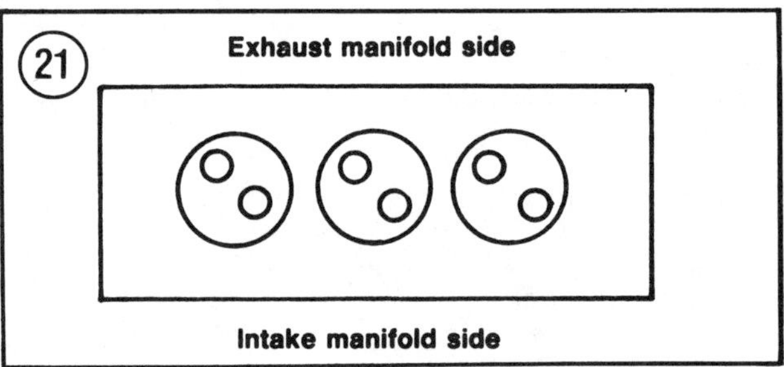

21

4. Install a new head gasket on the cylinder block dowel pins with the word "THIS SIDE UP" facing up.
5. Carefully lower the cylinder head in place on the dowel pins and gasket.
6. Coat the head bolt threads with sealing compound and install the bolts finger-tight.
7. Tighten the head bolts following the sequence shown in **Figure 20** to specifications (**Table 2**).
8. Reverse Steps 1-9 of *Removal* in this chapter.

VALVES AND VALVE SEATS

Servicing the valves, guides and valve seats requires special knowledge and expensive machine tools. A general practice among those who do their own service is to remove the cylinder head, perform all disassembly except valve removal and take the head to a dealer or machine shop for inspection and service. Since the cost is low relative to the required effort and equipment, this is usually the best approach, even for experienced mechanics.

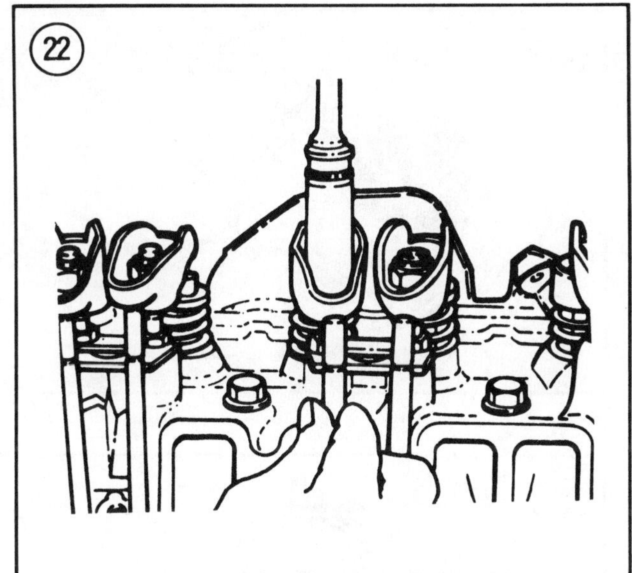

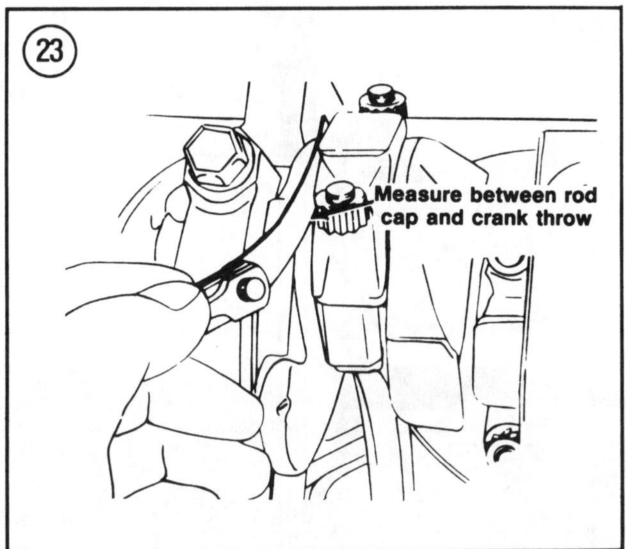

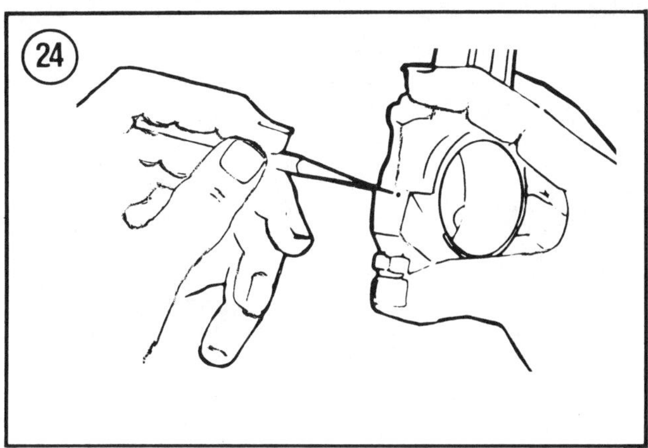

VALVE ADJUSTMENT

Valve lash adjustment is required only when the cylinder head or valve train has been disassembled. Adjust the valves with the lifter on the base circle of the camshaft lobe.

1. Rotate the crankshaft until the pulley notch aligns with the zero mark on the timing tab. This positions the No. 1 cylinder at TDC. This position can be verified by placing a finger on the No. 1 rocker arms as the pulley notch nears the zero mark. If the valves are moving, the engine is in the No. 4 firing position. Rotate the crankshaft pulley one full turn to reach the No. 1 firing position.
2. With the engine in the No. 1 firing position, adjust the No. 1, 2 and 3 exhaust valves and the No. 1, 5 and 6 intake valves. See **Figure 21**. Back off the adjusting nut until lash is felt at the pushrod, then turn the nut to remove all lash. When lash has been removed, the pushrod will not rotate (**Figure 22**). Turn the nut in another 1 1/2 turns to center the lifter plunger.
3. Rotate the crankshaft pulley one full turn to realign the pulley notch and the timing tab zero mark in the No. 4 firing position. Adjust the No. 4, 5, and 6 exhaust valves and the No. 2, 3 and 4 intake valves. See **Figure 21**.

5

PISTON/CONNECTING ROD ASSEMBLY

Piston/Connecting Rod Removal

1. Remove the cylinder head and oil pan as described in this chapter.
2. Rotate the crankshaft until one piston is at bottom dead center. Pack the cylinder bore with clean shop rags. Remove the carbon ridge at the top of the cylinder bores with a ridge reamer. These can be rented for use. Vacuum out the shavings, then remove the shop rags.
3. Rotate the crankshaft until one connecting rod is centered in the bore. Measure the clearance between the connecting rod and the crankshaft with a feeler gauge (**Figure 23**). If the clearance exceeds the specifications in **Table 1**, replace the connecting rod during reassembly. Repeat this step for all connecting rods.

NOTE

*Mark the cylinder number on the top of each piston with quick-drying paint. Check for cylinder numbers or identification marks on the connecting rod and cap. If they are not visible, make your own (**Figure 24**).*

4. Remove the nuts holding the connecting rod cap. Lift off the cap, together with the lower bearing insert.

NOTE
If the connecting rod caps are difficult to remove, tap the studs with a wooden hammer handle.

5. Use the wooden hammer handle to push the piston and connecting rod from the bore.
6. Remove the piston rings with a ring remover (**Figure 25**).

Piston Pin Removal/Installation

The piston pins are press-fitted to the connecting rods and hand-fitted to the pistons. Removal requires the use of a press and support stand. This is a job for a dealer or machine shop equipped to fit the pistons to the pins, ream the pin bushings to the correct diameter and install the pistons and pins on the connecting rods.

Piston Clearance Check

Unless you have precision measuring equipment and know how to use it properly, have this procedure done by a machine shop.

1. Measure the piston diameter with a micrometer (**Figure 26**). Measure just below the rings at a right angle to the piston pin bore.
2. Measure the cylinder bore diameter with a bore gauge (**Figure 27**). Measure at the top, center and bottom of the bore, in front-to-rear and side-to-side directions.
3. Subtract the piston diameter from the largest cylinder bore reading. If the clearance in any cylinder exceeds the specifications in **Table 1**, the cylinder must be rebored and an oversized piston installed.

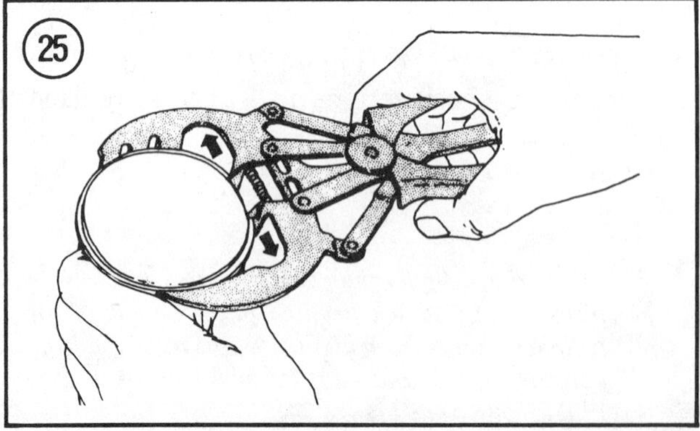

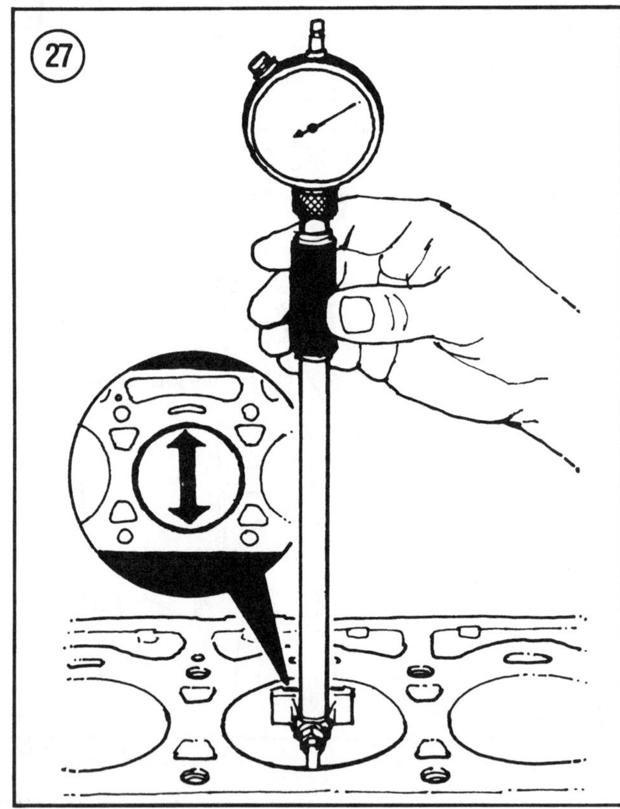

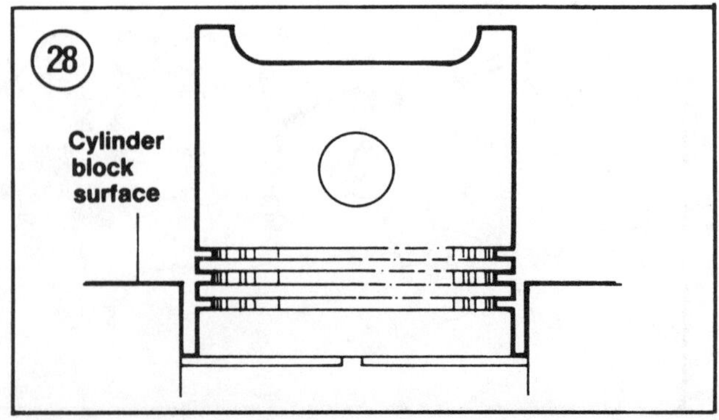

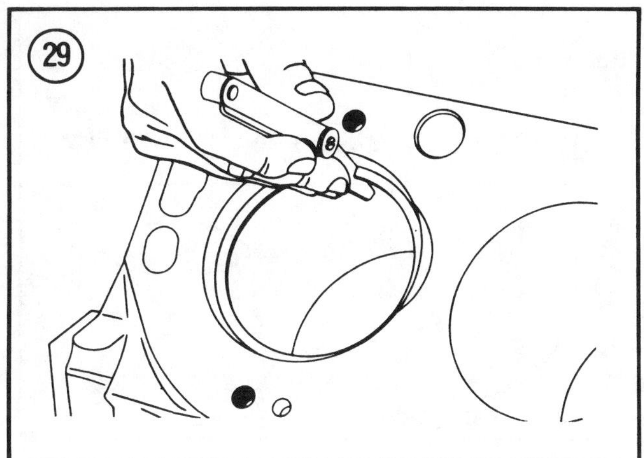

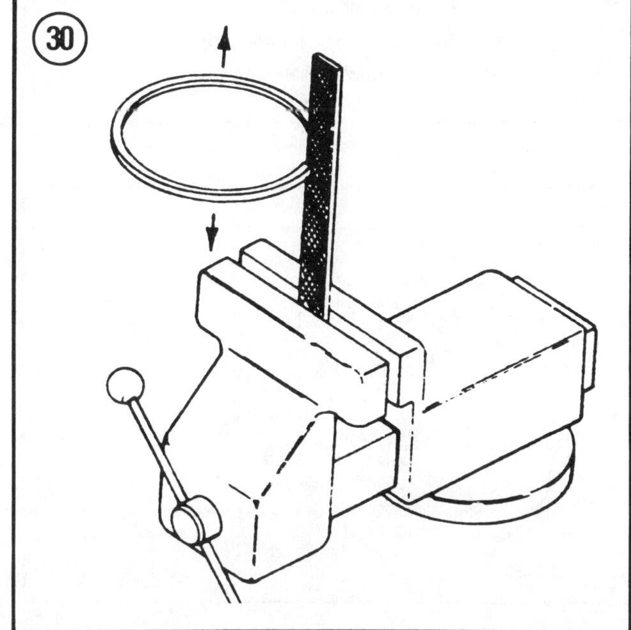

NOTE
Obtain the new piston and measure it to determine the correct cylinder bore oversize dimension.

Piston Ring Fit/Installation

1. Check the ring gap of each piston ring. To do this, position the ring at the bottom of the ring travel area and square it by tapping gently with an inverted piston. See **Figure 28**.

NOTE
If the cylinders have not been rebored, check the gap at the bottom of the ring travel, where the cylinder is least worn.

2. Measure the ring gap with a feeler gauge as shown in **Figure 29**. Compare with specifications in **Table 1**. If the measurement is not within specifications, the rings must be replaced as a set. Check gap of new rings as well. If the gap is too small, file the ends of the ring to correct it (**Figure 30**).
3. Check the side clearance of the rings as shown in **Figure 31**. Place the feeler gauge alongside the ring all the way into the groove. If the measurement is not within specifications (**Table 1**), either the rings or the ring grooves are worn. Inspect and replace as necessary.
4. Using a ring expander tool (**Figure 32**), carefully install the oil control ring, then the compression rings. Oil rings consist of 3 segments. The wavy segment goes between the flat segments to act as a spacer. Upper and lower flat segments are interchangeable. The second compression ring is tapered. The top of each compression ring is marked and must face up.

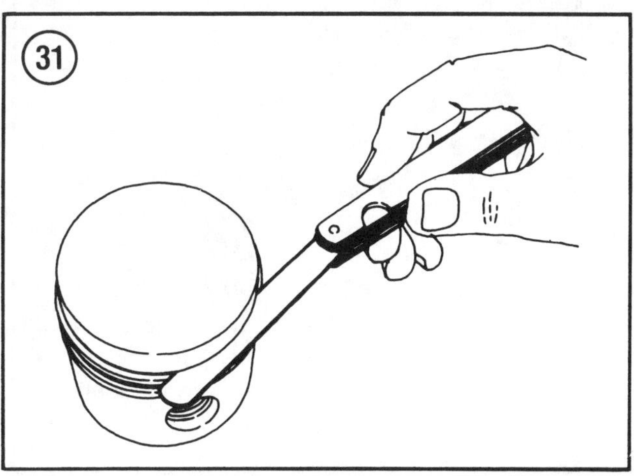

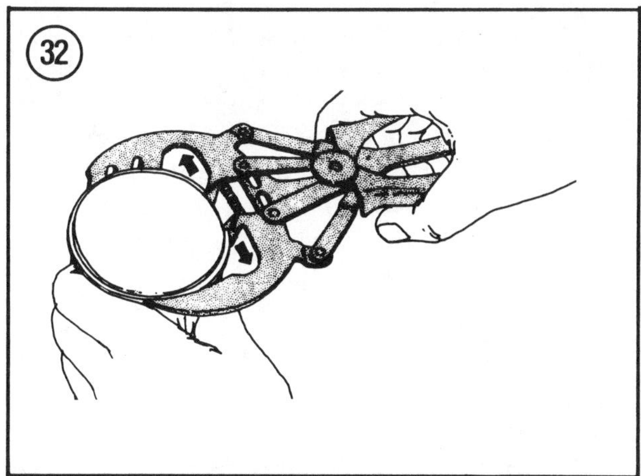

5. Position the ring gaps as shown in **Figure 33**.

Connecting Rod Inspection

Have the connecting rods checked for straightness by a dealer or a machine shop.

Connecting Rod Bearing Clearance Measurement

1. Place the connecting rods and upper bearing halves on the proper connecting rod journals.
2. Cut a piece of Plastigage the width of the bearing. Place the Plastigage on the journal, then install the lower bearing half and cap.

NOTE
Do not place Plastigage over the journal oil hole.

3. Tighten the connecting rod cap to specifications (**Table 2**). Do not rotate the crankshaft while the Plastigage is in place.
4. Remove the connecting rod caps. Bearing clearance is determined by comparing the width of the flattened Plastigage to the markings on the envelope (**Figure 34**). If the clearance is excessive, the crankshaft must be reground and undersize bearings installed.

Piston/Connecting Rod Installation

1. Make sure the pistons are correctly installed on the connecting rod. The machined hole or cast notch on the top of the piston (**Figure 35**) and the oil hole on the side of the connecting rod must both face the same way.
2. Make sure the ring gaps are positioned as shown in **Figure 33**.
3. Slip short pieces of hose over the connecting rod studs to keep them from nicking the crankshaft. Tape will work if you do not have the right diameter hose, but it is more difficult to remove.
4. Immerse the entire piston in clean engine oil. Coat the cylinder wall with oil.

CAUTION
Use extreme care in Step 5 to prevent the connecting rod from nicking the crankshaft journal.

5. Install the piston/connecting rod assembly in its cylinder with a piston installer tool as shown in

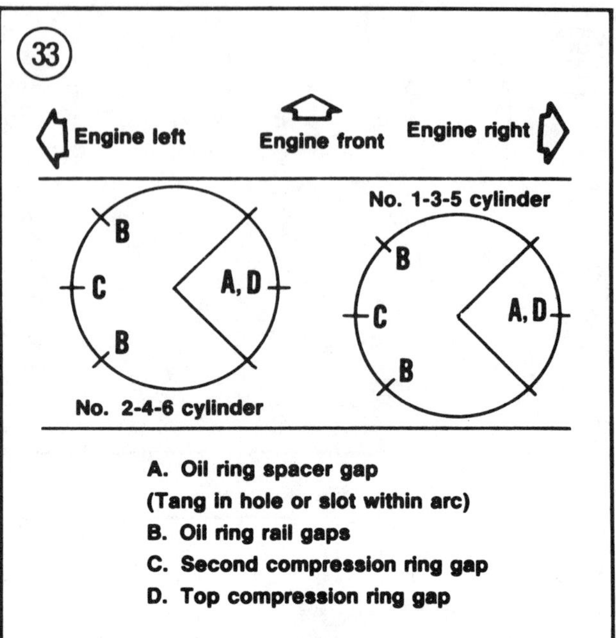

A. Oil ring spacer gap
(Tang in hole or slot within arc)
B. Oil ring rail gaps
C. Second compression ring gap
D. Top compression ring gap

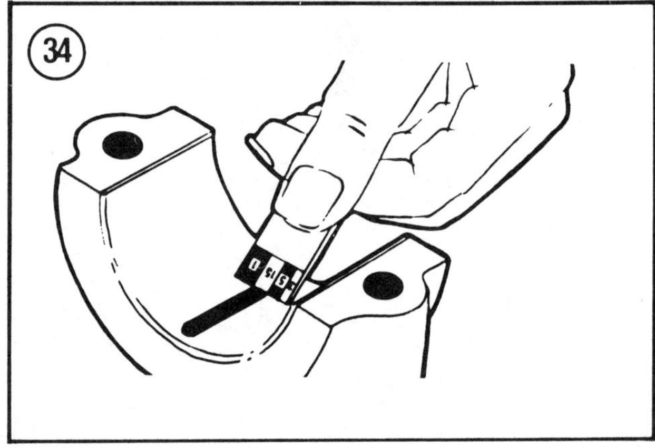

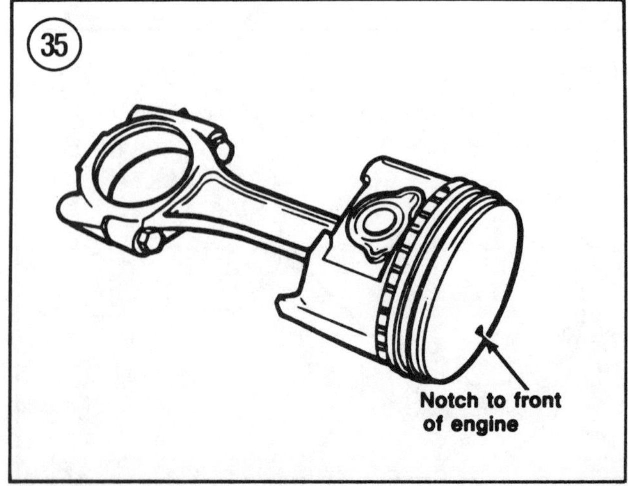

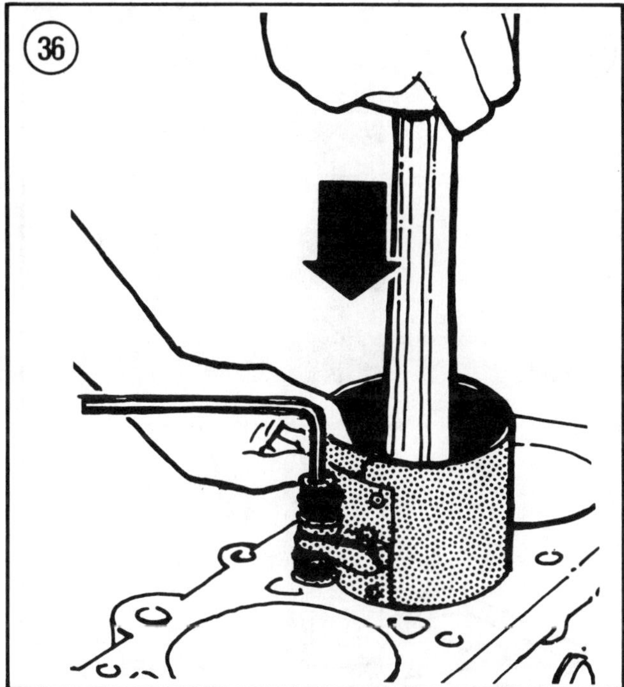

Figure 36. Tap lightly with a wooden hammer handle to insert the piston. Be sure the notch or hole at the top of the piston (**Figure 35**) faces toward the front of the engine. The piston number (painted on the top before removal) must correspond to the cylinder number, counting from the front of the engine.

6. Clean the connecting rod bearings carefully, including the back sides. Coat the journals and bearings with clean engine oil. Place the bearings in the connecting rod and cap.
7. Remove the protective hose or tape and install the connecting rod cap. Make sure the rod and cap marks align.
8. Lightly lubricate the connecting rod bolt threads with SAE 30W engine oil and install the rod caps.
9. Install the cap nuts finger-tight, then tighten the nuts to specifications (**Table 2**).
10. Check the connecting rod big-end play as described under *Piston/Connecting Rod Removal* in this chapter.

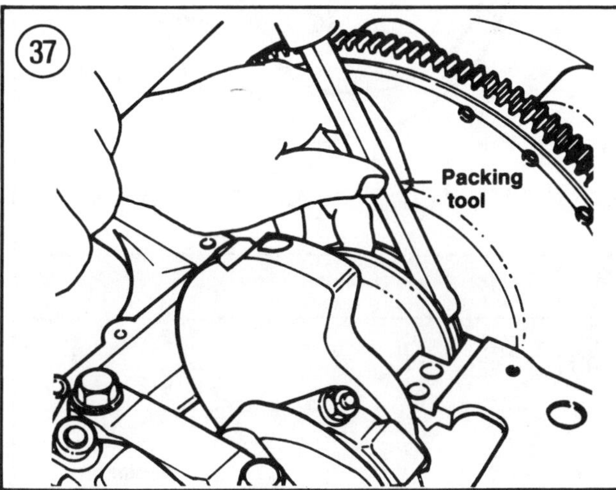

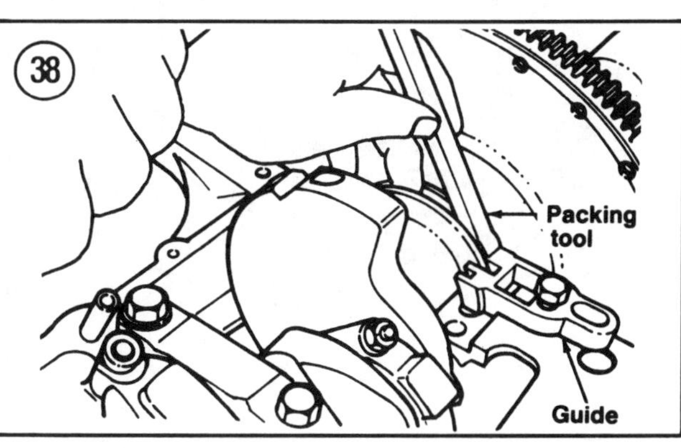

REAR MAIN OIL SEAL REMOVAL/INSTALLATION

A 2-piece rope type seal located under the rear main bearing cap is used on 1982-1984 engines. A 1-piece oil seal is used on 1985-on engines.

Rope Seal

This procedure requires the use of tools part No. J-29114-1, part No. J-29114-2 and part No. J-29590 for replacement.

1. Remove the engine from the vehicle as described in this chapter.
2. Remove the oil pan and oil pump as described in this chapter.
3. Unbolt and remove the rear main bearing cap.
4. Carefully drive the new upper seal into the block groove about 1/4 in. on both sides with tool part No. J-29114-2 (**Figure 37**).
5. Measure how far the seal was driven up on one side and add 1/16 in. to the distance. Carefully pry the old seal from the main bearing cap and cut that amount off it.
6. Repeat this step for the other side of the seal.
7. Install tool part No. J-29114-1 to the cylinder block (**Figure 38**). Use tool part No. J-29114-2 to

work the short pieces cut in Step 6 onto tool part No. J-29114-1. Oil the short pieces and pack into the block groove.

8. Install a new seal half in the main bearing cap. Position the seal with tool part No. J-29590, rotate the tool slightly and cut off each seal end flush with the block. See **Figure 39**.

9. Check rear main bearing clearance with Plastigage. See *Main Bearing Clearance Measurement* in this chapter.

10. Clean Plastigage from the journal and bearing. If bearing clearance is out of specifications, recheck seal ends for fraying and correct as required.

11. Apply a thin coat of anaerobic sealant to the rear bearing cap as shown in **Figure 40**. The sealant should not touch the seal or bearing.

12. Apply a thin coat of SAE 30W engine oil to the crankshaft surface that touches the seal.

13. Install the rear main bearing cap and tighten bolts to specifications (**Table 2**).

14. Install the oil pump and oil pan as described in this chapter.

15. Install the engine in the vehicle as described in this chapter.

One-piece Seal

The new seal comes attached to a disposable installation tool.

1. Remove the engine from the vehicle as described in this chapter.

2. Remove the oil pan and pump assembly.

3. Remove the crankshaft as described in this chapter.

4. Remove and discard the oil seal.

5. Clean all sealant residue from the cap, block and crankshaft seal area with solvent.

6. Coat the outer diameter of a new seal with a 0.04 in. (1 mm) bead of Loctite 515 sealer.

7. Install the seal installation tool on the rear of the crankshaft and align the tool so its arrow points as shown in **Figure 41**. Install crankshaft and tool in cylinder block. Align seal in case groove, then remove and discard the tool.

8. Lightly coat crankshaft journals with SAE 30W engine oil.

9. Apply a 0.08 in. (2 mm) bead of Loctite 515 sealer along the split-line surface (**Figure 40**) and install the rear main bearing cap with bearing insert. Install the remaining main bearing caps and tighten to specifications (**Table 2**).

10. Reverse Step 1 and Step 2 to complete the installation.

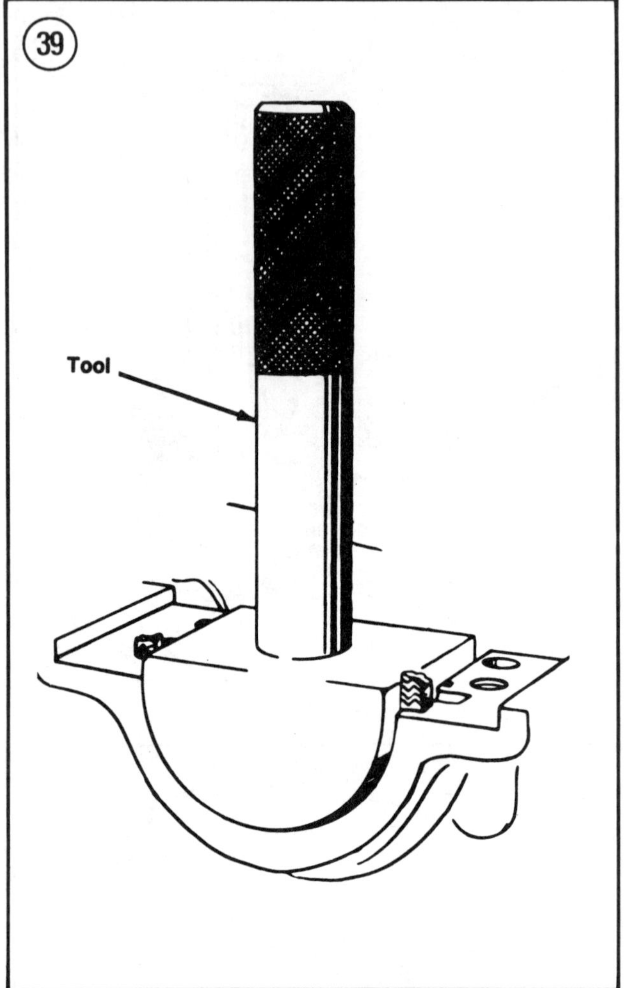

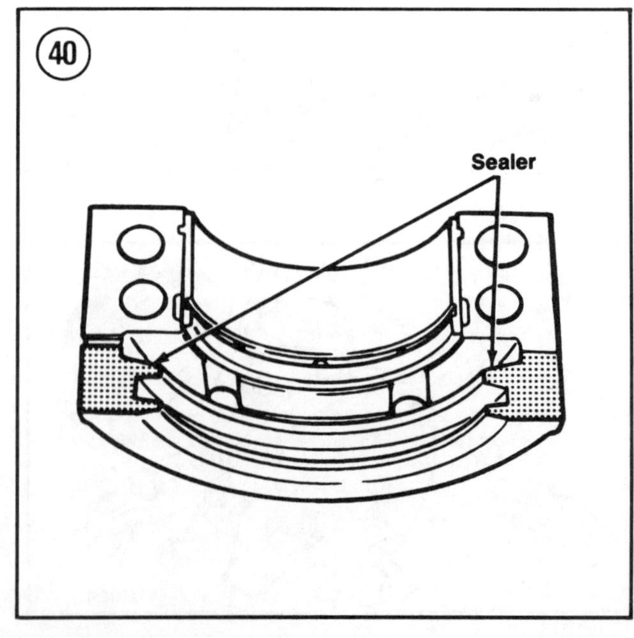

41

CAUTION: Retainer spring side of seal must face toward front of cylinder block.

42

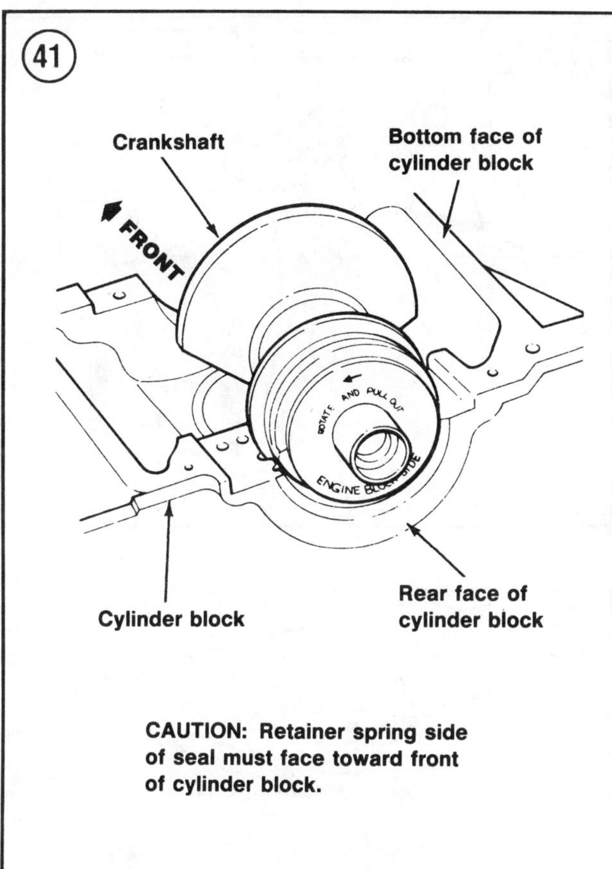

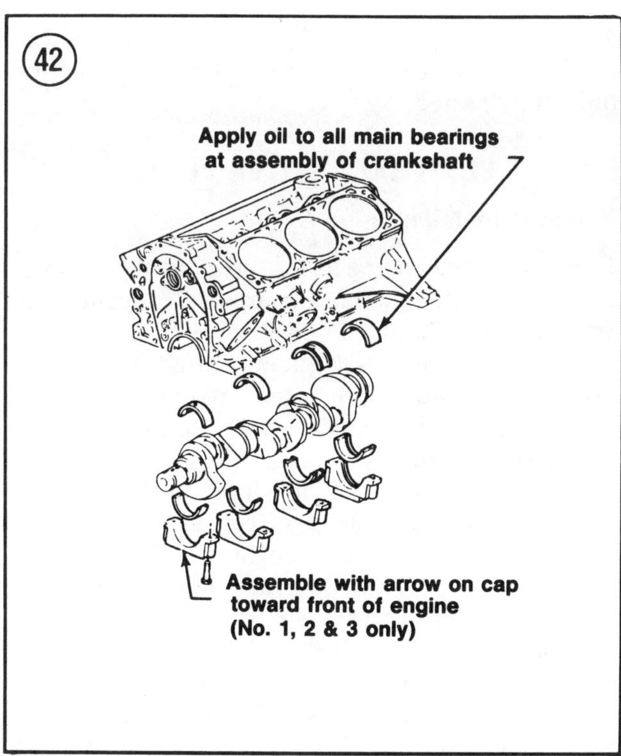

CRANKSHAFT

Removal

Refer to **Figure 42** for this procedure.

1. If it is necessary to remove the crankshaft sprocket, use puller part No. J-5825 or equivalent and install with tool part No. J-5590.
2. Remove the flywheel as described in this chapter.
3. Check the caps for identification numbers or marks. If none are visible, clean the caps with a wire brush. If marks still cannot be seen, make your own with quick-drying paint.
4. Unbolt and remove the main bearing caps and bearing inserts.

NOTE

If the caps are difficult to remove, lift the bolts partway out, then pry them from side to side.

5. Lift the crankshaft from the engine block and place it on a clean workbench.
6. Remove the bearing inserts from the block. Place the bearing caps and inserts in order on a clean workbench.

Inspection

1. Clean the crankshaft thoroughly with solvent. Blow out the oil passages with compressed air.

NOTE

If you do not have precision measuring equipment, have a machine shop perform Step 2.

2. Check the crankpins and main bearing journals for wear, scoring and cracks. Check all journals against specifications (**Table 1**) for out-of-roundness and taper. If necessary, have the crankshaft reground.

Main Bearing Clearance Measurement

Main bearing clearance is measured with Plastigage in the same manner as the connecting rod bearing clearance, described in this chapter. Excessive clearance requires that the bearings be replaced, the crankshaft be reground or both.

Installation

1. Install the main bearing inserts in the cylinder block. Bearing oil holes must align with block oil

holes and bearing tabs must seat in the block tab slots.

NOTE
Check cap bolts for thread damage before reuse. If damaged, replace the bolts.

2. Lubricate the bolt threads with SAE 30W engine oil.
3. Install the cap bearing shells.
4. Install the crankshaft in the block.
5. Install the bearing caps in their marked positions with the arrows pointing toward the front of the engine. See **Figure 42**.
6. Tighten all bolts finger-tight, then tighten all main bearing caps *except* the No. 3 main cap bolts to 70 ft.-lb. (95 N•m). Tighten the No. 3 main cap bolts to 11 ft.-lb. (15 N•m).
7. Tap crankshaft back and forth with a plastic mallet to align rear main bearing and crankshaft thrust surfaces. Retighten *all* cap bolts to 70 ft.-lb. (95 N•m).
8. Rotate the crankshaft to make sure it turns smoothly at the flywheel rim. If not, remove the bearing caps and crankshaft and check that the bearings are clean and properly installed.
9. Install the flywheel as described in this chapter.

End Play Measurement

1. Pry the crankshaft to the front of the engine with a large screwdriver.
2. Measure the crankshaft end play at the front of the No. 3 main bearing with a flat feeler gauge (**Figure 43**). Compare to specifications in **Table 1**.
3. If the end play is excessive, replace the No. 3 main bearing. If less than specified, check the bearing faces for imperfections.

Pilot Bearing

The pilot bearing is located inside the rear end of the crankshaft. It supports the transmission input shaft on manual transmission vehicles.
1. Check the bearing for visible wear or damage. Turn the bearing with a finger and make sure it turns easily. If wear, damage or stiff movement are found, remove the bearing with a puller. These are available from rental dealers.

CAUTION
Do not tap too hard during the next step or you will damage the bearing.

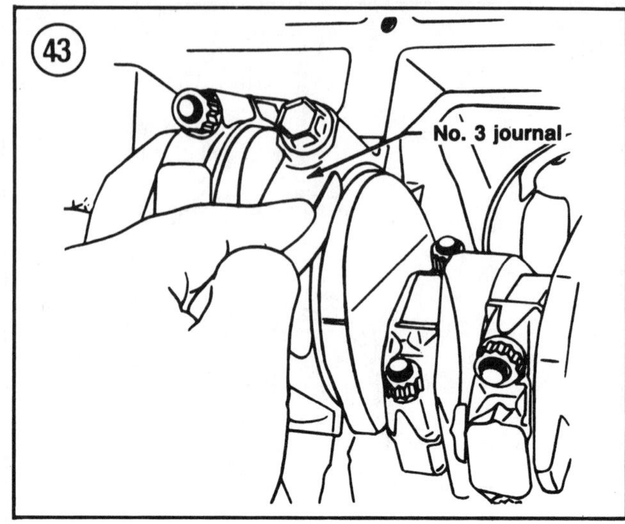

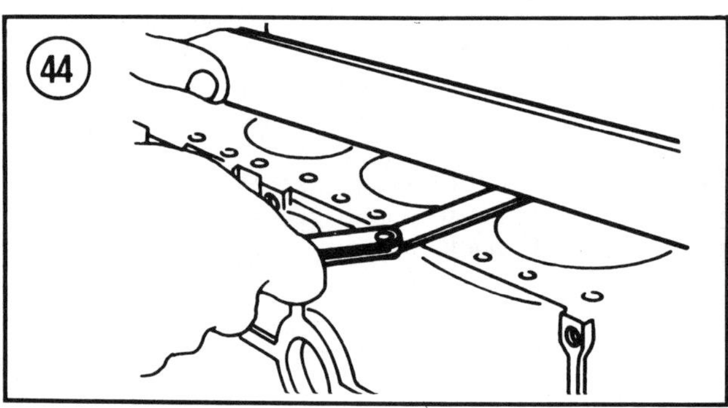

2. Tap a new bearing in place with a suitable drift until fully seated.

FLYWHEEL/DRIVE PLATE

Removal/Installation

1. Remove the engine as described in this chapter.
2. Remove the clutch on manual transmission vehicles. See Chapter Nine.
3. Unbolt the flywheel (manual transmission) or drive plate (automatic transmission) from the crankshaft. Remove the bolts gradually in a diagonal pattern.
4. Visually check the flywheel or drive plate surfaces for cracks, deep scoring, excessive wear, heat discoloration and checking. If the surface is glazed or slightly scratched, have the flywheel/drive plate resurfaced by a machine shop.
5. Inspect the ring gear for cracks, broken teeth or excessive wear. If severely worn, check the starter motor drive teeth for similar wear or damage. Replace as required.

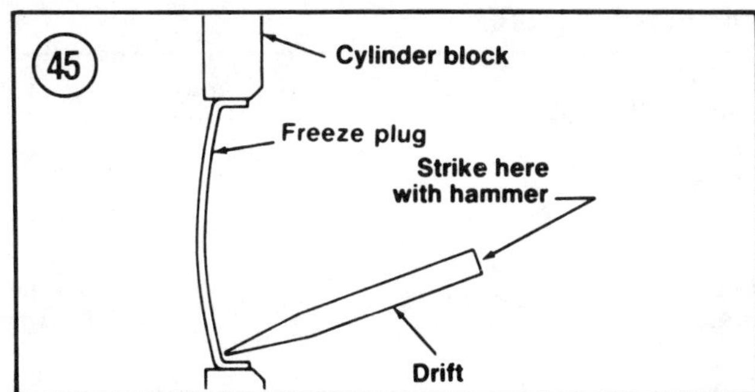

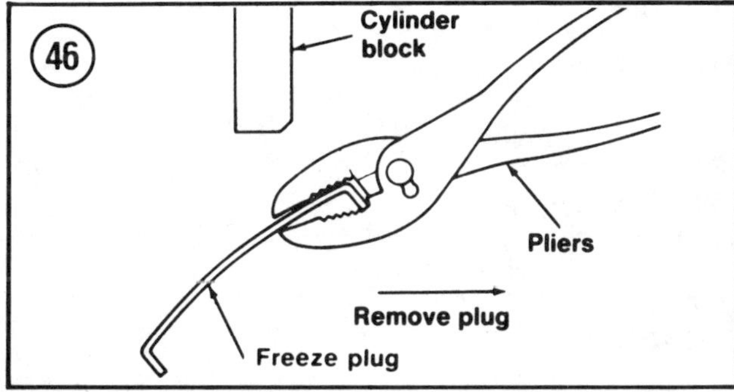

drive teeth for similar wear or damage. Replace as required.

6. Installation is the reverse of removal. Tighten bolts to specifications (**Table 2**) in a crisscross pattern. Wipe all oil, grease and other contamination from the flywheel surface before installing the clutch on manual transmission vehicles.

CYLINDER BLOCK

Cleaning and Inspection

1. Clean the block thoroughly with solvent. Remove any RTV sealant residue from the machined surfaces. Check all core plugs for leaks and replace any that are suspect. See *Core Plug Replacement* in this chapter. Remove any plugs that seal oil passages. Check oil and coolant passages for sludge, dirt and corrosion while cleaning. If the passages are very dirty, have the block boiled out by a machine shop. Blow out all passages with compressed air. Check the threads in the head bolt holes to be sure they are clean. If dirty, use a tap to true up the threads and remove any deposits.

2. Examine the block for cracks. To confirm suspicions about possible leak areas, use a mixture of 1 part kerosene and 2 parts engine oil. Coat the suspected area with this solution, then wipe dry and immediately apply a solution of zinc oxide dissolved in wood alcohol. If any discoloration appears in the treated area, the block is cracked and should be replaced.

3. Check flatness of the cylinder block deck or top surface. Place an accurate straightedge on the block. If there is any gap between the block and straightedge, measure it with a feeler gauge (**Figure 44**). Measure from end to end and from corner to corner. Have the block resurfaced if it is warped more than 0.0157 in. (0.4 mm). If it is warped more than this, replace the block.

4. Measure the cylinder bores with a bore gauge for out-of-roundness or excessive wear as described in Step 2, *Piston Clearance Check* in this chapter. If the cylinders exceed maximum tolerances, they must be rebored. Reboring is also necessary if the cylinder walls are badly scuffed or scored.

NOTE
*Before boring, install all main bearing caps and tighten the cap bolts to specifications in **Table 2.***

CORE PLUG REPLACEMENT

The condition of all core plugs in the block should be checked whenever the engine is out of the vehicle for service. If any signs of leakage or corrosion are found around one core plug, replace them all.

Removal/Installation

CAUTION
Do not drive core plugs into the engine casting. It will be impossible to retrieve them and they can restrict coolant circulation, resulting in serious engine damage.

1. Tap the bottom edge of the core plug with a hammer and drift. Use several sharp blows to push the bottom of the plug inward, tilting the top out (**Figure 45**).
2. Grip the top of the plug firmly with pliers. Pull the plug from its bore (**Figure 46**) and discard.
3. Clean the plug bore thoroughly to remove all traces of the old sealer.
4. Apply a light coat of Loctite Stud N' Bearing Mount or equivalent to the plug bore.
5. Install the new core plug with an appropriate size driver or socket. The sharp edge of the plug should be at least 0.02 in. (0.5 mm) inside the lead-in chamfer.
6. Repeat Steps 1-5 to replace each remaining core plug.

Table 1 V6 ENGINE SPECIFICATIONS

Type	60° V6
Displacement	2.8 liter (173 cid)
Bore	89 mm
Stroke	76 mm
Cylinder arrangement (front to rear)	
Right bank	1-3-5
Left bank	2-4-6
Firing order	1-2-3-4-5-6
Cylinder bore	
Diameter	88.992-89.070 mm
Out-of-round	0.02 mm max.
Taper (thrust side)	0.02 mm max.
Piston	
Clearance to cylinder	0.043-0.069 mm
Piston rings	
Ring groove clearance	
Top	0.030-0.070 mm
2nd	0.040-0.095 mm
Oil	0.199 mm max.
Ring gap	
Compression	0.25-0.50 mm
Oil	0.51-1.40 mm
Piston pin	
Diameter	22.9937-23.0015 mm
Clearance	0.0065-0.0091 mm
Fit in rod	0.0187-0.515 mm (press-fit)
Camshaft	
Lift	
Intake	5.87 mm
Exhaust	6.67 mm
Journal diameter	47.44-47.49 mm
Journal clearance	0.026-0.101 mm
Crankshaft	
Main journal	
Diameter	63.340-63.364 mm
Taper	0.005 mm max.
Out-of-round	0.005 mm max.
Main bearing clearance	0.044-0.076 mm
End play	0.05-0.17 mm
Crankpin	
Diameter	50.758-50.784 mm
Taper	0.005 mm max.
Out-of-round	0.005 mm max.
Connecting rod	
Bearing clearance	0.036-0.091 mm
Side clearance	0.16-0.44 mm
Valve system	
Lifter	Hydraulic (no adjustment needed)
Rocker arm ratio	1.5:1
Valve lash	1 1/2 turns from zero lash
Face angle	45°
Seat angle	46°
Seat runout	0.05 mm

(continued)

Table 1 V6 ENGINE SPECIFICATIONS (continued)

Valve system (cont'd)	
Seat width	
Intake	1.25-1.50 mm
Exhaust	1.60-1.90 mm
Stem clearance	0.026-0.068 mm
Valve spring	
Free length	48.5 mm
Load	
Intake and exhaust	
Closed	391 N @ 40 mm
Open	867 N @ 30 mm
Installed height	40 mm
Valve damper	
Free length	47.2 mm
Approximate number of coils	4

Table 2 V6 TIGHTENING TORQUES

Fastener	ft.-lb.	N•m
Air conditioning compressor		
Bracket-to-cylinder head	30-40	40-54
To bracket	20-30	27-40
Alternator		
Adjustment bolt	20-30	27-40
Bracket-to-cylinder head	30-40	40-54
Pivot bolt	20-30	27-40
Camshaft		
Cover	6-9	8-12
Sprocket	15-20	15-27
Clutch cover-to-flywheel	13-18	18-24
Connecting rod cap		
1982-1983	34-40	46-54
1984-on	34-44	46-60
Crankshaft		
Balancer	48-55	65-75
Pulley	20-30	27-40
Pulley hub	66-84	90-115
Cylinder head		
1982-1983	65-75	88-102
1984-on	55-77	74-108
Distributor hold-down bolt	20-30	27-40
Engine mount		
Bracket-to-block	30-40	40-54
Through bolt	53-66	72-90
To frame	35-48	48-65
Torque strut bracket	30-40	40-54
Exhaust manifold		
Bolt	20-30	27-40
Stud	24-35	32-48
Flex plate-to-torque converter	25-35	34-47
Flywheel	45-59	61-80

(continued)

Table 2 V6 TIGHTENING TORQUES (continued)

Fastener	ft.-lb.	N•m
Front cover		
1982-1983		
M8×1.25	13-18	18-24
M10×1.5	20-30	40-54
1984-on		
Bolt	13-22	18-30
Stud	24-35	32-48
Fuel pump	13-18	18-24
Intake manifold		
1982-1983	20-25	27-34
1984-on	13-25	18-34
Main bearing cap		
1982-1983	63-74	85-100
1984-on	63-83	85-112
Oil dipstick tube		
1982-1983	20-30	27-40
1984-on	13-18	18-24
Oil filter adapter	24-34	32-46
Oil pan		
Attaching bolts		
1982-1983		
M6×1.0	6-9	8-12
M8×1.25	14-22	19-30
1984-on		
M6×1.0	6-12	8-16
M8×1.25	14-26	19-35
Oil pressure switch	4-5	5-7
Oil pump		
Attaching screws	26-35	35-47
Cover	6-9	8-12
Rear lifting bracket	20-30	27-40
Rocker arm cover		
1982-1983	6-9	8-12
1984-on	6-12	8-16
Rocker arm stud		
1982-1983	43-49	58-66
1984-on	43-53	58-72
Timing chain tensioner	13-18	18-24
Water outlet (thermostat housing)	20-30	27-40
Water pump		
1982-1983		
M6×1.0	6-9	8-12
M8×1.25	13-18	18-24
M10×1.5	20-30	27-40
1984-on		
M6×1.0	6-9	8-12
M8×1.25	13-18	18-24
Nut	6-9	8-12
Water pump pulley	13-18	18-24

CHAPTER SIX

FUEL, EXHAUST AND EMISSION CONTROL SYSTEMS

This chapter consists of service procedures for the air cleaner, carburetor, throttle body, fuel pump, fuel tank and lines, fuel-related emission controls and exhaust system. Tightening torques are provided in **Table 1** at the end of the chapter.

THERMOSTATICALLY CONTROLLED (THERMAC) AIR CLEANER

A dry air cleaner containing a replaceable air filter element is standard on all engines. The filter element can be changed without removing the air cleaner housing from the engine. Many air cleaners also contain a replaceable crankcase ventilation filter element.

The air cleaner is attached to the top of the carburetor or throttle body. Various sensors, switches and a vacuum-operated control valve or door in the air cleaner snorkel control intake air temperature.

The air cleaner furnishes temperature-regulated air to the carburetor or throttle body to reduce emissions and improve driveability. The air cleaner snorkel is connected to a fresh air inlet hose and to a hot air hose/heat stove assembly surrounding the intake manifold. Air flow from these 2 sources is controlled by a valve in the snorkel. This valve is operated by a vacuum motor mounted on the snorkel. The door and motor are connected by mechanical linkage inside the snorkel. A temperature sensor inside the air cleaner housing modulates vacuum to the motor according to air cleaner air temperature. **Figure 1** shows the major components of the air cleaner system used on all engines.

When the engine is first started, the air cleaner draws hot air from near the exhaust manifold through the hot air hose (A, **Figure 2**). As the engine warms up, the control valve changes position to partially block off air from the hot air hose (B, **Figure 2**). Once the air cleaner temperature reaches a specified value, the control valve closes off the hot air hose completely. This allows the air cleaner to draw intake air through the snorkel from the fresh air inlet duct (C, **Figure 2**).

During periods of high engine compartment temperature, a hot idle compensator in the air cleaner opens to route air into the intake manifold. This prevents an excessively rich mixture that could result in a rough idle and high emissions.

1

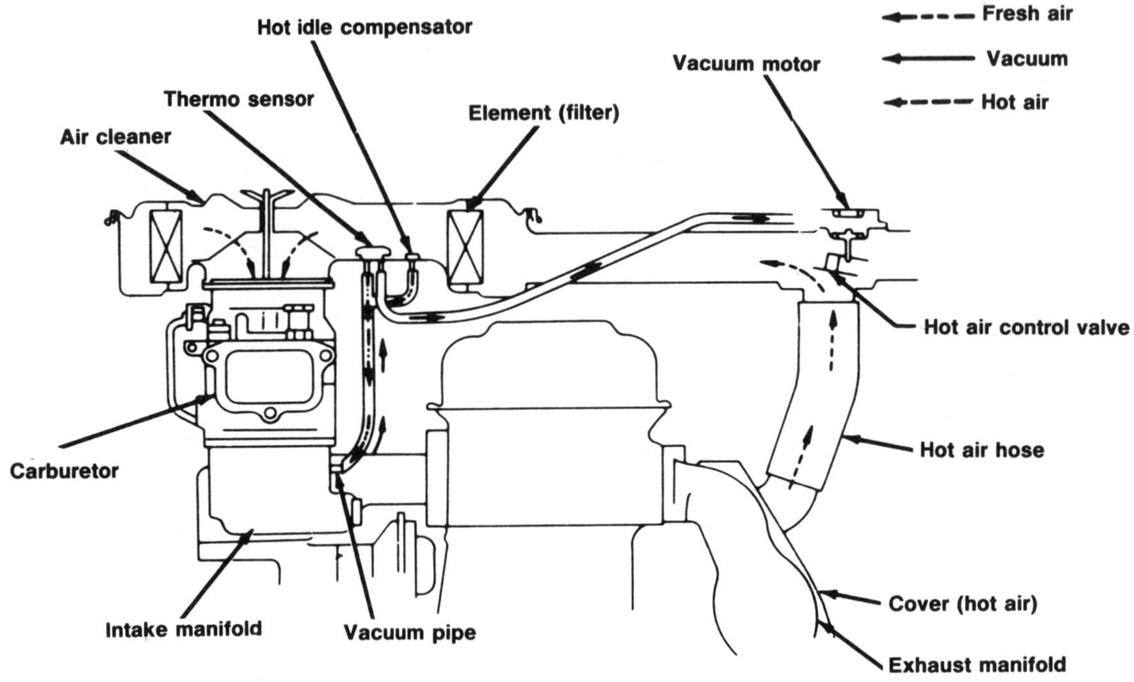

Fresh air
Vacuum
Hot air
Hot idle compensator
Vacuum motor
Thermo sensor
Element (filter)
Air cleaner
Hot air control valve
Carburetor
Hot air hose
Cover (hot air)
Intake manifold
Vacuum pipe
Exhaust manifold

Filter Replacement

Remove the air cleaner cover wing nut(s). Remove the cover and lift out the old filter. See **Figure 3** (typical). Wipe the inside of the air cleaner housing with a damp paper towel to remove dust, dirt and debris. Install a new filter. Reinstall the cover and tighten the wing nut(s) snugly.

Air Cleaner Removal/Installation

NOTE
Leave the filter element inside the air cleaner housing during removal. This will prevent dirt and debris from dropping into the carburetor

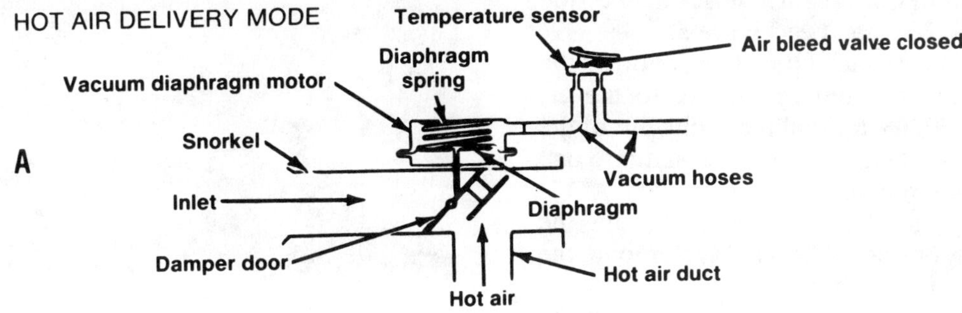
HOT AIR DELIVERY MODE
A
Temperature sensor
Air bleed valve closed
Diaphragm
spring
Vacuum diaphragm motor
Snorkel
Vacuum hoses
Inlet
Diaphragm
Damper door
Hot air duct
Hot air

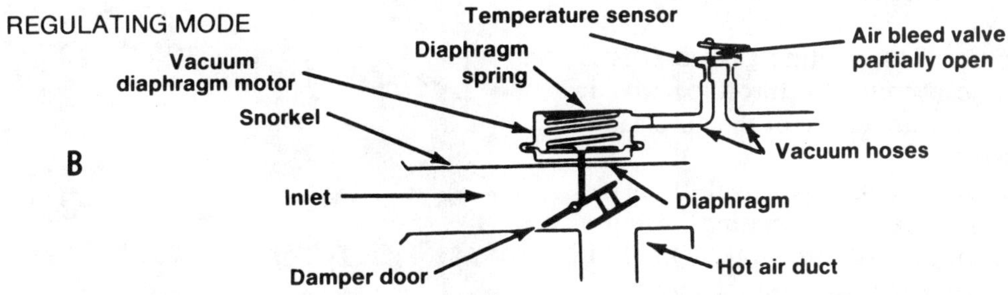
REGULATING MODE
B
Temperature sensor
Air bleed valve
partially open
Diaphragm
spring
Vacuum
diaphragm motor
Snorkel
Vacuum hoses
Inlet
Diaphragm
Damper door
Hot air duct

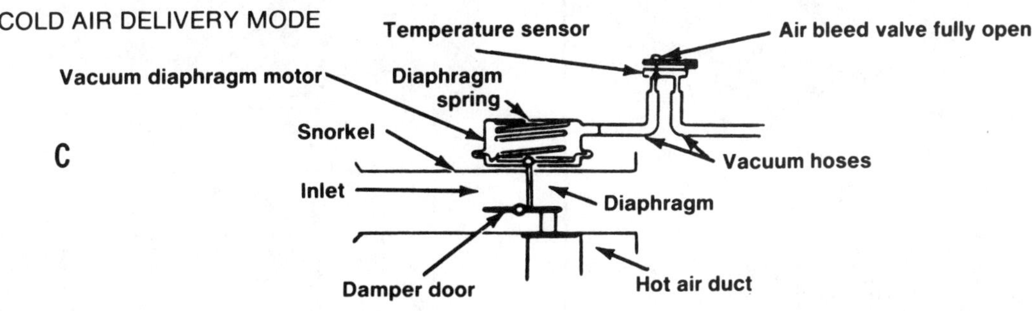
COLD AIR DELIVERY MODE
C
Temperature sensor
Air bleed valve fully open
Vacuum diaphragm motor
Diaphragm
spring
Snorkel
Vacuum hoses
Inlet
Diaphragm
Damper door
Hot air duct

6

Refer to **Figure 4** (typical) for this procedure.

1. Unscrew and remove the air cleaner cover wing nut(s).
2. Unsnap the intake duct clamp and remove the duct hose from the air cleaner snorkel.
3. Disconnect the hot air hose at the manifold heat stove.
4. Disconnect the PCV breather hoses at the side of the air cleaner housing. See **Figure 5**.
5. Remove the air cleaner filter, then remove the clamp holding the vacuum line fitting to the air cleaner housing (**Figure 6**). Pull the fitting out of the housing and reinstall the filter. Set the clamp to one side with the wing nut(s).
6. 4-cylinder engine—Remove the bolt from the snorkel support bracket (**Figure 7**). Remove the housing support bracket bolt.
7. Tilt the air cleaner housing and disconnect the line from the temperature sensor nipple on the underside (A, **Figure 8**). Disconnect any other lines connected to the housing.
8. Remove the air cleaner assembly and place it on a clean flat surface.
9. Check the air cleaner mounting gasket. If it is not found on the carburetor or throttle body, it may be attached to the underside of the air cleaner housing (B, **Figure 8**).
10. Installation is the reverse of removal. If the old mounting gasket is damaged or missing, install a new one to prevent a vacuum leak. On 1.9L engines, align the stamped arrows on the cover and housing. Install and tighten the wing nut(s) securely.

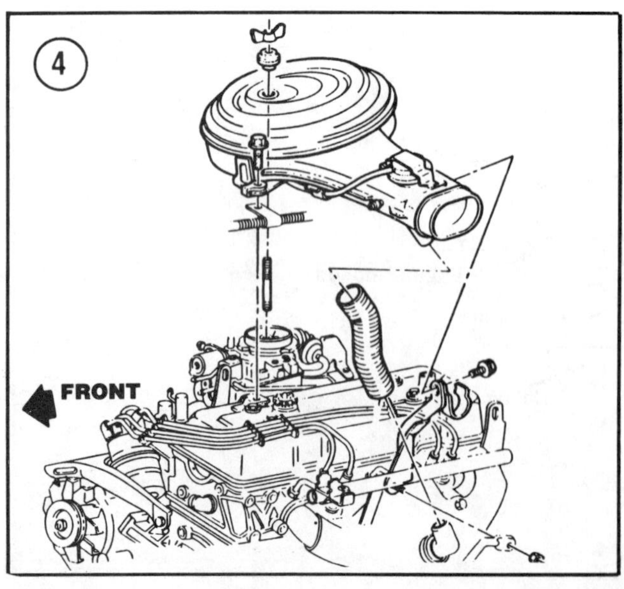

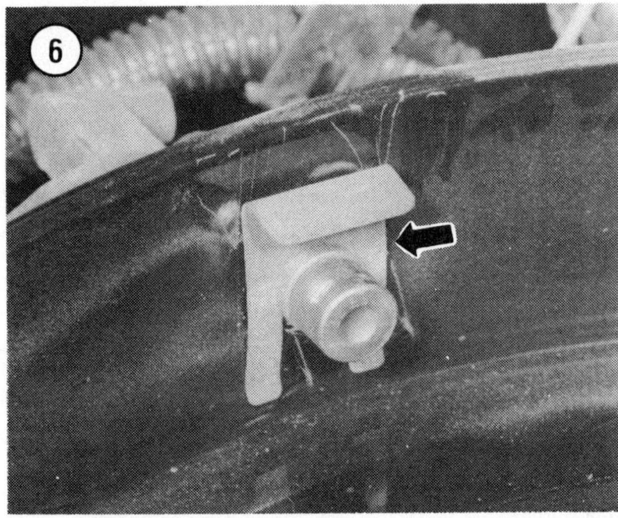

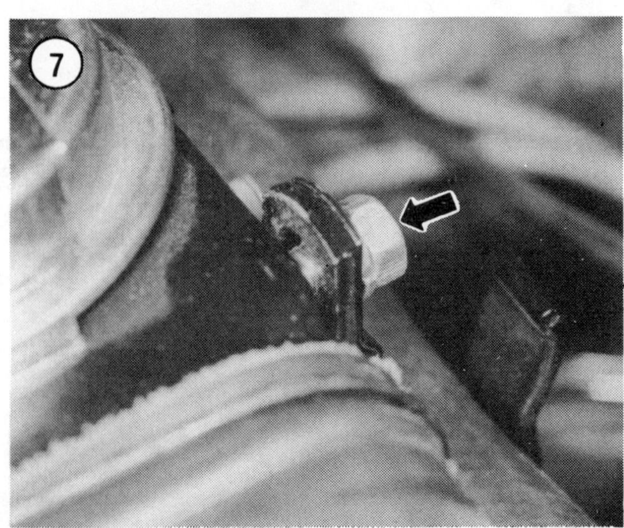

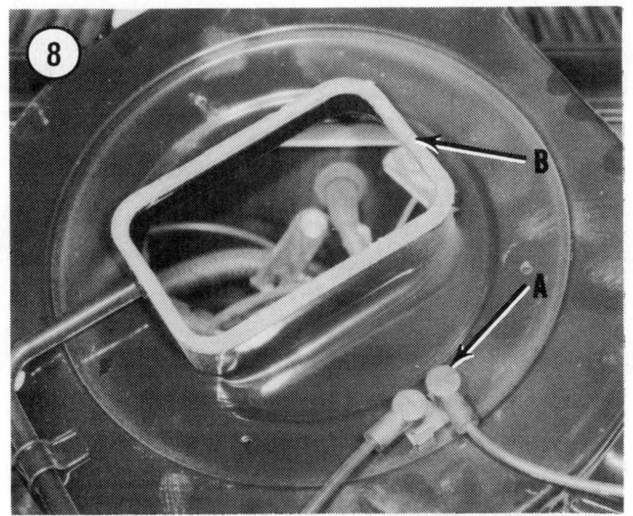

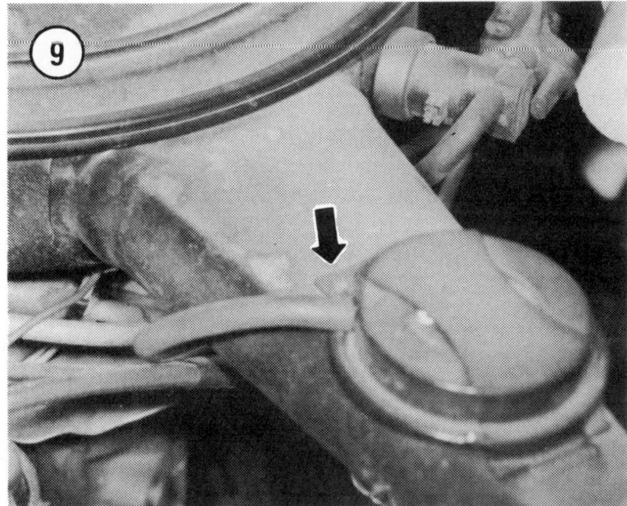

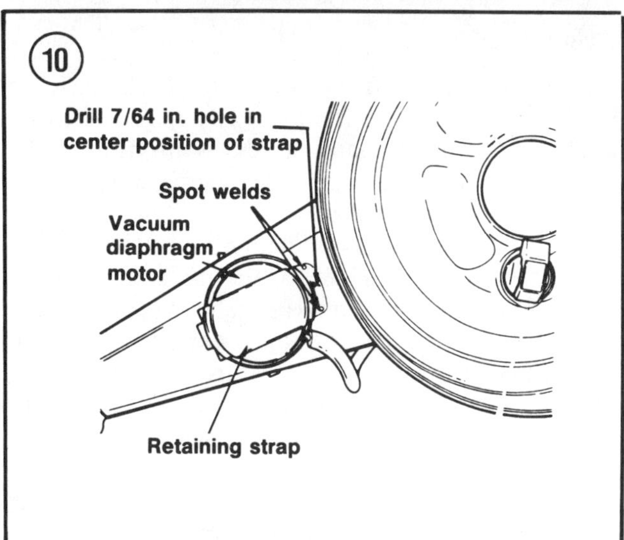

Control Valve Function Test

1. Unsnap the intake duct clamp and disconnect the duct hose from the air cleaner snorkel.
2. Disconnect the vacuum line at the vacuum motor (**Figure 9**). Connect a hand vacuum pump to the motor nipple.
3. Apply at least 7 in. Hg vacuum. The control valve should move to block off the snorkel passage completely.
4. Bend the vacuum pump hose to trap the vacuum. The control valve should remain closed. If it does not, check for binding linkage between the vacuum motor and valve.
5. If the linkage is not corroded and does not bind, replace the vacuum motor assembly.

Vacuum Motor Replacement

1. Remove the air cleaner from the engine as described in this chapter.
2. Place the air cleaner on a clean flat surface. Remove the cover and filter element.
3. Disconnect the vacuum line at the vacuum motor.

NOTE
Support the air cleaner housing and snorkel in Step 4 to prevent damage to the snorkel during drilling.

4. Drill the 2 spot welds holding the motor retaining strap (**Figure 10**) with a 1/16 in. drill bit. Enlarge the drill hole as required to remove the retaining strap.
5. Lift the vacuum motor up and tilt it as necessary to unhook the linkage from the control valve. Remove the motor.
6. Drill a 7/64 in. hole in the snorkel at the center of the retaining strap.
7. Install the new vacuum motor, tilting it to connect the linkage to the control valve.
8. Install the new retaining strap with the sheet metal screw provided with the new motor.

NOTE
Make sure the sheet metal screw does not interfere with control valve operation when installed. If it does, cut off the end of the screw.

9. Reconnect the vacuum motor line. Install the filter element and air cleaner cover.
10. Install the air cleaner on the engine as described in this chapter.

Air Cleaner Sensor Operational Check

NOTE
Perform this procedure with the engine off and cold.

1. Set the parking brake and block the rear wheels.
2. Unscrew and remove the air cleaner cover wing nut(s). Remove the cover and filter element.
3. Check the hot air and intake duct hoses for cracks or other damage. Repair or replace as necessary.
4. Disconnect the intake duct hose from the snorkel. Lift the air cleaner housing up enough to see into the snorkel.
5. Look inside the snorkel. The control valve should be in the open or full fresh air position (C, **Figure 2**).
6. Depress the control valve with one finger and check for binding or sticking.
7. Tape a candy thermometer as close as possible to the temperature sensor (**Figure 11**) on the air inlet side of the sensor. Install the air cleaner cover without the wing nut(s).
8. Start the engine. The control valve should move to the closed or full heat position (A, **Figure 2**). If it does not, shut off the engine, cool the temperature sensor with an ice pack and retest. If the valve still does not close, check the vacuum lines for leakage.

NOTE
Some temperature sensors incorporate a check valve in the vacuum line between the sensor and vacuum motor to delay control valve opening. The lower the temperature, the longer the delay.

9. If the control valve moves to the closed or full heat position, let the engine run for 5 minutes. Watch the control valve. When it starts to open, remove the air cleaner cover and note the thermometer reading. It should be approximately 111° F (44° C).
10. If the door does not move, remove the air cleaner cover and read the temperature. If the temperature is above 100° F (38° C), the sensor is defective.
11. A temperature of less than 100° F (38° C) is not sufficient to operate the valve. Install the air cleaner cover and let the engine continue to run. If the control valve still has not moved with the temperature above 100° F (38° C), replace the sensor.

Sensor Replacement

1. Remove the air cleaner as described in this chapter.
2. Disconnect the 2 vacuum lines at the sensor (A, **Figure 8**).
3. Pry open the sensor retaining clip tabs (**Figure 12**). Note the positioning of the old sensor and remove it from the air cleaner housing.
4. Install a new sensor in the same relative position. Press down on the sensor edges and install the retaining clip on the hose connectors.
5. Reconnect the 2 vacuum lines to the sensor nipples from which they were removed.
6. Reinstall the air cleaner as described in this chapter.

FUEL QUALITY

Gasoline

Gasoline blended with alcohol is widely available, although it is not legally required to be labeled as such in many states. A mixture of 10 percent ethyl alcohol and 90 percent unleaded gasoline is called gasohol.

Fuels with an alcohol content tend to absorb moisture from the air. When the moisture content of the fuel reaches approximately one percent, it combines with the alcohol and separates from the fuel. This water-alcohol mixture settles at the bottom of the fuel tank where the fuel pickup carries it into the fuel line to the carburetor or fuel injectors.

The greatest problem with gasohol is its cleaning effect on service station storage tanks, as well as the

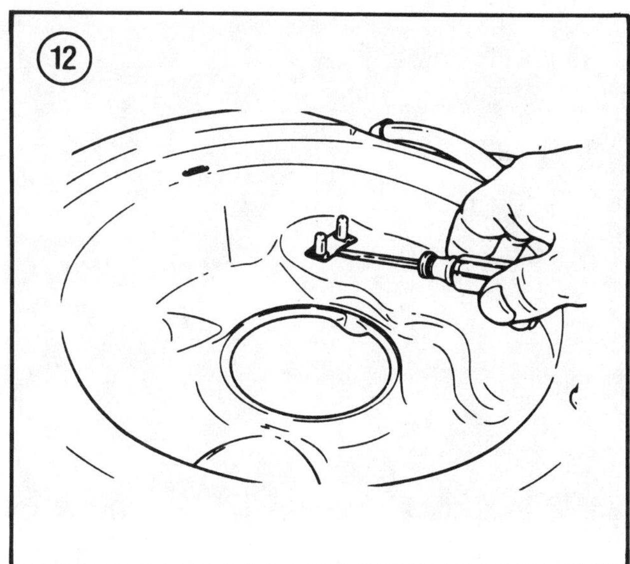

vehicle's fuel tank. As a result of this cleaning action, a combination of rust, a jelly-like sludge and metallic particles pass into the automotive fuel system. These substances cause reduced fuel flow through the filter and will eventually plug the carburetor or injector passageways.

Some methods of blending alcohol with gasoline now make use of "cosolvents" as a suspension agent to prevent the water-alcohol from separating from the gasoline. Regardless of the method used, however, alcohol mixed with gasoline in any manner can cause numerous and serious problems with an automotive fuel system, including:

a. Corrosion formation on the inside of fuel tanks, steel fuel lines, fuel pumps, carburetors and fuel injectors.
b. Deterioration of the plastic liner used in some fuel tanks, resulting in eventual plugging of the in-tank filter.
c. Deterioration and failure of synthetic rubber or plastic materials such as O-ring seals, diaphragms, inlet needle tips, accelerator pump cups and gaskets.
d. Premature failure of fuel line hoses.
e. Hot weather driveability problems.

The problem of gasoline blended with alcohol has become so prevalent around the United States that Miller Tools (32615 Park Lane, Garden City, MI 48135) and Kent-Moore (28635 Mound Road, Warren, MI 48092) now offer alcohol detection kits (Miller part No. C-4846; Kent-Moore part No. J-34353) so that owners can determine the quality of fuel being used.

The detection procedure is performed with water as a reacting agent. However, if cosolvents have been used as a suspension agent in alcohol blending, the test will not show the presence of alcohol unless glycol (automotive antifreeze) is used instead of water as a reacting agent. It is suggested that a gasoline sample be tested twice using the detection kit: first with water and then with ethylene glycol (automotive antifreeze).

The procedure cannot differentiate between types of alcohol (ethanol, methanol, etc.) nor is it considered to be absolutely accurate from a scientific standpoint, but it is accurate enough to determine whether or not there is enough alcohol in the fuel to cause the user to take precautions. Maintaining a close watch on the quality of fuel used can save hundreds of dollars in engine and fuel system repairs.

Diesel Fuel

Use only No. 2 diesel fuel when the ambient temperature is above 20° F. Use only winterized No. 2 diesel or No. 1 diesel fuel when the temperature is below 20° F. Never use any other diesel fuels and/or fuel additives.

Do not use ether or similar starting fluids in the diesel engine. The glow plugs may ignite the fluid and cause serious engine damage or personal injury.

Do not use diesel fuel which has been stored in a galvanized container. The zinc in the metal plating will be dissolved by the fuel and can cause serious damage if it gets into the injection pump or nozzles.

CARBURETOR

The 1.9L engine uses a Hitachi DCH 340 or DFP 340 2-barrel downdraft carburetor. The 2.0L and 1982-1985 2.8L engines use a Rochester 2SE (Federal) or E2SE (Computer Command Control) carburetor. Both Rochester models are 2-barrel, 2-stage downdraft carburetors.

The E2SE carburetor uses an electrically operated mixture control solenoid (MCS) which is mounted on the air horn. This solenoid extends into the carburetor float bowl and controls air and fuel metered to the idle and main metering systems upon command from the electronic control module (ECM). The ECM evaluates data from several sensors and cycles the solenoid plunger 10 times per second to control the air-fuel mixture for maximum performance and economy and minimum emissions.

A throttle position sensor (TPS) mounted on the carburetor signals the ECM whenever changes occur in the throttle position. The ECM holds the last-known air-fuel mixture ratio during throttle position changes.

An idle speed solenoid controls the carburetor idle speed on command from the ECM. Since the curb idle speed is programmed into the ECM, idle speed is automatic and cannot be adjusted.

NOTE
Do not attempt to adjust idle speed on the E2SE carburetor by adjusting the idle speed control screw.

A dual vacuum break system is used to control choke operation. The vacuum break adjustment screw is capped to prevent owner adjustment on carburetors manufactured prior to April 1, 1981.

The vacuum break rods are a non-bendable design and the choke cap is riveted to the housing. These tamper-resistant features are designed to prevent changes in the factory-adjusted choke setting.

The lean mixture screw in the float bowl requires the use of a special tool to turn it. The idle mixture screw in the throttle body and the TPS adjustment screw in the air horn are both recessed and sealed with a metal plug to prevent unauthorized changes in the factory adjustment.

WARNING
Tampering with the carburetor is a violation of Federal law. Choke, idle mixture and other sealed adjustments can legally be made only under specified circumstances. Adjustment of these systems should be left to a Chevrolet or GMC dealer.

Removal and installation procedures are provided for all carburetors. Carburetor specifications vary with model year and engine/transmission application. In some cases, specifications will differ depending upon whether the engine is a Federal (49-state), California or high altitude model. The necessary specifications are provided on instruction sheets accompanying overhaul kits, along with specific procedures required for proper adjustment. Such instruction sheets also incorporate any late changes authorized by the factory in adjustment specifications.

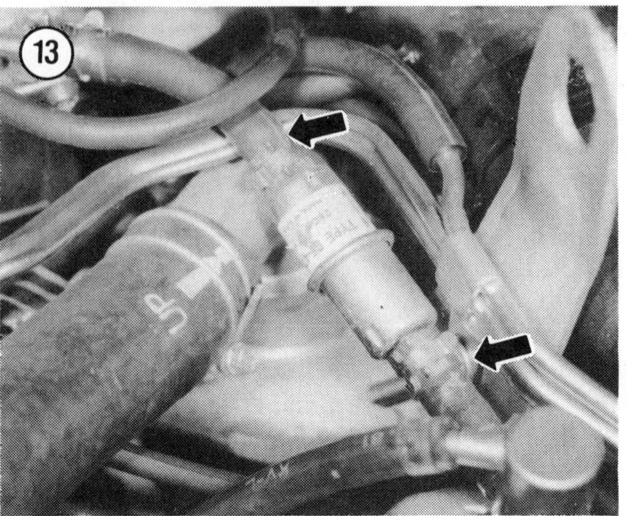

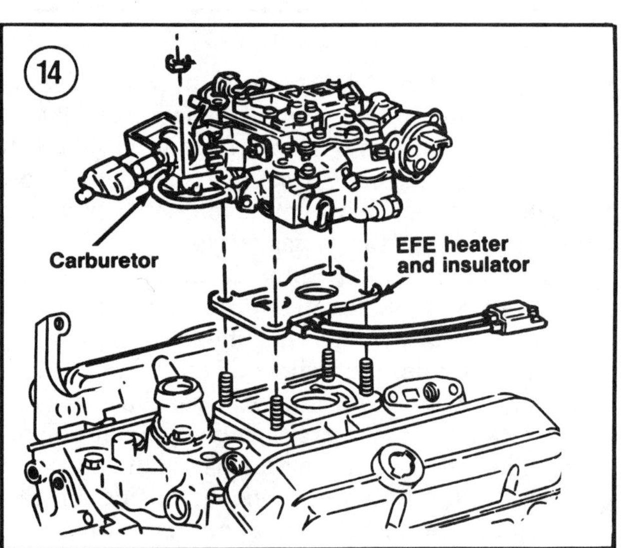

Removal/Installation (Hitachi DCH 340 and DFP 340)

1. Disconnect the negative battery cable.
2. Remove the air cleaner as described in this chapter.
3. Disconnect the throttle cable. Disconnect the cruise control cable and/or automatic transmission detent cable, if so equipped.

NOTE
Alphabetical code letters are cast into the carburetor vacuum fittings to assist in proper vacuum line reinstallation.

4. Label and remove all vacuum lines at the carburetor.

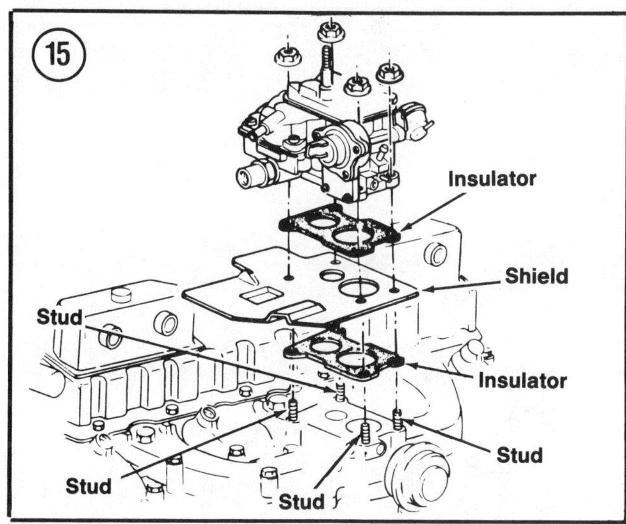

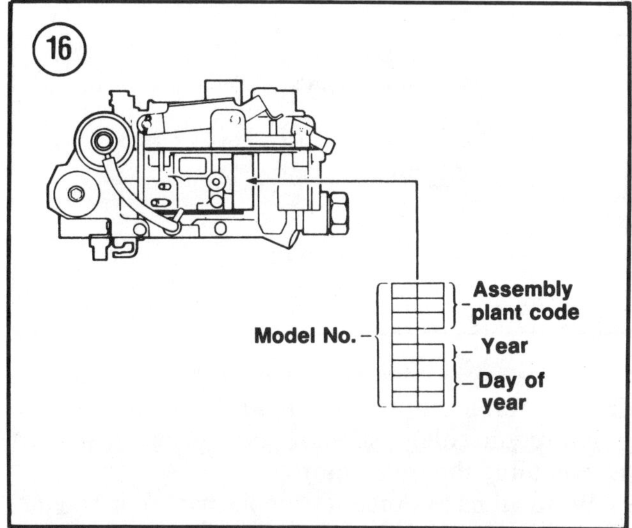

5. Unplug all electrical connectors at the carburetor.
6. Compress the fuel line clamp with a pair of pliers and slide it back on the hose about one inch. See **Figure 13**. Disconnect the fuel hose at the carburetor fitting. Plug the hose to prevent leakage.
7. Remove the 4 carburetor flange nuts and lockwashers. Remove the carburetor and gasket from the intake manifold. Discard the gasket.
8. Stuff a clean shop cloth in the intake manifold opening to prevent the entry of contamination.
9. Installation is the reverse of removal. Use a new gasket. Tighten attaching nuts in a clockwise direction to 14-20 ft.-lb. (18-28 N•m) to prevent carburetor base warpage. After installation, refer to Chapter Three for carburetor adjustments.

Removal/Installation (Rochester 2SE/E2SE)

Refer to **Figure 14** or **Figure 15** as required for this procedure.
1. Disconnect the negative battery cable.
2. Remove the air cleaner as described in this chapter.

NOTE
Alphabetical code letters are cast into the carburetor vacuum fittings to assist in proper vacuum line installation.

3. Label and disconnect all vacuum lines and electrical connectors.
4. Hold the fuel inlet nut with a suitable open-end wrench and use a second wrench to loosen the fuel linc fitting nut at the inlet nut. Disconnect the fuel line from the inlet nut. Plug the line to prevent leakage.
5. Disconnect the throttle cable. Disconnect the cruise control cable and/or automatic transmission detent cable, if so equipped.
6. Remove the 4 carburetor flange nuts. Remove the carburetor and EFE heater/insulator (**Figure 14**) or carburetor and insulator/shield sandwich (**Figure 15**) from the intake manifold.
7. Stuff a clean shop cloth in the intake manifold opening to prevent the entry of contamination.
8. Installation is the reverse of removal. If insulator is damaged, install a new one. Tighten attaching nuts in a clockwise direction to 13 ft.-lb. (18 N•m) to prevent carburetor base warpage. After installation, refer to Chapter Three for carburetor adjustments.

Identification (Rochester Models)

The model identification on Rochester 2SE/E2SE carburetor is stamped vertically on the float bowl next to the vacuum tube marked "B" (**Figure 16**). The basic part number for all Rochester 2SE/E2SE carburetors is 170. The other letters and numbers identify the specific model year and calibration. To obtain the correct carburetor overhaul kit, write down all information on this identification pad and give it to the parts department of any GM dealer or auto supply store.

Preparation for Overhaul

Before removing and disassembling any carburetor, be sure you have the proper overhaul kit, a sufficient quantity of fresh carburetor cleaner and the proper tools. Work slowly and carefully, follow the disassembly/assembly procedures, refer to the exploded drawing of your carburetor when necessary and do not apply excessive force at any time.

It is not necessary to disassemble the carburetor linkage or remove linkage adjusting screws when overhauling a carburetor. Solenoids, dashpots and other diaphragm-operated assist devices attached to the carburetor body should be removed, as carburetor cleaner will damage them. Wipe such parts with a cloth to remove road film, grease and other contamination.

Use carburetor legs to prevent throttle plate damage while working on the carburetor. If legs are not available, thread a nut on each of four 2 1/4 in. bolts. Install each bolt in a flange hole and thread another nut on the bolt. These will hold the bolts securely to the carburetor and serve the same purpose as legs.

WARNING
Tampering with the carburetor is a violation of Federal law. Choke, idle mixture and other sealed adjustments can legally be made only under specified circumstances. Adjustment of these systems should be left to a Chevrolet or GMC dealer.

Carburetors have riveted choke housings and plug seals over the idle mixture needles in accordance with Federal regulations. These adjustments are factory-set and should not be changed by the home mechanic. If the engine will not run properly after the carburetor is cleaned, reassembled and installed as described in this chapter, it is advisable to install a rebuilt carburetor.

Cleaning and Inspection

Dirt, varnish, gum or other contamination in or on the carburetor are often the cause of unsatisfactory performance. Gaskets and accelerating pump cups may swell or leak, resulting in carburetion problems. Efficient carburetion depends upon careful cleaning, inspection and proper installation of new parts. All parts provided in the carburetor overhaul kit (except the idle mixture needle) should be installed when overhauling the carburetor.

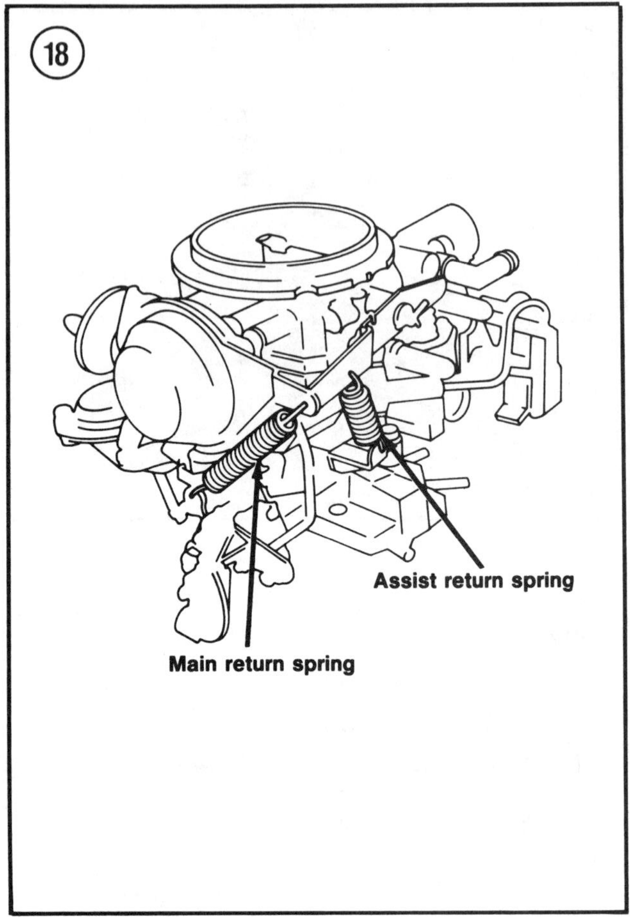

Wash all parts except the choke cap, diaphragms, dashpots, solenoids and other vacuum or electrically operated assist devices in a cleaning solvent. Immersion-type carburetor cleaners are often used to remove dirt, gum and varnish from carburetor parts, but the use of such cleaners can remove the sealing compound (dichromate finish) applied to the carburetor castings at the factory to prevent porosity. Cleaning with an aerosol type cleaner or with solvent and a brush will do the job without damage to the sealing compound.

If a commercial cleaning solvent is used, suspend the air horn in the cleaner to prevent the solution from reaching the riveted choke cap and housing. Do not leave any parts in the cleaning solution longer than necessary to avoid removal of the sealing compound.

Rinse parts cleaned in solvent with kerosene. Blow all parts dry with compressed air. Wipe all

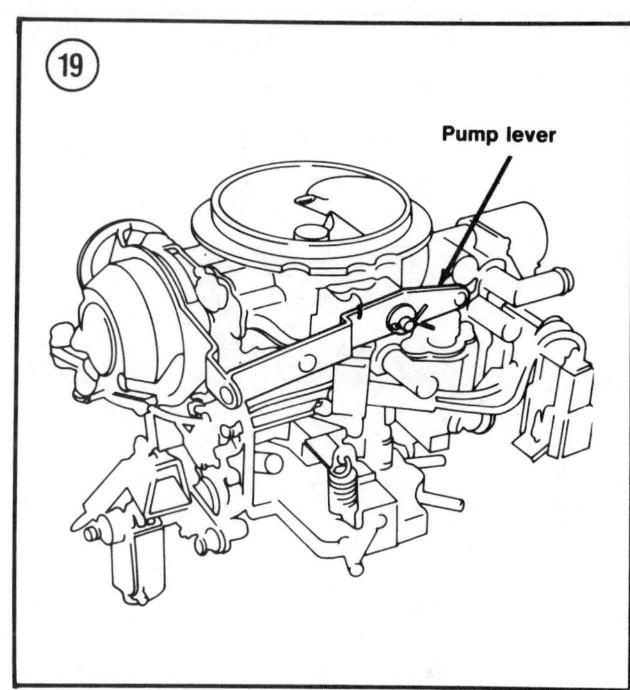

parts which cannot be immersed in solvent with a soft cloth slightly moistened with solvent, then with a clean, dry cloth.

Force compressed air through all passages in the carburetor.

CAUTION
Do not use a wire brush to clean any part. Do not use a drill or wire to clean out any opening or passage in the carburetor. A drill or wire may enlarge the hole or passage and change the calibration.

Check the choke and throttle plate shafts for grooves, wear or excessive looseness or binding. Inspect the choke and throttle plates for nicked edges or burrs which prevent proper closure. Choke and throttle plates are positioned during production and should not be removed unless damaged.

Clean all gasket residue from the air horn, main body and thottle body sealing surfaces with a putty knife. Since carburetor castings are aluminum, a sharp instrument should not be used to clean the gasket residue or damage to the carburetor assemblies may result.

Inspect all components for cracks or warpage. Check floats for wear on the lip and hinge pin. Check hinge pin holes in air horn, bowl cover or float bowl for wear and elongation.

Check brass floats (DCH 340 or DFP 340 carburetors) for leaks by holding them under water which has been heated to 200° F. Bubbles will appear if there is a leak.

Check composition floats (Rochester carburetors) for fuel absorption by gently squeezing and applying fingernail pressure. If moisture appears, replace the float.

Replace the float if the arm needle contact surface is grooved. If the float or floats are serviceable, gently polish the needle contact surface of the arm with crocus cloth or steel wool. Replace the float if the shaft is worn.

NOTE
Some gasolines contain additives that will cause the Viton tip on the fuel inlet needle to swell. If carburetor problems are traced to a deformed inlet needle tip, change brands of gasoline used.

Check the Viton tip of the fuel inlet needle for swelling or distortion. Discard the needle if the overhaul kit contains a new needle for assembly.

Replace all screws and nuts that have stripped threads. Replace all distorted or broken springs. Inspect all gasket mating surfaces for nicks or burrs.

Check the mixture control solenoid on E2SE models for sticking, binding or leakage. See *Mixture Control Solenoid Test* in this chapter.

If main body requires replacement, check float bowl casting. If marked "MW," be sure to replace the main body with one marked "MW." This stands for "machined pump well" and determines the type of pump used.

Reassemble all parts carefully. It should not be necessary to apply force to any parts. If force seems to be required, you are doing something wrong. Stop and refer to the exploded drawing for your carburetor.

Disassembly (Hitachi DCH 340 or DFP 340)

Refer to **Figure 17** as required for this procedure. Not all DCH 340 or DFP 340 carburetors will use all the parts shown in **Figure 17**.

1. Remove the main and assist return springs (**Figure 18**).
2. Disconnect the accelerator pump lever (**Figure 19**).

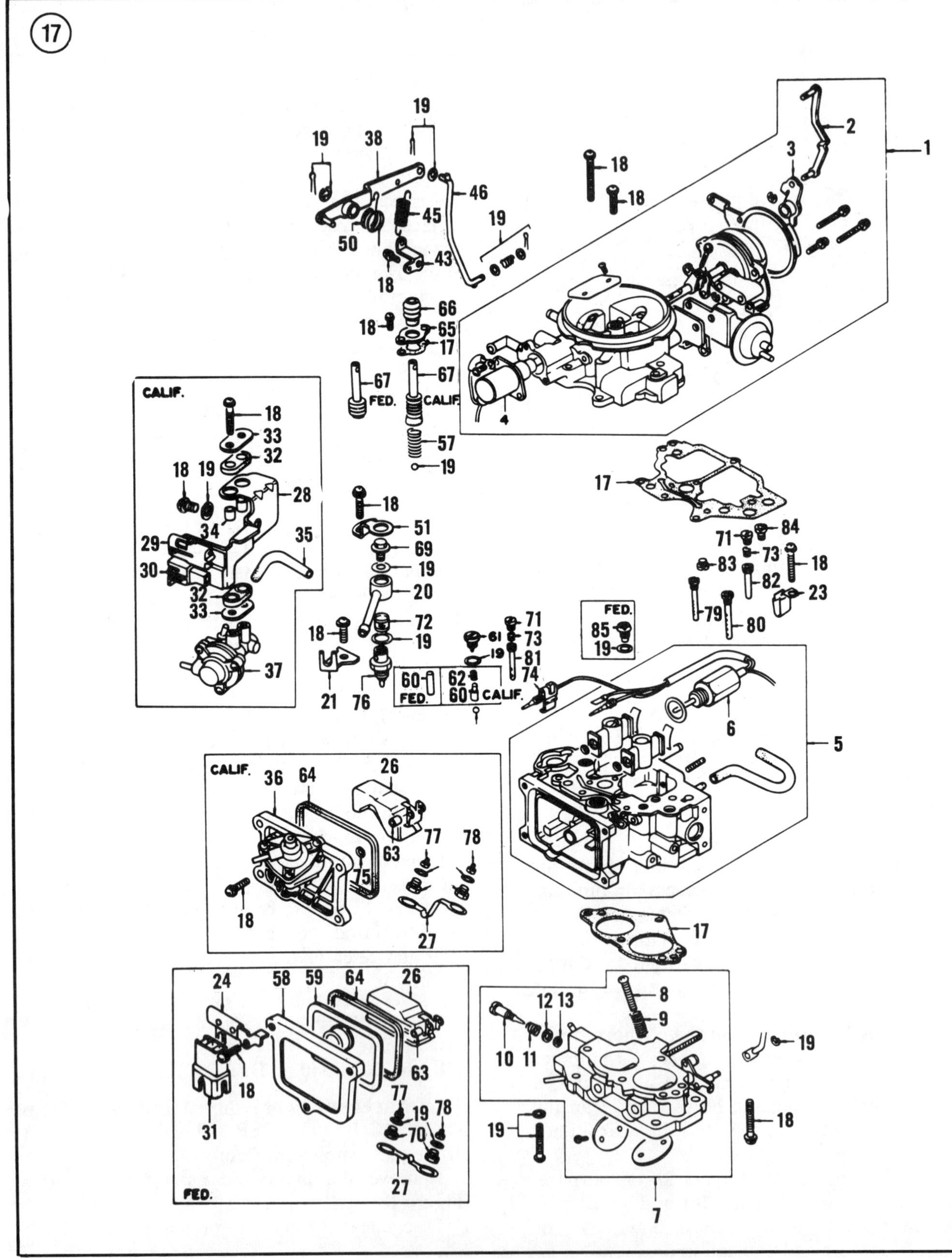
17
CALIF.
FED.
CALIF.
FED.
CALIF.
CALIF.
FED.
FED.

CARBURETOR (HITACHI DCH 340)

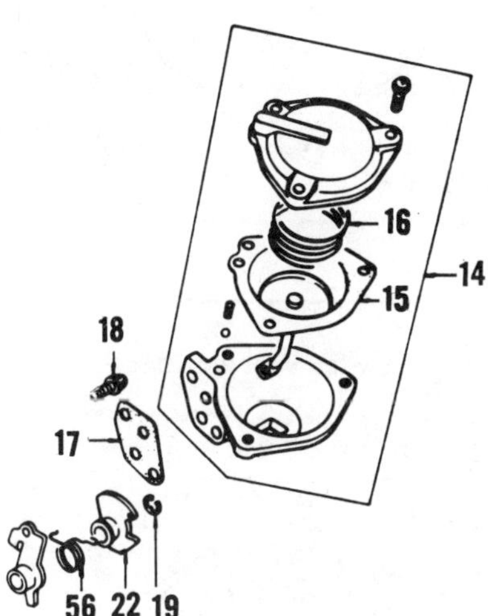

1. Choke chamber assembly
2. Choke connecting plate
3. Choke counter lever
4. Solenoid
5. Float chamber assembly
6. Slow cut solenoid
7. Throttle chamber assembly
8. Throttle adjusting screw
9. Spring
10. Idle adjusting screw
11. Spring
12. Washer
13. Seal
14. Diaphragm chamber assembly
15. Diaphragm
16. Spring
17. Gasket kit
18. Screw & washer kit (A)
19. Screw & washer kit (B)
20. Fuel nipple
21. Stopping plate
22. Fast idle cam
23. Lead wire holder
24. Connector hanger
25. Fast idle adjustment lever
26. Float
27. Lock plate
28. Connector hanger
29. Connector
30. Connector
31. Connector
32. Mounting rubber
33. Plate
34. Collar
35. Hose
36. Main actuator
37. Slow actuator
38. Pump lever
39. Accelerator lever
40. Cruise lever
41. Kick lever
42. Spring hanger "A"
43. Spring hanger "B"
44. Main spring
45. Assist spring
46. Pump rod
47. Sleeve
48. Shaft collar "A"
49. Shaft collar "B"
50. Pump lever spring
51. Lock lever
52. Return plate
53. Throttle spring "S"
54. Adjustment lever
55. Fast idle screw
56. Cam spring
57. Piston return spring
58. Level gauge cover
59. Level gauge
60. Injector weight
61. Screw
62. Spring
63. Collar "C"
64. Seal
65. Plate
66. Dust cover
67. Piston
68. Washer
69. Screw
70. Plug
71. Plug
72. Filter
73. Spring
74. Lead wire connector
75. O-ring
76. Needle valve
77. Main jet "P"
78. Main jet "S"
79. Main air bleed "P"
80. Main air bleed "S"
81. Slow jet "P"
82. Slow jet "S"
83. Slow air bleed "P"
84. Slow air bleed "S"
85. Power valve

3. Disconnect the rubber pipe from the slow actuator, if so equipped. See **Figure 20**.
4. Remove the throttle return spring(s). See **Figure 21**. Disengage the electrical lead wire from the harness clips under the choke housing and choke chamber.
5. Remove the electrical connector from its hanger. Disconnect the automatic choke lead wire at the connector. See **Figure 22**.
6. Remove the fuel nipple. Remove the strainer carefully to prevent distortion.
7. Disconnect the switch vent valve lead wire from the connector. See **Figure 23**.
8. Remove the circlip from the choke connecting rod at the counter lever (**Figure 24**).

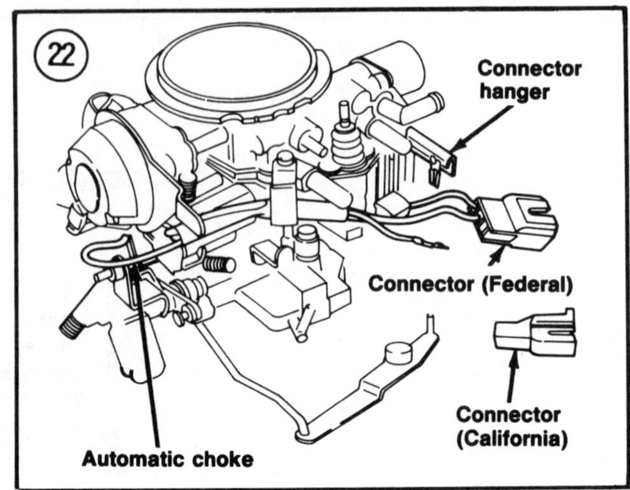

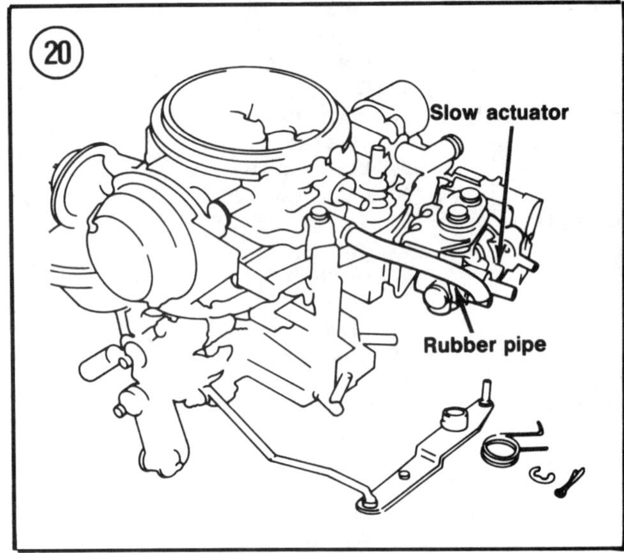

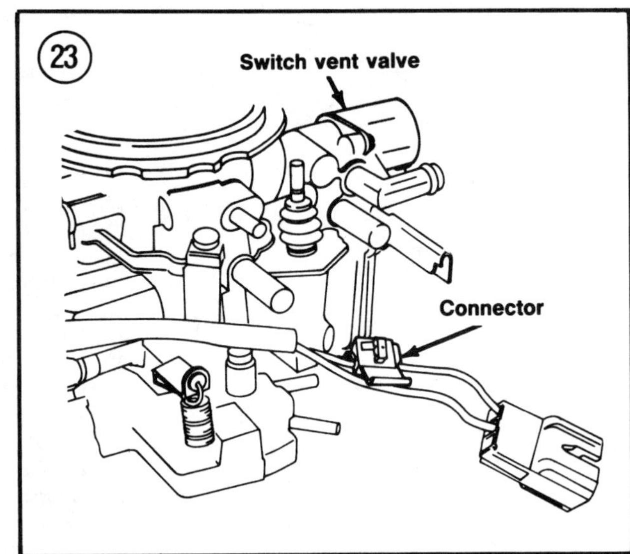

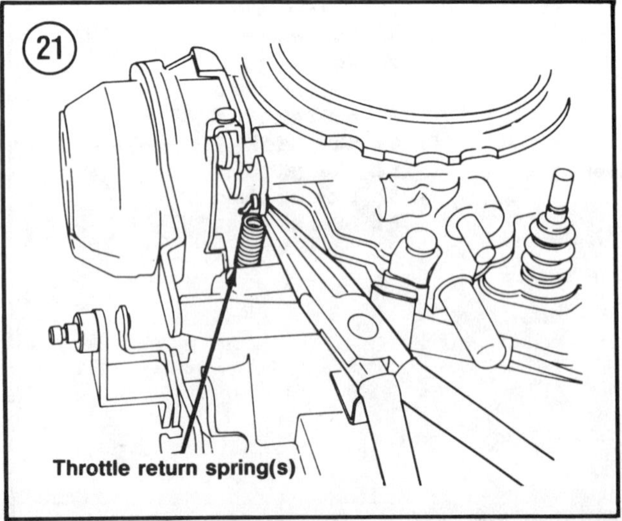

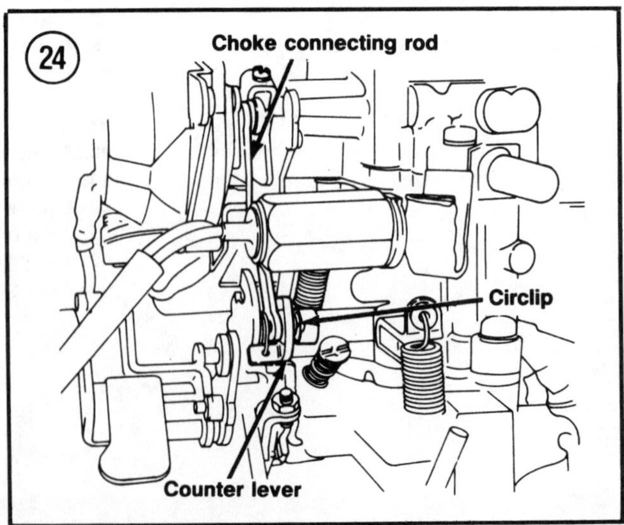

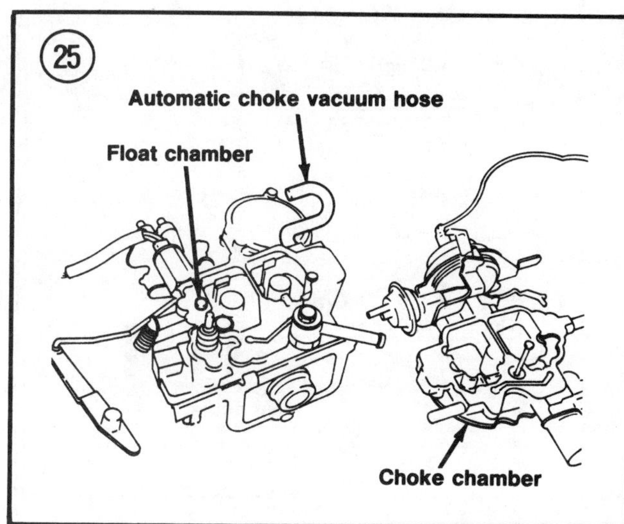

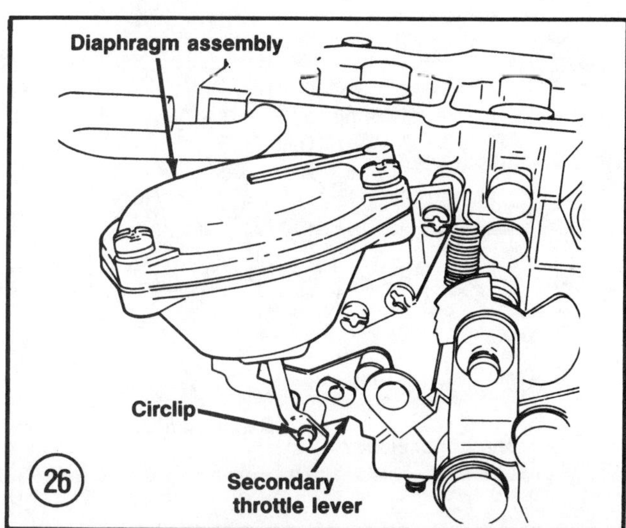

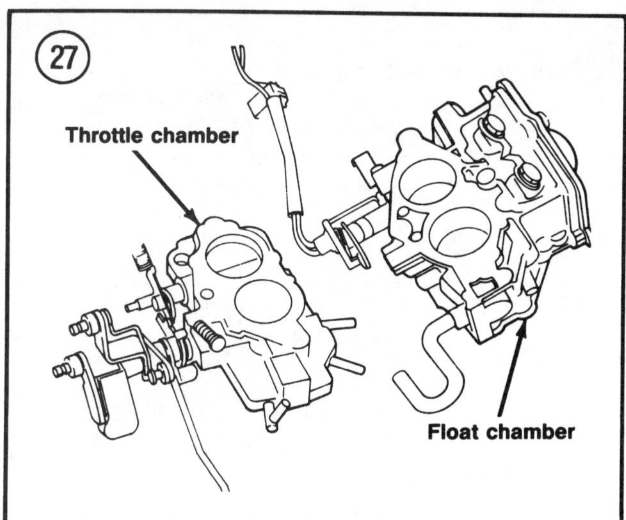

9. Disconnect the choke vacuum hose from the float chamber. Remove the choke chamber attaching screws. Remove the choke chamber. See **Figure 25**.

10. Remove the circlip holding the diaphragm arm to the secondary throttle lever (**Figure 26**).

11. Separate the throttle and float chambers (**Figure 27**).

12. Remove the slow actuator, if so equipped. See **Figure 28**.

13. Remove the accelerator pump plunger assembly (**Figure 29**).

14. Remove the float needle valve assembly. See **Figure 30**.

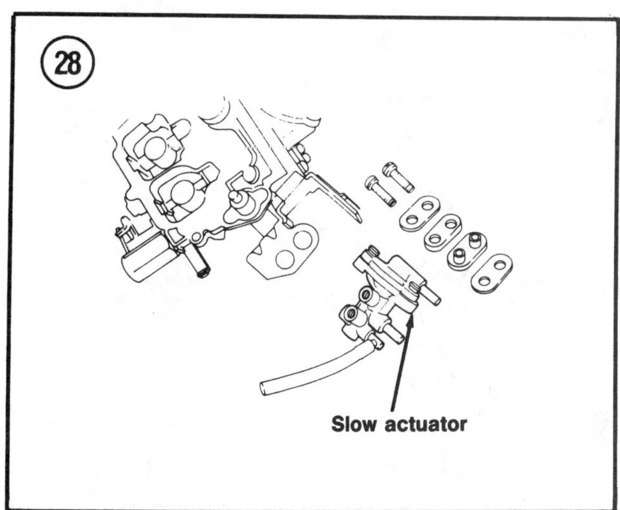

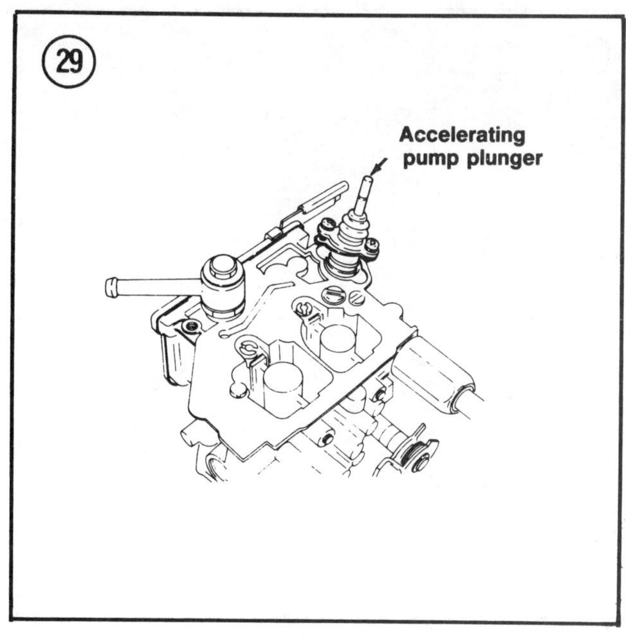

6

15A. Federal models—Remove 3 level gauge cover screws. Remove the level gauge, float and float collar (**Figure 31**).

15B. California models—Remove 4 main actuator cover screws. Remove the main actuator, float and float collar (**Figure 32**).

16. Remove the diaphragm cover screws. Separate the cover, spring and diaphragm. Do not lose the small ball and spring. See **Figure 33**.

17. Remove the jets shown in **Figure 34**.

18. Remove the injector weight plug, weight and check ball. California models also use an injector spring (**Figure 35**).

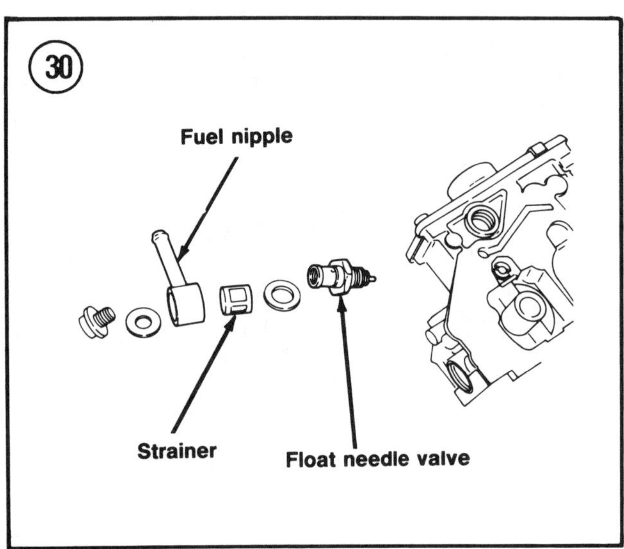

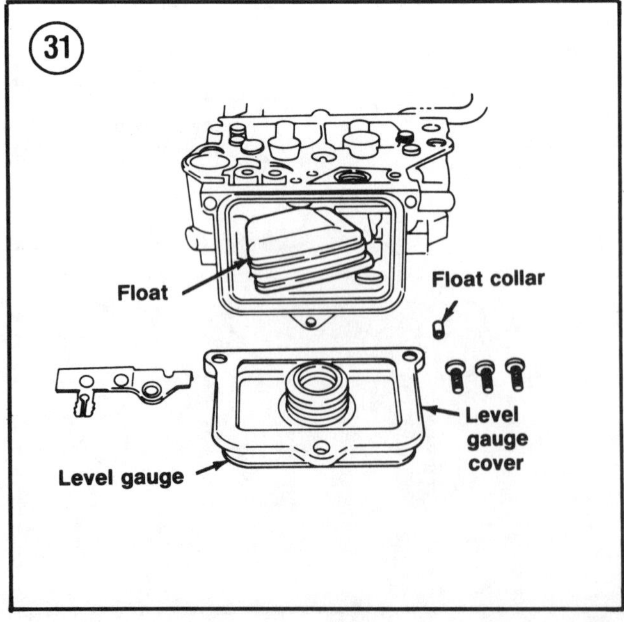

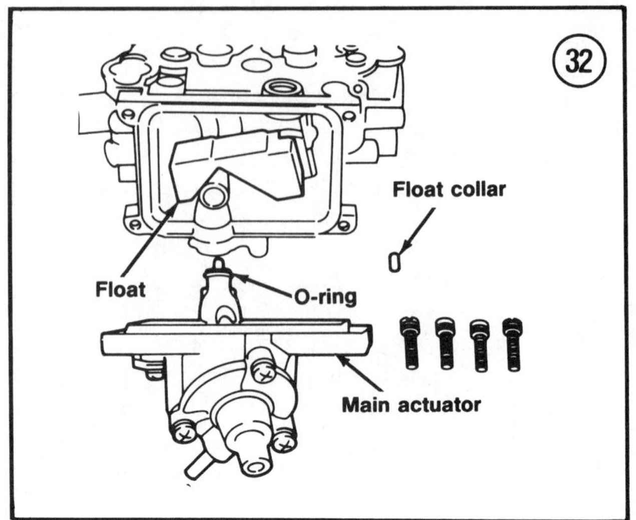

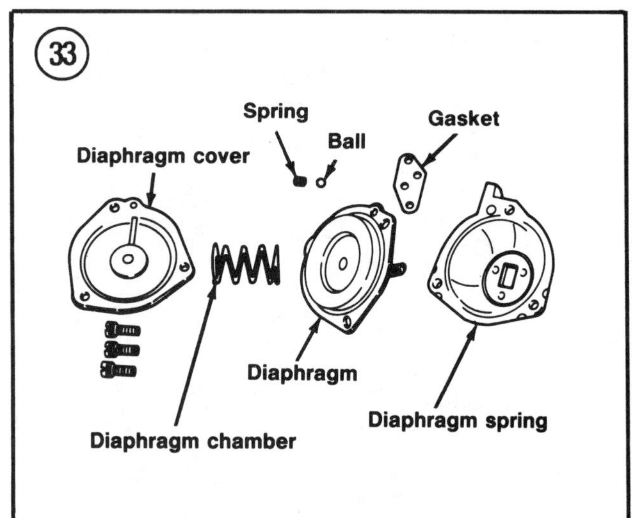

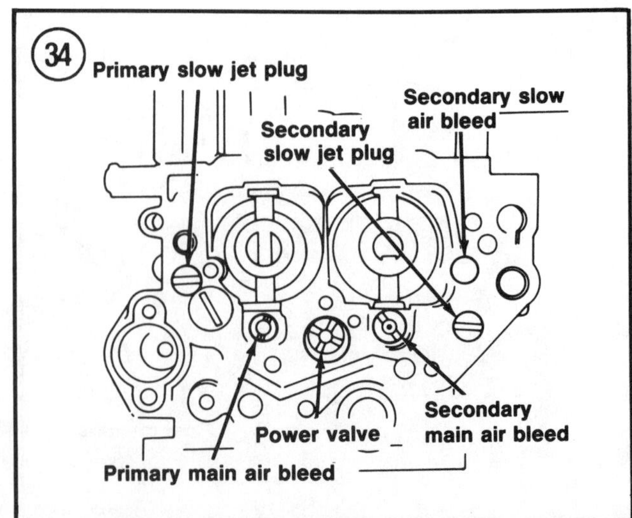

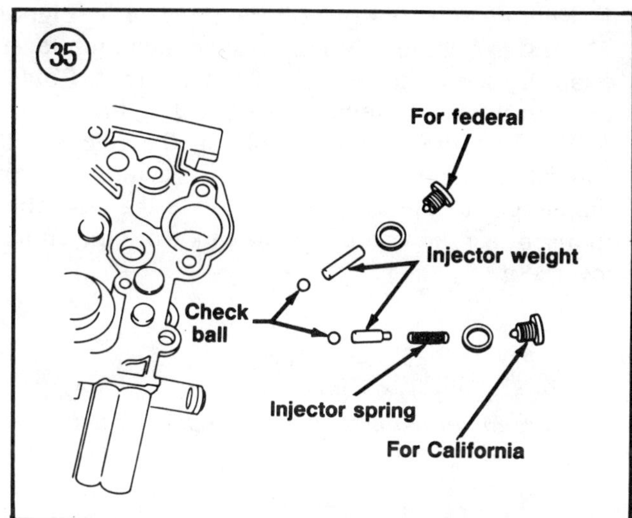

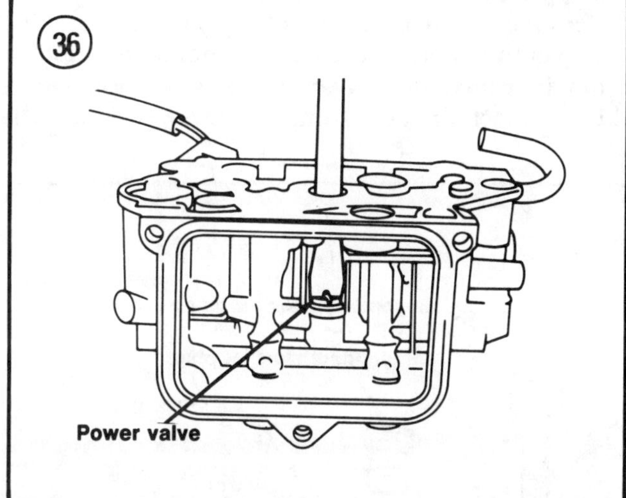

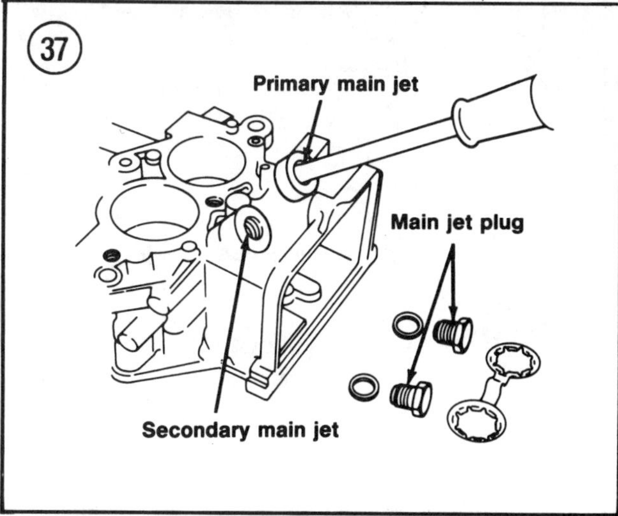

19. Remove the power valve with a wide-blade screwdriver as shown in **Figure 36**.
20. Remove the 2 main jet plugs. Remove the primary and secondary jets. See **Figure 37**.
21. Remove the primary slow air bleed from the choke chamber (**Figure 38**).
22. Clean and inspect all parts as described in this chapter.

Assembly
(Hitachi DCH 340 and DFP 340)

Assembly is the reverse of disassembly, plus the following. All parts should fit together easily without forcing. Refer to **Figure 17** as required. Refer to **Figure 39** for jet and air bleed identification.

1. Check replacement gaskets for proper punching by comparing them with old gaskets.
2. Federal models—Install the power jet valve carefully to prevent bending the valve rod.
3. Once accelerator pump assembly is completed, fill with fuel and operate pump. Injection should be smooth and consistent.

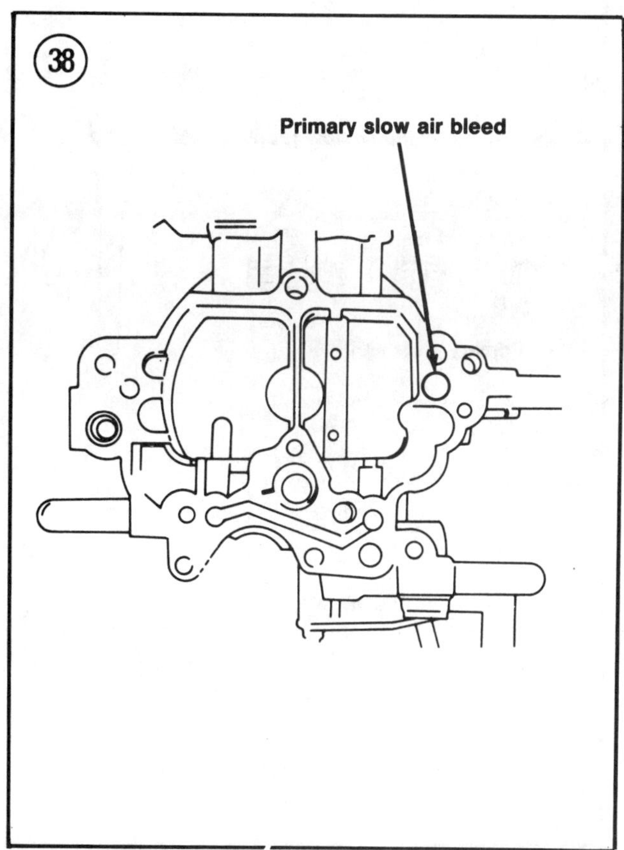

4. Lightly coat the main actuator O-ring with grease. Tighten actuator attaching screws with care to prevent the O-ring from cracking.
5. Adjust the float to specifications as described in this chapter. If specifications given in the overhaul kit instructions for your carburetor differ from those provided in this chapter, adjust the float to the overhaul kit specifications.

Disassembly (Rochester 2SE/E2SE)

The throttle shafts, secondary actuating lever and lockout lever on some carburetors are all coated with a special substance to reduce friction. The secondary throttle bore and valve are coated with a graphite compound to hold air leakage to a minimum. These coatings should not be damaged or removed during overhaul.

Refer to **Figure 40** (2SE) or **Figure 41** (E2SE) as required for this procedure. Not all 2SE/E2SE carburetors will use all the parts shown in **Figure 40** or **Figure 41**.

1. Remove the pump rod retaining clip (**Figure 42**). If it is a clipless design, remove the pump lever retaining screw and washer at the air horn. Rotate the pump lever to remove it from the pump rod.
2. Remove the 3 screws holding the idle speed control solenoid and primary vacuum break diaphragm to the carburetor. Rotate the assembly to disengage the vacuum break link from the choke lever slot.

NOTE
It is not necessary to remove the secondary vacuum break rod from the E2SE linkage unless the rod is damaged.

3. Remove the secondary vacuum break diaphragm and bracket screws, if so equipped. Remove the diaphragm and bracket.
4. Remove and discard the retaining clip holding the intermediate choke rod at the choke lever. Disconnect the rod from the lever. Remove the

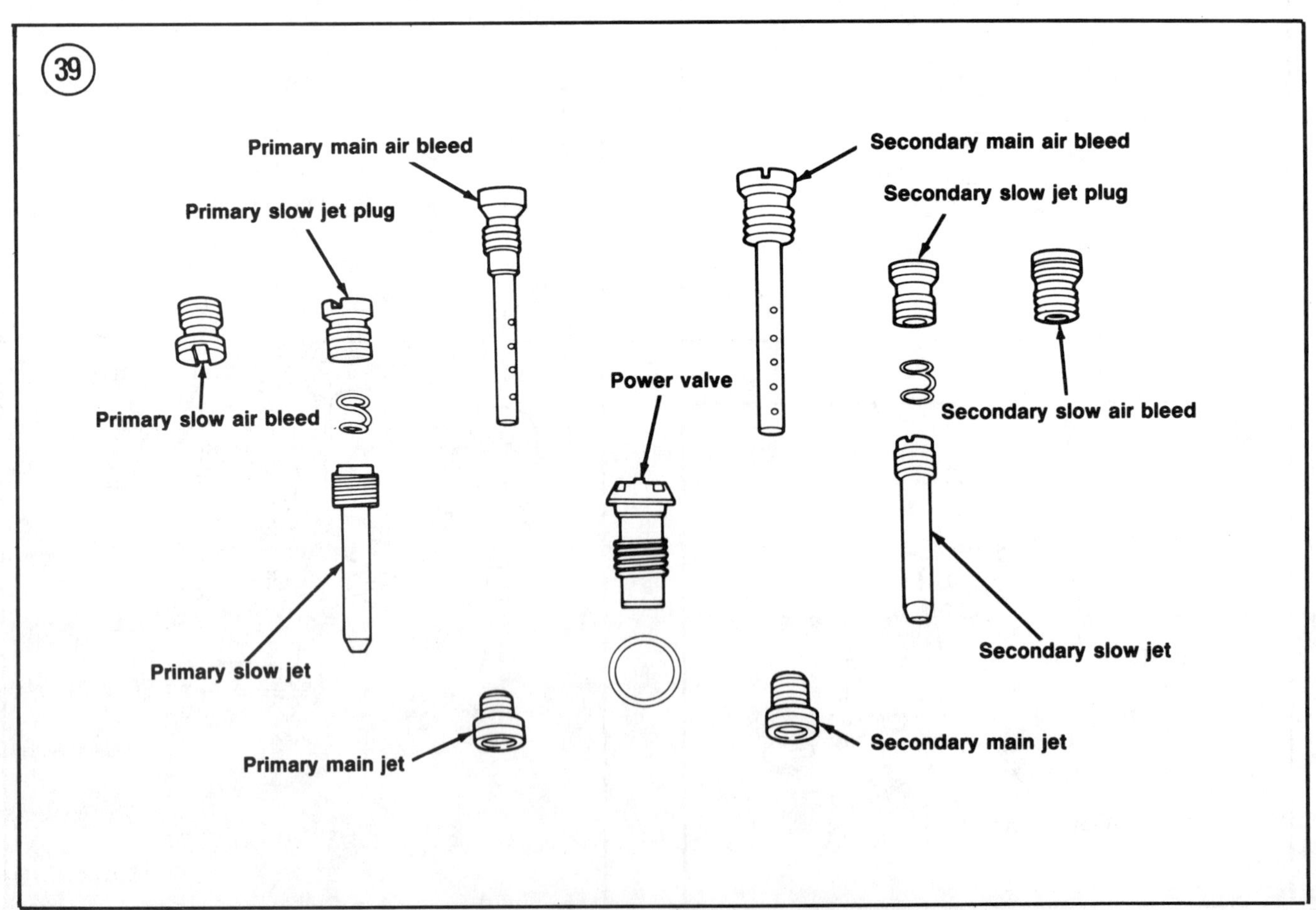

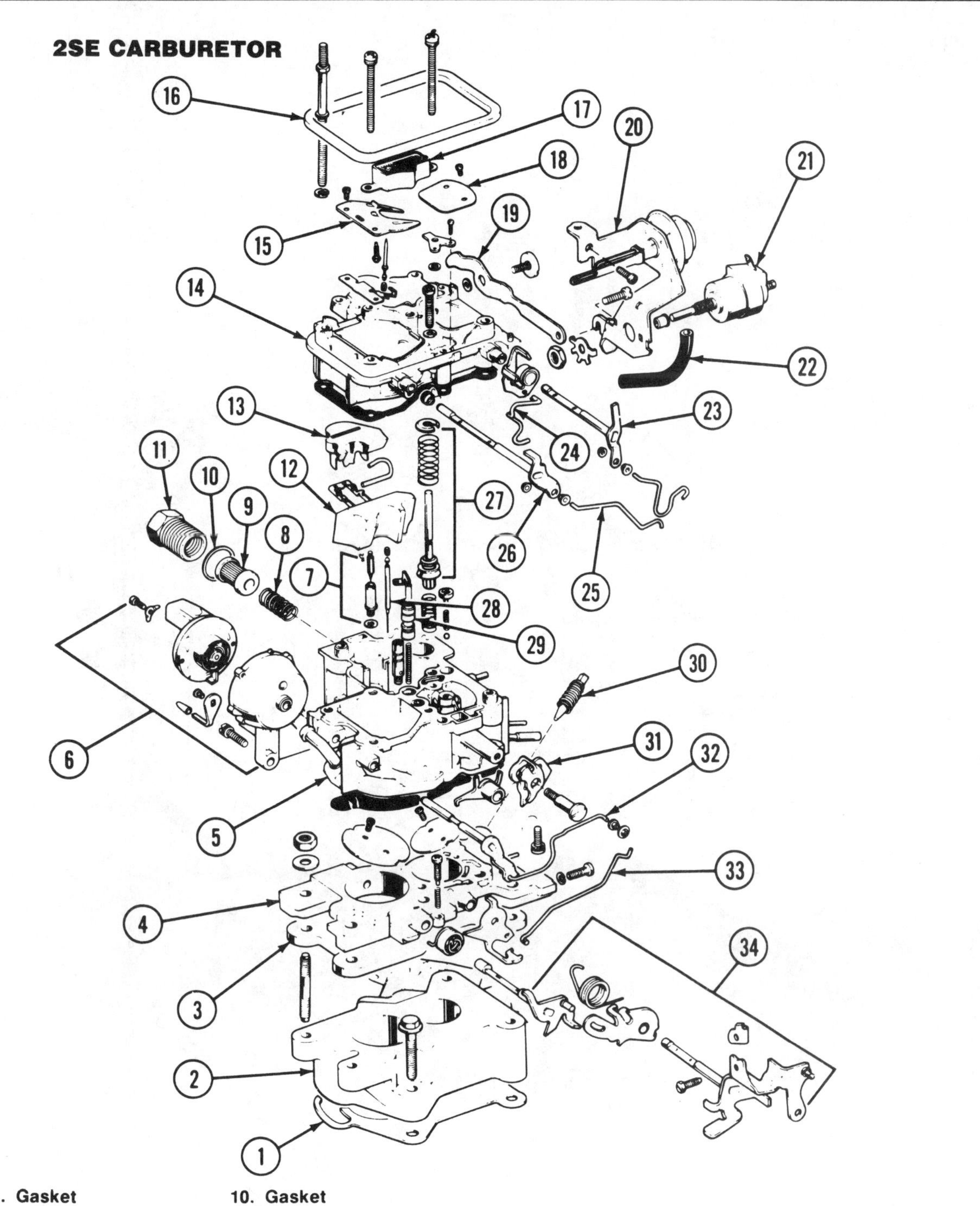

1. Gasket
2. Intake adapter
3. Insulator
4. Throttle body
5. Main body
6. Electric stat cover
7. Needle seat assembly
8. Spring
9. Fuel inlet filter
10. Gasket
11. Fuel inlet fitting
12. Float assembly
13. Float baffle
14. Air horn
15. Air valve
16. Air horn gasket
17. Vent screen
18. Choke valve
19. Pump lever
20. Vacuum break and bracket
21. Idle stop solenoid
22. Vacuum hose
23. Vacuum break lever
24. Choke link
25. Air valve rod
26. Air valve lever
27. Accelerator pump
28. Metering rod
29. Power piston
30. Idle needle and spring
31. Fast idle cam
32. Intermediate choke rod
33. Pump rod
34. Throttle lever assembly

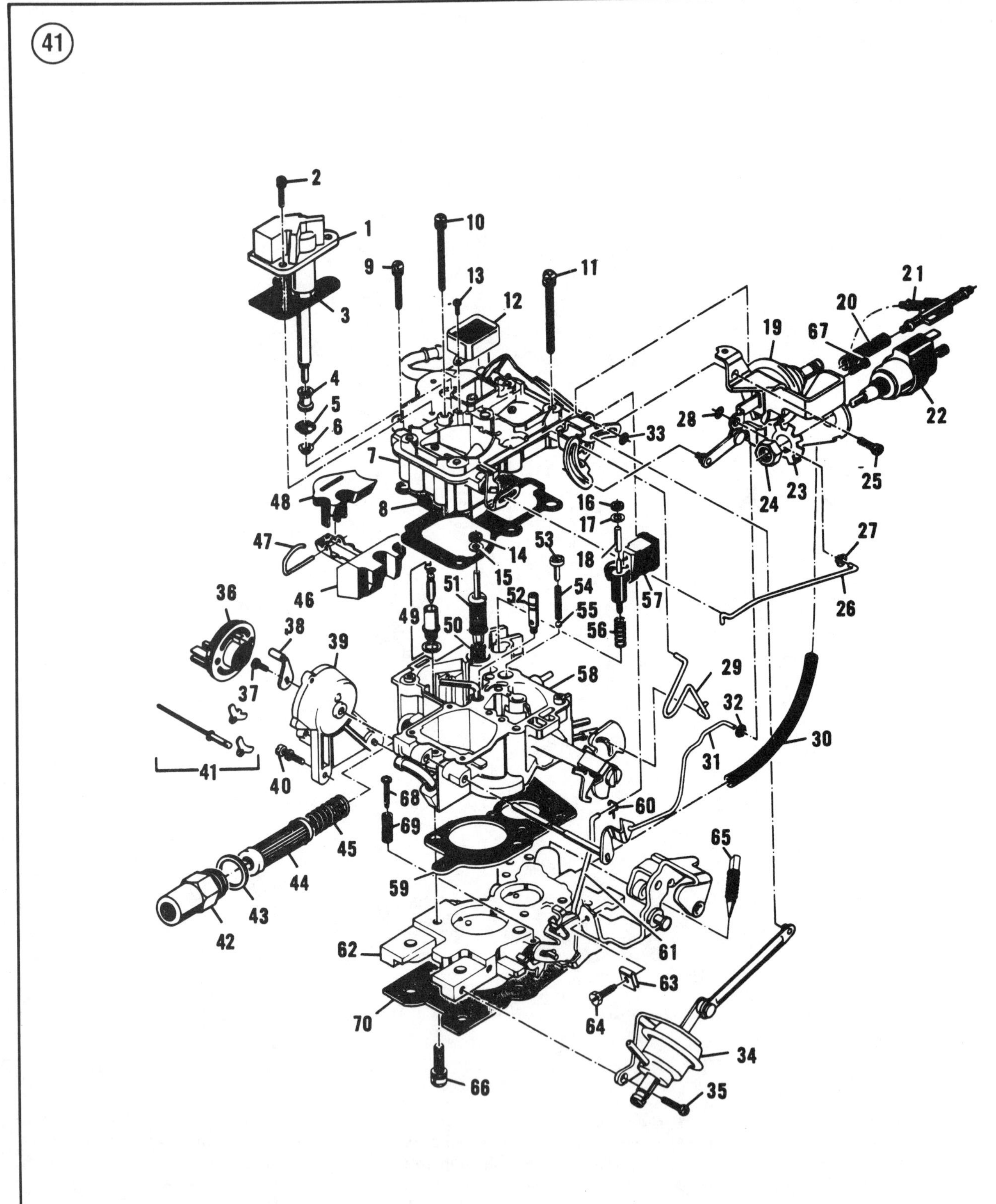
41
1
2
3
4
5
6
7
8
9
10
11
12
13
14
15
16
17
18
19
20
21
22
23
24
25
26
27
28
29
30
31
32
33
34
35
36
37
38
39
40
41
42
43
44
45
46
47
48
49
50
51
52
53
54
55
56
57
58
59
60
61
62
63
64
65
66
67
68
69
70

ROCHESTER E2SE CARBURETOR

AIR HORN PARTS:

1. Mixture control solenoid
2. M/C solenoid screw (3)
3. M/C solenoid gasket
4. M/C solenoid spacer
5. M/C solenoid seal
6. M/C solenoid seal retainer
7. Air horn assembly
8. Air horn gasket
9. Air horn screw—short (2)
10. Air horn screw—long (3)
11. Air horn screw—large
12. Vent stack
13. Vent stack screw (2)
14. Pump plunger seal
15. Pump plunger seal retainer
16. TPS plunger seal
17. TPS plunger seal retainer
18. TPS plunger (throttle position sensor)

CHOKE PARTS:

19. Primary vacuum break and bracket assembly
20. Vacuum break connecting hose
21. Vacuum break connecting tee
22. Idle speed solenoid
23. Idle speed solenoid retainer
24. Idle speed solenoid nut
25. Vacuum break bracket attaching screw
26. Air valve link
27. Air valve link bushing
28. Air valve link retainer
29. Fast idle cam link
30. Vacuum break hose
31. Intermediate choke shaft/lever/link assembly
32. Intermediate choke link bushing
33. Intermediate choke link retainer
34. Secondary vacuum break and bracket assembly
35. Vacuum break attaching screw (2)
36. Choke cover and coil assembly
37. Choke lever attaching screw
38. Choke lever and contact assembly
39. Choke housing
40. Choke housing attaching screw (2)
41. Stat cover retainer kit

FLOAT BOWL PARTS:

42. Fuel inlet
43. Fuel inlet nut gasket
44. Fuel inlet filter
45. Fuel filter spring
46. Float assembly
47. Float hinge pin
48. Float bowl insert
49. Needle and seat assembly
50. Pump return spring
51. Pump assembly
52. Metering jet
53. Pump spring and check ball retainer
54. Pump check ball spring
55. Pump check ball
56. TPS spring
57. TPS (Throttle Position Sensor)
58. Float bowl assembly
59. Float bowl gasket

THROTTLE BODY PARTS:

60. Pump rod clip
61. Pump rod
62. Throttle body assembly
63. Cam screw clip
64. Fast idle cam screw
65. Idle needle and spring
66. Throttle body attaching screw
67. Vacuum break bracket attaching screw (new)
68. Idle stop screw
69. Idle stop screw spring
70. Intake manifold gasket

plastic bushing from the choke lever and save for reuse. See **Figure 43**.

5. Model E2SE—Remove the 3 mixture control solenoid screws **(Figure 44)**. Lift the solenoid from the air horn with a twisting motion. Remove and discard the solenoid gasket.

6. Model E2SE—Remove and discard the solenoid stem seal and retainer **(Figure 45)**.

7. Remove the hot idle compensator valve screws and valve, if so equipped. See A, **Figure 46**. Remove and discard the seal.

8. Rotate the fast idle cam to its full-up position. Remove the retainer clip and disengage the fast idle cam link from the cam slot.

NOTE

The air horn screws have a Torx head. This is different from the usual Phillips head screw. Do not try to remove a Torx head screw with any tool other than a Torx head driver or the head will be damaged and require drilling out to remove the screw.

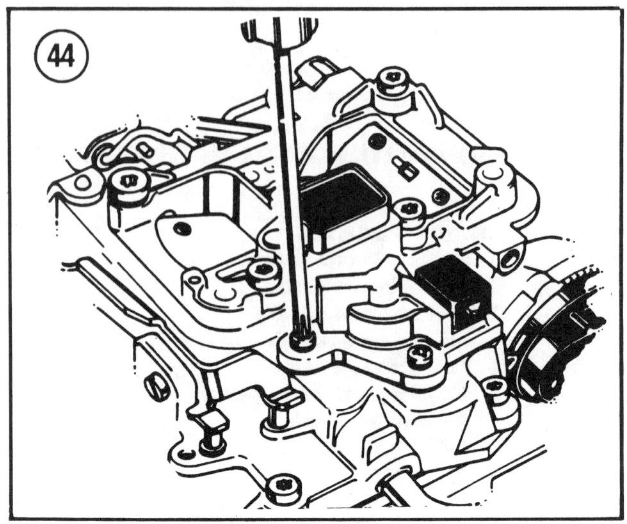

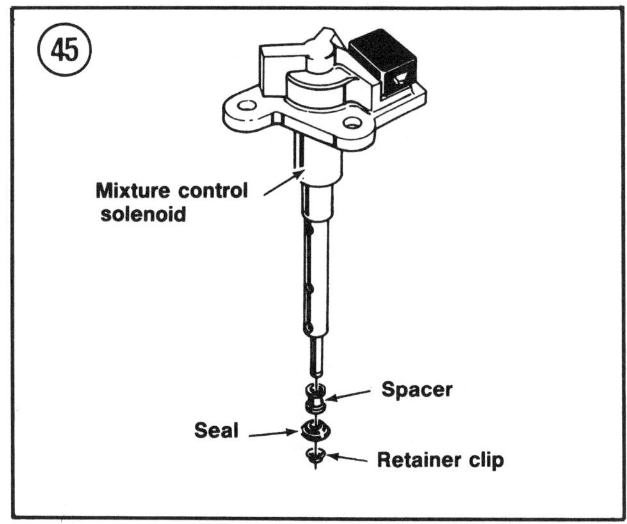

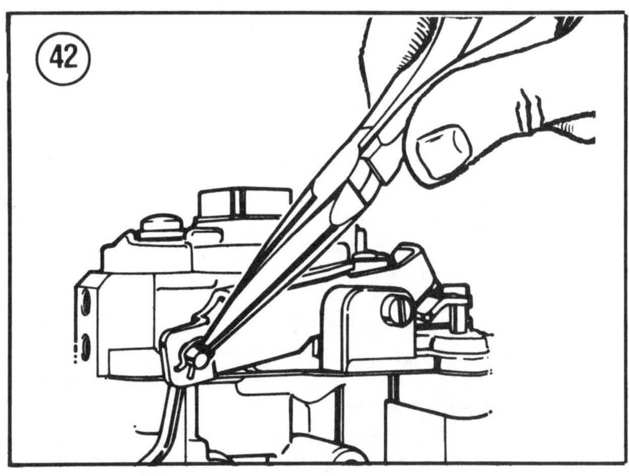

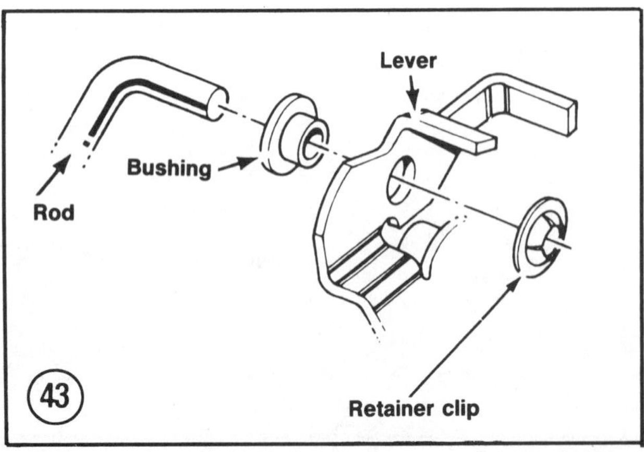

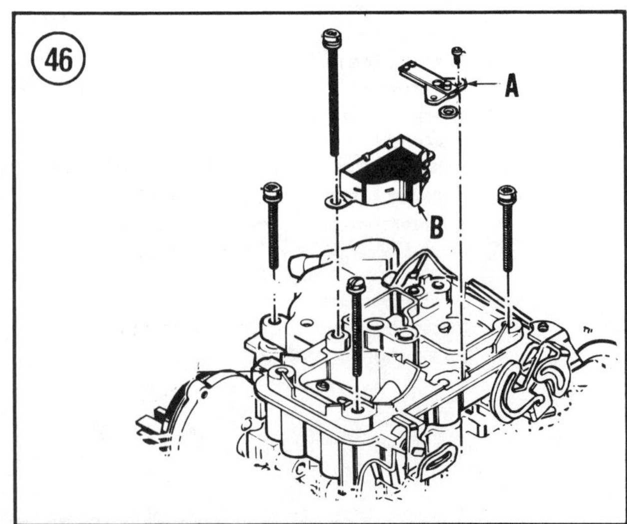

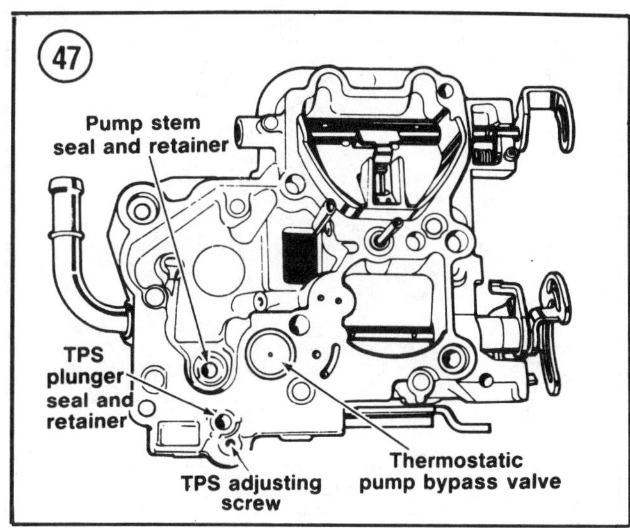

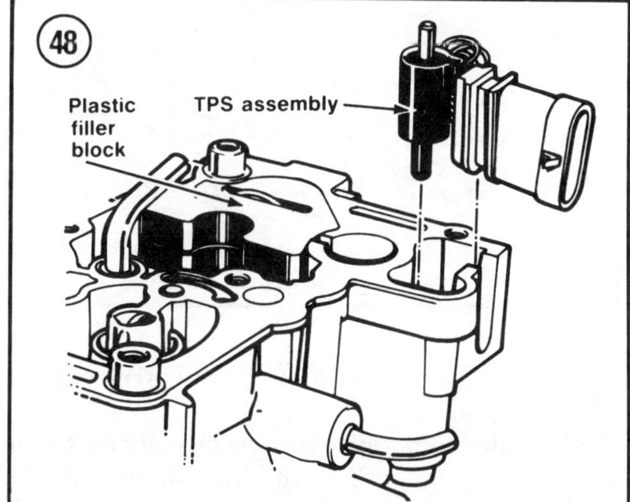

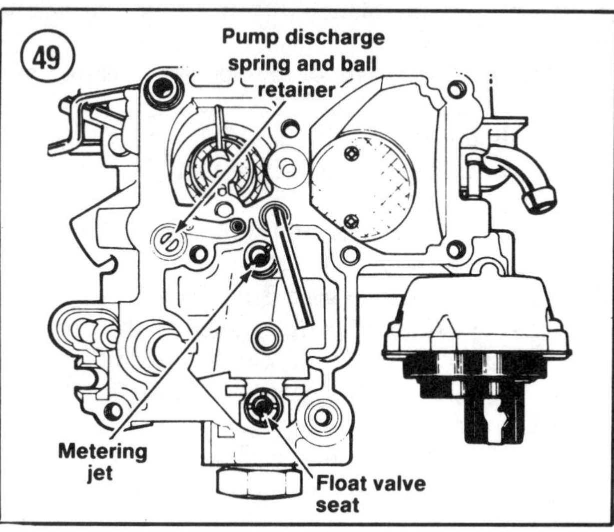

9. Remove the air horn attaching screws and lockwashers. Remove the vent stack (B, **Figure 46**).

10. Separate the air horn from the main body. It may be necessary to tap the air horn gently with a soft-faced hammer to break the gasket seal. Do *not* pry the air horn free of the main body or you may damage the aluminum mating surfaces.

11. Push the TPS plunger through the air horn seal and remove it.

12. Invert the air horn and use a small screwdriver to remove the TPS seal retainer staking. Remove and discard the retainer and seal (**Figure 47**).

NOTE
The accelerator pump plunger may remain in the air horn. If so, remove it before proceeding with Step 13.

6

13. Repeat Step 12 to remove the pump plunger retainer (**Figure 47**). Remove and discard the retainer and seal.

NOTE
*The thermostatic pump bypass valve (**Figure 47**) is permanently installed. Do not try to remove it. If defective, the entire air horn must be replaced.*

14. Model E2SE—Remove the vent stack/screen assembly (B, **Figure 46**).

NOTE
Do not remove the secondary metering rod from the air valve assembly. It is staked in place. Do not remove the idle air bleed screw cover plug. This adjustment is factory-set. If the metering rod, air bleed screw or air horn are defective, replace the air horn with a new one containing factory-set metering rod and air bleed screw.

15. Remove and discard the air horn gasket.

16. Remove the pump plunger and return spring from the pump well.

17. Model E2SE—Carefully push up on the bottom of the TPS electrical connector under the float bowl and remove the TPS and spring from the main body well. See **Figure 48**.

18. Remove the plastic float valve filler block.

19A. Model E2SE—Tilt the float to clear the vapor purge tube in the float bowl, then remove the float assembly.

19B. Model 2SE—Pull up on the retaining pin and remove the float assembly.

20. Remove the inlet valve seat (**Figure 49**) with a wide-blade screwdriver. Discard the seat gasket.

21. Model 2SE—Depress and release the power piston stem (**Figure 50**). The piston will snap free. Remove the piston and metering rod assembly.

NOTE
Do not remove or alter the adjustment of the calibration screw inside the E2SE metering jet. This is preset at the factory according to ECM calibration.

22. Remove the extended metering jet from the float bowl with a wide-blade (10 mm minimum width) screwdriver.

NOTE
Do not remove the plastic retainer in Step 23 with a punch or screwdriver. Such tools will damage the sealing beads on the bowl casting surface. If this happens, the entire float bowl assembly will have to be replaced.

23. Use needle nose pliers or a small slide hammer to remove the plastic retainer covering the pump discharge spring and check ball (**Figure 49**). Discard the retainer.
24. Invert the fuel bowl and catch the pump discharge spring and check ball in your hand.
25. Remove the fuel inlet fitting, gasket, check valve and filter/spring assembly.
26. Remove the throttle body attaching screws (**Figure 51**). Separate the throttle body from the main body. Remove and discard the insulator gasket.

NOTE
Further disassembly of the throttle body is not necessary for cleaning purposes. The primary and secondary throttle plate screws are staked in place and should not be removed. The throttle body and throttle plates are serviced as an assembly.

27. Clean and inspect all parts as described in this chapter.

Assembly (Rochester 2SE/E2SE)

Refer to **Figure 40** (2SE) or **Figure 41** (E2SE) as required for this procedure. Not all 2SE/E2SE carburetors will use all the parts shown in **Figure 40** or **Figure 41**. Check replacement gaskets for proper punching by comparing them with old gaskets.

1. Install the throttle body to the main body with a new insulator gasket and tighten the attaching screws securely. See **Figure 51**.

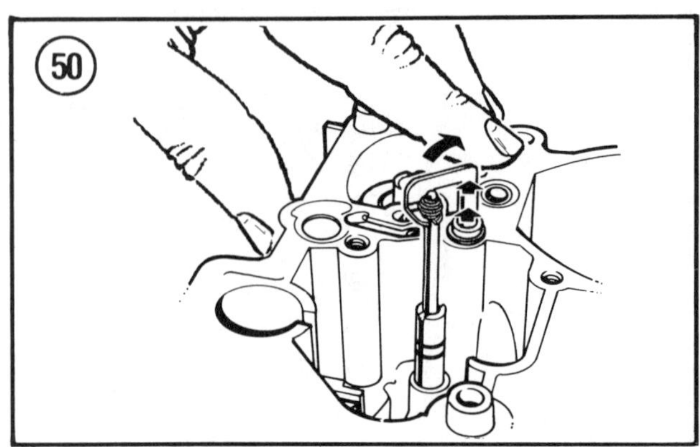

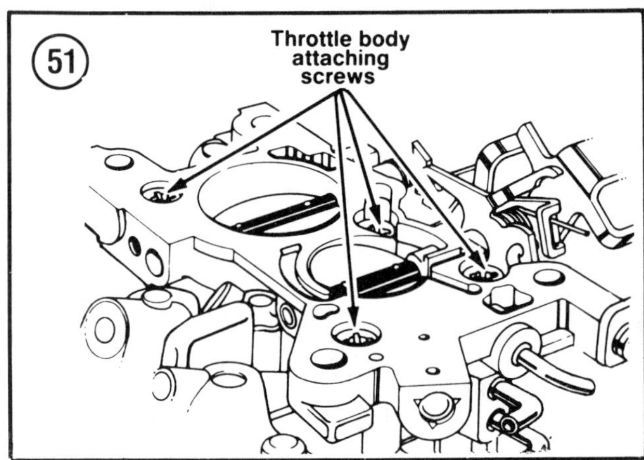

2. Install the fuel filter spring, filter, gasket and fuel inlet fitting in that order.
3. Drop the pump discharge check ball and spring in the discharge well, then install a new plastic retainer.
4. Install the extended metering jet in the float bowl with a wide-blade (10 mm minimum width) screwdriver.
5. Model 2SE—Install the power piston and metering rod assembly.
6. Install the inlet valve seat with a new gasket. Use a wide-blade screwdriver to tighten the seat securely.
7. Install the float assembly, then seat the plastic filler block in place.
8. Adjust the float to specifications as described in this chapter. If specifications given in the overhaul kit instructions for your carburetor differ from those provided in this chapter, adjust the float to the overhaul kit specifications.
9. Model E2SE—Install the TPS spring in the main body well, then carefully seat the TPS electrical connector.

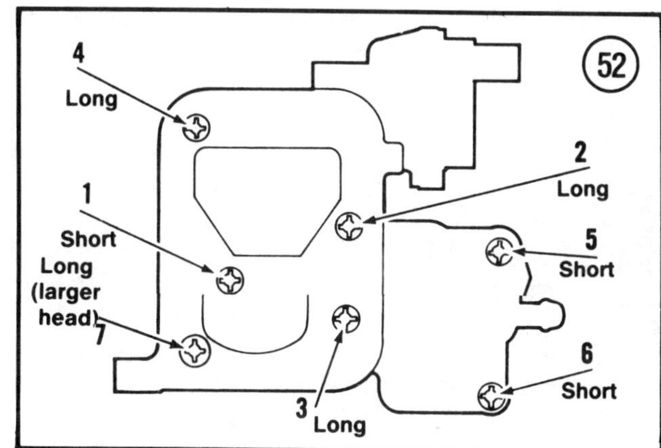

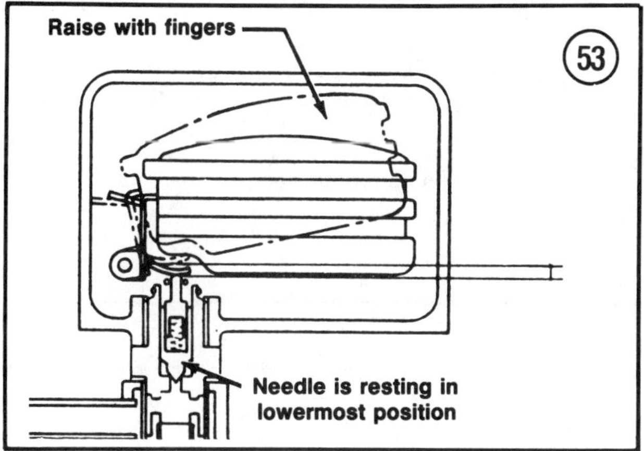

10. Install the pump return spring and plunger in the pump well.
11. Install a new air horn gasket.
12. Model E2SE—Install the vent stack/screen assembly on the air horn.
13. Install a new pump plunger retainer and seal. Stake in place with a small screwdriver.
14. Repeat Step 13 to install the TPS plunger retainer and seal.
15. Install the TPS plunger by pushing it through the air horn seal.
16. Install the air horn to the main body. Install and tighten the attaching screws (with lockwashers) following the sequence shown in **Figure 52**.
17. Rotate the fast idle cam to its full-up position. Insert the fast idle cam link in the cam slot and install the retainer clip.
18. Install the hot idle compensator with a new seal, if so equipped.
19. Model E2SE—Install a new seal on the mixture control solenoid plunger. Install the seal retainer on the solenoid plunger with a 3/16 in. socket and hammer. Drive retainer on stem just far enough to hold seal in place.
20. Model E2SE—Lubricate the mixture control solenoid plunger seal with silicone grease or light engine oil. Install solenoid to carburetor with a twisting motion to prevent seal damage or distortion.
21. Attach the intermediate choke rod to the choke lever with the plastic bushing. Install a new retaining clip.
22. Install the vacuum break diaphragm(s), if so equipped.
23. Connect the pump rod to the pump lever. Install the pump rod retaining clip, if used.

Mixture Control Solenoid Test (E2SE Carburetor)

Poor performance or poor fuel economy can result from a sticking, binding or leaking MCS solenoid. The solenoid can be removed with the carburetor on the engine.

1. Remove the 3 mixture control solenoid screws. Lift the solenoid from the carburetor air horn with a twisting motion. Remove and discard the solenoid gasket. Remove and discard the stem retainer and seal (**Figure 45**).
2. Connect a jumper lead between one of the solenoid terminals and the positive battery post.
3. Jumper the other solenoid terminal to a good ground.
4. Connect a hand vacuum pump to the solenoid stem and apply a minimum of 25 in. Hg vacuum.
5. Time the leakdown rate from 20 to 15 in. Hg vacuum. If leakage exceeds 5 in. in 5 seconds, replace the solenoid.
6. Remove the jumper lead from the positive battery terminal and note the vacuum pump reading. If it does not return to zero immediately (less than one second), replace the solenoid.

Float Level Adjustment

Hitachi DCH 340 and DFP 340

The fuel level should be within the range shown on the float chamber window glass when the engine is level and stationary. If the fuel level is above or below this line, bend the float seat as required to bring the fuel to the correct level in the sight glass.

The needle valve stroke should be about 0.059 in. (1.5 mm). To check the stroke, invert the carburetor and fully raise the float. See **Figure 53**.

6

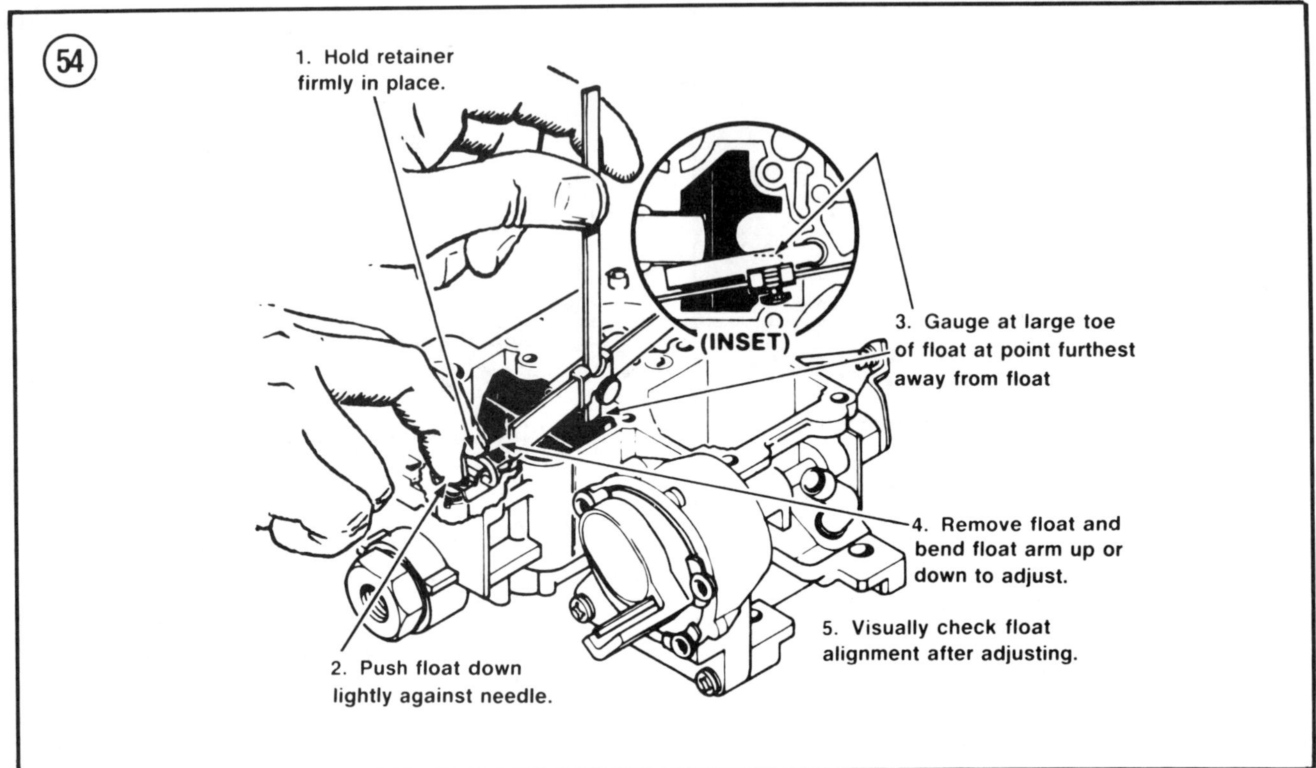

Rochester 2SE/E2SE

Follow the procedure shown in **Figure 54** to make the float adjustment. Unless specified otherwise in the overhaul kit instructions, all 2SE carburetors use a 7/16 in. (11.5 mm) float level setting, measured from the top of the float bowl casting surface to the top of the float toe. All E2SE carburetors use a 13/32 in. (10.3 mm) float level setting, measured at the same point.

The float level can also be checked on the vehicle with the help of a gauge pin kit (GM part No. J-9789-135). Refer to **Figure 55**. Use the blue gauge for 2SE and the white gauge for E2SE carburetors.

1. Remove the vent stack/screen assembly and the air horn screw as shown in **Figure 55**.
2. Start the engine and run at idle with the choke blocked wide open.
3. Carefully place the gauge in the air horn screw hole with its scale in the vent hole.

NOTE

Do not press down on the gauge. Let it float freely.

4. Sight the gauge at eye level and read the mark that aligns with the top of the vent hole casting. If the setting varies more than ±1.5 mm from the

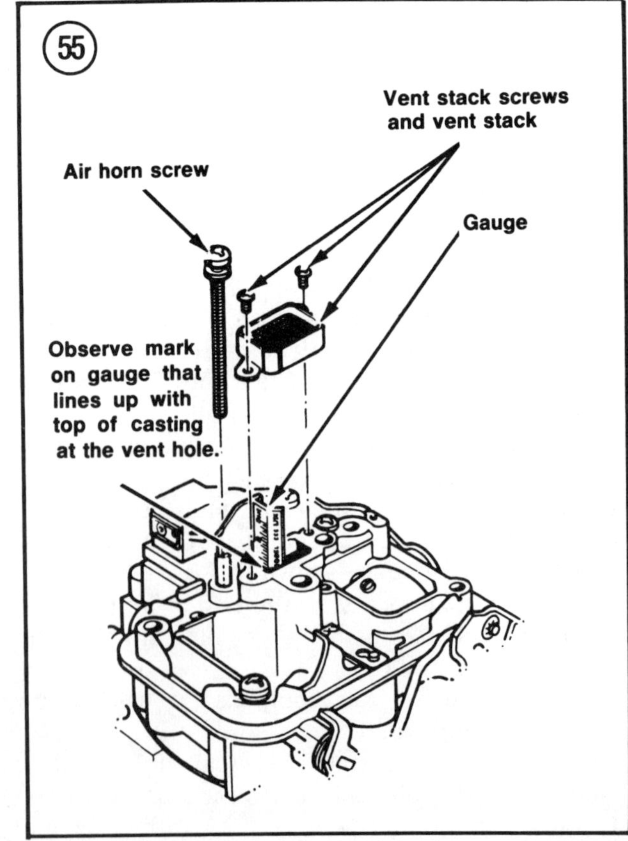

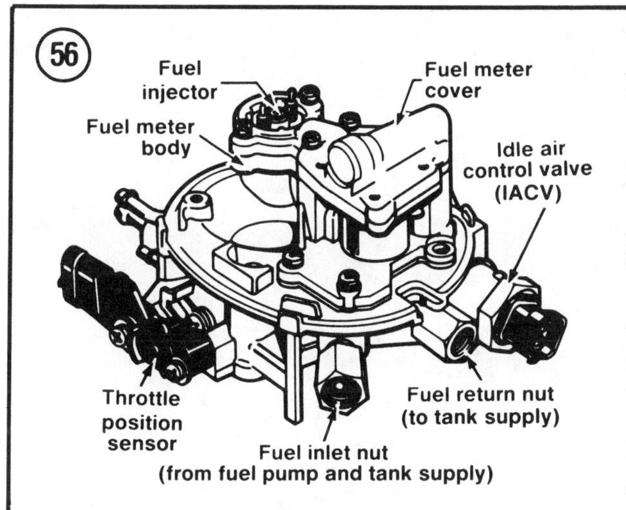

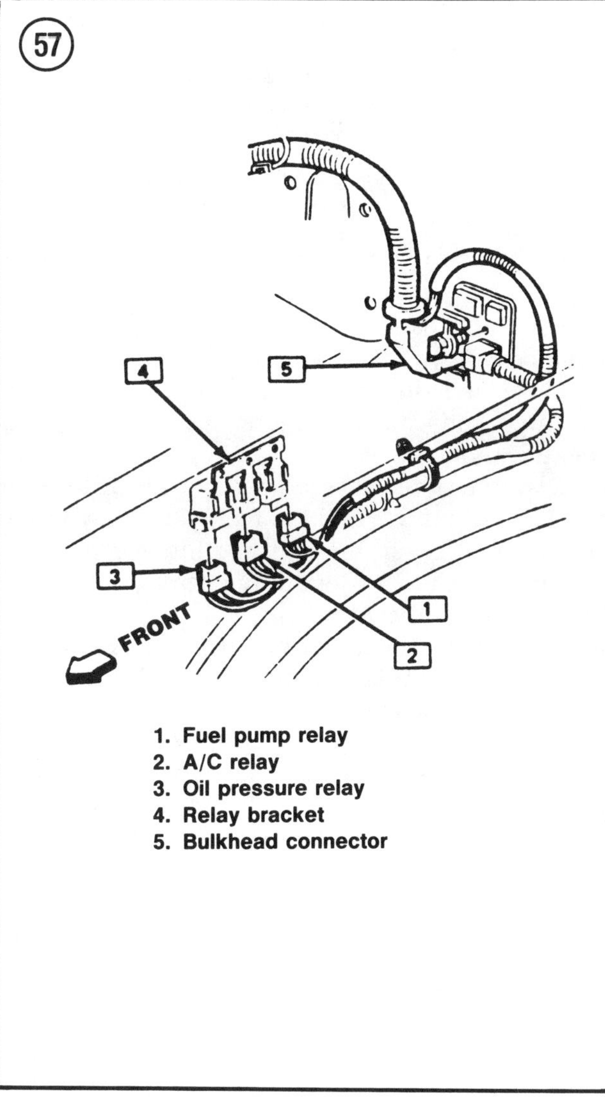

1. Fuel pump relay
2. A/C relay
3. Oil pressure relay
4. Relay bracket
5. Bulkhead connector

specified float setting, remove the air horn and adjust the float to specifications.

5. Install the air horn screw and vent stack/screen assembly.

THROTTLE BODY FUEL INJECTION

The 2.5L and 1986 2.8L V6 engines are equipped with throttle body fuel injection. The 2.5L engine uses a Rochester Model 300 throttle body injection (TBI) unit with a single injector; the 2.8L V6 uses a Model 220 with 2 injectors. **Figure 56** shows the Model 300 TBI unit; the Model 220 appearance is similar.

The TBI unit contains 1 (Model 300) or 2 (Model 220) electrically operated injectors that meter fuel into the intake air stream under the direction of the electronic control module (ECM). The ECM receives electrical signals from various sensors, refers to its stored program memory and calculates the precise amount and timing of fuel required by the engine. Fuel delivery time of the injector(s) is modified by the ECM to accomodate special engine conditions such as cranking, cold starts, elevation and acceleration or deceleration.

The basic TBI assembly consists of 2 major aluminum castings:

a. The throttle body containing a valve to control air flow.
b. A fuel meter body assembly containing an integral fuel pressure regulator and the injector(s).

6

System Operation

Filtered fuel is supplied to the TBI unit by an electric fuel pump mounted in the fuel tank. When the ignition switch is turned ON, a fuel pump relay located on the air conditioning relay bracket (**Figure 57**) activates the in-tank pump for 1.5-2 seconds to prime the injector. If the ECM does not receive a reference signal from the distributor within a certain time, it shuts down the fuel pump.

Fuel flow is controlled by varying the duration of injection according to signals from the ECM. Excess fuel passes through a pressure regulator and is then returned to the fuel tank. A throttle position sensor (TPS) informs the ECM of throttle valve position. An idle air control (IAC) assembly maintains a pre-programmed idle speed according to directions from the ECM.

Since the TBI system is electronically controlled, no attempt should be made to adjust the idle speed. Owner service should be limited to replacement only. If the TBI system is not working properly, take the vehicle to a Chevrolet or GMC dealer for diagnosis and adjustment.

System Pressure Relief

The Model 220 TBI unit has a bleed restriction in the fuel meter cover. This allows system pressure to bleed down as soon as the engine is shut off.

The Model 300 TBI unit does not have this feature. Before opening any fuel connection on the 2.5L TBI-equipped engine, the fuel pressure must be relieved to reduce the risk of fire and personal injury.

1. Place the transmission in PARK (automatic) or NEUTRAL (manual).
2. Set the parking brake and block the drive wheels.
3. Remove the fuel pump fuse from the fuse block.
4. Turn the ignition key to START. The engine will start and run for a few seconds until it runs out of fuel. Turn ignition key to START again and hold for another 3 seconds. This will dissipate fuel pressure and permit safe disconnection of the fuel lines.
5. Place a cloth under the line(s) to be serviced to catch any fuel spillage.
6. When fuel system service has been completed and all lines and components reconnected, install the fuel pump fuse in the fuse block.
7. Turn the ignition switch ON but do not start the engine. Inspect system components for leaks and repair if necessary before starting the engine.

Throttle Body Removal/Installation

1. 2.5L engine—Relieve system pressure as described in this chapter.
2. Remove the air cleaner as described in this chapter.
3. Disconnect the electrical connectors at the idle air control (IAC) and throttle position sensor (TPS).
4. Carefully disconnect the injector harness to prevent damage to the electrical connector pins.
5. Disconnect the throttle linkage and return spring. Disconnect the transmission TV (throttle valve) cable and cruise control cable, if so equipped.

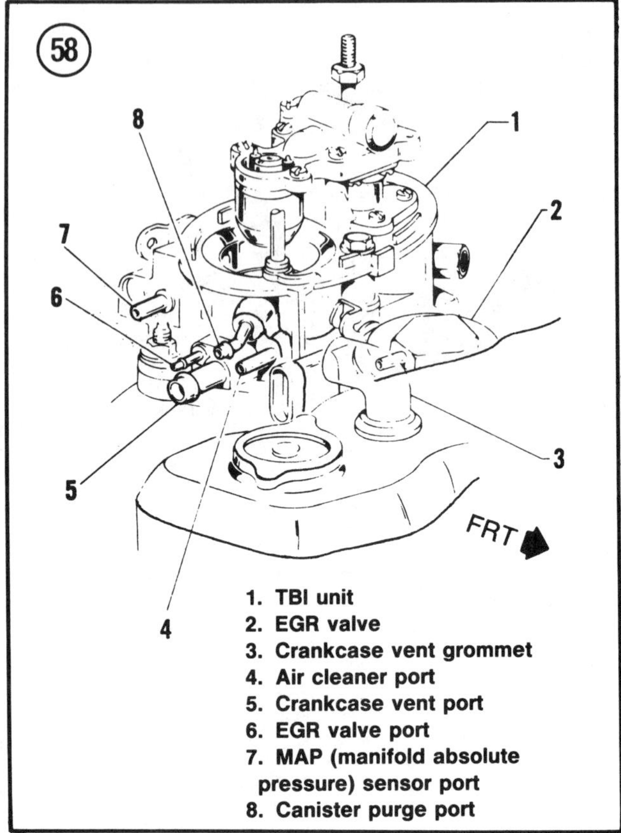

1. TBI unit
2. EGR valve
3. Crankcase vent grommet
4. Air cleaner port
5. Crankcase vent port
6. EGR valve port
7. MAP (manifold absolute pressure) sensor port
8. Canister purge port

6. Label and disconnect all vacuum lines at the throttle body. See **Figure 58** (typical) for identification.
7. Disconnect the fuel supply and return lines at the TBI assembly. Hold the fuel inlet nut with one wrench and loosen the fuel line fitting nut with a second wrench to prevent fitting damage. Plug both lines to prevent leakage.
8. Remove the fasteners holding the TBI unit to the intake manifold. Remove the TBI unit and flange mounting gasket. Discard the gasket.
9. Installation is the reverse of removal. Use a new gasket and tighten fasteners to 13 ft.-lb. (18 N•m) for 2.5L engines and 18 ft.-lb. (25 N•m) for 2.8L V6 engines. Tighten fuel and return line fittings to 19 ft.-lb. (26 N•m).

Throttle Body Disassembly

Refer to **Figure 59** (2.5L) or **Figure 60** (2.8L V6) for this procedure.

1. Remove the air cleaner studs from the throttle body assembly. Remove the 5 fuel meter cover

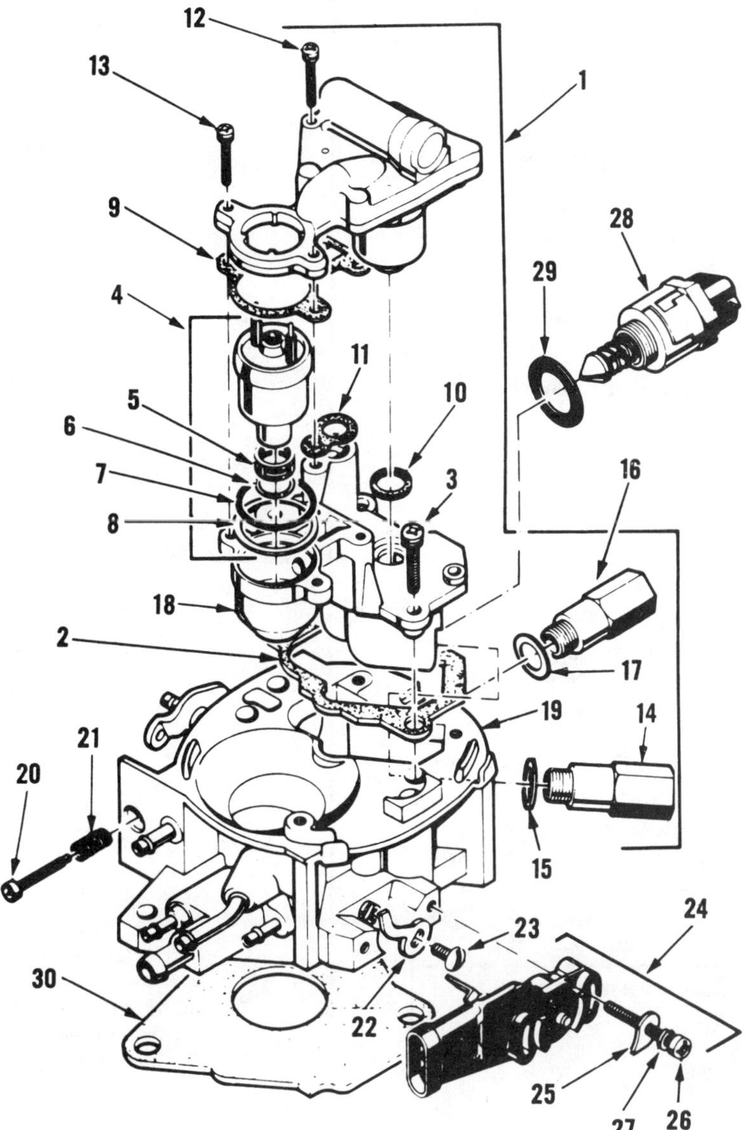

1. Fuel meter assembly
2. Fuel meter body gasket
3. Screw & washer assembly
4. Fuel injector kit
5. Fuel injector nozzle filter
6. Small O-ring seal
7. Large O-ring seal
8. Fuel injector backup washer
9. Fuel meter cover gasket
10. Pressure regulator dust seal
11. Fuel meter outlet gasket
12. Long (3) screw & washer assembly
13. Short (2) screw & washer assembly
14. Fuel inlet nut
15. Fuel inlet nut gasket
16. Fuel outlet nut
17. Fuel outlet nut gasket
18. Fuel meter body assembly
19. Throttle body assembly
20. Idle stop screw
21. Idle stop screw spring
22. TPS lever
23. TPS lever attaching screw
24. Throttle position kit sensor
25. TPS retainer (2)
26. TPS attaching screw (2)
27. TPS screw washer (2)
28. Idle air control valve
29. Control valve to throttle body gasket
30. Flange mounting gasket

6

screws and lockwashers (**Figure 61**). Lift the fuel meter cover and pressure regulator assembly from the throttle body.

WARNING
*Do not remove the 4 screws holding the pressure regulator to the fuel meter cover (**Figure 62**). The regulator contains a large spring under considerable tension which could cause serious personal injury if released accidentally. The pressure regulator is preset at the factory and is serviced (with the fuel meter cover) only as a complete assembly.*

2. Remove and discard the fuel meter cover gaskets.
3. Remove the pressure regulator dust seal from the fuel meter body (**Figure 61**).

NOTE
Do not immerse the fuel meter cover in carburetor cleaner, as it will damage the pressure regulator diaphragms and gaskets.

CAUTION
Use care in Step 4 to avoid damage to the electrical connecting pins on the top of the injector.

4. Reinstall the fuel meter gasket on the fuel meter body to protect the casting and pry the injector from the body with a screwdriver as shown in **Figure 63**. Repeat this step to remove the other injector on Model 220 units.

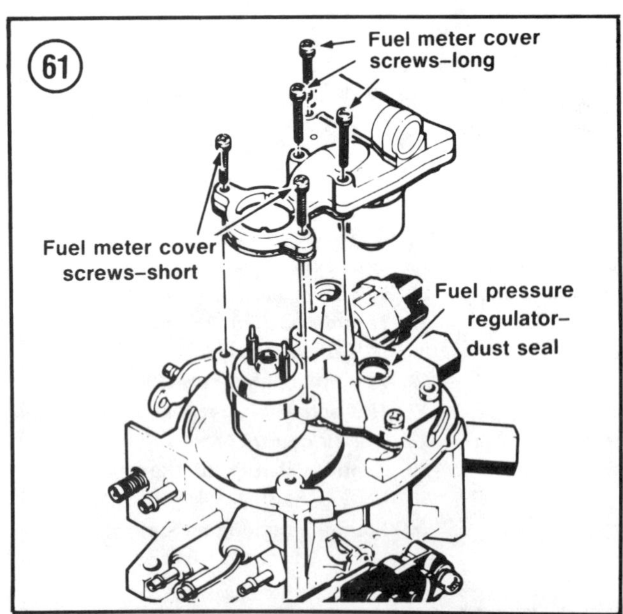

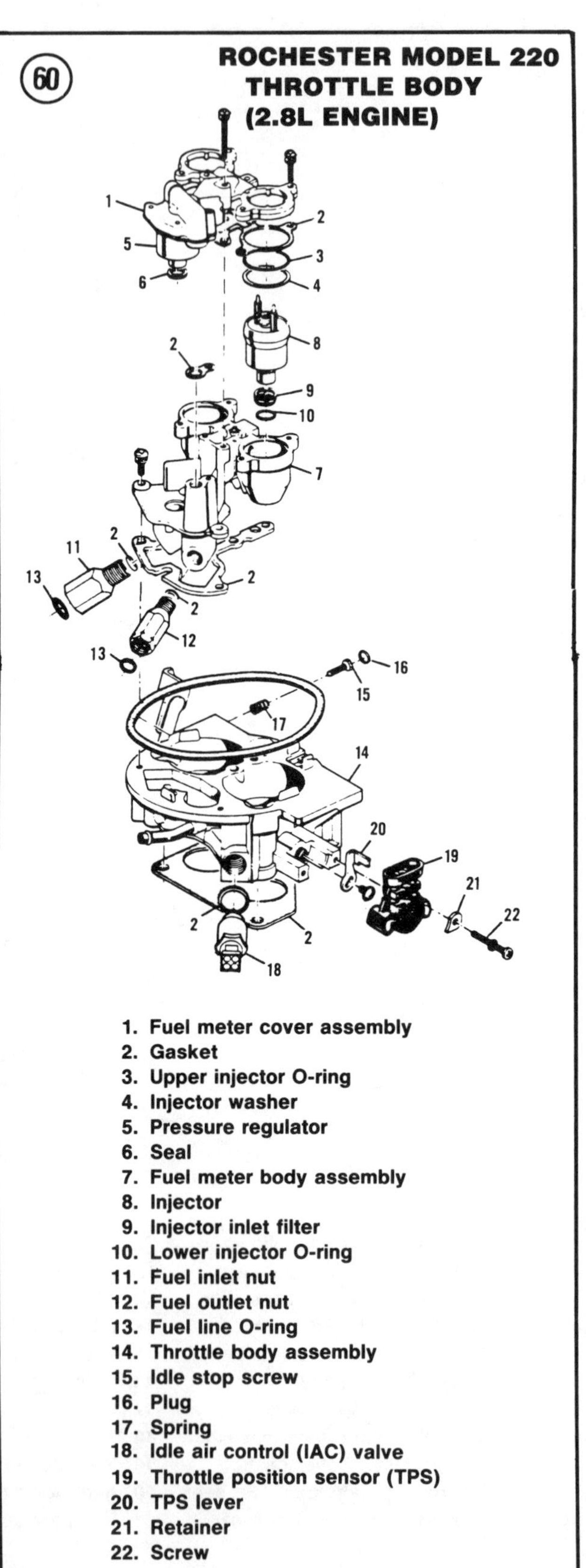

1. Fuel meter cover assembly
2. Gasket
3. Upper injector O-ring
4. Injector washer
5. Pressure regulator
6. Seal
7. Fuel meter body assembly
8. Injector
9. Injector inlet filter
10. Lower injector O-ring
11. Fuel inlet nut
12. Fuel outlet nut
13. Fuel line O-ring
14. Throttle body assembly
15. Idle stop screw
16. Plug
17. Spring
18. Idle air control (IAC) valve
19. Throttle position sensor (TPS)
20. TPS lever
21. Retainer
22. Screw

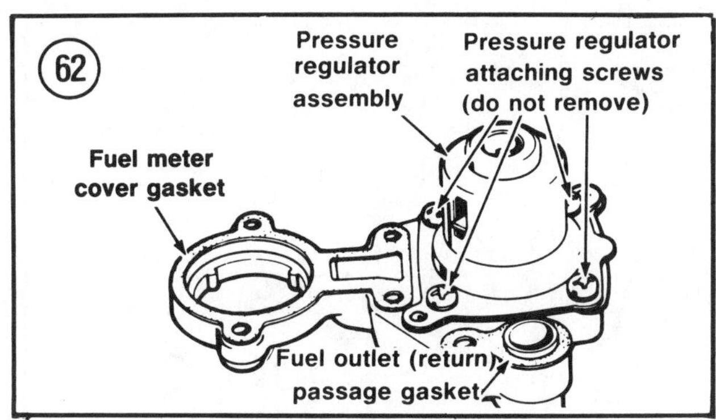

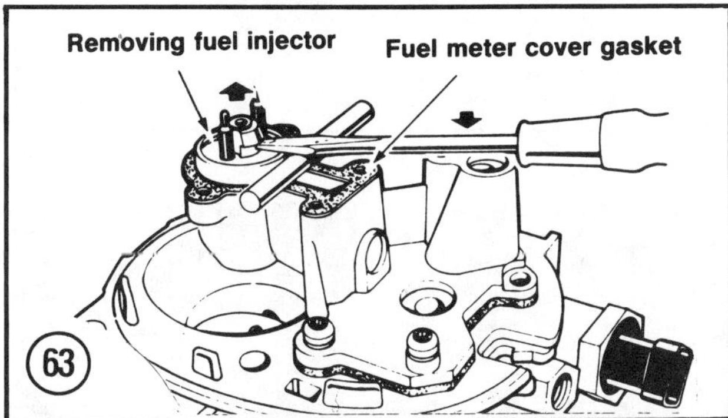

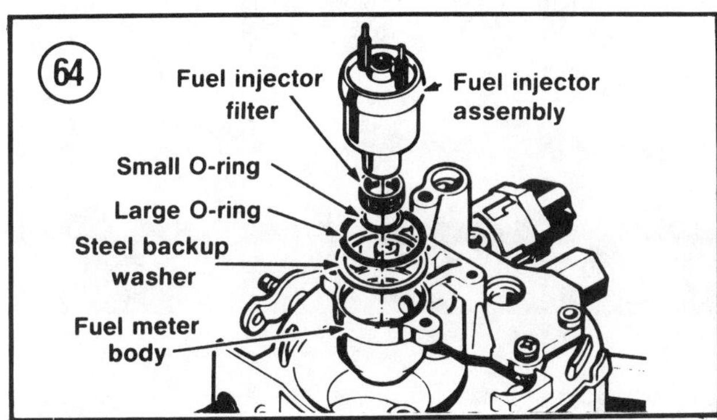

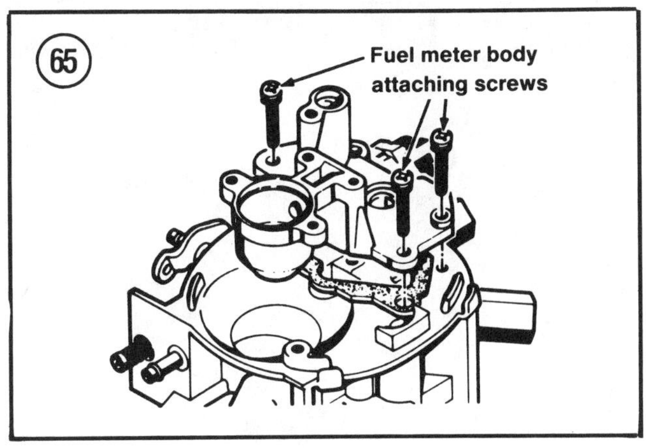

NOTE

The fuel injector is serviced as a complete assembly. Do not disassemble beyond Step 5 and Step 6. Do not immerse injector in any type of cleaner.

5. Rotate injector fuel filter with a back-and-forth motion and remove from the injector base. See **Figure 64**.
6. Remove the large O-ring and steel backup washer from the top of the injector cavity in the fuel meter body (**Figure 64**).
7. Remove the small O-ring from the bottom of the injector cavity.
8. Remove the fuel inlet/outlet nuts and gaskets from the fuel meter body.
9. Remove the 3 fuel meter body screws and lockwashers (**Figure 65**). Remove the fuel meter body and insulator gasket from the throttle body assembly.

NOTE

Do not remove the throttle position sensor or idle air control assembly from the throttle body. The TPS is factory-adjusted and the attaching screws are spot-welded to the throttle body to maintain its critical setting. Under normal service conditions, the throttle body need not be immersed in cleaner.

Cleaning and Inspection

1. Clean all metal parts thoroughly and blow dry with compressed air. Check all fuel passages to make sure they are free of burrs and dirt.
2. Inspect the casting mating surfaces for damage that might affect gasket sealing.
3. Discard all O-rings.
4. Check injector fuel filter for plugging or damage. Clean in gasoline or replace as required.

Throttle Body Assembly

Refer to **Figure 59** (2.5L) or **Figure 60** (2.8L V6) for this procedure.

1. Install a new fuel meter body gasket on the throttle body.

NOTE

Thread locking compound is included in overhaul kits. If necessary, Threadlock Adhesive X-10 or equivalent may be used in its place.

2. Install the fuel meter body to the throttle body. Apply a small quantity of thread locking compound to the fuel meter body screws. Install screws with lockwashers and tighten to 3.5 ft.-lb. (4 N•m).
3. Install fuel inlet/outlet nuts with new gaskets. Tighten nuts to 260 in.-lb. (29 N•m).
4. Install fuel filter to nozzle end of injector with a twisting motion. Large end of cone-shaped filter must face upward so the filter will cover the rib at the injector base.
5. Lubricate a new small O-ring with lithium grease or equivalent. Install O-ring on nozzle end of injector and press up against injector fuel filter.
6. Install steel washer in recess of injector cavity in fuel meter body.
7. Lubricate a new large O-ring with lithium grease or equivalent. Install O-ring above steel washer and seat in cavity recess. O-ring will be flush with top of fuel meter body casting surface when properly installed.
8. Install injector with a twisting/pushing motion. Nozzle O-ring must be centered in bottom of injector cavity and raised lug on injector base must be aligned with the cast-in notch in the fuel meter body cavity.
9. Push injector down as shown in **Figure 66** until fully seated in cavity. Electrical connector pin should be parallel with throttle shaft in throttle body.
10. Install a new dust seal in the fuel meter body recess.
11. Install a new gasket on the fuel meter cover.
12. Install fuel meter cover to fuel meter body. Apply a thread locking compound to cover attaching screws. Install screws with lockwashers as shown in **Figure 61** and tighten to 28 in.-lb. (3 N•m).

FUEL PUMP

The non-serviceable mechanical fuel pump used with carburetted engines is mounted above the distributor and to one side of the thermostat housing on the 1.9L engine (**Figure 67**). The 2.0L fuel pump is mounted on the right side of the block under the intake manifold. See **Figure 68**. Fuel pump location on the V6 engine is shown in **Figure 69**. The pump pushrod is actuated by an eccentric on the camshaft.

All fuel-injected engines use an electric fuel pump located in the fuel tank. The pump is

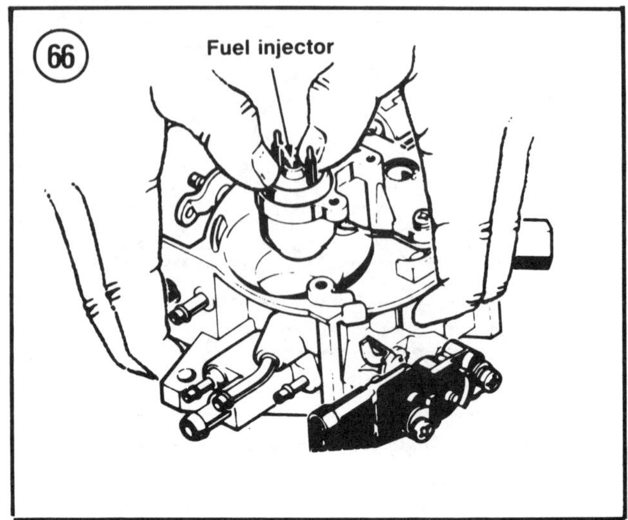

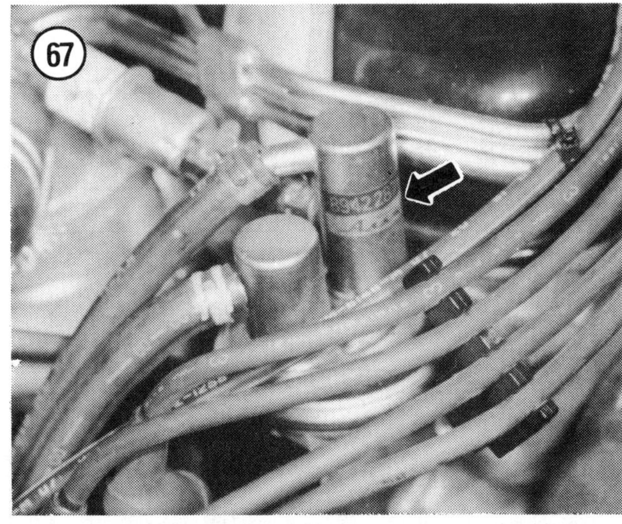

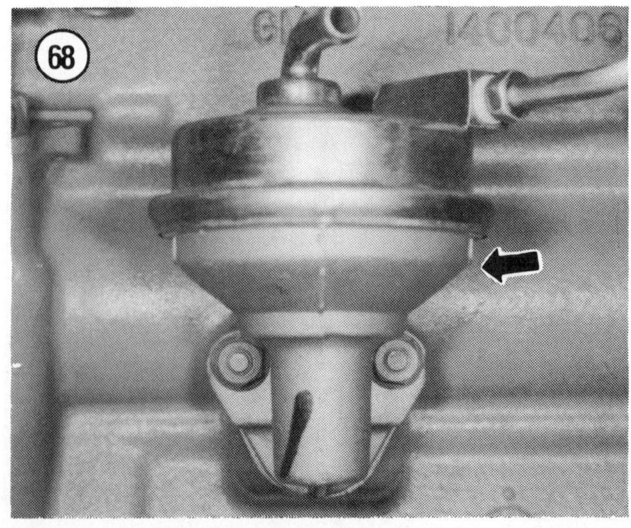

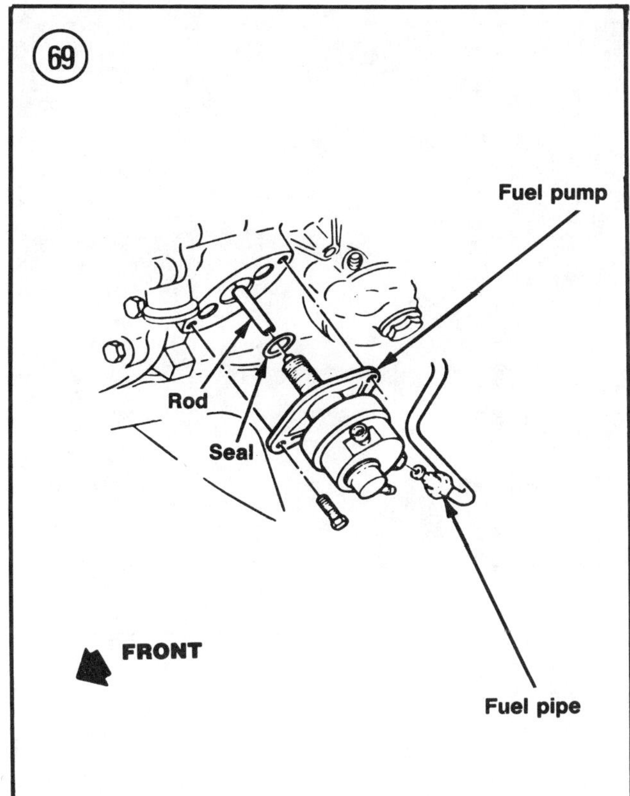

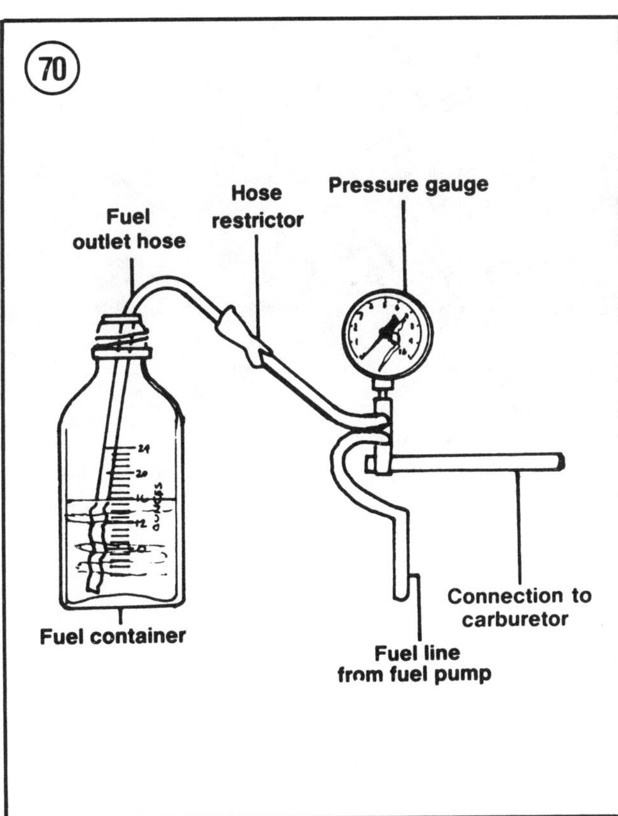

activated by a relay in the engine compartment (**Figure 57**).

The 2 most common fuel pump problems are incorrect pressure and low volume. Low pressure results in a too-lean mixture and too little fuel at high speeds. High pressure will cause flooding and result in poor mileage. Low volume also results in too little fuel at high speeds.

If a fuel system problem is suspected, check the fuel filter first as described in Chapter Three. If the filter is not clogged or dirty, test the fuel pump on carburetted engines as described below.

Incorrect fuel line pressure with fuel-injected engines may be caused by a defective fuel pressure regulator or the in-tank fuel pump. Because of the complexity of the TBI system, have a Chevrolet or GMC dealer perform the necessary fuel pump and pressure regulator tests.

Pressure Test (Carburetted Engine)

1. Remove the air cleaner as described in this chapter.
2. Disconnect the fuel line at the carburetor fuel filter.
3. Connect a pressure gauge and a flexible hose with a restrictor clamp between the fuel line and filter inlet, as shown in **Figure 70**.
4. Place the end of the line in a clean quart-size container.
5. Start the engine and let it idle. Vent the system into the container by opening and closing the restrictor.
6. Let the pressure stabilize and read the gauge. If it is below 4.5 psi, replace the fuel pump.

Flow Test (Carburetted Engine)

1. Perform Steps 1-4 of *Pressure Test, Carburetted Engine* described above.
2. Let the engine continue to idle and open the hose restrictor for 30 seconds, then close the restrictor.
3. Check the container. It should be approximately 1/2 full. If not, replace the fuel pump.
4. Disconnect the pressure gauge and restrictor line. Reconnect the fuel line to the carburetor fuel filter.

Replacement
(Carburetted Engine)

Refer to **Figure 71** (2.0L) or **Figure 69** (V6) for this procedure (the 1.9L is similar to the 2.0L).

1. Disconnect the negative battery cable.
2. 1.9L engine—Remove the distributor. See Chapter Eight.

3A. 1.9L engine—Slide the clamps on the inlet and outlet hoses back with pliers. Disconnect the hoses from the fuel pump fittings.

3B. 2.0L and V6 engine—Use 2 open-end wrenches to loosen the fuel line nut at the pump outlet fitting. Disconnect the outlet line and the inlet hose.

4. 1.9L engine—Remove the engine lift hook.
5. Remove the pump mounting fasteners.
6. Remove the pump. Remove and discard the gasket or seal.
7. Clean any gasket residue from the engine and pump mounting flanges with a putty knife.
8. Lubricate the pushrod with engine oil. Install the pushrod; if it does not fit all the way down in the engine, rotate the crankshaft pulley with a suitable wrench to position the camshaft eccentric at its low point.
9. Install the fuel pump to the block with a new gasket or seal. Tighten the mounting fasteners to 13-18 ft.-lb. (18-24 N•m).

10A. 1.9L engine—Connect the inlet and outlet hoses to the pump fittings. Slide the hose clamps over the pump fittings with pliers to secure the hoses in place.

10B. 2.0L and V6 engine—Connect the fuel pump outlet pipe and inlet hose. Use 2 open-end wrenches to tighten the fuel line nut at the pump outlet to 18 ft.-lb. (25 N•m).

11. Reconnect the negative battery cable.
12. Start the engine and let it run for 2 minutes. Check for fuel leaks at the pump base and inlet/outlet connections.

FUEL TANK AND LINES

The fuel tank is mounted to the left frame rail and crossover rail at the left rear. Two metal straps hold the tank in place. One end of each strap is secured by a bolt through the hinge. The other end is fastened by a nut and bolt assembly (**Figure 72**).

Fuel Tank
Removal/Installation

1. Disconnect the negative battery cable.

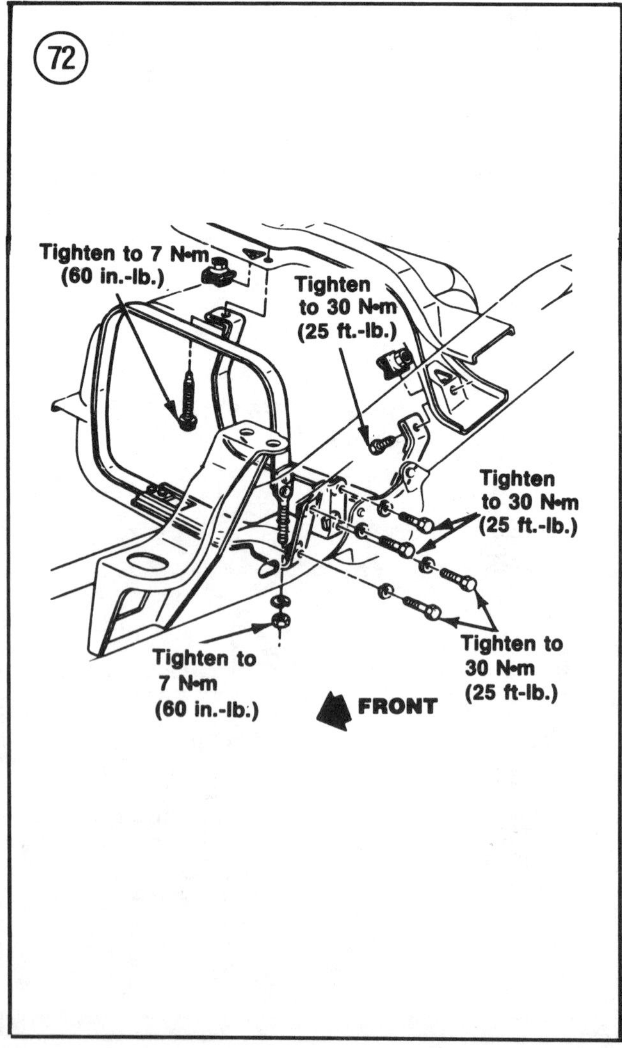

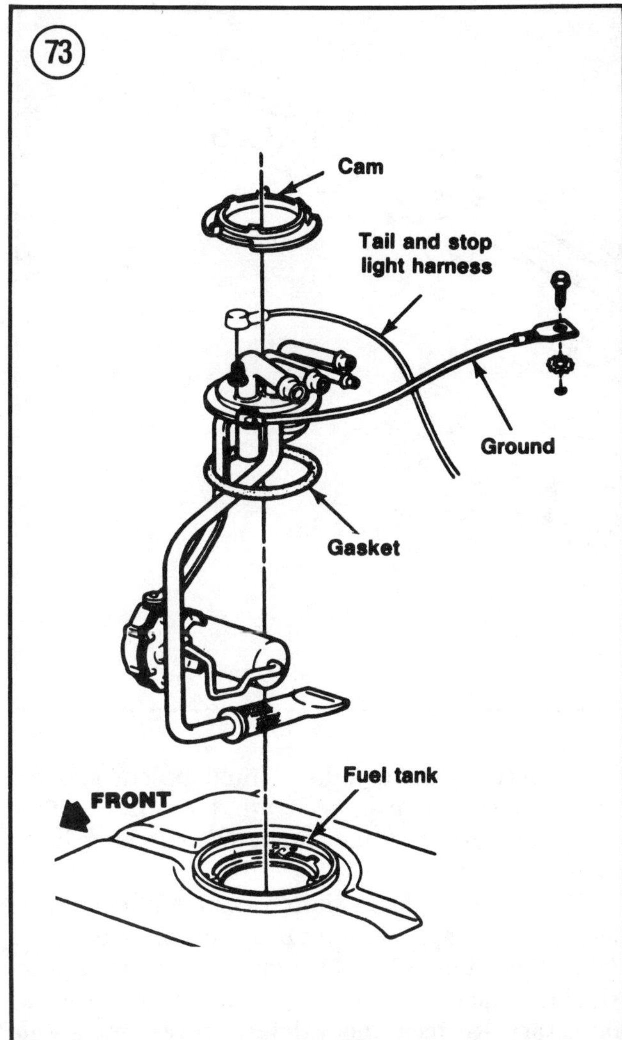

2. Remove the fuel tank filler cap.
3. Securely block both front wheels so the truck will not roll in either direction. Raise the vehicle with a jack and place it on jackstands.
4. Disconnect the fuel inlet line at the fuel pump.
5. Place a suitable container under the disconnected line. Siphon or pump the fuel through the inlet line into the container.

WARNING
Never store gasoline in an open container, since it is an extreme fire hazard. Store gasoline in a sealed metal container away from heat, sparks and flame.

6. Remove the fuel meter wire connector. Remove the fuel meter ground wire screw. See **Figure 73**.
7. Remove the filler pipe neck hose and vent hose (**Figure 74**). Disconnect the fuel lines at the hose connections.
8. Loosen the fuel tank strap rear support bolts. See **Figure 72**. Lower the tank enough to disconnect the fuel and vapor lines from the fuel meter. Remove the tank.
9. Installation is the reverse of removal.

6

Repairing Fuel Tank Leaks

Fuel tank leaks can be repaired by soldering.

WARNING
The fuel tank is capable of exploding and killing anyone nearby. Always observe the following precautions when repairing a tank.

1. Have the tank steam-cleaned *inside* and *outside*.

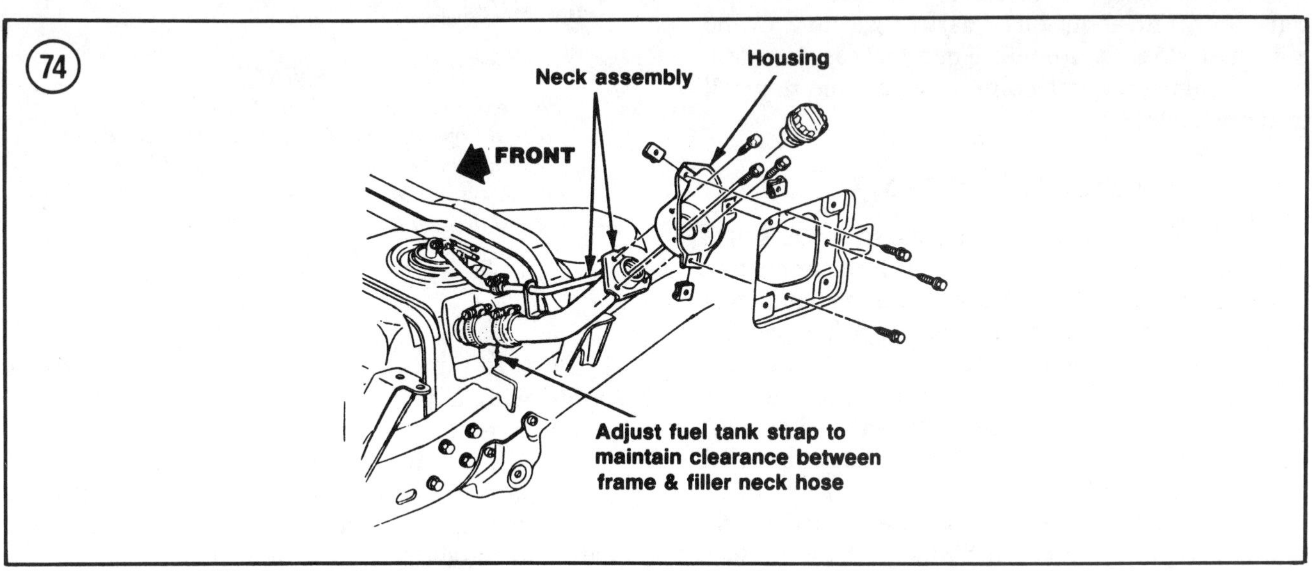

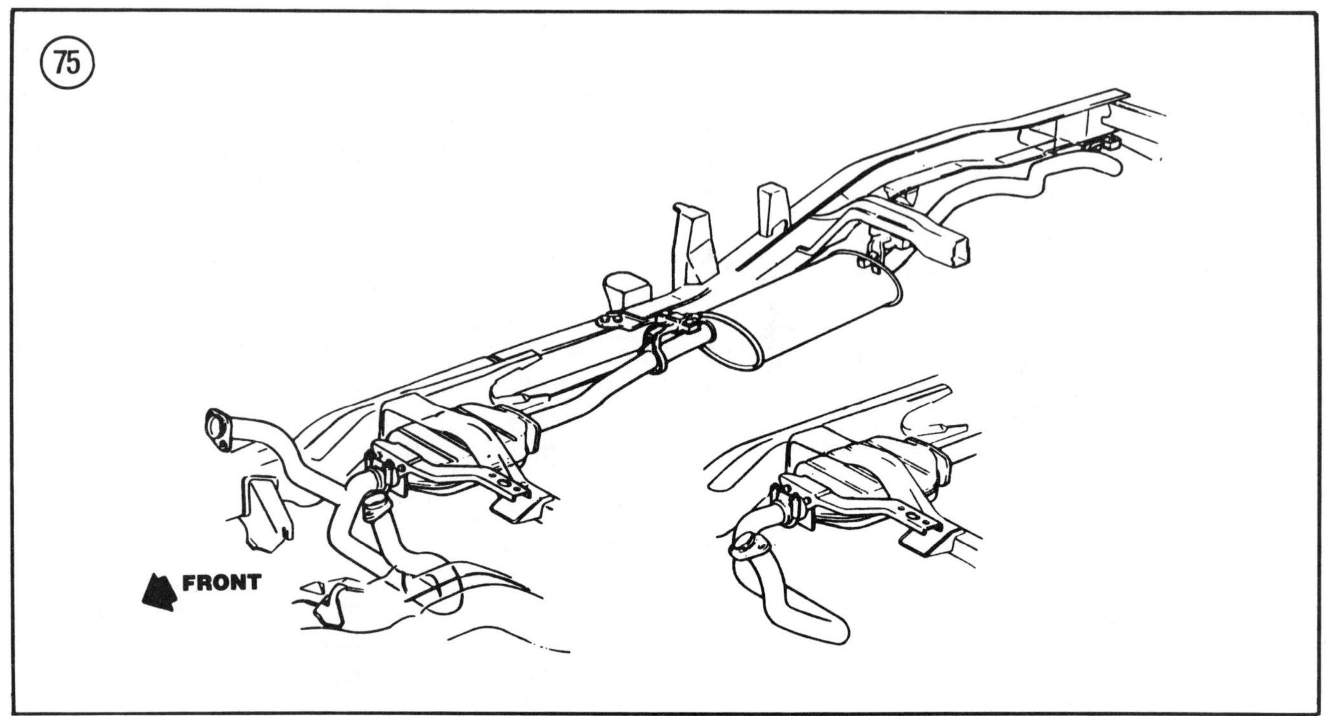

2. Fill the tank with inert gas such as nitrogen or carbon dioxide, or fill the tank *completely* with water. Gasoline residue on the tank walls can form a highly explosive vapor if allowed to mix with air.
3. Have a dry chemical (Class B) fire extinguisher close by.
4. Whenever the tank is cleaned, the fuel meter on the top of the tank should be removed (**Figure 73**) and the strainer screen cleaned with compressed air.

After making the necessary repairs, pour the water out, put about one quart of gasoline in the tank and slosh it around. Pour the gasoline out, blow the tank dry with compressed air and reinstall in the vehicle.

EXHAUST SYSTEM

The basic exhaust system consists of a single muffler, a single catalytic converter and connecting pipes. See **Figure 75**. A graphite-impregnated seal in the exhaust manifold-to-front pipe connection lets the engine move independently of the exhaust system. Chevrolet and GMC recommend that this seal and the pipe flange connecting nuts (**Figure 76**) be replaced whenever the pipe is disconnected from the manifold.

The muffler inlet/outlet pipes are welded to the muffler. Replace the tailpipe whenever the muffler is replaced. Welded joints should be cut and the new connections clamped with U-bolts. Coat all slip joints (except at the converter) with an exhaust system sealer.

The exhaust system should be free of corrosion, leaks, binding, grounding and/or excessive vibrations. Loose, broken or misaligned clamps, shields, brackets or pipes should be serviced as necessary to keep the exhaust system in a safe operating condition.

Removal/Installation

WARNING
The exhaust system is extremely hot under normal operating conditions. To avoid the possibillity of a bad burn, it is advisable to work on the system only when it is cool. Be especially careful around the catalytic converter on vehicles so equipped. It reaches temperatures in excess of 600° F after only a brief period of engine operation.

1. Prior to removal, soak all bolts, nuts and pipe joints with a penetrating oil such as WD-40 or Liquid Wrench.
2. Undo the required clamps and hanger brackets.
3. Replace worn, damaged or corroded component(s). Use new seals when installing a catalytic converter or manifold pipe.

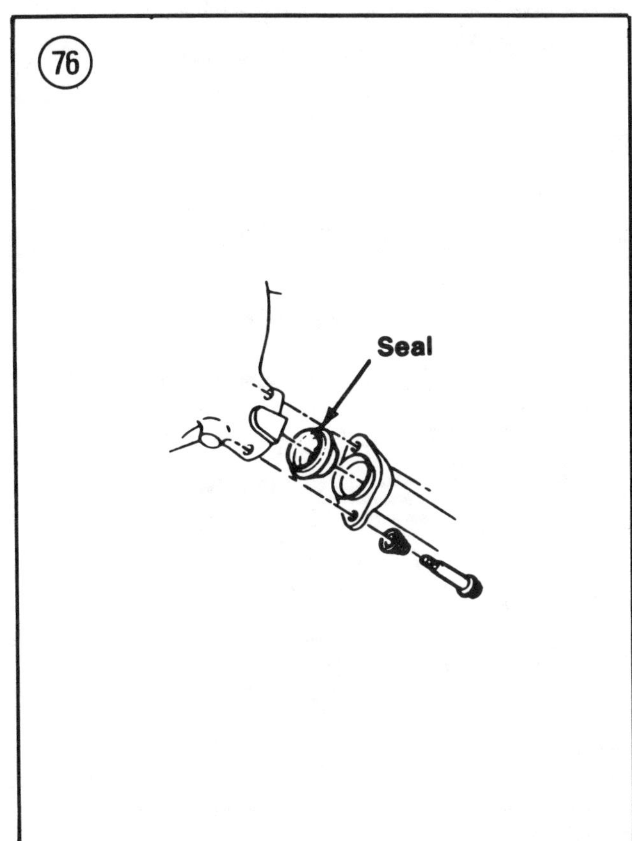

4. Clean manifold and clamp stud threads with a wire brush before installing new nuts.
5. Align the exhaust system. All components should have at least 3/4 in. clearance from the floor pan. Start at the front of the system and tighten all fasteners securely.

EMISSION CONTROL SYSTEMS

Figure 77 and **Figure 78** show typical vacuum line routing.

Computer Command Control (CCC) System

This electronically controlled system is used with all 2.0L and 2.5L engines, those carburetted V6 engines first sold in California and all TBI-equipped V6 engines. It monitors up to 15 different engine/vehicle functions and may control as many as 9 different operations through an electronic control module (ECM) and various sensors.

The ECM receives data signals concerning cooling system temperature, crankshaft and distributor rpm, throttle shaft position, manifold pressure and exhaust gas oxygen content. It

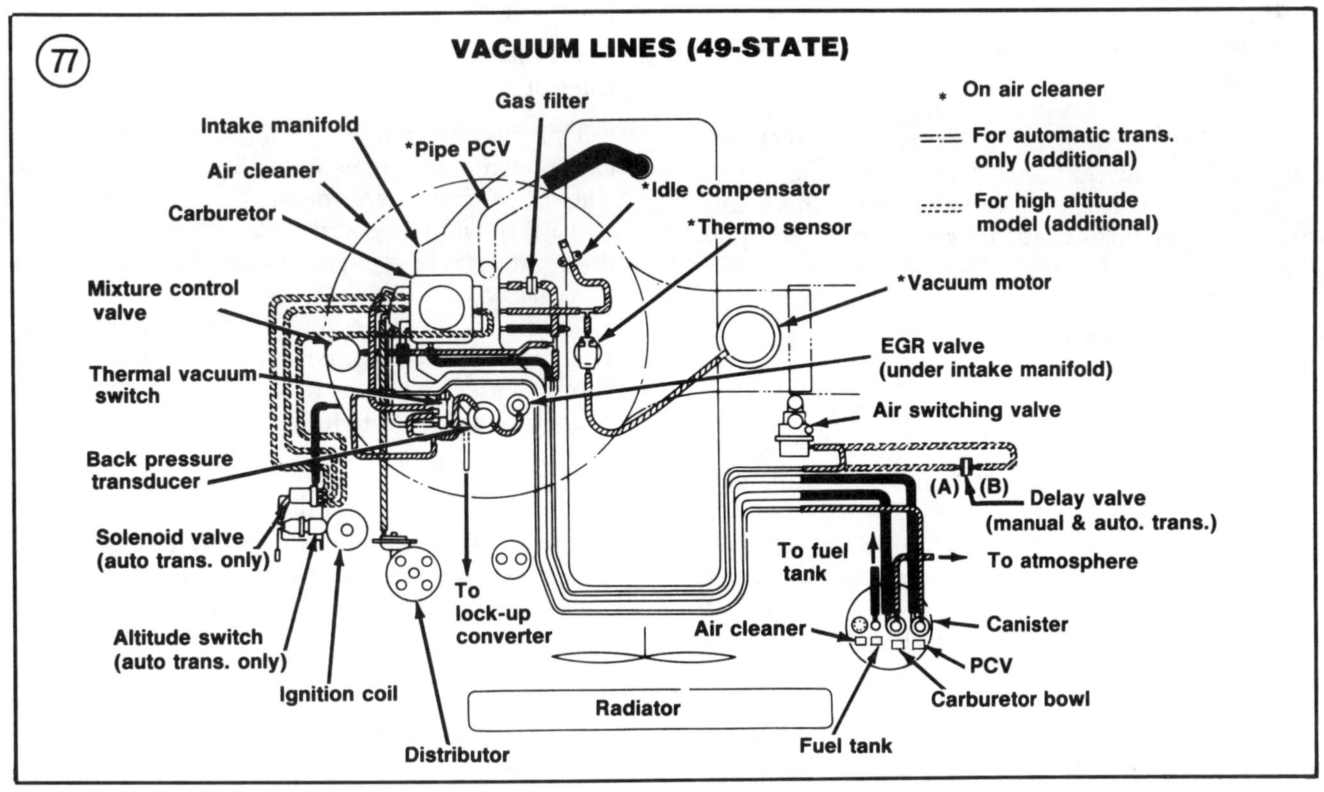

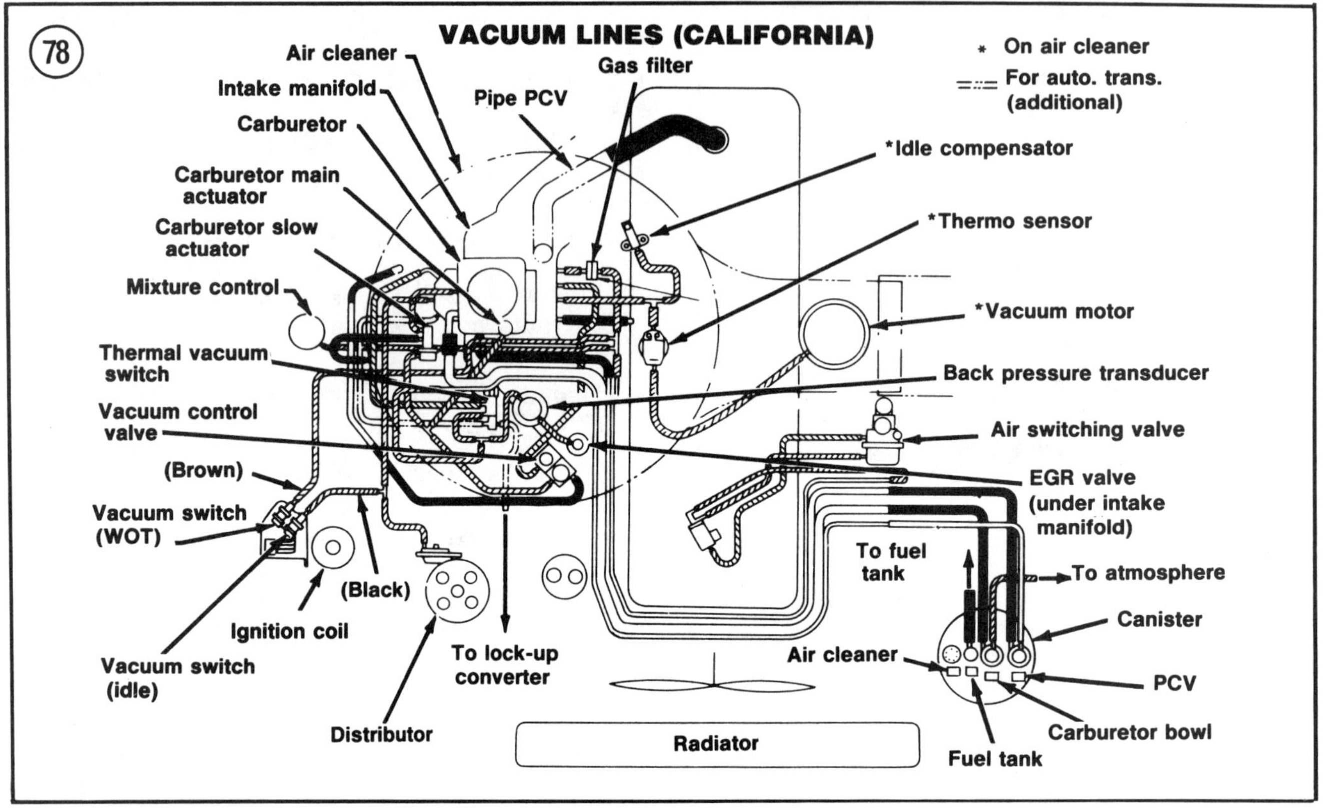

processes this information and sends back signals to control the air-fuel mixture, distributor advance, canister purge, air management system and other functions.

If a problem develops in the CCC system, a "Check Engine" lamp on the instrument panel with light. When this happens, return the vehicle to a GM dealer, who has the proper equipment and trained technicians to diagnose this complex system.

Closed Loop Emission Control System

The 1.9L engine uses a similar but less sophisticated engine control system in which the carburetor air-fuel ratio is controlled through a slow-cut solenoid valve on the carburetor. The electronic control module (ECM) interprets signals from the oxygen sensor in the exhaust manifold and operates a vacuum controller. The vacuum controller translates the electrical signals from the ECM into vacuum pulses to the slow-cut solenoid valve mounted on the carburetor. Adjustment of this system is not advised for the home mechanic and should be left to a GM dealer who has the required equipment and trained technicians to troubleshoot and correct any problems.

Evaporative Emission Control System

This system is used on all models to prevent gasoline vapors from escaping into the atmosphere. The ECM controls vacuum to a canister purge valve through a solenoid valve. If the purge valve does not operate properly, the entire canister must be replaced.

There is no scheduled maintenance of the system. Physical damage, leaks and missing components are the most common causes of evaporative system failures.

System inspection

1. Check the vapor lines for cracks or loose connections. Replace or tighten as necessary.
2. Check for a deformed fuel tank. Make sure the tank is not cracked and does not leak gasoline.
3. Inspect the carbon canister for cracks or other damage.
4. Check the vapor hoses and tubes to make sure they slope downhill from the carburetor to the canister.

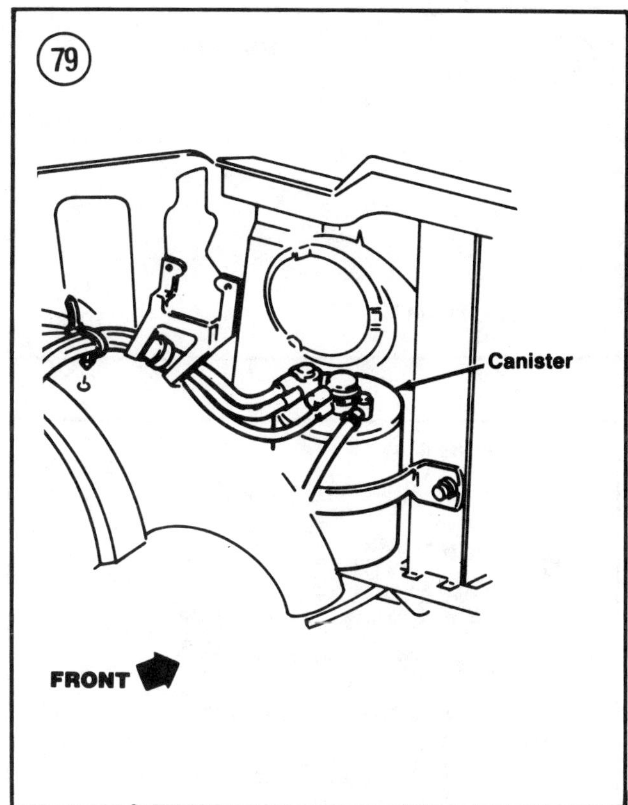

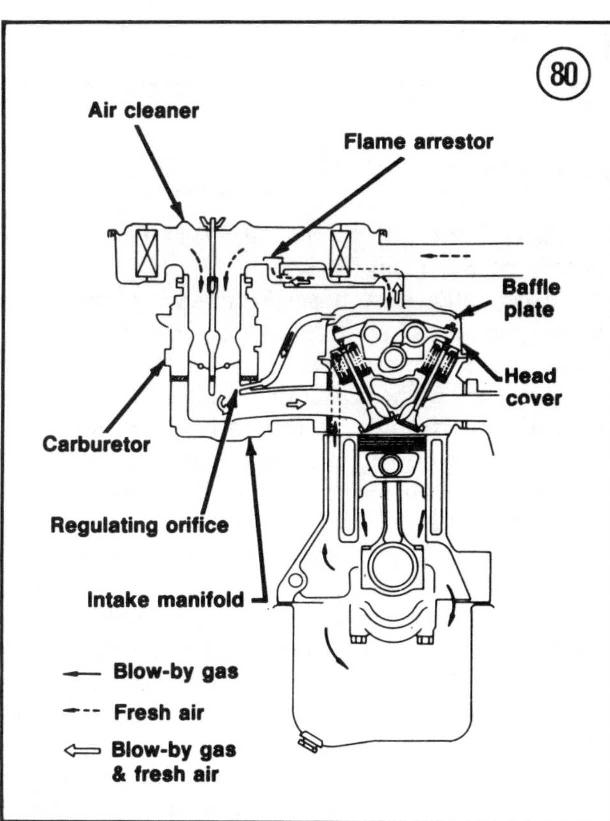

5. Check the fuel filler cap for a damaged gasket.

NOTE

Any damage or contamination which prevents the filler cap pressure-vacuum valve from working properly can result in deformation of the fuel tank.

Canister purge valve test

1. Disconnect the purge valve control vacuum line at the canister. There should be a vacuum signal from the line when the engine is operating above idle speed.
2. Connect a hand vacuum pump to the purge valve control diaphragm. Apply 7-10 in. Hg vacuum.
3. If the valve does not hold the vacuum, the purge valve is defective. Replace the entire canister assembly.

6

Canister replacement

Refer to **Figure 79** for this procedure.

1. Loosen the canister retaining bracket screw.
2. Loosen the air conditioning accumulator and pipe assembly attachments, if so equipped.

WARNING

Do not disconnect any air conditioning refrigerant lines.

3. Rotate the canister retainer. Remove the canister.
4. Transfer the canister hoses to the new canister one at a time to assure correct installation.
5. Install the canister in the retainer. Rotate the canister bracket over the canister and tighten the attaching screw.
6. Tighten the air conditioning accumulator and pipe assembly attachments, if loosened.

Positive Crankcase Ventilation (PCV) System

Gasoline engine

A closed crankcase ventilation system is used to recycle crankcase vapors into the combustion chambers for burning. A vent hose at the rear of the engine connects the crankcase to the valve cover. This provides a positive flow of air through the crankcase. Fresh air and crankcase vapors are draw into the intake manifold through a regulating orifice in the 1.9L engine (**Figure 80**) or a PCV valve in the valve cover of 2.0L, 2.5L and V6 engines (**Figure 81**).

The PCV system should be inspected and the PCV valve and air cleaner crankcase vent filter replaced at intervals specified in Chapter Three.

2.2L diesel engine

A baffle plate in the valve cover separates oil particles from blow-by gases. A vapor separator containing a PCV valve is installed in the valve cover and connected to the intake manifold by a connecting breather hose. The vapor separator is used as a safety feature to prevent oil from entering the combustion chamber. If the vapor separator system is disabled, the engine crankcase oil could cause the engine to run unrestricted and destroy itself. In such a case, even shutting off the fuel supply would not stop the engine.

There is no recommended service for the PCV system. However, it is a good idea to periodically check the system for restricted, plugged or deteriorated hoses. Whenever the valve cover is removed, clean the baffle with solvent and dry with compressed air.

Air Management System

The 1.9L engine air management system (**Figure 82**) consists of an air pump, air manifold, air switching valve, mixture control valve and one check valve. The system reduces hydrocarbon and carbon monoxide emissions by pumping fresh air into the exhaust ports near the valves during cold engine operation. This allows the hot exhaust gases to burn for a longer time. When required by engine operating conditions, the ECM switches air injection from the exhaust ports to the air cleaner (California) or atmosphere (Federal) by de-energizing the air switching valve.

The mixture control valve permits air to enter the intake manifold when there is a rapid increase in manifold vacuum during deceleration. This dilutes the air-fuel mixture and prevents an exhaust backfire.

The check valve prevents hot exhaust gases from reversing their flow in the system in case of a pump malfunction.

The 2.0L, 2.5L and V6 air management system operates in much the same way, except that engines equipped with CCC send air to the exhaust ports only when first started. Once the CCC system switches to closed loop operation, the air is diverted to the air cleaner.

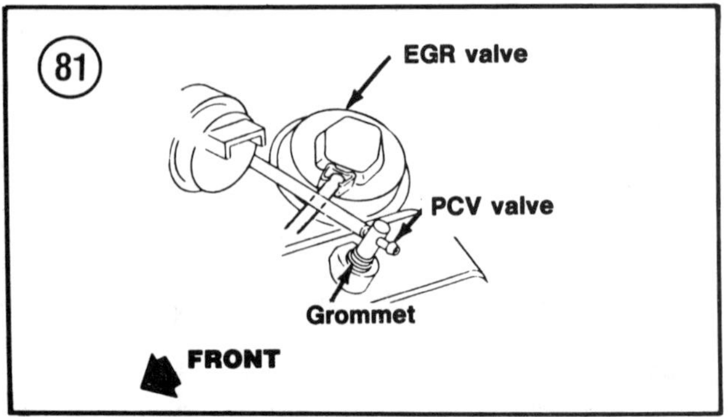

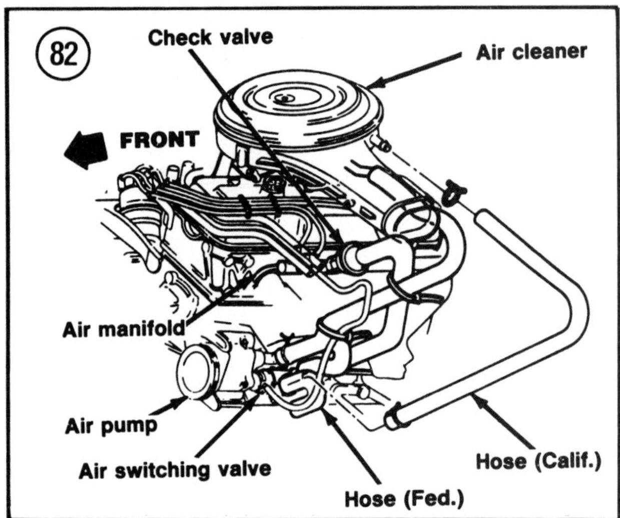

System test

1. Check and adjust the drive belt tension, if necessary. See Chapter Seven.
2. Inspect all system hoses for cracking, burning or loose connections. Replace hoses and tighten connections as necessary.
3. Start the engine. Disconnect the hoses at the air switching valve side of the check valve(s). There should be air flow to the exhaust port outlet of the valve for several seconds, then the air flow should switch to the air cleaner outlet side.
4. Increase engine speed to 1,500-2,000 rpm. Air flow should increase.
5. Reconnect the hoses. Increase engine speed to 2,000 rpm. Release the throttle quickly. If a backfire occurs, replace the mixture control valve.
6. Disconnect the check valve line (**Figure 83**) and remove the check valve.
7. Blow through both ends of the valve. Suck air through both ends. The valve should pass air in

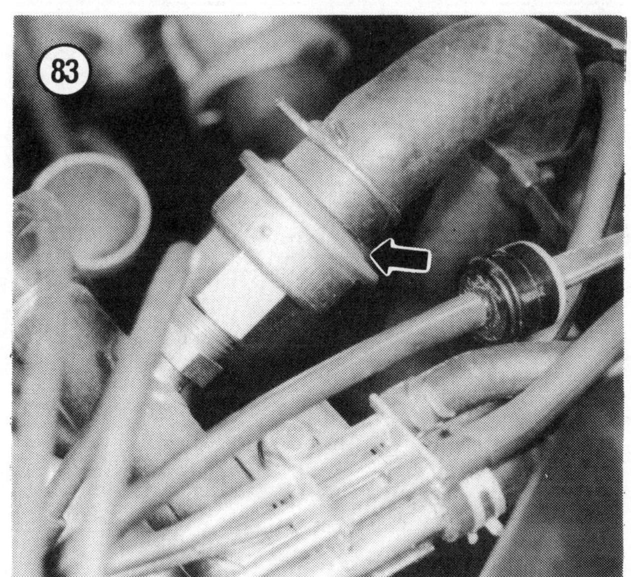

only one direction. If it passes air in both directions or does not pass air in either direction, install a new check valve.

Further air management system testing should be left to a dealer. Correct system operation is dependent on the ECM and its testing is best left to a qualified technician.

Exhaust Gas Recirculation

This system recirculates a small amount of exhaust gas into the incoming air-fuel mixture through a negative backpressure EGR valve. This lowers the combustion temperature and reduces oxides of nitrogen (NOx) emissions.

The EGR valve is attached directly to an adapter housing on the intake manifold on 1.9L engines (**Figure 84**). The 2.0L EGR valve is located beside

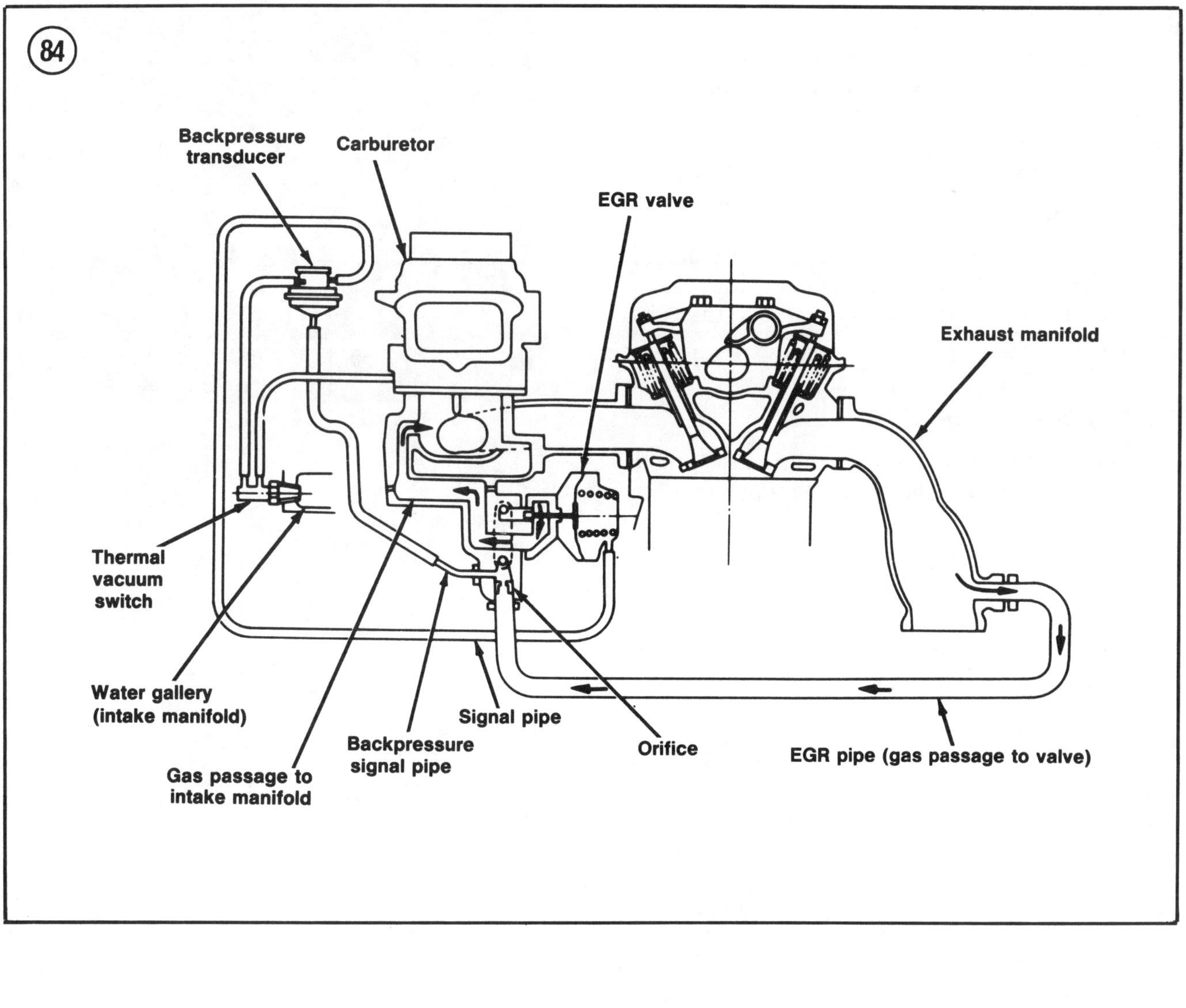

84

Backpressure transducer
Carburetor
EGR valve
Exhaust manifold
Thermal vacuum switch
Water gallery (intake manifold)
Signal pipe
Backpressure signal pipe
Orifice
EGR pipe (gas passage to valve)
Gas passage to intake manifold

the thermostat housing (**Figure 85**). The 2.5L EGR valve is installed on the intake manifold between the TBI unit and cylinder head; the V6 EGR valve is directly behind the carburetor or TBI unit on the intake manifold, hidden from view by the air management hoses (**Figure 86**).

Valve operation is controlled by vacuum received from a carburetor or TBI port and the amount of backpressure in the exhaust system.

System check

1. Start the engine and run at fast idle until the upper radiator hose is hot. Bring the engine speed back to a normal idle.
2. Tee a vacuum gauge into the vacuum line between the EGR valve and the carburetor or TBI vacuum port.
3. Increase engine speed to 3,000 rpm and note the vacuum gauge. It should read at least 3.9 in. Hg vacuum for the 1.9L engine or 5 in. Hg vacuum for the 2.0L, 2.5L or V6 engine.
4. Disconnect the vacuum line at the EGR valve. There should be an increase in engine rpm.
5. Reconnect the vacuum line at the EGR valve. The engine speed should decrease.
6. Depress and hold the EGR valve diaphragm. Plug the EGR valve vacuum nipple and release the diaphragm.
7. Time the leakdown rate. The diaphragm should require 20 seconds or more to close the valve. Replace the valve if it closes in less than 20 seconds.

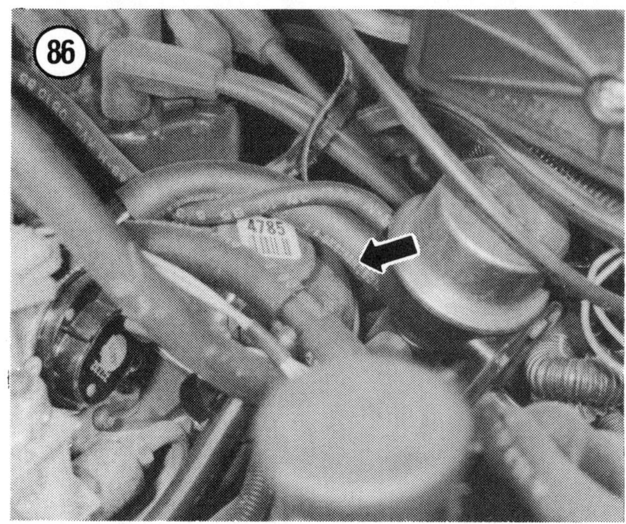

Cleaning and inspection

1. Remove the EGR valve from the intake manifold, thermostat adapter or manifold adapter.

CAUTION
Do not sandblast the valve or wash it in solvent.

2. Check the valve passages (**Figure 87**) for carbon buildup. Light deposits may be cleaned with careful use of a wire brush. If the deposits are heavy, replace the valve.
3. Depress valve diaphragm. Check valve seating and outlet areas. If not completely clean, repeat Step 2.
4. Clean intake manifold, thermostat adapter or manifold adapter and valve mounting surfaces. Install the EGR valve with a new gasket and tighten the attaching bolts to 25 ft.-lb. (34 N•m).

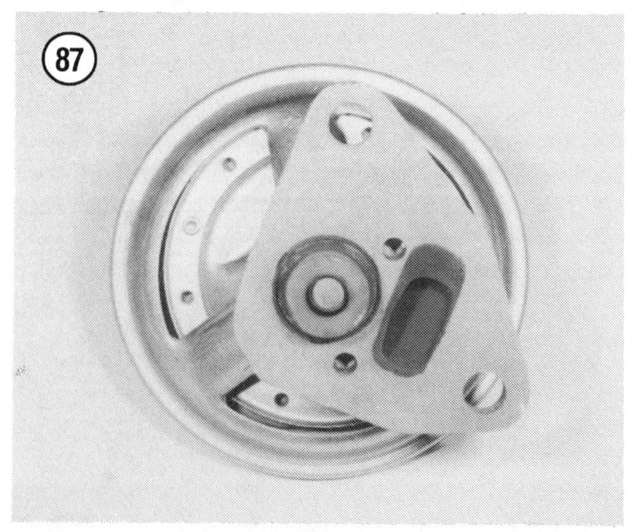

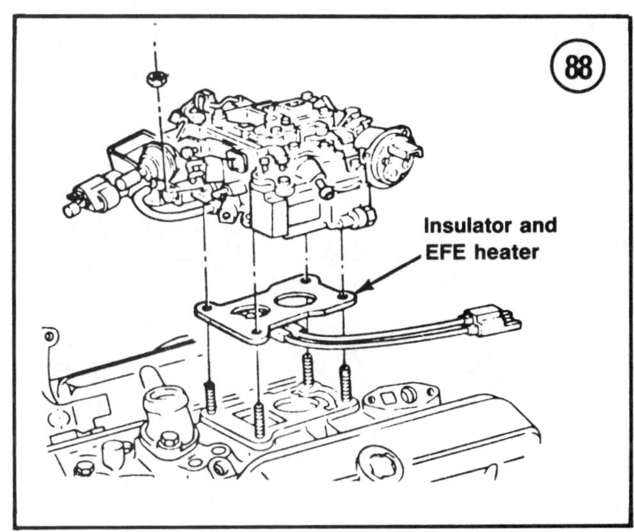

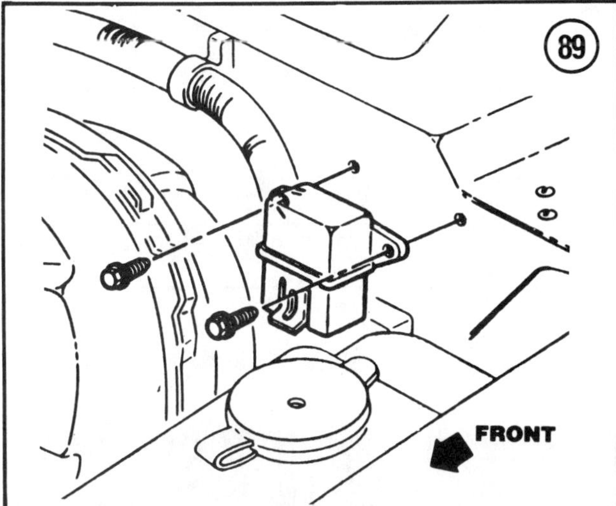

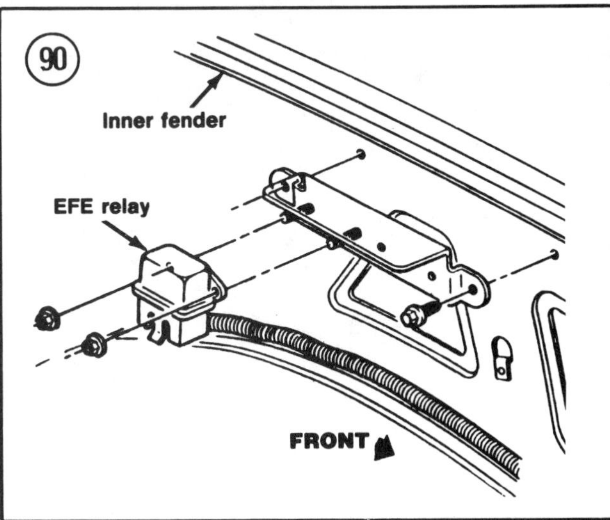

5. Check vacuum lines for damage or deterioration. Replace as required.

Catalytic Converter

The catalytic converter is mounted in the exhaust system between the manifold exhaust pipe and the muffler. See **Figure 75**.

Carbon monoxide and unburned hydrocarbons in the exhaust gas are oxidized as they pass through the converter. This process changes the harmful pollutants into harmless carbon dioxide and water. Oxides of nitrogen are reduced to pure nitrogen and oxygen. The converter requires no maintenance other than replacement of the heat shield, if damaged.

6

Early Fuel Evaporation (EFE) System

The EFE system is used on carburetted engines and consists of a ceramic heater grid contained within the rubber isolator between the carburetor and intake manifold (**Figure 88**). With the ignition ON and the coolant temperature low, voltage is applied to the EFE heater through a relay. See **Figure 89** for the 4-cylinder relay and **Figure 90** for the V6 relay. As coolant reaches a specified temperature, the coolant switch turns off the relay, shutting off the heater. See **Figure 91** for the

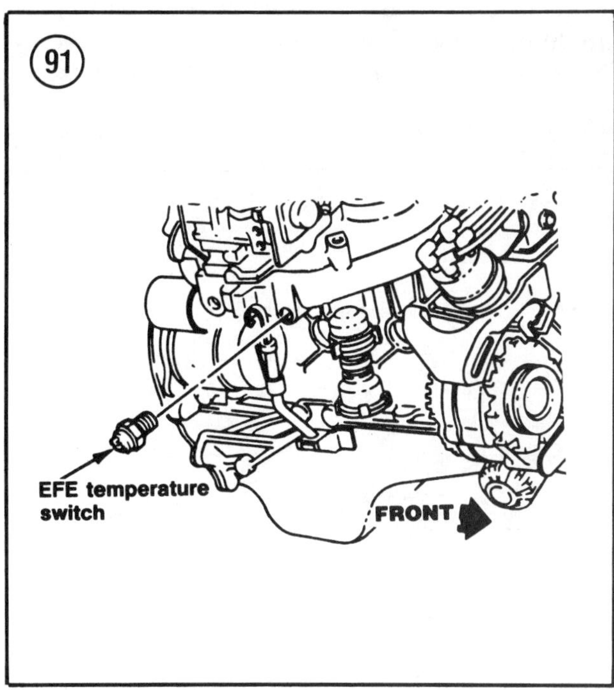

4-cylinder switch and **Figure 92** for the V6 switch. Diagnosis should be left to your Chevrolet or GMC dealer. No system maintenance is required.

Oxygen Sensor

An oxygen sensor installed in the exhaust manifold monitors the oxygen content of the exhaust gas and sends a voltage signal to the electronic control module (ECM). The ECM evaluates this signal and adjusts the carburetor mixture control solenoid or TBI injector duration accordingly. The use of leaded fuel or an attempt to measure the output voltage with a voltmeter will permanently damage an oxygen sensor.

Use the following procedure to replace a damaged sensor or transfer the sensor to a new manifold. Refer to **Figure 93** (1.9L) or **Figure 94** (all others) for this procedure.

1. Make sure the engine is warm. Removing a sensor when engine temperature is below 120° F (48° C) may damage the exhaust manifold or pipe threads.
2. Unplug the sensor electrical connector at the wiring harness.
3. Remove the sensor with tool part No. J-29533 or equivalent.
4. If installing the same sensor, wipe its threads with an electrically conductive anti-seize compound (part No. 5613695 or equivalent). New sensors are pre-coated.
5. Thread the sensor in place by hand and tighten to 30 ft.-lb. (41 N•m).
6. Reconnect the sensor electrical connector to the wiring harness.

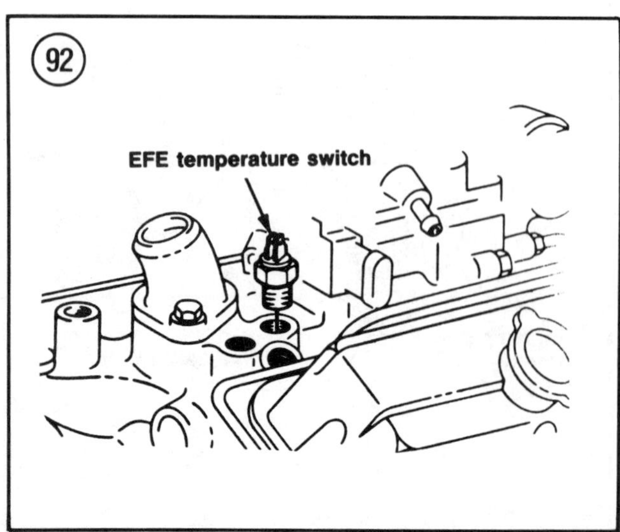

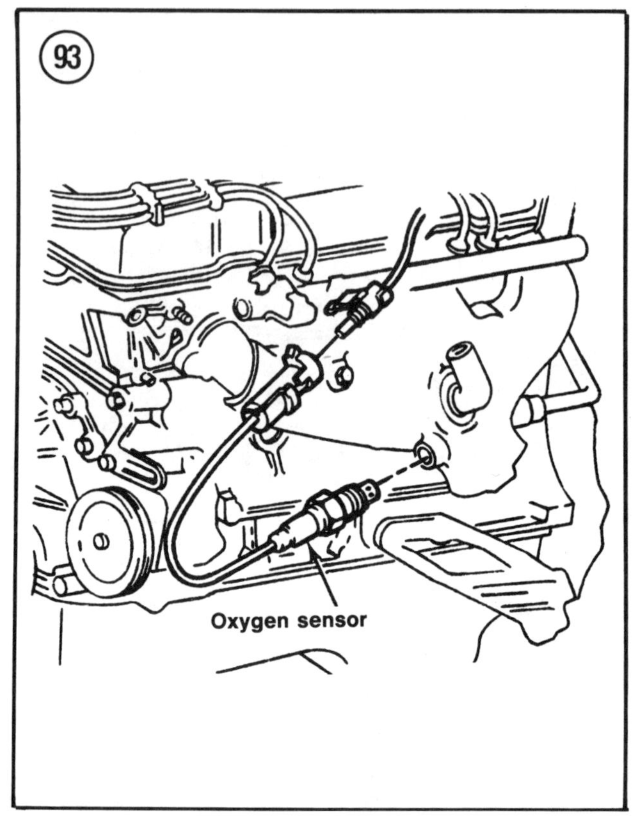

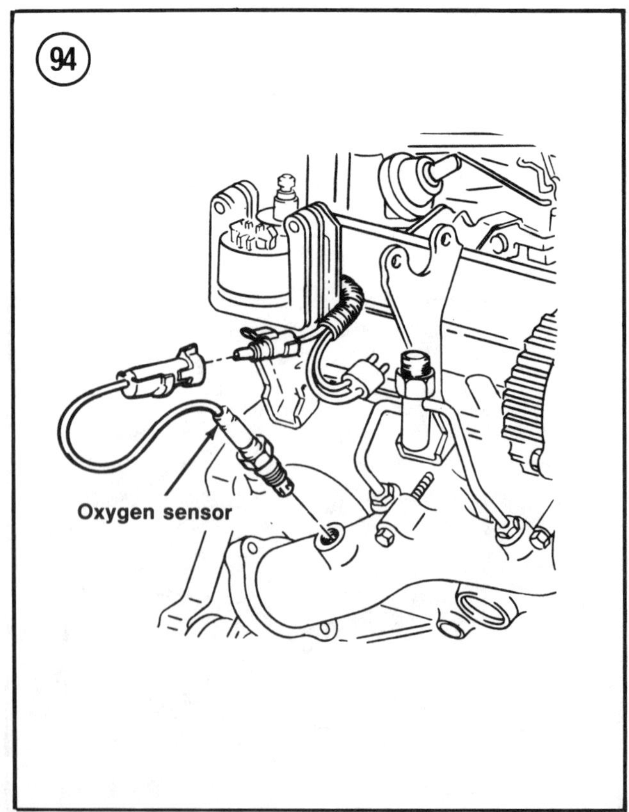

Table 1 TIGHTENING TORQUES

Fastener	ft.-lb.	N•m
Carburetor mounting nuts	12	16
Fuel inlet nut (2SE/E2SE)	25	34
Fuel line-to-fuel inlet (2SE/E2SE)	18	24
Fuel pump	13-18	18-24
EGR valve		
1.9L/2.0L	13-18	18-24
2.5L	15	22
V6 carburetted	25	35
V6 fuel injected	18	25
EFE heater bolts (V6)	14	18
EFE temperature switch	10	14
Exhaust pipe-to-manifold	15	20
Exhaust system		
U-bolts	35	47
Brackets	10-12	15-17
TBI fasteners		
2.5L	13	18
V6	18	25
TBI fuel line fittings	19	26
TBI fuel meter body screws	3.5	4
TBI fuel inlet/outlet nuts	21.5	29

CHAPTER SEVEN

COOLING, HEATING AND AIR CONDITIONING

All vehicles covered in this manual use a pressurized cooling system sealed with a pressure-type radiator cap. The higher operating pressure of the system raises the boiling point of the coolant. This increases the efficiency of the radiator. **Figure 1** shows a typical cooling system.

The cooling system consists of the radiator, water pump, cooling fan, thermostat, coolant recovery tank, temperature sensors and connecting hoses. The crossflow radiator is mounted on the engine compartment front body support panel. The water pump on the 1.9L gasoline, 2.2L diesel and the V6 engine is mounted to the front cover of the engine and coupled directly with the cooling fan. The water pump on the 2.0L and 2.5L engines is mounted in an offset housing at the front of the engine block.

The heater is a hot water type which circulates coolant through a small radiator (heater core) under the instrument panel.

The air conditioning system is a cycling clutch (intermittent) fixed orifice design and uses outside air at all times, except during MAX A/C operation.

This chapter includes service procedures for the radiator, thermostat, water pump, cooling fan, heater and air conditioner. Cooling system flushing procedures are also described. Torque values (**Table 1**) and drive belt tension (**Table 2**) are at the end of the chapter.

COOLING SYSTEM

A crossflow radiator (**Figure 2**) is used on all models. The crossflow radiator is constructed in a tube and slit-fin-core arrangement with the tubes positioned horizontally between the header tanks for crossflow of the coolant. The header tanks on each side of the radiator provide uniform distribution of the coolant to the crossflow tubes. One header tank contains the transmission oil cooler on automatic transmission models.

A coolant recovery system is incorporated in all cooling systems. This consists of a translucent plastic overflow reservoir connected to the radiator filler neck by a hose. See **Figure 3** (typical).

When coolant in the radiator expands to the overflow point, it passes through the filler neck and into the plastic reservoir. Once the coolant in the radiator cools down, it contracts. The vacuum created pulls coolant from the reservoir back into the radiator. This system prevents the radiator from boiling over. By remaining filled to capacity, cooling efficiency is maintained at all times.

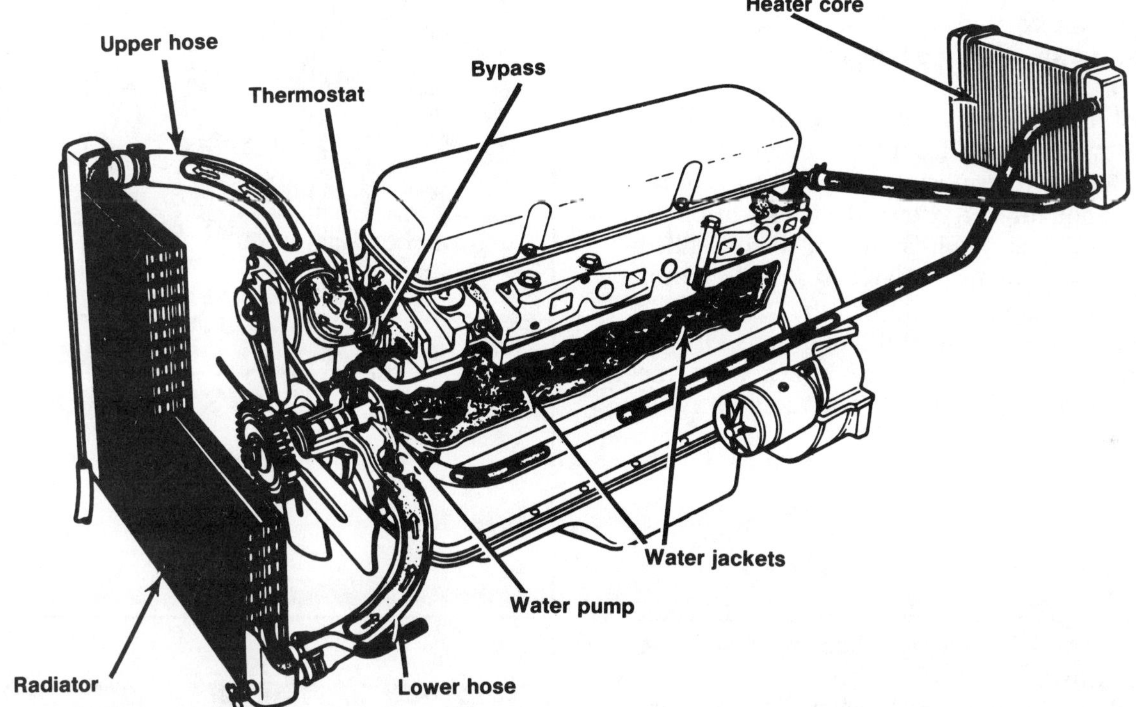
Heater core
Upper hose
Bypass
Thermostat
Water jackets
Water pump
Radiator
Lower hose
ARROWS DENOTE FLOW OF COOLANT

The recommended coolant is a 50/50 mixture of ethylene glycol antifreeze and low mineral content water, which provides a lower freezing point and higher boiling point than water alone.

The water pump circulates the coolant through the cooling system when the engine is running. When the engine is cold, the coolant is trapped inside the engine water jacket by the thermostat, which is located in the mouth of the hose leading to the radiator inlet tank. The thermostat remains closed until the coolant heats up to operating temperature. It then opens and the coolant flows through the hose into the radiator inlet tank. The coolant passes through the radiator tubes to the outlet tank, where it flows through the radiator outlet hose to the water pump inlet to start the cycle over again.

The cooling fan draws air through the radiator and removes excess heat from the coolant. Rigid or viscous clutch (thermostatic) fans are used, depending upon model year and air conditioning option. The viscous clutch fan uses a silicone-filled coupling that automatically increases or decreases fan speed according to temperature to provide proper engine cooling under all conditions.

Some models have a shroud attached to the radiator to funnel air through the radiator more efficiently.

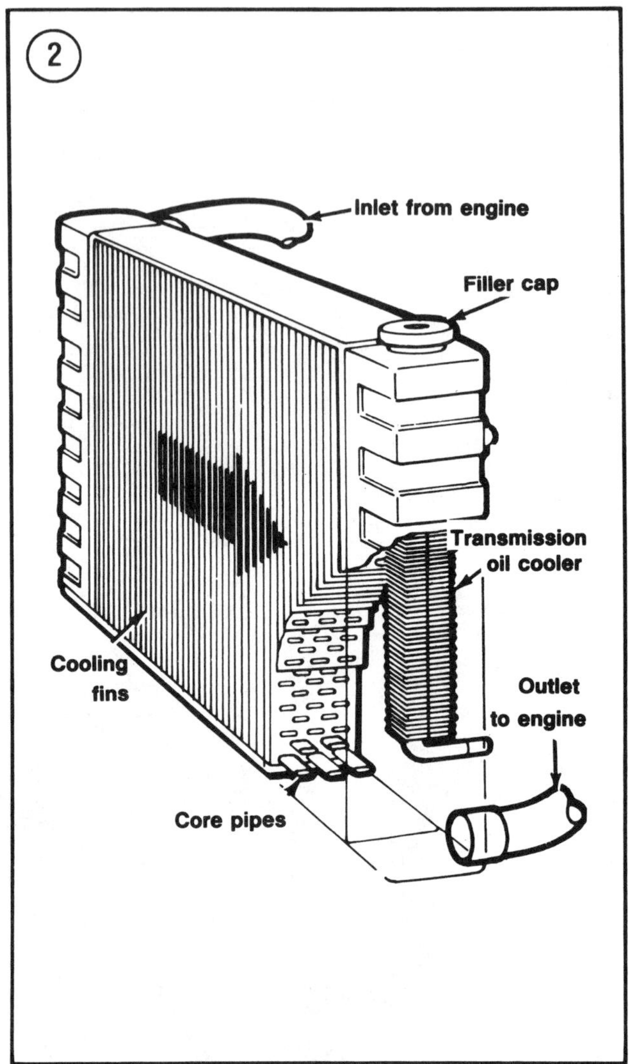

COOLING SYSTEM CHECKS

1. Visually inspect the cooling system and heater hoses for signs of cracking, checking, excessive swelling or leakage.
2. Check that all supporting brackets for hoses are properly positioned (if used) and that the hoses are correctly installed in the brackets.
3. Inspect the front and rear of the radiator core and tanks, all seams and the radiator drain valve for signs of seepage or leaks. See **Figure 4**.
4. Make sure all hose connections are tight and in good condition. Check the hoses carefully at their clamps for cuts or weakness. Overtightening strap-type clamps can cut the outer surface of a hose and weaken it.
5. Remove the radiator pressure cap. Check the rubber cap seal surfaces for tears or cracks (**Figure 5**). Check for a bent or distorted cap. Raise the vacuum valve and rubber seal and rinse the cap under warm tap water to flush away any loose rust or dirt particles.

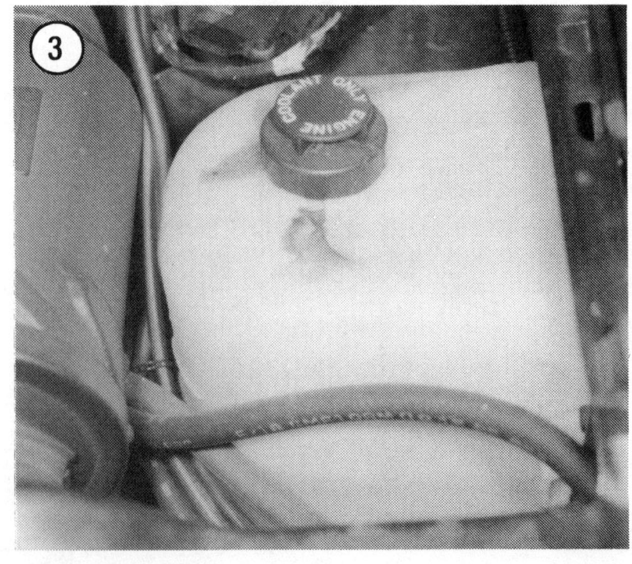

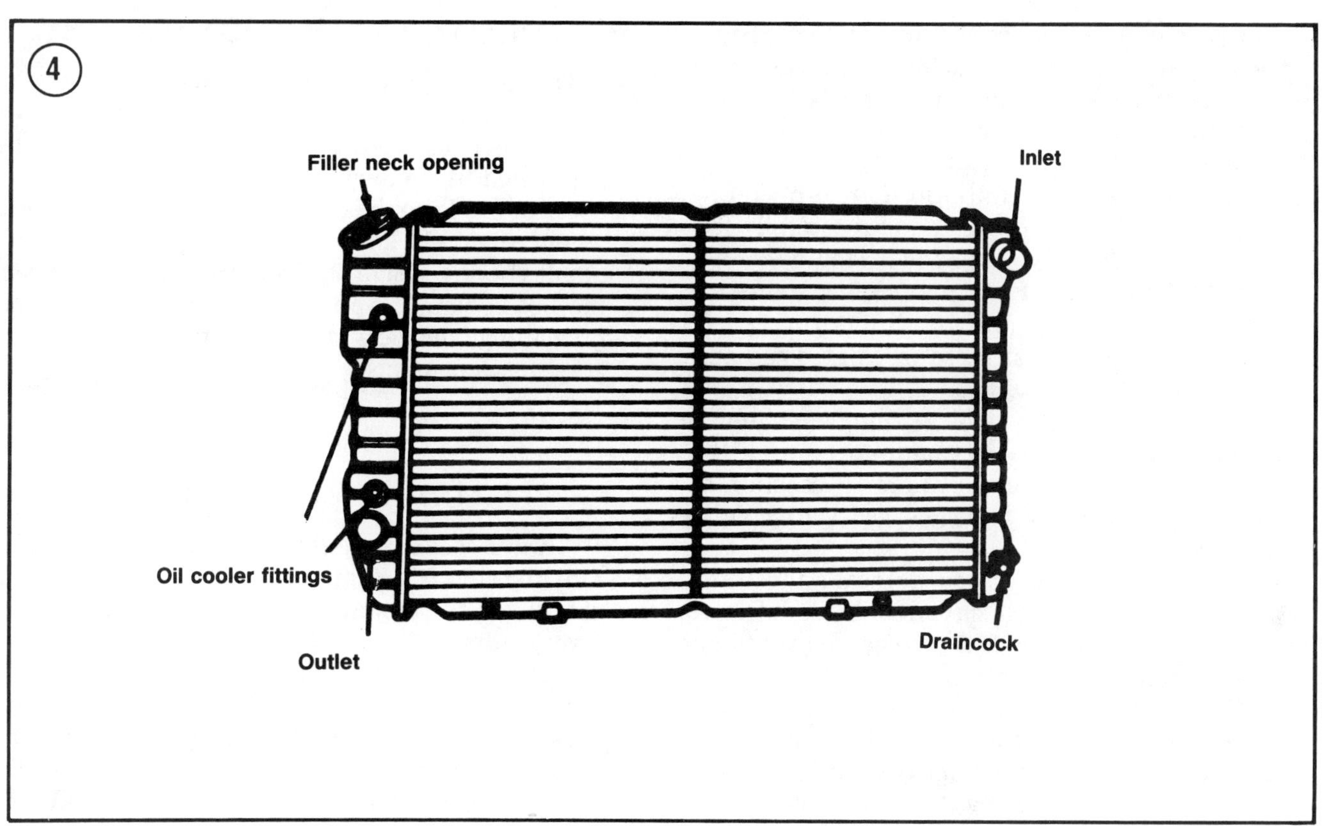

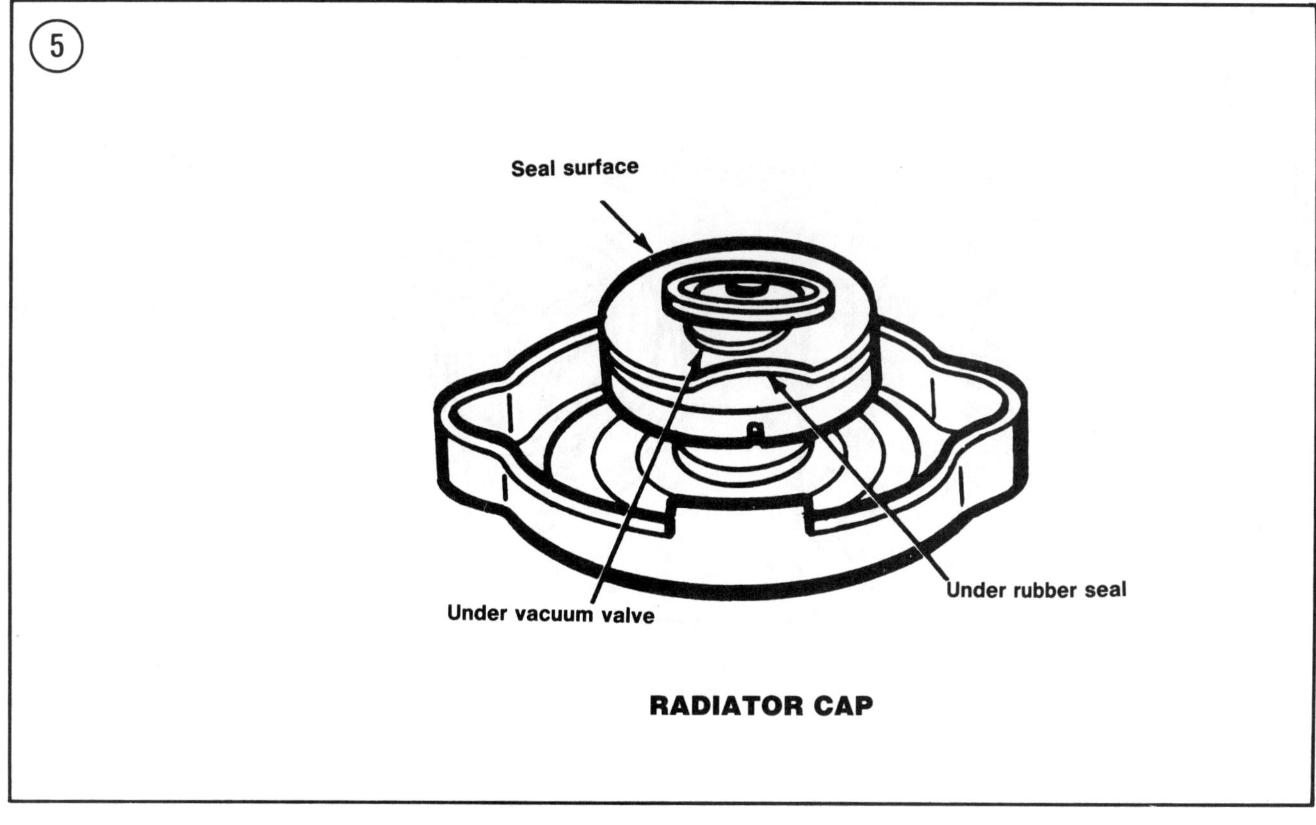

RADIATOR CAP

6. Inspect the filler neck seat and sealing surface (**Figure 6**) for nicks, dents, distortion or contamination. Wipe the sealing surface with a clean cloth to remove any rust or dirt. Install the cap properly.
7. Start the engine and warm to normal operating temperature. Shut the engine off and carefully feel the radiator. Crossflow radiators should be hot along the left side and warm along the right side with an even temperature rise from right to left. Cold spots indicate obstructed or clogged radiator sections.
8. Restart the engine and squeeze the upper radiator hose to check water pump operation. If a pressure surge is felt, the water pump is functioning properly. If not, check for a plugged vent hole in the pump.
9. Visually check the area underneath the water pump for signs of leakage or corrosion. A defective water pump will usually leak through the vent hole at the bottom of the pump.
10. Check the crankcase oil dipstick for signs of coolant in the engine oil. On automatic transmission models, check the coolant for signs of transmission fluid leaking from the oil cooler. Check the transmission lines which connect to the oil cooler.

COOLING SYSTEM LEAKAGE TEST

This test requires a reliable pressure tester and can be performed quickly and economically by your dealer or a radiator shop. The test should be performed if frequent additions of coolant are necessary to keep the cooling system topped up and your radiator is known to be in good condition. Small cooling system leaks are not easy to locate; the hot coolant evaporates as fast as it leaks out, preventing the formation of tell-tale rusty or grayish-white stains.

COOLANT LEVEL CHECK

Always check coolant level with the engine and radiator cold. Coolant expands as it is heated and checking a hot or warm system will not give a true level reading.

Cooling systems equipped with a coolant recovery feature are checked at the reservoir instead of the radiator. Remove the reservoir cap. Add coolant as required to bring the level in the reservoir to the "HOT FULL" or "COLD FULL" mark on the side of the reservoir, according to engine temperature. Install the reservoir cap.

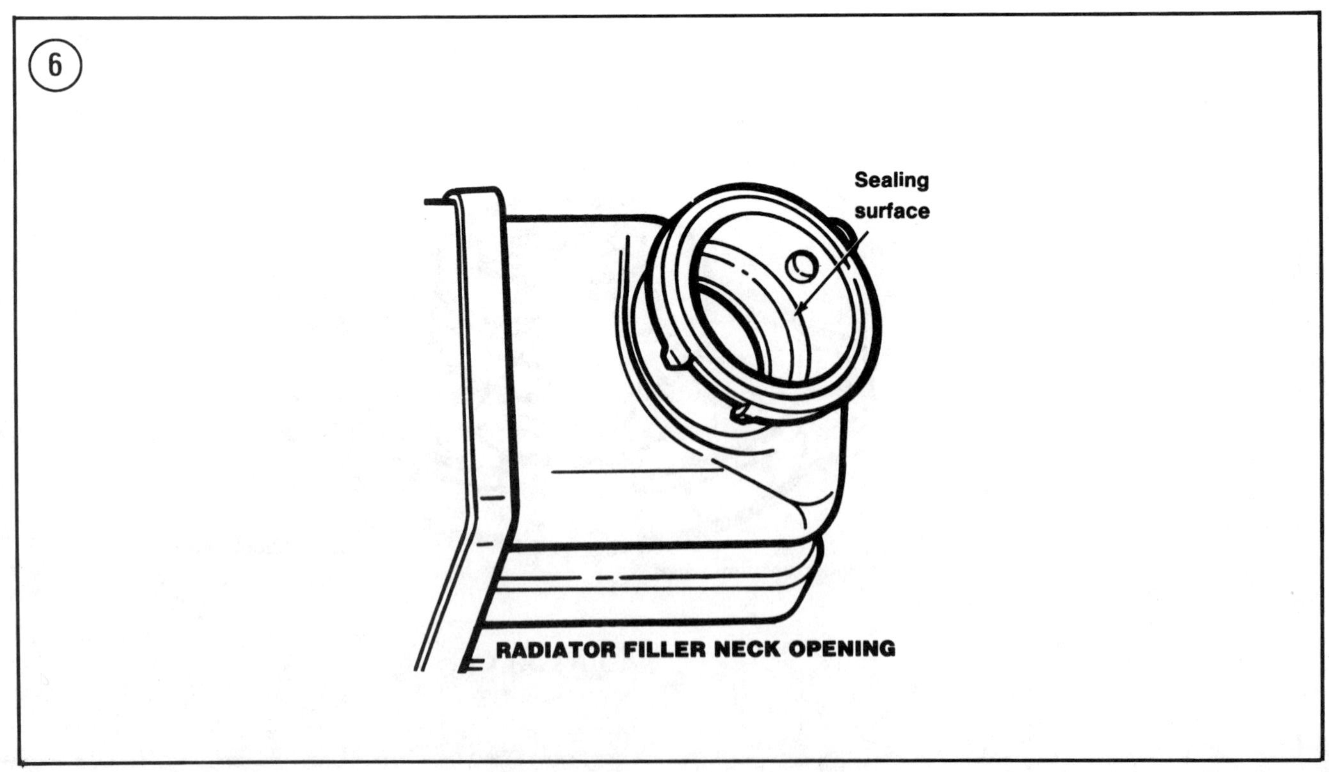

COOLING SYSTEM FLUSHING

The recommended coolant is a 50/50 mixture of ethylene glycol antifreeze and water. GM recommends that only an antifreeze containing a silicate inhibitor and meeting GM specification 1825-M be used. GM Cooling System Fluid (part No. 1052753) and Prestone II are recommended coolants which meet this specification.

Recommended coolants are designed to prevent corrosion of aluminum components used in late-model engines and cooling systems. The use of antifreeze without the silicate inhibitor which does not meet GM specifications may cause a thermo-chemical reaction resulting in serious radiator and engine damage.

The radiator should be drained, flushed and refilled at the intervals specified in Chapter Three. After initial filling, the coolant level may drop by as much as one quart after engine operation due to the displacement of entrapped air.

CAUTION
Under no circumstances should a chemical flushing agent be used. Flush the cooling system with clear water only.

1. Coolant can stain concrete and harm plants. Park the vehicle over a gutter or similar area.
2. Move the heater temperature control on the instrument panel to its maximum heat position.
3. Loosen the radiator cap to its first detent and release the system pressure, then turn the cap to its second detent and remove it from the radiator.
4. Remove the cap from the coolant recovery tank.
5. Open the draincock at the bottom of the radiator tank. See **Figure 4** (typical). Let the cooling system drain.
6. When the system has finished draining, open the engine drain tap(s). V6 engines have a drain tap on each side of the block. 4-cylinder engines have one drain tap at the left rear of the cylinder block. Let the engine block drain.
7. Loosen the clamp on the heater outlet hose at the water pump. Disconnect the hose and bend it down to aid in draining the heater.
8. Remove the thermostat as described in this chapter. Temporarily reinstall the thermostat housing.
9. Disconnect the top raditor hose from the radiator.
10. Disconnect the bottom hose from the water pump inlet.
11. Disconnect the heater inlet hose at the engine block.
12. Connect a garden hose to the heater hose nearest the front of the engine. This does not have to be a positive fit, as long as most of the water enters the heater hose. Run water into the heater hose until clear water flows from the other heater hose.
13. Insert the garden hose into the top radiator hose. Run water into the top hose until clear water flows from the bottom hose.
14. Insert the garden hose into the hose fitting at the bottom of the radiator. Run water into the radiator until clear water flows from the top fitting, then turn the water off.
15. Close the radiator draincock and engine drain taps.
16. Disconnect the coolant recovery tank hose (**Figure 3**). Remove and drain the tank. Flush the tank first with soapy water, then clean water. Drain and reinstall the tank. Connect the hose.
17. Reconnect all hoses to the water pump inlet, radiator and engine. Reinstall the thermostat.
18. Slowly pour 4 quarts of GM Cooling System Fluid or equivalent into the radiator.
19. Add sufficient water to bring the coolant level to within 1-1 1/2 in. of the cap seat seal in the filler neck. Do not install the radiator cap yet.
20. Fill the coolant recovery tank to the FULL mark with coolant, then install the recovery tank cap.
21. Set the parking brake and block the drive wheels.
22. Place the transmission in NEUTRAL (manual) or PARK (automatic). Start the engine and run at a fast idle until the upper radiator hose is hot. Return the engine to normal idle.
23. Check the coolant level and add sufficient coolant to bring it back to within 1-1 1/2 in. of the cap seat seal in the filler neck. Install the radiator cap, aligning the cap arrow with the overflow tube.
24. After the vehicle has been driven, recheck the coolant level in the recovery tank when the radiator is cold. Top up as required with coolant to bring the level within specifications.

THERMOSTAT

Coolant flow to the radiator is blocked by the thermostat when the engine is cold. As the engine warms up, the thermostat gradually opens, allowing coolant to circulate through the radiator.

The thermostat heat range used depends upon model year and engine application. Check the thermostat when removed to determine its opening point; the heat range should be stamped on the thermostat flange.

Removal and Testing

1. Make sure the engine is cool. Disconnect the negative battery cable.
2. Place a clean container under the radiator draincock (**Figure 4**). Remove the radiator cap and open the draincock. Drain sufficient coolant from the radiator to bring the coolant level below the thermostat housing. If the coolant is clean, save it for reuse.

7

8

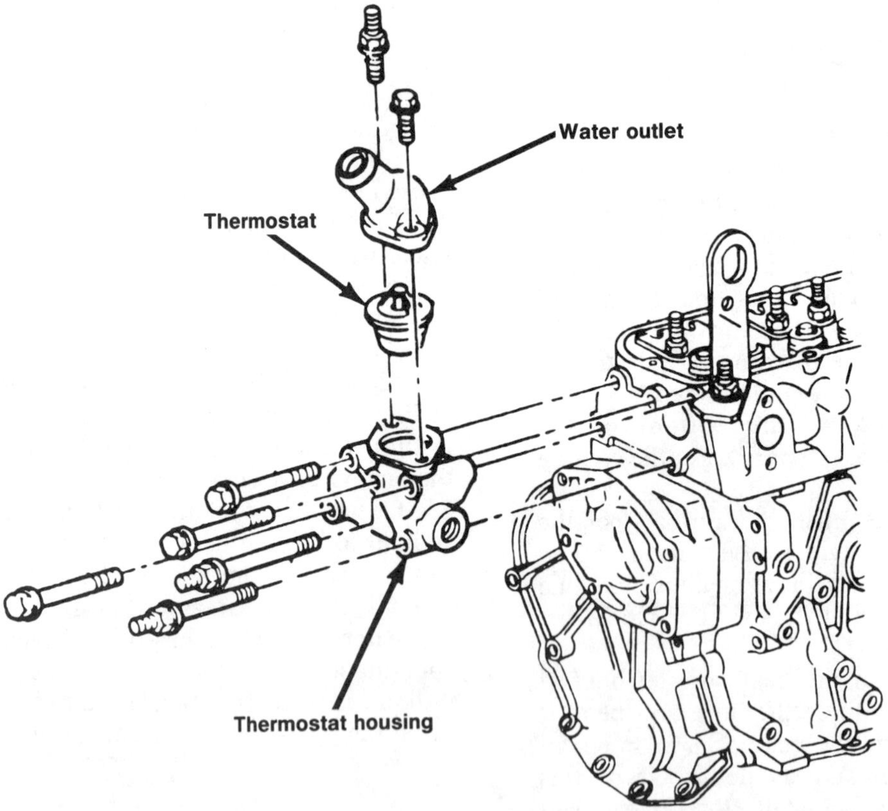

Water outlet

Thermostat

Thermostat housing

9

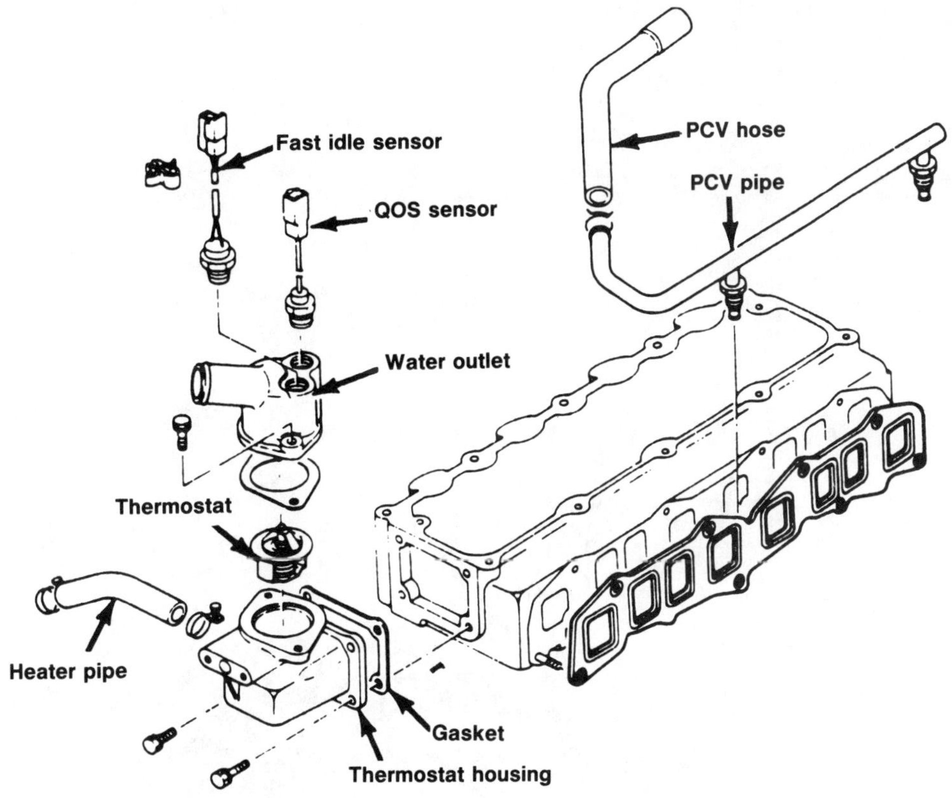

Fast idle sensor
QOS sensor
PCV hose
PCV pipe
Water outlet
Thermostat
Heater pipe
Gasket
Thermostat housing

10

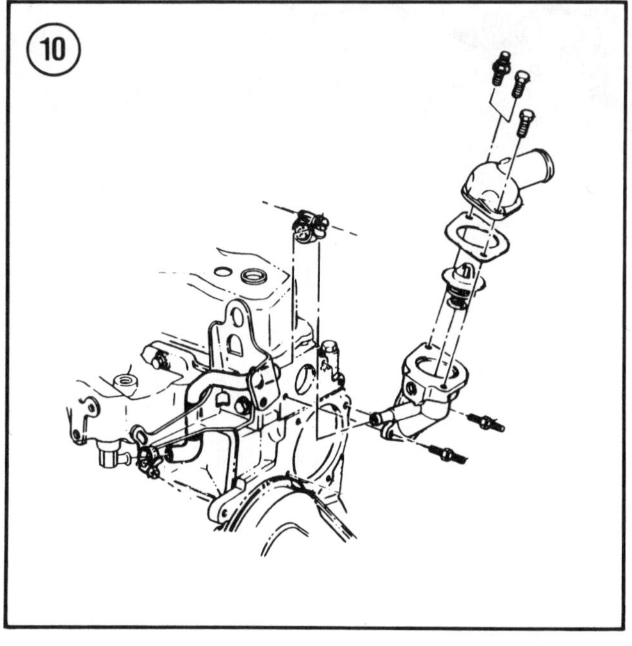

3. All 4-cylinder engines—Remove the air cleaner as described in this chapter.

4. 2.0L engine—Disconnect the AIR pipe at the upper check valve and water outlet bracket. Disconnect the coolant temperature switch leads.

5. 2.2L diesel—Remove the vacuum pump adjusting bracket and disconnect the sensor electrical leads.

6. 2.5L engine—Remove the thermal vacuum hose connections at the thermostat housing. Loosen the alternator and air conditioning compressor (if so equipped) enough to provide access to the housing retaining bolts.

7. Remove the thermostat housing cover/water outlet bolts. Lift the cover/outlet (with coolant hose attached) clear of the thermostat housing (2.0L and 2.2L diesel), cylinder head (2.5L) or intake manifold (1.9L and V6). See **Figure 7** (1.9L), **Figure 8** (2.0L), **Figure 9** (2.2L diesel), **Figure 10** (2.5L) or **Figure 11** (V6).

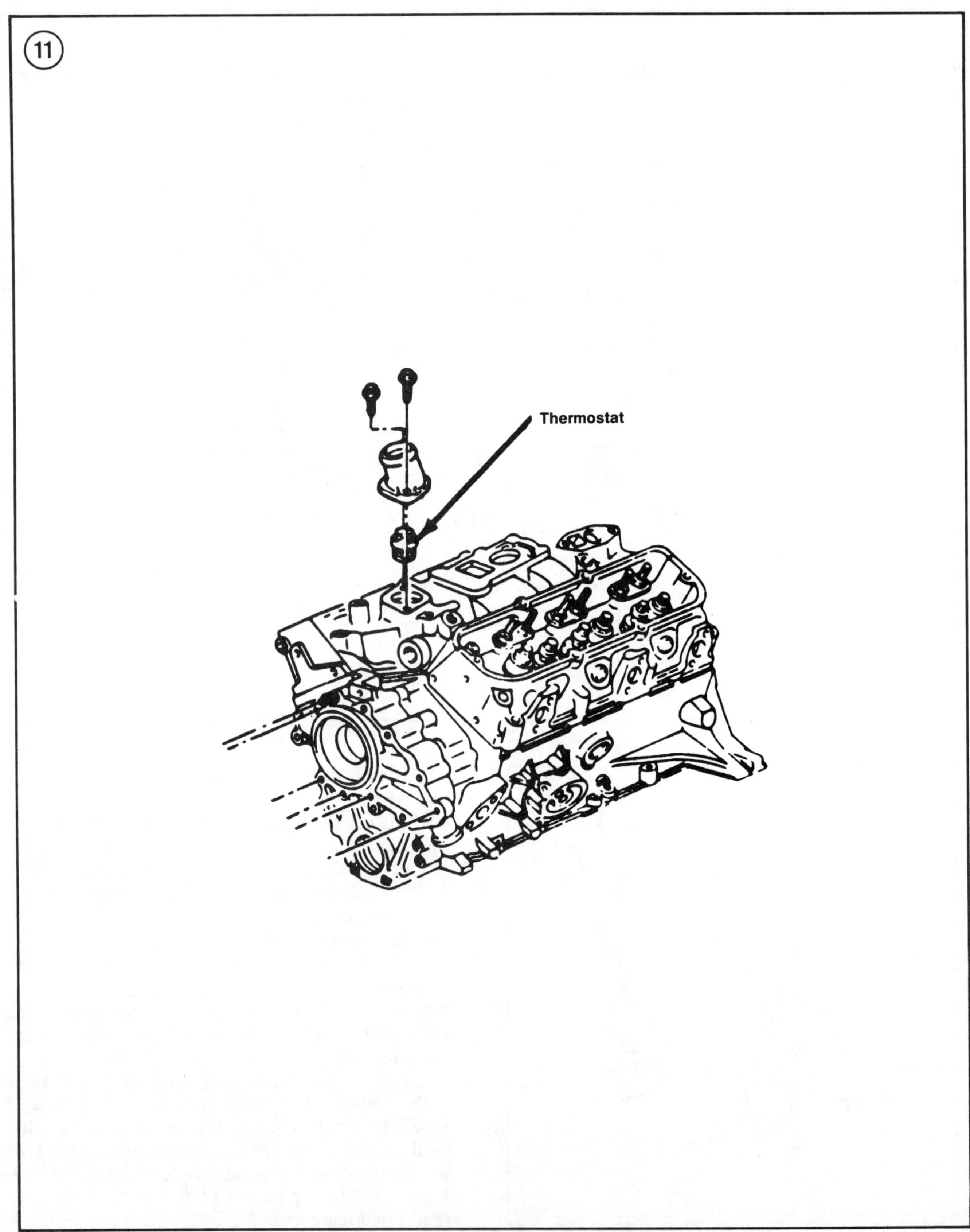
11
Thermostat

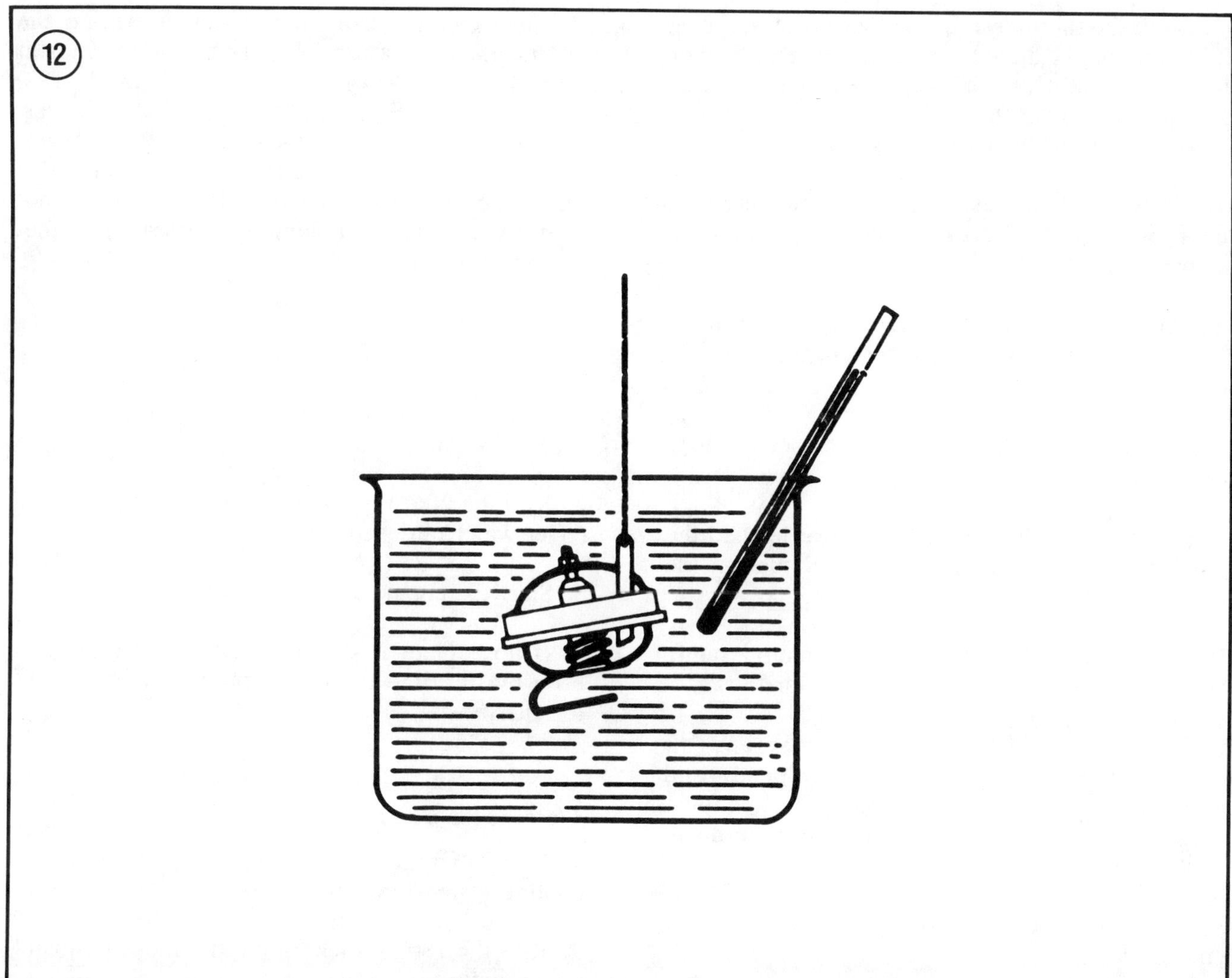

8. Remove the thermostat from the thermostat housing (2.0L and 2.2L diesel), cylinder head (2.5L) or intake manifold (1.9L and V6). Remove and discard the gasket.
9. Prepare a container of coolant mixed 1 part antifreeze to 2 parts water and suspend a thermometer in the container. See (**Figure 12**).

NOTE
Support the thermostat with wire so it does not touch the sides or bottom of the pan.

10. Heat the solution 25° F above the heat range stamped on the thermostat flange. Submerge the thermostat in the container of coolant and agitate the solution thoroughly. Replace the thermostat if the valve does not open fully.
11. Cool the solution 10° F below the temperature stamped on the thermostat flange. Replace the thermostat if the valve does not close completely.
12. Let the thermostat cool to room temperature. Hold it close to a light bulb and check for leakage. If light can be seen around the valve, the thermostat is defective.

Installation

1. If a new thermostat is being installed, test it as described in this chapter.
2. Stuff a clean shop cloth in the thermostat housing (2.0L and 2.2L diesel), cylinder head (2.5L) or intake manifold (1.9L and V6) to prevent gasket residue from entering the engine. Clean all gasket or RTV sealant residue from the mating surfaces with a putty knife.

3. Install the thermostat in the thermostat housing (2.0L and 2.2L diesel), cylinder head (2.5L) or intake manifold (1.9L and V6). The copper element should face toward the engine and the thermostat flange must fit in the recess provided.

4A. 1.9L and 2.2L diesel—Install a new gasket on the cylinder head (1.9L) or thermostat housing adapter (2.2L diesel).

4B. All others—Run a 3 mm (1/8 in.) bead of RTV sealant in the thermostat housing groove.

5. Install the thermostat housing cover/water outlet. Tighten the attaching bolts to specifications (**Table 1**).

6. 2.0L engine—Connect the electrical lead to the temperature switch. Connect the AIR pipe at the water outlet bracket and check valve.

7. 2.2L diesel—Reinstall the vacuum pump bracket and connect the electrical sensors.

8. 2.5L engine—Tighten the alternator and air conditioning compressor (if so equipped) and adjust the drive belts as described in this chapter. Reinstall the thermal vacuum hose connections to the thermostat housing.

9. 4-cylinder engine—Install the air cleaner. See Chapter Six.

10. Refill the cooling system to the specified level as described in this chapter.

11. Reconnect the negative battery cable.

12. Start the engine and check for leaks. Check coolant level and top up if required.

In-vehicle Testing

Thermostat operation can be tested without removing it from the engine. This procedure requires the use of 2 thermostat sticks available from Chevrolet or GMC dealers. A thermostat stick looks like a carpenter's pencil and is made of a chemically impregnated wax material which melts at a specific temperature.

This technique can be used to determine the thermostat's operation by marking the thermostat housing with 180 degree F (part No. J-24731-188) or 206 degree F (part No. J-24731-206) sticks, depending upon the problem. As the coolant reaches 180° F, the mark made by that stick will melt. The mark made by the 206° F stick will not melt until the coolant increases to that temperature.

Overheated engine

1. Carefully remove the radiator cap to relieve the cooling system pressure.

2. Rub the 206° F stick on the thermostat housing cover/water outlet.

3. Start the engine and run at a fast idle.

4. If no coolant flows through the upper radiator hose by the time the mark starts to melt, replace the thermostat.

Slow engine warmup

1. Carefully remove the radiator cap to relieve the cooling system pressure.

2. Rub the 180° F stick on the thermostat housing cover/water outlet.

3. Start the engine and run at a fast idle.

4. If coolant flows through the upper radiator hose before the mark starts to melt, replace the thermostat.

RADIATOR

A vacuum brazed aluminum design with nylon end tanks is used on some 1985 and later vehicles. All other models use a copper/brass core radiator with metal header tanks. Work carefully when removing or installing hoses to a nylon end tank. If excessive pressure is applied, the fitting may crack or break. If this happens, the radiator must be removed and the end tank replaced.

13

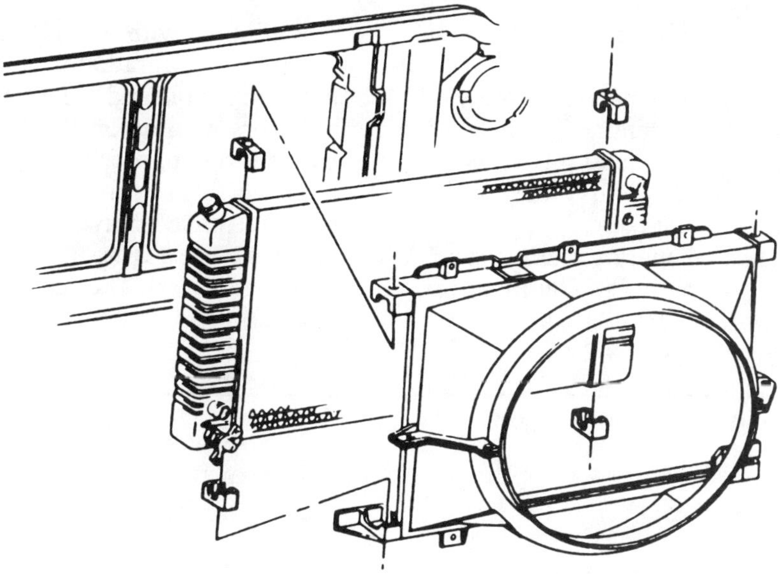

14

Removal/Installation

Refer to **Figure 13** (typical) for this procedure.

1. Make sure that the engine is cool enough to touch comfortably.
2. Coolant can stain concrete and harm plants. Park the vehicle over a gutter or similar area. Place a clean container under the drain valve.
3. Remove the radiator cap and open the draincock at the bottom of the radiator. See **Figure 4** (typical).
4. Disconnect the overflow tube at the radiator nipple (**Figure 14**). Remove overflow tube from fan shroud, if so attached.
5. If equipped with air conditioning, remove the air conditioning hose retainer clip.
6. Remove the screws holding the upper half of the fan shroud. Loosen the lower fan shroud screws (if

used) or lift shroud from its lower retainer clips. Move shroud back and drape it over the fan.
7. Disconnect the upper and lower hoses at the radiator.
8. If equipped with an automatic transmission, disconnect the 2 oil cooler lines at the radiator fittings. Cap the fittings and lines to prevent leakage.
9. 2.2L diesel—Repeat Step 7 to disconnect the engine oil cooler lines.
10. On some models with limited access, it may be necessary to remove the fan retaining bolts and loosen the alternator adjusting and pivot bolts. Remove the fan, spacer, water pump pulley, drive belt and fan shroud (if so equipped).
11. Remove the mounting panel or retainer arms from the upper radiator support. Remove the upper mounting pads.
12. Tilt the radiator back as required, then lift it up and out of the lower mounting pads.
13. Installation is the reverse of removal. Tighten all fasteners to specifications (**Table 1**).

Header Tank Removal

Radiators with metal header tanks should be serviced by a radiator shop equipped with the necessary tools and skills to do the job. Aluminum radiators with nylon header tanks can be serviced by the home mechanic. The header tanks are attached to the core by metal tabs with an O-ring gasket installed between the core and header tank as a seal. See **Figure 15**.
1. Remove the radiator as described in this chapter.

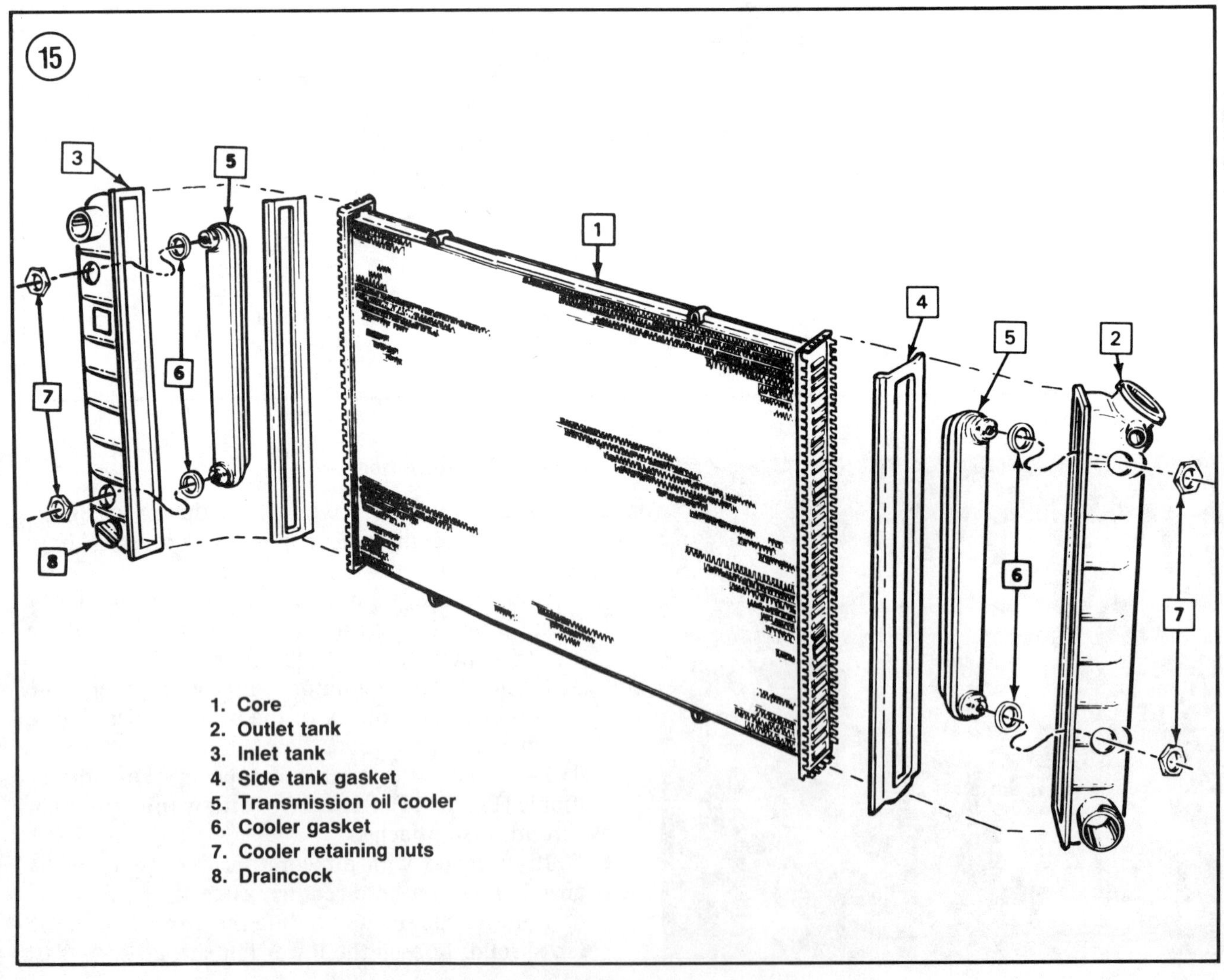

1. Core
2. Outlet tank
3. Inlet tank
4. Side tank gasket
5. Transmission oil cooler
6. Cooler gasket
7. Cooler retaining nuts
8. Draincock

2. Insert a screwdriver tip between the core and the end of the cinch tab, as shown in **Figure 16**. Carefully pry each cinch tab (except those under the inlet, outlet and filler necks) away from the core edge enough for tank removal.
3. Separate the core and header tank, then slide the tank out from under the remaining cinched tabs.
4. Remove and discard the tank gasket.

Header Tank and Core Inspection

Examine each header tank for cracks and damage to the mounting brackets, shroud bosses, gasket sealing surface and hose fittings. Replace any damaged tank.

Check the header gasket surface and tank sealing flange for signs of leakage. Clean surfaces to remove any dirt or other contamination.

Check the core for broken cinch tabs. Replace if more than 3 tabs on one side or 2 adjacent tabs are broken.

Header Tank Installation

1. Clean the gasket surface of the radiator core and header.
2. Dip a new O-ring gasket in engine coolant and install it on the header surface.
3. If the outlet tank is being replaced and it contains an oil cooler, transfer the cooler to the new tank as described in this chapter.
4. Fit the tank to the core header with the top and bottom of the new tank aligned with the other tank.

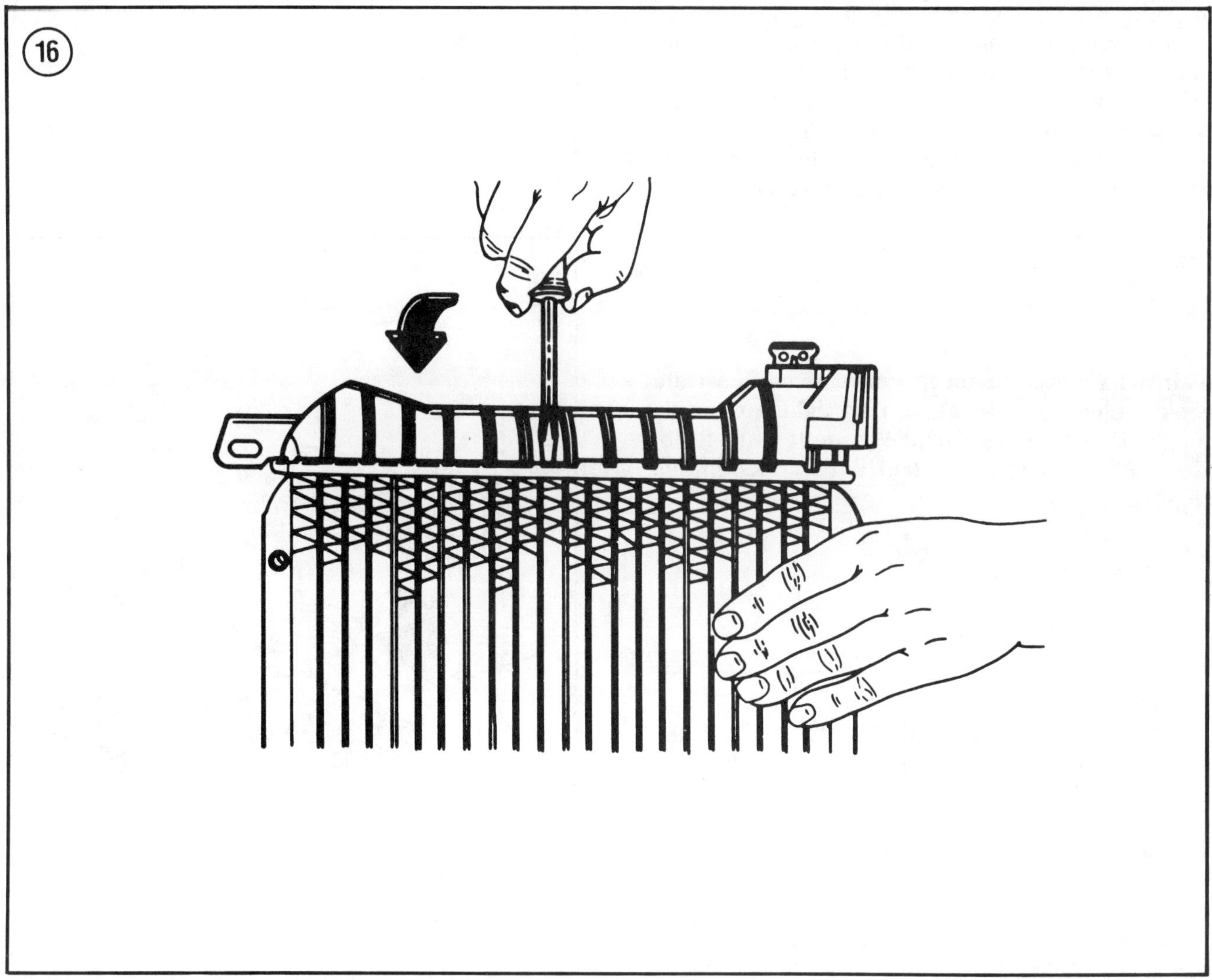

5. Attach the tank to the core by bending the 4 header cinch tabs shown in **Figure 17**.
6. Clamp the remaining cinch tabs around the header with pliers (**Figure 18**), following the sequence shown in **Figure 19**.
7. Leak test the radiator at 14-16 psi. Minor seal leaks can usually be corrected by recrimping the clamp tabs on both sides of the apparent leak.

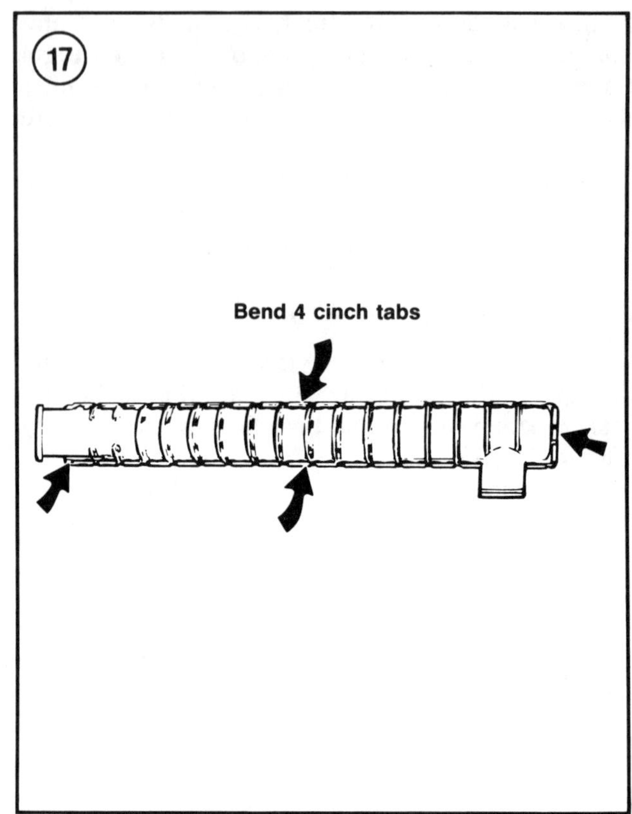

Oil Cooler Replacement

1. Remove the radiator and separate the outlet tank from the core header as described in this chapter.
2. Remove the oil cooler inlet and outlet connections. Lift the oil cooler and gaskets from the outlet tank.
3. If the cooler is defective, discard it. If the cooler is to be reused, remove and discard the neoprene gaskets from the inlet/outlet connections.
4. Clean and dry the gasket sealing areas, then install new gaskets on the cooler to be used.
5. Insert the oil cooler fittings through the tank holes. Make sure the gaskets are properly aligned.

CAUTION
Overtightening of the nuts in Step 6 can cut the gaskets and result in leakage.

6. Installation is the reverse of removal. Start the cooler connections by hand, then tighten the nuts snugly on the fittings. Tighten the nuts to 15 ft.-lb. (20 N•m) and reinstall the tank as described in this chapter.

Draincock Replacement

1. Remove the radiator as described in this chapter.
2. Turn the draincock until fully open and pull the stem from the radiator tank and draincock body. See **Figure 20**.
3. Squeeze the draincock body together with pliers and insert in the inlet tank opening until it locks in place.
4. Fit the stem into the body opening and push until the stem tabs engage with the draincock body. Turn the draincock stem until it is fully closed.

19
9
5
1
4
8
12
10
6
2
3
7
11

20
1
2
3
1. Stem
2. Seal
3. Body

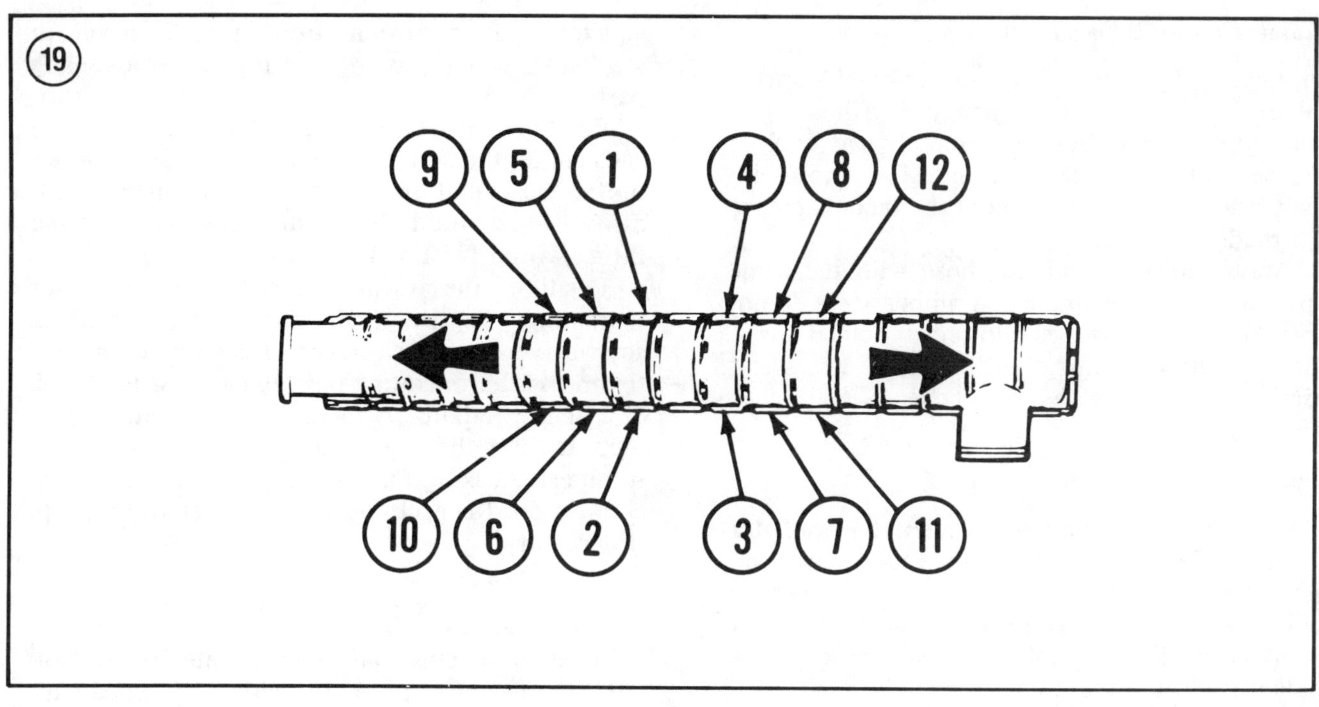

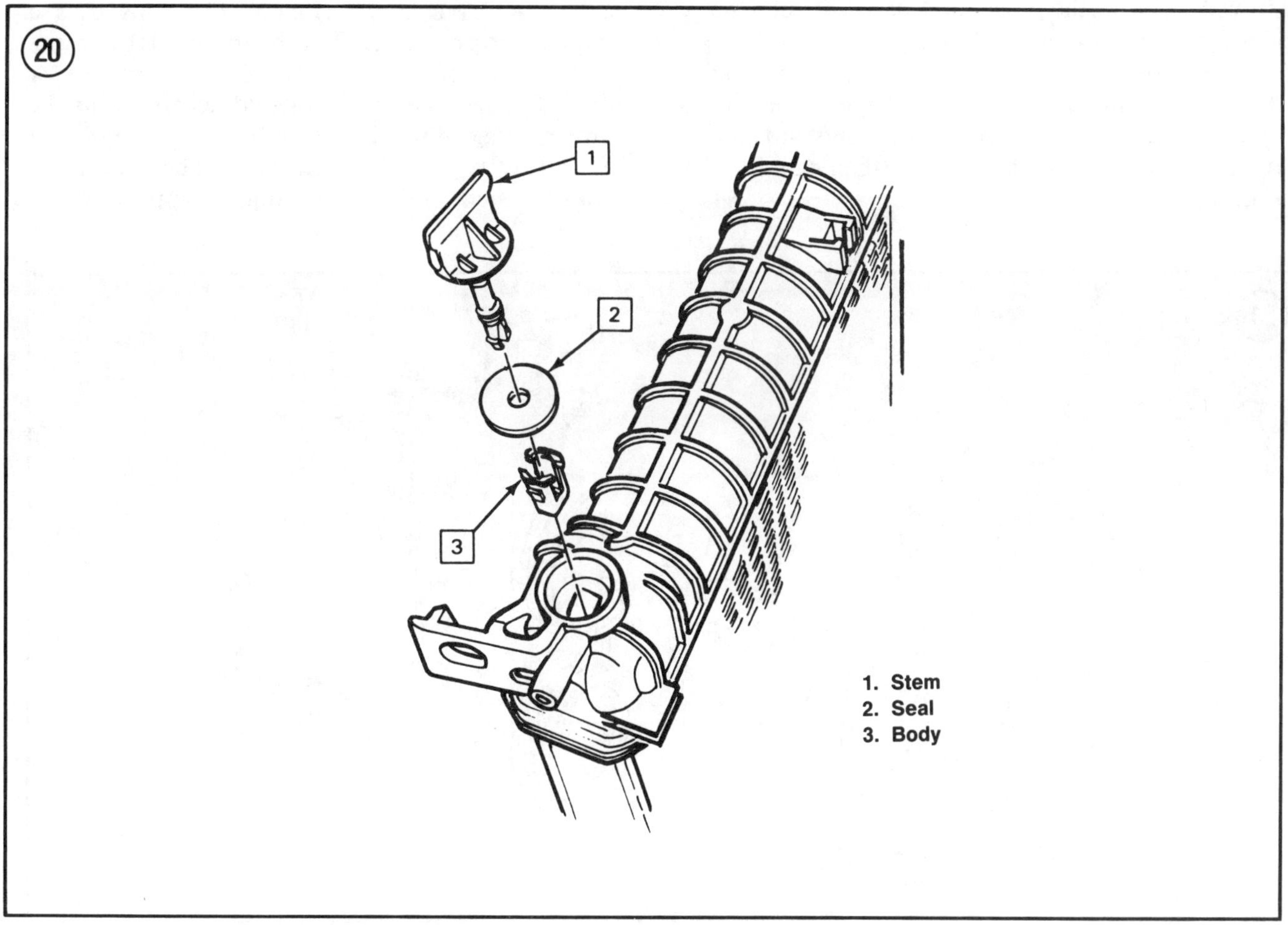

Radiator Hose Replacement

Replace any hoses that are cracked, brittle, mildewed or very soft or spongy. If a hose is in doubtful condition, but not definitely bad, replace it to be on the safe side. Even though the hoses are easily accessible, this will avoid the inconvenience of a roadside repair.

Always replace a radiator hose with the same type removed. Plain or pleated rubber hoses do not have the same strength as reinforced molded hoses. Check the hose clamp condition and, if necessary, install new clamps with a new hose.

Replacement

1. Place a clean container under the radiator draincock (**Figure 4**). Remove the radiator cap and open the draincock. Drain about one quart of coolant when replacing an upper hose. Completely drain the coolant to replace a lower hose. If the coolant is clean, save it for reuse.
2. Loosen the clamp at each end of the hose to be removed. Grasp the hose and twist it off the connection with a pulling motion.
3. If the hose is corroded to the fitting, cut it off with a sharp knife about one inch beyond the end of the fitting. Remove the clamp and slit the remaining piece of hose lengthwise, then peel it off the fitting.
4. Clean all corrosion from the fitting with sandpaper, then rinse the fitting to remove any particles.
5. Position the new clamps at least 1/4 in. from each end of the new hose. Wipe the inside diameter of the hose and the outside of the fitting with dishwashing liquid. Install the hose end on the fitting with a twisting motion.
6. Position the clamps for easy access for tightening. Tighten each clamp snugly with a screwdriver or nut driver. Recheck them for tightness after operating the vehicle for a few days.
7. Fill the radiator with the coolant removed in Step 1. Start the engine and operate it for a few minutes, checking for signs of leakage around the connection. Recheck the coolant level and top up, if necessary.

COOLING FAN

Fixed drive fans mate to the water pump hub with a spacer (**Figure 21**). A vehicle equipped with air conditioning or a heavy-duty cooling system has a fan drive clutch (**Figure 22**). This uses a temperature-controlled fluid coupling that permits use of a powerful fan without great power loss or noise. The fan speed is regulated according to the temperature of the air passing through the radiator core. The type of fan installed depends upon cooling system and air conditioning application.

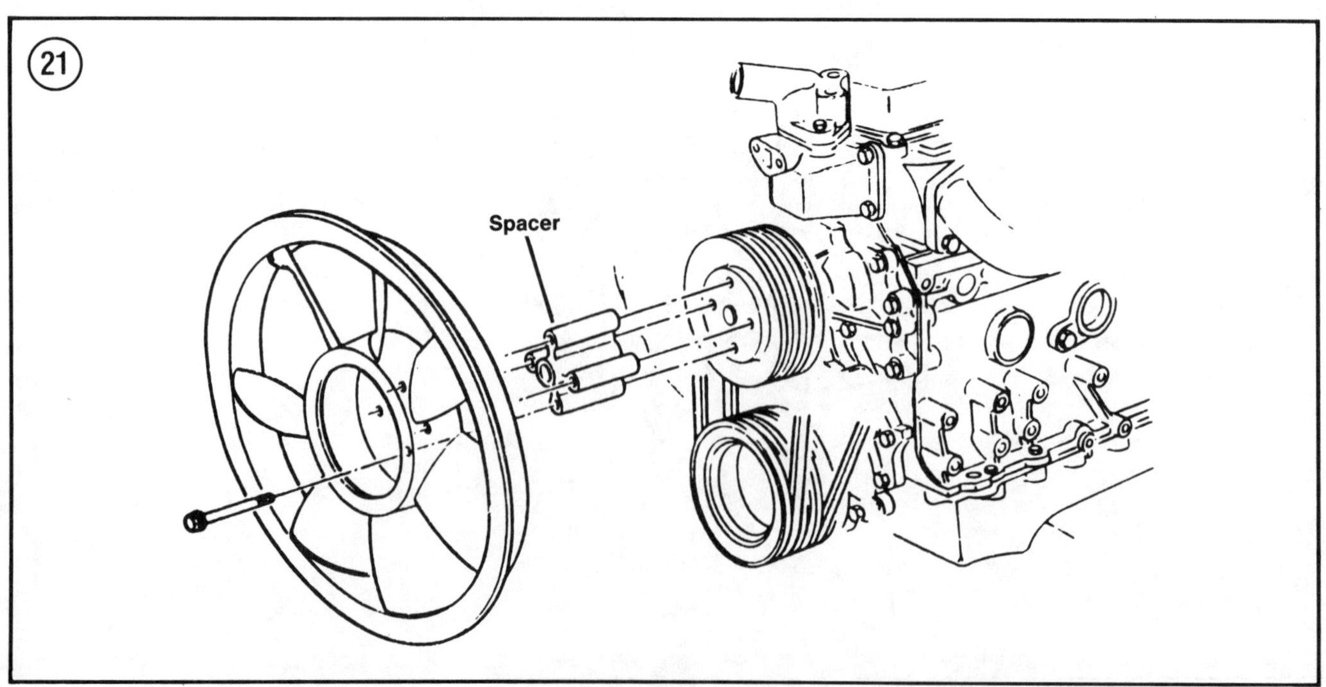

On some models, the fan must be removed from underneath the vehicle, while others require radiator removal prior to fan removal. The following generalized procedures can be used to remove any fan installation. Before attempting the procedure, however, it is a good idea to follow it visually while looking at the engine compartment.

CAUTION

Bent or damaged fans should not be reused, as any distortion will affect fan balance and operation. Damaged fans cannot be properly repaired and should be discarded.

Rigid Fan Removal/Installation

Refer to **Figure 21** (typical) for this procedure.

1. Disconnect the negative battery cable.
2. If necessary, remove the radiator and/or raise the front of the vehicle with a jack and place it on jackstands If the front of the vehicle is jacked up, securely block both rear wheels so the truck will not roll in either direction.
3. Check the fan mounting system to see if the drive belt tension should be relieved. If so, loosen the alternator adjusting and pivot bolts to relieve the drive belt tension.
4. Remove the fan blade retaining screws from the water pump hub or crankshaft damper (low-mount fan). Remove the fan blade and spacer.
5. Check the fan blade carefully for cracks, breaks, loose rivets or broken welds. Replace the fan if any defect is noted.
6. Installation is the reverse of removal. Tighten the fan blade screws to specifications (**Table 1**). Adjust the fan belt as described in this chapter, if necessary.

Fan Drive Clutch Removal/Installation

Refer to **Figure 22** (typical) for this procedure.

1. Disconnect the negative battery cable.
2. If necessary, remove the radiator and/or raise the front of the vehicle with a jack and place it on jackstands.
3. Check the fan mounting system to see if the drive belt tension should be relieved. If so, loosen the alternator adjusting and pivot bolts to relieve the drive belt tension.
4. Remove the upper radiator support and/or upper fan shroud as necessary.
5. Scribe balance marks on the fan clutch and water pump hub for proper alignment during installation.
6. Remove the attaching fasteners holding the fan clutch hub to the water pump hub.
7. Remove the fan clutch assembly.
8. Remove the capscrews and lockwashers holding the fan to the drive coupling. Separate the fan and coupling.
9. Place clutch assembly on work bench in an upright position to prevent silicone from draining into the fan drive bearing. If clutch is not going to be reinstalled immediately, store in an upright position.

7

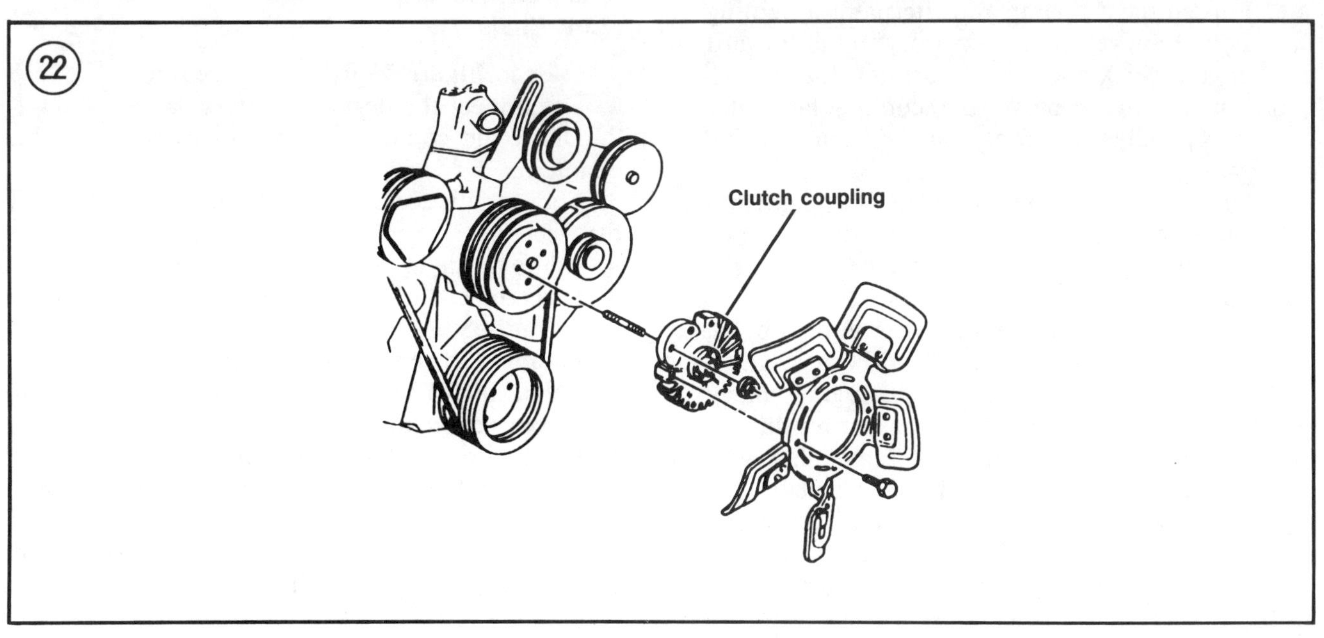

10. Check the fan blade carefully for cracks, breaks, loose rivets or broken welds. Replace the fan if any defect is noted.
11. Installation is the reverse of removal. Check fan drive clutch flange-to-water pump hub for proper mating. Align balance marks made in Step 5. Tighten attaching fasteners to specifications (**Table 1**). Adjust drive belts as described in this chapter.

WATER PUMP

A water pump may warn of impending failure by making noise. If the pump seal is defective, coolant may leak from behind the pump pulley. The water pump can be replaced on all models without discharging the air conditioning system. The pump is serviced as an assembly.

Removal/Installation (1.9L Engine)

1. Disconnect the negative battery cable.
2. Drain the cooling system as described in this chapter.
3. Remove the 4 bolts holding the lower cover. Remove the cover.
4. Loosen accessory units and remove the drive belts.
5. Non-air conditioned model—Remove the fan as described in this chapter.
6. Air conditioned model:
   a. Loosen the air pump and alternator mounting bolts. Swivel both accessory units toward engine block and remove drive belts.
   b. Unbolt and remove the cooling fan/water pump pulley assembly and air pump drive pulley.
   c. Unbolt and remove the fan set plate and pulley assembly.
7. Disconnect the radiator and heater hose at the water pump.
8. Remove the water pump mounting bolts. Remove the water pump and discard the gasket.
9. Clean the water pump and engine block mounting surfaces to remove all gasket residue.
10. Installation is the reverse of removal. Use a new gasket and tighten pump bolts snugly. No tightening specifications are provided by Chevrolet or GMC. Adjust drive belt tension as described in this chapter. Refill the cooling system and check for leaks.

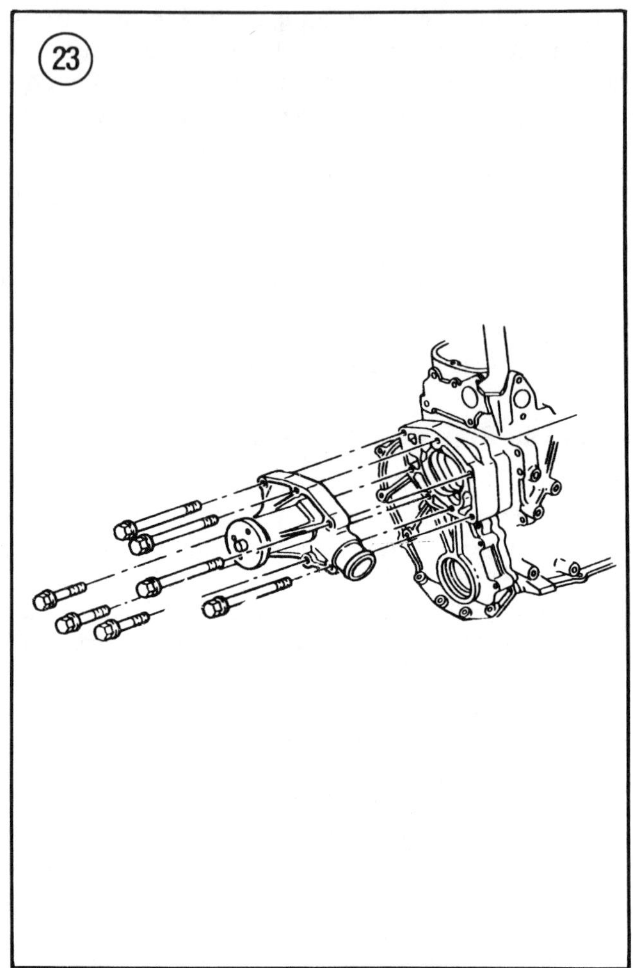

Removal/Installation (2.0L Engine)

Refer to **Figure 23** for this procedure.
1. Disconnect the negative battery cable.
2. Drain the cooling system as described in this chapter.
3. Loosen all accessory units and remove their drive belts.
4. Remove the upper radiator shroud.
5. Disconnect the radiator and heater hose at the water pump.
6. Unbolt and remove the water pump.
7. Clean all RTV sealant residue from the pump and front cover mounting surfaces.
8. Installation is the reverse of removal. Run a 3 mm (1/8 in.) bead of RTV sealant on the pump sealing surface. Tighten the bolts to specifications (**Table 1**). Adjust drive belt tension as described in this chapter. Refill the cooling system and check for leaks.

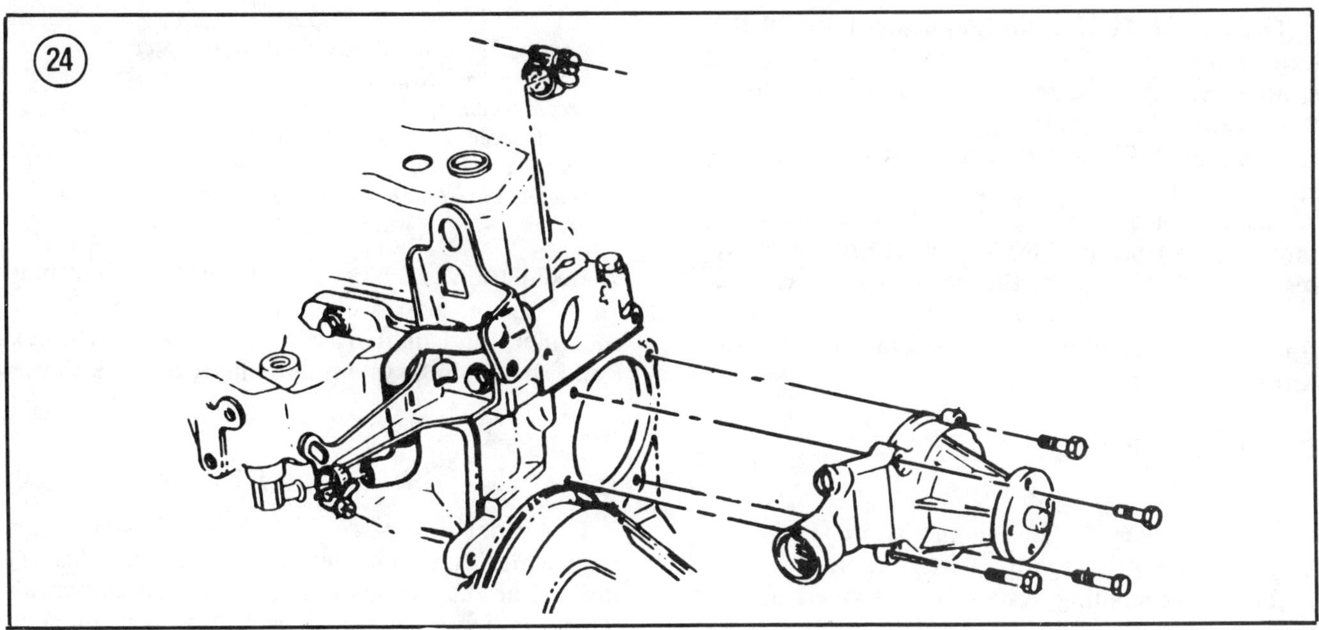

Removal/Installation (2.2L Diesel)

1. Disconnect the negative battery cable.
2. Drain the cooling system as described in this chapter.
3. Disconnect the power steering reservoir from the fan shroud and remove the upper shroud.
4. Loosen all accessory units and remove their drive belts.
5. Disconnect the radiator hose at the front cover.

WARNING
The air conditioning system contains pressurized refrigerant which can cause frostbite if it touches skin and blindness if it touches the eyes. If discharged near an open flame, the refrigerant forms poisonous gas. Never disconnect air conditioning system lines unless the system has been discharged and evacuated by a professional.

6. If equipped with air conditioning, remove the compressor without disconnecting any refrigerant lines and set to one side out of the way.
7. Disconnect the radiator and heater hoses on the right side of the water pump.
8. Disconnect the PCV hose at the valve cover.
9. Remove the air cleaner assembly. See Chapter Six.
10. Disconnect the heater pipe at the intake manifold.
11. Disconnect the heater hose on the left side of the water pump.
12. Disconnect the alternator bracket at the water pump.
13. Remove the water pump bolts. Remove the water pump and gasket. Discard the gasket.
14. Clean the water pump and engine block mounting surfaces to remove all gasket residue.
15. Installation is the reverse of removal. Use a new gasket and tighten pump bolts to specifications (**Table 1**). Adjust drive belt tension as described in this chapter. Refill the cooling system and check for leaks.

Removal/Installation (2.5L Engine)

Refer to **Figure 24** for this procedure.

1. Disconnect the negative battery cable.
2. Drain the cooling system as described in this chapter.
3. Loosen all accessory units and remove their drive belts.
4. Remove the upper fan shroud, fan and pump pulley.

5. Disconnect the radiator and heater hoses at the water pump.
6. Remove the water pump attaching bolts. Remove the water pump.
7. Clean all RTV sealant residue from the pump and front cover mounting surfaces.
8. Installation is the reverse of removal. Run a 3 mm (1/8 in.) bead of RTV sealant on the pump sealing surface. Tighten the bolts to specifications (**Table 1**). Adjust drive belt tension as described in this chapter. Refill the cooling system and check for leaks.

Removal/Installation (V6 Engine)

Refer to **Figure 25** for this procedure.
1. Disconnect the negative battery cable.
2. Drain the cooling system as described in this chapter.
3. Disconnect the heater hose at the water pump.
4. Remove the pump attaching fasteners. Remove the pump. Remove and discard the gasket, if used.

NOTE
Anaerobic sealant was used at the factory on 1982-1984 engines and is recommended for replacement pumps. A gasket is used on 1985 and later engines and is recommended for replacement pumps. If your pump uses sealant, clean all residue from the front cover and reinstall pump with a gasket.

5. Installation is the reverse of removal. Coat bolt threads with pipe sealant part No. 1052080 or equivalent and tighten to specifications (**Table 1**). Refill the cooling system and check for leaks.

DRIVE BELTS

The water pump/fan drive belt, as well as the belts which drive the alternator and other accessory units, should be inspected at regular intervals (Chapter Three) to make sure they are in good condition and are properly tensioned.

Worn, frayed, cracked or glazed belts should be replaced immediately. The components to which

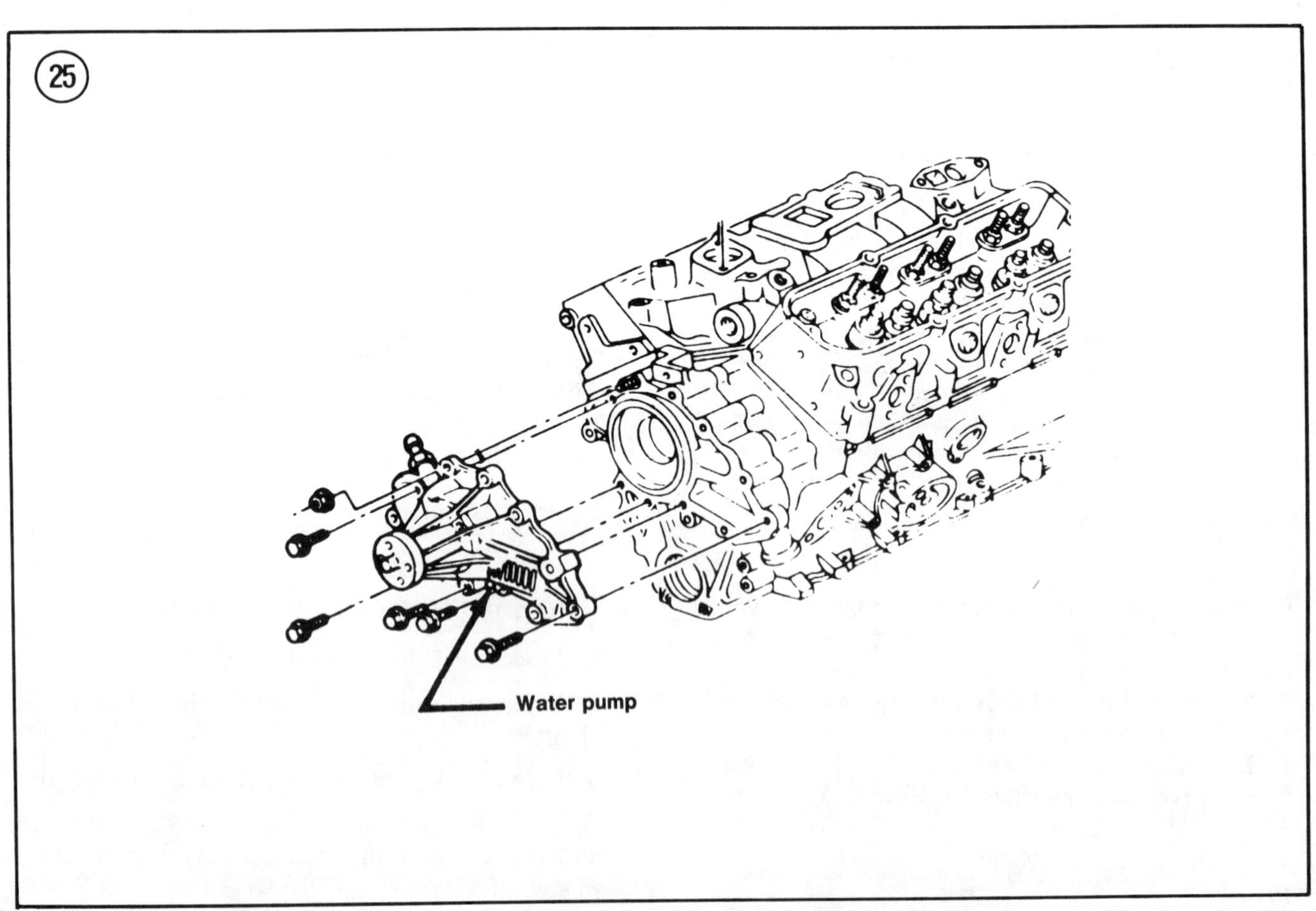

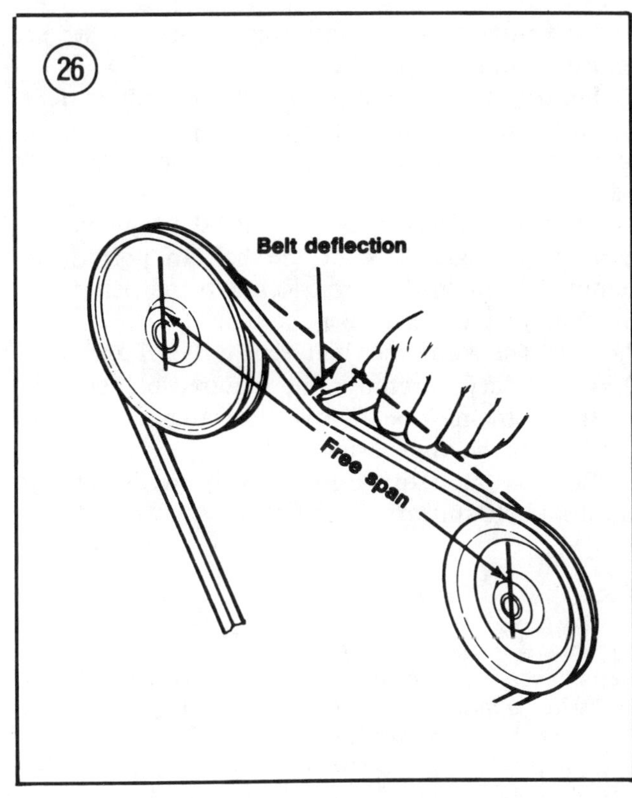

they direct power are essential to the safe and reliable operation of the vehicle. If correct adjustment is maintained on all belts, they will usually all give the same service life. For this reason and because of the effort involved in replacing an inner belt (requiring the removal of all outer belts), it is a good idea to replace all belts as a set. The added expense is small compared to the cost of replacing the belts individually and eliminates the possibility of a breakdown on the road which could cost far more in time and money.

A V-belt should be correctly tensioned at all times. If loose, the belt will not permit the driven components to operate at maximum efficiency. The belt will also wear rapidly because of the increased friction caused by slipping. Belts that are too tight will be overstressed and prone to premature failure. An excessively tight belt will also overstress the accessory unit's bearings, resulting in their premature failure.

7

Tension Adjustment

Drive belt tension can be checked according to belt deflection (**Figure 26**), but GM recommends the use of a belt tension gauge (**Figure 27**). Chevrolet and GMC recommend the use of a strand tension gauge (part No. J-23600 or equivalent) whenever possible as the most accurate means of setting belt tension. If access to the drive belt is limited, tension may be established by the deflection method. Drive belt specifications are provided in **Table 2**.

1A. To check tension by deflection, depress the belt at a point midway between the 2 pulleys (**Figure 26**). If the free span between the pulleys is less than 12 inches, the belt should deflect 1/8-1/4 in. when approximately 10 lb. pressure is applied. Drive belts with a greater span should deflect 1/8-3/8 in.

1B. To check belt tension with a tension gauge, install the gauge on the drive belt (**Figure 27**) and check tension according to the gauge manufacturer's instructions. Compare to the specifications in **Table 2**.

2. If adjustment is required, loosen the accessory pivot and adjustment bolts. Some engines equipped with power steering and air conditioning will use 2 pivot and 2 adjustment bolts.

3. Move the accessory unit toward or away from the engine as required.

CAUTION

*Do not pry on the accessory unit to reposition it. Most adjustment brackets have a slot provided for use of a breaker bar as a pry tool. See **Figure 28** (typical). To move the accessory, insert a suitable breaker bar in the bracket slot and reposition the unit as required.*

4. Tighten the adjustment bolt(s), release pressure on the accessory unit, then tighten the pivot bolt(s).
5. Recheck belt tension. If necessary, repeat the procedure to obtain the correct tension.

Removal

Vehicles equipped with power steering, air conditioning or an air pump require removal of accessory drive belts before the fan drive belt can be removed. Depending upon the positioning of the accessory unit, some steps of this procedure may have to be performed from underneath the vehicle. With some installations, it may be more convenient to remove the fan assembly before proceeding.

1. Determine which accessory belts must be removed and in what order.
2. Loosen the accessory pivot and adjustment bolts. Some engines equipped with power steering and air conditioning will use 2 pivot and 2 adjustment bolts.
3. Move the accessory unit toward the engine until there is enough slack in the belt to permit its removal from the pulleys. Remove the belt from the pulleys and lift it over the fan.
4. If replacing an inner belt, repeat Step 1 and Step 2 as necessary to remove the required belt(s).
5. Install the new belt(s) over the fan and fit in the grooves of the appropriate pulleys.
6. Pry the accessory unit away from the engine until its belt appears to be properly tensioned.

CAUTION

*Do not pry on the accessory unit to reposition it. Most adjustment brackets have a slot provided for use of a breaker bar as a pry tool. See **Figure 28** (typical). To move the accessory, insert a suitable breaker bar in the bracket slot and reposition the unit as required.*

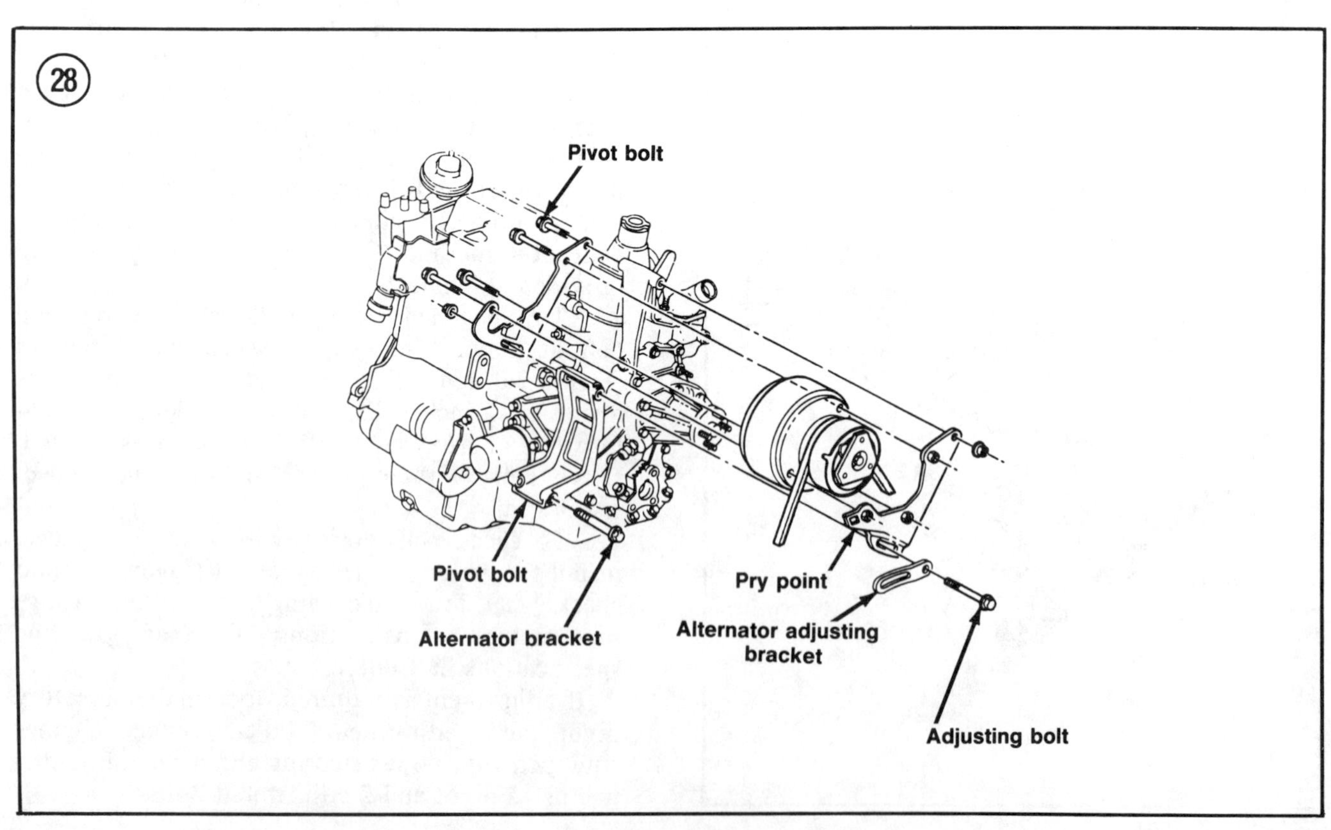

7. Tighten the adjustment bolt(s), release pressure on the accessory unit, then tighten the pivot bolt(s).
8. If outer belts were removed, repeat Step 6 and Step 7 to tension each remaining drive belt.
9. Recheck belt tension with the tension gauge. If necessary, repeat the procedure to obtain the correct tension.

HEATER

The heater system consists of a blower air inlet and a heater/defroster assembly. Power vent, heat and defrost functions are controlled by the heater/defroster assembly. The blower air inlet is connected to the front of the dash in the cab. The heater/defroster is fastened to the rear of the dash in the cab. Mounting gaskets on both components prevent air, water and noise from entering the passenger compartment. **Figure 29** shows the base heater system. **Figure 30** shows the optional system. The 2 differ primarily in ducting. The optional system is used in all vehicles equipped with air conditioning.

Troubleshooting

1. If the heater does not produce heat, make sure the engine will warm up in a reasonable amount of time. If the thermostat sticks in the open position, the engine will not completely warm up. Since hot engine coolant provides heat for the heater, a defective thermostat may be the problem.

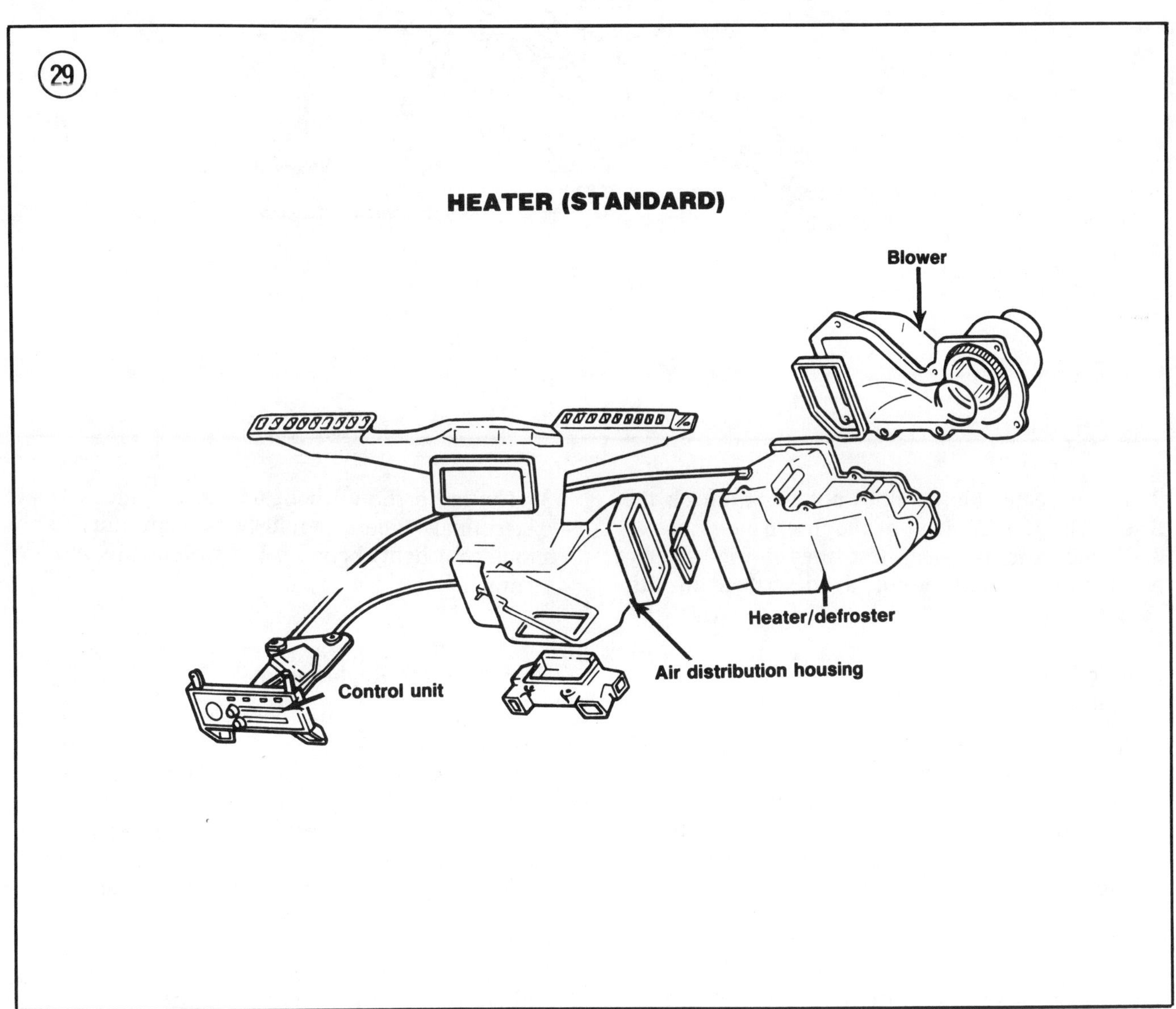

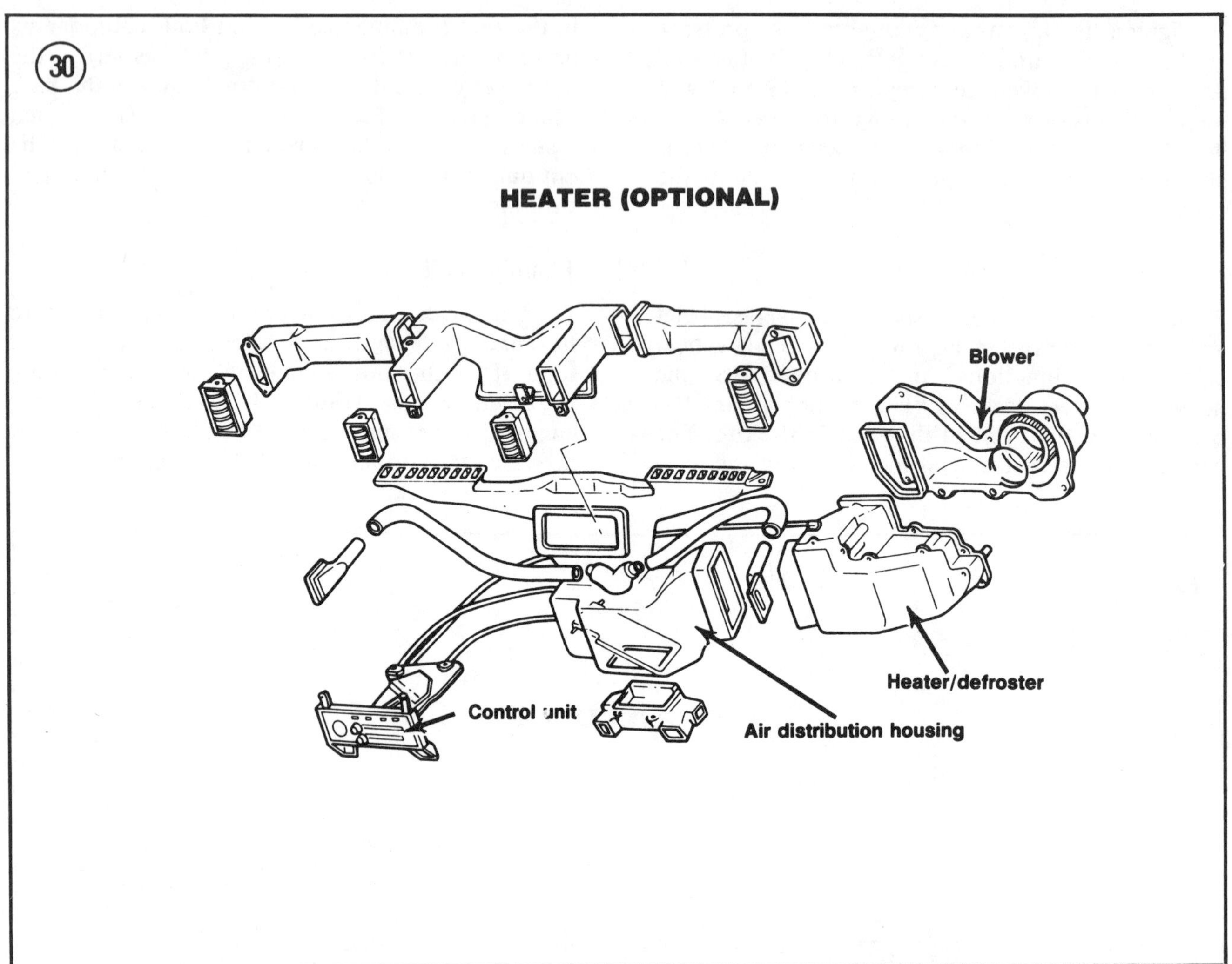

2. If the heater blower does not work, check the fuse in the H-AC cavity of the fuse panel.
3. If the fuse is good, test the blower switch, resistor block and motor as described in this chapter.

Blower Motor and Switch Testing

Power to the blower motor is provided through the ignition switch and a 25-amp fuse in the H-AC cavity of the fuse panel. Blower motor speed is controlled in all modes by the switch on the instrument panel control assembly.

1. Remove the control assembly as described in this chapter.
2. If the problem is in the blower speed, check for continuity between the 4 terminals of the fan switch at all 4 switch positions with a test lamp.
3. The lamp should light for each connected pair of terminals. There should be no continuity (lamp should not light) between the switch case and any terminal.

Blower Switch Replacement

1. Remove the control assembly as described in this chapter.
2. Carefully pry the switch knob off with a screwdriver.
3. Remove the fasteners holding the switch to the control assembly.
4. Align the pin on the new switch with the hole in the mounting bracket and install the fasteners securely.
5. Push the knob on the switch shaft as far as it will go. Reinstall the control assembly.

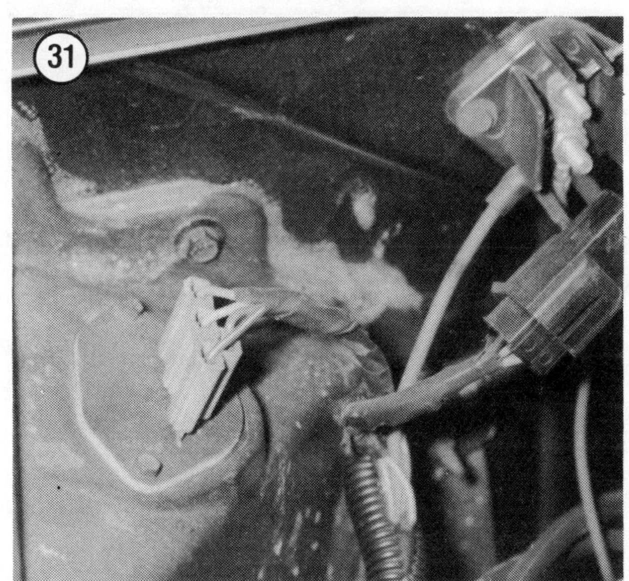

Resistor Block Test

The resistor block is mounted on the heater housing in the engine compartment. See **Figure 31** (typical).

1. Unplug the resistor block electrical connector.
2. Remove the resistor block retaining screws. Remove the resistor block.
3. Test the resistors for an open circuit with a self-powered test lamp. Replace resistor block if an open circuit is found.

Control Assembly

Refer to **Figure 32** for this procedure.

1. Disconnect the negative battery cable.
2. Remove the center bezel from the instrument panel. See *Instrument Panel Removal/Installation*, Chapter Thirteen.

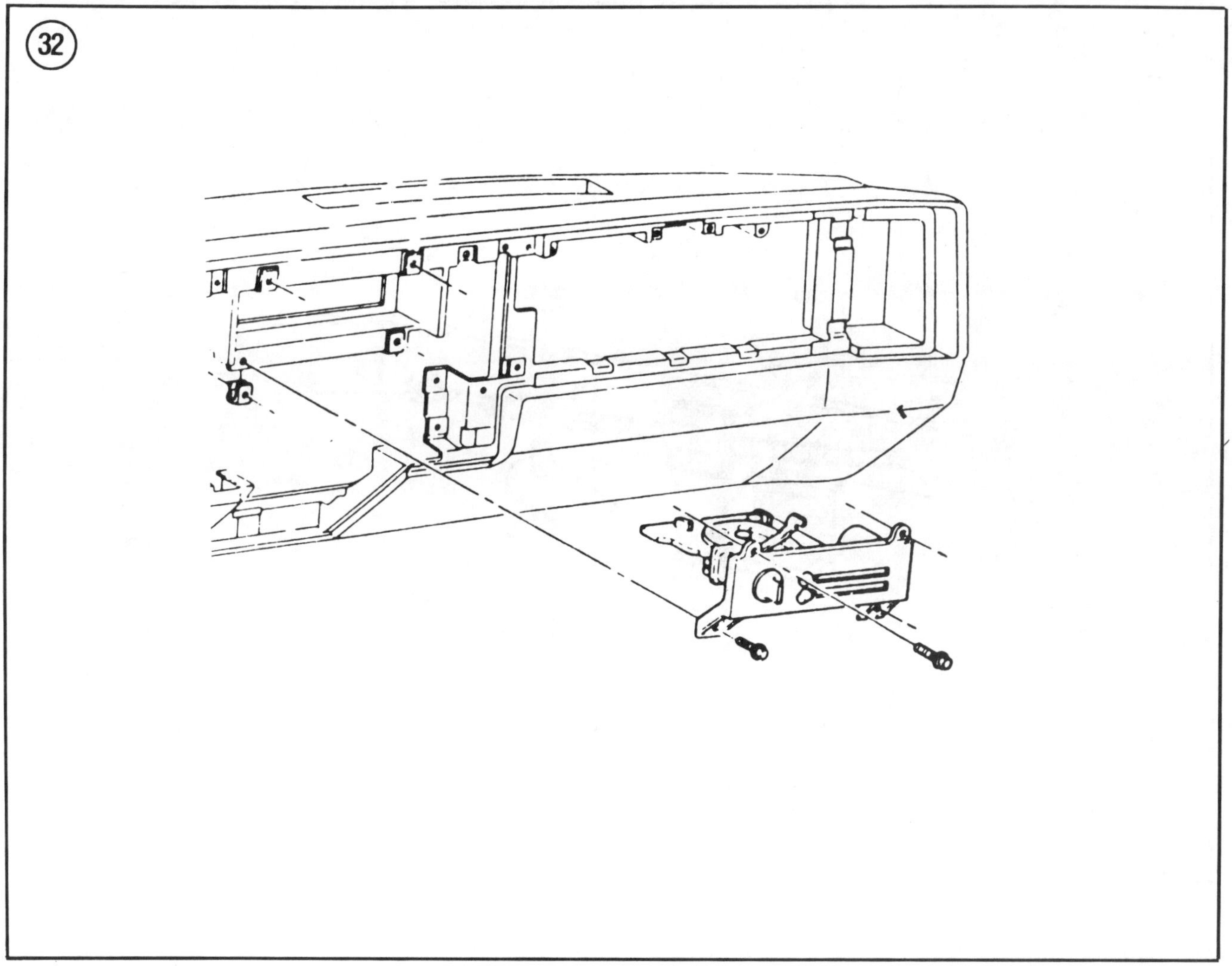

32

3. Remove the control assembly attaching screws. Pull the assembly out far enough to remove the clips holding the control cables to the module assembly crank arms (**Figure 33**).
4. Pry the cable retaining tabs from their holders (**Figure 33**).
5. Unplug the blower switch electrical connector at the switch.
6. Remove the control assembly from the instrument panel.
7. Installation is the reverse of removal.

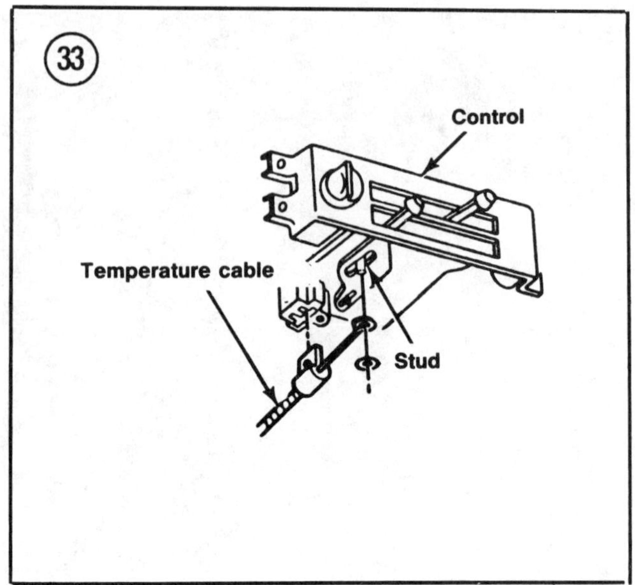

Control Cables

The control cables connect to the control assembly and heater crank arms by snap-on retaining tabs. See **Figure 33** (control assembly) and **Figure 34** (crank arm).

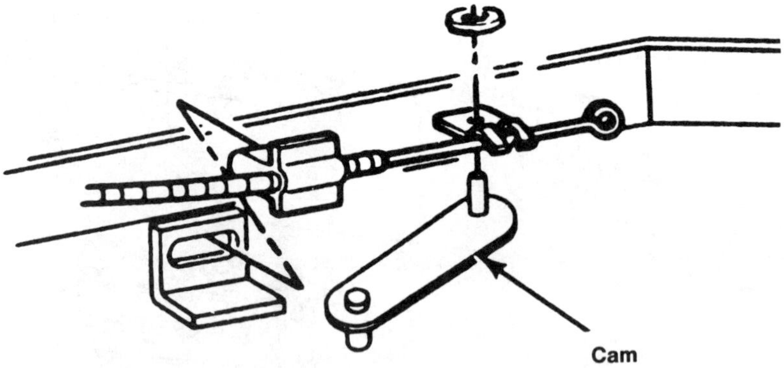

Cable Adjustment

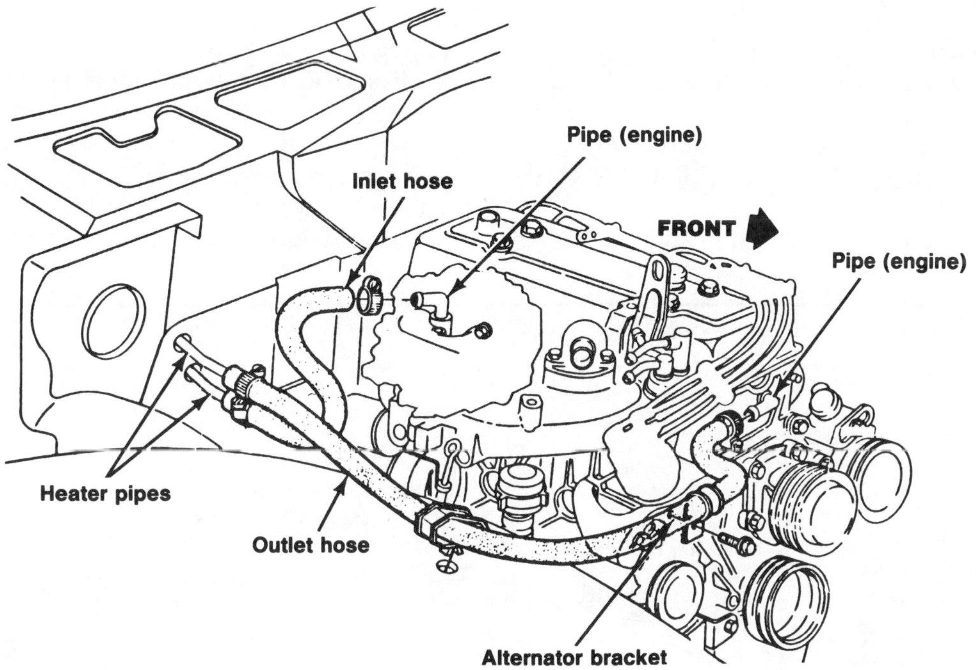

The temperature cable has a slider-type self-adjustment feature. As the temperature lever is moved through its full range of travel, the cable clip assumes a position to seat the temperature valve in both extreme positions. The vent/defrost cable requires no adjustment.

Blower Motor Removal/Installation

Refer to **Figure 35** (typical) for this procedure.

1. Disconnect the negative battery cable.
2. Disconnect the ground lead (A, **Figure 36**) on the motor housing.
3. Unplug the wiring connectors at the blower motor (B, **Figure 36**) and resistor block (**Figure 31**).
4. Remove the blower motor housing attaching screws. Remove the blower motor from the engine compartment.

5. Hold the blower motor cage and remove the nut holding the cage to the motor shaft. Remove the motor and cage.
6. Installation is the reverse of removal.

Modular Duct Removal/Installation

Refer to **Figure 37** (typical) for this procedure.

1. Drain the cooling system as described in this chapter.
2. Disconnect the heater inlet and outlet hoses at the firewall. See **Figure 38** (typical). Plug the core tubes.
3. Disconnect the radio suppression strap.
4. Remove the modular duct retaining screws. Remove the modular duct.
5. Installation is the reverse of removal.

Heater Core Removal/Installation

1. Drain the cooling system as described in this chapter.
2. Remove the modular duct as described in this chapter.
3. Remove the 2 attaching screws at each end of the core. Remove the heater core from inside the cab.
4. Installation is the reverse of removal.

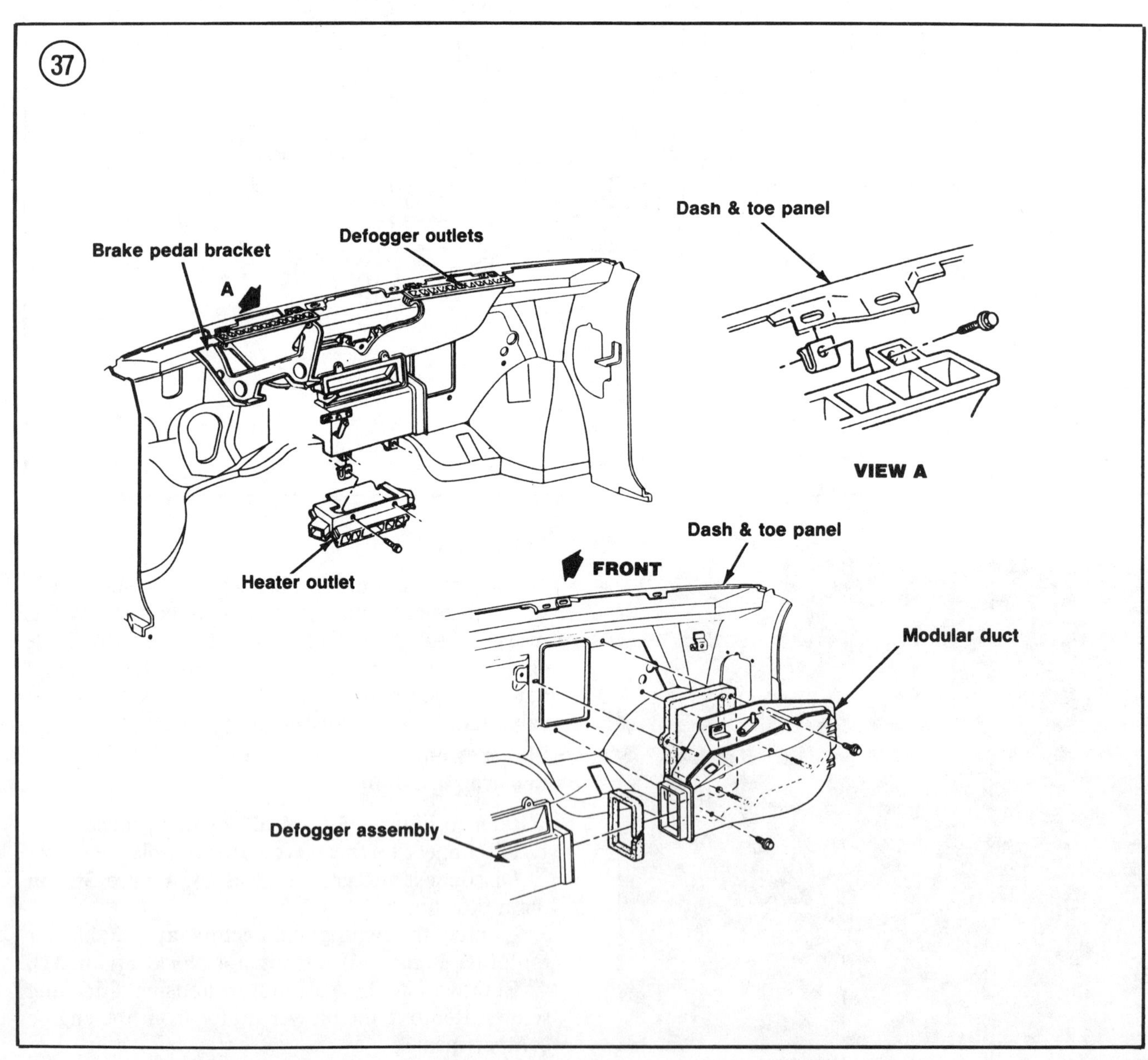

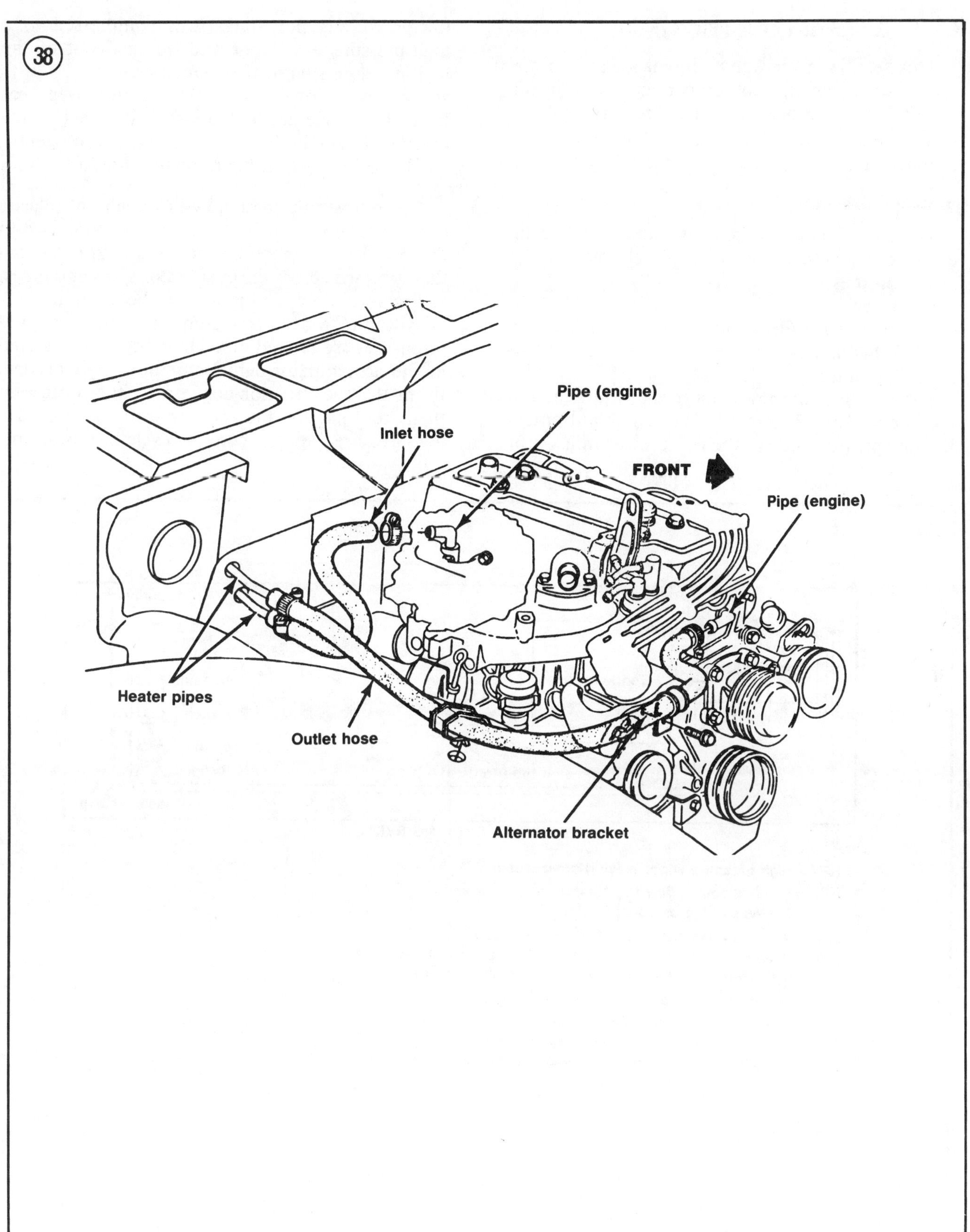
38
Pipe (engine)
Inlet hose
FRONT
Pipe (engine)
Heater pipes
Outlet hose
Alternator bracket

AIR CONDITIONING

This section covers the maintenance and minor repairs that can prevent or correct common air conditioning problems. Major repairs require special training and equipment and should be left to a dealer or air conditioning expert.

System Operation

There are 5 basic components common to the air conditioning system used with all vehicles.

a. Compressor.
b. Condenser.
c. Accumulator/dehydrator.
d. Orifice tube.
e. Evaporator.

For practical purposes, the cycle begins at the compressor. See **Figure 39**. The refrigerant enters the low-pressure side of the compressor in a warm low-pressure vapor state. It is compressed to a high-pressure hot vapor and pumped out of the high-pressure side to the condenser.

Air flow through the condenser removes heat from the refrigerant and transfers the heat to the outside air. As the heat is removed, the refrigerant condenses to a warm high-pressure liquid.

The refrigerant than flows through the plastic expansion tube with its mesh screen and orifice to the evaporator, where it removes heat from the cab that is blown across the evaporator's fins and tubes. Refrigerant flow continues to the accumulator/dehydrator, where moisture is removed and impurities are filtered out. The refrigerant is stored in the accumulator/dehydrator until it is needed. From the accumulator/dehydrator, the refrigerant then returns to the compressor as a warm low-pressure vapor, where the cycle begins again.

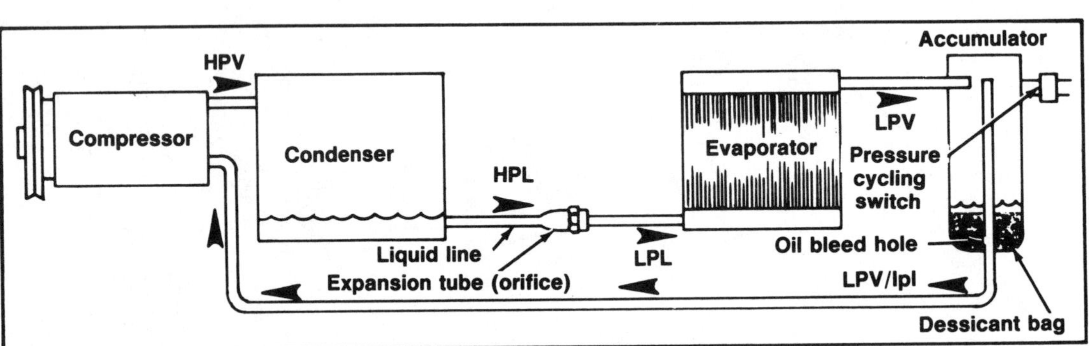

PRESSURE CYCLING SYSTEM

HPV—High pressure vapor leaving compressor.

HPL—Vapor is cooled down by condenser air flow and leaves as high pressure liquid.

LPL—Orifice meters the liquid R-12 into evaporator, reducing its pressure, and warm blower air across evaporator core causes boiling off of liquid into vapor.

LPV—Leaves evaporator as low pressure vapor and returns with the small amount of...

lpl—...low pressure liquid that didn't boil off completely back to the compressor to be compressed again.

Compressor

The compressor is located on the drive belt end of the engine, like the alternator, and is driven by a V-belt. The large pulley on the front of the compressor contains an electromagnetic clutch. This activates and operates the compressor when the air conditioning is switched on. A pressure relief valve opens to discharge refrigerant if operating pressure exceeds 440 psi (3036 kPa). Some systems may use a muffler to reduce compressor noise and high-pressure line vibrations.

Condenser

The condenser is mounted in front of the radiator. Air passing through the condenser tubes and fins removes heat from the refrigerant in the same manner it removes heat from the engine coolant as it passes through the radiator. The cooling fan also pulls air through the condenser.

Accumulator/dehydrator

The accumulator/dehydrator is a small tank-like unit, usually mounted near one of the wheel wells.

Orifice Tube

The plastic orifice tube is located inside the evaporator inlet pipe at the liquid line connection. It meters refrigerant into the evaporator.

Evaporator

The evaporator is mounted inside the blower motor assembly in the cab cooling unit beneath the instrument panel. Warm air is blown across the fins and tubes, where it is cooled and dried and then ducted into the cab.

Vacuum Tank

Air conditioning systems on diesels and some gasoline engines use a vacuum supply tank to store vacuum for use whenever manifold vacuum decreases, as during heavy acceleration. See **Figure 40**. The vacuum tank contains a check valve.

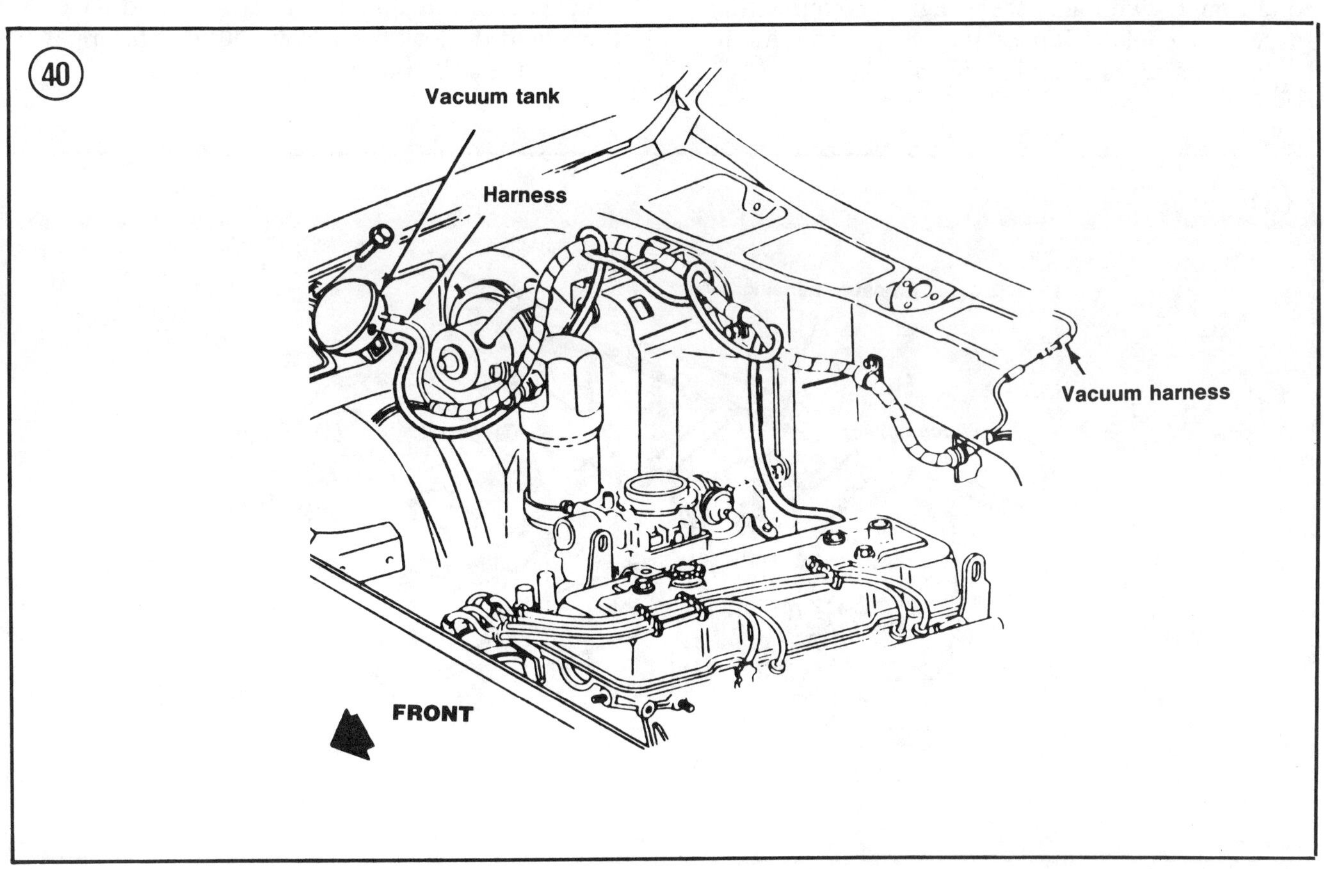

Pressure Sensing Switch

This switch, located at the accumulator/dehydrator (**Figure 41**) cycles on and off to prevent an evaporator freeze-up. Cycling of the compressor will cause occasional slight changes in engine speed and power under certain operating conditions; this should be considered normal.

ROUTINE MAINTENANCE

Basic maintenance of the air conditioning system is easy. At least once a month, even in cold weather, start your engine, turn on the air conditioner and operate it at each of the control settings.

Operate the air conditioner for about 10 minutes, with the engine running at about 1,500 rpm. This will ensure that the compressor seal does not deform from sitting in the same position for a long period of time. If deformation occurs, the seal is likely to leak.

The efficiency of the air conditioning system also depends in great part on the efficiency of the cooling system. If the cooling system is dirty or low on coolant, it may be impossible to operate the air conditioner without the engine overheating. Inspect the coolant. If necessary, flush and refill the cooling system as described in this chapter.

NOTE
Do not install a bug screen on vehicles with air conditioning. The screen reduces air flow and thus affects air conditioner efficiency. During hot weather, a bug screen can cause the engine to overheat.

Use an air hose and a soft brush to clean the radiator and condenser fins and tubes. Remove any bugs, leaves or other imbedded debris.

Check drive belt tension as described in this chapter.

If the condition of the cooling system thermostat is in doubt, test it as described in this chapter.

Once you are sure the cooling system is in good condition, the air conditioning system can be inspected.

Inspection

1. Clean all lines, fittings and system components with solvent and a clean rag. Pay particular attention to the fittings; oily dirt around connections almost certainly indicates a leak. Oil from the compressor will migrate through the system to the leak. Carefully tighten threaded connections, but do not overtighten and strip the threads. If the leak persists, it will soon be apparent as oily dirt will continue to accumulate.

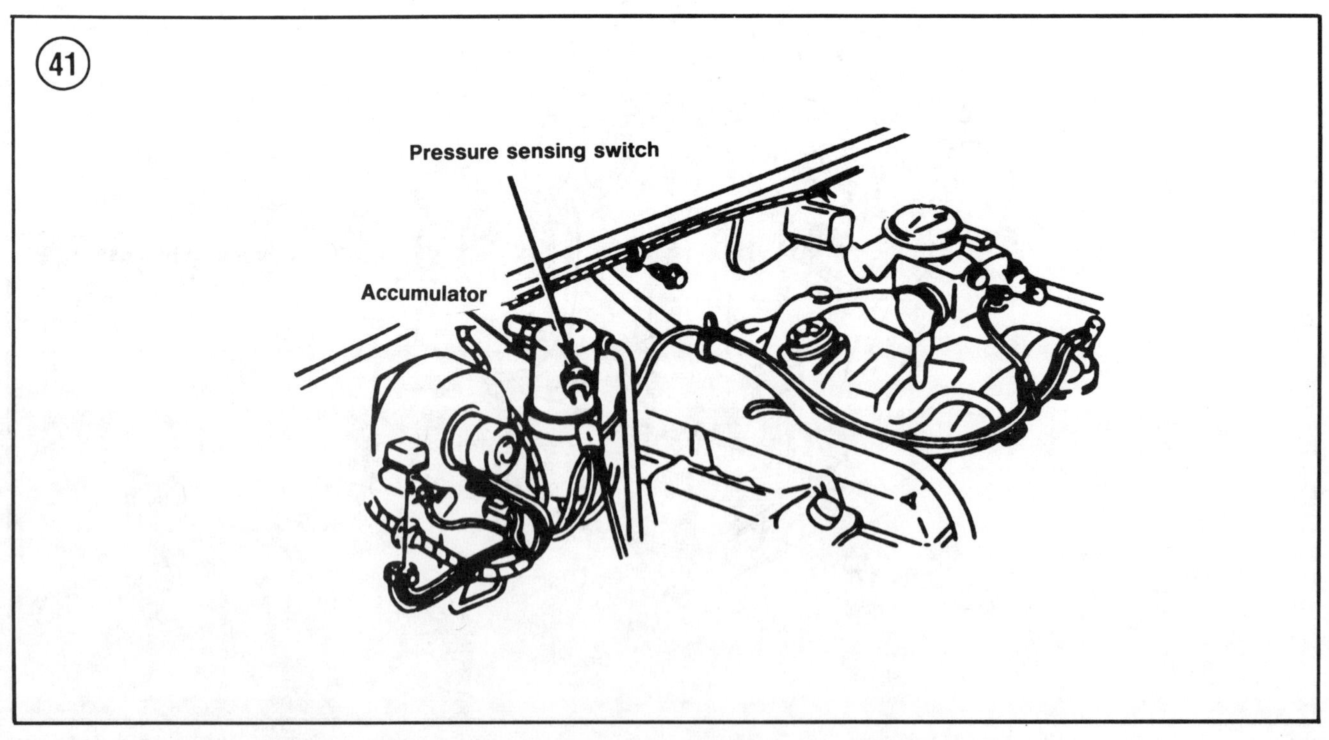

2. Clean the condenser fins and tubes with a soft brush and an air hose or with a high-pressure stream of water from a garden hose. Remove any bugs, leaves or other imbedded debris. Carefully straighten any bent fins with a screwdriver, taking care not to puncture or dent the tubes.
3. Start the engine and check the operation of the blower motor and the compressor clutch by turning the controls on and off. If either the blower or clutch fails to operate, shut off the engine and check the H-A/C fuse in the fuse panel. See *Electrical Circuit Protection*, Chapter Eight. If it is blown, replace it. If not, remove and clean the fuse holder contacts. Then check the clutch and blower operation again. If they still will not operate, take the vehicle to a dealer or air conditioning specialist.

REFRIGERANT

The air conditioning system uses a refrigerant called dichlorodifluoromethane, or R-12.

WARNING
Refrigerant creates freezing temperatures when it evaporates. This can cause frostbite if it touches skin, and blindness if it touches the eyes. If discharged near an open flame, R-12 forms poisonous gas. If the refrigerant can is hooked up to the pressure side of the compressor, it may explode. Always wear safety goggles and gloves when working with R-12.

Charging

This section applies to partially discharged or empty air conditioning systems. If a hose has been disconnected or any internal part of the system exposed to air, the system should be evacuated and recharged by a dealer or air conditioning shop. Recharge kits are available from auto parts stores. Be sure the kit includes a gauge set. Refer to **Figure 42** for this procedure.

WARNING
Wear gloves and safety goggles to prevent frostbite and blindness. Do not allow any open flame near the refrigerant or poisonous gas may be formed.

7

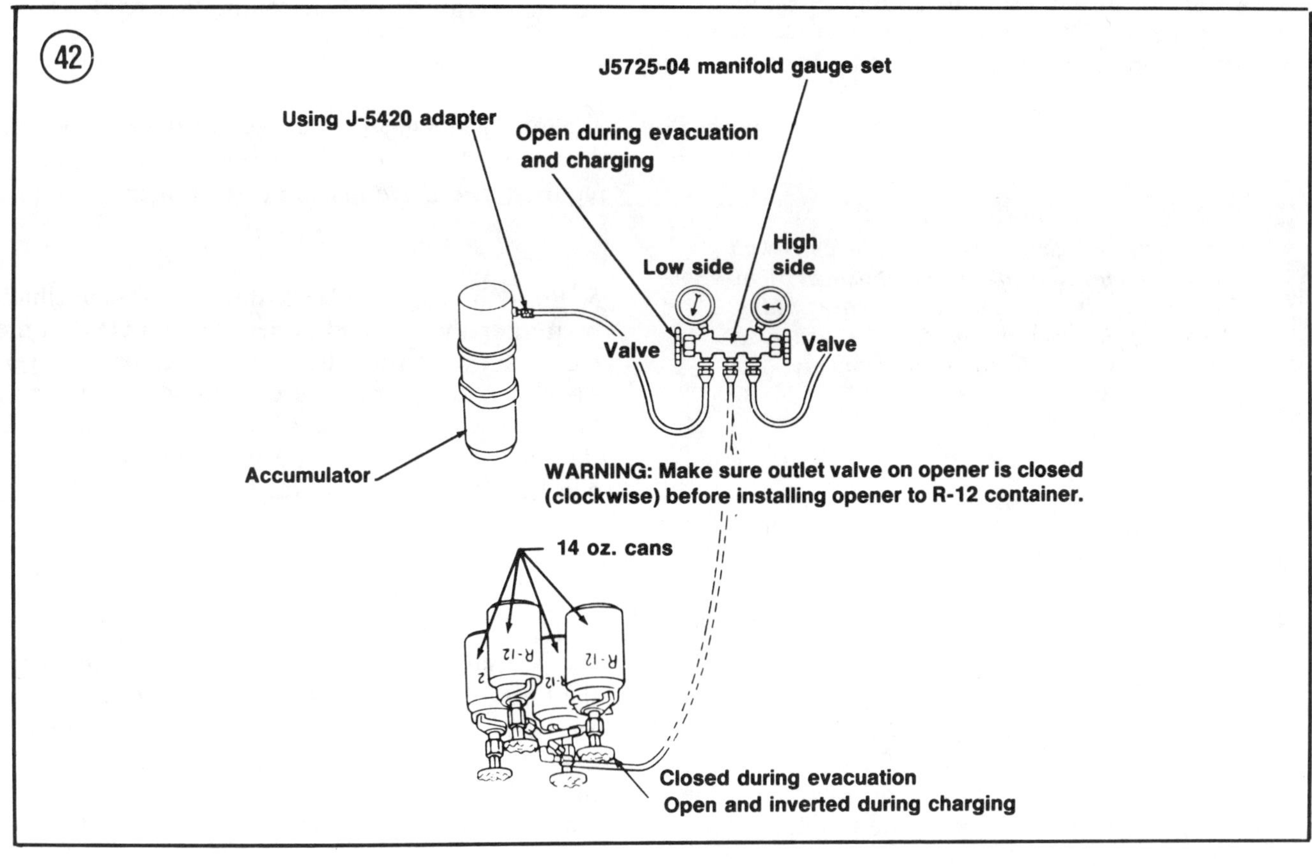

NOTE
The following procedure is for use with GM manifold gauge set part No. J-5725-04. Another gauge set may require a slightly different procedure. Carefully read and understand the gauge manufacturer's instructions before charging the system.

1. Carefully read and understand the gauge manufacturer's instructions before charging the system.
2. Connect the low pressure gauge of manifold gauge set part No. J-5725-04 to the accumulator fitting.
3. Connect the center gauge set hose to the R-12 can.
4. Start the engine and run at normal idle with the choke wide open.
5. Turn the A/C control lever OFF.
6. Open the R-12 source valve. Let one 14-oz. can of R-12 flow into the system through the accumulator fitting. Immediately engage the compressor by returning the A/C control lever to NORM and turning the blower on HI. This will draw the rest of the R-12 charge into the system.
7. Shut the R-12 source valve off. Run the engine for 30 seconds to clear the lines and gauges.

WARNING
Never remove a gauge line from its adapter with the line connected to the air conditioning system. Disconnect the line at the service fitting. Removing the charging hose at the gauge set while still connected to the accumulator can cause serious personal injury.

8. Remove the hose adapter at the accumulator quickly to prevent excessive R-12 loss. Install the protective cap on the accumulator fitting.
9. Check the system for leaks. Shut the engine off.

TROUBLESHOOTING

If the air conditioner fails to blow cold air, the following steps will help locate the problem.

1. First, stop the vehicle and look at the control settings. One of the most common air conditioning problems occurs when the temperature is set for maximum cold and the blower is set on LOW. This promotes ice buildup on the evaporator fins and tubes, particularly in humid weather. Eventually, the evaporator will ice over completely and restrict air flow. Turn the blower on HIGH and place a hand over an air outlet. If the blower is running but there is little or no air flowing through the outlet, the evaporator is probably iced up. Leave the blower on HIGH and turn the temperature control off or to its warmest setting and wait. It will take 10-15 minutes for the ice to start melting.

2. If the blower does not run at any speed, the fuse may be blown, there may be a loose wiring connection or the motor may be burned out. First, check the fuse panel for a blown or incorrectly seated fuse, then check the wiring for loose connections.

3. If the blower runs, but not on high speed, check for a blown fuse in the electrical wiring between the junction terminal and air conditioner relay.

4. Shut off the engine and inspect the compressor drive belt. If worn or loose, replace or tighten as required. See *Drive Belts* in this chapter.

5. Start the engine. Check the compressor clutch by turning the air conditioner ON and OFF. If the clutch does not activate, its fuse may be blown or the evaporator temperature-limiting switches may be defective. If the fuse is defective, replace it. If the fuse is not the problem, have the system checked by a dealer or an air conditioning specialist.

6. If the system appears to be operating as it should, but air flow into the cab is not cold, check the condenser for debris that could block air flow. Recheck the cooling system as described in this chapter. If the preceding steps have not solved the problem, take the vehicle to a dealer or air conditioning shop for service.

Table 1 TIGHTENING TORQUES

Fastener	ft.-lb.	N•m
Air conditioning compressor		
Bracket-to-cylinder head	30-40	40-54
To bracket	20-30	27-40
Alternator		
Adjustment bolt	20-30	27-40
Bracket-to-cylinder head	30-40	40-54
Pivot bolt	20-30	27-40
Coolant recovery tank	2	3
Cooling fan		
All except diesel	20	27
2.2L diesel		
Fan clutch-to-pulley	20-30	27-40
Fan-to-fan clutch	11-16	8-12
Plastic fan-to-pulley	20-30	27-40
Thermostat housing		
2.0L	12-20	16-27
2.2L diesel	10-17	14-23
2.5L	20	27
V6	21	28
Water pump		
1.9L	*	*
2.0L	13-18	18-24
2.2L diesel	10-17	14-23
2.5L	25	34
V6		
1982-1983		
M6×1.0	6-9	8-12
M8×1.25	13-18	18-24
M10×1.25	20-30	27-40
1984-on		
M6×1.0	6-9	8-12
M8×1.25	13-18	18-24
Nut	6-9	8-12
Water pump pulley		
2.0L and V6	13-18	18-24
Water outlet		
2.0L adapter	12-20	16-27
2.2L diesel	10-17	14-23
2.5L	25	34

* Torque specifications are not provided by General Motors for the 1.9L water pump.

Table 2 DRIVE BELT TENSION

	Tension in lb. New	Used*
1.9L engine		
Air conditioning	157	90
All others	135	67
2.0L engine		
Air conditioning	169	90
All others	146	67
2.2L diesel engine		
All belts	135	79
2.5L engine		
Air conditioning	169	90
Alternator		
With A/C	169	90
Without AC	90	67
Power steering/vacuum pump	146	67
2.8L V6		
Alternator and air conditioning	146	67
All others	135	67

* A belt is considered used after the engine had made more than one rotation and the belt has stretched or seated into the pulley groove.

CHAPTER EIGHT

ELECTRICAL SYSTEM

8

The vehicles covered in this manual are equipped with a 12-volt, negative-ground electrical system. Many electrical problems can be traced to a simple cause such as a blown fuse, a loose or corroded connection, a loose alternator drive belt or a frayed wire. While these are easily corrected problems which may not appear important, they can quickly lead to serious difficulty if allowed to go uncorrected.

Complete overhaul of electrical components such as the alternator, distributor or starter motor is neither practical nor economical. In many cases, the necessary bushings, bearings or other worn parts are not available for individual replacement.

If tests indicate a unit with problems other than those discussed in this chapter, replace it with a new or rebuilt unit. Make certain, however, that the new or rebuilt part to be installed is an exact replacement for the defective one removed. Also make sure to isolate and correct the cause of the failure before installing a replacement. For example, an uncorrected short in an alternator circuit will most likely burn out a new alternator as quickly as it damaged the old one. If in doubt, always consult an expert.

This chapter provides service procedures for the battery, charging system, starter, ignition system, lights, switches, turn indicators, horn, windshield wipers and washers, fuses and fusible links.

Table 1 and **Table 2** are at the end of the chapter.

BATTERY

The battery is the single most important part of in the automotive electrical system. It is also the one most frequently neglected. The battery should be cleaned and inspected at periodic intervals. In addition, the electrolyte level in unsealed batteries should be checked weekly (Chapter Three).

New vehicles are equipped with a sealed Freedom II battery (side terminal type) which requires no maintenance. See **Figure 1**. A test indicator (built-in hydrometer) is installed in one cell. It provides visual information of battery condition for testing only and should not be used to determine whether the battery is properly charged or discharged, good or bad.

When an unsealed (vent cap) battery is used as a replacement, it should be checked periodically for electrolyte level, state of charge and corrosion. During hot weather, check frequently. If the electrolyte level is below the bottom of the vent well in one or more cells, add distilled water as required. To assure proper mixing of the water and acid, operate the engine immediately after adding water. *Never* add battery acid instead of water—this will shorten the battery's life.

Maintenance-free batteries are completely sealed and never require the addition of water.

Using the Test Indicator

Make sure the battery is level and the test indicator sight glass is clean. If necessary, wipe the sight glass with a damp paper towel. A penlight is often useful in dim light to determine the indicator color. Look down into the sight glass and refer to **Figure 2**. If the dot appears green in color, the battery has a sufficient charge for testing. If it

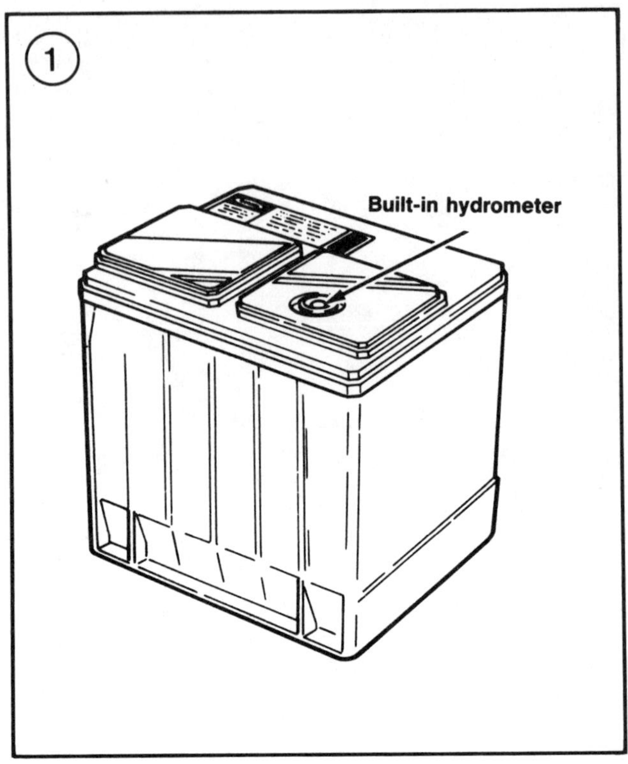

2

Battery top

Darkened indicator (with green dot)

MAY BE JUMP STARTED

Battery top

Light yellow or bright indicator

DO NOT JUMP START

Battery top

Darkened indicator (no green dot)

MAY BE JUMP STARTED

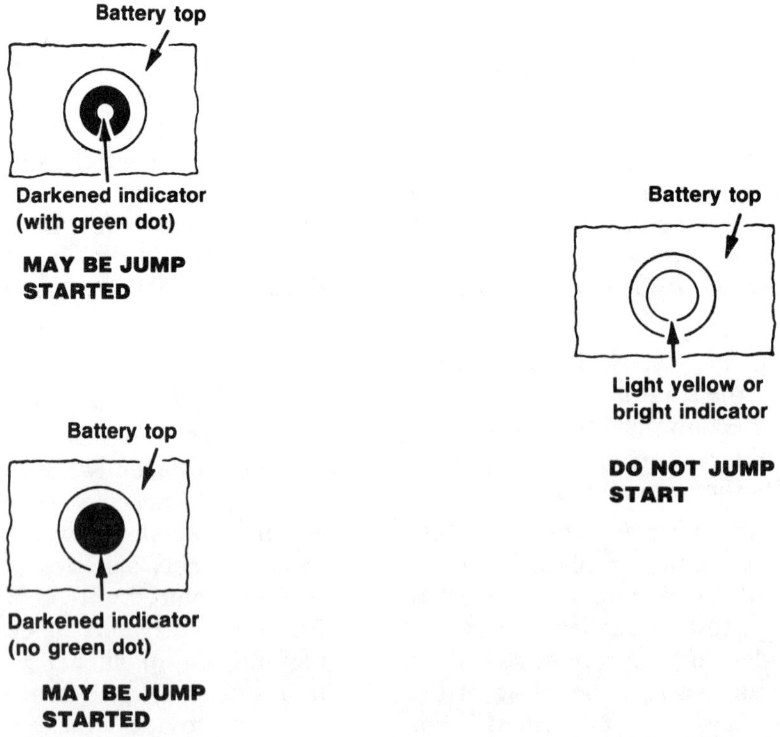

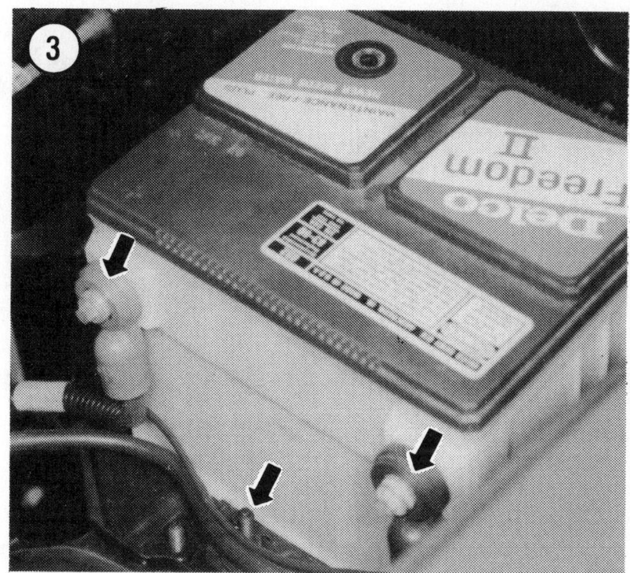

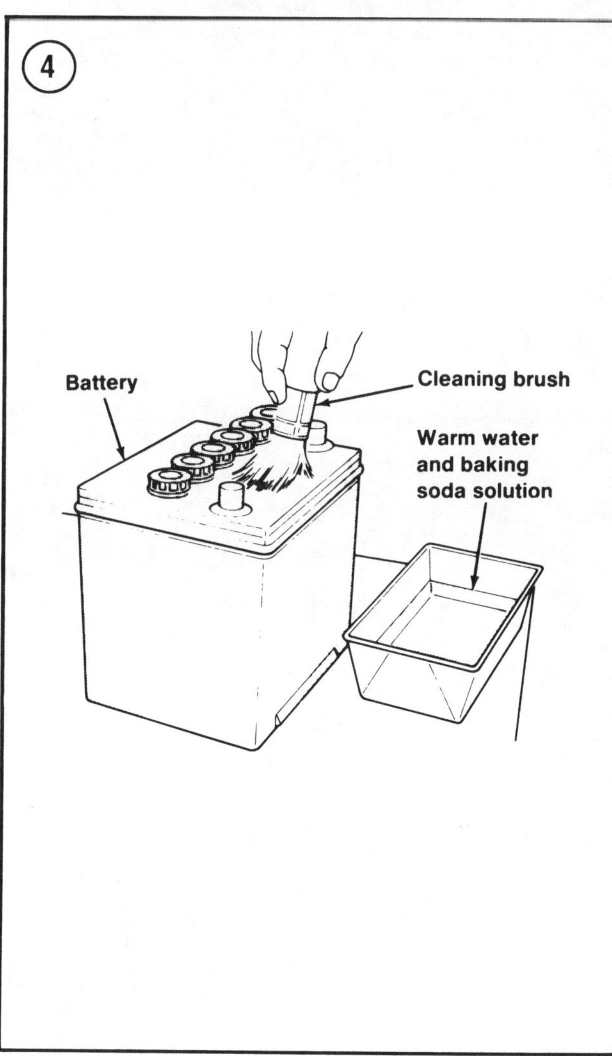

appears dark or black, charge the battery before testing. A clear or light yellow appearance indicates that the battery should be replaced and the charging system checked. Do not charge, test or jump start the battery when the sight glass appears light yellow in color.

Care and Inspection

1. Disconnect both battery cables and remove the batery hold-down clamp (**Figure 3**).
2. Attach a battery carrier or carrier strap and lift the battery from the engine compartment.
3. Check the entire battery case for cracks or other damage.
4. If the battery has removable vent caps, cover the vent holes in each cap with small pieces of masking tape.

CAUTION
Keep cleaning solution out of the battery cells in Step 5 or the electrolyte will be seriously weakened.

5. Scrub the top of the battery with a stiff bristle brush, using a baking soda and water solution (**Figure 4**). Rinse the battery case with clear water and wipe dry with a clean cloth or paper towels. Remove the masking tape from the filler cap vent holes, if so equipped.
6. Inspect the battery tray in the engine compartment for corrosion. Clean if necessary with the baking soda and water solution. Rinse with clear water and wipe dry.
7. Clean the battery cable clamps with a stiff wire brush or one of the many tools made for this purpose (**Figure 5**). The same tool is used for cleaning the threaded battery posts (**Figure 6**).
8. Reposition the battery on the battery tray and remove the carrier or strap. Engage the hold-down block lip in the slot on the battery case and tighten the bolt enough to hold the battery from moving; overtightening can crack the battery case.

CAUTION
Be sure the battery cables are connected to their proper terminals during the next step. Connecting the battery backwards will reverse the polarity and can damage the alternator.

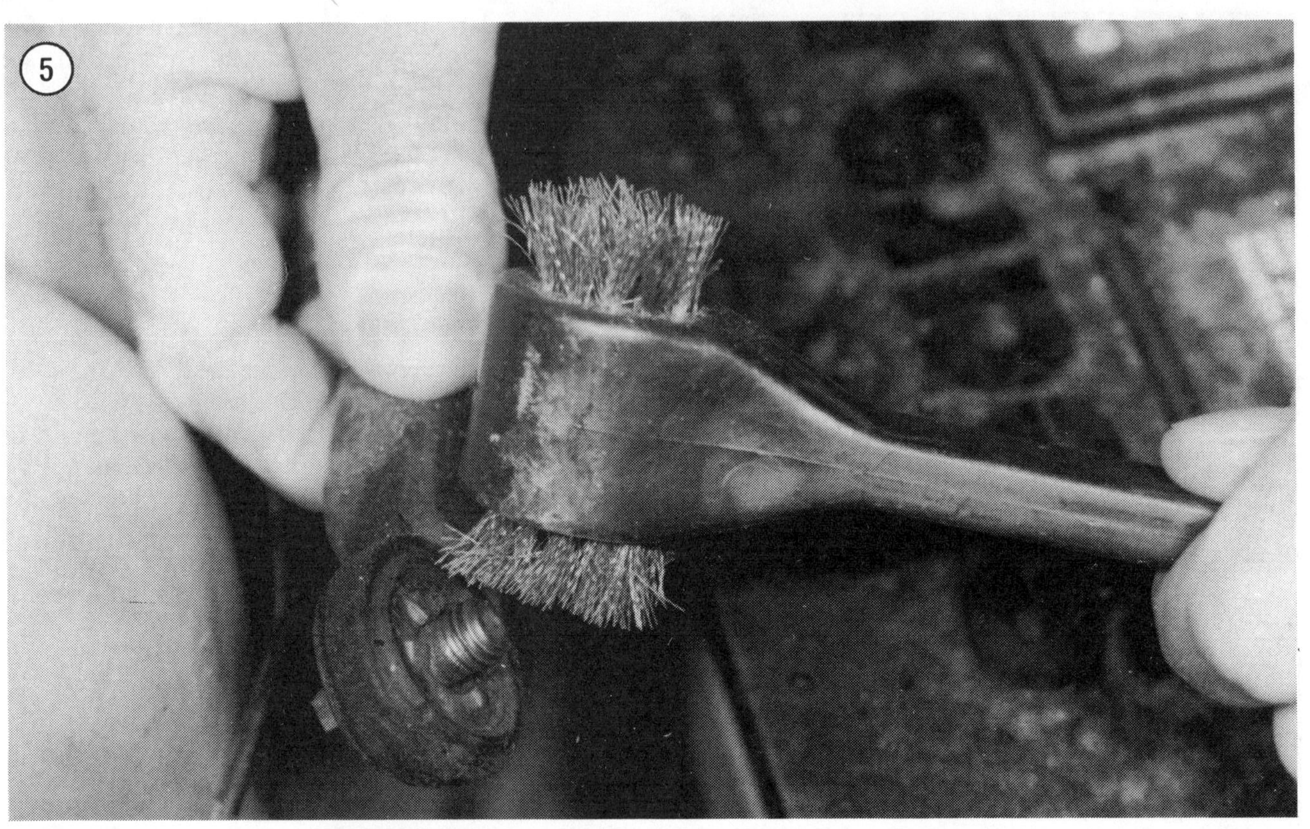
5

6

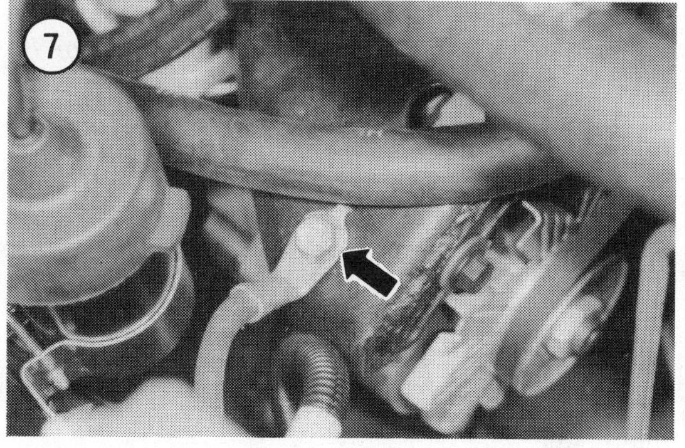

9. Reinstall the postive battery cable, then the negative battery cable. Some models use a ground connection at the alternator bracket (**Figure 7**). If so equipped, be sure the connection is clean and tight.

10. Tighten the battery cable connections (do not tighten excessively) and coat with a petroleum jelly such as Vaseline or a light mineral grease.

11. If the battery has removable filler caps, check the electrolyte level. The electrolyte should cover the battery plates by at least 1/4 in. (6 mm). See **Figure 8**. Top up with distilled water to the bottom of the fill ring in each cell, if necessary.

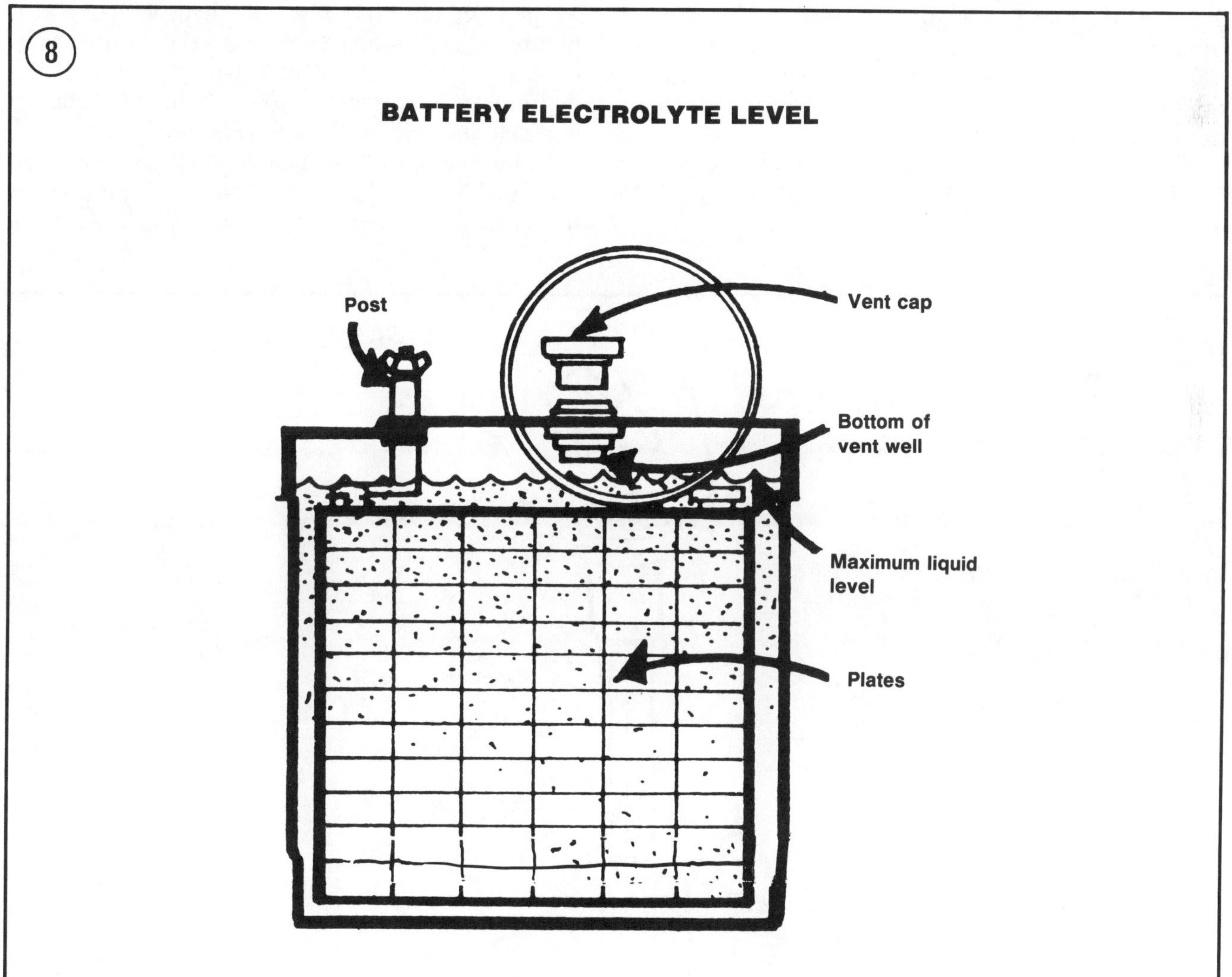

Open Circuit Voltage Test (Maintenance-free Batteries)

This procedure applies to sealed batteries without removable filler caps. The use of a digital voltmeter capable of reading to 1/100 volt is recommended to read open circuit voltage accurately. The relationship between open circuit voltage (OCV) and battery specific gravity is a direct one. To determine the state of charge or specific gravity of a maintenance-free battery, perform the test below and refer to **Table 1**.

1. The battery surface charge must be removed if the vehicle has just been driven. Turn the headlights on for 20 seconds.
2. Turn the headlights off and wait at least 5 minutes.
3. Connnect a digital voltmeter between the negative and positive battery terminals to determine open circuit voltage.
4. Compare the reading to **Table 1**. If the battery is at or near full charge, the voltmeter should read 12.5 volts or more.
5. If the battery open circuit voltage is below 9.6 volts at an approximate outside temperature of 70° F (21° C), charge the battery for 20 minutes at 35 amps and repeat the test. If the battery again fails the test, replace it.

Unsealed Battery Testing

This procedure applies to batteries with removable filler caps.

Hydrometer testing is the best way to check battery condition. Use a hydrometer with numbered gradations from 1.100-1.300 rather than one with just color-coded bands. To use the hydrometer, squeeze the rubber ball, insert the tip in a cell and release the ball (**Figure 9**).

Draw enough electrolyte to float the weighted float inside the hydrometer. Note the number in line with the surface of the electrolyte. This is the

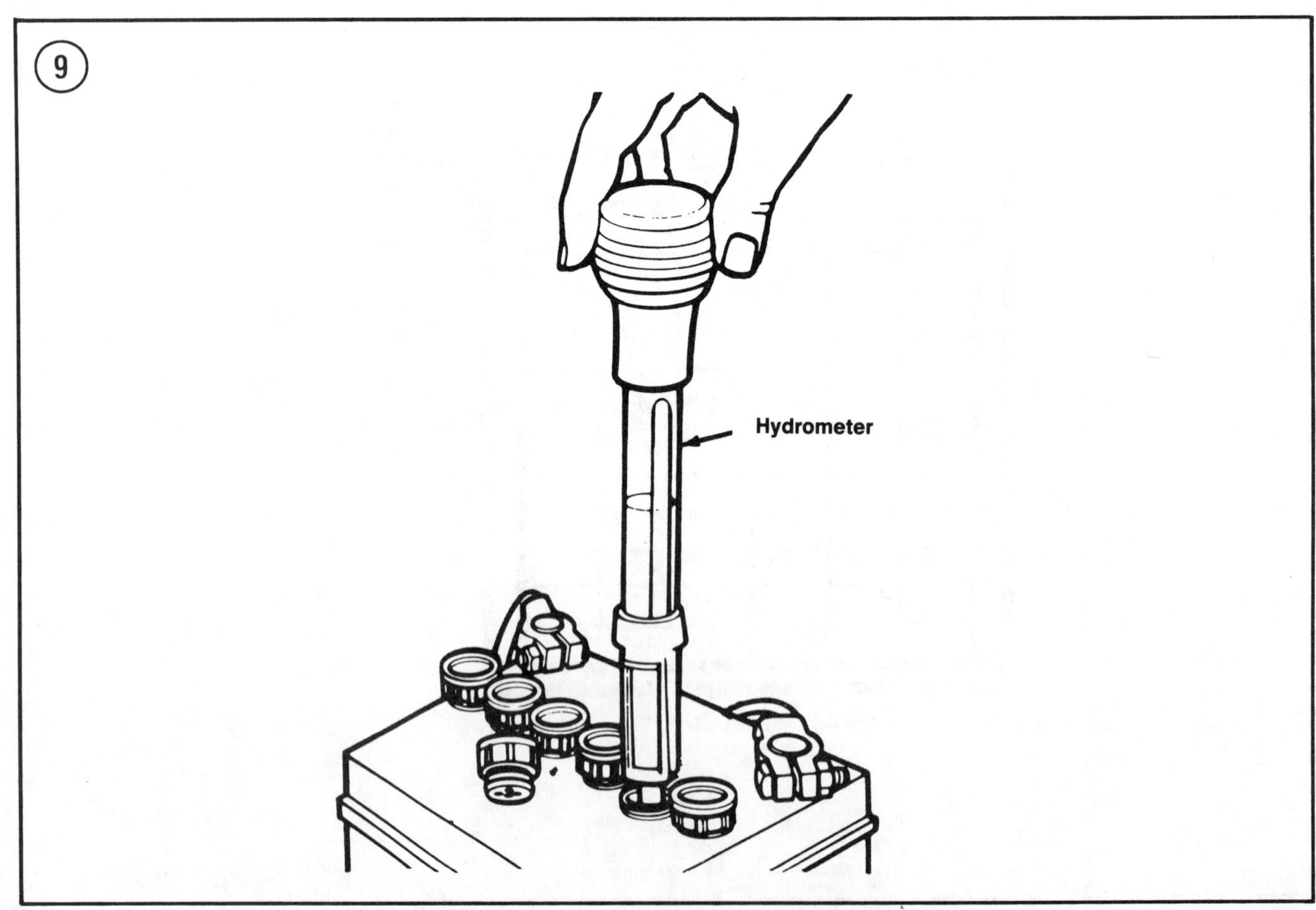

specific gravity for the cell. Return the electrolyte to the cell from which it came.

The specific gravity of the electrolyte in each battery cell is an excellent indicator of that cell's condition. A fully charged cell will read 1.260 or more at 68° F (20° C). If the cells test below 1.200, the battery must be recharged. Charging is also necessary if the specific gravity varies more than 0.050 from cell to cell.

NOTE
If a temperature-compensated hydrometer is not used, add 0.004 to the specific gravity reading for every 10° above 80° F (25° C). For every 10° below 80° F (25° C), subtract 0.004.

Safety Precautions

When working with batteries, use extreme care to avoid spilling or splashing the electrolyte. This solution contains sulfuric acid, which can ruin clothing and cause serious chemical burns. If any electrolyte is spilled or splashed on clothing or skin, immediately neutralize with a solution of baking soda and water, then flush with an abundance of clean water.

WARNING
Electrolyte splashed into the eyes is extremely dangerous. Safety glasses should always be worn while working with batteries. If electrolyte is splashed into the eyes, call a physician immediately, force the eyes open and flood with cool, clean water for approximately 5 minutes.

If electrolyte is spilled or splashed onto any surface, it should be immediately neutralized with a baking soda and water solution and then rinse with clean water.

While batteries are being charged, highly explosive hydrogen gas forms in each cell. Some of this gas escapes through filler cap openings (unsealed battery) or vent openings (sealed battery) and may form an explosive atmosphere in and around the battery. This condition can persist for several hours. Sparks, an open flame or a lighted cigarette can ignite this gas, causing an internal battery explosion and possible serious personal injury.

Take the following precautions to prevent an explosion:

1. Do not smoke or permit any open flame near any battery being charged or which has been recently charged.
2. Do not disconnect live circuits at battery terminals, since a spark usually occurs when a live circuit is broken. Take care when connecting or disconnecting any battery charger. Be sure its power switch is off before making or breaking connections. Poor connections are a common cause of electrical arcs which cause explosions.

Charging

A good state of charge should be maintained in batteries used for starting. Check the battery with a voltmeter as shown in **Figure 10**. Any battery that cannot deliver at least 9.6 volts under a starting

8

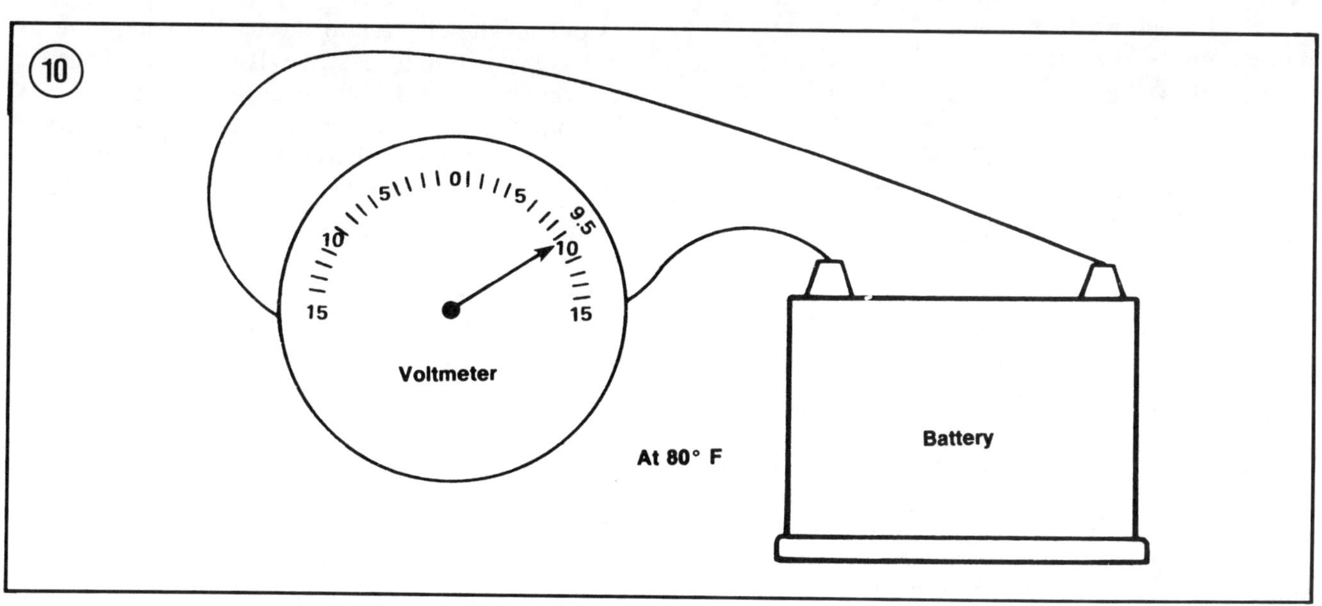

load should be recharged. If recharging does not bring it up to strength or if it does not hold the charge, replace the battery.

A cold battery will not accept a charge readily. If the temperature is below 40° F (5° C), the battery should be allowed to warm up to room temperature before charging.

The battery does not have to be removed from the vehicle for charging. Just make certain that the area is well-ventilated, the battery cables are disconnected and there there is no chance of sparks or flames occurring near the battery.

WARNING
Charging batteries give off highly explosive hydrogen gas. If this explodes, it may spray battery acid over a wide area.

Disconnect the negative battery cable first, then the positive cable. Install a pair of screw-in battery charging posts (**Figure 11**) or a charging strap adapter (**Figure 12**) to provide an adequate conductive surface for the charger leads.

On unsealed batteries, make sure the electrolyte is fully topped up. Remove the vent caps and place a folded paper towel over the vent openings to absorb any electrolyte that may spew as the battery charges.

Connect the charger to the battery—negative to negative, positive to positive. If the charger output is variable, select a high setting (30-40 amps), set the voltage selector to 12 volts and plug the charger in. Let the battery charge for 30 minutes, then reduce the charge rate to 5-10 amps.

Once the battery starts to accept a charge, the charge rate should be reduced to a level that will prevent excessive gassing and electrolyte spewing. This is especially important with sealed batteries, as excessive gassing will reduce the amount of electrolyte (which cannot be replaced) in the battery cells.

The length of time required to recharge a battery depends upon its size, state of charge and temperature. Generally speaking, the current input time should equal the battery amp-hour rating. For example, a 45 AH battery will require a 9-amp

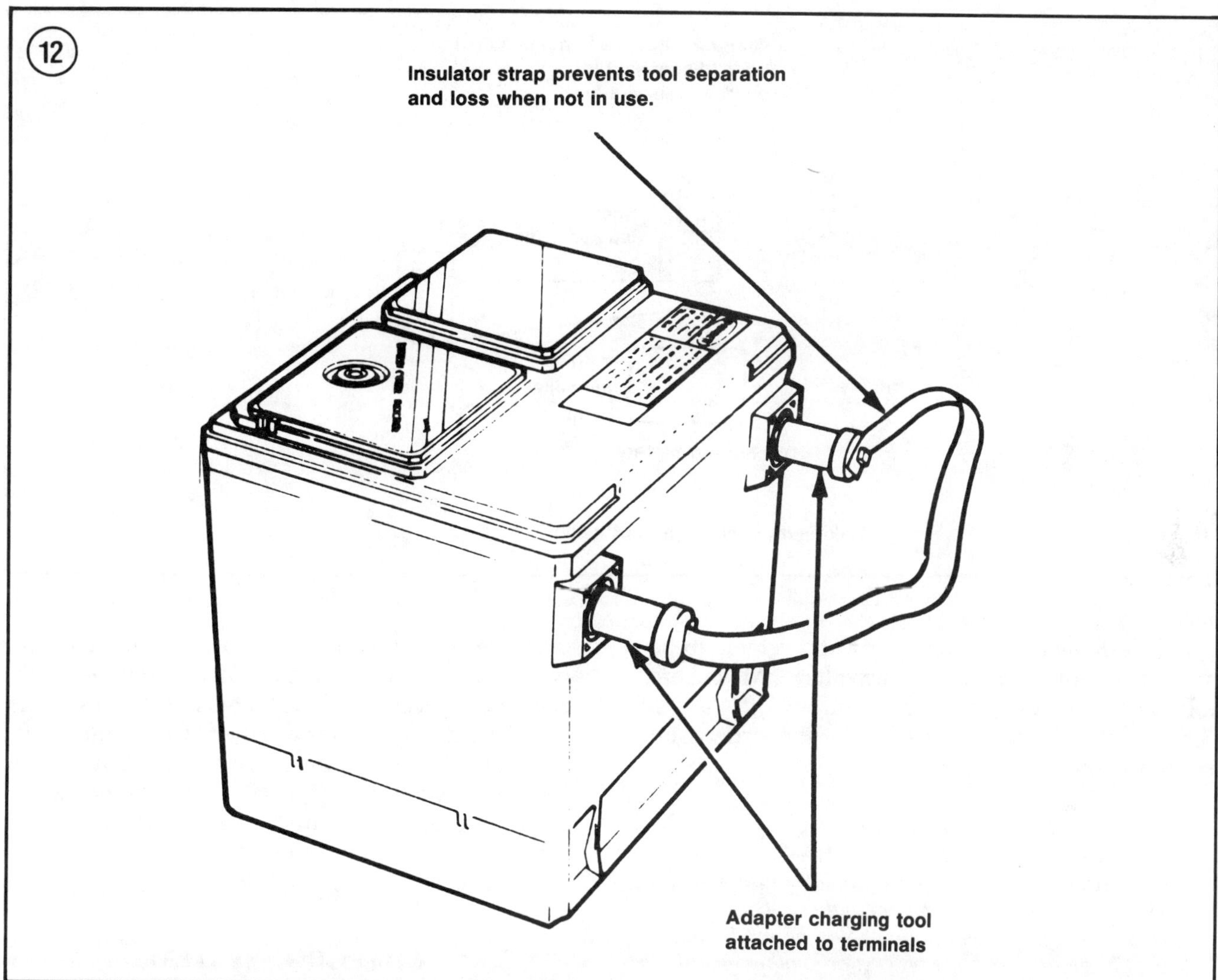

charging rate for 5 hours (9×5=45) or a 15-amp charging rate for 3 hours (15×3=45). On unsealed batteries, check charging progress with the hydrometer. **Table 2** gives approximate state of charge according to specific gravity.

Jump Starting

If the battery becomes severely discharged on the road, it is possible to start and run a vehicle by jump starting it from another battery. If the proper procedure is not followed, however, jump starting can be dangerous.

Before jump starting an unsealed battery when temperatures are 32° F (0° C) or lower, check the condition of the electrolyte. If it is not visible or if it appears to be frozen, do *not* attempt to jump start the battery, as the battery may explode or rupture. Do *not* jump start sealed batteries when the temperature is 32° F (0° C) or lower.

WARNING
Use extreme caution when connecting a booster battery to one that is discharged to avoid personal injury or damage to the vehicle.

1. Position the 2 vehicles so that the jumper cables will reach between batteries, but the vehicles do not touch. Set the parking brake on each vehicle.

CAUTION
Do not disconnect the battery of the vehicle to be started. This could damage the electronic ignition module or vehicle electrical system.

8

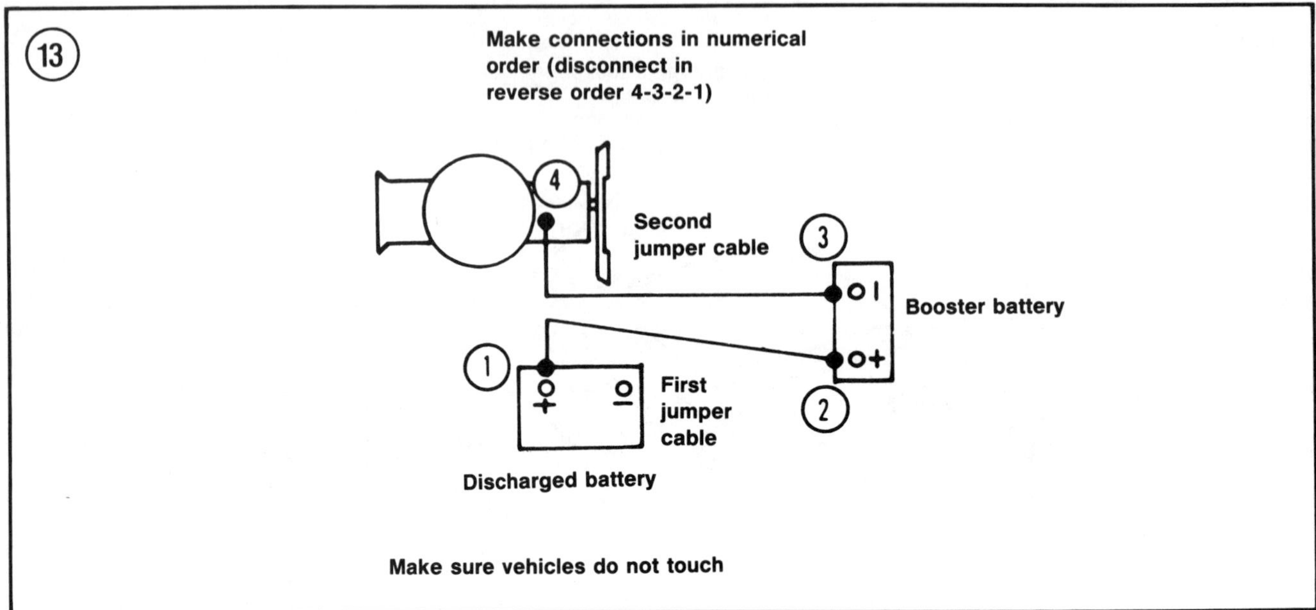

2. Turn the heater blower ON in the vehicle to be started to remove any transient voltage. Make sure all other switches and lights are turned off.
3. Connect the jumper cables in the order and sequence shown in **Figure 13**.

WARNING
An electrical arc may occur when the final connection is made. This could cause an explosion if it occurs near the battery. For this reason, the final connection should be made to the alternator mounting bracket or another good engine ground and not the battery itself.

4. Check that all jumper cables are out of the way of moving parts on both engines.
5. Start the vehicle with the good battery and run the engine at a moderate speed.
6. Start the vehicle with the discharged battery. Once the engine starts, run it at a moderate speed.

CAUTION
Racing the engine may cause damage to the electrical system.

7. Remove the jumper cables in the exact reverse order shown in **Figure 13**. Begin at point No. 4, then 3, 2 and 1.

Replacement Batteries

When replacing a battery, be sure to install one with sufficient power to handle the engine's cranking requirements. As a general rule, the battery's cold cranking capacity should equal the engine displacement in cubic inches. For example, the 173 cid V6 requires a battery with a minimum of 180 cold cranking amps. In winter climates, the battery's cold cranking specification should exceed the engine displacement by 50 percent, as battery efficiency can be reduced during cold weather.

CHARGING SYSTEM

The basic charging system consists of the battery, alternator, voltage regulator, ignition switch, charge indicator light or ammeter gauge, fusible link and connecting wiring. The various Delcotron alternators used on the vehicles covered in this manual differ primarily in output rating. The output rating is stamped on the Delcotron frame.

All alternator models use an integral solid-state voltage regulator. The regulator is serviced only by replacement.

Alternator

The alternator is a 3-phase current generator consisting of a stationary armature (stator), a rotating field (rotor) and a rectifying bridge of silicon diodes. See **Figure 14**. The alternator generates alternating current which is converted to direct current by the silicon diodes for use in the

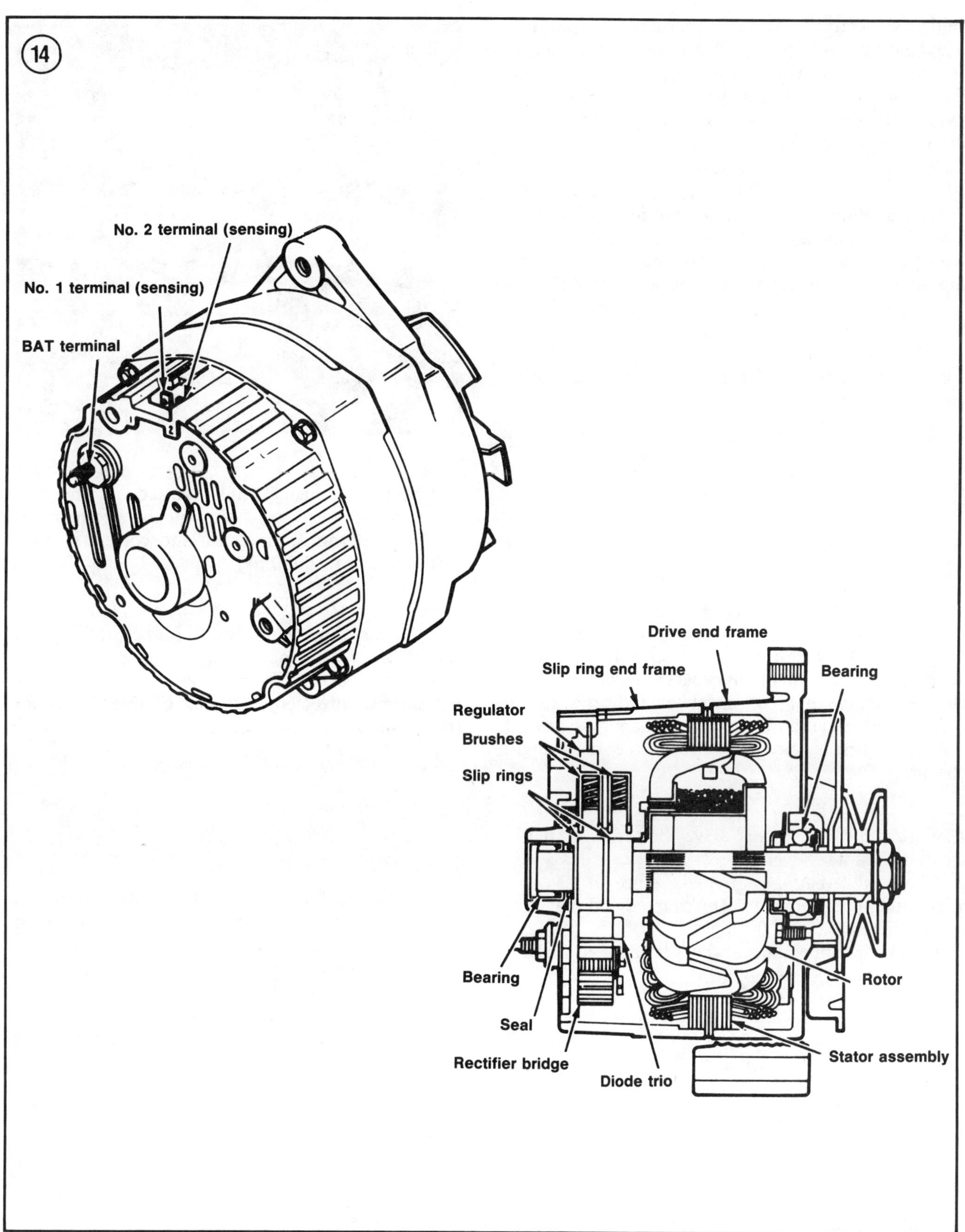
14
No. 2 terminal (sensing)
No. 1 terminal (sensing)
BAT terminal
Drive end frame
Slip ring end frame
Bearing
Regulator
Brushes
Slip rings
Bearing
Rotor
Seal
Stator assembly
Rectifier bridge
Diode trio

8

vehicle's electrical system. Alternator output is regulated by a voltage regulator to keep the battery charged. The alternator is mounted on the front of the engine and is belt-driven by the crankshaft pulley. **Figure 15** shows a typical alternator installation on the V6 engine; others are similar.

Make sure the connections are not reversed when working on the alternator. Current flow in the wrong direction will damage the diodes and render the alternator unserviceable. The alternator BAT or B terminal (**Figure 14**) must be connected to battery voltage. When charging the battery in the vehicle, disconnect the battery leads before connecting the charger. This is a precaution against incorrect current bias and heat reaching the alternator.

Testing

The first indication of charging system trouble is usually a slow engine cranking speed during starting or headlights that dim as engine speed decreases. This will often occur long before the charge warning light or ammeter indicates that there is a potential problem. When charging system trouble is first suspected, perform the following checks.

1. Check the alternator drive belt for correct tension (Chapter Seven).
2. Check the battery to make sure it is in satisfactory condition and fully charged and that all connections are clean and tight.
3. Check all connections at the alternator to make sure they are clean and tight.

NOTE
If locating the fusible link in Step 4 proved difficult in some engine compartments, connect a voltmeter between a good engine ground and the alternator BAT terminal. If the meter shows no voltage reading, the fusible link is probably burned out and should be replaced.

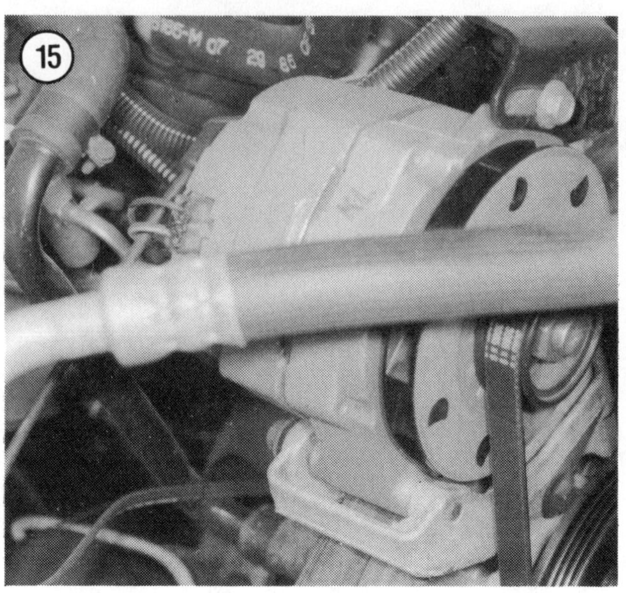

4. Check the fusible link located in the line between the starter solenoid and the alternator. If burned, determine the cause and correct it, then install a new fusible link.

If the charging system still is not performing as it should after each of the above points has been carefully checked and any unsatisfactory conditions corrected, refer to Chapter Two for troubleshooting procedures.

Removal/Installation

This procedure is generalized to cover all applications. On some models, the alternator is mounted low on the engine under other accessory units and can only be reached from underneath the vehicle. Access to the alternator is quite limited in some engine compartments and care should be taken to avoid personal injury during this procedure.

1. Disconnect the negative battery cable.
2. Unplug the connectors from the rear of the alternator.
3. Loosen the alternator adjusting and pivot bolts. See **Figure 16**.

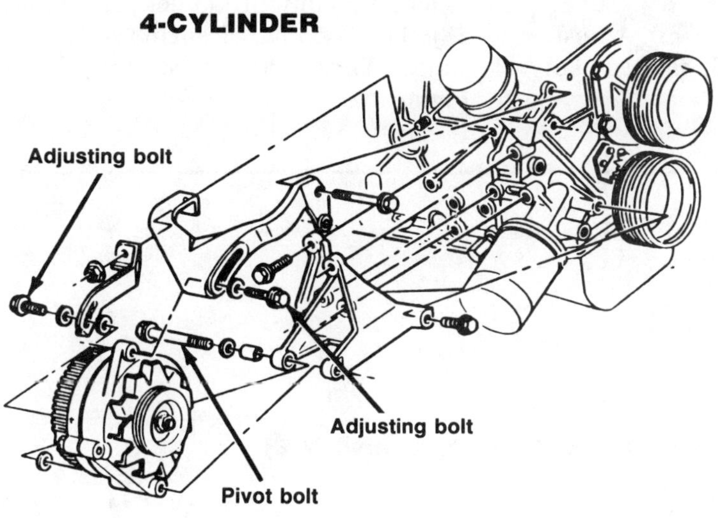
4-CYLINDER
Adjusting bolt
Adjusting bolt
Pivot bolt

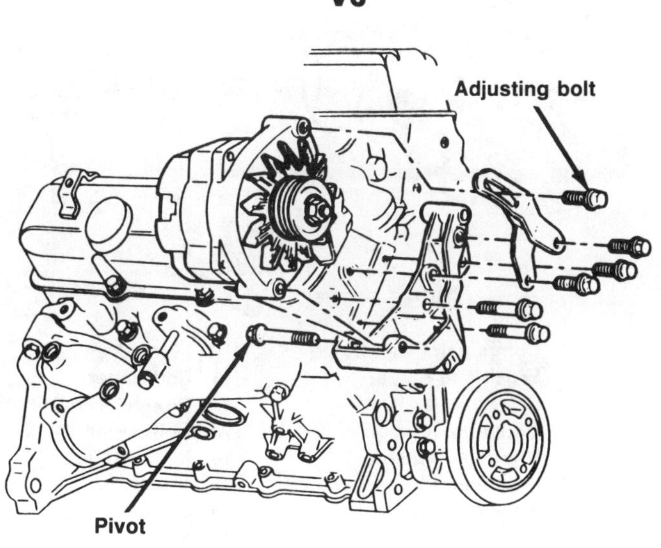
V6
Adjusting bolt
Pivot

4. Move the alternator toward the engine and remove the drive belt from the alternator pulley.
5. Support the alternator with one hand and remove the adjustment and pivot bolts. Remove the alternator.
6. Installation is the reverse of removal. Make sure the alternator connectors are properly installed before reconnecting the negative battery cable. Tighten the pivot bolt to 25 ft.-lb. (34 N•m). Adjust the belt tension (Chapter Seven) and tighten the adjusting bolt to 20 ft.-lb. (27 N•m).

STARTER

The Delco 5MT starter (**Figure 17**) is used with 2.0L, 2.5L and V6 engines. The starter solenoid is enclosed in the drive housing to protect it from exposure to dirt and adverse weather conditions. The starter used with the 1.9L engine is similar, differing mainly in the field coil mounting (**Figure 18**). The 2.2L diesel engine uses a gear reduction starter (**Figure 19**). The starting circuit is shown in **Figure 20**.

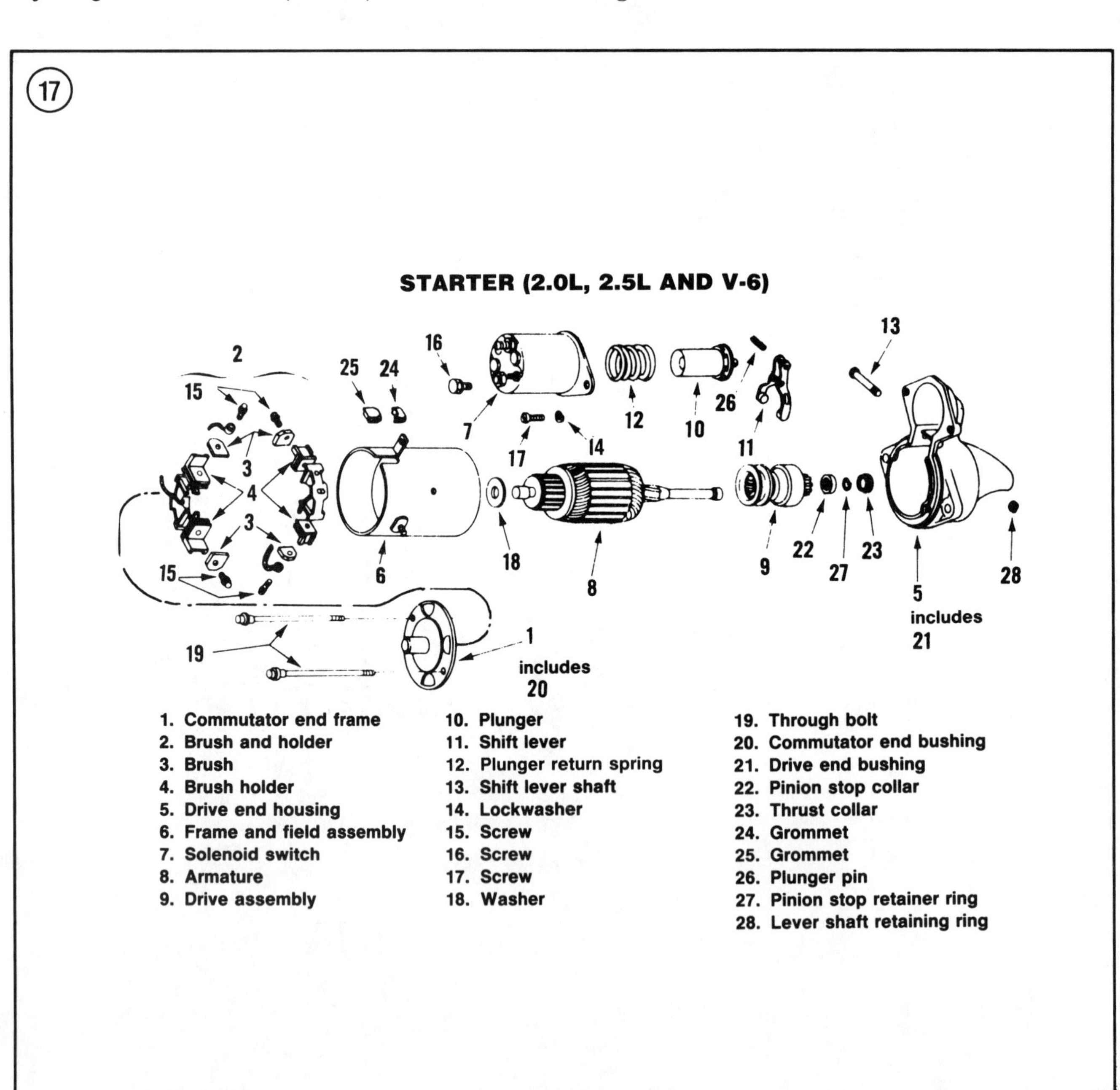

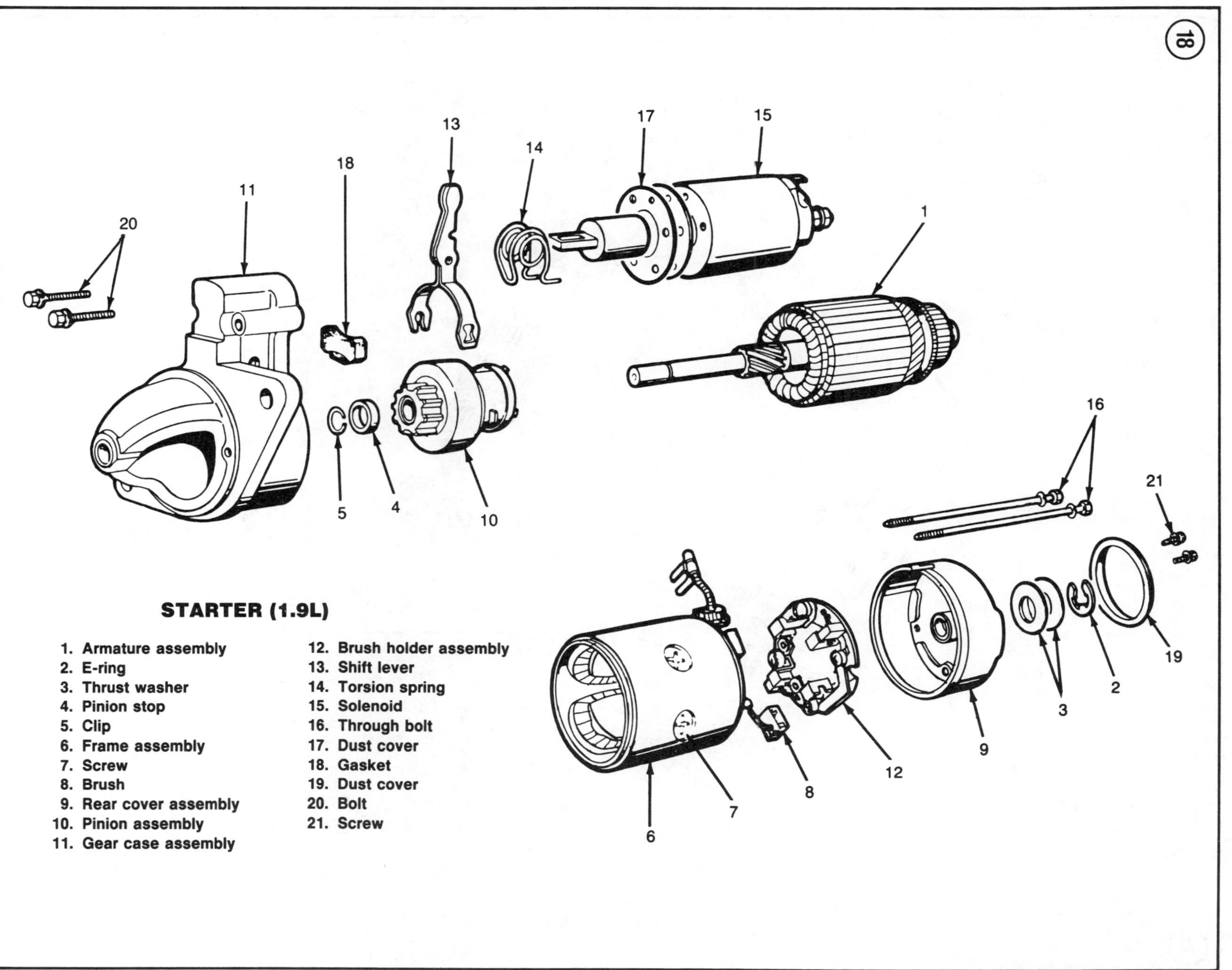
18
20
11
18
13
14
17
15
1
5
4
10
16
21
19
2
3
9
12
8
7
6
STARTER (1.9L)
1. Armature assembly
2. E-ring
3. Thrust washer
4. Pinion stop
5. Clip
6. Frame assembly
7. Screw
8. Brush
9. Rear cover assembly
10. Pinion assembly
11. Gear case assembly
12. Brush holder assembly
13. Shift lever
14. Torsion spring
15. Solenoid
16. Through bolt
17. Dust cover
18. Gasket
19. Dust cover
20. Bolt
21. Screw

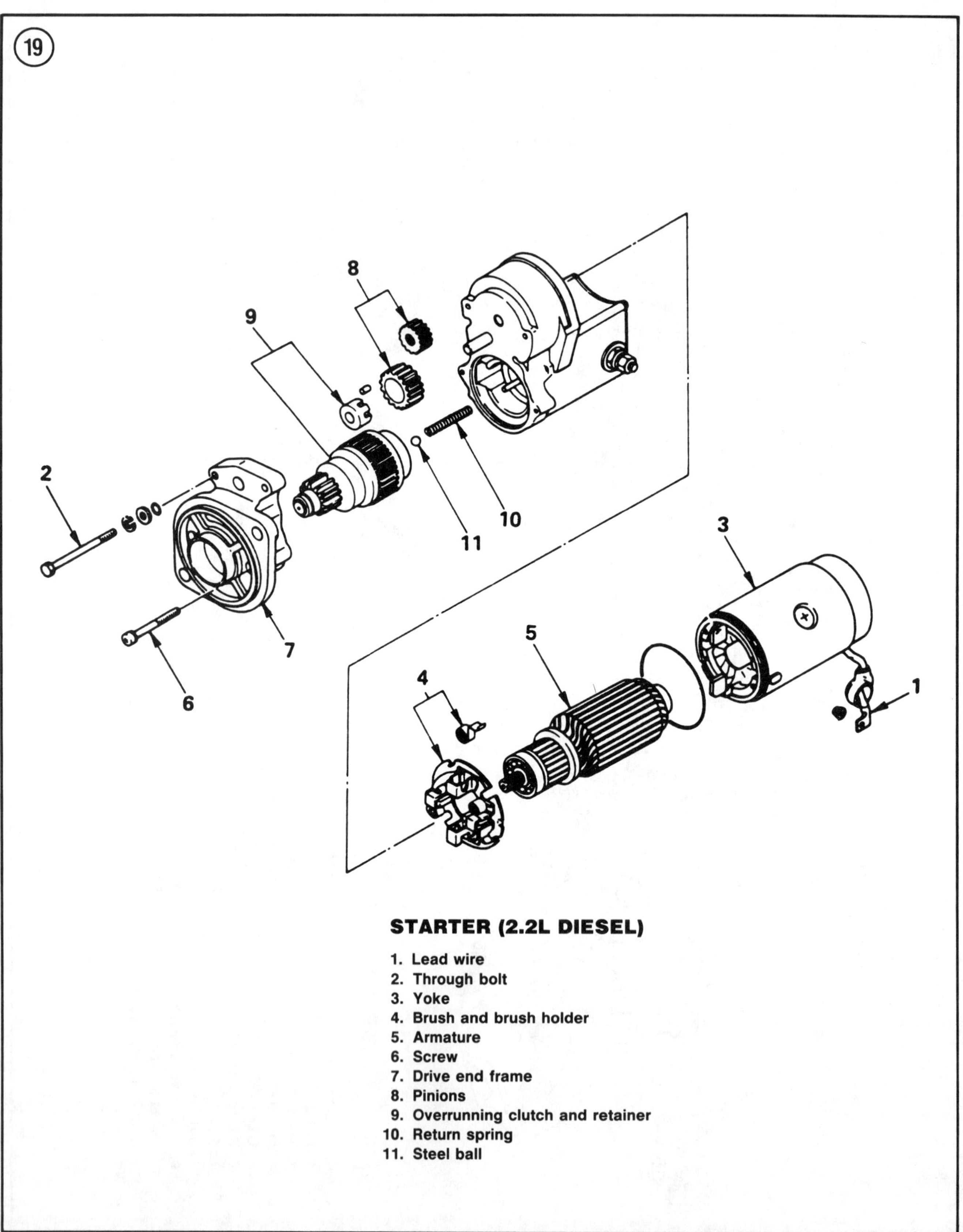

STARTER (2.2L DIESEL)

1. Lead wire
2. Through bolt
3. Yoke
4. Brush and brush holder
5. Armature
6. Screw
7. Drive end frame
8. Pinions
9. Overrunning clutch and retainer
10. Return spring
11. Steel ball

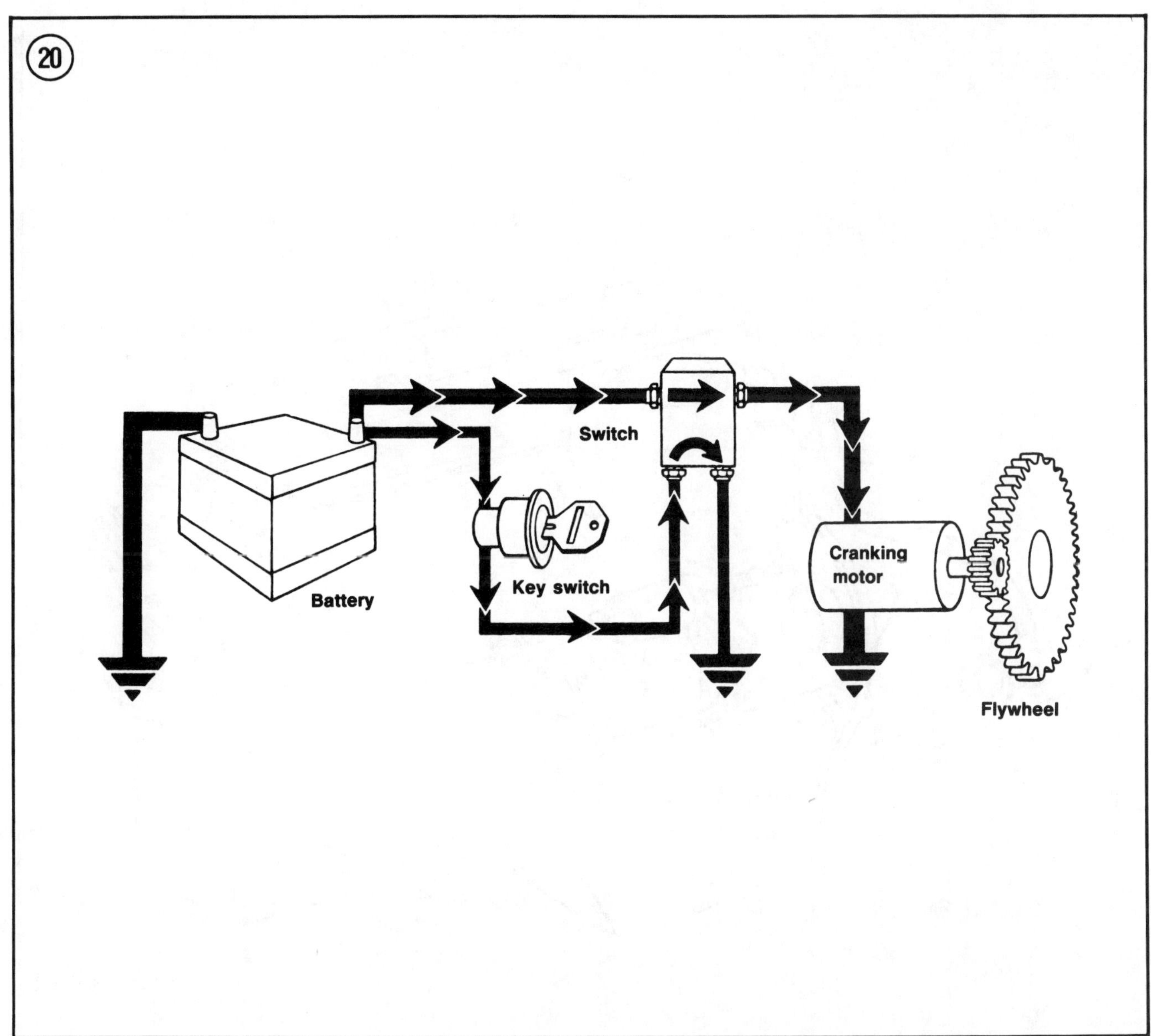

Starter service requires experience and special tools. Diagnostic procedures for troubleshooting the starter motor are given in Chapter Two. The service procedures described below consist of removal, installation and brush replacement. Any repairs inside the unit itself (other than brush replacement) should be done by a dealer or automotive electrical shop. Installation of a professionally rebuilt unit is generally more practical.

Starter Solenoid Replacement

1. Disconnect the negative battery cable.

2. Remove the plastic protective cover from the solenoid electrical connectors, if installed.

3. Disconnect the field strap at the starter from the motor terminal.

4. Remove the solenoid-to-drive housing screws and the motor terminal bolt.

5. Rotate the solenoid 90° and remove from the drive housing with the plunger return or torsion spring.

6. Installation is the reverse of removal.

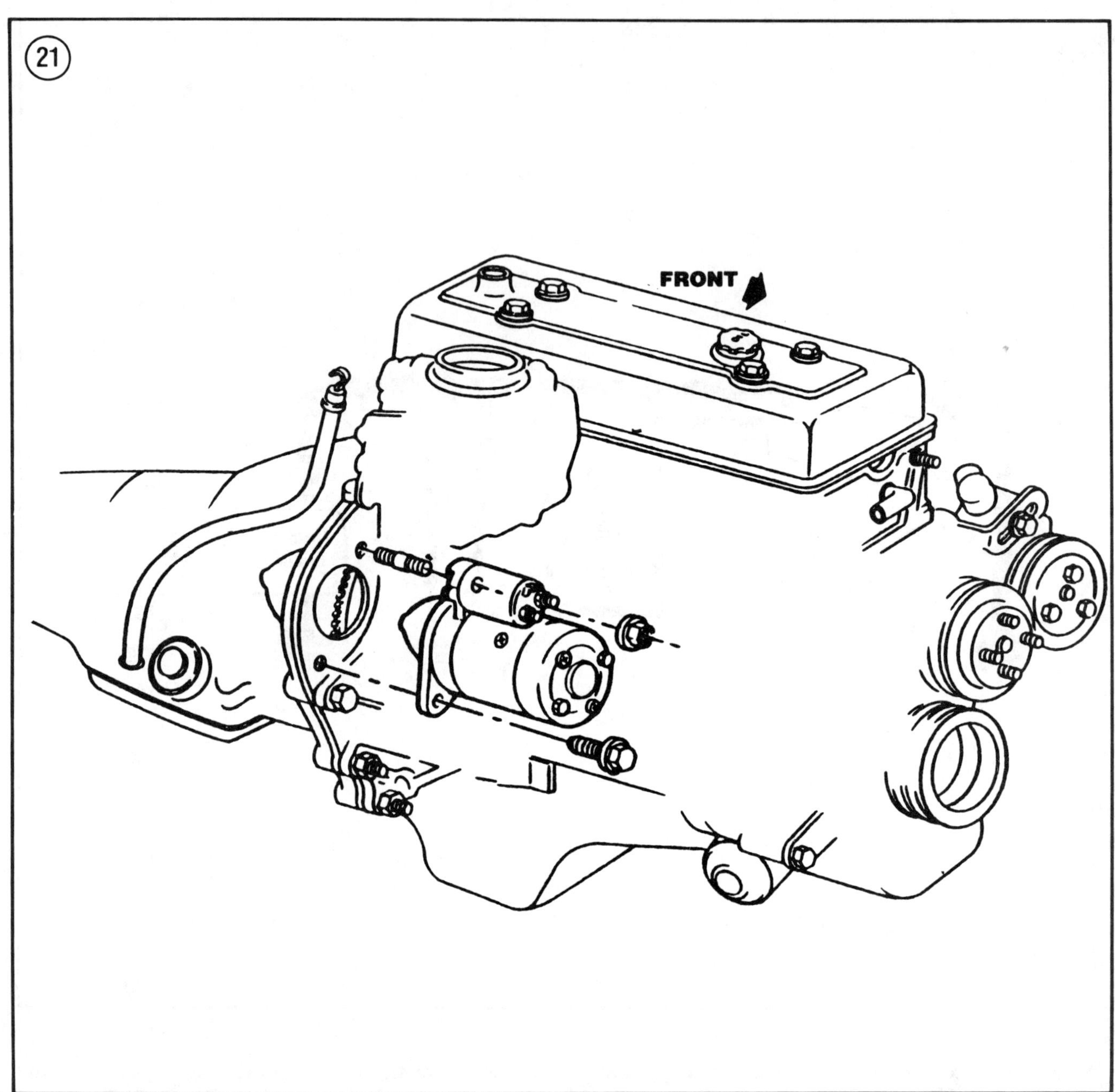

Starter Removal/Installation (1.9L Gasoline and 2.2L Diesel Engine)

Refer to **Figure 21** (1.9L gasoline) or **Figure 22** (2.2L diesel) for this procedure.

1. Disconnect the negative battery cable.
2. Set the parking brake and place the transmission in PARK or 1st gear.
3. Raise the front of the vehicle with a jack and place it on jackstands.
4. 1.9L engine—Unbolt the EGR pipe from the EGR valve and exhaust manifold. Remove the EGR pipe.
5. Disconnect the solenoid wiring.
6. Remove the fasteners holding the starter to the bell housing.
7. Remove the starter motor through the clearance under the intake manifold.
8. Installation is the reverse of removal. Tighten the fasteners to 30 ft.-lb. (41 N•m).

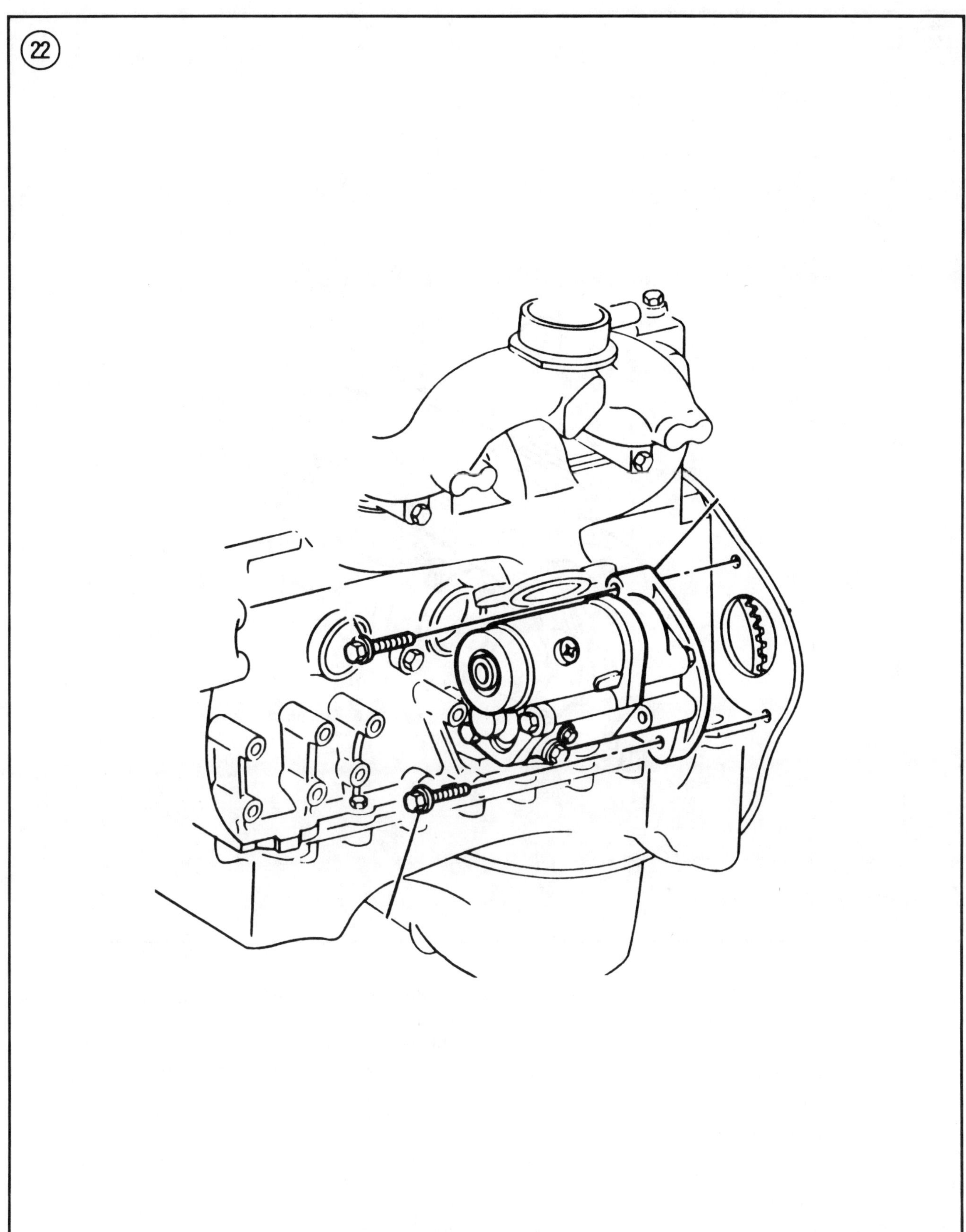
22

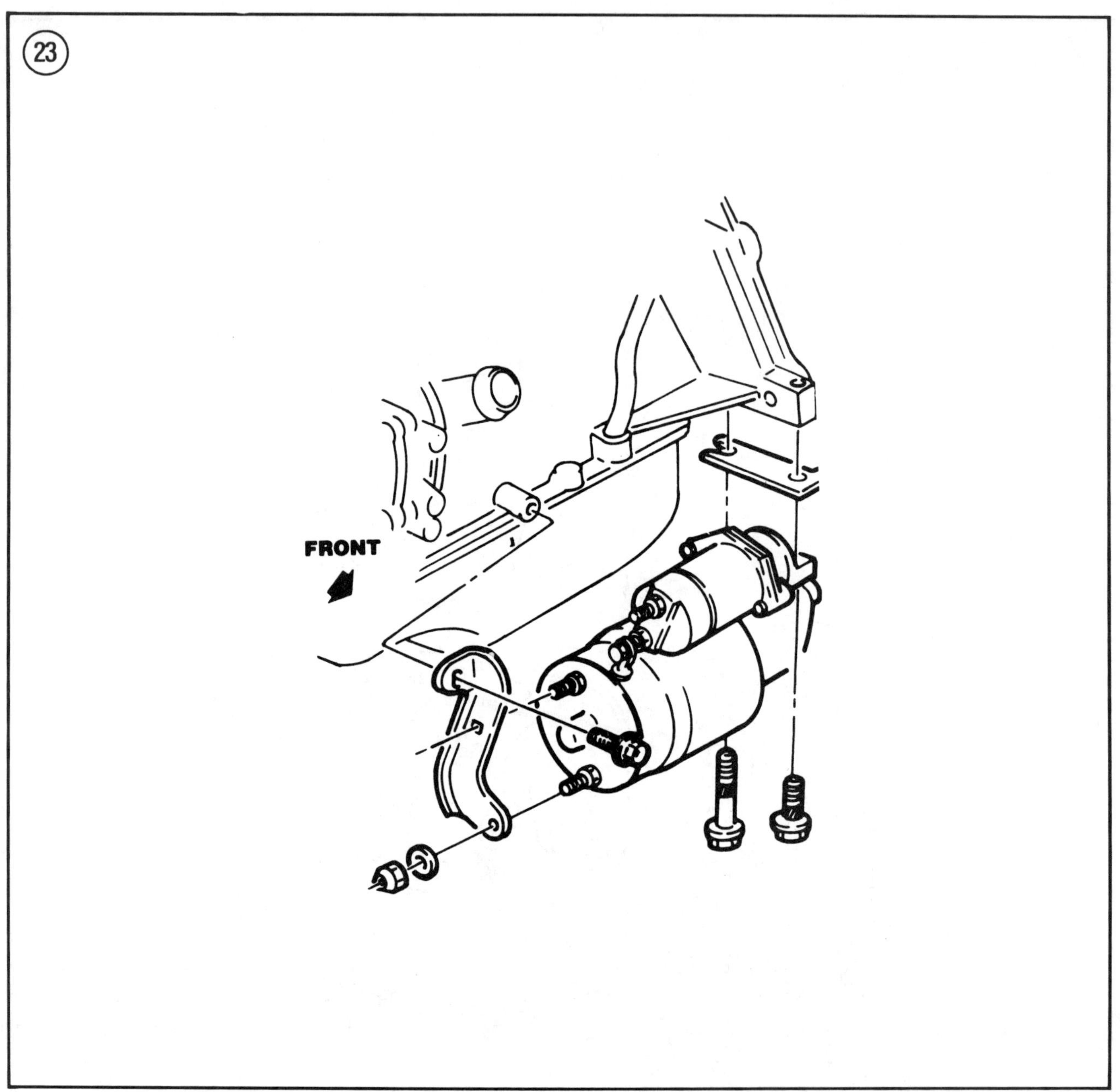

Starter Removal/Installation (2.0L, 2.5L and V6 Engine)

Refer to **Figure 23** (2.0L), **Figure 24** (2.5L) or **Figure 25** (V6) for this procedure.

1. Disconnect the negative battery cable.
2. Set the parking brake and place the transmission in PARK or 1st gear.
3. Raise the front of the vehicle with a jack and place it on jackstands.
4. Remove the plastic protective cover from the solenoid electrical connectors. Disconnect the starter cable and solenoid wires.
5. Remove the starter rear support bracket, if so equipped.
6. Remove the starter mounting bolts. Remove the starter.
7. Installation is the reverse of removal. Reinstall any shims that were removed to assure proper pinion-to-flywheel mesh. Tighten the mounting bolts to 26-37 ft.-lb. (36-50 N•m).

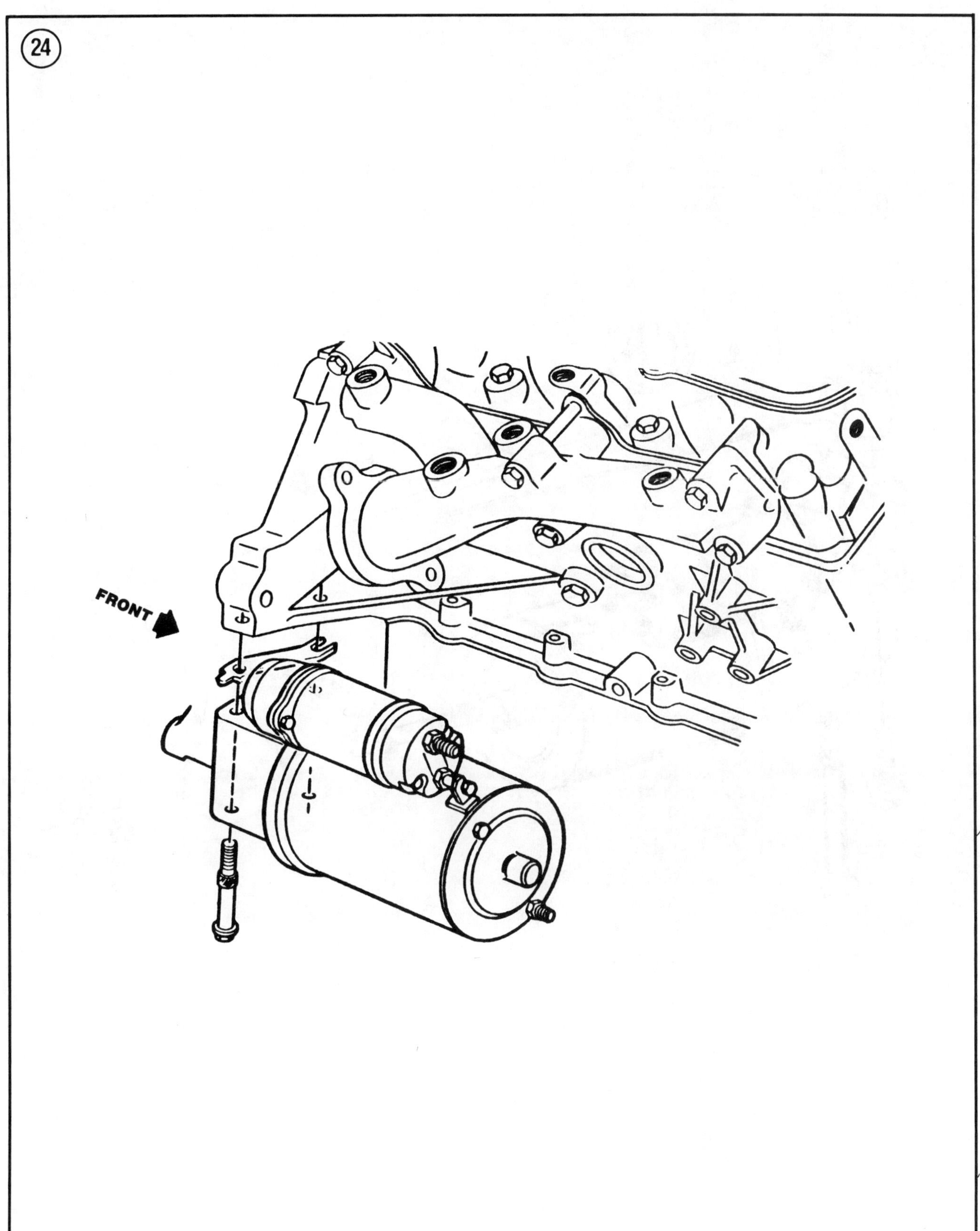

8

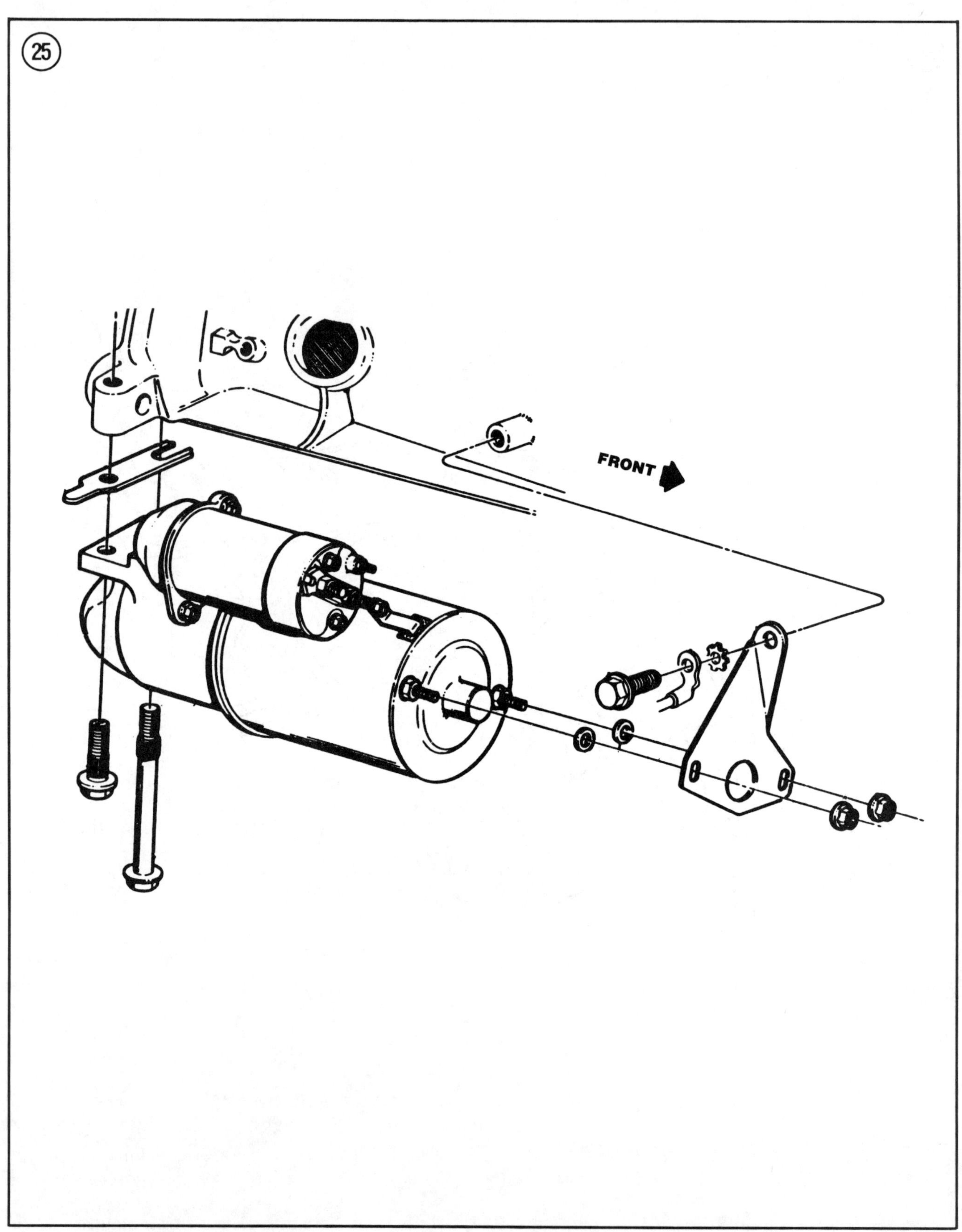
25
FRONT

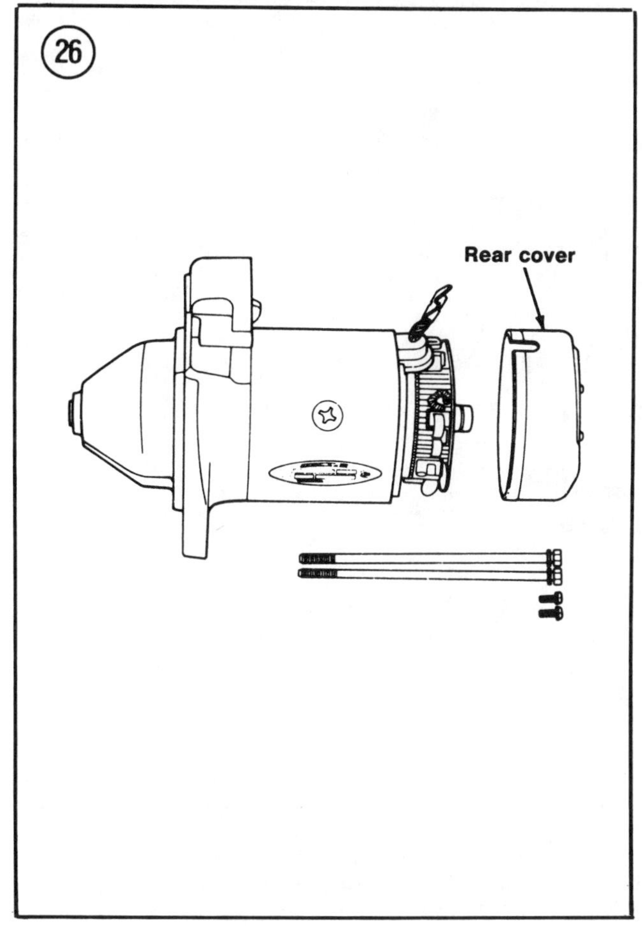

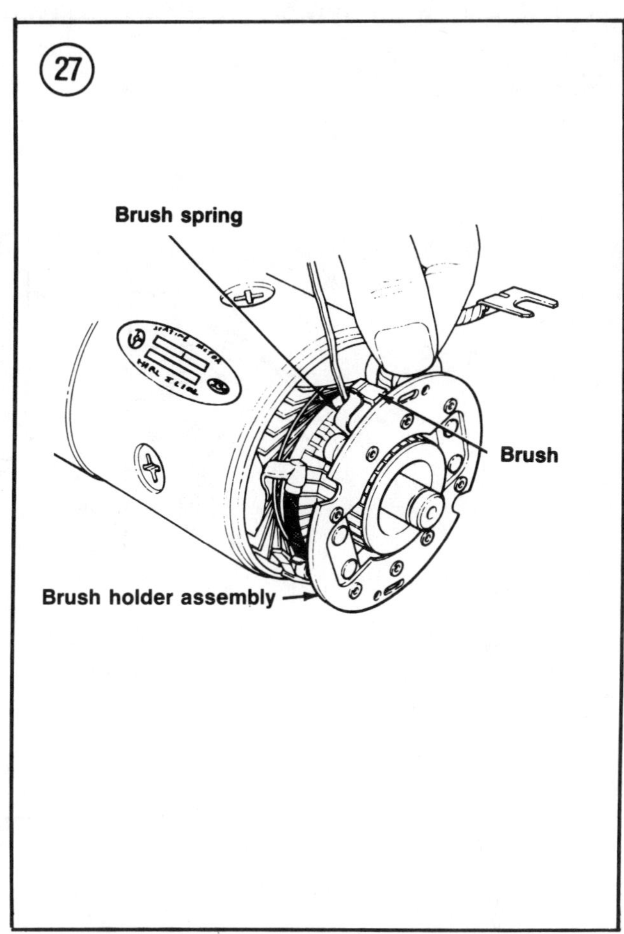

8

Starter Brush Replacement (1.9L Starter)

Refer to **Figure 18** for this procedure.

1. Remove the dust cover, circlip and thrust washer(s).
2. Remove the 2 short screws. Remove the 2 through-bolts.
3. Remove the rear cover assembly **(Figure 26)**.
4. Lift and hold each brush spring with a wire hook. Remove the brush from under the spring **(Figure 27)**.
5. Remove the brush holder assembly.
6. Check the brushes for length and condition. Replace all if any are worn to 0.47 in. (12 mm) or less.
7. Reverse Steps 1-5 to assemble the starter motor.

Starter Brush Replacement (2.0L, 2.5L and V6 Starter)

Brush replacement requires partial diassembly of the starter. Refer to **Figure 17** for this procedure.

1. Remove the 2 through-bolts, commutator end frame and insulator washer.
2. Separate the field frame from the drive housing. Remove the armature and washer.
3. Remove the brush holder from the brush support.
4. Remove the brush holder screw. Separate the brush and holder.
5. Inspect the plastic brush holder for cracks or broken mounting pads.
6. Check the brushes for length and condition. Replace all if any are worn to 1/4 in. or less in length.
7. Reverse Steps 1-4 to assemble the starter.

Starter Brush Replacement (2.2L Diesel Starter)

Refer to **Figure 19** for this procedure.

1. Disconnect the lead wire at the starter solenoid.
2. Remove the 2 through-bolts and separate the starter housing, armature and brush plate assembly

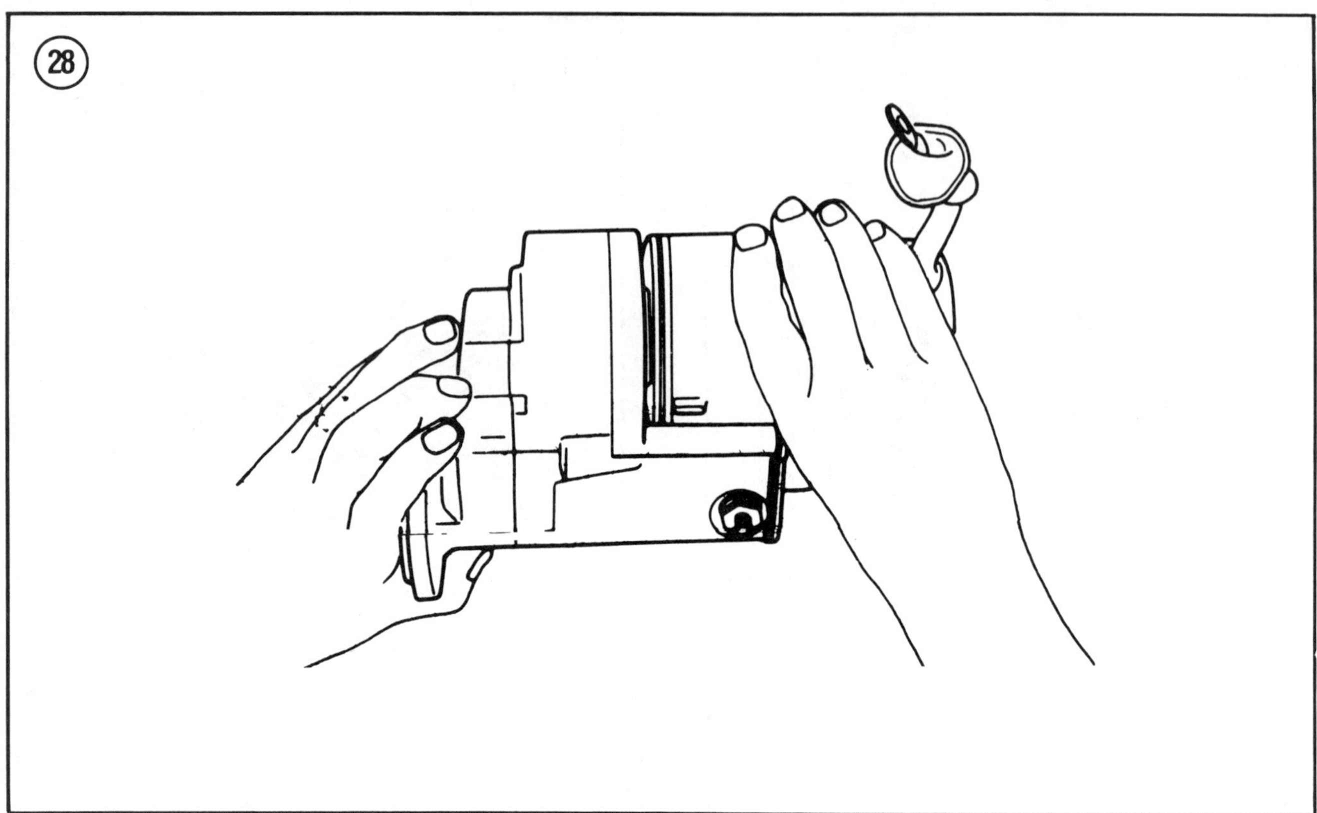

from the solenoid/drive gear assembly. See **Figure 28**. Discard the O-ring.

3. Remove the brushes from their holders on the brush plate with needlenose pliers (**Figure 29**), then remove the brush plate from the armature.

NOTE
The negative brushes and brush plate are serviced as an assembly.

4. Check the brushes for length and condition. Replace all if any are worn to 0.374 in. (9.5 mm) or less.
5. Connect an ohmmeter between the brush plate assembly and one positive brush holder to check insulation. There should be no continuity. Repeat this step to check the other positive brush holder.
6. If brush replacement is required, discard the brush plate. Cut the insulated brush leads as close as possible to the lead clamp. Straighten the clamp and insert the new brush lead, then bend the clamp to hold both leads (remainder of old lead and the new lead). Solder the brush leads in the clamp with rosin core solder and a 300-watt soldering iron.
7. Install the brush plate on the armature and insert each brush in its respective holder.
8. Install the drive housing to the starter frame with a new O-ring. Install and tighten the through-bolts. Connect the solenoid lead wire.

IGNITION SYSTEM

The ignition system consists of the battery, a breakerless distributor, ignition coil, ignition switch, ignition module, spark plugs and connecting primary/secondary wiring. Three slightly different ignition systems are used, depending upon the engine and point of first sale.

2.0L, 2.5L and V6 Engines

The Delco High Energy Ignition (HEI) system is used on these engines. Electronic spark timing (EST) is used on 1982-1983 California V6 and all 1984-on engines. The HEI-EST system differs from the standard HEI system on 1982-1983 Federal models in that the distributor has no vacuum or centrifugal advance mechanisms. Spark timing is controlled directly by the electronic control module (ECM).

The HEI distributor may use either a magnetic pick-up assembly or a Hall-effect switch.

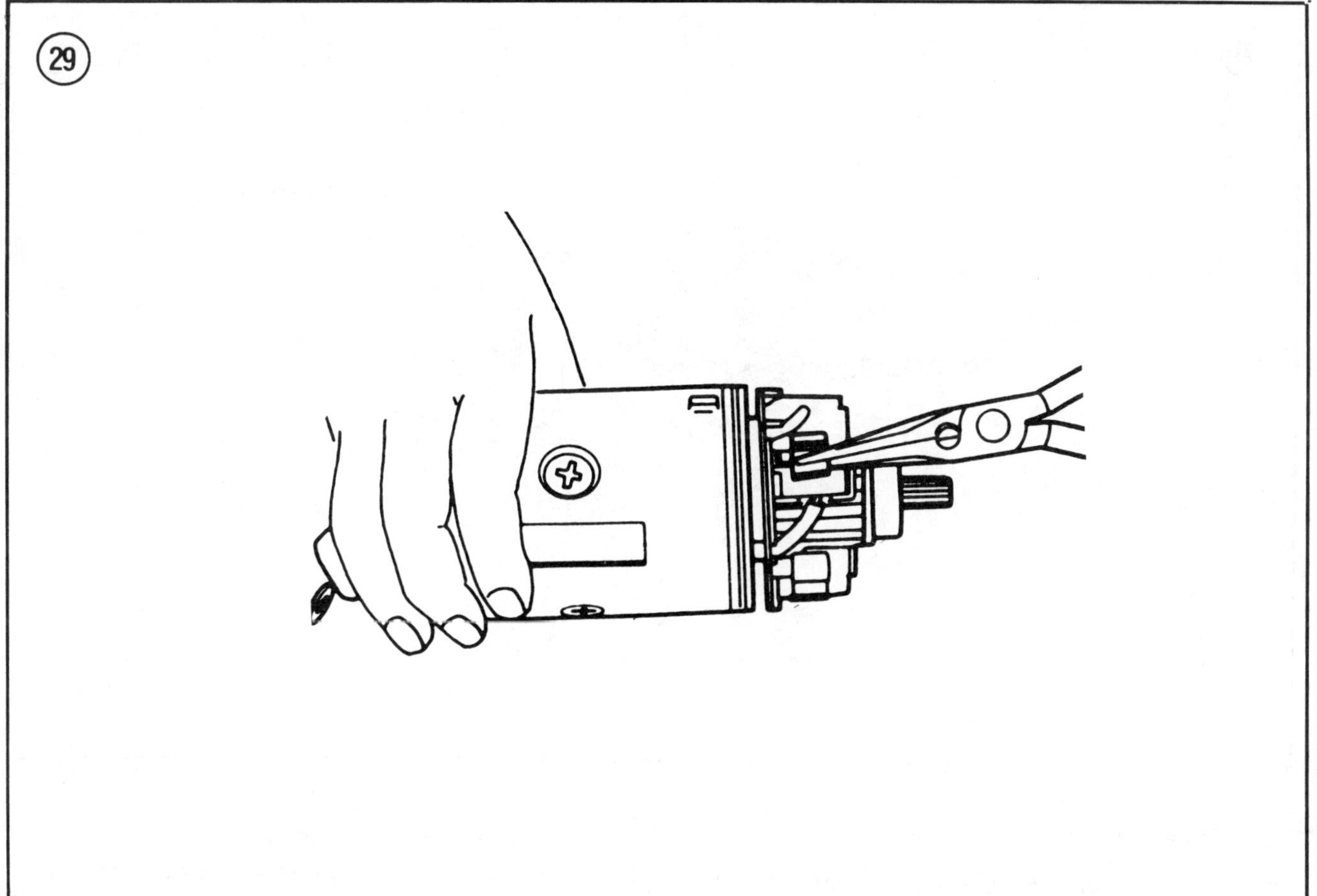

The magnetic pickup assembly contains a permanent magnet, a pole piece with internal teeth, and a pickup coil. A timer core with external teeth rotates inside the pole piece. When the timer core teeth align with the pole piece teeth, a voltage is induced in the pickup coil.

The Hall-effect switch consists of a plastic cup which contains 4 openings or windows and 4 vanes or solid portions (one for each cylinder). A permanent magnet is positioned on one side of the cups, with a Hall sensor on the other. As the cup rotates, the magnetic field varies according to the position of the window or vane between the sensor and magnet. When a vane passes between the sensor and magnet, a voltage signal is produced.

In both systems, this voltage signal is sent to an electronic module in the distributor. The module breaks the coil primary circuit, inducing a high voltage in the ignition coil secondary windings. This high voltage is sent to the distributor where it is directed to the appropriate spark plug by the rotor.

On engines with the HEI-EST ignition system, the ECM evaluates data from various engine sensors to calculate the required spark timing and directs the distributor accordingly. No vacuum or centrifugal advance mechanisms are used with the HEI-EST distributor and no changes can be made in the advance curve.

A radio noise suppression capacitor is located in the distributor.

1.9L Engine

The 1.9L engine ignition system functions in essentially the same way as the standard HEI ignition, but the distributor components differ somewhat. Instead of a timer core and pole piece, the 1.9L distributor contains a toothed reluctor which revolves in front of a magnetic pick-up. Movement of the reluctor teeth in front of the pick-up creates the voltage signal to trigger the ignition module.

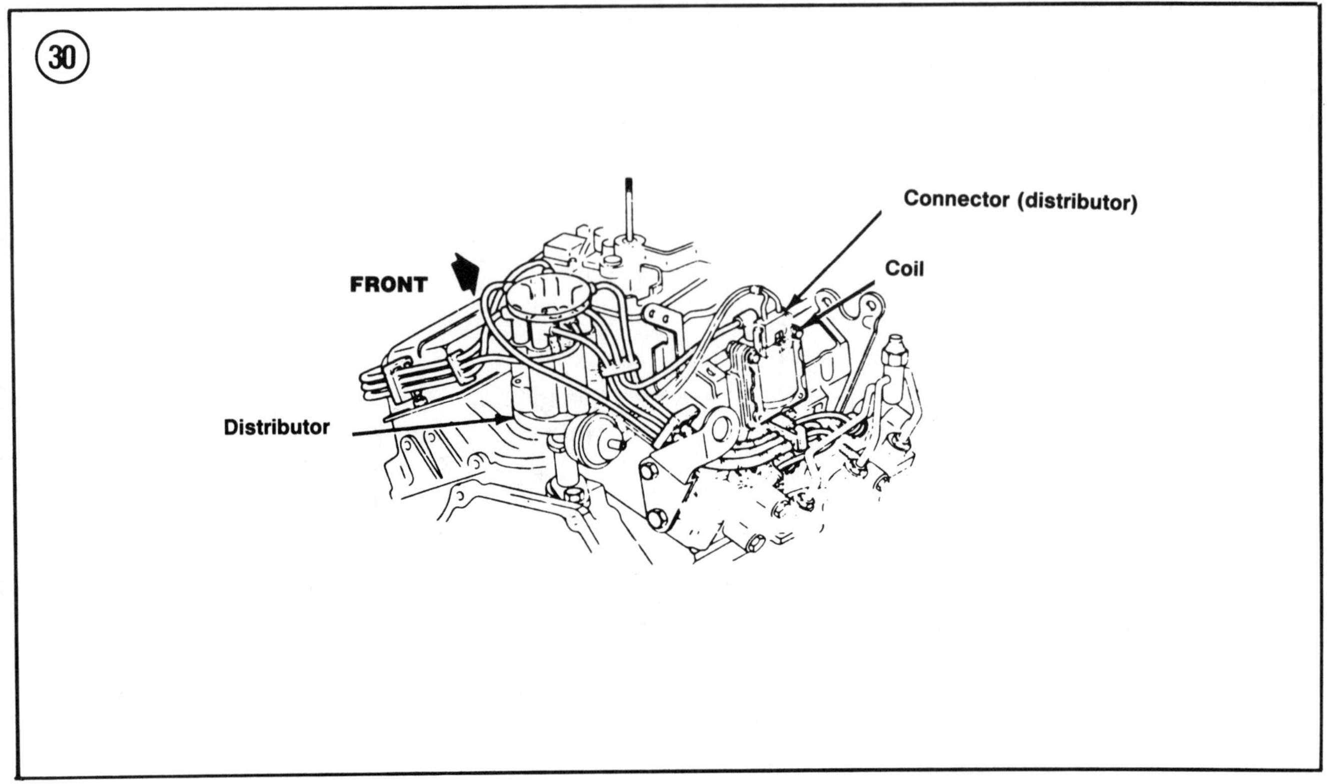

Distributor Removal/Installation

The 2.0L and V6 distributors are mounted vertically at the rear of the engine block. **Figure 30** shows the V6 distributor location; the 2.0L distributor location is similar. The 2.5L distributor is mounted below the coil on the passenger side of the engine at the rear as shown in **Figure 31**. A hexagon shaft installed in the end of the distributor shaft drives the oil pump on 2.0L, 2.5L and V6 engines.

The 1.9L distributor is mounted at the front of the engine block on the passenger's side (**Figure 32**). A projecting tang on the distributor shaft engages the oil pump drive shaft.

1. Disconnect the negative battery cable.
2. Turn the engine over by hand until the No. 1 cylinder is at top dead center on its compression stroke. The 0 degree mark on the timing tab will align with the notch scribed on the pulley and the distributor rotor will point to the No. 1 terminal in the distributor cap.
3. Disconnect the wiring harness at the distributor.

4A. All except 1.9L distributor—Release the coil connectors from the distributor cap.

4B. 1.9L distributor—Disconnect the ignition coil wire from the coil.

5A. All except 1.9L distributor—Rotate the 2 distributor cap latches counterclockwise with a screwdriver. Remove the cap and set it to one side out of the way.

5B. 1.9L distributor—Unsnap the clip on each side of the distributor cap. Remove the cap and set it to one side out of the way.

6. Mark the position of the distributor housing and block. Note the rotor position.
7. Remove the distributor hold-down nut or bolt and clamp. It may be necessary to retrieve the nut and clamp with a magnetic tool on the 2.0L and V6 engine.

NOTE

The oil pump drive shaft may come out with the distributor. Be sure to reinstall it when you reinstall the distributor.

8. Pull upward on the distributor with a rotating motion. As the drive gear disengages from the camshaft drive gear, the rotor will move slightly.
9. Installation is the reverse of removal. If the engine has been turned over with the distributor out, repeat Step 2. Align the distributor and block marks made in Step 6. When the distributor engages the camshaft drive gear, the rotor will turn

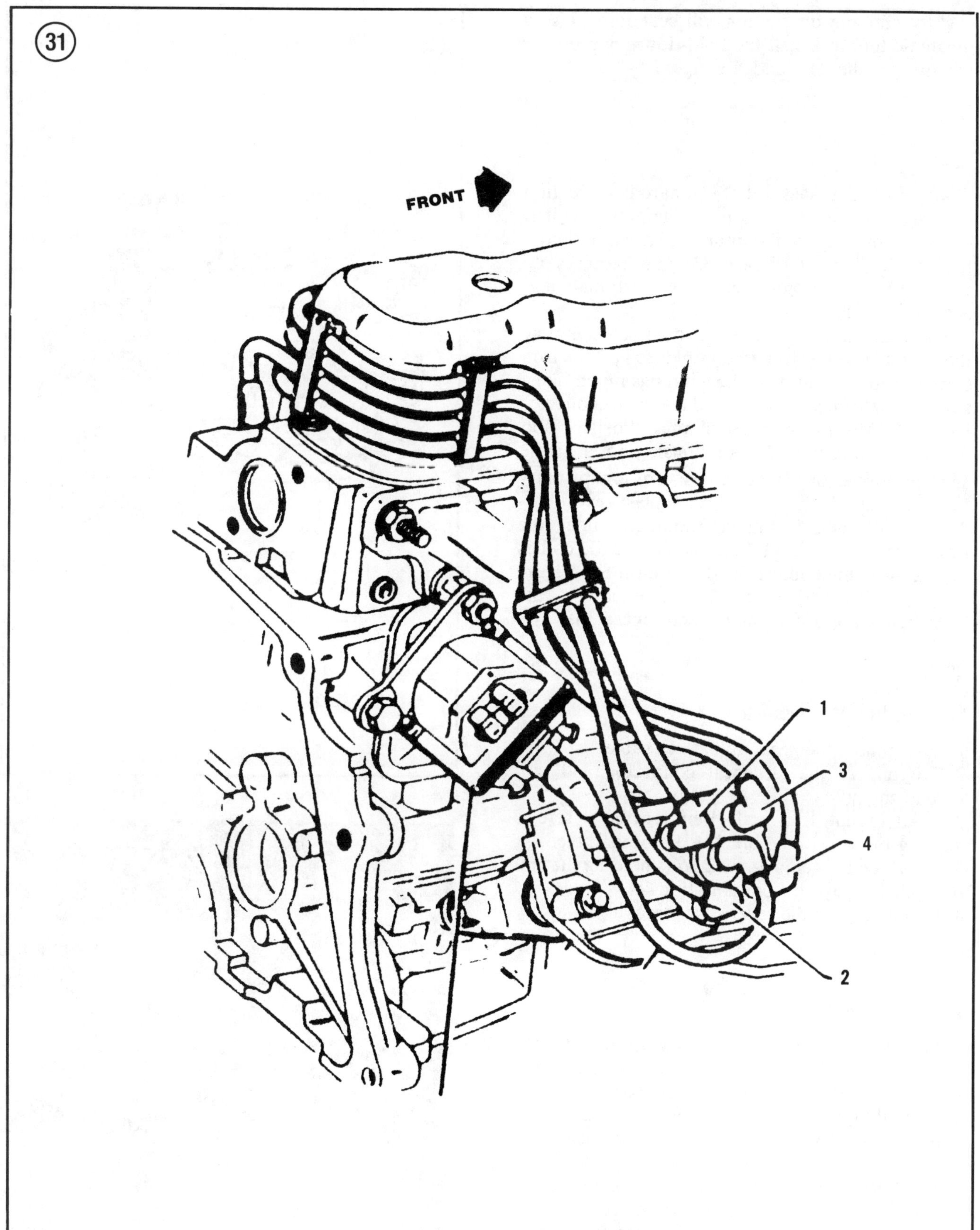
31
FRONT
1
3
4
2

slightly and the distributor will seat fully. Use a magnetic tool to install the hold-down clamp over the stud on the 2.0L and V6 engines.

Ignition Coil

An oil-filled, sealed coil of standard construction is used with the 1.9L ignition system. The coil is bracket-mounted to the inner right-hand fender behind the battery (**Figure 33**) and requires no special service beyond keeping the terminals and connections clean and tight.

The HEI ignition uses an "E-core" coil. Unlike the oil-filled coil, it is potted in plastic and the iron core is laminated around the windings much like a small transformer. The secondary lead connector looks like the top of a spark plug. Positive and negative primary leads are housing in a single snap-in connector. The coil has very low primary resistance and is used without a ballast resistor.

The 2.0L coil is bracket-mounted under the intake manifold. See **Figure 34**. The 2.5L coil is bracket-mounted above the distributor. See **Figure 31**. The V6 coil is bracket-mounted on the right-hand side of the engine. See **Figure 30**.

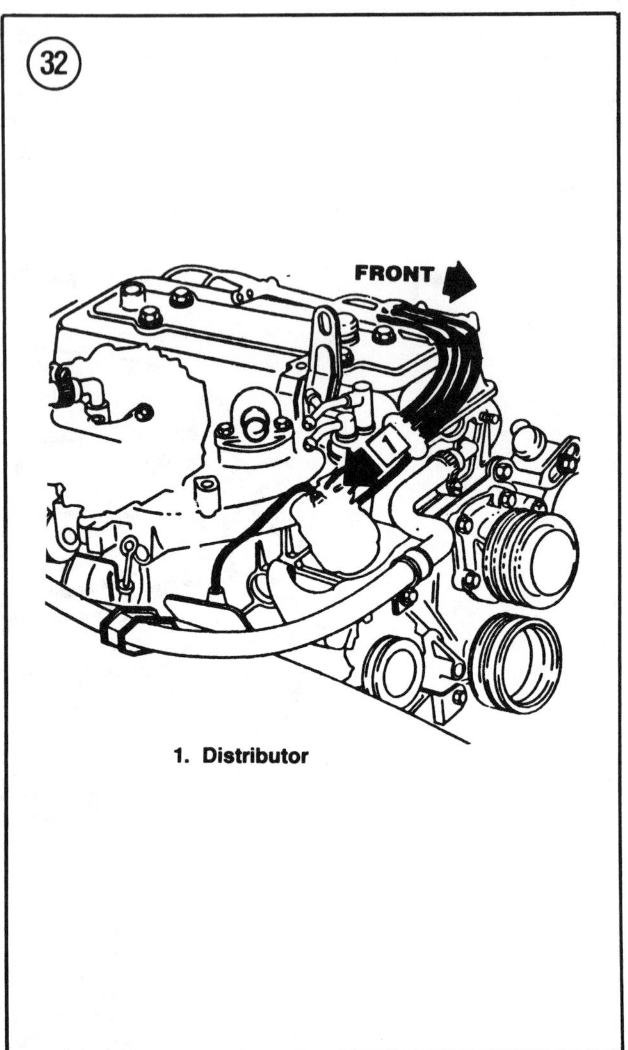

1. Distributor

Ignition Coil Replacement

1. Disconnect the negative battery cable.
2. Disconnect the electrical connector and coil wire at the coil.

3A. All except 1.9L coil—Remove the 4 screws holding the coil to the bracket. Remove the coil.

3B. 1.9L coil—Remove the 2 bolts holding the coil bracket. Remove the coil and bracket.

4. Installation is the reverse of removal.

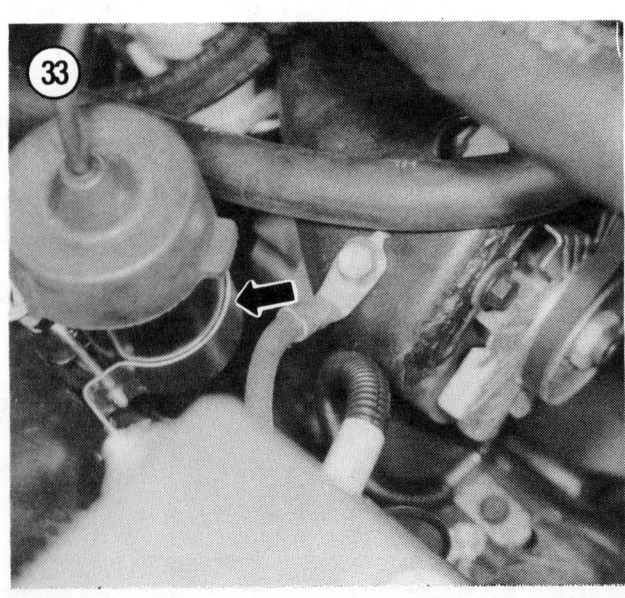

Ignition Module

The ignition amplifier module used with the breakerless ignitions is a solid-state, moisture-resistant unit which has its components permanently sealed to resist vibration and outside contaminants. The module is located inside the distributor. See **Figure 35** for the HEI module (all except 1.9L) and **Figure 36** for the 1.9L module.

All connections are waterproof. The HEI module has built-in reverse polarity and transient voltage

protection. The primary (low voltage) coil current is regulated by the magnetic pick-up or Hall-effect switch.

Replacement can be made with the distributor in the engine, but it will be far easier to remove the distributor for module replacement. Whenever a module is replaced, always install one bearing the same number stamped on top of the old module.

Ignition Module Replacement

1. Disconnect the negative battery cable.
2. Remove the distributor as described in this chapter.
3. Remove the distributor rotor. The HEI rotor (all except 1.9L) is held in place with 2 screws; the 1.9L rotor is simply pulled up and off the distributor shaft.

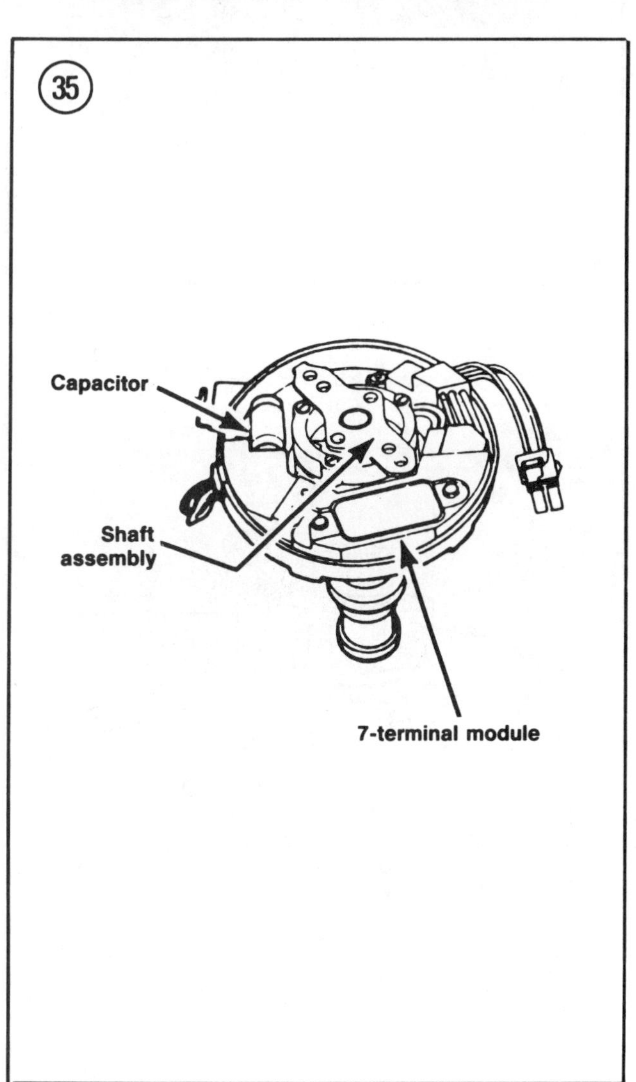

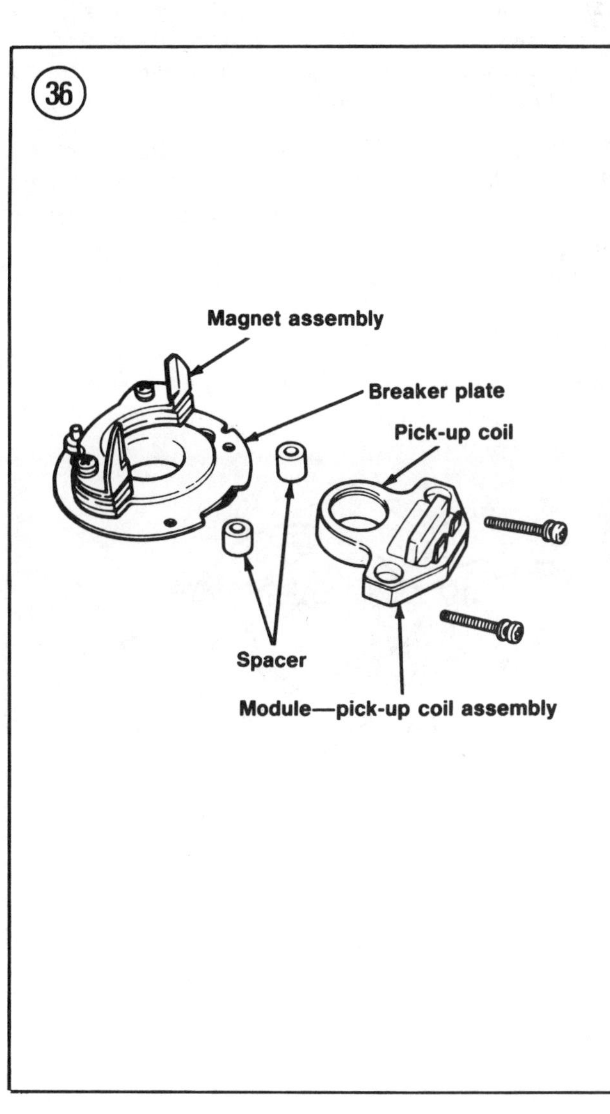

8

4. 1.9L distributor:
   a. Remove the dust cover (**Figure 37**).
   b. Remove the vacuum advance unit (**Figure 38**).
   c. Remove the wiring harness screw. Remove the harness (**Figure 39**).
   d. Pry the reluctor from the distributor shaft with 2 screwdrivers as shown in **Figure 40**.
   e. Remove the breaker plate screws and plate (**Figure 41**).
   f. Remove the module from the breaker plate (**Figure 42**).
5. HEI distributor—Disconnect the wiring connectors at each end of the module. Remove the 2 module screws. Remove the module.

NOTE
The module base which mates against the HEI distributor base is covered with silicone grease to protect the module from heat. Apply the packet of grease that comes with the new module to the module before installation.

6. HEI distributor—Wipe the distributor base and the module with a clean, dry cloth. Apply silicone grease to the distributor and module base before installing the new module.
7. Installation is the reverse of removal.

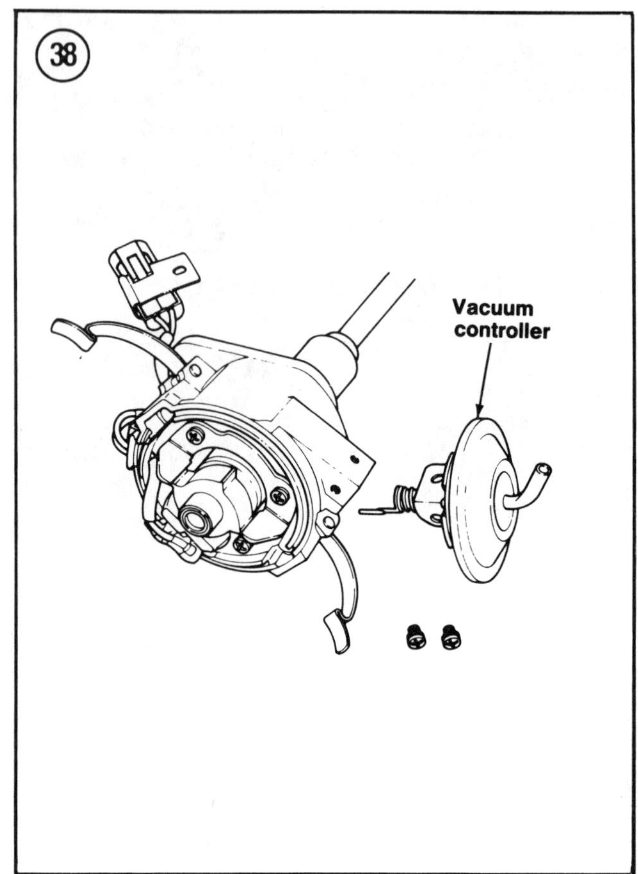

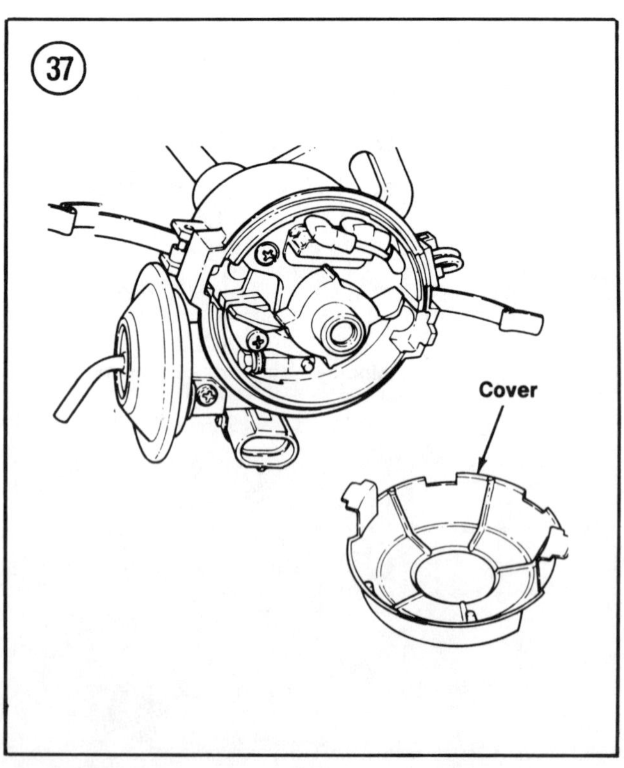

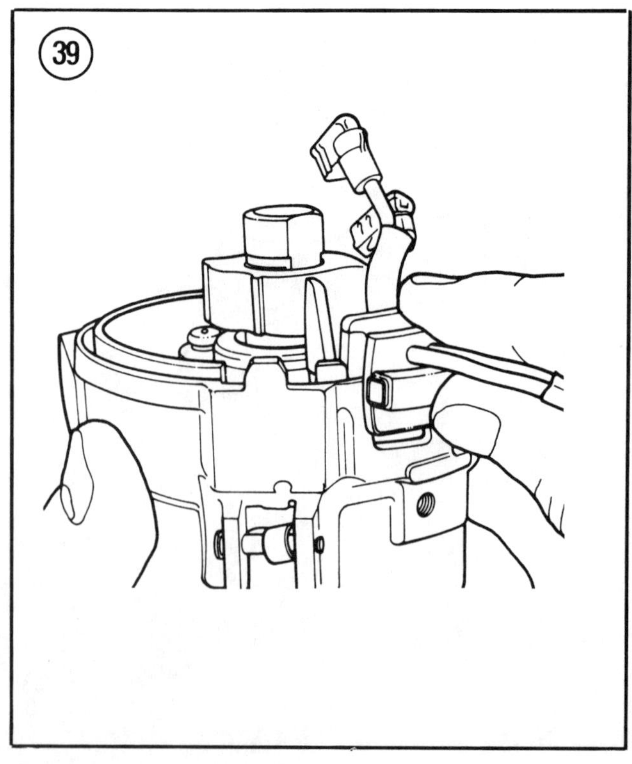

40

Reluctor

42

Magnet assembly
Breaker plate
Pick-up coil
Spacer
Module—pick-up assembly

8

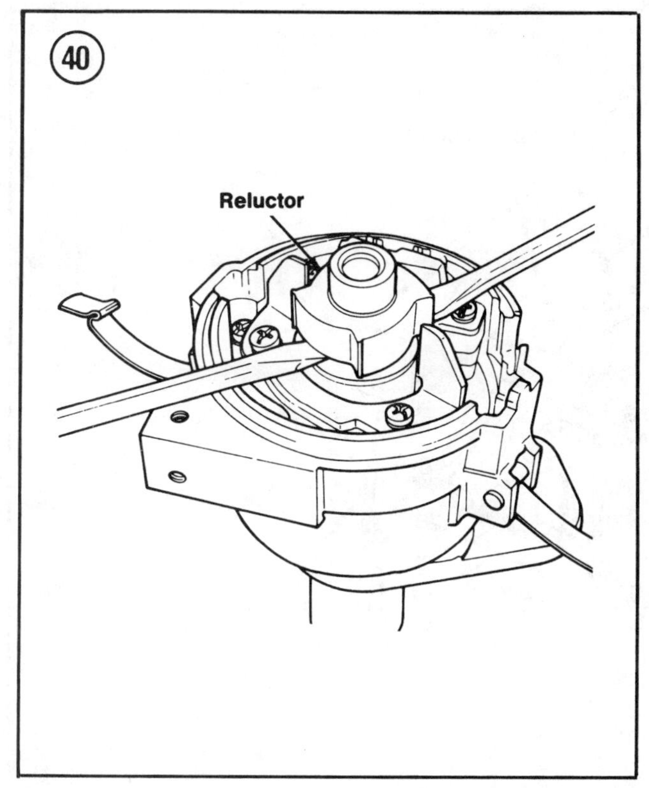

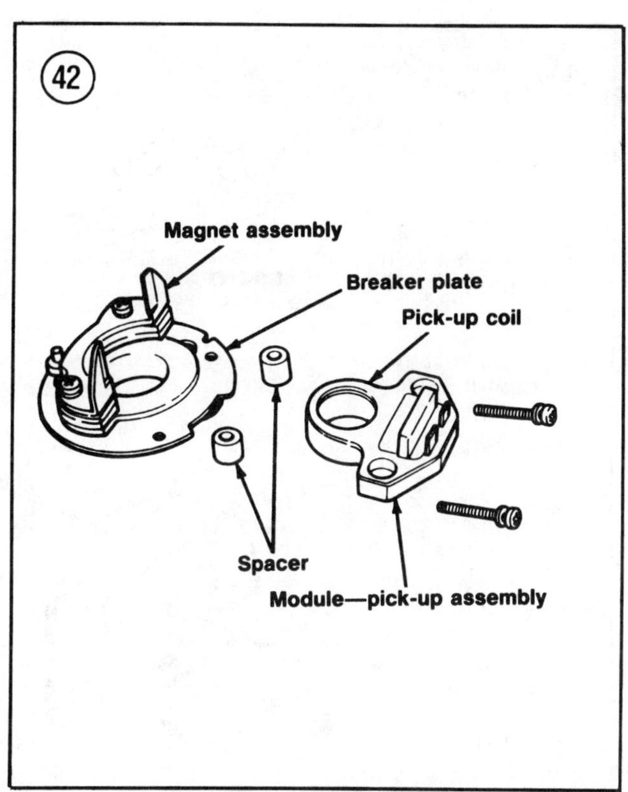

41

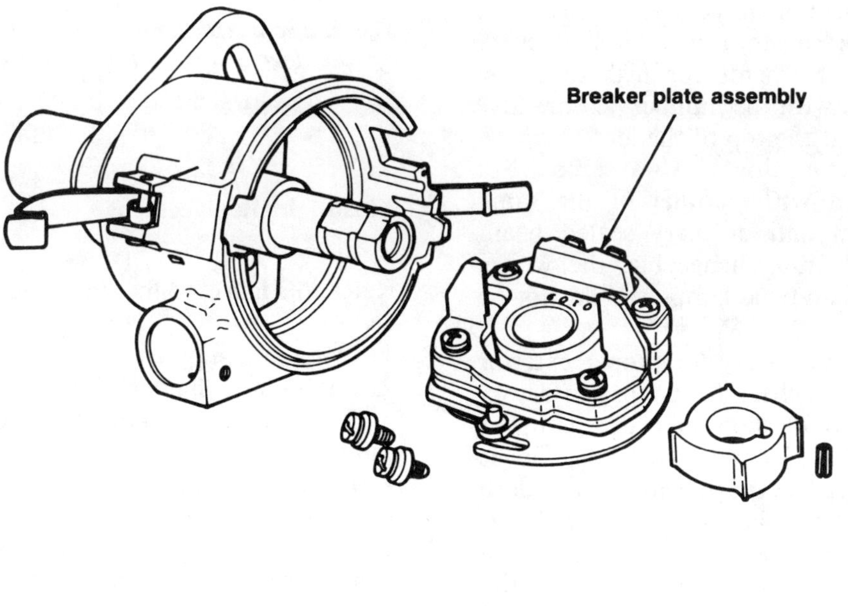

Breaker plate assembly

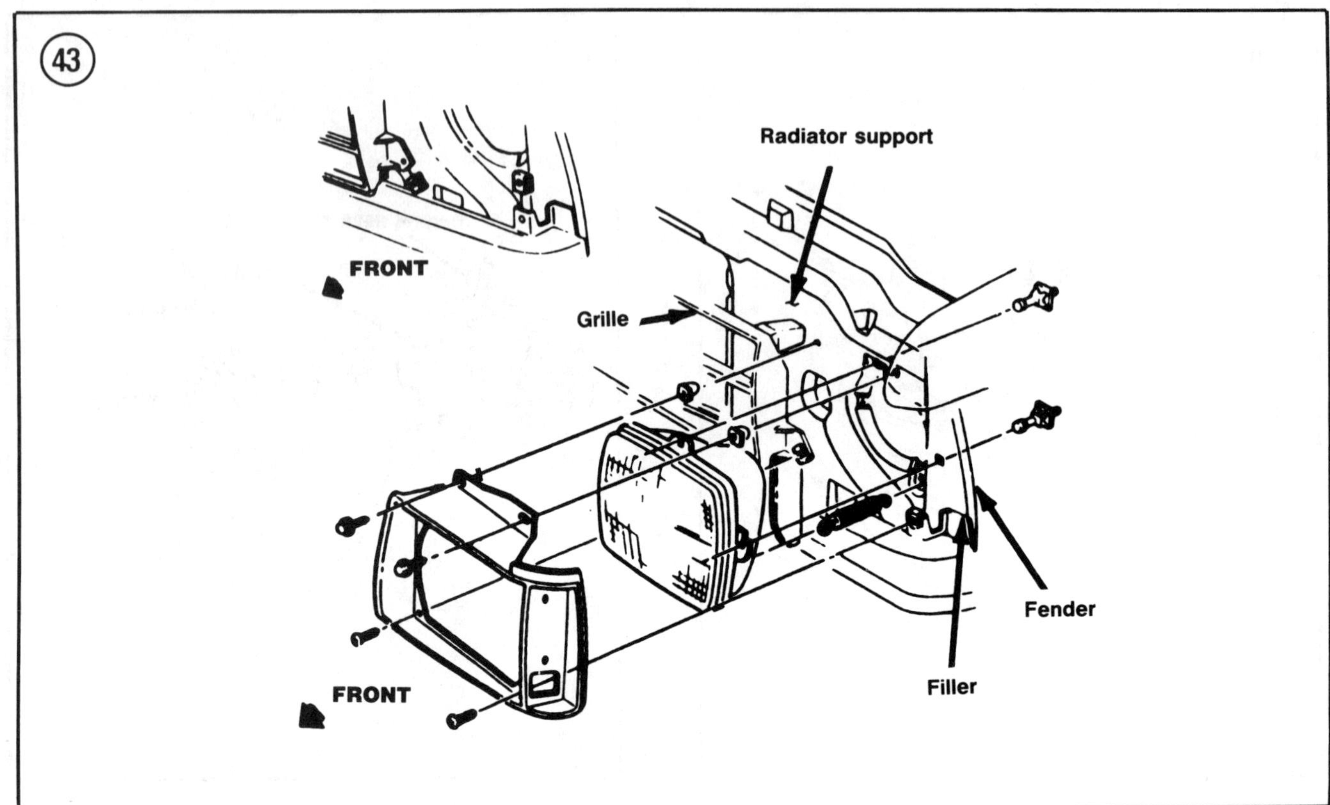

LIGHTING SYSTEM

The headlight system on all vehicles consists of a rectangular sealed-beam lamp on each side. Each lamp contains dual filaments for high and low beam and is marked with the number "2" or "2B" molded in the glass at the top of the lens.

Halogen lamps are optional. Always replace a burned-out headlight with another of the same type. While halogen and ordinary sealed beam lamps are physically interchangeable, the wiring circuitry is different and the lamps should not be interchanged.

A good ground is necessary for proper exterior light operation. Always check for an unsatisfactory ground first when troubleshooting a dim lamp or one that fails to light. Do not overlook a loose ground strap between the engine and body dash panel—this can affect headlight as well as instrument gauge operation. Failure of one circuit in the bulb requires replacement of the entire sealed beam unit.

NOTE
If both filaments in the lamp fail at the same time, the problem is generally a short in the wiring to that particular lamp. Check the fuse to make sure it is the correct amperage rating and replace it if it is not. Carefully inspect the wiring and connector for deterioration, chafing or other damage and correct as required.

Headlight Replacement

Refer to **Figure 43** for this procedure.

1. Open and support the hood.
2. Disconnect the negative battery cable.
3. Remove the 4 headlamp bezel screws. Remove the bezel.
4. Remove the 4 retaining ring screws. Remove the retaining ring.
5. Disconnect the headlight and side marker connectors from the rear of the bulb.
6. Remove the headlight from the vehicle.
7. Note the locating tabs molded in the new bulb. Position the bulb with the locating tabs in the retaining ring slots.
8. Reverse Steps 1-5 to install the new bulb.

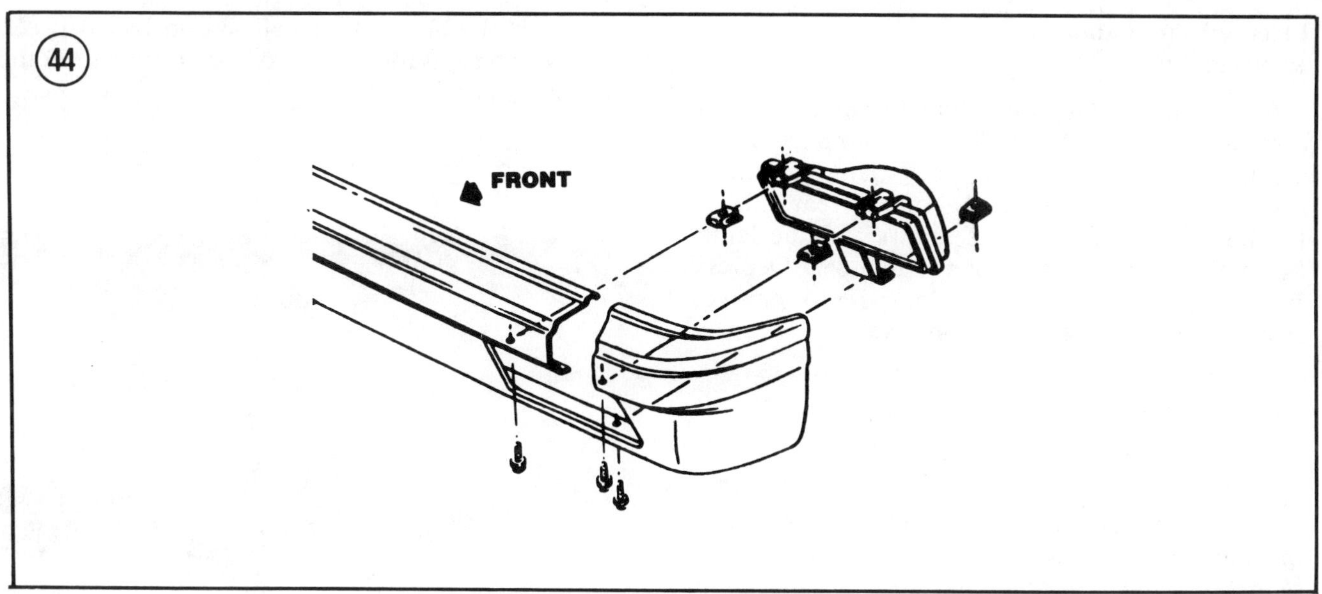

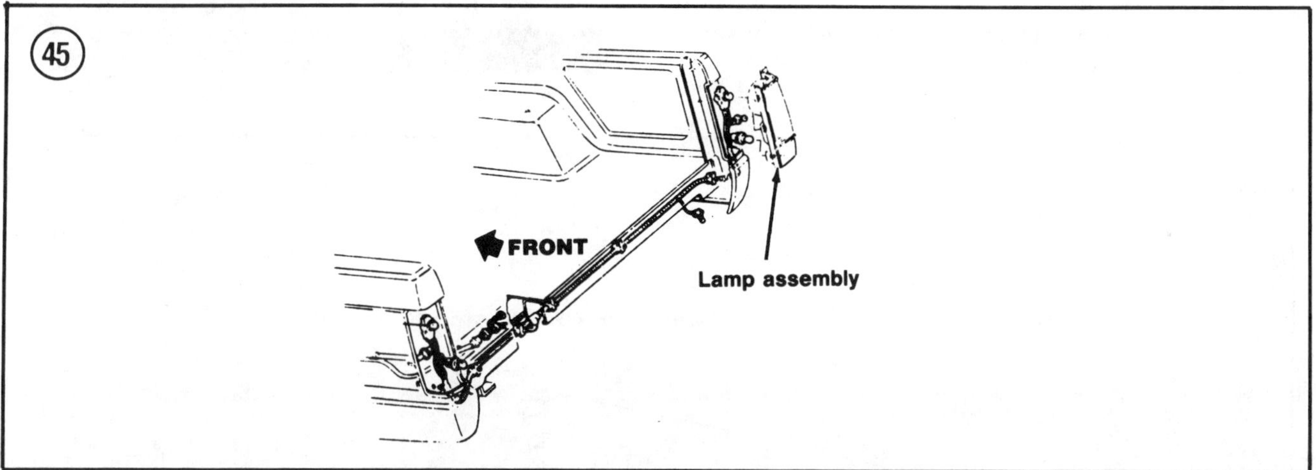

8

Front Park/Turn Signal Lamp Replacement

Refer to **Figure 44** for this procedure.

1. Reach under and behind the front bumper. Rotate the bulb socket counterclockwise and remove it from the lamp housing.
2. Depress the bulb and rotate it counterclockwise in the socket. Remove the bulb.
3. Installation is the reverse of removal.
4. If the lens requires replacement, remove the socket as described in Step 1. Remove the 2 attaching screws from the underside of the bumper. Remove the lamp housing.
5. Installation is the reverse of removal.

Side Marker Lamp and Lens Replacement

The side marker lamps use the same attachment method as the front park/turn signal lamps. The bulb socket is reached from the front under the front wheel well.

Rear Lamp Assembly Service

Refer to **Figure 45** for this procedure. All rear lamp bulbs are replaced by removing the retaining screws holding the lens housing to the vehicle. Once the lens housing has been removed, depress and turn the individual sockets counterclockwise to remove them from the lens housing. Replacement is the reverse of removal.

License Plate Lamp Replacement

Dual license plate lamps are installed, one on each side of the plate bracket. The lamp assembly is retained by 2 screws with spring clamp fasteners. **Figure 46** shows the fasteners on the rear side of the bumper. Remove the 2 screws and the lamp assembly from the front of the bumper. Depress the bulb and rotate it counterclockwise to remove. Installation is the reverse of removal.

Dome Lamp Replacement

Refer to **Figure 47** for this procedure.

1. Insert the blade of a small screwdriver between the lamp lens and housing. Press inward and down to unhook the lens retaining tab from the lamp housing. Remove the bulb.

2. If it is necessary to remove the lamp housing, remove the 2 attaching screws.

3. Insert the blade of a small screwdriver between the housing and roof bow. Pry the housing from the insulator pad.

4. Installation is the reverse of removal.

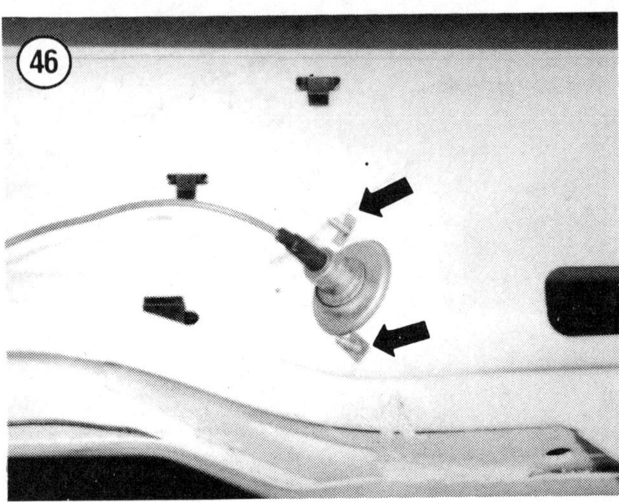

47

Wire assembly

Insulator pad

Bulb

FRONT

Lens

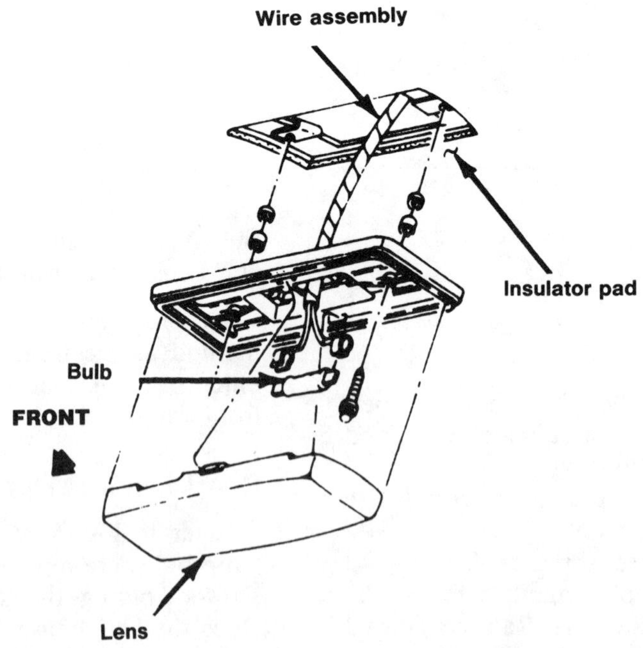

WITHOUT KEY RELEASE
KEY RELEASE

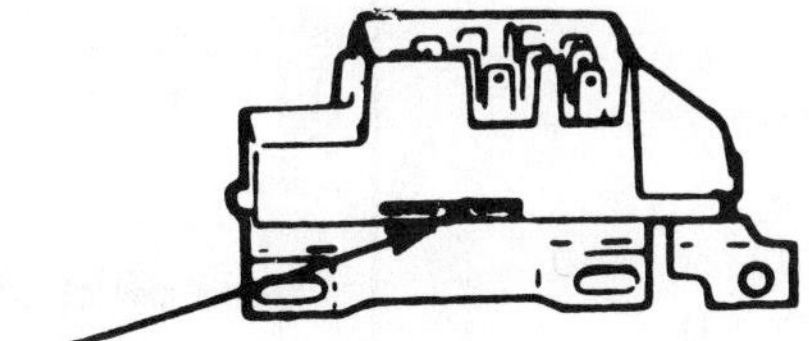

Move switch slider to extreme left (ACC) position. Then move slider two detents to the right to OFF-UNLOCK position.

KEY RELEASE

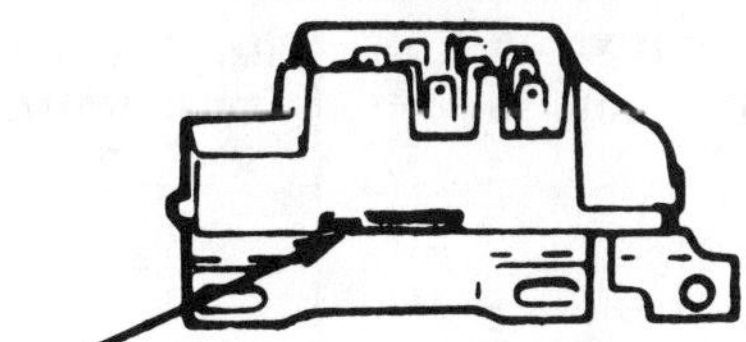

Move switch slider to extreme left (ACC) position.

Instrument Lights

The instrument cluster must be removed to replace any lamp. See *Instruments* in this chapter.

IGNITION SWITCH

A blade-type terminal switch with one multiple connector is used. The switch is attached to the steering column with a stud and screw. The dimmer light switch is attached in such a way that it must be removed in order to remove the ignition switch.

Removal

1. Disconnect the negative battery cable.
2. Remove the 2 lower protective shields under the steering column.
3. Remove the 3 support bracket bolts. Lower the steering column.
4. Unplug the ignition switch connector.
5. Remove the dimmer switch fasteners. Disengage the switch from its actuator rod and remove from the steering column.
6. Remove the ignition switch fasteners. Disengage the switch from its actuator rod and remove from the steering column.

Installation

1. Standard column—If equipped with key release feature, position the ignition switch slider to the extreme left as shown in **Figure 48**. If not equipped with key release feature, position the switch slider to the extreme left, then move it 2 detents to the right to the OFF-UNLOCK position (**Figure 48**).

2. Tilt column—If equipped with key release feature, position the switch slider to the extreme right, then move it 2 detents to the left to the OFF-UNLOCK position (**Figure 49**). If not equipped with key release feature, position the ignition switch slider to the extreme right (**Figure 49**).

3. Install the actuator rod in the switch slider hole.

4. Install the switch to the steering column and tighten the lower stud to 35 in.-lb. (3.9 N•m).

5. Install the dimmer switch and depress it sufficiently to insert a 3/32 in. drill bit as shown in **Figure 50**.

6. Move the dimmer switch upward to remove all lash, then tighten the attaching screws and nuts to 35 in.-lb. (3.9 N•m).

7. Reverse Steps 1-4 of *Removal* to complete installation.

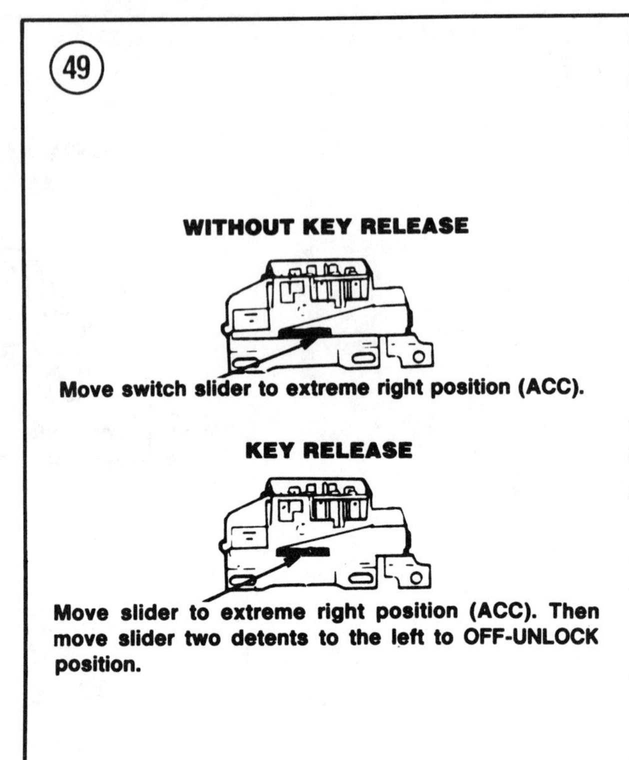

50

Dimmer switch asembly

3/32 in. drill

Dimmer switch rod

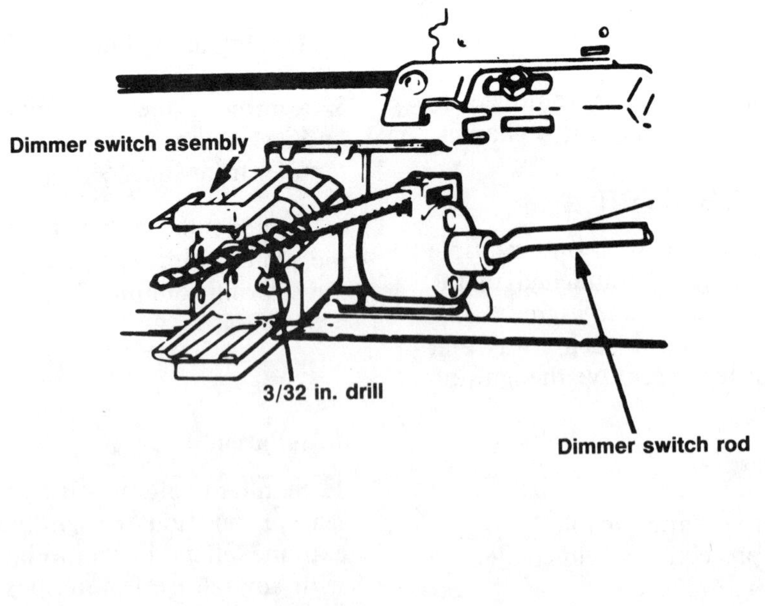

Testing

1. Perform Steps 1-4 of *Ignition Switch Removal* in this chapter.
2. Disconnect the ignition switch multiple connector.
3. Identify the terminals according to **Figure 51**.
4. Test the switch with an ohmmeter or a self-powered test lamp. There should be continuity as indicated in **Figure 51**.

HEADLIGHT SWITCH

The combination 3-position headlight switch is mounted in the lower left of the instrument panel. It controls circuits to the headlights, parking/marker and taillights, license plate, interior and instrument panel lights. Removal of the switch is recommended for ease in continuity testing.

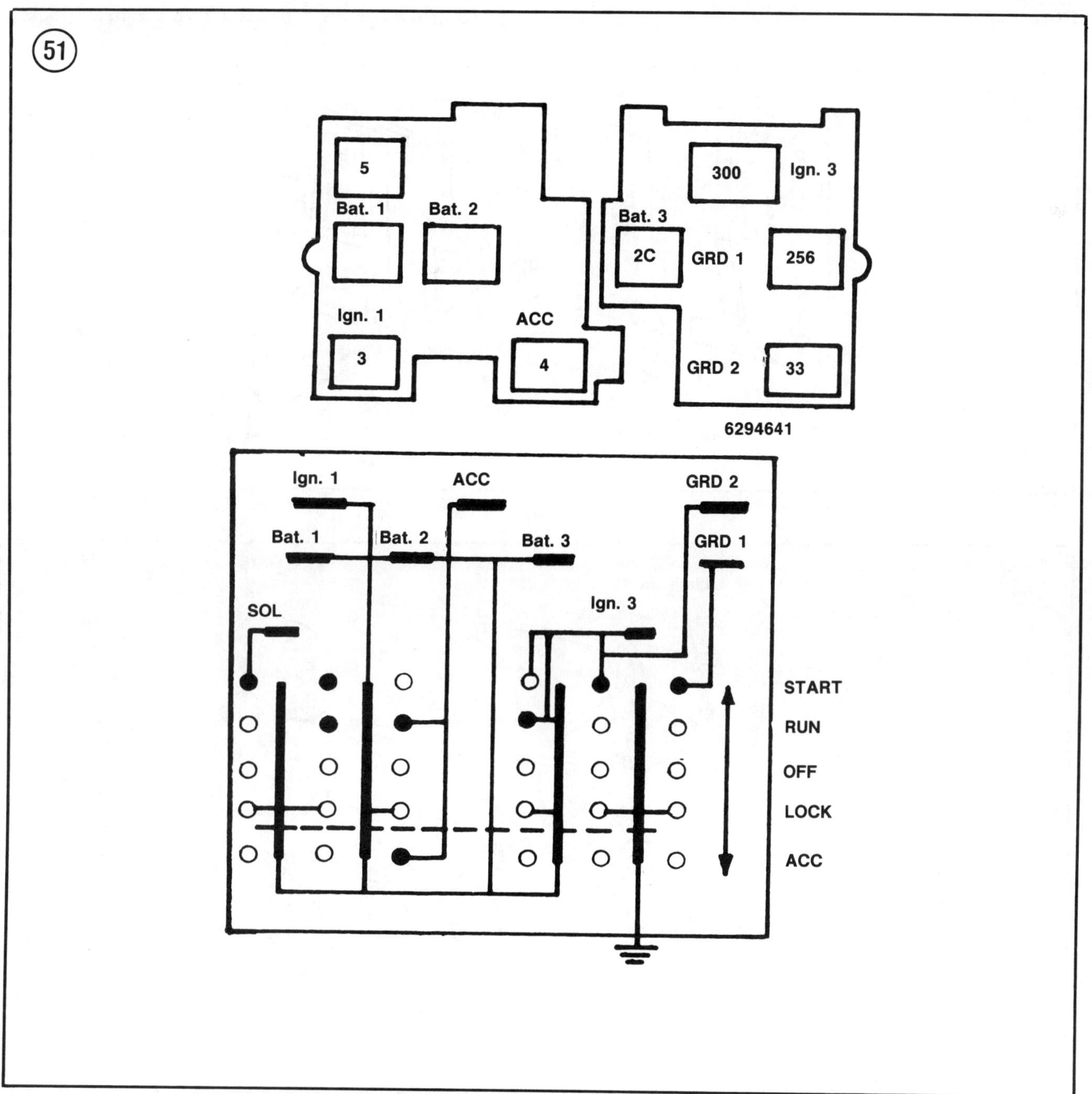

Removal/Installation (1982-1983)

Refer to **Figure 52** for this procedure.

1. Disconnect the negative battery cable.
2. Pull the switch knob out to its second detent position.
3. Reach under the instrument panel and depress the switch shaft retaining button while pulling forward on the shaft knob.
4. Remove the 3 trim plate screws. Remove the trim plate.
5. Unscrew the ferrule nut from the front of the instrument panel.
6. Disconnect the electrical connector from the bottom of the switch. Remove the switch.
7. Installation is the reverse of removal.

Removal/Installation (1984-on)

Refer to **Figure 53** for this procedure.

1. Disconnect the negative battery cable.
2. Remove the hush panel above the fuse block.

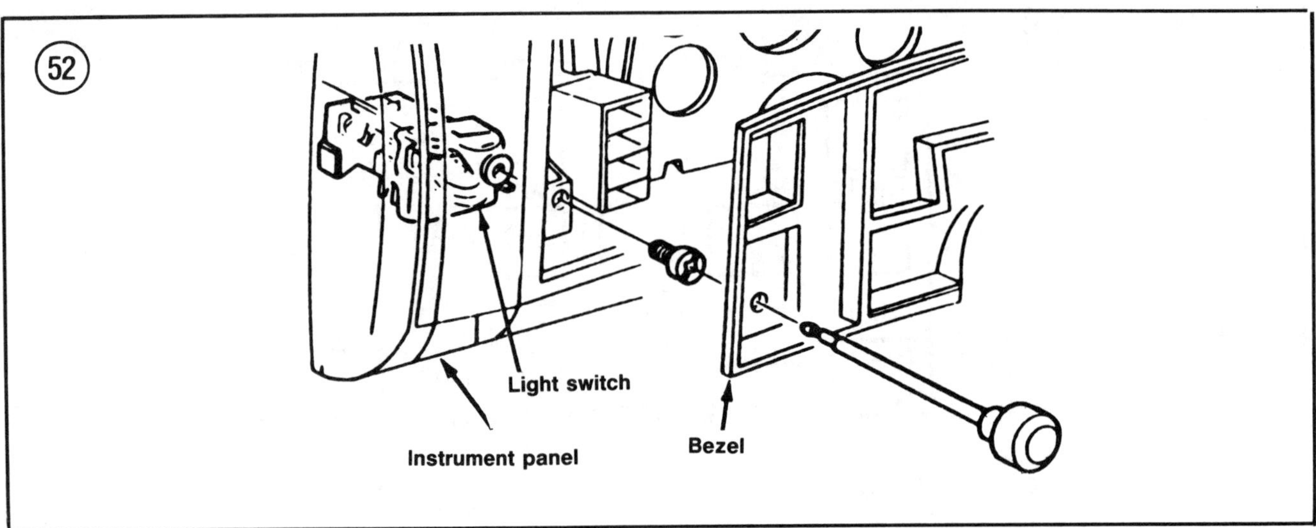

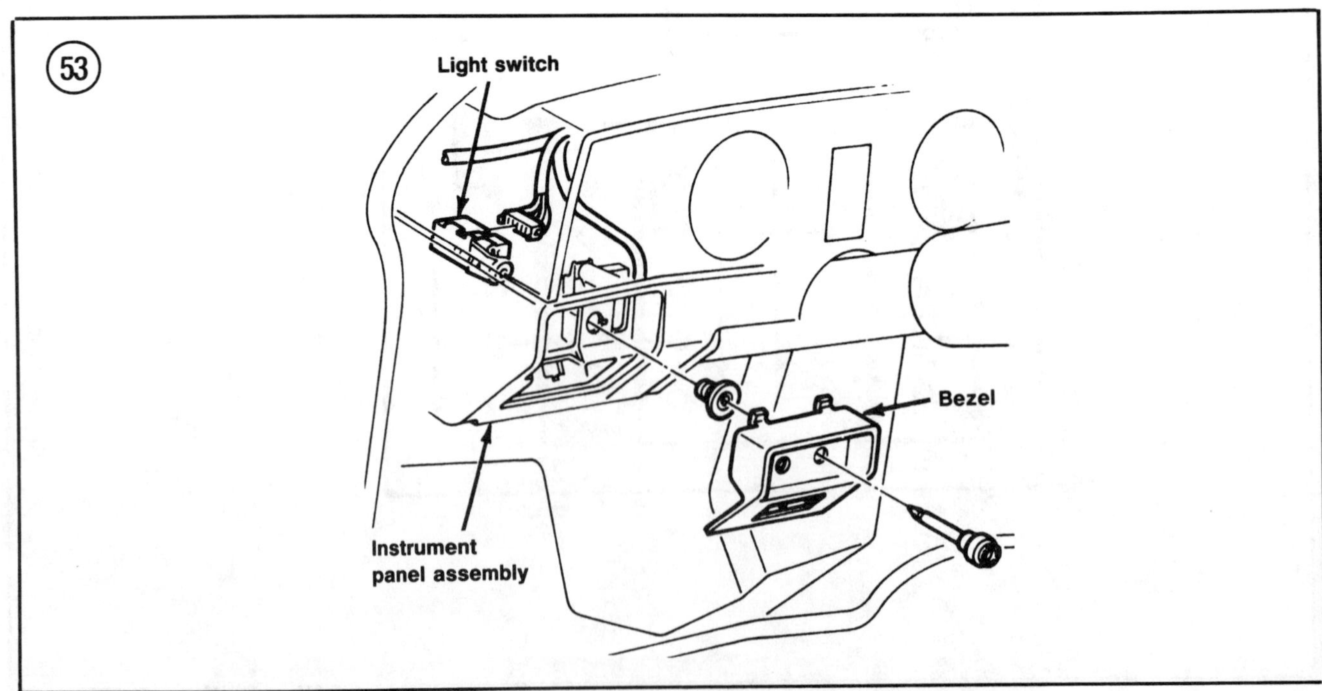

3. Remove the screws holding the hood release handle to the instrument panel.
4. Remove the lower steering column trim cover.
5. If equipped with cruise control, remove the module behind the instrument panel.
6. Remove the wiper delay switch knob and locknut.
7. Remove the headlamp switch knob and shaft.
8. Depress the tabs on the parking brake release handle. Remove the handle.
9. Disconnect the parking brake cable.
10. Remove the headlight switch bezel.
11. Remove the switch and disconnect the electrical connector.
12. Installation is the reverse of removal.

Testing

1. With the switch removed, identify the terminals according to **Figure 54**.
2. Test the switch with an ohmmeter or self-powered test lamp. There should be continuity as indicated in **Figure 54**.

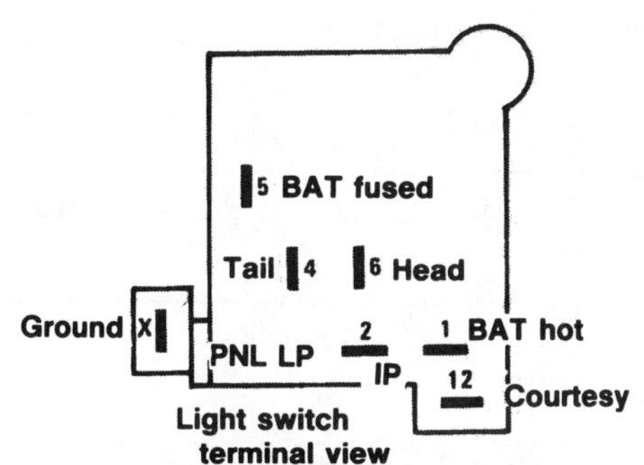

SWITCH POSITIONS

SWITCH TERMINALS	OFF	PARK	HEADLAMP
1 to X	Continuity	Continuity	Continuity
1 to 6	No cont.	No cont.	Continuity
1 to 5	No cont.	No cont.	No cont.
1 to 4	No cont.	No cont.	No cont.
2 to 5*	No cont.	Continuity	Continuity
4 to 5	No cont.	Continuity	Continuity
4 to 6	No cont.	No cont.	No cont.
5 to X	Continuity	Continuity	Continuity
5 to 6	No cont.	No cont.	No cont.
5 to 12	**	**	**

*Measure continuity with rheostat in full counterclockwise position. Test lamp should dim as rheostat is rotated clockwise.
**Continuity should only exist when rheostat is turned beyond detent is switch.

WIPER/WASHER SWITCH

Testing

Refer to **Figure 55** (1982-1984) or **Figure 56** (1985-on) for standard wiper switch; refer to **Figure 57** for pulse wiper switch.

1. Disconnect the switch connector at the wiper motor.
2. Check the continuity between the connector terminals. Either a test lamp or ohmmeter can be used with the standard switch. Only an ohmmeter should be used with the interval switch.

NOTE
If the terminals are not marked on the switch connector, refer to the appropriate illustration and identify the terminal by the wire color code.

3. Standard wiper:
   a. With the switch in the OFF position, there should be continuity only between terminals 4 and 3 or A and B.
   b. With the switch in the LO position, there should be continuity only between terminals 1 and 3 or B and D.
   c. With the switch in the HI position, there should be continuity only between terminals 1 and 2 or C and D.
4. Pulse wiper—Refer to **Figure 57** for continuity according to switch position.
5. Replace the switch if it does not perform as specified in Step 3 (standard wiper) or Step 4 (pulse wiper).

Removal/Installation

1. Remove the ignition and dimmer switches as described in this chapter.
2. Unplug the switch wiring connector.
3. Remove the switch actuator rack assembly.
4. Remove the pivot and switch assembly.
5. Installation is the reverse of removal. Assemble the rack with its first tooth between the first and second teeth of the sector.

COOLANT TEMPERATURE SWITCH

Vehicles with a standard cluster use a temperature warning lamp in the instrument panel. Those equipped with the optional gauge cluster

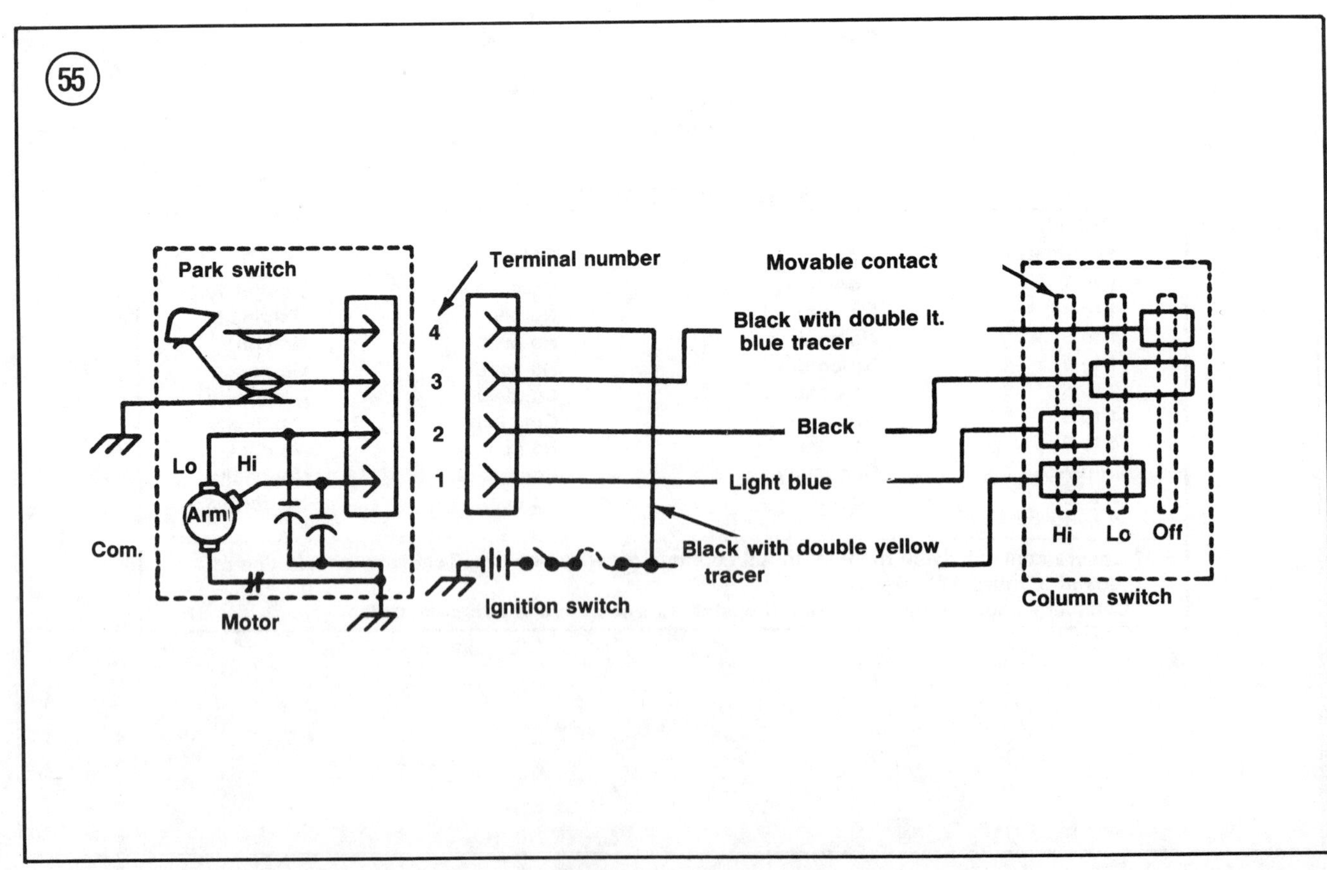

56

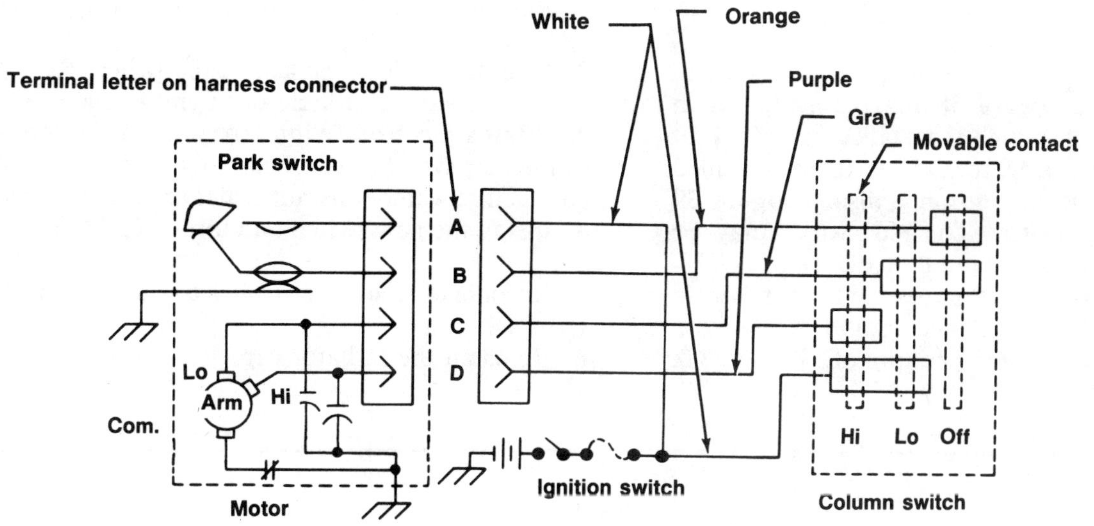

White
Orange
Terminal letter on harness connector
Purple
Gray
Movable contact
Park switch
A
B
C
D
Lo
Arm
Hi
Com.
Motor
Ignition switch
Hi
Lo
Off
Column switch

57

Bulkhead connector
Pulse circuitry
Park switch
360 ohms, 1/2 W
10K-500K ohms
IN4004
1
2
3
4
Arm.
Motor
Ignition switch
Arm.
Washer
Mist
Off
Pulse
Lo
Hi
Washer
Column switch

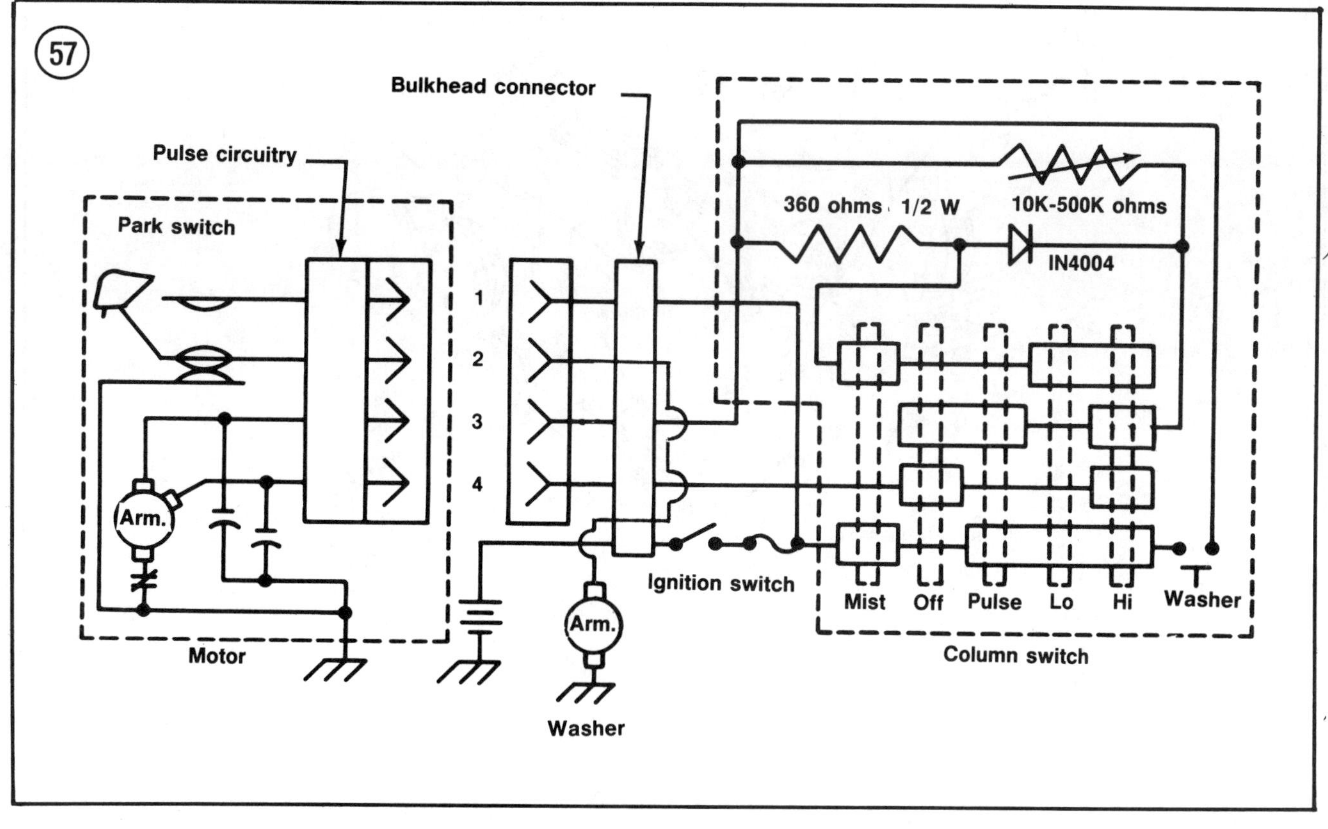

have a temperature gauge. Both types are controlled by a thermal switch in the thermostat housing which senses coolant temperature.

Testing

1. Remove the temperature switch as described in this chapter. See **Figure 58** for the 1.9L switch location. The 2.0L switch is installed in the top of the thermostat housing; the 2.5L switch is installed in the side of the thermostat housing. **Figure 59** shows the 2.5L switch. The V6 switch may be located as shown in **Figure 60** or **Figure 61**.
2. Measure the resistance across the terminals with an ohmmeter. The resistance should be between 4,114-4,743 ohms at a temperature of 59° F (15° C).

Replacement

1. Remove the radiator cap to relieve any pressure in the cooling system.
2. Unplug the electrical lead at the switch. Remove the switch with a suitable open-end wrench.
3. Wrap a piece of Teflon tape around the threads of the new switch. Teflon paste or other electrically conductive water-resistant sealers can also be used.
4. Install the new switch and torque to 72 in.-lb. (7 N•m).
5. Reconnect the electrical lead to the switch terminal.
6. Reinstall the radiator cap.

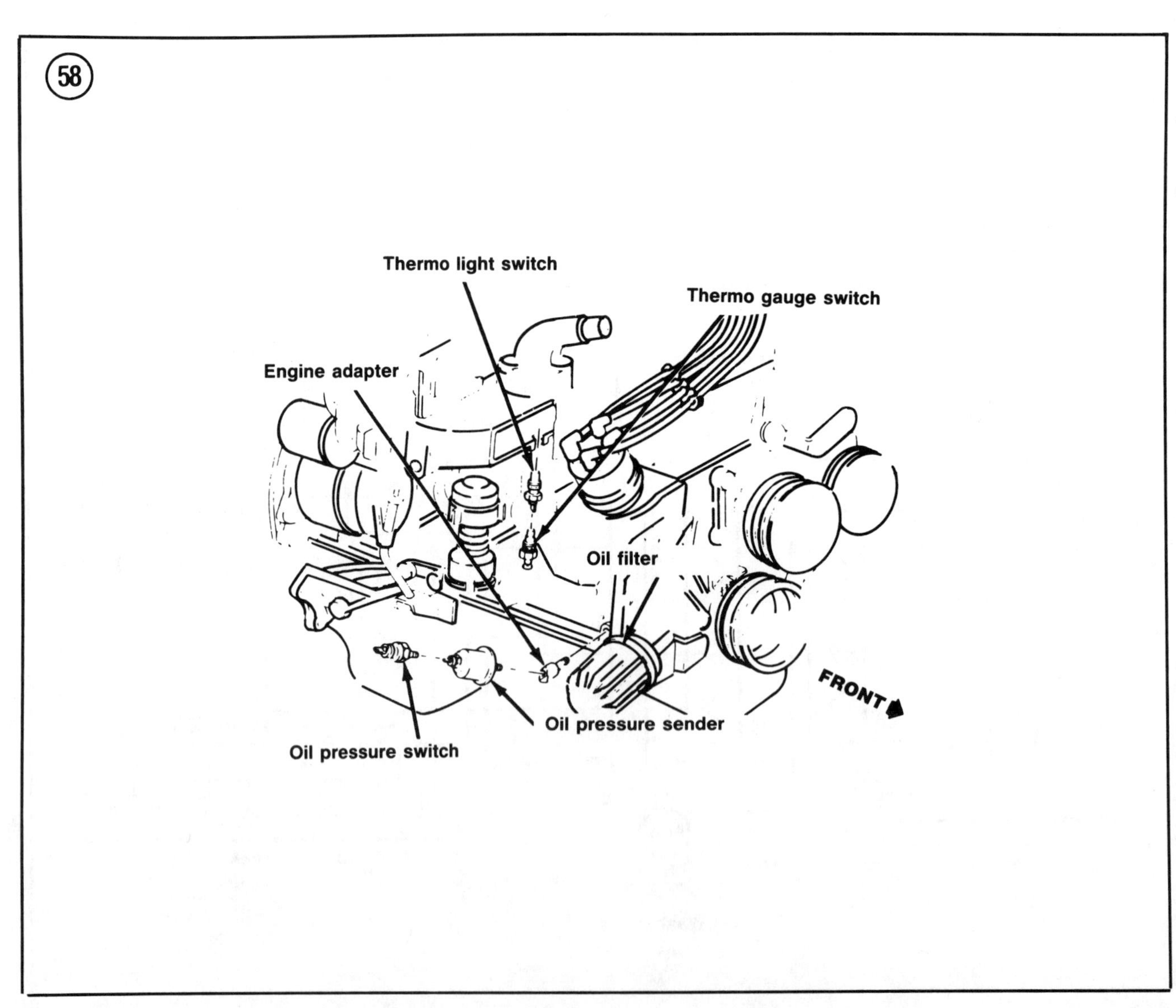

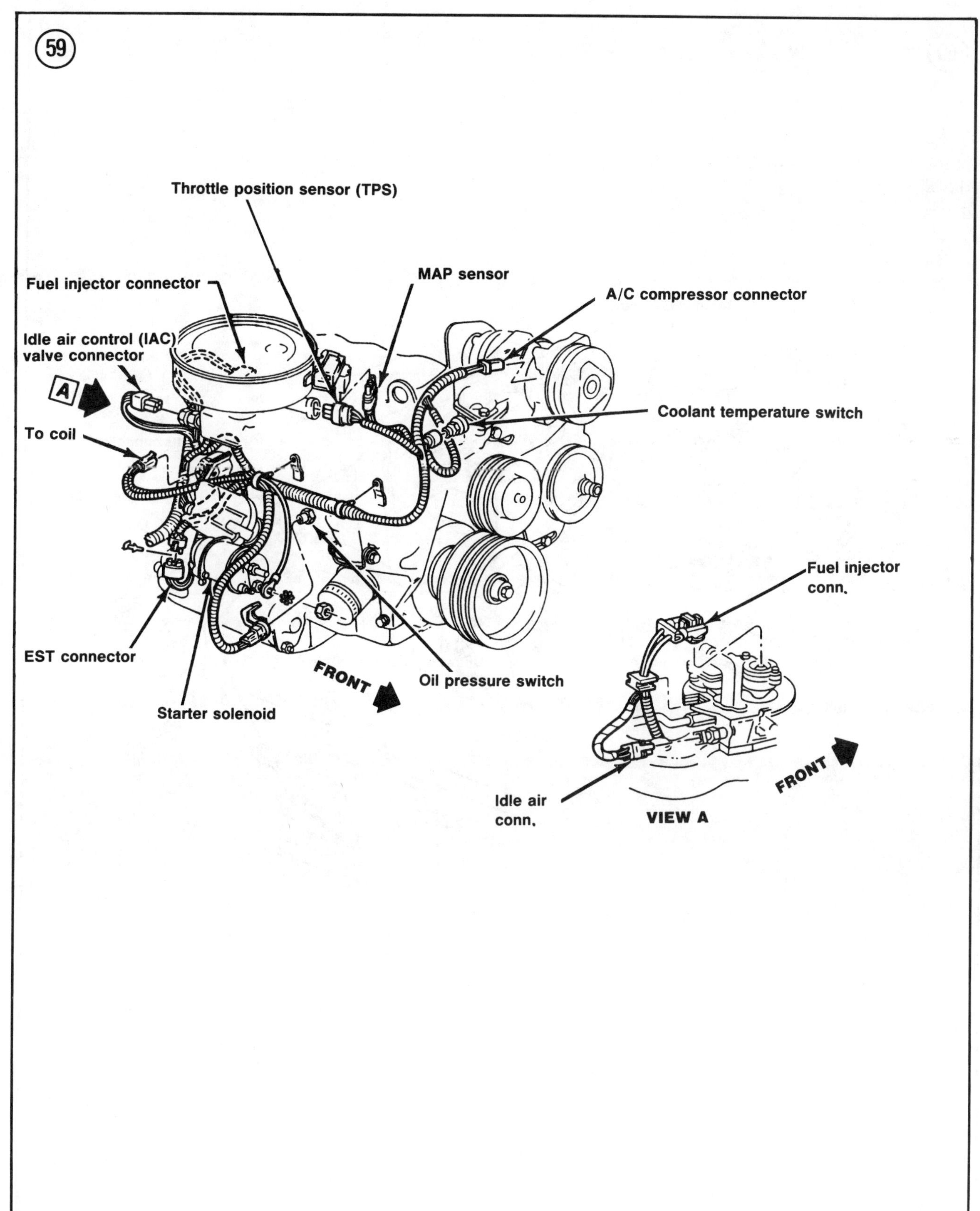
59
Throttle position sensor (TPS)
Fuel injector connector
MAP sensor
A/C compressor connector
Idle air control (IAC) valve connector
A
To coil
Coolant temperature switch
EST connector
FRONT
Oil pressure switch
Starter solenoid
Fuel injector conn.
Idle air conn.
VIEW A
FRONT

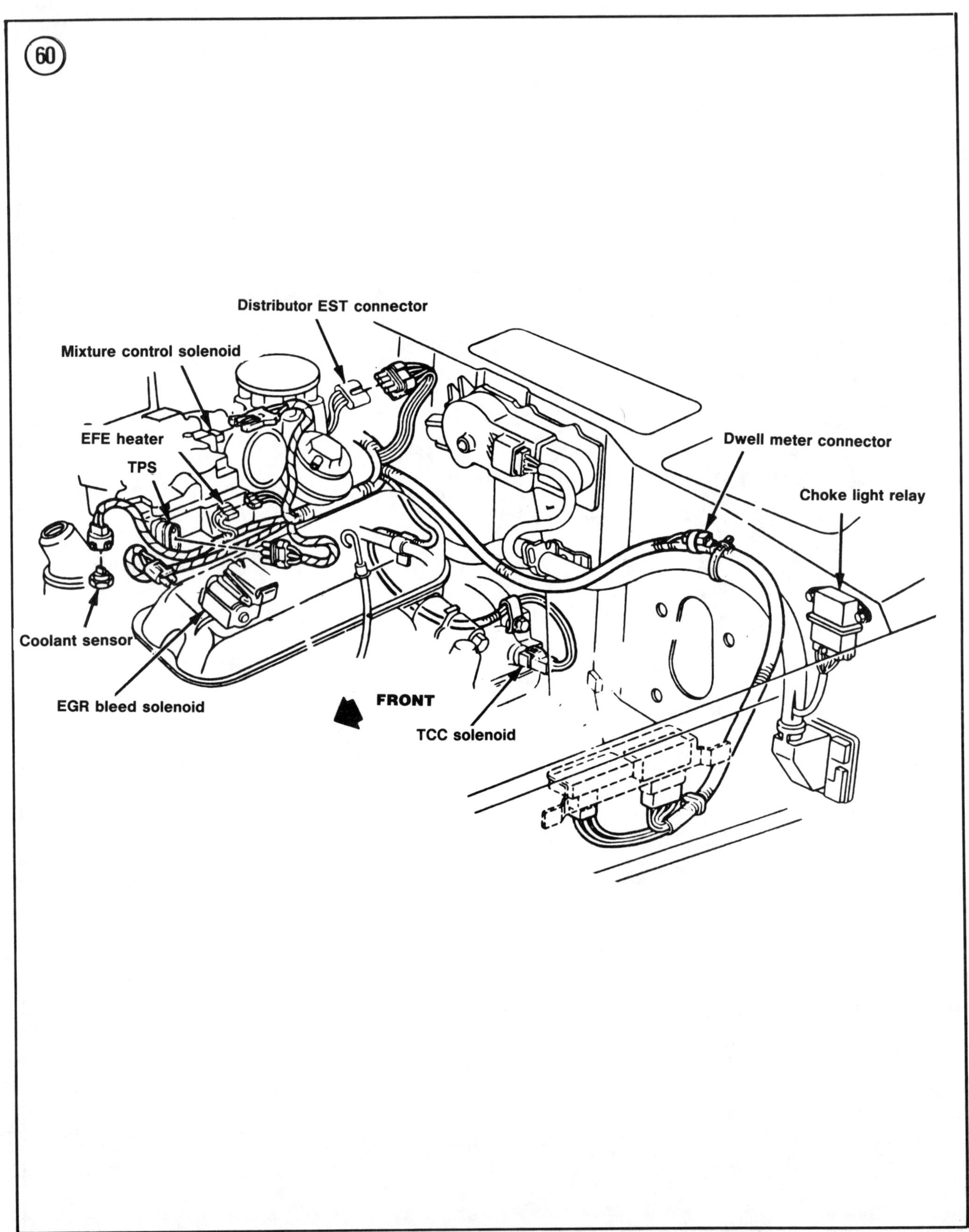
60
Distributor EST connector
Mixture control solenoid
EFE heater
TPS
Dwell meter connector
Choke light relay
Coolant sensor
EGR bleed solenoid
FRONT
TCC solenoid

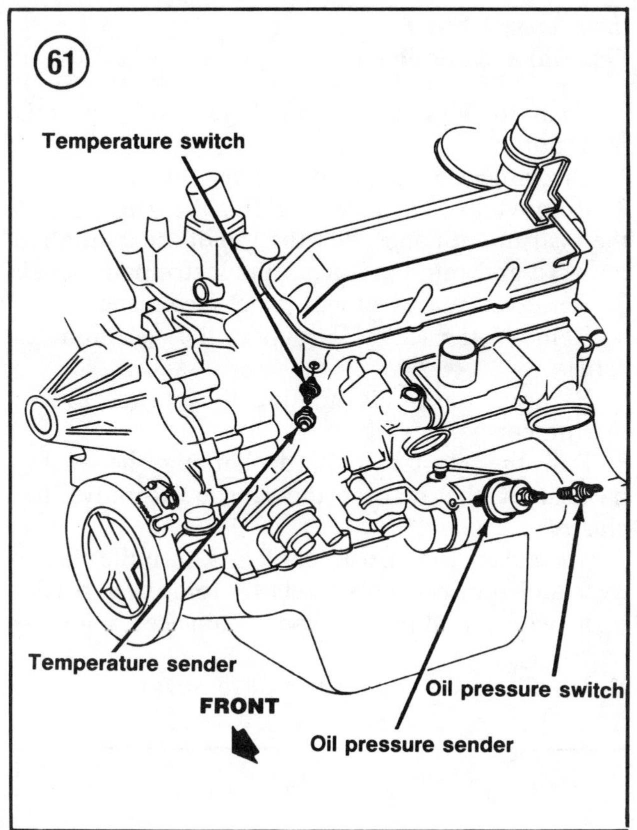

ELECTRIC CHOKE HEATER/ OIL PRESSURE SWITCH

A 2-terminal switch is used on carburetted engines with an oil pressure indicator light; a single terminal switch is used on all other engines. One circuit in the switch controls current flow to the electric choke heater; the other circuit operates the oil pressure warning light on the instrument panel in case of oil pressure loss. **Figure 62** is a schematic of the switch wiring.

Vehicles equipped wih an oil pressure gauge use a variable resistance sender unit.

Switch or sender unit location on gasoline engines is shown in **Figure 58** (1.9L), **Figure 63** (2.0L/2.5L) or **Figure 61** (V6). The switch/sender unit on diesel engines is installed in the block just in front of the oil filter adapter housing.

Testing

The oil pressure sending unit fitted to diesel engines and those gasoline-powered vehicles with an oil pressure gauge requires special equipment not commonly available to the home mechanic. Have the sending unit on such vehicles tested by a GM dealer.

8

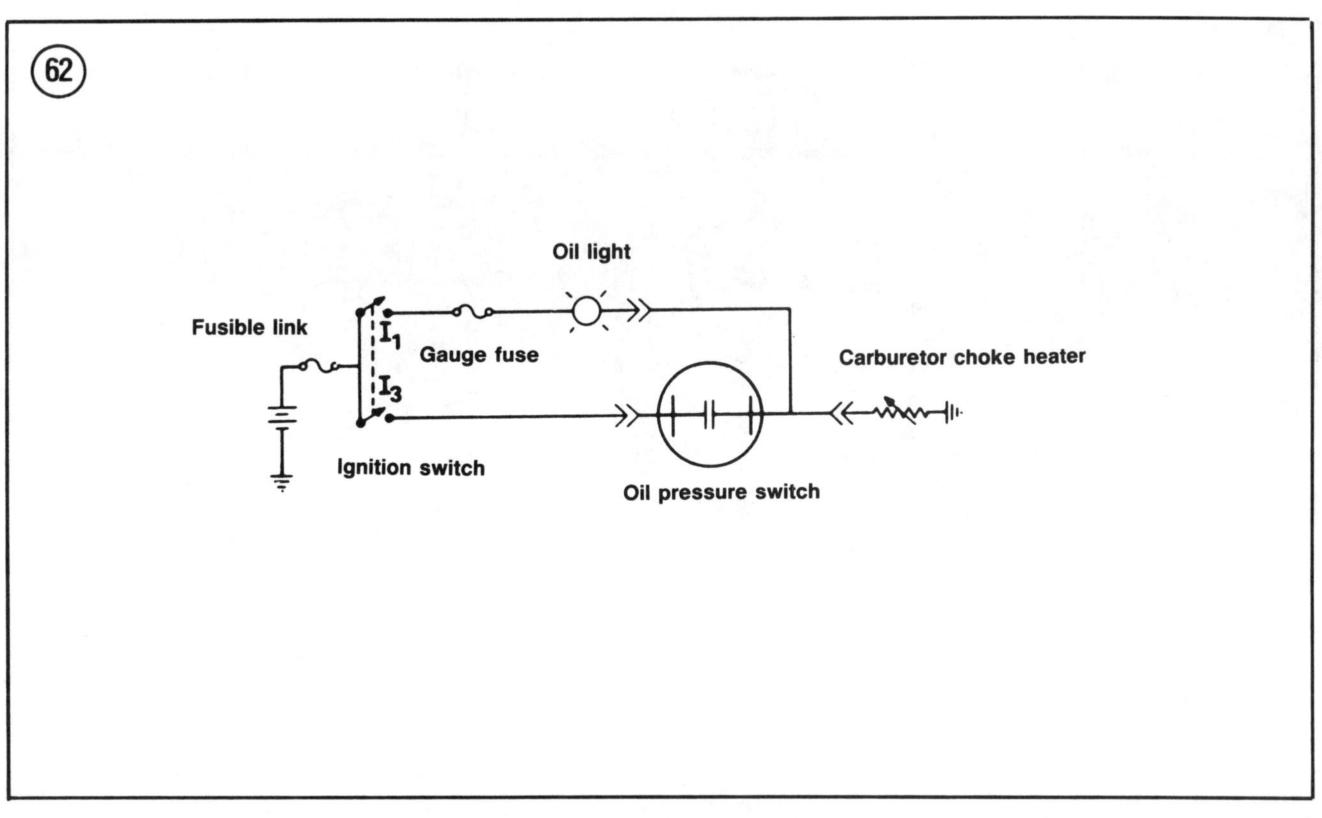

To test the switch used on non-diesel vehicles with an indicator light, turn the ignition switch ON but do not start the engine. The indicator light should come on. If it does not, disconnect the wire at the switch terminal and ground it with a jumper lead. If the indicator light comes on, replace the switch. If the light does not come on, check for a burned-out indicator bulb or an open circuit between the bulb and switch.

INSTRUMENTS

Current is supplied to the instrument cluster gauges and lamps by a printed circuit. This is made of copper foil bonded to a polyester base such as Mylar. There is no approved procedure for in-vehicle testing of the printed circuit. Using a probe may pierce the printed circuit or burn the copper conductor. If no damage seems apparent, check each circuit with a test light or ohmmeter. If an open or short circuit is found, replace the printed circuit board.

Instrument Cluster Removal/Installation

Refer to **Figure 64** and **Figure 65** for this procedure.

1. Disconnect the negative battery cable.
2. Remove the 5 fasteners holding the trim plate to the instrument panel. Pull the top of the trim plate outward and remove it from the instrument panel.
3. Remove the instrument panel face plate.
4. Remove the lens. Disconnect the speedometer cable.
5. Remove the studs holding the cluster to the instrument panel.
6. Pull the cluster forward. Unplug the wiring harness at the rear of the cluster. Remove the cluster.
7. To replace the instrument lights, turn the cluster over and remove the sockets by rotating a partial turn while pulling outward. Replace bulbs as necessary.
8. Installation is the reverse of removal.

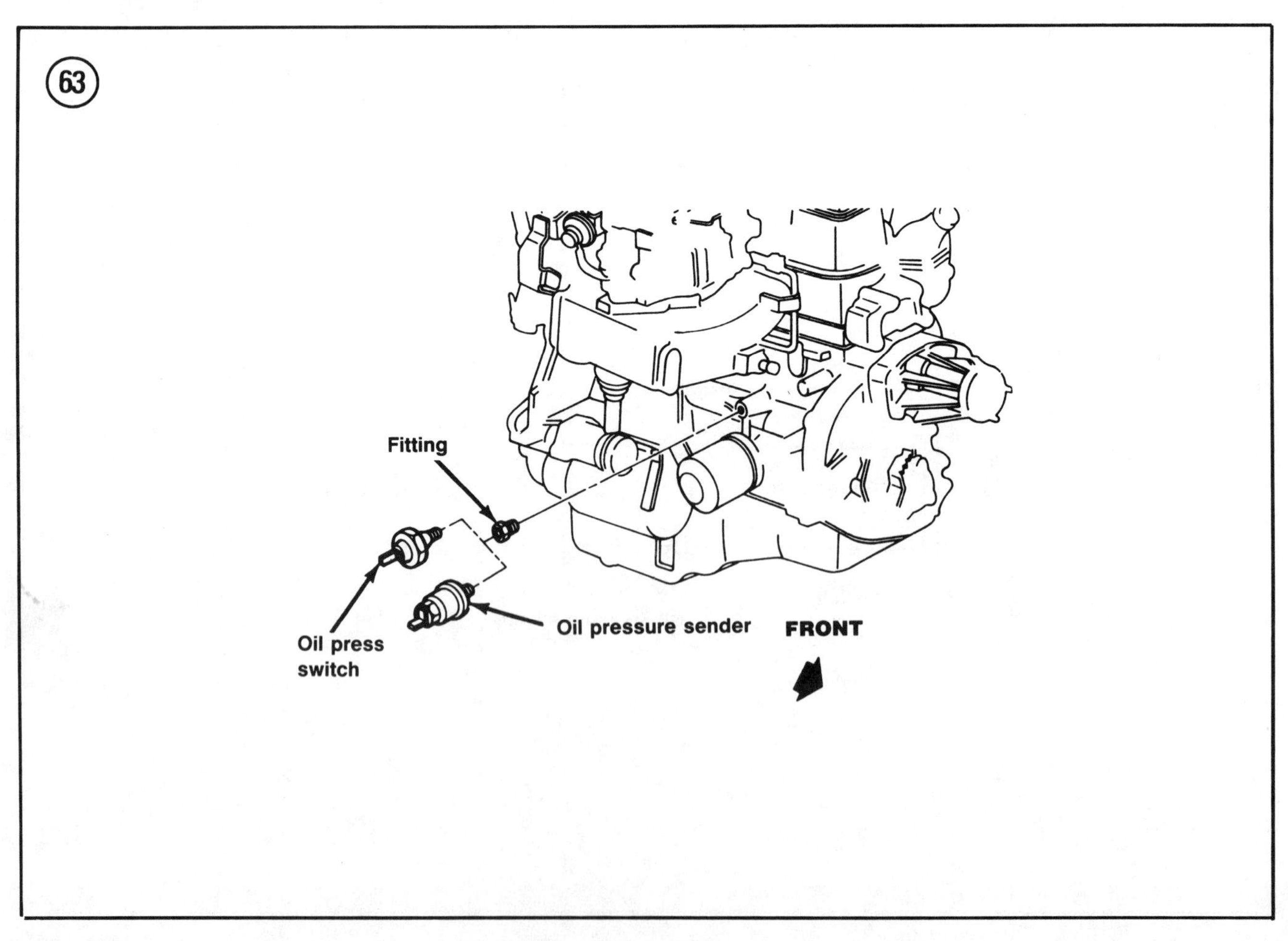

64

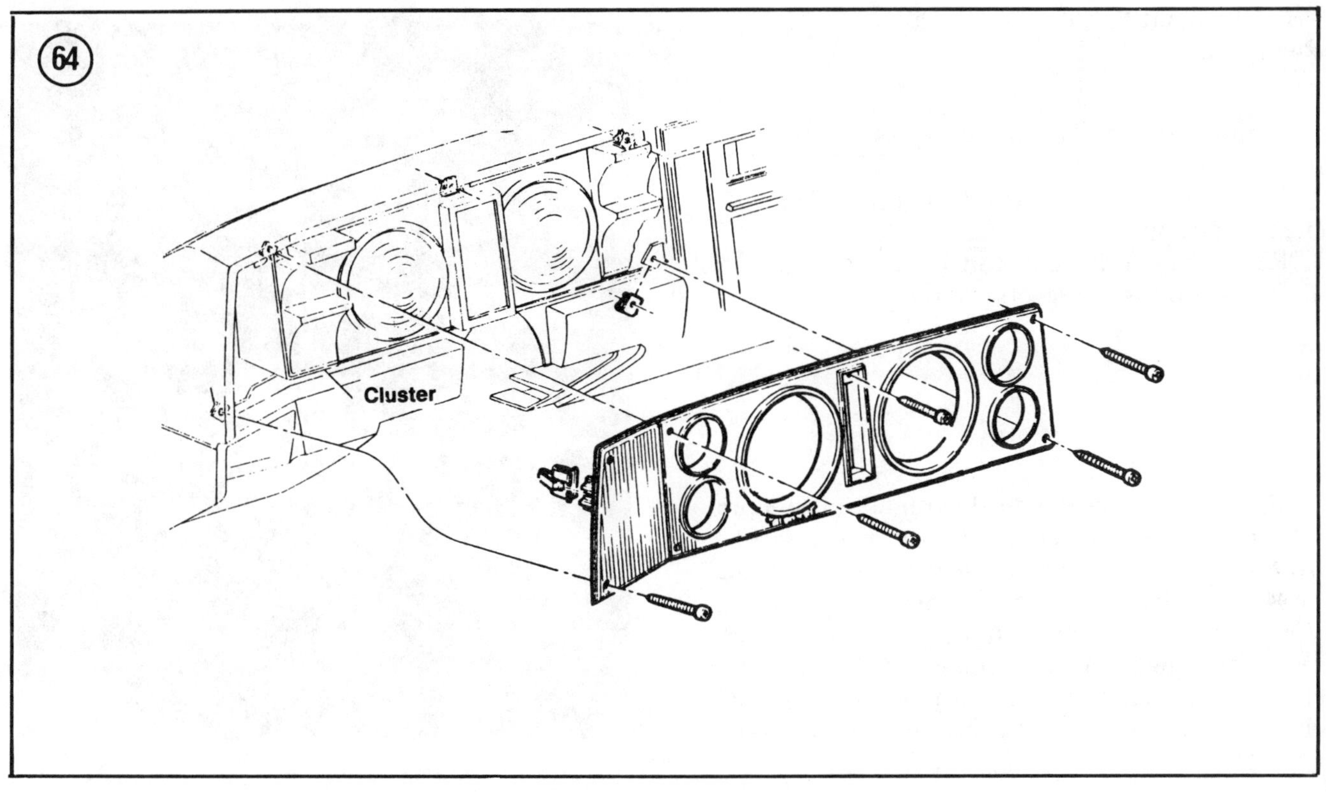

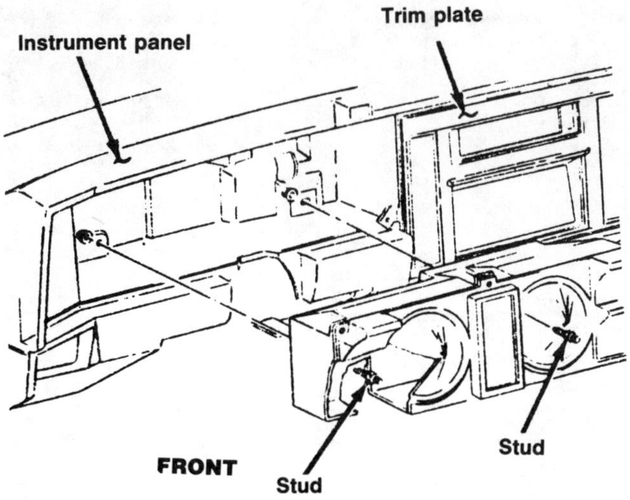

Cluster

65

Instrument panel
Trim plate
FRONT
Stud
Stud

8

Printed Circuit Board Replacement

1. Remove the instrument cluster as described in this chapter.
2. Remove all bulbs and retaining nuts from the cluster housing.
3. Remove the printed circuit.
4. Installation is the reverse of removal.

HORN

All vehicles are equipped with a single horn system. The horn is mounted on a bracket at the front of the engine compartment to the left of the fresh air intake duct. See **Figure 66** (typical). Voltage is applied to the horn relay at all times. Depressing the horn pad grounds the relay coil and closes its contacts. If the horn does not sound, check the 20-amp fuse in the fuse block cavity

66

67

marked HORN, then check the horn mounting screw. The screw provides a ground for the horn circuit. If corroded or loose, clean or tighten as required.

Testing

1. Ground the horn relay coil. The relay is located in the convenience center on the left-hand side of the dash panel near the fuse block.
2. If the horn sounds, disconnect the black relay lead. If the horn stops sounding with the lead disconnected, the horn switch is faulty. If the horn continues to sound, isolate the relay from the circuit.
3. Use a self-powered test lamp and check to see if the relay contacts are open. If they are, look for a short in the black wire. If they are not open, replace the relay.

Replacement

1. Disconnect the horn wire from the horn terminal.
2. Remove the horn bracket bolts.
3. Remove the horn and bracket from the engine compartment.
4. Remove the horn from the bracket.
5. Installation is the reverse of removal.

WINDSHIELD WIPERS AND WASHERS

The wiper system uses a 2-speed, positive park PM (permanent magnet) motor mounted in the center of the bulkhead. See **Figure 67** (typical). The motor housing is aluminum with a plastic cover. The wiper arms and blades park above the windshield lower molding. The washer reservoir (**Figure 68**) contains the pump and operates only when the wiper/washer lever is held in.

NOTE

The wiper motor uses locking-type connectors. Disconnect these carefully when motor testing or replacement is necessary.

Wiper Troubleshooting

1. If the wipers do not work, check the 20 amp fuse in the fuse block cavity marked "WIPERS." See *Electrical Circuit Protection* in this chapter.
2. If the wipers do not work with a good fuse, connect a jumper lead from the wiper motor housing to the vehicle body and test for ground. Ground is supplied by a ground strap and the

attaching screws. Check the screws and strap for a loose connection or corrosion. Clean or tighten as necessary.

3. If the wipers still do not work, check wiper switch continuity as described in this chapter.

4. If switch continuity is good, the problem is either a defective motor or an open circuit in the wiring.

Wiper Motor Current Draw Test

1. Remove the 20 amp fuse from the fuse block cavity marked "WIPERS." Connect an ammeter across the fuse cavity terminals.

2. Turn the ignition switch ON. Cover the windshield with newspapers to prevent damage to the glass, then run the wipers in high speed with the windshield dry. The normal current draw will fluctuate but not exceed 5 amps:

a. A current draw of less than 5 amps indicates that the internal circuit breaker is bad or that the brushes are bad.

b. A current draw in excess of 5 amps indicates binding linkage or a shorted or grounded armature. Disconnect the linkage and repeat the procedure. If the current draw is within specifications, correct the linkage binding. If current draw is still excessive, replace the motor.

Wiper Parking Test

Refer to **Figure 69** for this procedure.

1. Unplug the wire harness at the motor.

2. Connect a jumper lead between terminal No. 2 or C and terminal No. 3 or B. Connect a jumper lead between terminal No. 4 or A and the positive battery post. If the wipers do not work or do not park properly when the switch is turned ON, replace the motor.

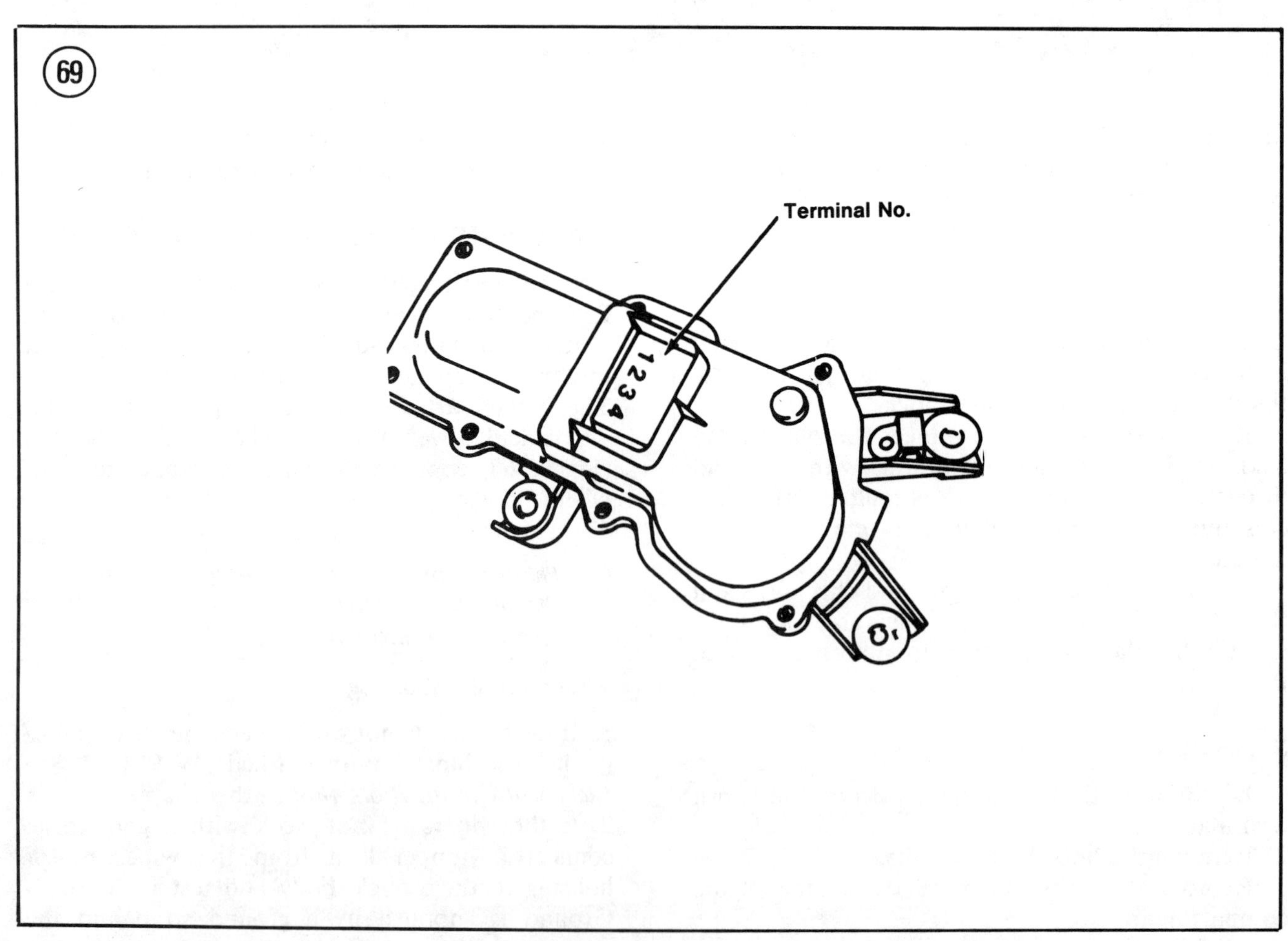

3. If the wipers operate and park properly, turn the wiper switch OFF. Disconnect the negative battery cable and check for continuity between terminal No. 2 or C and terminal No. 3 or B in the harness connector. Continuity indicates an open in the terminal No. 4 or A-to-fuse block circuit. If there is no continuity, look for an open in the circuit between terminal No. 3 or B and the wiper switch. If no open is found, replace the wiper switch.

Pulse Wiper Module Replacement

Refer to **Figure 70** for this procedure.

The pulse wiper module is mounted above the fuse block inner edge and is grounded by a screw to the steering column support outer leg. Disconnect the electrical connector, remove the ground screw and remove the module from its retainer.

Wiper Motor Replacement

CAUTION
The wiper motor contains ceramic permanent magnets. Handle the motor carefully and do not tap with a hammer or the magnets may be damaged.

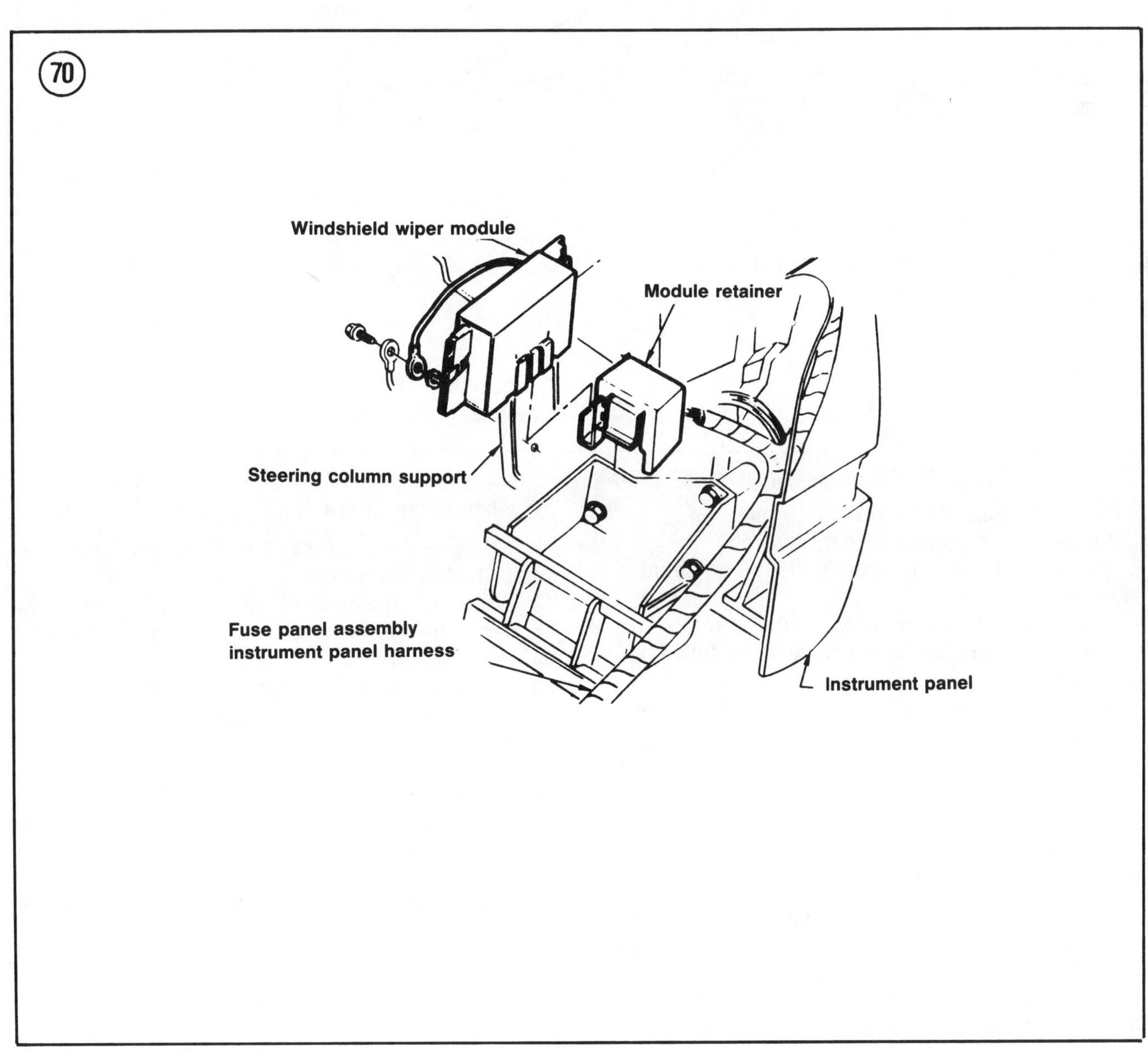

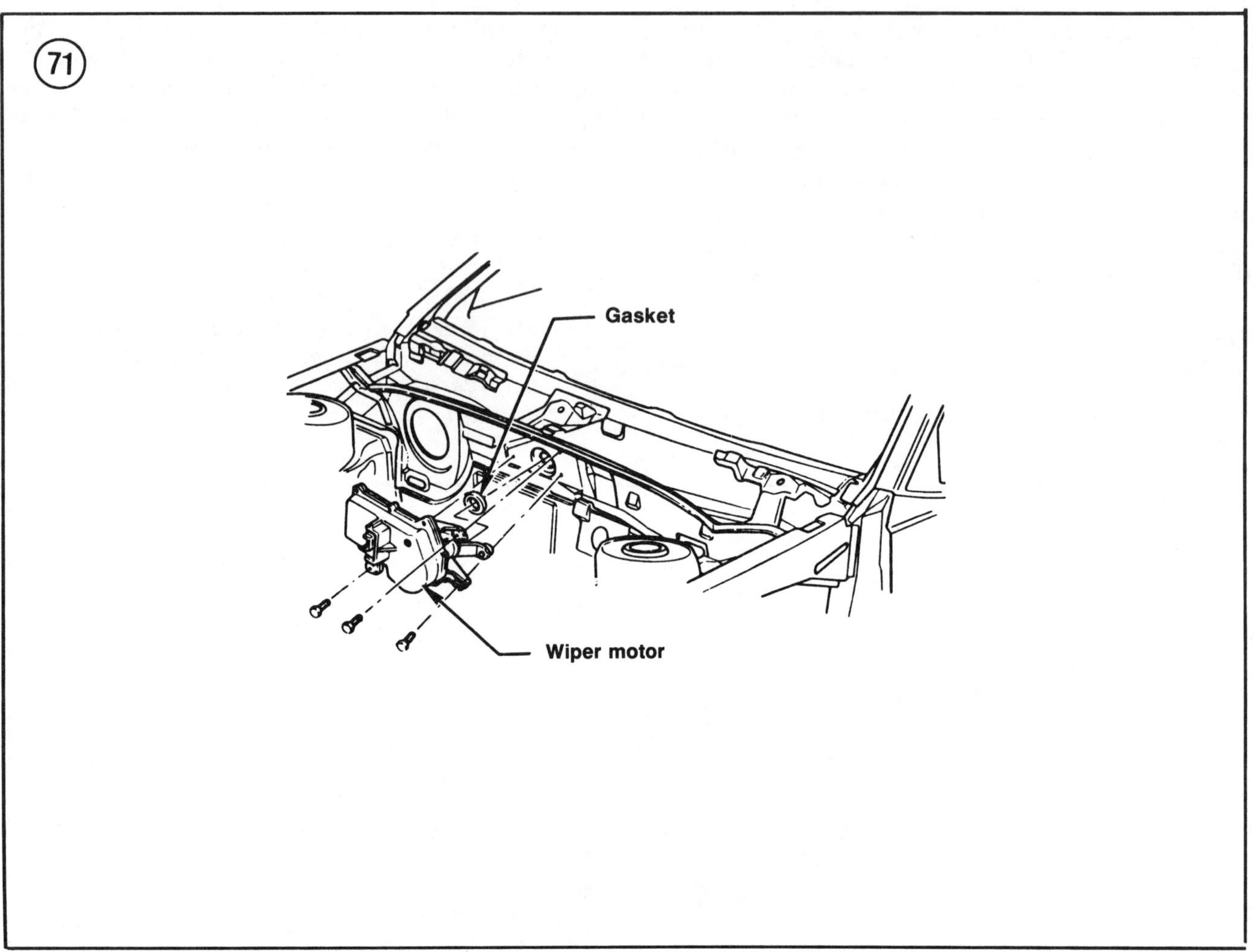

Refer to **Figure 71** for this procedure.

1. Disconnect the negative battery cable.
2. Remove the cowl vent grille. See Chapter Thirteen.
3. Loosen but do not remove the drive link to the motor crank arm nuts. Separate the drive link from the crank arm.
4. Remove the motor attaching screws and remove the motor.
5. Installation is the reverse of removal. Tighten the attaching screws to 51-73 in.-lb. (4.5-6.5 N•m).

Front Washer Pump and Reservoir Replacement

Figure 68 shows the front washer pump and reservoir assembly. To remove, disconnect the lock-tab connector and fluid hose. Remove the 2 retaining screws and lift the assembly from the fenderwell. Installation is the reverse of removal.

Washer Pump Motor Replacement

1. Remove the reservoir tank from the vehicle as described in this chapter.
2. Note the position of the pump motor. The replacement motor should be installed in the same position (**Figure 72**).
3. Insert a 7/8 in. (22 mm) socket and extension through the reservoir filler opening. Remove the pump motor.
4. Clean the reservoir before installing the new pump motor.
5. Installation is the reverse of removal. Tighten the retaining nut/screen assembly to 15-20 in.-lb. (1.8-3.6 N•m).
6. Install the reservoir assembly in the vehicle, fill with windshield washer fluid and check for leaks.

CAUTION

Do not operate the washer pump without fluid in the reservoir.

8

ELECTRICAL CIRCUIT PROTECTION

Electrical circuits are protected by a variety of devices: fuses, circuit breakers and fusible links. In addition, a convenience center located near the fuse block contains the headlight warning buzzer, horn relay and hazard flasher.

Fuses

A fuse is a "safety valve" installed in an electrical circuit which "blows" (opens) the circuit when excessive current flows through the circuit. This protects the circuit and electrical components such as the alternator from damage.

The fuse block is mounted on the bulkhead under the instrument panel to the left of the steering column. Fuse and circuit breaker identification is shown in **Figure 73**.

All vehicles use mini-fuses. This flat design has 2 blades connected by a metal link encapsulated in plastic. When the fuse is installed, the end of each metal blade is exposed, allowing the fuse condition to be checked with test probes. The plastic is color-coded according to amperage value. Some colors make it difficult to determine whether the fuse is good or bad. **Figure 74** shows the difference between a good and a blown mini-fuse.

Whenever a failure occurs in any part of the electrical system, always check the fuse first to see if it is blown. Usually, the trouble is a short circuit in the wiring. This may be caused by worn-through insulation or by a wire that has worked its way loose and shorted to ground. Occasionally, the electrical overload which causes a fuse to blow may occur in a switch or motor.

A blown fuse should be treated as more than a minor annoyance; it should serve as a warning that something is wrong in the electrical system. Before replacing a fuse, determine what caused it to blow and correct the problem. Always carry several spare fuses of the proper amperage values in the glovebox. Never replace a fuse with one of higher amperage rating than that specified for use. Failure to follow these basic rules could result in heat or fire damage to major parts or loss of the entire vehicle.

Fuse Replacement

To replace a mini-fuse, grasp the plastic covered top and pull the fuse from the fuse block. Insert a

73

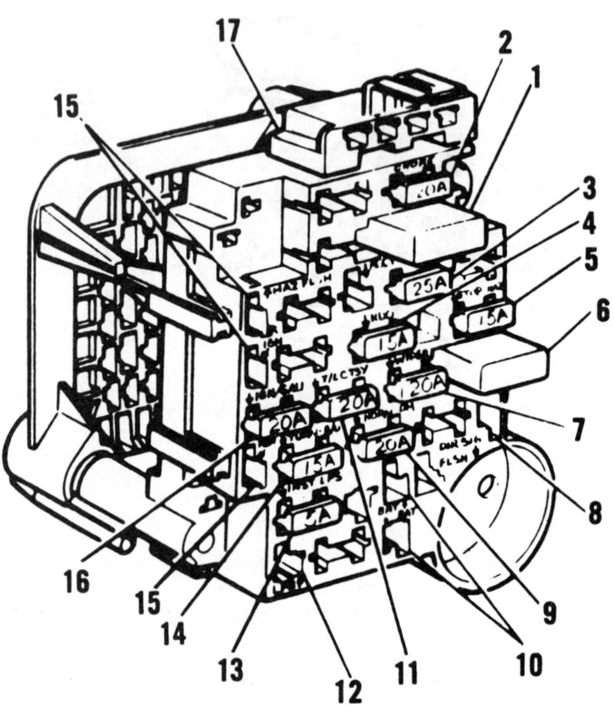

1. Circuit breaker
2. Fuse—choke
3. Fuse—heater or air conditioning
4. Fuse—radio
5. Fuse—stop, hazard lamps
6. Power accessory
7. Fuse—windshield wiper
8. Receptacle—power door locks
9. Fuse—horn
10. Receptacle—clock, courtesy lamp, dome lamp, instrument panel & headlamp warning
11. Fuse-tail & courtesy lamps
12. Receptacle—headlamp on warning
13. Fuse—instrument panel lamps
14. Fuse—turn & back-up lamps
15. Receptacle—cruise control & auto transmission
16. Fuse—ignition & gauges
17. Connector—seat belt warning buzzer & timer

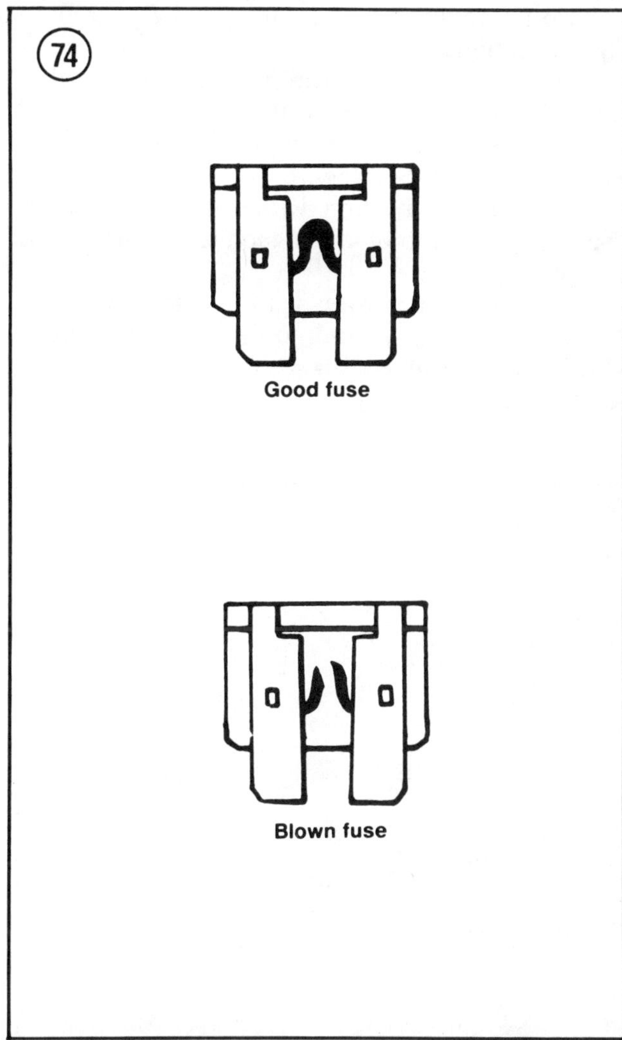

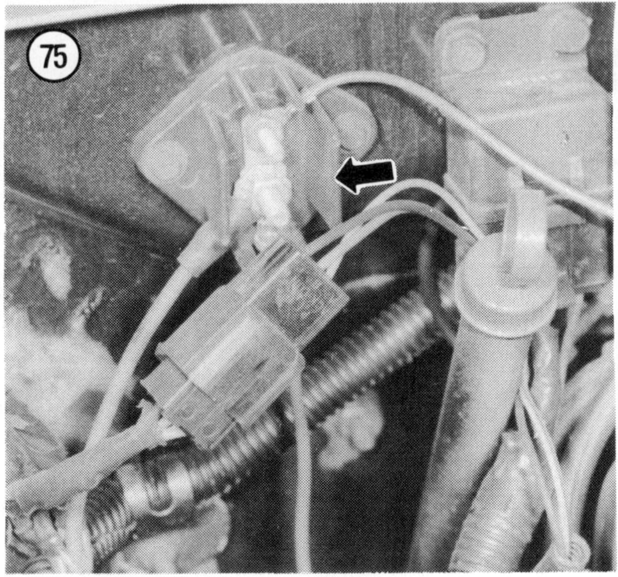

new one of the same amperage value (color) in its place.

Circuit Breakers

Some circuits are protected by circuit breakers. These may be mounted in the fuse block, installed in the circuit itself or located within the switch assembly. A circuit breaker conducts current through an arm made of 2 different types of metal connected together. If too much current passes through this bimetal arm, it heats up and expands. One metal expands faster than the other, causing the arm to move and open the contacts to break the current flow. As the arm cools down, the metal contracts and the arm closes the contacts, allowing current to pass. Cycling inline circuit breakers will repeat this sequence as long as power is applied or until the condition is corrected. Non-cycling circuit breakers use a coil around the bimetal arm to hold it in an open position until power is shut off or the condition is corrected.

8

Fusible Links

Fusible links are different than fuses. A fusible link is a short length of wire several gauges smaller than the circuit it protects. It is covered with a thick non-flammable insulation and is intended to burn out if an overload occurs, thus protecting the wiring harness and circuit components. All models use 3 fusible links. A 14-gauge red wire/molded splice is installed at the starter solenoid BAT terminal. A 16-gauge red wire is installed at the junction block (**Figure 75**) to protect all unfused 12-gauge or larger wiring. A 20-gauge red wire/molded splice installed at the junction block (**Figure 75**) protects the alternator warning light and field circuitry.

CAUTION
Always replace a burned fusible link with a replacement bearing the same color code or wire gauge. Never use ordinary wire, as this can cause an overload, an electrical fire and complete loss of the vehicle.

Burned-out fusible links can usually be detected by melted or burned insulation. When the link appears to be good but the starter does not work, check the circuit for continuity with an ohmmeter or self-powered test lamp.

Fusible Link Replacement

1. Obtain the proper service fusible link. Make sure the replacement link is a duplicate of the one removed in terms of wire gauge, length and insulation. .Do not substitute any other type or gauge of wire.
2. Disconnect the negative battery cable.
3. Disconnect the fusible link and/or eyelet terminal from the component to which it is attached.
4. Cut the harness behind the connector (**Figure 76**) to remove the damaged fusible link.
5. Strip approximately 1/2 inch from the harness wire insulation.
6. Install a connector on the end of the new fusible link. Fit the other end of the connector on the harness wire and crimp so that both wires are securely fastened. See **Figure 77**.
7. Solder the connection with rosin core solder. Use enough heat to obtain a good joint, but do not overheat.
8. Wrap all exposed wires with insulating tape.
9. Connect the fusible link to the component from which it was removed.
10. Reconnect the negative battery cable.

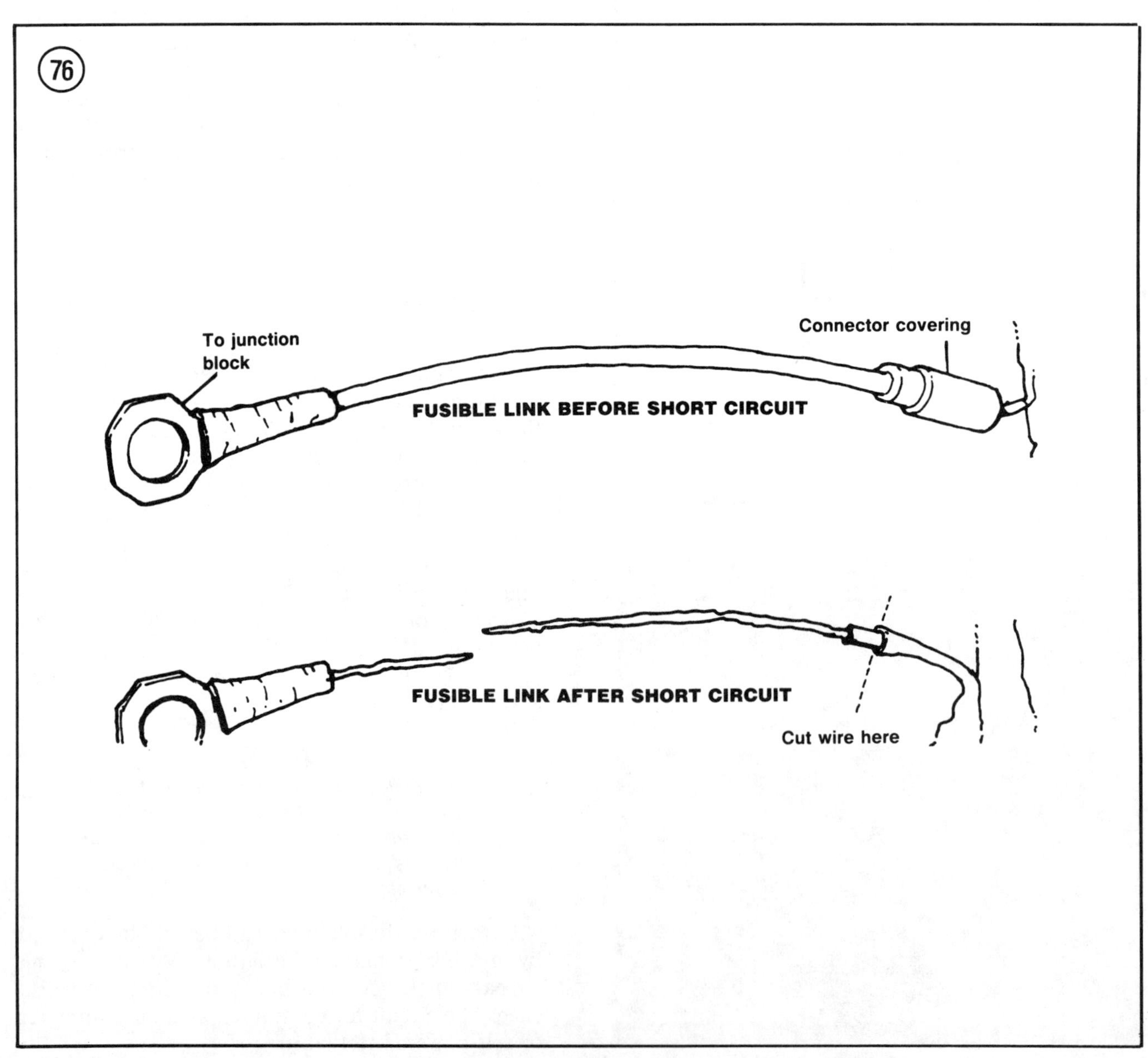

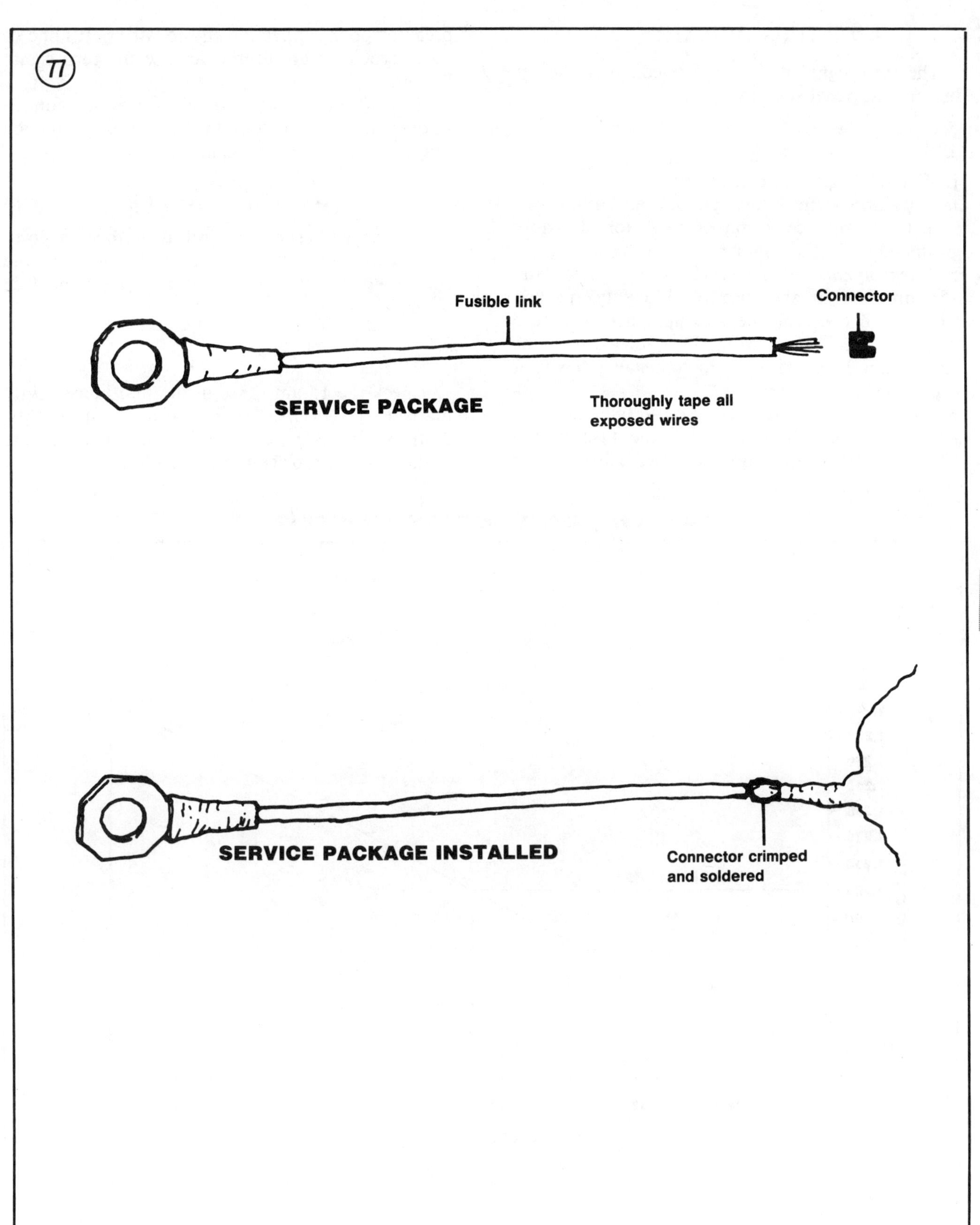
77
Fusible link
Connector
SERVICE PACKAGE
Thoroughly tape all exposed wires
SERVICE PACKAGE INSTALLED
Connector crimped and soldered

TURN SIGNALS

The turn signal flasher is located on the lower instrument panel support.

Testing

1. *One side flashes later than the other, or only one side operates*—Check for a burned-out bulb. Clean socket of any corrosion. Check for a badly grounded bulb. Check for breaks in the wiring.
2. *Turn signals do not work at all*—Check the 15-amp fuse in the fuse block cavity marked "T/LPS" by operating the back-up lights. If the fuse is good, check the wiring for a break or poor connection. If the wiring is good, install a new turn signal flasher unit.
3. *Lights flash slowly or stay on*—Make sure the battery is fully charged. Check the fuse in the "T/LPS" cavity for a poor contact. Check for a break or poor connection in the wiring. If none of these problems are found, replace the turn signal flasher.
4. *Lights flash too quickly*—Check for a burned-out bulb or disconnected wire. If none are found, replace the turn signal flasher.

HAZARD FLASHER

The hazard flasher is identical in appearance to the turn signal flasher. It is located in the convenience center wiring harness near the fuse block.

Testing

1. Check the 15-amp fuse in the fuse block cavity marked "STOP/HAZ" by operating the stop lights.
2. If the fuse is good and the turn signals operate on both sides, replace the hazard flasher.

Table 1 OPEN CIRCUIT VOLTAGE (STATE OF CHARGE)

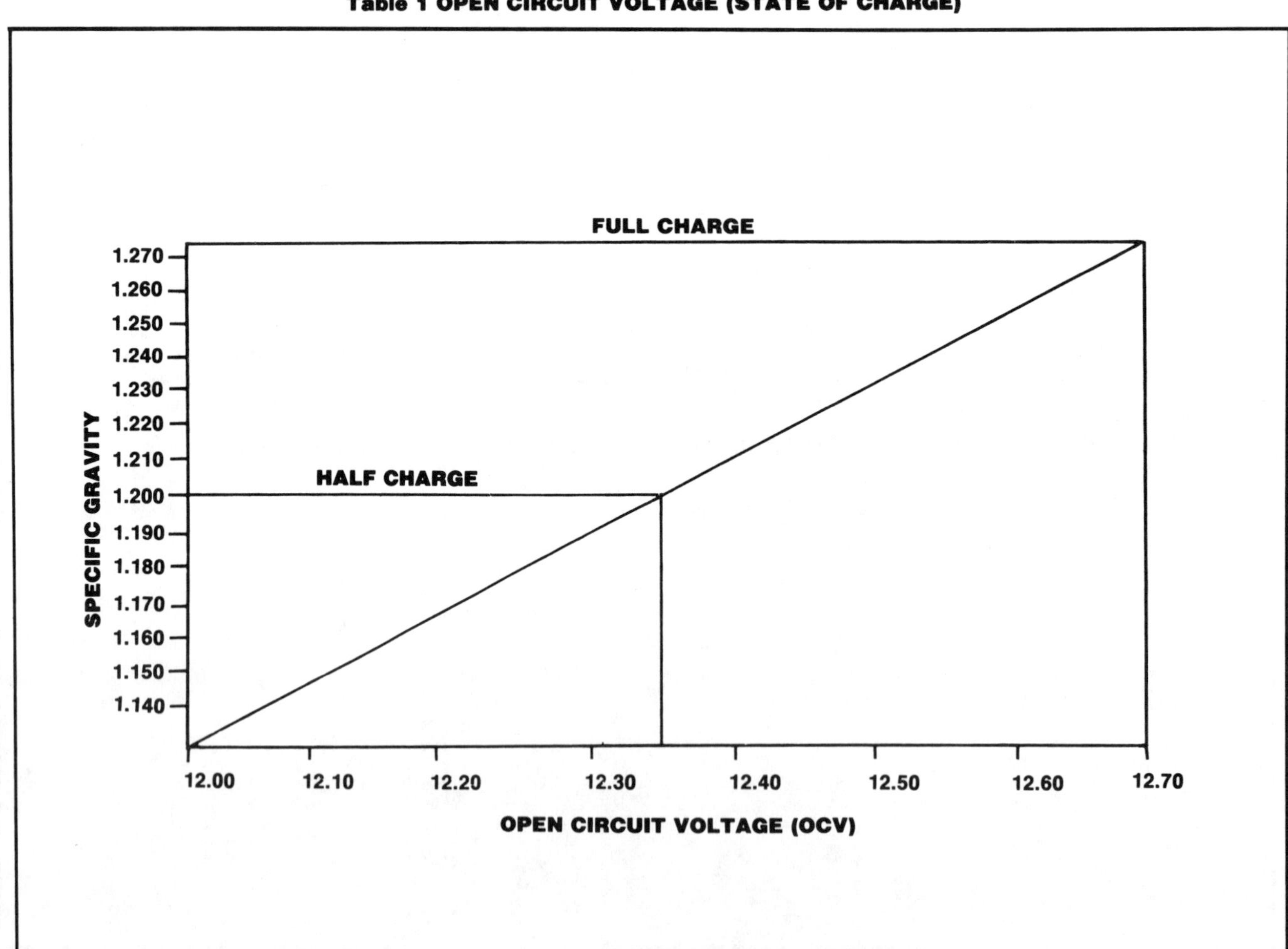

Table 2 BATTERY STATE OF CHARGE

Specific gravity 68°F (20°C)

1.280
1.260
1.240
1.220
1.200
1.180
1.160
1.140
1.120
1.100

10 20 30 40 50 60 70 80 90 100

BATTERY — State of charge (%)

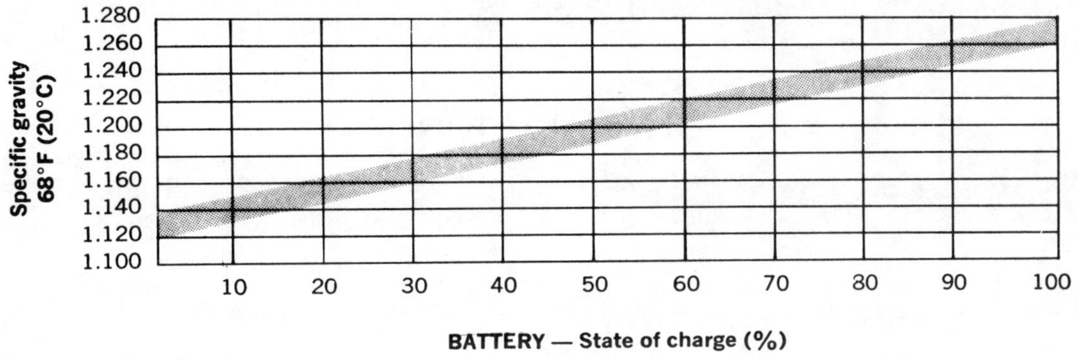

CHAPTER NINE

CLUTCH, TRANSMISSION AND TRANSFER CASE

The vehicles covered in this manual may be equipped with a 4-speed or 5-speed manual transmission. A 3-speed or 4-speed automatic transmission is optional.

Power is transmitted from the engine to the transmission, then to the differential or rear end where it is sent to the axle shafts which turn the wheel hubs. Manual transmissions are connected to the engine by the clutch; automatic transmissions are connected to the engine by a torque converter.

This chapter provides inspection, repair and replacement procedures for the clutch and manual transmission, as well as inspection and replacement procedures for the automatic transmission and transfer case.

Repair of the automatic transmission and transfer case requires special skills and tools and should be left to a dealer or other qualified shop. The inspection procedures will tell you if repairs are necessary. Tightening torques are provided in **Table 1** at the end of the chapter.

CLUTCH

Components

A mechanical clutch is used on 1982-1983 models; a hydraulic clutch system is used on 1984 and later models.

The major components of both clutch systems are the flywheel, driven plate or disc, pressure plate/cover assembly, clutch fork and clutch release bearing (**Figure 1**).

The mechanical clutch operating system consists of a release cable, clutch adjusting mechanism and pedal/bracket assembly (**Figure 2**). The hydraulic clutch operating system consists of the pedal/bracket assembly, fluid reservoir, master cylinder, slave cylinder and connecting tubing (**Figure 3**). An interlock switch prevents the starter from operating unless the clutch pedal is depressed.

Operation

The release cable transmits pedal pressure to the clutch release lever on a mechanical clutch. With a hydraulic clutch, the master cylinder changes

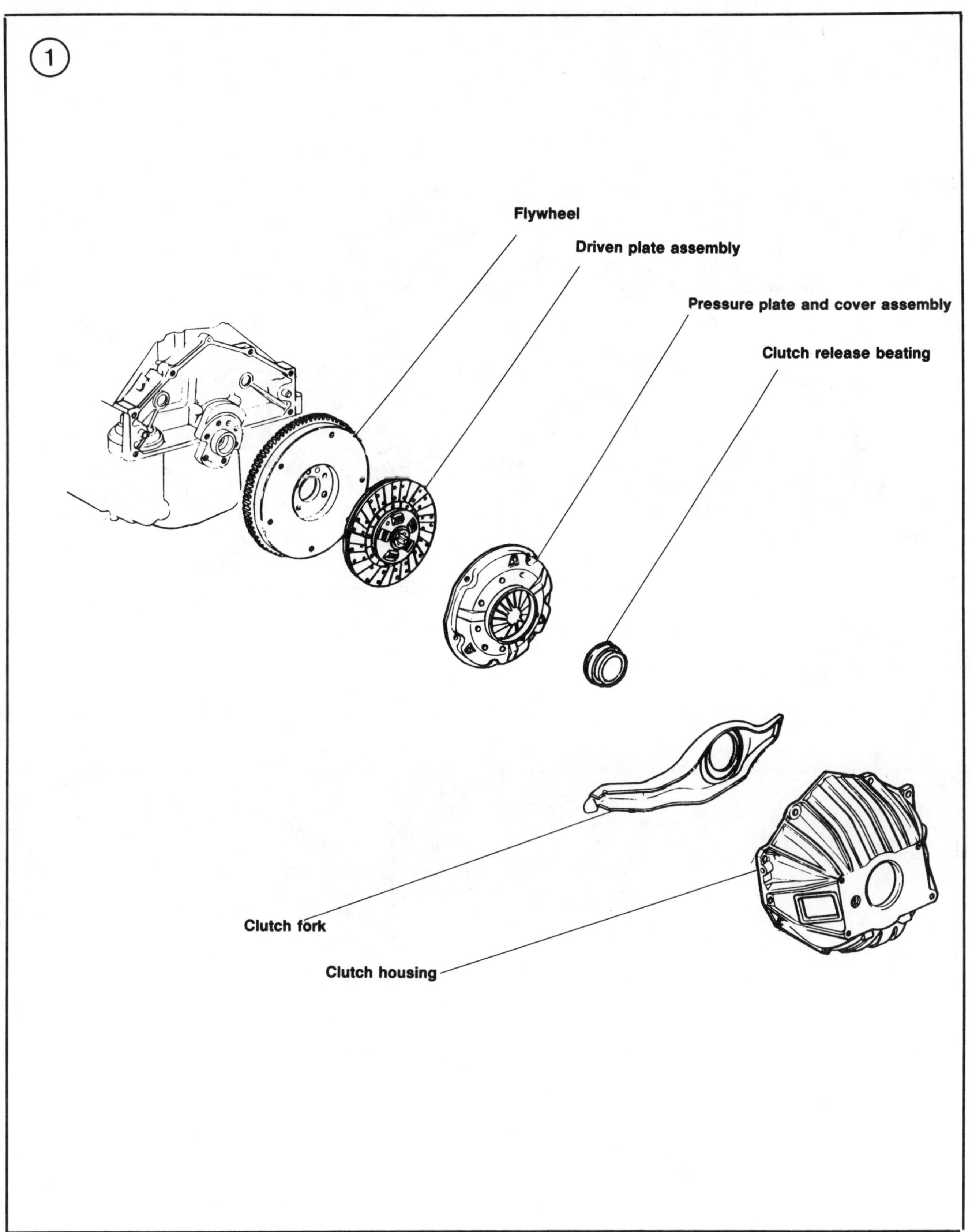
1
Flywheel
Driven plate assembly
Pressure plate and cover assembly
Clutch release beating
Clutch fork
Clutch housing

9

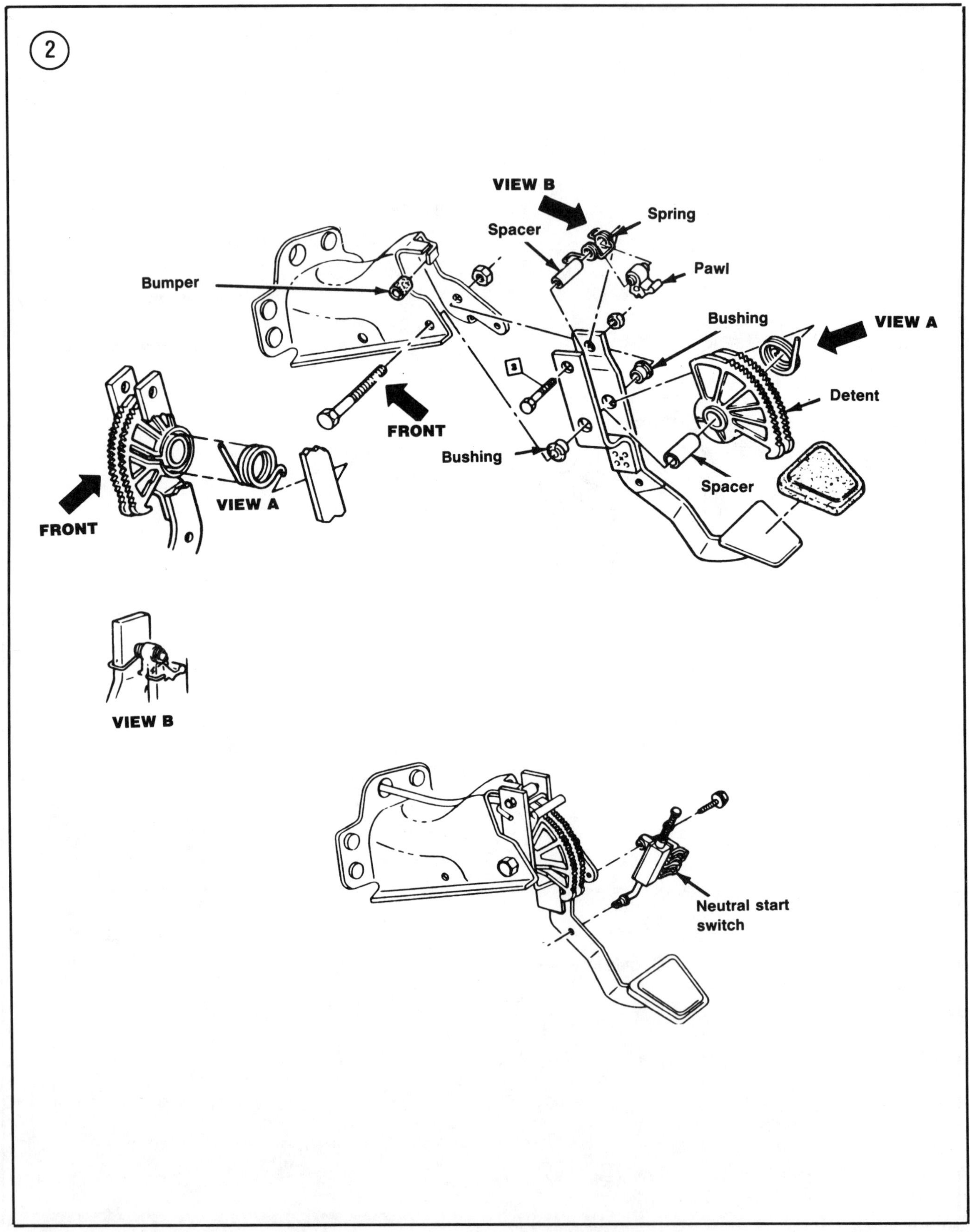
2
VIEW B
Spring
Spacer
Pawl
Bumper
Bushing
VIEW A
Detent
FRONT
Bushing
Spacer
VIEW A
FRONT
VIEW B
Neutral start switch

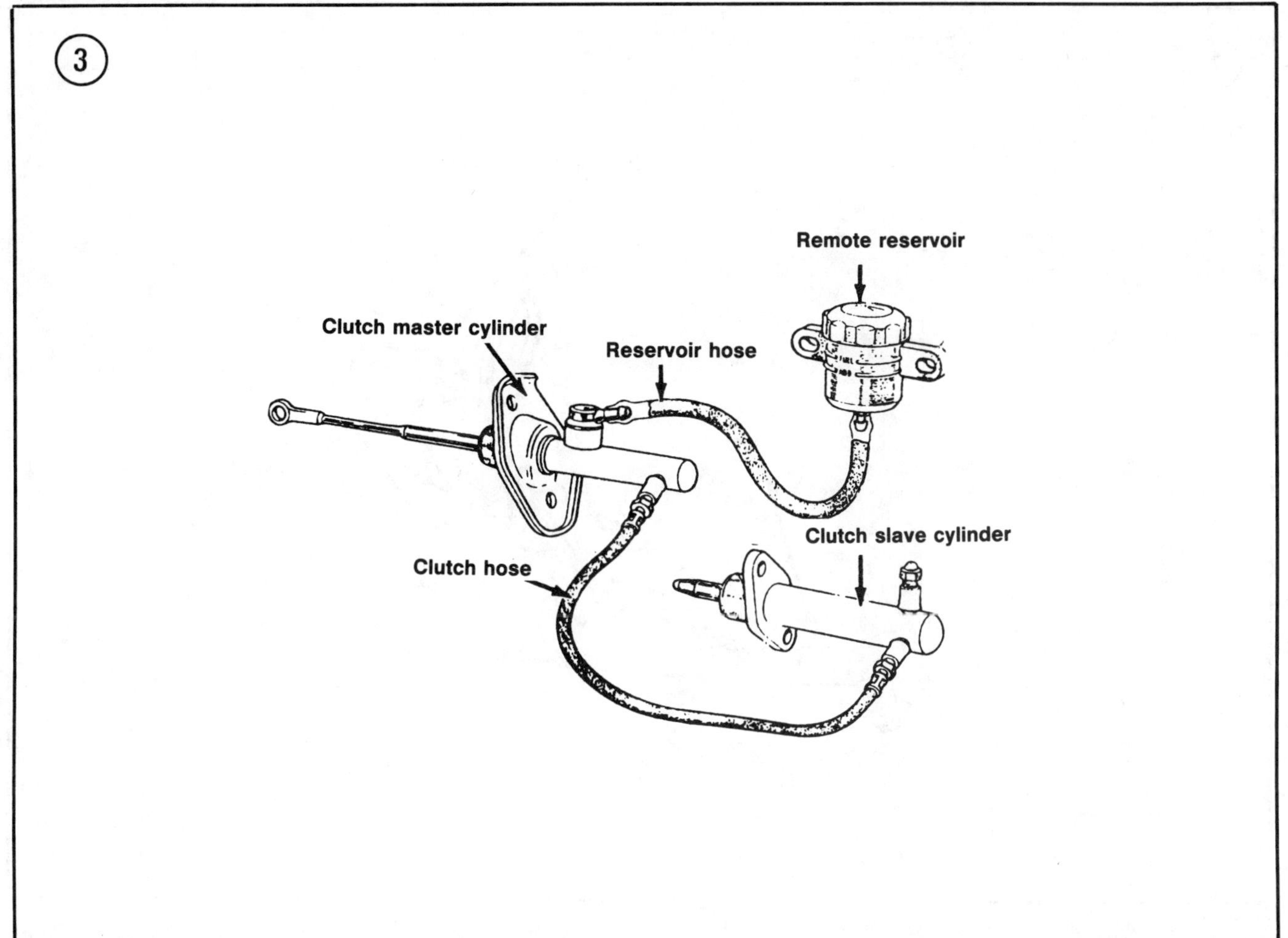

9

mechanical movement of the pedal into hydraulic fluid pressure. The slave cylinder mounted on the bellhousing changes the hydraulic pressure back to mechanical movement to operate the clutch release lever.

The remainder of the operational sequence is the same in both systems. As the clutch fork pivots on its shaft, the inner end pushes against the release bearing. The bearing in turn pushes against the release levers in the pressure plate/cover assembly, releasing the clutch.

The mechanical clutch release cable is connected to an adjusting detent mounted on the pedal/bracket assembly. Cable adjustment is required at 5,000 mile intervals.

The hydraulic clutch system locates the clutch pedal and provides automatic clutch adjustment. No routine service, beyond adding brake fluid to the clutch reservoir (Chapter Three), or adjustment of any kind is required or possible.

Parts Identification

Some clutch parts have 2 or more names. To prevent confusion, the following list gives part names used in this chapter and common synonyms.

a. Bellhousing—flywheel housing.
b. Clutch disc—driven plate.
c. Clutch fork—release fork, throw-out arm, withdrawal lever.
d. Clutch cover assembly—pressure plate, clutch cover, clutch plate.

NOTE
The clutch cover assembly is often referred to as the pressure plate or clutch cover. These items are 2 of the cover assembly's parts.

e. Release bearing—throw-out bearing.

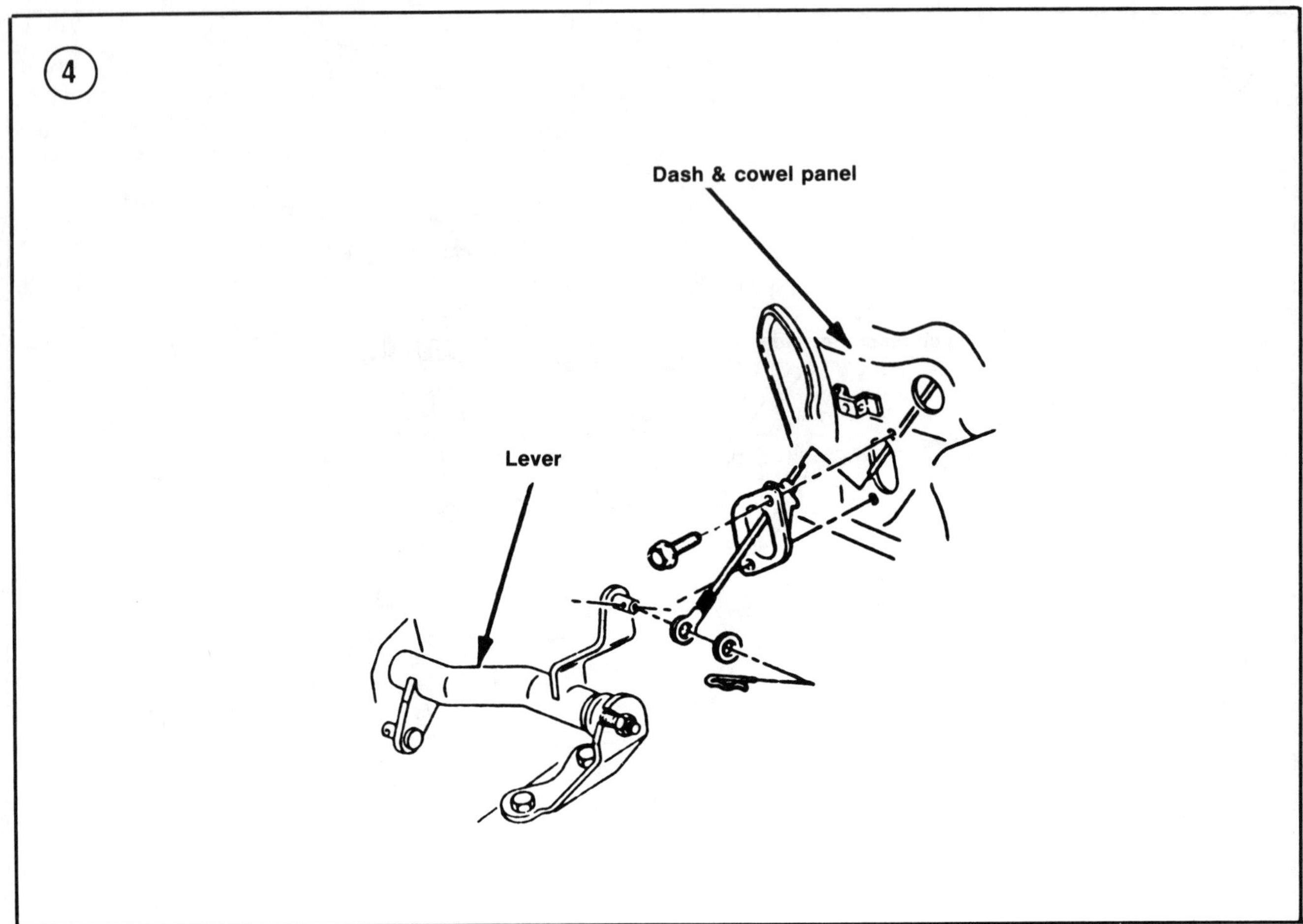

Mechanical Clutch Adjusting Mechanism

The clutch adjusting mechanism is mounted on the pedal/bracket assembly (**Figure 2**). The pawl rests against the bracket assembly stop, with its teeth meshed with those on the detent. The detent hub is spring-loaded to keep tension on the release cable. This holds the release bearing in contact with the clutch levers.

Depressing the pedal causes the pawl to drive the detent, which pulls on the cable to force the release bearing against the diaphragm springs. This action disengages the clutch. Releasing the pedal returns the detent to its original position.

As the clutch disc wears, the cable must be lengthened by pulling the pedal up to its rubber bumper stop. This forces the pawl to disengage from the detent and lets the cable extend until the detent position is balanced against the release bearing load. GM recommends this be done every 5,000 miles.

Mechanical Clutch Cable Replacement

Refer to **Figure 2** for this procedure.

1. Pull clutch pedal upward against the bumper stop and support in that position. This releases the pawl from the detent.

CAUTION
Do not allow the cable to snap backwards when disconnecting it in Step 2. This can damage the adjusting detent mechanism.

2. Raise the hood and disconnect the cable from the release lever at the transmission. See **Figure 4**.
3. Remove the hush panel from inside the passenger cab.
4. Disconnect the neutral start switch electrical lead, remove the bracket mounting screw, then disconnect and remove the neutral start switch

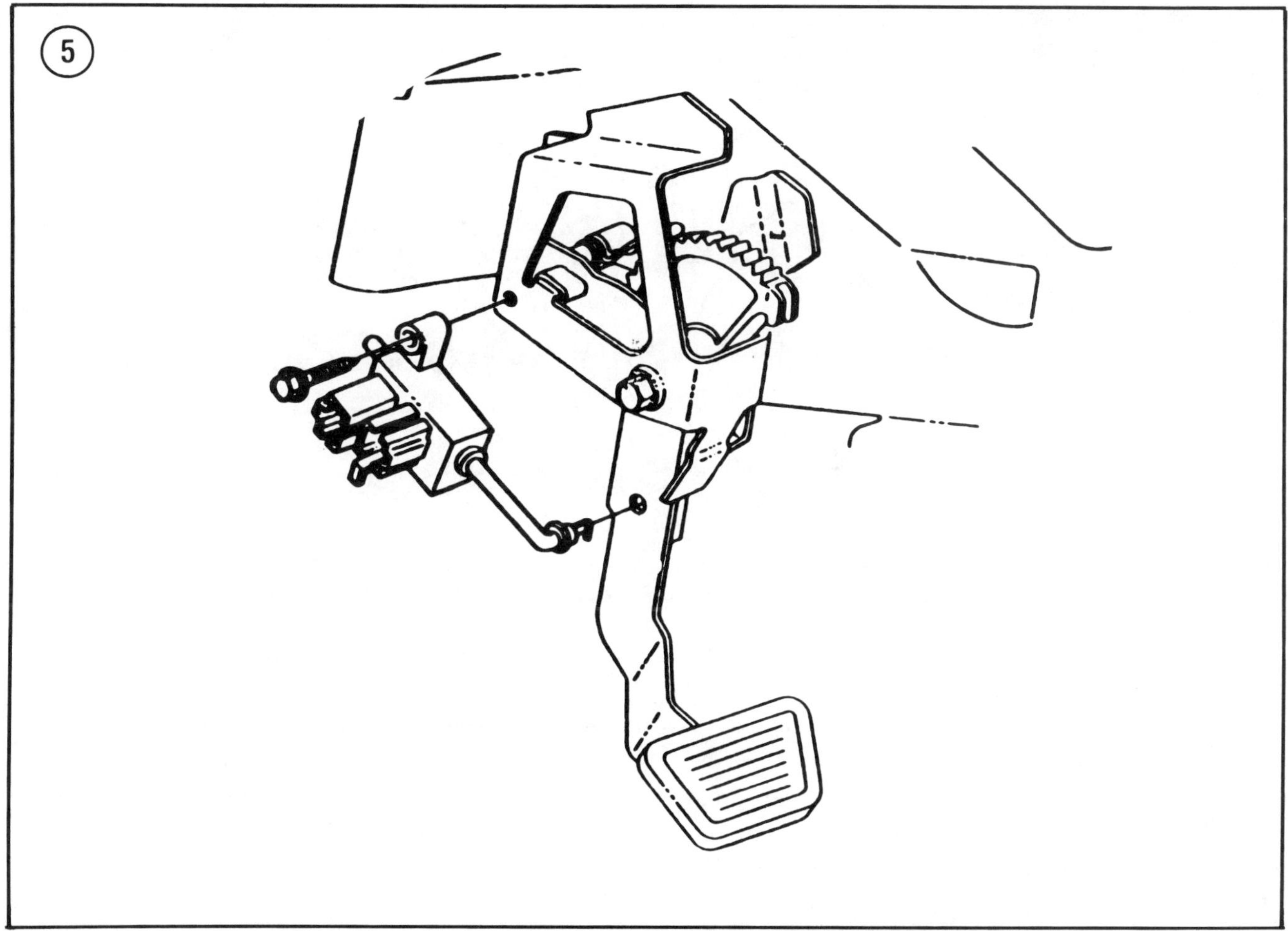

from the pedal/bracket assembly. See **Figure 5** (typical).

5. Remove the pedal stop-to-mounting bracket bolts.
6. Remove the pedal pivot bolt. Remove the pedal from the bracket.
7. Disconnect the cable from the detent. Move the pawl away from the detent and push the cable free of the detent/pawl mechanism.
8. Remove the cable retainer from the cowl panel (**Figure 4**).
9. Remove the cable from the engine compartment.
10. To reinstall, push the cable through the cowl from the engine compartment and install the cable retainer bolts.
11. Route the cable end between the pawl and detent, fitting the cable into the detent groove. Connect the cable end to the detent.
12. Install pedal in mounting bracket. Install pivot bolt and torque to 25 ft.-lb. (35 N•m).
13. Install pedal stop to bracket. Install french lock and bolts. Tighten bolts to 10 ft.-lb. (15 N•m). Bend lock tabs against the bolts.
14. Install the neutral start switch to the pedal/mounting bracket.
15. Install the hush panel.
16. Pull the clutch pedal upward against the bumper stop and support it in that position.
17. Attach the other end of the cable to the release lever at the transmission.
18. Lift the clutch pedal up to let the detent adjust the cable length. Slowly depress the pedal several times to engage the pawl with the detent teeth.

Hydraulic Clutch Inspection

1. Check the clutch master cylinder reservoir level and top up with DOT 3 brake fluid, if necessary.
2. Start the engine. Apply the parking brake. Apply the foot brake.
3. Hold the clutch pedal about 1/2 in. above the floor mat and shift the transmission from 1st to

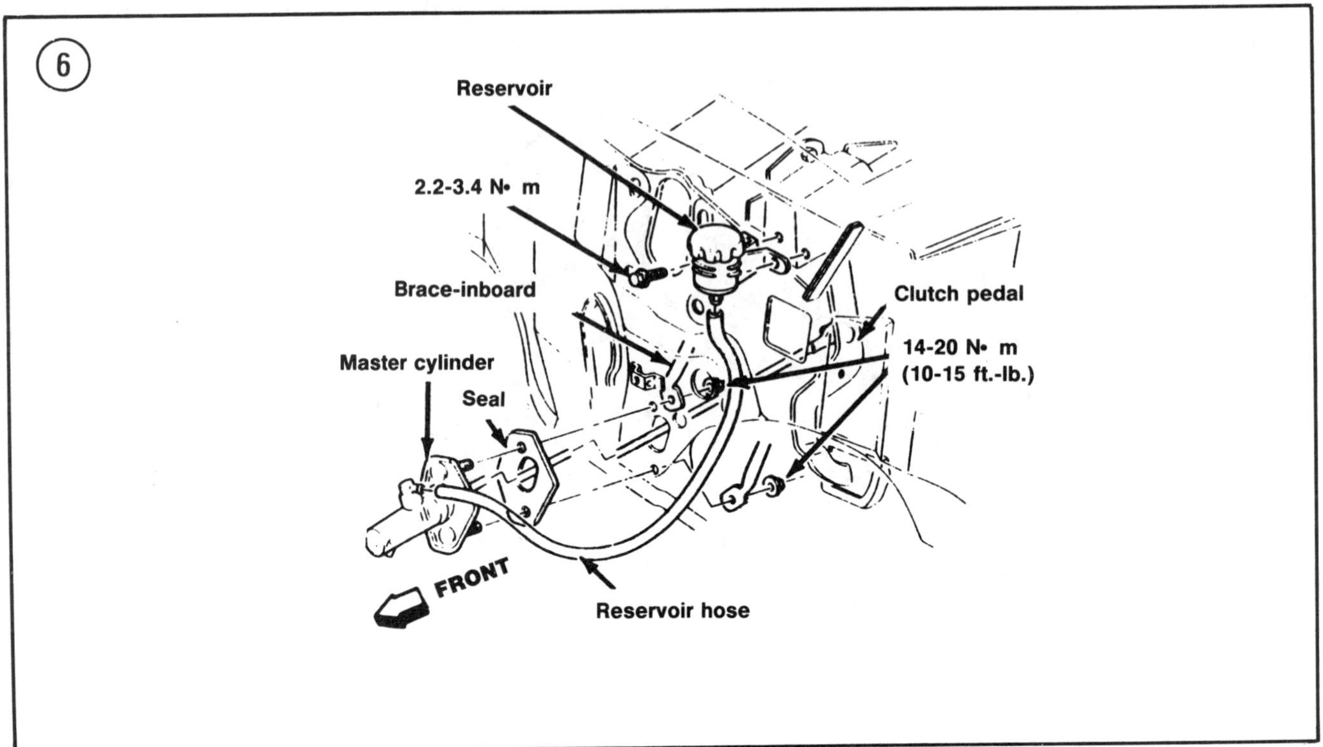

reverse several times. If this cannot be done smoothly, the clutch is not releasing fully.

4. Check the clutch pedal bushings for excessive wear or deformation.
5. Raise the vehicle with a jack and place it on jackstands.
6. Check the clutch fork for proper installation and lubrication. Correct as required.
7. Have an assistant depress the clutch fully and hold it in that position while you measure the slave cylinder pushrod travel. It should be a minimum of 0.624 in. (1.9L and 2.2L) or 0.832 in. (all others). The clutch pedal should move approximately 6 inches when fully depressed.
8. If the clutch does not perform as specified in Step 3 or Step 6, inspect the hydraulic system for leaks. If leakage is found, the problem is most likely in the hydraulic system. No leakage indicates a mechanical problem.

Hydraulic Clutch System Bleeding

This procedure requires handling brake fluid. Clean all dirt from the slave cylinder bleed valve before beginning. Two people are needed: one to operate the clutch pedal and the other to open and close the bleed valve.

1. Clean away any dirt around the clutch master cylinder reservoir. Remove the cover and top up the reservoir with brake fluid marked DOT 3 or DOT 4.

NOTE
DOT 3 means the brake fluid meets current Department of Transportation quality standards. If the fluid does not say DOT 3 somewhere on the label, buy a brand that does. DOT 4 brake fluid can also be safely used.

2. Set parking brake. Securely block both rear wheels so the truck will not roll in either direction. Raise the vehicle with a jack and place it on jackstands.
3. Clean all dirt and grease from the slave cylinder where it attaches to the bellhousing. Remove the slave cylinder attaching bolts.
4. Hold the slave cylinder at a 45-degree angle with the bleed valve at the highest point. Remove any dirt from around the bleed valve and remove the valve cap.
5. Have an assistant depress the clutch pedal fully and then open the bleed valve.
6. Close the bleed valve and have the assistant fully release the clutch pedal.

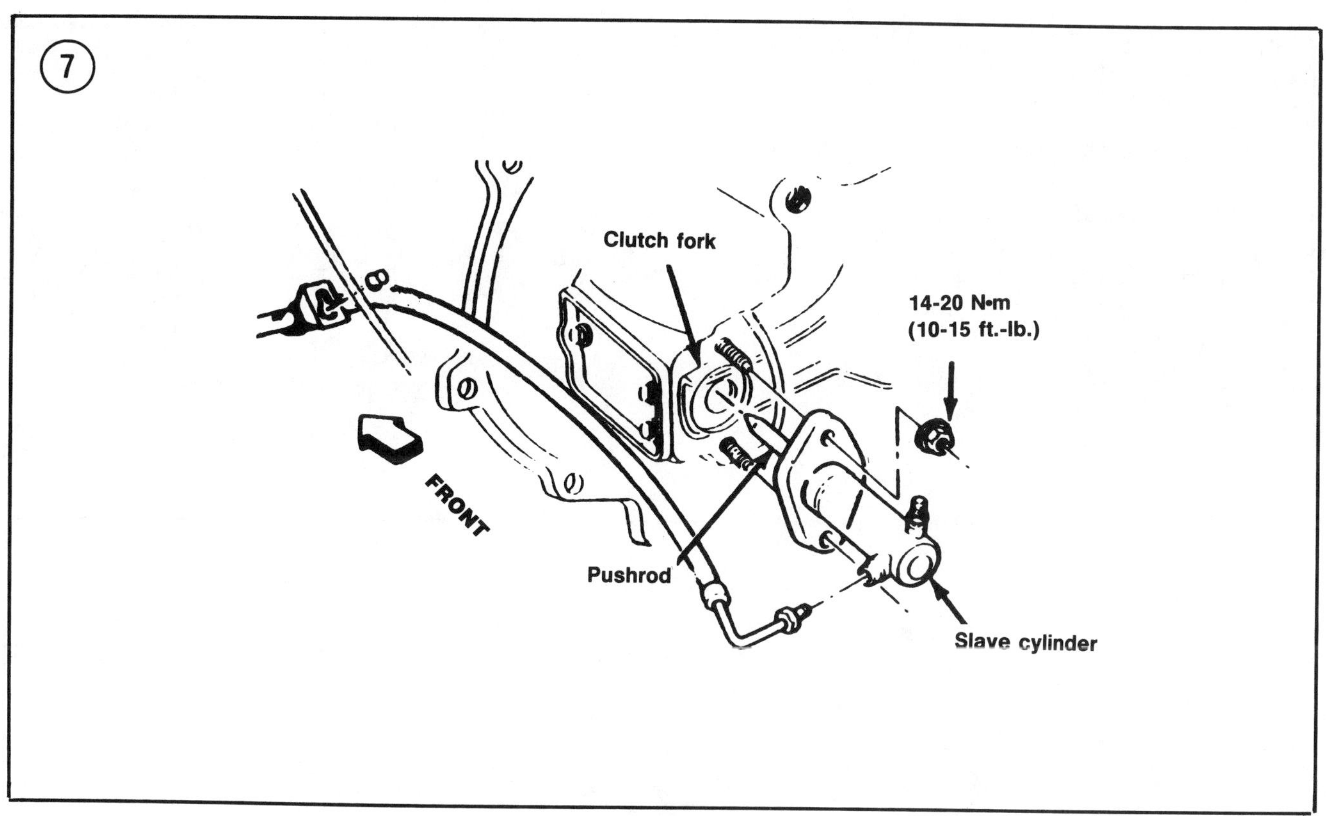

NOTE
Keep an eye on the fluid level in the reservoir during bleeding. If the fluid level is allowed to drop too low, air will enter the hydraulic lines and the entire bleeding process will have to be repeated.

7. Repeat Step 5 and Step 6 until the fluid leaving the bleed valve is free of air bubbles. Reinstall bleed valve cap.
8. Reinstall the slave cylinder to the bellhousing.
9. Remove the jackstands and lower the vehicle to the ground.
10. Top up the master cylinder reservoir with DOT 3 brake fluid as required and reinstall the reservoir cover.

Master Cylinder Removal/Installation (Hydraulic Clutch)

Refer to **Figure 6** for this procedure.

1. Remove the hush panel from inside the passenger cab.
2. Disconnect the master cylinder pushrod from the clutch pedal.
3. Remove the master cylinder attaching nuts.
4. Disconnect the reservoir line at the master cylinder.
5. Disconnect the slave cylinder hydraulic line at the master cylinder.
6. Remove the master cylinder.
7. Installation is the reverse of removal. Tighten the master cylinder attaching nuts to 10-15 ft.-lb. (14-20 N•m). Bleed the system as described in this chapter.

Slave Cylinder Removal/Installation (Hydraulic Clutch)

Refer to **Figure 7** for this procedure.

1. Raise the vehicle with a jack and place it on jackstands.
2. Disconnect the hydraulic line at the slave cylinder.
3. Remove the 2 nuts holding the slave cylinder to the bellhousing. Remove the slave cylinder.
4. Installation is the reverse of removal. Tighten the slave cylinder attaching nuts to 10-15 ft.-lb. (14-20 N•m). Bleed the system as described in this chapter.

Clutch Removal (All Vehicles)

1. Hydraulic clutch—Remove the slave cylinder as described in this chapter.
2. Remove the transmission as described in this chapter.
3. Hydraulic clutch:
   a. Remove the left body mounting bolts and loosen the radiator support bolt.
   b. Raise the left side of the cab with a jack enough to provide access to the upper bellhousing bolts.

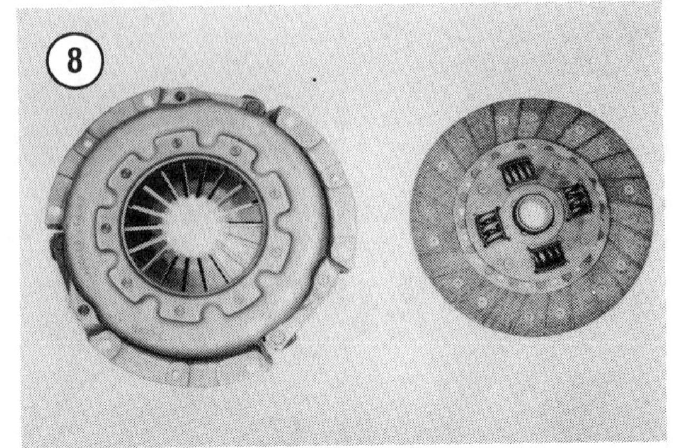
8

9

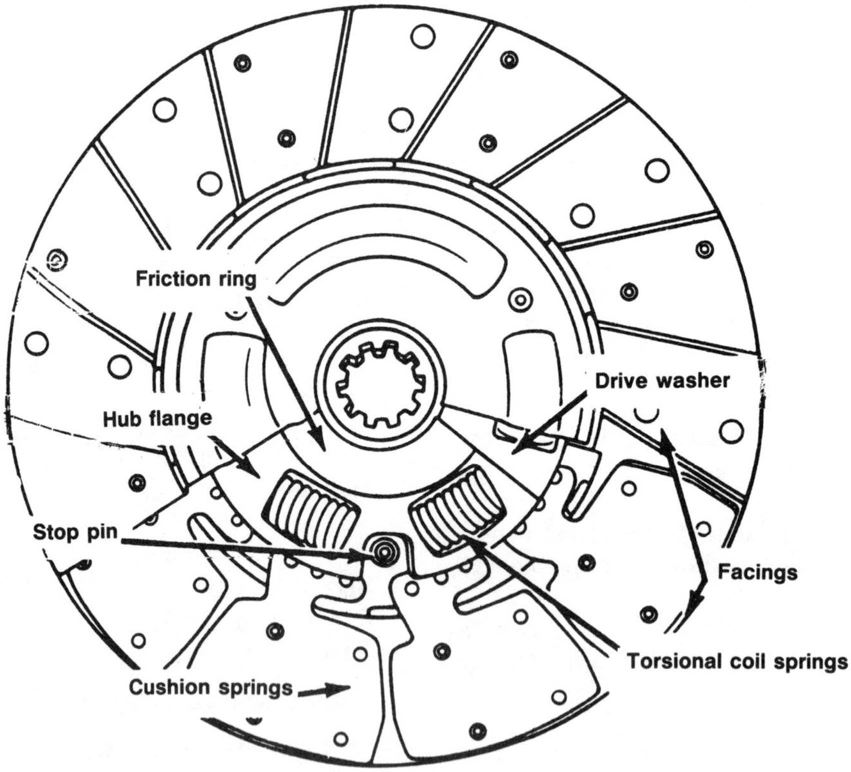

Friction ring
Drive washer
Hub flange
Stop pin
Facings
Torsional coil springs
Cushion springs

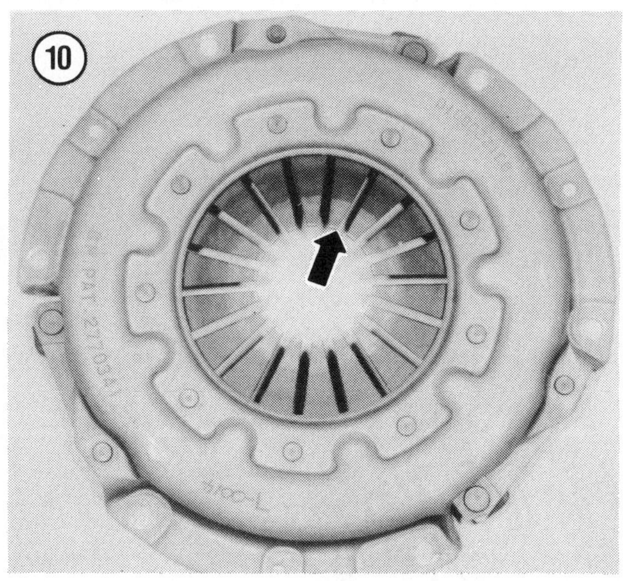

c. Place a suitable wooden block between the cab and frame for support.

4. Remove the bellhousing bolts. Remove the bellhousing.

5. Slide the clutch fork off the ball stud and remove fork from dust boot.

NOTE
If clutch cover assembly and flywheel are marked with a visible "X," omit Step 6.

6. Make reference marks on the clutch cover assembly and flywheel for reference during reassembly.

7. Install GM tool part No. J-33034 (1.9L or 2.2L engine) or tool part No. J-33169 (all others) or a dummy shaft made from an old input shaft through the clutch disc hub.

NOTE
An input shaft from a junk transmission can be used to make a dummy shaft. Inexpensive universal aligning bars can also be purchased from some auto parts stores which can be adapted. Some tool rental dealers and parts stores also rent universal aligning bars.

8. Unbolt the clutch cover assembly from the flywheel (**Figure 1**). Loosen the bolts in several stages using a diagonal pattern to prevent warping the cover.

9. Remove the clutch cover assembly and disc (**Figure 8**) from the flywheel.

Clutch Disc Inspection

Refer to **Figure 9** for this procedure.

1. Check the clutch disc for the following:
   a. Oil or grease on the facings.
   b. Glazed or warped facings.
   c. Loose or missing rivets.
   d. Broken springs.
   e. Loose fit or rough movement on the transmission input shaft splines.

2. Remove small amounts of oil or grease with aerosol brake cleaner and dress the facings with a wire brush, if necessary. However, if the facings are soaked with oil or grease, replace the disc. The disc must also be replaced if any of the other defects is present or if the facings are partially worn and a ncw prcssurc platc is bcing installed.

Clutch Cover Assembly Inspection

1. Check the pressure plate (part of the cover assembly) for:
   a. Scoring.
   b. Burn marks.
   c. Cracks.

2. Check the diaphragm spring (**Figure 10**) for wear or damage at the release bearing contact surface. Check for bent or broken spring fingers and, if found, replace the clutch cover assembly.

If the clutch trouble is still not apparent, take the cover assembly and disc to a competent machine shop. Have the disc and pressure plate checked for runout and the diaphragm spring checked for correct finger height. Do not attempt to dismantle the pressure plate or readjust the fingers yourself. This requires the proper tools and experience.

Clutch Installation

1. Be sure your hands are clean and free of oil or grease.

2. Make sure the disc facings, pressure plate and flywheel are free of oil, grease and other foreign material.

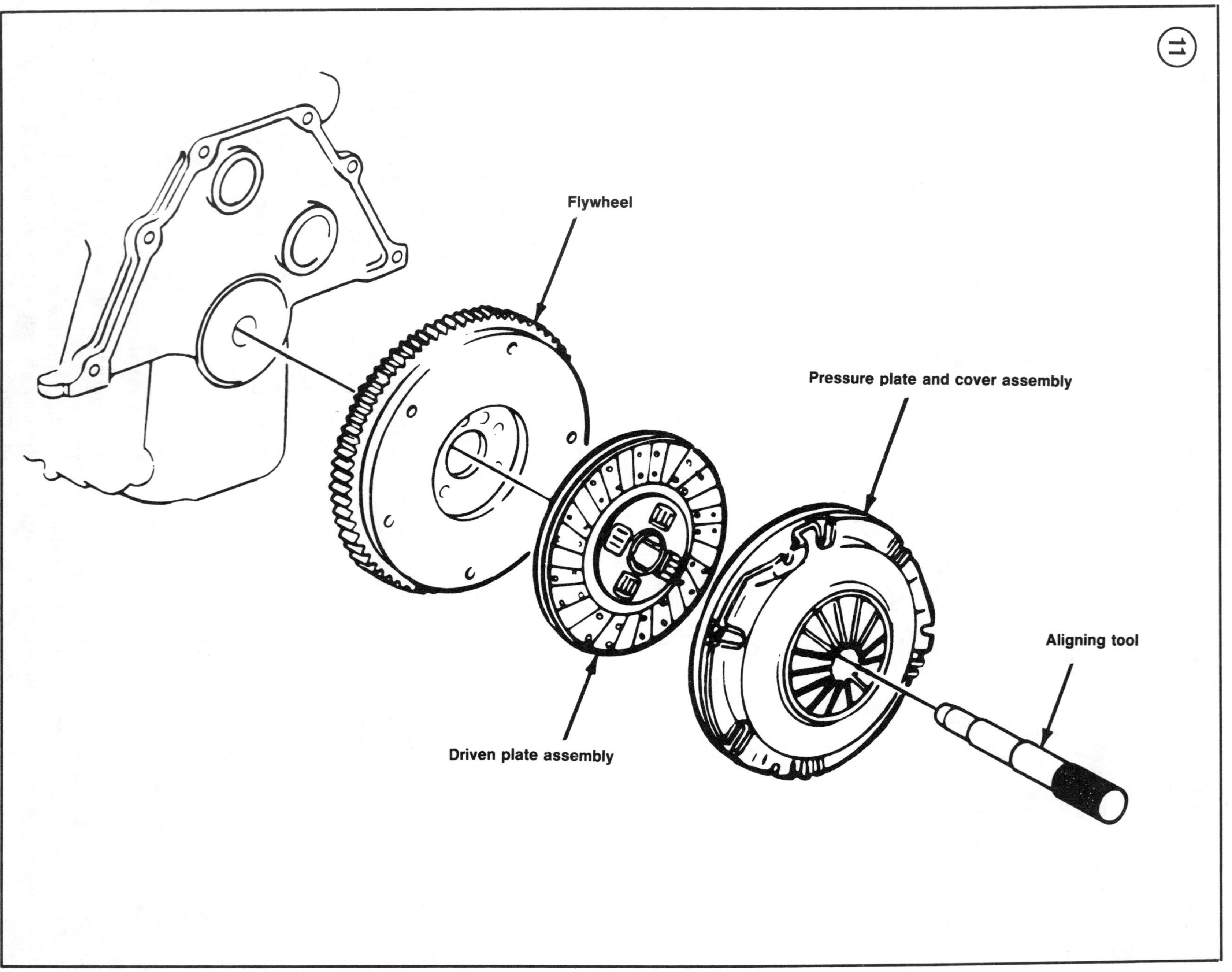
11
Flywheel
Pressure plate and cover assembly
Aligning tool
Driven plate assembly

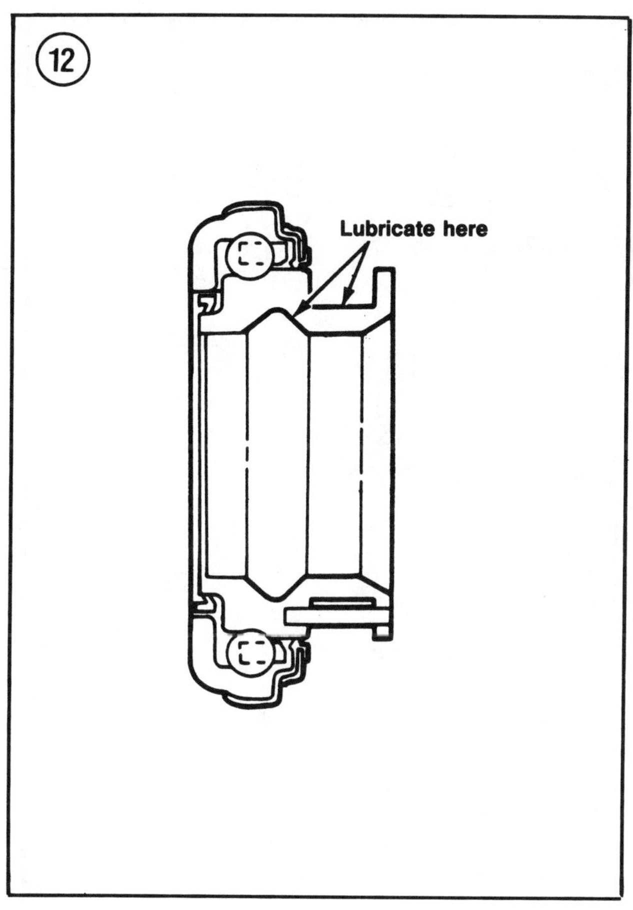

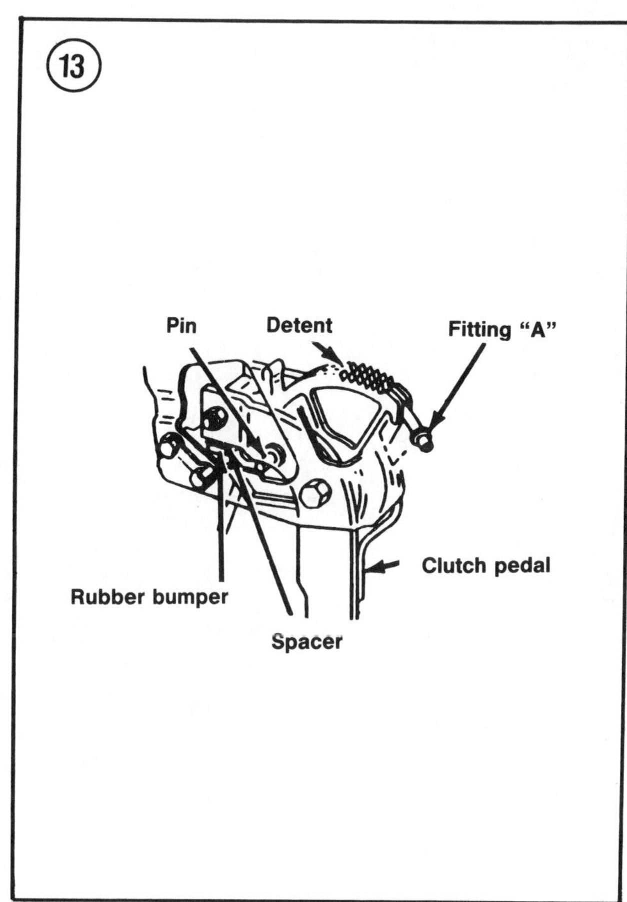

3. Place the clutch disc and cover assembly in position on the flywheel. The side of the disc stamped "FLYWHEEL" should face the flywheel with the damper springs facing the transmission when assembled.
4. Position the clutch cover assembly on the flywheel, aligning the clutch cover and flywheel "X" or alignment marks.
5. Start but do not tighten the cover bolts. Center the disc and pressure plate with GM tool part No. J-33034 (1.9L and 2.2L engine) or tool part No. J-33169 (all others), as shown in **Figure 11**. A dummy shaft can also be used for alignment.
6. Gradually tighten the cover bolts in a diagonal pattern to 20 ft.-lb. (25 N•m). Remove alignment tool.
7. Lubricate the outer diameter of the release bearing with E.P. multipurpose grease as shown in **Figure 12**. Pack the inner diameter recess of the bearing with E.P. multipurpose grease.
8. Lubricate the ball stud and the clutch fork fingers with graphite grease. Install fork on ball stud.
9. Install release bearing on clutch fork. Install bellhousing and tighten bolts to specifications (**Table 1**).
10. Hydraulic clutch:

a. Remove wooden block between frame and cab and the jack supporting the left side of the cab to return it to its normal position.

b. Install left body mounting bolts. Tighten these and the radiator support bolt loosened during *Clutch Removal* to 45-60 ft.-lb. (60-80 N•m).

11. Install transmission as described in this chapter.
12. Hydraulic clutch—Install and bleed the slave cylinder as described in this chapter.
13. Mechanical clutch:

a. Connect the clutch fork cable. Place a 0.18 in. (4.6 mm) spacer between the clutch pedal and rubber stop. Make sure pedal is seated firmly against the spacer. See **Figure 13**.

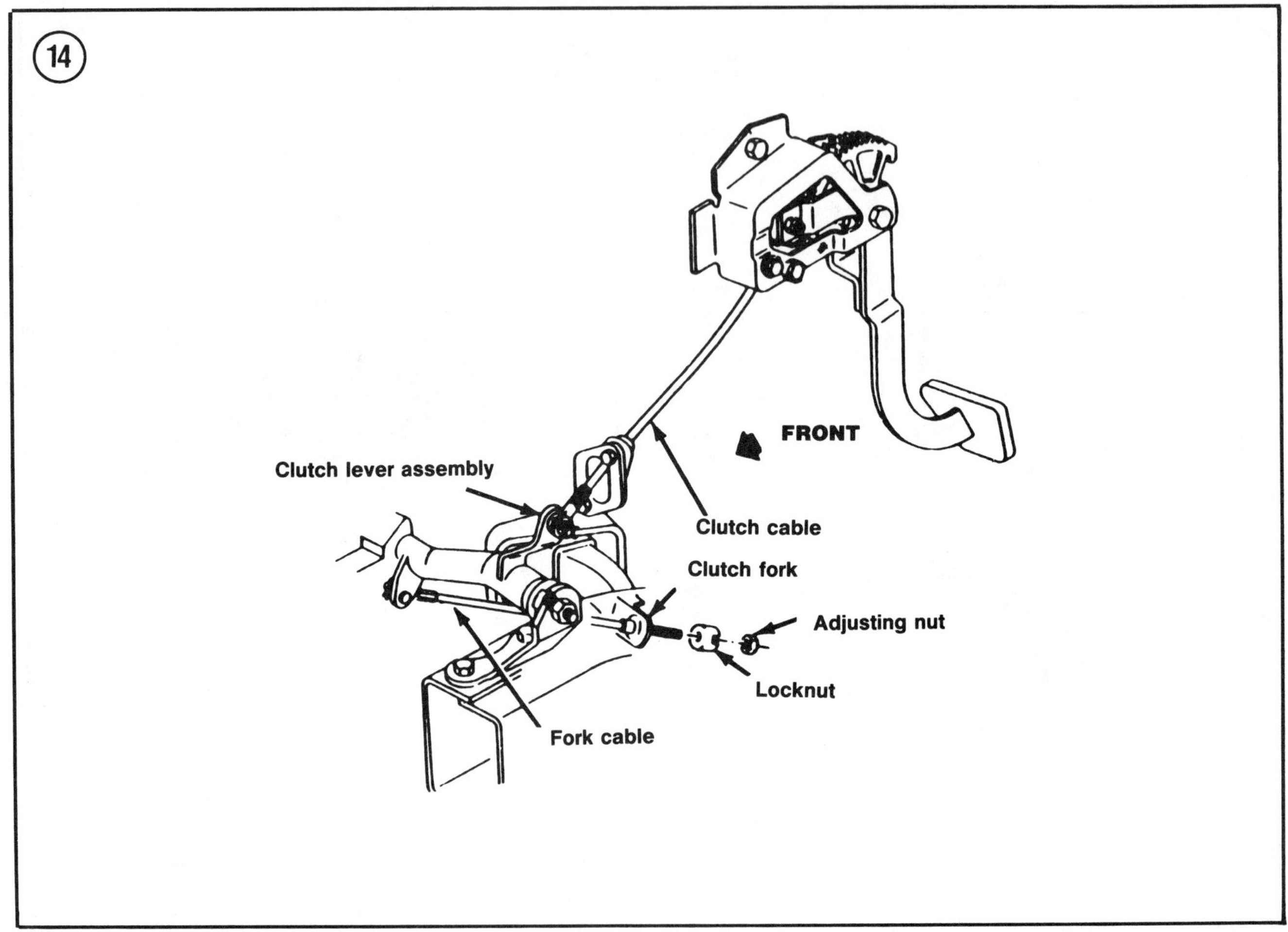

b. Pull the clutch fork forward until release bearing barely touches the cover diaphragm spring fingers.
c. Tighten the clutch fork adjusting nut (**Figure 14**) until all lash is removed. Tighten locknut against the adjusting nut.
d. Remove the spacer installed in Step a. Depress the pedal several times to engage the pawl and detent.

Clutch Release Lever Removal/Installation (Mechanical Clutch)

Refer to **Figure 15** for this procedure.

1. Pull the clutch pedal up against the bumper stop to release the pawl from the detent. Support the pedal in this position.
2. Disconnect the pedal cable at the clutch lever (**Figure 4**).
3. Remove the clutch fork cable at the lever.
4. Loosen the outer ball stud nut. Slide the stud from the frame bracket bolt.
5. Move the lever outward to clear the inner ball stud. Remove the lever.
6. Installation is the reverse of removal.

Clutch Release Bearing Removal/Installation (All Vehicles)

1. Hydraulic clutch—Remove the slave cylinder as described in this chapter.
2. Remove the transmission as described in this chapter.
3. Remove the release bearing from the fork assembly.

CAUTION

Do not place the bearing in a degreaser in Step 4. This can damage the seals.

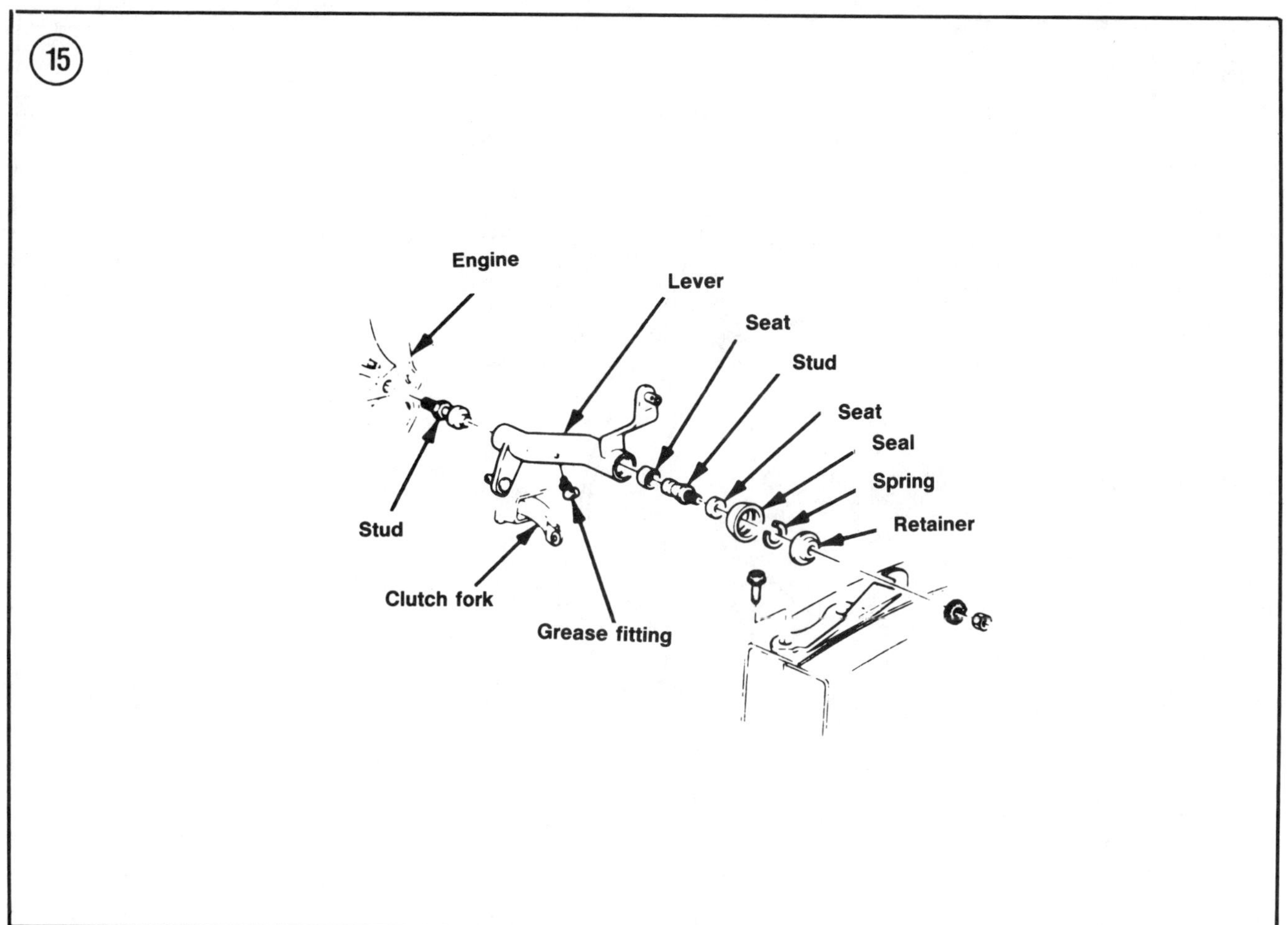

9

4. Clean and inspect the release bearing for excessive wear or other defects.
5. Lubricate the outer diameter of the release bearing with E.P. multipurpose grease as shown in **Figure 12**. Pack the inner diameter recess of the bearing with E.P. multipurpose grease.
6. Fit the release bearing to the clutch fork with both fork tangs engaging the bearing outer diameter groove.
7. Install the transmission as described in this chapter.
8A. Hydraulic clutch—Install and bleed the slave cylinder as described in this chapter.
8B. Mechanical clutch—Perform Step 13 of *Clutch Installation* in this chapter to adjust the cable.

Clutch Interlock Switch Removal/Installation

1. Remove the hush panel from inside the passenger cab.
2. Disconnect the neutral start switch electrical lead, remove the bracket mounting screw, then disconnect and remove the neutral start switch from the pedal/bracket assembly. See **Figure 16** (typical).
3. Installation is the reverse of removal.

Clutch Interlock Switch Adjustment

Adjustment should only be required when switch has been removed or replaced. Refer to **Figure 16** for this procedure.

1. Reinstall and connect switch as described in this chapter.
2. Move slider "A" forward on shaft B (**Figure 16**).
3. Set the switch by completely depressing the clutch pedal to the floor mat or carpet.
4. Reinstall hush panel.

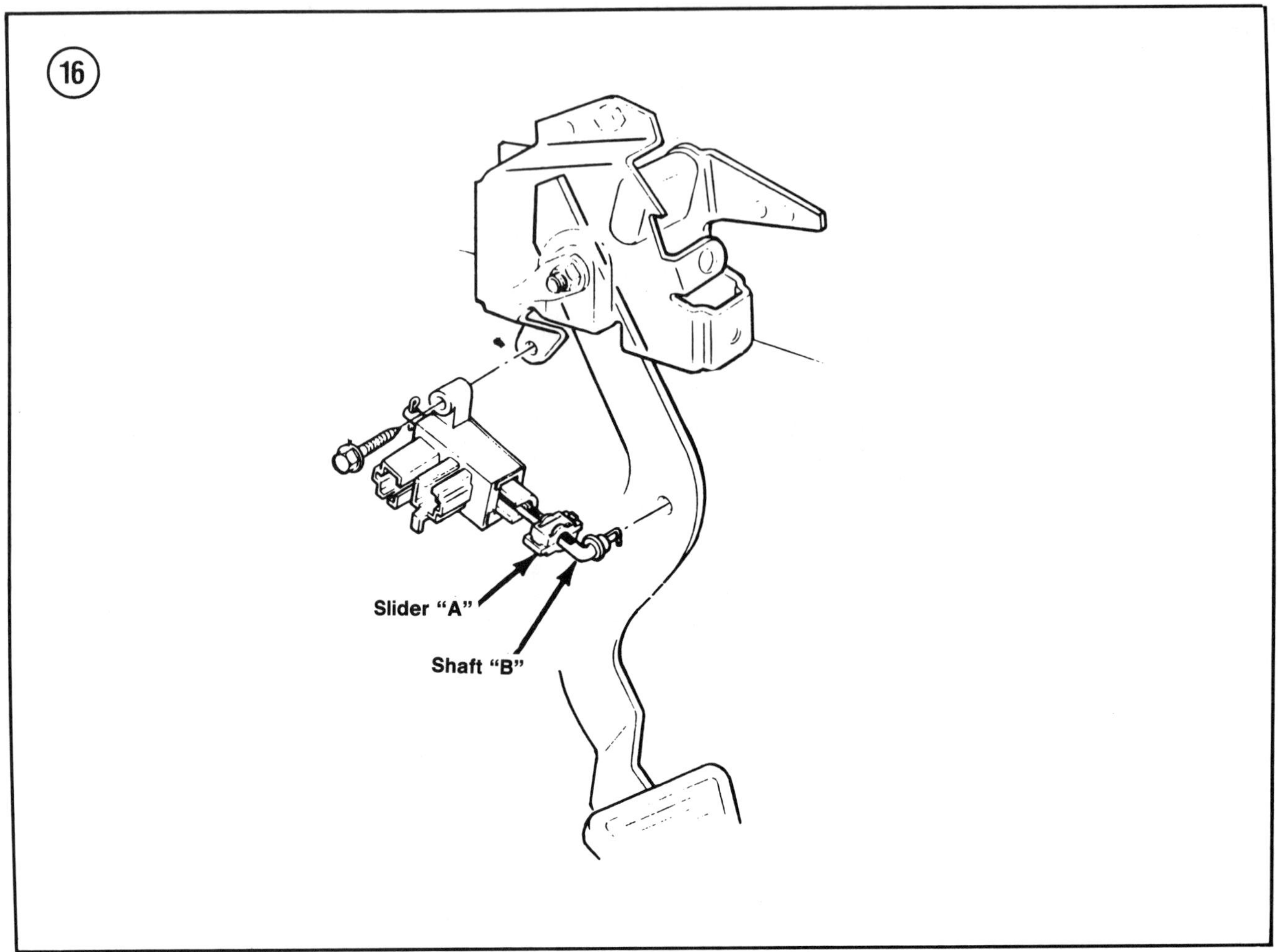

MANUAL TRANSMISSION

Two 4-speed manual transmissions are used: the Isuzu M150 77.5 mm and the Warner T4C 77 mm gearbox. The optional Warner T5 5-speed manual transmission is also designated as a 77 mm gearbox. The transmission designation in millimeters refers to the measured distance between the main shaft and countergear centerlines.

All 3 are floor-shifted, fully synchronized transmissions with blocker ring synchronizers and a sliding mesh type reverse gear. The gearshift lever assembly is mounted on top of the transmission extension housing and requires no adjustment.

The Isuzu M150 transmission consists of an integral clutch housing, center support and extension housing of aluminum. The Warner T4C 4-speed and T5 5-speed transmissions consists of an aluminum case and extension housing.

Transmission overhaul is not the best starting point for a beginning mechanic. However, it does not require special training or much special equipment. Overhaul does require patience and the ability to concentrate. The work area must be clean, well-lighted, free of distractions and inaccessible to pets and small children.

Before starting work, read this entire section. Obtain any necessary special tools or appropriate substitutes. Check the availability of parts with local suppliers.

A service identification or unit number is located on the driver's side of the extension housing. This unit number must be used when ordering replacement parts.

Parts Identification

Some manual transmission parts have 2 or more names. To prevent confusion, the following list gives parts names used in this chapter and common synonyms.

a. Output shaft—Main shaft.
b. Input shaft—Clutch shaft, clutch gear, input gear, drive gear.
c. Countershaft gear—Cluster gear.
d. Blocker ring—Blocking ring, synchronizer ring.
e. Synchronizer—Sliding clutch.

Safety Precautions

The use of a suitable holding fixture is highly recommended for transmission overhaul. Chevrolet and GMC have several different fixture designs available. While it may not prove economical to purchase a holding fixture just to overhaul your transmission on a one-time basis, obtaining one from a rental house is worth the small cost involved. It will save time, make the job easier and prevent damage to the transmission and possible personal injury to you.

The transmissions used in these vehicles are deceptive in appearance. Although small in size, they are extremely heavy and awkward to handle. You should not attempt to remove one from a vehicle without the use of an appropriate transmission jack, which can also be obtained from a rental house.

When handling the transmission, it is a good idea to wear heavy gloves to improve your grip on the transmission case and prevent possible injury from the sharp metal edges.

The use of safety goggles is highly recommended whenever you are removing snap rings. The snap rings used in transmission assemblies are extremely stiff and tend to be somewhat brittle. Safety goggles will protect your eyes from possible injury if the snap ring should break apart during removal or installation.

Cleaning and Inspection (All Models)

1. Wash the inside and outside of the transmission case and case components thoroughly with clean solvent to dissolve or loosen old lubricant and foreign material. Make sure the vent hole is open and clean. Blow dry with compressed air, if available.
2. Remove all gasket or sealant residue from mating surfaces.
3. Inspect the case and case components for cracks, worn or damaged bearing bores, damaged threads or other defects. If such defects are found, replace the case.
4. Check the front and rear case faces for burrs. If present, dress off with a fine mill file.
5. Check the condition of the extension housing oil seal and bushing. Remove and discard the seal. Install a new seal with a suitable installer tool.
6. Check the condition of all shift forks, rails and shafts. Replace as required if excessively worn or if any defects are noted.
7. Clean the ball bearings with solvent as follows:

   a. Place bearings in a wire basket and submerge in a suitable container of fresh solvent. The bottom of the basket should not touch the bottom of the container.

   b. Agitate the basket containing the bearings to loosen all grease, sludge and other contamination.

   c. Dry ball bearings with dry filtered compressed air, holding the bearing to prevent it from rotating.

   d. Lubricate the bearings with clean transmission lubricant. Turn each race slowly by hand and and check for loose, worn or damaged balls. Check for cracked, rough or worn races. Check bearings for rust, wear, scuffed surfaces, heat discoloration or other defects.

8. If needle bearings are to be reused, repeat Step 7, cleaning one set at a time to prevent any possible mixup. Check bearings for flat spots. If one needle bearing is defective or missing, replace the entire set.
9. Check all gears for chipped, worn or broken teeth. Replace the input shaft if the gear teeth are defective or if the cone surface is damaged.
10. Check the reverse gear and reverse idler gear bushings for wear or damage. If any defect is noted, replace as required.
11. Check all shafts and shaft splines for wear, scoring or an out-of-round condition.

12. Check the synchronizer sleeves for free movement on their hubs. Check the synchronizer rings for rounded teeth or enlarged index slots. Replace as required.
13. Check thrust washers for excessive wear and scoring or other surface damage. Replace as required.
14. Discard all snap rings and install new ones on assembly.

Shift Lever Removal/Installation

1. Disconnect the negative battery cable.
2. Remove the shift lever boot retainer screws. Slide the boot up the lever.
3. Remove the shift lever attaching bolts. Remove the lever.
4. Installation is the reverse of removal. Tighten the shift lever attaching bolts to 10 ft.-lb. (13 N•m).

Transmission Removal/Installation (All Models)

Remove the transfer case as described in this chapter, if equipped with 4-wheel drive.

1. Disconnect the negative battery cable.
2. Isuzu 4-speed—Remove the upper starter motor retaining nut.
3. Remove the shift lever as described in this chapter.
4. Isuzu 4-speed—Disconnect the electrical connector/clip at the shift tower.
5. Raise the front of the vehicle with a jack and place it on jackstands.
6. Remove the drive shaft. See Chapter Eleven.
7. Isuzu 4-speed—Disconnect the exhaust pipe at the manifold.

8A. 1982-1983—Disconnect the clutch cable at the transmission.

8B. 1984-on—Remove the slave cylinder as described in this chapter.

9. Disconnect the speedometer cable at the transmission extension housing.
10. Unplug all electrical connectors at the transmission.
11. Place a jack under the transmission for support. Remove the transmission mount bolts.
12. Remove the catalytic converter hanger, crossmember and dust cover bolts.
13. Isuzu 4-speed—Remove the lower starter mounting bolt. Remove the left body mounting bolts. Loosen the radiator support bolt.
14. Remove the bolts holding the transmission to the engine.

NOTE
Once the transmission is out of the vehicle, do not depress the clutch pedal or the clutch disc will fall out of position.

15. Pull the transmission to the rear until the input shaft clears the clutch housing, then lower the transmission to the floor with the jack and remove it from under the vehicle.
16. Installation is the reverse of removal, plus the following:

   a. Lightly lubricate the spline part of the transmission input shaft with high-temperature grease. Do not apply too much grease or the clutch disc can become contaminated during operation.
   b. Raise the transmission on a jack until the input shaft splines are aligned with the cluch disc splines. The clutch release bearing and hub must be properly positioned in the release lever fork.
   c. Install a guide stud in each lower clutch housing-to-transmission case bolt hole. Move the transmission forward on the guide studs until the input shaft enters the crankshaft pilot bearing and the case contacts the clutch housing. Install the upper mounting bolts, remove the guide studs and install the lower bolts.
   d. Tighten all fasteners to specifications (**Table 1**).
   e. Make sure the transmission drain plug is in place, then remove the fill plug and fill the transmission to the proper level with the recommended lubricant. See Chapter Three.
   f. 1982-1983—Adjust the clutch cable as described in this chapter.

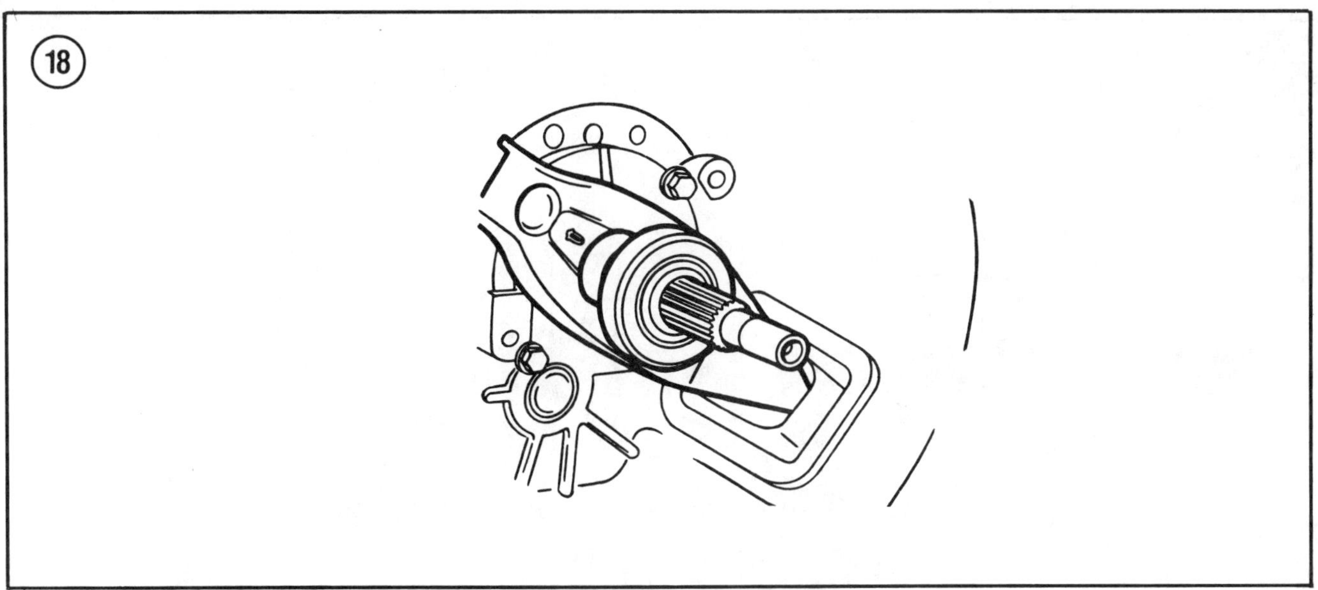

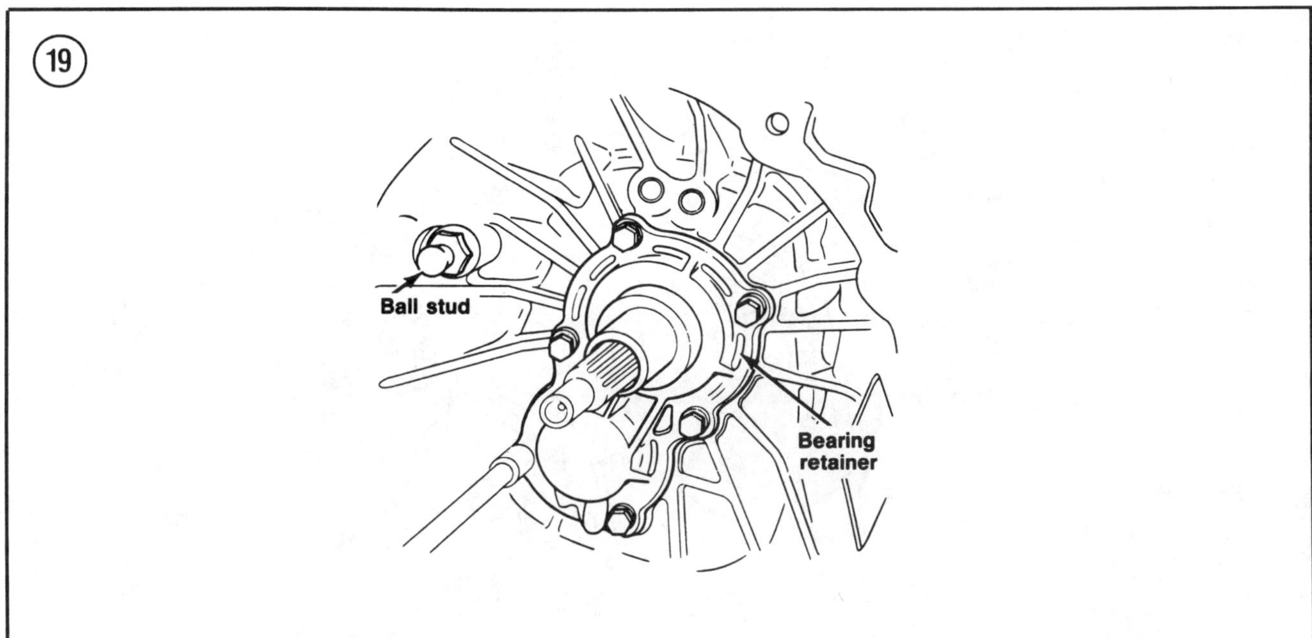

ISUZU M150 4-SPEED TRANSMISSION

Disassembly

Refer to **Figure 17** for this procedure.

1. Disconnect the retaining springs from the bearing side. Remove the bearing, boot and clutch fork. See **Figure 18**.
2. Remove the drain plug. Hold the transmission case over a clean container and drain the lubricant.
3. Remove the bearing retainer bolts. Remove the bearing retainer (**Figure 19**) and discard the gasket.
4. Remove the speedometer driven gear and the backup light switch.
5. Unbolt and remove the shifter cover.
6. Unbolt and remove the extension housing. Remove and discard the gasket.

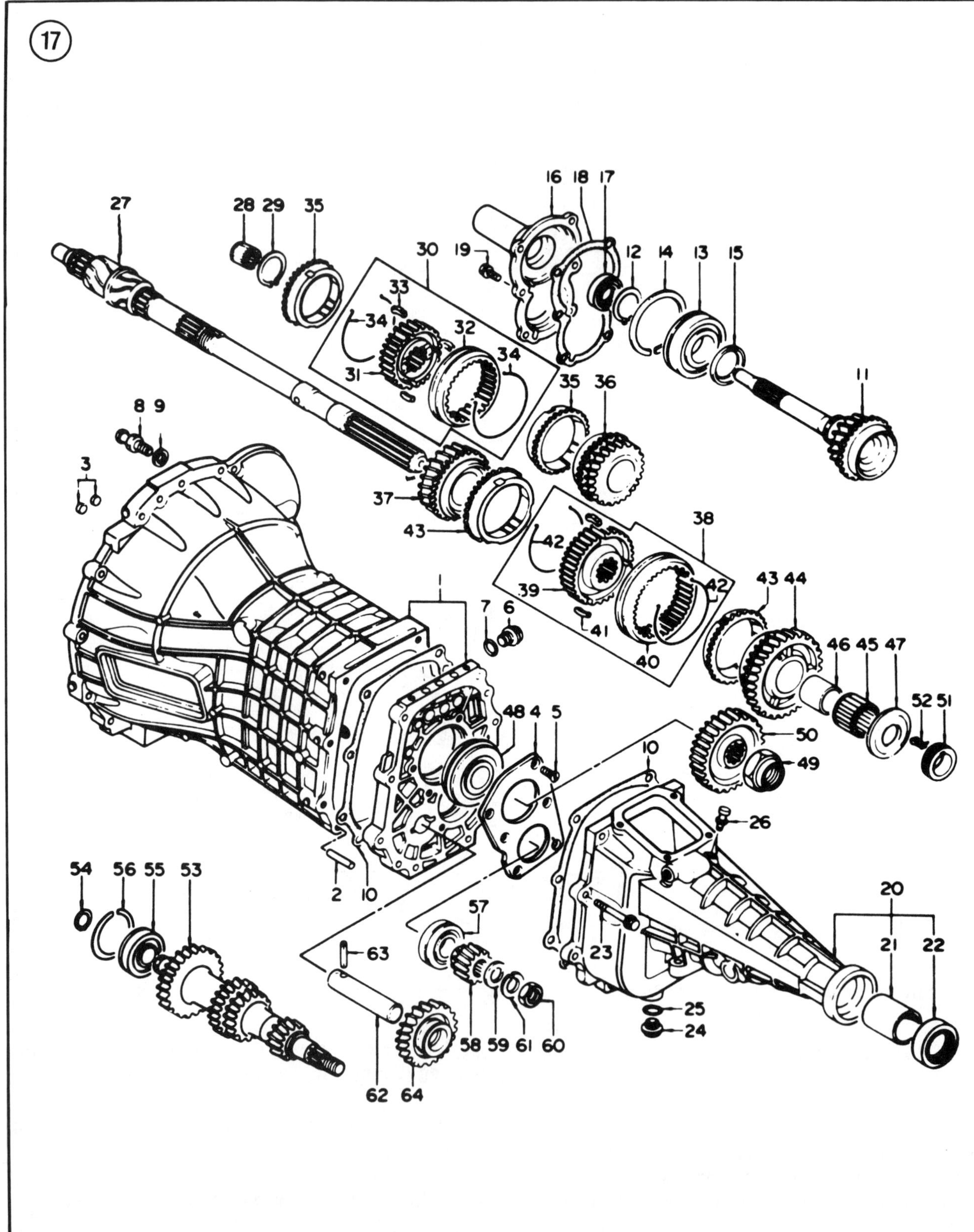
17
1
2
3
4
5
6
7
8
9
10
11
12
13
14
15
16
17
18
19
20
21
22
23
24
25
26
27
28
29
30
31
32
33
34
35
36
37
38
39
40
41
42
43
44
45
46
47
48
49
50
51
52
53
54
55
56
57
58
59
60
61
62
63
64

MANUAL TRANSMISSION (IZUZU 4-SPEED)

1. Transmission case and center support
2. Dowel
3. Plug
4. Rear bearing retainer
5. Screw
6. Oil filler plug
7. Gasket
8. Ball stud
9. Washer
10. Gasket
11. Drive gear shaft
12. Retaining ring
13. Bearing
14. Retaining ring
15. Spacer
16. Front bearing retainer
17. Oil seal
18. Gasket
19. Bolt and spring washer
20. Extension housing
21. Bushing
22. Rear oil seal
23. Bolt, plain washer and spring washer
24. Oil drain plug
25. Gasket
26. Ventilator
27. Mainshaft
28. Needle roller bearing
29. Retaining ring
30. 3rd-4th synchronizer
31. Clutch hub
32. Sleeve
33. Insert
34. Spring
35. Blocker ring
36. 3rd gear
37. 2nd gear
38. 1st-2nd synchronizer
39. Clutch hub
40. Sleeve
41. Insert
42. Spring
43. Blocker ring
44. 1st gear
45. Needle roller bearing
46. Bearing collar
47. Thrust washer
48. Bearing
49. Nut
50. Reverse gear
51. Speedometer drive gear
52. Clip
53. Counter shaft
54. Retaining ring
55. Bearing
56. Retaining ring
57. Bearing
58. Reverse gear
59. Plain washer
60. Nut
61. Spring washer
62. Reverse idler shaft
63. Spring pin
64. Reverse idler gear

7. Pry the speedometer drive gear retaining clip free as shown in **Figure 20**. Remove the drive gear.
8. Support the end of the reverse shift block with a piece of wood. Drive the pin from the shift block with a suitable punch (**Figure 21**).
9. Remove the bolts holding the reverse block. Remove the reverse shifter shaft, shift block, fork and reverse gear as an assembly. See **Figure 22**.
10. Remove the retaining snap rings from the drive gear and countershaft front bearing outer races (**Figure 23**). Discard the snap rings.
11. Remove the center support carefully to avoid hitting the front end of the drive shaft gear.
12. Support the shifter shafts with a block of wood and drive the pins from both forks with a punch (**Figure 24**).
13. Loosen the detent spring plate bolts. Remove the plate, gasket and springs.

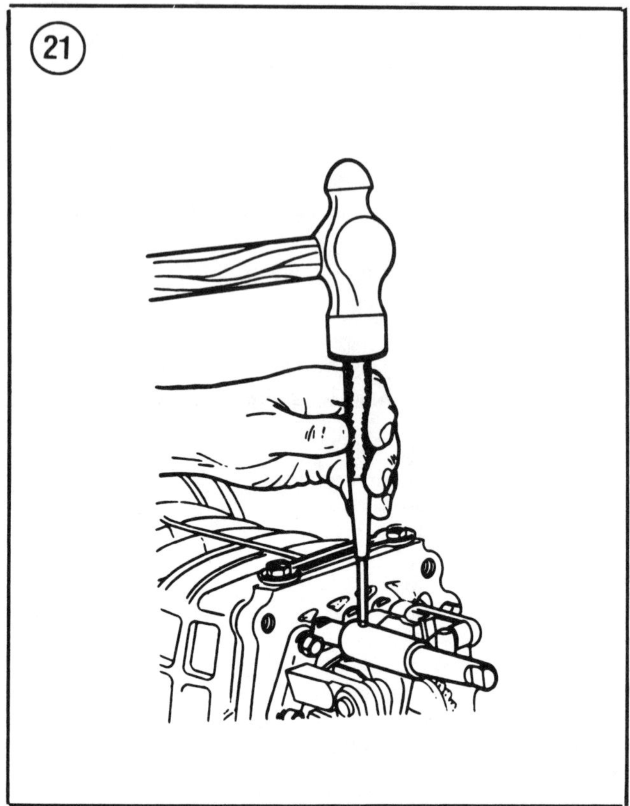

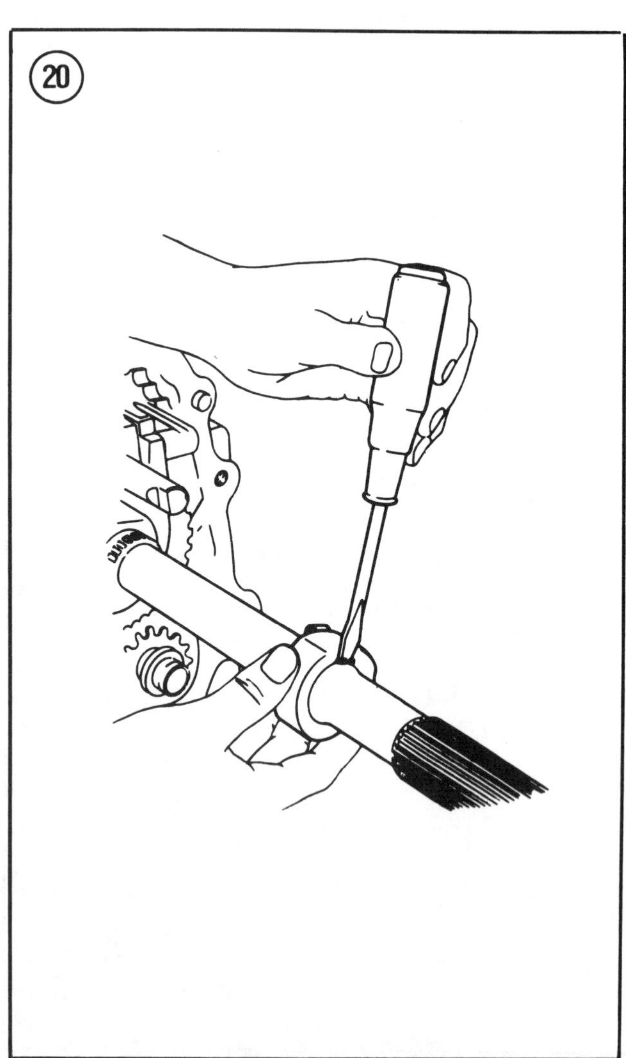

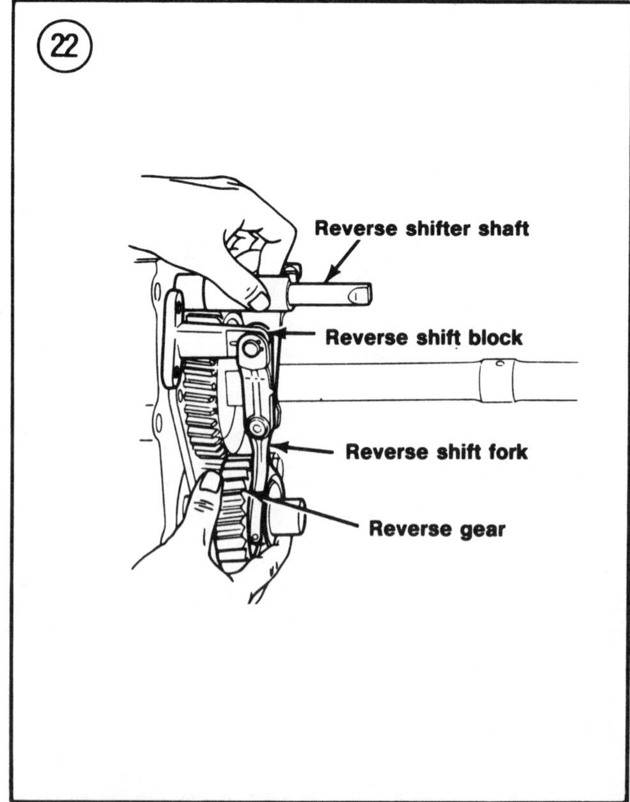

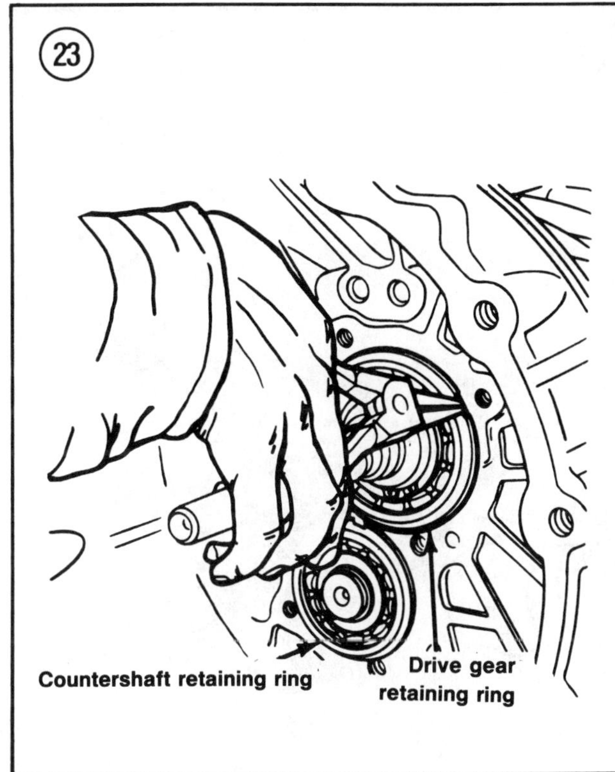

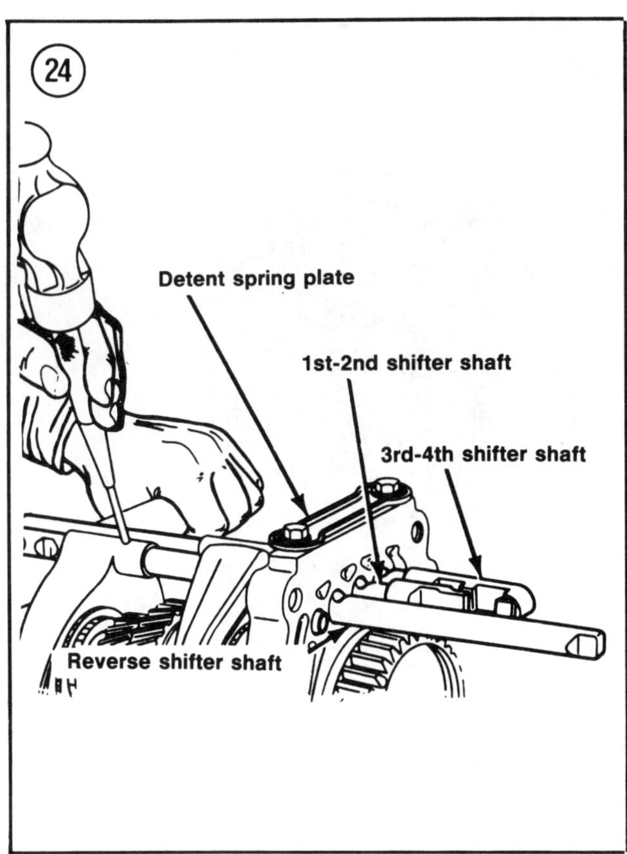

14. Position the 3 shift shafts in neutral. Remove the reverse, 1st/2nd and 3rd/4th shafts in that order, taking care not to lose the interlock pins and detent balls.

15. Remove the 2 interlock pins and 3 detent balls. Remove the shift forks.

16. Lock the synchronizers to prevent the main shaft from turning and temporarily reinstall the center support to the transmission case.

17. Unstake the main shaft rear nut with a punch (**Figure 25**). Remove the nut. Remove the reverse gear from the main shaft.

18. Remove the countershaft nut, spring washer, plain washer and reverse gear from the countershaft. Remove the center support from the transmission case.

19. Unlock the synchronizers and return the transmission to a neutral position. Remove the rear bearing retainer from the center support (**Figure 26**).

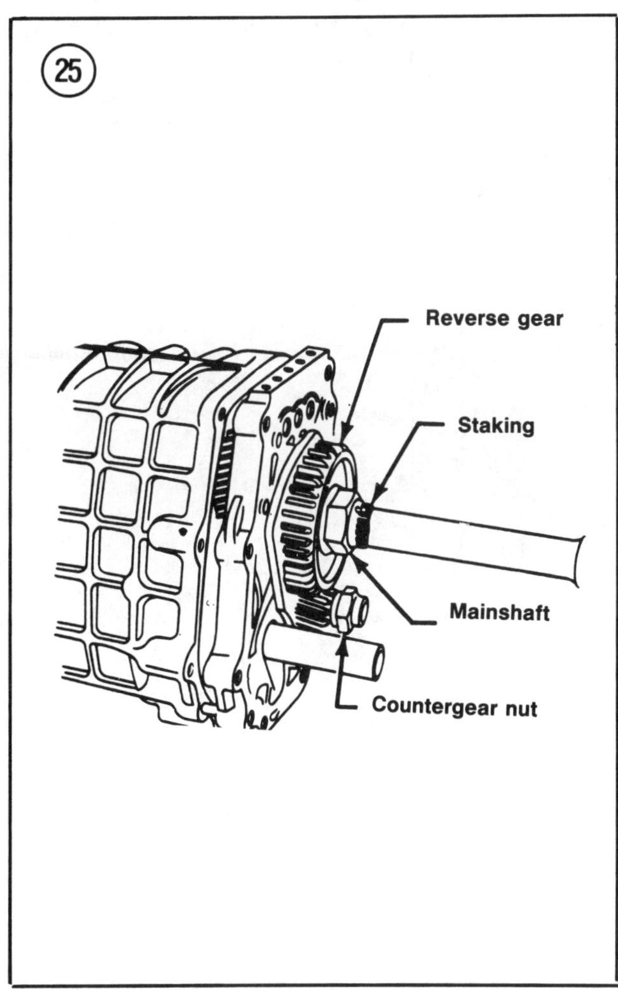

20. Move the countershaft back and forth to slide the rear bearing outer race to the rear. Remove the race with a pair of screwdrivers. See **Figure 27**.
21. Remove the countershaft and drive gear shaft. Remove the 4th gear blocker ring and needle roller bearing.
22. Clean and inspect all components as described in this chapter.

Assembly

Refer to **Figure 17** for this procedure.

1. Install the countershaft to the center support.
2. Install the rear bearing outer race to the countershaft from the rear side of the center support.
3. Install the bearing retainer to the center support. Clean the threaded holes in the support. Apply a coat of Loctite 242 or equivalent to the screw threads, then install and tighten to 15 ft.-lb. (20 N•m).
4. Lock the synchronizers to prevent the main shaft from moving. Temporarily install the center support to the transmission case.

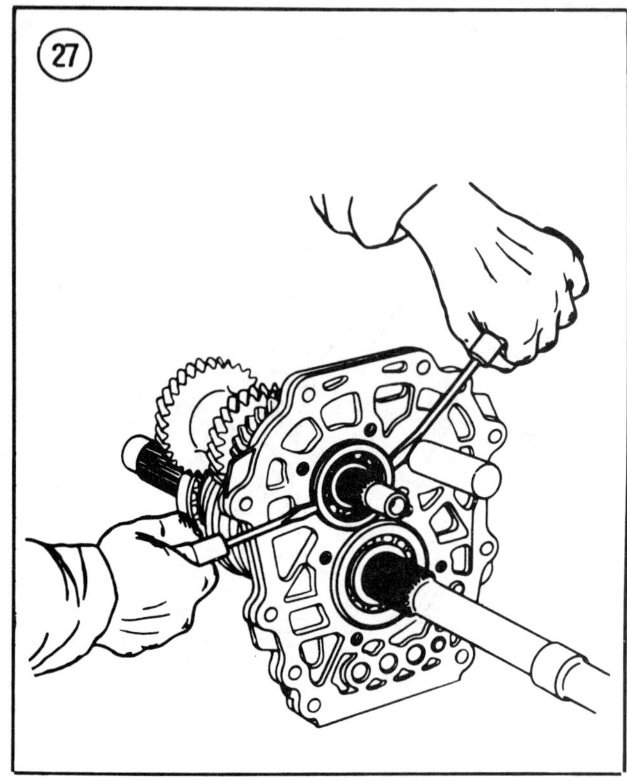

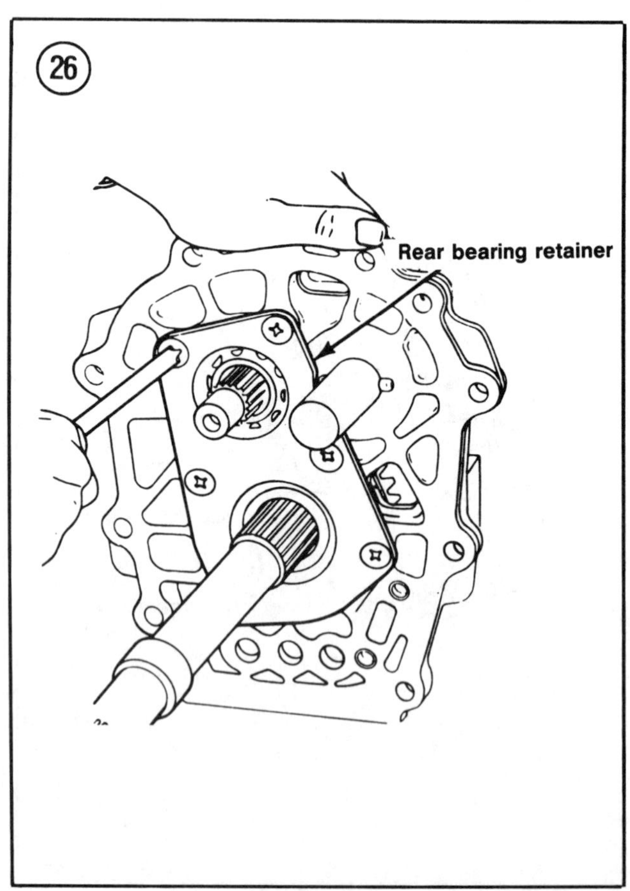

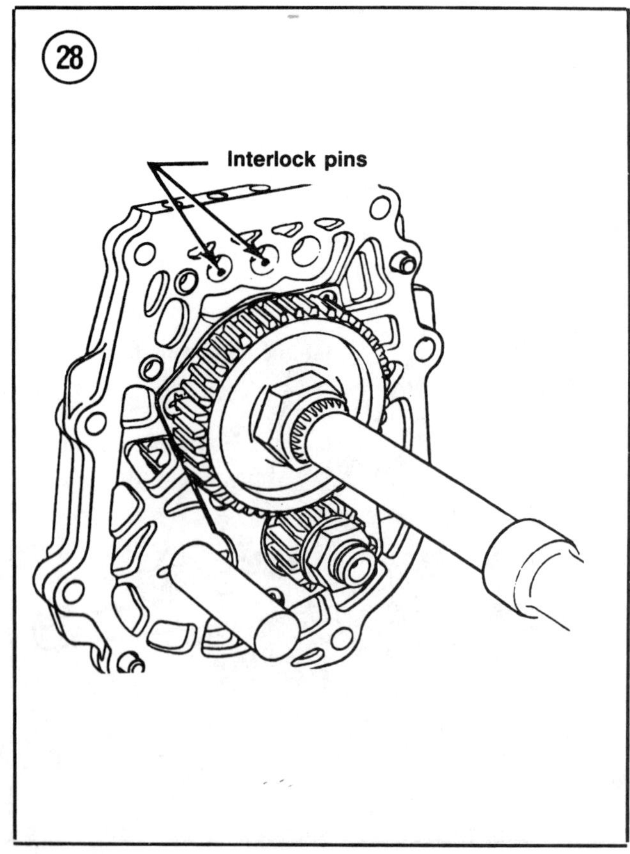

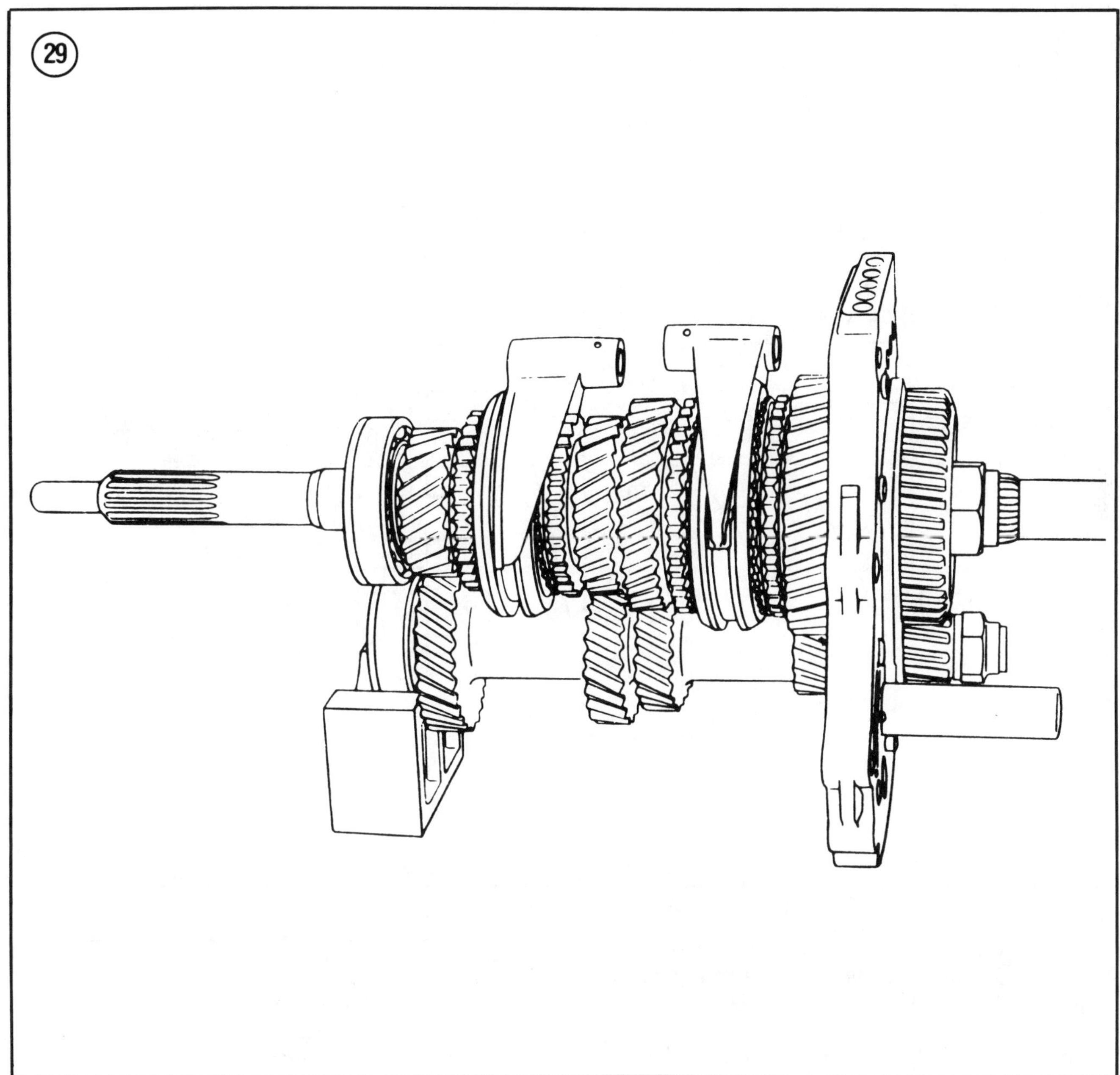

5. Install the countershaft reverse gear with the rounded edges facing to the rear of the shaft. Install the plain washer, spring washer and nut. Tighten the nut to 80 ft.-lb. (110 N•m).

6. Install the main shaft reverse gear with its rounded teeth facing the rear of the shaft. Install and tighten the nut to 95 ft.-lb. (130 N•m), then stake the nut in place with a punch.

7. Separate the case and center support. Coat the 2 interlock pins with grease and install in the center support. See **Figure 28**.

8. Install the 2 shift forks to the synchronizers as shown in **Figure 29**.

9. Install the 3rd/4th shift shaft to the center support and shift fork. Position the shaft in neutral.

10. Install the 1st/2nd and reverse shifter shafts to the center support. See **Figure 30**.

11. Support the end of the main shaft with a block of wood and install the roll pins in the shift forks with a punch.

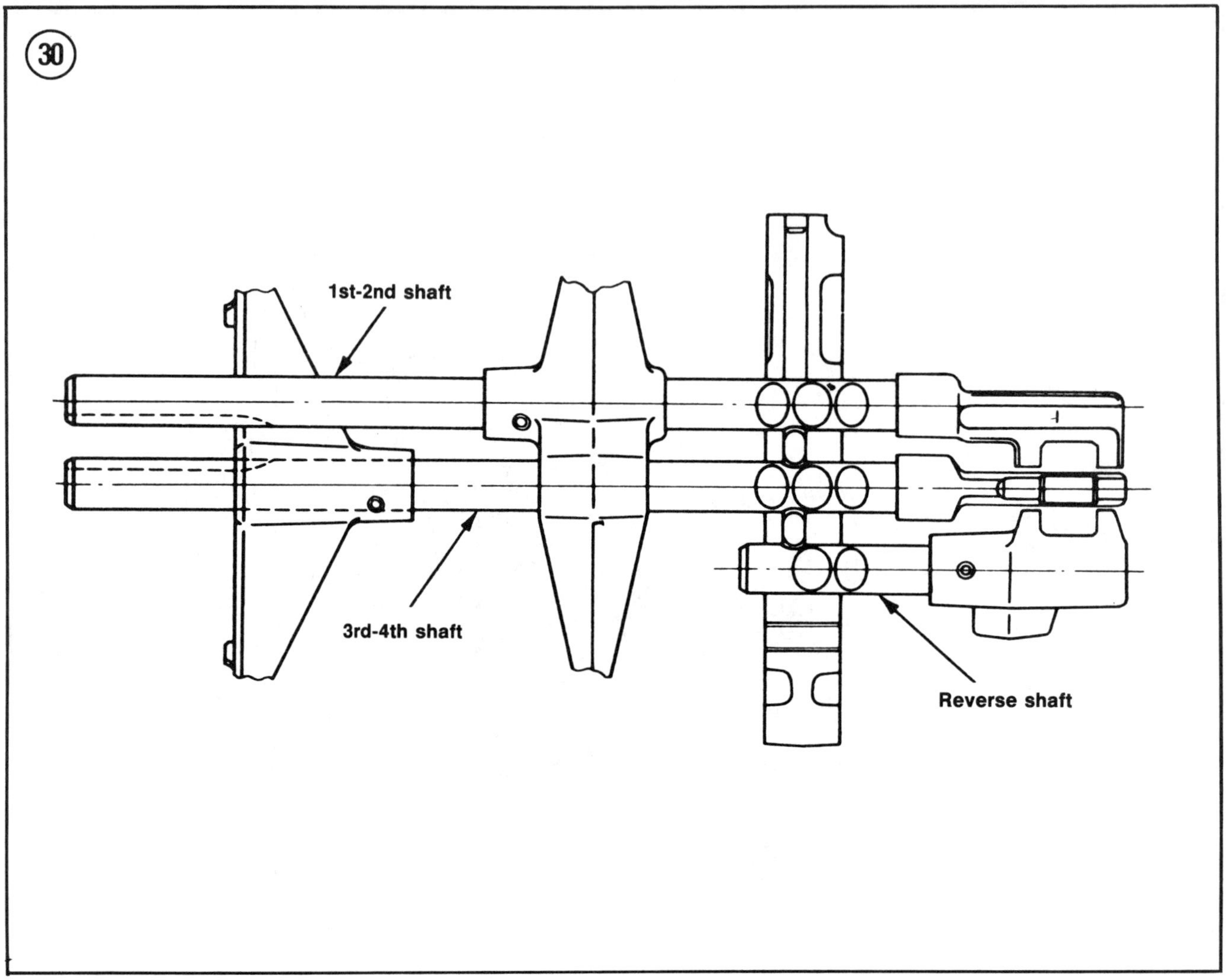

(30)

1st-2nd shaft

3rd-4th shaft

Reverse shaft

12. Install the 3 detent balls in the center support. Install the 3 detent springs as shown in **Figure 31**. Note that the reverse detent spring is shorter and must be positioned as shown.
13. Install the gasket and plate over the detent springs. Tighten the attaching bolts to 15 ft.-lb. (20 N•m).
14. Install the transmission case gasket. Use a light coat of grease to hold it in place, if necessary. Align the center support with the case and install it over the case dowels (**Figure 32**).
15. Install the drive gear and countershaft retaining rings.
16. Assemble the reverse shift block, reverse block and reverse shift fork with the pins and snap rings. Install the shift block assembly to the reverse shift fork, then install the fork in the reverse idler gear groove.

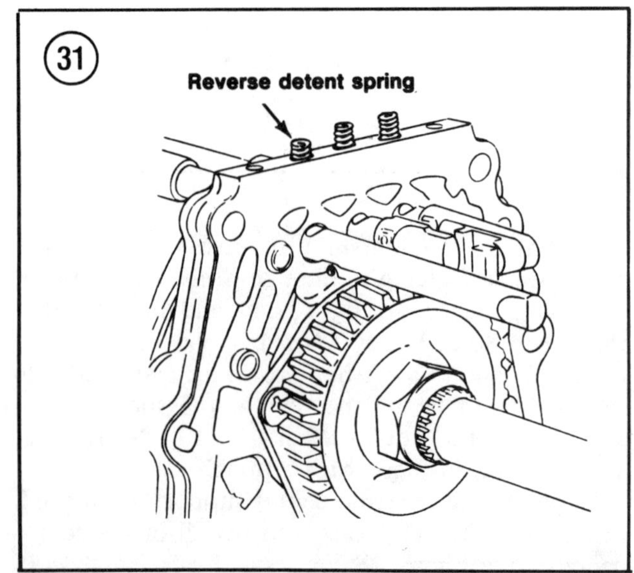

32

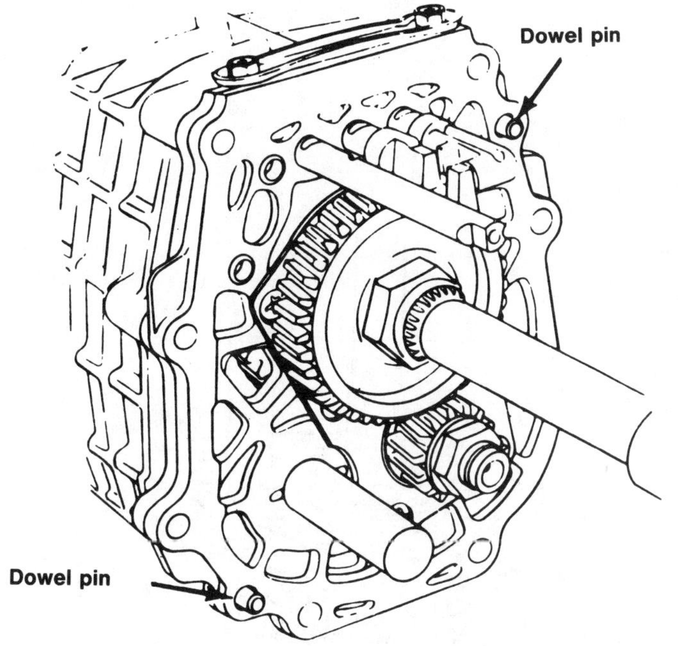

Dowel pin

Dowel pin

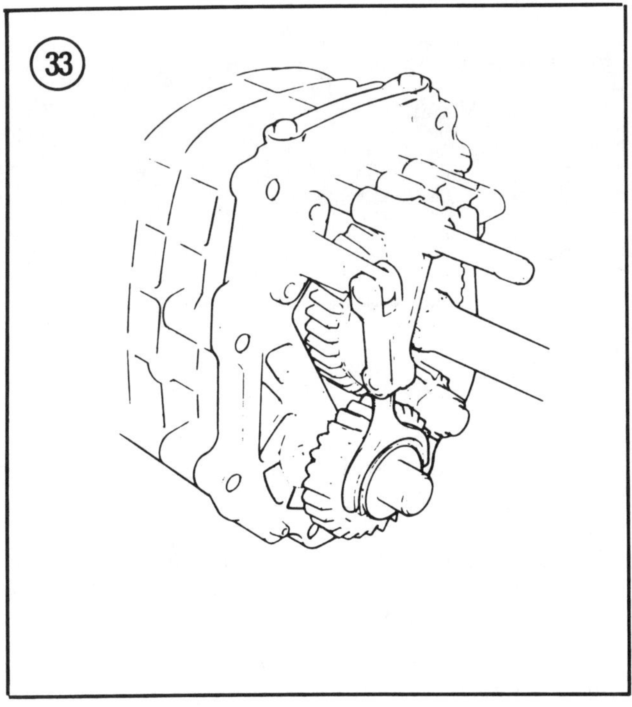

17. Install the reverse gear to the idler shaft and the reverse shift block to the shifter shaft (**Figure 33**).
18. Attach the reverse shift block to the shift shaft with the spring pin.
19. Fit the end of the speedometer retaining clip into the hole in the main shaft. Install the drive gear over the clip.
20. Install the center support gasket. Install the extension housing to the support. Tighten the bolts to 30 ft.-lb. (40 N•m).
21. Install the backup light switch and speedometer driven gear.
22. Install the shifter cover to the extension housing with a new gasket.
23. Install the front bearing retainer with a new gasket. Coat the bolt threads with Permatex No. 2 or equivalent. Install the bolts and tighten to 15 ft.-lb. (20 N•m).
24. Temporarily install the shift lever to the shifter cover and check the shift pattern for correct and smooth gear engagement.

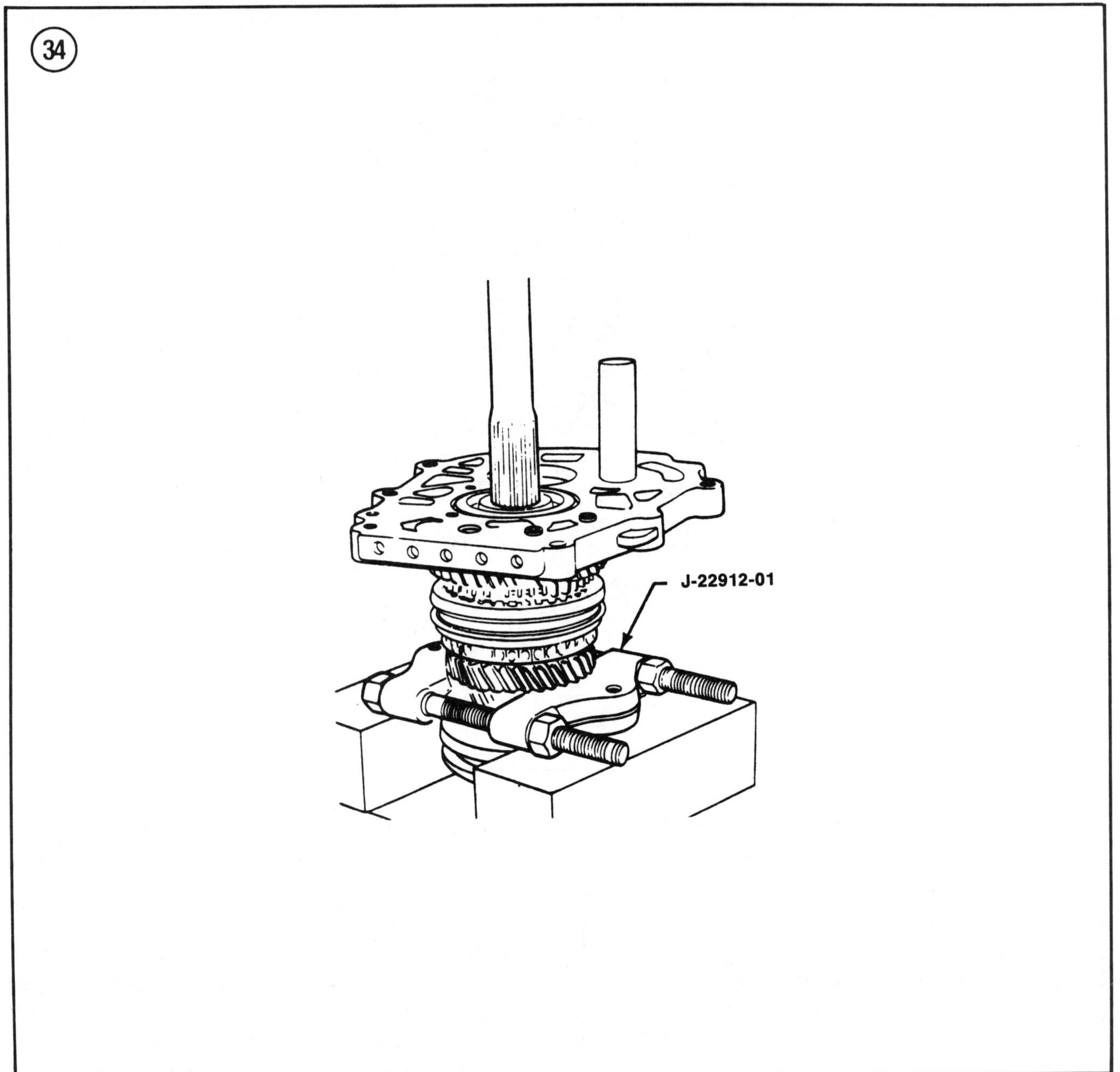

Main Shaft Disassembly/Assembly

The use of a hydraulic press and a universal bearing remover is required for this procedure.

1. Install the universal bearing remover at the face of the main shaft 2nd gear and press the main shaft from the center support (**Figure 34**).
2. Remove 2nd gear, the 1st/2nd synchronizer, 1st/2nd blocker ring, 1st gear needle roller bearing, bearing collar and thrust washer. See **Figure 17**.
3. Remove the main shaft rear bearing from the center support.
4. Remove the snap ring at the front of the main shaft. Discard the snap ring.
5. Install the universal bearing remover to the rear face of the 3rd gear. Press off 3rd gear, the 3rd gear blocker ring and the 3rd/4th synchronizer.
6. Assembly is the reverse of disassembly.

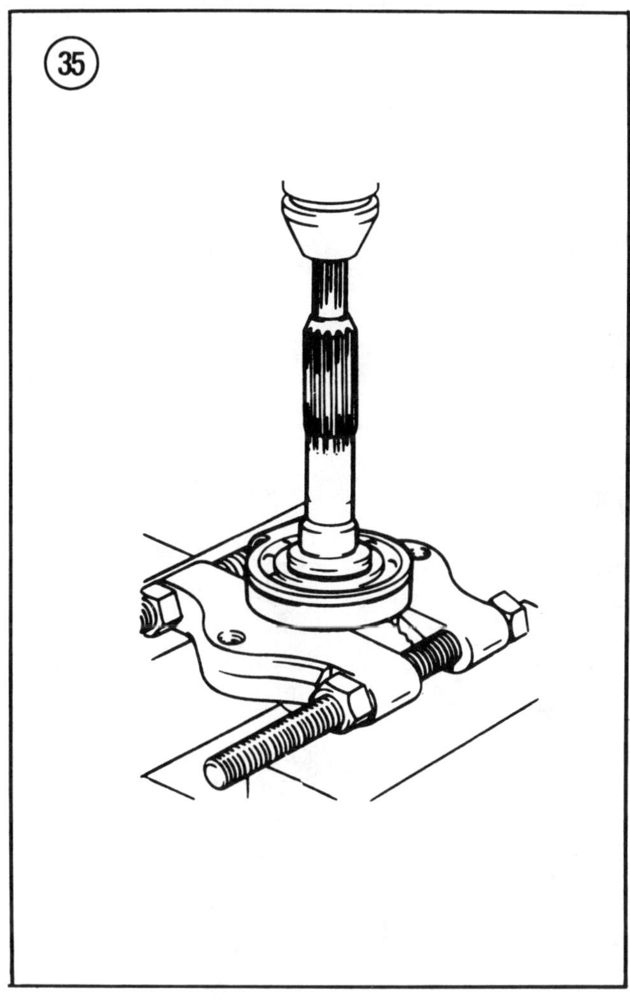

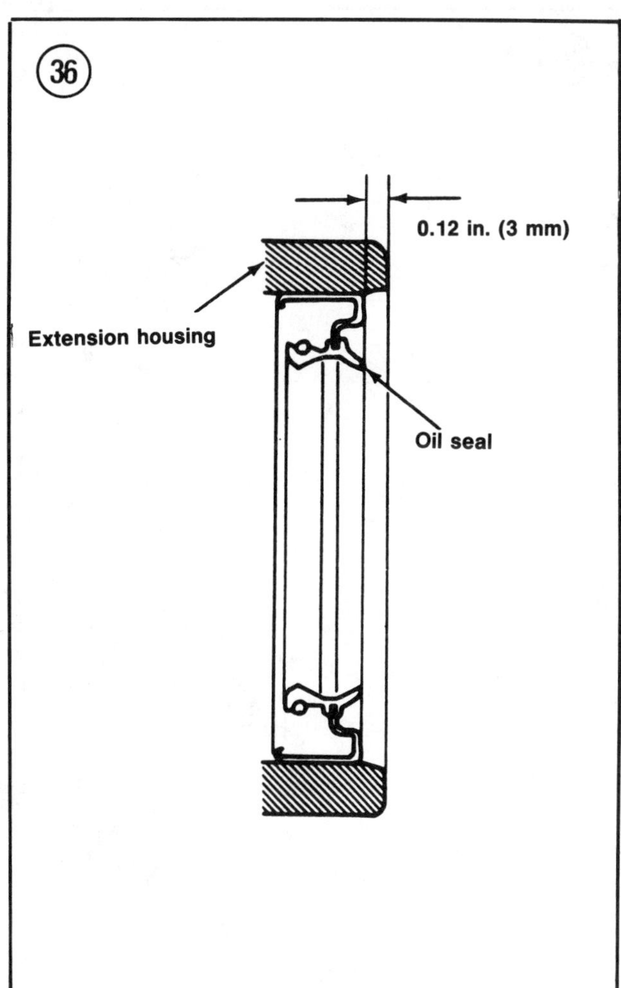

Drive Gear/Countershaft Bearing Replacement

The use of a hydraulic press and a universal bearing remover is required for this procedure.

1. Remove the snap ring from the drive gear or countershaft. Discard the snap ring.
2. Install the universal bearing remover and press the bearing off. **Figure 35** shows the drive gear bearing being pressed off.
3. Press the new bearing on the shaft with its snap ring groove facing away from the gear.
4. Install a new snap ring in the bearing groove.

Extension Housing/Front Bearing Retainer Oil Seal Replacement

1. Pry the old seal out with a screwdriver.
2. Clean all residue from the seal bore.
3. Coat the outer diameter of a new seal with Permatex No. 2 or equivalent.
4. Install the new seal with an appropriate driver. The extension housing seal should be installed until its face is recessed from the rear of the housing by 0.12 in. (3 mm). See **Figure 36**.

WARNER T4C AND T5 TRANSMISSION

Disassembly

Disassembly of these 2 transmissions is quite similar. Differences are pointed out in the following procedure where applicable. **Figure 37** is an exploded view of the Warner T4C 4-speed transmission. The Warner T5 5-speed is shown in **Figure 38**.

1. Remove the drain plug. Hold the transmission over a clean container and drain the lubricant.

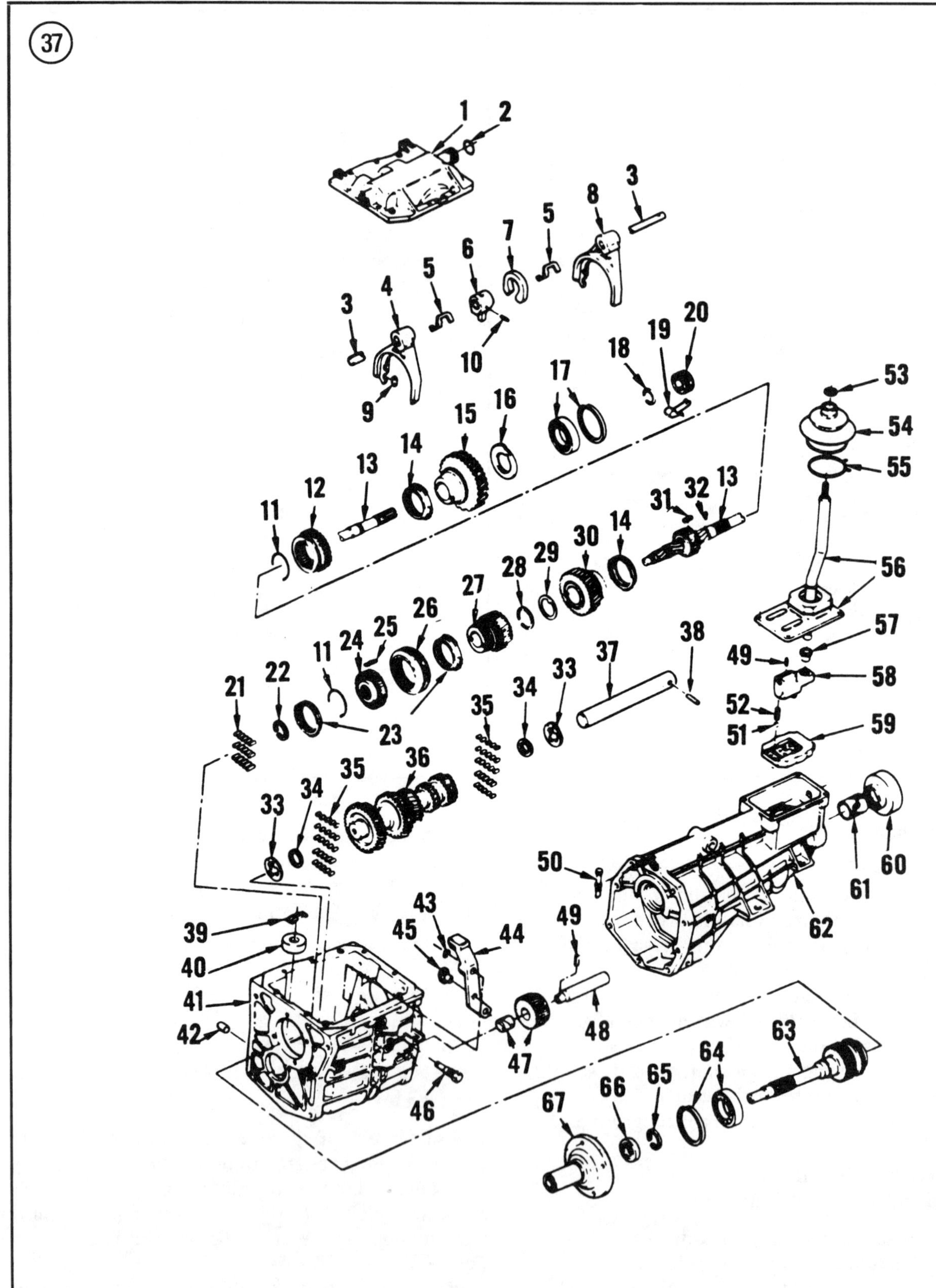
37
1
2
3
4
5
6
7
8
9
10
11
12
13
14
15
16
17
18
19
20
21
22
23
24
25
26
27
28
29
30
31
32
33
34
35
36
37
38
39
40
41
42
43
44
45
46
47
48
49
50
51
52
53
54
55
56
57
58
59
60
61
62
63
64
65
66
67

WARNER T4C 4-SPEED TRANSMISSION

1. Cover
2. O-ring
3. Shift shaft
4. 3rd and 4th shift fork
5. Shift fork plate
6. Control arm
7. Interlock plate
8. 1st and 2nd shift fork
9. Shift fork insert
10. Roll pin
11. Synchronizer spring
12. Reverse sliding gear
13. 1st and 2nd synchronizer shaft
14. 1st and 2nd synchronizer blocking ring
15. 1st gear
16. 1st gear thrust washer
17. Main shaft bearing
18. Retaining ring
19. Clip
20. Speedometer gear
21. Main shaft roller
22. Synchronizer retaining ring
23. 3rd and 4th synchronizer blocking ring
24. 3rd and 4th synchronizer hub
25. 3rd and 4th synchronizer key
26. 3rd and 4th synchronizer sleeve
27. 3rd gear
28. Retaining ring
29. Thrust washer
30. 2nd gear
31. 1st and 2nd synchronizer key
32. Retaining pin
33. Counter gear thrust washer
34. Counter gear spacer
35. Counter gear roller
36. Counter gear
37. Counter gear shaft
38. Spring pin
39. Spring nut
40. Magnet
41. Case
42. Fill and drain plug
43. Retaining ring
44. Reverse relay lever
45. Reverse shift lever fork
46. Pivot pin
47. Reverse idler gear
48. Reverse idler gear shaft
49. Pin
50. Ventilator
51. Steel ball
52. Detent spring
53. Boot retainer
54. Boot
55. Boot retainer
56. Lever control
57. Damper sleeve
58. Offset shift lever
59. Guide plate
60. Oil seal
61. Bushing
62. Extension housing
63. Main drive gear
64. Main drive gear bearing
65. Retaining ring
66. Oil seal
67. Retainer

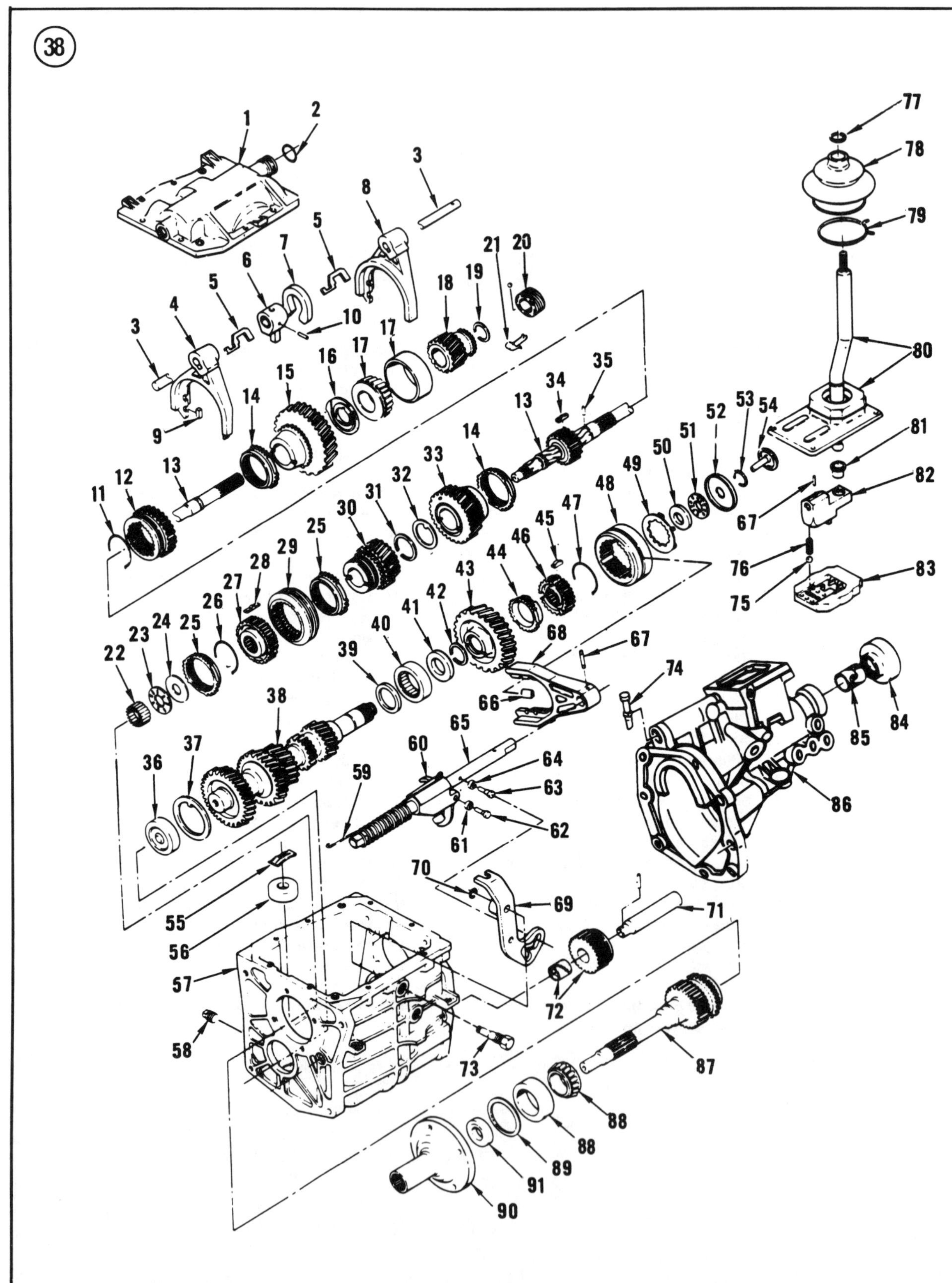
38

5-SPEED TRANSMISSION

1. Cover
2. O-ring
3. Shift shaft
4. 3rd and 4th shift fork
5. Shift fork plate
6. Control selector arm
7. Interlock plate
8. 1st and 2nd shift fork
9. Shift fork insert
10. Roll pin
11. Synchronizer spring
12. Reverse sliding gear
13. Output shaft/1st and 2nd synchronizer
14. Blocking ring
15. 1st gear
16. Thrust washer
17. Rear bearing
18. 5th driven gear
19. Snap ring
20. Speedometer drive gear
21. Clip
22. Main shaft bearing
23. Needle bearing
24. Bearing race
25. 3rd and 4th synchronizer ring
26. 3rd and 4th synchronizer spring
27. 3rd and 4th synchronizer hub
28. 3rd and 4th synchronizer key
29. 3rd and 4th synchronizer sleeve
30. 3rd gear
31. Snap ring
32. Thrust washer
33. 2nd gear
34. 1st and 2nd synchronizer key
35. Retaining pin
36. Bearing
37. Thrust washer
38. Counter gear
39. Spacer
40. Bearing
41. Spacer
42. Snap ring
43. 5th drive gear
44. 5th synchronizer ring
45. 5th synchronizer key
46. 5th synchronizer hub
47. 5th synchronizer spring
48. 5th synchronizer sleeve
49. Retainer
50. Bearing race
51. Thrust bearing
52. Bearing race
53. Snap ring
54. Funnel
55. Nut
56. Magnet
57. Case
58. Fill and drain plug
59. Reverse spring
60. Reverse fork
61. Fork roller
62. Reverse fork pin
63. Shift rail pin
64. Rail pin roller
65. 5th and reverse shift rail
66. Shift fork insert
67. Roll pin
68. 5th shift fork
69. 5th and reverse relay lever
70. Retaining ring
71. Reverse idler gear shaft
72. Reverse idler gear
73. Pin
74. Ventilator
75. Ball
76. Detent spring
77. Boot retainer
78. Boot
79. Boot retainer
80. Control lever
81. Damper sleeve
82. Offset shift lever
83. Detent and guide plate
84. Oil seal
85. Extension housing bushing
86. Extension housing
87. Main drive gear
88. Front bearing
89. Shim
90. Drive gear bearing retainer
91. Oil seal

2. Remove the roll pin holding the offset lever to the shift rail with a suitable punch. See **Figure 39**.
3. Remove the extension housing bolts. Remove the housing and offset lever as an assembly.
4. Remove the detent ball/spring from the offset lever (**Figure 40**). Remove the roll pin from the extension housing.
5. Remove the transmission shift cover bolts. Pry the shift cover loose and remove it from the case with the shift forks attached. **Figure 41** shows the 4-speed cover.
6. 5-speed—Remove the plastic funnel from the rear of the countershaft (**Figure 42**). Remove the race and thrust bearing (**Figure 43**).

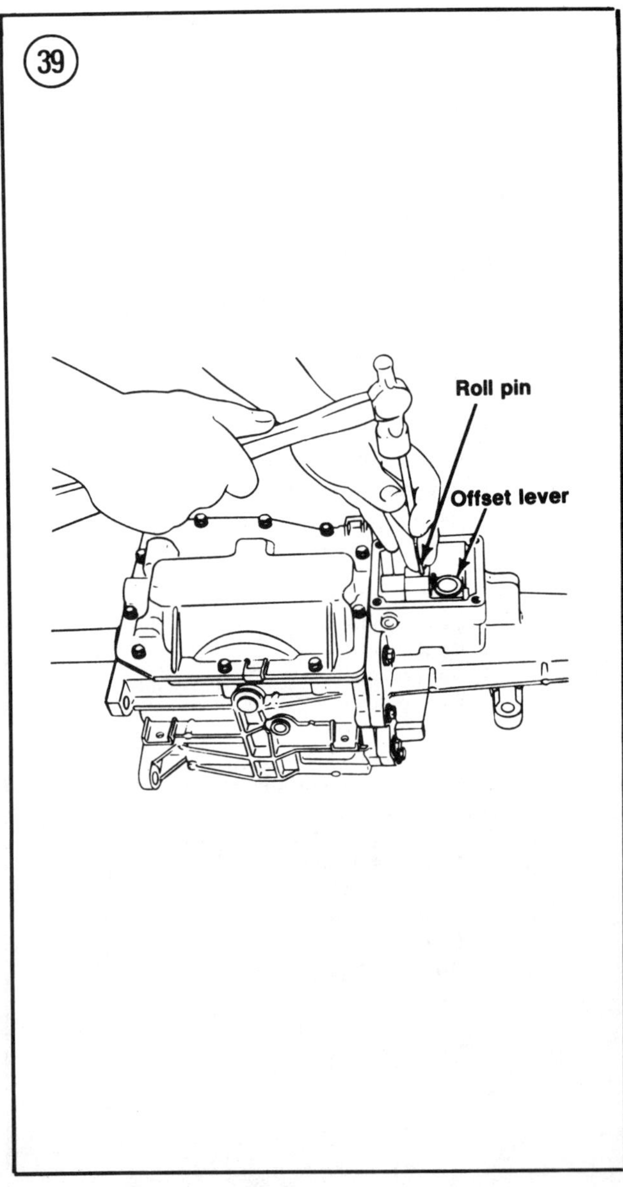

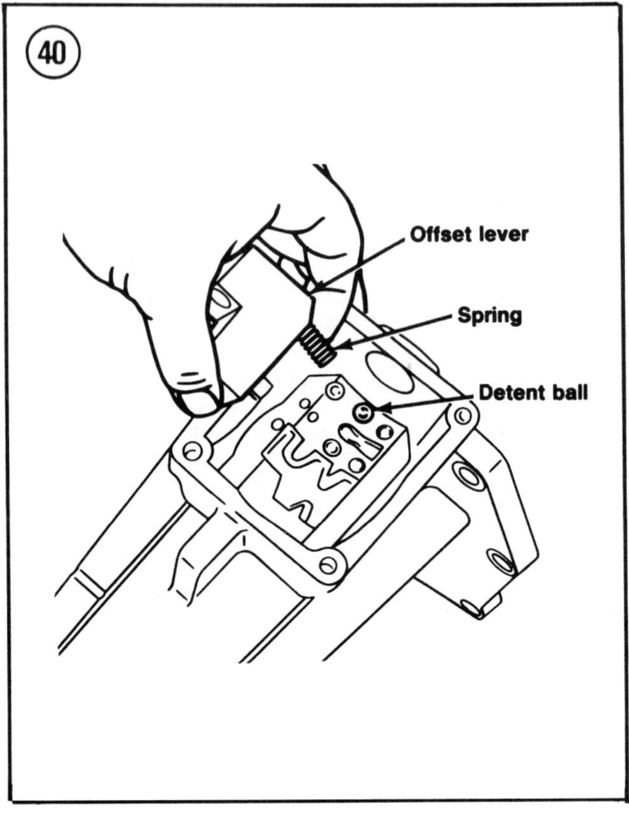

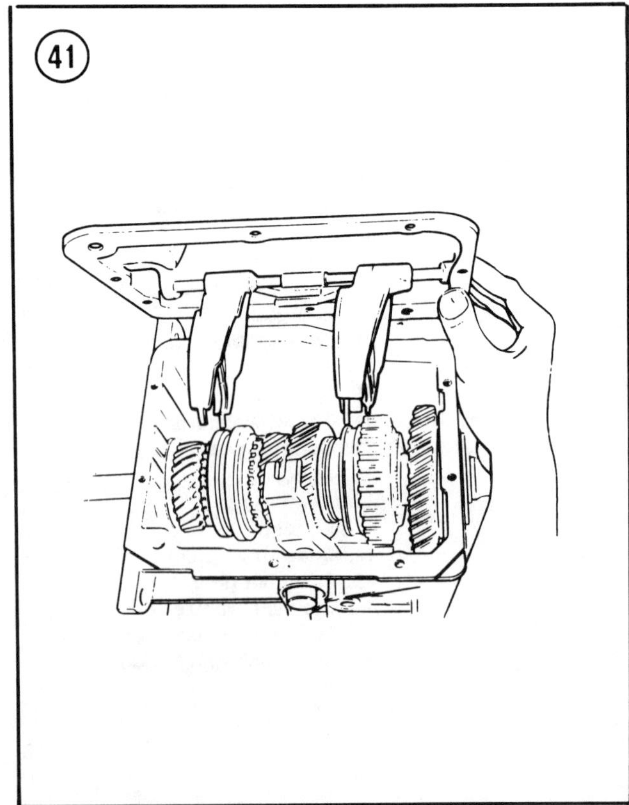

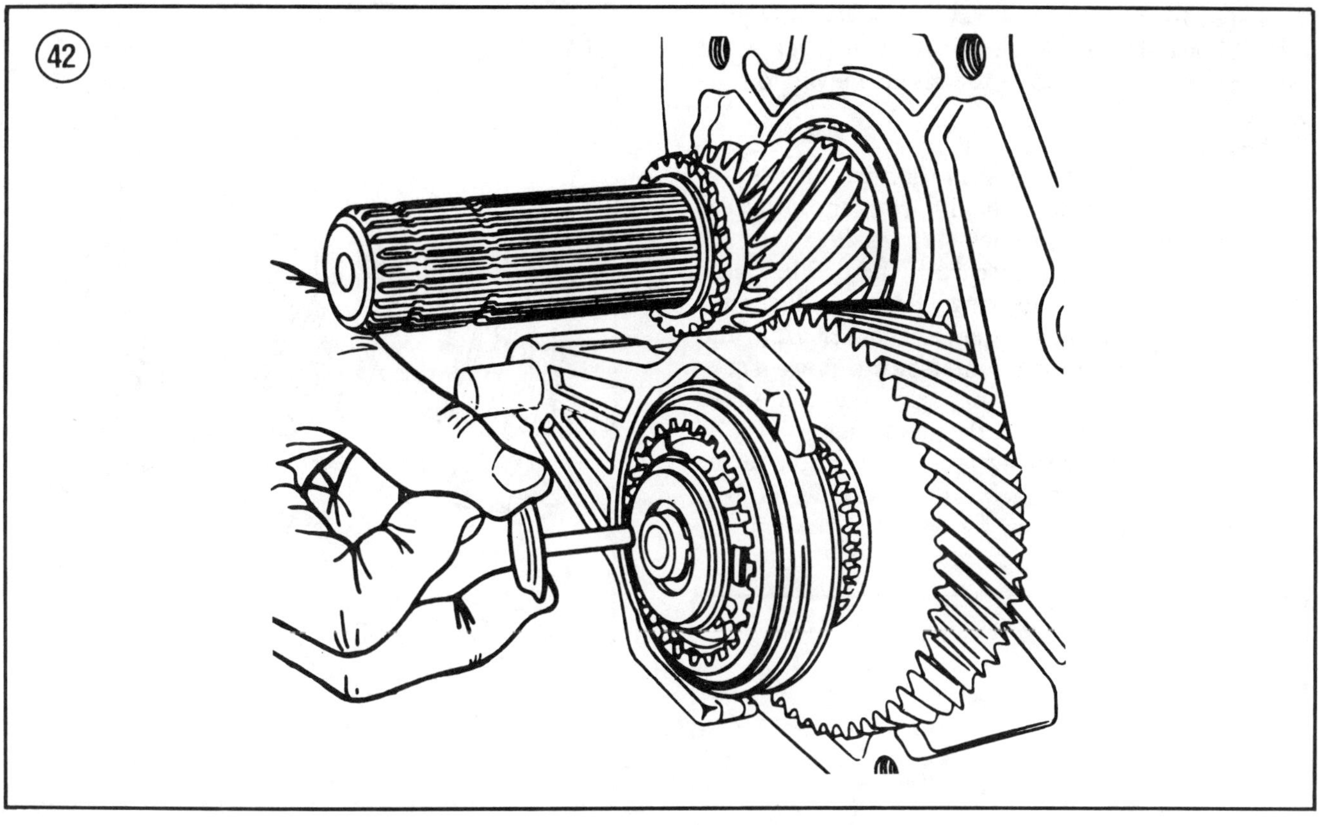
42

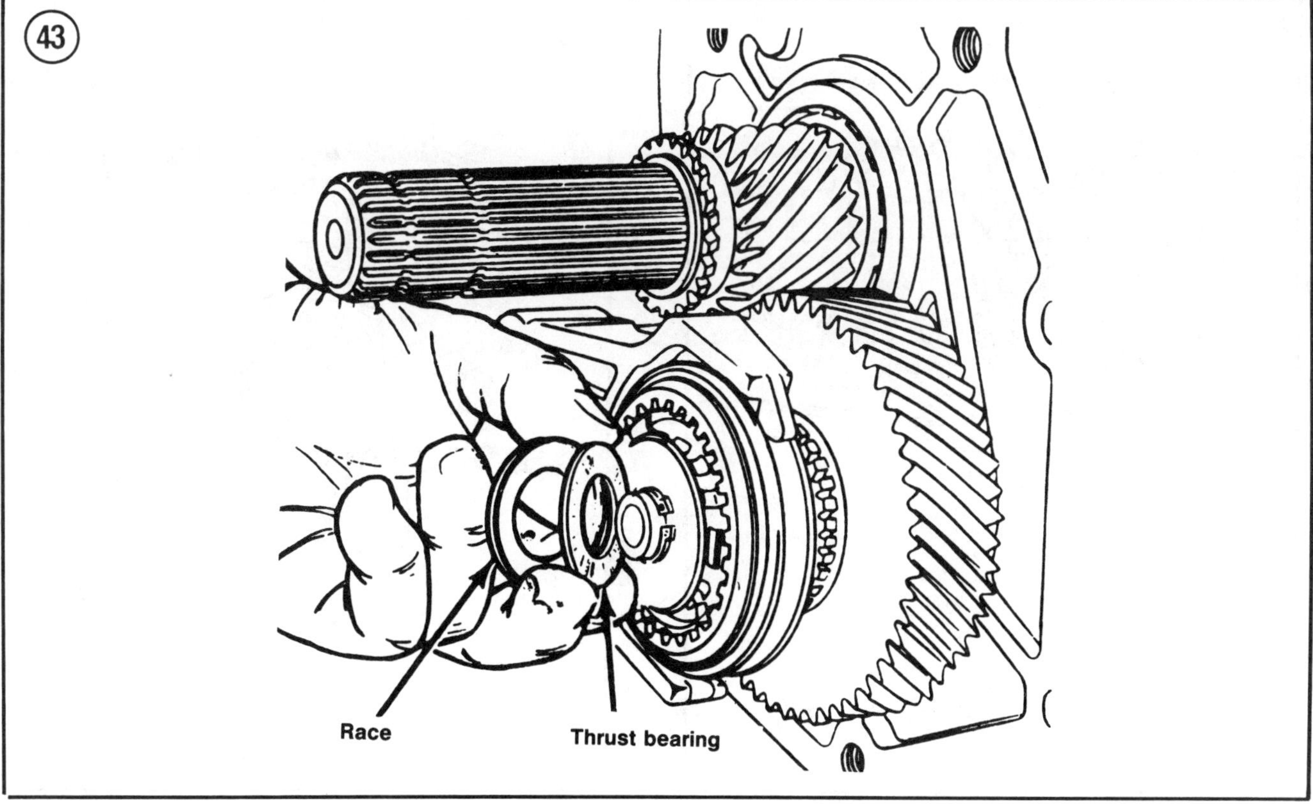
43
Race
Thrust bearing

7. 4-speed—Remove the reverse lever retaining clip (**Figure 44**). Remove the reverse lever pivot bolt (**Figure 45**). Remove the reverse lever/fork as an assembly.

8. 5-speed:

   a. Support the 5th gear shift shaft with a block of wood. Drive the roll pin from the 5th gear shift fork with a punch (**Figure 46**).
   b. Remove and discard the 5th gear synchronizer snap ring. Remove the shift fork, synchronizer sleeve, blocker ring and 5th gear from the countershaft (**Figure 47**).
   c. Remove the snap ring from the 5th speed driven gear. Discard the snap ring.

9. Mark the front bearing retainer position to the case with a punch as shown in **Figure 48**. Unbolt and remove the retainer.

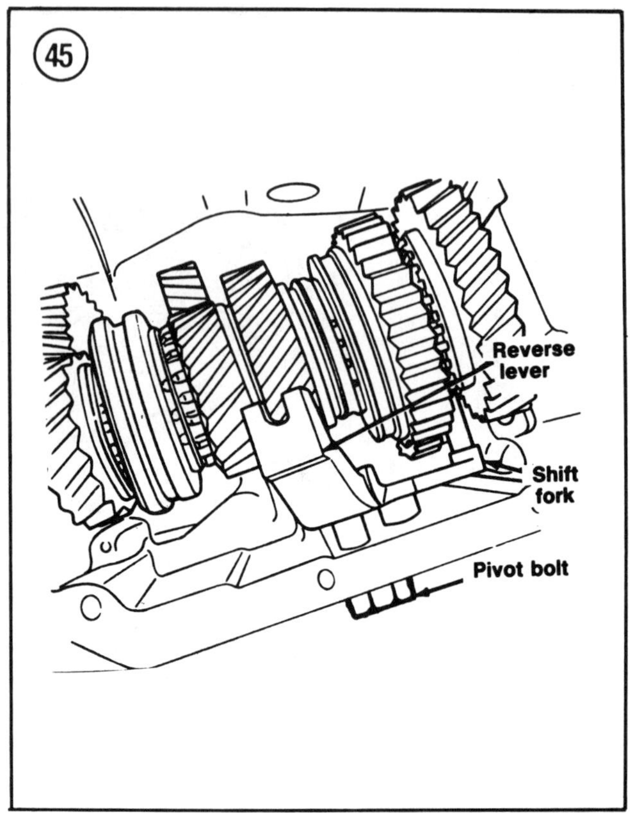

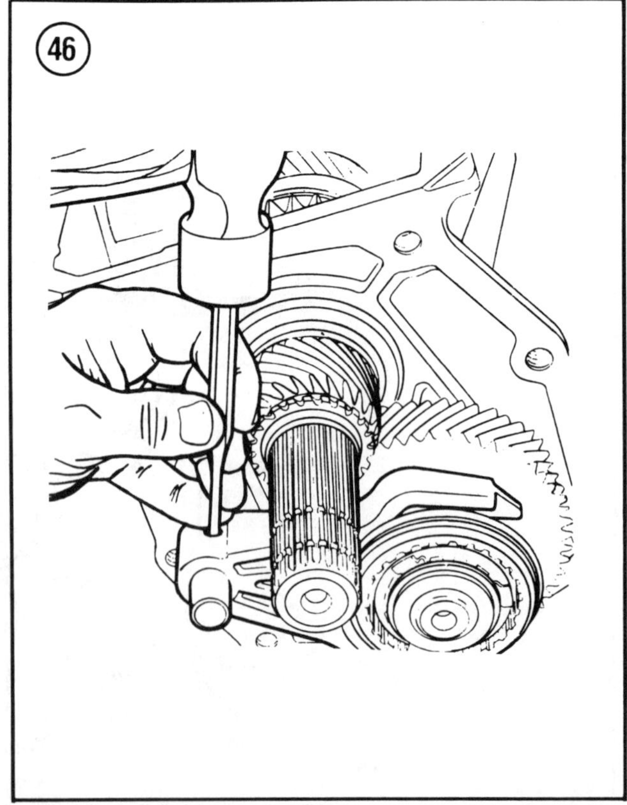

47

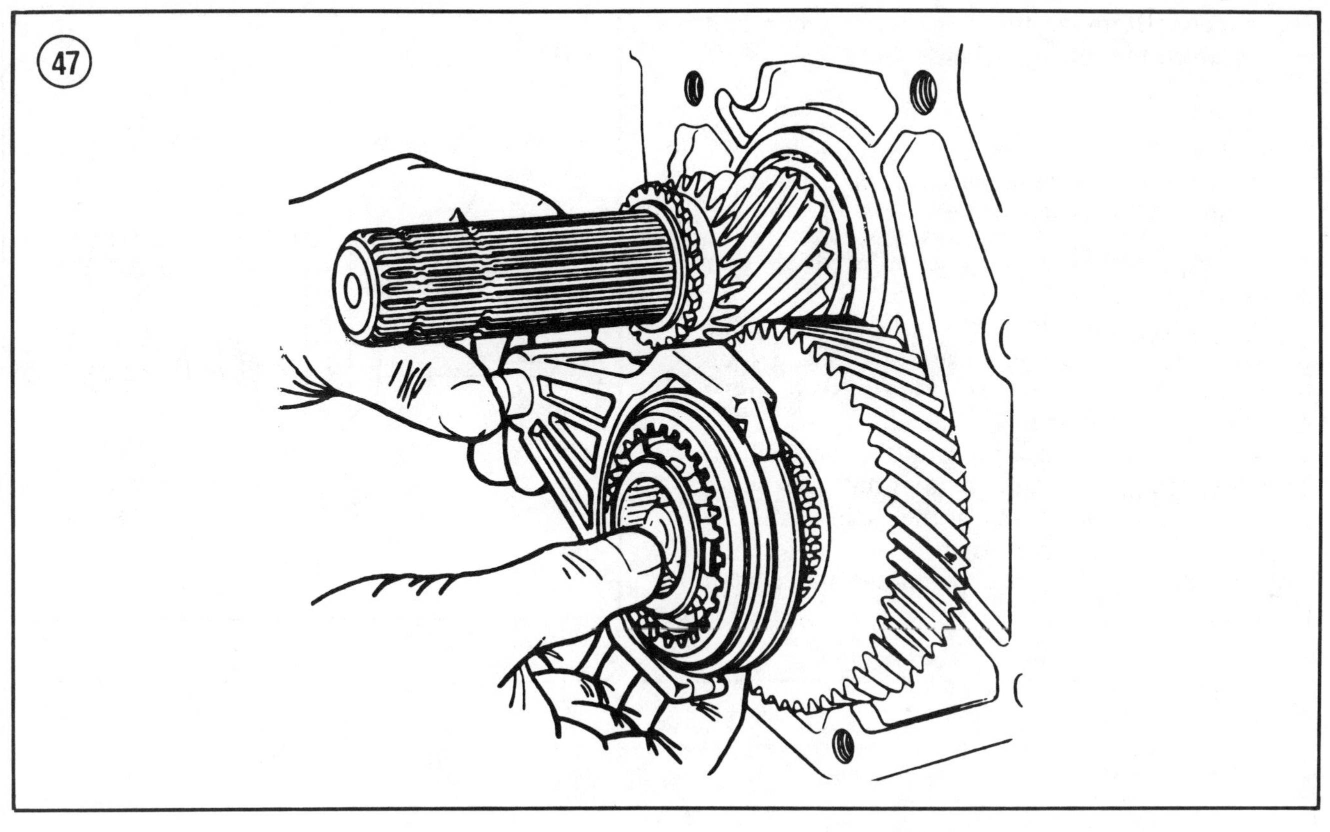

48

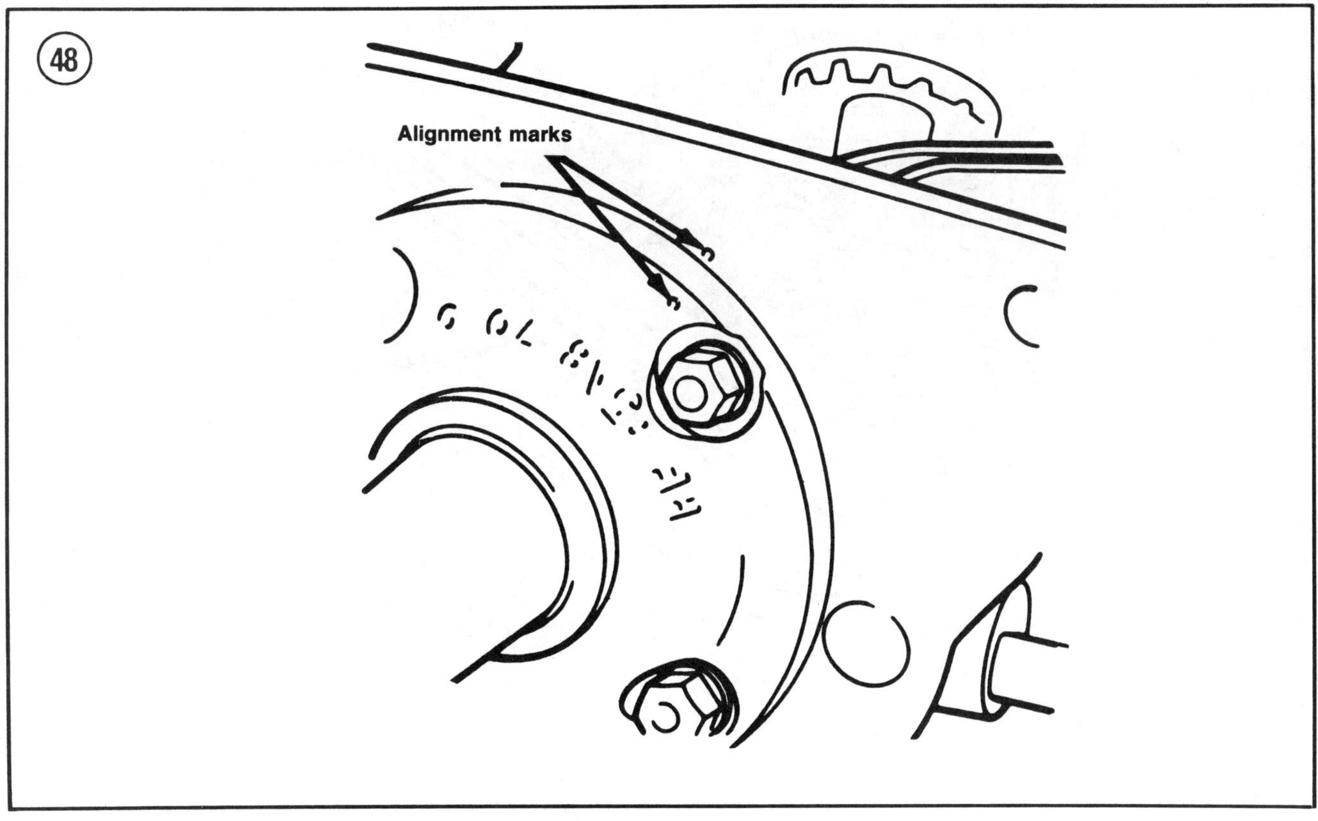

10. 5-speed—Remove the front bearing cup and shim(s) from the retainer (**Figure 49**).

NOTE

Steps 11-17 complete disassembly of the 4-speed transmission. For the remainder of the 5-speed disassembly, proceed to Step 18.

11. Remove and discard the 2 front drive gear bearing snap rings.
12. Install bearing puller part No. J-6654-01 on the front bearing. Install puller part No. J-8433-1 on the end of the drive gear. See **Figure 50**. Remove and discard the bearing.
13. Remove the rear bearing with the same puller. Two long bolts are required to install the puller correctly, due to the length of the main shaft. See **Figure 51**. Discard the bearing.
14. Separate the drive gear from the main shaft (**Figure 52**).

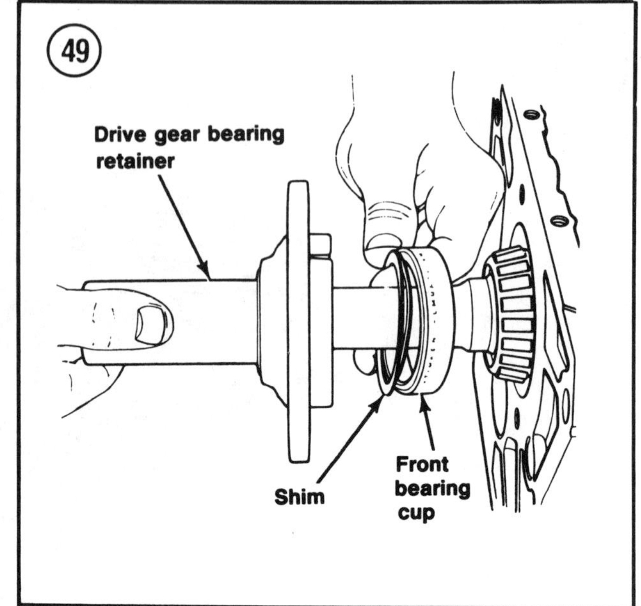

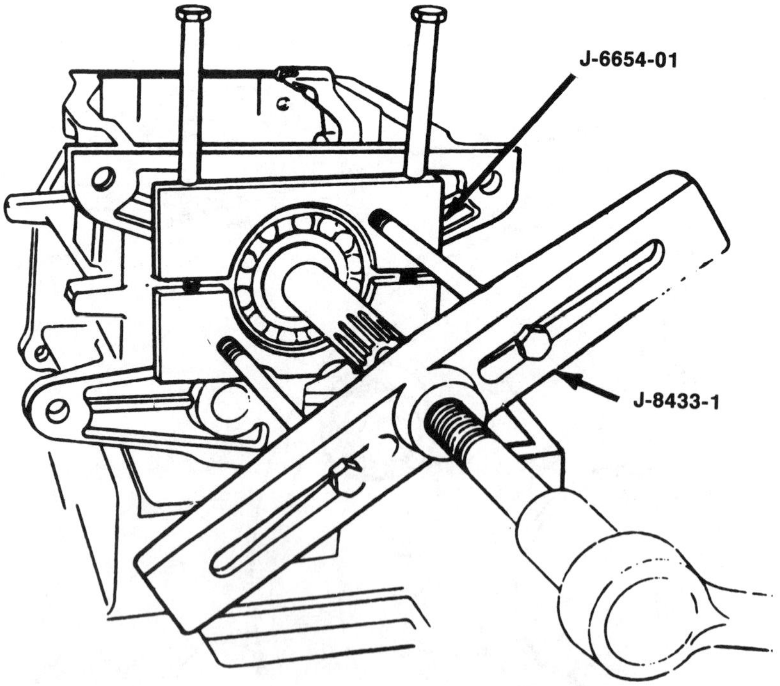

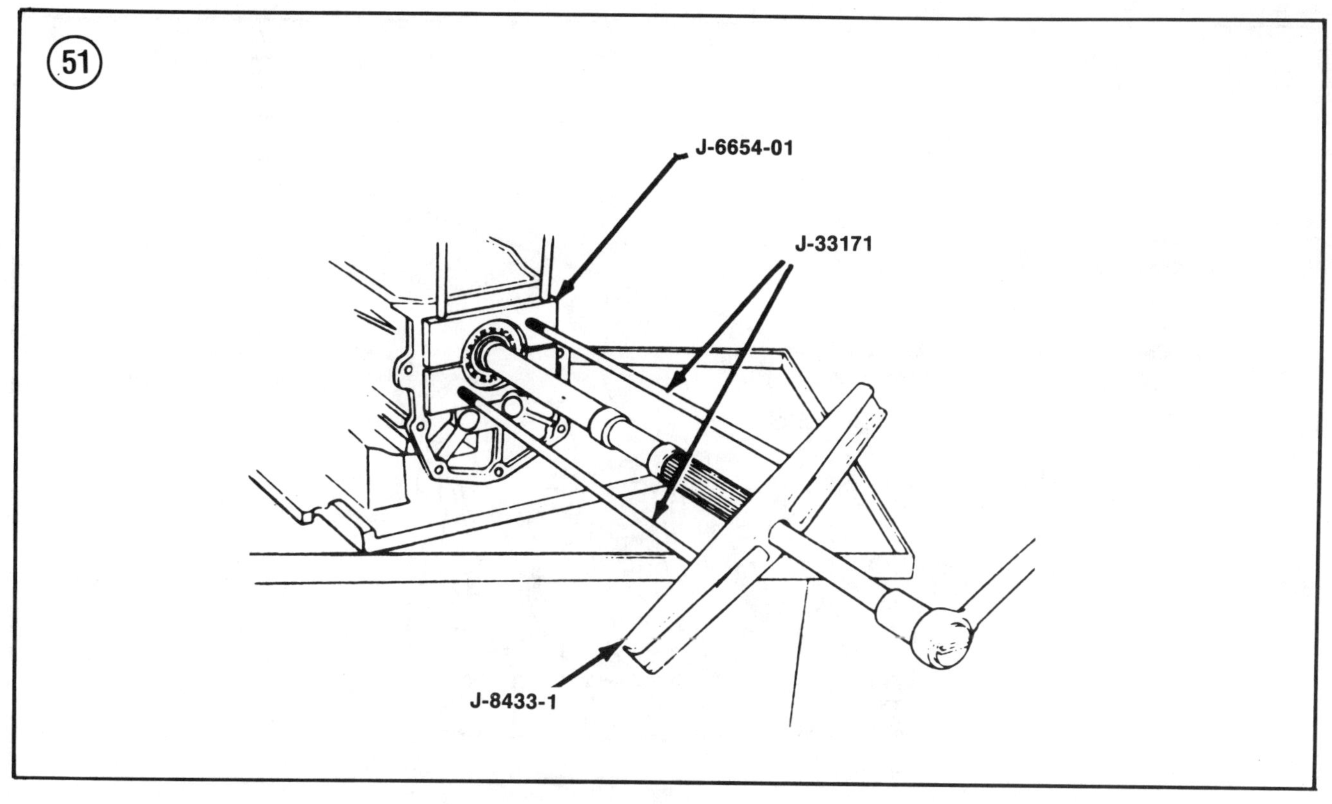

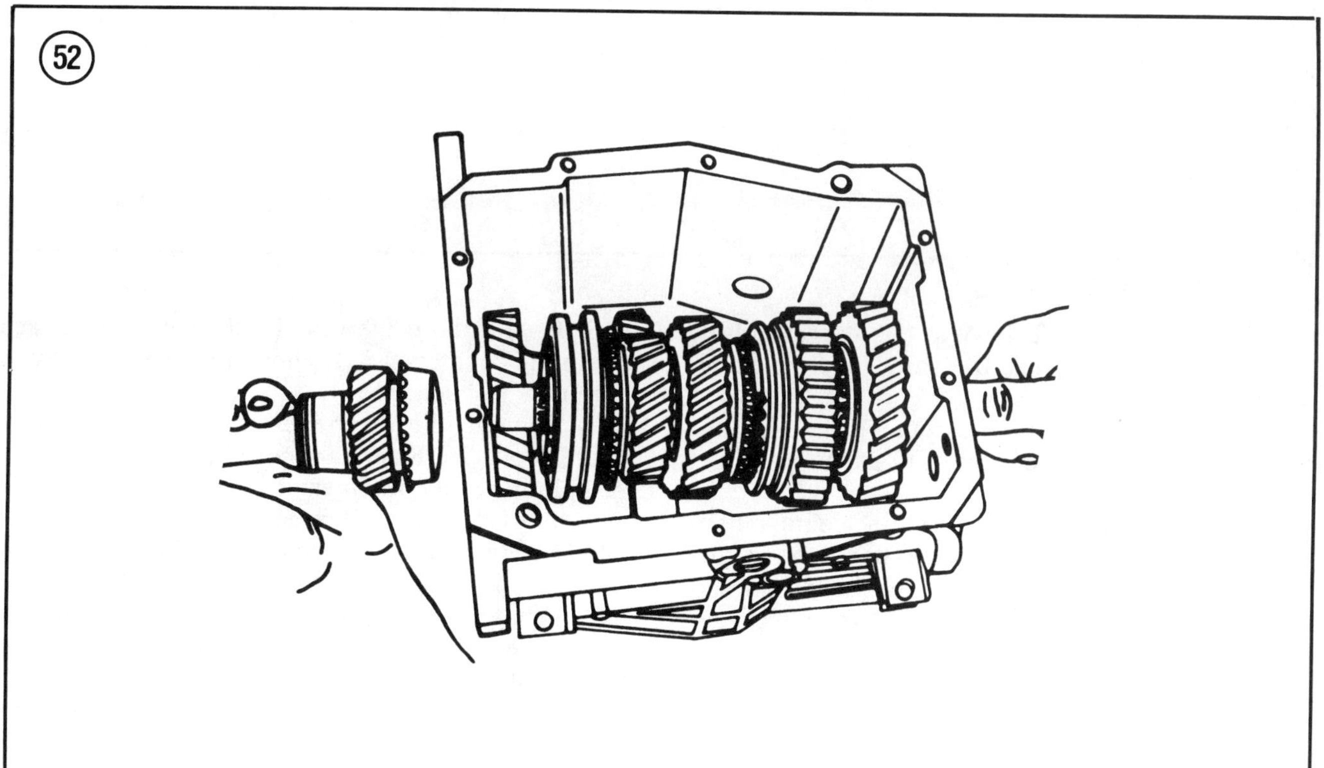

52

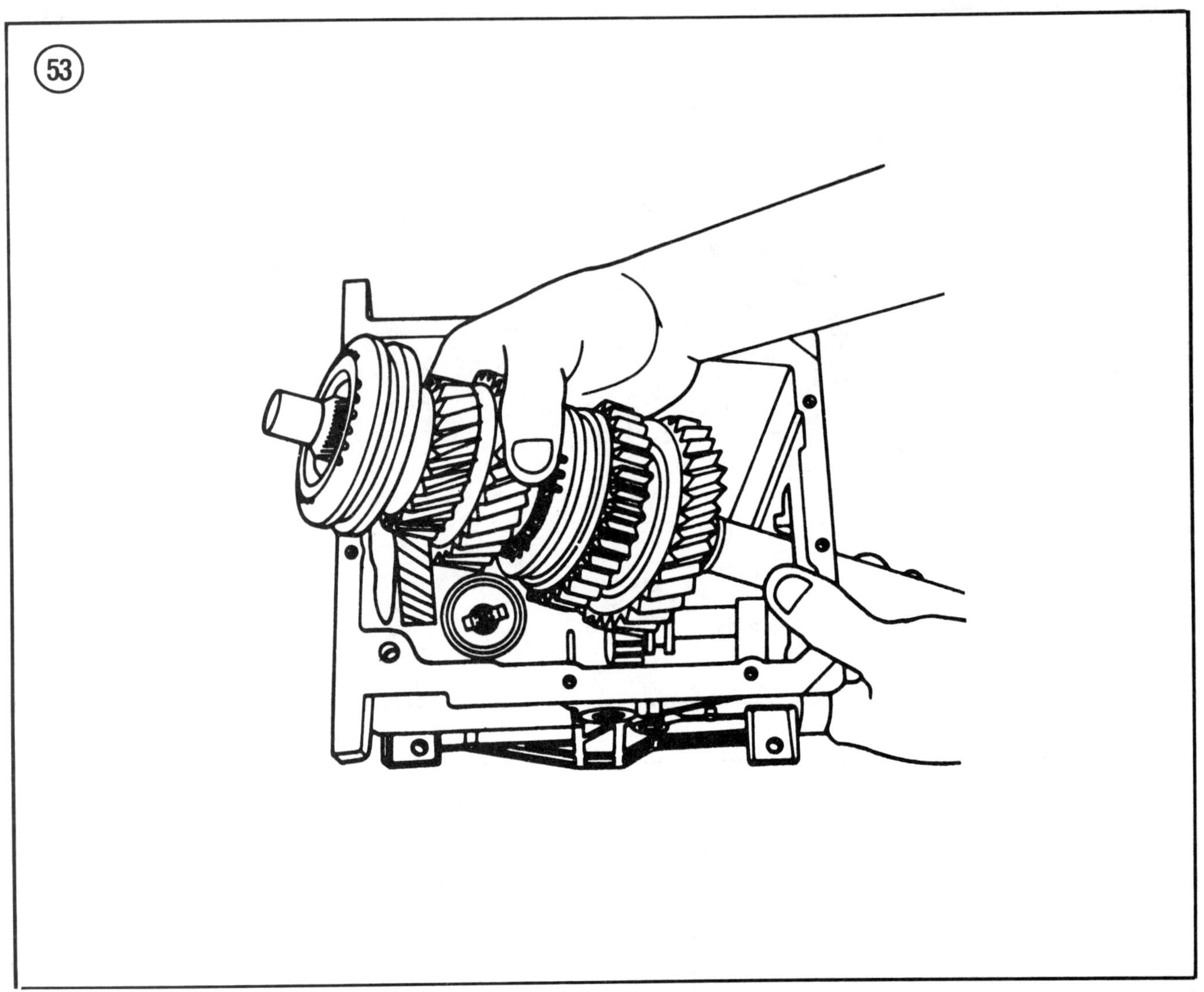

15. Tilt the main shaft down at the rear and lift it out of the case through the shift cover opening (**Figure 53**).
16. Use a suitable punch to remove the roll pin holding the reverse idler gear shaft in the case. See **Figure 54**.
17. Insert a dummy shaft through the countershaft opening at the front of the case and remove the countershaft/dummy shaft as an assembly from the rear of the case. This completes disassembly of the 4-speed gearbox.

NOTE
Steps 18-28 complete disassembly of the 5-speed transmission.

18. Rotate the drive gear to align its flat surface with the countershaft. Remove the drive gear from the case (**Figure 55**).
19. Remove the reverse lever retaining clip and pivot bolt. See **Figure 44** and **Figure 45**.
20. Remove the main shaft rear bearing race. Tilt the main shaft up and remove it from the case.
21. Disconnect the overcenter link spring from the front of the transmission case.
22. Rotate the 5th/reverse gear shift rail to disconnect it from the reverse lever. Remove the shift rail from the rear of the case.
23. Remove the reverse lever/fork assembly from the case.
24. Drive the roll pin from the front of the reverse idler shaft with a punch. Remove the reverse idler shaft, O-ring and gear from the case.

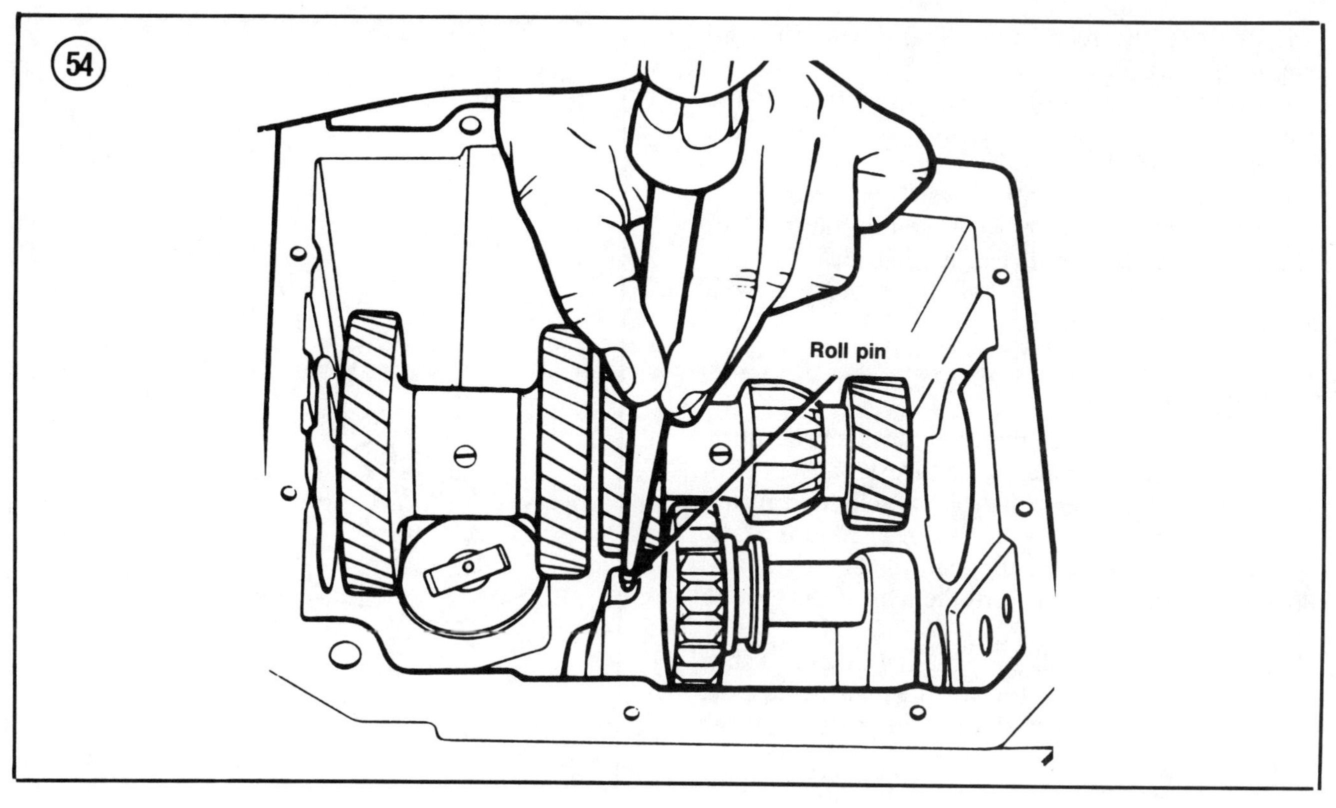

55

9

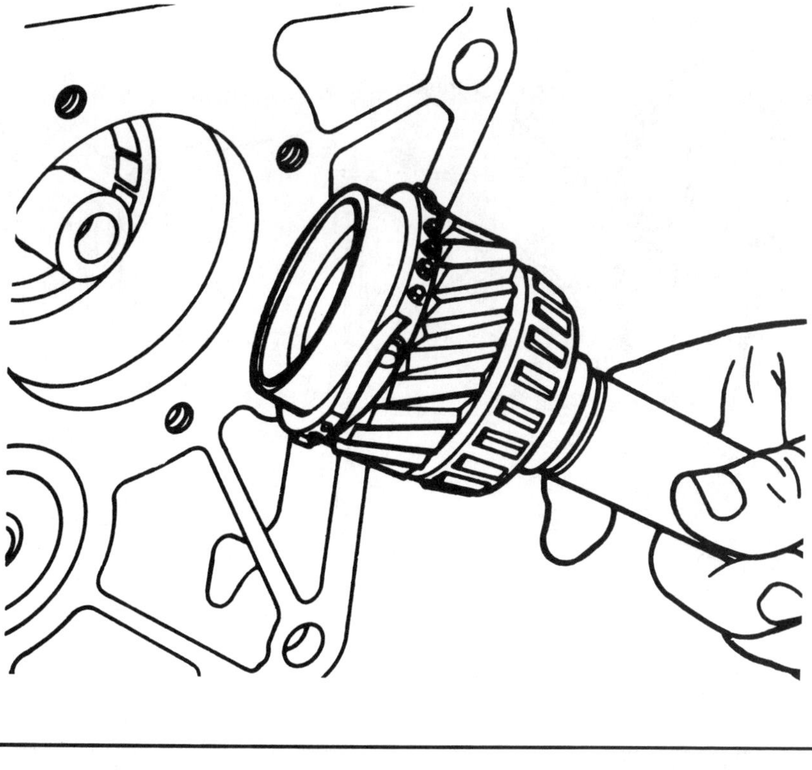

25. Remove the rear countershaft snap ring and spacer (**Figure 56**).
26. Insert a brass drift through the front of the case. Tap the drift carefully to move the countershaft to the rear of the case.
27. Tilt the countershaft upward and remove it from the rear of the case. Remove the countershaft front thrust washer and rear bearing spacer.
28. Remove the countershaft front bearing from the case with a hydraulic press.

Assembly (4-speed)

Refer to **Figure 37** as required for this procedure.
1. Wipe the countershaft gear thrust washers with a light coat of grease or petroleum jelly and install in the transmission case as shown in **Figure 57**.
2. Place the countershaft gear in the case and install the countershaft from the rear of the case to engage the gear.
3. Place the reverse idler gear in the case. The shift lever groove must face toward the rear of the case. Install the reverse idler shaft from the rear of the case.
4. Install the reverse idler shaft roll pin so it is centered in the shaft.

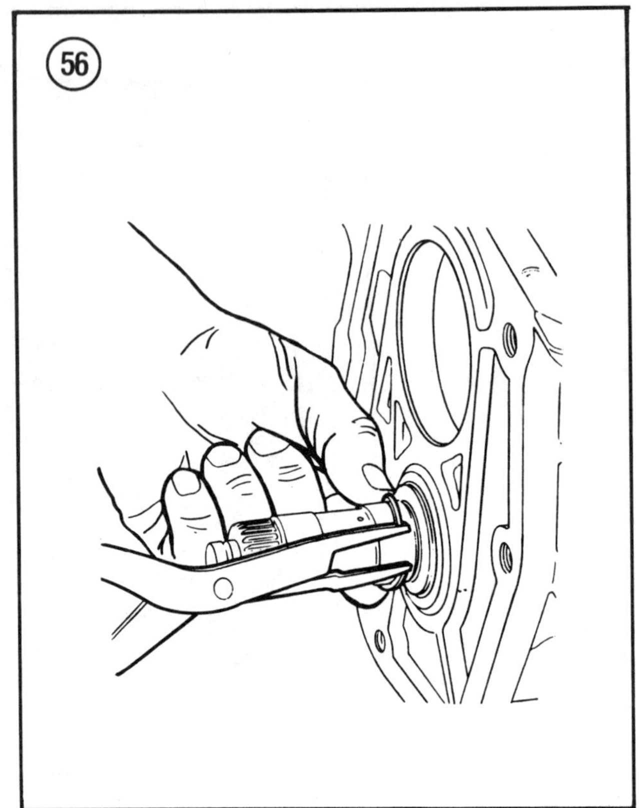

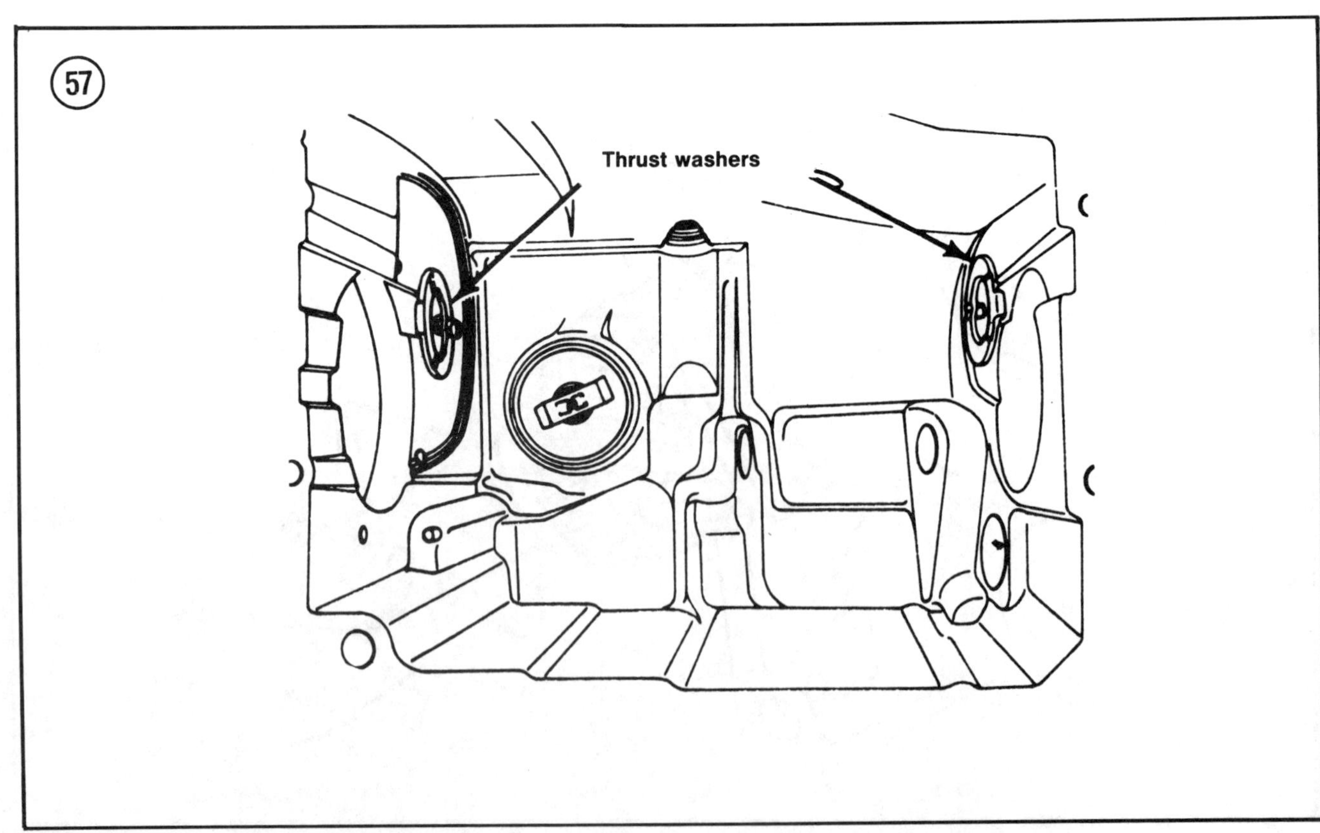

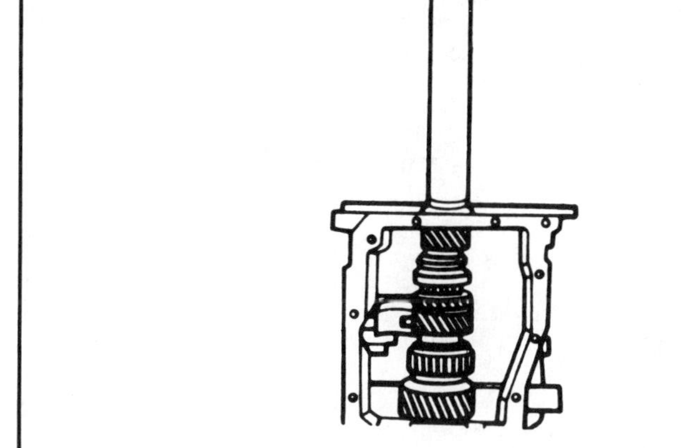

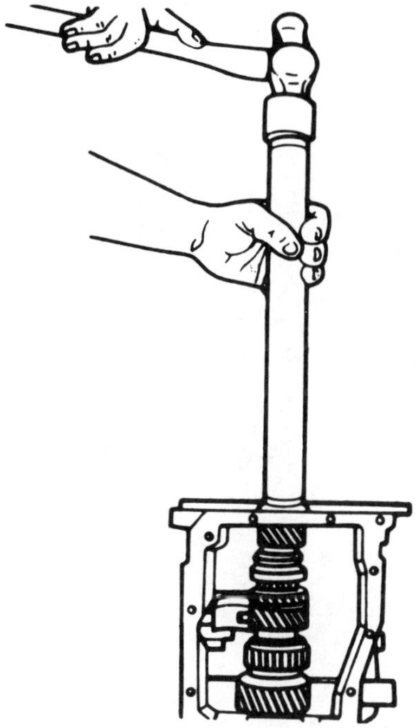

5. Install the main shaft in the case, taking care not to disturb the synchronizer assemblies.
6. Fit the 4th gear blocker ring in the 3rd/4th synchronizer sleeve. The synchronizer keys must engage the blocker ring notches.
7. Install the drive gear and connect it with the main shaft.
8. Hold the main shaft 1st gear against the rear of the case. Start a new front bearing on the drive gear, align the bearing with the case bore and drive into position as shown in **Figure 58**.
9. Install the front bearing retaining/locating snap rings.
10. Run a 1/8 in. (3 mm) bead of RTV sealant along the front bearing retainer mating surface. Install the retainer according to the alignment marks made during disassembly.
11. Coat the retainer bolt threads with a non-hardening sealer. Install and tighten bolt to 15 ft.-lb. (20 N•m).
12. Install the 1st gear thrust washer with its oil groove facing toward the main shaft 1st gear. Align the washer slot with the 1st gear roll pin (**Figure 59**).

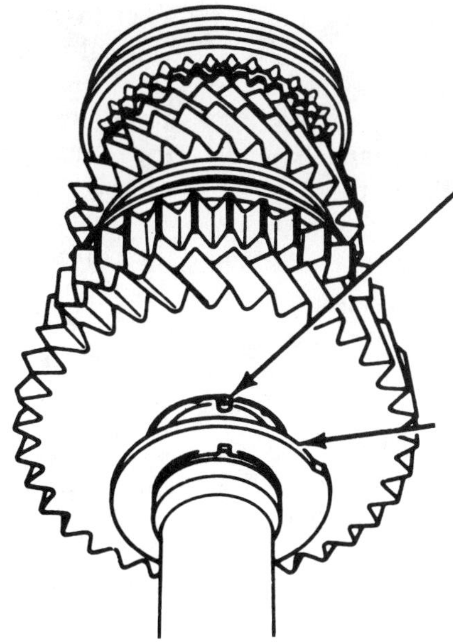

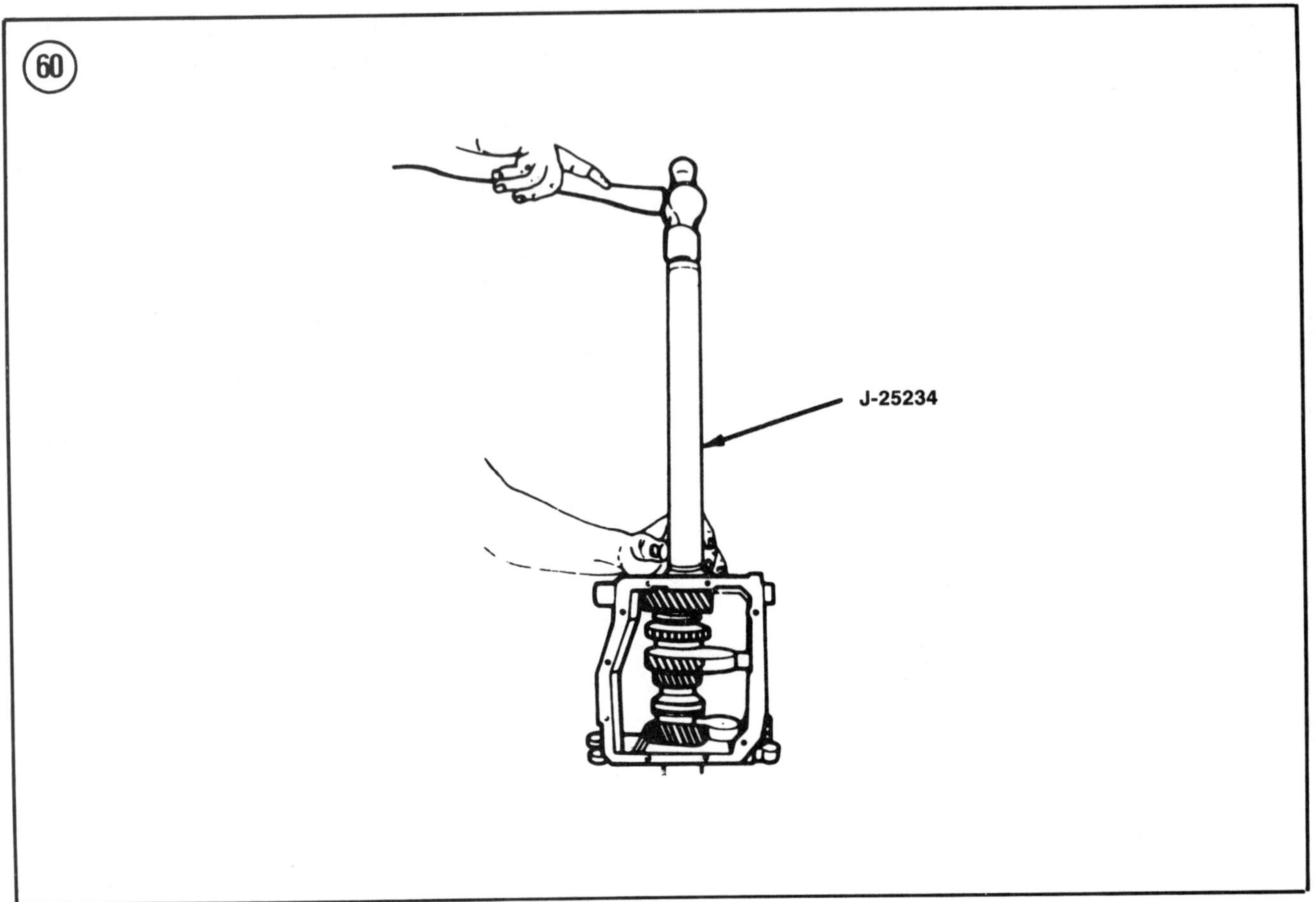

13. Install a new rear bearing on the main shaft. Align the bearing with the case bore and drive into position as shown in **Figure 60**.
14. Install the locating/retaining snap rings on the rear bearing.
15. Fit the speedometer clip tang in the main shaft hole and install the drive gear over the clip.
16. Coat the reverse lever pivot bolt threads with nonhardening sealer. Start bolt into case.
17. Fit the reverse lever fork in the reverse idler gear. Position the reverse lever on the pivot bolt. Tighten the bolt to 20 ft.-lb. (27 N•m). Install the retaining clip.
18. Rotate the drive and main shaft gears to check blocker ring action. If the rings stick on the gears, gently pry them off the cones with a screwdriver.
19. Run a 1/8 in. (3 mm) bead of RTV sealant on the transmission cover mating surface. Move the reverse lever into neutral and install the cover with the 2 dowel-type bolts.
20. Install the other cover bolts and tighten to 10 ft.-lb. (15 N•m).
21. Check the relationship of the offset lever-to-shift rail roll pin hole. It must be in a vertical position after cover installation.
22. Run a 1/8 in. (3 mm) bead of RTV sealant along the extension housing mating surface. Install the housing over the main shaft until the shift rail can be seen in the shift cover opening.
23. Install the offset lever detent spring. Position the ball in the neutral guide plate detent position.
24. Apply pressure to the offset lever and slide it onto the shift rail, then seat the extension housing on the case.
25. Install the extension housing bolts and tighten to 25 ft.-lb. (30 N•m).
26. Align the offset lever and shift rail roll pin holes. Install the roll pin.

Assembly (5-speed)

Refer to **Figure 38** as required for this procedure.

1. Wipe the countershaft front bearing bore with Loctite 601 or equivalent. Press the front countershaft bearing in the case until it is flush with the case surface.

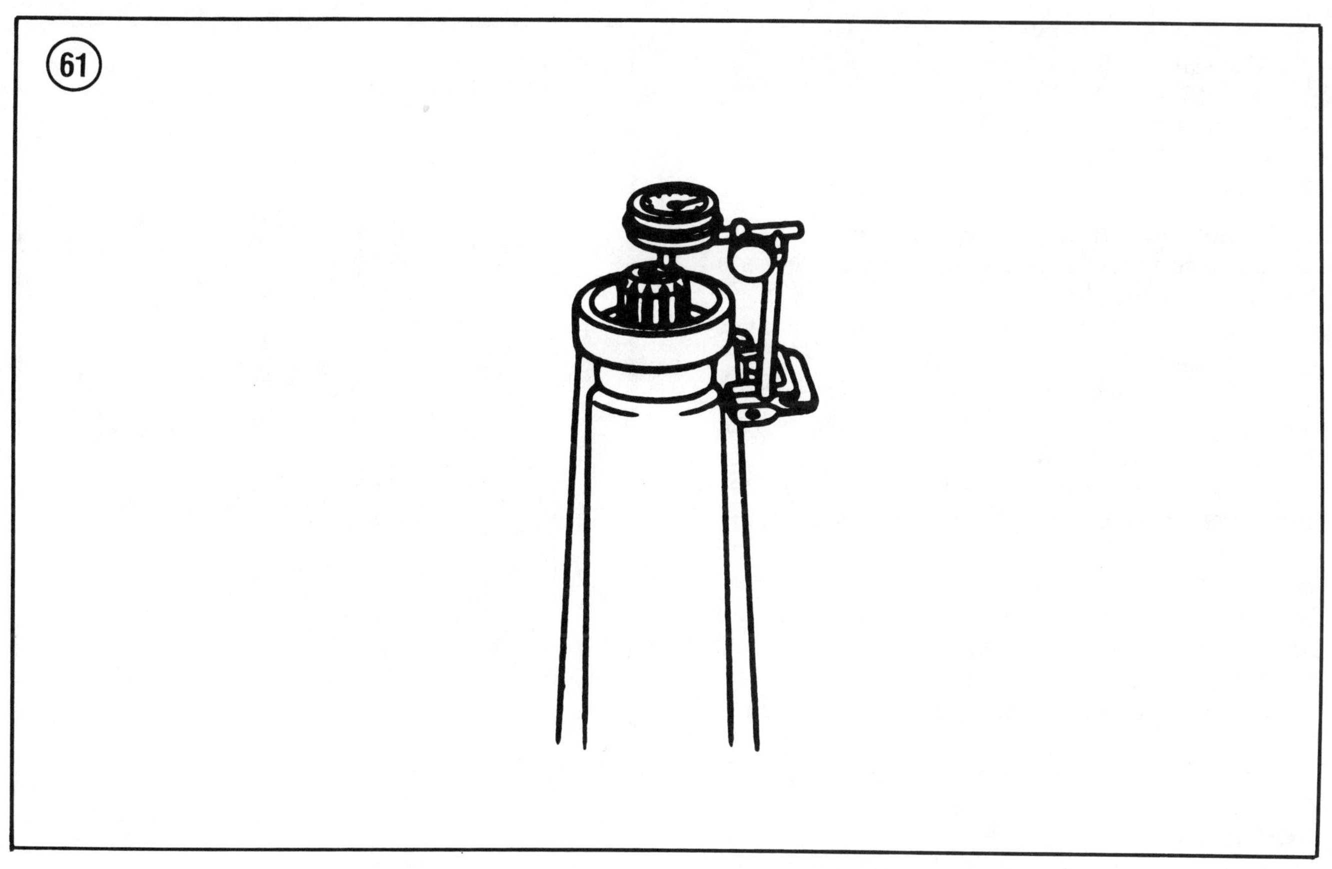

2. Wipe the countershaft tanged thrust washer with a coat of grease or petroleum jelly and install in the case with its tang engaging the case recess.
3. Place the transmission case on end and install the countershaft in the front bearing bore.
4. Install the countershaft rear bearing spacer. Wipe the rear bearing with grease and install it in the case so it extends 0.125 in. (3 mm) from the case surface.
5. Place the reverse idler gear in the case. Its shift lever groove must face to the rear of the case. Install the reverse idler shaft from the rear of the case. Install the roll pin in the idler shaft.
6. Install the main shaft in the case. Install the rear main shaft bearing race in the case.
7. Install the drive gear so it engages the 3rd/4th synchronizer sleeve and blocker ring.
8. Install the front bearing race in the retainer without the shims. Temporarily install the bearing retainer.
9. Coat the pivot bolt threads with a nonhardening sealer. Install the 5th/reverse lever, pivot bolt and retaining clip. The reverse lever fork must engage the reverse idler gear.
10. Install the countershaft rear bearing spacer and snap ring.
11. Install the countershaft 5th gear. Insert the 5th/reverse shift rail from the rear of the case and engage with the 5th/reverse lever. Connect the spring to the front of the case.
12. Place the 5th gear shift fork on the 5th gear synchronizer. Install the synchronizer on the countershaft and the shift fork on the shift rail. Make sure the roll pin holes align.
13. Support the 5th gear shift rail with a block of wood and install the roll pin through the fork/rail.
14. Install the thrust race to the 5th gear synchronizer hub. Install the snap ring.
15. Install the thrust bearing against the countershaft race. Lubricate the bearing and race with petroleum jelly.
16. Install the lipped thrust race over the needle-type thrust bearing. Install the plastic funnel in the end of the countershaft gear.
17. Temporarily install the extension housing and mount a dial indicator as shown in **Figure 61**.
18. Rotate the main shaft and zero the dial indicator. Pull up on the main shaft until end play is removed. Read the indicator gauge.

NOTE
The main shaft bearings require a 0.001-0.005 in. (0.03-0.13 mm) preload. Select a shim pack which measures this much more than the dial indicator reading.

19. Remove the front bearing retainer. Separate the race from the retainer and intall the appropriate shim pack. Reinstall the race and run a 1/8 in. (3 mm) bead of RTV sealant along the retainer mating surface.
20. Install the retainer so that the marks made during disassembly are aligned. Install and tighten the bolts to 15 ft.-lb. (20 N•m).
21. Remove the extension housing. Position the shift forks on the cover in neutral. Run a 1/8 in. (3 mm) bead of RTV sealant along the transmission case cover mating surface.
22. Install the cover with the shift forks and synchronizer sleeves aligned. Install the 2 dowel-type bolts.
23. Install the remaining cover bolts and tighten to 10 ft.-lb. (15 N•m).
24. Check the offset lever-to-shift rail roll pin hole position. It should be vertical after cover installation.
25. Run a 1/8 in. (3 mm) bead of RTV sealant along the extension housing mating surface. Install the housing over the main shaft until the shift rail just enters the shift cover opening.
26. Install the offset lever detent spring. Position the ball in the neutral guide plate detent position.
27. Apply pressure to the offset lever and slide it onto the shift rail, then seat the extension housing on the case.
28. Install and tighten the extension housing bolts to 25 ft.-lb. (30 N•m).
29. Align the offset lever and shift rail roll pin holes. Install the roll pin.

Main Shaft Disassembly/Assembly

Refer to **Figure 37** (4-speed) or **Figure 38** (5-speed) as required for this procedure.

1. Scribe an alignment mark on the 3rd/4th synchronizer hub and sleeve.
2. Remove and discard the snap ring (**Figure 62**). Install a universal puller behind 3rd gear as shown in **Figure 63** and press the 3rd/4th synchronizer and 3rd gear from the main shaft.

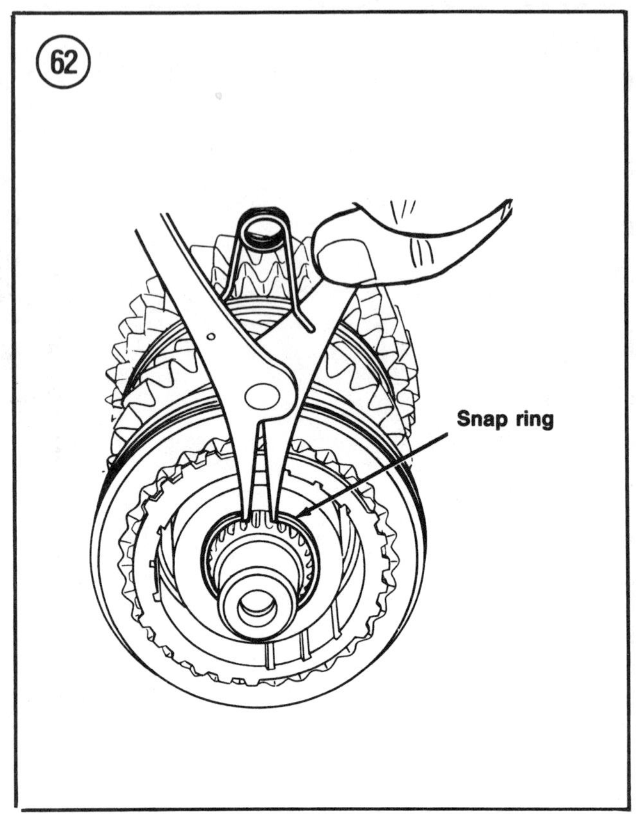

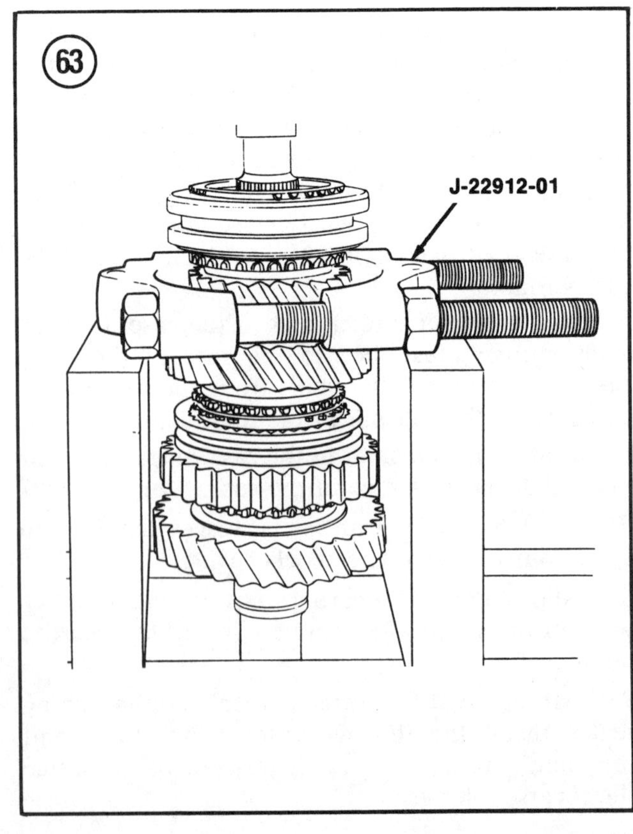

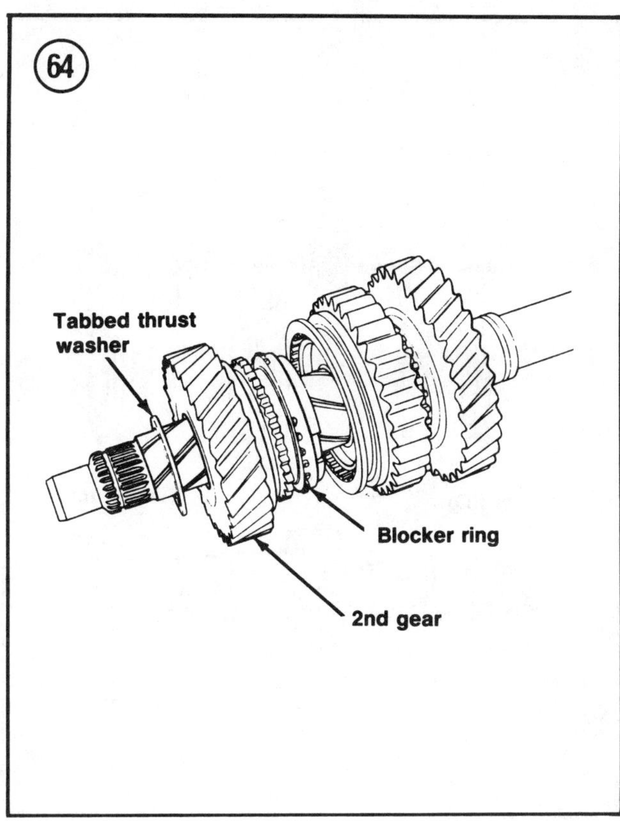

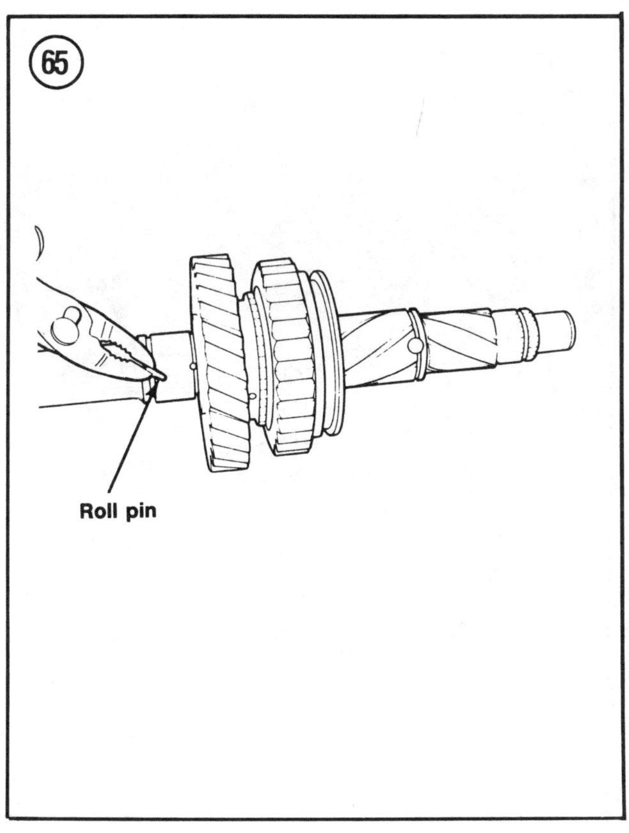

3. Remove and discard the 2nd gear snap ring. Remove the tabbed thrust washer, 2nd gear and blocker ring. See **Figure 64**.
4. 5-speed—Press 5th gear and the rear bearing from the main shaft.
5. Remove the 1st gear thrust washer. Pull the roll pin out with pliers (**Figure 65**).
6. Remove 1st gear and the blocker ring from the main shaft (**Figure 66**).
7. Scribe an alignment mark on the 1st/2nd synchronizer hub and sleeve.

NOTE
The 1st/2nd synchronizer hub is machined as a part of the 4-speed main shaft. The 1st/2nd/reverse hub is machined as a part of the 5-speed main shaft. Neither hub can be removed.

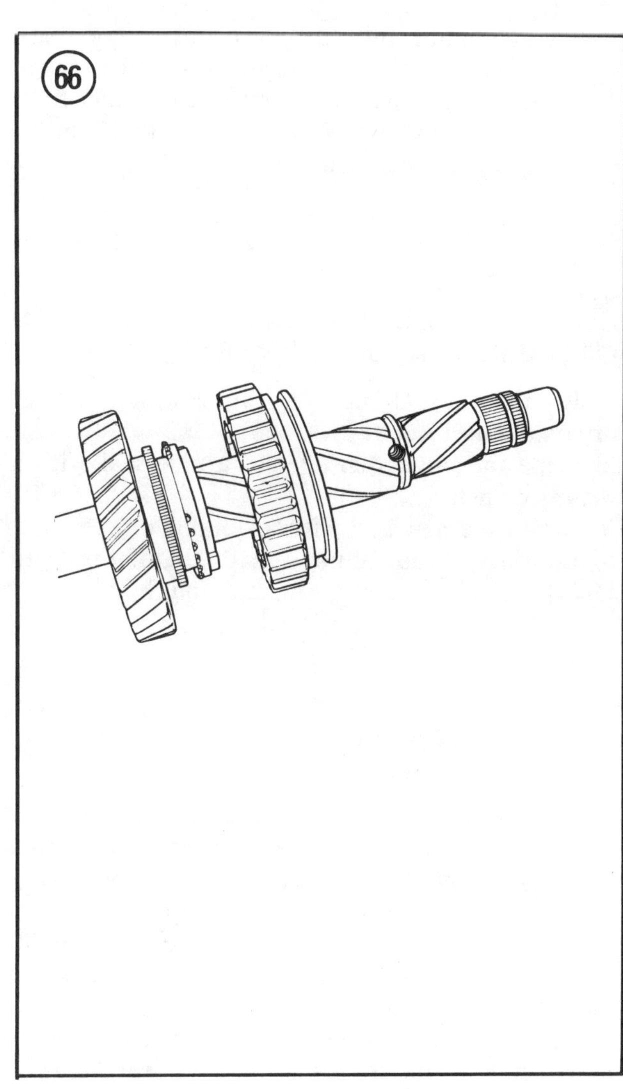

9

8. 4-speed—Remove the springs and keys from the 1st/2nd synchronizer sleeve. Remove the sleeve from the main shaft. See **Figure 67**.
9. 5-speed—Remove the springs and keys from the 1st/2nd synchronizer sleeve. Remove the sleeve and 1st/reverse sliding gear from the main shaft.
10. Clean and inspect all components as described in this chapter.
11. Assembly is the reverse of disassembly, plus the following:
   a. Install the synchronizer keys and springs with the tanged spring end in the same key, but with the open spring ends positioned to face away from each other. See **Figure 68**.
   b. Measure 2nd gear end play with a flat feeler gauge. Insert the gauge between the gear and thrust washer. If end play exceeds 0.014 in. (0.35 mm), replace the thrust washer and snap ring.
   c. Measure the 3rd/4th synchronizer end play with a flat feeler gauge. Insert the gauge between the snap ring and synchronizer hub. If end play exceeds 0.014 in. (0.35 mm), replace the snap ring.

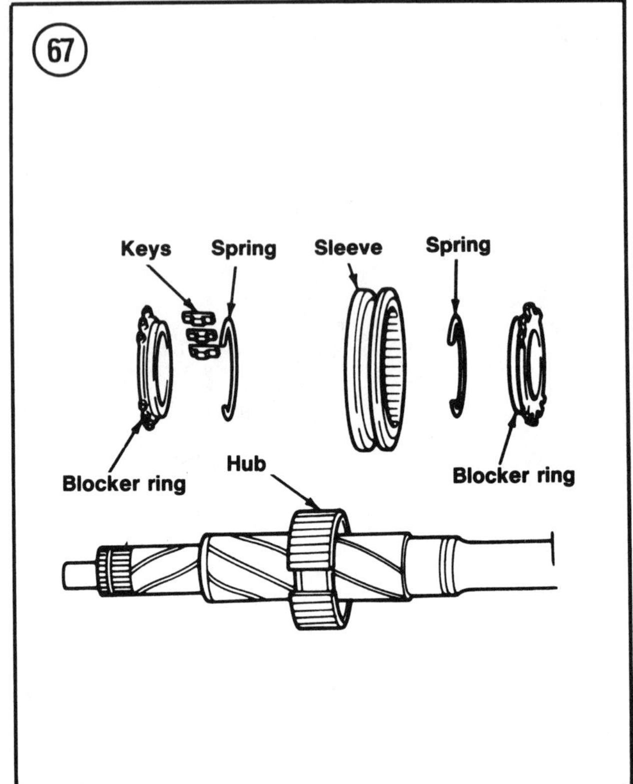

Extension Housing/Drive Gear Oil Seal Replacement

1. Pry the old seal out with a suitable screwdriver or small chisel.
2. Wipe the outer diameter of a new seal with a sealing cement.
3. Install the new seal with a suitable driver.
4. Lubricate the inner seal diameter with DEXRON II automatic transmission fluid.

Drive Gear/Countergear Shaft Bearing Replacement

The 4-speed and 5-speed drive and 5-speed countergear shafts use roller bearings which must be pressed off the shaft (**Figure 69**). The 4- and 5-speed drive and 4-speed countergear shafts use needle roller bearings inside the shaft (**Figure 70**). These are installed with a light coat of grease or petroleum jelly to hold them in place, then a dummy shaft is inserted in the shaft to retain the bearings until the transmission is reassembled.

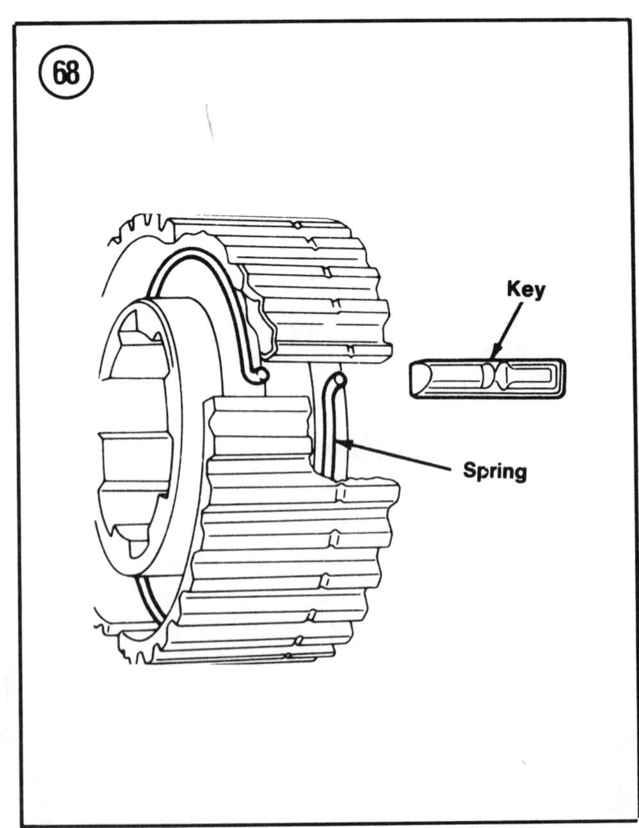

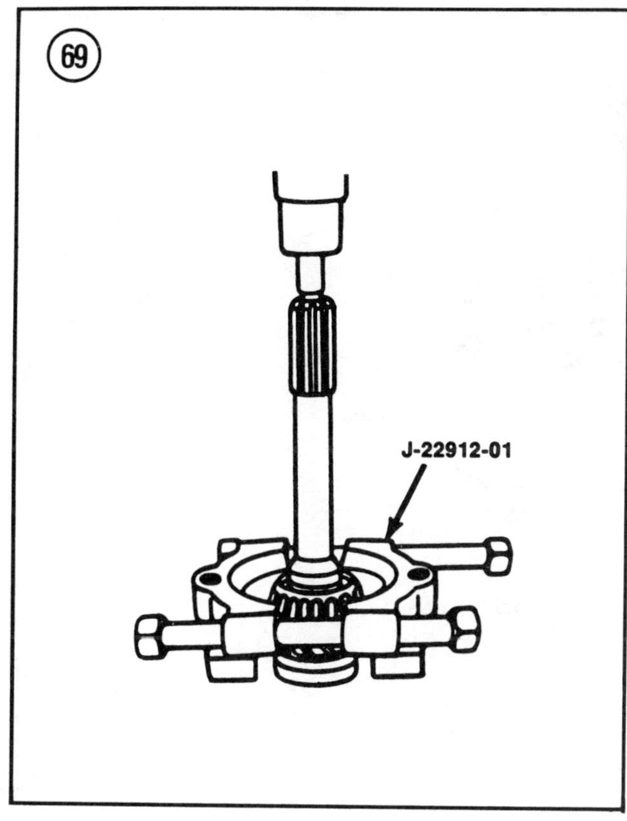

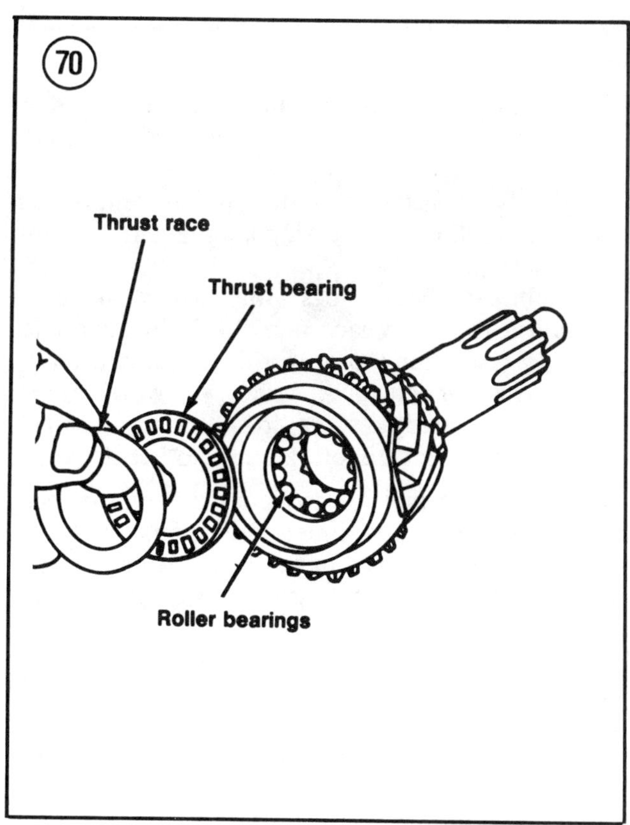

TRANSFER CASE

A transfer case mounted behind the transmission directs the driving torque from the engine and transmission to the front and rear driving axles of 4-wheel drive vehicles.

This section provides removal, installation and overhaul procedures for the New Process 207 transfer case and adapter.

Tightening torques are provided in **Table 1** at the end of the chapter.

Transfer case overhaul is not the best starting point for a beginning mechanic. However, it does not require special training or much special equipment.

Before starting work, read this entire section. Obtain any necessary special tools or appropriate substitutes. Check the availability of parts with local suppliers.

Safety Precautions

The use of a suitable holding fixture is highly recommended for transfer case overhaul. Chevrolet and GMC have several different fixture designs available. While it may not prove economical to purchase a holding fixture just to overhaul your transmission on a one-time basis, obtaining one from a rental house is worth the small cost involved. It will save time, make the job easier and prevent damage to the transfer case and possible personal injury to you.

The transfer case used in these vehicles are deceptive in appearance. Although small in size, they are extremely heavy and awkward to handle. You should not attempt to remove one from a vehicle without the use of an appropriate transmission jack, which can also be obtained from a rental house.

When handling the transfer case, it is a good idea to wear heavy gloves to improve your grip on the transfer case and prevent possible injury from the sharp metal edges.

The use of safety goggles is highly recommended whenever you are removing snap rings. The snap rings used in transfer case assemblies are extremely stiff and tend to be somewhat brittle. Safety goggles will protect your eyes from possible injury if the snap ring should break apart during removal or installation.

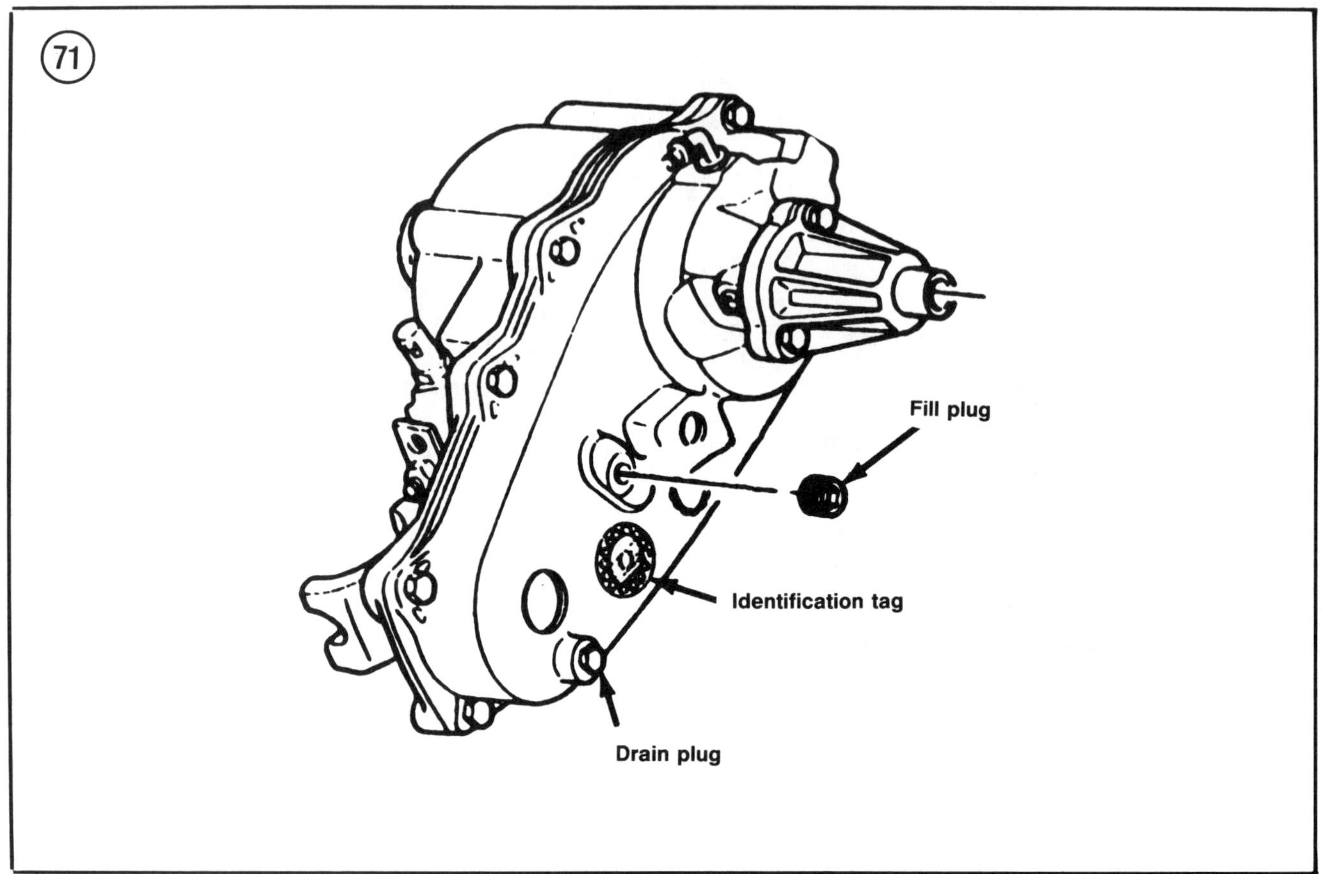

Cleaning and Inspection

1. Wash the inside and outside of the transfer case and case components thoroughly with clean solvent to dissolve or loosen old lubricant and foreign material. Make sure the vent hole and all oil feed ports or channels are open and clean. Blow dry with compressed air, if available.
2. Remove all gasket or sealant residue from mating surfaces.
3. Inspect the case and case components for cracks, worn or damaged bearing bores, damaged threads or other defects. If such defects are found, replace the case.
4. Check the front and rear case faces for burrs. If present, dress off with a fine mill file.
5. Check the condition of all shift forks and nylon wear tips, shift rails and shafts. Replace as required if excessively worn or if any defects are noted.
6. Clean the ball bearings with solvent as follows:
   a. Place bearings in a wire basket and submerge in a suitable container of fresh solvent. The bottom of the basket should not touch the bottom of the container.
   b. Agitate the basket containing the bearings to loosen all grease, sludge and other contamination.
   c. Dry ball bearings with dry filtered compressed air, holding the bearing to prevent it from rotating.
   d. Lubricate the bearings with clean transfer case lubricant. Turn each race slowly by hand and and check for loose, worn or damaged balls. Check for cracked, rough or worn races. Check bearings for rust, wear, scuffed surfaces, heat discoloration or other defects.
7. If needle bearings are to be reused, repeat Step 6, cleaning one set at a time to prevent any possible mixup. Check bearings for flat spots. If one needle bearing is defective or missing, replace the entire set.
8. Check all gears for chipped, worn or broken teeth.
9. Check the drive chain for wear or damage.
10. Check the input and output shafts and shaft splines for wear, scoring or an out-of-round condition.

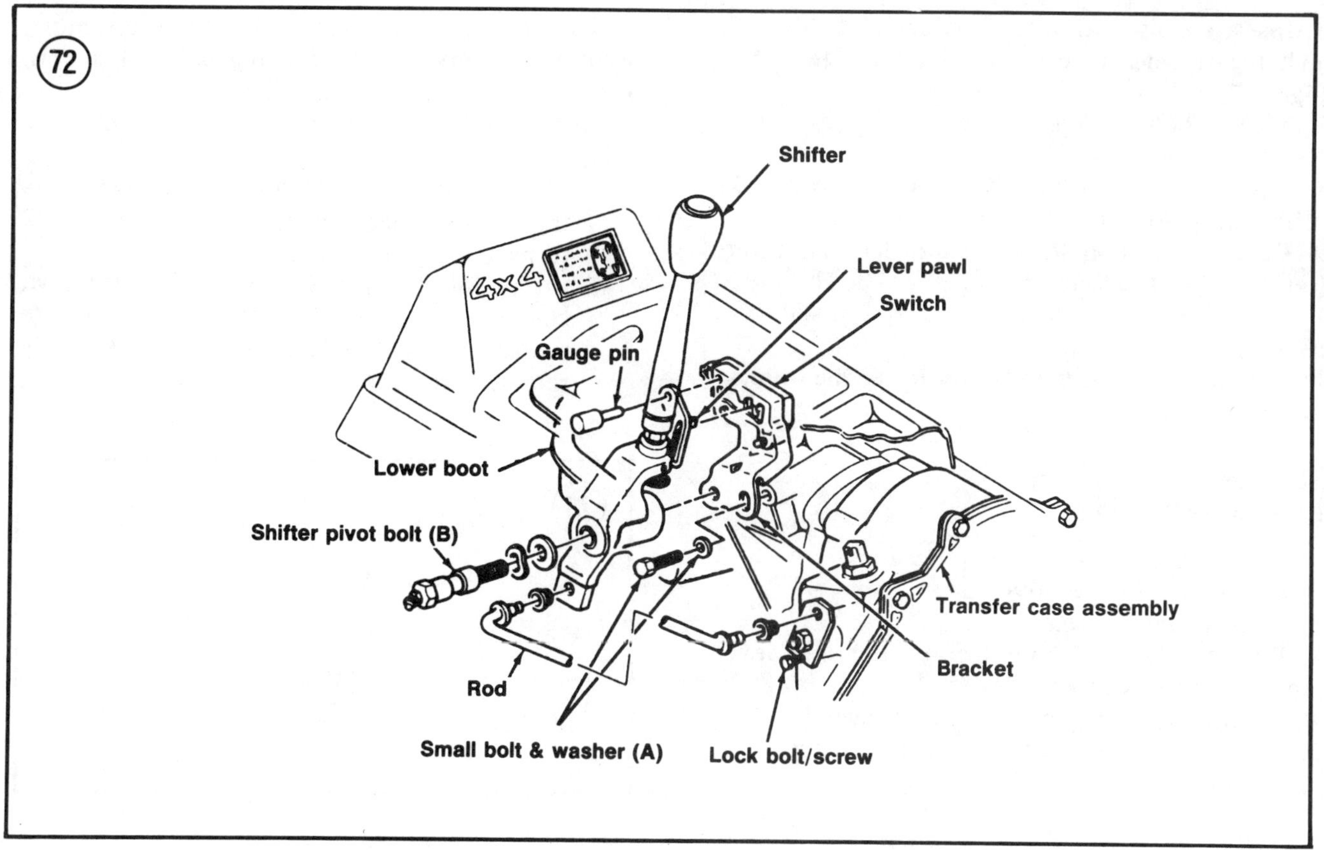

11. Check front case lockplate hub and teeth for signs of excessive wear, cracks, chips or other damage. If replacement is required, install new lockplate attaching bolts.
12. Check thrust washers for excessive wear and scoring or other surface damage. Replace as required.
13. Discard all snap rings and install new ones on assembly.

NEW PROCESS 207 TRANSFER CASE

This part-time 4-speed transfer case is used on all 4-wheel drive vehicles. The New Process 207 has 4 shift lever positions:

a. 4L (low gear, all wheels).
b. N (neutral).
c. 2H (high gear, rear wheels).
d. 4H (high gear, all wheels).

The 2-piece aluminum case contains front and rear output shafts, 2 drive sprockets, a drive chain, shift mechanism and a planetary gear assembly. The 3-pinion carrier and annulus gear provide the 4L range when engaged.

A service identification tag is attached to the rear case half (**Figure 71**). The model number, low range reduction ratio and assembly number are stamped on this tag. This information must be used when ordering replacement parts. If the tag becomes detached from the case half during overhaul, reaffix it with Loctite 312 or equivalent.

Linkage Adjustment

Refer to **Figure 72** for this procedure.

1. Remove the console.
2. Securely block both front wheels so the truck will not roll in either direction. Raise the vehicle with a jack and place it on jackstands.
3. Loosen the bolt and pivot bolt marked A and B in **Figure 72**.
4. Place the transfer case shifter in the 4 HI position.
5. Pull the shifter boot upward and insert an 8 mm gauge pin or 5/16 in. drill bit through the shifter and into the bracket (**Figure 72**).

9

6. Insert a bolt at the transfer case shift lever to lock the transfer case in the 4 HI position. See **Figure 73**.
7. Tighten bolt A (**Figure 72**) to 25-35 ft.-lb. (34-48 N•m).
8. Tighten the pivot bolt (B, **Figure 72**) to 88-103 ft.-lb. (120-140 N•m).
9. Remove the bolt from the transfer case lever. Remove the gauge pin or drill bit at the shifter.
10. Pull the shifter boot down and install the console.
11. Remove the jackstands and lower the vehicle to the ground.

Shift Lever Removal/Installation

Refer to **Figure 74** for this procedure.

1. Disconnect the negative battery cable.
2. Remove the console.
3. Remove the shift boot. Loosen the shift lever jam nut and unscrew the lever.
4. Remove the transfer case selector switch.
5. Raise the vehicle with a jack and place it on jackstands.
6. Disconnect the shift rod at the shifter assembly. Remove the pivot and adjusting bolts (A and B, **Figure 72**). Remove the shift lever.
7. Installation is the reverse of removal, plus the following:
   a. Tighten shift lever down until the pawl clears the bracket, then tighten an additional 1 1/2 turns and tighten the jam nut.
   b. Install selector switch with shift lever pawl contacting the switch contact carrier. Route switch wiring under the boot assembly retainer bridge.

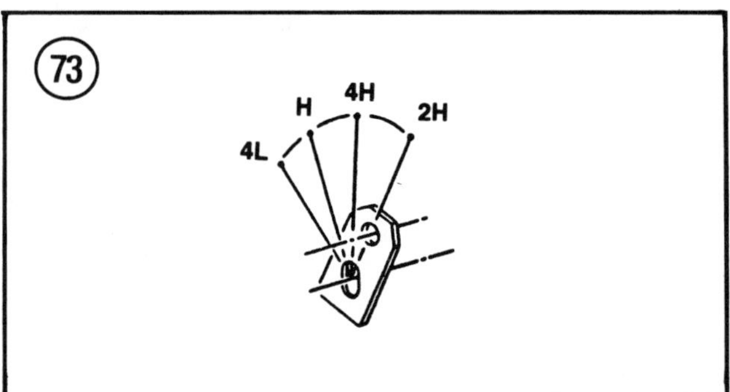

74

AUTOMATIC TRANSMISSION

Adapter

View A

Detent

MANUAL TRANSMISSION

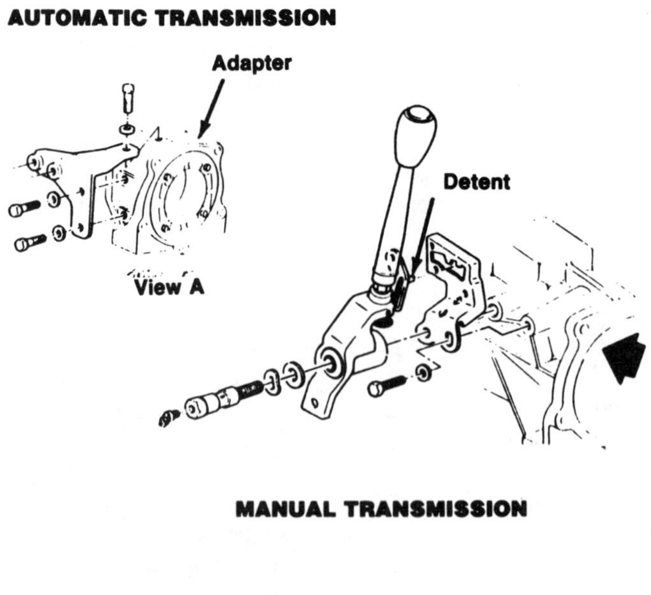

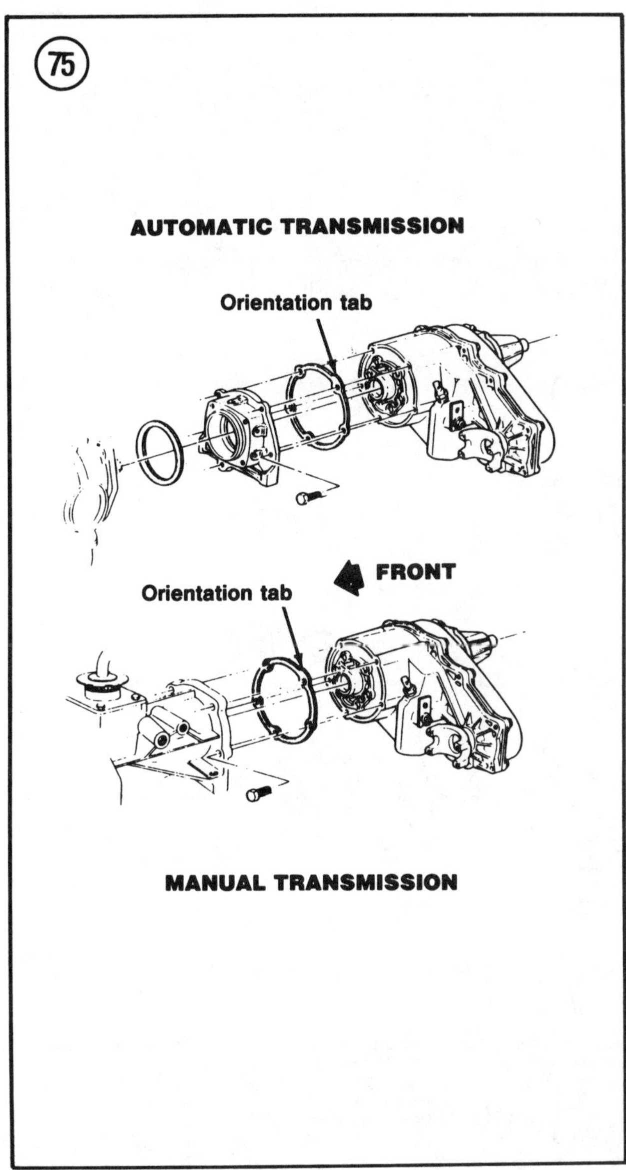

c. Adjust the shift linkage as described in this chapter before lowering the vehicle to the ground.

Transfer Case Removal/Installation

1. Shift the transfer case into the 4 HI position.
2. Disconnect the negative battery cable.
3. Securely block both front wheels so the truck will not roll in either direction. Raise the vehicle with a jack and place it on jackstands.
4. Unbolt and remove the skid plate, if so equipped.
5. Place a suitable container under the transfer case and remove the drain plug (**Figure 71**). Let the fluid drain, then reinstall the drain plug.
6. Mark the front and rear drive shaft and yoke assemblies for reassembly reference. Disconnect the front drive shaft from the transfer case. Disconnect and remove the rear drive shaft from the vehicle. See Chapter Eleven.
7. Disconnect the vacuum harness and speedometer cable from the transfer case.
8. Remove the shift lever as described in this chapter.
9. Remove the catalytic converter hanger bolts at the converter.
10. Support the transmission with a jack. Raise the transmission and transfer case slightly, then remove the transmission mount bolts. Remove the transmission mount and converter hanger. Lower the transmission and transfer case back to their normal position.
11. Support the transfer case with a jack, then remove the transfer case attaching bolts. If equipped with an automatic transmission, remove the shift lever bracket (**Figure 74**) for access to the upper left transfer case bolt.
12. Unbolt the transfer case from the automatic transmission adapter or manual transmission extension housing. Remove the transfer case from under the vehicle. Remove and discard the gasket (**Figure 75**).
13. Installation is the reverse of removal, plus the following:
   a. Use a new gasket. See **Figure 75**.
   b. Align the input shaft splines with the transmission and slide the transfer case forward until fully seated against the transmission or adapter.
   c. Tighten attaching bolts to 19-29 ft.-lb. (26-40 N•m).
   d. Remove fill plug (**Figure 71**) and fill transfer case with DEXRON II automatic transmission fluid to the edge of the fill hole opening. Tighten drain and fill plugs to 30-40 ft.-lb. (40-54 N•m).
   e. Road test vehicle to make sure transfer case shifts and operates properly in all ranges.

9

Transfer Case Disassembly

Refer to **Figure 76** for this procedure.

1. Clean all dirt and grease from the outside of the transfer case.

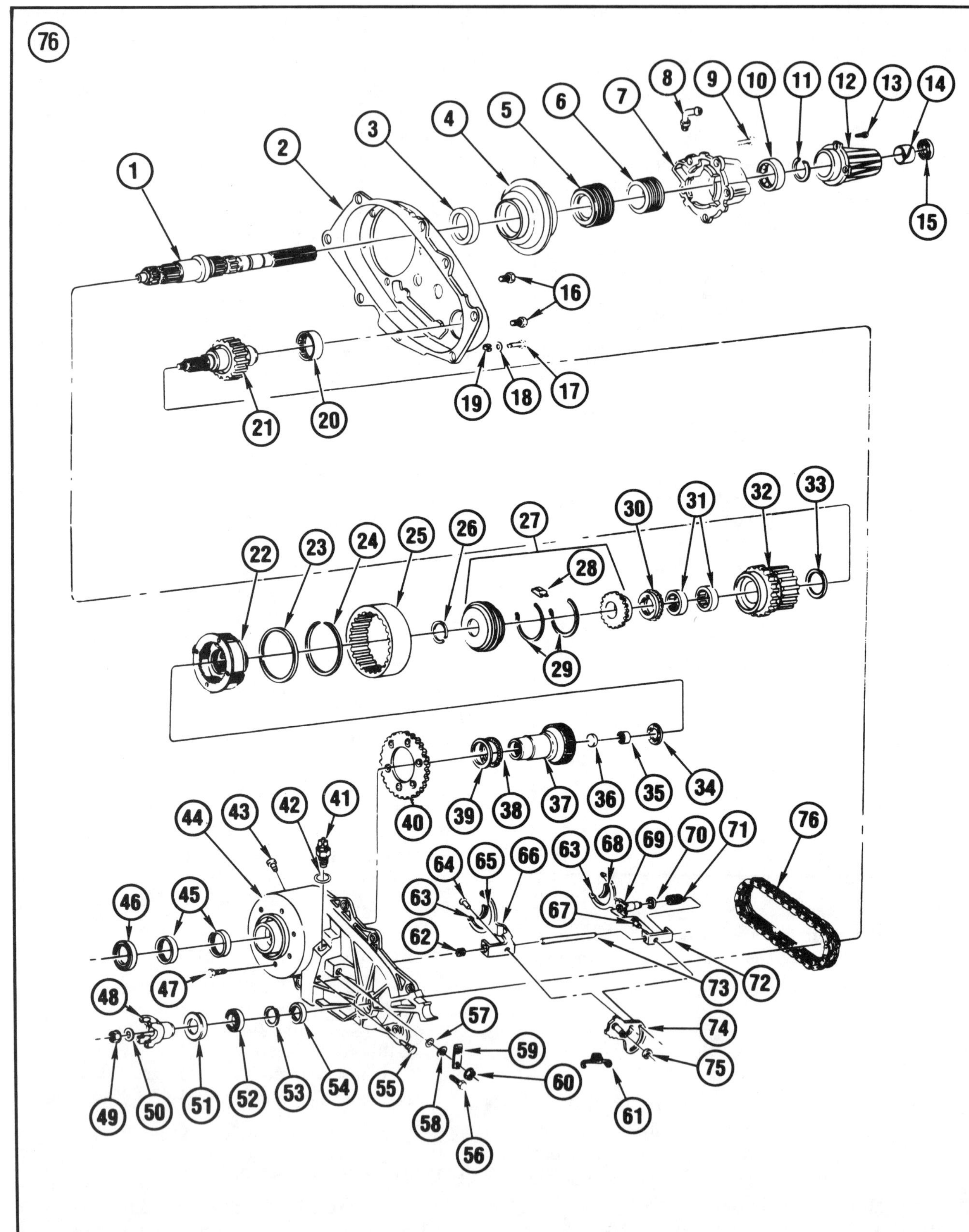
76

NEW PROCESS 207 TRANSFER CASE COMPONENTS

1. Main drive shaft
2. Case housing
3. Oil pump seal
4. Oil pump housing
5. Oil pump
6. Speedometer drive gear
7. Rear bearing retainer
8. Case vent connector
9. Bolt
10. Rear bearing
11. Rear bearing snap ring
12. Extension housing
13. Hex head bolt
14. Extension housing bushing
15. Extension housing seal
16. Drain/fill plugs
17. Hex head bolt
18. Dowel washer
19. Dowel
20. Front output shaft pilot bearing
21. Front output shaft
22. Planetary gear carrier assembly
23. Thrust washer
24. Snap ring
25. Annulus gear
26. Snap ring
27. Synchronizer assembly
28. Synchronizer strut
29. Synchronizer strut spring
30. Stop ring
31. Sprocket bearing
32. Sprocket
33. Sprocket thrust washer
34. Main drive gear thrust washer
35. Input drive gear pilot bearing
36. Cup plug
37. Input main drive gear assembly
38. Input drive gear thrust bearing
39. Input drive gear thrust washer
40. Low range lock plate
41. 4WD indicator light switch
42. Switch seal
43. Oil access hole plug
44. Front case half
45. Input drive bearing
46. Seal
47. Hex bolt
48. Front output shaft yoke
49. Yoke nut
50. Yoke washer
51. Yoke deflector
52. Front output shaft seal
53. Snap ring
54. Front output shaft bearing
55. Shift sector spring screw
56. Screw
57. Sector and shaft oil seal
58. Sector and shaft retainer
59. Shift shaft lever
60. Nut
61. Shift sector spring assembly
62. Range fork bushing
63. Fork wear pad
64. Range shift fork pin
65. Rang shift fork center pad
66. Range shift fork assembly
67. Mode shift fork bracket pin
68. Mode shift fork center pad
69. Mode shift fork assembly
70. Mode shift fork spring cup
71. Mode shift fork spring
72. Mode shift fork bracket assembly
73. Shift fork shaft
74. Shift sector
75. Shift sector shaft spacer
76. Drive chain

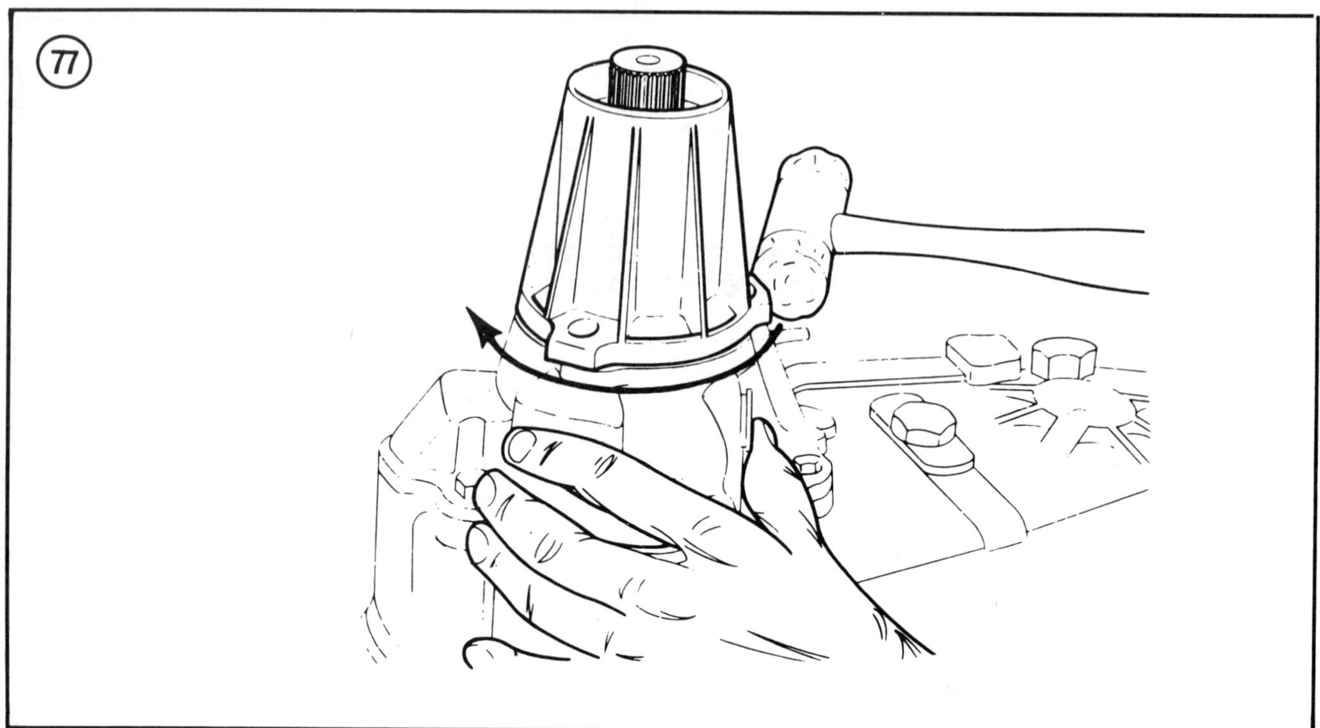

2. Remove the drain and fill plugs (**Figure 71**).
3. Use a flange holding tool and loosen the front output shaft yoke nut. Remove the nut, washer and yoke. Discard the washer and nut.
4. Position the front half of the case on wooden blocks and shift the transfer case into 4L.
5. Remove the extension housing bolts and tap the housing shoulder as shown in **Figure 77** to break the sealant loose. Remove the extension housing.
6. Remove and discard the main shaft rear bearing snap ring.
7. Unbolt the rear retainer and tap the retainer shoulder to break the sealant loose. Remove the rear retainer and pump housing assemblies from the transfer case (**Figure 78**).
8. Remove the speedometer drive gear and pump gear from the main shaft.
9. Remove the bolts holding the 2 case halves together.
10. Pry the case halves apart by inserting a suitable flat-bladed screwdriver in the housing pry slots (**Figure 79**). Separate the case halves and remove the magnetic chip collector from the bottom of the case half.
11. Raise the main shaft slightly to allow the front output shaft to clear the case (**Figure 80**), then remove the output shaft and drive chain as an assembly.

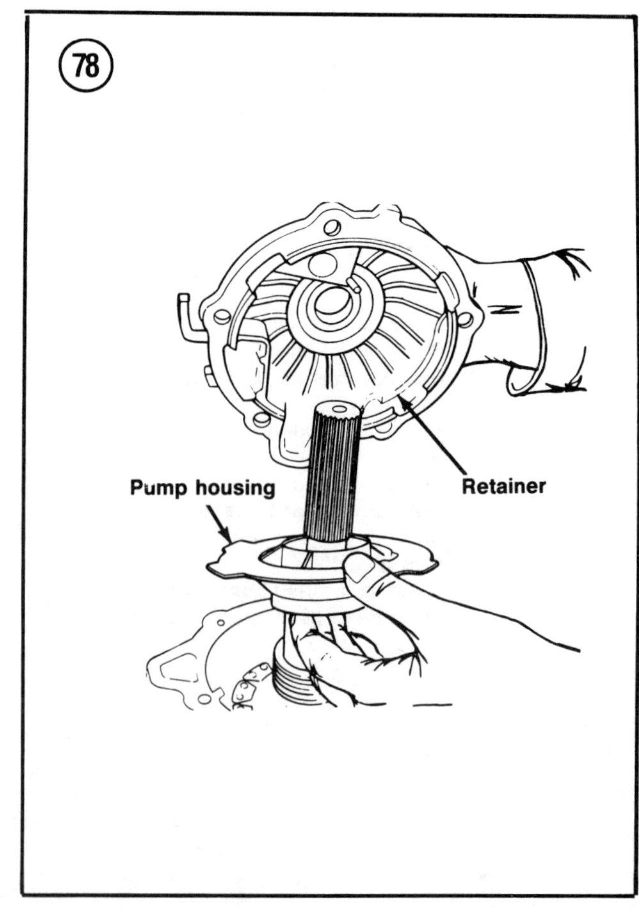

79

80

Front output shaft
Drive chain

9

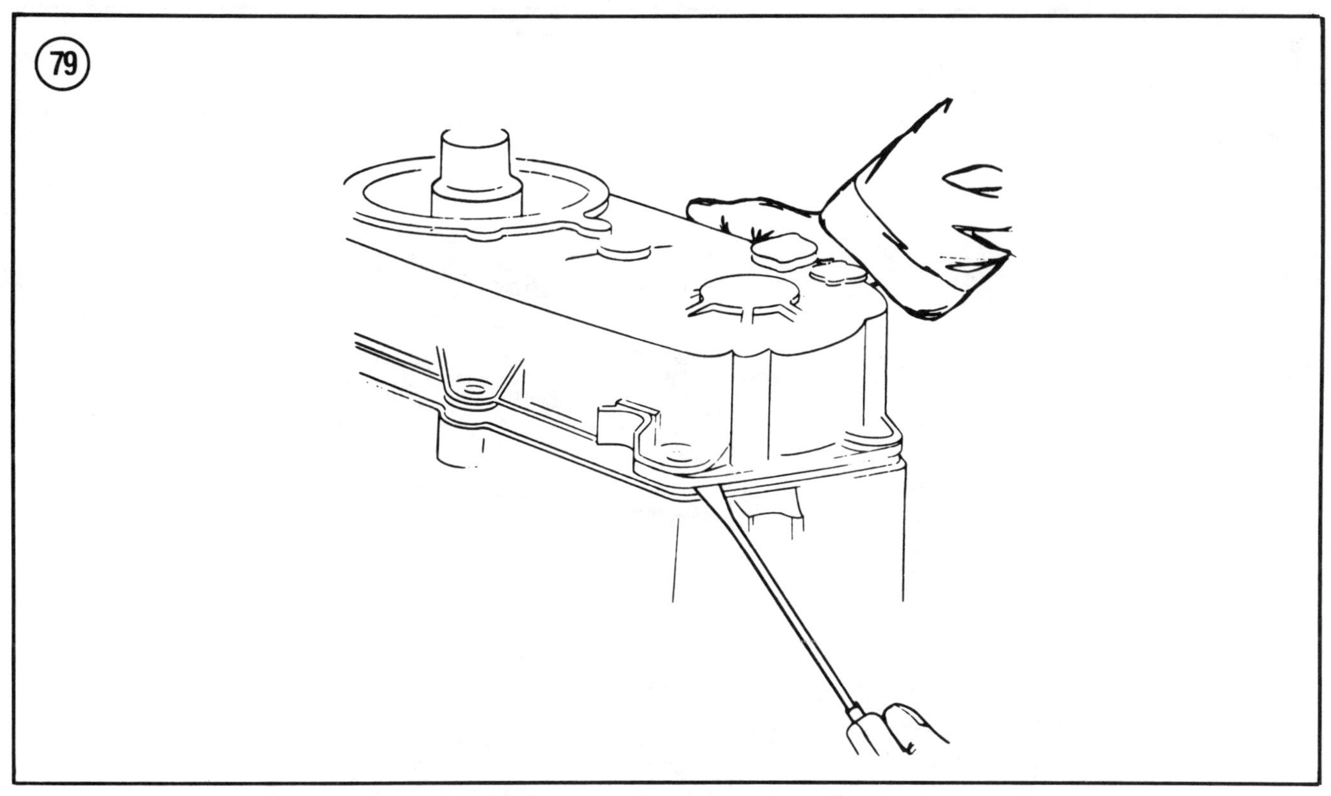

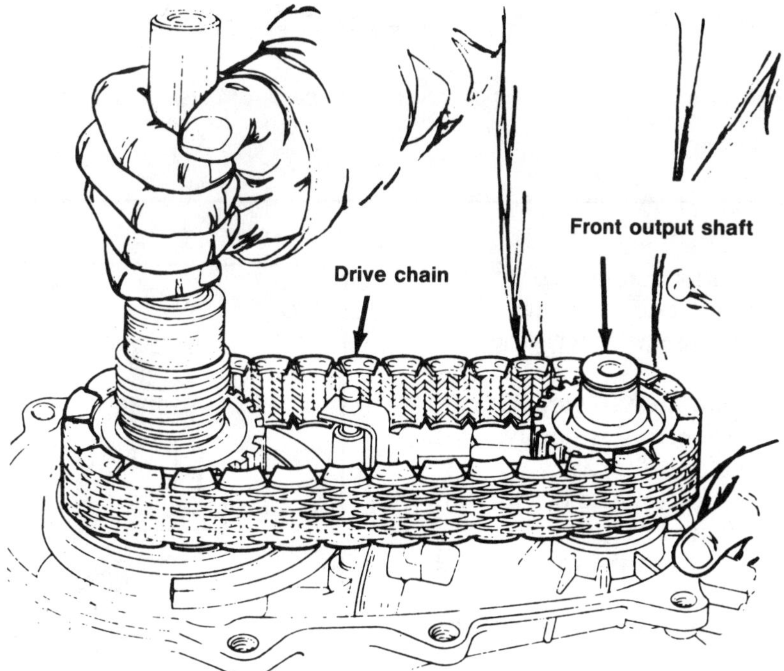

(81)

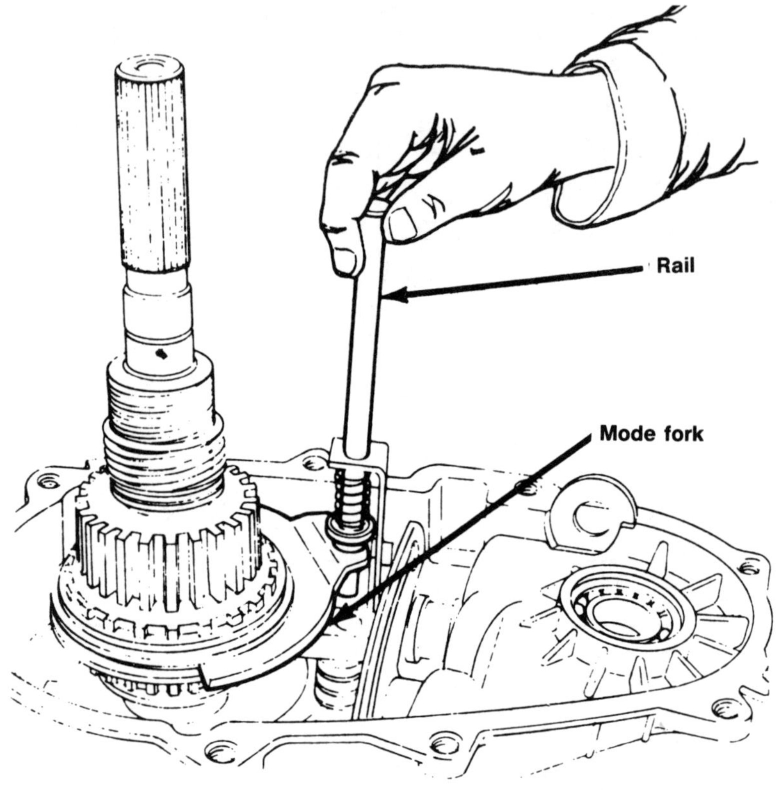

Rail

Mode fork

12. Pull upward on the mode fork rail until it clears the range fork, then rotate and remove the mode fork and rail from the transfer case. See **Figure 81**.
13. Pull upward on the main shaft **(Figure 82)** until it separates from the planetary assembly, then remove the shaft from the transfer case.
14. Remove the planetary assembly and range fork from the transfer case **(Figure 83)**.
15. Remove the input gear from the transfer case. Remove the planetary thrust washer, input gear thrust bearing and front thrust washer. See **Figure 84**.
16. Remove the shift sector detent spring and retaining bolt.

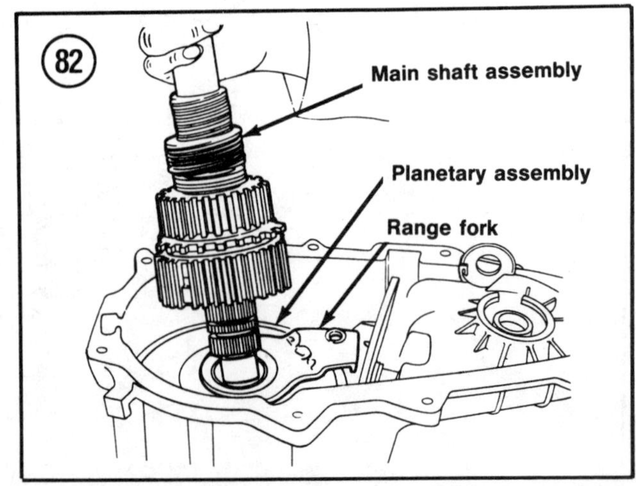

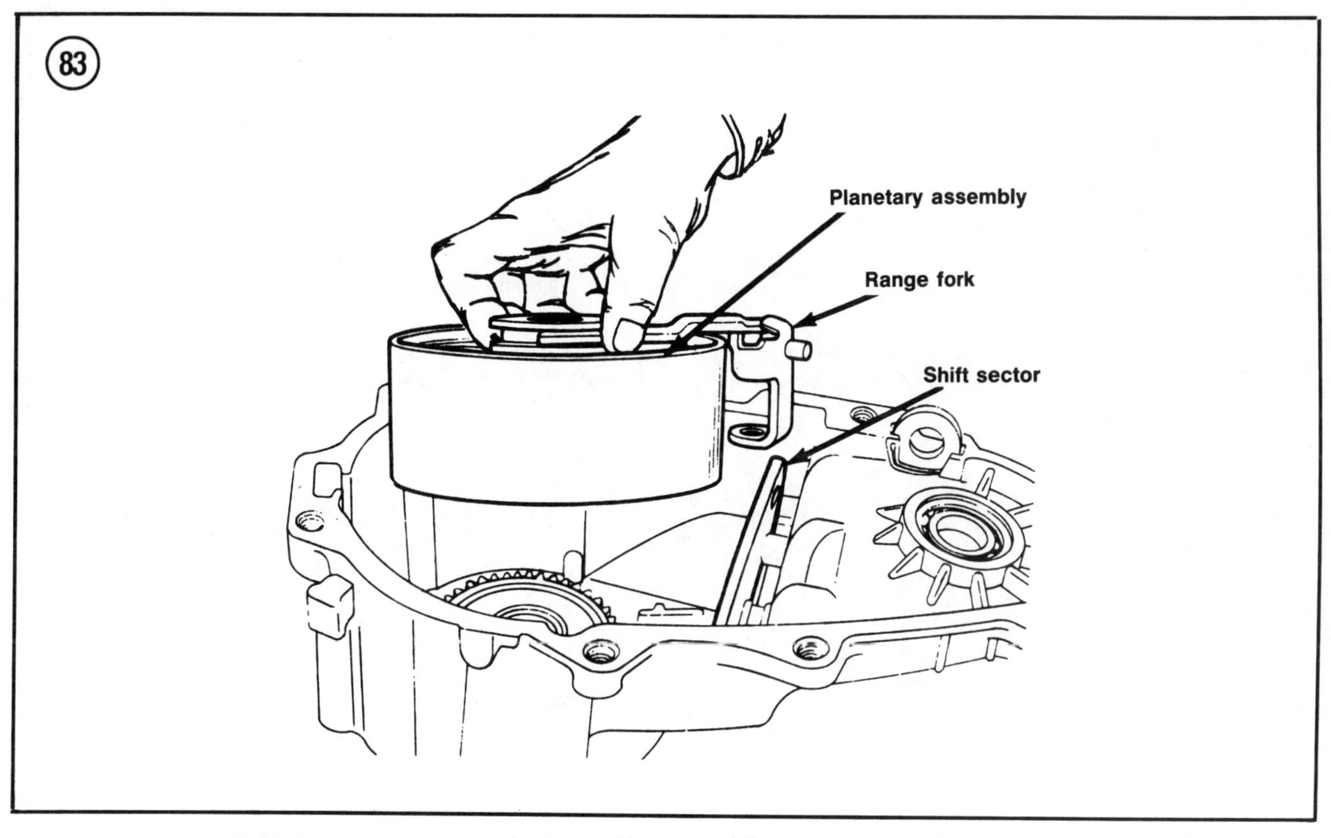
83
Planetary assembly
Range fork
Shift sector

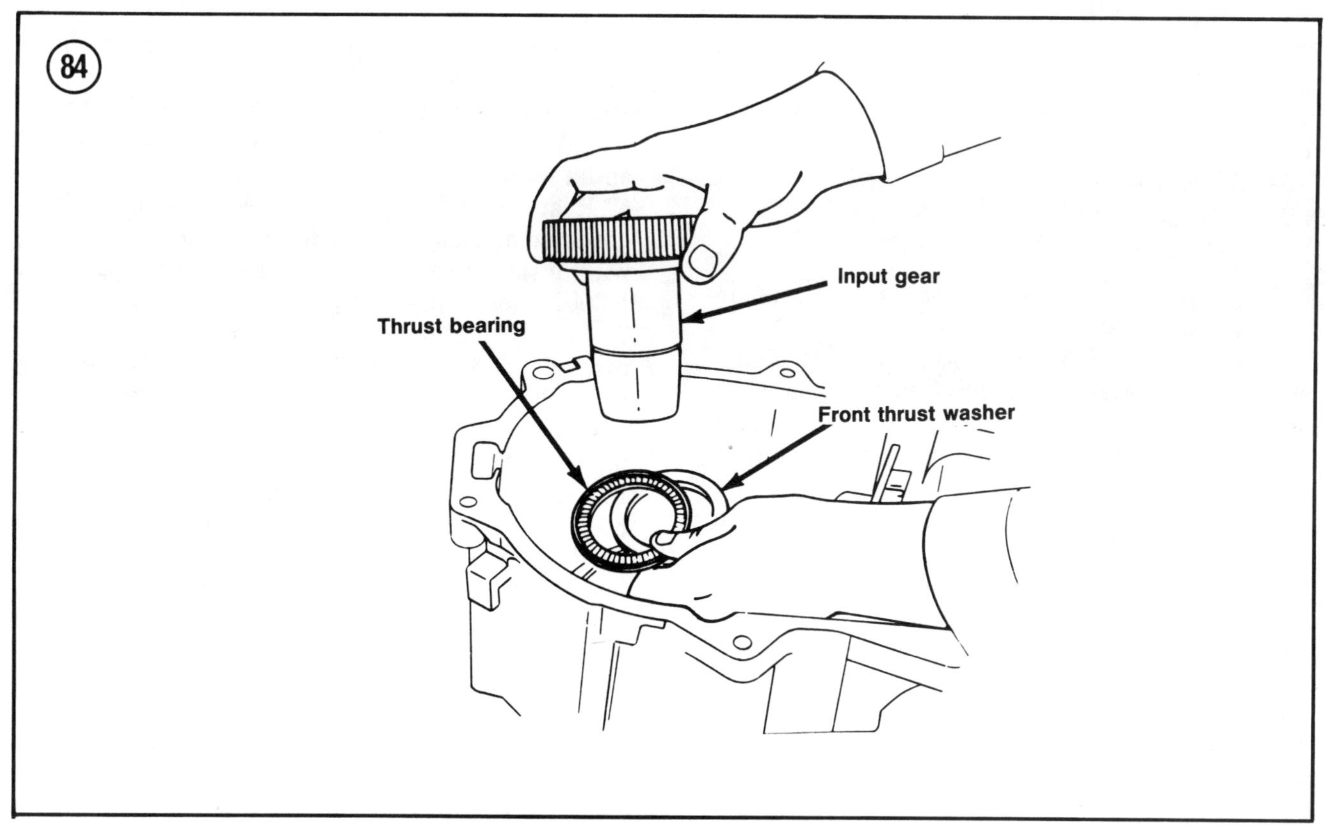
84
Input gear
Thrust bearing
Front thrust washer

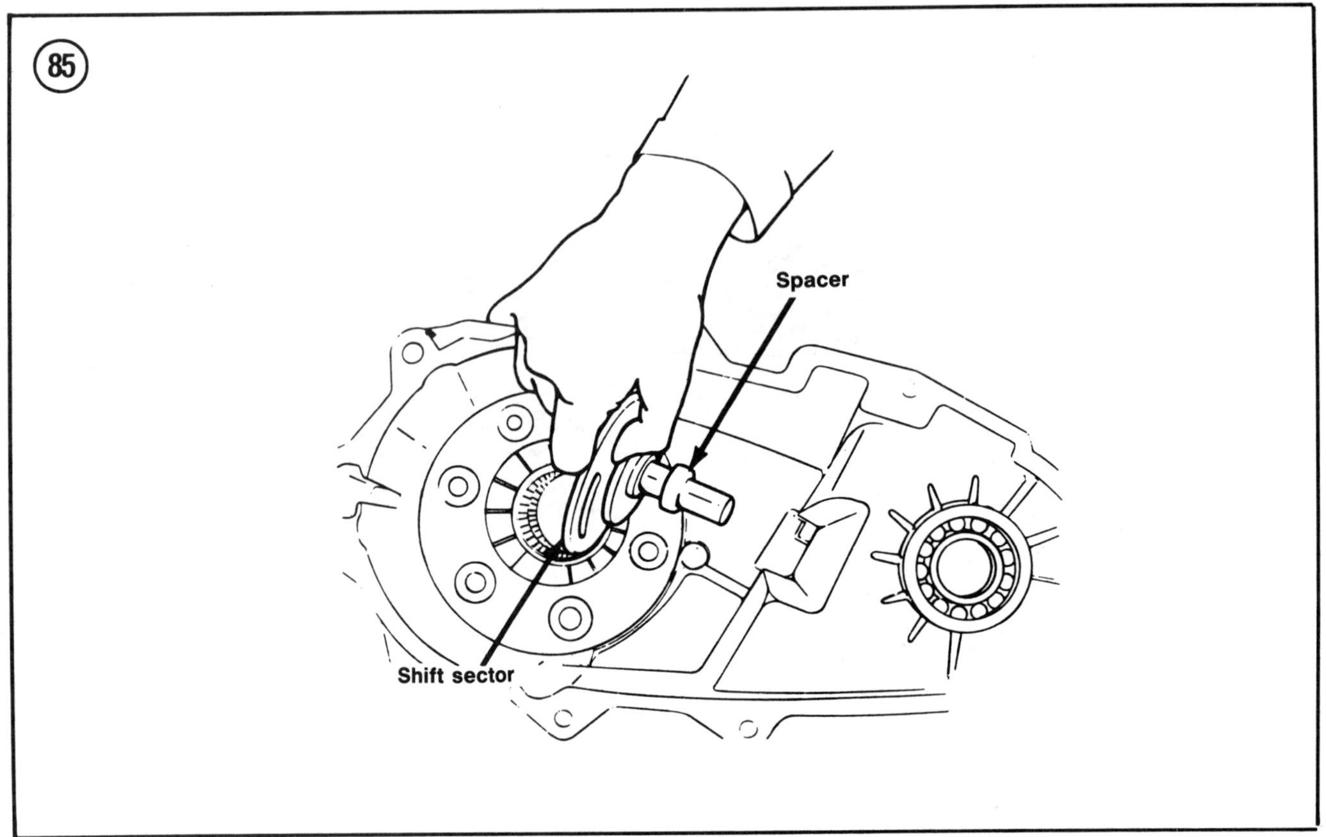

17. Remove the shift sector, shaft and spacer from the transfer case. See **Figure 85**.
18. Unbolt and remove the locking plate from the transfer case (**Figure 86**).

Bearing, Bushing and Seal Replacement

1. Disassemble the transfer case as described in this chapter.
2. Input gear pilot bearing—Remove with puller part No. J-29369-1 (or equivalent) and a slide hammer. Install a new bearing with installer part No. J-33829, handle part No. J-8092 and a hydraulic press.
3. Input shaft gear roller bearings—Remove with remover part No. J-33841, handle part No. J-8092 and a hydraulic press. Install new bearings installer part No. J-33830, handle part No. J-8092 and a hydraulic press.
4. Front output shaft rear bearing—Remove with puller part No. J-29369-2 and a slide hammer. Install a new bearing with installer part No. J-33832, handle part No. J-8092 and a hydraulic press.
5. Extension housing bushing—Remove with remover part No. J-33839, handle part No. J-8092 and a hydraulic press. Install a new bushing with installer part No. J-33826, handle part No. J-8092 and a hydraulic press.
6. Rear main shaft bearing—Remove with a hammer and suitable drift. Install a new bearing with installer part No. J-33833, handle part No. J-8092 and a hydraulic press.
7. Front output shaft bearing—Remove and discard the bearing snap ring. Drive the bearing from the case with a hammer and suitable drift. Install a new bearing with tool part No. J-33833, handle part No. J-8092 and a hydraulic press. Install a new bearing snap ring.
8. Seals—Pry the seal from its bore with a suitable flat-bladed screwdriver. Install new seals with installer part No. J-33832 (input shaft), part No. J-33843 (extension housing), part No. J-33835 (pump) or part No. J-33834 (front input shaft).

Main Shaft Disassembly/Assembly

Refer to **Figure 87** for this procedure.

1. Remove the speedometer gear.

86

Lock plate

87

Speedometer gear
Pump gear
Synchronizer hub
Main shaft
Drive sprocket
Blocker ring

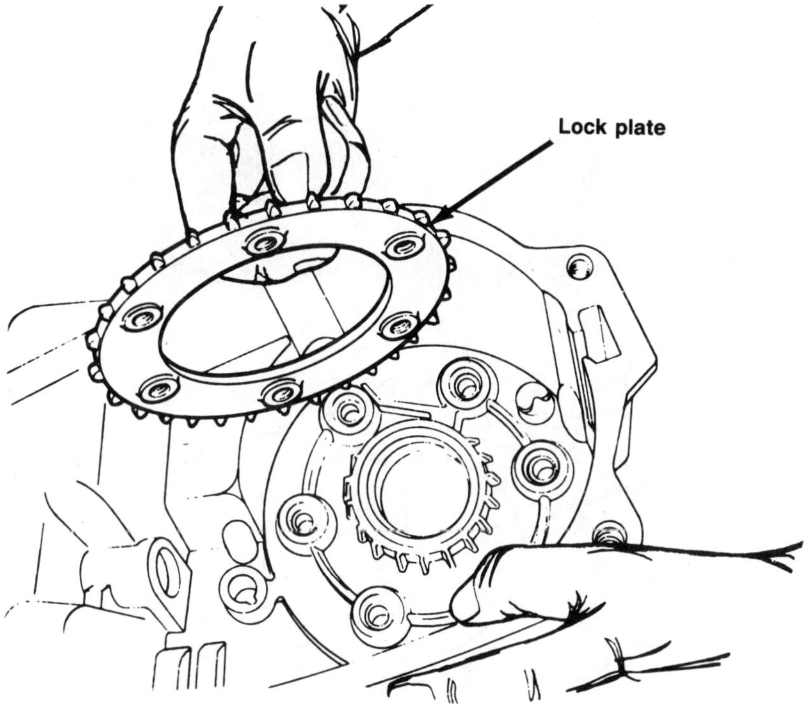

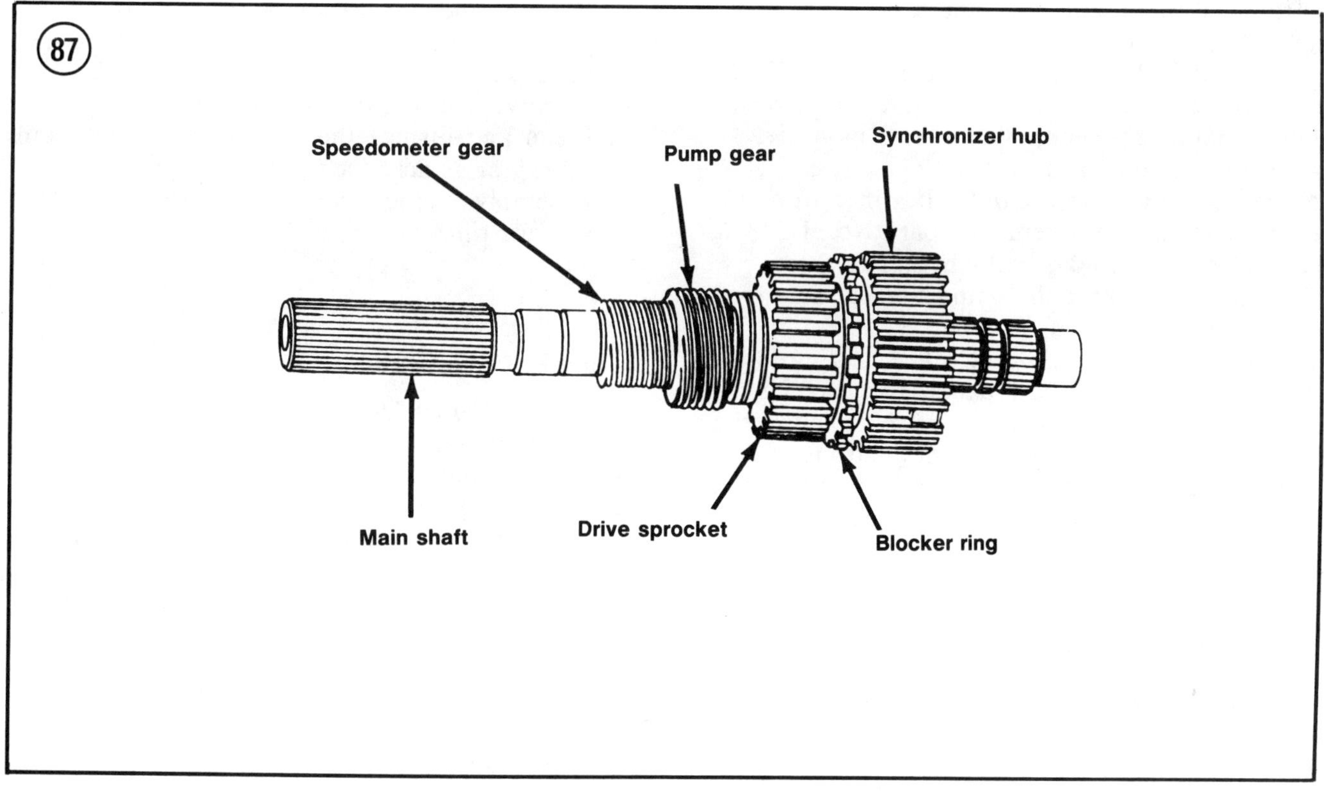

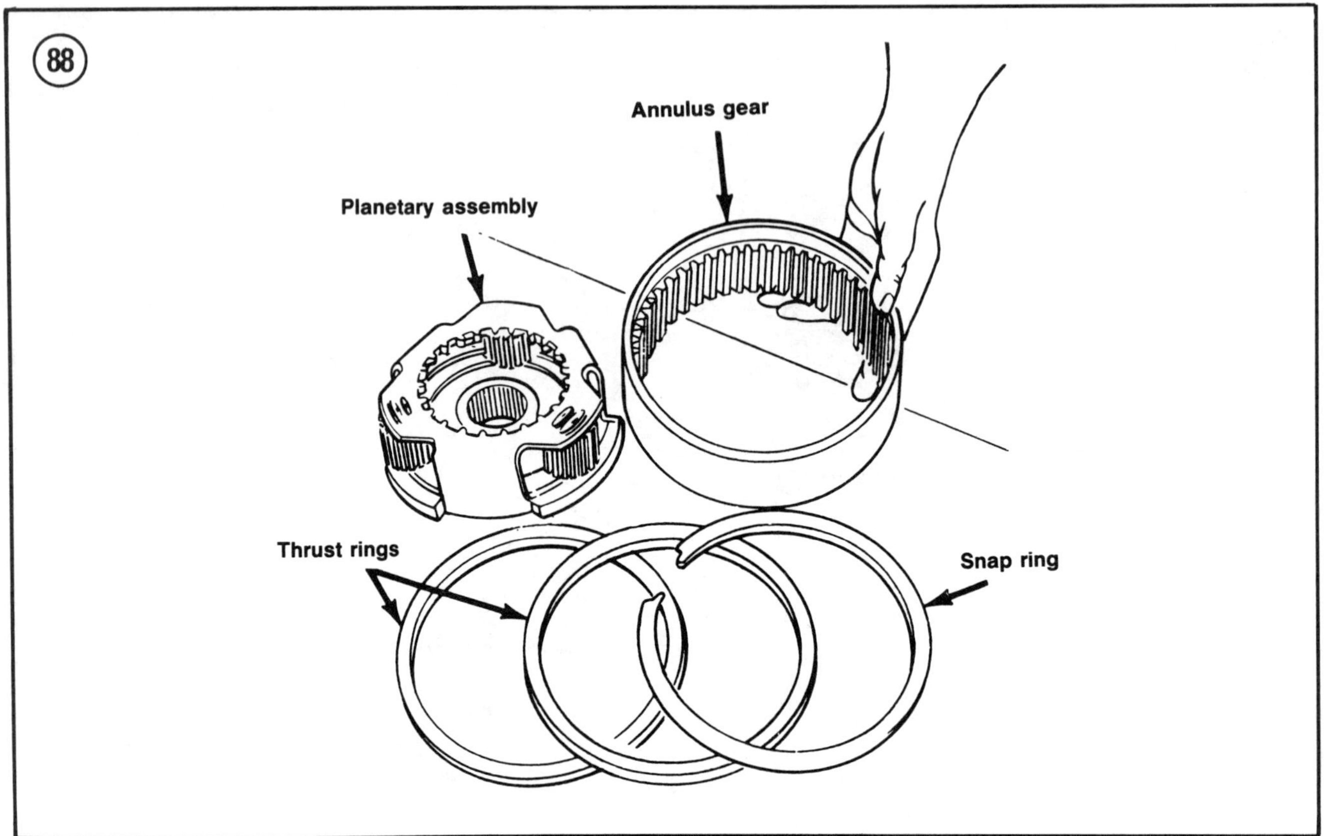

2. Pry the pump gear from the main shaft with a suitable screwdriver.
3. Expand and remove the snap ring holding the synchronizer hub to the main shaft. Remove the hub by tapping it gently with a brass hammer.
4. Remove the drive sprocket.
5. Remove the 2 caged roller bearings from the drive sprocket with remover part No. J-33826, handle part No. J-8092 and a hydraulic press.
6. Clean and inspect all components as described in this chapter.
7. Install the drive sprocket roller bearings with installer part No. J-33828, handle part No. J-8092 and a hydraulic press. When properly installed, the front bearing should be flush with the front surface and the rear bearing should be recessed in its bore.
8. Reverse Steps 1-4 to complete assembly. Install a new snap ring.

Planetary Gear Disassembly/Assembly

Refer to **Figure 88** for this procedure.

1. Remove the snap ring holding the planetary assembly in the annulus gear.
2. Remove and discard the outer thrust ring.
3. Separate the planetary assembly from the annulus gear.
4. Remove and discard the inner thrust ring.
5. Clean and inspect the planetary assembly and annulus gear as described in this chapter.
6. Assembly is the reverse of disassembly. Use new thrust rings.

Transfer Case Assembly

Refer to **Figure 76** for this procedure.

1. Lubricate all components with DEXRON II automatic transmission fluid.
2. Apply a light coat of Loctite 515 (or equivalent) to the lock plate mating surface in the transfer case and around the lock plate bolt holes. Position the lock plate in the case (**Figure 86**) and tighten the bolts to specifications (**Table 1**).
3. Fit the spacer on the shift sector shaft, then install sector in the transfer case (**Figure 85**). Install the shift lever with retaining nut and tighten to specifications (**Table 1**).

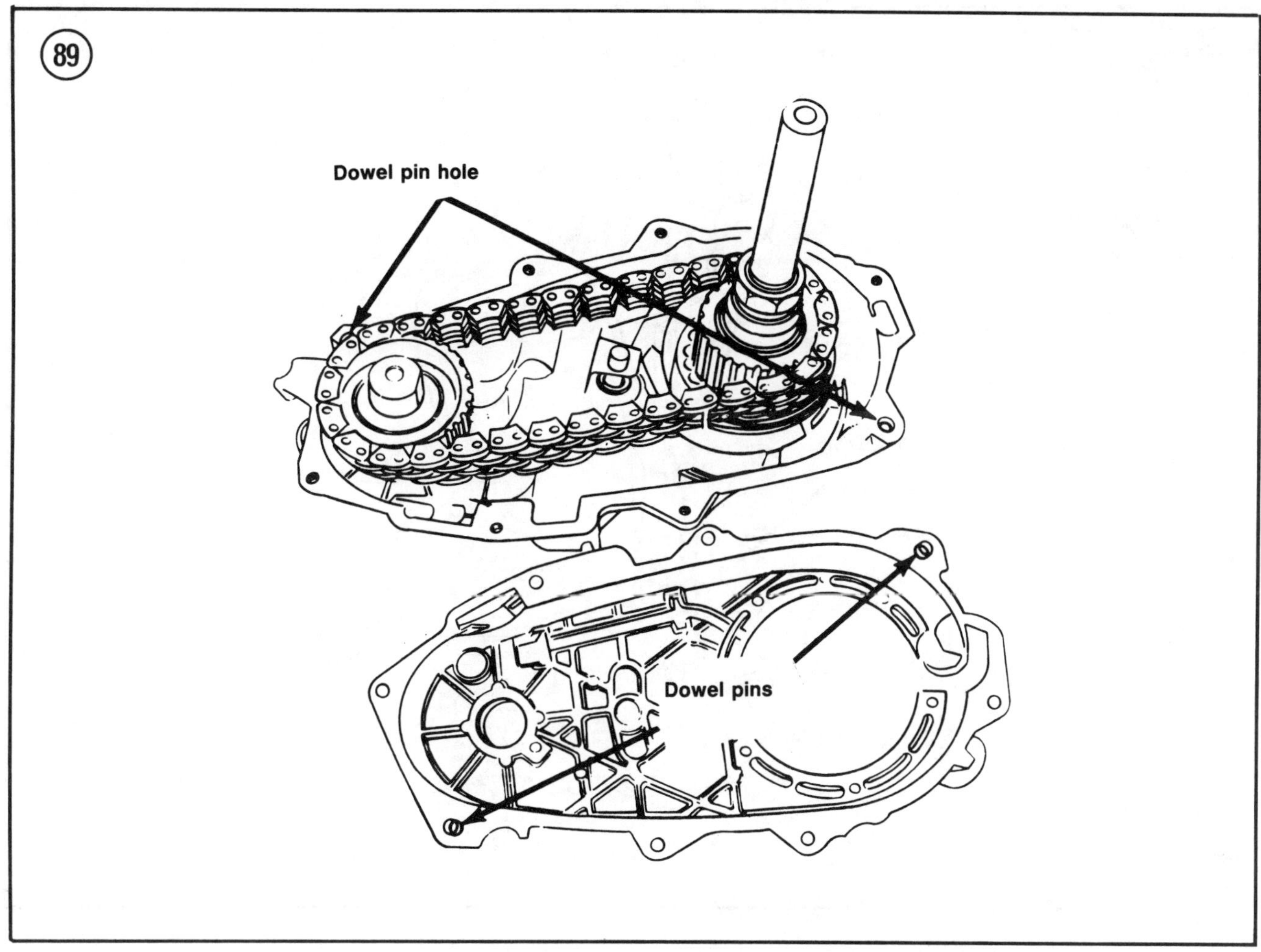

4. Install the shift sector detent spring with retaining bolt.

5. Install the input gear front thrust bearing and input gear in the case (**Figure 84**).

6. Fit the planetary gear thrust washer on the input gear. Make sure the nylon wear tips are installed on the range fork. Align the fork with the planetary assembly and install both in the transfer case (**Figure 83**).

7. Make sure the thrust washer aligns with the input gear and planetary assembly, then install the main shaft in the case (**Figure 82**).

8. Make sure the nylon wear tips are installed on the mode fork, then position the fork on the synchronizer sleeve, rotating until it aligns with the range fork. Insert the mode fork rail through the range fork until it seats in the transfer case bore (**Figure 81**).

9. Fit the drive chain around the front output shaft drive sprocket. Install front output shaft in transfer case while lifting main shaft slightly to seat the output shaft and fit the drive chain around the main shaft sprocket (**Figure 80**).

10. Reinstall the magnetic chip collector in the slot provided in the case half.

11. Run a 1/8 in. (3 mm) bead of Loctite 515 (or equivalent) along the front case mating surface. Lower the rear case half onto the front case half. The dowel pin holes in the rear case must engage the dowel pins in the front case. See **Figure 89**. Install and tighten the housing bolts to specifications (**Table 1**).

12. Wipe pump housing tabs with petroleum jelly and install housing in the rear retainer.

13. Run a 1/8 in. (3 mm) bead of Loctite 515 (or equivalent) along the rear retainer mating surfaces. Position retainer on transfer case. Install and tighten bolts to specifications (**Table 1**).

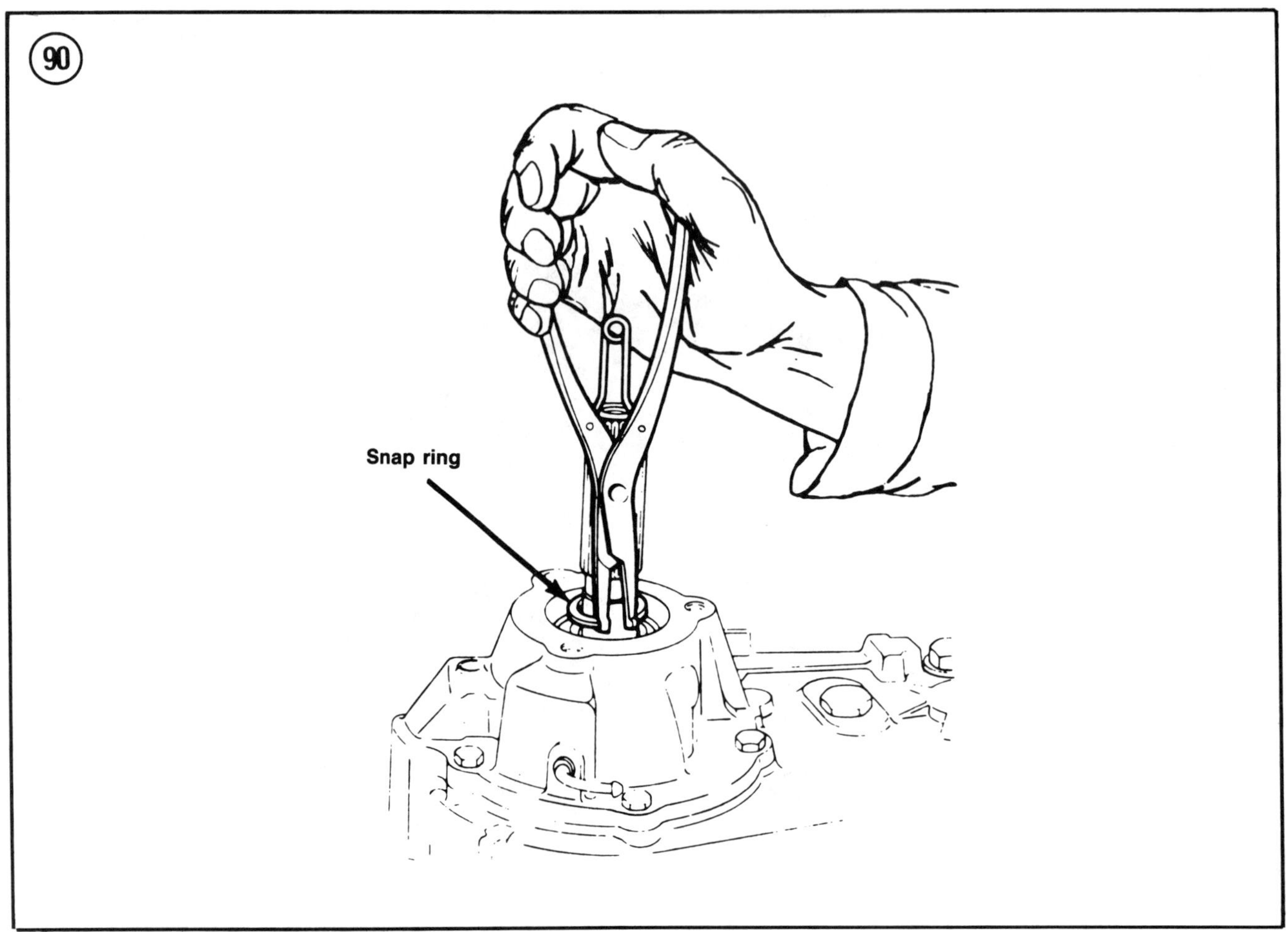

14. Expand and install a new main shaft snap ring. Lift up on the main shaft and seat the snap ring in its groove (**Figure 90**).
15. Run a 1/8 in. (3 mm) bead of Loctite 515 (or equivalent) to the extension housing mating surface. Position extension housing on transfer case. Install and tighten bolts to specifications (**Table 1**).
16. Fit the front yoke on the output shaft. Install a new washer and yoke nut. Hold yoke with a flange holding tool and tighten yoke nut to specifications (**Table 1**).
17. Install the drain and fill plugs. Tighten to specifications (**Table 1**).

AUTOMATIC TRANSMISSION

The vehicles covered in this manual may be equipped with either a 3-speed Turbo-Hydramatic 200C or a 4-speed Turbo-Hydramatic 700R4 automatic transmission.

Both transmissions use DEXRON II automatic transmission fluid. Use of a transmission fluid other than that specified can result in a transmission malfunction and/or premature failure.

To determine the transmission type, check the transmission code on the vehicle certification label attached to the driver's side front door lock face panel or door pillar. A transmission nameplate is attached or stamped on the transmission at one of the points shown in **Figure 91**. This nameplate contains the transmission model, model year and serial number. This information is required for ordering replacement parts.

This section includes checks and adjustment procedures to be performed with the transmission in the vehicle. Many problems can be corrected with the adjustment procedures provided here. Automatic transmission overhaul, however, requires professional skills, many special tools and extremely high standards of cleanliness. Although

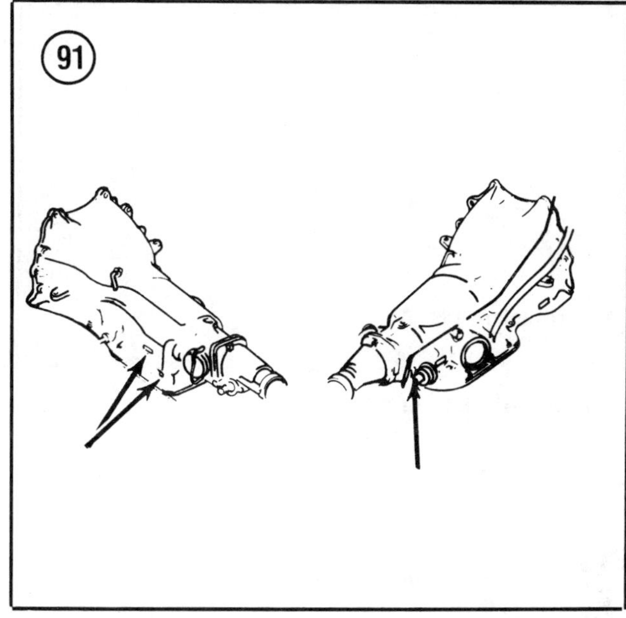

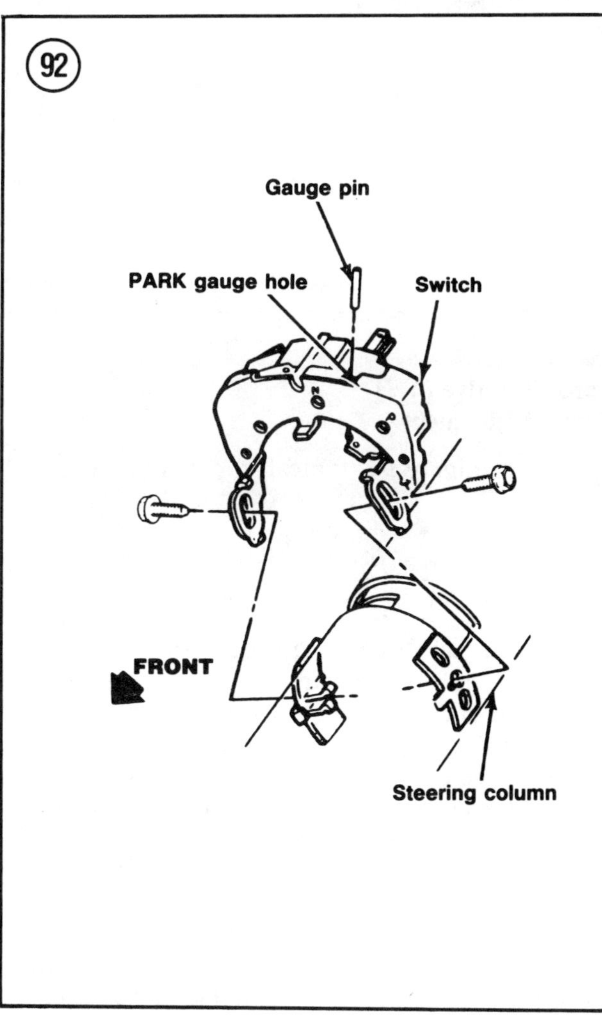

procedures for removal and installation are included in this chapter, disassembly and overhaul should be left to a Chevrolet or GMC dealer or a competent automatic transmission repair shop.

Checking Procedure

1. Park the vehicle on a level surface.
2. Make sure the engine starts only when the shift lever is in NEUTRAL or PARK. If it will start in any other position, check the neutral start/backup light switch as described in this chapter.
3. Make sure the backup lights go on when the transmission is shifted to REVERSE.
4. Make sure the truck moves forward in DRIVE and backward in REVERSE.
5. Make sure the shift selector indicator points to the correct range. If the indicator is out of alignment, adjust the shift linkage as described in this chapter.
6. Check fluid level. See Chapter Three.
7. Shut the engine off. Check the throttle lever and cable bracket on the side of the carburetor or throttle body for damage. Correct or replace as required.

Neutral Start/Backup Light Switch Testing

9

This switch is attached to the steering column.

1. Unplug the wiring connector from the switch.
2. Connect a self-powered test lamp between the connector and switch terminals.
3. Turn the ignition switch ON, but do not start the engine.
4. Move the gearshift lever through the gear range and check for continuity in each position. There should be continuity only when the lever is in PARK or NEUTRAL. If the test lamp lights in any other position, adjust the switch as described in this chapter.

Neutral Start/Backup Light Switch Adjustment

Refer to **Figure 92** for this procedure.

1. Move the shift lever into NEUTRAL.
2. Loosen the attaching bolt/screw.
3. Rotate the switch to insert a 0.096 in. gauge pin to a depth of 3/8 in.
4. Tighten the attaching bolt/screw.

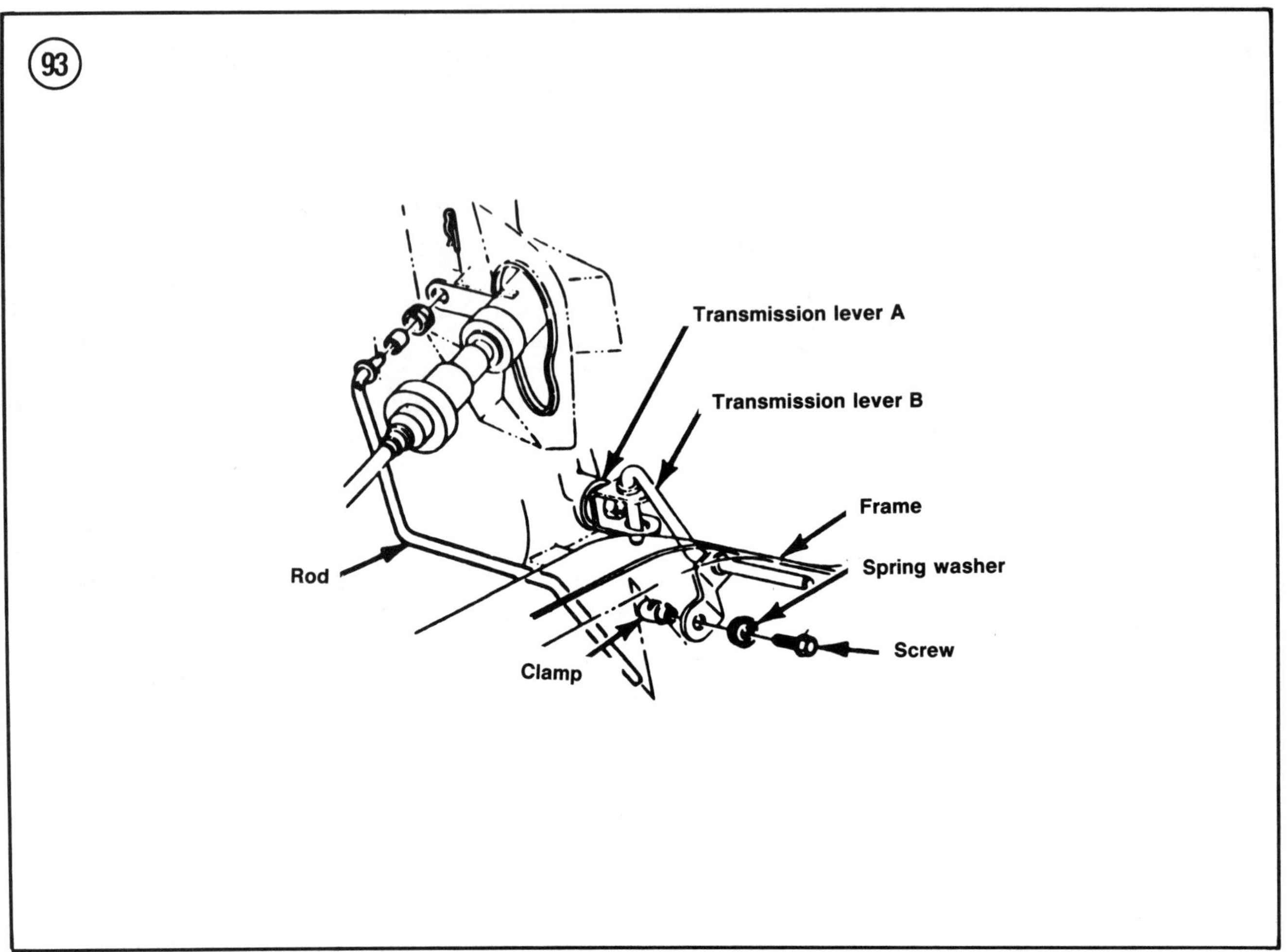

the switch. It should enter the hole to a depth of 3/8 in.

7. If the 0.089 in. pin enters the hole freely, the switch adjustment is correct. If it does not enter freely, repeat Steps 1-6.

Shift Linkage Adjustment

Refer to **Figure 93** for this procedure.

1. Move the shift lever to NEUTRAL.
2. Place lever A in the neutral detent position.
3. Assemble the clamp spring washer and screw to lever B and the control rod.
4. Hold the clamp tightly against lever B and tighten the clamp screw against the rod.
5. Tighten the clamp screw securely.
6. Move the shift lever through the gearshift range. The pointer will align properly if the adjustment is correct. If it does not align, repeat Steps 1-5.

Throttle Valve (TV) Cable Adjustment

Refer to **Figure 94** (typical) for this procedure.

NOTE
Do not depress the TV cable lock tab during adjustment.

1. Open the carburetor or throttle body lever to the full throttle stop position. This automatically adjusts the slider on the cable to its correct setting. Release the carburetor or throttle body lever to complete the adjustment. **Figure 95** shows the TV cable at the carburetor when properly adjusted; the throttle body cable position is similar.
2. If readjustment is necessary because the lock tab was accidentally depressed, depress and hold it again. See **Figure 96**. Move the slider away from the carburetor or throttle body until it stops against the fitting. Release the lock tab and repeat Step 1.

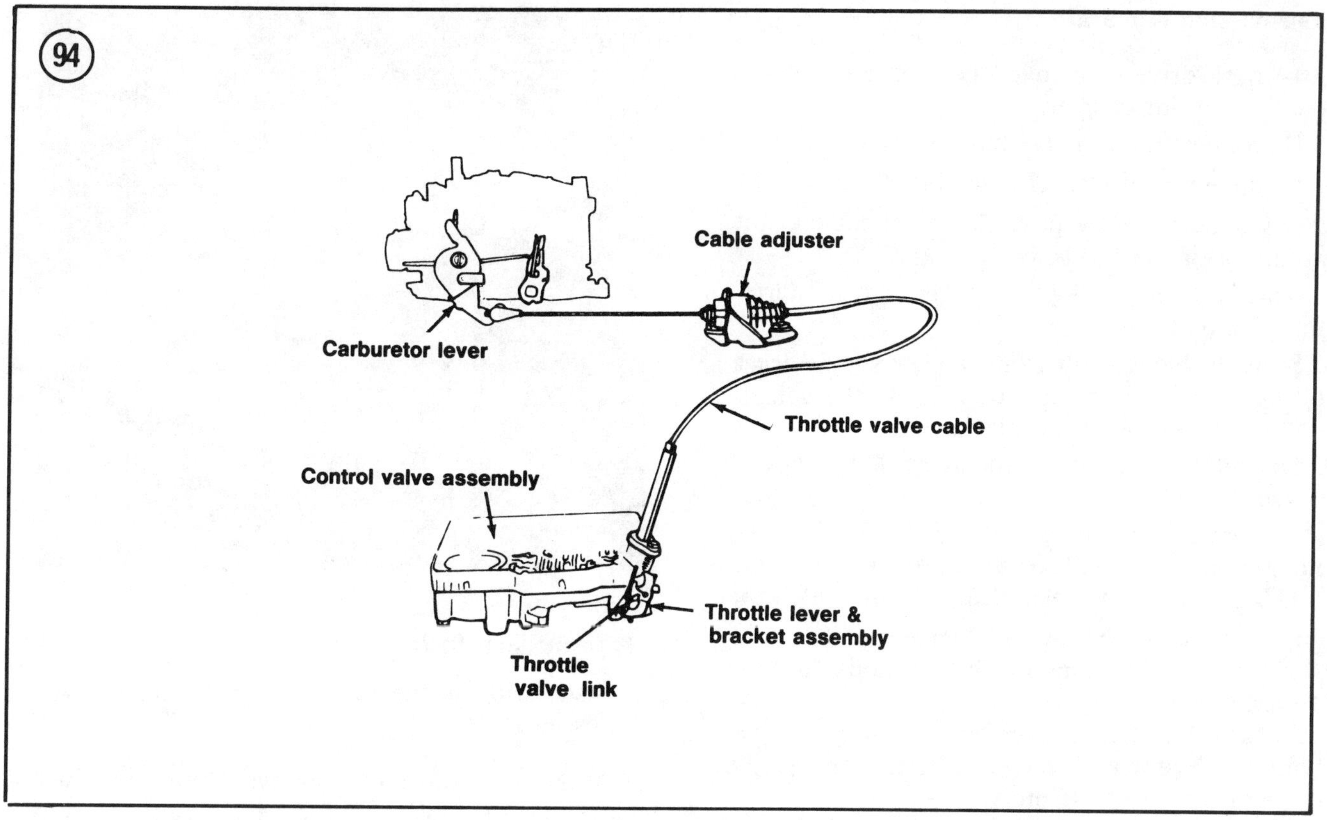

94
Cable adjuster
Carburetor lever
Throttle valve cable
Control valve assembly
Throttle lever &
bracket assembly
Throttle
valve link

95
Carburetor
Throttle valve
cable terminal
Throttle valve cable
(closed position)

96
Re-adjust tab
Fitting
Throttle
lever
Re-adjust
direction
Slider
Detent cable

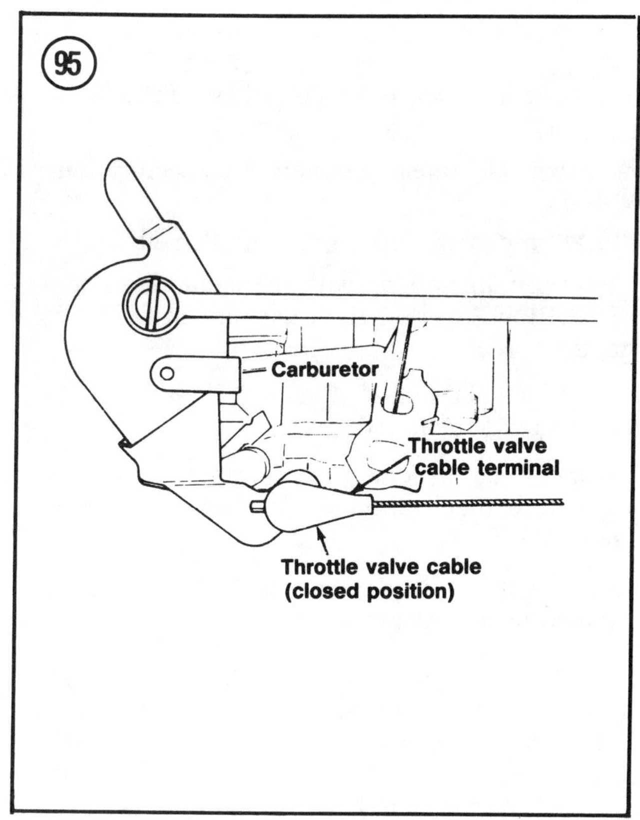

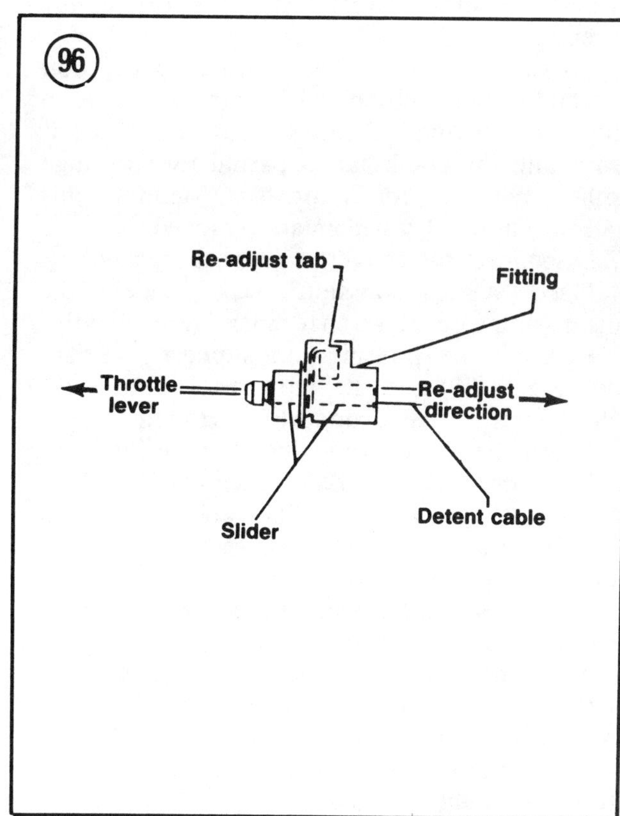

Transmission Removal

1. 4-wheel drive—Remove the transfer case as described in this chapter.
2. Disconnect the negative battery cable.
3. Remove the air cleaner assembly (Chapter Six).
4. Disconnect the TV (throttle valve) cable at the carburetor or throttle body.
5. 4-cylinder engine—Remove the upper starter mounting bolt.
6. Securely block both front wheels so the truck will not roll in either direction. Raise the vehicle with a jack and place it on jackstands.
7. Disconnect and remove the drive shaft (Chapter Eleven).
8. Disconnect the speedometer cable (**Figure 97**) and shift linkage (A, **Figure 98**) at the transmission.
9. Disconnect all electrical leads at the transmission. See B, **Figure 98** (typical).
10. Remove the support brace bolts at the converter, if so equipped.
11. Disconnect the exhaust crossover pipe. Remove the pipe and converter bolts. Remove the pipe and converter assembly.
12. Remove the converter cover. Mark the flywheel and torque converter for reassembly reference.
13. Install a wrench on the crankshaft pulley bolt to rotate the crankshaft and gain access to a converter attaching bolt/nut. Remove the fastener, then rotate the crankshaft a partial turn to align another bolt/nut for removal. Continue this procedure until all fasteners are removed.
14. Disconnect the converter support bracket.
15. Place a transmission jack under the transmission case. Raise the transmission slightly.
16. Remove the transmission support-to-mount bolts (**Figure 99**) and the support-to-frame bolts. Slide the transmission support to the rear.
17. Lower the transmission slightly with the jack.
18. Disconnect the oil cooler lines and TV cable at the transmission. Plug the lines and cap the oil cooler fittings to prevent leakage or entry of contamination.
19. Support the engine with another jack. Remove the transmission-to-engine bolts.
20. Move the transmission back slightly and install a holding fixture or strap to prevent the torque converter from falling out.
21. Lower the transmission carefully and remove it from under the vehicle.

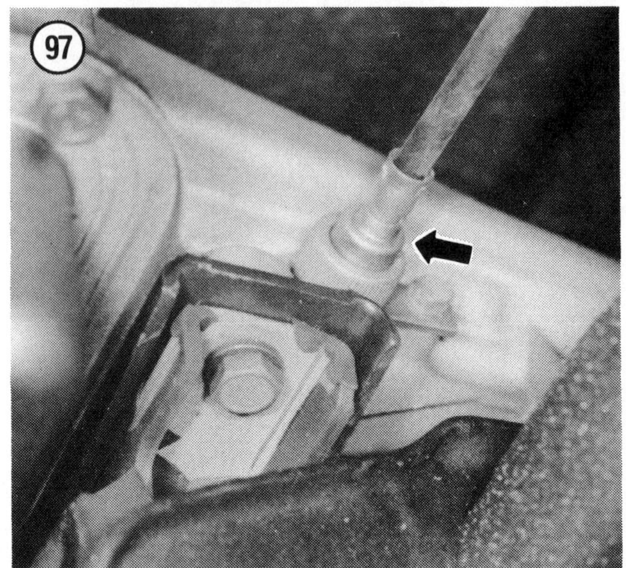

Transmission Installation

Installation is the reverse of removal, plus the following:

1. Make sure the converter weld nuts are flush with the flex plate before installing the flex plate-to-converter bolts. The converter should rotate freely in this position.
2. Tighten the flex plate-to-converter bolts by hand, then retighten to specifications (**Table 1**) to ensure proper converter alignment.
3. Tighten all other fasteners to specifications (**Table 1**).
4. Install a new oil seal on the oil filler tube.
5. Fill the transmission with the required amount of DEXRON II automatic transmission fluid. See Chapter Three.
6. Check the fluid level (Chapter Three). Add or remove fluid as required.
7. Warm the engine to normal operating temperature, then recheck the fluid level and adjust as required.
8. Adjust the shift linkage and TV cable as described in this chapter.
9. Road test the vehicle. Make sure the transmission shifts smoothly, makes no abnormal noises and holds the vehicle when in PARK (parking brake should be applied). After road testing, check for fluid leaks.

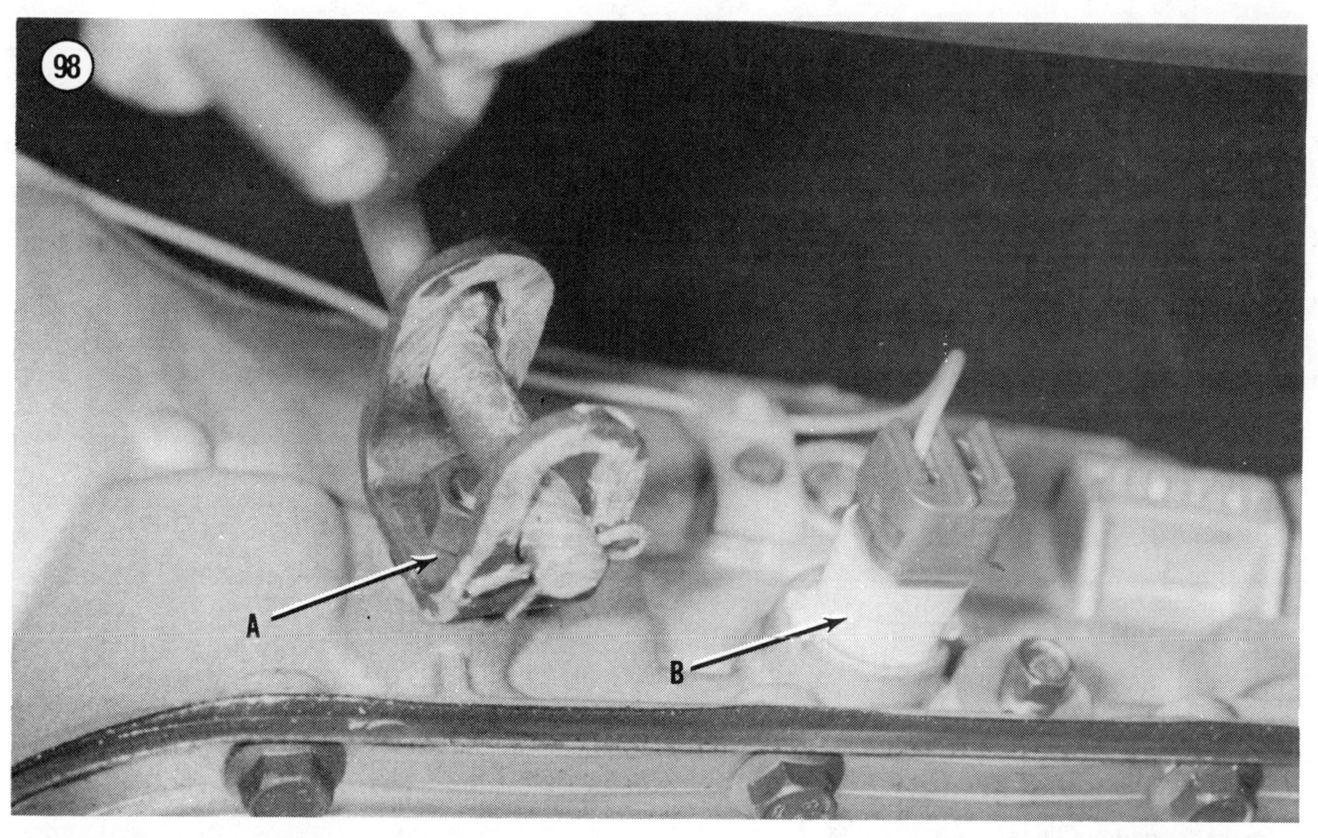
98
A
B

99

Table 1 TIGHTENING TORQUES

Fastener	ft.-lb.	N•m
	CLUTCH	
Clutch fork cable locknut	2	3
Flywheel		
Inline engine	70	95
V6 engine	50	70
Flywheel housing-to-engine	55	75
Master cylinder attaching nuts	10-15	15-20
Neutral start switch	2	3
Pawl-to-clutch pedal	7	10
Pedal bumper stop	10	15
Pedal-to-mounting bracket	25	35
Pressure plate-to-flywheel	20	25
Slave cylinder attaching nuts	10-15	15-20
	M150 MANUAL TRANSMISSION	
Body mount bolts	45-60	60-80
Clutch ball stud	30	40
Clutch housing cover bolts	7	10
Countershaft rear nut	80	110
Detent spring plate bolts	15	20
Extension housing bolts	30	40
Fill/drain plugs	30	40
Front bearing retainer bolts	15	20
Gearshift quadrant bolts	15	20
Main shaft rear nut	95	130
Radiator support bolts	45-60	60-80
Rear bearing retainer screws	15	20
Transmission-to-engine bolts		
Inline engine	25	35
V6 engine	55	75
Transmission mount bolts		
Crossmember-to-frame	25	30
Mount-to-transmission bolts	35	50
Mount-to-crossmember nuts	25	30
	T4C/T5 MANUAL TRANSMISSION	
Crossmember-to-frame	25	30
Extension housing bolts	25	30
Front bearing retainer	15	20
Fill/drain plugs	20	27
Reverse pivot bolt-to-case	20	27
Shift cover-to-case	10	15
Transmission-to-engine bolts	55	75
Transmission mount		
To transmission	35	50
To crossmember	25	30

(continued)

Table 1 TIGHTENING TORQUES (continued)

Fastener	ft.-lb.	N•m
NEW PROCESS 207 TRANSFER CASE		
Adapter-to-transfer case	19-29	26-40
Extension housing-to-transfer case	19-29	26-40
Fill/drain plugs	30-40	40-54
Front output yoke nut	90-130	122-176
Lock plate bolts	20-30	27-40
Rear retainer bolt	15-20	20-27
Shift brakcet bolt	47-62	65-85
Shift lever		
Adjusting bolt	25-35	34-48
Nut	15-20	20-27
Pivot bolt	88-103	120-140
Vacuum switch	15-25	20-34
AUTOMATIC TRANSMISSION		
Converter cover		
Inline engine	7	10
V6 engine	25	30
Crossmember-to-frame	25	30
Flywheel-to-converter	35	50
Oil cooler lines		
At radiator	25	30
At transmission	12	16
Oil pan bolts		
200C	7-10	9-13
700R4	12	16
Transmission		
Braces	35	50
Mount-to-crossmember	25	30
Mount-to-transmission	35	50
Transmission-to-engine		
Inline engine	25	35
V6 engine	55	75

9

CHAPTER TEN

FRONT SUSPENSION, AXLES, DIFFERENTIAL AND STEERING

All vehicles use an independent front suspension with upper and lower control arms, ball-joint assemblies and cast steering knuckles. Front wheel relationship is maintained by 2 tie rods connected to an intermediate or relay rod and steering arms on the knuckles.

Two-wheel drive vehicles use coil springs mounted between the lower control arms and spring housings on the frame/front end sheet metal. Four-wheel drive vehicles use torsion bars connected to the lower control arms and rear crossmember.

Tubular shock absorbers provide ride control. The upper end of each shock absorber extends through the upper control arm frame brackets and is retained with rubber bushings and a nut. The lower shock absorber end is attached to the lower control arm. A spring steel stabilizer shaft controls front suspension side roll. The stabilizer ends are connected to the lower control arms by link bolts.

The upper control arm is connected to a cross shaft, which is bolted in turn to frame brackets. A ball-joint is riveted to the outer end of the control arm and pre-loaded by a rubber spring for proper ball seating in the socket.

The inner ends of the lower control arm contain pressed-in bushings and are attached to the frame with bolts. The lower ball-joint is pressed into the lower control arm.

Figure 1 shows the major components of the 2-wheel drive front suspension, including the brake caliper, rotor and wheel bearings. **Figure 2** shows the 4-wheel drive front suspension.

Tightening torques (**Table 1**) and alignment specifications (**Table 2**) are provided at the end of

FRONT SUSPENSION

Shock Absorber Replacement

Always use new rubber insulators/bushings when installing new shock absorbers. Refer to **Figure 3** for this procedure.

1. Set the parking brake. Place the transmission in PARK (automatic) or 1st gear (manual).
2. Raise the front of the vehicle with a jack and place it on jackstands.
3. Hold the upper end of the shock absorber from turning with an open-end wrench. Remove the upper retaining nut with a second wrench. Remove the retainer and rubber bushing.

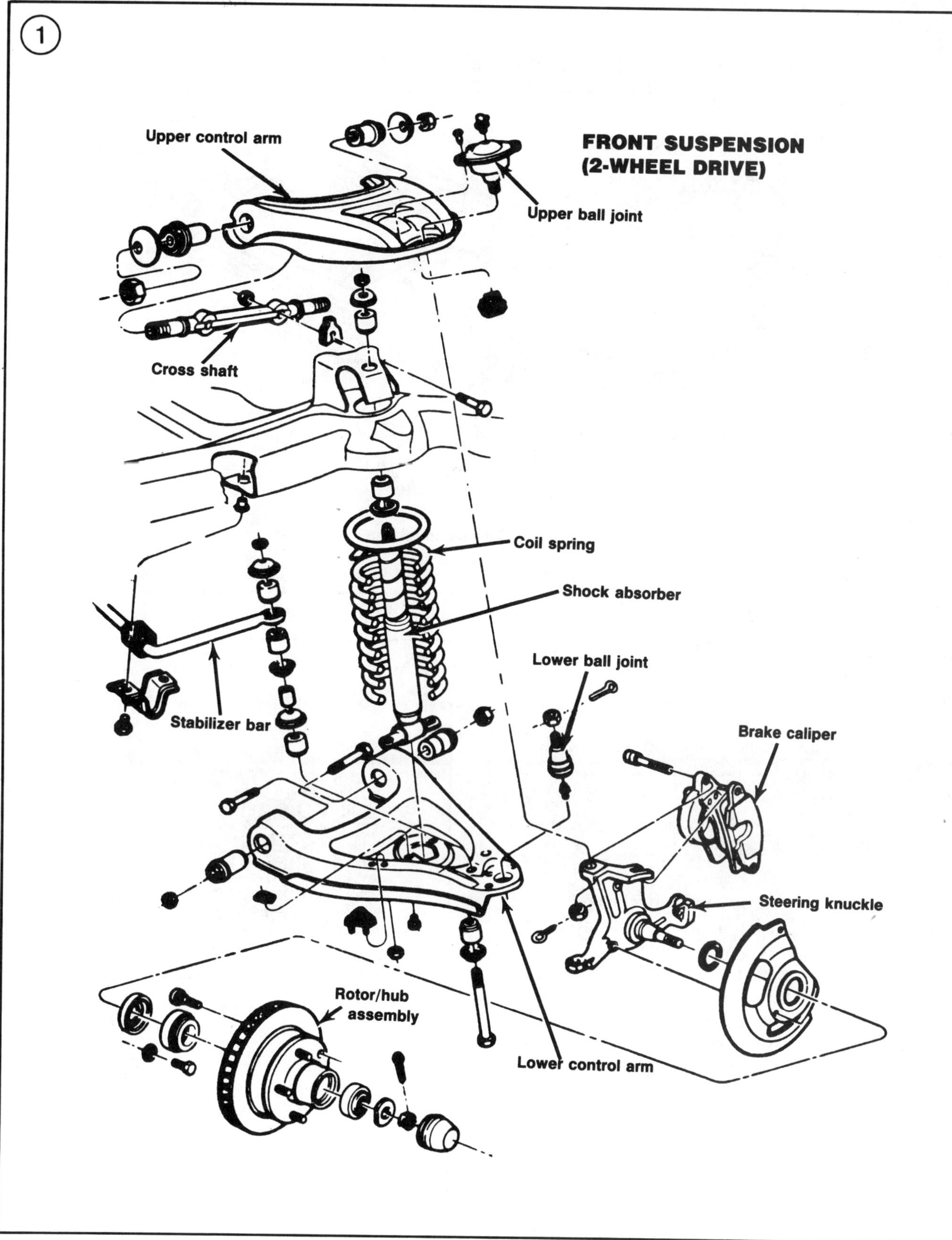
1
FRONT SUSPENSION
(2-WHEEL DRIVE)
Upper control arm
Upper ball joint
Cross shaft
Coil spring
Shock absorber
Lower ball joint
Stabilizer bar
Brake caliper
Steering knuckle
Rotor/hub
assembly
Lower control arm

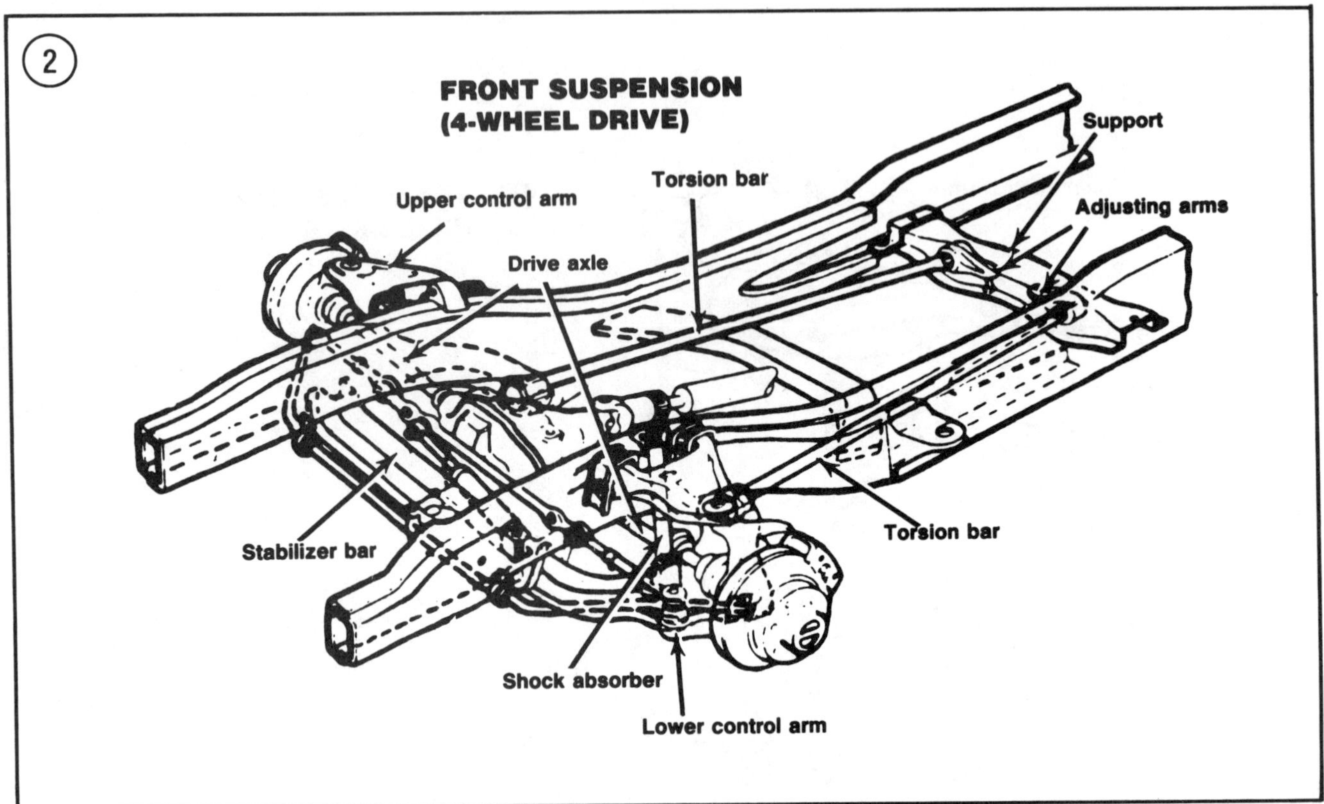

4. Remove the 2 bolts holding the lower pivot to the control arm. Pull the shock absorber out from the bottom.
5. Installation is the reverse of removal. Tighten the upper nut and lower bolts to specifications (**Table 1**). Remove the jackstands and lower the vehicle to the ground.

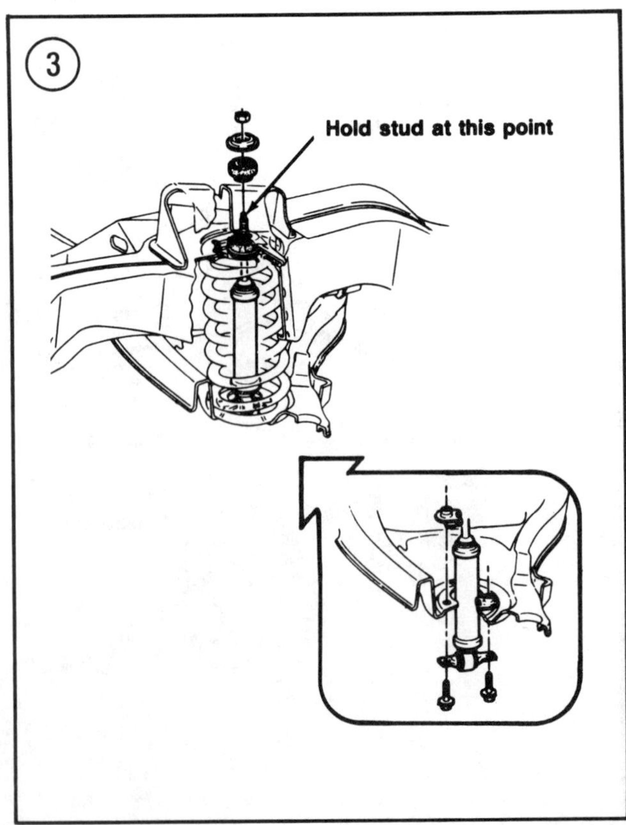

Shock Absorber Operational Check

Shock absorbers can be routinely checked while installed on the vehicle. Bounce the front of the vehicle up and down several times and release. Repeat this action with the rear of the vehicle. In either case, the vehicle should not continue to bounce more than twice. Excessive bouncing is an indication of worn shock absorbers. This test is not conclusive, since the spring stiffness of the vehicle makes it difficult to detect marginal shock absorbers.

If there is any doubt about their serviceability, remove the shock absorbers and perform the following procedure. If a shock absorber is found to be defective, replace all shocks on that end of the vehicle at the same time. If one shock absorber has

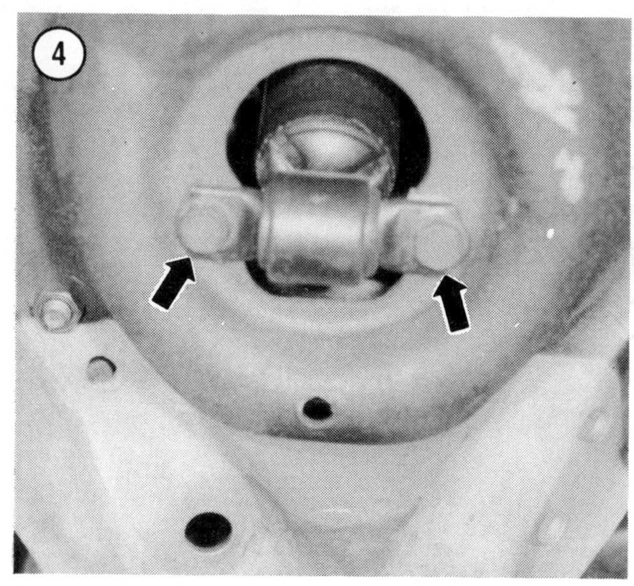

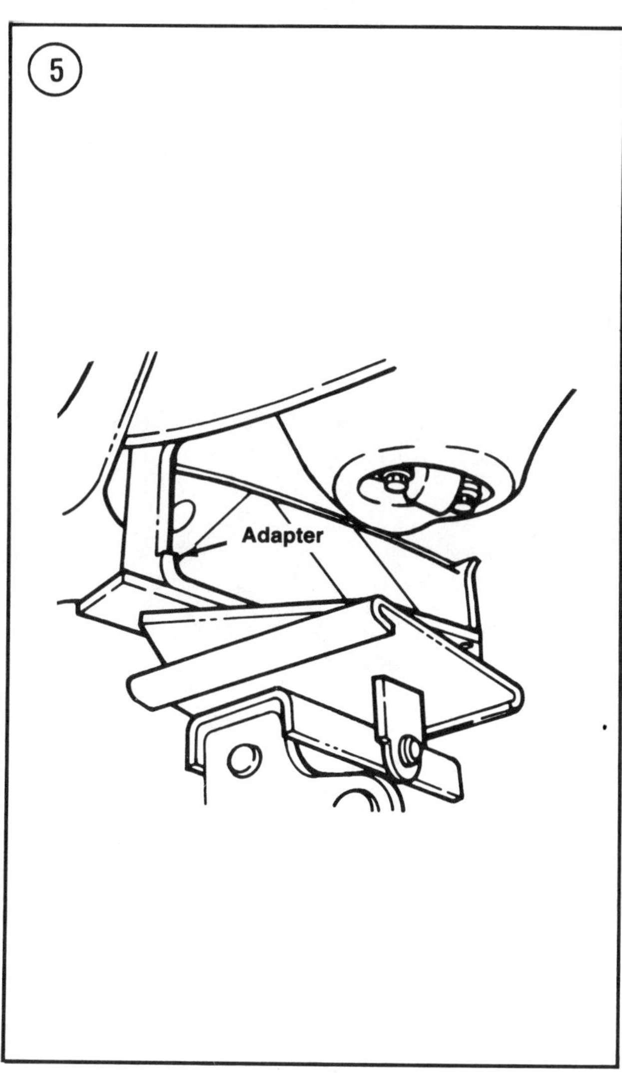

failed because of physical damage, both should be replaced at the same time, even if the remaining shock appears to be satisfactory.

NOTE
Comparison of a used shock absorber believed to be good with a new shock absorber is not a valid test. The new shock absorber will tend to offer more resistance due to the greater friction of the new rod seal.

1. Inspect the shock absorber piston rod for bending, galling and abrasion. Discard the shock absorber if any of these conditions are noted.
2. Check the outside of the shock absorber for fluid leakage. A light film of fluid on the rod is normal, but severe leakage requires replacement.
3. Holding the shock absorber in the installed position, completely extend the rod, then invert the shock and completely compress the rod. Repeat this step several times to expel any trapped air.
4. Secure the lower end of the shock absorber in a vise with protective jaws. If protective jaws are not available, place the shock between soft wooden blocks or wrap it in shop cloths before clamping it in the vise.
5. Compress and extend the piston rod as rapidly as possible and check the damping action. The resistance should be smooth and uniform throughout each stroke, and the resistance felt during extension should be greater than during compression. Repeat this step with the other shock absorber. Both shock absorbers in a pair should feel the same.
6. If the damping action is erratic or resistance to rapid extension/compression is very low (or the same in both directions), replace the shock absorbers as a set.

Coil Spring Replacement (2-wheel Drive Models)

The use of adapter part No. J-23028 is recommended to protect the inner bushings during this procedure.

1. Set the parking brake. Place the transmission in PARK (automatic) or 1st gear (manual).
2. Raise the front of the vehicle with a jack and place it on jackstands.
3. Remove the lower shock absorber mounting bolts. See **Figure 4**. Push the shock absorber upward to compress it.
4. Install tool part No. J-23028 to the hydraulic jack and position it as shown in **Figure 5**.

5. Remove the stabilizer from the lower control arm as described in this chapter.
6. Raise the jack to relieve any tension on the control arm pivot bolts. Install a chain through the spring and control arm as a safety precaution.
7. Remove the rear pivot bolt (A, **Figure 6**). Remove the front pivot bolt (B, **Figure 6**).
8. Lower the jack slowly to lower the control arm and relieve the spring compression. Remove the safety chain and spring from the control arm.
9. Installation is the reverse of removal. Install the spring with the tape at the lowest position (A, **Figure 7**). The end of the spring must cover all or part of one inspection drain hole (B, **Figure 7**) when properly installed.

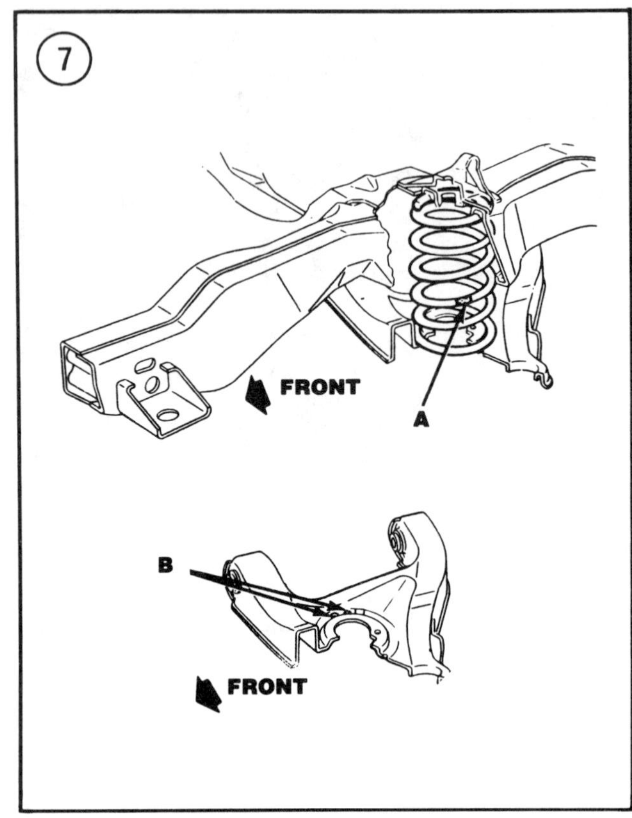

Stabilizer Bar Replacement

1. Set the parking brake. Place the transmission in PARK (automatic) or 1st gear (manual).
2. Raise the front of the vehicle with a jack and place it on jackstands.
3. Remove the link bolt holding each end of the stabilizer bar to the lower control arm (**Figure 8**). Remove the spacer, retainers and rubber bushings.
4. Remove the bracket mounting bolts at each side of the frame (**Figure 8**). Remove the brackets, rubber bushings and stabilizer bar.
5. Installation is the reverse of removal. Align the rubber bushings in their brackets with the bushing slit facing the front of the vehicle. Tighten the link nuts and bracket bolts to specifications (**Table 1**).

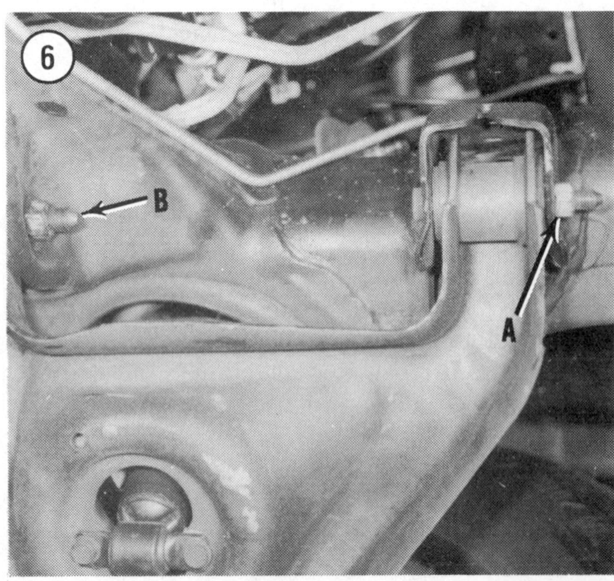

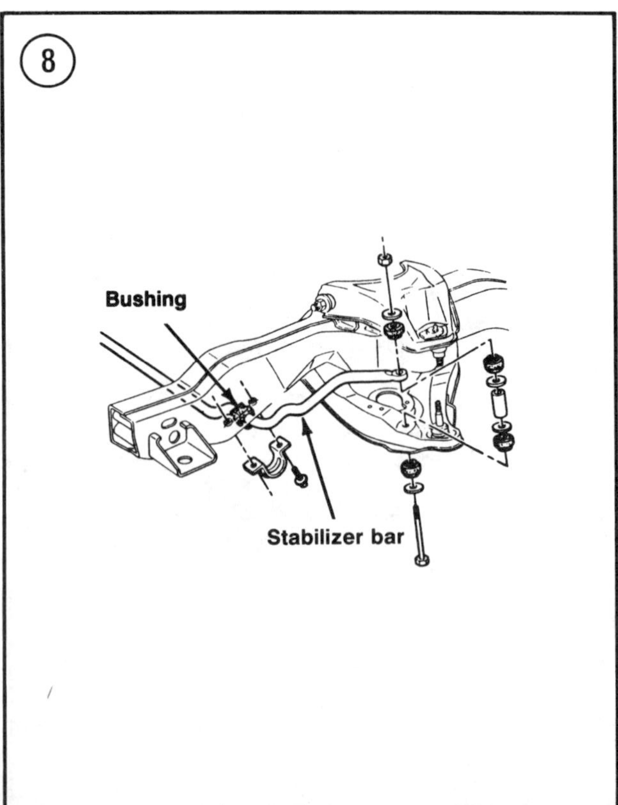

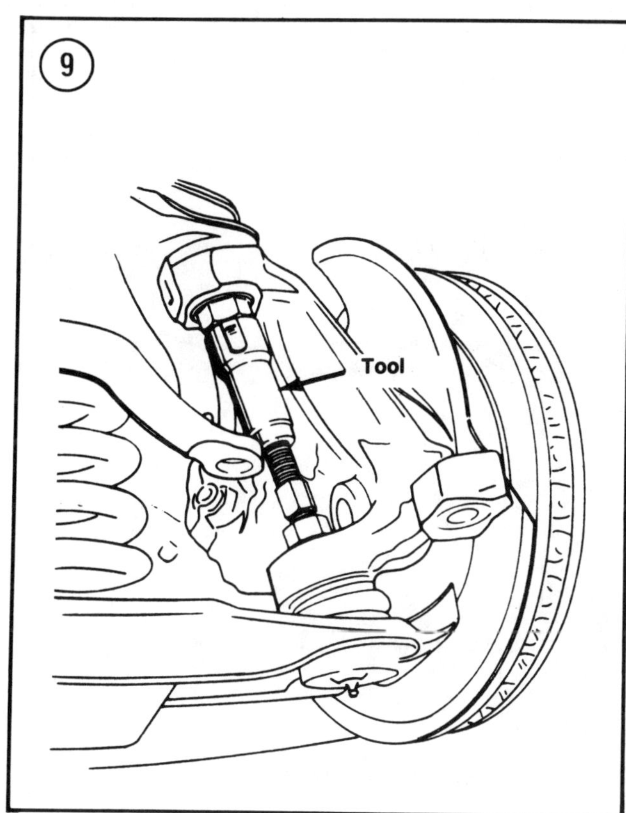

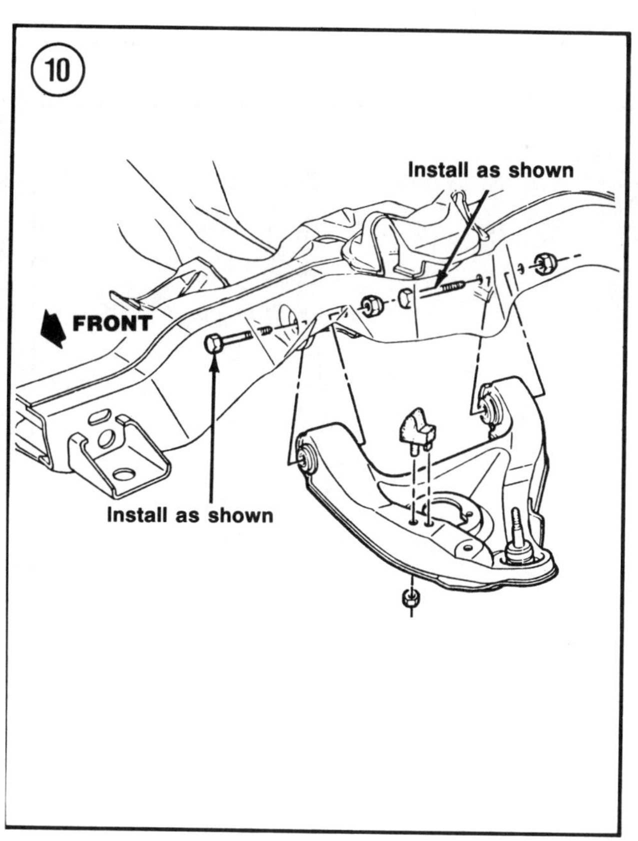

Lower Control Arm Removal/Installation

This procedure requires the use of ball-joint remover part No. J-23742.

1. Set the parking brake. Place the transmission in PARK (automatic) or 1st gear (manual).
2. Loosen the front wheel lug nuts.
3. Raise the front of the vehicle with a jack and place it on jackstands. Position the jackstands under the frame jack pads to the rear of the front wheels.
4. Remove the front wheel/tire assembly.
5. Remove the coil spring as described in this chapter.
6. 4-wheel drive—Disconnect the torsion bar at the control arm.
7. Separate the lower ball-joint stud from the steering knuckle with tool part No. J-23742 (**Figure 9**).
8. Remove the control arm.
9. Installation is the reverse of removal. Install the front leg of the arm into the crossmember before installing the rear leg in the frame bracket. Install both pivot bolts with their heads facing the front of the vehicle and tighten to specifications (**Table 1**). See **Figure 10**.

Lower Ball-joint Inspection

The lower front suspension ball-joint is pressed into the lower control arm. The ball-joint contains a visual wear indicator (**Figure 11**). Ball-joint inspection is done with the vehicle on the ground so that its weight will load the ball-joints properly.

Ball-joint wear is indicated by the position of the grease fitting nipple. On a new ball-joint, this nipple will project 0.050 in. (1.27 mm) below the surface of the ball-joint cover. As normal wear occurs, the nipple will gradually move up into the cover.

To inspect the ball-joint, clean the grease fitting and nipple to remove all dirt, grease and contamination. Scrape the cover with a screwdriver. If the nipple is flush with or inside the cover surface, replace the ball-joint.

Lower Ball-joint Replacement

This procedure requires the use of ball-joint remover tool part No. J-23742.

1. Remove the lower control arm as described in this chapter.

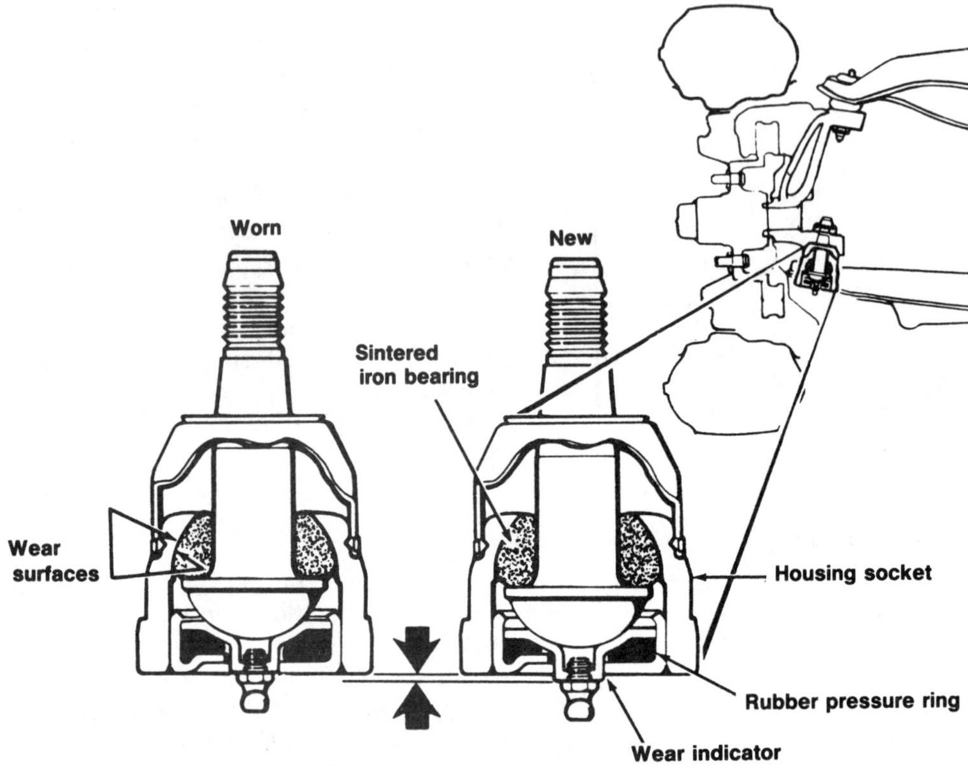

2. Remove the grease fitting.
3. Install a C-clamp with appropriate receivers as shown in **Figure 12** and press the ball-joint from the control arm.
4. Press a new ball-joint into the control arm.
5. Install the control arm as described in this chapter. Tighten the ball stud nut to 90 ft.-lb. (120 N•m), then tighten enough more to align the nut slot with the stud hole. Install a new cotter pin and lubricate the ball-joint grease fitting (Chapter Three).

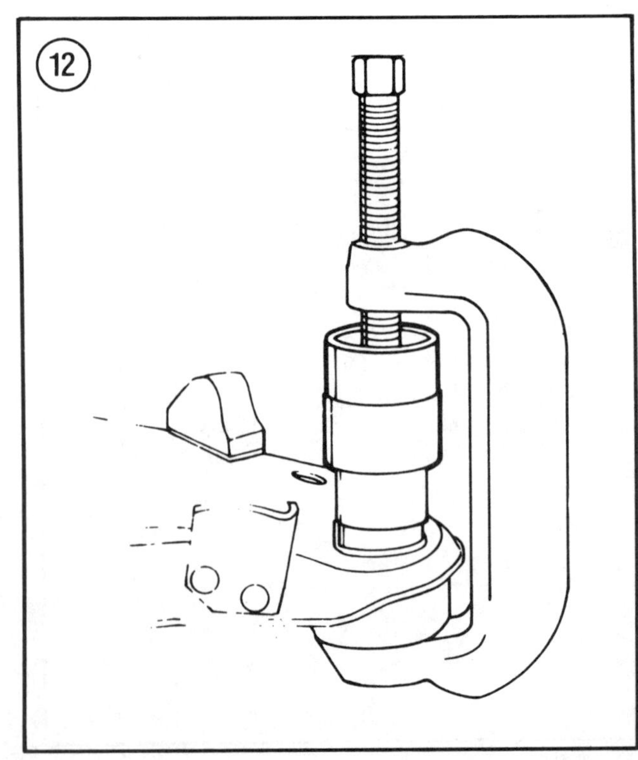

Lower Control Arm Bushing Replacement

Front and rear bushing replacement requires many special tools and should be referred to a dealer or qualified specialist.

Upper Control Arm Removal/Installation

1. Set the parking brake. Place the transmission in PARK (automatic) or 1st gear (manual).

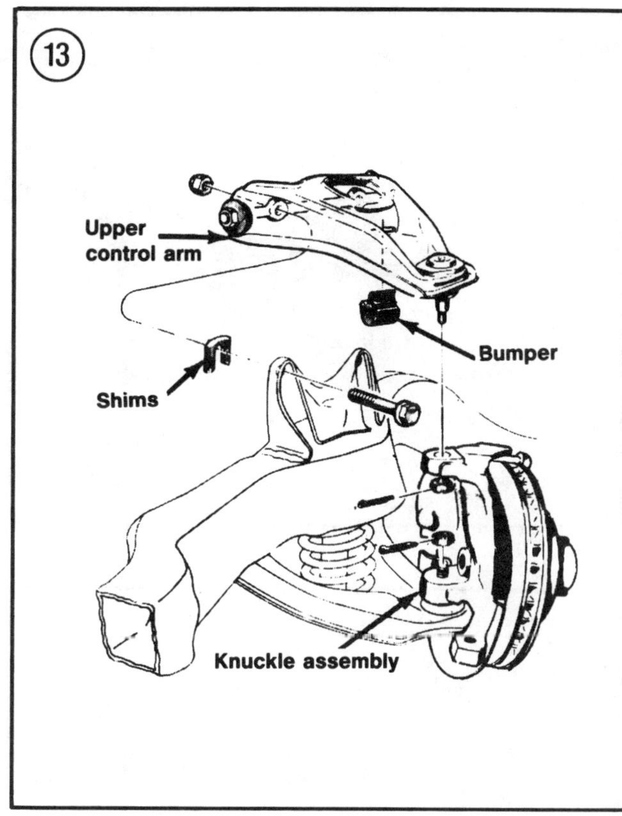

2. Loosen the front wheel lug nuts.
3. Note the position of the shims (**Figure 13**); they must be reinstalled in the same position from which they were removed. Remove the nuts and shims.
4. Raise the front of the vehicle with a jack and install jackstands between the spring seats and ball-joints of the lower control arms.
5. Remove the wheel/tire assembly.
6. Remove and discard the upper ball-joint cotter pin. Remove the castellated nut. Separate the ball-joint stud from the steering knuckle with tool part No. J-23742 or equivalent. See **Figure 14**.
7. Support the hub to prevent damage to the brake hose.
8. Remove the upper control arm bolts. Remove the control arm.
9. Installation is the reverse of removal. Tighten all fasteners to specifications (**Table 1**).

Upper Ball-joint Inspection

Refer to **Figure 15** for this procedure.
1. Set the parking brake. Place the transmission in PARK (automatic) or 1st gear (manual).
2. Raise the front of the vehicle with a jack. Install jackstands under each control arm as close as possible to the lower ball-joint.

NOTE
*The control arm bumper (**Figure 13**) must not touch the frame.*

3. Install a dial indicator against the wheel rim as shown in **Figure 15**.
4. Grasp the front wheel and push in on the bottom of the tire while pulling out on the top. Read the dial indicator. Reverse the push-pull procedure and reread the dial indicator.

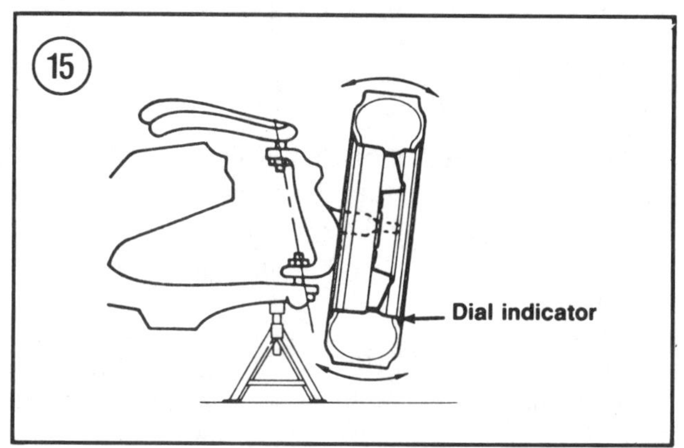

5. If the indicator reading exceeds 0.125 in. (3.18 mm), replace the ball-joint as described in this chapter.

Upper Ball-joint Replacement

1. Set the parking brake. Place the transmission in PARK (automatic) or 1st gear (manual).
2. Loosen the front wheel lug nuts.
3. Raise the front of the vehicle. Install jackstands between the spring seats and lower control arm ball-joints to relieve spring tension on the upper control arm.
4. Remove the wheel/tire assembly.
5. Remove and discard the upper ball-joint cotter pin. Remove the castellated nut. Separate the ball-joint stud from the steering knuckle with tool part No. J-23742 or equivalent. See **Figure 14**.
6. Drill the 4 rivets 1/4 in. deep with a 1/8 in. diameter drill bit (**Figure 16**).
7. Drill the rivet heads off with a 1/2 in. drill bit (**Figure 17**).
8. Remove the rivets with a suitable punch (**Figure 18**). Remove the ball-joint.
9. Install the new ball-joint with 4 attaching bolts and nuts as shown in **Figure 19**. Tighten the nuts to specifications (**Table 1**).
10. Reverse Steps 1-5 to complete installation. Tighten the castellated nut to 65 ft.-lb. (90 N•m), then tighten it enough more to align the nut slot with the stud hole. Install a new cotter pin. Install and lubricate the ball-joint grease fitting.

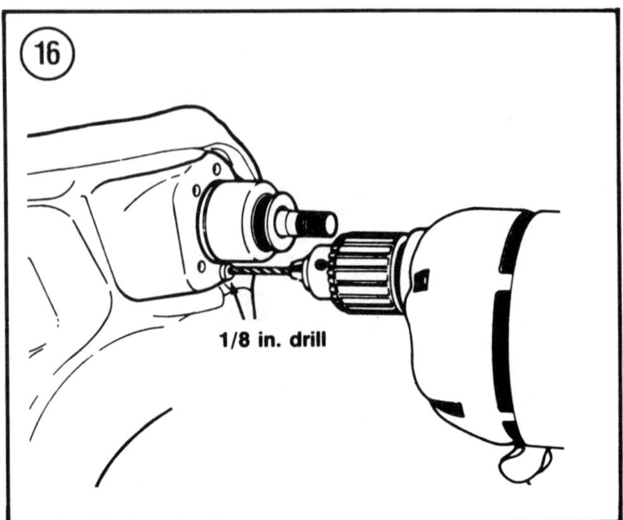

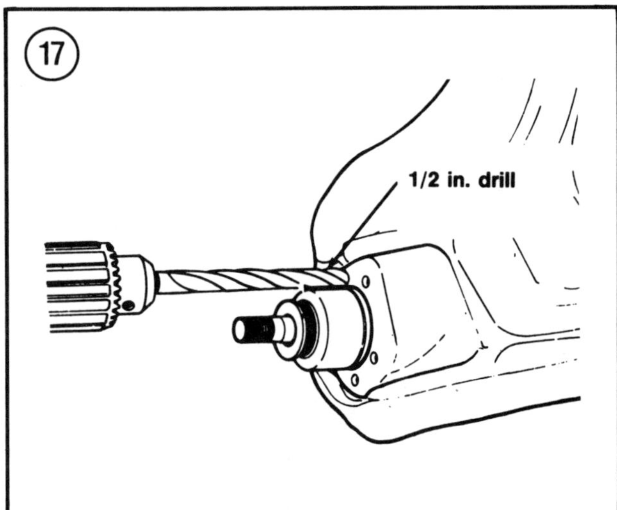

Upper Control Arm Bushing Replacement

Bushing replacement requires many special tools and should be referred to a dealer or qualified specialist.

Torsion Bar Removal/Installation

Refer to **Figure 20** for this procedure.

1. Set the parking brake. Place the transmission in PARK (automatic) or 1st gear (manual).
2. Raise the vehicle with a jack and place it on jackstands.
3. Install puller part No. J-22517-02 or equivalent so that it will contact the end of the adjusting arm. Tighten puller screw sufficently to remove tension from the torsion bar adjusting screw.

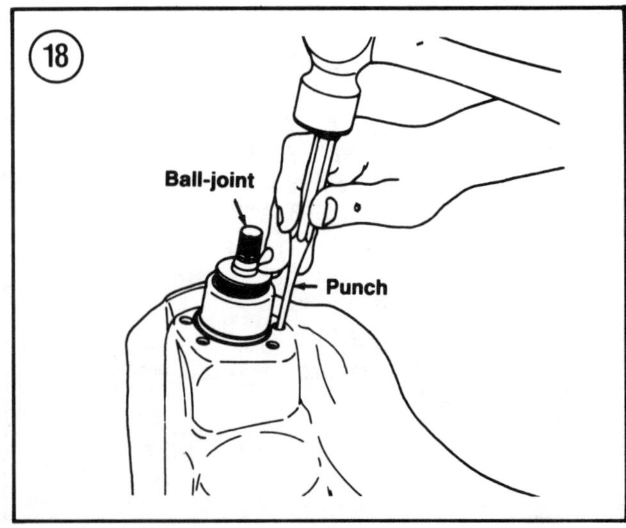

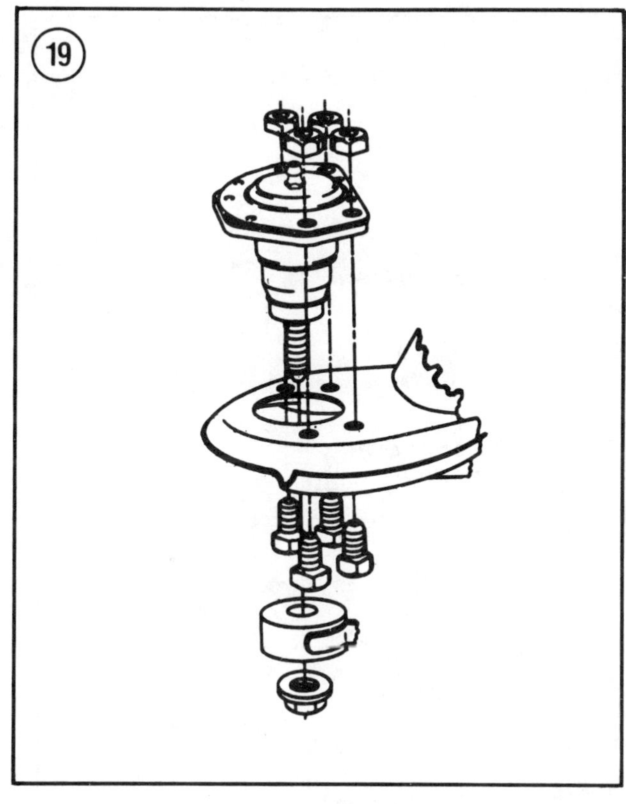

4. Remove the adjusting screw, noting the number of turns required for reinstallation reference.
5. Remove the support retainer nuts and bolts.
6. Slide the torsion bar toward the front of the vehicle until it clears the support, then pull downward on the bar and remove it from the lower control arm.
7. Installation is the reverse of removal. Lubricate the top of the adjusting arm, adjusting bolt and hex ends of torsion bar with Lubriplate or equivalent to ease installation. Tighten all fasteners to specifications (**Table 1**).

4-WHEEL DRIVE FRONT AXLE AND DIFFERENTIAL

A Central Disconnect System eliminates the need for locking hubs on 4-wheel drive models. With the vehicle in 2-wheel drive, power to the front axle is disengaged and a central disconnect in the front axle lets the axle shafts freewheel. When 4-wheel drive is engaged, a vacuum actuator applies vacuum to the central disconnect mechanism, providing power to drive the front wheels.

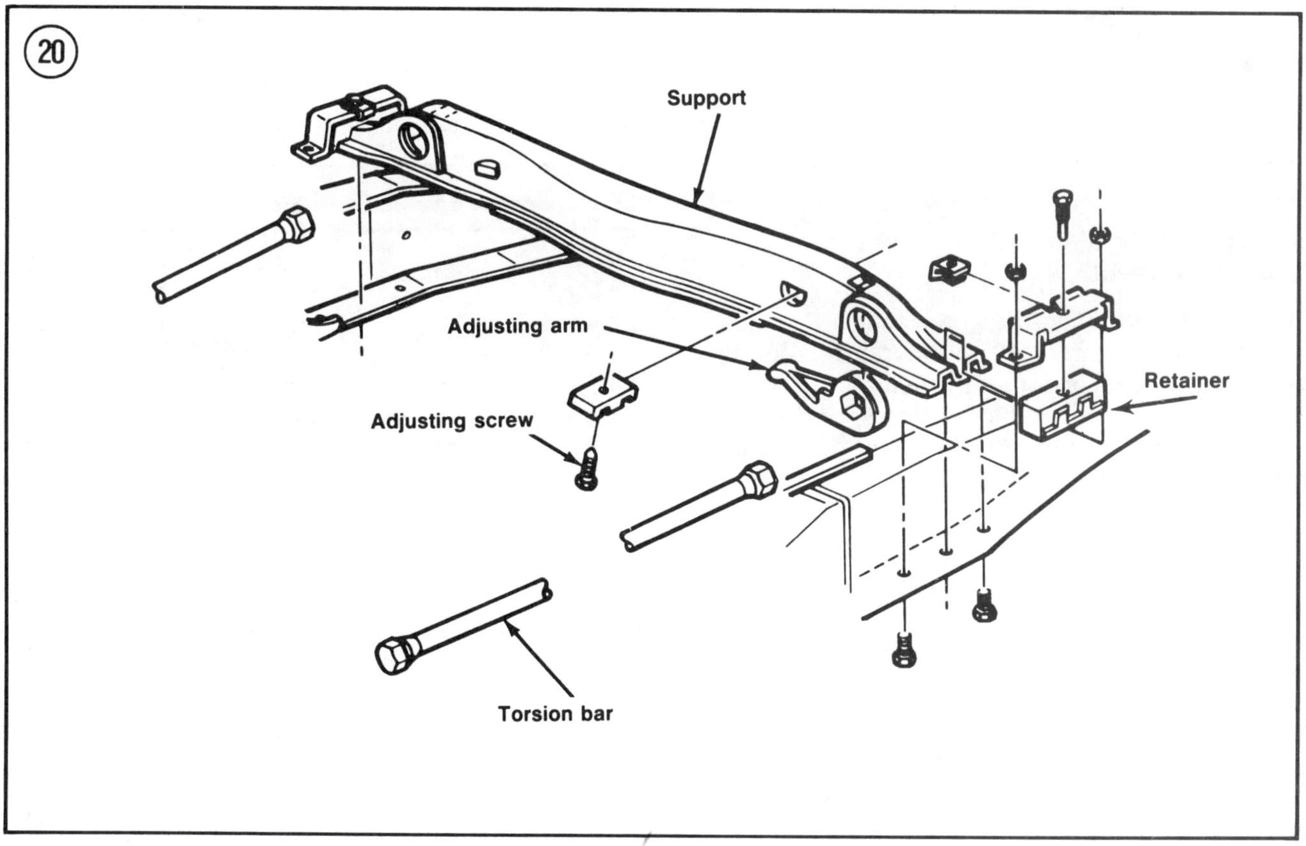

20

Support
Adjusting arm
Retainer
Adjusting screw
Torsion bar

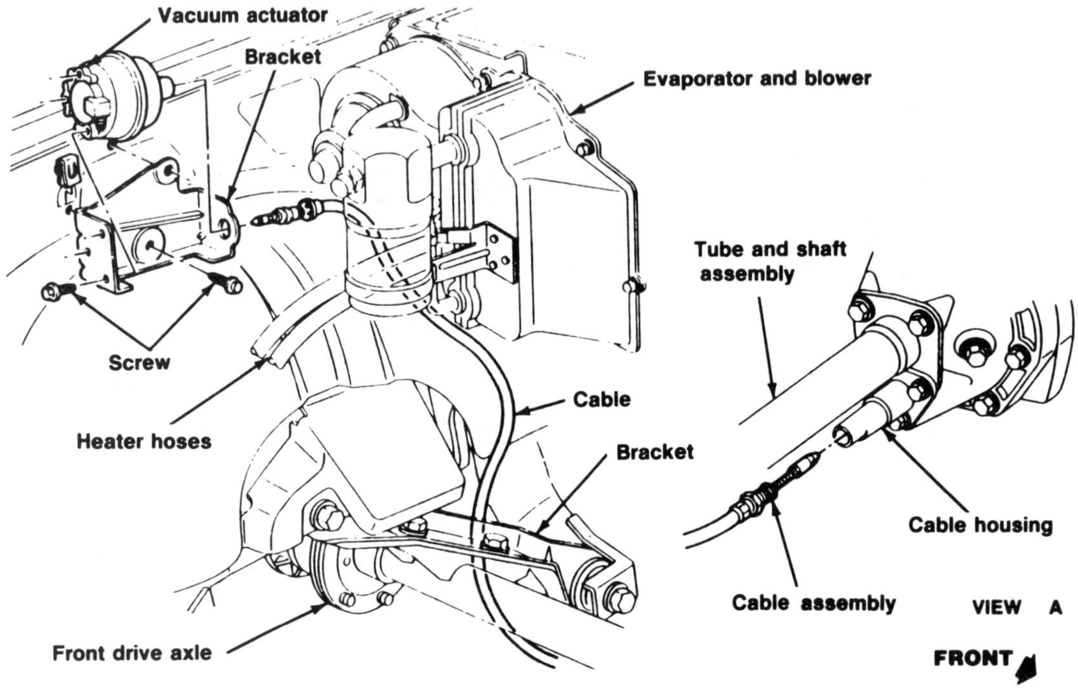

Vacuum Actuator Shift Cable Replacement

Refer to **Figure 21** for this procedure.

1. Set the parking brake. Place the transmission in PARK (automatic) or 1st gear (manual).
2. Disengage the shift cable locking spring at the vacuum actuator and push the actuator diaphragm inward to release the cable.
3. Squeeze the cable locking fingers with pliers and pull cable from the bracket.
4. Raise the front of the vehicle with a jack and place it on jackstands.
5. Remove the bolts holding the cable and switch housing to the differential carrier. Pull the switch housing away from the carrier to provide access to the cable locking spring. Lift the spring over the shift fork slot and disconnect the cable.
6. Unscrew the cable from the housing and remove from the vehicle.

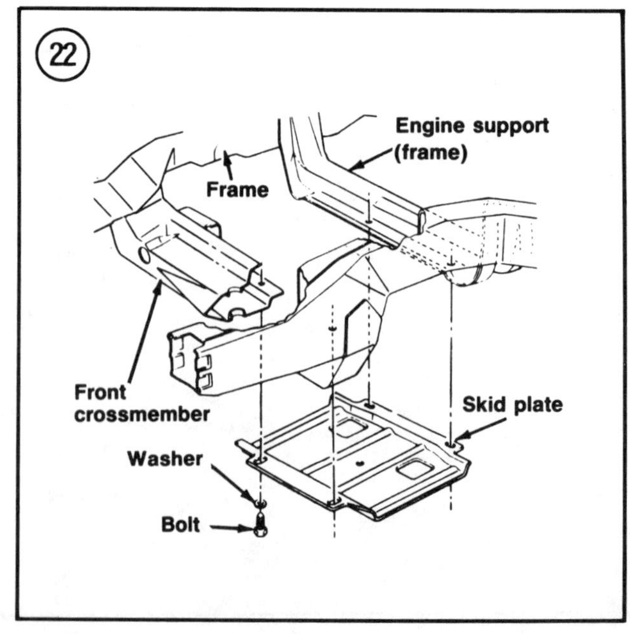

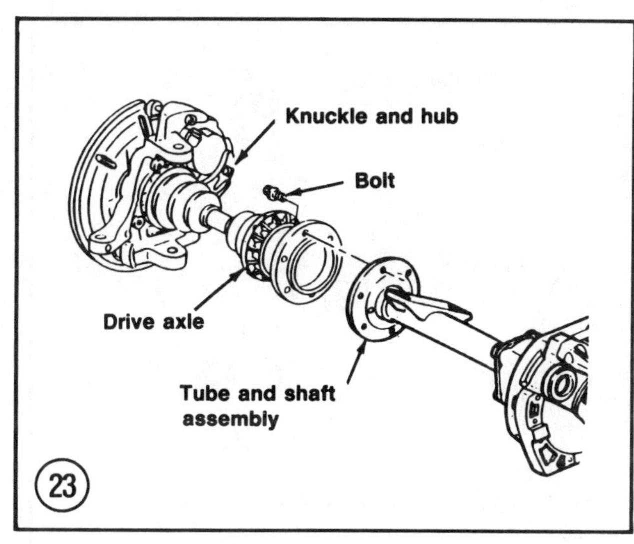

7. Route the new cable according to **Figure 21**. Install the cable housing to the carrier and tighten the bolts to 30- 40 ft.-lb. (40-55 N•m).
8. Fit the cable through the housing into the fork shaft hole. Push the cable inward until it snaps in place. Start the coupling nut by hand, then tighten to 71-106 in.-lb. (8-12 N•m).
9. Remove the jackstands and lower the vehicle to the ground.
10. Press the cable into the vacuum actuator bracket hole until it snaps in place.
11. Check cable operation.

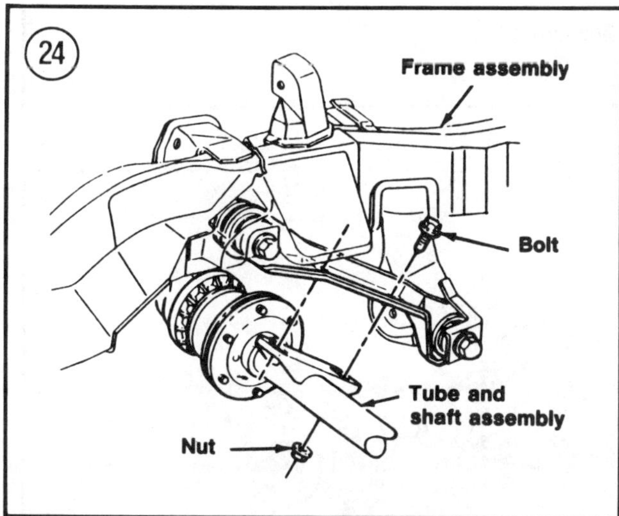

Tube and Shaft Assembly

1. Set the parking brake. Place the transmission in PARK (automatic) or 1st gear (manual).
2. Disconnect the negative battery cable.
3. Disconnect the shift cable from the vacuum actuator as described in this chapter.
4. Loosen the front wheel lug nuts.
5. Raise the front of the vehicle with a jack and place it on jackstands.
6. Remove the front wheel/tire assemblies.
7. Remove the engine drive belt shield.
8. Remove the front axle skid plate (**Figure 22**).
9. Support the lower control arm with a jack and disconnect the upper ball-joint as described in this chapter. Remove the jack and allow the control arm to hang freely.
10. Insert a drift through the brake caliper opening into a brake rotor vane to prevent the drive axle from turning, then disconnect the drive axle shaft from the tube assembly (**Figure 23**).
11. Disconnect the 4-wheel drive indicator switch leads.
12. Remove the cable and switch housing at the carrier. Lift the cable spring over the shift fork slot to disconnect the cable from the shaft.
13. Remove the bolts holding the tube bracket to the frame (**Figure 24**).
14. Remove the bolts holding the tube assembly to the carrier.
15. Remove the tube assembly carefully to prevent the sleeve, thrust washers, connector and output tube from falling out of the carrier.
16. Installation is the reverse of removal. Apply Loctite 514 or equivalent on the tube-to-carrier surface. Install the thrust washer with grease as shown in **Figure 25**. Use tool part No. J-33799 as

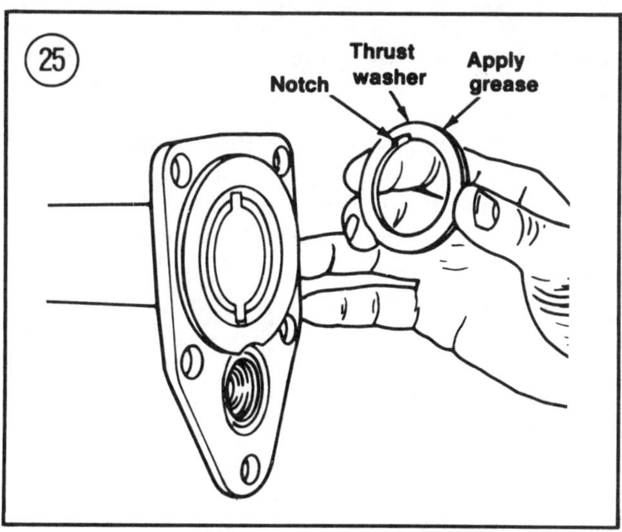

10

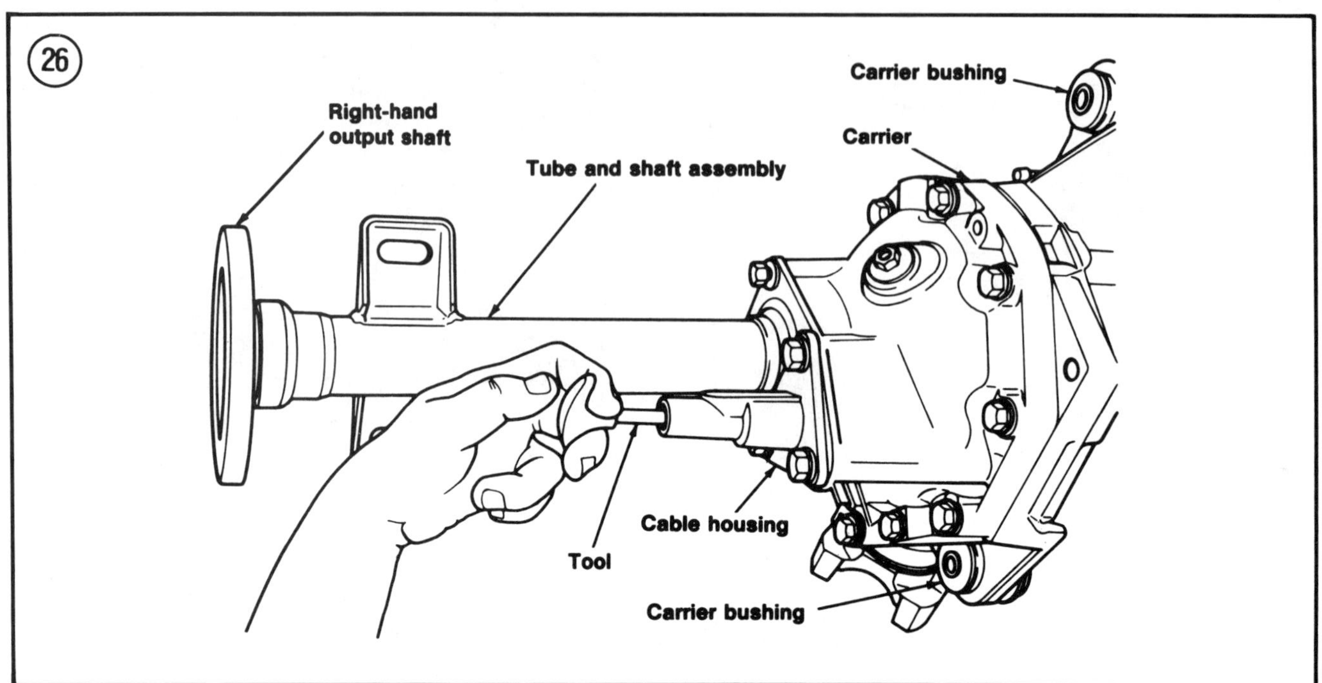

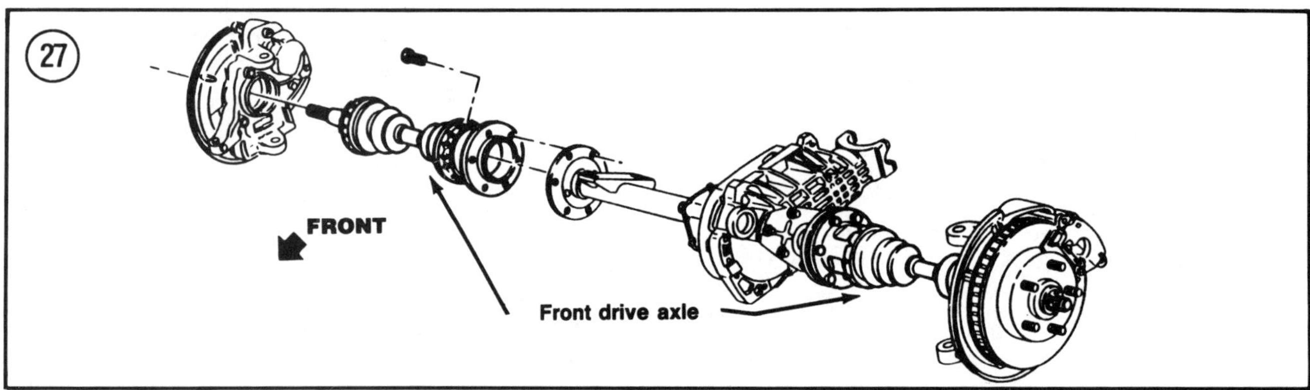

shown in **Figure 26** to check 4-wheel drive operation before installing the cable to the cable housing. Tighten the cable and switch housing to 30-40 ft.-lb. (40-55 N•m), drive axle-to-output shaft bolts to 53-63 ft.-lb. (72-85 N•m) and the output shaft tube bracket-to-frame bolts to 45-60 ft.-lb. (60-80 N•m).

Front Drive Axle Removal/Installation

Drive axles on 4-wheel drive vehicles are flexible assemblies consisting of an axle shaft with inner and outer constant velocity (CV) joints. The left-hand drive axle connects directly to the front differential carrier. The right-hand drive axle is connected to the tube and shaft assembly. See **Figure 27**.

1. Set the parking brake. Place the transmission in PARK (automatic) or 1st gear (manual).
2. Loosen the front wheel lug nuts.
3. Raise the front of the vehicle with a jack and place it on jackstands.
4. Remove the wheel/tire assemblies.
5. Remove the engine drive belt shield and front axle skid plate.
6. Remove the cotter pin, retainer, nut and washer from the axle stub (**Figure 28**).
7. Support the lower control arm with a jack. Disconnect the upper ball-joint and remove the jack to allow the control arm to hang unsupported.

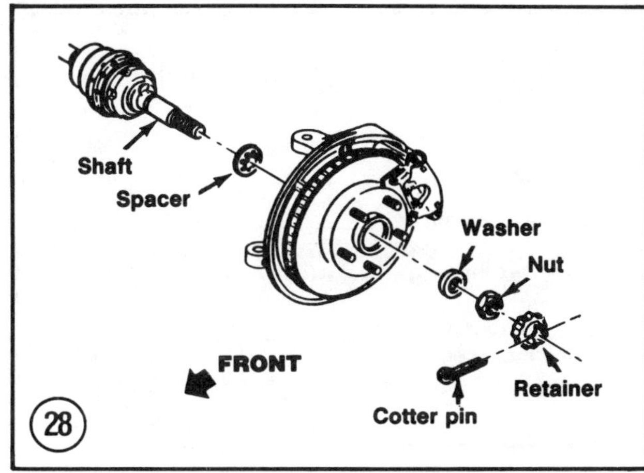

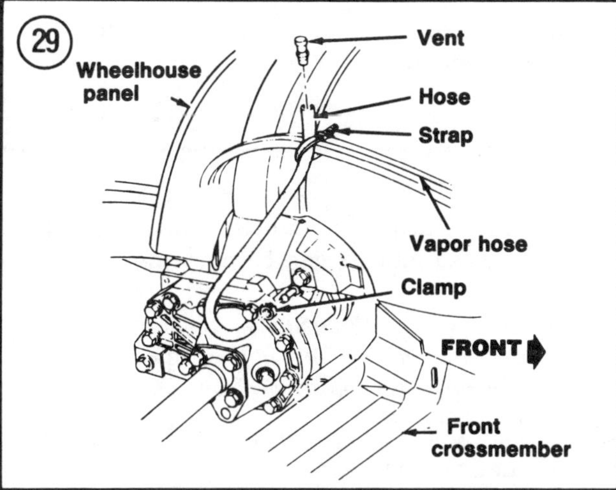

8. Disconnect the drive axle shaft from the tube assembly (right-hand side) or differential housing (left-hand side).
9. Pull the drive axle shaft from the steering knuckle and remove the spacer (**Figure 28**).
10. Installation is the reverse of removal. Tighten the drive axle shaft attaching bolts to specifications (**Table 1**).
11. Adjust the wheel bearings as described in this chapter.

Front Differential Removal/Installation

1. Set the parking brake. Place the transmission in PARK (automatic) or 1st gear (manual).
2. Raise the front of the vehicle with a jack and place it on jackstands.
3. Remove the tube and shaft assembly as described in this chapter.
4. Remove the bolt holding the steering stabilizer to the frame.
5. Mark the idler arm location. Unbolt and remove the idler arm from the frame as described in this chapter. Push the steering linkage toward the front of the vehicle.
6. Disconnect the axle vent hose from the carrier. See **Figure 29**.
7. Disconnect the left-hand drive axle shaft as described in this chapter.
8. Disconnect the drive shaft at the transfer case and differential. See **Figure 30**.

10

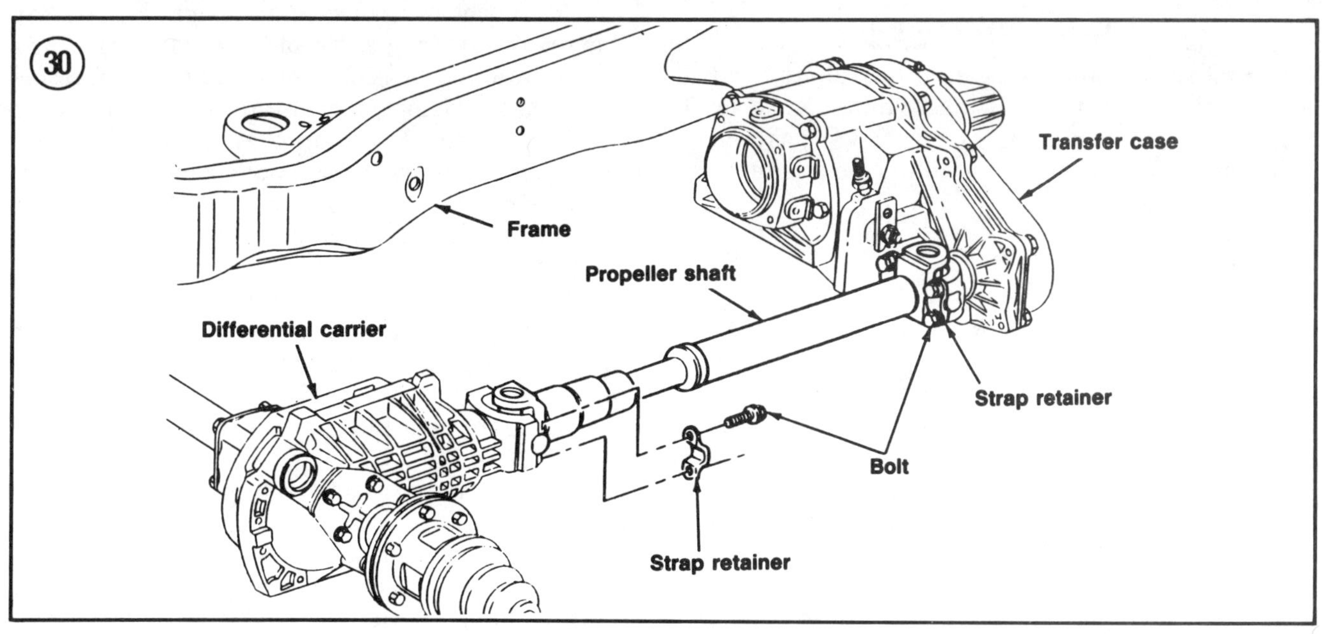

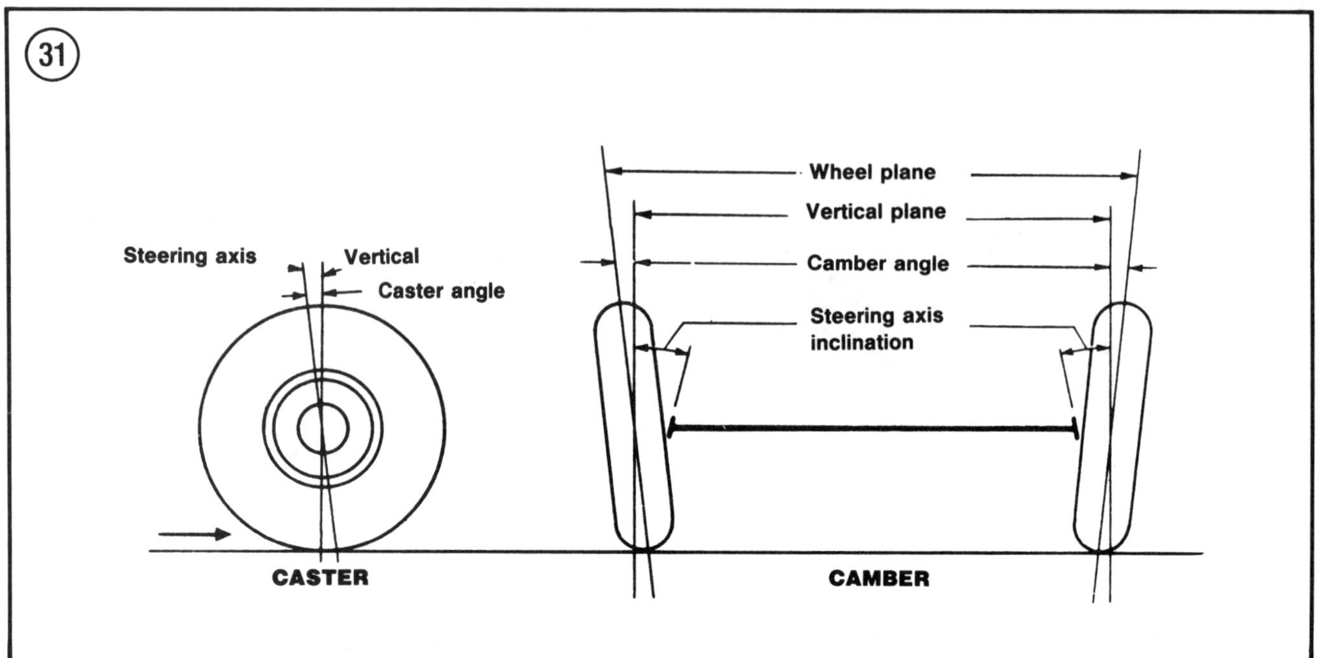

9. Remove the bolts holding the carrier to the frame.
10. Tip the differential housing counterclockwise while lifting it up to clear the mounting ears, then remove from the vehicle.
11. Installation is the reverse of removal. Tighten all fasteners to specifications. Check axle lubricant level and fill to level of fill plug hole if necessary with lubricant specified in Chapter Three.

WHEEL ALIGNMENT

Several suspension angles affect the running and steering of the front wheels. These angles must be properly aligned to prevent excessive wear, as well as to maintain directional stability and ease of steering. The angles are:

a. Caster.
b. Camber.
c. Toe.
d. Steering axis inclination.
e. Steering lock angles.

Steering axis inclination and steering lock angles are built in and cannot be adjusted. These angles are measured to check for bent suspension parts. Caster and camber should not be adjusted without the use of an alignment rack. Toe can be adjusted at home as described in this section, but, the procedure given should be used only as a temporary measure to allow you to drive the vehicle to a dealer or alignment shop where accurate measurements can be made and set.

WARNING
Do not attempt to adjust alignment angles by bending or twisting suspension or steering linkage components.

Pre-Alignment Check

Adjustment of the steering and various suspension angles is affected by several factors. For this reason, steering and handling problems which may seem to be caused by misalignment can result from other factors which are easily corrected without expensive equipment. The following procedure should be carried out whenever steering, handling or tire wear problems exist. It should also be performed before having the alignment checked or prior to adjusting the toe setting.

1. Check tire pressure (with tires cold) and adjust to the specified pressure, if necessary. Both front tires should be the same size, ply rating and load range.
2. Check tire condition. See *Tire Wear Analysis*, Chapter Two.
3. Check the radial and lateral runout of both front tires with a dial indicator. Place the indicator plunger against the tire tread and slowly rotate the wheel. Then position the indicator against the outer sidewall of the tire and slowly rotate the

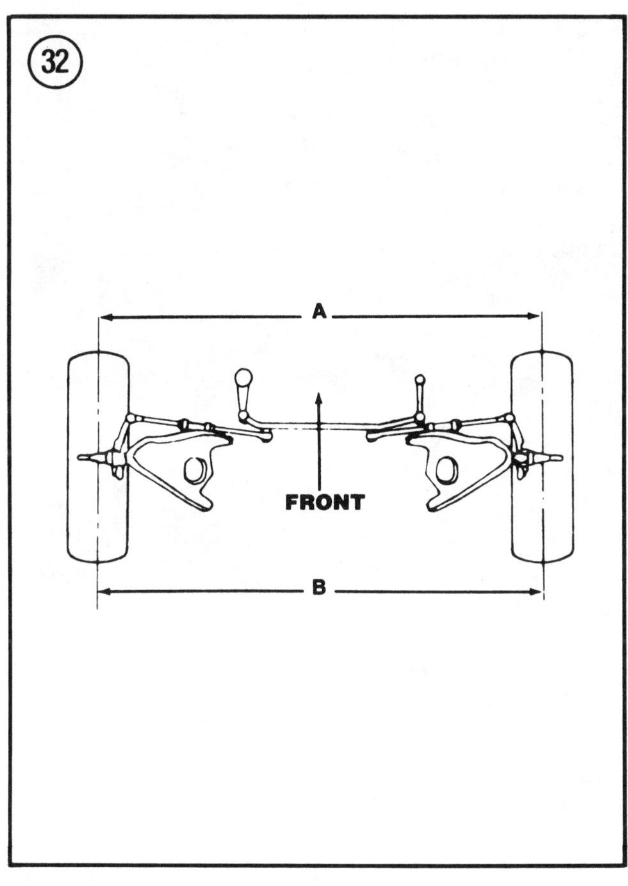

wheel. If either the radial or lateral runout exceeds 0.080 inch:

a. Deflate the tire.
b. Rotate the tire 90° on the rim.
c. Lubricate the rim with liquid soap.
d. Reinflate the tire to the specified pressure.
e. Recheck runout.

4. Check all suspension components, steering components and linkage for wear, damage or improper adjustment. Replace if required as described in this chapter.
5. Check the steering gearbox mounting bolt torque. Retighten as required.
6. Make sure the suspension is properly lubricated. See Chapter Three.
7. Check brakes for proper operation. See Chapter Twelve.
8. Check the shock absorbers for proper operation as described in this section.
9. Check wheels and balance as required.
10. Check rear suspension for looseness.

Front tire wear problems can indicate alignment problems. These are covered under *Tire Wear Analysis*, Chapter Two.

Caster and Camber

Caster is the inclination from vertical of the line through the ball-joints (**Figure 31**). Positive caster shifts the wheel forward; negative caster shifts the wheel rearward. Caster causes the wheels to return to a straight-ahead position after a turn. It also prevents the wheels from wandering due to wind, potholes or uneven road surfaces.

Camber is the inclination of the wheel from vertical (**Figure 31**). With positive camber, the top of the tire leans outward. With negative camber, the top of the tire leans inward. Excessive camber causes tire wear. Negative camber wears the inside of the tire; positive camber wears the outside.

Toe

Since the front wheels tend to point outward when the vehicle is moving in a forward direction, the distance between the front edges of the tire (A, **Figure 32**) is generally slightly less than the distance between the rear edges (B, **Figure 32**) when the vehicle is at rest.

Toe Adjustment

Although toe adjustment requires only a simple homemade tool, it usually is not worth the trouble for home mechanics. Alignment shops include toe adjustment as part of the alignment procedure, so you probably will not save any money by doing it yourself. The procedure described here can be used for an initial toe setting after spindle or ball-joint replacement.

1. With the steering wheel centered, roll the vehicle forward about 15 ft. on a smooth, level surface.
2. Mark the center of the tread at the front and rear of each tire.
3. Measure the distance between the forward chalk marks (A, **Figure 32**). Use 2 pieces of telescoping aluminum tubing. Telescope the tubing so each end contacts a chalk mark. Using a sharp center scribe, mark the small diameter tubing where it enters the large diameter tubing.
4. Measure between the rear chalk marks with the telescoping tubes. Make another mark on the small tube where it enters the large one. The distance between the 2 scribe marks is the toe-in and must be divided in half to determine the amount of toe at each wheel.

5. If toe-in is incorrect, loosen the clamp bolts on each end of the tie rod adjusting sleeve (**Figure 33**) at each wheel.
6. Rotate each adjusting sleeve as required until correct toe alignment is obtained.
7. Reposition the clamps if necessary. They should be located 3/16 in. from the end of the sleeve with the nut end of the bolt facing the front of the vehicle.
8. When the toe is correctly set, tighten the clamp bolts to specifications (**Table 1**).

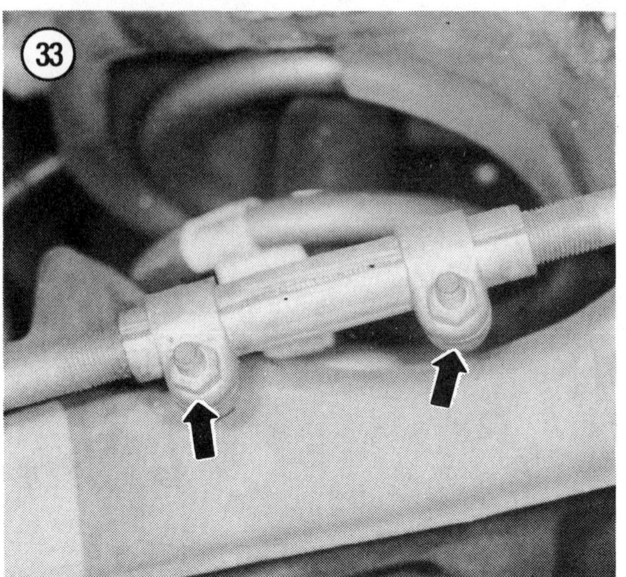

Steering Axis Inclination

Steering axis inclination is the inward or outward lean of the line through the ball-joints. It is not adjustable on S- and T-series vehicles.

Steering Lock Angles

When a vehicle turns, the inside wheel makes a smaller circle than the outside wheel. Because of this, the inside wheel turns at a greater angle than the outside wheel. These angles are not adjustable, but are measured to check for bent suspension and steering parts.

WHEEL BEARINGS

The front wheels use adjustable tapered roller bearings which must be cleaned, repacked with grease and adjusted at periodic intervals. A grease retainer at the inner end of the hub prevents lubricant from leaking onto the brake rotor. A retainer locknut and cotter pin hold the entire assembly on the spindle.

The factory-recommended service intervals (Chapter Three) refer to vehicle usage in dry weather on good roads. If the vehicle is used off-road (but not in water), a service interval of 6,000-10,000 miles is more appropriate. For vehicles operated in deep water or mud, the bearings should be serviced daily.

The rear wheel bearings are sealed and receive their lubrication from the oil carried in the rear differential. There is no adjustment required for the rear bearings.

Front Wheel Bearing Adjustment

1. Set the parking brake. Place the transmission in PARK (automatic) or 1st gear (manual).
2. Raise the front of the vehicle with a jack and place it on jackstands.
3. Remove the wheel cover, if so equipped.
4. Carefully pry the grease cap from the hub and wipe the grease from the end of the spindle.
5. Remove and discard the spindle nut cotter pin.
6. Rotate the wheel in a forward direction while tightening the spindle nut to 12 ft.-lb. (16 N•m).
7. Back the spindle nut off until it reaches the "just loose" position, then tighten the nut finger-tight.
8. Loosen the spindle nut enough to align a slot in the nut with either spindle hole (but not more than 1/2 flat) and install a new cotter pin without bending the ends of the pin over. This should provide a bearing end clearance of 0.001-0.005 in. (0.03-0.13 mm).
9. Install a dial indicator and measure the hub assembly end play. If properly adjusted, the indicator gauge should read within the specification provided in Step 7. If the wheel is still loose, its rotation is noisy or rough or the indicator reading is not within specifications, remove the bearings and cups to check for dirt, damage or excessive wear.
10. When bearing adjustment is satisfactory, bend the ends of the cotter pin over to lock it in place and reinstall the grease cap.
11. Lower the vehicle to the ground and install the wheel covers, if so equipped.

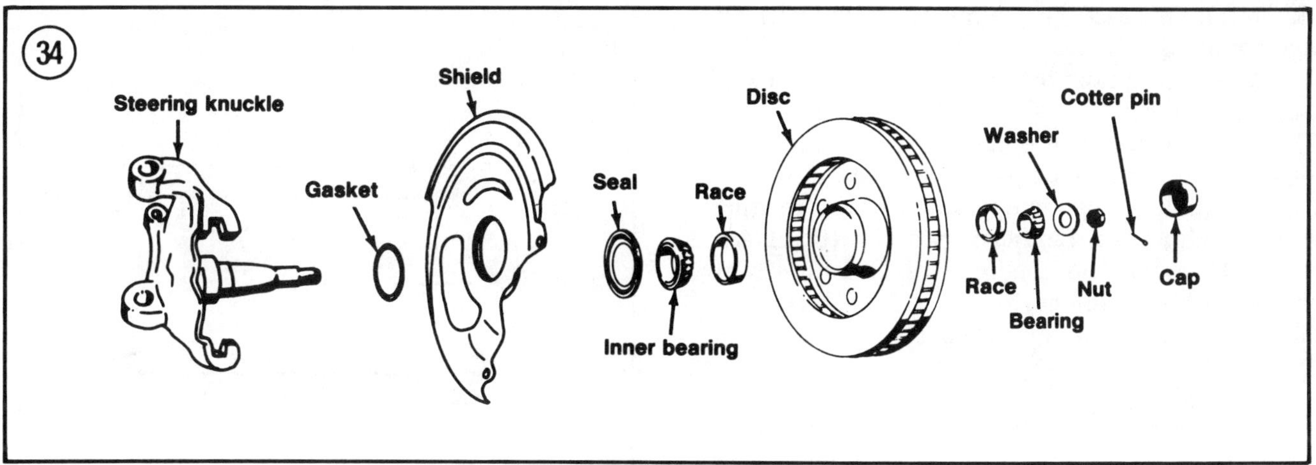

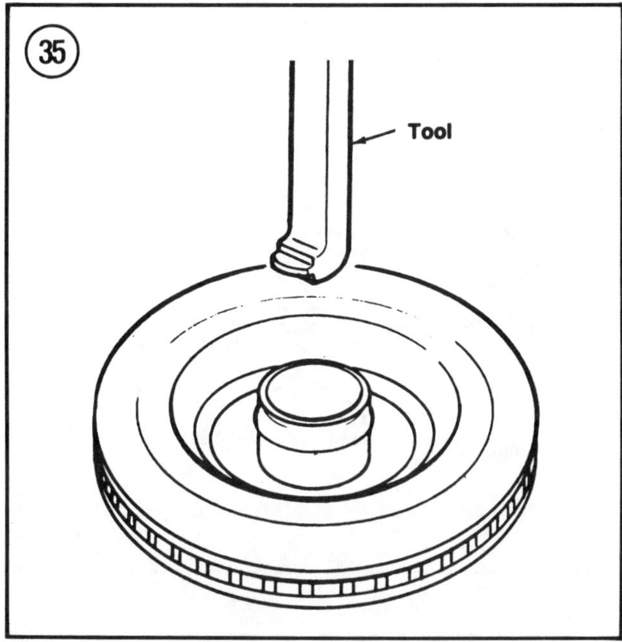

Front Wheel Bearing Replacement

If rough and noisy operation or looseness is not eliminated by adjustment, the wheel bearings should be removed, cleaned, inspected and repacked with the specified lubricant or replaced as required. A lithium-base grease such as GM Lubricant part No. 1051344 or equivalent should be used. Do not use other types of grease, as they are not compatible and can result in premature bearing failure.

Refer to **Figure 34** for this procedure.

1. Set the parking brake. Place the transmission in PARK (automatic) or 1st gear (manual).
2. Remove the wheel cover, if so equipped. Loosen the front wheel lug nuts.
3. Raise the front of the vehicle with a jack and placc it on jackstands.
4. Remove the wheel/tire assemblies.
5. Remove the brake caliper. See Chapter Twelve.
6. Carefully pry the grease cap from the hub and wipe the grease from the end of the spindle.
7. Remove and discard the spindle nut cotter pin.
8. Remove the spindle nut and washer from the spindle.
9. Grasp the brake disc/hub assembly and pull it outward enough to loosen the outer wheel bearing. Remove the outer wheel bearing from the spindle.
10. Pull the brake disc/hub assembly straight off the spindle to prevent damage to the inner bearings or spindle.
11. Remove and discard the grease seal. Remove the inner bearing assembly from the hub.
12. Insert tool part No. J-29117 or equivalent behind the bearing races in the hub assembly (**Figure 35**) and drive the races out.

WARNING

Do not spin bearings with compressed air in Step 12; it is capable of rotating the bearings at speeds far in excess of those for which they were designed. The bearing could disintegrate, causing damage and injury.

13. Thoroughly clean the bearings, races and inside of the hub with solvent. Blow dry with compressed air.
14. Check the bearing rollers and cups for scoring, pitting, cracking, scratching or excessive wear. If any of these defects are found, replace the bearings and cups as an assembly.

15. Install new races in the hub assembly with an appropriate driver.
16. Carefully clean the spindle with a cloth moistened in solvent.
17. Lightly grease the spindle at the outer and inner bearing seats, the shoulder and seal seat with a good quality, high-temperature wheel bearing grease, such as GM Lubricant part No. 1051344.
18. Pack the inside of the hub with GM Lubricant part No. 1051344 or equivalent until it is level with the inside diameter of the outer bearing cups (**Figure 36**).
19. If installing the original bearings, thoroughly pack the bearing assemblies with GM Lubricant part No. 1051344 or equivalent. If a bearing packer is not available, work the lubricant in carefully by hand.
20. Lightly coat the inner cone with the same lubricant and install the inner bearing assembly in the inner cup.
21. Place a new seal in the hub. Cover with a flat plate or a block of wood and tap into place until the seal is flush with the hub. Wipe a thin coat of grease across the seal lip.
22. Install the wheel on the spindle, keeping the hub centered to prevent damage to the seal.
23. Install the outer wheel bearing assembly and thread the spindle nut in place.
24. Adjust the wheel bearings as described in this chapter.

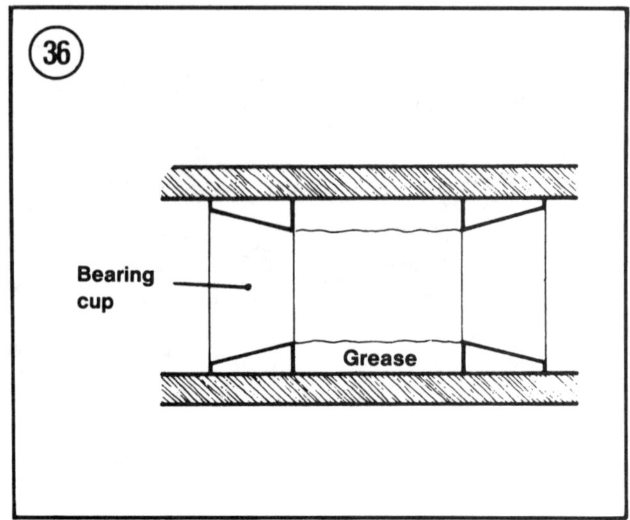

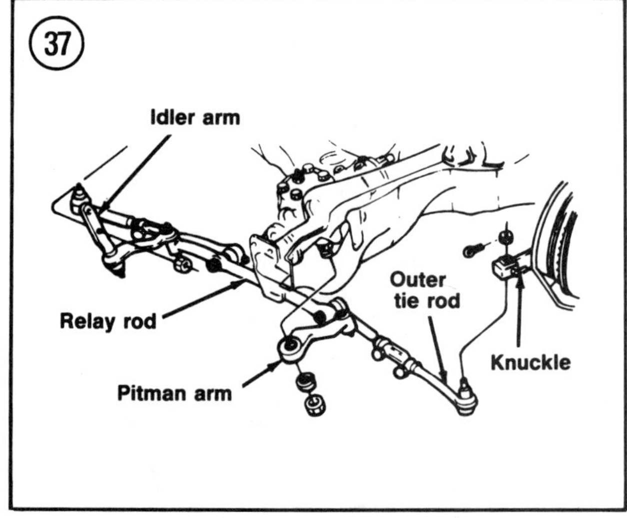

STEERING SYSTEM

Vehicles may be equipped with manual (non-power) steering or integral power steering. The steering system on all models is a parallelogram type which connects both front wheels to the steering gear by a Pitman arm and idler arm. The 2 tie rods are connected to the steering arms and relay rods by ball studs. The left end of the relay rod is supported by the Pitman arm, which is driven by the steering gearbox sector shaft. The right end of the relay rod is supported by an idler arm, which pivots on a support connected to the frame rail. **Figure 37** shows the major steering linkage components.

Bent, distorted or otherwise damaged steering linkage should never be straightened and reused. Such components should be replaced with new ones. Any linkage with excessively loose ball-joints should also be replaced.

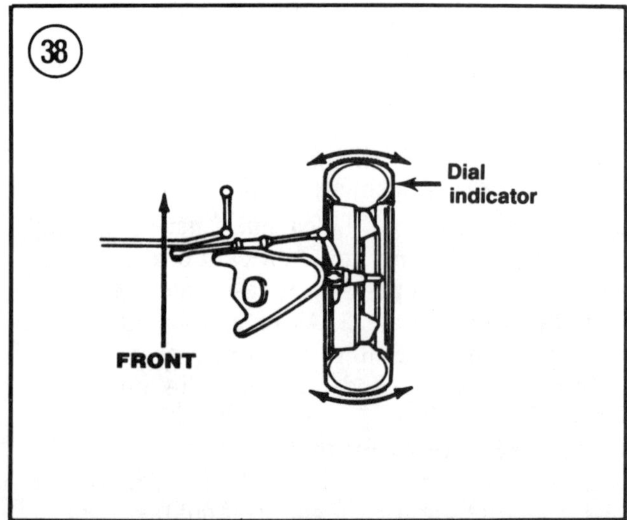

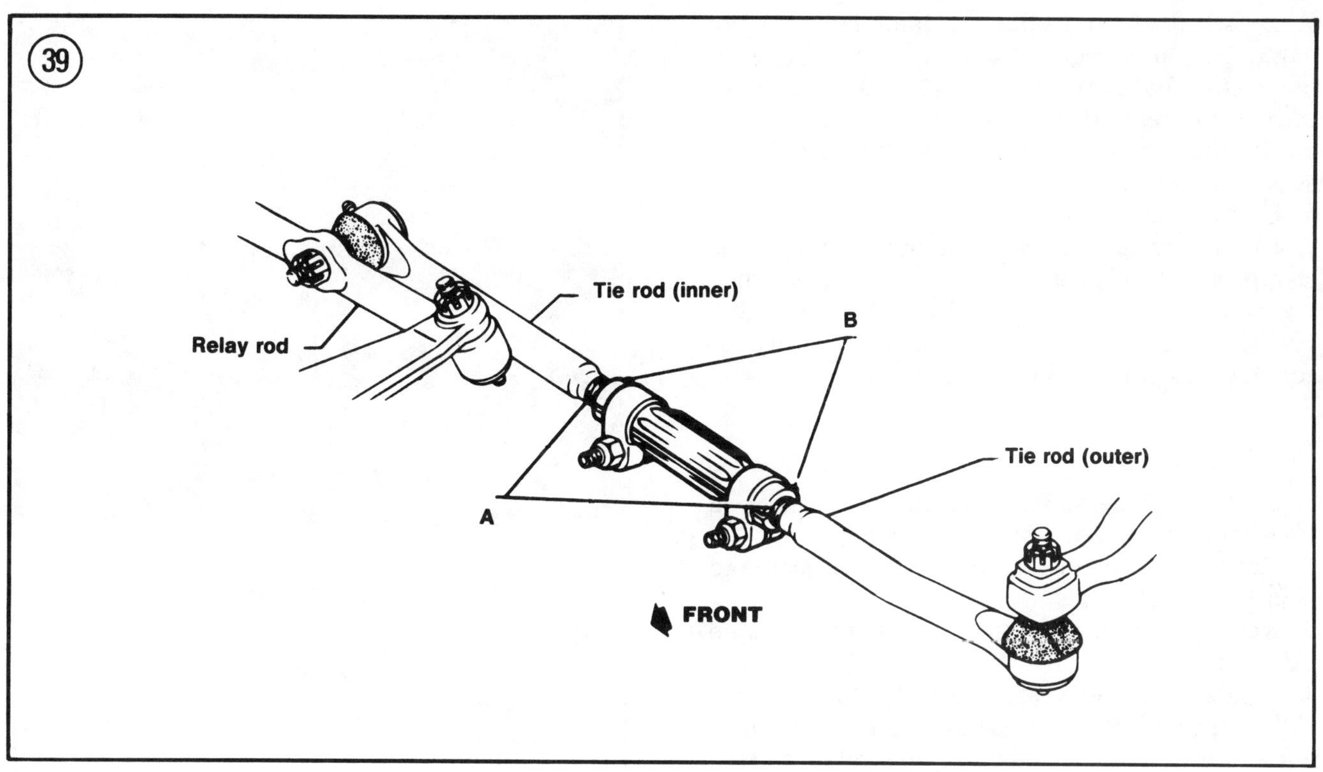

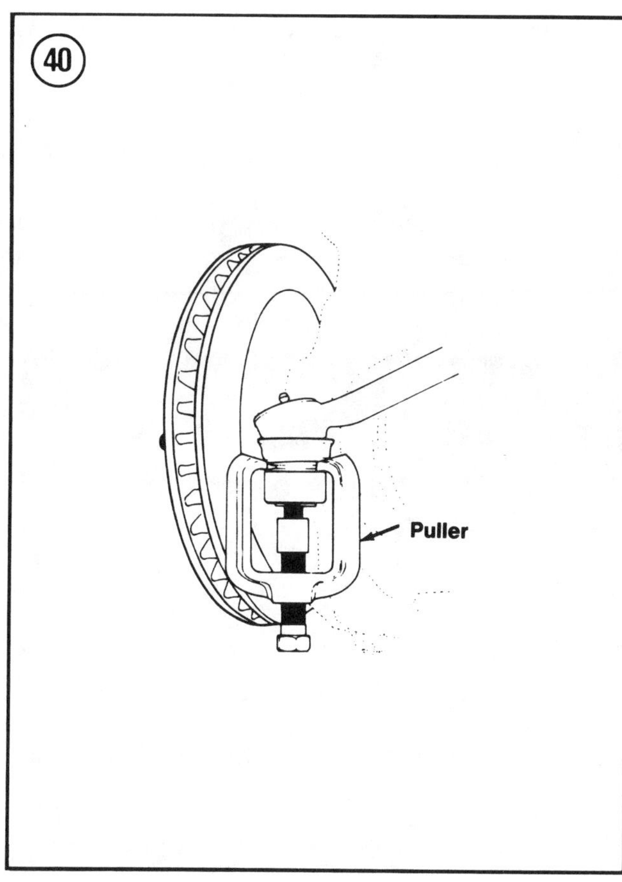

Steering Linkage/Suspension Check

1. Set the parking brake. Place the transmission in PARK (automatic) or 1st gear (manual).
2. Raise the vehicle on one side with a jack until the tire is about one inch off the ground.
3. Install a dial indicator as shown in **Figure 38**.
4. Place the steering wheel in the locked position.
5. Grasp the front wheel at each side and move the wheel in and out at the back.
6. The dial indicator should read 0.108 in. (2.74 mm) or less. If the reading exceeds this specification, inspect all linkage pivots and ball studs for looseness. Replace as necessary.

Tie Rod Replacement

Refer to **Figure 39** for this procedure.
1. Set the parking brake. Place the transmission in PARK (automatic) or 1st gear (manual).
2. Raise the front of the vehicle with a jack and place it on jackstands.
3. Remove and discard the ball stud cotter pins.
4. Remove the ball stud nuts. Separate the ball studs from the steering knuckle or relay rod as required with tool part No. J-6627 or equivalent. See **Figure 40**.

5. Loosen the tie rod adjusting clamp bolts (**Figure 33**). If the torque required to remove the nuts from the clamp bolts exceeds 7 ft.-lb. (9 N•m) after breakaway, discard the nuts and bolts and use a penetrating oil to loosen the clamps. Install new nuts and bolts during reassembly.
6. Unscrew the tie rod ends.
7. Installation is the reverse of removal. The sleeve clamps must be positioned between the locating dimples at either side of the sleeve (B, **Figure 39**). The distance at each end of the sleeve must be equal within 3 threads (A, **Figure 39**).

Pitman Arm Removal/Installation

1. Set the parking brake. Place the transmission in PARK (automatic) or 1st gear (manual).
2. Raise the front of the vehicle with a jack and place it on jackstands.
3. Remove the nut from the Pitman arm ball stud (A, **Figure 41**).
4. Separate the relay rod from the Pitman arm with a Pitman arm puller. These are available from rental dealers. Pull down on the relay rod to remove it from the stud.
5. Remove the Pitman arm nut from the sector shaft (B, **Figure 41**).

CAUTION
Do not hammer on the puller in Step 5 to separate the Pitman arm from the sector shaft. This can cause internal damage to the steering gearbox.

6. Mark the Pitman arm-to-sector shaft relationship. Separate the Pitman arm from the sector shaft with a puller as shown in **Figure 42**.
7. Installation is the reverse of removal. Tighten all fasteners to specifications (**Table 1**).

Idler Arm Replacement

1. Set the parking brake. Place the transmission in PARK (automatic) or 1st gear (manual).
2. Raise the front of the vehicle with a jack and place it on jackstands.
3. Remove the idler arm-to-relay rod ball stud nut (A, **Figure 43**).
4. Separate the idler arm from the relay rod with a suitable puller.
5. Remove the nuts, washers and bolts holding the idler arm to the frame (B, **Figure 43**).
6. Remove the idler arm.

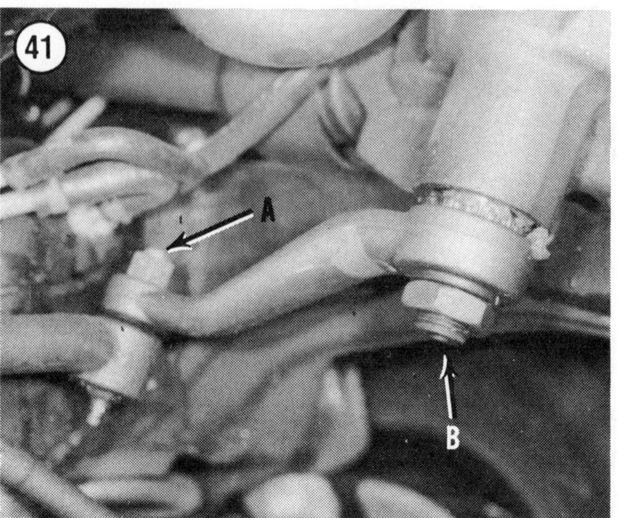

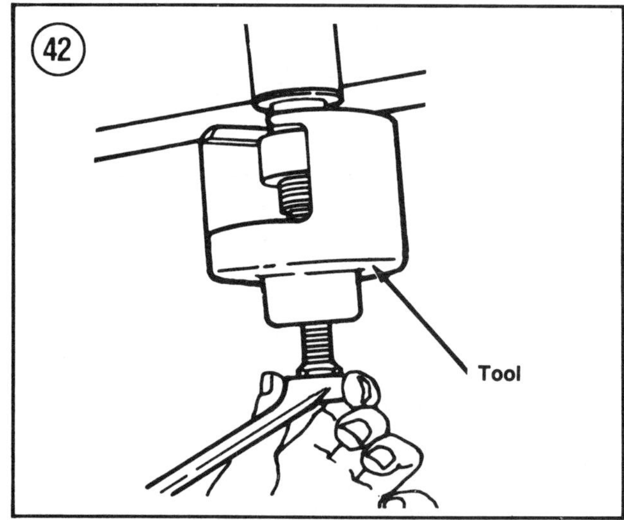

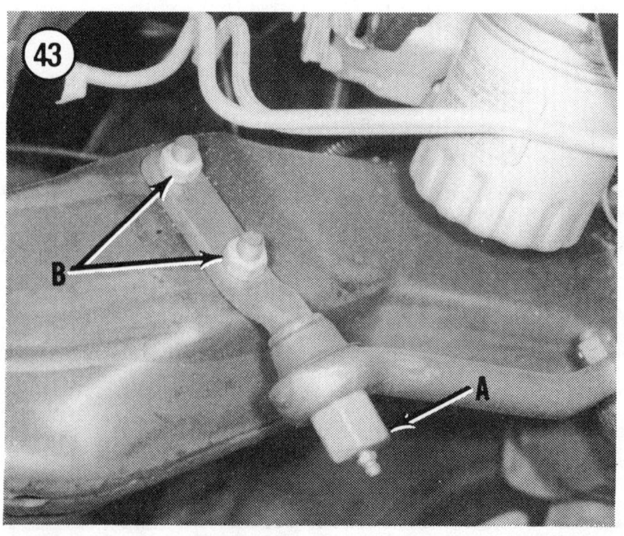

44

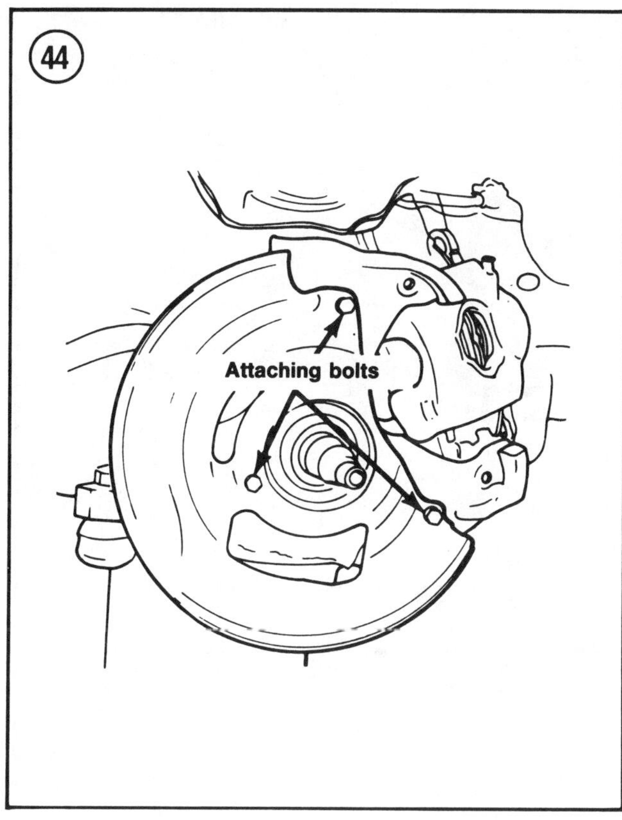

45

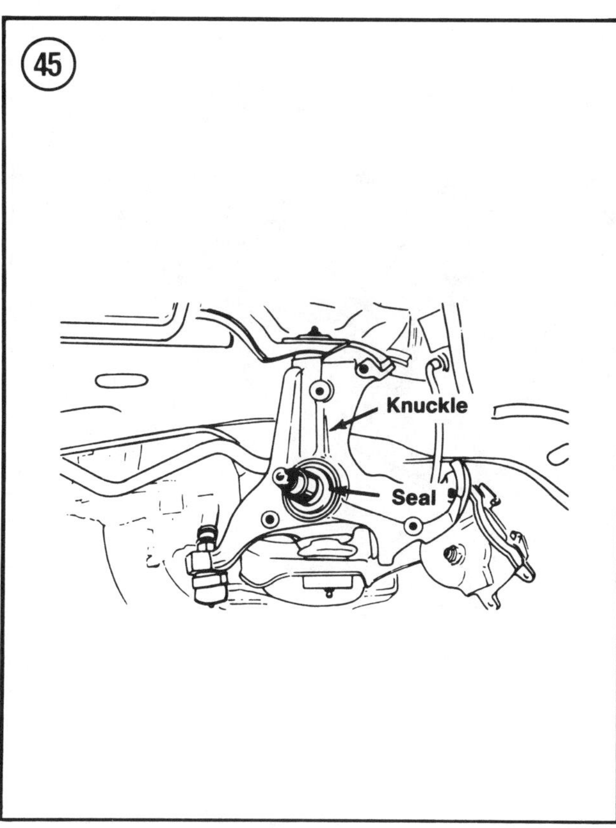

7. Installation is the reverse of removal. Tighten all fasteners to specifications (**Table 1**).

Relay Rod Replacement

1. Set the parking brake. Place the transmission in PARK (automatic) or 1st gear (manual).
2. Raise the front of the vehicle with a jack and place it on jackstands.
3. Disconnect the inner tie rod ends from the relay rod as described under *Tie Rod Replacement* in this chapter.
4. Remove the relay rod ball stud nut (A, **Figure 41**).
5. Disconnect the relay rod from the Pitman arm with a suitable puller. Move the steering linkage back and forth, if necessary, to separate the rod and arm.
6. Remove the idler arm nut (A, **Figure 43**) and separate the idler arm and relay rod with a suitable puller.
7. Remove the relay rod.
8. Installation is the reverse of removal. Tighten all fasteners to specifications (**Table 1**).

Steering Knuckle Replacement

1. Set the parking brake. Place the transmission in PARK (automatic) or 1st gear (manual).
2. Remove the wheel cover, if so equipped. Loosen the wheel lug nuts.
3. Raise the front of the vehicle with a jack and place it on jackstands.
4. Remove the wheel/tire assembly.
5. Remove the brake caliper. See Chapter Twelve.
6. Remove the brake disc/hub assembly as described under *Front Wheel Bearing Replacement* in this chapter.
7. Remove the shield attaching bolts and shield (**Figure 44**).
8. Separate the tie rod end from the steering knuckle with tool part No. J-6627 or equivalent (**Figure 40**).
9. Remove the knuckle seal (**Figure 45**). Save it for reuse if the same steering knuckle is to be reinstalled; discard it if a new knuckle will be installed.
10. Remove the ball studs from the steering knuckle as described in *Ball-joint Replacement* in this chapter.
11. Place a hydraulic jack under the lower control arm near the spring seat. Raise the jack until it supports the control arm.

12. Raise the upper control arm to disconnect the ball-joint stud from the knuckle.
13. Raise the knuckle from the lower ball-joint stud. Remove the knuckle.
14. Installation is the reverse of removal. Tighten all fasteners to specifications (**Table 1**).

Manual Steering Gearbox Removal/Installation

Refer to **Figure 46** for this procedure.

1. Disconnect the negative battery cable.
2. Remove the coupling shield, if so equipped.
3. Remove the retaining nuts, lockwashers and bolts holding the steering coupling to the steering shaft flange.
4. Remove the Pitman arm as described in this chapter.
5. Remove the bolts holding the steering gearbox to the frame. Remove the gearbox.
6. Installation is the reverse of removal. Tighten all fasteners to specifications (**Table 1**).

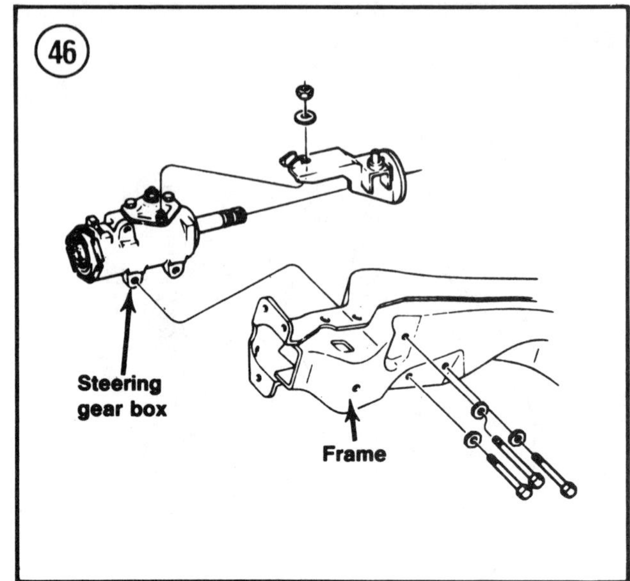

Manual Steering Gearbox Seal Replacement

Steering gearbox seal replacement requires special tools and skills and should be done by a Chevrolet or GMC dealer. If inspection indicates that solid grease is oozing from the gearbox seal area, you can save much of the repair cost by removing the gearbox yourself and taking it to a dealer for seal replacement.

Power Steering Gearbox Removal/Installation

The power steering gearbox is attached to the vehicle in the same manner as the manual gearbox and is removed using the same procedure after the pressure and return hoses have been disconnected. See **Figure 47**.

After installation, fill the power steering pump reservoir with power steering fluid recommended in Chapter Three. Start the engine and run for several seconds, then recheck the fluid level and top up if necessary. Repeat this procedure until the fluid level remains constant after running the engine. With the engine running, turn the steering wheel lock-to-lock several times and recheck the fluid level. Top up if necessary, then shut the engine off.

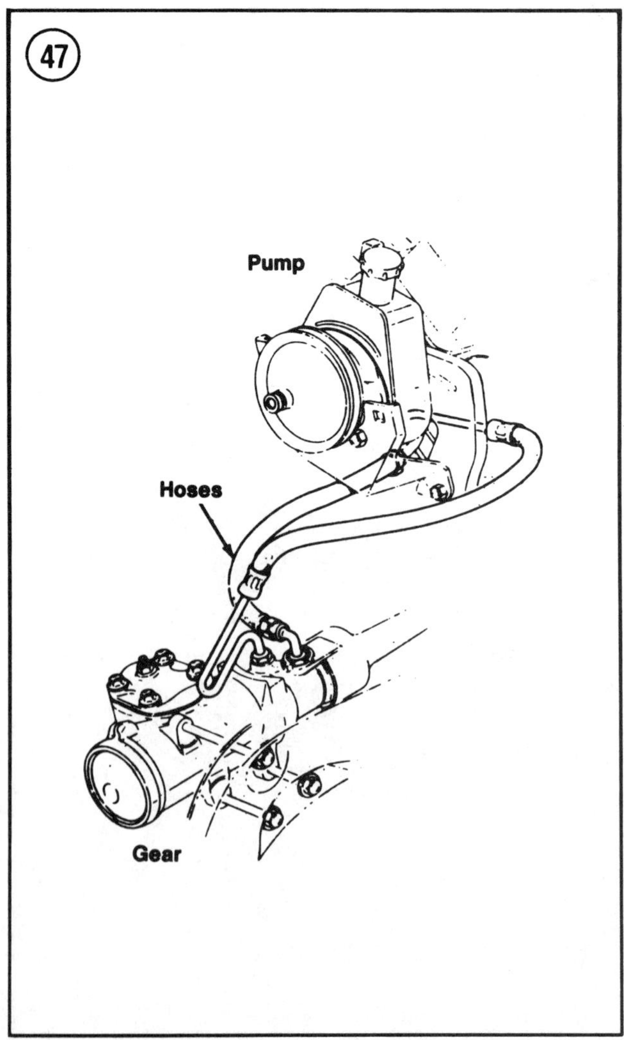

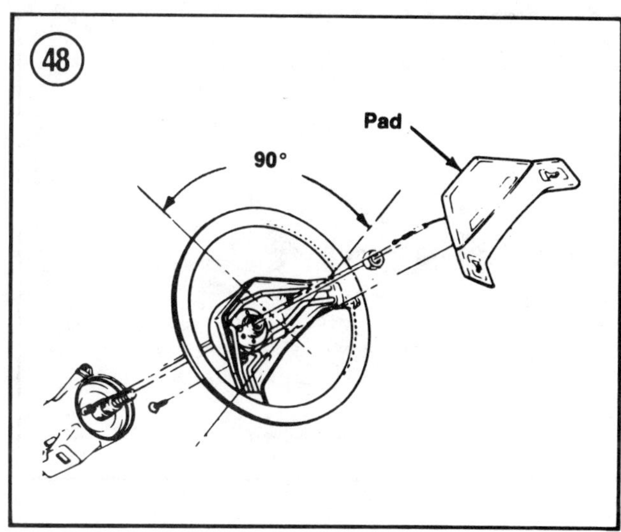

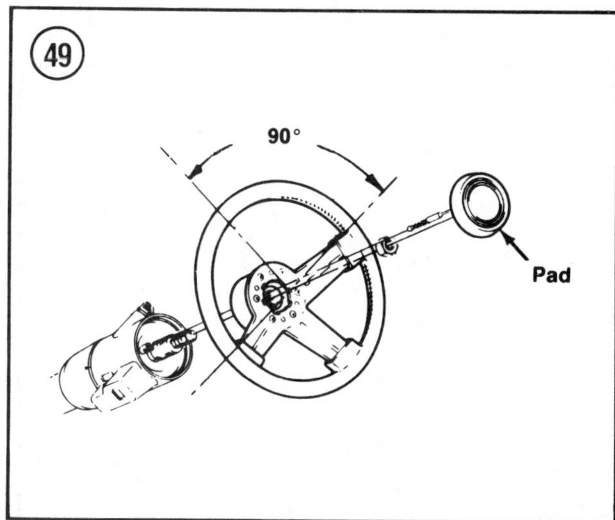

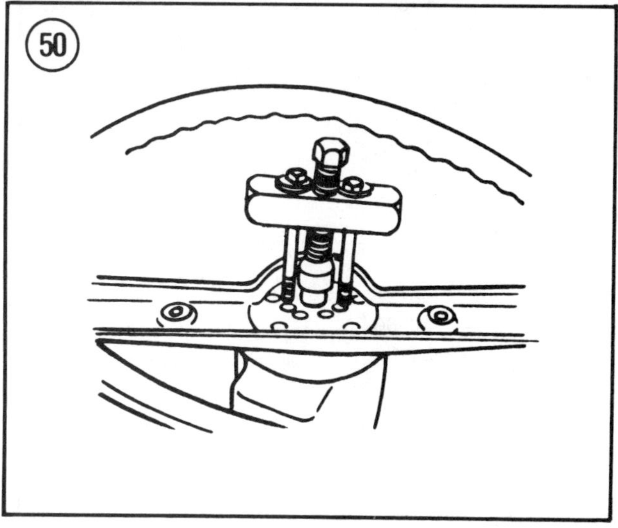

Steering Wheel Removal/Installation

WARNING
Use of a puller other than part No. J-1859-03 or equivalent can shear or loosen the plastic fasteners used to maintain steering column rigidity.

1. Tilt wheel—Position the wheel in its full up position.
2. Make sure the steering wheel and front wheels are in the staight-ahead position.
3. Disconnect the negative battery cable.
4A. Standard wheel—Remove 2 screws from the underside of the horn pad. Rotate the pad 90° and remove (**Figure 48**).
4B. Sport wheel—Remove the horn button by depressing and rotating 90° (**Figure 49**).
5. Remove and discard the steering wheel nut.
6. Scribe an alignment mark on the steering wheel and shaft for reinstallation reference.
7. Install wheel puller part No. J-1859-03 or equivalent as shown in **Figure 50** and remove the steering wheel.
8. Installation is the reverse of removal. Make sure the front wheels are in the straight-ahead position, then align the steering wheel and shaft marks scribed before removal. Engage the wheel and shaft serrations and fit the wheel onto the shaft. Install a new wheel nut and tighten to specifications (**Table 1**).

Steering Column Removal/Installation

WARNING
The steering column is very susceptible to damage during and after removal from the vehicle. Hammering, dropping or leaning on the column can damage internal plastic injections used to maintain rigidity.

This procedure applied to both standard and tilt-wheel columns.

1. Disconnect the negative battery cable.
2. Unplug the wiring connectors at the steering column jacket.
3. Remove the steering wheel as described in this chapter.

4. Remove the steering column bracket attaching nuts.
5. Remove the cover and seal at the base of the column against the firewall.
6. Remove the protective cap from the steering column/intermediate shaft coupling in the engine compartment.
7. Remove the bolt/screw and nut from the coupling (A and B, **Figure 51**).
8. Grasp the steering column assembly and pull it rearward to disconnect the lower stub shaft from the flexible coupling.
9. Remove the steering column from the vehicle.
10. Installation is the reverse of removal. Tighten all fasteners to specifications (**Table 1**).

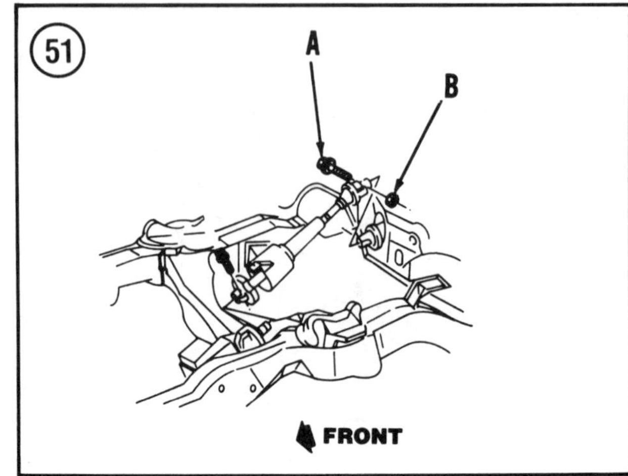

Table 1 TIGHTENING TORQUES

Fastener	ft.-lb.	N•m
Ball-joint-to-upper control arm		
2-wheel drive	8	11
4-wheel drive	15	20
Ball-joint stud nut		
2-wheel drive		
Upper	65	90
Lower	90	120
4-wheel drive		
Upper	50	68
Lower	83	113
Brake caliper mounting bolt		
1982-1983	21-35	28-47
1984-on	30-45	41-61
Control arm		
2-wheel drive		
Upper arm-to-frame nut	45	60
Lower arm-to-frame nut	65*	85*
Pivot shaft nut	85	115
4-wheel drive		
Upper arm-to-frame nut	70	95
Lower arm-to-frame nut	92*	125*
Front wheel drive (4-wheel drive only)		
Differential carrier-to-frame	60-74	80-100
Drive axle nut-to-hub/bearing	174	235
Drive axle-to-output shaft flange	53-63	72-85
Front output shaft strap retainer	12-17	16-23
Hub/bracket-to-knuckle bolt	77	105
Left hand output shaft cover	15-20	20-27
Output shaft tube bracket	45-60	60-80
Skid plate	20-28	27-38
Tie rod-to-knuckle nut	35	48
Torsion bar crossmember retainer	25	34

(continued)

Table 1 TIGHTENING TORQUES (continued)

Fastener	ft.-lb.	N•m
Idler arm		
To relay rod	40	54
To frame	60	80
Intermediate shaft-to-steering gearbox pinch bolt	45	60
Lower control arm bumper	20	27
Pitman arm		
To relay rod	40	54
To sector shaft	180	250
Power steering lines-to-gearbox	20	27
Stabilizer bar		
2-wheel drive		
Link nut	13	18
Bracket-to-frame	24	33
4-wheel drive		
Link nut	23	32
Bracket-to-frame	30	40
Steering gearbox		
To frame		
Manual (non-power)	63	85
Power	80	100
Steering knuckle		
Splash shield	10	14
To tie rod	40	54
Shock absorber		
2-wheel drive		
Upper attaching nut	8	11
To control arm	20	27
4-wheel drive		
Upper and lower nuts	52	70
To control arm	66	90
Tie rod		
Clamp nut	14	19
To relay rod	40	54
Wheel lug nuts		
Base wheel		
2-wheel drive	80	110
4-wheel drive	100	140
Optional wheel (2-wheel drive)	100	140

* Tighten with vehicle weight resting on wheels.

Table 2 ALIGNMENT SPECIFICATIONS

Caster	+2° ±0.5°
Camber	+0.8° ±0.5°
Toe-in (degrees per wheel)	+0.15° ±0.05°

CHAPTER ELEVEN

REAR SUSPENSION, DIFFERENTIAL AND DRIVE SHAFT

This chapter provides service procedures for the rear suspension, the rear axle assembly, drive shaft and differential. Tightening torques are provided in **Table 1** at the end of the chapter.

REAR SUSPENSION

Semi-elliptic leaf springs are used for the rear suspension on all vehicles. The number of leaves depends upon the vehicle and load capacity. The eye at the front of each spring is bolted to a frame side member bracket; the rear eye is shackled to a frame side member bracket. This allows the spring to change its length while the vehicle is in motion.

Two U-bolts are used to attach the center of each spring to the semi-floating rear axle housing. Ride control is provided by tubular shock absorbers which are angle-mounted between the frame and lower U-bolt anchor plate. **Figure 1** shows the major components of the rear suspension.

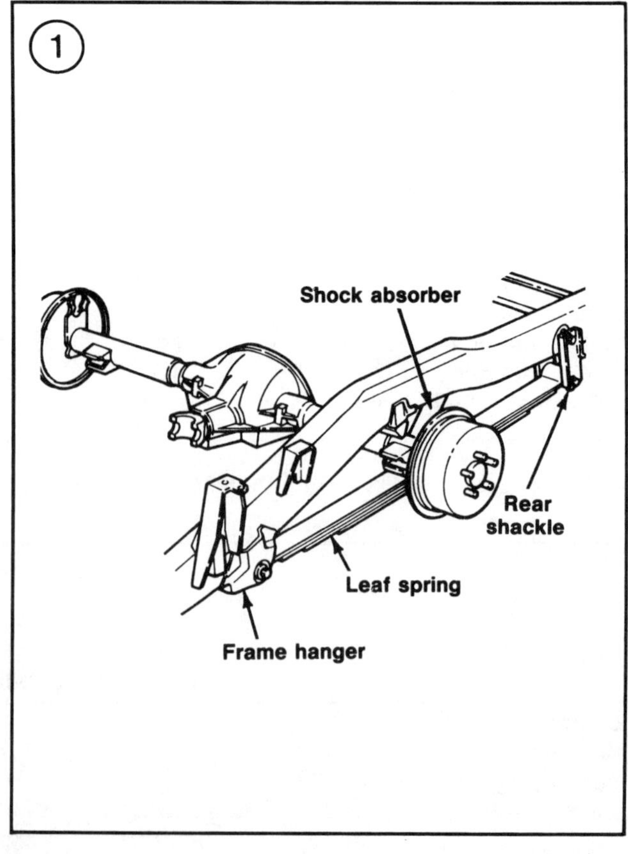

Shock Absorber Removal/Installation

Always use new rubber insulators/bushings when installing new shock absorbers. Refer to **Figure 2** for this procedure.

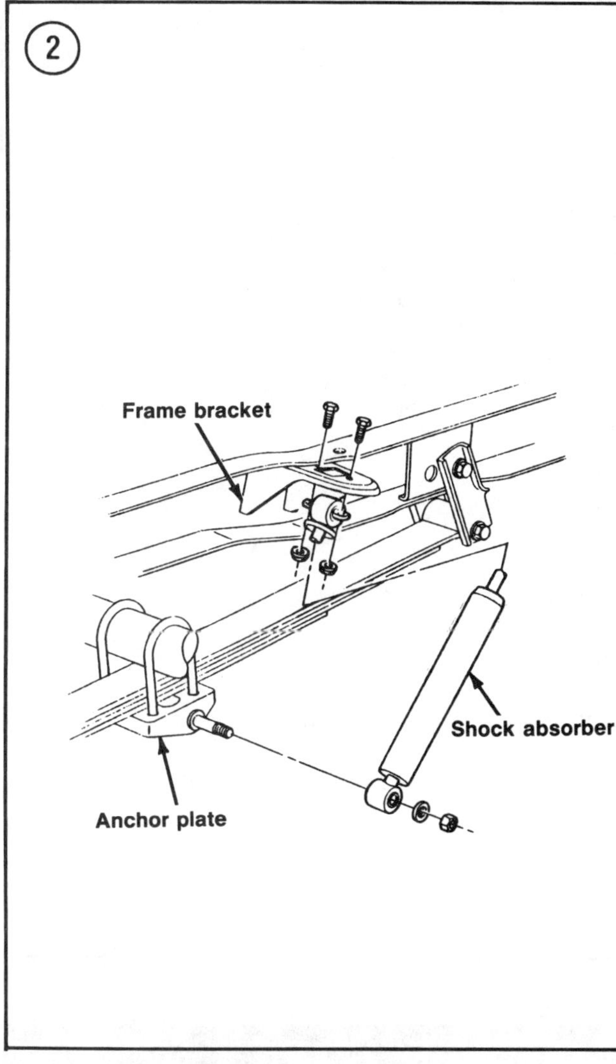

1. Securely block both front wheels so the truck will not roll in either direction.
2. Raise the rear of the vehicle with a jack and place it on jackstands.
3. Place a hydraulic jack underneath the axle housing. Raise the axle to remove its weight from the springs.
4. Disconnect the shock absorber at the upper frame bracket (**Figure 3**).
5. Remove the nut and washer from the lower shock absorber mount at the anchor plate (A, **Figure 4**).
6. Remove the shock absorber from the vehicle.
7. Fit the insulator/bushing and washer on the shock absorber upper stud. Install the shock absorber to the frame bracket and loosely thread the nuts on the attaching bolts.
8. Slide the lower shock eye over the anchor plate mounting stud and install the nut.
9. Tighten the upper and lower shock absorber fasteners to specifications (**Table 1**).
10. Remove the jackstands and lower the vehicle to the ground.

Leaf Spring Removal/Installation

Refer to **Figure 5** for this procedure.

1. Securely block both front wheels so the truck will not roll in either direction.
2. Raise the vehicle with a jack and place it on jackstands. Support the body/chassis and axle separately to relieve the load on the springs.

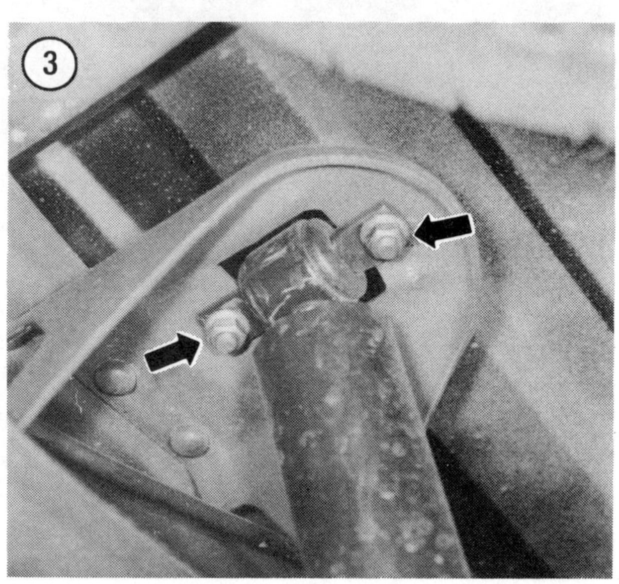

11

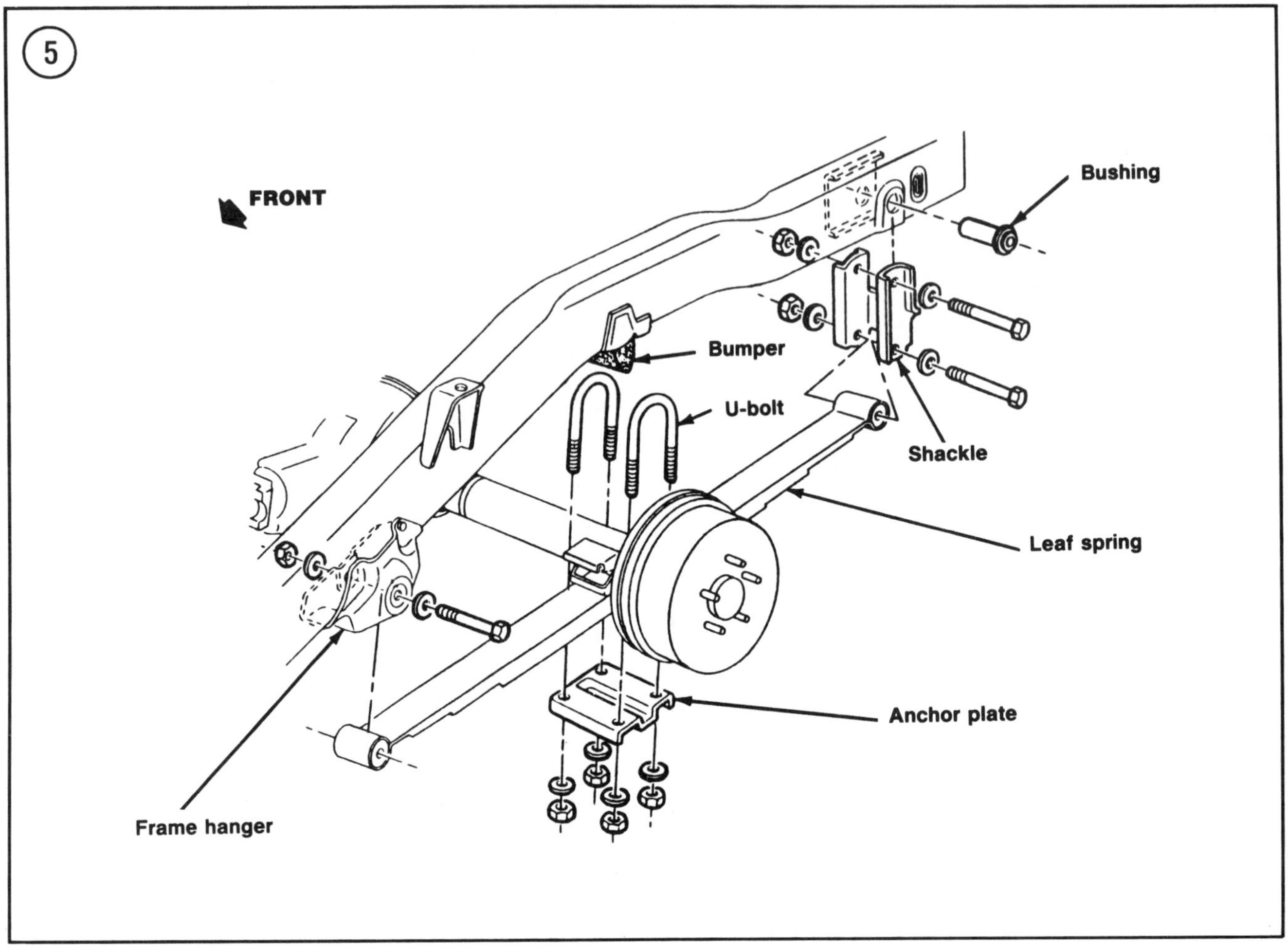

5

FRONT

Bushing

Bumper

U-bolt

Shackle

Leaf spring

Anchor plate

Frame hanger

3. Loosen but do not remove the spring-to-shackle retaining nut (A, **Figure 6**).
4. Remove the U-bolt retaining nuts (B, **Figure 4**). Drive the U-bolts from the anchor plate.
5. Rotate the anchor plate on the shock absorber until it clears the spring.

WARNING
Use caution in Step 5 and restrain the spring to prevent it from rotating on the front hanger bolt.

6. Remove the bolt/nut holding the shackle to the frame (B, **Figure 6**).
7. Remove the front hanger bolt/nut (**Figure 7**).
8. Remove the spring and shackle from the vehicle.
9. To reinstall, reattach the shackle to the rear spring eye, if removed. The open end of the shackle must face toward the front of the vehicle.
10. Position the spring to the axle and install the spring plate and U-bolts. Install U-bolt nuts lightly.

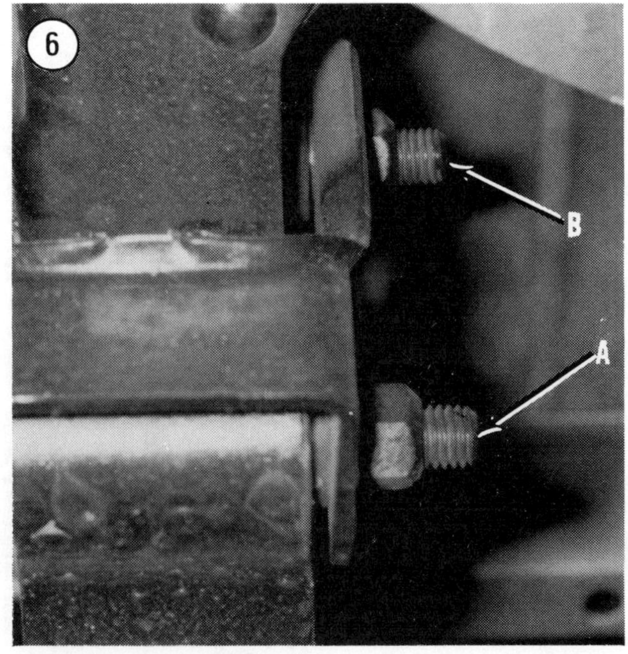

11. Align spring and shackle with spring hangers, then loosely install shackle bolt and nut.
12. Reposition spring as required to align its front eye with the hanger, then install the front eye bolt and nut.
13. Remove the jackstands and lower the vehicle enough to place its weight on the suspension, then tighten all fasteners to specifications (**Table 1**). Tighten the U-bolt nuts uniformly in a diagonal pattern to assure that the anchor plate remains perpendicular to the U-bolt axis. Remove the jack and lower the vehicle to the ground.

Leaf Spring Bushing Replacement

1. Remove the spring from the vehicle as described in this chapter.
2. Press the old bushing from the spring eye with a suitable driver and hydraulic press.
3. Press the new bushing into the spring eye with a suitable driver and hydraulic press.
4. Reinstall the spring as described in this chapter.

Shackle Replacement

Refer to **Figure 4** for this procedure.

1. Securely block both front wheels so the truck will not roll in either direction.
2. Raise the rear of the vehicle with a jack. Support the body/chassis and axle housing separately with jackstands to relieve the load on the spring.
3. Loosen but do not remove the spring-to-shackle retaining bolt (A, **Figure 6**).
4. Remove the shackle-to-frame retaining bolt (B, **Figure 6**). Remove the shackle bolt from the spring eye. Remove the shackle assembly from the vehicle.
5. If shackle-to-frame bushing requires replacement, drive old bushing out with a suitable punch and hammer. Carefully drive a new bushing in place with the same tools.
6. Position shackle to spring eye (open end facing the front of the vehicle) and loosely install the bolt and nut.
7. Engage spring eye in shackle and loosely install the bolt and nut.
8. Remove the jackstands and lower the vehicle enough to place its weight on the suspension, then tighten all fasteners to specifications (**Table 1**).
9. Remove the jack and lower the vehicle to the ground.

DRIVE SHAFT

A drive shaft asssembly is used to transmit torque from the transmission to the rear axle. The drive shaft connects to the transmission with a single cardan universal joint.

Vehicles with a standard bed use a 1-piece drive shaft (**Figure 8**). In the 1-piece design, a universal joint and splined slip yoke are located on the

11

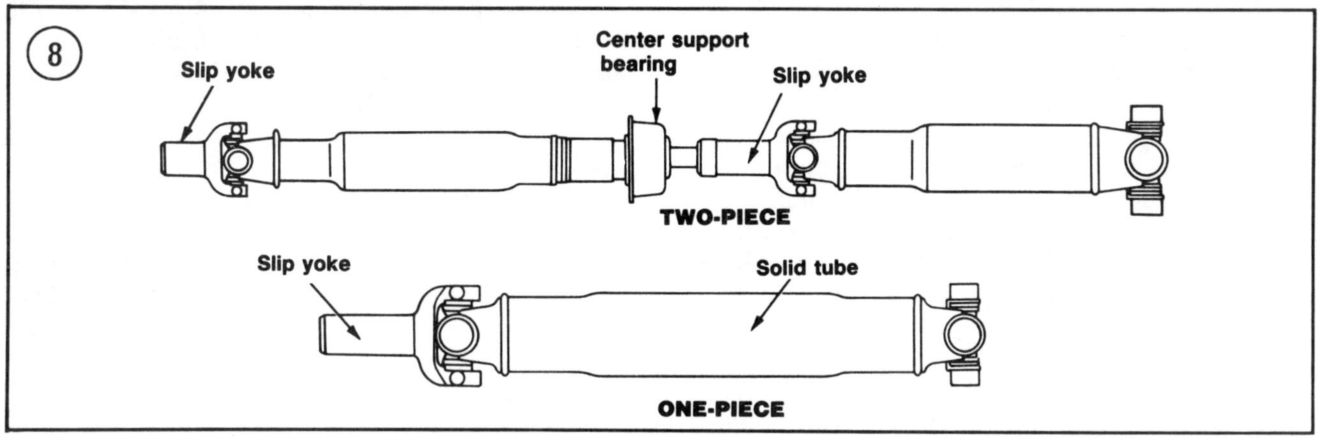

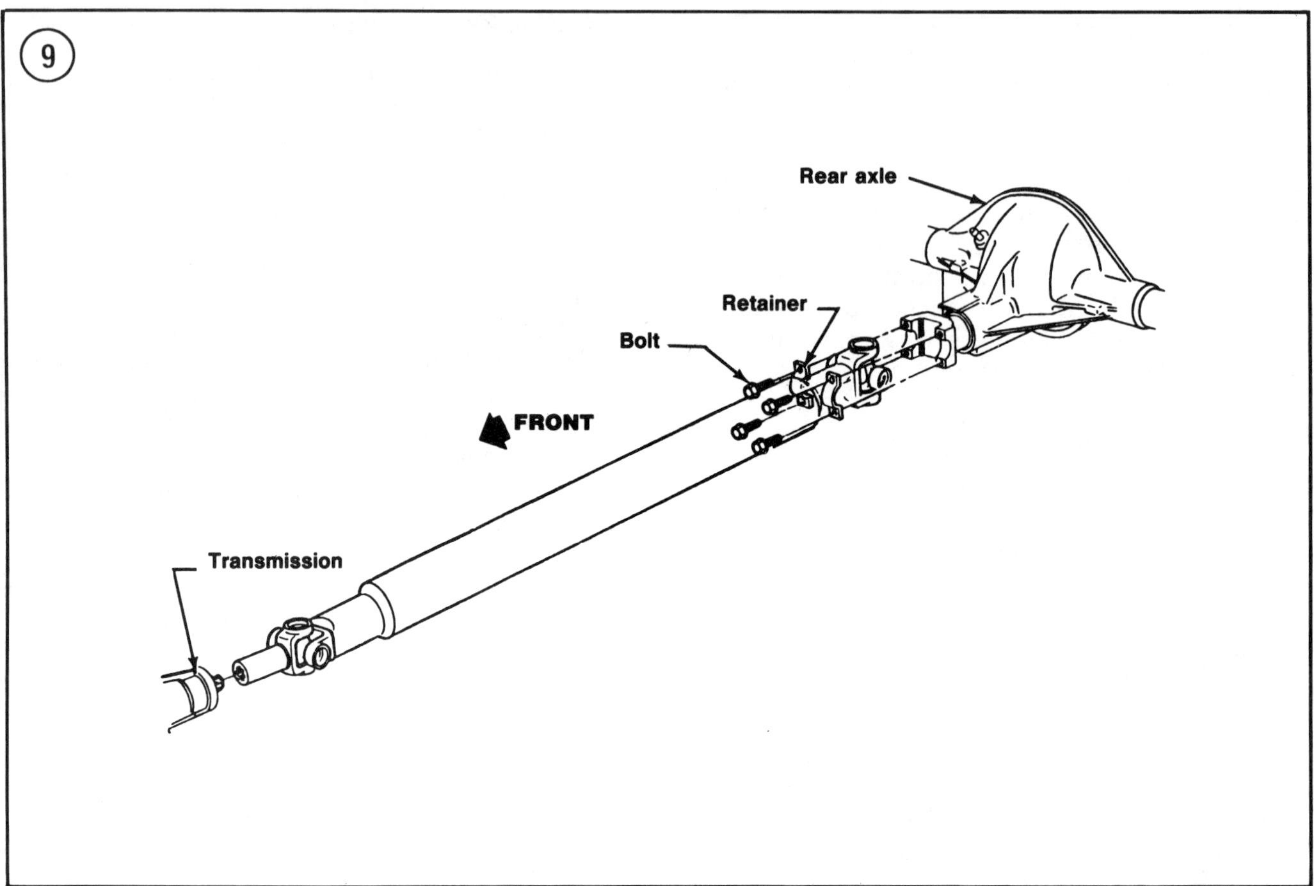

transmission end of the shaft. A universal joint on the other end of the shaft connects to the differential companion flange with retainer straps.

If equipped with the long bed, the vehicle uses a 2-piece drive shaft to the rear axle (**Figure 8**). The 2-piece drive shaft is supported near its splined end in a bracket-mounted center support attached to a frame crossmember. This center support contains a rubber cushioned ball bearing which is permanently lubricated and sealed.

Four-wheel drive vehicles use a one-piece drive shaft between the front differential and transfer case.

All drive shafts are tubular and use needle bearing type universal joints. The universal joints are factory-lubricated and cannot be lubricated while on the vehicle. A repair kit is available containing a new spider with bearing assemblies and snap rings to overhaul worn universal joints.

Drive shafts and coupling shafts are balanced assemblies and must not be painted or undercoated. Correct alignment is required when a drive shaft is removed and reinstalled to prevent drive line vibration. Correct phasing is also required. This means that the U-joints must be installed on the shafts in the same plane.

Removal

If the drive shaft must be disconnected but need not be removed from the vehicle, perform Steps 1-3 and wire the end of the shaft to the underbody for support. Do not pound on the yoke ears while removing or installing the drive shaft, as this can fracture the nylon injection rings used in the factory-installed universal joints.

Refer to **Figure 9** or **Figure 10** as required for this procedure.

1. Block wheels at whichever end of the truck is not being raised so the truck will not roll. Raise the front or rear of the vehicle with a jack according to the drive shaft being removed. Place the vehicle on jackstands.
2. Scribe or chalk alignment marks on the shaft and transfer case or differential pinion flange for reassembly reference.

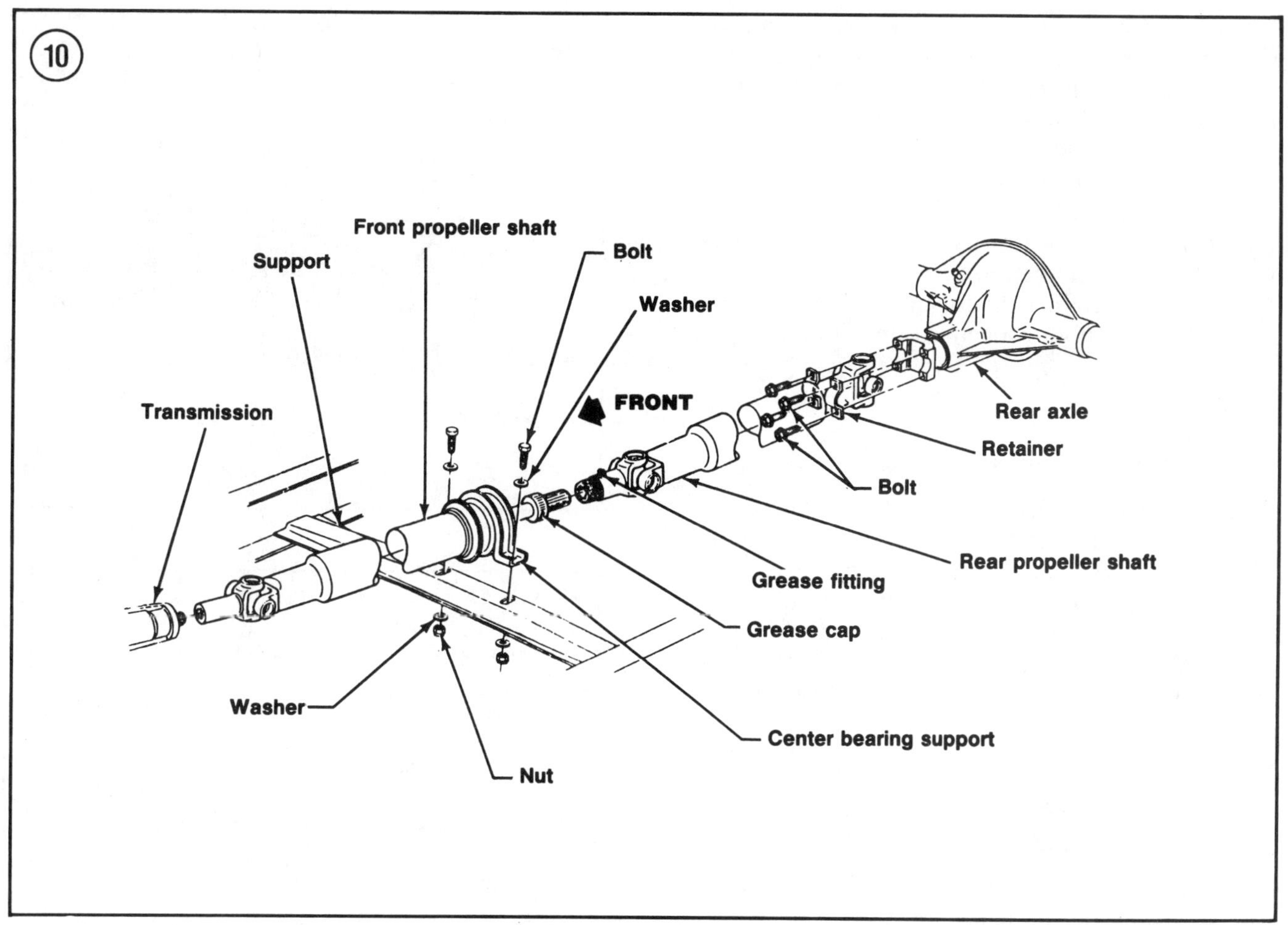

3. Remove the nuts holding the retainer straps at the pinion flange.
4. On front axle drive shafts, disengage the shaft from the transfer case and remove it from the vehicle.
5. On 2-piece drive shafts, remove the center bearing support-to-hanger retaining bolts.
6. Slide the drive shaft forward to disconnect the trunnion from the axle flange.
7. Move the drive shaft to the rear and pass it under the axle housing to disengage it from the transmission.
8. Remove the drive shaft from the vehicle.

Installation (1-piece Drive Shaft)

Refer to **Figure 9** for this procedure.
1. Apply chassis lubricant to the drive shaft slip yoke splines. Engage the slip yoke in the transmission extension housing.
2. Align the rear universal joint with the rear axle pinion flange. Make sure the bearings are properly seated in the pinion flange yoke and that the alignment marks scribed during removal are aligned.
3. Install the retainer straps. Install the strap bolts and tighten evenly to specifications (**Table 1**).

Installation (2-piece Drive Shaft)

Refer to **Figure 10** for this procedure.
1. Apply chassis lubricant to the front drive shaft slip yoke splines. Engage the slip yoke in the transmission extension housing.

NOTE
Make sure the drive shaft is fully forward in the transmission before proceeding to Step 2.

2. Install the center support to the crossmember and tighten the nuts to specifications (**Table 1**).

3. Rotate the drive shaft to position the front universal joint trunnion as shown in **Figure 11**. A key in the output spline of the front drive shaft must align with a missing spline in the rear yoke.
4. Install the rear drive shaft. Align the rear universal joint with the rear axle pinion flange. Make sure the bearings are properly seated in the pinion flange yoke and that the alignment marks scribed during removal are aligned.
5. Install the retainer straps. Install the strap bolts and tighten evenly to specifications (**Table 1**).

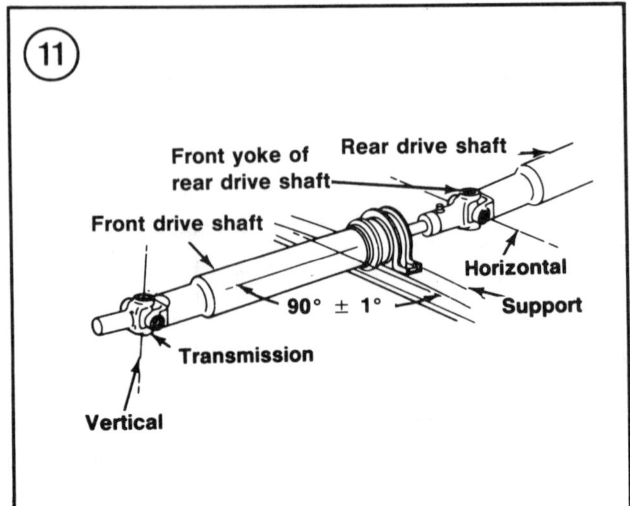

Installation
(Front Axle Drive Shaft)

1. Slide the drive shaft into the transfer case.
2. Align the universal joint with the axle pinion flange. Make sure the bearings are properly seated in the pinion flange yoke and that the alignment marks scribed during removal are aligned.
3. Install the retainer straps. Install the strap bolts and tighten evenly to specifications (**Table 1**).

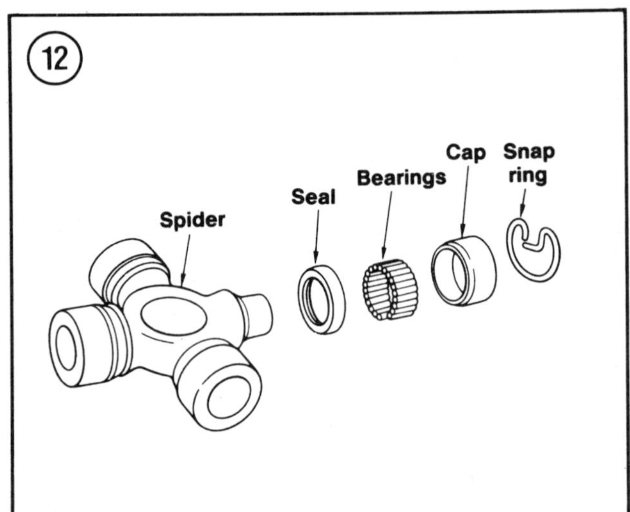

UNIVERSAL JOINTS

The single cardan joint consists of a single spider and 4 sets of needle bearings, bearing seals, caps and cap retainers. Replacement universal joint kits may be of the internal snap ring type (**Figure 12**) or external snap ring type (**Figure 13**).

Disassembly
(Factory Installed Joint)

Production universal joints are retained by nylon injected rings. Removal of the universal joint destroys the nylon ring and the universal joint must be discarded.

1. Support the lower ear of the drive shaft yoke on a 1 1/8 in. socket on the base plate of a hydraulic press.
2. Install a cross press such as tool part No. J-9522-3 over the open horizontal bearing cup (**Figure 14**) and press the lower bearing cup from the yoke ears.
3. Rotate the drive shaft 180° and repeat Step 1 and Step 2 to press the opposite bearing cup from the yoke.
4. Remove the spider from the yoke.

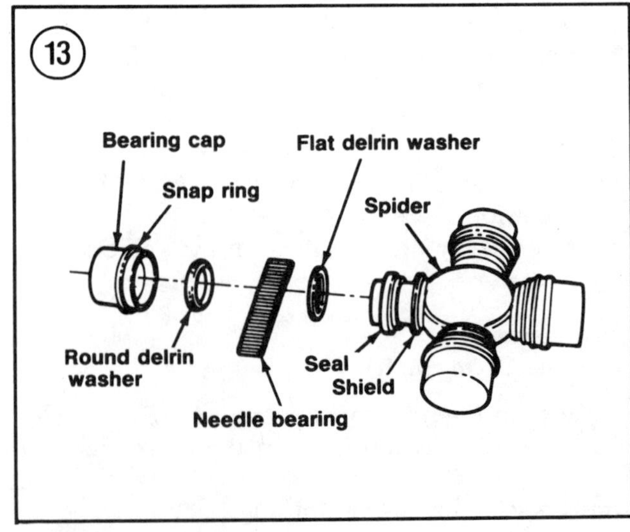

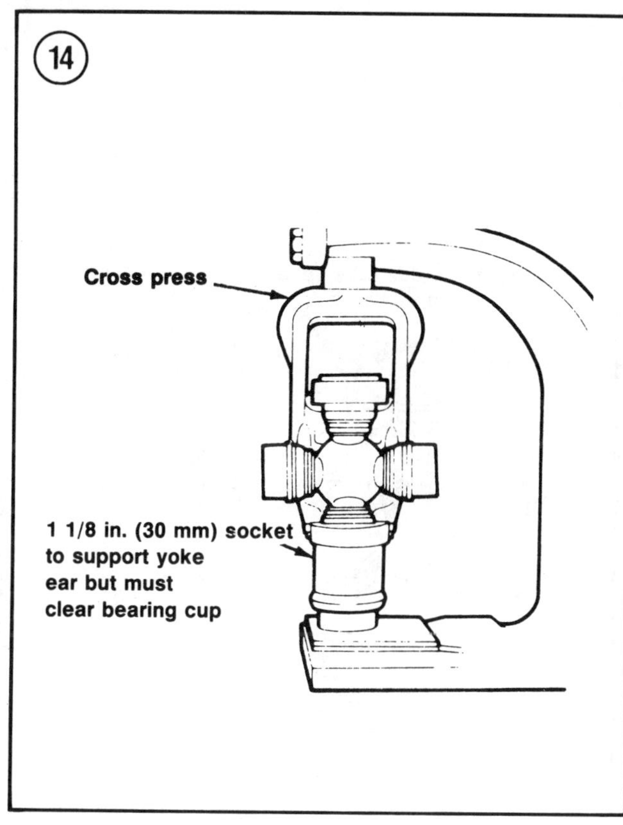

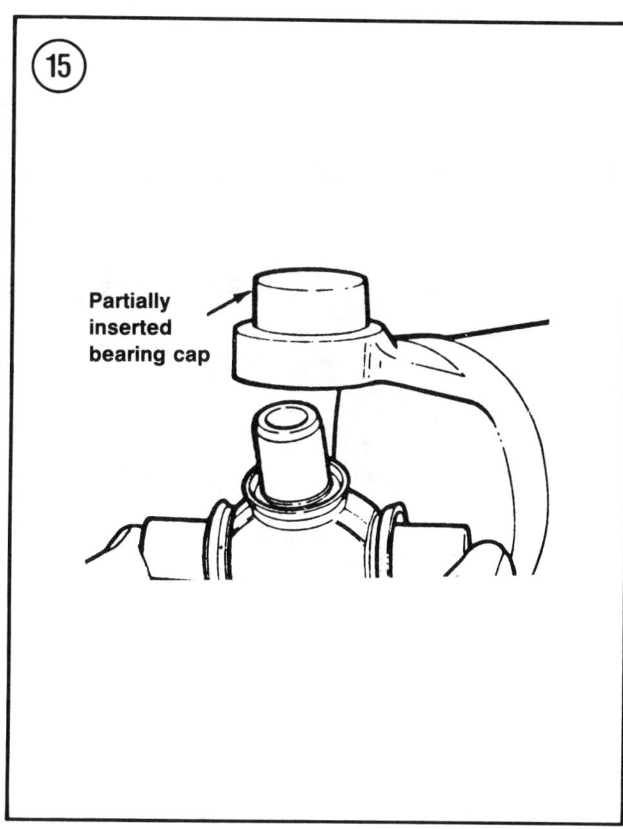

Disassembly (Service Replacement Joint)

1. Paint alignment marks on the drive shaft and slip yoke for reassembly reference. Remove the slip yoke from the drive shaft.
2. Remove the loose bearing caps from the spider. Apply liberal quantities of penetrating oil to the bearing caps in the shaft yoke.

CAUTION
Clamp only the forged portion of the slip yoke or drive shaft yoke in the vise in Step 3. Clamping the drive shaft tube in a vise can distort the tube and result in drive line vibration after installation.

3. Clamp the drive shaft yoke or slip yoke in a vise with protective jaws. If protective jaws are not available, wrap the yoke in shop cloths.
4. Remove the snap rings or retaining rings from opposite bearing caps with pliers. If necessary, tap the ends of the bearing caps with a hammer to relieve any pressure on the snap rings.
5. Tap the end of one bearing cap with a hammer and drive the opposite cap from the yoke. Remove the bearing cap.
6. Repeat Step 5 to remove the other bearing cap.
7. Remove the drive shaft yoke or slip yoke from the spider.
8. Unclamp and reposition the yoke in the vise. Repeat Steps 4-6 to remove the remaining bearing caps. Remove the spider from the yoke.

Cleaning and Inspection

1. If replacing original universal joints that used nylon injected retaining rings, remove any remaining sheared plastic from the yoke grooves.
2. Clean the yoke bearing cap bores with solvent and a wire brush.
3. Wash the bearing caps, bearings and spider in solvent. Wipe dry with a clean shop cloth.
4. Check the caps, bearings and spider for brinneling, flat spots, scoring, cracks or excessive wear. Replace the entire assembly if any part(s) show such conditions.

Assembly

1. Lubricate all components with chassis grease. Wipe the outside of the bearing caps with a thin film of chassis grease.
2. Install the bearing cap seals on the spider.
3. Partially install a bearing cap and needle bearing assembly in the shaft yoke (**Figure 15**).

4. Place the spider in the shaft yoke. Install the opposite bearing cap and needle bearing assembly in the yoke bore.
5. Support the yoke on the vise jaws. Seat both caps in the yoke by tapping lightly with a hammer. See **Figure 16**.
6. Install the bearing cap snap rings or retaining rings (**Figure 17**). If retaining rings are used, tape the caps on the spider to hold them in place until the drive shaft is reinstalled.
7. Reposition the shaft yoke in the vise and install the 2 remaining bearing cap and needle bearing assemblies. Install the bearing cap snap rings or retaining rings. If retaining rings are used, tape the caps on the spider to hold them in place until the drive shaft is reinstalled.

CAUTION

Do not reinstall the drive shaft if the universal joints show any signs of binding when checked in Step 8 or drive line vibration and possible damage may result.

8. Check the assembled joint for free movement. If misalignment during installation has caused a bind, tap the drive shaft ears sharply with a hammer. If this does not relieve the binding condition, disassemble the joint as described in this chapter and locate the cause of the problem.

Center Support Bearing Replacement

The center support bearing is a prelubricated, sealed unit that does not require periodic lubrication. The bearing is serviced by replacement only. Whenever it is removed, clean the assembly by wiping it with a cloth moistened in solvent and check for rough action or wear by rotating the inner race while holding the outer race. If wear or roughness is noted, replace the bearing assembly.
1. Remove the drive shaft as described in this chapter.
2. Remove the retaining strap bolts. Remove the support bracket.
3. Separate the rubber cushion from the bearing.
4. Press the old bearing from the shaft.
5. Install the inner deflector tightly on the drive shaft.
6. Pack lithium soap grease into the cavity between the inner dust shield and the bearing.
7. Fit the bearing and slinger assembly onto the drive shaft journal.

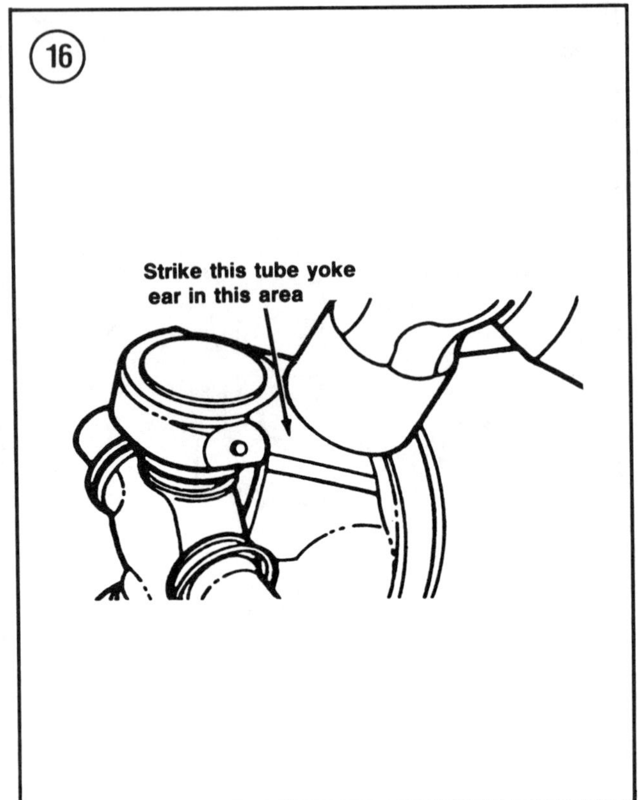

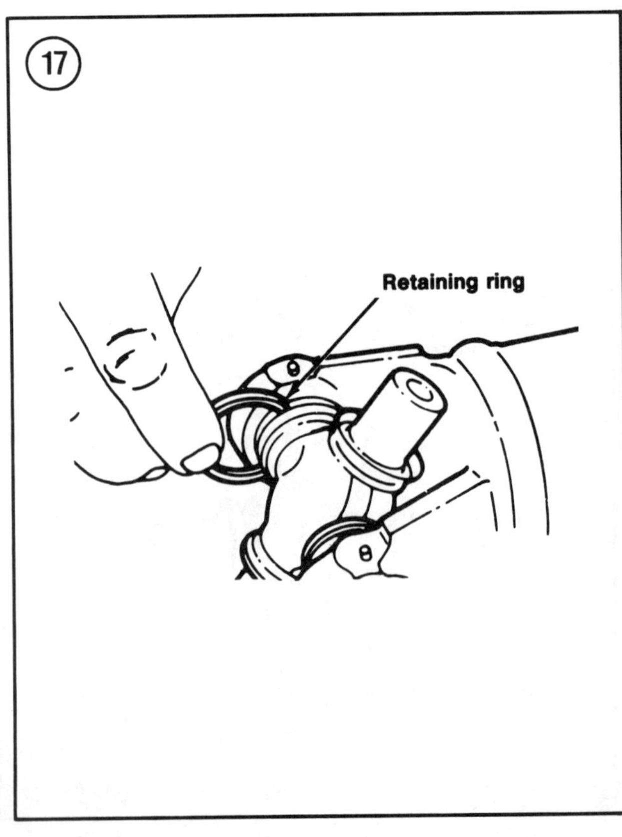

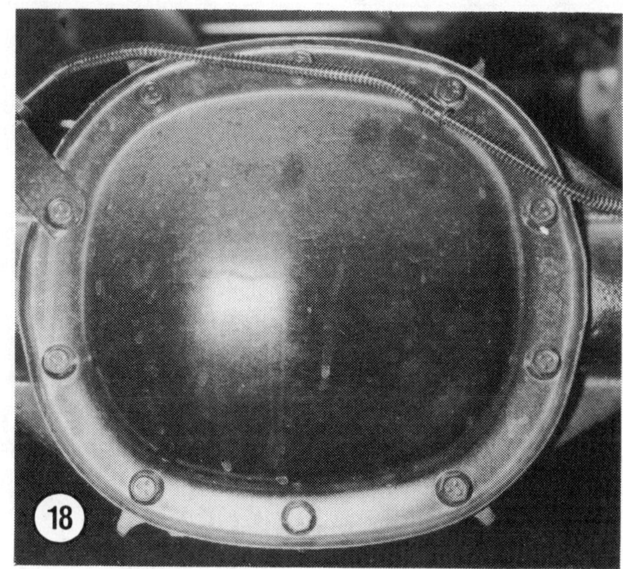

18

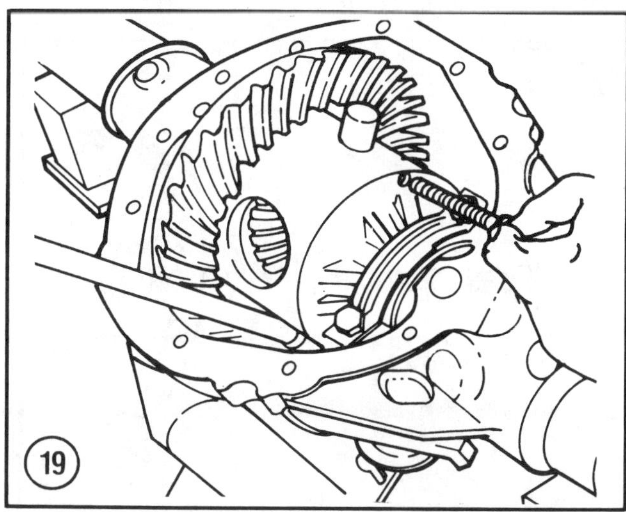

19

8. Support the drive shaft and install the bearing and inner slinger against the shaft shoulder with a press.
9. Install the bearing retainer. Install the rubber cushion on the bearing.
10. Install the bracket to the cushion. Install the retaining strap. Install the drive shaft as described in this chapter.

REAR AXLE AND AXLE SHAFTS

A semi-floating rear axle is used with five different axle ratios available, depending upon engine and transmission usage. The Eaton positive locking differential is also available in 5 different ratios as an option.

This section includes removal, installation and inspection procedures for the standard rear axle and axle shafts. Rear axle repair requires special skills and many expensive special tools. The inspection procedures will tell you if repairs are necessary. Refer service on locking rear axles to your dealer.

Carrier Cover Gasket Replacement

1. Raise the vehicle with a jack and place it on jackstands.
2. Place a clean container underneath the carrier housing.
3. Remove the cover bolts (**Figure 18**).

NOTE
One carrier cover bolt holds the brake line junction block to the cover; a second bolt attaches a brake line holder to the cover. Lift the line up and place it on top of the axle housing to prevent any possible damage.

4. Pry the cover loose with a screwdriver and let the lubricant drain into the container.
5. Remove the cover. Remove and discard the gasket.
6. Clean the gasket sealing surfaces on the cover and carrier.
7. Install the cover with a new gasket.
8. Install the cover bolts and tighten to specifications (**Table 1**) in a crosswise pattern to assure a uniform draw on the gasket.
9. Remove the fill plug and fill the carrier with the recommended type and quantity of lubricant (Chapter Three) to within 3/8 in. of the fill plug hole. Reinstall the fill plug and tighten to 20ft.-lb. (27 N•m).
10. Remove the jackstands and lower the vehicle to the ground.

Axle Shaft Removal/Installation

1. Remove the wheel cover, if used. Loosen the rear wheel lug nuts.
2. Securely block both front wheels so the truck will not roll in either direction. Raise the vehicle with a jack and place it on jackstands.
3. Remove the wheel/tire assembly and brake drum (Chapter Twelve).
4. Remove the carrier cover and drain the lubricant as described in this chapter.
5. Remove the rear axle pinion shaft lock screw and pinion shaft (**Figure 19**).

6. Push the flanged end of the axle shaft in toward the center of the vehicle. Remove the C-lock from the shaft (**Figure 20**).
7. Carefully withdraw the axle shaft from the carrier housing to prevent damage to the oil seal.
8. Installation is the reverse of removal.

Axle Shaft Oil Seal/ Bearing Replacement

1. Remove the axle shaft as described in this chapter.
2. Pry the seal from the housing with a suitable tool.
3. Install a bearing removal tool to a slide hammer, as shown in **Figure 21**.
4. Insert the tool in the bore and engage its tangs with the bearing outer race. Remove the bearing.
5. Lubricate a new bearing with gear lubricant.
6. Install the bearing with an installer tool as shown in **Figure 22**. The tool must bottom against the housing shoulder to properly seat the seal.
7. Lubricate the seal lips with gear lubricant.
8. Fit the seal in the housing bore and tap in place with a seal installer until it is flush with the axle tube.
9. Reinstall the axle shaft as described in this chapter.

Rear Axle Removal/Installation

1. Securely block both front wheels so the truck will not roll in either direction. Remove the wheel covers, if used. Loosen the rear wheel lug nuts.
2. Raise the vehicle with a jack. Support the vehicle with jackstands placed at the frame. Install the jack under the rear axle housing.
3. Disconnect the lower ends of the shock absorbers at the spring anchor plates as described in this chapter.
4. Disconnect the drive shaft from the pinion flange as described in this chapter. Wire the shaft up and out of the way.
5. Remove the brake line junction block bolt at the axle housing (**Figure 23**). Disconnect and cap the brake lines at the junction block.
6. Remove the spring U-bolts and spring anchor plates on each side of the housing tube.
7. Remove the wheel/tire assemblies and brake drums (Chapter Twelve).
8. Lower the axle housing as required to remove the lower spring shackle bolts.

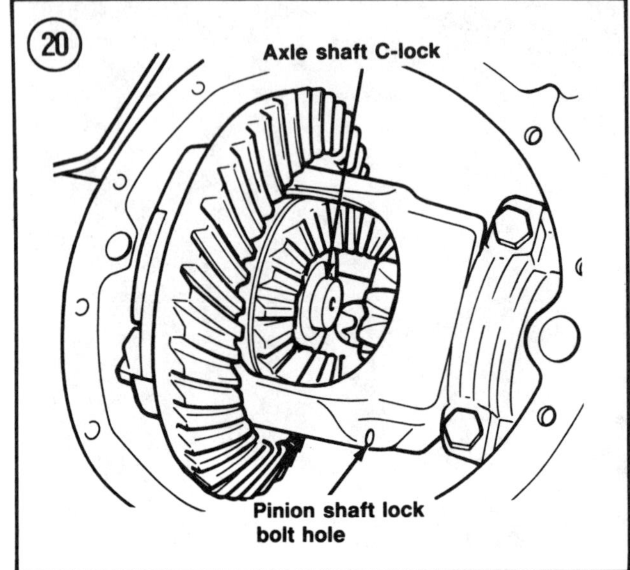

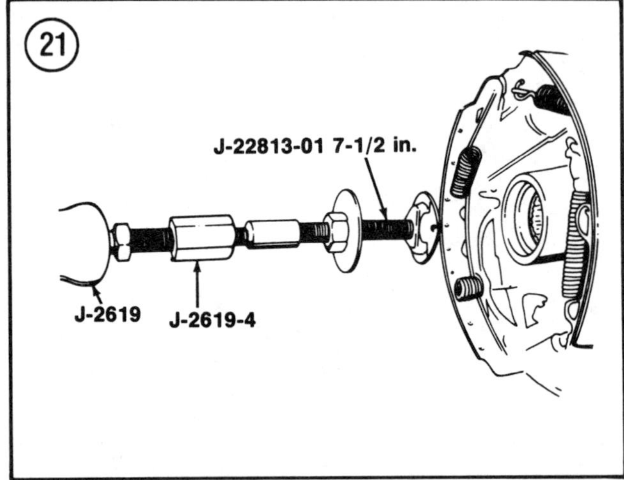

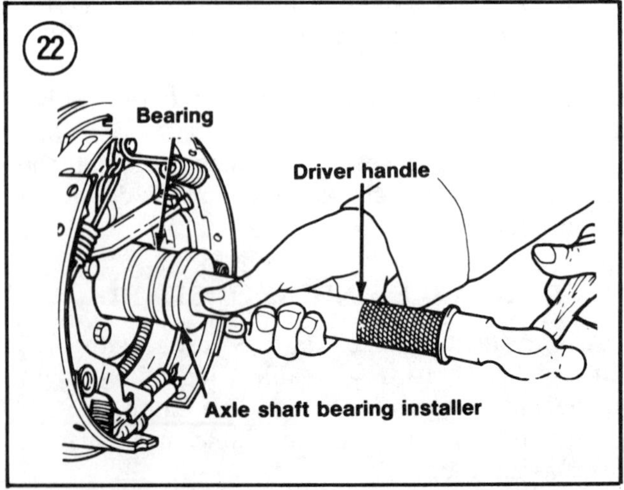

9. Remove the carrier cover as described in this chapter.
10. Remove the axle shafts as described in this chapter.
11. Disconnect the brake lines from the axle housing clips.
12. Remove the brake backing plates.
13. Lower the axle housing to the ground with the jack and remove it from under the vehicle.
14. Installation is the reverse of removal, plus the following:
    a. Tighten all fasteners to specifications (**Table 1**).
    b. Fill the axle with the specified lubricant (Chapter Three).
    c. Bleed the brakes (Chapter Twelve).
    d. Adjust the parking brake (Chapter Twelve).

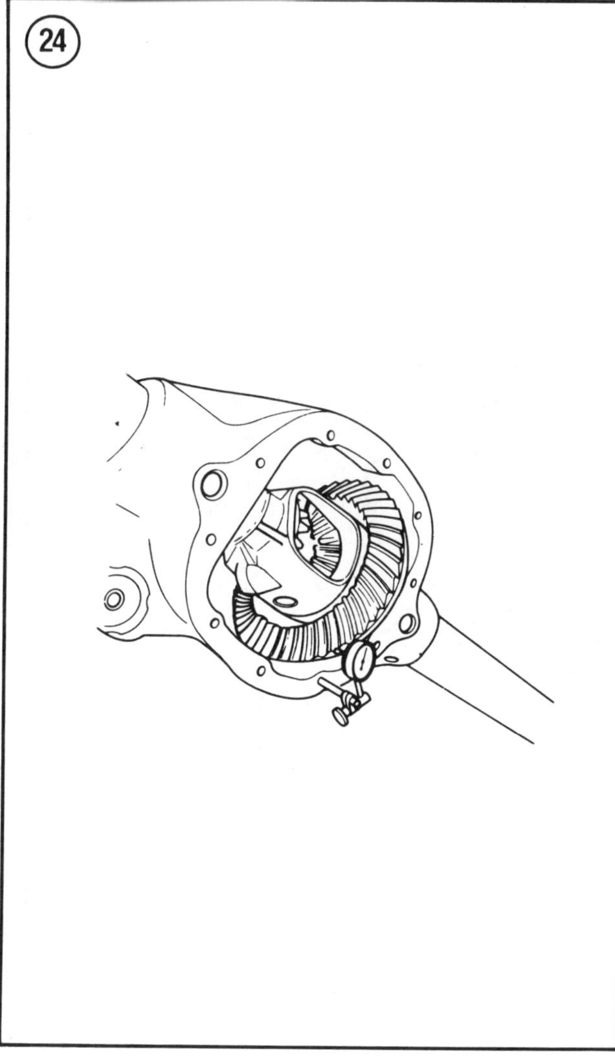

Differential Inspection

Inspection of the differential case and drive pinion assembly before removal from the carrier housing can be helpful in determining the cause of a differential problem.

1. Wipe as much lubricant as possible from the internal components. Use paper towels or clean lint-free cloths.
2. Mount a dial indicator on the housing as shown in **Figure 24** to measure ring gear backlash. The indicator plunger should touch the drive side of a ring gear tooth at right angles to the tooth. Hold the pinion from turning with one hand and rotate the ring gear against the dial indicator with the other. Backlash should be 0.005-0.009 in. (0.13-0.23 mm). If not, have the differential disassembled and adjusted.
3. Measure ring gear runout. It should not exceed 0.002 in. (0.05 mm). If it does, have the differential repaired.
4. Rotate the ring gear and check for broken, chipped or worn teeth. Check the differential for rough movement. Have the differential repaired if these conditions are found.
5. Inspect all bearings and cups for pitting, galling, flat spots or cracks. Replace as required.
6. Check the differential case for an elongated or enlarged pinion mate shaft bore.
7. Inspect the machined thrust washer surface area for nicks, gouges, cracks or burrs.
8. Check the case for cracks or other damage. Replace the case if any of these conditions are found.

11

Differential Removal/Installation

1. Inspect the differential housing as described in this chapter.
2. Remove the axle housing as described in this chapter.
3. Mark the differential bearing caps wtih a centerpunch for reassembly alignment reference.
4. Remove the differential bearing cap bolts.
5. Pry the rear axle case from the carrier as shown in **Figure 25**. Work carefully to prevent damage to the gasket sealing surface.
6. Tie the left and right bearing shims and outer races in sets for proper reinstallation.
7. Installation is the reverse of removal. Tighten all fasteners to specifications.

Tooth Contact Pattern Test

1. Wipe all oil from the axle housing. Clean each ring gear tooth carefully.
2. Apply a light coat of gear marking compound to the drive side of the ring gear teeth (**Figure 26**).
3. Rotate the ring gear slowly in both directions. Compare the contact pattern pressed into the marking compound with those shown in **Figure 27**.
4. The desired tooth contact pattern under a light load is shown in **Figure 27**. If the pattern is not correct, have the differential disassembled and adjusted.

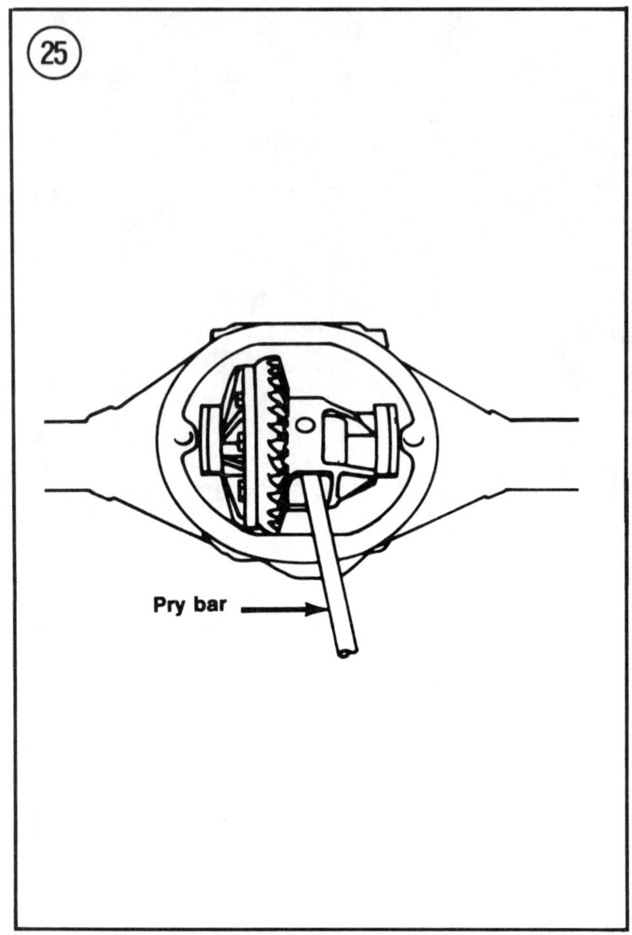

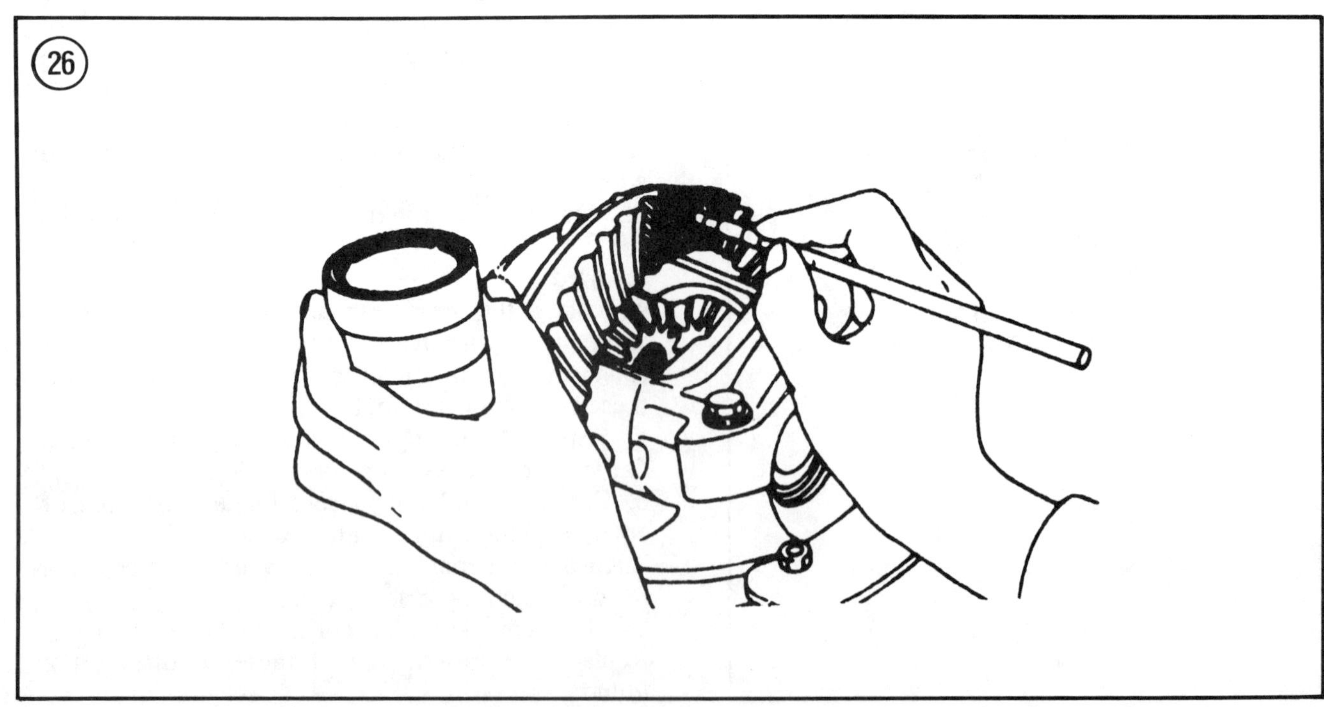

27

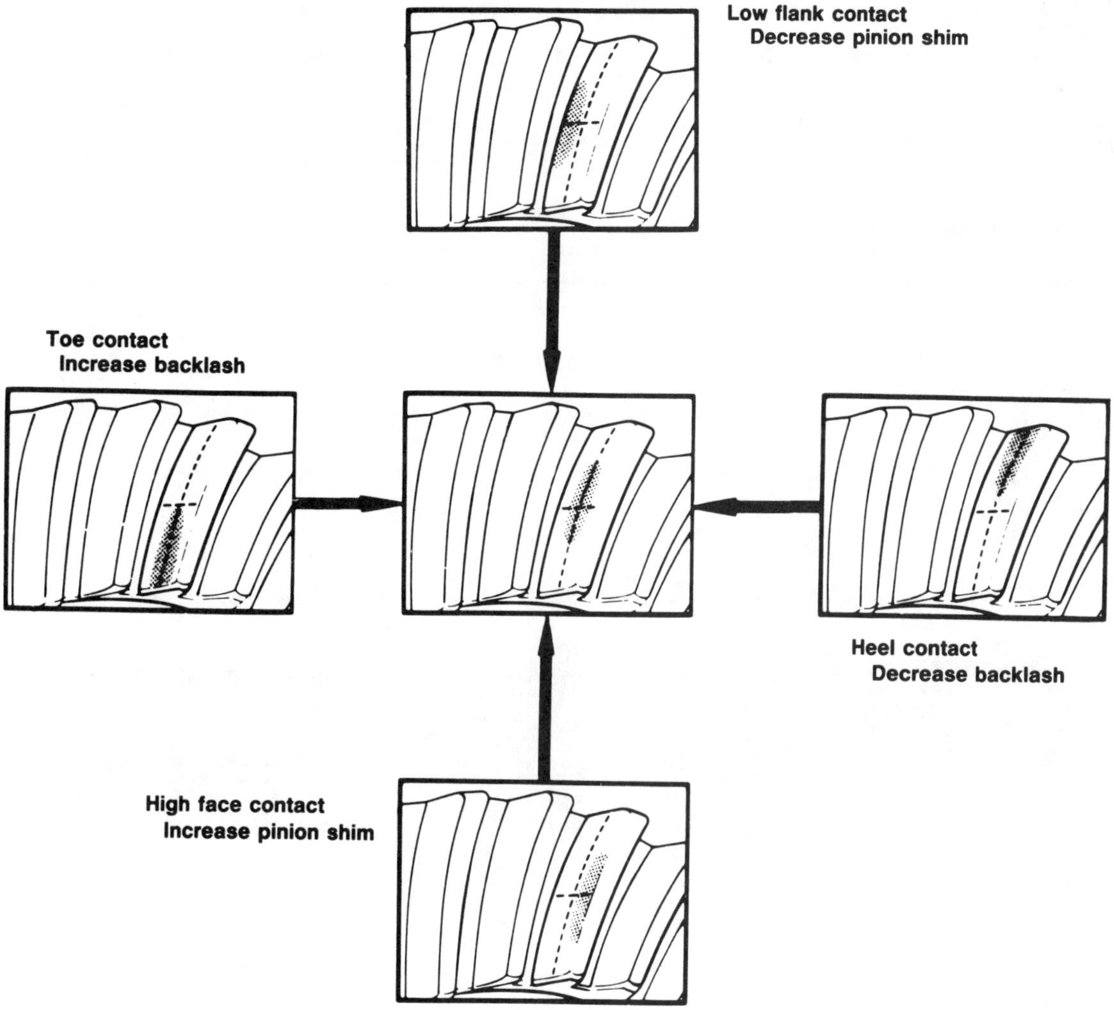

Low flank contact
Decrease pinion shim

Toe contact
Increase backlash

Heel contact
Decrease backlash

High face contact
Increase pinion shim

11

Table 1 TIGHTENING TORQUES

Fastener	ft.-lb.	N•m
Drive shaft		
Retainer-to-pinion flange	13-17	17-23
Center support	20-30	27-40
Leaf spring		
Front/rear bushing bolt	88	120
Rear shackle-to-frame	88	120
Pinion shaft lock bolt	25	34
Rear axle carrier cover	20	27
Shock absorber		
Upper attachment	15	20
Lower nut-to-stud	50	70
Spring-to-axle U-bolt nuts	85	115
Wheel lug nuts		
Base wheel		
2-wheel drive	80	110
4-wheel drive	100	140
Optional wheel (2-wheel drive)	100	140

CHAPTER TWELVE

BRAKES

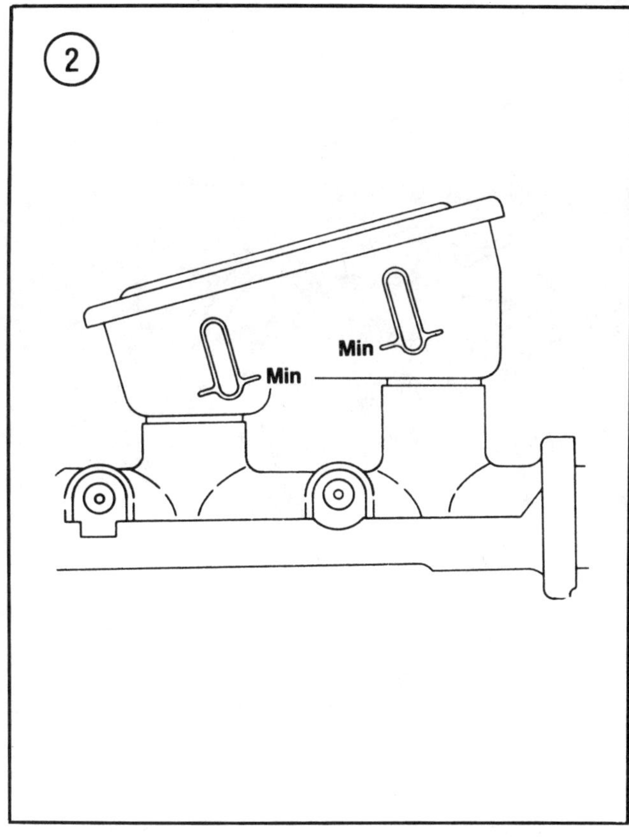

Front disc brakes and self-adjusting rear drum brakes are standard on all models. All vehicles use a dual hydraulic brake system with 2 independent circuits. See **Figure 1** (typical). A failure in one circuit leaves the other circuit intact and functional. One circuit operates the front brakes and the other circuit operates the rear brakes. Failure of one of the brake circuits will normally be indicated by the instrument panel brake warning light turning on. However, if the light is burned out or the wiring is faulty, the first indication of a brake failure may occur when the brakes are applied, requiring much more pedal pressure than normal.

Rear drum brakes are the single anchor, duo-servo design.

A dual reservoir master cylinder (**Figure 2**) is used, with the smaller front reservoir connected to the rear drum brakes. The larger rear reservoir is connected to the front disc brakes.

A combination valve is bracket-mounted to the master cylinder (**Figure 3**) and contains metering and proportioning sections. The pressure differential warning switch in the combination valve compares front and rear brake pressure. If a pressure loss occurs in either brake system, the instrument panel warning light comes on to alert

1

TYPICAL DISC/DRUM BRAKE SYSTEM
Rear wheel cylinder
Master cylinder
Rear brake hose
Combination valve
Front brake hose
Front brake caliper

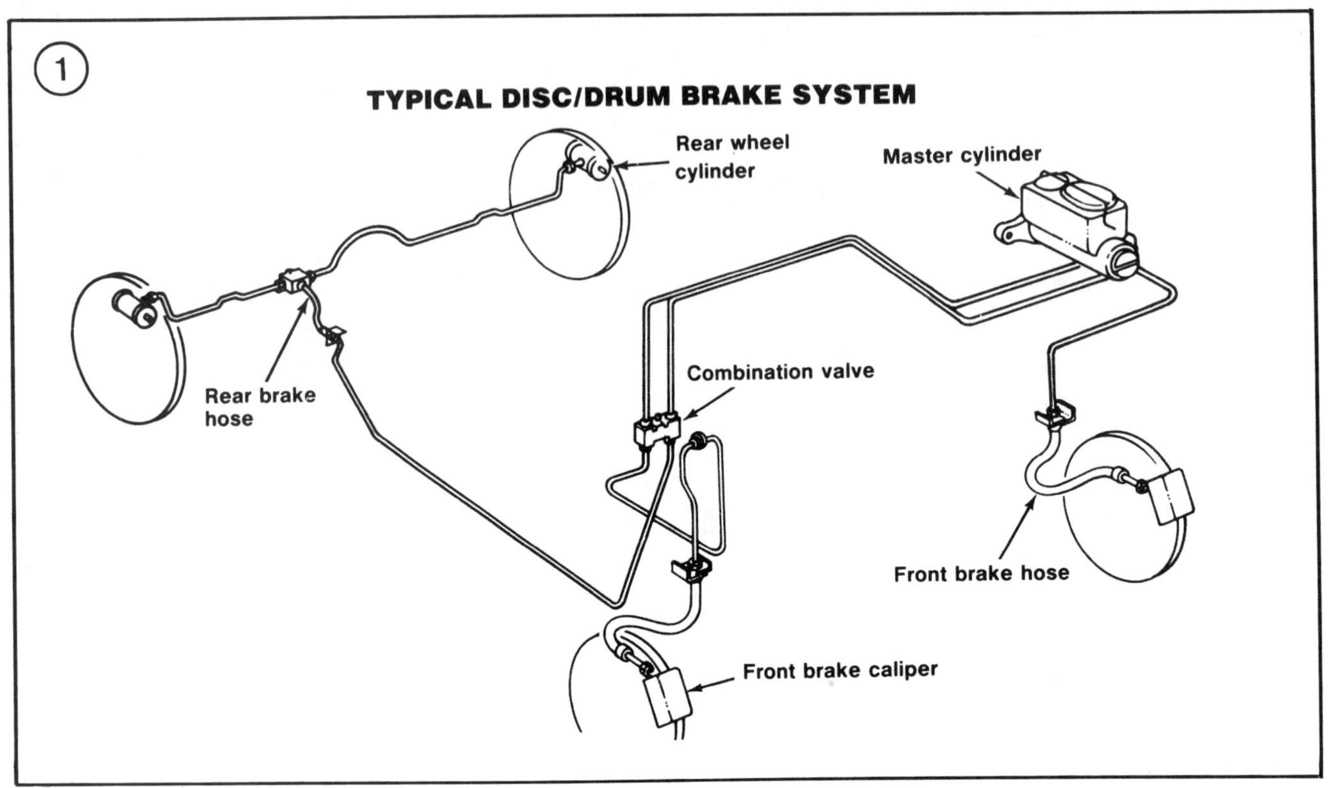

3

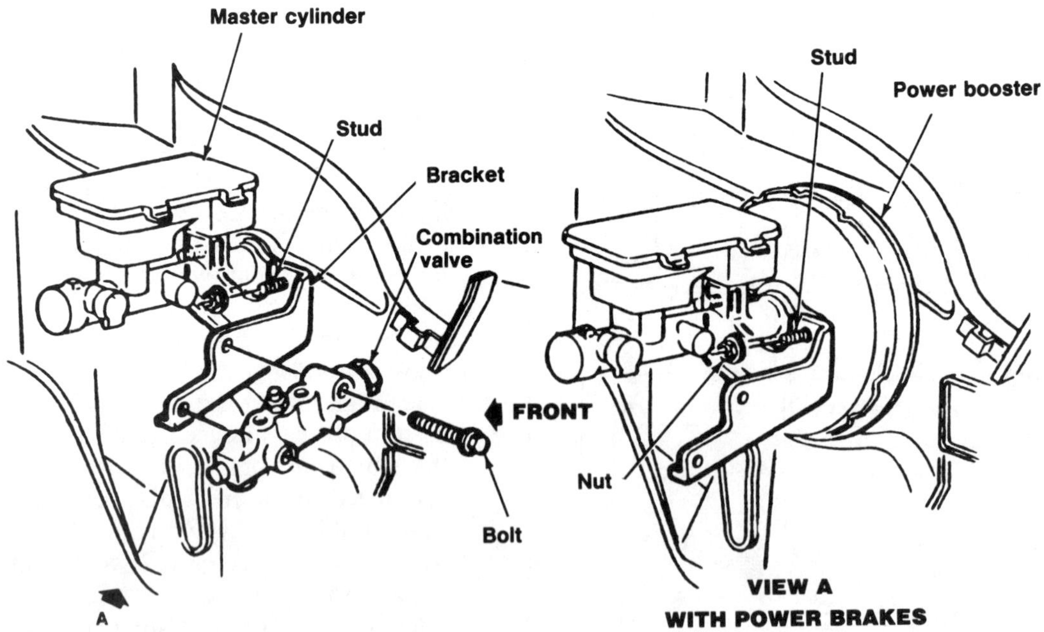

Master cylinder
Stud
Bracket
Combination valve
FRONT
Bolt
A
Stud
Power booster
Nut
VIEW A
WITH POWER BRAKES

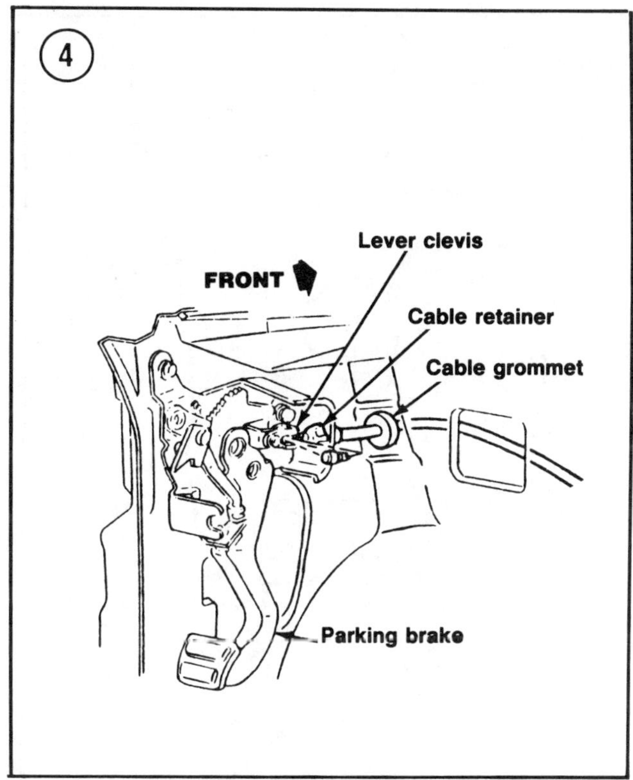

the driver. The light shuts off when the system is serviced, bled and the brake pedal depressed to center the piston.

The proportioning section of the valve balances braking pressure between the front and rear brakes to minimize rear wheel skidding during hard braking.

An optional power brake booster utilizes engine intake manifold vacuum (gasoline engine) or vacuum from a belt-driven pump and atmospheric pressure for its power.

A ratchet-type foot-operated parking brake lever is mounted at the left side of the cab (**Figure 4**) and is connected to the rear wheel brakes through a series of cables underneath the floor pan.

Tightening torques are provided in **Table 1** at the end of the chapter.

FRONT DISC BRAKES

The front disc brake assembly uses a single piston Delco pin slider caliper. The caliper is located on abutment surfaces machined on the leading and trailing edges of the caliper anchor bracket. No return spring is used in the caliper piston bore. Lining wear is compensated for by increased piston extension and the lateral sliding motion of the caliper.

Before replacing disc brake pads, remove the master cylinder cover and use a large syringe to remove and discard about 50 percent of the fluid from the rear reservoir. This wil prevent the master cylinder from overflowing when the caliper piston is compressed for reinstallation. *Do not drain the entire reservoir* or air will enter the system. Recheck the reservoir when the pads have been reinstalled and top up as required with fresh DOT 3 or DOT 4 brake fluid. If no hydraulic line is opened, it should not be necessary to bleed the brake system after pad replacement.

Pad Inspection

An integral spring clip on the front disc brake pads serves as an audible wear indicator. As lining wear reaches the point where replacement is required, the clip touches the rotor and produces a warning sound. See **Figure 5**.

1. Set the parking brake. Place the transmission in 1st gear (manual) or PARK (automatic).
2. Loosen the front wheel lug nuts.
3. Raise the front of the vehicle with a jack and place it on jackstands.

4. Remove the front wheel/tire assemblies.
5. Visually check the thickness of the inboard lining through the inspection hole in the center of the caliper. Check the thickness of the lining at both ends of the outboard pads. See **Figure 6**.
6. If the lining is worn to within 1/32 in. of the pad on bonded linings or to within 1/32 in. of the rivet heads on riveted linings, replace the pads as a set on both front wheels. See **Figure 7**.
7. Install the wheel/tire assemblies. Install the lug nuts finger-tight, then remove the jackstands and lower the vehicle to the ground.
8. Tighten the wheel lug nuts to specifications (**Table 1**) in an alternating pattern.

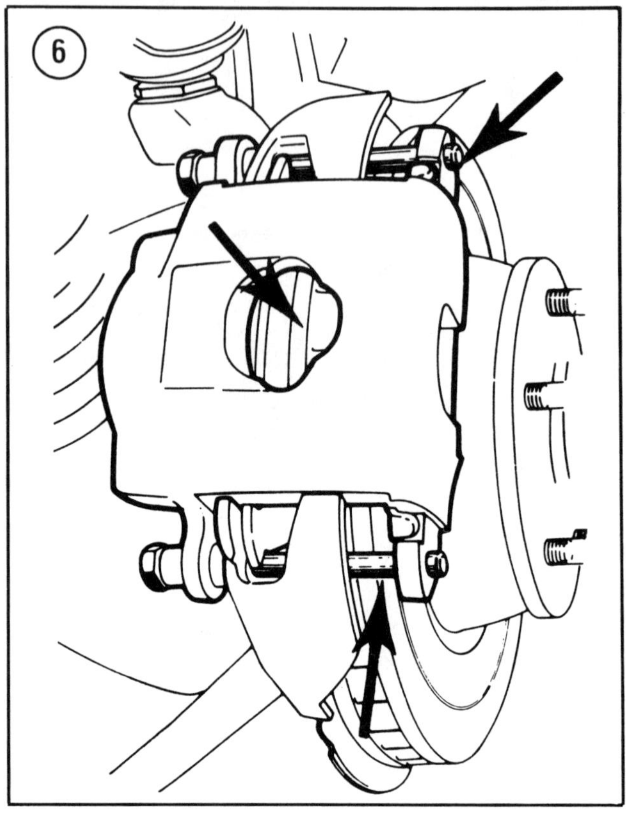

Pad Replacement

1. Set the parking brake. Place the transmission in 1st gear (manual) or PARK (automatic).
2. Loosen the front wheel lug nuts.
3. Remove the master cylinder cover and use a large syringe to remove about half the brake fluid in the rear reservoir.

WARNING
Discard this brake fluid. Do not reuse.

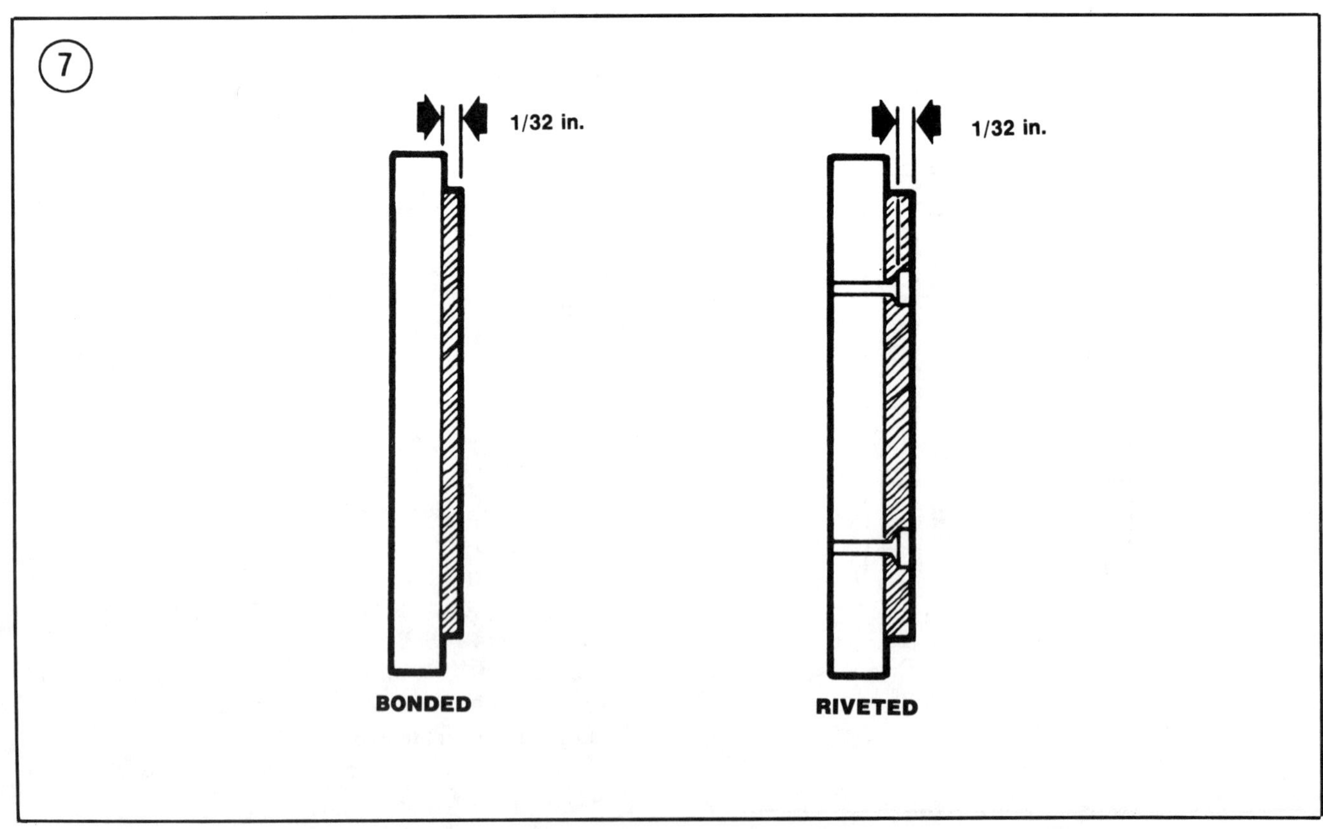

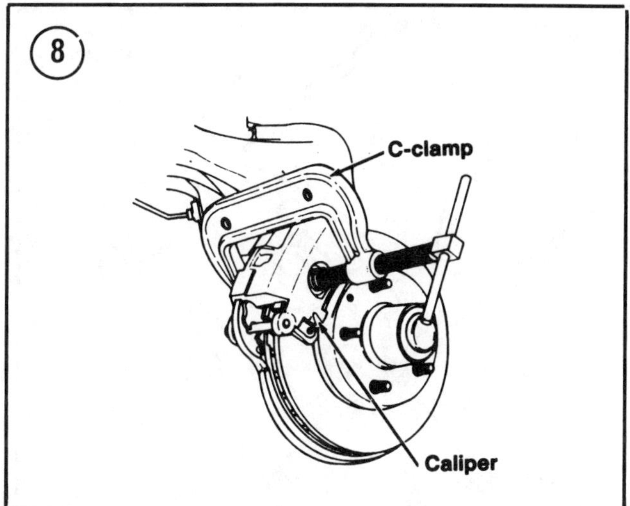

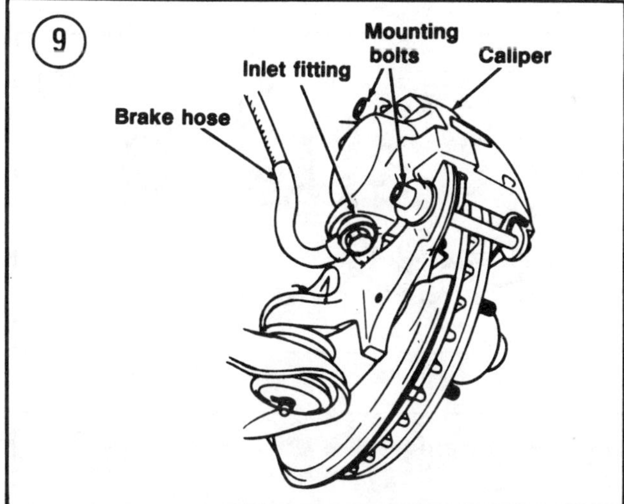

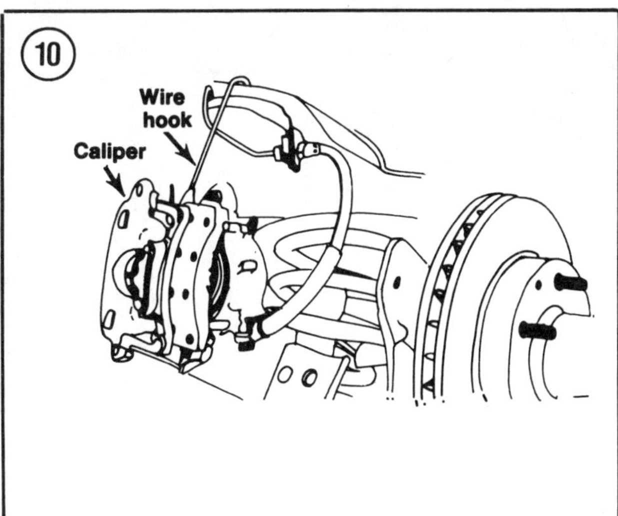

4. Raise the front of the vehicle with a jack and place it on jackstands.
5. Remove the front wheel/tire assemblies.
6. Install a C-clamp as shown in **Figure 8** and tighten until the piston bottoms in the bore.
7. Remove the C-clamp. Remove the 2 Allen head mounting bolts (**Figure 9**).

WARNING
If the bolts are corroded, discard and install new ones when the caliper is reinstalled.

8. Remove the caliper with an upward rotating motion. Suspend it from the coil spring with a wire hook to prevent stressing the brake hose. See **Figure 10**.
9. Remove the pads from the caliper.
10. Remove the sleeves from the caliper bolt holes. Remove the bushings from the bolt hole grooves. See **Figure 11**.
11. Inspect the pads. Light surface dirt, oil or grease stains may be sanded off. If oil or grease has penetrated the surface, replace the pads. Since brake fluid will ruin the friction material, pads must be replaced if any brake fluid has touched them.

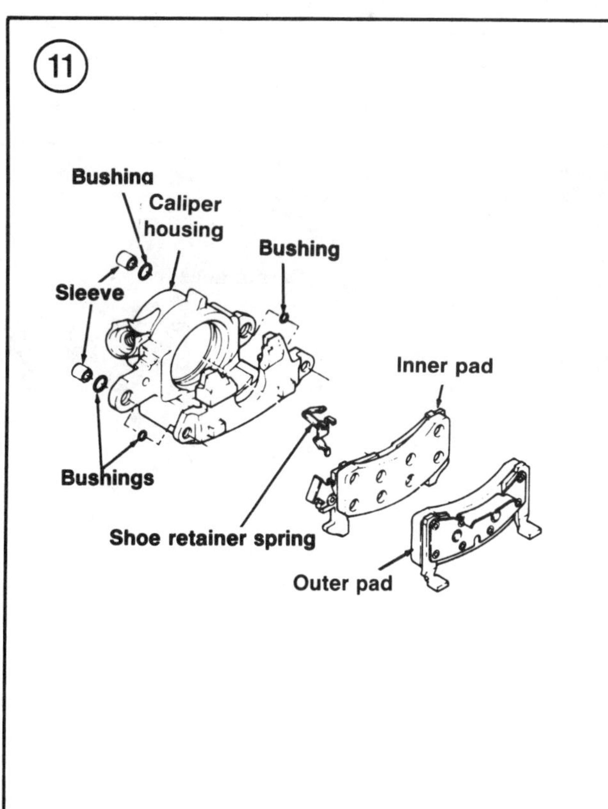

12. Check the caliper piston seal and boot area for brake fluid leaks. If brake fluid has leaked from the caliper housing, replace the caliper. If the leak appears to come from the seal area, rebuild the caliper as described in this chapter.
13. Inspect the brake rotor as described in this chapter.
14. Lubricate new sleeves and rubber bushings, the caliper bushing grooves and the end of the mounting bolts with Delco Moraine Silicone Lubricant or equivalent.
15. Install the bushings in the caliper bolt hole grooves. Install the sleeves in the bolt holes until their ends are flush with the inside machined surface of the lugs. See **Figure 12**.
16. Install the retainer spring on the inner pad (**Figure 13**) with a rotating motion.
17. Install the inner pad carefully (**Figure 14**). If the inner pad retainer clip is bent during installation, the brakes may rattle.
18. Install the outer pad in the caliper.
19. Install the caliper over the brake rotor with a rotating motion, holding the outer pad against the rotor braking surface to prevent pinching the piston boot. Align the holes in the caliper lugs with the holes in the caliper mounting bracket.
20. Insert the mounting bolts through the sleeves in the inboard mounting lugs and make sure the bolts pass under the ears on the inboard brake pad

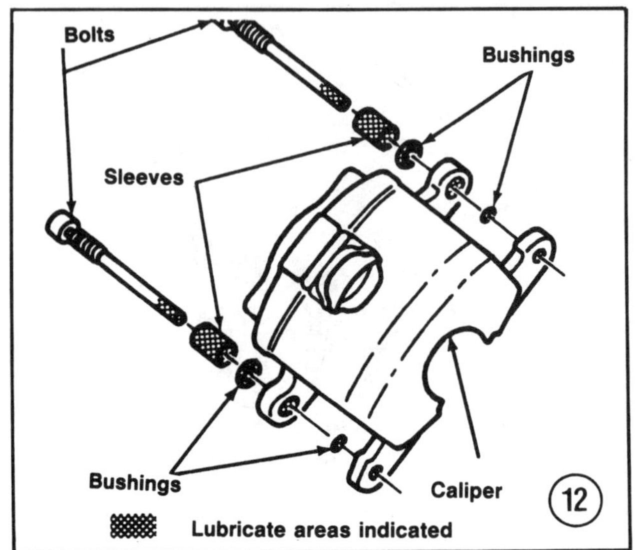

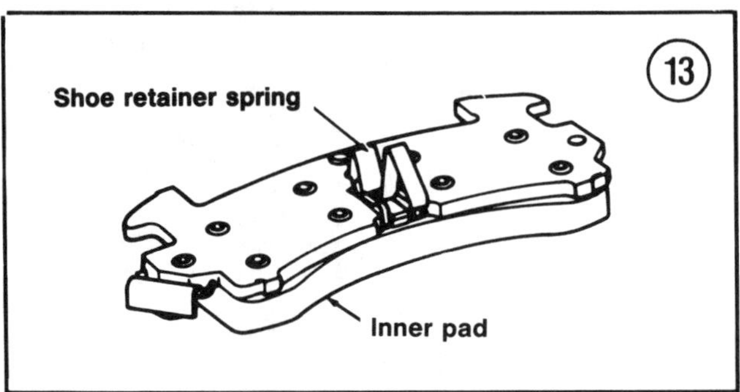

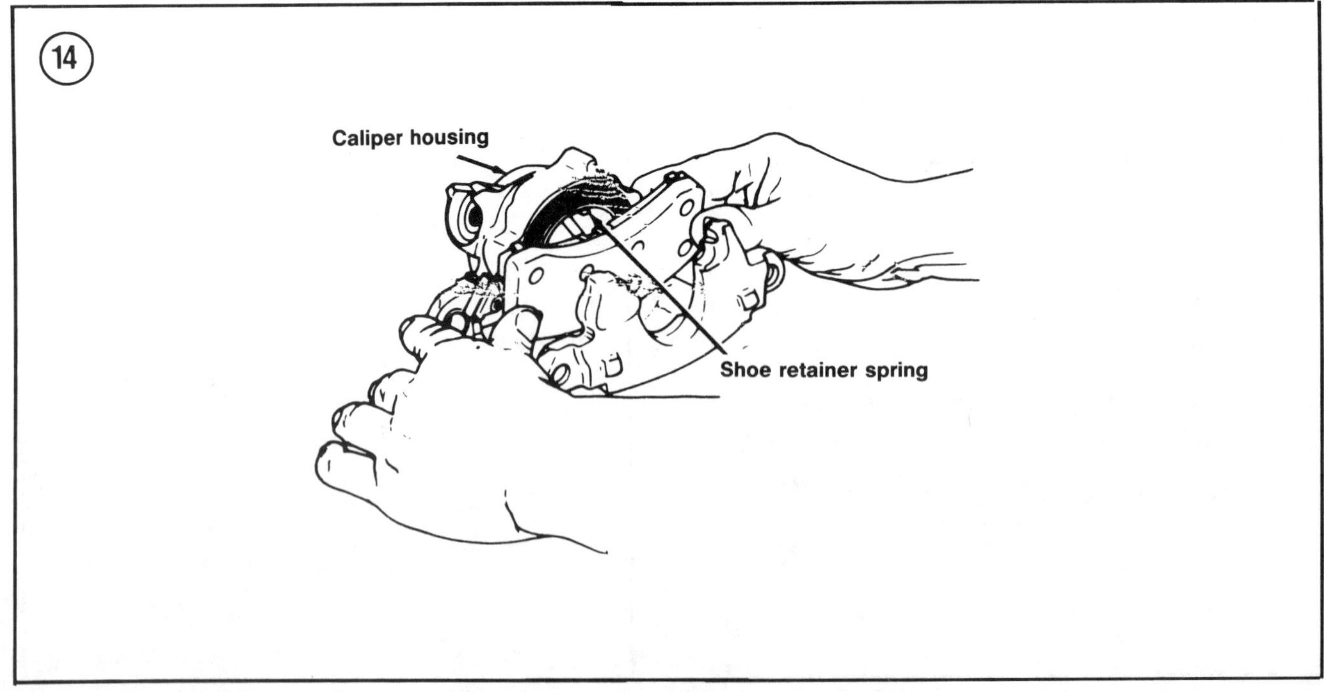

15

Note end of bolt passes under retaining ear

(**Figure 15**). Guide the bolts through to engage the holes in the outboard shoe and the outboard lugs on the caliper. Tighten bolts to specifications (**Table 1**).

21. Use a pair of channel lock pliers to tightly cinch the outer pad ears to the caliper. See **Figure 16**.
22. Install the wheel/tire assemblies. Install the lug nuts finger-tight, then remove the jackstands and lower the vehicle to the ground.
23. Tighten the wheel lug nuts to specifications (**Table 1**) in an alternating pattern.

WARNING
Do not use brake fluid from a previously opened container in Step 24. Brake fluid absorbs moisture from the air and moisture in the hydraulic lines can result in erratic or slow braking.

24. Fill the master cylinder to within 1/4 in. of the divider in the reservoir. Use fresh DOT 3 or DOT 4 brake fluid from an unopened container.
25. Install the reservoir cover and check for leaks around the caliper and hoses.
26. Depress the brake pedal several times to position the caliper and pads.
27. Check for firm pedal pressure. Road test the vehicle to make sure the brakes operate properly.

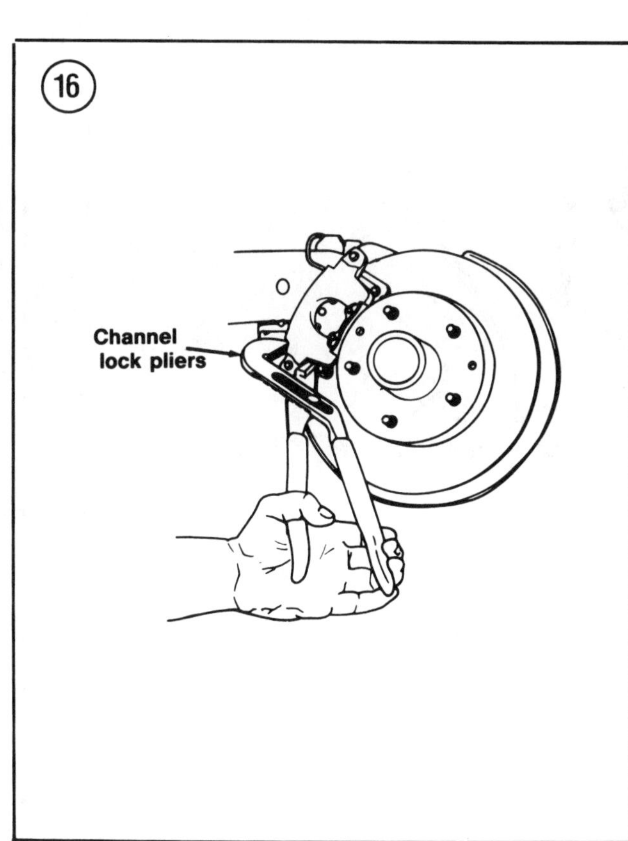

Caliper Removal

1. Perform Steps 1-7 of *Pad Replacement* in this chapter.
2. Have an assistant carefully depress the brake pedal. This should hydraulically push the piston from the caliper bore. Remove the piston.
3. Disconnect the brake hose from the caliper at the inlet fitting (**Figure 9**) and discard the copper washers. Plug the caliper inlet port and hose outlet to prevent dirt from entering.
4. Mark the left and right calipers for identification if both are removed.

Caliper Overhaul

Refer to **Figure 17** for this procedure.

1. Drain and discard any fluid in the caliper.
2. Remove the pads from the caliper. Remove the sleeves from the caliper bolt holes. Remove the bushings from the bolt hole grooves.

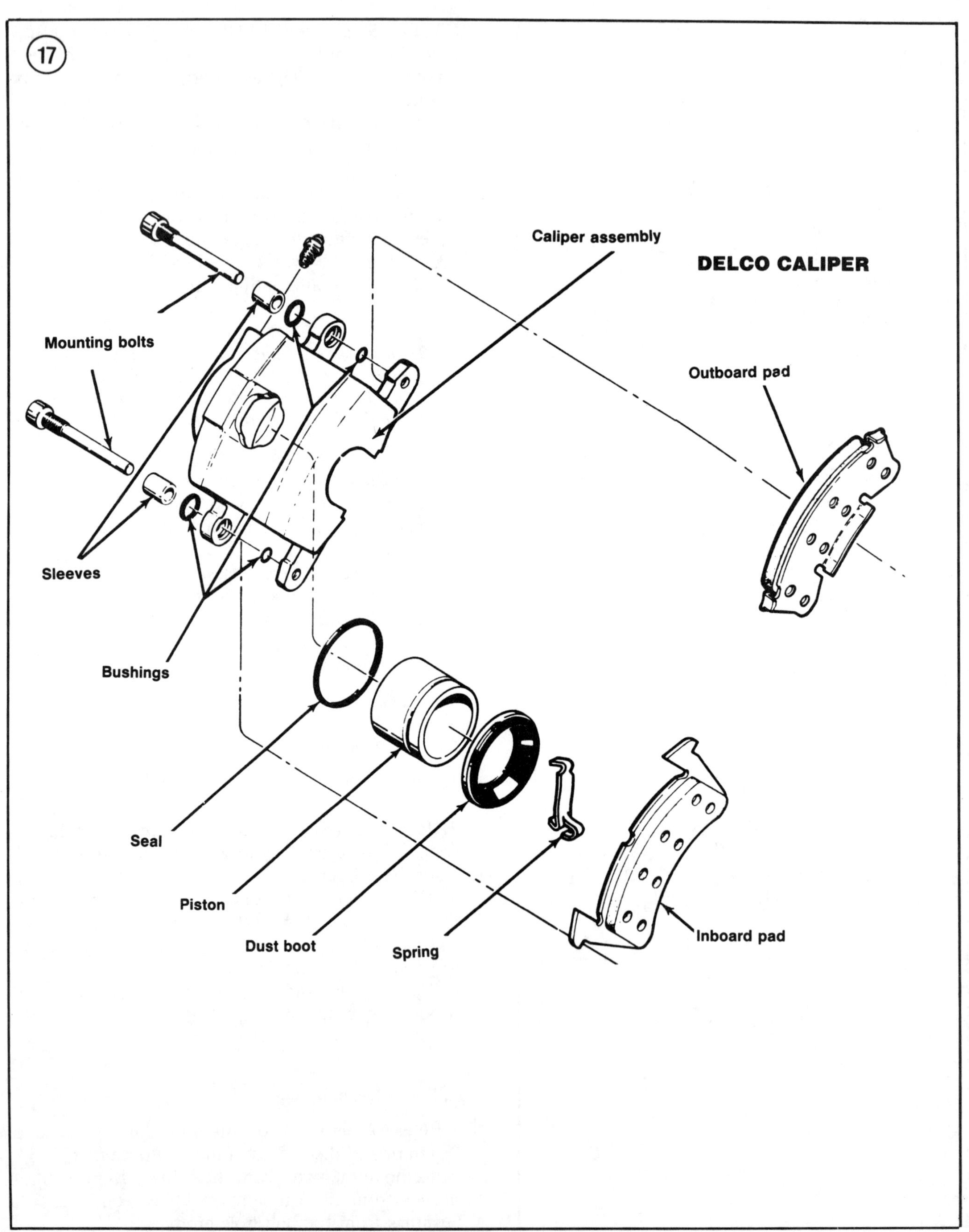
17
Caliper assembly
DELCO CALIPER
Mounting bolts
Outboard pad
Sleeves
Bushings
Seal
Piston
Dust boot
Spring
Inboard pad

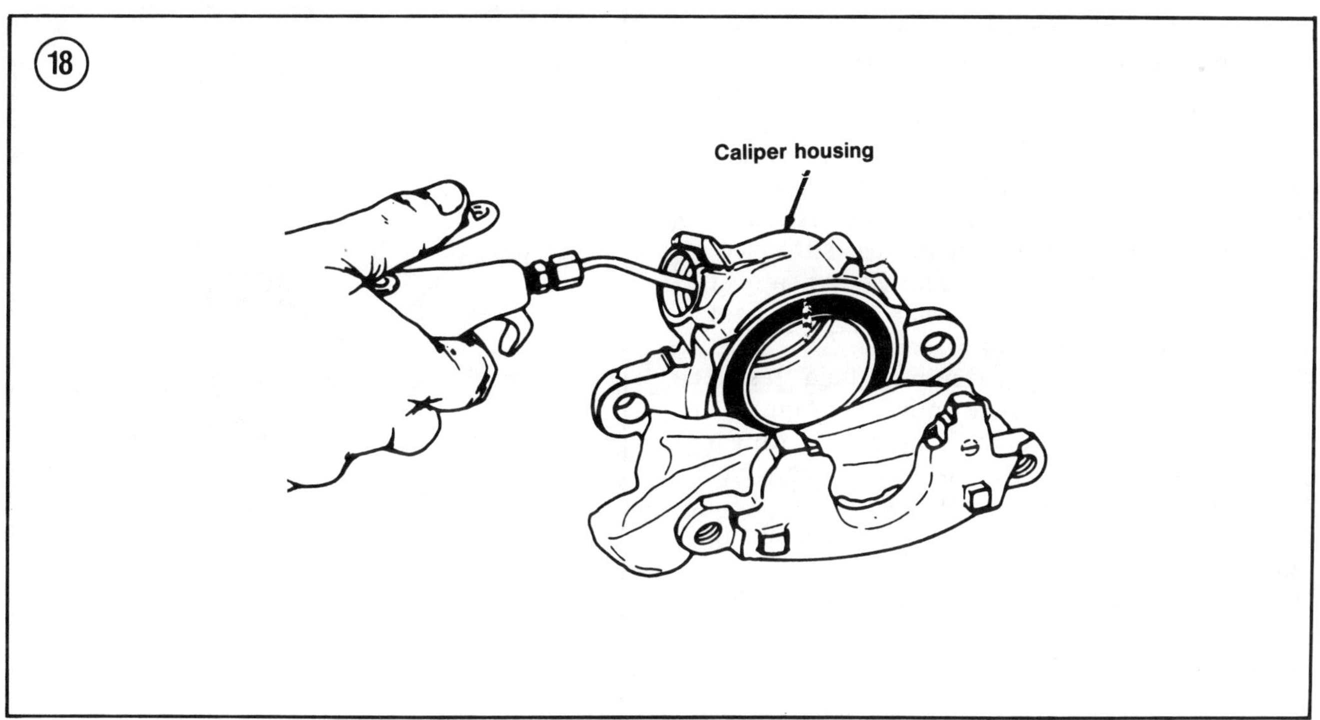

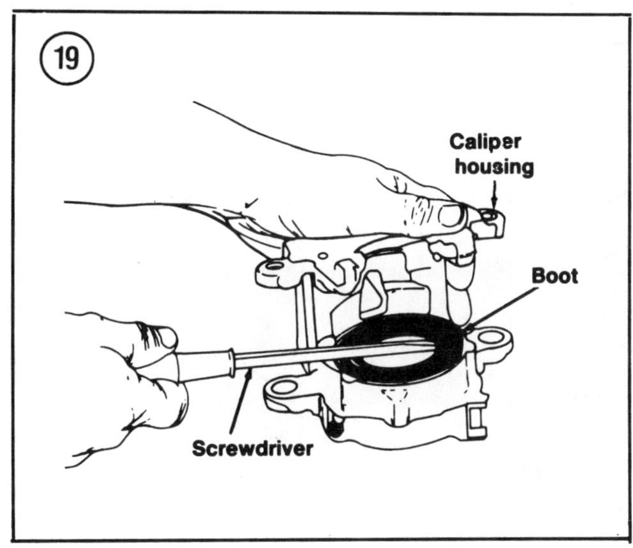

3. Mount the caliper in a vise with protective jaws. If protective jaws are not available, wrap the caliper in shop cloths.

WARNING
Do not attempt to remove the piston in Step 4 by catching it with your fingers or by applying high air pressure. The piston can be ejected with enough force to cause serious personal injury and damage to the piston.

4. If the piston was not removed hydraulically during caliper removal, pad the inside of the caliper with shop cloths and direct a stream of low-pressure compressed air into the caliper inlet hole **(Figure 18)** to remove the piston.
5. If the piston is cocked or seized in its bore and does not come out of its bore far enough for removal in Step 4, rap the edge of the piston sharply with a brass hammer, then reapply air pressure as in Step 4 and remove the piston.
6. Remove and discard the caliper dust boot **(Figure 19)**.

NOTE
Use a plastic or wooden dowel for seal removal in Step 7. Do not pry seal out with a screwdriver or other metal tool. This can scratch the piston bore or burr the seal groove edge.

7. Remove and discard the piston seal. Remove the bleed screw.
8. Clean all rust and corrosion from the caliper boot groove and the machined surfaces of the caliper housing and steering knuckle mount with a wire brush.
9. Clean the caliper housing and piston with rubbing alcohol or clean brake fluid. Make sure all grooves and passages are clean, then blow dry with compressed air.

10. Inspect the caliper bore and piston for pitting or scoring. Replace the piston if pitted or scored. Replace the caliper if bore corrosion cannot be removed with crocus cloth.
11. Coat a new piston seal with clean brake fluid and install it in the caliper bore groove. Use clean fingers to work the seal into the groove; make sure the seal is properly seated and not twisted or rolled.
12. Coat the cylinder bore and lubricate a new dust boot with clean brake fluid. Install the dust boot over the piston as shown in **Figure 20**.
13. Coat the piston with clean brake fluid. Install the piston in the caliper bore until it bottoms.
14. Drive the boot into the caliper bore with a boot installer tool (part No. J-26267 or part No. J-22904) as shown in **Figure 21**.
15. Install the bleed screw and tighten to specifications (**Table 1**).
16. Install the caliper as described in this chapter.

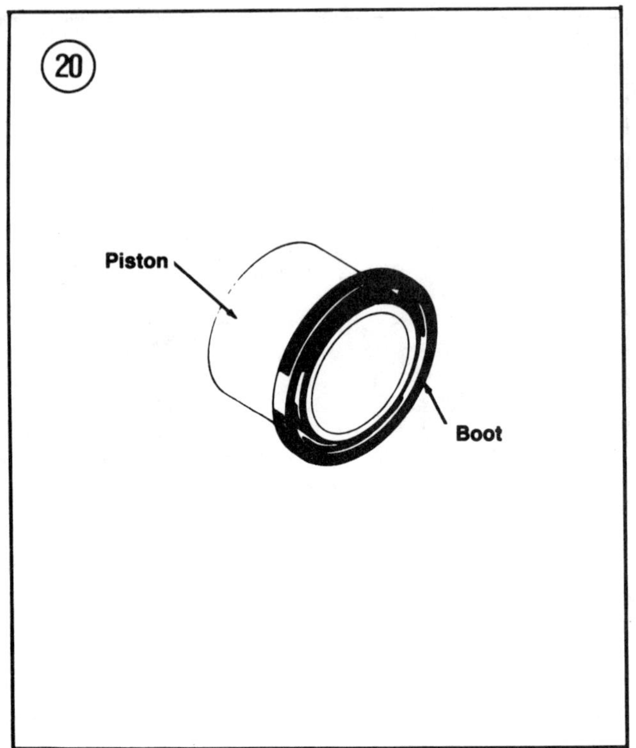

Caliper Installation

1. Install the caliper over the brake rotor with a rotating motion, holding the outer pad against the

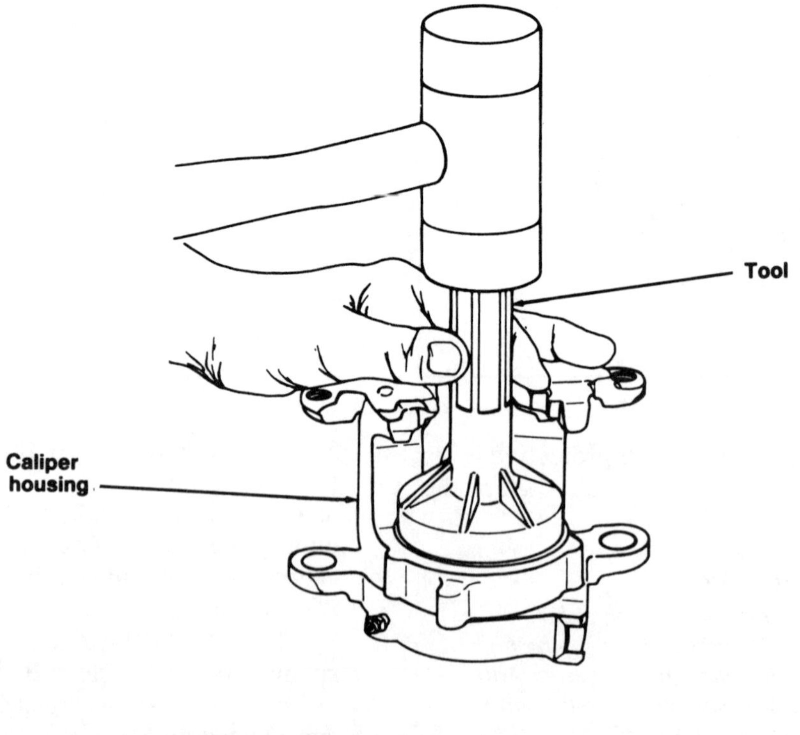

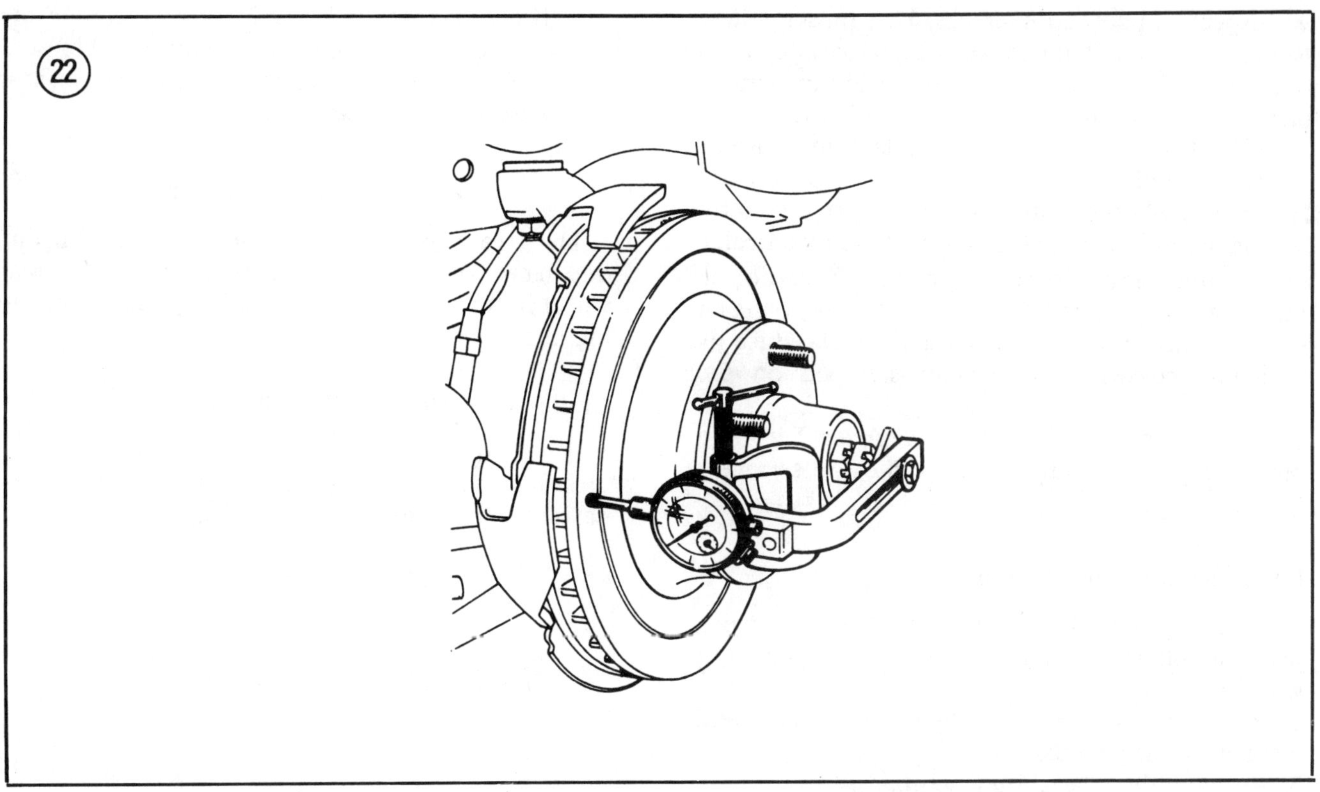

rotor braking surface to prevent pinching the piston boot. Align the holes in the caliper lugs with the holes in the caliper mounting bracket.

2. Insert the mounting bolts through the sleeves in the inboard mounting lugs and make sure the bolts pass under the ears on the inboard brake pad (**Figure 15**). Guide the bolts through to engage the holes in the outboard shoe and the outboard lugs on the caliper. Tighten bolts to specifications (**Table 1**).
3. Install the brake hose to the inlet fitting with new copper washers.
4. Perform Steps 21-27 of *Pad Replacement* in this chapter to complete installation.

Rotor Inspection

1. Securely block both front wheels so the truck will not roll in either direction. Loosen the front wheel lug nuts.
2. Raise the front of the vehicle with a jack and place it on jackstands.
3. Remove the wheel/tire assemblies.
4. Tighten the wheel bearings just enough to remove all bearing free play.
5. Attach a dial indicator to some part of the suspension so that the indicator stylus touches the rotor surface approximately one inch from the outer edge of the rotor. See **Figure 22**.
6. Set the dial indicator to zero, then slowly turn the brake rotor one complete revolution to check runout. Note the high and low readings on the indicator gauge. If the total between the two readings exceeds 0.004 in. (0.10 mm), have the rotor resurfaced by a dealer or replace it if the wear is excessive.

NOTE

If the rotor is resurfaced, its finished thickness should not be less than 24.84 mm. This minimum dimension is cast on the rotor.

7. Check the rotor for parallelism (thickness variation) with a micrometer at 12 equal points on the rotor. Take each reading with the micrometer positioned one inch from the edge of he rotor. If measurements vary more than 0.0005 in. (0.013 mm), resurface or replace the rotor.
8. Use the micrometer to measure the thickness of the rotor at several points around the circumference and at varying distances from the center. If the rotor measures less at any point than the minimum stamped on the rotor, replace it.

9. Inspect the rotor for cracks, rust or scratches. Replace the rotor if cracked. Light rust can be removed with crocus cloth or medium emery paper. Light scoring of the rotor which does not exceed 0.015 in. (0.38 mm) results from normal operation and does not affect brake operation. Heavy rust or deep scratches should be removed by resurfacing the rotor. This can be done by a dealer or machine shop. However, the rotor must not be machined more than 0.020 in. (0.508 mm) on each side. Replace the rotor if resurfacing will reduce its thickness below the minimum stamped on the rotor.
10. Adjust the wheel bearings (Chapter Ten) and reverse Steps 1-3 to return the vehicle to service.

Rotor Removal/Installation

1. Securely block both front wheels so the truck will not roll in either direction. Loosen the front wheel lug nuts.
2. Raise the front of the vehicle with a jack and place it on jackstands.
3. Remove the wheel/tire assemblies.
4. Remove the brake caliper as described in this chapter but do not disconnect the brake hose. Suspend the caliper from the suspension with a length of wire to prevent stressing the brake hose.

CAUTION
Do not damage or deform the hub grease cap by removing it with pliers in Step 5. Work carefully with a screwdriver and pry the cover off.

5. 2-wheel drive:
   a. Remove the hub grease cap.
   b. Remove and discard the cotter pin.
   c. Remove the wheel bearing nut.
   d. Grasp the hub and rotor assembly in both hands and pull it off the spindle. The outer wheel bearing and washer will slide out when the hub is removed. The inner wheel bearing and grease seal will remain in the hub. See **Figure 23**.
6. 4-wheel drive—Grasp the rotor in both hands and pull it off the spindle. See **Figure 24**.
7. 2-wheel drive:
   a. Mark rotor to hub position, then unbolt the rotor and hub assembly.
   b. Remove and discard the hub grease seal.
8. Installation is the reverse of removal, plus the following:
   a. If a new rotor is being installed, remove the protective coating with carburetor degreaser.
   b. 2-wheel drive—Adjust the wheel bearings as described in this chapter.

REAR DRUM BRAKES

The rear drum brakes are a self-adjusting duo-servo design. The drums fit over the rear wheel hub studs and are retained by the wheel/tire lug nuts.

Brake Drum Removal/Installation

If the drum and lining on one side require cleaning and dressing, this service should be carried out on the opposite side also.

WARNING
Do not inhale brake dust. It contains asbestos, which can cause lung cancer.

1. Securely block both front wheels so the truck will not roll in either direction. Set the parking brake and block the front wheels.
2. Loosen the rear wheel lug nuts.
3. Raise the rear of the vehicle with a jack and place it on jackstands.
4. Remove the wheel/tire assembly. Remove the drum.
5. If the brake drum will not come off easily, remove the access hole plug from the support plate. Insert a narrow screwdriver through the adjusting hole, disengage and hold the adjusting lever away from the adjusting screw. Back off the screw with a brake adjusting tool. Be careful not to damage notches in the adjusting screw; otherwise, the self-adjusting mechanism will not function properly. If adjustment is backed off, make sure adjuster lever seats properly in the shoe web.
6. If a new drum is being installed, remove the protective coating with carburetor degreaser.
7. Install the brake drum. Install the wheel/tire assembly. Install the wheel lug nuts finger-tight.
8. Lower the vehicle to the ground and tighten the lug nuts to specifications (**Table 1**) in an alternating pattern.
9. If brake adjustment was backed off to remove the drum, adjust the brakes as described in this chapter.

23

Steering knuckle
Shield
Gasket
Seal
Race
Inner bearing
Disc
Washer
Cotter pin
Race
Bearing
Nut
Cap

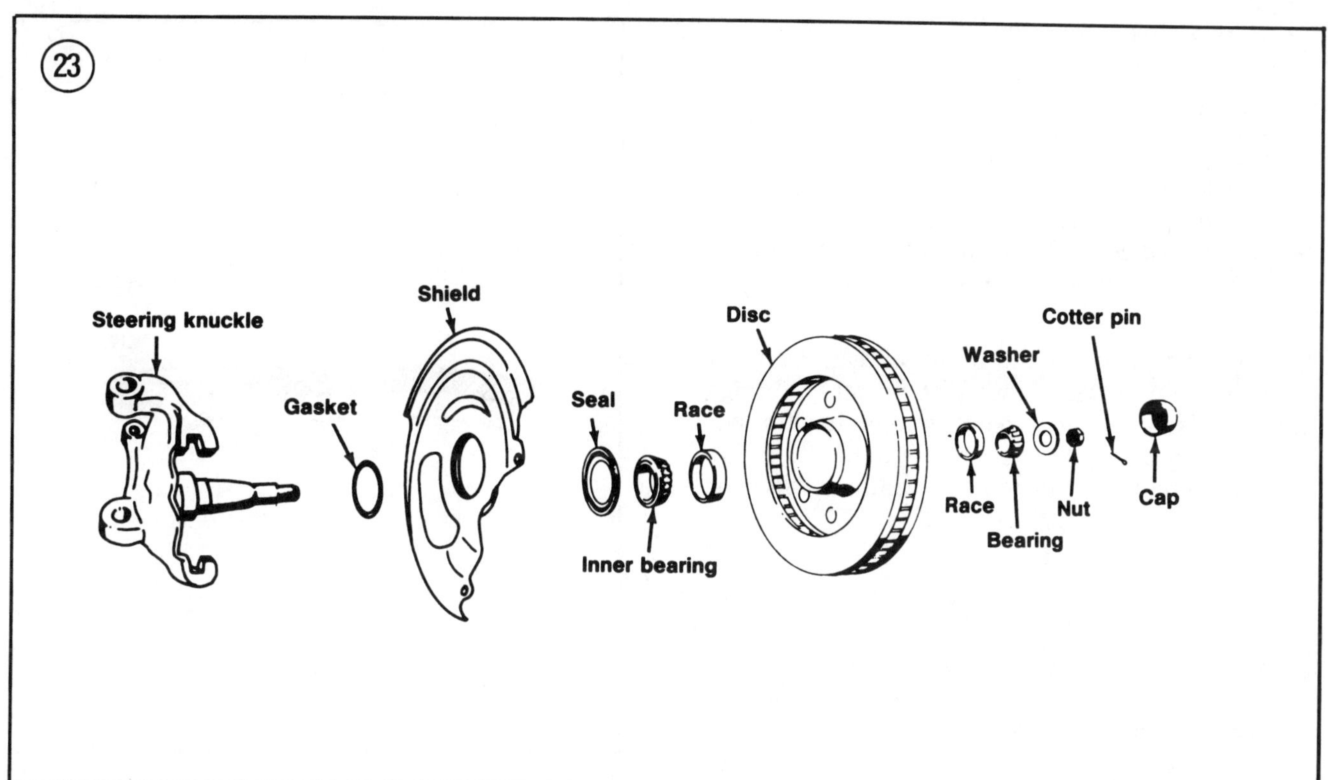

24

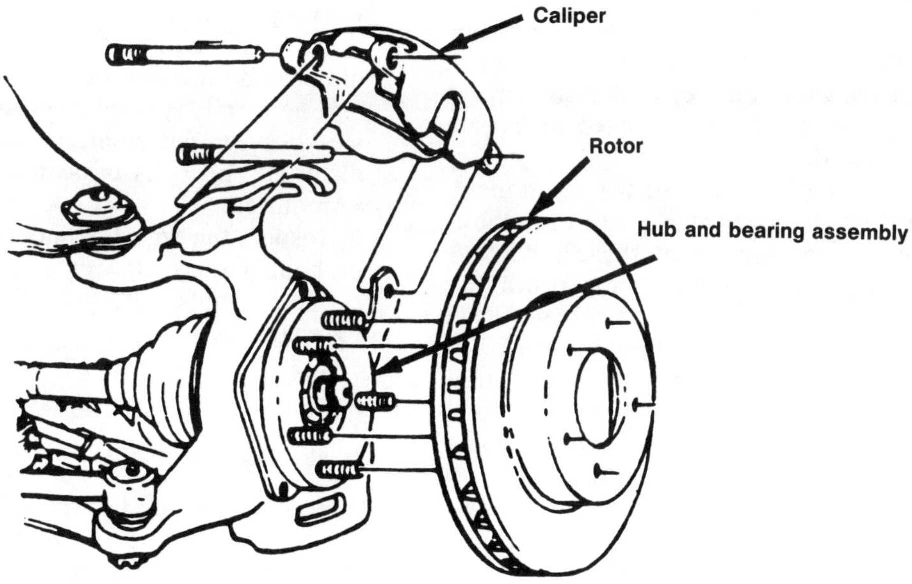

Caliper
Rotor
Hub and bearing assembly

Drum and Shoe Inspection

WARNING

Do not clean brake drum or shoe assembly with compressed air in Step 1. Brake linings contain asbestos and the dust can be hazardous to your health. If the drum or shoe assembly is extremely dirty, clean with a vacuum cleaner or use an old paint brush and wear a painter's mask over your nose and mouth.

1. Wipe the inside of the drum with a clean dry cloth to remove any sand, dirt or other foreign matter. Clean all other parts (except the linings) with aerosol brake cleaner or new brake fluid. Do not use gasoline, kerosene or solvent as a cleaning agent.

CAUTION

If cleaning with brake fluid, keep it off the lining surfaces. Brake fluid will ruin the linings and they will have to be replaced.

2. Check drum for visible scoring, excessive or uneven wear, corrosion or glazed heat spots. Any scoring sufficiently deep to snag a fingernail is reason enough for having the drums turned and the linings replaced. Minor scratches or scoring can be removed with fine emery cloth. If this is done, clean thoroughly with compressed air to remove any abrasive. If heat spots (blue-tinted areas) are noted, replace the drum.
3. If you have precision measuring equipment, measure the drum for wear and out-of-roundness. If you do not have the equipment, this can be done by a dealer or machine shop. If the drum has surface damage or runout exceeds 0.007 in. (0.178 mm), have it resurfaced on a lathe by a dealer or machine shop. However, the inside diameter after resurfacing must not exceed the maximum wear specification cast in the drum. If the drum would have to be cut larger than this to correct it, it must be replaced.
4. Inspect the lining material on the brake shoes. Make sure it is not cracked, unevenly worn or separated from the shoes. Dirt and foreign particles that are imbedded in the lining can often be removed with a wire brush, but lining replacement is recommended instead. Light surface oil or grease stains may be sanded off. If oil or grease has soaked beneath the surface, replace the shoes. Since brake fluid will ruin the linings, the shoes must be replaced if brake fluid has touched them. Shoes must also be replaced if the lining material has worn to within 1/32 in. of a rivet (riveted lining) or the shoe (bonded lining). **Figure 25** shows the wear dimension on riveted shoes.

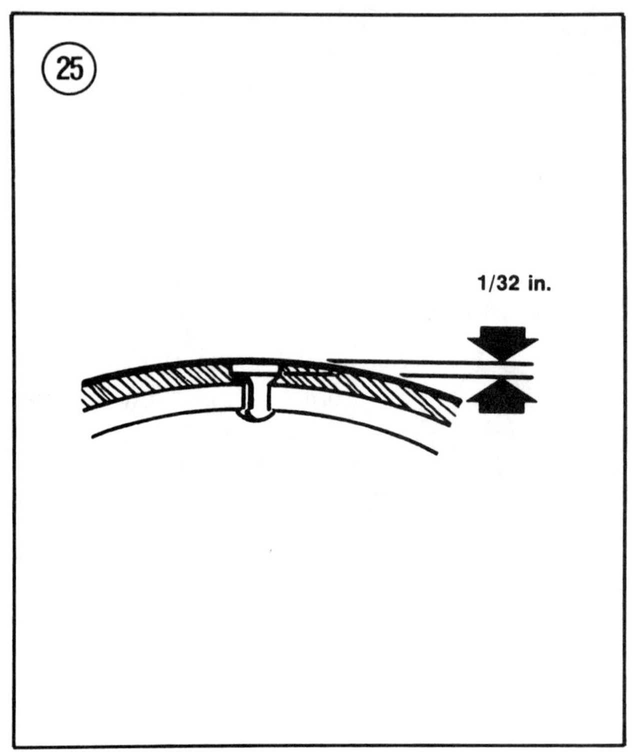

5. Check all springs for signs of overheating, weakness or deformation (paint discoloration or distorted end coils indicate overheating). Replace as required.
6. Inspect the wheel cylinders for signs of leakage or boot damage. If wet areas are found near the cylinder boots, the wheel cylinder should be overhauled.

Brake Disassembly

Brakes should be reconditioned at least in pairs—both front or both rear—or all 4 wheels at the same time. In addition, new linings should be arced to the contour of the drums. This is a job for a dealer or automotive brake specialist.

Refer to **Figure 26** for this procedure.

1. Remove the brake drum as described in this chapter.

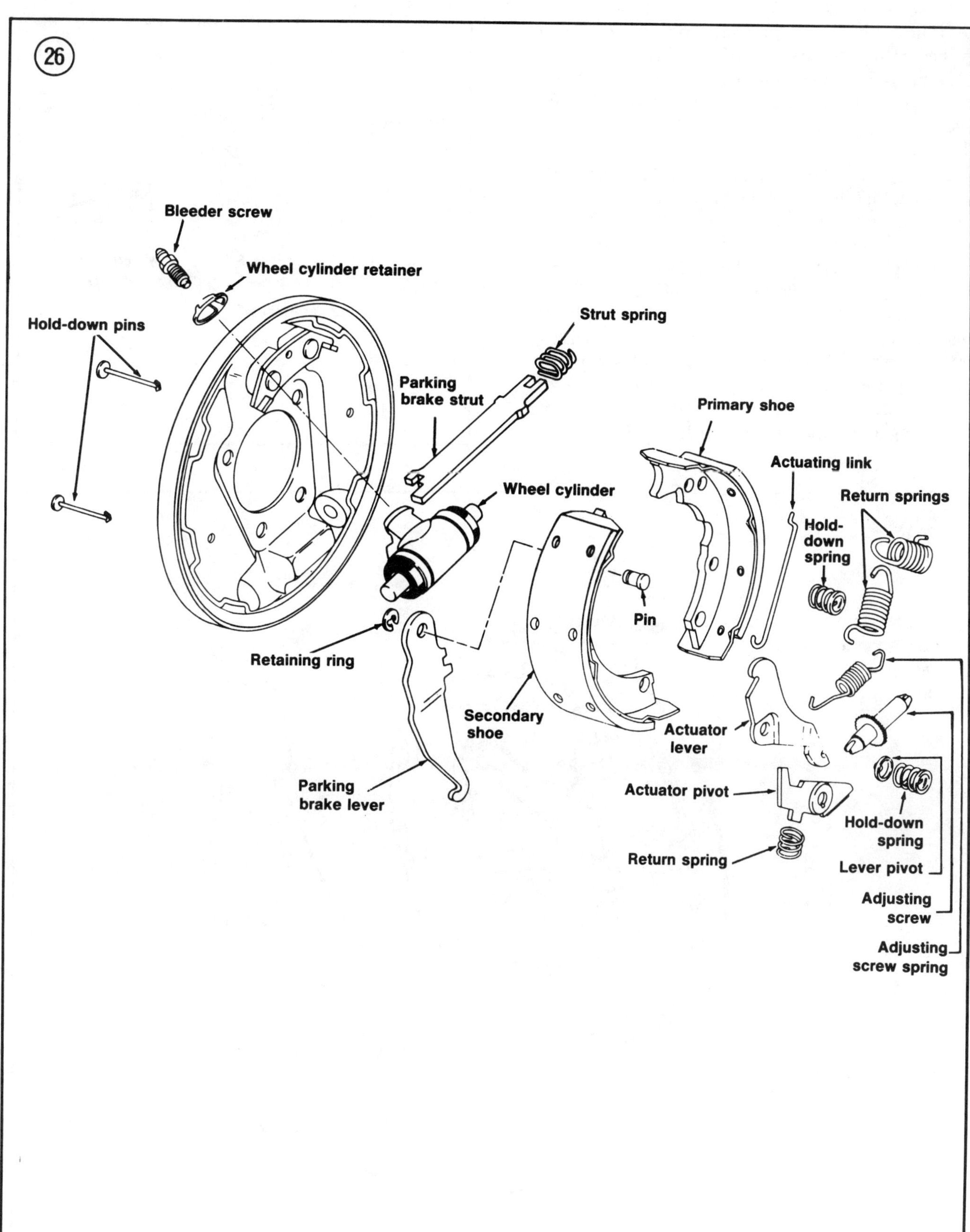
26
Bleeder screw
Wheel cylinder retainer
Hold-down pins
Strut spring
Parking brake strut
Primary shoe
Actuating link
Wheel cylinder
Return springs
Hold-down spring
Pin
Retaining ring
Secondary shoe
Actuator lever
Parking brake lever
Actuator pivot
Hold-down spring
Return spring
Lever pivot
Adjusting screw
Adjusting screw spring

2. Unhook the primary and secondary shoe return springs with a brake tool or large pliers.
3. Depress the shoe hold-down spring cups and remove from the hold-down springs along with the lever pivot. Remove the hold-down pins. See **Figure 27**.
4. Lift up on the actuator and disconnect the actuating link from the anchor pin. Remove the link, lever, pawl and return spring (**Figure 28**).
5. Spread the shoes enough to clear the wheel cylinder connecting links. Disconnect and remove the parking brake strut and spring (**Figure 29**).
6. Expand the shoes until they clear the axle flange. Disconnect the parking brake cable at the parking brake lever and remove the shoe assembly from the backing plate.
7. Note the adjuster spring position, then remove the spring and adjuster screw (**Figure 30**).

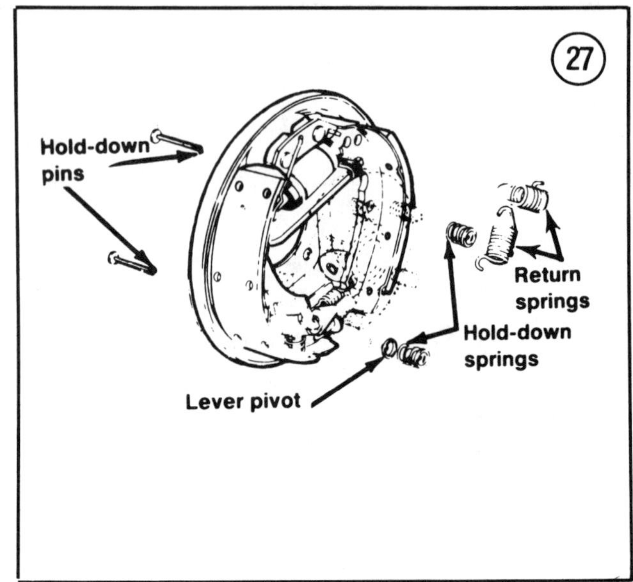

28

Shoe retainer
Actuating link
Actuator lever
Actuator pivot
Return spring

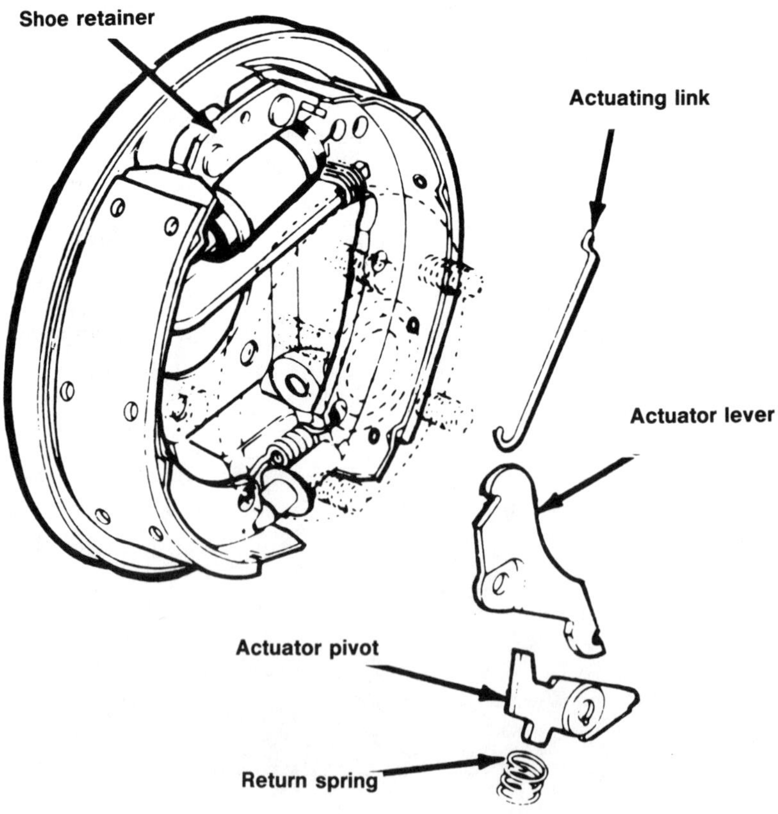

29

Strut spring
Parking brake strut

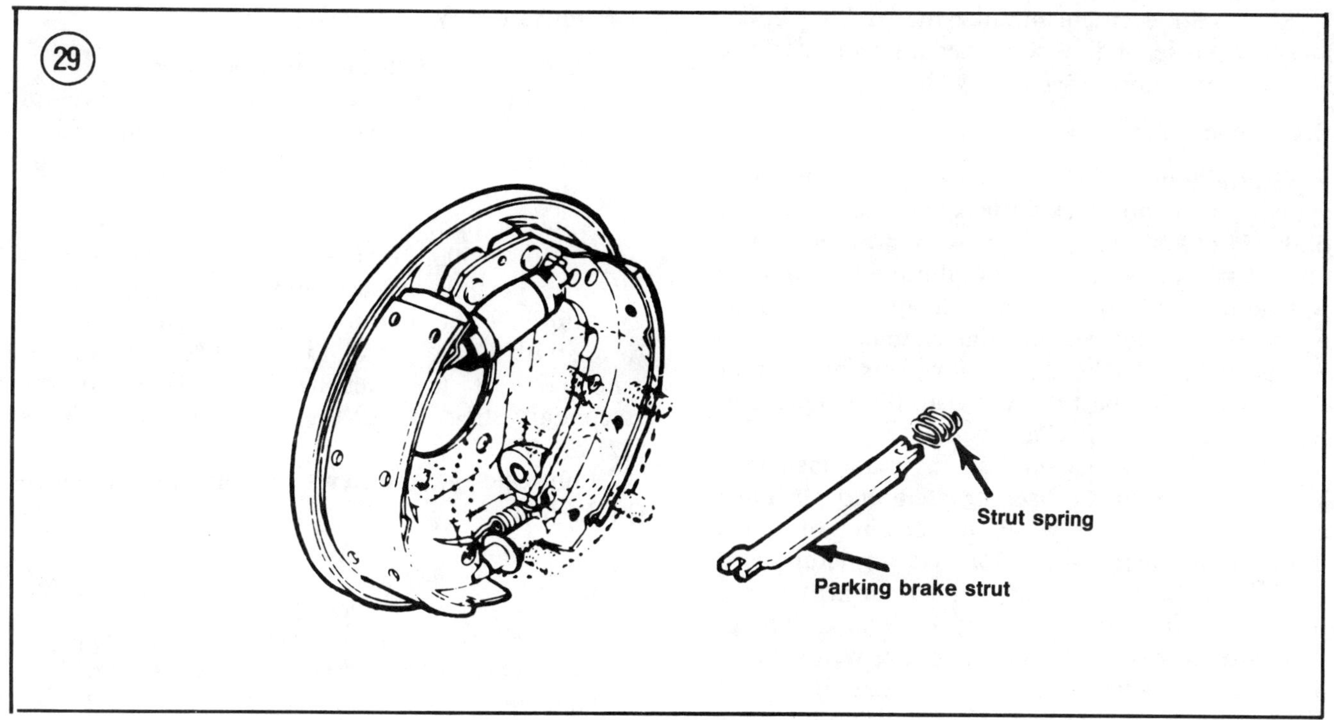

30

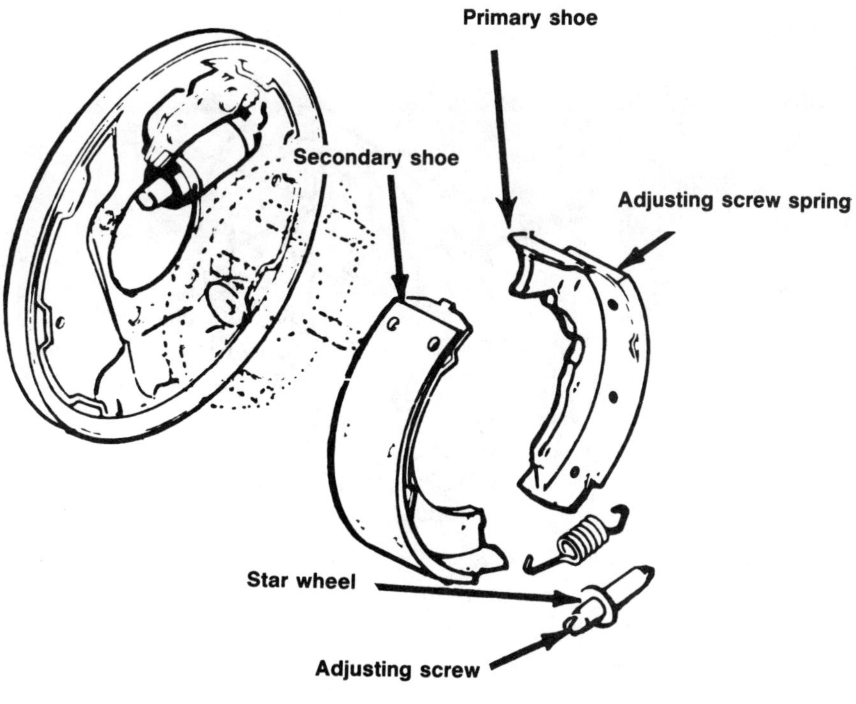

Primary shoe
Secondary shoe
Adjusting screw spring
Star wheel
Adjusting screw

8. Remove the circlip holding the parking brake lever to the secondary shoe. Separate the parking brake lever from the secondary shoe.

Brake Inspection

1. Carefully pry back the lower edge of each wheel cylinder boot and check for leakage. A slight film of brake fluid on the piston rods is normal, but if there is an excessive amount of fluid in the boots or wet stains outside the cylinder, it should be rebuilt or replaced as described in this chapter.
2. Inspect the backing plate for signs of oil that may have leaked past the axle seal. If oil is present, replace the seals. See Chapter Eleven.
3. Check and tighten the backing plate fasteners. Thoroughly clean the backing plate and all brake components. Use only rubbing alcohol or brake fluid as a cleaner—do not use mineral-based detergents. Clean the shoe contact surfaces to the bare metal with emery cloth. Make certain all loose dirt, rust, corrosion and abrasives are removed.
4. Check the adjuster screw operation. If it does not turn smoothly, disassemble, clean and lubricate it.

Brake Assembly

Refer to **Figure 26** for this procedure.
1. Check the new linings to make sure they are not nicked or burred. If they are bonded linings, check for and remove any excess bonding cement along the edges.
2. Apply a light coat of Delco Brake Lubricant (part No. 5450032) or equivalent to the support plate at the shoe contact points. See **Figure 31**.
3. Lubricate the fulcrum end of the parking brake lever with Delco Brake Lubricant (or equivalent) and connect the parking brake lever to the secondary shoe. Install the circlip retainer (**Figure 32**).
4. Lubricate the adjuster screw threads with clean brake fluid.

NOTE
Adjuster screw spring coils must not be positioned over the starwheel in Step 5. Left- and right-hand adjuster springs differ and should not be interchanged. The right-hand thread adjusting screw must go on the left support plate

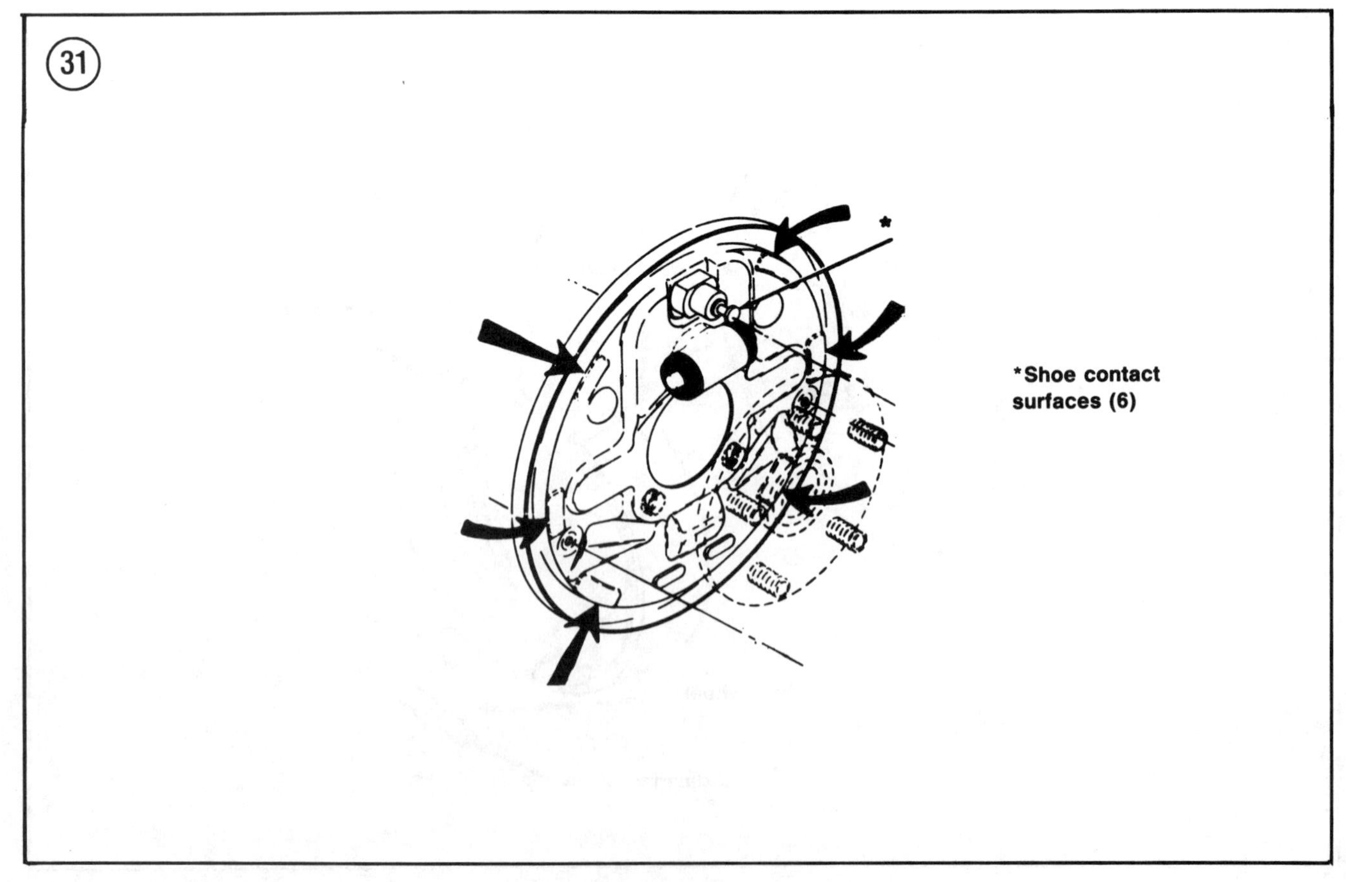

and the left-hand thread screw on the right support plate. The adjuster starwheel must face the secondary shoe and align with the access hole in the support plate.

5. Reassemble the adjuster (if disassembled for cleaning). See **Figure 33**. Turn the adjuster screw into the adjusting pivot nut to the limit of the threads, then back off 1/2 turn.
6. Position the brake shoes to the support plate. Install the adjuster screw and spring as shown in **Figure 33**.
7. Spread the shoes enough to install the parking brake strut and spring. The spring end of the strut should engage the primary shoe.
8. Install the actuator pivot, lever and return spring.

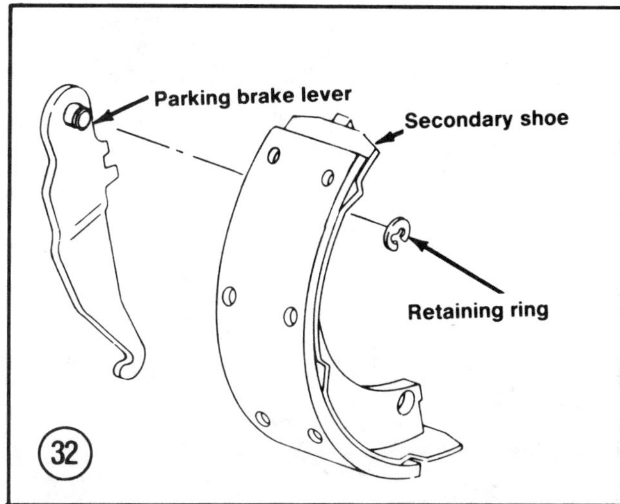

9. Install the actuator link in the shoe retainer. Lift up on the lever and connect the link and lever.
10. Insert the hold-down pins through the backing plate and shoes. Install the lever pivot on the secondary shoe. Install the hold-down spring and cup assemblies over the pins. Depress the cups with the brake tool and rotate 90°.
11. Install and connect the primary and secondary return springs.
12. Make sure that all components connected to the anchor pin are stacked flat on the pin.
13. Once both brakes on the axle have been assembled, make a preliminary adjustment. Pull the adjuster lever away from the adjusting screw starwheel just far enough to disengage it. Rotate the starwheel to expand the brakes far enough so the drum can be installed with a slight drag, then back the starwheel off 1 1/4 turns to slightly retract the shoes.
14. If the adjuster does not operate properly, check the following points:
    a. Make sure the cable ends are not pulled out of their crimped collars. If they are, replace the cable.
    b. Make sure the lever hook is square and parallel with the lever. If it is not, it may be possible to bend it slightly to correct the condition. If not, replace the lever.
    c. Make sure the adjusting screw socket is seated in the secondary shoe notch.
15. Install the drums and wheel/tire assemblies as described in this chapter.
16. Adjust the parking brake as described in this chapter.

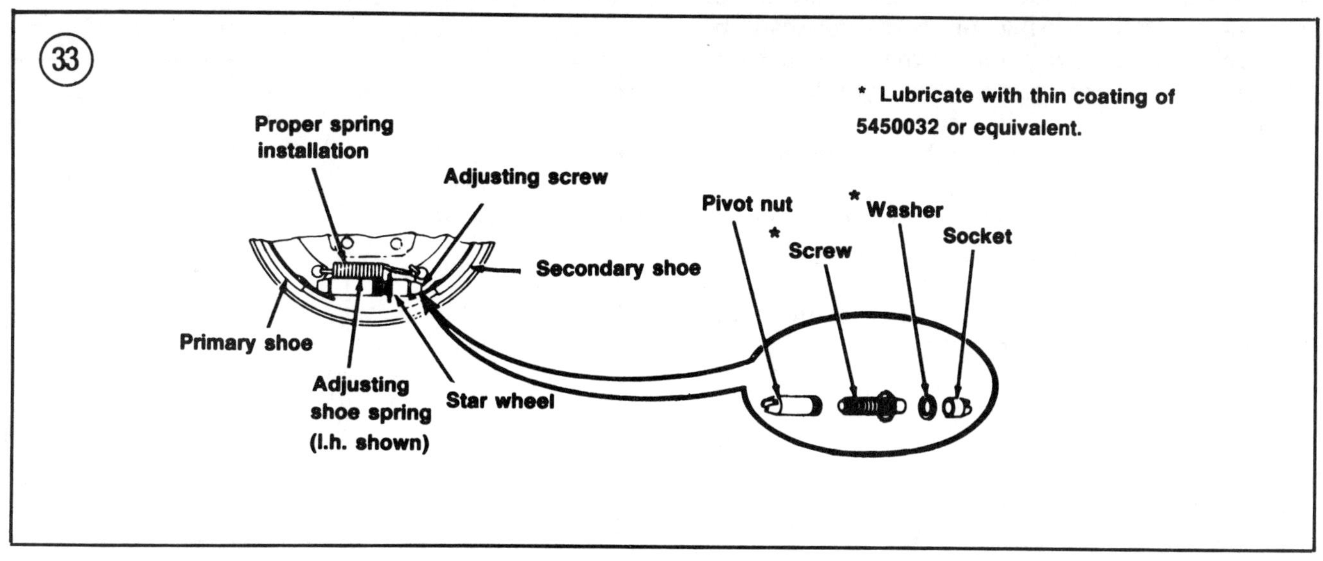

17. Make a final brake adjustment by repeatedly driving the vehicle backward and forward and stopping with firm pedal pressure until the pedal height and resistance are satisfactory.

Wheel Cylinder Overhaul

1. Remove the brake drum and shoes as described in this chapter.

CAUTION

Do not bend the brake line away from the wheel cylinder after unscrewing the nut in Step 2. Bending the brake line will make it difficult to reconnect and may cause it to crack. The wheel cylinder will separate from the brake line when it is removed from the backing plate.

2. Clean all dirt and contamination from the brake line fitting at the rear of the support plate. Disconnect the brake line and cover the end of the line with a clean, lint-free cloth to prevent contamination from entering the hydraulic system.
3. Pry the wheel cylinder retainer from the support plate with 2 awls as shown in **Figure 34**. Remove the wheel cylinder.
4. Remove the bleed screw.
5. Remove the boots, piston cups, expanders and spring from the wheel cylinder bore (**Figure 35**).
6. Discard all rubber parts. Clean the cylinder and pistons with rubbing alcohol. Do not use gasoline, kerosene or solvents. These leave a residue which can cause rubber parts to soften and swell.
7. Check the pistons for scratches, scoring or other damage. Replace if necessary.
8. Inspect the cylinder bore for scoring or corrosion. Light scoring or corrosion can be removed with crocus cloth. If the bore is badly scored or pitted, replace the wheel cylinder.
9. If the cylinder bore is resurfaced with crocus cloth, clean it a second time with rubbing alcohol and blow dry with compressed air.
10. Coat the piston cups with clean brake fluid and install the return spring/expander, cups and pistons in the cylinder bore.
11. Install a boot over each end of the cylinder and thread the bleed screw into the cylinder. Tighten the screw to specifications (**Table 1**).
12. Install the wheel cylinder to the support plate. Place a wooden block between the cylinder and axle flange.
13. Position a new retainer over the wheel cylinder stud and install by pressing in place with a 1 1/8 in.

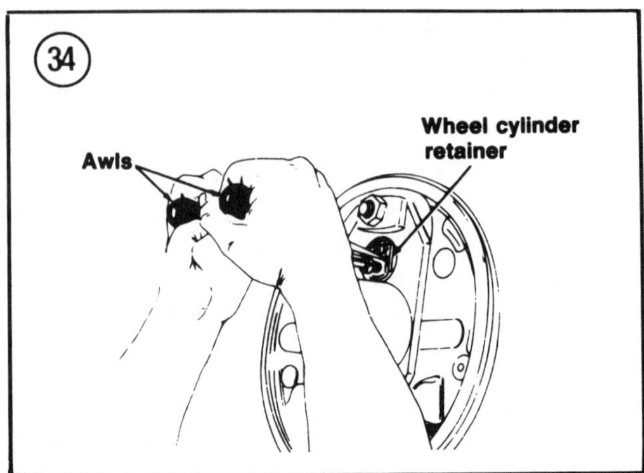

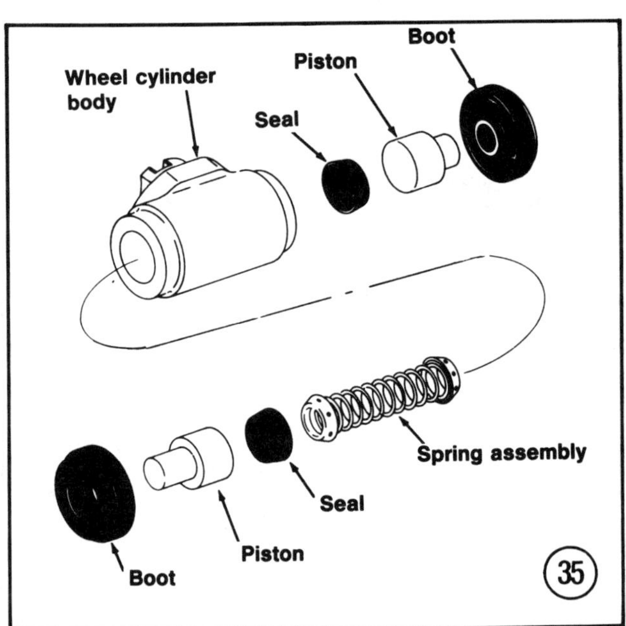

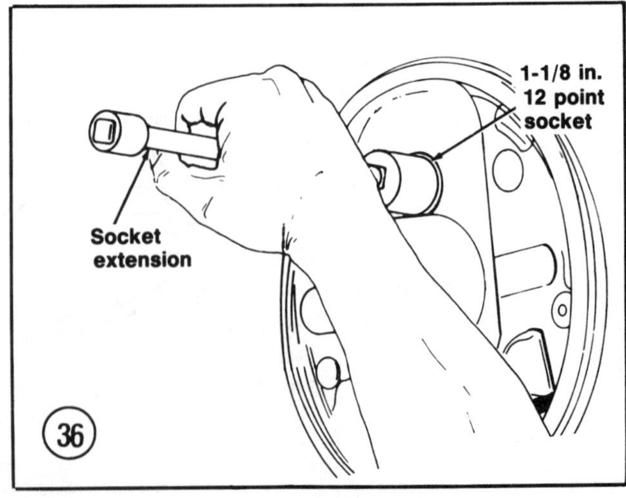

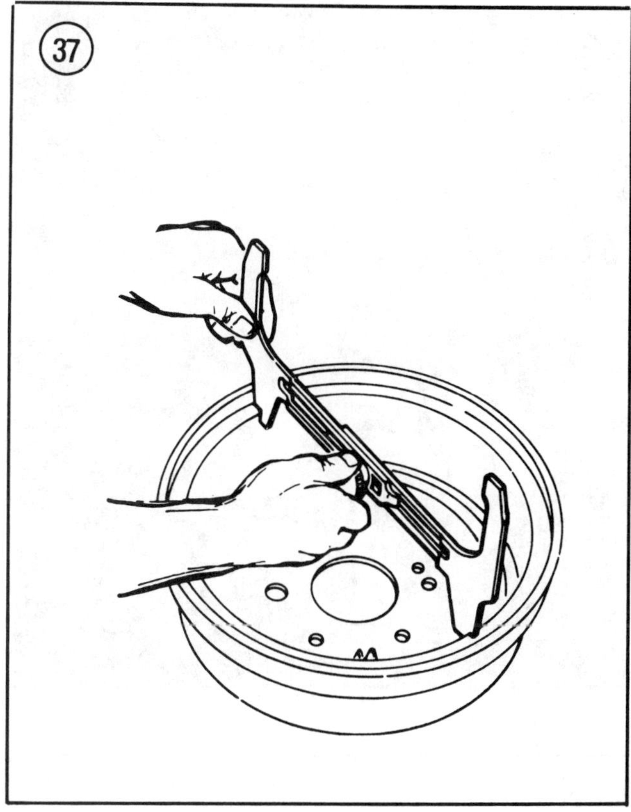

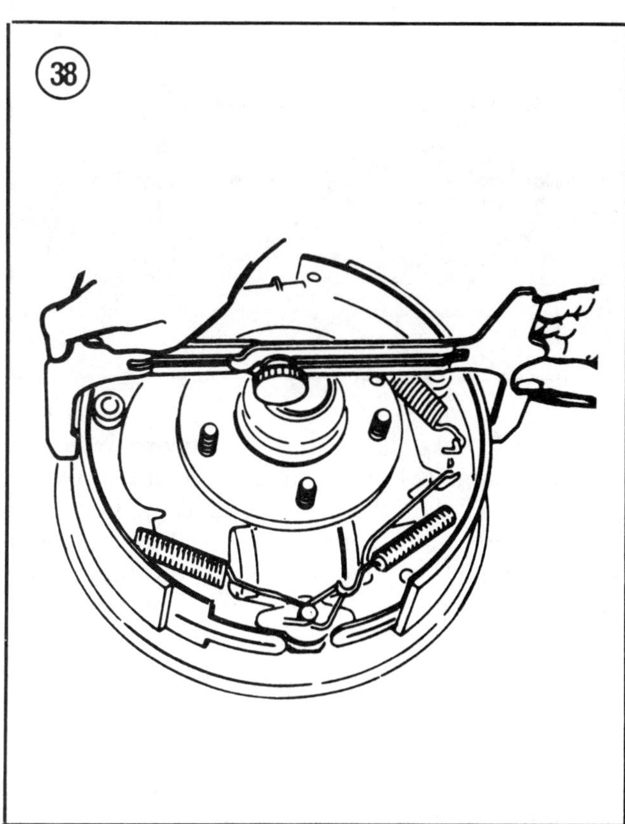

12-point socket and extension (**Figure 36**). Remove the wooden block.

14. Connect the brake inlet tube to the wheel cylinder and tighten the tube nut to specifications (**Table 1**).

BRAKE ADJUSTMENT

Disc Brakes

Disc brakes are automatically adjusted. No adjustment procedure is necessary or provided.

Drum Brakes

Drum brakes are self-adjusting. Adjustment occurs when the vehicle is driven in reverse and the brakes are applied. If the brake pedal can be pushed within a few inches of the floor, the brakes should be adjusted by backing the vehicle up several times and sharply applying the brakes. Test the adjustment by driving the vehicle at about 20 mph and braking to a smooth stop. If the pedal travel is still too great, repeat the procedure as required.

NOTE
Brake drums should be cold when adjusting the shoes. If the shoes are adjusted when the drums are hot and expanded, they may drag when the drums cool and contract.

Manual adjustment is unnecessary unless the brakes have been serviced.

Recommended procedure

1. With the brake drum off, disengage the actuator lever from the starwheel.
2. Measure the inner diameter of the brake drum with clearance gauge part No. J-21177 or part No. J-22364. See **Figure 37**.
3. Using the opposite side of the tool, position it against the linings (**Figure 38**) and rotate the starwheel with a small screwdriver blade as required until the tool just fits over the linings.
4. Install the brake drum as described in this chapter.

Alternate procedure

If the brake clearance gauge is not available, the brake drum can be used as an adjustment tool.

1. Rotate the starwheel with a small screwdriver blade as required until the drum slides over the linings with a slight drag.
2. Rotate the starwheel another 1 1/4 turns to retract the shoes. This will give enough clearance for final adjustment by driving the vehicle as described in this chapter.
3. Install the brake drum as described in this chapter.
4. Repeat the procedure on the opposite wheel.
5. Install the wheel/tire assemblies.
6. Remove the jackstands and lower the vehicle to the ground.
7. Make a final brake adjustment by repeatedly driving the vehicle backward and forward and stopping with firm pedal pressure until the pedal height and resistance are satisfactory.

Parking Brake

Chevrolet and GMC specifies the use of a proper calibrated cable tension gauge for this procedure.
1. Depress the parking brake pedal 8 notches (2-wheel drive except Blazers) or 10 notches (4-wheel drive and all Blazers) and lock the pedal to the mounting bracket by inserting a pin through the indicator hole in the pedal arm.
2. Raise the vehicle with a jack and place it on jackstands.
3. Clean the equalizer connector nut and threads (**Figure 39**). Lubricate the threads with brake fluid.
4. Install the cable tension gauge on the left rear cable (2-wheel drive except Blazers) or right rear cable (4-wheel drive and all Blazers) as close as possible to the equalizer.
5. Tighten the cable adjustment nut until the gauge reads 200-220 lb. (2-wheel drive except Blazers) or 140-150 lb. (4-wheel drive and all Blazers) tension. The cables should not be adjusted tight enough to cause brake drag when rotating the wheels.
6. Remove the lock pin from the parking brake pedal and release the brake.
7. Remove the jackstands and lower the vehicle to the ground.

MASTER CYLINDER

The aluminum master cylinder uses a plastic reservoir with a single reservoir cover. The master cylinder is attached to the power booster (with power brakes) or to the cowl (non-power brakes). **Figure 40** shows the power brake installation.

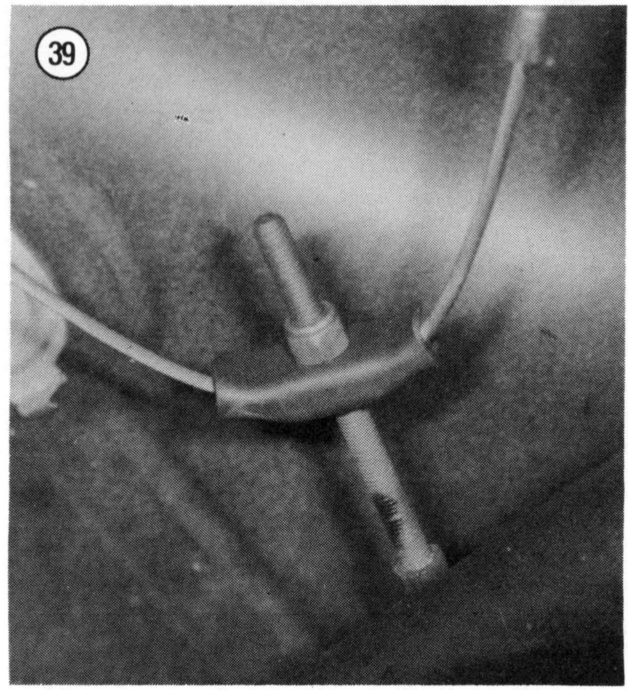

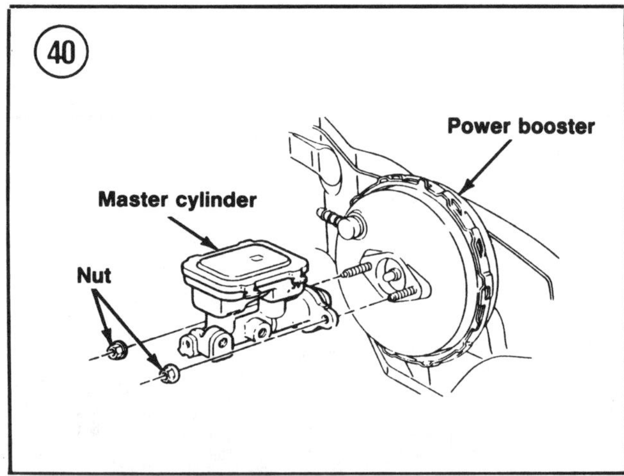

A quick take-up feature is incorporated to provide a large volume of fluid to the disc brakes at low pressure when the brake pedal is applied. This low-pressure fluid accomodates caliper seal and spring retraction requirements during initial braking effort.

Removal/Installation

Refer to **Figure 40** (typical) for this procedure.
1. Power brakes—With the engine stopped, depress the brake pedal to expel any vacuum remaining in the brake booster system.

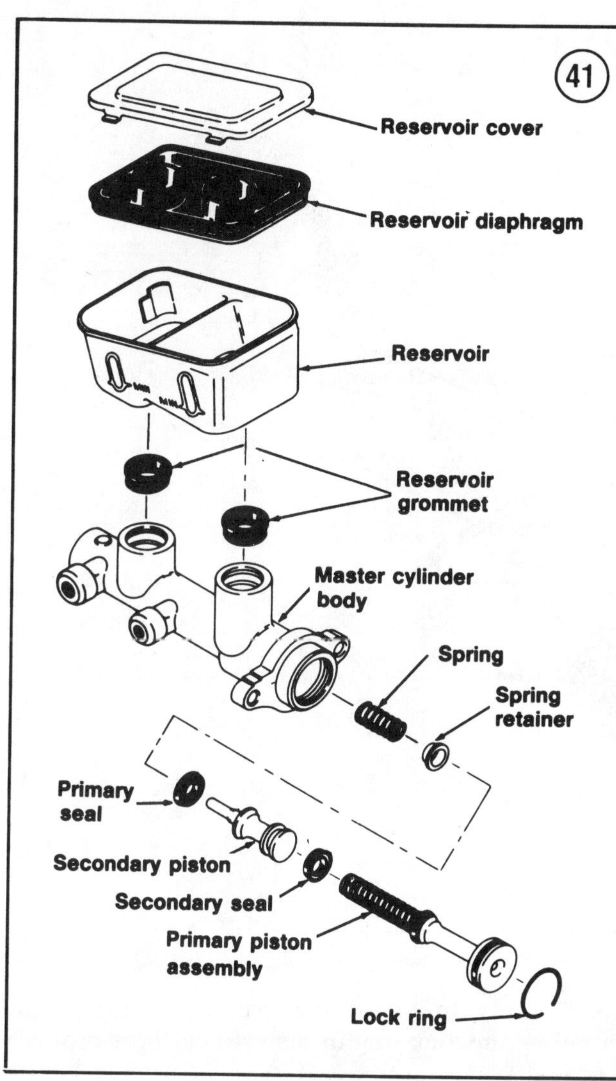

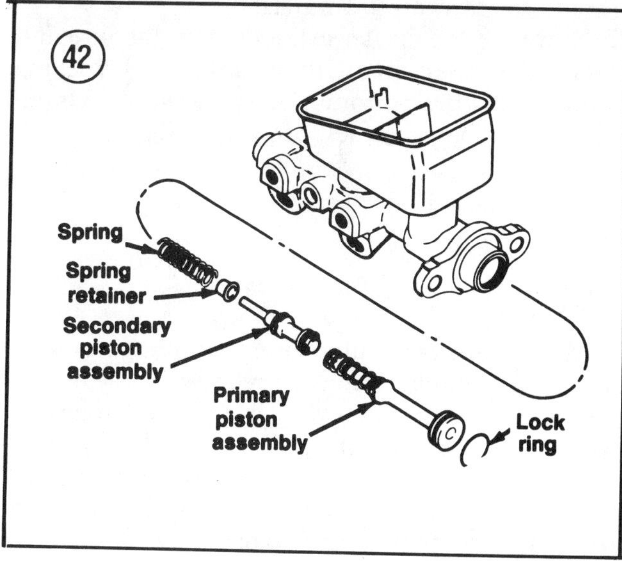

2. Disconnect the negative battery cable.

CAUTION
Brake fluid will damage paint. Wipe up any spilled fluid immediately, then wash the area with soap and water.

3. Disconnect the electrical leads and hydraulic lines at the master cylinder. Cap the lines and plug the master cylinder ports.
4. Non-power brakes—Working inside the cab, disconnect the master cylinder pushrod from the brake pedal.
5. Remove the 2 attaching nuts from the booster unit studs (power brakes) or cowl (non-power brake).
6. Remove the master cylinder.
7. Installation is the reverse of removal. Tighten all fasteners to specifications (**Table 1**). Fill the master cylinder reservoir to within 1/4 in. of the divider with clean DOT 3 or DOT 4 brake fluid. Bleed the brakes as described in this chapter. Start the engine and depress the brake pedal to set the warning light in position. Check for external leaks.

Overhaul

Refer to **Figure 41** for this procedure.
1. Clean the outside of the master cylinder with clean brake fluid or rubbing alcohol.
2. Remove the reservoir cover and diaphragm. Drain the reservoir and discard the fluid.
3. Clamp the master cylinder by one mounting flange in a vise with protective jaws. If protective jaws are not available, protect it with soft pieces of wood placed on each side of the housing or wrap the master cylinder in shop cloths.
4. Depress and hold the primary piston. Remove the lock ring.
5. Withdraw the primary piston from the bore. Cover the bore with a shop cloth and use compressed air to remove the secondary piston. See **Figure 42**.

NOTE
Do not disassemble the primary piston. This is factory-set and must be replaced if defective.

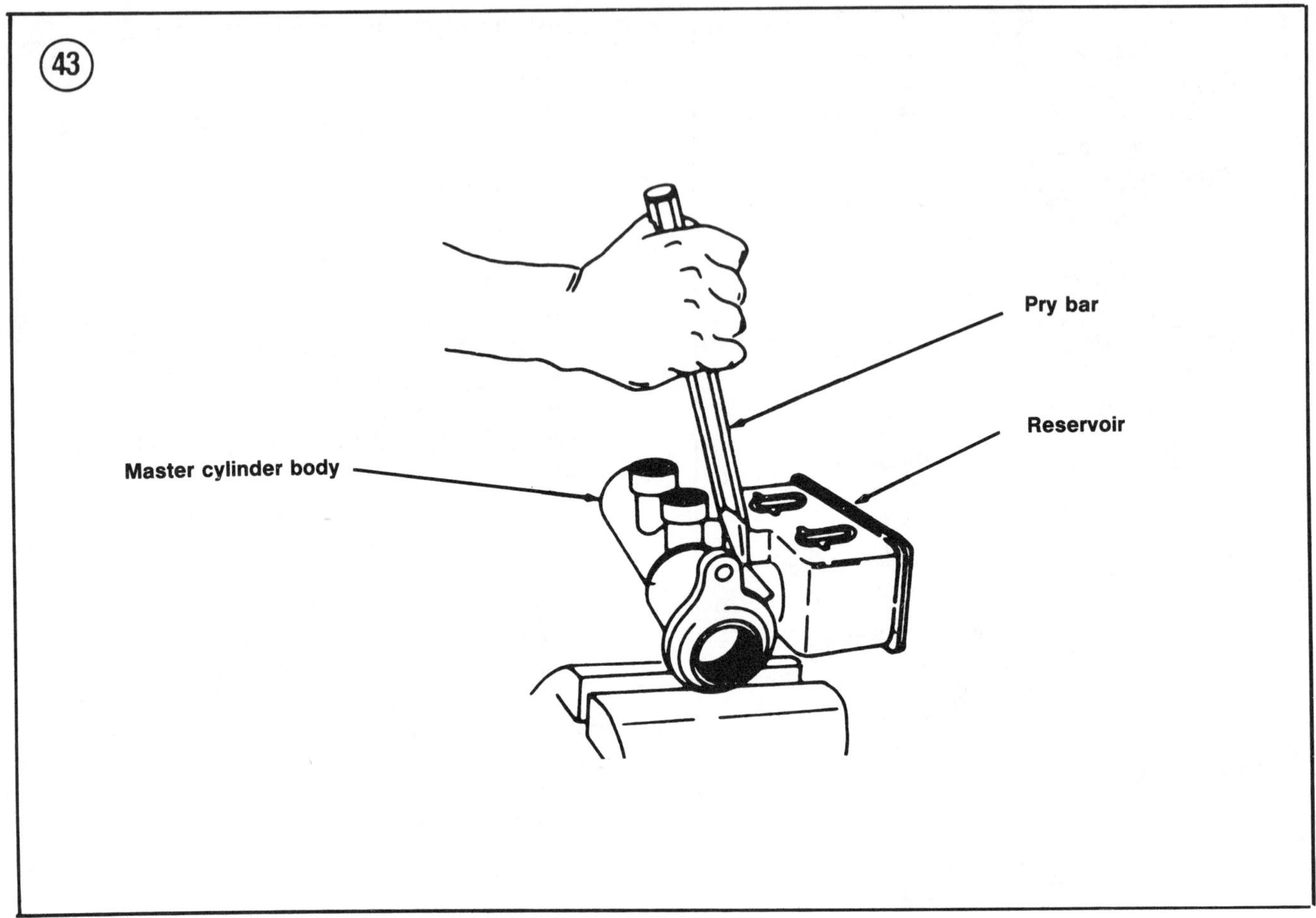

6. Use a pry bar as shown in **Figure 43** to remove the reservoir.
7. Remove the 2 reservoir grommets. Remove the quick take-up valve snap ring and valve from the rear reservoir bore.
8. Clean all metal parts in brake fluid. Do not clean with gasoline, kerosene or solvents. These leave a residue which can cause rubber parts to soften and swell.
9. If the rebuild kit includes piston assemblies, discard the old ones. If not, remove the old piston cups and install new ones. Be sure the new cups face in the same direction as the old ones.
10. Check the cylinder bore for wear, scoring, pitting or corrosion. Since the master cylinder is aluminum and the bore is anodized, it cannot be honed. If any defect is found, replace the master cylinder.
11. Lubricate all parts in clean brake fluid and insert the secondary piston and return spring assembly in the cylinder bore.
12. Install the primary piston assembly.
13. Depress and hold the primary piston while installing the lock ring in the cylinder bore groove. Make sure the snap ring is completely seated.
14. Install the quick take-up valve and snap ring. Install the reservoir grommets.
15. Remove the master cylinder from the vise and install the reservoir with a downward rocking motion until the bottom of the reservoir seats on the top of each grommet. See **Figure 44**.

Bleeding

Perform this procedure before installing a new or professionally rebuilt master cylinder.

1. Clamp the master cylinder by one mounting flange in a vise with protective jaws. If protective jaws are not available, protect it with soft pieces of wood placed on each side of the housing or wrap the master cylinder in shop cloths.

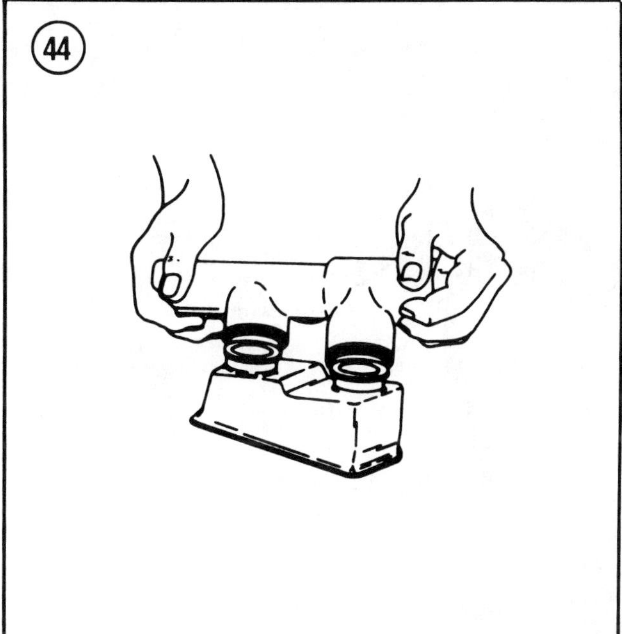

2. Fill the master cylinder with fresh DOT 3 or DOT 4 brake fluid.

WARNING
Do not use fluid from a previously opened container that is only part full. Brake fluid absorbs moisture and moisture in the master cylinder or brake lines can reduce braking efficiency.

3. Loosely install plugs in the front and rear brake outlet bores.
4. Tighten the front outlet plug and bleed the rear brake system first.
5. Slowly depress and hold the primary piston to force air out of the master cylinder, then tighten the plug.
6. Repeat Step 5 until no air bubbles appear in the brake fluid at the outlet port.
7. Loosen the front outlet plug and repeat Step 5 and Step 6 to bleed the front brake system.
8. With both plugs tightened, try to depress the piston. If it moves easily or if significant piston travel remains, there is still air in the master cylinder. Repeat Steps 4-7 until piston travel is restricted.
9. Refill the master cylinder reservoir as required. Install the cover and diaphragm assembly. Be sure that the cover is securely snapped in place.
10. Remove the plugs and install the master cylinder as described in this chapter.

BRAKE BLEEDING

After long usage, brake fluid absorbs enough atmospheric moisture to significantly reduce its boiling point and make it prone to vapor lock during repeated hard braking applications, such as mountain driving. While no hard and fast rule exists for changing the fluid in the system, it should be checked at least annually by bleeding fluid from one of the wheel cylinders and inspecting it for signs of moisture. If moisture is present, the brake fluid should be replaced. To do this, follow the procedure for bleeding the brakes. Continue adding new fluid to the master cylinder and bleeding fluid at each wheel until fresh, new fluid appears at each wheel.

The hydraulic system should be bled whenever air enters it. Air in the brake lines will compress, rather than transmitting pedal pressure to the brake operating parts. If the pedal feels spongy or if pedal travel increases considerably, brake bleeding is usually called for. Bleeding is also necessary whenever a brake line is disconnected.

This procedure requires handling brake fluid. Be careful not to get any fluid on brake discs, pads, shoes or drums. Clean all dirt and contamination from the bleed valves before beginning. Two people are needed: one to operate the brake pedal and the other to open and close the bleed valves.

Since the brake system consists of 2 individual systems (front and rear), each system should be bled separately. Bleeding should be conducted in the following order: master cylinder, right rear, left rear, right front, left front.

NOTE
Do not allow the master cylinder reservoirs to run dry during bleeding.

If the vehicle has power brakes, exhaust the vacuum reserve by applying the brakes several times.

Omit Steps 2-4 if the master cylinder was bench-bled before installation.

1. Clean away all dirt around the master cylinder. Remove the cover and diaphragm assembly. Top up the reservoirs with brake fluid rated DOT 3 or DOT 4. Leave the cover off the reservoirs and place a clean shop cloth over the top of the master cylinder to prevent any contamination from entering the fluid.

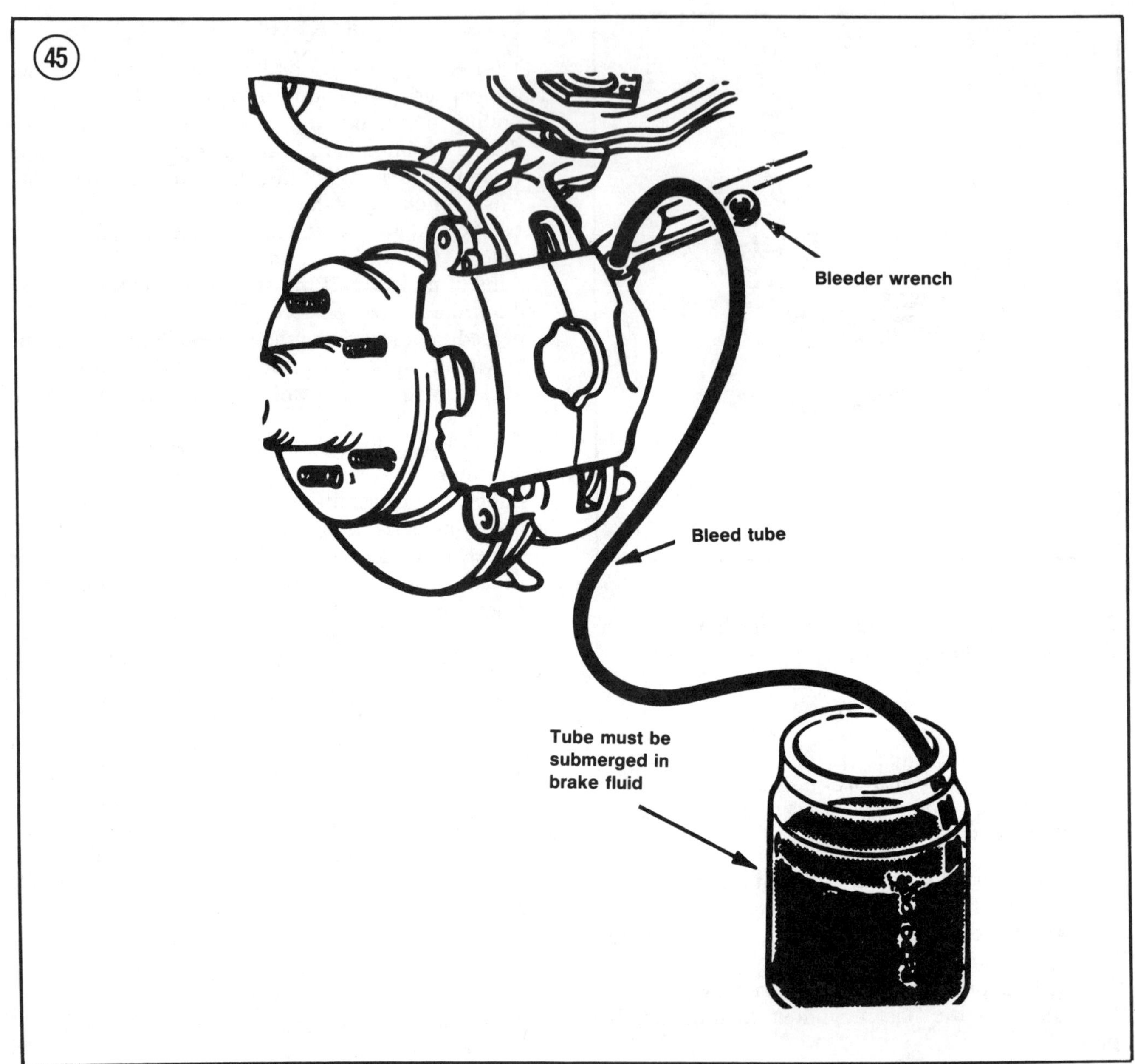

NOTE

DOT 3 means that the brake fluid meets current Department of Transportation quality standards. If the fluid does not say DOT 3 somewhere on the label, buy a brand that does. DOT 4 brake fluid can also be safely used.

2. Loosen the master cylinder hydraulic line nuts and place a shop cloth under the fittings to catch any leaking fluid.
3. Have an assistant slowly depress the brake pedal by hand until it reaches the floorboard and hold it there while you tighten the master cylinder hydraulic line nuts loosened in Step 2.
4. Repeat Step 2 and Step 3 as required until the brake pedal is firm and no air escapes from the fittings.
5. Fit an appropriate size box-end wrench over the bleed screw on the right rear wheel and attach a length of plastic or rubber tubing to the bleed screw. Be sure the tubing fits snugly on the screw. Submerge the other end of the tubing in a container partially filled with clean DOT 3 or DOT 4 brake fluid. See **Figure 45**.

NOTE
Do not allow the end of the tubing to come out of the brake fluid during bleeding or the fluid level in the reservoirs to run dry. Either could allow air to enter the system and require that the bleeding procedure be repeated.

6. Open the bleed screw about 3/4 turn and have the assistant slowly depress the brake pedal to the floorboard. When the pedal reaches the floorboard, close the bleed screw. After the screw is closed, have the assistant slowly release the pedal.
7. Wait 15 seconds and repeat Step 6 until the fluid entering the jar from the tubing is free of air bubbles.
8. Repeat this procedure at each of the remaining bleed screws. Top up the master cylinder after bleeding each wheel to prevent the reservoirs from running dry.
9. Road test the vehicle to make sure the brakes operate correctly. If the brake warning light remains on after the system has been bled and the braking action is satisfactory, center the pressure differential valve as described in this chapter.

POWER BRAKE VACUUM BOOSTER

The vehicles covered in this manual use either a single or tandem diaphragm Bendix vacuum booster unit mounted to the engine compartment cowl. The booster unit uses intake manifold vacuum (gasoline engine) or vacuum from a belt-driven pump (diesel engine) and atmospheric pressure to reduce braking effort. The power booster can be serviced if defective. Since the procedure is complex and requires the use of many special tools, it is best left to a dealer.

Testing

1. Check the brake system for signs of a hydraulic leak. Make sure the master cylinder reservoirs are filled to within 1/4 in. of the top of the divider.
2. Start the engine and let it idle for about 2 minutes, then shut it off. Place the transmission in NEUTRAL and set the parking brake.
3. Depress the brake pedal several times to exhaust any vacuum remaining in the system.
4. When the vacuum is exhausted, depress and hold the pedal. Start the engine. If the pedal does not start to fall away under foot pressure (requiring less pressure to hold it in place), the vacuum booster unit is not working properly.
5. Disconnect the vacuum line at the booster check valve (A, **Figure 46**). Connect a vacuum gauge with a tee fitting to gasoline engines. Connect a vacuum gauge directly to the vacuum line on diesel engines. Start the engine and check the gauge reading at idle:

   a. Gasoline engine—If the gauge does not read at least 18-21 in. Hg (at sea level), tune the engine. See Chapter Three. If tuning the engine does not solve the problem, there is a vacuum leak in the system.

   b. Diesel engine—If the gauge does not read at least 21 in. Hg (at sea level), check the vacuum pump drive belt tension (Chapter Seven) and make sure that the fast idle speed is within specifications (Chapter Three). If these are correct, replace the vacuum pump as described in this chapter.

6. Diesel engine—Remove the vacuum gauge from the line and reconnect the gauge with a tee fitting to restore the system operation. Start the engine and run at idle, watching the vacuum gauge. If the reading drops by more than 3 inches, there is a vacuum leak in the system.

47

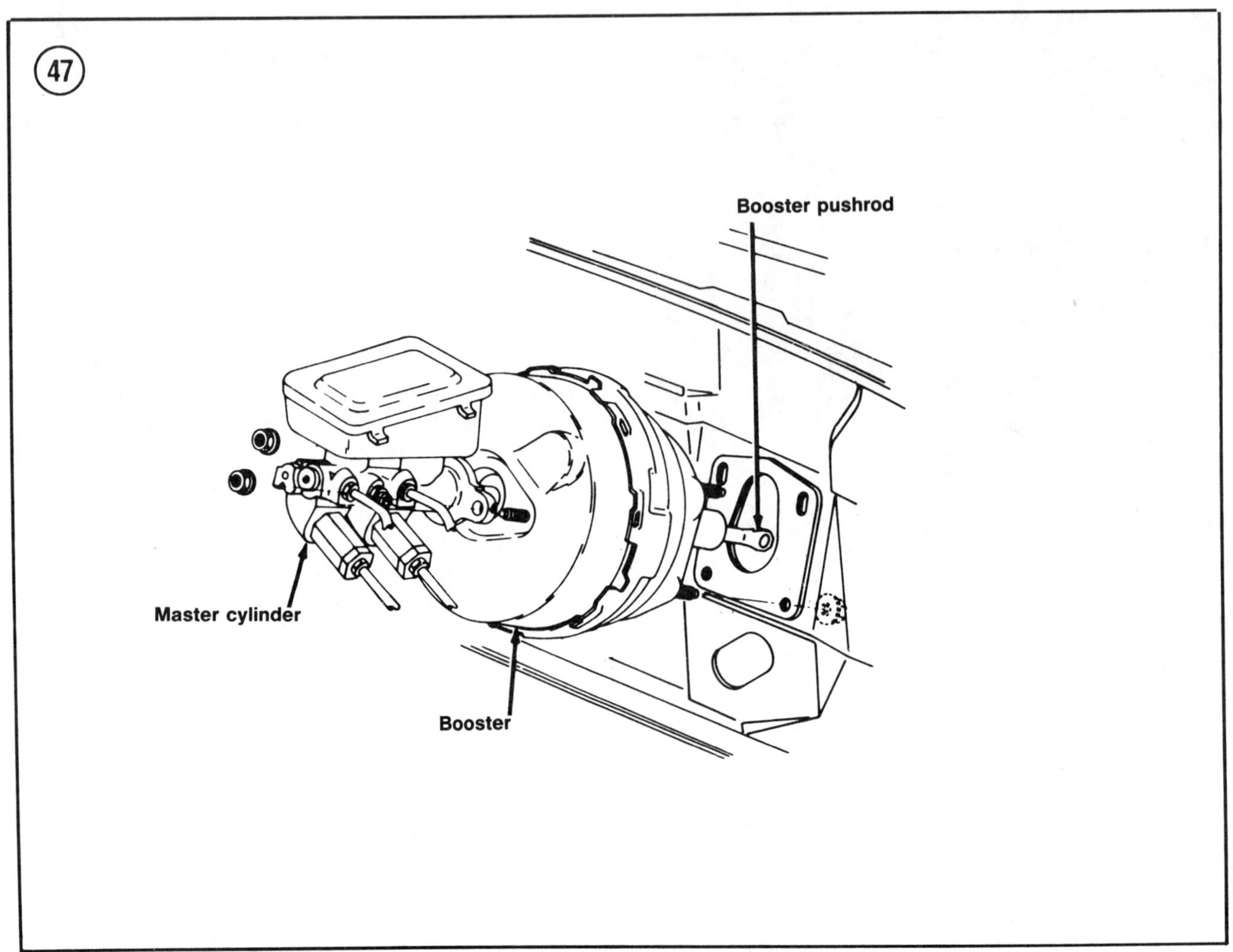

7. Shut the engine off and watch the vacuum gauge. If the reading drops by more than one inch in one minute, replace the check valve.
8. With the engine off, the vacuum gauge connected and the system holding vacuum as specified in Step 5, depress and hold the brake pedal for several seconds, then release it. If the vacuum reading drops to zero, replace the booster.
9. Run the engine for at least 10 minutes at fast idle. Shut the engine off and let it stand for 10 minutes. Depress the brake pedal with about 20 lb. of force. If the pedal feel is not the same as it was with the engine running, replace the vacuum unit.

Vacuum Hose, Check Valve and Charcoal Filter Inspection

1. Check the vacuum hose between the booster unit and the charcoal filter (B, **Figure 46**) for leaks or a loose connection. Replace or tighten as required.
2. Disconnenct the hose and remove the check valve from the booster unit (A, **Figure 46**). If should be possible to blow air into the brake booster end of the valve, but not into the intake manifold end. If air flows both ways or neither way, replace the check valve.
3. Repeat Step 2 to test the charcoal filter (B, **Figure 46**).

Booster Removal/Installation

Refer to **Figure 47** (typical) for this procedure.

1. With the engine stopped, depress the brake pedal to expel any vacuum remaining the brake booster system.
2. Install a prop under the master cylinder for support.

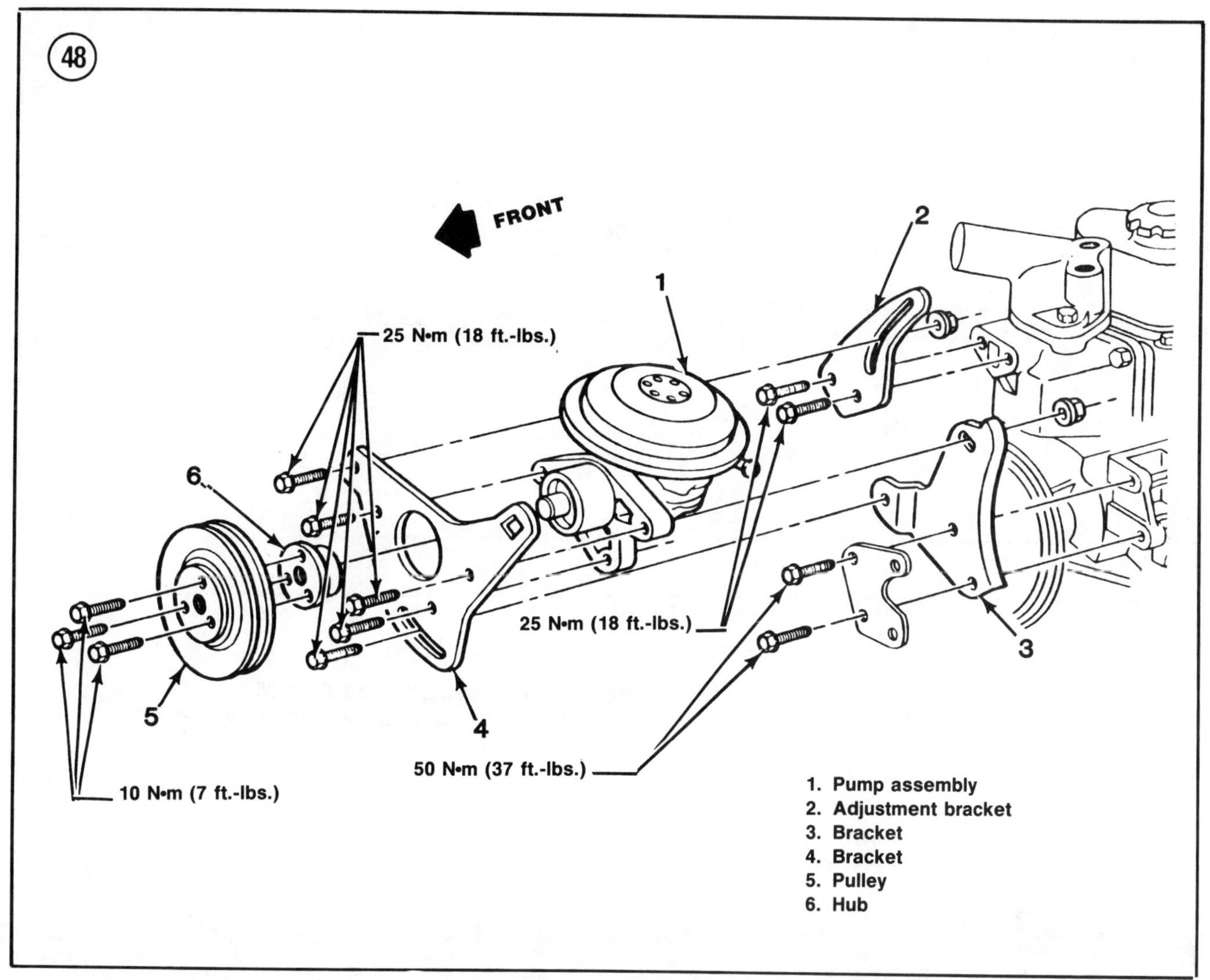

3. Loosen the clamp holding the charcoal filter vacuum line to the booster check valve (A, **Figure 46**). Disconnect the line at the check valve. Remove the valve from the booster unit.

CAUTION
Move the master cylinder carefully in Step 4 to prevent bending or stressing the hydraulic lines.

4. Remove the nuts and lockwashers holding the master cylinder to the booster unit. Carefully pull the master cylinder from the booster studs and move it to one side to provide room for booster removal. Make sure the prop supports the master cylinder.
5. Working inside the cab, disconnect the booster pushrod from the brake pedal. Remove the nuts holding the booster unit to the firewall.
6. Remove the booster unit from the engine compartment.
7. Installation is the reverse of removal. Since the master cylinder lines are not disconnected during this procedure, it is not necessary to bleed the brake system. Start the engine and check brake operation. Road test the vehicle to make sure the brakes operate properly.

BRAKE BOOSTER VACUUM PUMP (DIESEL ENGINE)

A diesel engine does not produce enough vacuum to power a vacuum brake booster unit. The necessary vacuum is provided by a belt-driven diaphragm pump. See **Figure 48**. The pump is non-serviceable and must be replaced if it does not function properly.

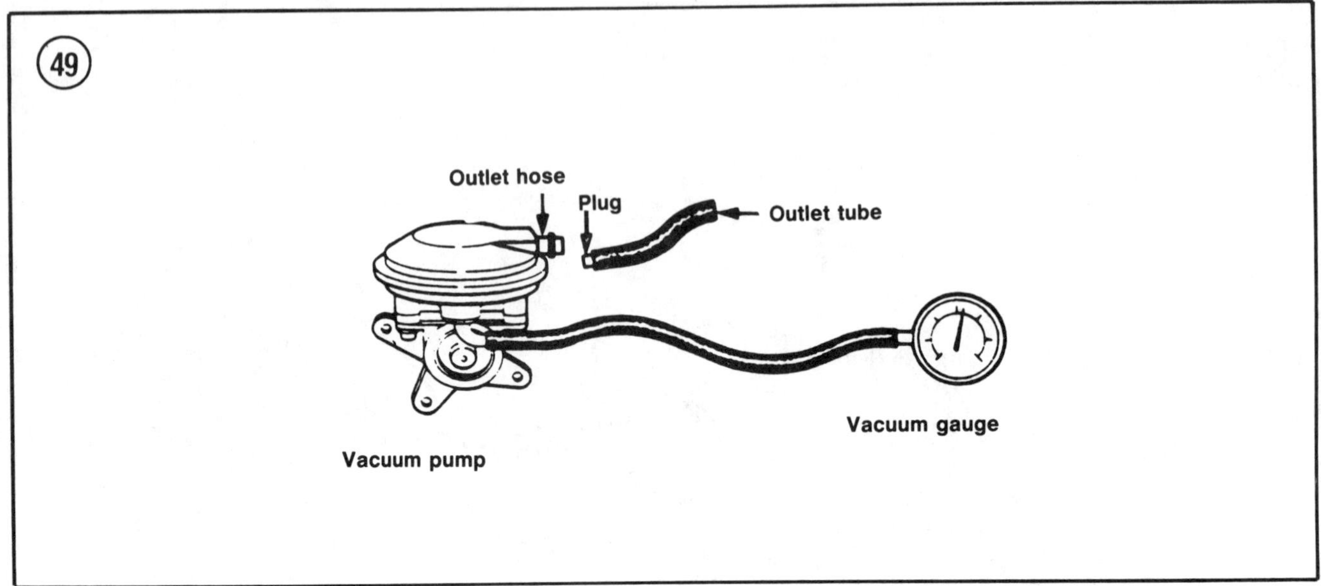

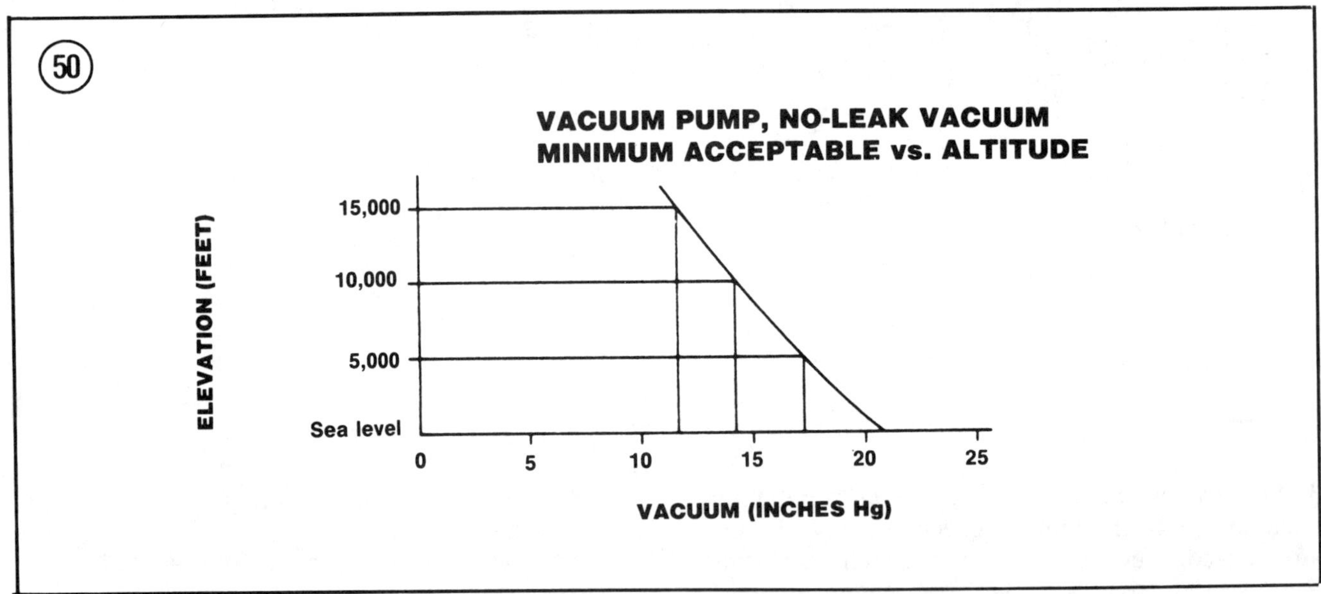

Diagnosis

1. Set the parking brake and block the rear wheels.
2. Place the transmission in NEUTRAL (manual) or PARK (automatic).
3. Start the engine and let it idle. Disconnect the hose at the vacuum pump outlet fitting and plug the hose. Connect a vacuum gauge to the pump inlet fitting. See **Figure 49**. The gauge should read 21 in. Hg vacuum (at sea level) within 30 seconds. See **Figure 50** for readings at other elevations.
4. If the gauge does not read as specified in Step 3, check the drive belt tension (Chapter Seven) and make sure the fast idle speed is within specifications (Chapter Three). If these are correct, replace the vacuum pump as described in this chapter.
5. If the gauge reads as specified in Step 3, unplug and reconnect the outlet hose to the vacuum pump. Remove and reconnect the vacuum gauge with a tee as shown in **Figure 51**. If the vacuum reading is less than 18 in. Hg (at sea level) after one minute, check the vacuum lines for leaks. If none are found, replace the vacuum pump.

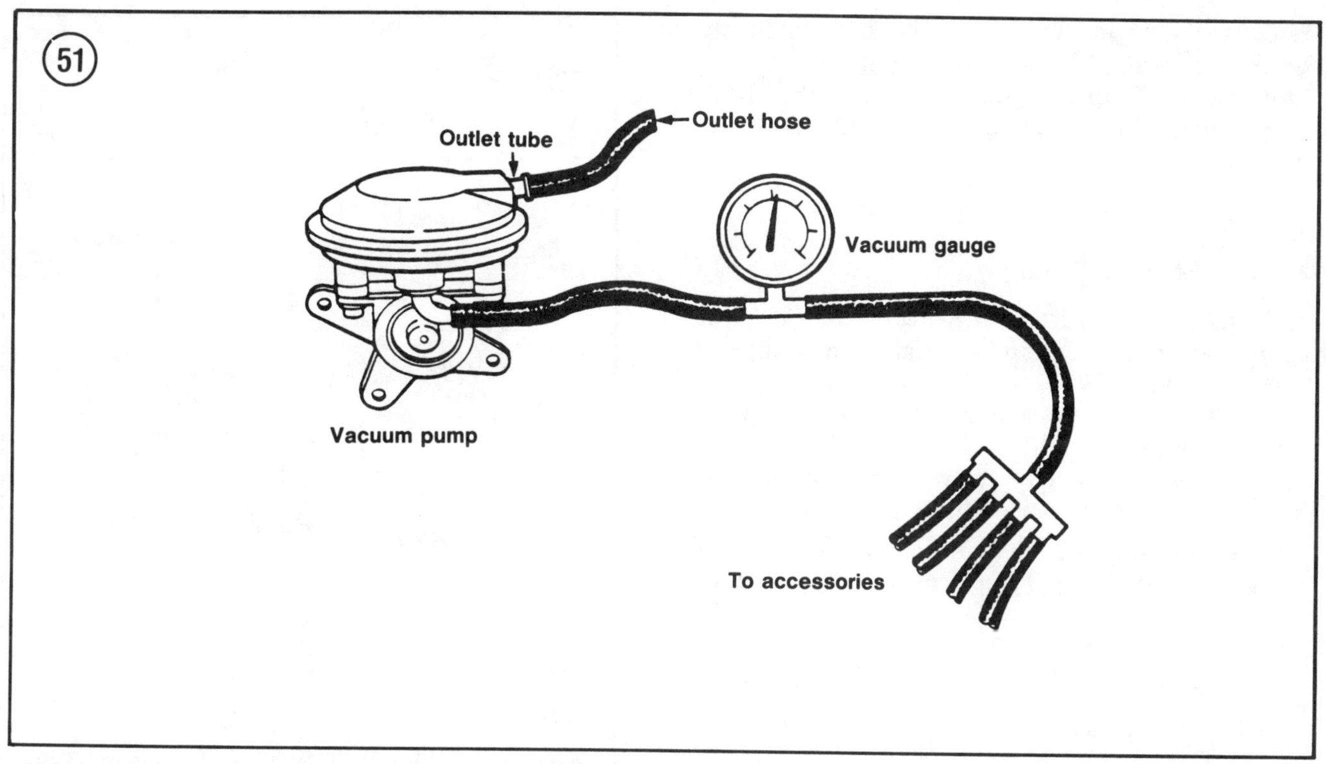

Removal/Installation

Refer to **Figure 48** for this procedure.

1. Disconnect the negative battery cable.
2. Disconnect the vacuum hose at the pump.
3. Loosen and remove the vacuum pump drive belt.
4. Remove the bolts holding the pump pulley to the vacuum pump hub.
5. Unbolt and remove the pump and bracket from the engine.
6. Separate the pump from the bracket.
7. If the pump is being replaced, remove the hub from the old pump with a hydraulic press. Install the hub on the new pump with the press.
8. Installation is the reverse of removal. Adjust the drive belt tension (Chapter Seven).

COMBINATION VALVE AND WARNING LIGHT SWITCH

The combination valve and warning light switch are combined into a single unit bracket-mounted beside the master cylinder (**Figure 52**).

If hydraulic pressure drops severely in either the front or rear brake system, the valve operates the switch which in turn activates the instrument panel warning light. The combination valve is not serviceable and must be replaced if any of its 3 functions do not work properly.

12

Centering

The combination valve must be centered whenever the brakes are bled. To do so, turn the ignition switch to the ACC or ON position, but do not start the engine. Depress the brake pedal firmly until the warning light goes out (if it was illuminated). Turn the ignition switch OFF. Check brake operation to make sure a firm pedal is obtained.

Electrical Circuit Testing

1. Squeeze the plastic locking ring on the electrical connector at the combination valve and pull the connector off.
2. Connect the electrical connector to ground with a jumper lead.
3. Turn the ignition ON; the warning lamp should light. If the lamp does not light, check for a burned-out bulb or a short in the circuit wiring. If these are satisfactory, replace the combination valve.

Warning Light Switch Test

1. Connect a suitable length of hose to a rear brake bleed screw. Place the other end of the hose in a container partially filled with clean brake fluid.
2. Remove the master cylinder cover and diaphragm. Make sure both reservoirs are full to within 1/4 in. of the divider. If not, top up as required with clean DOT 3 or DOT 4 brake fluid.
3. Turn the ignition ON. Open the bleed screw while an assistant applies moderate pressure to the pedal. The warning lamp on the instrument panel should light.
4. Close the bleed screw. Have the assistant apply moderate-to-heavy pressure on the pedal. The instrument panel should go out.
5. Repeat Steps 1-4 with a front brake bleed screw and look for the same results.
6. If the warning lamp does not light during Step 3 and Step 4, connect the switch terminal to ground with a jumper lead. If the lamp lights, the warning light switch in the combination valve is defective. Replace the combination valve.

Combination Valve Replacement

1. Unplug the electrical connector at the combination valve.
2. Disconnect and plug the hydraulic lines at the combination valve.

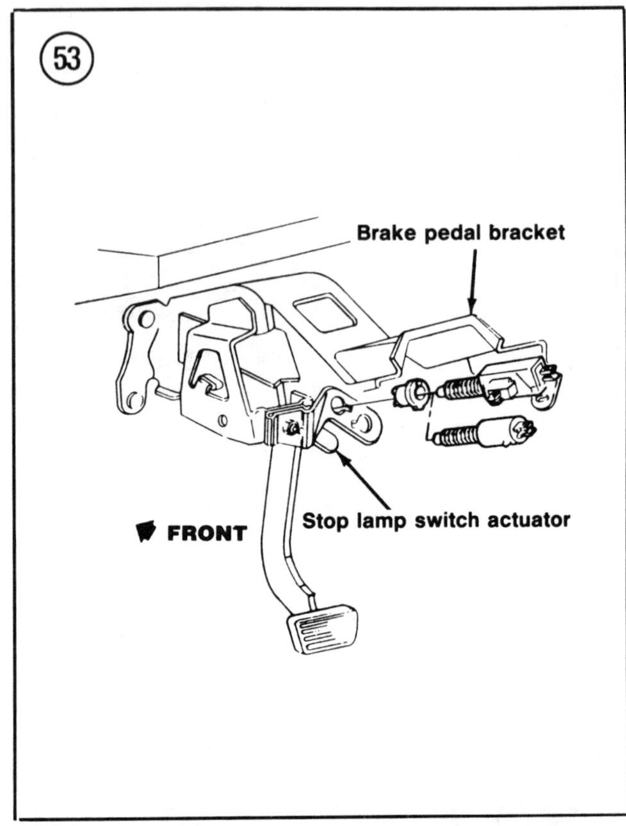

3. Remove the bolts holding the valve to its mounting bracket. Remove the valve.
4. Installation is the reverse of removal. Tighten the mounting bolts to specifications (**Table 1**). Bleed the brakes as described in this chapter.

STOPLIGHT SWITCH

The stoplight switch is mounted on the brake pedal arm with a tubular clip (**Figure 53**).

Replacement

1. Unplug the wiring harness connector at the switch.
2. Rotate the switch and tubular clip to align the clip tang with the bracket slot.
3. Remove the switch.
4. Installation is the reverse of removal.

Adjustment

1. Push the switch into the tubular clip.
2. Pull the brake pedal up just enough to reach the normal released position. This automatically adjusts the switch.

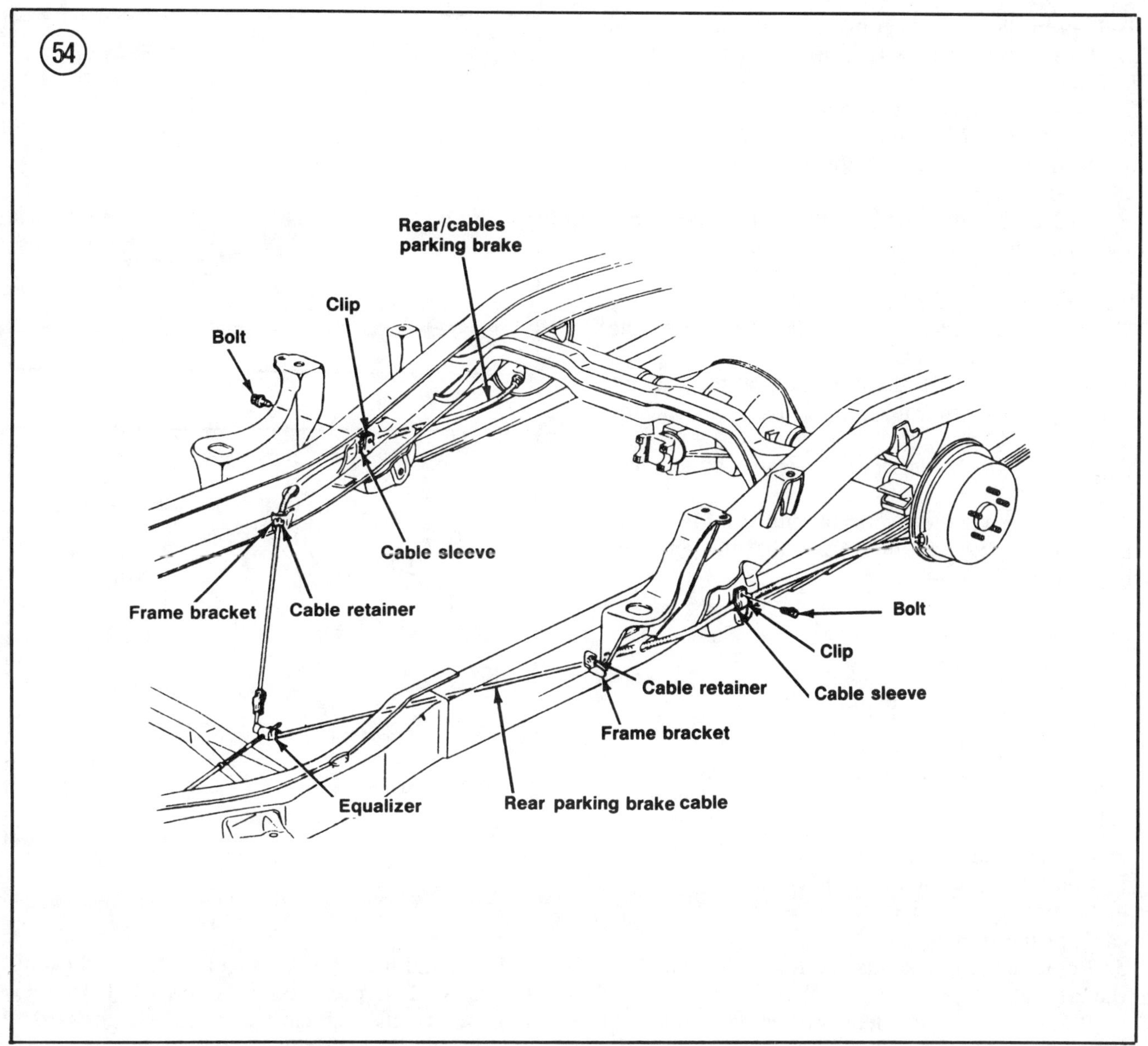

3. Rotate the switch 1/2 turn counterclockwise to prevent it from holding the brake pedal on after adjustment.

4. Check for free play between the pedal and switch by pulling the pedal upward. Electrical contact should be made when the pedal is depressed 0.53 in. (13.5 mm) from its fully released position.

5. If further adjustment is required, rotate or pull the switch in its clip until contact is made as specified in Step 4.

PARKING BRAKE

All models use a manually operated parking brake assembly. A cable connected to the parking brake pedal is routed to the equalizer. Separate cables connected to the equalizer are routed to each rear wheel. **Figure 54** shows the parking brake cable system.

Rear Cable Removal/Installation

Refer to **Figure 54** for this procedure. The following steps can be used to replace either the right- or left-hand cable.

1. Loosen the rear wheel lug nuts.
2. Raise the vehicle with a jack and place it on jackstands.
3. Mark the wheel/tire assembly relationship to the axle flange. Mark the brake drum relationship to the axle flange. Remove the wheel/tire assembly and brake drum.
4. Loosen the equalizer adjusting nut (**Figure 55**) and disconnect the cable at the center retainer.
5. Squeeze the plastic retainer fingers and remove the retainer from the frame bracket.
6. Remove the rear brake shoes. Disconnect the cable from the secondary shoe.
7. Depress the cable retaining tangs at the backing plate. Remove the cable fitting from the backing plate.
8. Remove the cable from the frame attachment point.
9. Installation is the reverse of removal. Make sure the cable is properly routed and that the retainers hold the cable securely.

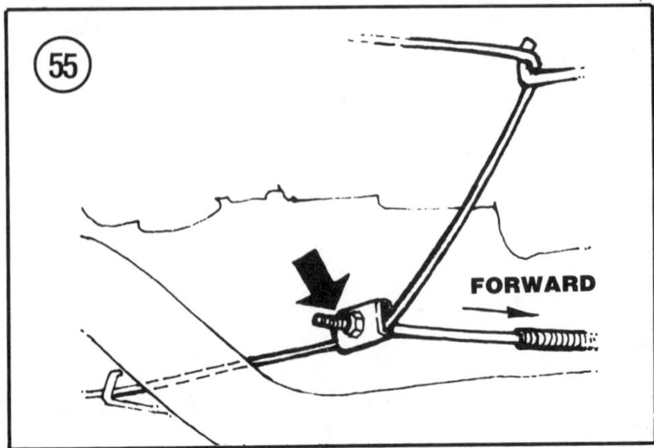

Front Cable Removal/Installation

Refer to **Figure 56** for this procedure.

1. Shift the transmission into NEUTRAL.
2. Raise the vehicle with a jack and place it on jackstands.
3. Loosen the equalizer nut (**Figure 36**). Disconnect the cable from the connector.
4. Compress the retainer tangs and loosen the cable at the frame.
5. Remove the jackstands and lower the vehicle to the ground.
6. Remove the windshield washer reservoir from the engine compartment.
7. Working in the cab, disconnect the cable at the parking brake pedal.
8. Compress the retainer tangs and withdraw the cable from the engine compartment.
9. Installation is the reverse of removal. Adjust the parking brake as described in this chapter.

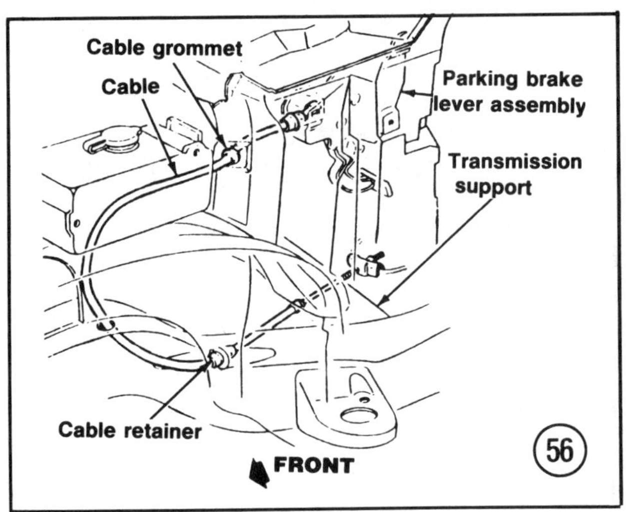

BRAKE PEDAL

The pedal height and travel are fixed and cannot be adjusted. If pedal travel exceeds 2 1/4 in. (57 mm), drive the vehicle backward and forward to activate the brake adjuster. If this does not bring pedal travel within specifications, bleed the brakes as described in this chapter. Adjust the parking brake as described in this chapter. Check for hydraulic fluid leaks and correct if found. Inspect the front and rear brake linings and replace if excessively worn.

Table 1 TIGHTENING TORQUES

Fastener	ft.-lb.	N•m
Cable clip-to-frame bolt	9-12	11-16
Caliper		
Bleed screw	8-12	9-16
Brake hose	18-30	24-40
Mounting bolts		
1982-1983	21-25	28-47
1984-on	30-45	41-61
Combination valve attaching bolt	6-9	8-11
Drum brake inlet tube nut	10-15	14-20
Equalizer locknut	9-12	11-16
Master cylinder attaching nuts	22-33	30-45
Pedal bracket bolt	22-30	30-40
Power booster-to-cowl	22-33	30-45
Vacuum pump		
Adjustment bracket bolts	18	25
Bracket-to-block bolts	37	50
Bracket-to-pump bolts	18	25
Pulley-to-hub screws	7	10
Wheel cylinder bleed screw	2-4.5	3.4-7.9
Wheel lug nuts		
Base wheel		
2-wheel drive	80	110
4-wheel drive	100	140
Optional wheel (2-wheel drive)	100	140

CHAPTER THIRTEEN

BODY

This chapter provides service procedures for the bumpers, hood, grille, fenders, cowl vent grille, doors, door handles, door windows, seats, glove box, instrument panel and console. No special tools are required for these procedures. Other body repairs require many special skills and tools and should be left to a dealer or body shop.

BUMPERS

Front Bumper Replacement

Refer to **Figure 1** for this procedure.

1. Remove the parking lamps from the right and left lamp housings in the bumper. See Chapter Eight.
2. Remove the air deflector attaching bolts at each side of the lower front fender flange.
3. Support the bumper with a jack or wooden blocks.
4. Remove the bumper brace-to-frame bolts. Remove the brace at each side of the bumper.
5. Remove the attaching bolts holding the bumper bracket at each side of the bumper.
6. Lower the bumper to the ground.
7. Installation is the reverse of removal.

Rear Bumper Replacement

Refer to **Figure 2** for this procedure.

1. Remove the license plate housing.
2. Disconnect the wiring clips from the bumper (**Figure 3**).
3. Support the bumper with a jack or wooden blocks.
4. Remove the bolts holding the bumper at each bumper brace.
5. Lower the bumper to the ground.
6. Installation is the reverse of removal.

HOOD

Hood hinges are bolted to the hood and to a fender bracket. Adjustment can be made at the hinge-to-hood attaching fasteners.

Adjustment

1. To move the hood forward, to the rear or from side-to-side, loosen the hinge-to-hood bolts on each side (**Figure 4**).

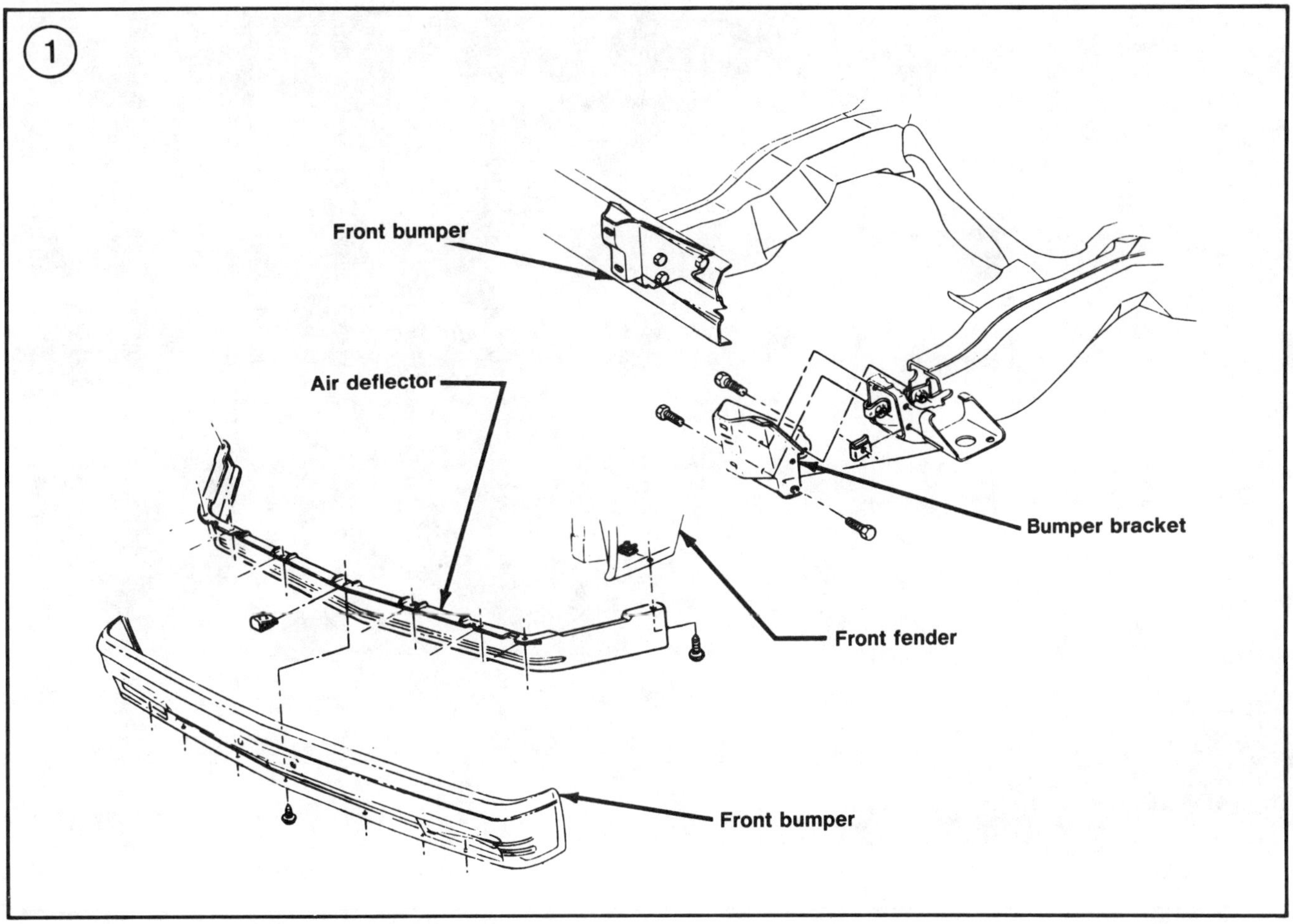

1
Front bumper
Air deflector
Bumper bracket
Front fender
Front bumper

2
Brace

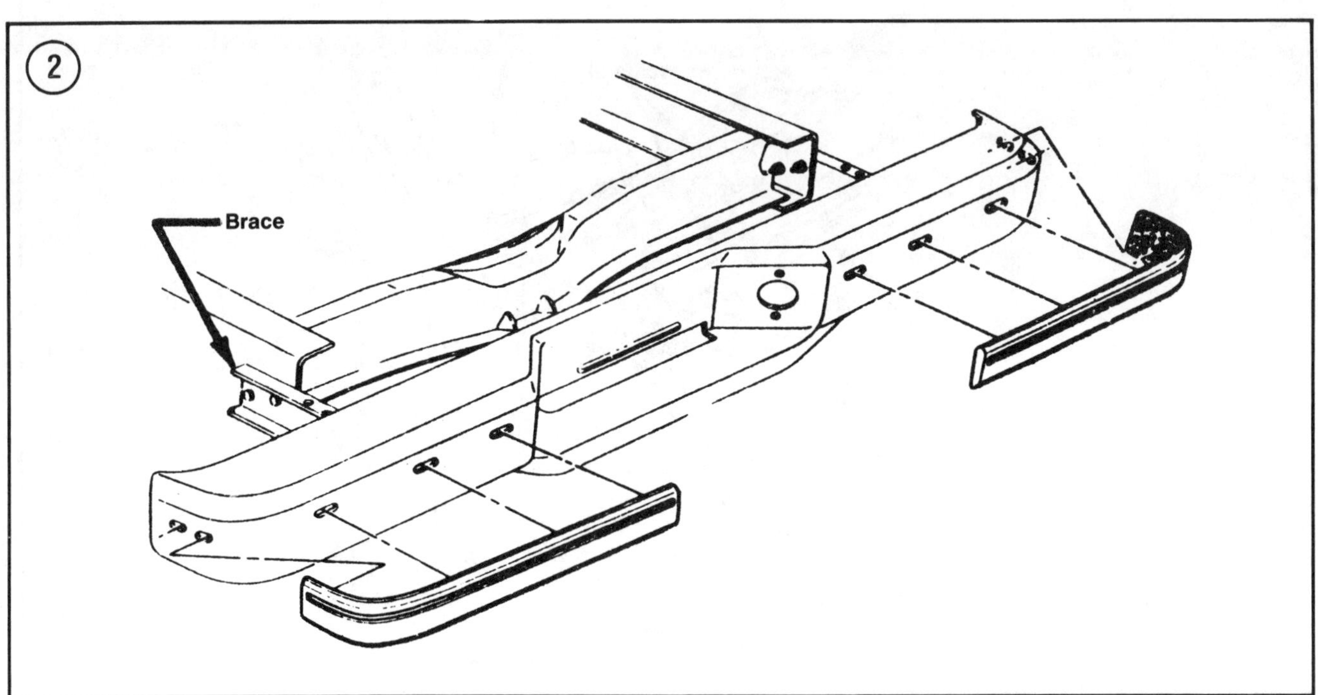

3

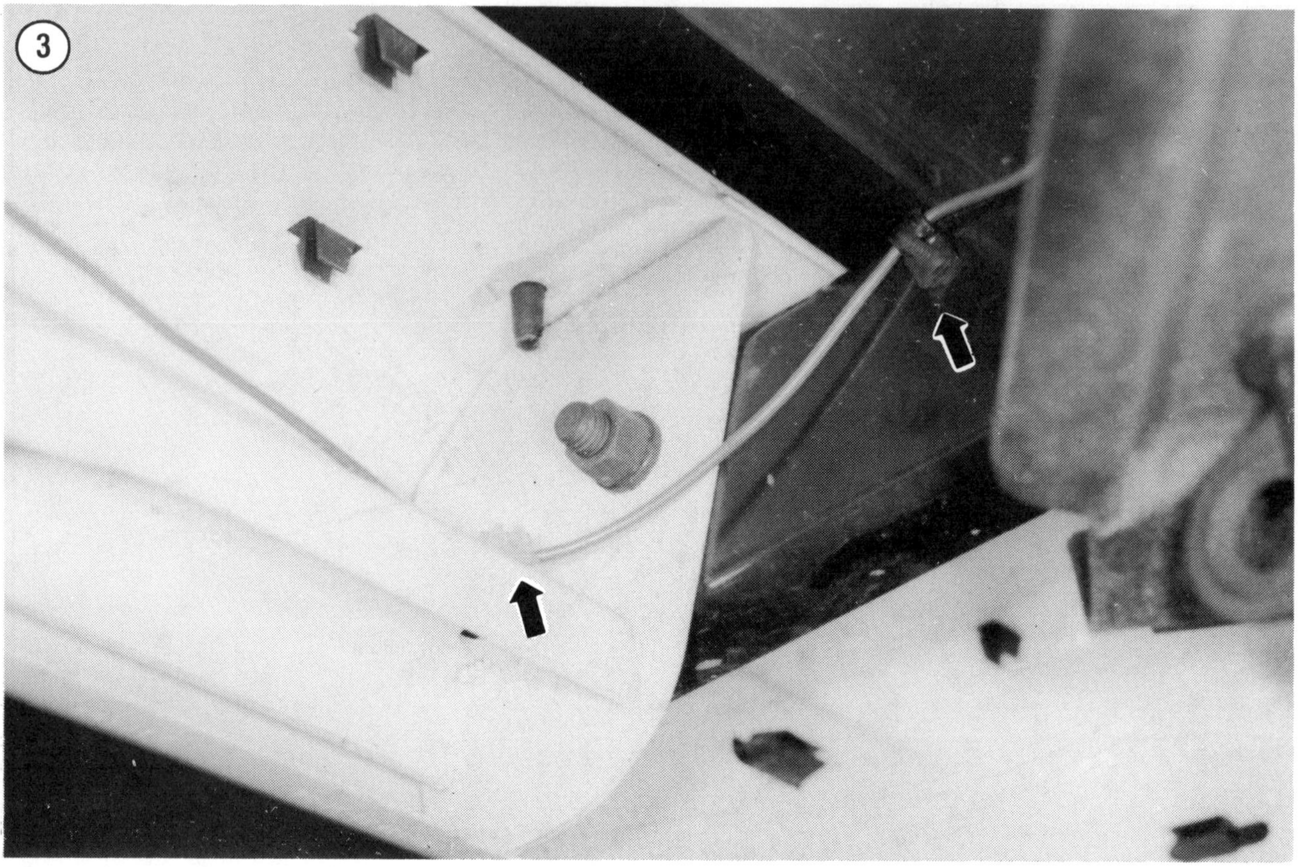

4

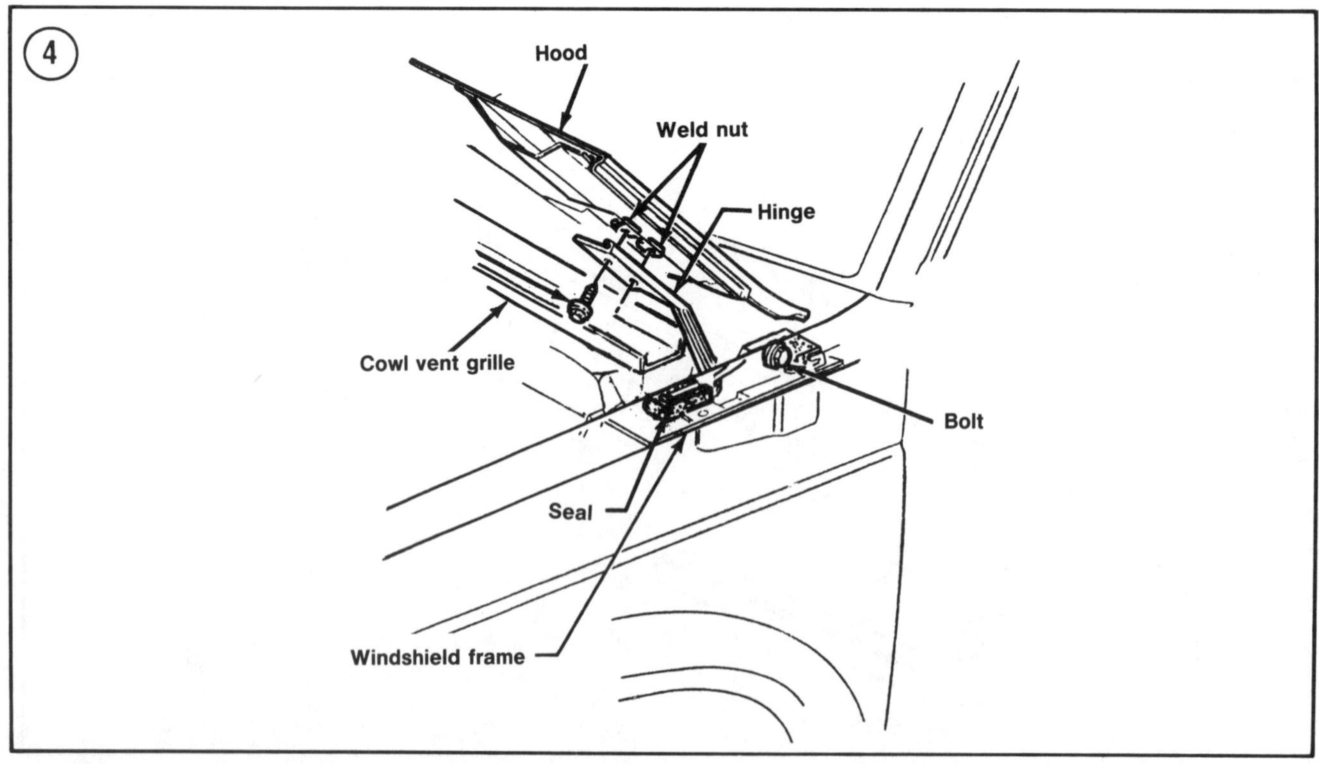
Hood
Weld nut
Hinge
Cowl vent grille
Bolt
Seal
Windshield frame

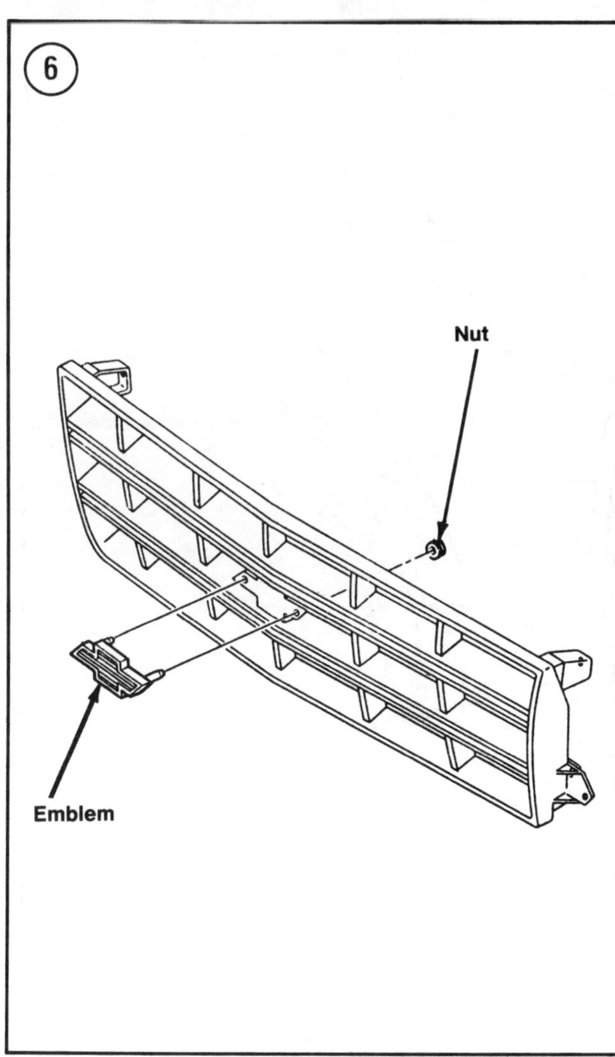

2. Align the hood as necessary, then tighten the bolts to 15-25 ft.-lb. (20-34 N•m).
3. To align the hood vertically with the fenders, loosen the hood bumper locknuts located on either side of the radiator support (**Figure 5**). Turn the bumpers to raise or lower them. Once properly adjusted, the hood should be tight when latched. If the hood rattles or moves downward when hand pressure is applied, readjust the bumpers higher. If the hood will not latch properly, readjust the bumpers lower. Once adjustment is correct, tighten the bumper locknuts.

Removal/Installation

This procedure requires the help of an assistant.
1. Raise the hood and place a blanket or towels between the hood and cowl vent grille to prevent damage to the paint.
2. Disconnect the underhood lamp wire, if so equipped.
3. Use a soft lead pencil to make alignment marks around the hinges directly on the hood. The marks will make installation easier.
4. Place a protective cover over the windshield. Place a block of wood between the hood and windshield to prevent a sudden rearward movement of the hood.
5. While an assistant supports one side of the hood, remove the hinge-to-hood bolts. See **Figure 4**.
6. Support your side of the hood while the assistant removes the other hinge-to-hood bolts. Lift the hood off and place it out of the way.

NOTE
Do not place the hood flat on the floor or ground. Lean it up against a wall or other solid object to prevent the possibility of damage.

7. Installation is the reverse of removal. Align the marks made before removal. If necessary, adjust the hood as described in this chapter. Tighten the attaching bolts to 15-25 ft.-lb. (20-34 N•m).

GRILLE

Refer to **Figure 6** for this procedure.
1. Remove the left and right headlight bezels. See Chapter Eight.
2. Remove the 4 grille-to-radiator support screws.
3. Remove the grille from the vehicle.
4. Installation is the reverse of removal.

FRONT FENDERS

Left Front Fender Replacement

Refer to **Figures 7-9** for this procedure.

1. Remove the right and left headlight bezels. See Chapter Eight.
2. Remove the grille as described in this chapter.
3. Remove the front bumper as described in this chapter.
4. Remove the radiator coolant recovery reservoir.
5. Remove the windshield washer reservoir.
6. Remove the hood lock cable.
7. Remove the windshield wiper arms.
8. Remove the cowl vent grille as described in this chapter.

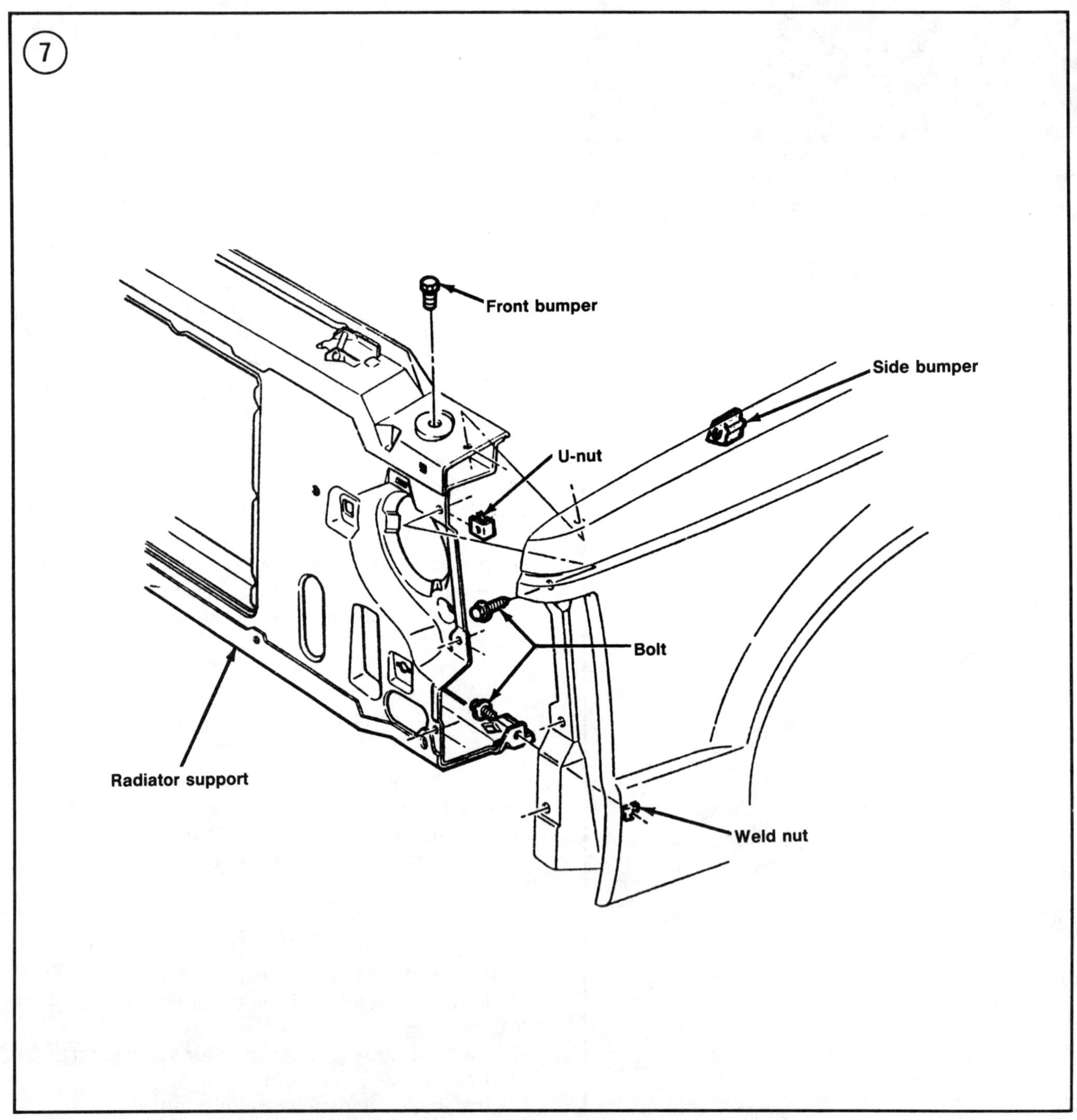

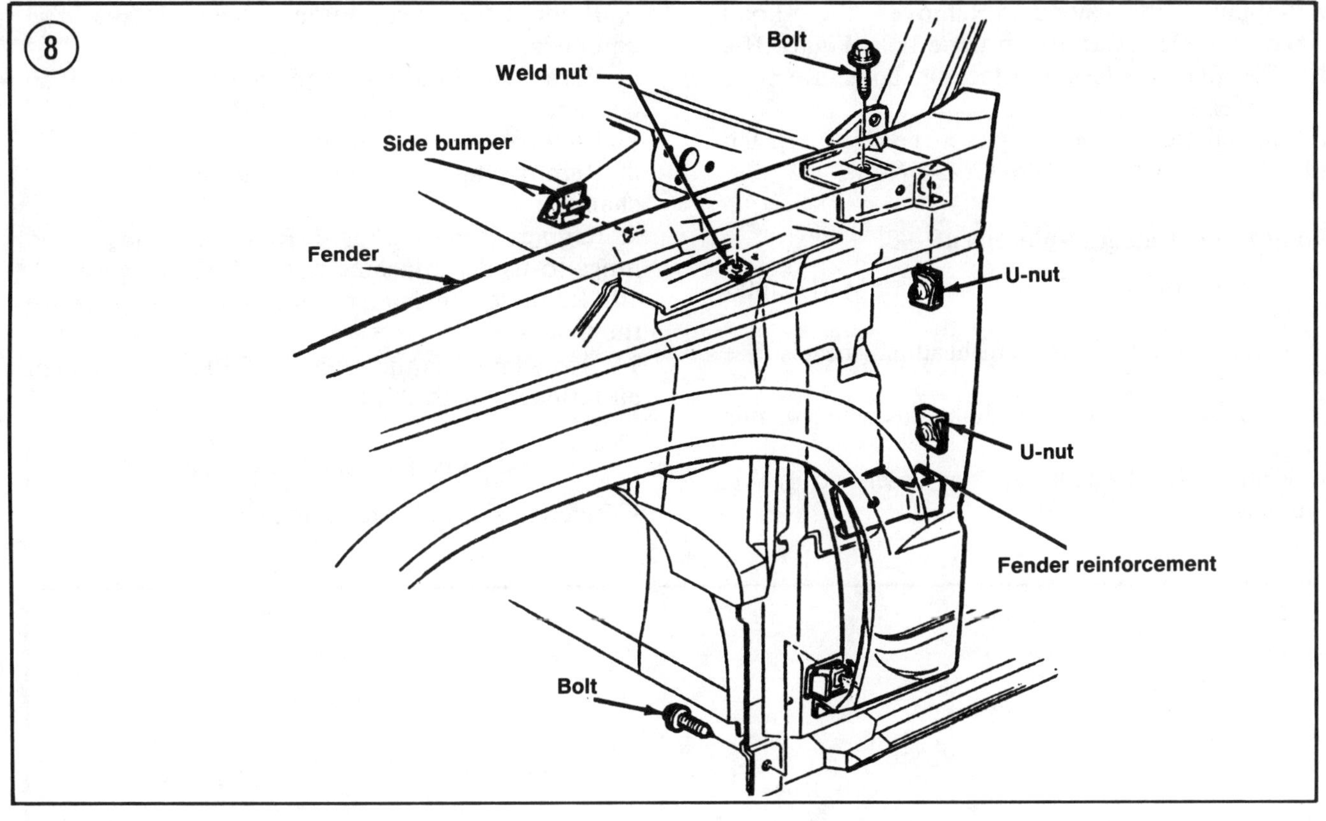
8
Bolt
Weld nut
Side bumper
Fender
U-nut
U-nut
Fender reinforcement
Bolt

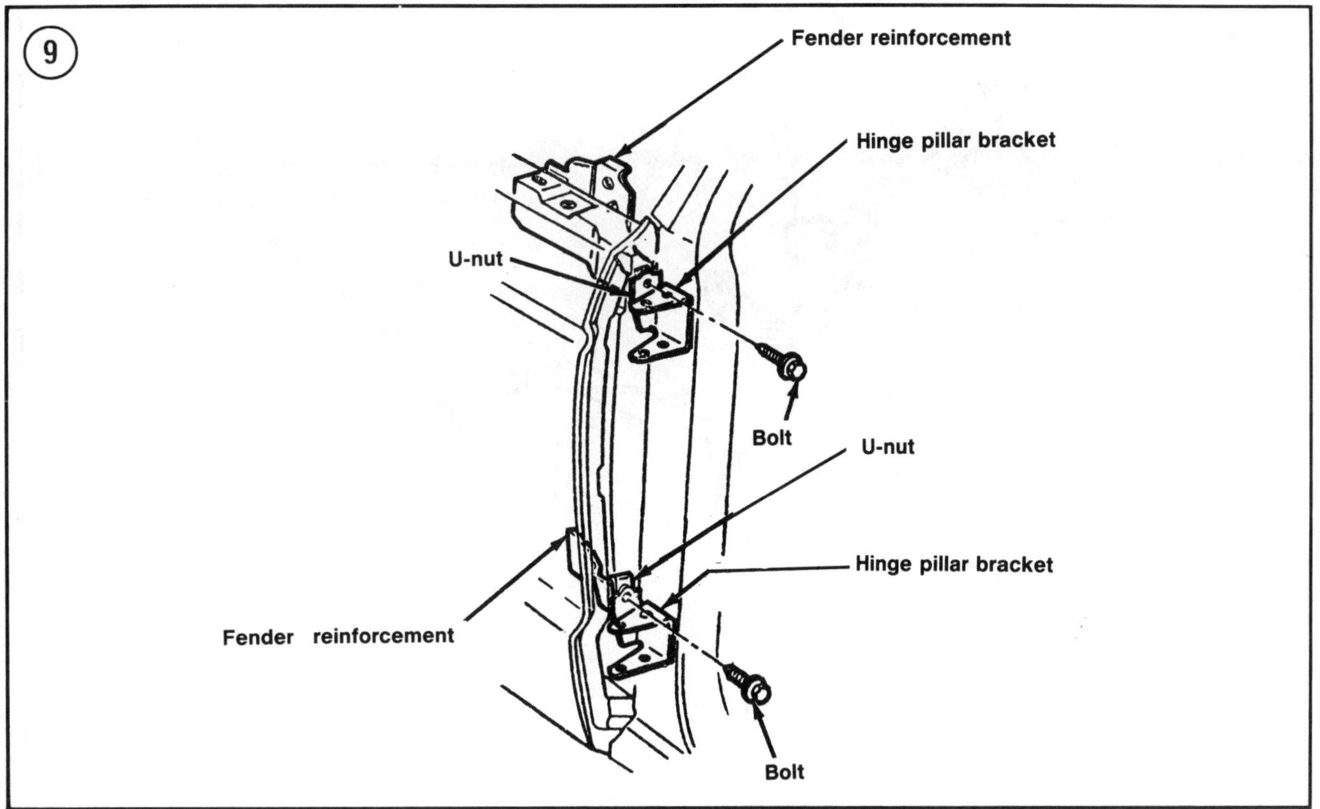
9
Fender reinforcement
Hinge pillar bracket
U-nut
Bolt
U-nut
Hinge pillar bracket
Fender reinforcement
Bolt

13

9. Support the hood. Remove the hood hinge-to-fender attaching nut and bolt (**Figure 10**).
10. Remove the fender attaching bolts. Remove the fender.
11. Installation is the reverse of removal. Tighten all fasteners to 15-25 ft.-lb. (20-34 N•m).

Right Front Fender Replacement

1. Remove the battery and battery tray (Chapter Eight).
2. Remove the left and right headlight bezels. See Chapter Eight.
3. Remove the radiator grille as described in this chapter.
4. Remove the front bumper as described in this chapter.
5. Remove the air conditioning vacuum tank, if so equipped.
6. Remove the radio antenna mast and base, if so equipped.
7. Remove the windshield wiper arms.
8. Remove the cowl vent grille as described in this chapter.
9. Support the hood. Remove the hood hinge-to-fender attaching nut and bolt (**Figure 10**).
10. Remove the fender attaching bolts. Remove the fender.
11. Installation is the reverse of removal. Tighten all fasteners to 15-25 ft.-lb. (20-34 N•m).

COWL VENT GRILLE

Refer to **Figure 11** for this procedure.

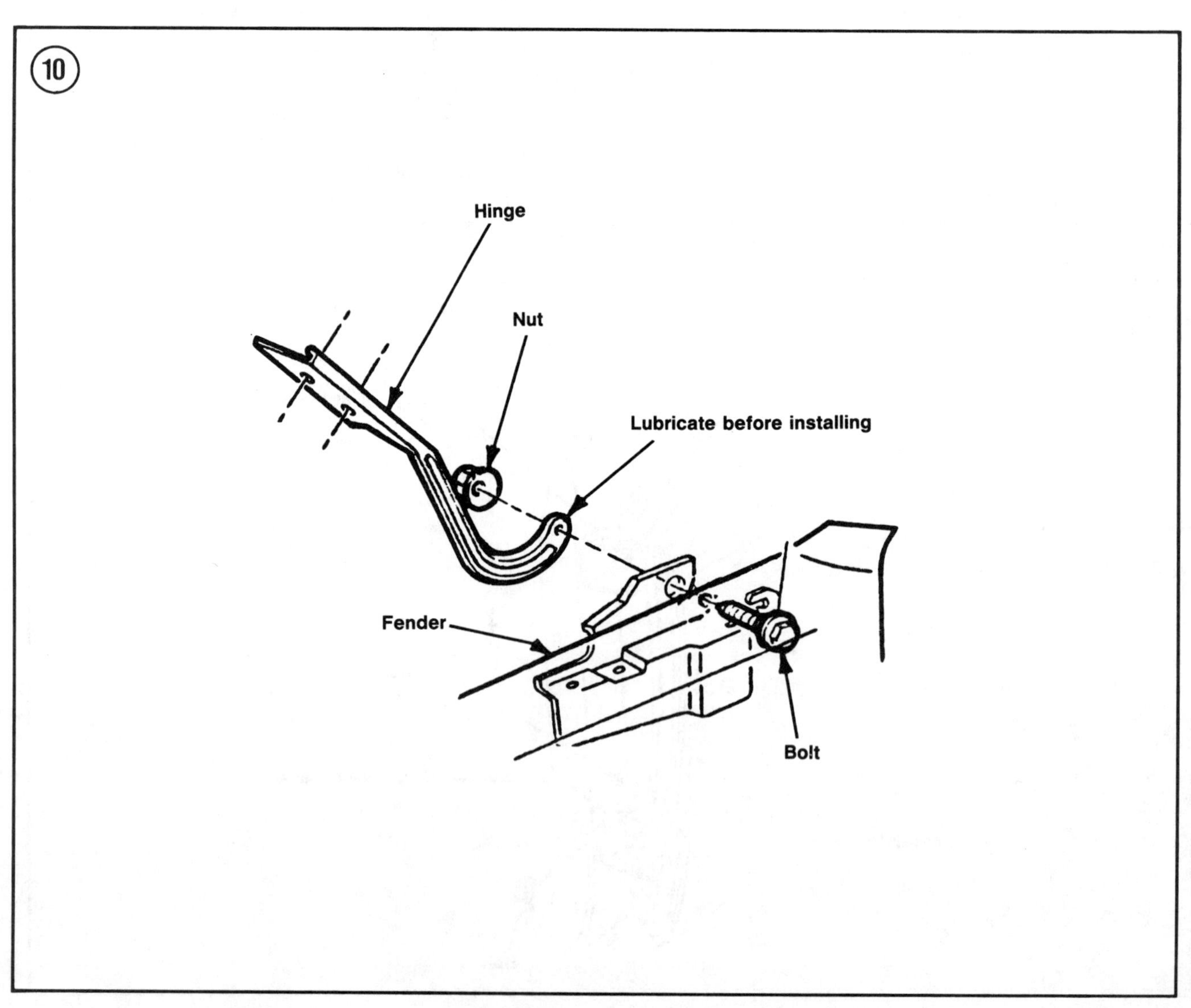

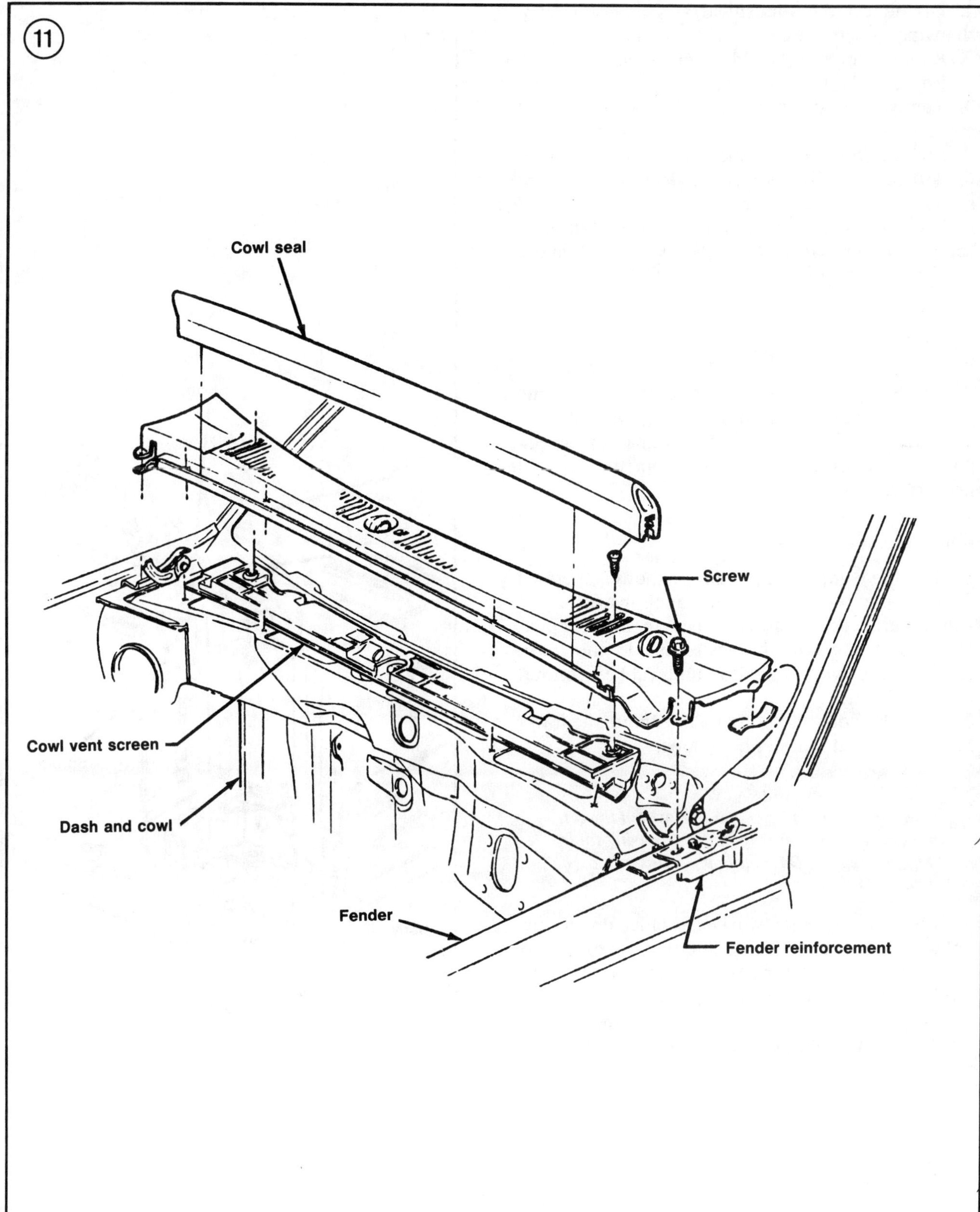
11
Cowl seal
Screw
Cowl vent screen
Dash and cowl
Fender
Fender reinforcement

1. Disconnect the windshield washer hoses from the wiper assemblies.
2. Remove the windshield wiper arms.
3. Remove the cowl top seal.
4. Remove the screws holding the vent grille to the cowl.
5. Lift the front edge of the vent grille and pull it toward the front of the vehicle. Remove the vent grille.
6. Installation is the reverse of removal. Make sure the vent grille is installed underneath the 2 fender reinforcement clips.

DOORS

The door hinges are welded to the door panel and the body hinge pillars (**Figure 12**). No adjustment is possible. A removable hinge pin allows the door to be removed from the body, if necessary.

Removal

1. If the door contains power-operated components, remove the trim panel, insulator pad and water deflector as described in this chapter. Disconnect the wire harnesses inside the door. Remove the wire harnesses and rubber conduit from the door.
2. Tape the door and body pillars above the lower hinge with cloth-backed body tape.

WARNING

*Cover the door spring (**Figure 12**) with a towel to prevent it from snapping out and causing injury during Step 3. Do not apply pressure to the hold-down link.*

3. Insert a long screwdriver blade under the hold-down link pivot point and over the top of the spring. Cover the spring with a towel and lift the screwdriver to disengage the spring.
4. Spread the hinge pin barrel clip (**Figure 13**) with 2 small screwdrivers and move the clip above the pin recess.

NOTE

The clip will fall free when the hinge pin is removed.

5. Have an assistant support the door. Remove the lower hinge pin with locking pliers and a soft-faced hammer.

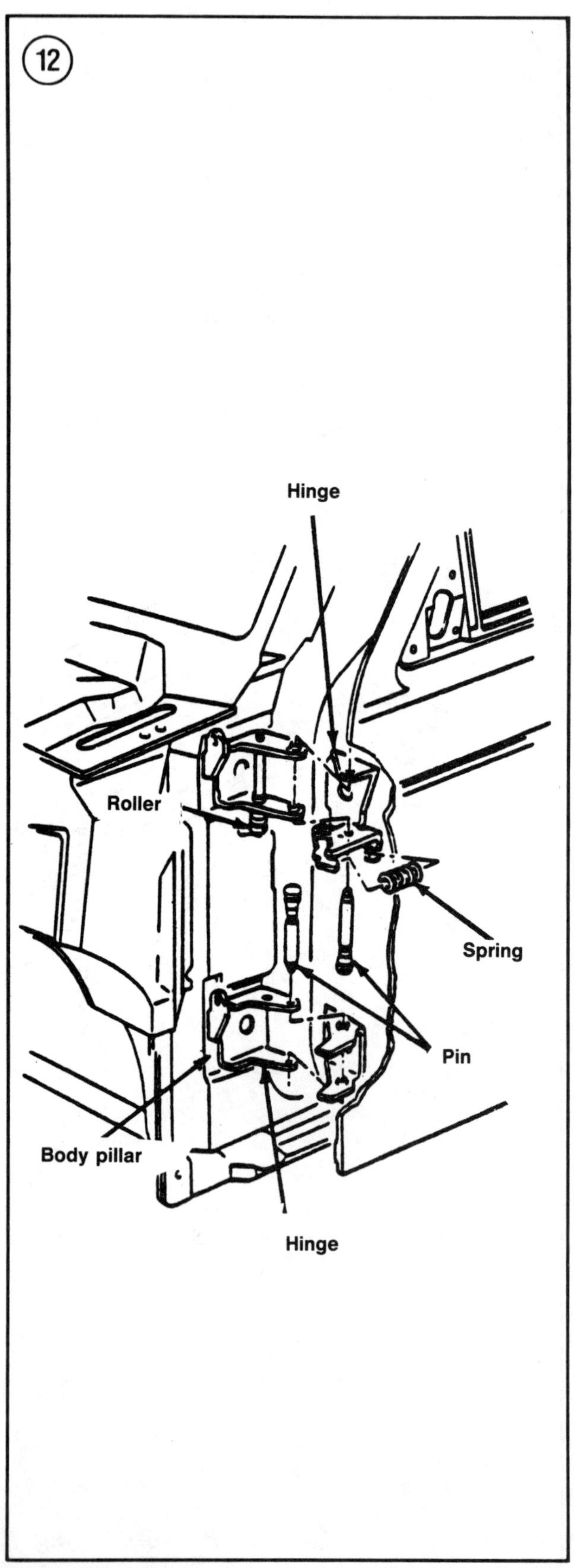

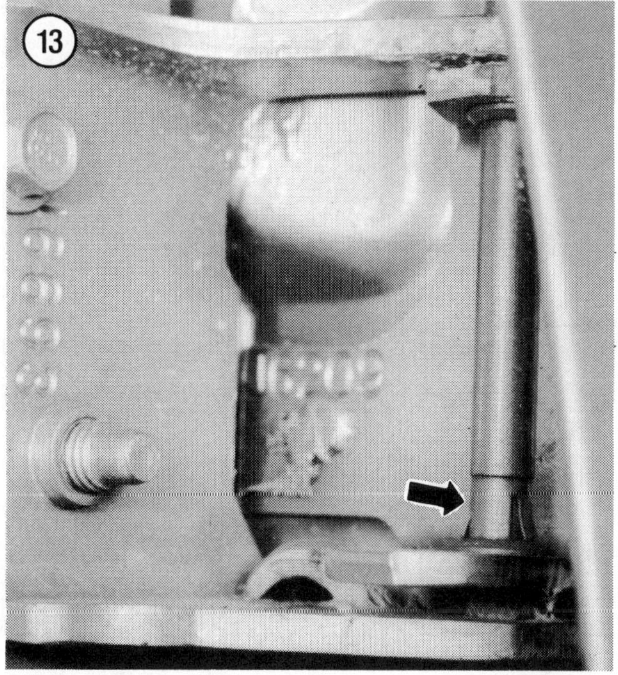

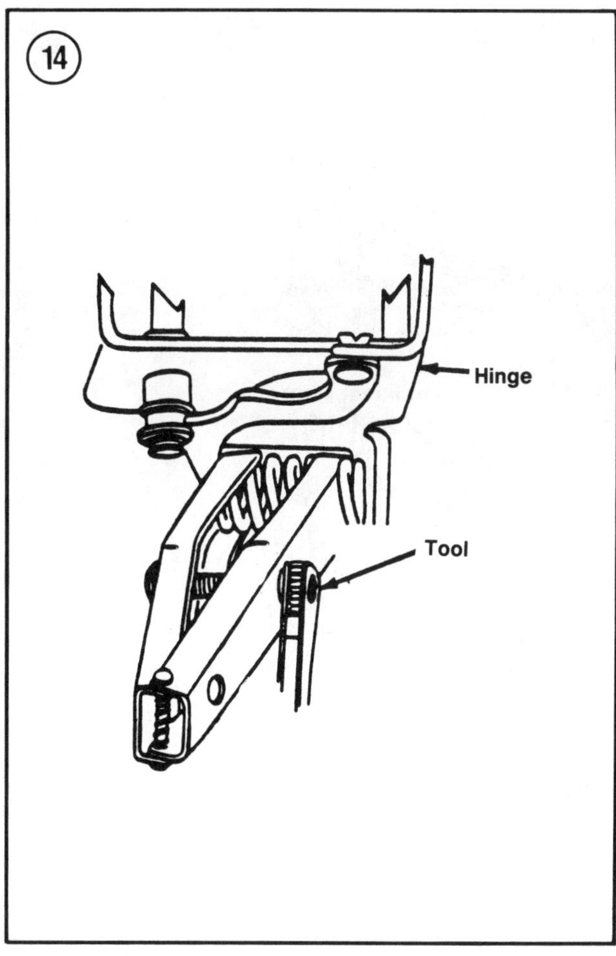

6. When the lower hinge pin is removed, install a bolt in its place to maintain door position while removing the upper pin.
7. Remove the upper hinge pin. Remove the bolt from the lower hinge. Remove the door.

Installation

A special spring compressor tool (GM part No. J-28625-A) is required for this procedure. Refer to **Figure 14**.

1. Have an assistant position the door to the body. Install a bolt in the lower hinge pin hole.
2. Install the barrel clips on the hinge pins. Install the upper hinge pin with its pointed end facing upward and the lower pin with its pointed end facing down.
3. Insert the door spring in the spring compressor part No. J-28625-A. Compress the spring and tool in a vise and install the tool bolt to hold the spring compressed.
4. Remove the tool and spring from the vise. Install the tool and spring in the lower door hinge. The slot in one tool jaw fits over the hold-down link. The hole on the other jaw fits over the bubble.
5. Remove the tool bolt and tool. Open and close the door to check proper spring operation.
6. If the door contains power-operated components, install the wire harnesses and conduit. Connect the wire harnesses and install the door trim panel as described in this chapter.

Trim Panel Removal/Installation

Standard trim panels are a 1-piece unit; custom trim panels are a 2-piece assembly. Both are removed in essentially the same manner. Door armrests are fastened to the trim panel with screws. Since trim designs differ between the various vehicle models and trim levels, carefully inspect the panel to be removed for screw location before beginning this procedure. Some screws are hidden from sight under pop-off caps. This procedure applies to all models in a general way. If some steps are not applicable to the vehicle being serviced, proceed to the next step.

1. If equipped with window regulator handles, insert a door clip remover tool behind the regulator

15

Tool J-9886
Retaining spring disengaged
Push tool in direction of arrow
Inside handle

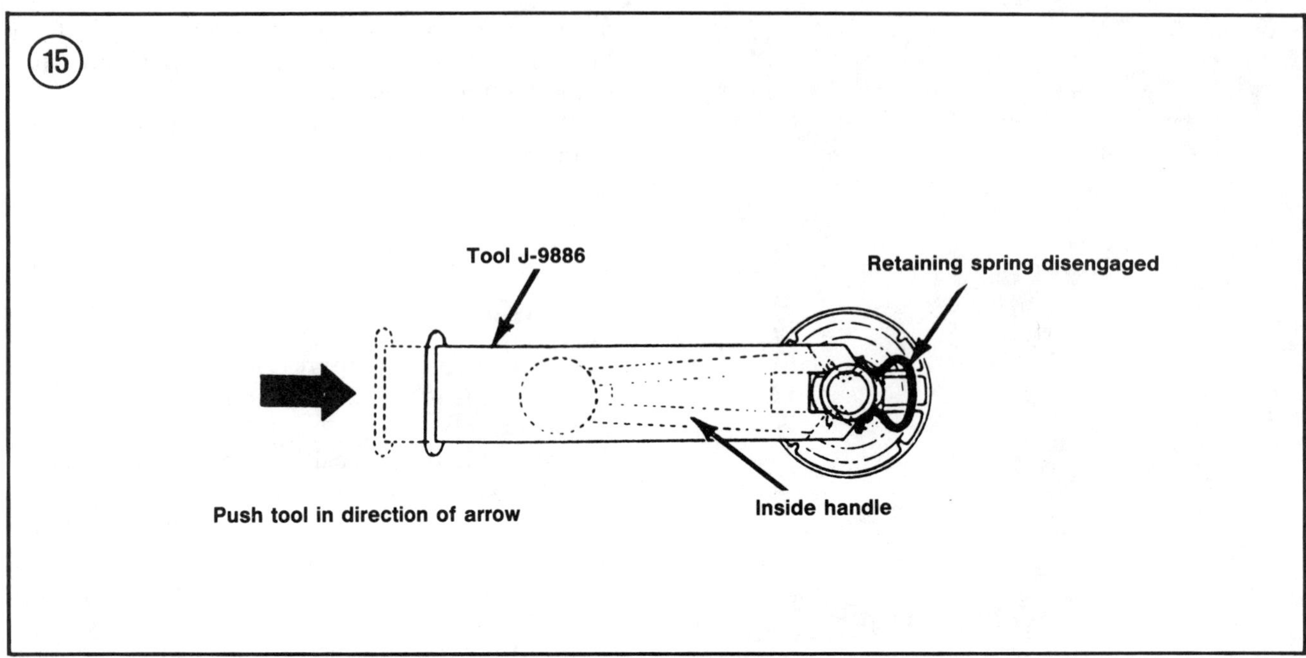

16

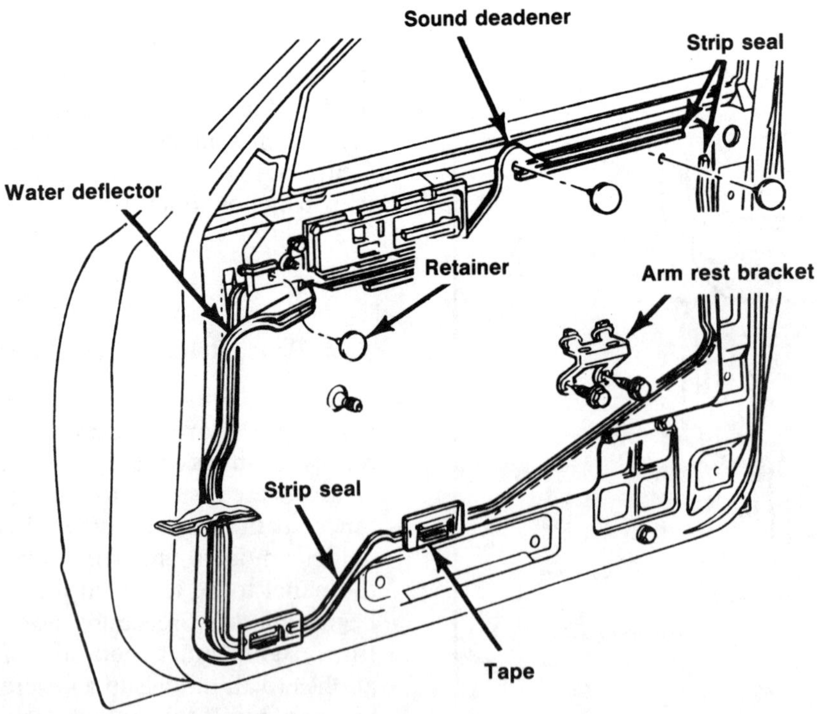

Sound deadener
Strip seal
Water deflector
Retainer
Arm rest bracket
Strip seal
Tape

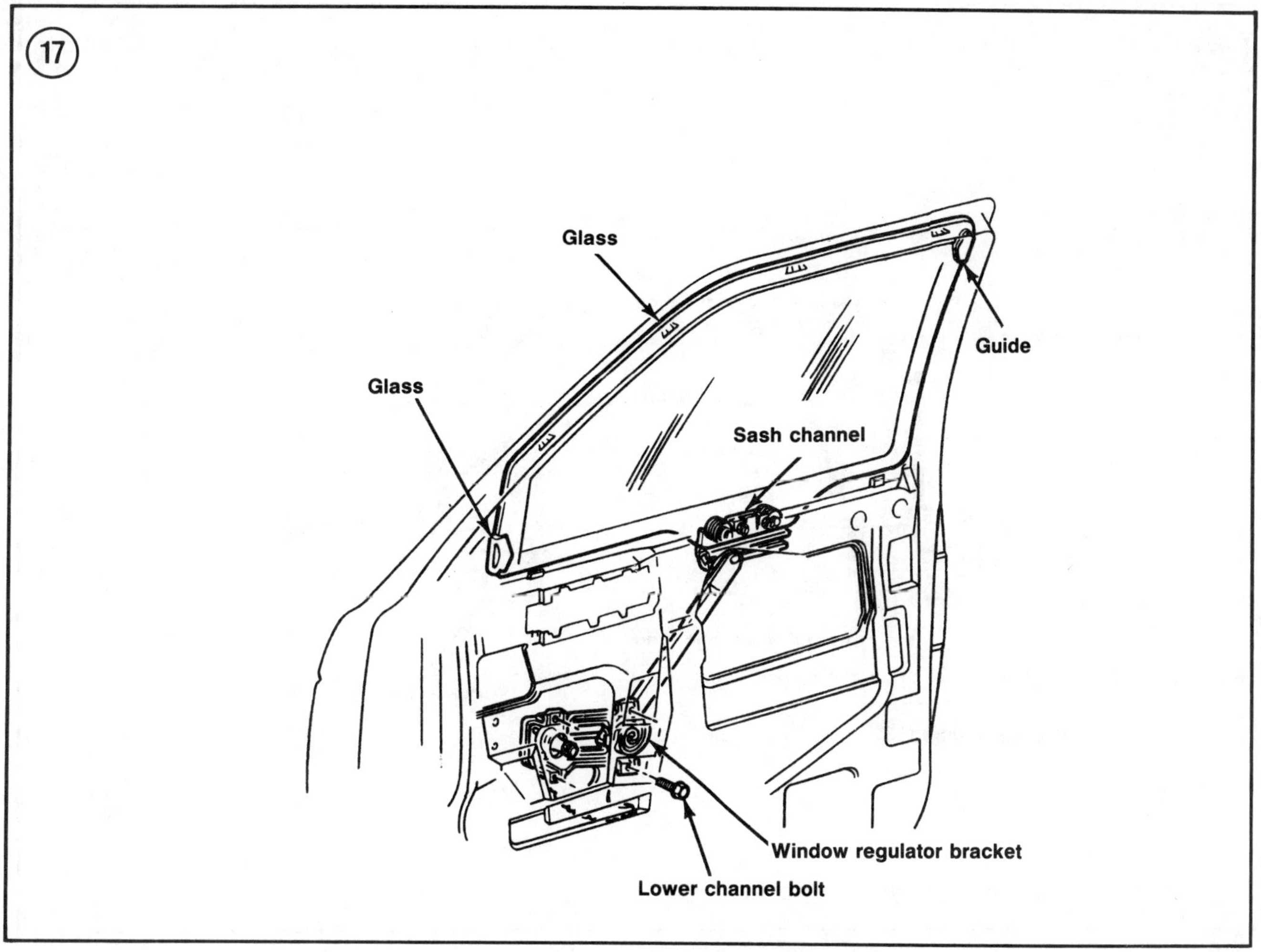

bezel (**Figure 15**) and push the retaining clip off the spindle. Remove the handle.
2. If equipped with a pull cup opener, remove the bezel retaining screws. Pry the lock knob off the lock rod. Slide the knob forward and remove it from the rod.
3. Pry power switches from the trim panel and unplug the wire harnesses.
4. Remove the upper trim panel on custom trim models.
5. Remove all armrest-to-inner door panel screws.
6. Use a putty knife, a wide-blade screwdriver or a door panel trim stick to pry the trim panel retaining pins from the edges of the inner door panel.

NOTE
The water deflector may be cemented to the inner door panel or retained in place with plastic nails.

7. Carefully remove the water deflector with a putty knife, if so equipped. See **Figure 16**.
8. Installation is the reverse of removal. Make sure the armrest retaining clips are properly positioned on the inner door panel before installing the water deflector. Use a silicone gasket sealer to attach the water deflector and repair any tears with duct tape.

Window Replacement

The window assembly consists of an unframed piece of glass with guide clips attached. The glass is attached to the window regulator sash with screws. The glass and sash channel are removed from the door as an assembly. The sash channel is removed and installed on the replacement glass.

Refer to **Figure 17** for this procedure.

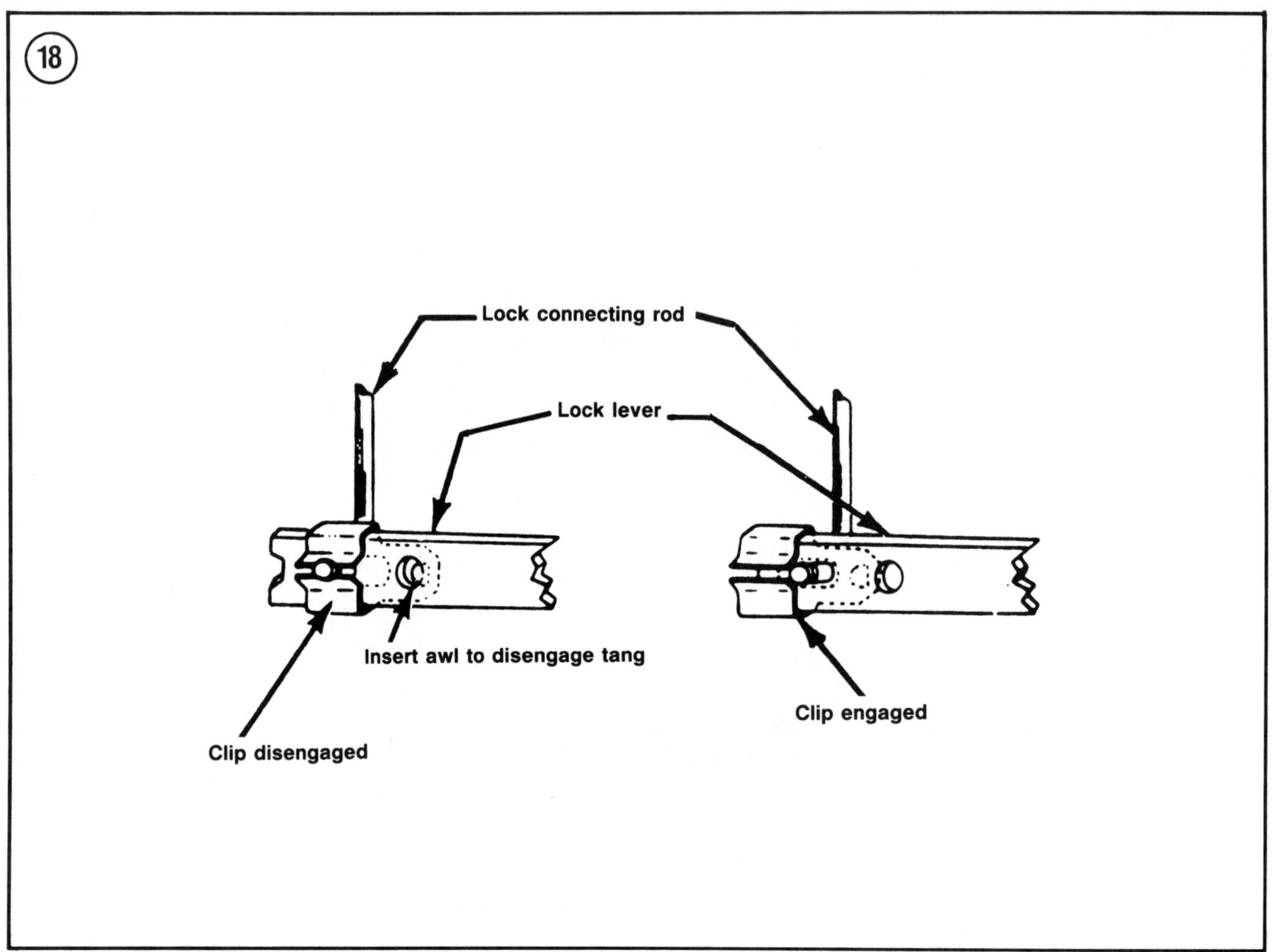

1. Remove the door trim panel, water deflector and armrest bracket as described in this chapter.
2. Raise the glass approximately 3 in. (75 mm) above the beltline.
3. Remove the screws holding the window regulator in the sash channel.
4. Rotate the glass forward and disengage the regulator roller from the sash channel.
5. Lower the glass into the door. Disengage the rear guide clip on the glass from the rear run channel.
6. Carefully raise the glass, tilt it forward and remove from the inside of the upper door frame.
7. Installation is the reverse of removal.

Lock Replacement

NOTE

*Spring clips are used to retain linkage connections inside the door. A slot in the clip allows it to be disengaged with a screwdriver when disconnecting linkage. To disengage a spring clip, use a screwdriver or awl as shown in **Figure 18**. To install a clip, reverse the removal procedure.*

1. Raise the window glass to its full up positon.
2. Remove the door trim panel as described in this chapter.
3. Disconnect the lock rod from the lock cylinder.

CAUTION

Wear gloves to prevent injury when removing the cylinder retainer by hand in Step 4.

4. Slide the cylinder retainer forward to disengage it from the cylinder body. Remove the lock cylinder and gasket.
5. Installation is the reverse of removal. Lubricate with WD-40 or equivalent spray lubricant.

FRONT SEATS

Seats are secured to adjuster mechanisms. The adjuster/seat assembly fits over studs welded to the floor pan anchor plates and is retained by nuts. See **Figure 19** for bucket seats and **Figure 20** for bench seats.

Removal/Installation

1. Draw the seat to its full-forward position.
2. Remove the adjuster rear foot covers and/or track covers to provide access to the attaching nuts. Remove the rear attaching nuts.
3. Move the seat to its full-rearward position.
4. Remove the front foot or track covers, as necessary. Remove the front attaching nuts.
5. Remove the seat assembly from the vehicle.
6. Installation is the reverse of removal. Tighten attaching nuts to 15-21 ft.-lb. (20-28 N•m). Check seat operation for smooth and complete travel.

GLOVE BOX REPLACEMENT

Refer to **Figure 21** for this procedure.

1. Open the glove box door. Remove the 5 screws holding the glove box to the instrument panel pad.
2. Pull the glove box out far enough to disconnect the glove box light. Remove the glove box.
3. If the door requires removal, remove the retaining screws.
4. Installation is the reverse of removal.

INSTRUMENT PANEL

Removal/Installation

This procedure covers removal of the entire instrument panel assembly. To remove just the gauge cluster, see *Instruments*, Chapter Eight. Refer to **Figure 22**.

1. Disconnect the negative battery cable.
2. Remove the trim panel and glove box.
3. Remove the radio speakers and grille, if so equipped.
4. Remove the center and left trim panels.
5. Remove the heater or heater/AC control assembly. See *Control Assembly Removal/Installation*, Chapter Seven.
6. Remove the instrument cluster trim plate.
7. Disconnect the speedometer cable and remove the cluster housing. See *Instruments*, Chapter Eight.
8. Remove the steering column trim cover and lower trim plate.
9. Remove both windshield garnish moldings.
10. Remove the hood release bracket and cable.
11. Unplug all electrical connectors. Remove the instrument panel.
12. Installation is the reverse of removal. If installing a new instrument panel, remove all components from the old one and install them on the new panel.

CONSOLE REPLACEMENT

Refer to **Figure 23** for these procedures.

Automatic Transmission

1. Remove the console front ash tray. Remove 2 Torx-head fasteners from under the ash tray.
2. Lift the front of the trim plate assembly, disconnect the wiring harness and remove the trim plate. Remove the 3 screws located under the trim plate.
3. Remove the rear ash tray. Remove the screw located under the ash tray. Lift the console off and remove it from the vehicle.
4. Installation is the reverse of removal.

Manual Transmission

1. Move the shift lever to NEUTRAL. Set the parking brake.
2. Remove the console front ash tray. Remove the 2 screws from under the ash tray.
3. Loosen the set screw at the base of the shift knob. Remove the shift knob.
4. Remove 2 screws from the console base at the rear. Lift the console off and remove it from the vehicle.
5. Installation is the reverse of removal.

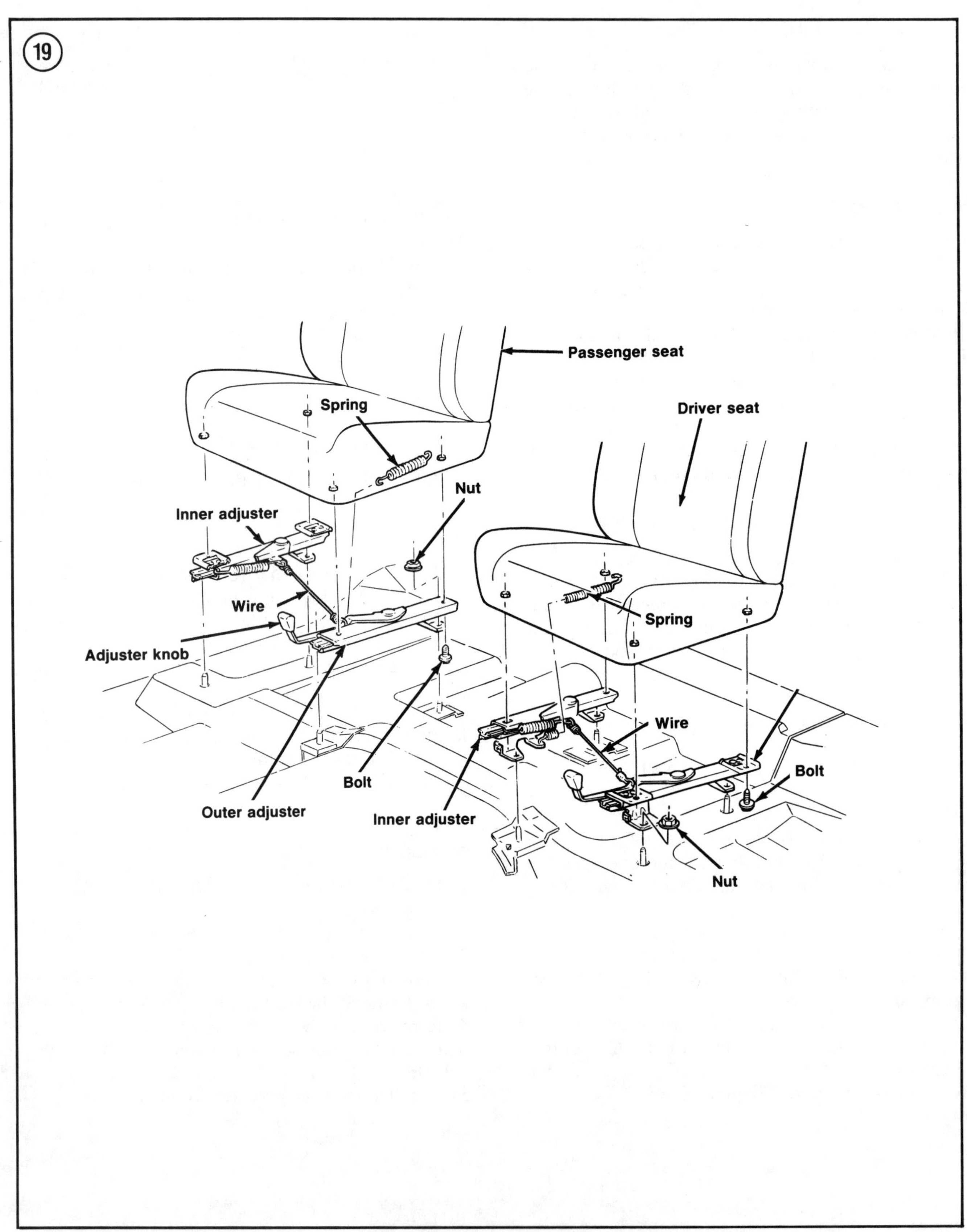
19
Passenger seat
Spring
Driver seat
Nut
Inner adjuster
Wire
Adjuster knob
Spring
Wire
Bolt
Bolt
Outer adjuster
Inner adjuster
Nut

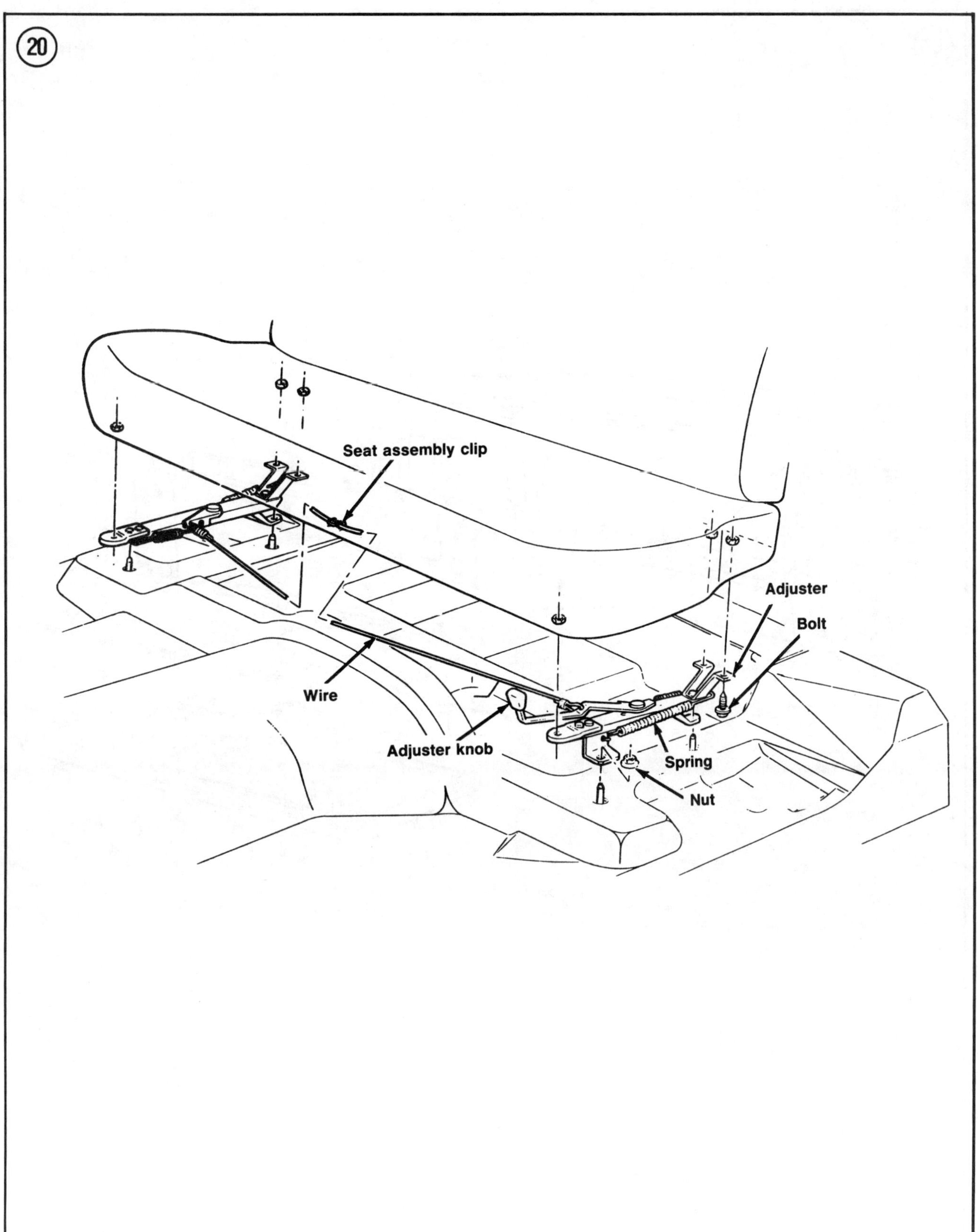
20
Seat assembly clip
Adjuster
Bolt
Wire
Adjuster knob
Spring
Nut

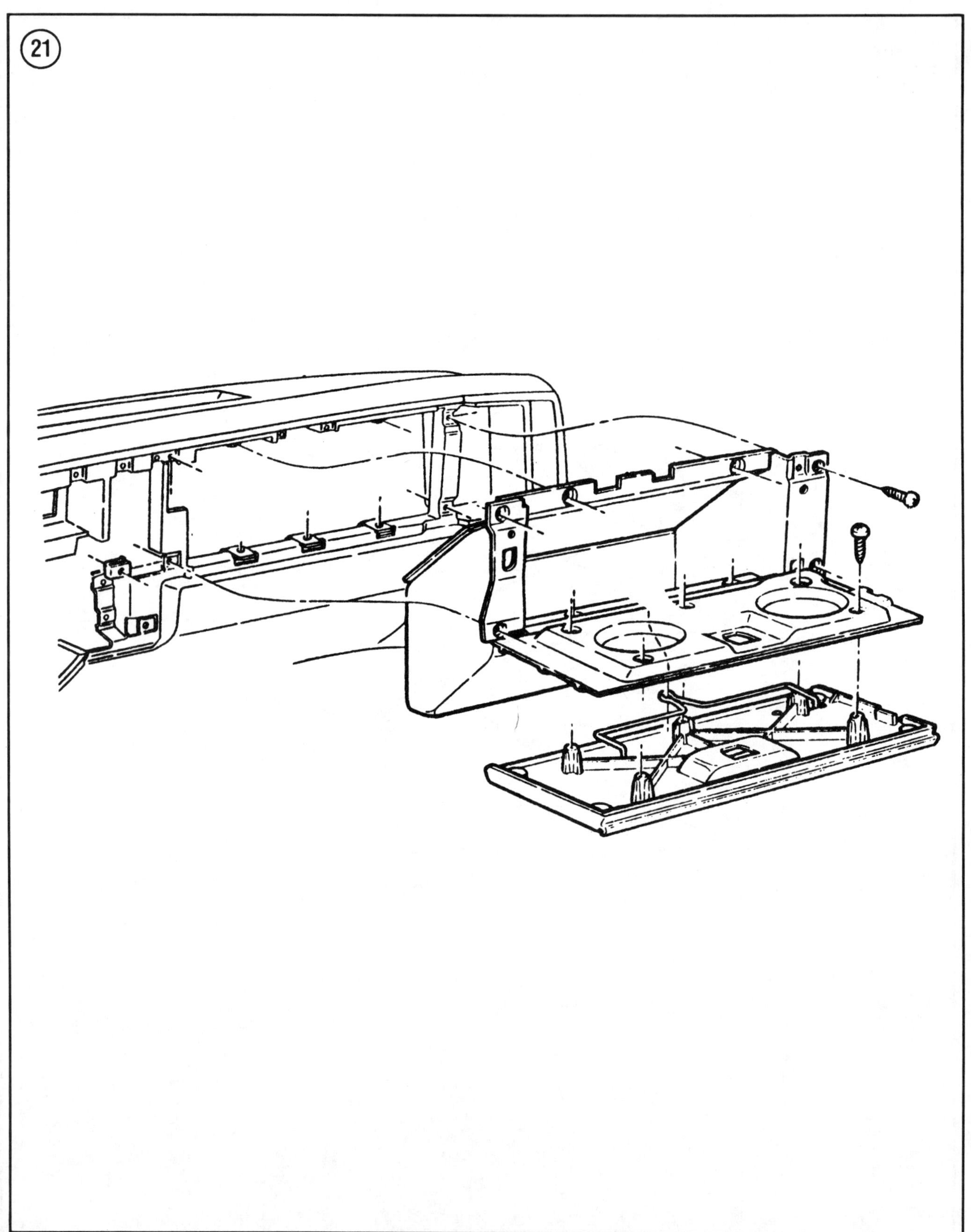
21

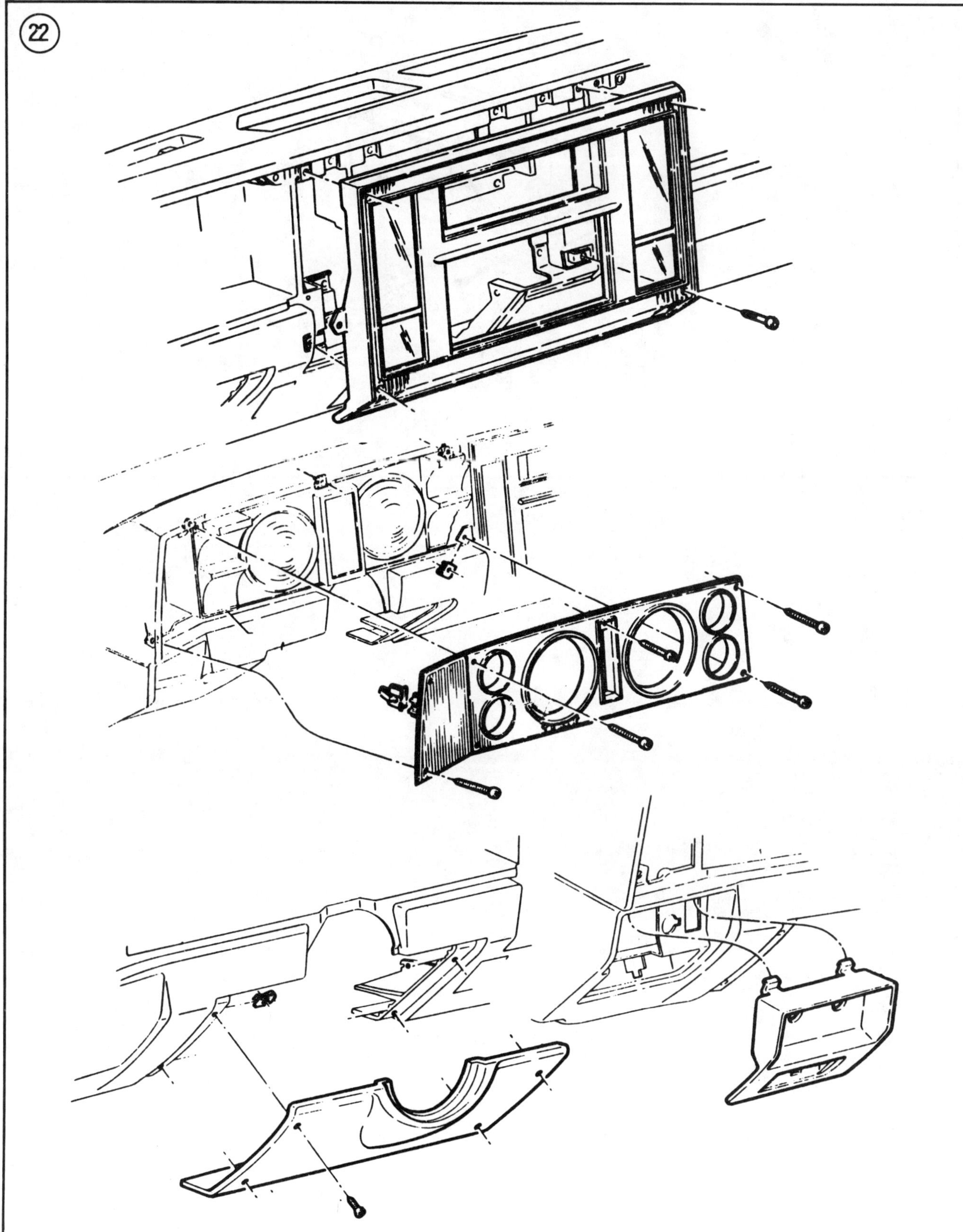
22

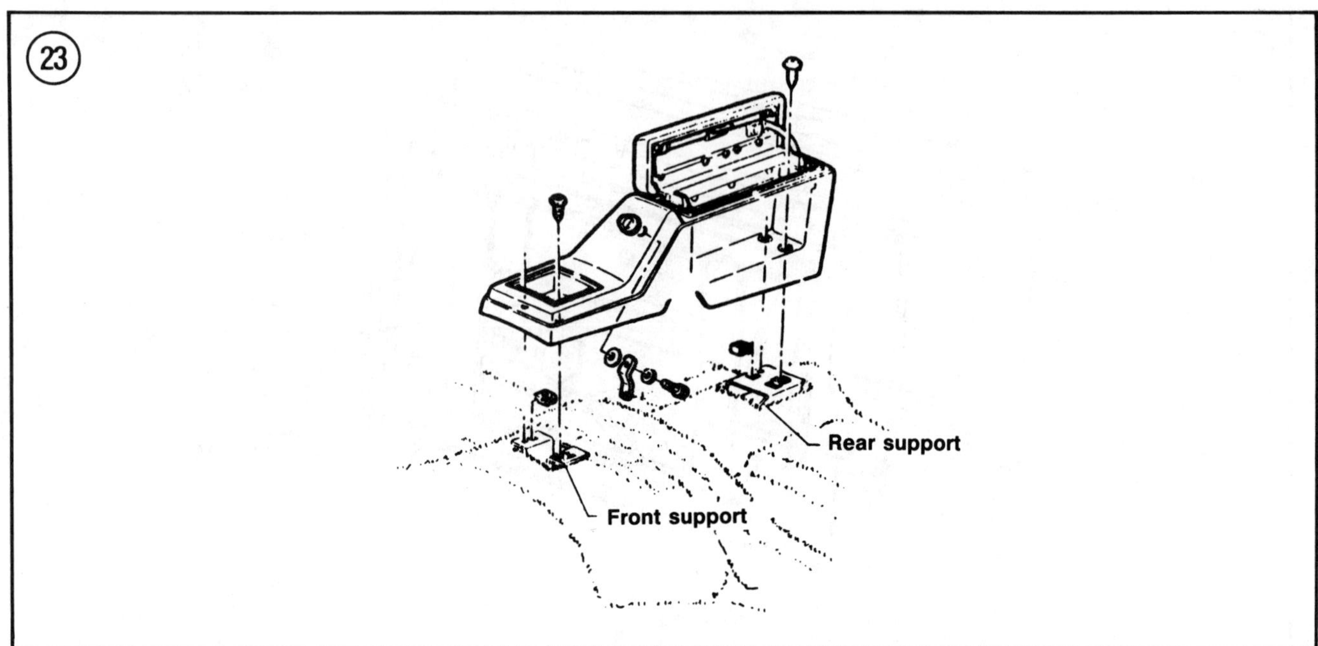
23
Rear support
Front support

INDEX

QUICK INDEX

A

B

C

14

F

G

H

I

J

L

M

O

P

R

CLYMER LABOR, TIME AND PARTS PRICING GUIDE

The time estimates, price information and skill level data that follow were prepared in conjunction with Mitchell Information Services, the leader in providing this material to professional mechanics, garages and fleet operators.

This section will tell you 3 vital things about 116 different jobs on the Chevy/GMC S- and T-Series pickups and Blazer:

How long the job takes.
How complicated the job is.
How much the parts should cost.

1. How long the job takes: This is the same time figure used by dealers and independent shops to estimate labor charges. Times are shown in tenths of an hour (6-minute intervals). For example, a labor time of 0.3 is 3 tenths of an hour or 18 minutes.

These times are estimates which generally reflect the needs of an average trained auto mechanic using factory recommended tools and following factory recommended procedures. They include allowances for repair preparation, normal cleanup associated with repair, road testing, mechanic personal needs, preventive measures and any other service that would normally accompany an individual operation.

Times do not include allowances for diagnosis, machine operations or obtaining substitutes for factory recommended special tools.

Estimated labor time can be used in 2 ways:

a. If you decide to have a job done professionally, you can compare the time specified in this chart with the shop's labor estimate for the same work.
b. If you decide to do a job yourself, you can use the estimated time, together with the job's skill level, to estimate how long it will take you.

WARNING
Unless you are a professional mechanic with a fully equipped shop, you should expect a job to take you longer than the estimated time. Since the skills and equipment possessed by home mechanics vary widely, it is impossible to estimate how long a job should take a home mechanic. Use the estimated labor times as a rough guide only. Never hurry a job, trying to finish within the estimated time. You may damage the vehicle or injure yourself.

2. How complicated the job is: Each job is placed in one of 4 skill levels:

A. HIGHLY SKILLED—Requires the use of precision measuring tools and highly specialized measuring equipment. Also requires thorough knowledge of complicated systems and strong diagnostic ability. Some jobs in this category can be done by home mechanics. Often, money can be saved by removing and installing a part yourself and having a shop do only the part of a job which requires special training and equipment. The manual will tell which of these jobs can be done by home mechanics.

B. SKILLED—Requires the use of basic tools and simple measuring devices. Accurate diagnosis is required using special test equipment. Must have basic knowledge of complex systems. Many skilled jobs can be done by a beginner using the Clymer manual. Often it is faster and more economical to have the job done by a shop, and the manual will point out such instances.

C. SEMI-SKILLED—Diagnosis is limited to a single possible cause of a problem. Must have basic knowledge of component or system operation. Can be done by a beginner using the Clymer manual.

D. LOW SKILLED—Repair consists of part replacement only. Can be done by a beginner using the Clymer manual.

The letter indicating skill level follows each job description.

3. How much the parts should cost: These are manufacturer's suggested retail prices as of the date this guide was prepared. These prices can be used for comparison. Chevy and GMC dealerships are independent businesses and may charge more or less than the manufacturer's suggested retail prices.

In comparing current parts prices with prices listed here, be sure to allow for time that has passed since the table was prepared.

Model Identification

Vehicles in this list are identified by model year, model code and date of manufacture. To identify your vehicle's model year and model code, refer to the vehicle identification plate in the engine compartment. Date of manufacture is usually listed on a plate on the driver's doorjamb.

Abbreviations

Several abbreviations are used in this guide. They are:

a. R&R: Remove and replace. Includes removal of part or assembly from vehicle, transfer of attached parts to new part or assembly and installation of new part or assembly on vehicle. Includes any alignment necessary to reposition new part or assembly.

b. R&I: Remove and install. Includes removal of part or assembly from vehicle and installation of same part or assembly on vehicle. Includes any alignment necessary to reposition part or assembly.

* Indicates item is part of General Motors Target Marketing Program and does not have a manufacturer's suggested retail price. The listed price is an approximation.

CLYMER LABOR, TIME AND PARTS PRICING GUIDE

ABBREVIATIONS

For full explanation of abbreviations, see the first page of this section.

Skill levels:
- A. Highly skilled
- B. Skilled
- C. Semi-skilled
- D. Low skilled

R&R: Remove and replace

R&I: Remove and install

Prices: These are manufacturer's suggested retail prices as of the date this guide was prepared.

* Indicates item is part of General Motors Target Marketing Program and does not have a manufacturer's suggested retail price. The listed price is an approximation.

1. Accelerator cable R&R (D)
Labor time ... 0.6

2. Air conditioner belt replacement (B)
Labor time
Diesel ... 0.3
Gasoline
1.9L engine
Non-power steering ... 0.5
Power steering ... 0.7
2.0L, 2.5L engines ... 0.5
V6 engine
Non-power steering ... 0.5
Power steering ... 0.7
Additional time:
Where air pump interferes, add 0.2.
Where power steerig interferes, add 0.2.

3A. Air filter element R&I (carburetor) (D)
Labor time ... 0.5
Filter price
A391 type ... $10.48
A826 type ... $12.72

3B. Air filter element R&I (fuel injection) (C)
Labor time ... 0.3
Element price ... $10.48

4. Air pump R&R (C)
Labor time ... 0.6
Pump price
1982-1985
1.9L engine ... $258.00
2.0L engine ... $148.74
2.8L engine ... $148.84
1986 ... see local supplier.

5. Alternator belt replacement (D)
Labor time
Four
Diesel
With a/c ... 0.5
Without a/c ... 0.3
Gasoline
With a/c ... 0.6
Without a/c ... 0.3
V6 ... 0.3
Additional time:
Where air pump interferes, add:
1982-1984 V6 ... 0.2.
1985-1986 V6 ... 0.1.
Where power steering interferes, add 0.2.

6. Alternator R&R (D)
Labor time
Diesel ... 0.5
Gasoline
1.9L engine ... 0.8
2.0L, 2.5L engines ... 0.5
2.8L engine ... 0.6
Alternator price
1982 ... $228.30

6. Alternator R&R (D) (cont.)
Alternator price (cont.)
1983
1.9L engine ... $228.30
2.0L, 2.8L engines
37 amp ... $205.70
66, 78 amp ... $204.70
1984-1985
55, 66, 78 amp
Except 1.9L engine ... $204.70
1.9L engine ... $232.25
94 amp ... $211.05
1986 ... $128.45

7. Automatic choke overhaul
Not applicable.

8. Automatic transmission R&I and overhaul (A)
Labor time
THM 200 w/o overdrive
1982-1984 2-wheel drive ... 10.3
1982-1984 4-wheel drive ... 11.1
THM700 R-4
1982-1984
2-wheel drive ... 9.7
4-wheel drive ... 11.9
1985-1986
2-wheel drive ... 10.2
4-wheel drive ... 11.1
Additional time .. With 4-wheel drive skid plate add 0.2.

9. Automatic transmission shift linkage adjustment (B)
Labor time ... 0.6

10. Automatic transmission neutral safety switch R&R (C)
Labor time ... 0.5

11. Battery test (C)
Labor time ... 0.5

12. Battery R&R (C)
Labor time
One ... 0.6
Both ... 0.8

13. Brake booster R&R (C)
Labor time ... 1.6
Booster price
1982
Single diaphragm ... $173.20
Dual diaphragm ... $271.25
1983-1984
Diesel ... $271.25
Gasoline
1.9L, 2.8L engines
Single diaphragm ... $174.75
Dual diaphragm ... $271.25
2.0L engine ... $271.25
1985-1986
Single diaphragm ... $174.25
Dual diaphragm ... $271.25

14. Breaker point R&R (C)
Not applicable.

15. Camshaft R&R (A)
Labor time
Diesel ... 8.3
Gasoline
1.9L engine ... 1.3
2.0L engine
2-wheel drive ... 6.3
4-wheel drive ... 7.4
2.5L engine ... 5.9
2.8L engine ... 6.4
Camshaft price
Diesel ... $204.00
Gasoline
1.9L engine ... $172.00
2.0L engine ... $127.00
2.5L engine ... $118.00
2.8L engine ... $113.00

16. Carburetor R&I and overhaul (B)
Labor time ... 2.7

17. Carburetor and/or gasket R&R (B)
Labor time
Isuzu ... 1.0
Rochester ... 0.8
Carburetor price ...... See local supplier.

18. Charging system test (B)
Labor time ... 0.6

19. Clutch plate or disc R&R (C)
Labor time
2-wheel drive
Isuzu transmission
Four ... 4.1
V6 ... 3.6
Warner transmission ... 3.2
4-wheel drive ... 5.1
Additional time:
With catalytic converter, add 0.4.
With skid plate add 0.4.

CLYMER LABOR, TIME AND PARTS PRICING GUIDE (continued)

19. Clutch plate or disc R&R (C) (cont.)
Pressure plate price
1982-1984
Diesel $153.00
Gasoline
1.9L engine
With paint stripe $137.00
Without paint stripe $114.00
2.0L engine
1983 .... $153.00
1984 .... $135.00
V6
1982-1983 .... $151.99*
1984 .... $146.00
1985-1986
Diesel $153.00
Gasoline
1.9L engine $137.00
2.5L engine $135.00
V6 .... $135.00
Disc price
1982-1984
Four
Diesel $117.00
Gasoline
1.9L engine $89.25
2.0L engine $119.00
V6 .... $123.43*
1985-1986
Four
Diesel $117.00
Gasoline
1.9L engine $89.25
2.5L engine $85.75
V6 .... $85.75

20. Clutch pedal adjustment (C)
Labor time 0.5

21. Clutch bleeding (C)
Labor time
1984 .... 0.5
1985-1986 .... 0.7

22. Clutch release bearing R&R (C)
Labor time
2-wheel drive
Isuzu
Four 3.7
V6 .... 3.2
Warner 2.5
4-wheel drive 4.4
Additional time:
With catalytic converter, add 0.4.
With skid plate, add 0.4.
Bearing price
1982-1984
Cable type $29.35
Hydraulic type $30.50
1985-1986 .... $23.85

ABBREVIATIONS

For full explanation of abbreviations, see the first page of this section.
Skill levels:
A. Highly skilled
B. Skilled
C. Semi-skilled
D. Low skilled
R&R: Remove and replace
R&I: Remove and install
Prices: These are manufacturer's suggested retail prices as of the date this guide was prepared.
* Indicates item is part of General Motors Target Marketing Program and does not have a manufacturer's suggested retail price. The listed price is an approximation.

23. Clutch master cylinder R&R (C)
Labor time
1984 .... 0.7
1985-1986 .... 1.0
Master cylinder price
1984 .... $48.75
1985-1986 .... see local supplier.

24. Clutch slave cylinder R&R (C)
Not available.

25. Compression test (C)
Includes: clean and adjust spark plugs.
Labor time
Four 0.6
V6 .... 0.8
Additional time:
Where air pump interferes, add 0.3.

26. Connecting rod and piston assembly R&I (A)
Labor time
1982-1983
1.9L engine
2-wheel drive
One 8.6
All 10.1
4-wheel drive
One 9.5
All 11.0
2.0L engine
2-wheel drive
One 8.5
All 10.0
4-wheel drive
One 9.5
All 11.0
V6 engine
1982
One 10.5
One each side 12.1
All 14.9

26. Connecting rod and piston assembly R&I (A) (cont.)
Labor time (cont.)
1982-1983 (cont.)
V6 engine (cont.)
1983
2-wheel drive
One 11.2
One each side 12.7
All 14.9
1984-1986
1.9L engine
2-wheel drive
One 9.0
All 10.5
4-wheel drive
One 9.9
All 11.4
2.0L engine
2-wheel drive
One 8.9
All 10.4
4-wheel drive
One 9.9
All 11.4
2.5L engine
2-wheel drive
One 7.3
All 9.5
4-wheel drive
One 10.0
All 12.5
V6 engine
2-wheel drive
One 11.5
One each side 13.6
All 15.8
4-wheel drive
One 11.2
One each side 13.6
All 15.2

Additional time:
Where air conditioning interferes, add:
1.9L engine .... 0.4.
2.0L engine .... 0.3.
2.5L engine .... 0.2.
V6 engine (one side or both) .... 0.2.
Where electronic engine control system interferes, add 0.5.
With skid plate, add 0.2.
Where cruise control interferes, add 0.2.
With auto trans (2WD) add 0.4.
Where power steering interferes, add:
1.9L engine .... 0.4.
2.0L engine .... 0.3.
2.5L engine (4WD) .... 0.1.
V6 engine .... 0.2.

CLYMER LABOR, TIME AND PARTS PRICING GUIDE (continued)

26. Connecting rod and piston assembly R&I (A) (cont.)
Connecting rod price
1982-1985
1.9L engine $53.50
2.0L engine $44.50
2.5L engine $39.50
V6 .... $36.50
1986
Four $39.50
V6 .... $36.50

27. Connecting rod bearing R&R (B)
Labor time
1.9L engine
2-wheel drive
One 5.0
All 6.0
4-wheel drive
One 6.1
All 8.4
2.0L engine
2-wheel drive
One 6.0
All 7.1
4-wheel drive
One 4.9
All 5.9
2.5L engine
2-wheel drive
One 3.0
All 4.2
4-wheel drive
One 5.8
All 6.9
V6
2-wheel drive
One 3.1
All 4.6
4-wheel drive
One 4.8
All 6.3
Standard bearing price
1.9L engine $12.80
2.0L engine $7.50
2.5L engine $11.25*
2.8L engine $10.87*

28. Cooling system flushing (D)
Labor time 0.7

29. Crankshaft R&R (A)
Labor time
1.9L engine
2-wheel drive 9.2
4-wheel drive 10.5
2.0L engine
2-wheel drive 9.2
4-wheel drive
1983 .... 10.2
1984 .... 12.3

ABBREVIATIONS

For full explanation of abbreviations, see the first page of this section.
Skill levels:
A. Highly skilled
B. Skilled
C. Semi-skilled
D. Low skilled
R&R: Remove and replace
R&I: Remove and install
Prices: These are manufacturer's suggested retail prices as of the date this guide was prepared.
* Indicates item is part of General Motors Target Marketing Program and does not have a manufacturer's suggested retail price. The listed price is an approximation.

29. Crankshaft R&R (A) (cont.)
Labor time (cont.)
2.5L engine
2-wheel drive
Standard trans 7.8
Auto trans 8.1
4-wheel drive
Standard trans 8.7
Auto trans 9.0
V6 engine
2-wheel drive
Standard trans 10.0
Auto trans 10.4
4-wheel drive
Standard trans 13.0
Auto trans 11.0
Additional time:
Where air conditioning interferes, add:
1.9L, 2.5L engines .... 0.4.
2.0L engine .... 0.3.
V6 .... 0.5.
Where cruise control interferes, add 0.2.
Where power steering interferes, add:
Four .... 0.4.
V6 .... 0.3.
Where electronic engine control system interferes, add 0.5.
With skid plate, add 0.3.
Crankshaft price
1982-1985
1.9L engine $333.00
2.0L engine $285.00
2.5L engine $313.00
2.8L engine $336.00
1986
Four $313.00
V6 .... $336.00

30. Crankshaft damper or pulley R&R (C)
Not available.

31. Crankshaft rear seal R&R (B)
Includes: pack and add only for upper rope seal. If necessary to replace upper seal use crankshaft R&R.
Labor time
1.9L engine
2-wheel drive 5.2
4-wheel drive 6.0
2.0L engine
1983
2-wheel drive 6.0
4-wheel drive 4.9
1984
Circular type seal
2-wheel drive 8.1
4-wheel drive 10.9
Split type seal
2-wheel drive 6.0
4-wheel drive 4.9
2.5L engine
2-wheel drive
Standard trans 3.2
Auto trans 3.6
4-wheel drive
Standard trans 4.9
Auto trans 4.5
V6 engine
1982-1984
2-wheel drive 6.8
4-wheel drive
Standard trans 5.0
Auto trans 5.3
1985
5.5 mm thick[1]
2-wheel drive
Standard trans 8.7
Auto trans 9.0
4-wheel drive
Standard trans 11.6
Auto trans 9.6
11 mm thick[2]
2-wheel drive
Standard trans 4.0
Auto trans 4.3
4-wheel drive
Standard trans 4.8
Auto trans 5.0
1986
2-wheel drive
Standard trans 3.8
Auto trans 4.9
4-wheel drive
Standard trans 4.8
Auto trans 5.0

1. Includes R&I engine and crankshaft.
2. Includes R&I transmission and flywheel or drive plate.

CLYMER LABOR, TIME AND PARTS PRICING GUIDE (continued)

31. Crankshaft rear seal R&R (B) (cont.)
Additional time:
Where air conditioning interferes, add:
1.9L engine .... 0.4.
2.0L engine .... 0.3.
V6 .... 0.2.
Where cruise control interferes, add 0.2.
Where power steering interferes, add:
1.9L, 2.0L engines .... 0.4.
2.5L engine (4-wheel drive) .... 0.1.
V6 .... 0.2.
Where electronic engine control system interferes, add 0.5.
With skid plate, add:
1983-1984 4-wheel drive .... 0.2.
1985-1986 1.9L, 2.0L engines .... 0.2.
1985-1986 2.5L engine .... 0.3.
Seal price
1982-1985
1.9L engine $16.45
2.0L engine
5.5 mm thick $15.73
11 mm thick $14.30
2.5L engine $7.52
V6
1982-1983 .... $3.30
1984-1985
O-ring (cap) $0.16
Seal kit $15.73
1986
Four $7.52
V6 .... $14.30

32. Cylinder head gasket R&I (C)
Labor time
1982-1983
1.9L engine 5.2
2.0L engine 5.5
V6
One side 6.1
Both 7.7
Right side 8.5
1984-1986
1.9L engine 5.2
2.0L engine 5,5
2.5L engine 5.8
V6
2-wheel drive
Right side 6.5
Left side 6.3
Both 8.9
4-wheel drive
Right side 6.5
Left side 6.6
Both 9.2

ABBREVIATIONS
For full explanation of abbreviations, see the first page of this section.
Skill levels:
A. Highly skilled
B. Skilled
C. Semi-skilled
D. Low skilled
R&R: Remove and replace
R&I: Remove and install
Prices: These are manufacturer's suggested retail prices as of the date this guide was prepared.
* Indicates item is part of General Motors Target Marketing Program and does not have a manufacturer's suggested retail price. The listed price is an approximation.

32. Cylinder head gasket R&I (C) (cont.)
Additional time:
Where air conditioning interferes, add:
1.9L engine .... 0.8.
2.0L engine .... 0.3.
2.5L engine .... 0.5.
V6 right side .... 0.2.
V6 left side or both .... 0.5.
Both .... 0.4.
Where cruise control interferes, add 0.2.
Where power steering interferes, add:
1.9L engine .... 0.4.
V6 (1982-1984) .... 0.2.
V6 (1985-1986) .... 0.5.
Cylinder head gasket price
1982-1985
1.9L engine $18.50
2.0L engine $12.90
2.5L engine $9.55
2.8L engine $4.15
1986
Four $9.55
V6 .... $4.15

33. Differential R&I and overhaul, front axle (A)
Labor time 7.9

34. Differential R&R (C)
Labor time .... 5.2.

35. Distributor cap R&R (C)
Labor time
Four .... 0.3.
V6 .... 0.5
Distributor cap price
1982-1985
1.9L engine $11.25
2.0L engine $17.77*
2.5L engine $17.77*

35. Distributor cap R&R (C) (cont.)
Distributor cap price (cont.)
1982-1985 (cont.)
V6
1982-1984 .... $19.85
1985
California $9.48
Non-California 19.85
1986
Four $17.77
V6 .... $19.85

36. Distributor R&R (C)
Includes: adjust ignition timing.
Labor time
1.9L engine .... 0.5.
2.0L, 2.5L engines .... 0.8.
V6 .... 0.8.
Distributor price
1982
Four $224.00
V6
California $263.00
Non-California $245.12
1983-1985
1.9L engine $224.00
2.0L engine $252.70
2.5L engine $268.30
V6
California
1983 .... $243.40
1984 .... $214.05
1985 .... $176.35
Non-California
1983-1984 .... $243.40
1985
Standard trans
High altitude $210.95
Low altitude $211.25
Auto trans $210.95
1986
Four $268.30
V6 .... $221.05

37. Drag link R&R (B)
Not applicable.

38. Drive plate R&I (C)
Labor time
THM200 .... add 0.3 to automatic transmission R&I.
THM700-R4 .... add 0.2 to automatic transmission R&I.
Additional time:
With skid plate, add 0.1.
Drive plate price
1982-1985
1.9L engine $73.25
2.0L engine $50.50
2.5L engine $64.75
V6 .... $67.50

CLYMER LABOR, TIME AND PARTS PRICING GUIDE (continued)

38. Drive plate R&I (C) (cont.)
Drive plate price (cont.)
1986
Four $64.75
V6 .... $67.50

39. Drive shaft R&I (C)
Labor time
One piece driveline
To front axle 0.6
To rear axle 0.5
Two-piece driveline
Front shaft
With slip yoke) 0.6
Without slip yoke 0.7
Rear shaft 0.5

40. Drive shaft center bearing R&R (B)
Labor time
With slip joint 0.7
Without slip joint 0.8
Bearing price
Except Dana $45.65
Dana
ID No. 2108654-X $42.45
ID No. 211115-1X $23.95

41. EGR valve R&R (C)
Labor time
1.9L engine 1.0
2.0L engine 0.5
2.5L engine 0.7
V6 .... 0.5

42. Engine mount R&R (D)
Labor time
Four
One side 0.7
Both 1.0
V6
One side 1.3
Both 2.0
Mount price
1982-1985
Four $26.75
V6 .... $30.25
1986
Four $26.75
V6 .... $27.25

43. Engine oil and filter change (gasoline) (D)
Labor time 0.3
Filter price
1.9L engine $10.08*
2.0L engine
1983 .... $7.22
1984 .... $7.32
2.5L engine $7.32
V6
1982-1983 .... $7.22*
1984-1985 .... $7.32*
1986
2-wheel drive $7.08
4-wheel drive $7.32

ABBREVIATIONS

For full explanation of abbreviations, see the first page of this section.
Skill levels:
A. Highly skilled
B. Skilled
C. Semi-skilled
D. Low skilled
R&R: Remove and replace
R&I: Remove and install
Prices: These are manufacturer's suggested retail prices as of the date this guide was prepared.
* Indicates item is part of General Motors Target Marketing Program and does not have a manufacturer's suggested retail price. The listed price is an approximation.

44. Engine oil and filter change (diesel) (D)
Labor time 0.3
Filter price $14.30

45. Engine R&I and overhaul (A)
Includes: Replace rings, main and rod bearings and crankshaft; remove cylinder ridge and burnish cylinders, clean and test hydraulic lifters, grind valves and adjust idle speed, timing and valves where applicable.
Labor time
1.9L engine
2-wheel drive 18.6
4-wheel drive 19.8
2.0L engine
2-wheel drive 20.3
4-wheel drive
1983 .... 21.1
1984 .... 25.5
2.5L engine
2-wheel drive
Standard trans 19.1
Auto trans 19.5
4-wheel drive
Standard trans 20.0
Auto trans 20.3
V6
2-wheel drive
Standard trans 25.1
Auto trans 25.4
4-wheel drive
Standard trans 27.8
Auto trans 26.4

Additional time:
Where air conditioning interferes, add:
1.9L, 2.0L 0.4
2.5L 0.5
V6 .... 0.2

45. Engine R&I and overhaul (A) (cont.)
Additional time (cont.):
Where cruise control interferes, add 0.2.
Where power steering interferes, add:
1.9L, 2.0L 0.4
2.5L 0.3
V6 .... 0.2
With transmission oil cooler, add 0.2.
With skid plate, add 0.3.

46. Engine assembly R&I (C)
Includes: R&I only those components necessary for the removal of the complete engine assembly.
Does not include transfer of parts or tune engine.
Labor time
1.9L engine
2-wheel drive 4.7
4-wheel drive 5.6
2.0L engine
2-wheel drive 5.4
4-wheel drive
1983 .... 6.1
1984 .... 8.4
2.5L engine
2-wheel drive
Standard trans 4.8
Auto trans 5.1
4-wheel drive
Standard trans 5.6
Auto trans 5.9
V6
2-wheel drive
Standard trans 7.6
Auto trans 7.9
4-wheel drive
Standard trans 10.6
Auto trans 8.8
Additional time:
Where air conditioning interferes, add:
1.9L, 2.0L 0.4
2.5L 0.5
V6 .... 0.2
Where cruise control interferes, add 0.2.
Where power steering interferes, add:
1.9L, 2.0L 0.4
2.5L 0.3
V6 .... 0.2
With transmission oil cooler, add 0.2.
With skid plate, add 0.3.

47. Engine short block R&R (A)
Labor time
1.9L engine
2-wheel drive 11.5
4-wheel drive 12.3
2.0L engine
2-wheel drive 13.5

CLYMER LABOR, TIME AND PARTS PRICING GUIDE (continued)

47. Engine short block R&R (A) (cont.)
Labor time (cont.)
2.0L engine (cont.)
4-wheel drive
1983 .... 14.4
1984 .... 17.2
2.5L engine
2-wheel drive
Standard trans 12.4
Auto trans 12.7
4-wheel drive
Standard trans 13.5
Auto trans 13.8
V6
2-wheel drive
Standard trans 16.3
Auto trans 16.7
4-wheel drive
Standard trans 19.5
Auto trans 17.6
Additional time:
Where air conditioning interferes, add:
1.9L, 2.0L 0.4
2.5L 0.5
V6 .... 0.2
Where cruise control interferes, add 0.2.
Where power steering interferes, add:
1.9L, 2.0L 0.4
2.5L 0.3
V6 .... 0.2
With transmission oil cooler, add 0.2.
With skid plate, add 0.3.

48. Evaporative emission canister R&R (C)
Labor time 0.5

49. Flywheel R&I (C)
Labor time .... add 0.3 to job No. 19.
Flywheel price
1982-1985
1.9L engine $138.00
2.0L engine $142.00
2.5L engine $159.00
V6 .... $159.00
1986 .... $159.00

50. Float and/or needle seat R&R (B)
Includes: adjust float level and idle speed.
Labor time
Isuzu 1.0
Rochester 1.1

51. Fuel filter R&R (D)
Labor time
In carb 0.5
In line 0.3
Filter price
1982-1985
Isuzu $0.55
Rochester $3.88*

ABBREVIATIONS
For full explanation of abbreviations, see the first page of this section.
Skill levels:
A. Highly skilled
B. Skilled
C. Semi-skilled
D. Low skilled
R&R: Remove and replace
R&I: Remove and install
Prices: These are manufacturer's suggested retail prices as of the date this guide was prepared.
* Indicates item is part of General Motors Target Marketing Program and does not have a manufacturer's suggested retail price. The listed price is an approximation.

51. Fuel filter R&R (D) (cont.)
Filter price (cont.)
1986
Four
In line $18.60
Meter body $13.85
V6 .... $16.02

52. Fuel pump R&R (B)
Does not include: test.
Labor time
Mechanical 0.8
Electric (in tank)
1982-1984 .... 0.9
1985-1986 .... 1.8
Fuel pump price
1982
Four $76.00
V6 .... $58.43*
1983-1984
1.9L engine $76.00
2.0L engine $34.63
V6
2-wheel drive
1983 .... $58.43*
1984 .... $41.08
4-wheel drive
1983 .... $51.78
1984 .... $31.30
1985
1.9L engine $76.00
2.5L engine
Blazer $56.88
Cab
50 liter tank $58.90
76 liter tank $56.88
V6 .... Not available.
1986
13.2 gal. tank $58.90
20 gal. tank $56.88

53. Front shock absorber R&R (C)
Labor time
2-wheel drive
One side 0.5
Both 0.8
4-wheel drive
One side 0.7
Both 1.0
Shock absorber price
2-wheel drive $24.40
4-wheel drive
1983-1985
Except extended cab $26.43
Extended cab $40.63
1986 .... Not available.

54. Front coil spring R&R (B)
Does not include: alignment.
Labor time
One side 1.0
Both 1.9

55. Front hub and rotor R&R (C)
Labor time
2-wheel drive
One side 0.9
Both 1.6
4-wheel drive
Hub
One side 1.0
Both 1.8
Rotor
One side 0.7
Both 1.1
Hub and rotor price
2-wheel drive $100.00
4-wheel drive
Rotor $70.10
Hub with bearings $208.15

56. Front wheel bearing R&R (C)
Labor time
2-wheel drive
One side 0.9
Both 1.6
4-wheel drive
One side 1.0
Both 1.8
Bearing price
Inner
2-wheel drive $9.43
4-wheel drive .... Serviced in front wheel hub.
Outer
2-wheel drive $11.50
4-wheel drive .... Serviced in front wheel hub.

57. Front axle shaft R&R (4WD) (C)
Labor time
One side 1.8
Both 2.9

CLYMER LABOR, TIME AND PARTS PRICING GUIDE (continued)

58. Free wheel hub R&R (4WD) (C)
Labor time
One side 0.5
Both 0.9
Hub price
Automatic $192.00
Manual .... serviced in components

59. Free wheel hub R&I and overhaul (4WD) (C)
Labor time
One side 0.7
Both 1.3

60. Front brake pad R&R (C)
Labor time 1.1
Pad price (2 wheels) $43.33

61. Front brake caliper R&R (C)
Includes: bleed system and replace pads if necessary.
Labor time
One side 0.9
Both sides 1.5
Caliper price
2-wheel drive
Right $148.45
Left $137.00
4-wheel drive $137.00

62. Front brake caliper overhaul (B)
Labor time
One side 1.4
Both 2.5
Seal package price $8.40
Piston price $10.80

63. Fuel pump pressure test (B)
Labor time 0.6

64. Headlight replacement (D)
Does not include: adjustment.
Labor time
One side 0.3
Both 0.4
Bulb price
Except halogen $19.95
Halogen $36.25

65. Headlight switch R&R (B)
Labor time
1982-1983 .... 0.6
1984-1986 .... 0.8
Switch price $16.12

66. Heater hose replacement (D)
Labor time
With a/c (one or all) 0.5
Without a/c
One 0.4
All 0.5

67. Heater core R&R (A)
Labor time
Diesel
With a/c
1982-1984 .... 1.5
1985 .... 2.0
Without a/c .... -1.5

ABBREVIATIONS

For full explanation of abbreviations, see the first page of this section.
Skill levels:
A. Highly skilled
B. Skilled
C. Semi-skilled
D. Low skilled
R&R: Remove and replace
R&I: Remove and install
Prices: These are manufacturer's suggested retail prices as of the date this guide was prepared.
* Indicates item is part of General Motors Target Marketing Program and does not have a manufacturer's suggested retail price. The listed price is an approximation.

67. Heater core R&R (A) (cont.)
Labor time (cont.)
Gasoline
With a/c
1982-1984 .... 1.5
1985-1986 .... 2.0
Without a/c 1.5

68. Horn R&R (D)
Labor time 0.3
Horn price
High note (A) $22.62
High note (C) $26.95
Low note (D) $24.65
Low note (F) $22.62

69. Idle mixture adjustment
Not available.

70. Idle speed adjustment
Not available.

71. Igniter R&R
Not applicable.

72. Ignition coil R&R (C)
Includes: test coil.
Labor time
1.9L engine 0.5
2.0L engine
With a/c 3.4
Without a/c 2.7
2.5L engine 0.8
V6 .... 1.0
Coil price
1982-1984
1.9L engine $40.75
2.0L engine $47.81
V6 .... $47.81
1985
1.9L engine $40.75
2.5L engine $38.25
V6 .... $38.25
1986 .... Not available.

73. Ignition switch R&R (B)
Labor time 0.7
Switch price
Fixed wheel $11.02
Tilt wheel $11.25

74. Ignition timing adjustment (C)
Labor time 0.5

75. Load sensing valve R&R
Not applicable.

76. Lower and upper ball-joint R&R (B)
Labor time
2-wheel drive
Upper
One side 1.1
Both 2.0
Lower
One side 0.8
Both 1.1
4-wheel drive
Upper
One side 1.1
Both 2.0
Lower
One side 1.5
Both 2.7
Ball-joint price
Upper $34.75
Lower $36.22*
1984-1986

77. Lower suspension arm R&R (B)
Labor time
2-wheel drive 1.5
4-wheel drive 2.0
Suspension arm price
2-wheel drive $159.00
4-wheel drive $213.00

78. Lower suspension arm shaft R&R (B)
Includes: Replace bushings.
Labor time
2-wheel drive 1.6
4-wheel drive 1.9

79A. Manifold gasket R&R, intake (C)
Labor time
Carburetor
1982
Four 2.7
V6 .... 3.9
1983-1986
1.9L engine 2.3
2.0L engine 2.6
2.5L engine 5.1
V6
1983-1984 .... 3.6
1985 .... 5.0
Fuel injection
Four 3.1
V6 .... 5.0

CLYMER LABOR, TIME AND PARTS PRICING GUIDE (continued)

79A. Manifold gasket R&R, intake (C) (cont.)
Additional time:
To replace carburetor manifold, add:
1.9L engine ... 0.3
2.0L, 2.5L engine ... 0.2
V6 ... 0.3
To replace fuel injection manifold, add:
Four ... 0.2
V6 ... 0.3
Where air conditioning interferes, add:
Carburetted S10 V6 ... 0.2
All fuel injected ... 0.2
Where cruise control interferes, add 0.2.
Where electronic engine control system interferes, add 0.5
Manifold price
1982
Four ... $105.00
V6 ... $139.00
1983-1985
1.9L engine ... $105.00
2.0L engine ... $177.00
V6 ... $139.00
1986 ... Not available.

79B. Manifold removal/installation, exhaust (C)
Labor time
1.9L, 2.0L engine ... 1.3
2.5L engine ... 0.9
V6
Right ... 0.8
Left ... 1.1
Additional time:
Where air conditioning interferes, add:
1.9L engine ... 0.8
2.5L engine ... 0.4
Where power steering interferes, add:
1.9L engine ... 0.4
V6 left side (1982-1984) ... 0.2
V6 left side (1985-1986) ... 0.3
Where electronic engine control system interferes, add 0.5.
Manifold price
1982
Four ... $97.50
V6 ... $97.50
1983-1984
Four ... $97.50
V6
Right ... $97.50
Left
California ... $94.75
Non-California ... $97.50
1986
Four ... $93.75
V6
Right ... $70.00
Left ... Not available.
Right ... $100.23

ABBREVIATIONS

For full explanation of abbreviations, see the first page of this section.
Skill levels:
A. Highly skilled
B. Skilled
C. Semi-skilled
D. Low skilled
R&R: Remove and replace
R&I: Remove and install
Prices: These are manufacturer's suggested retail prices as of the date this guide was prepared.
* Indicates item is part of General Motors Target Marketing Program and does not have a manufacturer's suggested retail price. The listed price is an approximation.

80. Master cylinder R&R, brakes (C)
Includes: bleed system.
Labor time ... 0.8
Master cylinder price ... $171.05

81. Master cylinder R&I and overhaul, brakes (B)
Includes: bleed system.
Labor time ... 1.6
Kit price
1982-1984
Non-power brakes ... $20.80
Power brakes
1982 ... $20.80
1983-1984 ... $22.75
1985-1986
Non-power brakes ... $20.80
Power brakes ... $22.75

82. Oil pan and/or gasket R&R (C)
Labor time
1.9L engine
2-wheel drive ... 4.8
4-wheel drive ... 5.8
2.0L engine
2-wheel drive ... 5.4
4-wheel drive ... 4.3
2.5L engine
2-wheel drive ... 2.4
4-wheel drive ... 5.3
V6
2-wheel drive
Standard trans ... 6.1
Auto trans ... 6.5
4-wheel drive ... 4.5
Additional time:
Where air conditioning interferes, add:
1.9L engine ... 0.4
2.0L engine ... 0.3
V6 2-wheel drive ... 0.2

82. Oil pan and/or gasket R&R (C) (cont.)
Additional time:
Where power steering interferes, add:
1.9L, 2.0L engines ... 0.4
2.5L engine (4-wheel drive) ... 0.1
V6 (2-wheel drive) ... 0.2
Where electronic engine control system interferes, add 0.5.
Where cruise control interferes, add 0.2.
Oil pan price
1982-1985
1.9L engine
2-wheel drive ... $84.75
4-wheel drive ... $76.00
2.0L engine ... $55.25
2.5L engine ... $47.50
V6 ... $53.50
1986
Four ... $47.50
V6 ... $53.50

83. Oil pump R&R (C)
Labor time
1.9L engine
2-wheel drive ... 4.9
4-wheel drive ... 5.0
2.0L engine
2-wheel drive ... 5.5
4-wheel drive ... 4.5
2.5L engine
2-wheel drive ... 2.7
4-wheel drive ... 5.4
V6
2-wheel drive
Standard trans ... 6.3
Auto trans ... 6.6
4-wheel drive ... 4.5
Oil pump price
1.9L engine ... $67.50
2.0L engine
2-wheel drive ... $95.50
4-wheel drive ... $71.75
2.5L engine ... $64.08*
V6
1982-1985 ... $85.75
1986 ... $82.28

84. Power steering belt R&R (D)
Labor time
Diesel ... 0.3
Gasoline
1.9L, 2.0L engine ... 0.5
2.5L engine
With a/c ... 0.7
Without a/c ... 0.5
V6 ... 0.6

85. Piston and rod assembly R&I, all (A)
Labor time: to job No. 26, add 0.4 per piston.

CLYMER LABOR, TIME AND PARTS PRICING GUIDE (continued)

86. PCV valve R&R (C)
Labor time 0.3
PCV valve price
1982
Four .... Not available.
V6 .... $4.10
1983-1985
2.0L, 2.8L engines $4.10
2.5L engine $6.02
1986
Four $6.02
V6 .... Not available.

87. Pitman arm R&R (B)
Does not include: alignment.
Labor time
2-wheel drive 0.7
4-wheel drive 0.9
Pitman arm price $44.00

88. Power steering pump R&R (B)
Labor time
Diesel 1.0
Gasoline
Four 1.0
V6
1982-1984 .... 1.3
1985-1986 .... 1.0
Additional time
Where air conditioning interferes, add 0.2.
Pump price
Four $199.00
V6
1982 .... $187.00
1983-1986 .... $199.00

89. Power steering pump R&I and overhaul (B)
Labor time
Diesel 1.7
Gasoline
Four 1.7
V6
1982-1984 .... 1.8
1985-1986 .... 1.6

90. Radiator R&R (D)
Labor time
Standard trans 0.9
Auto trans 1.1

91. Radiator hose R&R (D)
Labor time
Upper or lower 0.5
Both 0.7
Upper hose price
1982-1985
Four
1982 .... $9.65
1983-1985
1.9L engine $10.10
2.0L engine $10.60
2.5L engine $9.25

ABBREVIATIONS
For full explanation of abbreviations, see the first page of this section.
Skill levels:
A. Highly skilled
B. Skilled
C. Semi-skilled
D. Low skilled
R&R: Remove and replace
R&I: Remove and install
Prices: These are manufacturer's suggested retail prices as of the date this guide was prepared.
* Indicates item is part of General Motors Target Marketing Program and does not have a manufacturer's suggested retail price. The listed price is an approximation.

91. Radiator hose R&R (D) (cont.)
Upper hose price (cont.)
1982-1985 (cont.)
V6
1982 .... $9.65
1983-1985 .... $9.25
1986 .... $9.25
Lower hose price
1982
Four
With a/c
Non-power steering $10.00
Power steering
At pump $2.00
At radiator $6.30
Without a/c $10.00
V6 .... $10.00
1983-1985
Diesel $14.90
Gasoline
1.9L engine
2-wheel drive
With a/c
Non-power steering $10.00
Power steering
At pump $2.00
At radiator $6.50
Without a/c $9.50
4-wheel drive
With a/c
At pump $2.00
At radiator $6.50
Without a/c $9.50
2.0L engine $10.60
2.5L engine $9.50
1986 .... $9.50

92. Rear axle housing R&R (B)
Labor time 5.7

93. Rear axle shaft R&R (C)
Labor time
One side 1.2
Both 1.8
Axle shaft price
2-wheel drive $109.00
4-wheel drive $172.42

94. Rear wheel bearing R&R (C)
Labor time
One side 1.0
Both 1.4
Bearing price $16.80

95. Rear brake drum R&R (C)
Non-separable drum 1.3
Separable drum 0.6
Brake drum price $72.75

96. Rear brake shoe R&R (C)
Includes: Bleed system and adjust brakes and parking brake where necessary.
Labor time (2 wheels) 1.6
Shoe price (2 wheels) $43.33

97. Rear wheel cylinder R&R (B)
Includes: Bleed system and replace shoes if necessary.
Labor time: to job No. 96, add 0.3.
Wheel cylinder price
1982 .... $31.05
1983-1984
2-wheel drive
Non-power brakes $31.05
Power brakes $30.20
4-wheel drive
1983 .... $31.05
1984 .... $30.20
1985-1986
2-wheel drive $31.05
4-wheel drive $30.20

98. Rear wheel cylinder overhaul (B)
Includes: Bleed system and replace shoes if necessary.
Labor time: to job No. 96, add 0.4.
Kit price
1982-1983 .... $7.75
1984-1986 .... $12.55

99. Regulator R&R (B)
Incudes: test
Labor time
1.9L engine 1.1
2.0L, 2.5L engine 1.0
V6 .... 1.1
Regulator price
1982-1984
Non-integral regulator $32.79*
Integral regulator $23.68*
1985-1986 .... See local supplier.

100. Rings, piston R&R
Labor time .... to job No. 26, add 0.3 per piston.

CLYMER LABOR, TIME AND PARTS PRICING GUIDE (continued)

100. Rings, piston R&R (cont.)
Ring set price
1982-1985
1.9L engine
1982 .... $16.65
1983-1985 .... $18.85
2.0L engine $14.95
2.5L engine $17.95
V6
1982-1984 .... $15.50
1985 .... $16.90
1986
Four $17.95
V6 .... $16.90

101. Rocker assembly and shaft R&R (B)
Not available.

102. Shock absorber R&R, rear (D)
Labor time
One side 0.6
Both 0.9
Shock absorber price
1982-1985
2-wheel drive $24.68
4-wheel drive
With Off Road Package
Blazer $92.08
Cab $40.63
Without Off Road Package
Blazer
1983-1984 .... $26.43
1985 .... $24.68
Cab
Regular (1983) $26.43
Regular (1984-1985) $24.68
Extended $40.63
1986
With Off Road Package $92.08
Without Off Road Package ... $24.68

103. Spark plugs, clean or replace (C)
Labor time
Four 0.5
V6 .... 0.6
Additional time:
Where air pump interferes, add 0.3.

104. Spring R&R, rear (C)
Labor time
One side 0.9
Both 1.6

105. Stabilizer bar and/or bushings R&R (C)
Labor time
1982
2-wheel drive 0.7
4-wheel drive 0.8
1983-1986 .... 0.8
Stabilizer bar price
Except 25 mm diameter $44.75
25 mm diameter $43.25

ABBREVIATIONS
For full explanation of abbreviations, see the first page of this section.
Skill levels:
A. Highly skilled
B. Skilled
C. Semi-skilled
D. Low skilled
R&R: Remove and replace
R&I: Remove and install
Prices: These are manufacturer's suggested retail prices as of the date this guide was prepared.
* Indicates item is part of General Motors Target Marketing Program and does not have a manufacturer's suggested retail price. The listed price is an approximation.

106. Starter R&R (D)
Labor time
1.9L engine 0.8
2.0L engine 1.0
2.5L engine
2-wheel drive 1.0
4-wheel drive 2.3
V6
2-wheel drive 1.1
4-wheel drive 1.9
Additional time:
With skid plate, add 0.2.
Starter price
1982-1983
Diesel $454.10
1.9L engine $239.00
V6
ID No. 1109535 .... $208.85
ID No. 1998243 .... $217.50
ID No. 1998245 .... $247.65
ID No. 1998427 .... $185.45
1984-1985
Diesel $413.00
1.9L engine $239.00
2.0L engine $189.85
2.5L engine $185.45
V6 .... $185.45
1986
Four $177.15
V6 .... $187.60

107. Starter circuit check (B)
Labor time 0.5

108. Steering damper R&R
Not applicable.

109. Steering gear R&R (C)
Labor time
2-wheel drive 0.8
4-wheel drive 1.0
Steering gear price $266.00

110. Steering knuckle R&R (B)
Includes: replace ball-joints on 4-wheel drive only.
Does not include: alignment.
Labor time 1.6
Steering knuckle price
2-wheel drive $117.00
4-wheel drive $158.00

111. Tension strut R&R
Not applicable.

112. Thermostat and/or outlet R&R (D)
Labor time
Four
Diesel 0.6
Gasoline 0.7
V6
1982 .... 0.7
1983-1986 .... 0.5
Thermostat price
1982-1984
Diesel $12.70
1.9L engine $12.70
2.0L engine $5.93*
2.5L engine $7.15
V6 engine $5.93
1985 .... Not available.
1986
Four $7.15
V6 .... $5.93

113. Tie rod and/or ends R&R (B)
Includes: .... Adjust toe-in only.
Deduct 0.4 if alignment is also performed.
Labor time
2-wheel drive
One side
Inner or outer 0.9
Inner and outer 1.0
Both
Inner or outer 1.2
Inner and outer 1.4
4-wheel drive
One side
Inner or outer 0.8
Inner and outer 0.9
Both
Inner or outer 1.1
Inner and outer 1.3

114. Timing chain R&R (B)
Labor time
1.9L engine 7.1
2.0L engine 2.7
V6
1982-1984 .... 2.8
1985-1986 .... 3.1
Additional time:
Where air conditioning interferes, add:
1.9L engine 0.4
2.0L engine 0.1
V6 .... 0.2.

CLYMER LABOR, TIME AND PARTS PRICING GUIDE (continued)

114. Timing chain R&R (B) (cont.)
Additional time (cont.):
Where power steering interferes, add:
1.9L engine 0.4
With skid plate, add 0.4.
Timing chain price
1982-1985
1.9L engine $40.50
2.0L engine $30.50
V6 .... $30.00
1986 (2.8L engine) $30.00
See local supplier for applications not listed.

115. Toe-in adjustment (B)
Labor time 0.7

116. Torsion bar R&R
Not applicable.

117. Transfer case R&I and overhaul (B)
Labor time 4.6
Additional time:
With skid plate, add 0.4.

118. Transfer case R&I (C)
Labor time 2.0
With skid plate, add 0.4.

119A. Transmission R&I, automatic (C)
Labor time
1982-1984
THM200
2-wheel drive 3.3
4-wheel drive 4.1
THM700-R4
2-wheel drive 3.5
4-wheel drive 4.4
1985-1986
2-wheel drive 3.5
4-wheel drive 4.4
Additional time:
With transfer case skid plate, add 0.4.

119B. Transmission R&I, manual (C)
Labor time
4-speed
2-wheel drive
Isuzu
Four 3.5
V6 .... 3.0
Warner 2.3
4-wheel drive 4.2
5-speed
2-wheel drive 2.3
4-wheel drive 4.2

120. Transmission overhaul, manual (B)
Labor time
4-speed
Isuzu
Four 5.4
V6 .... 5.0
Warner 4.7

ABBREVIATIONS

For full explanation of abbreviations, see the first page of this section.
Skill levels:
A. Highly skilled
B. Skilled
C. Semi-skilled
D. Low skilled
R&R: Remove and replace
R&I: Remove and install
Prices: These are manufacturer's suggested retail prices as of the date this guide was prepared.
* Indicates item is part of General Motors Target Marketing Program and does not have a manufacturer's suggested retail price. The listed price is an approximation.

120. Transmission overhaul, manual (B) (cont.)
Labor time (cont.)
5-speed
2-wheel drive 4.9
4-wheel drive 6.4
Additional time:
With catalytic converter, add 0.4.
With skid plate, add 0.4.

121. Tune-up (B)
Labor time
Four 1.3
V6 .... 1.5
Distributor cap price
1982-1985
1.9L engine $11.25
2.0L engine $17.77*
2.5L engine $17.77*
V6
1982-1984 .... $19.85
1985
California $9.48
Non-California $19.85
1986
Four $17.77
$19.85
Rotor price
1982-1985
1.9L engine $2.95
2.0L engine $9.08*
2.5L engine $8.20
V6
1982-1984 .... $9.08*
1985
California .... Not available.
Non-California $9.08
1986
Four $8.20
V6 .... $9.08

122. Universal joint R&R (B)
Labor time
One piece driveline
To front axle
Front joint 0.8
Rear joint 1.5
Both 1.8
To rear axle
Front joint 0.9
Rear joint 0.7
Both 1.1
Two piece drive line (to rear axle)
One joint
Front 0.9
Intermediate 0.8
Rear 0.7
Two joints
Front and intermediate 1.5
Intermediate and rear 1.1
Three joints 1.6
Universal joint price
Saginaw
With lube fitting $40.17*
Without lube fitting $32.50
Spicer
21/32 in. finger dia.
2 31/32 in. span $24.65
3 3/8 in. span $28.50
49/64 in. finger dia.
Except 3 3/8 in. span $17.45
3 3/8 in. span $28.25*
50/64 in. finger dia. $22.84

123. Upper ball-joint R&R (B)
See job No. 110.

124. Upper suspension arm R&R (B)
Does not include: alignment.
Labor time
2-wheel drive 1.0
4-wheel drive 1.2
Suspension arm price
2-wheel drive $97.75
4-wheel drive $129.00

125. Upper suspension arm shaft R&R (B)
Does not include: alignment.
Labor time 1.5
Shaft kit price
2-wheel drive $33.75
4-wheel drive .... Not available.

126. Valve grind, complete (A)
Labor time
1982-1983
1.9L engine 7.5
2.0L engine 7.6
V6
One side 8.1
Both sides 11.1
1984-1986
1.9L engine 7.5
2.0L engine 7.6

CLYMER LABOR, TIME AND PARTS PRICING GUIDE (continued)

126. Valve grind, complete (A) (cont.)
Labor time (cont.)
1984-1986 (cont.)
2.5L engine 8.2
V6
1984
One side 8.4
Both 11.1
1985-1986
Right side 9.4
Left side 0.9
Both 13.1

Additional time:
Where air conditioning interferes, add:
1.9L engine .... 0.8.
2.0L engine .... 0.3.
2.5L engine 0.5
V6 (right side) .... 0.2.
V6 (left side or both) .... 0.3.
Where cruise control interferes, add 0.2.
Where electronic engine control system interferes, add 0.5.
Where power steering interferes, add:
1.9L engine .... 0.4.

ABBREVIATIONS

For full explanation of abbreviations, see the first page of this section.
Skill levels:
A. Highly skilled
B. Skilled
C. Semi-skilled
D. Low skilled
R&R: Remove and replace
R&I: Remove and install
Prices: These are manufacturer's suggested retail prices as of the date this guide was prepared.
* Indicates item is part of General Motors Target Marketing Program and does not have a manufacturer's suggested retail price. The listed price is an approximation.

127. Water pump R&R (C)
Labor time
1.9L engine 0.9
2.0L, 2.5L engine 1.1
V6
1982-1983 .... 1.0
1984-1986 .... 1.6

127. Water pump R&R (C) (cont.)
Additional time:
Where air conditioning interferes, add 0.2.
Where power steering interferes, add:
2-wheel drive 0.232

Water pump price
1982-1985
Diesel $94.50
Gasoline
1.9L engine $75.33
2.0L engine $78.25
2.5L engine $59.50
V6 .... $78.25
1986
Four $59.50
V6 .... $78.25

128. Wiper motor R&R (C)
Labor time 0.7
Wiper motor price
1982-1984 .... $105.00
1985-1986
With intermittent wiper $132.65
Without intermittent wiper . $105.00

CLYMER OFFICIAL SERVICE HINTS

This section contains a feature exclusive to Clymer manuals—troubleshooting and service tips based on factory service bulletins. Specific problems and exact solutions are listed, together with simple, easy-to-understand repair procedures.

The section is organized by subject area. Problems, the models they apply to and solutions are described. Repair procedures are given, together with illustrations where necessary.

CHASSIS

Problem: clutch "clunk"

Models affected: 1984 S/T truck with hydraulic clutch

Condition and Cause

Some 1984 S/T trucks with a hydraulic clutch may emit a "clunk" type of noise when the pedal is depressed. This may occur if the clutch does not hit the rubber bumper stop.

Repair

Refer to **Figure 1** for this procedure. Install a new bumper stop (part No. 14040582).

ENGINE

Subject: new rocker arm cover gasket

Models affected: 1982-1984 with 2.8L engine

Service Information

A new composition gasket (part No. 14089252) is available for service use on 1982-1984 models equipped with 2.8L engines. The gasket replaces RTV sealant and is to be used for repair of rocker arm cover oil leaks and general service procedures. A small amount of GM sealer must be applied at the cylinder head-to-intake manifold split line prior to gasket installation. Tighten the rocker arm cover attaching bolts to 75-90 INCH-pounds (8.5-10.0 N•m).

FUEL SYSTEM

Problem: hard start or poor choke operation

Models affected: All 1982-1984 carburetted with vacuum break

Condition and Cause

All General Motors models up to 1984 equipped with a vacuum break on the carburetor may start

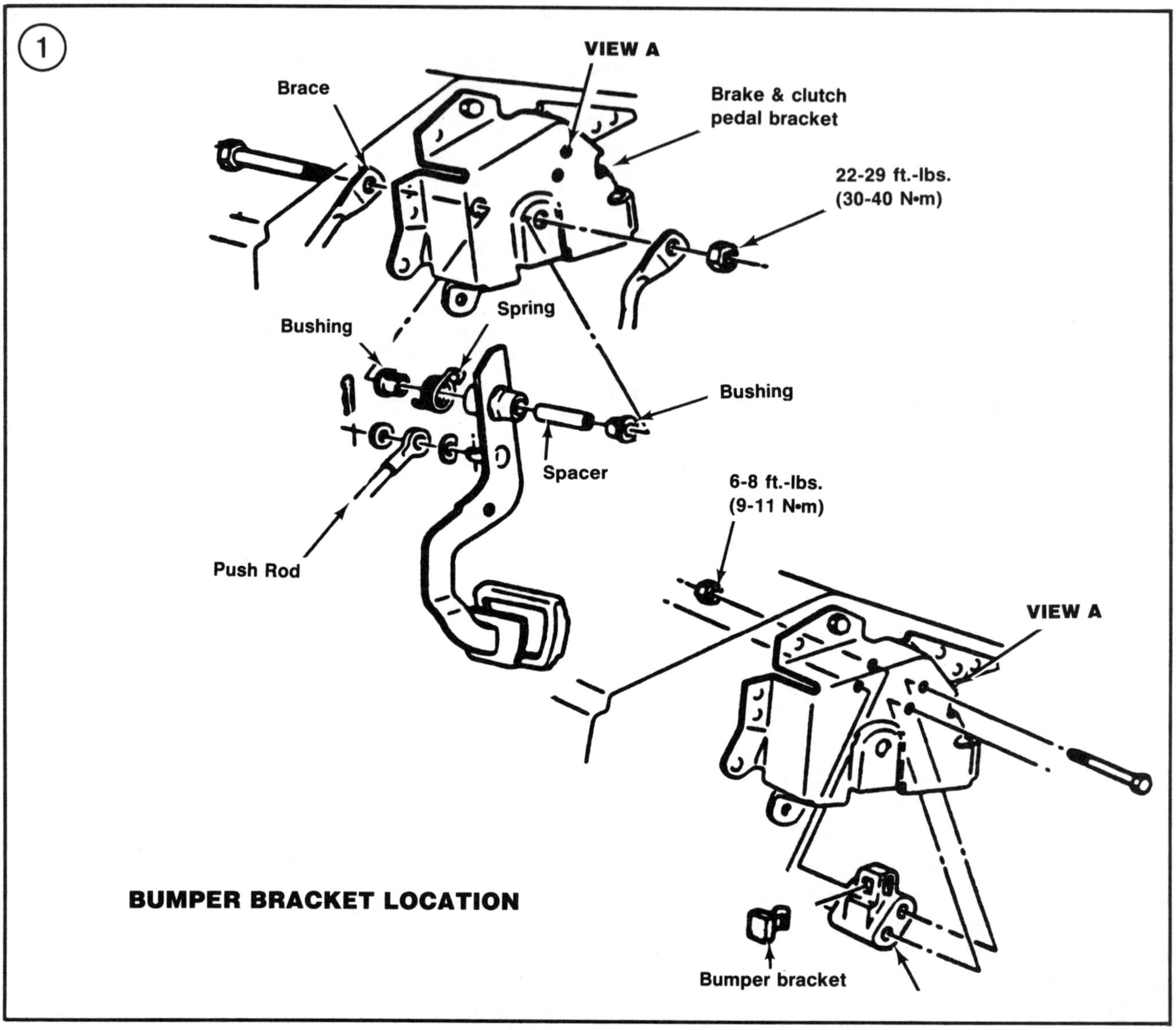

1
VIEW A
Brace
Brake & clutch
pedal bracket
22-29 ft.-lbs.
(30-40 N•m)
Spring
Bushing
Bushing
Spacer
6-8 ft.-lbs.
(9-11 N•m)
Push Rod
VIEW A
BUMPER BRACKET LOCATION
Bumper bracket

2
LOCATION OF VACUUM BREAK AIR BLEED
HOLES
Place valve
stem seal
over hole
Tape hole
in tube
Tape end
of cover

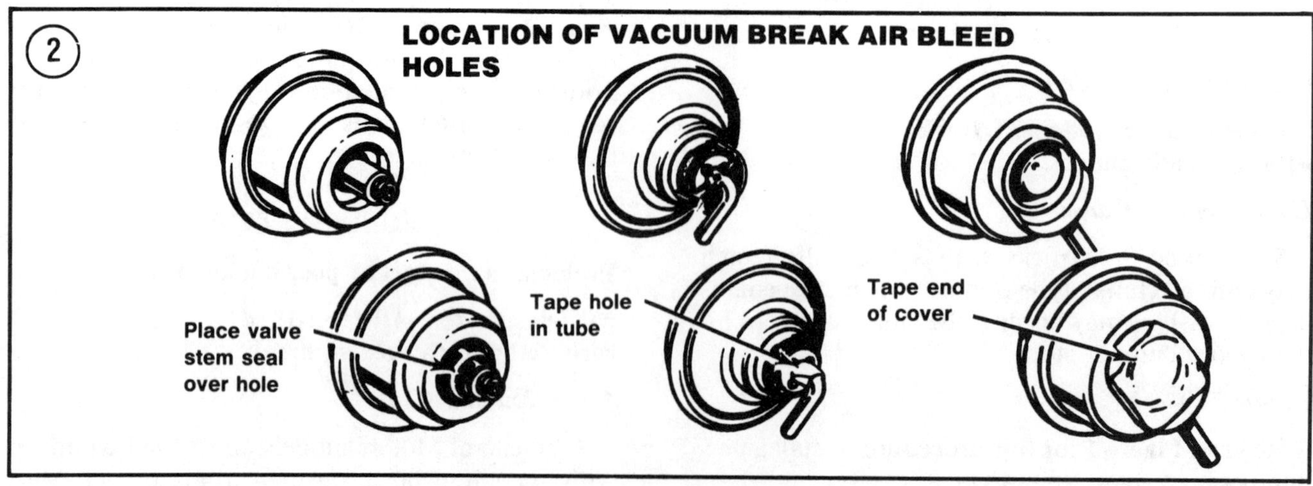

hard or have poor cold operation. This condition may be caused by a faulty vacuum break (choke pull-off).

Diagnosis

Refer to **Figure 2** for this procedure.

Plug the air bleed hole on the vacuum break, if equipped. Apply 15 in. Hg vacuum to the vacuum break. Ensure the vacuum break moves to full travel. Vacuum break diaphragm should hold vacuum for a minimum of 20 seconds. Replace the vacuum break if it does not test good.

GENERAL SERVICING

Problem: water pump leaks

Models affected: All with diesel engine

Condition and Cause

All General Motors vehicles with diesel engines may experience a water pump leak at the mounting area. This condition may be caused by improper sealing of the water pump gasket.

Repair

Remove the water pump from the vehicle. Clean mating surfaces. If present, DO NOT grind the 2 raised areas between bolt holes. Apply RTV sealer to each side of gasket and install water pump.

Subject: limited slip lubricants

Models affected: All with limited slip differential

Service Information

If special limited slip lubricant (part No. 1050010) is called for but is not available, use lubricant part No. 1052271 in conjunction with 3 oz. of additive (part No. 1052358) in limited slip axles. Limited slip lubricant (part No. 1050001) may also be used in non-limited slip applications.

HEATING AND AIR CONDITIONING

TRANSMISSION

Problem: overheating

Models affected: All with THM700-R4 transmission

Condition and Cause

Some THM700-R4 transmissions may overheat when the vehicle is operated in 4th gear (overdrive) and the torque converter clutch is not operational. Under heavy load conditions, so much heat is generated in the torque converter that the transmission cooler cannot adequately cool the transmission.

Diagnosis

The following conditions may lead to transmission overheating:

1. The speedometer may not be working properly on ECM controlled units.
2. A disconnected speedometer cable on ECM controlled units.
3. The transmission electrical connector is disconnected.
4. The torque converter clutch is inoperative.
5. The ECM unit is inoperable.

NOTE

To prevent possible transmission overheating, it is recommended that the THM700-R4 transmission never be operated in 4th gear when the torque converter clutch is non-operational. If the TCC is non-operational, vehicle should be operated in 3rd gear range until it can be serviced.

Problem: buzzing noise and possible delayed upshifts

Models affected: 1982 with THM700-R4

Condition and Cause

Some THM700-R4 transmissions may emit a buzzing noise and experience delayed upshifts. This condition may be caused by use of a 1983 THM700-R4 control valve-to-spacer plate and spacer plate-to-case gasket that has been installed on the 1982 transmission. The condition may also be caused by the control valve assembly spacer plate itself.

Repair

When servicing 1982 THM700-R4 transmissions, always replace the control valve-to-spacer plate and spacer plate-to-case gasket with gasket service kit part No. 8642974. Check the control valve assembly spacer plate identification. If the plate is identified by the letter

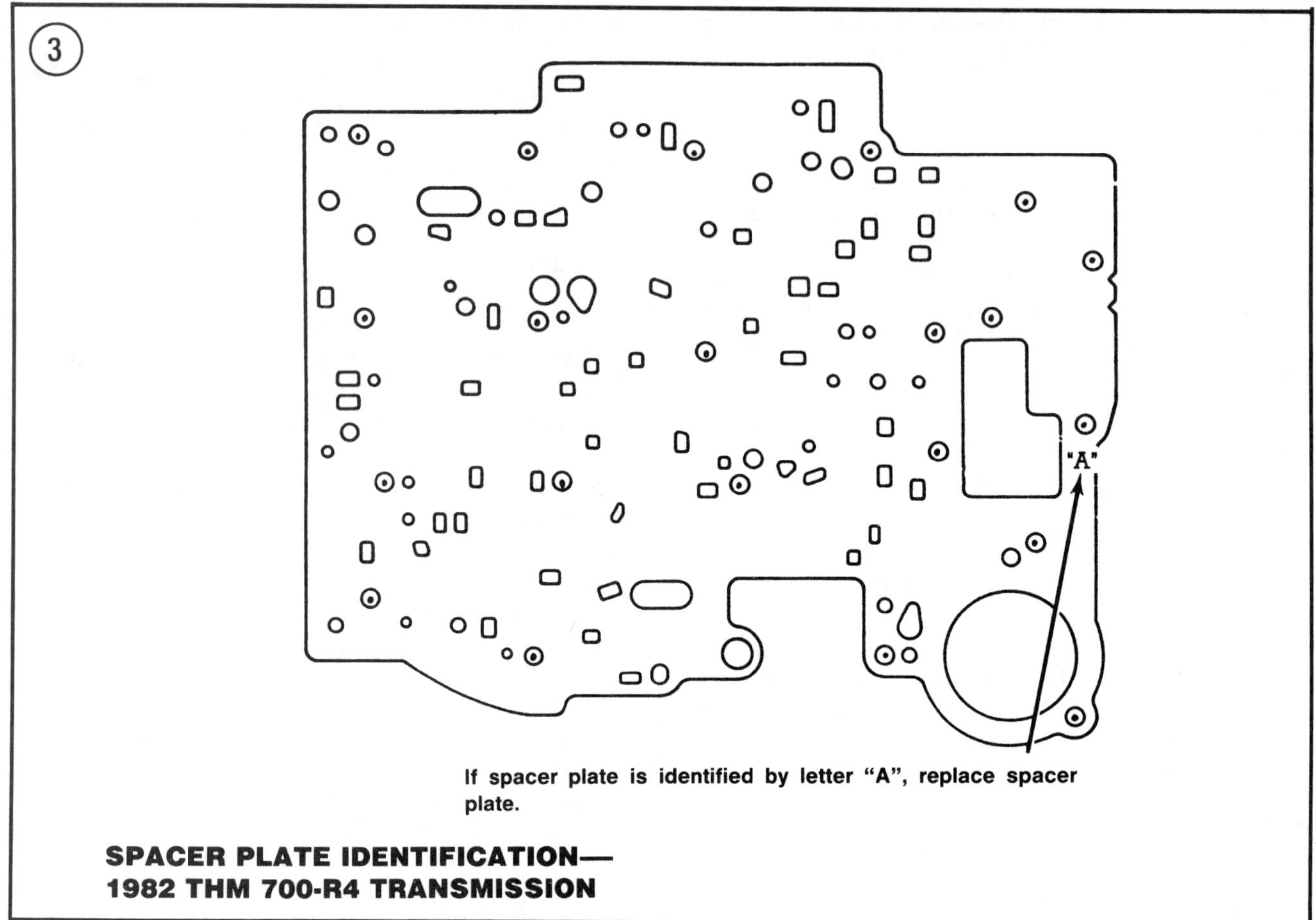

**SPACER PLATE IDENTIFICATION—
1982 THM 700-R4 TRANSMISSION**

"A," replace the spacer plate with service unit. See **Figure 3**.

Problem: oil leaks at transfer case adapter

Models affected: 1982-1983 4-wheel drive models with THM700-R4 transmission

Condition and Cause

Some 1982-1983 4-wheel drive models equipped with THNM700-R4 transmission may exhibit an oil leak at the transmission case-to-transfer case adapter. This condition may be caused by a lack of compression of the O-ring seal that is used on the transfer case adapter.

Repair

To correct the oil leak condition, install 2 O-rings (part No. 1358899) on the transfer case adapter to correct the oil leak.

Problem: gear clash

Models affected: 1984 T trucks with 207 transfer case

Condition and Cause

Some 1984 T trucks may experience a gear clash condition when shifting from 2-wheel drive to 4-wheel drive, while the vehicle is in motion. This condition may be caused by the drive chain sprocket.

Repair

To correct this condition, replace the drive chain sprocket with a new sprocket (part No. 14075350).

TUNE-UP AND EMISSIONS

Problem: false setting of trouble code 42

Models affected: 1984 S/T truck with 2.8L California engine

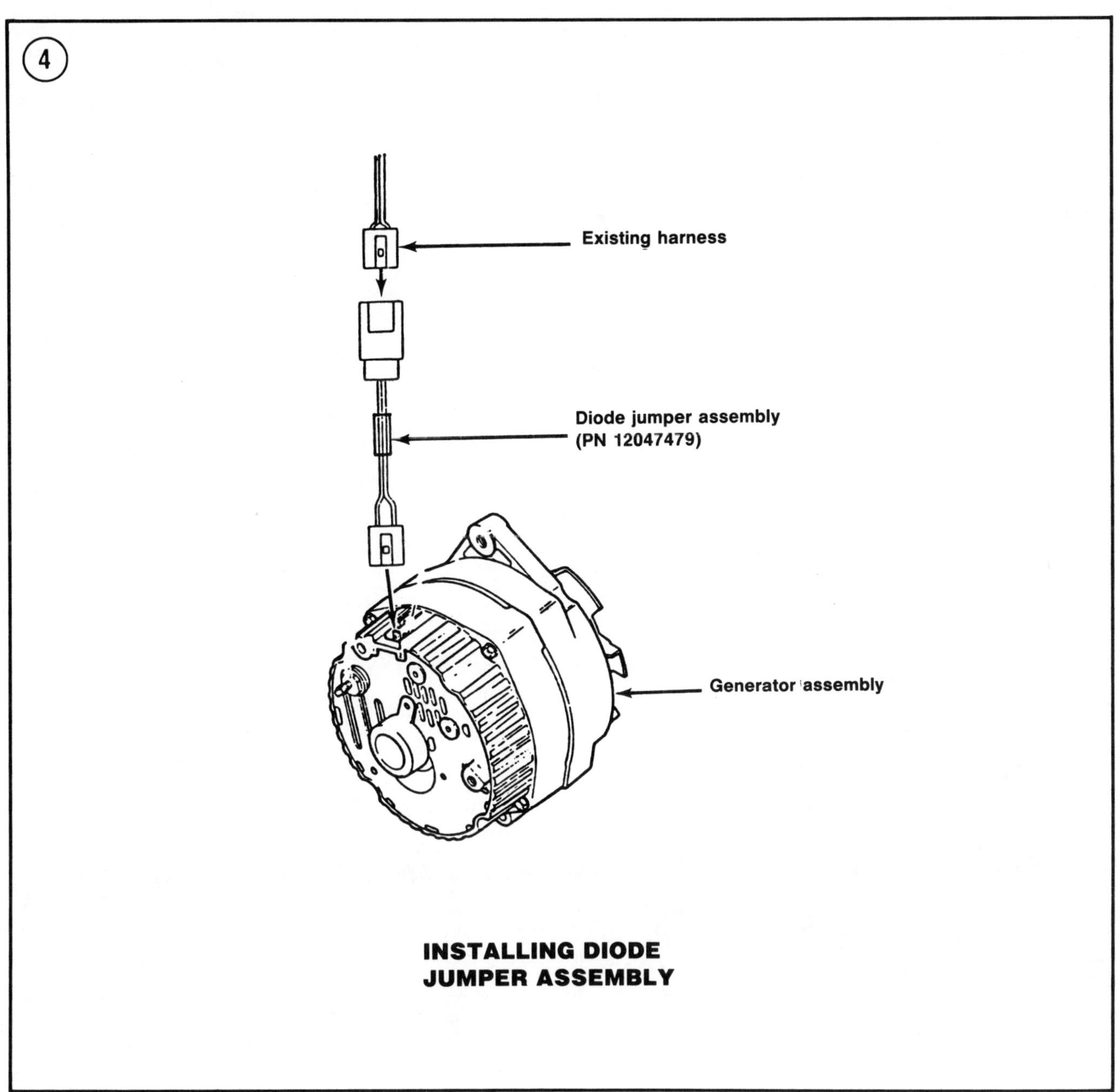

INSTALLING DIODE JUMPER ASSEMBLY

Condition and Cause

Some 1984 S/T trucks with 2.8L California engine may set a false trouble code 42. This condition may be caused by electrical feedback from the generator light circuit back to the electronic control module.

Repair

NOTE

This procedure requires diagnosis of the electronic spark timing control system and should be done by a General Motors dealer or other qualified specialist.

Always determine that the trouble code is false, and not a legitimate electronic spark timing problem, using regular diagnostic procedures. If the trouble code proves false, install a diode jumper assembly (part No. 12047479) between the generator and the existing harness. See **Figure 4**.

NOTES

NOTES

NOTES

NOTES

NOTES

NOTES

NOTES

NOTES

NOTES